W9-ACX-167

Why We Remember

United States History Through Reconstruction

A Total Teaching Package

Why We Remember

An Interview with Dr. Herman Viola

by Ms. Bonnie White
Buzz Aldrin School
Reston, Virginia

Ms. White: When did you become interested in American history?

Dr. Viola: *I began to get interested in American history in elementary school. Both my parents were Italian immigrants who came to America as young adults. Neither of them had more than an eighth grade education, but they loved their adopted country even though they knew little about its past. I was the one who answered their questions about famous historical figures and explained the significance of our patriotic holidays. As I read about American history in school, I liked to go home and tell my family the stories I was learning about the country they had chosen to make their home.*

Ms. White: Many people enjoy reading about history. Why did you decide to make it your life's work?

Dr. Viola: *For me, history is like an endless detective story. As a history major in college, I loved the challenge of finding facts in little-known archival records, letters, diaries, and other sources. With that information, I would try to answer questions about historical events or individuals.*
My first job after college was as a reference specialist at the National Archives. To me, the National Archives is a historian's paradise. It is filled with literally millions of documents created by ordinary citizens. Throughout my years at the Archives and later at the Smithsonian, I have never grown tired of searching for pieces of historic puzzles and putting those pieces together to create snapshots of history.

Ms. White: You've written many books and articles over the years. Why do you like to write?

Dr. Viola: I have always liked to tell stories. Even before I finished my college training in history, I would tell history stories to anyone who wanted to listen. I learned that often people who said they hated history, like my Navy buddies, enjoyed listening to stories about the past.

As I became a more seasoned historian, I knew that if I wanted to share my history stories with a wider range of people, I needed to write them down. So I started to write books based on the stories. One book just seemed to lead to another.

Ms. White: Writing a textbook for young adolescents seems very different from writing books for adults. Why did you decide to write *Why We Remember*?

Dr. Viola: I guess it goes back to my Navy days. Most of those teenagers told me they hated history. I always hoped one day to write a textbook that was more than names, dates, and facts. I wanted to tell stories to make youngsters love their country's past as much as I do.

I decided I could employ some of the storytelling skills I use in trade book writing and in teaching to help solve the problem of uninspired history in textbooks. My goal in writing this text program has been to help students understand the intrigue and pleasure of history, as well as to help them learn the common core of knowledge that all Americans should know.

Ms. White: Some people contend that in our technological age learning history is not very important. Why do you think history is a meaningful study for young people?

Dr. Viola: The best answer to that question is an inscription on a statue in front of the National Archives: "The Past is Prologue." For me, this epitomizes the reason every young person should leave school with a sense of the heritage that is his or hers as an American citizen. Without a grounding in the past—a knowledge of how we've gotten where we are—the next generations will not continue the legacy that our ancestors have passed along to us.

Dr. Herman Viola

Ph.D. in American history, Indiana University
Nationally recognized authority on American Indians, the West, and the Civil War
Founder of the National Archives scholarly journal *Prologue*
Former Director of the National Anthropological Archives at the Smithsonian Institution
Curator of *Seeds of Change* and *Magnificent Voyager*, two highly acclaimed exhibitions at the Smithsonian Museum of Natural History
Author of more than 15 books and many articles on the history of the United States

Teaching the History You Want Students to Remember—

In Ways They'll Never Forget!

Student Text

Provides the young adolescent with a visual and conceptual road map for understanding and remembering our nation's past.

Teacher's Edition

Point-of-use information in a convenient format helps you bring new life to your history classroom.

Addison-Wesley

Why We Remember

United States History
Through Reconstruction

Teacher's Edition

Herman Viola

Take-Home Planner

For each chapter in a unit,
an easy-to-carry guide previews
content and teaching resources,
describes options for in-class activities,
and provides answers for grading.

Teacher's Resource Package

Thoughtfully planned supplementary
materials help ensure that students
comprehend basic information *and* gain
an in-depth understanding of history.

Additional Resources

Special resources,
designed specifically
to be used with
Why We Remember,
are available for
purchase.

Wall
Time Line

Vital Links™
Multimedia
Program

Transparency
Package

SelecTest
Testing Software

Why We Remember
Video Series

Teaching Tools for *Why We Remember*

Chapter Planning Guide

The **Chapter Planning Guide** is your at-a-glance starting point for teaching each chapter of *Why We Remember*. The guide appears in both the Teacher's Edition and the Take-Home Planner. It highlights major teaching opportunities in the Student Text, Teacher's Edition, Teacher's Resource Package, and Take-Home Planner.

Glance across the rows to see the teaching opportunities for each chapter section.

Glance down the columns to review the highlights of each program component.

Graphic symbols help you locate specific teaching opportunities in the Student Text, Teacher's Edition, and Teacher's Resource Package.

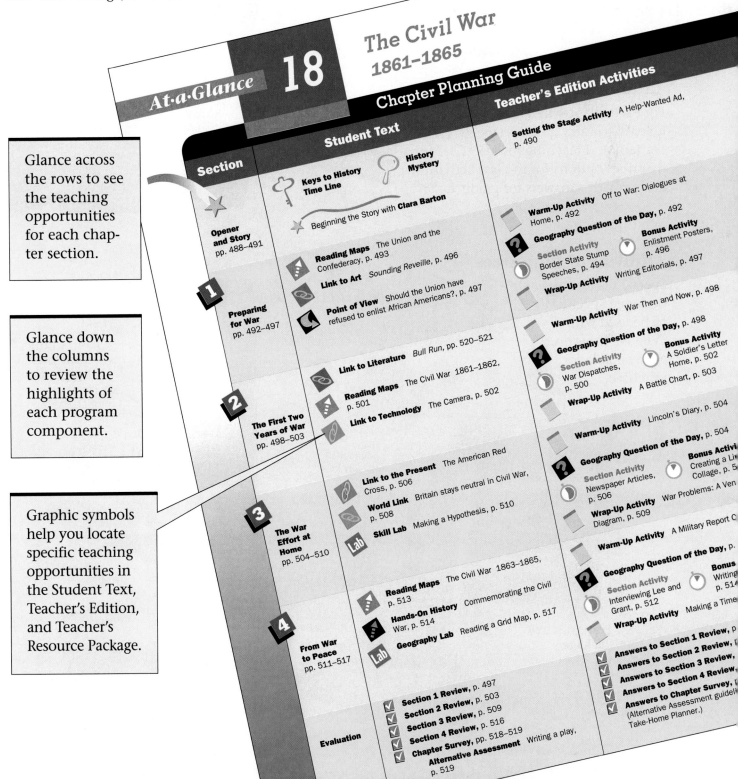

At-a-Glance 18 The Civil War 1861–1865

Chapter Planning Guide

Student Text

Section

Keys to History Time Line · History Mystery

Opener and Story pp. 488–491

Beginning the Story with **Clara Barton**

1 Preparing for War pp. 492–497

Reading Maps The Union and the Confederacy, p. 493
Link to Art Sounding Reveille, p. 496
Point of View Should the Union have refused to enlist African Americans?, p. 497

2 The First Two Years of War pp. 498–503

Link to Literature Bull Run, pp. 520–521
Reading Maps The Civil War 1861–1862, p. 501
Link to Technology The Camera, p. 502

3 The War Effort at Home pp. 504–510

Link to the Present The American Red Cross, p. 506
World Link Britain stays neutral in Civil War, p. 508
Skill Lab Making a Hypothesis, p. 510

4 From War to Peace pp. 511–517

Reading Maps The Civil War 1863–1865, p. 513
Hands-On History Commemorating the Civil War, p. 514
Geography Lab Reading a Grid Map, p. 517

Evaluation

Section 1 Review, p. 497
Section 2 Review, p. 503
Section 3 Review, p. 509
Section 4 Review, p. 516
Chapter Survey, pp. 518–519
Alternative Assessment Writing a play, p. 519

Teacher's Edition Activities

Setting the Stage Activity A Help-Wanted Ad, p. 490

Warm-Up Activity Off to War: Dialogues at Home, p. 492
Geography Question of the Day, p. 492
Section Activity Border State Stump Speeches, p. 494 · Bonus Activity Enlistment Posters, p. 496
Wrap-Up Activity Writing Editorials, p. 497

Warm-Up Activity War Then and Now, p. 498
Geography Question of the Day, p. 498
Section Activity War Dispatches, p. 500 · Bonus Activity A Soldier's Letter Home, p. 502
Wrap-Up Activity A Battle Chart, p. 503

Warm-Up Activity Lincoln's Diary, p. 504
Geography Question of the Day, p. 504
Section Activity Newspaper Articles, p. 506 · Bonus Activity Creating a Li[...] Collage, p. 5[...]
Wrap-Up Activity War Problems: A Ven[...] Diagram, p. 509

Warm-Up Activity A Military Report O[...]
Geography Question of the Day, p. [...]
Section Activity Interviewing Lee and Grant, p. 512 · Bonus Writing [...] p. 51[...]
Wrap-Up Activity Making a Time[...]

Answers to Section 1 Review, p[...]
Answers to Section 2 Review, [...]
Answers to Section 3 Review,[...]
Answers to Section 4 Review[...]
Answers to Chapter Survey,[...]
(Alternative Assessment guideli[...]
Take-Home Planner.)

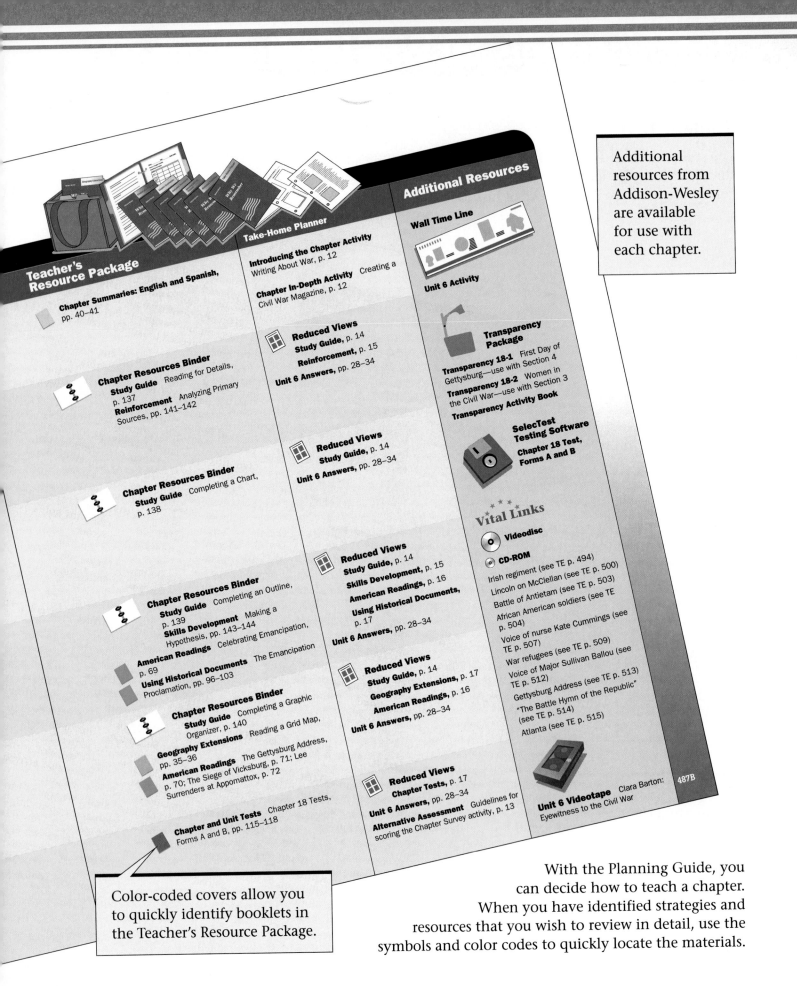

Additional resources from Addison-Wesley are available for use with each chapter.

Teacher's Resource Package

Chapter Summaries: English and Spanish, pp. 40–41

Chapter Resources Binder
Study Guide Reading for Details, p. 137
Reinforcement Analyzing Primary Sources, pp. 141–142

Chapter Resources Binder
Study Guide Completing a Chart, p. 138

Chapter Resources Binder
Study Guide Completing an Outline, p. 139
Skills Development Making a Hypothesis, pp. 143–144
American Readings Celebrating Emancipation, p. 69
Using Historical Documents The Emancipation Proclamation, pp. 96–103

Chapter Resources Binder
Study Guide Completing a Graphic Organizer, p. 140
Geography Extensions Reading a Grid Map, pp. 35–36
American Readings The Gettysburg Address, p. 70; The Siege of Vicksburg, p. 71; Lee Surrenders at Appomattox, p. 72

Chapter and Unit Tests Chapter 18 Tests, Forms A and B, pp. 115–118

Take-Home Planner

Introducing the Chapter Activity
Writing About War, p. 12

Chapter In-Depth Activity Creating a Civil War Magazine, p. 12

Reduced Views
Study Guide, p. 14
Reinforcement, p. 15
Unit 6 Answers, pp. 28–34

Reduced Views
Study Guide, p. 14
Unit 6 Answers, pp. 28–34

Reduced Views
Study Guide, p. 14
Skills Development, p. 15
American Readings, p. 16
Using Historical Documents, p. 17
Unit 6 Answers, pp. 28–34

Reduced Views
Study Guide, p. 14
Geography Extensions, p. 17
American Readings, p. 16
Unit 6 Answers, pp. 28–34

Reduced Views
Chapter Tests, p. 17
Unit 6 Answers, pp. 28–34
Alternative Assessment Guidelines for scoring the Chapter Survey activity, p. 13

Additional Resources

Wall Time Line

Unit 6 Activity

Transparency Package
Transparency 18-1 First Day of Gettysburg—use with Section 4
Transparency 18-2 Women in the Civil War—use with Section 3
Transparency Activity Book

SelecTest Testing Software
Chapter 18 Test, Forms A and B

★★★ Vital Links ★★★

⊙ **Videodisc**

⊙ **CD-ROM**

Irish regiment (see TE p. 494)
Lincoln on McClellan (see TE p. 500)
Battle of Antietam (see TE p. 503)
African American soldiers (see TE p. 504)
Voice of nurse Kate Cummings (see TE p. 507)
War refugees (see TE p. 509)
Voice of Major Sullivan Ballou (see TE p. 512)
Gettysburg Address (see TE p. 513)
"The Battle Hymn of the Republic" (see TE p. 514)
Atlanta (see TE p. 515)

Unit 6 Videotape Clara Barton: Eyewitness to the Civil War

487B

Color-coded covers allow you to quickly identify booklets in the Teacher's Resource Package.

With the Planning Guide, you can decide how to teach a chapter. When you have identified strategies and resources that you wish to review in detail, use the symbols and color codes to quickly locate the materials.

Teaching Tools for *Why We Remember*

Student Text

The student text of *Why We Remember* guides the young adolescent through history by identifying key people, events, and ideas—then connecting them to build a core of historical knowledge.

Each page organizes information conceptually and visually for maximum student retention.

State-of-the-art computer-generated maps enhance the chapter narrative while improving map-reading skills.

Frequent primary source excerpts are clearly identified with large quotation marks.

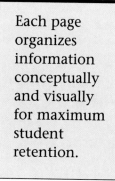

Jamestown and Plymouth 1620

QUEBEC

Abnaki

Algonkin

NEW ENGLAND

Huron

Massachuset
Mahican · Cape Cod
Plymouth · Wampanoag
Pequot Narragansett

Iroquois

ATLANTIC OCEAN

Delaware

0   200 mi
0   200 km
Transverse Mercator Projection

Powhatan
Jamestown · *Chesapeake Bay*
James River
Roanoke Island

Roanoke R.

VIRGINIA
Tuscarora

English land grants

Pee Dee River

Reading Maps

What Indian tribes lived in the area where the English colonists built Jamestown?

Virginia, the First Colony

Merchants founded the first permanent English colony in Virginia. They hoped to find precious metals and other raw materials that England needed.

Establishing a colony was expensive and risky. Thus, the merchants organized the Virginia Company of London. It was a **joint-stock company**—a business that raised money by selling shares, called stock, to investors. The profits were to be divided among the investors according to the number of shares each had.

In a document called a charter, the king, James I, granted the Virginia Company the right to "plant," or establish, colonies in Virginia. Investors eagerly bought stock. As a result, the company was able to buy the ships and supplies it needed to launch a colony.

Building Jamestown In the spring of 1607, 105 men and boys sailed up a broad river in Chesapeake Bay. They named the river the James and their settlement James-town in honor of their king.

From the first, Jamestown was in trouble. Ignoring orders from the Virginia Company, the leaders located their settlement on low, swampy ground. The only drinking water was salty, and the area swarmed with mosquitoes. Disease spread rapidly.

Then, instead of planting crops, the colonists rushed off to search for gold. As Captain John Smith later wrote:

❝There was no talk, no hope, no work, but dig gold, wash gold, refine gold, load gold.❞

Too late did they learn that their gold was really fool's gold.

Hard times During the first 7 month[s] in Jamestown, 73 colonists died of hung[er] and disease. The rest owed their lives to [the] inspired leadership of John Smith and the friendship of Pocahontas.

After Smith took control of the colo[ny] 1608, he forced the settlers to plant c[rops.] He declared, "He that will not work, not eat." More supplies also arrived England. So did more colonists.

A year later, Smith was burned in powder explosion and returned to E[ngland.] Without him, the colony fell into dis[order.] supplies ran out, people ate rats to s[urvive.] The winter of 1609–1610 became [known as] the "starving time." When spri[ng came] only 60 of 500 colonists were still [alive.]

Changes in Virginia

Hope for survival of the colony came from tobacco, an American "weed" that had become very popular in Europe. The soil of Virginia was ideal for growing tobacco, and in 1612 John Rolfe, husband of Pocahontas, developed a method of drying it for shipment to England.

Tobacco exports soared. **Exports** are goods sent out of one country to sell in another. The Virginia Company was pleased by the new tobacco trade. However, life in Jamestown was very hard, and few English people wanted to live there.

To stir up interest in Virginia, in 1616 the company brought Pocahontas and John Rolfe to England. Everywhere Pocahontas went, she caused a sensation. Merchants, church leaders, and even the king and queen were eager to meet her.

To attract more settlers, the Virginia Company also made several important changes in the colony. First, in 1618 the company gave colonists the right to own land. Until then, the company had owned all land in Virginia. Now people who paid their own way to the colony were granted 50 acres. They received another 50 acres for each new settler they brought with them.

Indentured servants To encourage settlers who could not afford to pay their own way to Virginia, the company allowed

No one knows what Jamestown looked like in 1607 because some of the site has been washed away by the James River. This artist's view shows how the colonists might have built a protective wall around their tents and huts.

1600–1750 Chapter 5 • **123**

Take-Home Planner

A unique **Take-Home Planner** enables you to make teaching plans for each chapter in a unit and to grade students' work without carrying home the Teacher's Edition.

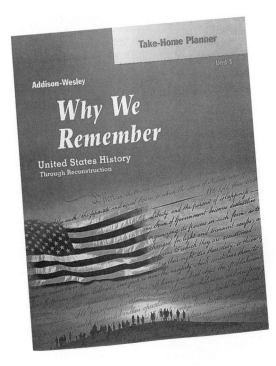

For each chapter, the Take-Home Planner provides

- a replica of the Chapter Planning Guide in the Teacher's Edition

- directions for
  - an introductory chapter activity
  - an in-depth chapter activity
  - scoring the chapter's alternative assessment

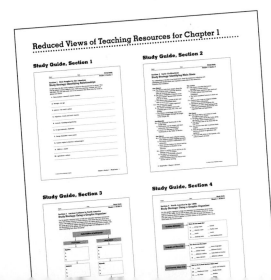

- reduced views of all activity sheets and tests for the chapter

- answers to all activity sheets and tests for the chapter

Teacher's Edition

The wraparound Teacher's Edition is designed for classroom use. Side columns provide instructional suggestions to guide daily teaching. Top margins provide organizational and background information, as well as suggestions for meeting special student needs.

✠ Connections to Language Arts

Around the year 1000 the Aztecs began compiling codices—book-like written records consisting of pages stitched together. Painting on paper made from fig tree bark, artists used pictures and symbols to show daily life, royal history, religious practices, and tribute records. Aztec storytellers who passed down knowledge to students orally used codices as memory aids.

See the Reinforcement activity in **Chapter Resources Binder,** pp. 5–6.

tribute in the form of gold, cotton, turquoise, feathers, incense, and food. Tribute also included human beings for sacrifice to the Aztec sun god. The Aztecs believed that unless the sun god was fed hearts and blood, the world would come to an end. At one especially bloody four-day celebration, 20,000 prisoners had their hearts cut out.

The Aztecs were very successful at agriculture. Farmers grew crops on irrigated hillside terraces around Lake Texcoco. They also cultivated vegetables and flowers in *chinampas* (chee-NAHM-pahs), farm plots built by digging ditches in the lakeshore to channel the water and then piling up the fertile mud into raised beds.

Aztec trade, like Aztec agriculture, showed careful organization and government direction. Merchants traveled through the empire

and beyond to Central America and north into the present-day United States. They brought a great variety of goods to Tenochtitlán. Orderly markets displayed meat, vegetables, cloth, rope, pottery, precious metals, jade, feathers, and animal skins.

The Incas

Far to the south, the Inca empire rivaled the Aztecs in size and power. Beginning in the early 1400s, the Incas dominated much of the Pacific Coast of South America. Their capital was the city of Cuzco (KOOS-kō), located high in the Andes Mountains. The supreme ruler, the Sapa Inca, had total control of his subjects. Priests and nobles helped him rule his empire.

The well-organized Incas could communicate over a vast area. They built a road system

Discussion

Checking Understanding

1. What made the Aztecs so powerful? (A strong army and a well-structured government.)

2. Why did the Aztecs sacrifice humans to their sun god? (They believed the world would end without the sacrifices.)

Stimulating Critical Thinking

3. What was the Mayas' most important accomplishment? Support your opinion. (Answers might include writing, because it gave a means of recording information; developing the concept of zero, because the concept is important to mathematical processes; and the development of an accurate calendar.)

Teaching the

〰 Hands-On —— HISTORY

To provide a model, display items from each category, such as a small figurine or painting, an heirloom ring, a political poster or sign, a religious pin or pendant, a favorite pen or cup. Explain their significance to you.

For European descriptions of Tenochtitlán and Cuzco, see **Using Historical Documents,** pp. 8–12.

⏱ Bonus Activity

Enlistment Posters

To help students understand why northerners and southerners were willing to fight in the war, have pairs create enlistment posters. Assign half the pairs to imagine they are recruiters for the Union army, and the other half that they are Confederate recruiters. They should focus on emotional appeals, using persuasive language and eye-catching images. Conclude by comparing persuasive techniques in the posters.

Teaching the

✏ Link to Art

Point out that drummers not only awakened soldiers and called them to meals but also communicated orders on smoke-filled battlefields. Drummers often became the target of enemy fire because of their importance in the field. They also cooked, cared for horses, and carried wounded soldiers. After analyzing this painting, display a book containing other war paintings by Homer if possible. Ask students to suggest how the paintings are similar and different. **Discussion Answers:** It depicts tents where the soldiers lived, and shows soldiers sitting around campfires and taking care of their equipment.

✠ History Footnote

Several women served as spies in the war. Harriet Tubman knew many secret routes on the Underground Railroad, and she recruited other former slaves to find Confederate camps and report them to Union officers. She and the others were able to give information about the location of Confederate explosives to Colonel James Montgomery in South Carolina during a Union gunboat raid in 1863.

Another Union spy, Elizabeth Van Lew, lived in a mansion in Richmond. She provided hiding places in her home for Union soldiers who had escaped from Confederate prisons.

Rose O'Neal Greenhow was a society hostess in Washington, D.C., who spied for the South. She learned of the Union's planned attack on Manassas in 1861 and sent coded information to General Beauregard, who won an important victory at Manassas.

〰 HISTORY

Creating a temple treasure Ordinary activities sometimes [lead to] extraordinary discoveries. In Mexico City in 1978, a worker [digging a] trench came upon the buried ruins of *el Templo Mayor*—the [great "temple"] of the Aztecs.

[Arch]aeologists uncovered the temple, they [found thou]sands of items the Aztecs had buried [close] to their gods. These included turtle [shells, snak]e skins, jaguar skeletons, crocodile [bones, and] the remains of sacrificed humans.

[There were] wonderful treasures too: gemstones, [gold mas]ks, musical instruments, knives, [statue]s of gods, and carvings of animals.

[Some] were made by Aztec artists. Others were antiques from [civil]izations like the Olmecs. Most came from peoples the [Aztecs] conquered.

El Templo Mayor model

[Acti]vity Suppose you wanted to bury a "treasure chest" [containing] items of special value to you. Make a list of what you [would put] in the chest. Include at least one item from each of [these three] categories: artworks, antiques or heirlooms, items with [special] religious meaning, and special everyday objects. [Explain e]ach of your choices.

✏ Link to Art

Sounding Reveille (1865) Almost every family North and South had someone in uniform. People at home were desperate for news of their loved ones. "Special artists" helped satisfy that demand. Hired by illustrated newspapers, special artists went to battlefields and camps to sketch what they saw. The most gifted of these artists was Winslow Homer, who worked for *Harper's Weekly* newspaper. In this painting of a Union camp by Homer, a bugler and two drummers sound reveille, a signal to wake the soldiers each morning.
Discuss In what ways does this painting show the everyday life of soldiers?

Although the Union and the Confederacy had rules banning boys from enlisting, many managed to join. Historians estimate that between 10 and 20 percent of all soldiers— 250,000 to 420,000—were 16 years old or younger. John Mathew Sloan of the 9th Texas was only 13 when he lost a leg in battle. He claimed his only regret was that "I shall not soon be able to [shoot] at the enemy."

Women soldiers Hundreds of women, too, fought for the cause. Their exact number will never be known, for they had to change their names and disguise themselves as men. Rosetta Wakeman, who joined the 153d Regiment New York State Volunteers, called herself "Lyons Wakeman" and wore men's clothing. Some women even wore fake mustaches or charcoal "whiskers."

Teaching Resources

Take-Home Planner 1, pp. 2–9

Chapter Resources Binder

Study Guide, p. 3

Reinforcement

Skills Development

Geography Extensions, pp. 1–2

American Readings, p. 3

Using Historical Documents

Transparency Activities

Chapter and Unit Tests

Teacher's Resource Package

The Teacher's Resource Package has two kinds of resources—basic chapter teaching activities to ensure student comprehension, and fresh, innovative, in-depth activities to motivate and engage your students.

A **Chapter Resources Binder** conveniently organizes three basic resources by chapter:

- Study Guides
  - Reinforcement Activities
    - Skills Development Activities and Teaching Transparencies

Six separate booklets provide in-depth options for extending and assessing student learning

- Geography Extensions
  - American Readings
    - Using Historical Documents from National Archives
      - Interdisciplinary Projects
        - Chapter Summaries in English and Spanish
          - Chapter and Unit Tests

Customize your own instructional notebook by removing activities from the in-depth booklets and inserting them into the Chapter Resources Binder.

Additional Resources

Available for purchase are five special resources specifically designed to add more instructional depth and student interest as you teach *Why We Remember.*

Wall Time Line

A 12-foot-long, laminated, foldable time line enables your students to create their own class time line of United States history. An activities guide suggests many creative ideas for continual use of the time line.

Douglas DC-3

Transparency Package

Thirty-eight color transparencies, two for each chapter, help illustrate your lectures and stimulate discussion. The activities book contains suggestions for using transparencies to extend content.

SelecTest Testing Software

This computerized testing system (Macintosh and IBM) allows you to customize your own tests. The test file book contains a printed version of all test questions.

Vital Links Multimedia Program

See page T26 for information on this multimedia United States history program.

Why We Remember Video Series

Six videotapes, one per unit, provide a motivational way to introduce each unit's content by engaging students in the story of one person from the time period. Videos can also be used for review and assessment.

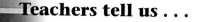

Teachers tell us . . .

"We want a U.S. history program that helps students to learn about important people, events, and ideas—the core history of our nation—and to understand their significance today."

Why We Remember responds . . .

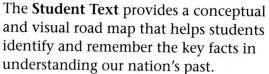

Keys to History

1862
September
Battle of Antietam

1862
March
Monitor vs. *Merrimac*

1861
July
First Battle of Bull Run

1861   1862

Looking Back   World Link

488

Lincoln elected President
1860

Britain stays neutral in Civil War
1861–1865

The **Student Text** provides a conceptual and visual road map that helps students identify and remember the key facts in understanding our nation's past.

Every entry in the **chapter time line** is a carefully chosen Key to History.

Teacher's Edition time line notes help you reinforce key learning.

As students read the chapter, they see the keys highlighted in **bold headings**, with their importance emphasized in the text.

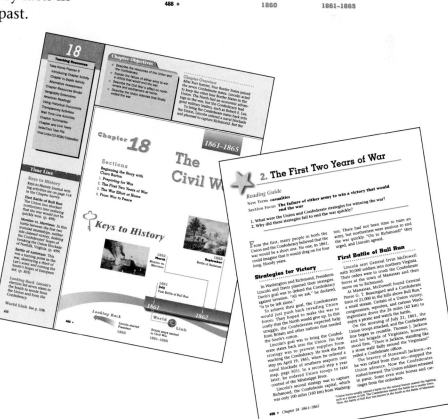

Each chapter ends with a **"Why We Remember" conclusion** explaining the significance of the time period for Americans today.

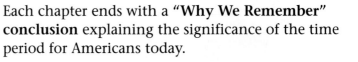

In a **journal writing activity** in the **Chapter Survey**, students describe in their own words the importance of the chapter's Keys to History.

The **Chapter Resources Binder** provides

- **Study Guides** that teach students a variety of study skills as they learn key information.

- **Reinforcement** activities that give students additional help in understanding and remembering key information.

The **Chapter Summaries** supplement offers

- a one-page summary of each chapter

- Summaries in Spanish as well as English

Chapter Tests assess student recall and comprehension of key information.

. . . the first step to historical literacy.

Teachers tell us . . .

"Students at this age respond best when history is told through stories of people. They like to know about the famous and the ordinary, the young and the old, the good and the not-so-good."

Why We Remember responds . . .

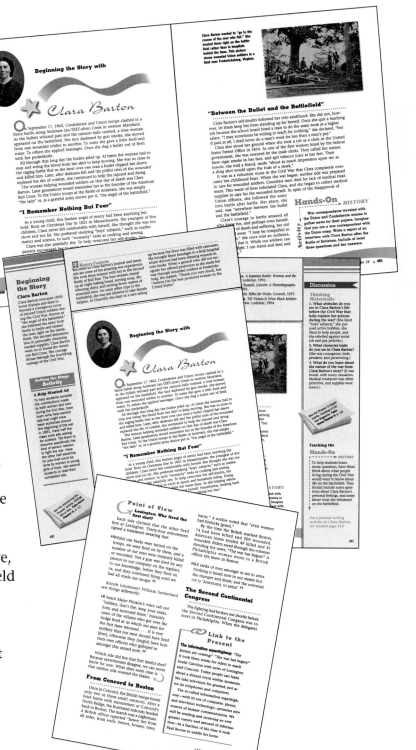

In the **Student Text**, each chapter begins with an **introductory story** about a real person from the time period.

- The story tells a dramatic incident from the person's life.

- It focuses on an important decision the person had to make, often when he or she was an adolescent.

- The person reappears throughout the chapter and in the conclusion, putting a human face on historical events.

History Footnotes in the **Teacher's Edition** provide background information to help you personalize history. **Thinking Historically** questions help students put themselves in the place of people of the past.

Each chapter includes a **Point of View** feature, which helps students see that people have held differing opinions throughout our history.

- Focuses on issues of significance

- Incorporated into the ongoing text, so that students will not skip it

Scores of American voices are heard in the numerous **primary sources** woven throughout the narrative.

- Primary-source excerpts drawn from a wide range of historic figures
- Excerpts easily identified by large quotation marks

For every chapter, the **American Readings** supplement offers two or more opportunities for students to read firsthand what Americans have written about our past.

- Journal and diary entries and letters
- Excerpts from historical fiction and poetry
- Oral history

A unique *Why We Remember* Video Series offers a 12- to 15-minute video for each unit. Videos can be used to preview the unit content and to engage students by introducing them to a person from the time period.

- Each video tells a story of the time period through the eyes of a person from the era.
- Videos dramatize key events that students will read about as they study the unit.
- A video guide suggests strategies for using the videos for learning and motivation.

. . . *that enables students to trace their American heritage.*

Getting students involved . . .

Teachers tell us . . .

"We want students to like history—to see history as interesting, intriguing, and fun. We want to turn students on to history."

Why We Remember responds . . .

In the **Student Text**, each chapter begins with a **History Mystery**, which students can solve only by reading the chapter.

Hands-On History activities, two in each chapter, engage students in "doing history."

- Stimulate students' imaginations about the past.
  - Link past events with the present.
    - Encourage students to take responsibility for their own learning.

How Do We Know? Scholar's Tool Kits are a unique feature designed to help students learn about the "tools" historians use to understand history.

- Stories describe how historians use archaeology, maps, public records, pictures, oral history, and memoirs to learn about and interpret history.
- **Scholar at Work** activities let students become historians by practicing the use of historians' tools.

The **Teacher's Edition** helps you involve students in their learning.

■ **Discussion questions** enable you to monitor student comprehension and stimulate critical thinking.

■ A **Section Activity** and a **Bonus Activity** for each section give you the option of a full-period or a short activity each teaching day.

■ Activities are innovative, practical, and engaging.

Options allow you flexibility in meeting student needs as well as time constraints.

In the **Take-Home Planner** you will find two important activity options.

■ An **Introducing the Chapter Activity** motivates students to dig into the upcoming chapter.

■ A **Chapter In-Depth Activity** enables students to study a significant topic from the chapter in greater detail.

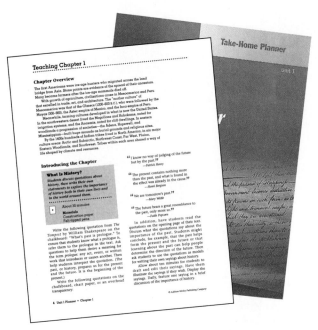

The **Teacher's Resource Package** offers even more resources for getting students involved.

■ For example, **Using Historical Documents from National Archives** lets students analyze reproductions of actual documents from national archives in Washington, D.C.

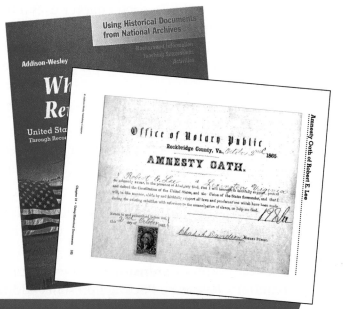

. . . in discovering the excitement and mystery of history!

Building geography knowledge . . .

Teachers tell us . . .

"Students this age need geography instruction combined with history."

Why We Remember responds . . .

A **Prologue** in the student text introduces the land as it was before humans lived on it, and gives an overview of how the land was changed by the people who came.

A **Geography Lab** in each chapter uses a historical topic, often described through primary source readings, to help students achieve the geographic competencies detailed in the **National Standards for Geography**. In the labs students learn

- the geographic areas—"places"—where history happened
- why maps are important in understanding history
- how "mental maps" are essential to historical literacy

The **Teacher's Edition** offers a **Geography Question of the Day** to encourage continual geographic learning.

The **Geography Extensions** supplement in the **Teacher's Resource Package** presents additional geography learning opportunities that expand history understanding.

Applying social studies skills . . .

Teachers tell us . . .

"Students need practice in applying social studies skills to real problem-solving situations."

Why We Remember responds . . .

Skill Labs, one per chapter, systematically provide experiences in applying critical social studies skills as identified by the National Council for the Social Studies. Labs develop competencies in:

- Acquiring Information
  - Thinking Critically
    - Using Information

Each lab requires students to apply one or more skills to investigate an issue or question.

Throughout the text, students use **charts, diagrams, graphs,** and **maps** as they learn history.

To assist students who need review or remediation in social studies skills, the **Teacher's Resource Package** provides a series of **skills development activities** with accompanying **skills teaching transparencies** for you to use.

Particular attention is given to developing **citizenship skills** throughout the program. In a special **journal writing activity** for each chapter, students are challenged to think about how people throughout history have practiced citizenship.

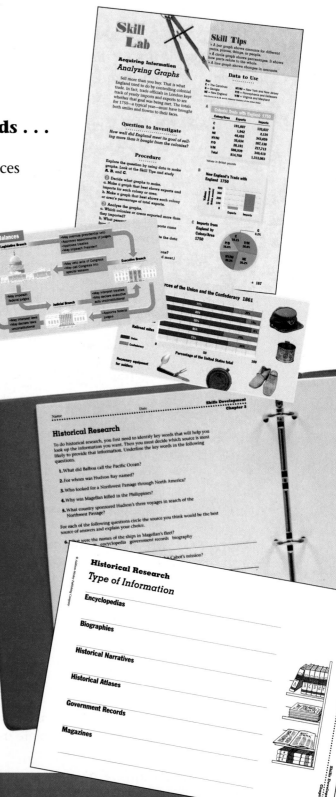

. . . to develop knowledgeable and competent young citizens.

Linking history to life . . .

Teachers tell us . . .

"We want students to understand how history relates to other subjects and to their everyday lives."

Why We Remember responds . . .

In the **Student Text**, each chapter presents a **Link to Art**, a **Link to the Present**, and a **World Link**.

The **Teacher's Edition** offers innovative strategies for using these links to broaden students' understanding of the world.

Links to Technology offer diagrams and cutaway drawings for students to examine as they study the role of technology in our nation's history.

Literature as a way of knowing history is beautifully illustrated in each unit's **Link to Literature** selection, carefully chosen to stimulate interest in reading the book from which the selection is taken.

Why We Remember offers two options for **interdisciplinary projects.**

- Each **Unit Survey** provides an **interdisciplinary project** that students can complete individually or in groups.

- The **Interdisciplinary Projects** supplement in the **Teacher's Resource Package** provides all the resources and directions needed to direct four major interdisciplinary projects—peak learning experiences that students will never forget.

Assessing student performance . . .

Teachers tell us . . .

"We want options in how we assess students so that we can choose the best assessment for the chapter content and for the students."

Why We Remember responds . . .

Traditional Assessment Options

Section Reviews allow frequent comprehension checks.

Chapter and Unit Surveys provide a combination of comprehension and critical thinking questions appropriate for either teacher evaluation or student self-evaluation.

Chapter and Unit Tests, in the **Teacher's Resource Package,** enable you to assess levels of student understanding from factual recall to higher-order thinking. Two forms are provided for each test.*

Also available as a computer software program, **SelecTest.*

The convenient **Take-Home Planner** lets you grade all student work without taking home the larger Teacher's Edition.

Alternative Assessment Options

Ideal for Portfolio Assessment, the **Writing in Your History Journal** activities in each **Chapter Survey** provide a continuous record of student comprehension and understanding.

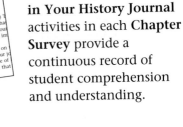

Alternative Assessment activities in each **Chapter Survey** and each **Unit Survey** offer opportunities to evaluate students' understanding through valid, reliable, performance-oriented assessment techniques.

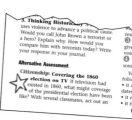

For those teachers with limited experience in alternative assessment, the **Take-Home Planner** provides information on structuring each alternative assessment, developing appropriate evaluation criteria, and setting up a scoring rubric.

. . . to make history relevant to today's students.

Vital Links

Vital Links is a project-based multimedia United States history program. It blends leading-edge technologies with sound instructional design to stimulate adolescent minds and meet unique learning needs. Each unit uses components to address different learning modes and expand opportunities for all students.

The Vital Links multimedia components include historical photographs, video, animation, and audio to capture students' attention and make learning history engaging and relevant. With Vital Links, teachers create a real-world learning environment. Available in Macintosh and Windows versions.

Vital Links is correlated through bar codes and CD-ROM address references throughout the Teacher's Edition of *Why We Remember.*

 Each videodisc includes the Explore database of that unit's historical time period, giving students access to hundreds of video and audio primary sources. It also contains a Video Introduction of the unit themes.

 Videotapes also provide the Video Introduction portion of the program, so that all classrooms have the technology to introduce unit themes to students.

 Vital Links Chronicle **newspapers** include articles, editorials, graphs, time lines, charts, and more for off-line historical reading and research.

CD-ROMs provide content and tools, including

Explore, a database with over 400 primary sources and an abundance of historical data.

Write, a desktop publishing tool that easily combines text and imported images into student documents.

Analyze, a spreadsheet tool for inputting, graphing, and evaluating historical and current data.

Present, a multimedia tool for producing dynamic video presentations with rich images and sound.

Vital Links U.S. Heritage Music **audio-cassettes** provide 70 minutes of U.S. history through beautiful music and songs that span all time periods covered by the Vital Links program.

Enjoy the best of two worlds with the Why We Remember *basal text program and Vital Links multimedia.*

Why We Remember

"A people without history is like wind on the buffalo grass."

—*Lakota/Dakota proverb*

"One of the ways of helping to destroy a people is to tell them they don't have a history, that they have no roots."

—*Archbishop Desmond Tutu*

"We are tomorrow's past."

—*Mary Webb*

"Those who cannot remember the past are condemned to fulfill it."

—*George Santayana*

About the Author

Dr. Herman J. Viola, curator emeritus with the Smithsonian Institution, is a distinguished historian, author, and curator. Dr. Viola received his Ph.D. in American history from Indiana University. He founded the scholarly journal *Prologue* at the National Archives. Dr. Viola also served as director of the National Anthropological Archives at the Smithsonian Institution. There he organized two major historical exhibitions: *Seeds of Change,* highlighting the cultural and biotic exchange after the Columbus voyages, and *Magnificent Voyagers,* chronicling the journey of the U.S. Exploring Expedition of 1838–1842, which sailed around the world and discovered Antarctica.

A nationally recognized authority on American Indians, the history of the American West, and the Civil War, Dr. Viola is the author of many historical works for both adults and young readers.

Books written or edited by Herman J. Viola

Thomas L. McKenney: Architect of America's Early Indian Policy

The Indian Legacy of Charles Bird King

Diplomats in Buckskins

The National Archives of the United States

Magnificent Voyagers: The U.S. Exploring Expedition, 1838–1841

Exploring the West

After Columbus: The Smithsonian's Chronicle of the Indians of North America Since 1492

Seeds of Change: A Quincentennial Commemoration

Ben Nighthorse Campbell: An American Warrior

The Memoirs of Charles Henry Veil

For young readers

Andrew Jackson

Giuseppe Garibaldi

Sitting Bull

After Columbus: The Horse's Return to America

Osceola

Addison-Wesley

Why We Remember

United States History
Through Reconstruction

Herman J. Viola

Contributing Author
Diane Hart

Addison-Wesley Publishing Company

Menlo Park, California • Reading, Massachusetts • New York • Don Mills, Ontario
Wokingham, England • Amsterdam • Bonn • Paris • Milan • Madrid • Sydney
Singapore • Tokyo • Seoul • Taipei • Mexico City • San Juan

Contributing Author

Diane Hart is a writer and consultant specializing in history and social studies. A former teacher and Woodrow Wilson Fellow, Ms. Hart remains deeply involved in social studies education through her active participation in both the National and California Councils for the Social Studies. She has written a number of textbooks for middle school students.

Reviewers and Consultants

Dr. Pedro Castillo
Associate Professor of History and American Studies and Co-Director, Chicano/Latino Research Center, University of California, Santa Cruz

Dr. David Barry Gaspar
Professor of History, Duke University, Durham, North Carolina

Dr. Joseph E. Harris
Professor of History, Howard University, Washington, D.C.

LaDonna Harris
President, Americans for Indian Opportunity, Bernalillo, New Mexico

Tedd Levy
Teacher, Nathan Hale Middle School, Norwalk, Connecticut

Dr. Glenn Linden
Associate Professor of History and Education, Southern Methodist University, Dallas, Texas

Charlene Pike
Teacher, L'Ance Creuse Middle School South, Harrison Township, Michigan; past president, National Middle School Association

Esther Taira
Multicultural Advisor, Division of Instruction, Los Angeles Unified School District, Los Angeles, California

Dr. Ralph E. Weber
Professor of History and Chair, Department of History, Marquette University, Milwaukee, Wisconsin

Dr. Helen Wheatley
Assistant Professor of History, Seattle University, Seattle, Washington

Acknowledgments

Susan P. Viola, literature consultant, is librarian at The Langley School in McLean, Virginia. She received her M.S.L.S. from The Catholic University of America.

Dr. Viola wishes to acknowledge the assistance of Ronald E. Grim of the Library of Congress Geography and Map Division and Howard W. Wehman of the National Archives in preparing the Scholar's Tool Kits on pages 85 and 173, respectively. He also acknowledges the research and editorial assistance of Jan Shelton Danis. Ms. Danis, a graduate of Emory University and former archivist with the National Archives and Records Administration, is an editor and indexer specializing in books on American history and politics.

Acknowledgments of permission to reprint copyrighted materials appear on page R102.

ISBN 0-201-86937-3

2 3 4 5 6 7 8 9 10 - VH - 99 98 97 96

Table of Contents

Prologue: The Land   P1

Unit 1   Three Worlds Meet   Beginnings–1610   4

Chapter 1   The First Americans   Beginnings–1492   6
Beginning the Story with the Stone Seekers   8
1. First Peoples in the Americas   10
2. Early Civilizations   14
3. Ancient Cultures in North America   19
4. North America in the 1400s   25
Why We Remember   30

Chapter 2   Africa, Asia, and Europe in the 1400s   1400–1460   34
Beginning the Story with Prince Henry the Navigator   36
1. Trading Empires of Africa   38
2. The Wealth of Asia   44
3. Europe Looks Outward   49
Why We Remember   54

Chapter 3   Voyages of Exploration   1450–1610   58
Beginning the Story with Christopher Columbus   60
1. The Quest for Trade Routes by Sea   62
2. Seeds of Change   68
3. The Race for Discovery   73
Why We Remember   78

Unit 2   Newcomers in the Americas   1500–1750   88

Chapter 4   The Conquest of the Americas   1500–1700   90
Beginning the Story with Bartolomé de Las Casas   92
1. Spain Carves Out an American Empire   94
2. Spanish America   101
3. Challenges to Spain   108
Why We Remember   113

Chapter 5   Planting English Colonies   1600–1750   116
Beginning the Story with Pocahontas   118
1. The First English Colonies   120
2. Puritan Colonies in New England   128
3. Later English Colonies   133
Why We Remember   138

Chapter 6   Life in the English Colonies   1600–1750   142
Beginning the Story with Benjamin Franklin   144
1. Different Ways of Life   146
2. Diversity in the Colonies   154
3. Colonial Government   162
Why We Remember   166

Unit 3   A New Nation Begins   1750–1791   176

Chapter 7   The Years of Conflict   1754–1774   178
Beginning the Story with George Washington   180
1. The French and Indian War   182
2. Growing Pains   186
3. The Road to Revolution   194
Why We Remember   198

Chapter 8 The War of Independence 1775–1783   **202**
Beginning the Story with Joseph Martin 204
1. The War Begins 206
2. The Issue of Independence 211
3. The War in the North 216
4. The End of the War 221
Why We Remember 225

Chapter 9 Creating the Constitution 1776–1791   **230**
Beginning the Story with James Madison 232
1. The Nation's Shaky Start 234
2. The Constitutional Convention 241
3. The Struggle for Ratification 246
4. An Enduring Framework 250
Why We Remember 253

Unit 4   The Early Years 1789–1824   **260**

Chapter 10 The First Years of the Republic 1789–1801   **262**
Beginning the Story with Abigail Adams 264
1. The First Difficult Years 266
2. Conflicts at Home and Abroad 272
3. The Birth of Political Parties 279
Why We Remember 284

Chapter 11 The Jefferson Era 1801–1815   **288**
Beginning the Story with Tecumseh 290
1. The New Republican President 292
2. Troubles at Sea 300
3. The War of 1812 303
Why We Remember 308

Chapter 12 The Confident Years 1816–1830   **314**
Beginning the Story with the Mill Girls 316
1. A Revolution in Industry 318
2. New Forms of Transportation 322
3. A Bold Foreign Policy 328
4. Strains on National Unity 332
Why We Remember 336

Unit 5   Expansion and Reform 1820–1850   **344**

Chapter 13 The Age of Jackson 1824–1840   **346**
Beginning the Story with Andrew Jackson 348
1. The New Spirit of Democracy 350
2. Jackson Takes Charge 356
3. Jackson's Indian Policy 359
4. "The Bank War" and Its Effects 364
Why We Remember 368

Chapter 14 The Westward Movement 1820–1850   **372**
Beginning the Story with John and Jessie Frémont 374
1. Trappers and Traders Blaze the Way 376
2. The Republic of Texas 380
3. Trails West 385
4. Manifest Destiny Triumphs 393
Why We Remember 398

Chapter 15 Americans at Mid-Century 1830–1850   **402**

Beginning the Story with Frederick Douglass 404
1. Life in the North and the South 406
2. African American Life 414
3. Workers and Immigrants 419
Why We Remember 422

Chapter 16 Religion and Reform 1820–1850   **428**

Beginning the Story with Sojourner Truth 430
1. Revival and Reform 432
2. Movements to End Slavery 440
3. Working for Women's Rights 447
4. American Voices 452
Why We Remember 455

Unit 6 Civil War and Reconstruction 1850–1905   **462**

Chapter 17 The Gathering Storm 1846–1861   **464**

Beginning the Story with Abraham Lincoln 466
1. Efforts to Save the Union 468
2. The Failure of Compromise 472
3. On the Brink of War 478
Why We Remember 484

Chapter 18 The Civil War 1861–1865   **488**

Beginning the Story with Clara Barton 490
1. Preparing for War 492
2. The First Two Years of War 498
3. The War Effort at Home 504
4. From War to Peace 511
Why We Remember 516

Chapter 19 Reconstruction 1865–1905   **522**

Beginning the Story with Susie King Taylor 524
1. Rebuilding the Union 526
2. The South Under Reconstruction 532
3. The Legacy of Reconstruction 538
Why We Remember 544

Epilogue: Continuing the Story 1860s to 1990s   **549**

Reference Center   **R1**

Atlas R2

Gazetteer R12

The States R19

The Presidents R24

Key Events in United States History R30

The Declaration of Independence R32

Constitution Handbook R34

Glossary R74

Index R80

Acknowledgments R102

Getting to Know This Textbook

This book tells the story of our country from its beginnings to about 100 years ago. To help you learn—and remember—this important history, the book has many special features. These features are explained on this page and the pages that follow.

Keys to History Time Line

As you glance through this text, you will see that each chapter begins with a two-page time line that shows the time period covered in the chapter.

Each time line entry is a **Key to History**—an important event, person, or idea from the period. The key symbol highlights these keys to the past.

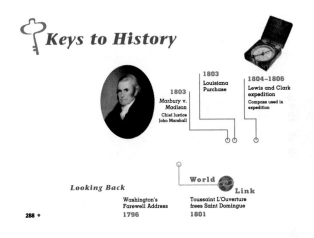

Keys to History

1803
Marbury v. Madison
Chief Justice John Marshall

1803
Louisiana Purchase

1804–1806
Lewis and Clark expedition
Compass used in expedition

Looking Back
Washington's Farewell Address
1796

World Link
Toussaint L'Ouverture frees Saint Domingue
1801

288 ●

History Mystery

Historians sometimes think of history as a series of mysteries to be unraveled. The magnifying glass symbol at the start of each chapter points out a **History Mystery** feature. Read the feature and look for clues in the chapter to help you unravel the mystery.

HISTORY
Mystery

After a terrible first winter at Plymouth, the Pilgrims were rescued by an English-speaking Indian. Where had the Indian come from, and how had he learned English?

Citizenship Skills

Americans study our country's past to be better citizens today. In the Chapter Survey at the end of each chapter, you will see a star symbol. It points out an activity in which you can practice **Citizenship Skills** by applying information that you learned in the chapter.

Scholar's Tool Kit

How Do We Know?

How do we know what we know about history? Where does our knowledge of history come from? In this book you will learn about six different "tools" that historians use to uncover information about the past. Each tool is featured in a Scholar's Tool Kit, which comes before a new unit. You can recognize the tool kits by their notebook design.

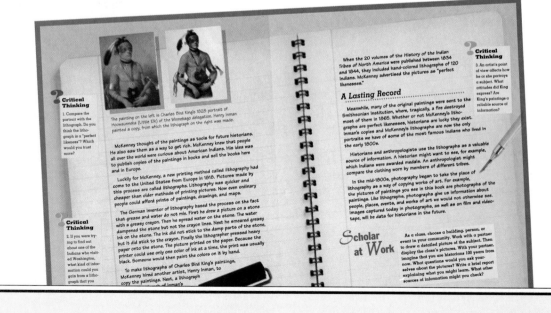

How Do We Know?

Young Omahaw, War Eagle, Little Missouri, and Pawnees, (1821), by Charles Bird King

Scholar's Tool Kit
Pictures

Imagine walking down the dusty, unpaved streets of Washington, D.C., in the early 1800s and coming upon groups of Indians, some in buckskins and some in suits and ties. Indian leaders often visited Washington to meet with government officials. In November 1821 a delegation of Plains Indians—Pawnees, Omahas, Kansas, Otos, and Missouris—arrived. Officials showed them the sights and gave them friendship medals bearing the likeness of President James Monroe.

One official was particularly eager to meet the visitors. He was Thomas McKenney, superintendent of Indian trade, and later the head of the Bureau of Indian Affairs. Because McKenney believed that settlers were destroying the Indians' ways of life, he was trying to preserve information about them. He collected clothing, weapons, samples of medicine, and other objects Indians used.

"Perfect Likenesses"

McKenney also wanted a record of how the Indians looked and dressed. In the days before photography, drawings and paintings were the usual way to record how people looked. So McKenney persuaded the delegates to have their portraits painted. He asked artist Charles Bird King to make "perfect likenesses," showing not only the faces of his subjects, but also their clothing and the way they wore their hair. King made many paintings of the Plains delegation. He sent a portrait home with each delegate and McKenney kept eight to hang in his office. These were the first of many paintings McKenney would collect.

• 257

A Note from the Author	P8
Introducing Scholar's Tool Kits	
Archaeology	1
Ozette: A Buried Village	
Maps	85
The Strait of Magellan	
Public Records	173
Revolutionary War Pension Files	
Pictures	257
Portraits of Indian Leaders	
Oral History	341
Life Under Slavery	
Memoirs	459
The Battle of Gettysburg	

Critical Thinking

1. Compare the portrait with the lithograph. Do you think the lithograph is a "perfect likeness"? Which would you trust more?

The painting on the left is Charles Bird King's 1828 portrait of Hoowaunneka (Little Elk) of the Winnebago delegation. Henry Inman painted a copy, from which the lithograph on the right was made.

McKenney thought of the paintings as tools for future historians. He also saw them as a way to get rich. McKenney knew that people all over the world were curious about American Indians. His idea was to publish copies of the paintings in books and sell the books here and in Europe.

Luckily for McKenney, a new printing method called lithography had come to the United States from Europe in 1818. Pictures made by this process are called lithographs. Lithography was quicker and cheaper than older methods of printing pictures. Now even ordinary people could afford prints of paintings, drawings, and maps.

The German inventor of lithography based the process on the fact that grease and water do not mix. First he drew a picture on a stone with a greasy crayon. Then he spread water on the stone. The water dampened the stone but not the crayon lines. Next he smeared greasy ink on the stone. The ink did not stick to the damp parts of the stone, but it did stick to the crayon. Finally the lithographer pressed heavy paper onto the stone. The picture printed on the paper. Because the printer could use only one color of ink at a time, the print was usually black. Someone would then paint the colors on it by hand.

To make lithographs of Charles Bird King's paintings, McKenney hired another artist, Henry Inman, to copy the paintings. Next, a lithographer...

Critical Thinking

2. If you were trying to find out about one of the Indians who visited Washington, what kind of information could you gain from a lithograph that you...

When the 20 volumes of the *History of the Indian Tribes of North America* were published between 1834 and 1844, they included hand-colored lithographs of 120 Indians. McKenney advertised the pictures as "perfect likenesses."

A Lasting Record

Meanwhile, many of the original paintings were sent to the Smithsonian Institution, where, tragically, a fire destroyed most of them in 1865. Whether or not McKenney's lithographs are perfect likenesses, historians are lucky they exist. Inman's copies and McKenney's lithographs are now the only portraits we have of some of the most famous Indians who lived in the early 1800s.

Historians and anthropologists use the lithographs as a valuable source of information. A historian might want to see, for example, which Indians were awarded medals. An anthropologist might compare the clothing worn by members of different tribes.

In the mid-1800s, photography began to take the place of lithography as a way of copying works of art. For example, the pictures of paintings you see in this book are photographs of the paintings. Like lithographs, photographs give us information about people, places, events, and works of art we would not otherwise see. Images captured today in photographs, as well as on film and videotape, will be data for historians in the future.

Critical Thinking

3. An artist's point of view affects how he or she portrays a subject. What attitudes did King express? Are King's paintings a reliable source of information?

Scholar at Work

As a class, choose a building, person, or event in your community. Work with a partner to draw a detailed picture of the subject. Then display the class's pictures. With your partner, imagine that you are historians 100 years from now. What questions would you ask yourselves about the pictures? Write a brief report explaining what you might learn. What other sources of information might you check?

• ix

Beginning the Story with

Most students find that stories about people are the most interesting part of history. Each chapter in this book begins with the story of a person or group of people. Some of the people are famous; some are not. Most of the stories tell something about the people when they were near your age. All the people in the stories are representative of those who lived during the time period. Remembering their stories will help you remember the significance of that period in history.

The Stone Seekers	8
Prince Henry the Navigator	36
Christopher Columbus	60
Bartolomé de Las Casas	92
Pocahontas	118
Benjamin Franklin	144
George Washington	180
Joseph Martin	204
James Madison	232
Abigail Adams	264
Tecumseh	290
The Mill Girls	316
Andrew Jackson	348
John and Jessie Frémont	374
Frederick Douglass	404
Sojourner Truth	430
Abraham Lincoln	466
Clara Barton	490
Susie King Taylor	524

Link to Art

Throughout our history, artists have expressed themselves in works that give us a sense of what life in America was like. Their drawings, paintings, sculpture, architecture, and other creations reflect America as they knew it, from important events to broad themes to images of daily life. The Link to Art feature found in each chapter provides us with a window on the past.

Link to Art

Landscape with a Lake (1804) During Jefferson's presidency, American painting entered the Romantic period. Romantic artists celebrated the beauty of nature. Their work reflected feelings of hope and nationalism as Americans expanded into new lands. During his painting career, Washington Allston developed a "love for the wild and marvelous." In this painting, he contrasts the majesty of nature with the tiny human figure. **Discuss** Do you think the artist intended to depict nature as friendly or dangerous? Explain your answer.

On his return home, Pike wrote a popular book about his journey. In it he praised the Spanish settlers in New Mexico for their "heaven-like qualities of hospitality and kindness." Pike also described the sea of grass that covered much of the whole region, calling it a desert. Later, mapmakers would label the Great Plains as desert. For the next half century, settlers would avoid this region.

296 • Chapter 11 1801–1815

⭐ 1. Section Review

1. Define **judicial review.**
2. What reasons did the United States have for purchasing Louisiana?
3. **Critical Thinking** How might a map of the United States look different today if all Presidents had followed a strict construction of the Constitution?

Emergence of the Clowns by Roxanne Swentzell	21
Benin Bronze	42
Inuit Man and Woman with Child by John White	75
Church of Santa Clara, Tunja, Colombia	103
The Peaceable Kingdom by Edward Hicks	137
Sarah Furman Warner's Quilt	149
The Bloody Massacre by Paul Revere	191
Washington Crossing the Delaware by Emanuel Leutze	217
Signing the Constitution by Howard Chandler Christy	243
The Federal Style	268
Landscape with a Lake by Washington Allston	298
The War of Independence by Juan O'Gorman	329
Bull Dance, Mandan O-Kee-Pa Ceremony by George Catlin	360
The Trapper's Bride by Alfred Jacob Miller	378
Harriet Powers's Bible Quilt	415
Landscape with Rainbow by Robert S. Duncanson	454
John Brown Going to His Hanging by Horace Pippin	481
Sounding Reveille by Winslow Homer	496
Aspects of Negro Life: From Slavery through Reconstruction by Aaron Douglas	541

World Link

This book is primarily about United States history. Yet the history of our nation has always been linked to happenings in other parts of the world. In each chapter you will learn how events or people in other countries affected our nation's history.

The Spread of Agriculture	13
Polynesian Navigators	47
Expulsion of Jews from Spain	65
Cimarrons	111
Huguenots Flee France	134
War Between England and France	164
The British in India	185
Spanish Settlers in California	218
The China Trade	238
Kamehameha Unifies Hawaii	275
Haiti Breaks Free	296
Russia Claims Much of Pacific Northwest	331
The Panama Congress	351
"Golden Mountain"	397
The Great Famine in Ireland	421
Britain Abolishes Slavery	442
Freedom for Russian Serfs	483
Britain Stays Neutral in Civil War	508
Europeans Divide Up Africa	542

Link to the Present

Have you ever asked, "What does history have to do with my life?" As you read each chapter, you will find a Link to the Present that provides one example of how the past has influenced life today.

Indian as a Term	10
The Appeal of Spices	50
Tomorrow's Explorers	76
Lost Treasure Ships	96
Lost Settlement Found	124
Gullah	160
Boycotts	190
The Information Superhighway	207
The 27th Amendment	248
New Columbia?	282
Sea Piracy Today	300
Women in the Work Force	320
The Cherokee Nation	363
Santa Fe Then and Now	379
Buxton Reunions	417
The Environmental Movement	436
Election Campaigns Today	480
The American Red Cross	506
Juneteenth	529

Point of View

Today's news reports often feature people expressing conflicting points of view. In the past, too, people had different opinions on the issues of the day. Furthermore, historians often disagree about how to interpret past events. In each chapter's Point of View feature, you will read about different perspectives on a historical issue.

When did the first settlers migrate to America? 11

Why did the Chinese voyages stop? 48

How did the slave trade affect Africa? 71

How should Spaniards treat Indians? 103

Are there limits to liberty? 130

How should children be educated? 156

Did the colonies owe obedience to Britain? 188

Lexington: Who fired the first shot? 207

Should the Constitution be ratified? 247

Are there limits to freedom of the press? 282

Did the Court attack the President's power? 294

Was the Missouri Compromise good for the nation? 335

Can a state disobey the federal government? 357

Why did Texans declare their independence? 383

Who is a true American? 421

What did women think about the vote? 450

Is secession ever justifiable? 482

Should the Union have refused to enlist African Americans? 497

Were Jim Crow laws to be taken seriously? 541

Hands-On HISTORY

History is not just a subject for you to read. It is also something you can "do." The activities described in each Hands-On History feature will give you a chance to recreate or interact with some aspect of our nation's past. In addition to the Hands-On Histories listed here, you will also find them at the beginning of each unit and in the "Beginning the Story with . . ." feature at the start of each chapter.

Recreating a Temple Treasure	17
Designing a Book	52
Simulating the Spread of Smallpox	69
Planning a Modern-Day Entrada	97
Advertising the Colonies	136
Writing Rules of Conduct	152
Classifying Types of Protest	196
Promoting the Declaration of Independence Exhibit	212
Proposing an Amendment	251
Designing Political Party Symbols	283
Designing a Peace Medal	297
Making Compromises	335
Planning an Inauguration	354
Making Decisions on the Trail	388
Analyzing How You Use Space	416
Speaking to Persuade	435
Creating an Advertisement for Kansas	475
Commemorating the Civil War	514
Getting Out the Vote	533

Skill Lab

In science classes, you participate in labs where you practice skills used in scientific study. In this book, the Skill Lab in each chapter gives you a chance to learn and apply skills used by historians. The labs will help you develop skills in acquiring information, thinking critically, and using information. You can use these skills in everyday problem solving and decision making as well as in your study of history.

Acquiring Information

Time Lines	31
Reading History	43
Historical Research	79
Analyzing a Painting	107
Analyzing Statistical Tables	139
Analyzing Graphs	167

Thinking Critically

Primary and Secondary Sources	193
Statements of Fact and Opinions	210
Point of View	249
Cause and Effect	285
Detecting Bias	309
Generalizations	337
Recognizing Stereotypes	369
Determining Credibility	392
Identifying Evidence	423
Historical Interpretations	446

Using Information

Asking Historical Questions	477
Making a Hypothesis	510
Making Decisions	537

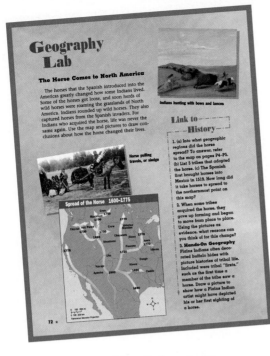

Geography Lab

You cannot fully understand history without also understanding geography. When you think of geography you may think of maps, but geography is much more than reading maps. The Geography Lab in each chapter has readings and pictures as well as maps to help you learn how geography influenced history—and how history influenced geography.

The Colorado Plateau — 24
Comparing Historical and Modern Maps — 55
The Horse Comes to North America — 72
Reading a Terrain Map — 100
The Coastal Lowlands — 127
The Atlantic Slave Trade — 161
Colonial Communication — 199
Reading a War Map — 220
The Central Lowlands — 240
Reading a Population Density Map — 271
The Rocky Mountains — 299
Steamboats and Westward Expansion — 327
From Forest to Farm — 355
Basins and Ranges — 399
Reading Climate Maps — 413
The First Big City Park — 439
The Appalachian Mountains — 485
Reading a Grid Map — 517
The Civil War and Southern Agriculture — 545

Alternative Assessment

As you study history, you and your teacher will want to know how much you are learning. Your teacher will probably give you paper-and-pencil tests to assess your knowledge and skills. In the Chapter Survey, you will also have the opportunity to demonstrate what you have learned through an alternative assessment activity. To receive a good evaluation of your work, you will need to be sure to meet the criteria provided.

Preparing a Museum Exhibit	33
Teaching a Class at Sagres	57
Holding a Debate	81
Recalling a Life	115
Planning a Colony	141
Creating a Mural	169
Role-Playing the Continental Congress	201
Acting Out Opposing Roles	227
Creating a Constitution Exhibit	255
Campaigning for President	287
Creating a Front Page	311
Writing About Current Events	339
Journal Writing	371
Planning a Western	401
Planning a Time Capsule	425
Working for Reform	457
Covering the 1860 Election on TV	487
Writing a Play	519
Improving on Reconstruction	547

Link to Literature

Just as artists give us visual pictures of the past, writers of literature give us word pictures of the past. Sometimes works of literature are based on true events, but often they are fiction. In each unit, you will read a short segment of a work of literature that will help you better understand the time period. Perhaps the segment will make you want to read the whole book from which it was taken.

Morning Girl by Michael Dorris — 82

The Witch of Blackbird Pond by Elizabeth George Speare — 170

April Morning by Howard Fast — 228

The Journals of Lewis and Clark — 312

Nightjohn by Gary Paulsen — 426

Bull Run by Paul Fleischman — 520

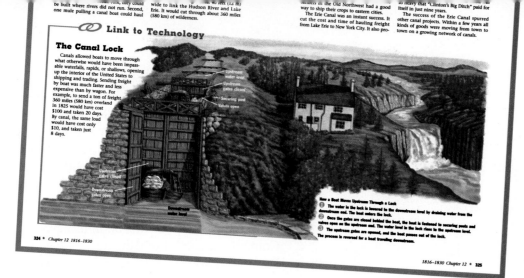

(Chapter 12 spread, pages 324–325)

Link to Technology

The Canal Lock

Canals allowed boats to move through what otherwise would have been impassable waterfalls, rapids, or shallows, opening up the interior of the United States to shipping and trading. Sending freight by boat was much faster and less expensive than by wagon. For example, to send a ton of freight 360 miles (580 km) overland in 1825 would have cost $100 and taken 20 days. By canal, the same load would have cost only $10, and taken just 8 days.

be built where rivers did not run. Second, one mule pulling a canal boat could haul

wide to link the Hudson River and Lake Erie. It would cut through about 360 miles (580 km) of wilderness.

way to ship their crops to eastern cities. The Erie Canal was an instant success. It cut the cost and time of hauling freight from Lake Erie to New York City. It also pro-

so heavy that "Clinton's Big Ditch" paid for itself in just nine years.
The success of the Erie Canal spurred other canal projects. Within a few years all kinds of goods were moving from town to town on a growing network of canals.

Upstream water level
Upstream gates closed
Securing post
Valves open

Upstream gates closed
Downstream gates open
Downstream water level

How a Boat Moves Upstream Through a Lock
1 The water in the lock is lowered to the downstream level by draining water from the downstream end. The boat enters the lock.
2 Once the gates are closed behind the boat, the boat is fastened to securing posts and valves open on the upstream end. The water level in the lock rises to the upstream level.
3 The upstream gates are opened, and the boat passes out of the lock.
The process is reversed for a boat traveling downstream.

Link to Technology

Some of the most dramatic changes in our nation have resulted from technological inventions. In each unit you will learn about one advance in technology, illustrated by diagrams or cutaway drawings.

The Birchbark Canoe 26
A Colonial Sawmill 151
Minting a Coin 237
The Canal Lock 324
The Telegraph 408
The Camera 502

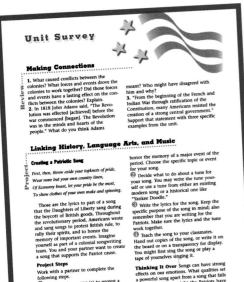

Unit Survey

Making Connections

Review:

1. What caused conflicts between the colonies? What forces and events drove the colonies to work together? Did those forces and events have a lasting effect on the conflicts between the colonies? Explain.
2. In 1818 John Adams said, "The Revolution was effected [achieved] before the war commenced [began]. The Revolution was in the minds and hearts of the people." What do you think Adams

meant? Who might have disagreed with him and why?
3. "From the beginning of the French and Indian War through ratification of the Constitution, many Americans resisted the creation of a strong central government." Support that statement with three specific examples from the unit.

Linking History, Language Arts, and Music

Project:

Creating a Patriotic Song

First, then, throw aside your topknots of pride,
Wear none but your own country linen,
Of Economy boast, let your pride be the most,
To show clothes of your own make and spinning.

Those are the lyrics to part of a song that the Daughters of Liberty sang during the boycott of British goods. Throughout the revolutionary period, Americans wrote and sang songs to protest British rule, to rally their spirits, and to honor the memory of important events. Imagine yourself as part of a colonial songwriting team. You and your partner want to create a song that supports the Patriot cause.

Project Steps

Work with a partner to complete the following steps.
1 Plan to write a song (a) to protest a British action against the colonies, (b) to rally the Continental Army's spirits when things look grim during the war, or (c) to

honor the memory of a major event of the period. Choose the specific topic or event for your song.
2 Decide what to do about a tune for your song. You may write the tune yourself or use a tune from either an existing modern song or a historical one like "Yankee Doodle."
3 Write the lyrics for the song. Keep the specific purpose of the song in mind; also remember that you are writing for the Patriots. Make sure the lyrics and the tune work together.
4 Teach the song to your classmates. Hand out copies of the song, or write it on the board or on a transparency for display. You might first sing the song or play a tape of yourselves singing it.

Thinking It Over Songs can have strong effects on our emotions. What qualities set a powerful song apart from a song that fails to move us? How might the Patriots have felt when they heard your song? How might the Loyalists have felt?

256 •

Interdisciplinary Projects

Although this is a history book, you will discover that much of the information you learn relates to other subjects, such as science, math, and music. In each Unit Survey, you will find an interdisciplinary project that links history to one or more of these other subjects.

Healthy Foods from Around the World 84
Reconstructing the Jamestown Fort 172
Creating a Patriotic Song 256
Inventing a New Gadget 340
Writing and Illustrating Historical Fiction 458
Your State in the Civil War 548

Maps

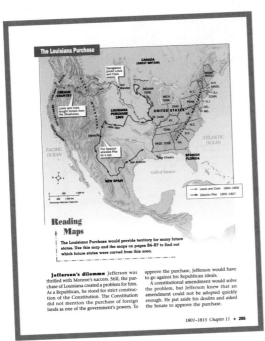

Maps are the constant companions of historians. Maps are also tools you will use in everyday life. For many centuries maps were drawn by hand. Recently, however, map makers have begun to make maps with computers.

Most of the maps in this book have been created especially for this book using computers. Computers make it possible to include all the latest geographic information and reflect the most precise detailing possible. They also enable map makers to include color and explanations that are difficult to achieve with hand-drawn maps.

Migration Routes of First Americans	11
Indian Civilizations	16
Indian Culture Areas and Tribes	29
Trade in Africa 1450	39
Trade in Asia 1450	45
Trade in Europe 1450	51
Portuguese Voyages 1420–1460	53
Voyages of Dias and da Gama	64
Voyages of Columbus 1492–1503	66
Spread of the Horse 1600–1775	72
Voyage of Magellan 1519–1521	74
Search for the Northwest Passage 1497–1610	77
Spanish Exploration in North America	98
Route of Cortés 1519	100
Spanish America 1542	101
The Spanish Borderlands	105
New France	109
Jamestown and Plymouth 1620	122
New England 1660	131
The Thirteen Colonies 1760	135

Products of the Thirteen Colonies 1760   147
Settlers from Many Lands 1770   155
Atlantic Slave Trade   161
The French and Indian War 1754–1763   183
European Claims 1750   187
European Claims 1763   187
Colonial Roads 1775   199
The War in the North 1776–1778   220
The War in the South and West 1778–1781   223
North America 1783   224
The United States 1790   235
United States Population Density 1790   271
Western Settlement 1795   277
The Louisiana Purchase   295
The Barbary States   301
The War of 1812   306
Roads and Canals 1830–1850   323
The Western Hemisphere 1825   330
The Missouri Compromise 1820   334
Election of 1824   353
Election of 1828   353
Forced Migration of Eastern Indians   362
The Texas War for Independence   384
Trails to the West   387
The Mexican-American War 1846–1848   395
The United States 1853   396
Products of the North and South Mid-1800s   407
Railroads 1850   410
Railroads 1860   410
Growing Season   413
Average Annual Precipitation   413
The Underground Railroad   444
The Spread of Slavery   474
   The Missouri Compromise 1820
   The Compromise of 1850
   The Kansas-Nebraska Act 1854

Maps

Election of 1860	482
The Union and the Confederacy	493
The Civil War 1861–1862	501
The Civil War 1863–1865	513
Gettysburg National Military Park	517
African Americans in Congress 1876 and 1896	540
The World: Political	R2
United States: Physical	R4
United States: Political	R6
Natural Vegetation of the United States	R8
Land Use in the United States	R9
Territorial Growth of the United States	R10
Population Density in the United States Today	R11
Seats in the House of Representatives	R38

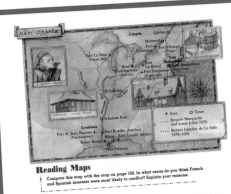

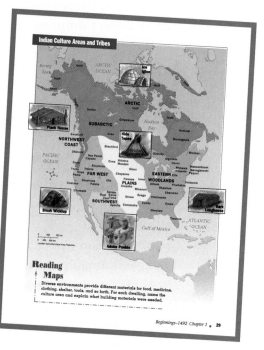

Charts, Graphs, and Diagrams

Some information is easier to undersand when it is presented in charts, graphs, and diagrams rather than in words. Throughout this book you will find these kinds of graphics. Like the maps in the text, these features are computer-generated and represent the latest techniques in data presentation.

Steps Toward the American Revolution 1763–1774

British Law	What It Did	Colonial Reaction
Proclamation of 1763	Prohibited settlement west of the Appalachians	Protests, defiance
Sugar Act (1764)	Lowered duties on molasses, but first time duties used to collect revenue; denied jury trial to accused smugglers	Protests, petitions
Stamp Act (1765)	Required all written materials to be printed on stamped paper; first direct tax to get revenue (repealed in 1766)	Stamp Act Congress, petitions, boycotts, demonstrations
Declaratory Act (1766)	Declared Parliament's right to impose any laws on colonies	Little notice because of Stamp Act repeal
Townshend Acts (1767)	Taxed tea, lead, glass, paint, and paper; governors to be paid by Parliament (most repealed in 1770)	Boycotts, riots, demonstrations
Tea Act (1773)	Required that only East India Company may import and sell tea	Boycotts, Boston Tea Party
Coercive Acts (1774) ("Intolerable Acts")	Closed Boston port until destroyed tea paid for; suspended town meetings; appointed military governor of Massachusetts; permitted trials of government officials to be in England	Other colonies sent food and money to Massachusetts; call for Continental Congress

Source: Oxford Book of Reference on English History

1754–1774 Chapter 7 • **197**

The Columbian Exchange	70
Population by Colony 1680	139
The Way People Describe Themselves 1990s	161
Colonial Trade with England 1750	167
New England's Trade with England 1750	167
Imports from England by Colony/Area 1750	167
The Jamestown Fort	172
Steps Toward the American Revolution 1763–1774	197
Land Ordinance Survey System	235
From the Articles to the Constitution	245
Federalism	250
Checks and Balances	252
Federal Court System 1789	267
The First Political Parties	280
Steamboats in the West	327
Population 1810–1860	327
Voter Participation 1824, 1828	352
An African American Yard in North Carolina 1914	416
Compromise of 1850	471
Comparing Resources of the Union and the Confederacy 1861	494
Reconstruction Begins and Ends	534
Amount of Farmland 1850–1880	545
Total Value of Farms 1850–1880	545
United States Overseas Areas	R10
Checks and Balances: How the Veto Works	R42
Limits on State and Federal Power	R47
Vice-Presidents Who Have Taken Over for Presidents	R48
The President's Many Roles	R51
The Amendment Process	R56
The Bill of Rights	R59
Electing a President	R63
Sources of Federal Income 1995	R66

Epilogue

This book focuses on the story of our nation from the time the first Americans arrived on the continent to about 1876. The Epilogue brings our country's story up to the present. It gives you an overview of each decade in pictures and words. The Epilogue ends with a project in which you and your classmates predict, based on the past and present, what the future holds for our nation and for you.

Introduction	**549**
Continuing the Story with . . .	
1865–1889	550
1890–1899	551
1900–1909	552
1910–1919	553
1920–1929	554
1930–1939	555
1940–1949	556
1950–1959	557
1960–1969	558
1970–1979	559
1980–1989	560
1990–present	561
To the Year 2025: A Wrap-Up Activity	**562**

Constitution Handbook

In this text you will read about many important documents in our country's history. No document is as important for you to understand, though, as the United States Constitution. The Constitution Handbook includes the complete text of the Constitution as well as information that can help you better understand it and appreciate its importance in your life today.

Introducing the Constitution Handbook	**R34**
The Preamble to the Constitution	**R36**
Articles of the Constitution	**R37**
Amendments to the Constitution	**R59**

Prologue
The Land

"Wilderness is the raw material out of which man has hammered . . . civilization."

Aldo Leopold

The land is the stage upon which human history unfolds. It provides people with the basic necessities of life—food, clothing, and shelter. Beyond that, the varied landscape captures our imagination and inspires us. Before there were people in the Americas, there was the land—a vast wilderness of forests, grasslands, mountains, valleys, plains, deserts, and swamps.

As the first peoples came into the Americas thousands of years ago, they learned to use the land's gifts. The land not only affected how they lived day to day, but also how they thought about their place in nature. "The earth is our mother," wrote an Abnaki Indian a centry ago. "She nourishes us. That which we put into the ground she returns to us."

Over the centuries Americans have altered the land. They have carved out farms and ranches. They have constructed dams and mines. They have built towns of brick and timber and cities of concrete and steel, linking them with steel railroads, asphalt highways, and invisible electronic networks. Even though most Americans today live in towns and cities, they still depend on the land for resources, recreation, and inspiration. To understand the story of the United States and its people, we need to start by looking at the land.

In this Prologue, students explore the features of the land that became the United States and reflect upon ways these features have both shaped and been shaped by human history. To introduce the Prologue, bring to class books and magazines with pictures of different places and regions in the United States. Invite students to look at the photos, noting the vast geographic diversity. Have them point out photos that illustrate the quotation from Aldo Leopold on the student page: "Wilderness is the raw material out of which man has hammered . . . civilization."

Setting the Stage
Activity

Relating to the Land

To focus students' attention on their relationship with the land, make a chart on the chalkboard. In the first column, have volunteers list activities during a typical day. In the second column, have them describe how each activity affected or was affected by the land. Examples: "Got dressed," "Cotton for clothes grown in cotton fields"; "Took a shower," "Water from dammed river"; "Took the bus to school," "Used fossil fuel." Discuss why understanding their relationship with the land might be important, such as to ensure protection of resources.

The American Landscape

Have students work in small groups to compile lists of the types of terrain and other features indicated on the map on these pages (for example, mountains, forests, lakes and rivers, deserts, and plains). Ask a representative from one group to share its list with the class. Ask representatives of the other groups to add to the list as needed. Invite students to share experiences they may have had with the areas or types of terrain listed.

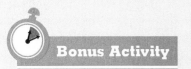

Bonus Activity

Naming the Land

To help students recognize that at one time the land had no people and thus no names, have them give their own names to parts of what is now the United States. Give students outline maps (see **Geography Extensions** in Teacher's Resource Package) or have them trace the map on these pages. Have them indicate ten geographic features on their maps (for example, areas, rivers, lakes, mountain ranges, or peaks) and label them with names of their choosing. Have the class compare their maps and the names they have given.

* Geography Footnote

Writer John Steinbeck, in his book *America and Americans,* makes a connection between the landscape and the people of the United States who have come together from all over the world:

> Something happened in America to create the Americans. Perhaps it was the grandeur of the land—the lordly mountains, the mystery of deserts, the ache of storms, cyclones—the enormous sweetness and violence of the country which, acting on restless, driven peoples from the outside world, made them taller than their ancestors, stronger than their fathers—and made them all Americans.

The American Landscape

Throughout this book you will be using many kinds of maps to help you see where things happened, what the land was like, and how geography and history are linked.

The picture map on these pages shows what the land that is now the United States looked like at the time people first arrived. As you can see, it was remarkably beautiful and varied. It was also a landscape without names.

Geography Footnote

Below are some statistical comparisons.

• Mount McKinley, in Alaska, is the highest peak in North America at 20,320 feet (6,194 m) above sea level. There are many higher peaks in South America and Asia. Mount Everest, at over 29,000 feet (8,839 m), is the highest in the world.

• With a length of 3,710 miles (5,971 km), the combined Mississippi–Missouri River system is the third longest in the world, after the Nile and the Amazon.

• Together, the Great Lakes comprise the largest body of fresh water in the world.

• The U.S., with a total area of nearly four million square miles, is among the largest countries in the world. Canada and China are larger, and Russia, with more than six million square miles, is by far the largest.

Using Map Skills

To get the most out of maps, you need to use a variety of map skills. These skills include reading keys, locating features, estimating distances, and interpreting visual patterns. Locate the following features on this map. Then use the physical map of the United States on pages R4–R5 to name each feature.

1. The longest mountain chain
2. The five largest bodies of fresh water
3. The longest river
4. An island chain
5. The largest area of flat land
6. The easternmost mountain range

● **P3**

Checking Understanding

1. What kind of information is included on this map? (Physical features of the land, such as mountains, forests, lakes, and plains.)

2. Why are there boxes around two areas? (To show that they are not positioned accurately in relation to the larger land mass and that they are not drawn to the same scale.)

Stimulating Critical Thinking

3. Why do you think that some of the features of this map, such as trees, mountains, and buffalo, are out of proportion? (The map is meant to provide information about the landscape, not about the size of the features.)

4. How else might you represent the information on this map? (Students may suggest a three-dimensional model, or a collection of photographs.)

Using Map Skills
Answers

1. Rocky Mountains
2. Lakes Michigan, Superior, Huron, Erie, and Ontario
3. Mississippi River
4. Hawaii
5. Great Plains
6. Appalachian Mountains

Teaching
Geographic Regions

Using a wall map or a rough outline of the continental United States drawn on the chalkboard, point to different areas and ask students to attach a label to each. Elicit responses that reflect position ("northeast"), geographic features ("coast"), political divisions ("Florida"), and other characteristics. Ask if students are familiar with terms such as "Rust Belt" (an older industrialized area, such as the Northeast) or "Sun Belt" (the South/Southwest).

Point out that geographers use many different labels, depending on what aspects they wish to describe. The regions labeled on this map are widely accepted, but are not the only ones applied to the United States.

Bonus Activity

Writing a Poem

To focus on the characteristics of American geographic regions, have students write descriptive poems or brief essays. Poems may rhyme or be in blank verse. Have each student choose a geographic region from the map to write about. To help them get started, show photographs of the landscape. Suggest that they include descriptive words and phrases as well as feelings the region inspires. They might illustrate their poems and combine their efforts into an anthology.

P4

Names of states with roots in Indian words that describe the terrain include:
- *Connecticut,* from Mohican and Algonquin words for "long river place."
- *Michigan,* from the Chippewa *mici gama,* or "great water" (Lake Michigan).
- *Minnesota,* from the Dakota Sioux word meaning "cloudy water" or "sky-tinted water" (the Minnesota River).
- *Mississippi,* from the Chippewa words *mici* and *zibi* ("great river").
- *Nebraska,* from the Omaha or Otos word for "flat river" or "broad water," referring to the Platte River.
- *Ohio,* from an Iroquois word meaning "fine or good river."
- *Wyoming,* from an Algonquin word meaning "large prairie place."

Geographic Regions

Geographers divide the United States into regions in order to study geographic patterns. They describe a region as an area with some feature or features that set it apart from other areas.

A region may be defined by natural features, such as climate or types of vegetation. A region can also be defined by human features, such as cultural heritage or main industry. The regions shown on this map are geographic regions, defined according to the physical characteristics of the land.

Rocky Mountains

Western Plateaus

Pacific Mountains and Valleys

Basins and Ranges

Western Plateaus

Great Plains

P4 ●

Geography Footnote

The Basin and Range region is known for its extremes. The lowest land elevation in the Western Hemisphere is at Badwater, in California's Death Valley. It lies 282 feet (86 m) below sea level. Death Valley was named by a group of gold seekers who mistakenly entered the valley in 1849 and lost one of their party to the extreme conditions there. Rainfall averages about two inches (5.08 cm) a year, and temperatures, among the highest in the world, have exceeded 130°F (54°C). Only 75 miles (120 km) from Death Valley rises Mt. Whitney. At 14,494 feet (4,418 m), it is the highest point in the continental United States.

Canadian Shield

Central Lowlands

Interior Highlands

Appalachian Highlands

Coastal Lowlands

Developing a Mental Map

A mental map is a picture you carry in your head of how an area looks and where things are located. You use a mental map to find your way around your school and community. This year you will be expanding your mental map of the United States, beginning with your region.

1. Which region of the United States do you live in?

2. What features seem to set your region apart from those around it?

3. Based on your own mental map, list five features of your region.

Ask students to imagine that the United States is located on a tropical island. How might the nation have developed differently? What types of industry might have been developed? Could the nation have become a world political power? As students look at the photographs on this page, discuss the role that the geography of the country—including its size and its varied topography and resources—may have played in its political and social development.

Bonus Activity

Cause-Effect Chains

To illustrate the relationship between geography and history, have small groups create cause-and-effect chains or webs. First, they should identify geographic characteristics of your region. (They may define the region broadly, for instance as "Pacific Mountains and Valleys," or more narrowly, as "Central Valley of California.") Then they identify how the geography and human activities have affected each other. An example, using California's Central Valley, might be: *Causes:* fertile land, lack of rainfall, San Joaquin River. *Effect:* canals dug to bring river water. *Effect:* successful farms. *Effect:* attracted more settlers, who dammed rivers, built towns and cities. Discuss the completed chains with the class as a whole.

✴ Geography Footnote

John Muir, a naturalist and writer, had an important influence on the history of the American landscape. Muir spent years exploring and writing about the mountains of California. In the early 1870s his articles describing the natural beauties of Yosemite Valley attracted thousands of tourists there. By 1889, however, tourism and overgrazing by sheep and cattle were threatening to destroy the area. Muir and Robert Underwood Johnson, an editor of *Century* magazine, campaigned to save Yosemite. In lectures and articles Muir urged the public to support the protection of Yosemite. Meanwhile, Johnson was in Washington fighting the opposition of ranchers and tour companies. Muir and Johnson were victorious: In 1890 Congress passed legislation creating Yosemite National Park.

Geography and History

Geography and history are closely linked. The land is the geographic setting for the human drama we call history. It provides the raw materials out of which humans shape their cultures and civilizations. The way people use these materials changes over time as different players set foot on the stage of history.

Rocky Mountains

Western Plateaus

Basins and Ranges

Pacific Mountains and Valleys

Western Plateaus

Great Plains

Gold mining in California

Rancheros in Texas

✳ Geography Footnote

The Dust Bowl of the 1930s is an example of how changes in human behavior can affect geography. Until World War I, the area of the Oklahoma and Texas panhandles and bordering sections of Kansas, Colorado, and New Mexico was largely grazing lands. New farm machinery, combined with rising wheat prices during the war, encouraged farmers to plow up the grasslands and plant wheat. When a severe drought struck between 1934 and 1937, the soil, deprived of its anchoring grass root system, was swept away. Dust blackened the sky, choked cattle, and forced more than half of the population to flee their ruined farms. Millions of acres suffered damage. As a result of the disaster, new farming methods were adopted, including contour plowing to retain water and anchoring the soil with grass and trees.

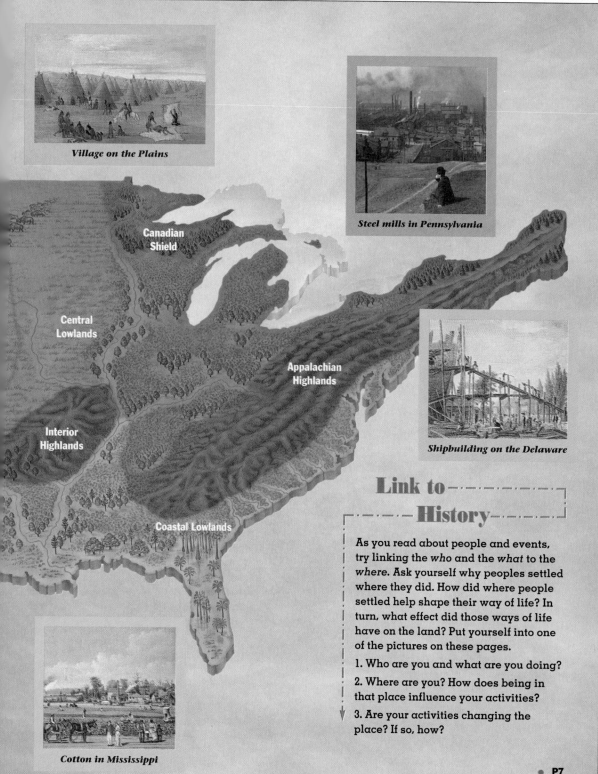

Village on the Plains

Steel mills in Pennsylvania

Canadian Shield

Central Lowlands

Appalachian Highlands

Interior Highlands

Shipbuilding on the Delaware

Coastal Lowlands

Cotton in Mississippi

Link to History

As you read about people and events, try linking the *who* and the *what* to the *where*. Ask yourself why peoples settled where they did. How did where people settled help shape their way of life? In turn, what effect did those ways of life have on the land? Put yourself into one of the pictures on these pages.

1. Who are you and what are you doing?

2. Where are you? How does being in that place influence your activities?

3. Are your activities changing the place? If so, how?

● **P7**

(Top) Dr. Viola in his home office, and (bottom) seeking out clues to history in the Congressional Cemetery.

A Note from the Author . . .

Introducing Scholar's Tool Kits

Did you ever wonder how historians are able to write about the past? It is not a secret. Anyone who has a curious mind, likes to solve mysteries, and knows how to use the "tools" of historical scholarship can "do" history.

Historians build knowledge much like carpenters build houses, only their tools are unlike anything a carpenter would use. A scholar's tools are ancient bones, pots, jewelry, and sculpture. They are drawings, maps, lithographs, and photographs. They are stories and remembrances passed down from person to person. They are letters, diaries, and newspapers. They are, in fact, anything that helps unlock the mysteries of history.

A scholar's tools, you will see, are easy to learn about and fascinating to use. The six Scholar's Tool Kits in this book each tell about how one tool is used, and give you a chance to try out "doing" history.

As you read the stories and information in this or any history book, think about the tools the historian who wrote the book used to learn about the past. What questions are still unanswered? What tools would you use to answer them? You will soon see that you, too, can use the tools of history to recreate the past.

Sincerely,

Herman J. Viola

Herman J. Viola

Objectives

★ Describe the tools and methods used by archaeologists.

★ Identify the kinds of information that archaeologists can acquire from artifacts and ruins.

★ Explain how historians can use archae-ological information to draw conclusions about past cultures.

How Do We Know?

Scholar's Tool Kit
Archaeology

You can see the archaeologists' camp in this photo of the Ozette site.

The rain had been falling for days—far more heavily than usual. Nearby creeks overflowed. The ground, with its tangle of trees, shrubs, and vines, was soaked. In the little seaside village of Ozette, the people stayed home, carving, weaving, and repairing tools for fishing and whale hunts.

The mudslide came suddenly. The water-soaked soil on the hill behind the houses gave way, and tons of dirt, rocks, trees, and brush poured into the village. Mud and debris flowed over eight houses, sealing up all their contents. There the houses stayed, buried and undisturbed, for almost 500 years.

Using Science to Unlock the Past

The mudslide was a disaster for the people of Ozette, a Makah Indian village in what is now the state of Washington. To historians and to today's Makahs, though, the site is a priceless treasure. Because the early Makahs left no written records, historians knew little about how they lived—until scientists unearthed the buried village. There they found hundreds of clues to how the Makah people had lived in the past.

Anthropologists are scientists who study human beings and how they live in groups. Anthropologists who search for clues to how human beings lived in the past are called **archaeologists**. Among the clues that archaeologists study are **artifacts**—objects made by human work—as well as remains of bones and teeth. Archaeologists also look for larger pieces of evidence, such as ruins of buildings.

● 1

Introducing
How Do We Know?

Archaeology

Check what students already know about archaeology by asking what the term calls to mind. List answers on the chalkboard. Then explain what archaeology is and ask students how it relates to history. Have them think of some types of things people of the past might have left and how those things might serve as evidence of how they lived.

By reading about the Ozette site, students will follow a case study in how historians use archaeology as a tool. Before the site was discov-ered, historians had little knowledge of the way of life of early Makahs. The ancient Makahs left no written records. Historians used the physical evidence archaeology provided to draw conclusions about the history of the Makahs in Ozette.

Setting the Stage
Activity

Imagining a Dig Site

Have students imagine the ruins of their town being uncovered by future archaeologists 500 years from now. Have them list objects that are likely to survive and consider what conclusions future archae-ologists might draw from that evidence. They should note the ways the evidence might be misinterpreted.

Critical Thinking
Answers

1. Students might identify berry-stained dishes and baskets, berries, roots, paste made from roots, and sea plants as evidence that the Makahs ate these foods.

2. Evidence of trade might include foods or goods made from resources not found in the natural environment around Makah villages.

3. Responses will vary, depending on the presence of archaeological sites near the students' communities. If there are nearby sites, students should identify the following: the location of the site, the peoples who inhabited the site in the past, the artifacts found, and the goals of the archaeologists investigating the site.

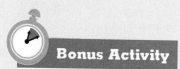

Bonus Activity

Sketching Ozette

To help students synthesize information about the Ozette community, have them draw the village and its environment. Have them refer to the description in the section titled "Telling the Story of an Ancient People." Students might display their sketches and tell why they included certain details.

✳ History Footnote

At Ozette, archaeologists were surprised to find steel knives and chisels. Never before were steel tools found in sites that predated European or American contact with Indians. Where did the steel tools come from? Archaeologists have identified Japan as a possible source. From written Japanese records and their own examination of the tools, they know that the composition of the steel is like that of primitive steel from Japan. How did the Makahs acquire the tools? Historians know of disabled Japanese junks that drifted across the ocean and came ashore in the Americas. Maybe the tools were taken from one of these junks. Perhaps the Makahs traded for tools with other coastal Americans who had some link with Japan. The source of the tools and how the Makahs acquired them remain a mystery.

Archaeologist Richard Daugherty and Makah crew member Meri Flinn carefully open a fragile basket. Even the contents of the carrying basket—rolls of cedar bark—were preserved by the mud.

❓ Critical Thinking

1. Peoples along the Northwest Coast relied heavily on the sea for survival. As an archaeologist, what evidence would you look for at Ozette to show that the Makahs relied on the sea? Why?

Dating artifacts To help figure out the age of their findings, archaeologists use many methods. The most common method of dating the remains of ancient plants, animals, and human beings is **radiocarbon dating**. This technique is based on the fact that all living things absorb radiocarbon from the atmosphere. This radiocarbon decays at a steady rate, even after the plant or animal dies. By measuring the amount of radiocarbon remaining in an item, scientists can figure out its age.

Searching for Clues

❓ Critical Thinking

2. Some tribes were involved in trade up and down the Northwest Coast. What would you look for as evidence of extensive trading? Why?

When the Makah Tribal Council asked archaeologist Richard D. Daugherty to study Ozette, he eagerly agreed. Daugherty put together a team of scientists aided by students, some of whom were Makah Indians. First the team took photographs and made a map. Then they began the long, delicate process of excavating—uncovering—the site inch by inch. Because the artifacts were so fragile, the excavators used a fine spray of water rather than metal tools. Team members made a record of everything they found and carefully protected the artifacts.

This wooden owl club was likely used in ceremonies.

In all, the archaeologists found more than 55,000 artifacts at Ozette—timbers and benches from houses, nets, cedar bark baskets, sleeping mats, cradles, tools used for woodworking, carved cedar boxes, wooden dishes, and paddles. These items were beautifully preserved by the mud.

Connections to Science

The Ozette artifacts had absorbed water from the mud. Archaeologists faced the challenge of preserving the fragile artifacts so they could study and display them. They placed them in a chemical solution that penetrated the items and replaced the molecules of water. After a month of soaking, the artifacts were hard enough to be handled without damaging them.

By using radiocarbon dating and other dating techniques, the scientists learned that the mudslide at Ozette took place between 300 and 500 years ago—perhaps about the same time that the explorer Christopher Columbus reached the Americas.

Telling the Story of an Ancient People

Using the findings at Ozette as well as the knowledge of Makah tribal elders, archaeologists have pieced together a picture of the lives of the early Makah people. For example, we know that the sea was all-important to the Makah way of life. Houses faced the beach, where canoes could be landed. Tools included devices used to hunt whales and seals, to fish for halibut and salmon, and to collect clams, crabs, and other shellfish. Evidence also showed that the Makahs relied on the forests nearby for cedar to build houses and make tools and ceremonial objects. Three looms and the folded remains of a blanket woven of dog hair, cattail fluff, feathers, and cedar bark show that early Makahs were weavers.

Archaeologists' discoveries at Ozette changed some old theories and raised new questions about the lives of early coast Indian people. They also gave today's Makahs fresh insight into their own past.

Scholar at Work

Imagine that your classroom has been buried in a mudslide. It is now 500 years in the future, and archaeologists have discovered the burial and excavated it.

Make an excavation map of the site (your classroom) by making a string grid across the room. List the artifacts that an archaeologist would find within each grid square. What hypotheses might these scientists make about the date of the slide and about the people who "inhabited" this site?

? Critical Thinking

3. Is there an archaeological site in or near your community? If so, describe the site. What do the archaeologists hope to learn? What kind of artifacts have they found?

Checking Understanding

1. Why did the Makahs and the archaeologists value the Ozette ruins? (They discovered important information about the way of life of early Makah people.)

2. What characteristics of radiocarbon enable scientists to use it to date artifacts? (Radiocarbon decays at a known, steady rate.)

3. What evidence provides information that the early Makahs hunted sea life? (Tools used to hunt and collect sea life were found.)

4. How did archaeologists determine when the mudslide occurred? (Archaeologists based their determination on the radiocarbon dates of artifacts buried by the slide.)

Teaching the Scholar at Work

Students can work together to create the grid in the classroom, using masking tape and kite string. They should identify each grid section by letter. Then assign students to investigate specific sections. In examining a section, each student should study all surfaces including walls and floors as well as the artifacts. If you are unable to grid the classroom, have students make a scale drawing of the room on graph paper. Before students draw conclusions about the artifacts, have them imagine which objects future archaeologists might not be familiar with.

Introducing the Unit

Navajo Rock Painting

The painting depicts a procession of Spanish cavalry across Navajo land. It is thought that the painting shows soldiers led by Lieutenant Antonio Narbona, who attacked the Navajos at Massacre Cave in 1805.

Throughout this unit, students study the quest for trade that led to European exploration. This exploration resulted in the presence of armed Europeans in America and forever altered the way of life of American Indians.

Teaching the
Hands-On
- - - - - - - ► *HISTORY*

To help students retell the story, focus attention on the elements of the rock painting by asking questions such as: **Where do you think the group is going?** Point out that the central figure in black may have been the leader of the group. Ask: **Why might the painter have depicted the leader differently from the others?** You may wish to have groups of students work together in choosing a method of storytelling and preparing a story. Several stories might be presented to the class, followed by discussion on similarities and differences between them.

Unit Overview

For thousands of years, diverse cultures developed in the Americas, independent of European, Asian, or African cultures. The unit focuses on what led to the first contacts between Europe, Africa, and the Americas.

By the 1400s Muslim traders controlled overland trade routes between Europe, Asia, and Africa. China traded directly with India, Africa, and the Middle East before withdrawing its fleet. Seeking direct trade with Africa and Asia, Portugal explored Africa's west coast in the mid 1400s.

Spain sponsored Columbus's quest for a western route. His voyages led to an exchange of plants, animals, diseases, and people that would impact both sides of the Atlantic. They also spurred a race between Spain, England, the Netherlands, and France for a water route west to Asia.

Unit 1

Beginnings–1610

Chapters

1. **The First Americans**

2. **Africa, Asia, and Europe in the 1400s**

3. **Voyages of Exploration**

Hands-On
- - - - - - - - - ► *HISTORY*

Activity

People tell stories in many ways—with spoken words and written words, in song, dance, puppetry, and pantomime, to name a few. Pictures also tell stories. The pictures you see here were made on red sandstone walls just above a narrow ledge in Canyon de Chelly. They tell the story of the arrival of a group of Spaniards accompanied by an Indian. Suppose that you want to pass the story down to younger people. Choose a different method of storytelling and retell the story as you see it.

Navajo mural, Canyon de Chelly, Arizona

4 ●

See the Unit 1 activity in **Wall Time Line Activities.**

See the Unit 1 activity in **Wall Time Line Activities.**

Three Worlds Meet

Checking Understanding

1. **What are the riders carrying?** (Guns)

2. **What animals other than horses does the painting show?** (Dogs)

Stimulating Critical Thinking

3. **Why do you think the artist chose to depict the Spanish riders?** (Students may indicate that the painter chose the subject because of the strong impact of the Spanish intruders on the Navajos.)

4. **Why do you think the artist decided to paint on rock rather than paper?** (Accept logical responses, such as the fact that rock painting was traditional for Navajos.)

For an in-depth unit project on musical fusion, see **Unit Interdisciplinary Projects,** pp. 1–18.

5

1

The First Americans
Beginnings–1492

Chapter Planning Guide

Section	Student Text	Teacher's Edition Activities
Opener and Story pp. 6–9	**Keys to History Time Line** **History Mystery** Beginning the Story with **the Stone Seekers**	**Setting the Stage Activity** Stones and Survival, p. 8
1 First Peoples in the Americas pp. 10–13	**Link to the Present** *Indian* as a term, p. 10 **Reading Maps** Migration Routes of First Americans, p. 11 **Point of View** When did the first settlers migrate to America? p. 11 **World Link** The spread of agriculture, p. 13	**Warm-Up Activity** Migration Then and Now, p. 10 **Geography Question of the Day,** p. 10 **Section Activity** Digging for Artifacts, p. 12 **Bonus Activity** Making a Food Web, p. 12 **Wrap-Up Activity** Cause-Effect Chains, p. 13
2 Early Civilizations pp. 14–18	**Reading Maps** Indian Civilizations, p. 16 **Hands-On History** Recreating a temple treasure, p. 17	**Warm-Up Activity** Analyzing a Visual, p. 14 **Geography Question of the Day,** p. 14 **Section Activity** Recording Aztec Tribute, p. 16 **Bonus Activity** Creating a Date System, p. 15 **Wrap-Up Activity** Comparing Civilizations, p. 18
3 Ancient Cultures in North America pp. 19–24	**Link to Art** *Emergence of the Clowns*, p. 21 **Geography Lab** The Colorado Plateau, p. 24	**Warm-Up Activity** Clues from Pottery, p. 19 **Geography Question of the Day,** p. 19 **Section Activity** Identifying Mound Artifacts, p. 22 **Bonus Activity** Making Cliff Dwelling Models, p. 20 **Wrap-Up Activity** Making a Culture Bar Graph, p. 23
4 North America in the 1400s pp. 25–31	**Link to Technology** The Birchbark Canoe, p. 26 **Reading Maps** Indian Culture Areas and Tribes, p. 29 **Skill Lab** Time Lines, p. 31	**Warm-Up Activity** Identifying Tribes, p. 25 **Geography Question of the Day,** p. 25 **Section Activity** Designing Shelters, p. 28 **Bonus Activity** Identifying Environments, p. 26 **Wrap-Up Activity** Making Concept Webs, p. 30
Evaluation	✓ **Section 1 Review,** p. 13 ✓ **Section 2 Review,** p. 18 ✓ **Section 3 Review,** p. 23 ✓ **Section 4 Review,** p. 30 ✓ **Chapter Survey,** pp. 32–33 **Alternative Assessment** Preparing a museum exhibit, p. 33	✓ **Answers to Section 1 Review,** p. 13 ✓ **Answers to Section 2 Review,** p. 18 ✓ **Answers to Section 3 Review,** p. 23 ✓ **Answers to Section 4 Review,** p. 30 ✓ **Answers to Chapter Survey,** pp. 32–33 (Alternative Assessment guidelines are in the Take-Home Planner.)

Teacher's Resource Package

 Chapter Summaries: English and Spanish, pp. 6–7

 Chapter Resources Binder
Study Guide Identifying Relationships, p. 1

 Chapter Resources Binder
Study Guide Identifying Main Ideas, p. 2
Reinforcement Identifying Characteristics, pp. 5–6
American Readings The Quest for Corn, pp. 1–2
Using Historical Documents European descriptions of Tenochtitlán and Cuzco, pp. 8–12

 Chapter Resources Binder
Study Guide Using a Graphic Organizer, p. 3
Geography Extensions Grand Canyon of the Colorado, pp. 1–2
American Readings Finding the Center, p. 3

 Chapter Resources Binder
Study Guide Using a Graphic Organizer, p. 4
Skills Development Creating a Time Line, pp. 7–8
American Readings A Zuni Poem, p. 4

Chapter and Unit Tests Chapter 1 Tests, Forms A and B, pp. 5–8

Take-Home Planner

Introducing the Chapter Activity
What Is History?, p. 4

Chapter In-Depth Activity Modeling Uses of the Environment, p. 5

 Reduced Views
Study Guide, p. 6
Skills Development, p. 7
Unit 1 Answers, pp. 28–34

 Reduced Views
Study Guide, p. 6
Reinforcement, p. 7
American Readings, p. 8
Using Historical Documents, p. 9
Unit 1 Answers, pp. 28–34

 Reduced Views
Study Guide, p. 6
Geography Extensions, p. 9
American Readings, p. 8
Unit 1 Answers, pp. 28–34

 Reduced Views
Study Guide, p. 6
Skills Development, p. 7
American Readings, p. 8
Unit 1 Answers, pp. 28–34

 Reduced Views
Chapter Tests, p. 9
Unit 1 Answers, pp. 28–34
Alternative Assessment Guidelines for scoring the Chapter Survey activity, p. 5

Additional Resources

Wall Time Line

Unit 1 Activity

Transparency Package

Transparency 1-1 Mound painting—use with Section 3
Transparency 1-2 Archaeologists at Work—use with Section 3
Transparency Activity Book

 **SelecTest Testing Software**
Chapter 1 Test, Forms A and B

★★★ Vital Links

 Videodisc

○ **CD-ROM**

Anasazi Indians (see TE p. 20)
Cahokia mound city (see TE p. 22)
American Indians fishing for salmon (see TE p. 27)
Mohawk Indians farming (see TE p. 28)

5B

Teaching Resources

Take-Home Planner 1
  Introducing Chapter Activity
  Chapter In-Depth Activity
  Alternative Assessment
Chapter Resources Binder
Geography Extensions
American Readings
Using Historical Documents
Transparency Activities
Wall Time Line Activities
Chapter Summaries
Chapter and Unit Tests
SelecTest Test File
Vital Links CD-ROM/Videodisc

Time Line

Keys to History

Keys to History journal writing activity is on page 32 in the Chapter Survey.

Earliest inhabitants The first people to migrate to the Americas followed herds of large animals across a land bridge from Siberia. (pp. 10–11)

Agriculture begins in the Americas This development was a turning point, leading to settled life and faster population growth. (p. 13)

Mayan civilization The Mayas built one of the most advanced civilizations in the Americas. (pp. 15–16)

Looking Back The Pleistocene Epoch was marked by periods of glaciation and nonglaciation. The Pleistocene Epoch and its last ice age ended about 10,000 years ago.

World Link See p. 13.

6

Chapter Objectives

★ Identify how scientists think people first came to the Americas.
★ Identify and describe early civilizations in Mesoamerica and South America.
★ Identify and describe the ancient cultures in North America.
★ Compare American Indian cultures in the 1400s.

Chapter Overview
The first Americans were ice-age hunters who migrated across the land bridge from Asia. Stone points are evidence of the spread of their ancestors. Many became farmers after the ice-age mammals died off.

With growth of agriculture, civilizations arose in Mesoamerica and Peru that excelled in trade, art, and architecture. The "mother culture" of Mesoamerica was that of the

Beginnings–1492

Chapter **1**

The First Americans

Sections

Beginning the Story with the Stone Seekers
1. **First Peoples in the Americas**
2. **Early Civilizations**
3. **Ancient Cultures in North America**
4. **North America in the 1400s**

Keys to History

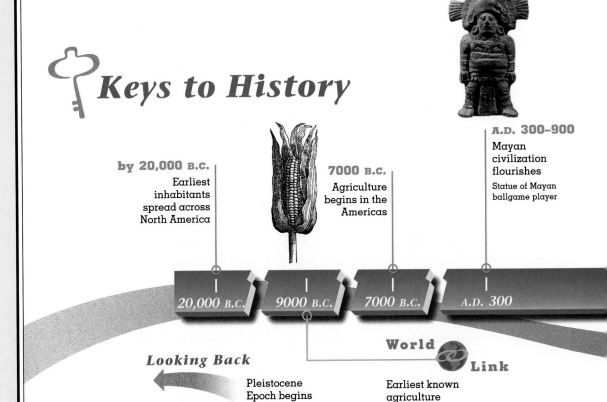

by 20,000 B.C.
Earliest inhabitants spread across North America

7000 B.C.
Agriculture begins in the Americas

A.D. 300–900
Mayan civilization flourishes
Statue of Mayan ballgame player

20,000 B.C.   9000 B.C.   7000 B.C.   A.D. 300

Looking Back
Pleistocene Epoch begins
2,000,000 B.C.

World Link
Earliest known agriculture
9000 B.C.

Olmecs (1200–600 B.C.), who were followed by the Mayas (300–900), the Aztec empire of Mexico, and the Inca empire of Peru.

Meanwhile, farming cultures developed in what is now the United States. In the southwestern desert lived the Mogollons and Hohokams, noted for irrigation systems, and the Anasazis, noted for cliff dwellings. In eastern woodlands a progression of societies—the Adena, Hopewell, and Mississippian—built huge mounds as burial grounds and religious sites.

By the 1400s hundreds of Indian tribes lived in North America, in six major culture areas: Arctic and Subarctic, Northwest Coast, Far West, Plains, Eastern Woodlands, and Southwest. Tribes within each area shared a way of life shaped by climate and resources.

Teaching the HISTORY Mystery

Students will find further information on pp. 21–23. See Chapter Survey, p. 32, for additional information and questions.

Time Line

Cahokia Cahokia, in present-day Illinois, was the largest Indian town in what is now the United States. At its peak around 1100, it had at least 10,000 people. (p. 23)

Anasazis The Anasazis of the Southwest built roads, irrigation canals and dams, and cliff dwellings. (pp. 20–21)

Aztecs The Aztec empire controlled most of what is now central Mexico. The site of Tenochtitlán is within present-day Mexico City. (pp. 16–17)

Incas The Inca empire of Peru was among the richest in the Americas. (pp. 17–18)

Looking Ahead The arrival of Columbus in 1492 marked the beginning of a lasting European impact on life in the Americas.

HISTORY Mystery

This photo shows an aerial view of a mound created by Indians thousands of years ago. It measures a quarter mile (390 m) long and five feet (1.5 m) tall. Why do you think people built the mound? Read the chapter to learn more about such mounds.

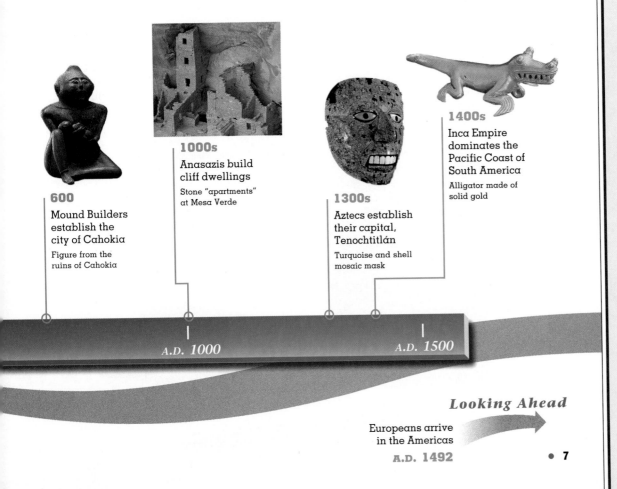

600
Mound Builders establish the city of Cahokia
Figure from the ruins of Cahokia

1000s
Anasazis build cliff dwellings
Stone "apartments" at Mesa Verde

1300s
Aztecs establish their capital, Tenochtitlán
Turquoise and shell mosaic mask

1400s
Inca Empire dominates the Pacific Coast of South America
Alligator made of solid gold

A.D. 1000

A.D. 1500

Looking Ahead
Europeans arrive in the Americas
A.D. 1492

Beginning the Story

The Stone Seekers

Some scientists think that Indians like the stone seekers in this story traveled as much as 200 miles (322 km) from their home base in present-day New Mexico to an ancient quarry in what is now Wyoming. There they found beautiful multicolored stones from which their people could fashion spear points and other tools. This is one explanation of why spear points found in New Mexico match the stones in a Wyoming quarry.

Setting the Stage
Activity

Stones and Survival

To help students focus on why sharpened stones were important, ask them to imagine being alone in the wilderness. Have them fill in a chart with columns titled "With Sharpened Stones" and "Without Sharpened Stones," listing options they would have for food and protection in each case.

See the Introducing the Chapter activity, What Is History? **Take-Home Planner 1**, p. 4.

✳ **History Footnote**

Scientists have developed many methods for understanding ancient Indian cultures. One method is to re-create stone, antler, and bone tools and use them in the same ways as Paleo-Indians did. A team of Smithsonian scientists, including Dennis Stanford, were given an elephant that died of natural causes in a zoo. They used re-creations of ancient tools to butcher the animal. Recording their movements with modern instruments, they rated the tools' usefulness.

This hands-on experience gave the researchers valuable insights. They were able to determine the amount of wear on tools, the labor intensity of butchering activities, and the practicality of bone versus stone tools.

Beginning the Story with

The Stone Seekers

The hair on the back of the young man's neck prickled. He could hear them out there, just beyond the light of the dying campfire. The dim shapes looming in the darkness were dire wolves, great shaggy beasts that sometimes hunted humans. The young man looked across the fire at the old man, his leader on this long journey away from the People. The old man nodded. At this signal, both grabbed burning sticks from the fire and charged at the wolves. The beasts scattered. Even so, it would be a nervous night for the stone seekers.

The Long Journey

The two men had been walking for days—as many as the fingers of three hands. They had left the People to journey north to the place of the multicolored stone. The stone at this distant quarry was the best—better than any

Archaeologist Dennis Stanford, a leader in research on the earliest Americans, demonstrates how the stone seekers might have made flaked stone points. The points below date to around 11,500 years ago and show the beauty and workmanship of such tools.

History Bookshelf

Sneve, Virginia Driving Hawk. *The Nez Percé*. Holiday House, 1994. In *The Nez Percé*, Virginia Driving Hawk Sneve retells the creation story of the Nez Percé Indians and recounts the history and customs of the people. This beautifully illustrated book was chosen as a 1994 Notable Children's Trade Book in Social Studies.

Also of interest:

De Armond, Dale. *The Boy Who Found the Light: Eskimo Folktales*. Little, Brown, 1989.

Lee, Martin. *Seminoles*. Franklin Watts, 1989.

Mayo, Gretchen Will. *Earthmaker's Tales: North American Indian Stories about Earth Happenings*. Walker, 1988.

the People could find near their hunting grounds. The old man explained why. The rock there was striped with the colors of the earth—red, yellow, black, and white. The stone was extremely smooth. Spear points made from this stone would have the sharpest, most deadly edge.

The young man was pleased to have been chosen for the journey. He had already proven himself as a hunter. Now he was recognized as a man by the People, though he was only 15 and not yet married.

At the age of 35, the old man's hunting days were nearly over. Good hunters needed more strength and agility than he seemed to have now. No one, however, could equal his skill in making sharp stone points for spears. A hunter armed with such a spear could bring down a woolly mammoth or long-horned bison. A few of the old man's points were so perfect they were never used for hunting. Instead, they were brought out during ceremonies when the People prayed for—or celebrated—a successful hunt.

During the long journey, the young hunter listened carefully to the old man's stories about the landmarks on their route. They had already crossed the wide river and were nearing the red bluffs. In a few more days they would reach the quarry where they would find the special stones. The young man knew that the stories would help him remember the way to the quarry in future years. To the old man's tales he would add his own story of their frightening encounter with the dire wolves near the hidden spring.

The Special Stones

Once the two men arrived at the quarry, the hard work began. With great care they broke off large chunks of stone with just the right grain and no flaws. A careless slip of a tool could shatter a stone into a dozen useless pieces. They filled their leather sacks with as many stones as they could carry. Then, bending under their heavy burdens, they began retracing their route back to the People. Luckily, the old stone seeker said to himself, the young man was strong.

On the return journey, the young stone seeker thought of the months ahead. Now that he was a man, he would join the other men hunting. After a good hunt, the People would celebrate by feasting on the meat. Between hunts, he would work with the other men to make and repair their stone-tipped tools and weapons. They would replace broken points with new ones chipped out of the precious stones he himself had carved out of the distant quarry.

Hands-On → HISTORY

Activity

The points made by the stone seekers were precious to them—precious enough for them to walk hundreds of miles to select just the right stones. Write a description for a future historian of an object in your life that you value both for its usefulness and its beauty. Tell how you use the object and why you consider it beautiful. How did you acquire the object? Finally, tell what you expect to do with the object ultimately—will you save the item, discard it, or pass it along to someone else? Be prepared to bring the object to class.

Discussion

Thinking Historically

1. How did the young stone seeker benefit from the experience of the older stone seeker? (He learned where to find and collect stones for hunting tools.)

2. How did the efforts of the stone seekers help maintain their people's way of life? (Stones were used to create and repair hunting spears. Some stone points were used in ceremonies. The journey was a way to transfer knowledge from one generation to another.)

3. What similarities are there to the way young and older people help one another today? (The young learn from their elders' skill and experience. Older people benefit from the strength of the young.)

See the Chapter In-Depth Activity, Modeling Uses of the Environment, **Take-Home Planner 1**, p. 5.

Teaching the

Hands-On

→ HISTORY

Point out that the object students choose should have practical as well as aesthetic value. For example, students might choose a CD-ROM because of its technological features and physical appearance.

For a journal writing activity on the stone seekers, see student page 33.

Introducing the Section

Vocabulary

migration (p. 10) movement from one region to another

glaciers (p. 10) vast slow-moving masses of ice

nomads (p. 11) people with no permanent home who move in search of food

culture (p. 13) way of life

Warm-Up Activity

Migration Then and Now

Ask how many students have moved. Point out that moving has been part of life for as long as 50,000 years. Have students list reasons why people move today and possible reasons why they moved thousands of years ago.

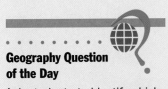

Geography Question of the Day

Ask students to identify which continents touch each other by placing names within a map oval according to position on the globe, then drawing lines between names of continents that touch. They can refer to pages R2–R3. This activity can lead in to the topic of Beringia.

Teaching the

Link to the Present

Ask: **Why do you think most Indians prefer to be called by their tribe's name?** (To recognize each tribe has its own identity.)

Section Objectives

★ Identify when and how humans came to the Americas.

★ Summarize why archaeologists have different views about human habitation in the Americas.

★ Explain how the development of agriculture changed the way of life of early Americans.

Teaching Resources

Take-Home Planner 1, pp. 2–9

Chapter Resources Binder

Study Guide, p. 1

Reinforcement

Skills Development

Geography Extensions

American Readings

Using Historical Documents

Transparency Activities

Chapter and Unit Tests

1. First Peoples in the Americas

Reading Guide

New Terms **migration, glaciers, nomads, culture**

Section Focus **The beginnings of human history in the Americas**

1. How did humans come to live in the Americas?
2. How did agriculture change the way of life of early Americans?

The stone seekers in the story are imaginary. However, the beautiful points really exist, and the quarry has been found in Wyoming. America's ancient hunters who used stone tools are called *Paleo-Indians*, meaning "ancient Indians." Little is known about these people, but what we do know is that their ancestors migrated from Asia. A **migration** is a movement of people from one region to another. Over the course of thousands of years, Paleo-Indians spread throughout North and South America.

Beringia

The arrival of human beings in the Americas took place during the last ice age, when a third of the earth was locked in ice two miles (3.2 km) thick in some places. It was a time when nature's bulldozers, vast slow-moving masses of ice called **glaciers,** transformed huge areas of the earth's surface as they gouged and crushed everything in their path.

So much water turned into ice that it lowered the water level of the oceans. The lowered waters exposed a bridge of land as much as 1,000 miles (1,600 km) wide linking the continents of Asia and North America. Geologists call this land bridge Beringia (bayr-IN-jee-uh). Across Beringia came bison,

musk oxen, elephants, caribou, and other large animals. Behind them followed small groups of hunters who depended on these animals for their very existence.

 **Link to the Present**

***Indian* as a term** Europeans of the 1400s used the term *Indies* to refer to India, China, Japan, and the other Asian lands. When Christopher Columbus landed in the Bahamas in 1492, he was certain he had reached the Indies. He called the native people he met *Indians.*

Although Columbus was wrong about where he had landed, the name *Indian* stuck. Today, many descendants of America's earliest people prefer *Indian* over terms like *Amer-Indian* or even *Native American.* However, the first preference for most is to be called by the name of their tribe or nation, such as Arapaho, Cherokee, Mandan, or Zuni. In most Indian languages, the tribal name means "the people."

The Paleo-Indians who made and used Folsom and Clovis points probably attached the points to wooden shafts. Some shafts may have been heavier for thrusting directly into animals. Other stone points may have been attached to light, arrow-like shafts that hunters could throw from a distance with enough force to penetrate the thick hides of large animals.

See the Study Guide activity in **Chapter Resources Binder**, p. 1.

Checking Understanding

1. What evidence is there that humans lived in the Americas at the same time as extinct animals? (Sharpened stone points were found near ancient animal bones.)

Stimulating Critical Thinking

2. Why do you think evidence of ice-age people in the Americas was not found hundreds of years ago? (Perhaps fewer people were looking for such evidence; changes in the land's surface over time hid evidence; and sites are in remote areas.)

Teaching the

↑ **Reading Maps**

Have students identify the estimated ages of sites. Point out that question marks indicate estimates that fewer archaeologists accept. Ask: **Why do you think the older dates for South American sites are being questioned?** (Archaeologists who believe the first migration was from north to south over land would expect northern sites to be older.) **Answers to Reading Maps: 1.** The large ice sheet indicates a much colder climate. **2.** Probably not, because they had not crossed an ocean.

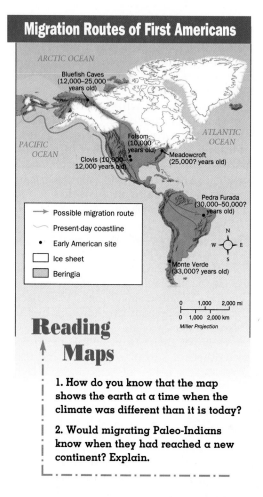

Migration Routes of First Americans

ARCTIC OCEAN

Bluefish Caves (12,000–25,000 years old)

PACIFIC OCEAN

ATLANTIC OCEAN

Folsom (10,000 years old)

Clovis (10,000–12,000 years old)

Meadowcroft (25,000? years old)

Pedra Furada (30,000–50,000? years old)

Monte Verde (33,000? years old)

→ Possible migration route
⌒ Present-day coastline
• Early American site
☐ Ice sheet
▨ Beringia

0   1,000   2,000 mi
0   1,000   2,000 km
Miller Projection

Reading Maps

↑

1. How do you know that the map shows the earth at a time when the climate was different than it is today?

2. Would migrating Paleo-Indians know when they had reached a new continent? Explain.

Although scholars disagree about when these hunters first arrived, by 20,000 B.C. descendants of the hunters had spread across North America. They eventually spread throughout South America as well. These small groups of people lived as **nomads,** people with no permanent home who move in search of food. To survive, the hardy nomads hunted animals and birds and gathered nuts, berries, and edible plants. They used fire for cooking and comfort, and wore clothes made of animal skins and furs.

Folsom and Clovis People

Paleo-Indian families used a variety of tools, such as stone knives, hammers, and scrapers, and bone needles. Today their best-known tools are their stone points, like the ones made by the stone seeker.

The person who discovered the first of these points was a cowboy named George McJunkin. In 1926, while looking for stray cattle near Folsom, New Mexico, McJunkin noticed the sun-bleached bones of a large animal peeping through the dirt. The bones proved to be those of a type of buffalo or bison that roamed the earth 10,000 years ago. With the bones archaeologists found several stone points.

The discovery of the points with the bones excited scientists and historians. It was the first proof that humans had lived in the Americas at the same time as ice-age mammals. In 1932 a similar discovery near Clovis, New Mexico, thrilled archaeologists. Since then, the points—referred to as Clovis points—have been found all over North America and even in parts of South America.

The land bridge disappears About 10,000 years ago, the earth began to warm. Glaciers melted, oceans rose, and the land bridge disappeared beneath the Bering Strait. All that remains of the land bridge today are a few islands in a channel 50 miles (80 km) wide between Alaska and Russia.

☾ Point of View

➔ **When did the first settlers migrate to America?**

Archaeologists and anthropologists who first studied Clovis points believed that Clovis people were the first Americans and that they came about 11,500 years ago. Yet recent research dates the migration anywhere from 20,000 to even 50,000 years ago.

Teaching the

C Point of View

Have students contrast Meltzer's and Guidon's explanations for where the pieces of charcoal came from. Ask why two scientists might interpret the same evidence differently.

Digging for Artifacts

Have small groups create and analyze "dig sites." In a box filled with shredded paper, dirt, or packing peanuts, each group buries present-day artifacts such as tools, clothing, toys, and art objects, including some partial or broken objects. Exchanging boxes, they role-play archaeologists in the year 3000 who dig up and categorize the artifacts, drawing conclusions about life in the 1990s.

Making a Food Web

To reinforce understanding of food sources, have students draw a simple food web that includes ice-age mammals and Paleo-Indians. Provide a food web example: plants use the sun's energy to produce food; plant-eating animals gain energy from plants they eat; meat-eating animals gain energy from their diet.

12

✠ Connections to Science

The charcoal that Guidon found at sites in South America is too old for its age to be determined by the traditional method of radiocarbon dating (see p. 2). However, archaeologists now have another tool for estimating the ages of some artifacts. With some substances, such as charcoal, they can measure the amount of light energy trapped inside. The older the artifact, the more light it has been exposed to. To determine how much light is trapped inside, scientists release the light energy by heating the object to a very high temperature. The amount of light energy released—called thermoluminescence—helps scientists estimate the artifact's age.

While firm evidence of pre-Clovis people exists, certain finds have stirred debate. For example, in Pedra Furada, Brazil, French archaeologist Niéde Guidon has found artifacts she says are at least 30,000 and perhaps 50,000 years old. Some archaeologists question these dates.

One problem is proving that stone "tools" are in fact human-made and not formed by nature. As for burned remains, archaeologist David Meltzer raises this question: "How do you know it was a piece of charcoal touched by human hands and not just a piece of burned tree?" Guidon responds, "If they had been left by forest fires, carbon deposits would have been found scattered across a wide area." Instead, the charcoal is often ringed by stones, a sign that these were fires made by humans.

If humans got to South America even by 13,000 years ago, they would have had to cross Beringia many thousands of years before. At that time ice sheets would have blocked the path south. Archaeologists are still looking for explanations. Guidon's own answer is controversial. She thinks that the immigrants might have come to South America in boats from Asia.

Archaeologists who study the first Americans continue to dig and search, to study and disagree. As archaeologist Dennis Stanford of the Smithsonian Institution puts it, "This is a hot area of research. Man's origin in the New World [the Americas] is one of the major unanswered questions of archaeology."

Beginnings of Agriculture

Soon after the land bridge disappeared, ice-age mammals in the Americas began to die off. Climate change might have been the cause, or perhaps over-hunting by the Paleo-Indians.

Whatever the reason, people began to seek other ways to survive. Plants and fish

Archaeologist Tom Dillehay's team works at Monte Verde, Chile, a site that made scientists question the Clovis theory. Unusual natural conditions preserved not only stone and bone artifacts, but also organic materials such as mastodon meat, potatoes, and even seaweed from the Pacific coast. Radio-carbon dating shows these materials to be 12,500 years old.

World  Link

The spread of agriculture How did the practice of agriculture spread throughout the world? Did the first farmers teach their neighbors, who then taught *their* neighbors? Or did people in different places get the same idea at about the same time? The answer is: both.

The earliest farming took place about 9000 B.C. in the Middle East and spread outward from there. The first farmers in northern Africa, southern Europe, and India all got the idea from their neighbors in the Middle East.

In eastern Asia, agriculture started about 7500 B.C., with farmers planting rice and millet. Agriculture in the Americas started about 7000 B.C., in what is now Mexico. Historians can find no evidence that the first farmers in eastern Asia or in the Americas had any contact—either direct or indirect—with Middle Eastern farmers. Instead, they seem to have developed agriculture on their own, and at about the same time.

replaced meat at the center of their diet. As a result, smooth rocks for crushing nuts and grinding wild grains replaced spear points in their tool kits. People learned to weave baskets from plant fibers and to make clay pots for storing seeds, flour, and berries.

Over time, people learned that certain plants grew better and faster than others, so they devoted more attention to those plants. In this way agriculture got its start. As long ago as 7000 B.C., people in what is today central Mexico began to experiment

with wild maize (corn) in order to grow larger cobs. At the same time, groups living in what is now the eastern United States began to grow beans and squashes.

Agriculture brings change The development of agriculture was a major turning point in history. Once people began to grow their own food, they settled down in one place to tend their fields. In good crop years these farming villages could produce extra food and store it for the future. People were healthier and lived longer, and populations began to grow.

Farming changed the way of life—also known as **culture**—of these communities. Culture includes people's arts, beliefs, inventions, traditions, and language. With a good supply of food, not everyone had to farm. People with special skills or talents could become weavers or potters or healers. Individuals' special roles and jobs became a part of the culture of the community.

In addition, the goods people made and the extra food farmers grew could be sold to people outside the community. Trade began, and villages grew into larger towns and then into cities. As you will see, city life paved the way for even greater changes.

1. Section Review

1. Define **migration, glaciers, nomads,** and **culture.**
2. How did people come to live in the Americas?
3. What evidence pointed scientists to the dates of early humans in America?
4. Critical Thinking The culture of a group of people is said to include ideas, customs, skills, and arts. Choose one of these aspects of culture and explain how it might have changed with the shift from nomadic life to farming life.

Warm-Up
Activity

Analyzing a Visual

To preview Mayan civilization, have students write three statements about Mayan daily life, supporting each with evidence from the mural on p. 15. Some possible characteristics: division of labor, variety of clothing, outdoor cooking, water transportation, and fish as a probable source of food.

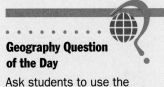

Geography Question of the Day

Ask students to use the map on p. 16 to estimate the length of the Inca Empire (about 2,500 miles, or 4,020 km) and how long it would take Inca runners to relay a message from one end to the other at a rate of 125 miles (200 km) per day (about 20 days).

Section Objectives

★ Describe characteristics of ancient civilizations in Mesoamerica and South America.
★ Explain how scientists have learned about these early civilizations.
★ Identify the major achievements of these early civilizations.

Teaching Resources

Take-Home Planner 1, pp. 2–9
Chapter Resources Binder
  Study Guide, p. 2
  Reinforcement, pp. 5–6
  Skills Development
Geography Extensions
American Readings, pp. 1–2
Using Historical Documents, pp. 8–12
Transparency Activities
Chapter and Unit Tests

2. Early Civilizations

Reading Guide

New Terms civilization, tribute

Section Focus The advanced civilizations that arose in Mesoamerica and South America

1. What civilizations arose in the Americas after the development of agriculture?
2. How do we know about ways of life of early American civilizations?
3. What were some major achievements of early civilizations in the Americas?

As agriculture flourished and populations grew, cities became centers of government and religious life. Some people became officials or priests. Others studied science and developed systems of writing. Artists and craftspeople created a variety of products.

With the development of cities came the beginnings of civilization. A **civilization** is a society in which a high level of art, technology, and government exists. Over the centuries several civilizations rose and fell in the Americas. The largest civilizations arose in what is now Peru, and in *Mesoamerica*, a term archaeologists use for the part of Mexico and Central America that had civilizations before A.D. 1500.

The Olmecs

A people called the Olmecs created the earliest great civilization in Mesoamerica. It flourished between 1200 B.C. and 600 B.C. along the Gulf Coast in what are now the Mexican states of Veracruz and Tabasco. In this rainy, swampy lowland, people can grow corn and other crops year-round. Olmec civilization is now known as the "mother culture" of Mesoamerica because later societies built on Olmec ideas.

Religion and art Much of what we know about the Olmecs comes from discoveries at places where they held religious ceremonies. Huge statues and beautiful carvings show that the Olmecs worshiped many gods, including a jaguar god and gods of rain, fire, corn, and fertility. These gods were important in all later Mesoamerican religion and art.

The Olmecs had a highly organized society that was ruled by priests. Their elaborate religious centers featured large earthen mounds topped with temples, broad plazas,

Colossal Olmec heads are thought to be either individual portraits of Olmec rulers or stylized portraits of Olmec gods. In addition to huge carvings, Olmec artists crafted lovely small figurines as well, often using prized green stones such as jade.

Teotihuacán was a planned city, built over hundreds of years. Within its boundaries were hundreds of pyramids and workshop areas and about 2,000 apartment complexes, all laid out in a grid. Each area had its own plazas. There were different neighborhoods for production of different goods, such as pottery and cloth. The city's elaborate irrigation system enabled farmers to produce enough food to feed its huge population.

The city thrived largely because it was a center of trade. It was located on a major trade route and controlled the major sources of obsidian, highly valued by Olmec and Mayan stone workers for making sacrificial knives and mirrors. The city was also a major site for religious ceremonies.

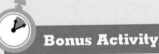
and carved altars. For such monuments, the Olmecs dragged stone over long distances. At one site colossal heads, carved from black stone called basalt, weigh as much as 20 tons. Amazingly, Olmecs dragged the basalt through miles of dense jungle to the site. We know that the Olmecs carried on trade because their pottery and sculpture have been found at sites throughout Mesoamerica.

Science Olmec scientists invented a calendar based on their study of the movement of the earth in relation to the sun, moon, and planets. They used a system of bars and dots to record dates of astronomical and historical events. Archaeologists say that this system was an early form of writing.

We know very little about how and why Olmec civilization disappeared. After the decline of the Olmec "mother culture," though, several other city centers rose to power in Mesoamerica.

Teotihuacán

The largest and most influential city center was Teotihuacán (TAY-ō-TEE-wah-KAHN). Located in the Valley of Mexico—where Mexico City is today—Teotihuacán drew people from small farms. At its peak in A.D. 500 it had a population of 200,000, making it the sixth largest city in the world at that time. Not only was Teotihuacán big, it also was powerful, dominating its neighbors through trade and warfare.

Teotihuacán's orderly city plan took over 500 years to carry out. The city covered over 8 square miles (21 square km) and was orga-

This Mayan mural, from a temple wall in the city of Chichén Itzá, shows village life. What can you infer about Mayan daily life from the scene?

nized around a religious center. Visitors to Mexico City today can still visit Teotihuacán's Pyramid of the Sun, an awesome structure of stone and dirt.

Around the middle of the 600s, fire destroyed Teotihuacán. Was the fire caused by rebellion against a hated ruler or by invasion? Historians still debate the answer.

The Mayas

After the decline of Teotihuacán, power in Mesoamerica shifted south to the energetic Mayan city-states. Located in tropical lowlands of present-day Yucatán, Guatemala, Belize, and Honduras, Mayan civilization flourished from A.D. 300 to 900.

Many historians believe the Mayas created the most advanced early civilization in the Americas. Like the Olmecs, the Mayas built hundreds of religious centers, such as Palenque (pah-LENG-kay), Uxmal (ooz-MAHL), Tikal (tee-KAHL), and Copán (kō-PAHN). Dramatic temples crowned stepped pyramids. Intricate carvings covered palaces and monuments.

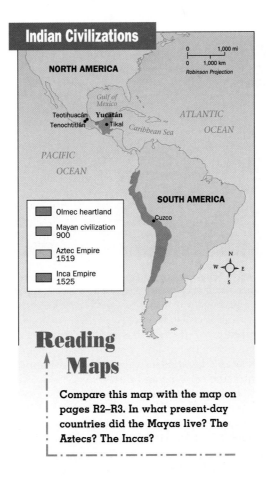

Indian Civilizations

NORTH AMERICA

Gulf of Mexico

Teotihuacán Yucatán
Tenochtitlán • Tikal Caribbean Sea

ATLANTIC OCEAN

PACIFIC OCEAN

SOUTH AMERICA
• Cuzco

0   1,000 mi
0   1,000 km
Robinson Projection

- Olmec heartland
- Mayan civilization 900
- Aztec Empire 1519
- Inca Empire 1525

Reading
↑ Maps

Compare this map with the map on pages R2–R3. In what present-day countries did the Mayas live? The Aztecs? The Incas?

Every ceremonial center had an observatory, and the Mayas excelled at mathematics and astronomy. They understood the concept of zero and had a symbol for it long before the rest of the world. Their calendar was far more accurate than those used in Europe hundreds of years later. In addition, the Mayas developed a written language.

A mysterious collapse Like Teotihuacán, the Mayan civilization collapsed suddenly and mysteriously. Perhaps enemies invaded or the city-states fought among themselves. A drought or overpopulation might have damaged the environment, making it hard for people to survive. Some his-

torians think that the Mayas wore out their soil for farming, leading to a food shortage.

The collapse of Mayan civilization may be a mystery, but the Mayan people themselves have survived. About 700,000 Mayas live in the Mexican state of Chiapas. Nearly 5 million more live on the Yucatán Peninsula and in Central America. Most of them live in villages and tend small farms. They speak the Mayan language and some still use the ancient calendar.

The Aztecs

To the north of the fading Mayan empire, the powerful Aztec empire began to rise. In the 1100s or 1200s the Aztecs migrated into the Valley of Mexico. By 1345 they had set up their island capital of Tenochtitlán (teh-NŌCH-tee-TLAHN) in marshy Lake Texcoco (tes-KŌ-kō). In the following century, the Aztecs' strong army and well-organized government enabled them to extend their power throughout central Mexico.

The Aztec army was bent on gaining land and collecting **tribute**—forced payment—from conquered peoples. Aztecs collected

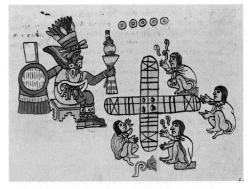

The Aztec writing system used pictures and symbols to represent ideas and sounds. This page from an Aztec book shows men playing a game. The curved symbols by two of the men represent speech.

See the Reinforcement activity in **Chapter Resources Binder**, pp. 5–6.

⚔ **Connections to Language Arts**

Around the year 1000 the Aztecs began compiling codices—book-like written records consisting of pages stitched together. Painting on paper made from fig tree bark, artists used pictures and symbols to show daily life, royal history, religious practices, and tribute records. Aztec storytellers who passed down knowledge to students orally used codices as memory aids.

tribute in the form of gold, cotton, turquoise, feathers, incense, and food. Tribute also included human beings for sacrifice to the Aztec sun god. The Aztecs believed that unless the sun god was fed hearts and blood, the world would come to an end. At one especially bloody four-day celebration, 20,000 prisoners had their hearts cut out.

The Aztecs were very successful at agriculture. Farmers grew crops on irrigated hillside terraces around Lake Texcoco. They also cultivated vegetables and flowers in *chinampas* (chee-NAHM-pahs), farm plots built by digging ditches in the lakeshore to channel the water and then piling up the fertile mud into raised beds.

Aztec trade, like Aztec agriculture, showed careful organization and government direction. Merchants traveled through the empire

and beyond to Central America and north into the present-day United States. They brought a great variety of goods to Tenochtitlán. Orderly markets displayed meat, vegetables, cloth, rope, pottery, precious metals, jade, feathers, and animal skins.

The Incas

Far to the south, the Inca empire rivaled the Aztecs in size and power. Beginning in the early 1400s, the Incas dominated much of the Pacific Coast of South America. Their capital was the city of Cuzco (KOOS-kō), located high in the Andes Mountains. The supreme ruler, the Sapa Inca, had total control of his subjects. Priests and nobles helped him rule his empire.

The well-organized Incas could communicate over a vast area. They built a road system

Hands-On ➤ *HISTORY*

Recreating a temple treasure Ordinary activities sometimes lead to extraordinary discoveries. In Mexico City in 1978, a worker digging a trench came upon the buried ruins of *el Templo Mayor*—the "Great Temple" of the Aztecs.

As archaeologists uncovered the temple, they found thousands of items the Aztecs had buried as offerings to their gods. These included turtle shells, snake skins, jaguar skeletons, crocodile heads—and the remains of sacrificed humans. There were wonderful treasures too: gemstones, jewelry, masks, musical instruments, knives, pottery, statues of gods, and carvings of animals. Some items were made by Aztec artists. Others were antiques from previous civilizations like the Olmecs. Most came from peoples the Aztecs had conquered.

El Templo Mayor model

➤ **Activity** Suppose you wanted to bury a "treasure chest" containing items of special value to you. Make a list of what you would put in the chest. Include at least one item from each of these four categories: artworks, antiques or heirlooms, items with political or religious meaning, and special everyday objects. Explain each of your choices.

▸ **Discussion**

Checking Understanding

1. What made the Aztecs so powerful? (A strong army and a well-structured government.)

2. Why did the Aztecs sacrifice humans to their sun god? (They believed the world would end without the sacrifices.)

Stimulating Critical Thinking

3. What was the Mayas' most important accomplishment? Support your opinion. (Answers might include writing, because it gave a means of recording information; developing the concept of zero, because the concept is important to mathematical processes; and the development of an accurate calendar.)

Teaching the Hands-On
┌ - - - - ➤ *HISTORY*

To provide a model, display items from each category, such as a small figurine or painting, an heirloom ring, a political poster or sign, a religious pin or pendant, a favorite pen or cup. Explain their significance to you.

For European descriptions of Tenochtitlán and Cuzco, see **Using Historical Documents**, pp. 8–12.

Comparing Civilizations

To review characteristics of early civilizations, provide ten minutes for small groups to compare civilizations in terms of religion, agriculture, and technology. Have a member of each group summarize the group's discussion.

Section Review
Answers

1. Definitions: *civilization* (14), *tribute* (16)

2. Olmecs: rulers were also religious leaders; Mayas: cities were religious centers; Aztecs: offered sacrifices to their gods; Incas: built great temples.

3. The Aztecs used terraces on hillsides and chinampas near lakes. The Incas used terraces on mountainsides.

4. Answers may include Olmecs: art, calendar, writing; Mayas: excellence in math and astronomy, written language; Aztecs: well-organized government, writing system, strong army; Incas: architecture, advances in agriculture and medicine.

5. A culture can be a simple or a complex way of life. Paleo-Indians had a simple hunting and gathering culture. A civilization is a culture with advanced art, technology, and government, such as the Olmecs, Mayas, Aztecs, and Incas.

✠ Connections to Civics

In the highly structured Inca society, the rights of the community took precedence over the rights of individuals. For example, strict laws prevented common people from owning luxury goods, and the rulers and nobles controlled the lives of the common people in many ways. Laws also required adult males to provide labor to the state each year. The laborer might farm state-owned land, build roads, construct buildings, or serve in the army. Our own system of government places great importance on protecting individual rights. The Bill of Rights in the Constitution identifies specific rights of individuals but does not limit rights to those listed.

The Incas built the city of Machu Picchu in the Andes on a narrow ridge some 8,000 feet (2,400 m) above sea level. This small Inca town was not only considered a strategic site on the edge of the empire but also a sacred place in Inca myths. Here you can see the intricate stone structures and terraced ledges used for farming on steep mountainsides.

that stretched 2,500 miles (4,000 km) from present-day Ecuador to central Chile. Swift runners carried messages. Because the Incas did not have a written language, runners memorized the messages. They also carried *quipu* (KEE-poo), cords tied with knotted strings of different colors. The colors and knots were a code for complex information such as financial accounts.

Inca technology The Incas are known for their monumental architecture, much of which still stands. Although they did not have iron tools, the wheel, or large animals, they built temples, palaces, and forts from huge stone blocks. The force of gravity, not cement, holds the stones together, their fit so snug that a knife cannot slip between them. During earthquakes, the blocks slide but do not tumble apart.

The Incas also made great advances in agriculture and medicine. Inca engineers built a system of terraces for farmers to grow potatoes and other crops on steep mountainsides. Inca doctors performed brain surgery, opening the skulls of patients even without metal instruments.

By the late 1400s the Incas were at the height of their power. They had created a vast, well-organized empire with extensive trade and great riches. As you will read, in the 1500s both the Aztecs and Incas fell prey to a new enemy: conquerors from faraway Spain. Hungry for riches, these ruthless conquerors were to shatter the last great civilizations of Mesoamerica and Peru.

★ 2. Section Review

1. Define **civilization** and **tribute**.

2. Choose two civilizations and explain how we know that religion was an important part of the society of each.

3. Give two examples of how farmers adapted to their environments in early civilizations.

4. List two accomplishments for each of these civilizations: Olmecs, Mayas, Aztecs, and Incas.

5. Critical Thinking Explain how a civilization differs from a culture. Give examples to support your answer.

Section Objectives

★ Explain how the desert farmers adapted to the environment in the Southwest.
★ Identify how the Mound Builders of the East provided for their basic needs.

Teaching Resources

Take-Home Planner 1, pp. 2–9
Chapter Resources Binder
  Study Guide, p. 3
  Reinforcement
  Skills Development
Geography Extensions, pp. 1–2
American Readings, p. 3
  Using Historical Documents
Transparency Activities
  Chapter and Unit Tests

3. Ancient Cultures in North America

Reading Guide

New Term irrigation

Section Focus **Ancient cultures that rose and fell in North America**

1. What ways of life developed among the ancient societies of the Southwest?
2. What were some characteristics of ancient Indian societies of the Eastern Woodlands?

At the same time that mighty civilizations were developing in Mesoamerica and Peru, complex cultures existed north of Mexico. Archaeologists have found evidence of several early farming cultures in the lands that became the United States.

Desert Farmers

Thousands of years after the Paleo-Indians of the Southwest made their famous spear points, three desert societies lived in the same lands. The Mogollons, the Hohokams, and the Anasazis settled into permanent villages and towns to grow corn, beans, squash, cotton, and tobacco.

Mogollons The name Mogollon (MUG-ee-YŌN) means "mountain people." It refers to the mountains of New Mexico and Arizona where these people once lived.

By around 100 B.C. the Mogollons were growing corn and beans in their desert environment by building dams and terraces on hillsides to make use of the small amount of rain. This system of **irrigation**—supplying land with water by use of dams, ditches, and channels—was very important because it provided a steady source of food.

The Mogollons crafted many kinds of objects for religious and personal use, such as tobacco pipes, masks, and stone and shell beads. However, they are best known for their pottery painted with striking red-on-white and black-on-white designs.

Hohokams The Hohokams (hō-HŌ-kahmz) lived mostly in the Sonoran Desert to the west of the Mogollon people. They are noted for their elaborate irrigation system.

The Mogollons often placed pots in graves along with the dead. They punched holes in the bottom of the pots, perhaps to "kill" the pots or release the spirits of the painted figures (here a frog and a turkey).

Warm-Up Activity

Clues from Pottery

To focus on pottery as an artifact, ask students to imagine themselves as archaeologists uncovering the two pots shown here from a Mogollon grave. Tell them the diameters and depths (about 10 by 4 inches and 7 by 3 inches). Then have them write down their thoughts about why these pots were made and what they reveal about the Mogollons.

Geography Question of the Day

To orient students before discussing Southwest desert farm cultures, ask them to draw a rough outline map of North America and to label Arizona, New Mexico, and Mexico. If necessary, they can refer to the political maps on pp. R2–R3 and R6–R7.

Making Cliff Dwelling Models

To help students understand Anasazi architecture, have them make clay models of Cliff Palace as it might have looked when the Anasazis inhabited it. After students study the photo on this page, provide modeling clay and other supplies. Have small groups work together to create models. They may wish to research information about Anasazi cliff dwellings before beginning their models.

See the Study Guide activity in **Chapter Resources Binder**, p. 3.

★ ★ ★
Vital Links

🔘 **Anasazi Indians (Movie)**
Unit 1, Side 2, Search 11687, Play to 13007

||||||||||

🔘 **See also Unit 1 Explore CD-ROM location 85.**

✳ **History Footnote**

The Hohokams built a remarkable network of irrigation canals in the Gila River and Salt River valleys of Arizona. They had built over 150 miles (241 km) of canals in the Salt River Valley by the end of the 1300s. Some were rebuilt and put back into use in the 1900s. In addition, some canals that supply water to Phoenix, Arizona, were built over those of the Hohokams.

They built hundreds of miles of canals criss-crossing their desert homeland.

The Hohokams traded widely with people in Mesoamerica, and their artifacts show strong Mexican influences. They used mirrors made in Mesoamerica, kept tropical birds as pets, and imported rubber balls to play a Mesoamerican game. Their craftsmen imitated Mesoamerican jewelry styles.

No one knows for sure why the Hohokams disappeared. Perhaps their irrigation system let salt into the soil, killing their crops. Perhaps they were overcome by a drought in the Southwest in the 1200s.

Some scholars believe that the Hohokams, weakened by food shortages and attacks, scattered to small villages, surviving to become ancestors of today's Pima (PEE-muh) and Papago (PAH-puh-Gō) Indians of Arizona. Indeed, the name Hohokam comes from a Pima word meaning "many things used up" or "the vanished ones."

Anasazis The Anasazis (AH-nuh-SAH-zeez) lived in the high desert country of the Colorado Plateau of northern Arizona and New Mexico. By about A.D. 700 they had found ways to grow corn, squash, and beans in their dry environment. At first they lived in pit houses like the Mogollons. Later they built large apartment-like communities made of stone, wood, and sun-dried mud called *adobe* (uh-DŌ-bee).

After about A.D. 1000, the Anasazis began building their villages in high canyon walls as protection from their enemies. For this reason the Anasazis are sometimes referred to as cliff dwellers. Some Anasazi structures had as many as 200 rooms and 20 *kivas* (KEE-vuhz)—round underground rooms

Anasazis built this dwelling, called Cliff Palace, under a protective overhang in what is today Mesa Verde National Park in Colorado. Builders began at the back, and as the apartments grew out and up, the dark first rooms became storage areas. On top of the underground kivas were courtyards. You can see the round kivas, now roofless, in this aerial view.

Roxanne Swentzell uses the traditional Pueblo method of coiling and scraping clay into figures. She winds long rolls of clay in circular layers. Once the coils are in the shape she wants, she scrapes and smoothes the clay. She then fires her work in a kiln. *Emergence of the Clowns* is in the permanent collection of the Heard Museum in Phoenix, Arizona.

Have students read an Indian origin story. **American Readings,** p. 3.

〰️ **Link to Art**

Emergence of the Clowns (1988) Today Pueblo peoples continue the Anasazi tradition of artworks in clay. Sculptor Roxanne Swentzell (b. 1962) lives in Santa Clara, a Tewa pueblo in northern New Mexico. This sculpture shows clowns called *koshares,* who act out the Tewa story of where humans came from. Swentzell says these koshares "came out of the earth first and brought the rest of the people to the surface." The sculpture's message? "Remember where you came from." **Discuss** What emotions do the koshares show? Why do you think they are experiencing these feelings?

used by the men of the community for religious ceremonies.

The Anasazis began leaving their cliff dwellings in the late 1200s to establish new communities in the Rio Grande Valley. The reason they moved may have been a drought or attacks by warlike Indians such as the Apaches (uh-PACH-eez) and Navajos (NAV-uh-hōz). Some historians believe that the Indians the Spanish later met in Arizona and New Mexico were descendants of the Anasazis. The Spanish called these Indians the Pueblo (PWEB-lō) Indians. *Pueblo* is the Spanish word for "town."

The Mound Builders

In the eastern part of what is now the United States, archaeologists have found rich evidence of ancient cultures inside

To reinforce understanding of Mound Builder cultures, have each student prepare a presentation on an excavation of an Adena, Hopewell, or Mississippian mound. It will include a large cross-section diagram identifying locations of artifacts, and a script describing each artifact and explaining what it might reveal about the people who built the mound. Several students might present reports orally, perhaps role-playing talks by archaeologists who excavated sites of the three cultures. In fact, the painting on this page was commissioned by an archaeologist for use with his lectures.

Vital Links

Cahokia mound city (Picture) Unit 1, Side 1, Search 06461

See also Unit 1 Explore CD-ROM location 72.

※ **History Footnote**

The first person to do a scientific dig of a mound may have been Thomas Jefferson. He heard rumors that Indians had collected all their dead at certain times and reburied them together, or that mounds were warrior graves. He decided to study a mound near his Virginia home "to satisfy myself whether any, and which of these opinions were just."

In 1781 he wrote a report of how he carefully measured the site, recorded locations of bones and artifacts, and drew conclusions. Finding a child's jawbone, he decided it was not solely a warrior grave site. Discovering layers of bones separated by stones and dirt, he concluded that the burials did not take place at one time. Recognizing his scientific approach, some have called him "the father of American archaeology."

thousands of earthen mounds. These mounds still exist in a vast region stretching from Kansas in the west to the Appalachian Mountains in the east, and from the Great Lakes in the north to the Gulf of Mexico in the south.

Scholars call the Indians who created these mounds the Mound Builders. The best-known Mound Builder cultures are the Adena (1000 B.C.–A.D. 200), the Hopewell (300 B.C.–A.D. 700), and the Mississippian (A.D. 700–1500).

Many of the huge earthen mounds mark the graves of dead leaders, but some were used for religious ceremonies. Some mounds look like mythological or real creatures, such as the gigantic 1,300-foot (390 m) Great Serpent Mound near present-day Cincinnati, Ohio. (See photo on page 7.)

Adenas The Adenas lived in the woodlands of Ohio, Kentucky, Indiana, Pennsylvania, and West Virginia. They got most of their food from hunting and gathering in their rich environment. In fact, even though they did very little farming, they could still settle down in one place without using up the food resources around them.

In their burial mounds the Adenas included grave goods—items buried with the dead—that tell archaeologists about their lives. For example, stone pipes show that the Adena smoked tobacco, which they grew. Beads made of seashells and bracelets made of copper from Michigan show that the Adenas carried on trade. The fact that some graves held more luxurious goods than others is a sign that certain people had a higher rank in society than others.

This cross section of a burial mound in Louisiana was painted in the mid-1800s. Several Mound Builder burial sites were excavated in the early to mid-1800s, though modern research has shed more light on these cultures. This painting shows the different levels in the burial site.

Each group of the Mississippian culture was headed by a chief ruler. The family of the ruler helped make important decisions and enjoyed an elevated status. They lived in houses atop the mounds, wore better clothing and jewelry, and ate better and more varied foods than the common population. Farmers, hunters, and gatherers all worked in part to support the family of the ruler.

Hopewells Hopewell culture gradually replaced the Adena after about 300 B.C. This culture had many of the same elements as Adena culture, but on a grander scale. The architecture of Hopewell mounds is more elaborate and their art is more refined.

With a larger population, the Hopewells were more dependent on farming than the Adenas. They also had a greater trading network. Rich burial sites contained obsidian from the Black Hills and the Rockies, mica from the Appalachians, and even alligator skulls from Florida and grizzly bear teeth from the far west.

Over time, the Hopewell culture spread over a vast area. From its core in the Ohio and Illinois River valleys, it stretched out across much of the present-day midwestern and eastern United States.

What became of the Hopewell culture? As with many Mesoamerican and Southwest cultures, historians have a variety of theories about why it vanished. The reason might have been climate changes or invasion, but no one knows for sure. Whatever the reason, another culture soon came to dominate the area: the Mississippian.

Mississippians The Mississippian people lived in the fertile valleys of the Ohio and Mississippi River basins. They grew corn, beans, squash, and pumpkins in the rich soil there. They also fished, gathered wild plants, and hunted deer, raccoons, and wild turkeys for meat. This way of life, a combination of agriculture and hunting-gathering, supported their large population.

Most Mississippian people lived in villages and on farms clustered around central towns, where religious and government leaders lived. Some of these towns grew quite large. For example, Cahokia (kuh-HŌ-kee-uh), in present-day Illinois, was the largest Indian town in what is now the United States. Established in A.D. 600, Cahokia had at least 10,000 inhabitants at its peak between 1050

and 1250. Its "downtown" covered five square miles (13 square km).

Farmers came to towns like Cahokia to trade, to take part in religious ceremonies, and for protection in times of war. In turn, leaders probably required the farmers to pay taxes in the form of crops or labor to build and maintain the massive mounds.

Like the Adenas and the Hopewells, the Mississippians built mounds. However, Mississippian mounds were even more massive, with temples and leaders' houses on top. The center of Cahokia had nearly 100 temple and burial mounds arranged around central plazas.

Grave goods from the mounds show that the Mississippians had an extensive network of trade. Scholars believe that the Mississippian people even had contact with Mesoamericans, either through trade or migration. They point to the similarities in their temples and villages, art styles, religious symbols, and farming practices.

By the time Europeans arrived in the early 1500s, Mississippian population had dropped off dramatically, leaving only a shadow of the culture's former splendor. Perhaps diseases had spread through their crowded towns, which lacked good sanitation. Later tribes in the region—the Cherokees, Creeks, Seminoles, Choctaws, and Chickasaws—are believed to be descendants of the Mississippians.

★ 3. **Section Review**

1. Define **irrigation.**
2. How did the desert farmers adapt to their environment?
3. What common characteristics did Mound Builder cultures share?
4. **Critical Thinking** Why do you think it is hard for archaeologists to find out why an ancient society collapsed?

Closing the Section

Making a Culture Bar Graph

To compare the number of years various North American cultures lasted, have students create a bar graph for six cultures. On the chalkboard, begin the graph by drawing a bar to represent the years the Mogollon culture lasted (1,700). Give figures for the Anasazis (1,400) and Hohokams (1,100). Have students refer to p. 22 to find data for the Adenas (1,200), Hopewells (1,000), and Mississippians (800). Conclude by having them compare the time spans of these cultures with the age of our nation, beginning in 1776.

Section Review
Answers

1. Definition: *irrigation* (19)
2. To make the best use of low rainfall, the Mogollans built dams and terraces, and the Hohokams built irrigation canals. The Anasazis used stone, wood, and sun-dried mud for building homes. They later made use of cliffs as natural protective sites for their dwellings.
3. All three cultures farmed, traded with other groups, created art, and built earthen mounds for religious ceremonies or burial sites.
4. Answers might include the lack of written records and physical evidence that can be used to explain the collapse of an ancient society.

Major Powell, a Civil War veteran who lost part of his right arm from wounds suffered at Shiloh, made his first exploratory trip into the Rocky Mountain region in 1867. In 1869 he led an expedition on a hazardous journey down the Colorado River and through the Grand Canyon. Later, Powell was appointed to head the United States Geographical and Geological Survey of the Rocky Mountain Region. In his explorations, he observed the Indians of the West and developed a system for classifying Indian languages. He also served as director of the Smithsonian's Bureau of Ethnology as well as of the U.S. Geological Survey.

Teaching the Geography Lab

To help students focus on general characteristics of a plateau (high elevation, mostly flat terrain), ask them to distinguish it from a mountain range (high elevation, steep terrain) and from a prairie (low elevation, flat terrain). To help them picture how a deep canyon can be created within a plateau, draw a simple cross section on the chalkboard showing a canyon in relation to the plateau surface and the surrounding lowlands.

Developing a Mental Map
Answers

1. Utah, Colorado, Arizona, and New Mexico.

2. Comparisons will vary. For example, Rhode Island is about 1/100 the size of the plateau.

3. Highest point: 12,700 feet (3,870 m); average elevation: 5,000 feet (1,525 m).

4. Dry, desert-like; evidence includes dry grass, lack of trees, yucca plant.

5. A wilderness of rock, deep gorges, rivers, cliffs, towers, pinnacles, strangely carved forms, and mountains.

6. Letters will vary but may include descriptions of physical landscape and plant and animal life.

See activity on the Grand Canyon in **Geography Extensions,** pp. 1–2.

Geography Lab

The Colorado Plateau

The Anasazis made their home in the region we call the Colorado Plateau. What was their environment like?

A **plateau** is a large expanse of high, flat land. The Colorado Plateau covers nearly 150,000 square miles (390,000 square km) and stretches over parts of four western states.

Although the plateau is mostly flat, wind and water have carved deep canyons and oddly beautiful rock formations into its surface. In 1869 Major John Wesley Powell surveyed the plateau's most famous canyon—the Grand Canyon—and found it to be more than a mile deep in places.

Look at the photograph of Mesa Verde on page 20 and at the illustrations and the words of Powell, below, to help you picture the Colorado Plateau region.

Sheep herding on the Colorado Plateau

Yucca, a dry-region plant

Basket of yucca fibers

Developing a Mental Map

Use the maps on pages P4–P5, R4–R5, and R6–R7 to help answer the questions.

1. The Colorado Plateau covers parts of which states?

2. Compare the area of the Colorado Plateau with the area of your state.

3. How high is the plateau?

4. What do the photographs tell you about the climate? Explain.

5. What features of the landscape did John Wesley Powell describe? List at least four.

6. **Hands-On Geography** Imagine that you and your family are camping on the Colorado Plateau. Write a letter to a friend describing the trip. What do you see? What does the air feel like? Will you be glad or sorry to leave? Why?

John Wesley Powell's Report

"Wherever we look there is but a wilderness of rocks—deep gorges where the rivers are lost below cliffs and towers and pinnacles, and ten thousand strangely carved forms in every direction, and beyond them mountains blending with the clouds."

Section Objectives

★ Identify factors that helped determine where North American Indians lived.

★ Describe how Indian groups in different culture areas adapted to their environments.

Teaching Resources

Take-Home Planner 1, pp. 2–9

Chapter Resources Binder

  Study Guide, p. 4

  Reinforcement

  Skills Development, pp. 7–8

  Geography Extensions

  American Readings, p. 4

  Using Historical Documents

  Transparency Activities

Chapter and Unit Tests, pp. 5–8

4. North America in the 1400s

Reading Guide

New Term **diversity**

Section Focus **Indian societies of North America at the time Europeans arrived**

1. What factors determined where North American Indians lived?
2. How did different Indian groups adapt to their environments?

The first Europeans to reach the Americas met members of only a few Indian groups. These Europeans had no idea that they had reached two enormous continents. Nor did they know the numbers and **diversity**—variety—of people who lived in North and South America. For on these two continents lived as many as a thousand different Indian groups—descendants of the hunters who migrated across the land bridge from Asia thousands of years earlier.

Population Distribution

Even today our knowledge of the peoples of North America around 1500 is incomplete. Certain facts about the population are clear, however. Fewer Indians lived in what is today Canada and the United States (around 2 million people) than in Mexico, Central America, and South America (around 40 million people).

We also know that the food available in a certain area helped determine the population size. In North America, more people lived along the coast, with its steady supply of seafood, than lived inland. More lived on the Pacific coast, where the climate was mild and food abundant, than on the Atlantic coast. More lived in the south than in the north, where harsh winters limited farming and other food supplies.

Where Indians lived by farming, their population was much larger than in nonfarming areas. As you have seen, farming made it possible for people to settle down and for their population to grow. One exception to this pattern was in the Northwest Coast area, where seafood was so abundant that Indians there had plenty to eat without farming.

Language and Ways of Life

In language and ways of life, the peoples of North America were as different from each other as the peoples of Europe. It is misleading, therefore, to speak about *the* American Indian. Indians were not—and are not—one people with a single culture.

For example, in 1492, the year Europeans first arrived in the Americas, the peoples of North America spoke nearly 550 different languages. Even tribes who lived near each other sometimes had to use sign language in order to communicate. Today, North American Indians still use about 200 of these languages.

From region to region across North America, Indian groups had very different ways of life. Some lived in wooden houses, while others made houses of animal skins. Some dug out wooden boats. Others built boats of bark or animal hides. Some wore

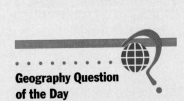

Teaching the

Link to
Technology

Point out that the advantage of the birchbark canoe is that it provides a lightweight, swift means of transportation. Ask: **What parts of trees were used to build the canoe shown? What two types of trees are specifically identified in the labels?** (Tree bark, roots, branches, and gum were used. Spruce and birch trees are identified.)

Bonus Activity

Identifying Environments

To identify environments and materials available for building shelters, have students examine the maps on pages P2 and P3 and the map on page 29. Based on their examination, students should write a description of the environments in which Indians built each of the shelters pictured on page 29.

See the Study Guide activity in **Chapter Resources Binder, p. 4.**

copper armbands; others tattooed their faces. In some groups men did the weaving; in others women were the weavers. Some Indian tribes honored their warriors. Others considered war a terrible thing and violence a form of insanity.

Tribes that lived near each other and shared a similar way of life are said to have shared the same culture. The region in which they lived is known as a *culture area.*

North American Culture Areas

The map on page 29 shows the locations of major culture areas at the time Europeans reached the Americas. Refer to the map as you read about North American cultures.

Arctic and Subarctic The Arctic area was home to the Aleuts (AHL-ee-oots) and the Inuits (IN-oo-wits). Few in number, they lived in a vast and harsh land, some of it covered with ice all year long. The weather was too cold for farming, so people survived on fish, shellfish, birds, and marine mammals such as whales, seals, and walrus.

Arctic peoples lived in small family groups. Many were nomads, traveling to follow food. They had no organized governments, but lived by general rules. The most important rule was that everyone cooperate to survive. Their arts included music, storytelling, and ivory carving.

South of the Arctic region lay the dense forests of the Subarctic. With a climate too cold for farming, Subarctic peoples such as the Crees, Chipewyans (CHIP-uh-WĪ-uhns),

Link to Technology

The Birchbark Canoe

The birchbark canoe originated among the Indians of the Great Lakes region, who used the canoes to glide along shallow rivers and creeks. When they needed to cross land, they simply lifted the lightweight canoes and carried them to the next waterway. The canoes were also easy to repair using materials from the forest—tree bark, spruce gum, and roots. When Europeans arrived in the region they quickly adopted this technology, allowing them to travel deep into the continent of North America.

Seams sewn
with spruce roots

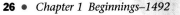

History Footnote

Archaeologists have found evidence that people hunted sea mammals, birds, and fish off the Pacific Northwest Coast as early as 7000 B.C. No one knows what type of boats the earliest people of the area used, but people later made wooden boats. The forests in the area offered an abundant supply of redwood, cedar, and fir trees. The Indians used controlled burning to harvest the trees.

They then split the trees with wedges and cutting tools and hollowed them out by using stone tools or by burning. These boats enabled hunters and fishers to help feed the people. The rich resources of the sea and the forests contributed to the prosperity of the Northwest Coast communities.

and Kaskas relied on animals and plants of the forest for food. Most migrated to follow the caribou, and also hunted moose, bear, and smaller animals. They used bones and hides of animals to make sleds and snowshoes. They glided along the rivers and lakes in birchbark canoes.

Northwest Coast In the region of the Pacific Northwest, warm ocean currents swirled along the coast, creating a mild, moist climate. Deer and bears roamed forests rich with roots and berries. Rivers swarmed with salmon. With so much food available, people here were able to live in large, permanent settlements even though they were not farmers.

In this rich land, the Tlingits (TLING-gits), Kwakiutls (KWAH-kee-OOT-uhls), Chinooks (chi-NOOKS), Coos, and other tribes developed complex cultures. Skilled at carpentry, they built large wood-planked houses from the region's giant trees. They carved *totems*, large posts displaying the animal spirits of their clan. They also hollowed out 60-foot (18-m) canoes to travel to other seaside villages for trade and to follow schools of halibut and cod far out to sea.

These Pacific people enjoyed a life of wealth and comfort. One of their most interesting customs was the *potlatch*, meaning "to give away." A potlatch was a celebration of abundance at which the hosts showered their guests with gifts of food, woven cloth and baskets, canoes, and furs. A family's rank and status were judged by how much wealth it could give away.

Discussion

Checking Understanding

1. What goods did the Arctic and Subarctic Indians produce to make traveling in their region easier? (Sleds, snowshoes, and canoes.)

2. Why were the Northwest Coast peoples able to live in large communities even though they did not farm? (The environment had an abundance of wild game, fish, and roots and berries.)

Stimulating Critical Thinking

3. What did the Subarctic and Arctic peoples and the Northwest Coast peoples have in common? (They relied on the natural environment to provide for their needs; they were not farmers; seafood was a major part of their diets.)

4. Why do you think more people lived in Central and South America than in North America? (Answers might include warmer climate and the ability of advanced civilizations to support large populations.)

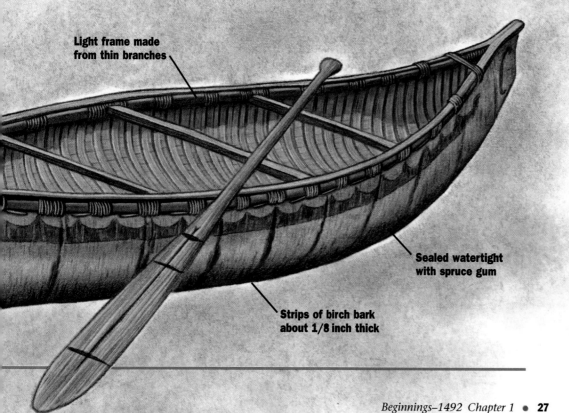

Light frame made from thin branches

Sealed watertight with spruce gum

Strips of birch bark about 1/8 inch thick

★ ★ ★
Vital Links

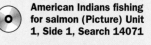
American Indians fishing for salmon (Picture) Unit 1, Side 1, Search 14071

See also Unit 1 Explore CD-ROM location 126.

The Algonquian cultures are good examples of use of natural resources. From plants and trees they created homes, clothing, containers, firewood, dugout canoes, and medicines (bitterroot: chewed for sore throat; fuchsia: leaves applied to sores; gum plant: fluid used for stomachache, poison ivy rash, and toothache; watercress: leaves or juice used to treat acne and gallstones).

Section Activity

Designing Shelters

To reinforce understanding of the relationship between shelters and environment, have students design a home using local natural resources. Discuss the natural environment around your community. For example, if you live in Wichita, Kansas, the natural environment is fairly dry plains with many different grasses and few trees. Ask students to draw a diagram of a shelter that they could build using only resources from the natural environment. Have them label the diagram in the way that the canoe shown on pages 26–27 is labeled.

★★★
Vital Links

Mohawk Indians farming (Picture) Unit 1, Side 1, Search 14049

See also Unit 1 Explore CD-ROM location 122.

Far West The Far West included three culture areas: California, Plateau, and Great Basin. The Great Basin and parts of the Plateau area are mountainous and dry, which made farming difficult and life hard. The people of the Great Basin—the Paiutes (PĪ-yoots), Shoshones (shō-SHŌ-neez), and Utes (YOOTS)—traveled in small groups to find food. They gathered acorns, seeds, and roots, and caught fish, insects, and rodents.

In California, with its warm summers and mild winters, life was not so hard. Food was abundant. People there ate small game, fish, and berries. Oak trees grew nearly everywhere, and acorns were a main source of food for the Hupas, Pomos, Chumashes, and other semi-nomadic tribes.

Indians of the Far West are known for weaving some of the world's finest baskets. The baskets, used as tools and containers, are both beautiful and practical. Some were so watertight Indians used them to cook stew.

Plains Indians of the Plains culture area relied mainly on the buffalo (bison), for survival. In these dry grasslands, buffalo gave the Plains Indians meat for food, skins for blankets and cone-shaped shelters called *tepees*, and horn and bone for tools.

Following the great herds meant a nomadic way of life for tribes such as the Kiowas (KĪ-ō-wahz) and Comanches (kuh-MAN-cheez). Along the Missouri River the Mandans and Hidatsas (hi-DAH-tsuhz) settled in earth lodges and raised crops. Still, they hunted buffalo every spring after planting and every autumn after harvest.

Plains Indians hunted buffalo on foot, for there were no horses in the Americas at that time. Their clever hunting methods included stampeding buffalo over cliffs and trapping them in ice at winter waterholes. There the hunters could kill the beasts with spears and arrows. Women and children did the butchering.

Once Plains tribes such as the Sioux, Cheyenne, and Comanche obtained horses, which came to America after Columbus, they became mighty enemies of the Europeans who later invaded their homeland.

Eastern Woodlands The many Indian groups in the large Eastern Woodlands region lived on the rich resources of the forests and coasts. They gathered wild plants and mollusks and hunted bears and deer as well as small animals such as rabbits, squirrels, birds, and turtles.

Still, farming provided the staples of the Eastern Indians' diet—corn, beans, and squash. Men cleared trees to make fields, probably using fire. Women planted, tended, and harvested the crops. If nutrients in the soil got used up after 10 or 20 years, the group would move its village a few miles and clear new fields. They built their houses from thin saplings, covering the frame with bark, animal hides, or mats made of plant fibers.

Eastern villages were often surrounded by tall fences to keep out wild animals and human enemies. War was fairly common, especially among the Iroquoian (IR-uh-KWOY-uhn) and Algonquian (al-GAHN-kee-uhn) groups in the Northeast. Algonquians such as the Narragansetts, Algonkins, Massachusets, and Delawares, and Iroquoians such as the Mohawks, Eries, Iroquois, and Hurons were among the first Indians to meet European explorers and settlers.

Southwest Indians of the dry Southwest culture area adapted to the environment much as the earlier Anasazis had. All the groups in the area did some farming, although certain groups also moved to follow animals they hunted.

Pueblo Indians such as the Hopis (HŌ-peez) and Zunis (ZOO-neez) had stable towns that lasted for hundreds of years. While the Pueblo Indians themselves were

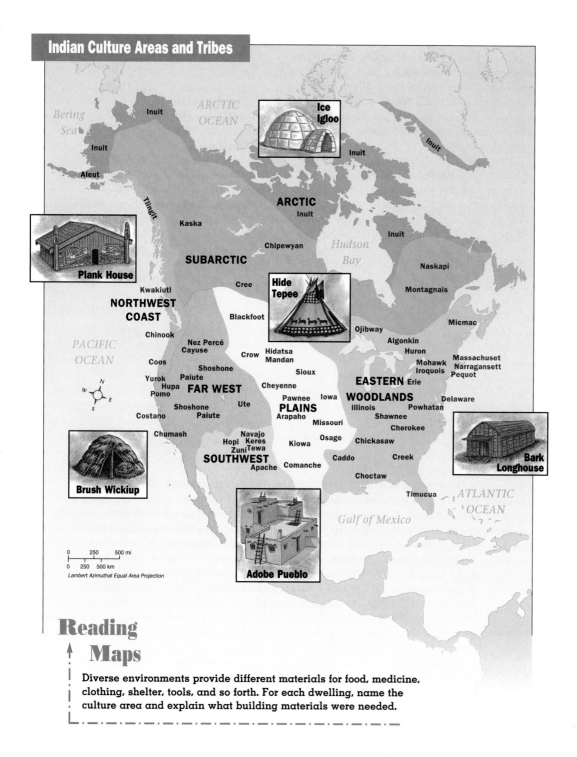

Connections to Language Arts

American Indians have a rich oral tradition of tales of creation and the Indian way of life and values. Many Northwest Coast Indians tell stories that involve Raven, who sometimes acts as a hero and sometimes a trickster. The Navajos of the Southwest culture area relate their stories in chants. They combine the chants with dancing in their ceremonies.

Have students read a Zuni poem. **American Readings,** p. 4.

Indian Culture Areas and Tribes

Ice Igloo

Plank House

Hide Tepee

Brush Wickiup

Bark Longhouse

Adobe Pueblo

Bering Sea
ARCTIC OCEAN
Inuit
Inuit
Aleut
Tlingit
Kaska
SUBARCTIC
Chipewyan
ARCTIC
Inuit
Hudson Bay
Inuit
Inuit
Naskapi
Montagnais
Cree
Kwakiutl
NORTHWEST COAST
Blackfoot
Chinook
Nez Percé
Cayuse
Crow
Hidatsa
Mandan
Ojibway
Algonkin
Huron
Micmac
PACIFIC OCEAN
Coos
Shoshone
Paiute
Sioux
Mohawk
Iroquois
Massachuset
Narragansett
Pequot
Yurok
Hupa
Pomo
FAR WEST
Cheyenne
EASTERN WOODLANDS
Erie
Shoshone
Paiute
Ute
Pawnee
Iowa
Delaware
PLAINS
Illinois
Powhatan
Costano
Arapaho
Missouri
Shawnee
Chumash
Navajo
Hopi Keres
Zuni Tewa
SOUTHWEST
Kiowa
Osage
Chickasaw
Cherokee
Caddo
Creek
Apache
Comanche
Choctaw
Timucua
ATLANTIC OCEAN
Gulf of Mexico

0 250 500 mi
0 250 500 km
Lambert Azimuthal Equal Area Projection

N
W   E
S

Reading Maps

Diverse environments provide different materials for food, medicine, clothing, shelter, tools, and so forth. For each dwelling, name the culture area and explain what building materials were needed.

Discussion

Checking Understanding

1. How did the Plains Indians use buffalo to meet basic needs? (Meat used as food; skins used for clothing and shelters.)

2. How was labor divided between men and women in the Plains? Eastern Woodlands? (Plains: men hunted and women butchered. Eastern Woodlands: men cleared land and women tended crops.)

Stimulating Critical Thinking

3. How did environment affect Indian ways of life? (Availability of usable natural resources.)

4. Do you think farming life was more advanced than nomadic hunting and gathering? Why or why not? (Some may see farming as more advanced because it involves controlling the environment and more structured societies. Others may say cultures that changed to farming did so only out of necessity. Hunting and gathering was actually easier, as long as supply was adequate.)

Teaching the Reading Maps

Have students identify which culture area they would be living in if they were Indians at the time Europeans reached North America. **Answers to Reading Maps:** Igloo: Arctic, ice; plank house: Northwest Coast, wood planks; tepee: Plains, animal hides; wickiup: Far West, brush; pueblo: Southwest, adobe clay; longhouse: Eastern Woodlands, bark.

Making Concept Webs

To review characteristics of American Indian culture areas, have students create concept webs. Display a model web on the chalkboard. Draw a circle with lines radiating from it and other circles at the ends of the lines. Write the name of a culture area in the center circle. Write specific characteristics, such as food and housing, in the circles radiating from the center. Ask students to use your model to develop webs for other culture groups.

Section Review
Answers

1. Definition: *diversity* (25)

2. Areas with abundant natural food supplies or where people farmed had larger populations.

3. In areas with large supplies, people hunted and gathered. In areas with few natural food sources, they were migratory or turned to farming.

4. Evidence would indicate that the people were settled. Pottery indicates food was stored. Stone buildings would indicate that the people were organized and perhaps settled. Traces of canals indicate irrigation for farming.

To check understanding of "Why We Remember," assign Thinking Critically question 3 on page 32.

30

✳ **History Footnote**

The Apaches, living in what is now Arizona, New Mexico, and northern Mexico, earned a reputation as fierce fighters that dates back many centuries. For over 250 years they staged guerrilla raids against Spanish settlements. Later, in the 1800s, they rigorously opposed attempts by the United States to place them on reservations. Their resistance continued until the late 1800s.

peaceful, they built large adobe apartment houses to give them shelter from attack by outsiders. The center of their village life was ceremony and ritual, which took place in the kivas and central plazas. Today, some Pueblo groups still practice a yearly cycle of ritual drama.

Other Southwestern Indian groups migrated to the region. While both the Navajos and the Apaches at first raided Pueblo settlements, eventually the Navajos took up farming and adapted many crafts, skills, and beliefs from their Hopi neighbors. The nomadic Apaches continued to raid neighboring groups and came to be feared as fierce warriors.

4. Section Review

1. Define **diversity**.
2. How did the supply of food affect the population distribution of Indians in North America?
3. In what ways did the way of life of different Indian groups reflect the region in which they lived?
4. **Critical Thinking** At one archaeological site bits of pottery, the foundation of a large stone building, and traces of an irrigation canal have been found. Would you hypothesize that the people who lived here were nomadic or settled? Explain.

Why We Remember

The First Americans

Today we find it hard to picture the America the Paleo-Indians knew. Had you traveled with the stone seekers, you would have seen no paved roads, no cars, no signs, no power lines, no tall buildings. The land would have seemed almost empty of people. Yet over thousands of years the descendants of the Paleo-Indians spread out across North and South America.

The first Americans lived well on the resources of the land. From the frozen Arctic shores to the steamy lowlands of Mesoamerica, they developed ways of life well-suited to the land's varied environments. Some peoples lived by harvesting natural riches of the forests, plains, or seas. Others were farmers. Making good use of water, often through complex irrigation systems, they grew food crops known only in the Americas. As you will read, these foods were some of the first Americans' greatest gifts to the world.

The descendants of the Paleo-Indian hunters who crossed the land bridge created rich cultures and splendid civilizations. Many of these cultures have endured over thousands of years. We remember the first Americans not only because they shaped the history of the Americas for countless centuries, but also because their cultures still help define what it means to be an American.

3. Questions about summary statements will vary. Most will probably focus on possible cause-effect relationships. Some examples: "Did people in North America learn how to grow corn from people in Mesoamerica?" "Why did pottery develop so much earlier in South America than in North America?"
4. Answers will vary. Answering the question on corn would require information on types of corn found at dig sites in North America and Mesoamerica. It could not be answered from the time line, which provides no information on contacts between people in those regions.

For further application, have students do the Applying Skills activity in the Chapter Survey (p. 32).

Skill Lab

Acquiring Information
Time Lines

Skill Tips

Keep in mind:
- Begin and end both of your parallel time lines with the same dates.
- Divide the time lines into equal units of time. (But see the next skill tip.)
- If the time lines cover a very long period of time, use jagged lines to show that a particular time span has been left out.

One group built dwellings of stone and clay along the sides of cliffs. Another created a city—complete with markets, temples, and an emperor's palace—on an island in the middle of a lake. Only a thousand miles and a few hundred years separated the Anasazis and the Aztecs. Yet their cultures, like others throughout the Americas, differed greatly.

Question to Investigate

How did some early American cultures differ in their development?

Procedure

One way to compare developments in different cultures is by using **time lines.** A time line is a chart that shows when, and in what order, events occurred in the past. Two or more time lines that cover the same time span but different sets of events are called **parallel time lines.**

❶ With **B** as a model, make two parallel time lines. Refer to **A, B,** and **C** for events.

❷ Look for similarities and differences. Write three summary statements, such as "__ was made in South America before it was made in North America."

❸ For each summary statement, write down two questions that it raises in your mind. For example, "Did people in __ learn about __ from people in __?"

❹ For each question you wrote, tell what else you would need to know in order to answer it. Explain why you cannot answer it just from the information on the time line.

Data to Use

A Make a list of the events and their dates given in the chapter time line and throughout Chapter 1.

B

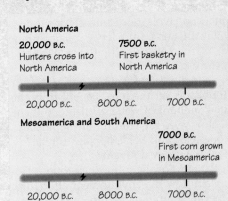

North America

20,000 B.C. Hunters cross into North America

7500 B.C. First basketry in North America

20,000 B.C.   8000 B.C.   7000 B.C.

Mesoamerica and South America

7000 B.C. First corn grown in Mesoamerica

20,000 B.C.   8000 B.C.   7000 B.C.

C Additional Events and Dates

3150 B.C.	First pottery in South America
2000	First pottery in North America
2000	First potatoes grown in South America
1500	First metalwork in South America
A.D. 750	Pueblos built in North America
800	First use of bow and arrow in North America
1000	First use of bow and arrow in Mesoamerica

Introducing the Skill Lab

In discussing how to interpret time lines, point out how the purpose of parallel time lines differs from the purpose of a regular time line. Also, have students consider what types of inferences are valid or invalid based solely on the information provided in the time line. For instance, they should recognize that the fact that one event occurs before another does not necessarily mean that the first event caused the second. Students should consider what additional information they would need in order to draw reasonable conclusions about cause-effect relationships.

Skill Lab
Answers

1. Time lines that students create should include the events shown in the sample labeled B, the ones listed in C, events from the chapter time line, and relevant dates from the chapter narrative.
2. Some examples: "The bow and arrow was used in North America before it was used in South America." "Pottery was created in South America before it was created in North America." "Corn was grown in Mesoamerica before it was grown in North America."

(Answers continued in top margin)

Reviewing Vocabulary

Definitions are found on these pages: *migration* (10), *glaciers* (10), *nomads* (11), *culture* (13), *civilization* (14), *tribute* (16), *irrigation* (19), *diversity* (25).

Reviewing Main Ideas

1. They followed animals that they hunted for food.

2. (a) Increased food supply, making it possible to live longer and increase population. (b) Not necessary for every person to farm; people could specialize. (c) Surplus food and goods could be traded.

3. Objects made or owned by one group might be found in sites inhabited by others. Objects made by different groups may be similar. Examples vary.

4. Answers may include (a) science: calendar (Olmecs, Mayas), astronomy (Olmecs, Mayas); (b) agriculture: irrigated terraces (Aztecs); (c) architecture: religious centers with large monuments (Olmecs); Pyramid of the Sun (Teotihuacán), pyramids with temples and palaces (Mayas), Great Temple (Aztecs).

5. Irrigation systems.

6. All built mounds, traded, farmed, hunted, and gathered. They occupied different areas. Mounds differed in size and complexity. Adenas were less dependent on farming. Hopewells and Mississippians had larger trade networks.

7. (a) Cold Arctic could not support farming, so Inuits hunted and fished. (b) Warm, moist climate of Northwest enabled Chinooks to fish, hunt, and gather. (c) Shoshones lived on mountainous and semi-arid land where they gathered plants and hunted and

(Answers continued in top margin)

---

fished. (d) Dry Great Plains grasslands made farming difficult, so Comanches relied on buffalo. (e) Iroquois lived in rich eastern woodlands where they hunted, gathered, and farmed.

Thinking Critically

1. It is hard to date artifacts or tell if made by humans. Archaeologists, anthropologists, geologists, and biologists might all work to

determine origins.

2. Unlike most North American cultures, Mesoamerican and Incan civilizations had widespread empires, large cities, complex governments, and massive architecture. Accept logical explanations.

3. Answers might include to learn how the land was used, to learn how to live harmoniously with it, to appreciate their cultures

---

Chapter Survey ★

Reviewing Vocabulary

Define the following terms.
1. migration
2. glaciers
3. nomads
4. culture
5. civilization
6. tribute
7. irrigation
8. diversity

Reviewing Main Ideas

1. Why did the ancestors of the Paleo-Indians travel across Beringia?
2. How did farming make each of the following possible? (a) larger populations (b) people specializing in one kind of work (c) development of trade
3. Tell one way historians know that some early groups carried on trade with other groups. Give an example of such trade.
4. Describe one achievement of Meso-american civilizations in each of the following areas. (a) science (b) agriculture (c) architecture. Identify the civilization in each case.
5. How did the Mogollons and the Hohokams get the most benefit from the small amount of water available to them?
6. How were the cultures of the Adenas, Hopewells, and Mississippians similar? How were they different?
7. For each of the following groups, explain how the environment affected the way the group obtained food. (a) Inuits (b) Chinooks (c) Shoshones (d) Comanches (e) Iroquois

Thinking Critically

1. **Analysis** Why is it so difficult to know for sure when people first came to live in the Americas? What different scientists might need to work together to help determine human origins in the Americas?
2. **Analysis** List three differences between most North American cultures and those of

Mesoamerica and Peru around 1500. Why do you think the differences developed?

3. **Why We Remember: Synthesis** The "Why We Remember" on page 30 explains why we study the lives of the first Americans. State one reason in your own words and give three supporting examples from the text or your own observations.

Applying Skills

Creating time lines Use what you learned on page 31 and work with your family to create parallel time lines. Show (1) major events in the United States and (2) important events in your family during a certain time period, such as the last fifty years. Does there seem to be a relationship between major events and events in your family? If so, describe the relationship. If not, tell why you think there is no obvious relationship.

History Mystery

The Great Serpent Mound
The reasons for building the Great Serpent Mound shown on page 7 and the meaning of the design remain a mystery. While some mounds were burial sites, no burial remains have been found within this mound. The age of the mound is also unknown, though scholars believe it to be Adena. Why do you think people who could not view the mound from the air created the structure?

Writing in Your History Journal

1. Keys to History (a) The time line on pages 6–7 has seven Keys to History. In your journal, list each key and describe why it is important to know about. (b) Look back over the chapter and find other important places,

and achievements, and to recognize that today's Indians have a rich heritage.

Applying Skills

Some students may see relationships, such as military service coinciding with a war. Others may find little connection, especially if the family recently immigrated.

History Mystery

Information on the mounds is found on page 22. The purpose remains a mystery. Answers might include that it honored a god who might see it from above, or symbolized a god who would look favorably on the people.

Writing in Your History Journal

1. (a) Explanations should be similar to the
(Answers continued in side margin)

time line notes on teacher pages 6–7.(b) Some examples are information about different culture areas.

2. Stories will vary, but explanations should be plausible. They might include the idea that stones were quarried at the site but used after people moved.

3. Opinions will vary. Responses should consider the balance between individual property rights and the public interest.

Reviewing Geography

1. (A) Arctic—Inuit, Aleut; (B) Subarctic—Kaska, Cree, Chipewyan, Naskapi, Montagnais; (C) Northwest Coast—Kwakiutl, Chinook, Coos; (D) Far West—Nez Percé, Cayuse, Shoshone, Paiute, Yurok, Hupa, Pomo, Ute, Costano, Chumash; (E) Plains—Blackfoot, Crow, Hidatsa, Mandan, Sioux, Cheyenne, Iowa, Pawnee, Arapaho, Missouri, Osage, Kiowa, Comanche; (F) Eastern Woodlands—Micmac, Ojibway, Algonkin, Huron, Mohawk, Iroquois, Massachuset, Narragansett, Pequot, Erie, Delaware, Powhatan, Illinois, Shawnee, Cherokee, Chickasaw, Caddo, Creek, Choctaw, Timucua; (G) Southwest—Navajo, Hopi, Keres, Tewa, Zuni, Apache.

2. Answers might include Aztec terraces and chinampas for farming; Anasazi cliff dwellings for protection; trees for houses, totems, and canoes in Northwest. Accept all reasonable present-day examples, such as roads, housing, and dams.

Alternative Assessment

Teacher's Take-Home Planner 1, p. 5, includes suggestions and scoring rubrics for the Alternative Assessment activity.

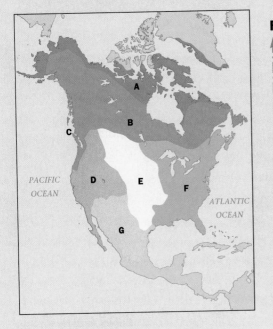

Reviewing Geography

1. For each letter on the map, write the name of the culture area and the name of one tribe that lived in that culture area around 1500.

2. **Geographic Thinking** Natural settings affect the way people live. For example, people who live in the Arctic dress differently from people who live in deserts. However, people also affect their natural settings. Identify two examples of changes that Indians made in their natural settings. Tell who the Indian groups were and why they made the changes. Then give two examples of how people have changed the natural setting where you live.

groups, or ideas. Add them to the list in your journal, along with why you think they are important to remember.

2. **The Stone Seekers** The story on pages 8 and 9 gives one explanation of how the spear points from an ancient quarry in Wyoming might have ended up in New Mexico—over 200 miles (320 km) away. In your journal, write your own short story explaining how the stone might have traveled such a long distance.

3. **Citizenship** Suppose a person finds an ancient artifact or bone in his or her backyard. Does the person have the right to keep it? Should the person turn it over to a museum, the government, or some other authority? Does it make a difference if the person finds the item on public property, such as at a park, or on his or her own property? Write your responses in your journal, and explain why you feel as you do.

Alternative Assessment

Preparing a museum exhibit Imagine that your class is the staff of a history museum planning a new wing called "The First Americans." With a group of other staff members, prepare an exhibit on one of the cultures or civilizations described in the chapter. Your exhibit might include artifacts, drawings, models, and audiotapes, as well as written material like labels and captions. Start with the information in the chapter and do additional research as needed to make the culture or civilization come alive for museum visitors.

Your exhibit will be evaluated on whether:
• it shows such aspects of the culture or civilization as daily life, interaction with the environment, and achievements
• it provides information that is accurate
• it presents the information in clear, inviting ways

Chapter Planning Guide

Section	Student Text	Teacher's Edition Activities
Opener and Story pp. 34–37	**Keys to History Time Line** **History Mystery** Beginning the Story with **Prince Henry the Navigator**	**Setting the Stage Activity** Maps vs. Oral Directions, p. 36
1 Trading Empires of Africa pp. 38–43	**Reading Maps** Trade in Africa 1450, p. 39 **Link to Art** Benin bronze, p. 42 **Skill Lab** Reading History, p. 43	**Warm-Up Activity** Trading Goods, p. 38 **Geography Question of the Day,** p. 38 **Section Activity** Practicing the Oral Tradition, p. 41 **Bonus Activity** Reporting on a Muslim Pilgrimage, p. 40 **Wrap-Up Activity** History Trivia, p. 42
2 The Wealth of Asia pp. 44–48	**Reading Maps** Trade in Asia 1450, p. 45 **World Link** Polynesian navigators, p. 47 **Point of View** Why did the Chinese voyages stop?, p. 48	**Warm-Up Activity** Inferring from a Picture, p. 44 **Geography Question of the Day,** p. 44 **Section Activity** Making a Cutaway Drawing of a Junk, p. 46 **Bonus Activity** Describing the Exotic, p. 46 **Wrap-Up Activity** Writing a Diary Entry, p. 48
3 Europe Looks Outward pp. 49–55	**Link to the Present** The appeal of spices, p. 50 **Reading Maps** Trade in Europe 1450, p. 51; Portuguese Voyages 1420–1460, p. 53 **Hands-On History** Designing a book, p. 52 **Geography Lab** Comparing Historical and Modern Maps, p. 55	**Warm-Up Activity** Imagining a Peasant's Choice, p. 49 **Geography Question of the Day,** p. 49 **Section Activity** Making a Spice Chart, p. 50 **Bonus Activity** Using a Compass, p. 52 **Wrap-Up Activity** Creating Tableaux, p. 54
Evaluation	☑ **Section 1 Review,** p. 42 ☑ **Section 2 Review,** p. 48 ☑ **Section 3 Review,** p. 54 ☑ **Chapter Survey,** pp. 56–57 **Alternative Assessment** Teaching a class at Sagres, p. 57	☑ **Answers to Section 1 Review,** p. 42 ☑ **Answers to Section 2 Review,** p. 48 ☑ **Answers to Section 3 Review,** p. 54 ☑ **Answers to Chapter Survey,** pp. 56–57 (Alternative Assessment guidelines are in the Take-Home Planner.)

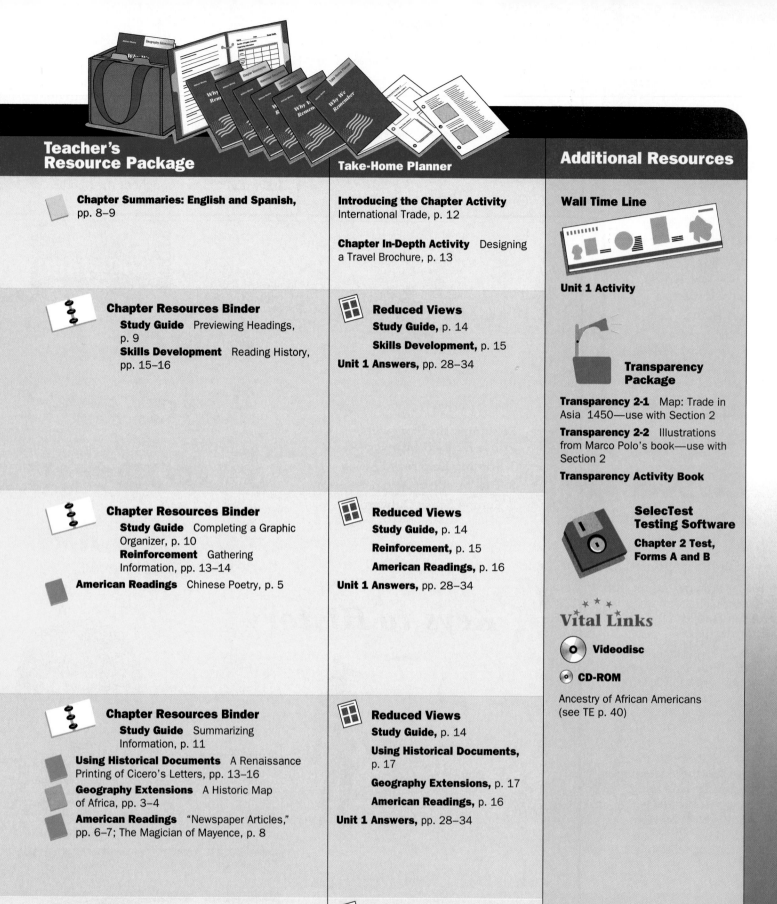

Teacher's Resource Package

Chapter Summaries: English and Spanish, pp. 8–9

Chapter Resources Binder
Study Guide Previewing Headings, p. 9
Skills Development Reading History, pp. 15–16

Chapter Resources Binder
Study Guide Completing a Graphic Organizer, p. 10
Reinforcement Gathering Information, pp. 13–14
American Readings Chinese Poetry, p. 5

Chapter Resources Binder
Study Guide Summarizing Information, p. 11
Using Historical Documents A Renaissance Printing of Cicero's Letters, pp. 13–16
Geography Extensions A Historic Map of Africa, pp. 3–4
American Readings "Newspaper Articles," pp. 6–7; The Magician of Mayence, p. 8

Chapter and Unit Tests Chapter 2 Tests, Forms A and B, pp. 9–12

Take-Home Planner

Introducing the Chapter Activity International Trade, p. 12

Chapter In-Depth Activity Designing a Travel Brochure, p. 13

Reduced Views
Study Guide, p. 14
Skills Development, p. 15
Unit 1 Answers, pp. 28–34

Reduced Views
Study Guide, p. 14
Reinforcement, p. 15
American Readings, p. 16
Unit 1 Answers, pp. 28–34

Reduced Views
Study Guide, p. 14
Using Historical Documents, p. 17
Geography Extensions, p. 17
American Readings, p. 16
Unit 1 Answers, pp. 28–34

Reduced Views
Chapter Tests, p. 17
Unit 1 Answers, pp. 28–34
Alternative Assessment Guidelines for scoring the Chapter Survey activity, p. 13

Additional Resources

Wall Time Line

Unit 1 Activity

Transparency Package

Transparency 2-1 Map: Trade in Asia 1450—use with Section 2
Transparency 2-2 Illustrations from Marco Polo's book—use with Section 2

Transparency Activity Book

SelecTest Testing Software
Chapter 2 Test, Forms A and B

Vital Links

Videodisc

CD-ROM

Ancestry of African Americans (see TE p. 40)

2

Teaching Resources

Take-Home Planner 1
  Introducing Chapter Activity
  Chapter In-Depth Activity
  Alternative Assessment
Chapter Resources Binder
Geography Extensions
American Readings
Using Historical Documents
Transparency Activities
Wall Time Line Activities
Chapter Summaries
Chapter and Unit Tests
SelecTest Test File
Vital Links CD-ROM/Videodisc

Time Line

Keys to History

Keys to History journal writing activity is on page 56 in the Chapter Survey.

Fall of Roman Empire The empire's fall led to division within Europe and a decline in trade. (p. 49)

Crusades Christian Europeans unsuccessfully fought to gain control of Palestine in a series of military expeditions against the Muslim Turks. (p. 50)

Looking Back As the ice age ended, the sea level rose, covering the land bridge over which the first people came to North America.

World Link See p. 47.

Chapter Objectives

★ Describe the world links that Africa had by the 1400s.
★ Identify the impact of Asian ideas and goods on the world by the 1400s.
★ Explain how European interest in trading developed and led to exploration.

Chapter Overview

By the 1400s Africa had long been part of a great trade network linking it to the Middle East and Asia. Trade led to the growth of rich empires and trade centers and to the exchange and sharing of ideas. Most West Africans valued community life, music, and communication.

Arab traders help spread the goods of India and China throughout the Middle

---

1400–1460

Chapter 2

Sections

Beginning the Story with Prince Henry the Navigator
1. **Trading Empires of Africa**
2. **The Wealth of Asia**
3. **Europe Looks Outward**

Africa, Asia, and Europe in the 1400s

Keys to History

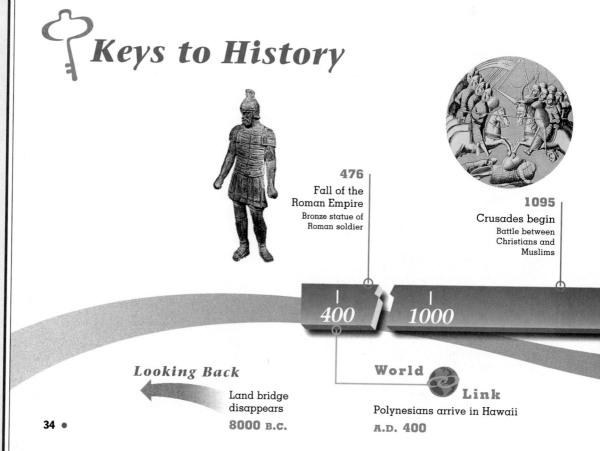

476
Fall of the Roman Empire
Bronze statue of Roman soldier

1095
Crusades begin
Battle between Christians and Muslims

400

1000

Looking Back
Land bridge disappears
8000 B.C.

World Link
Polynesians arrive in Hawaii
A.D. 400

East and Africa. China became a rich and powerful country because of its technological advances, navy, and goods such as silk and porcelain. The Silk Road was its overland trade route to the Middle East, and its ships sailed trade routes throughout Asia and to Africa. In the early 1500s, the Chinese ended their sea trade.

After the fall of the Roman Empire, Europe was divided into many small warring kingdoms. As the people relied on the protection of lords for survival, a feudal system of government developed. Christianity was a unifying force among Europeans. The Crusades helped introduce Europeans to African and Asian goods. In the 1300s and 1400s the growth of nations and the Renaissance fueled European interest in trade and exploration. Portugal led the way as it explored the African coast.

Teaching the HISTORY Mystery

Students will find possible solutions on p. 48. See Chapter Survey, p. 56, for questions related to the History Mystery. Some of Zheng He's ships were four times longer than the *Santa María*, which was 85 feet (26 m) long.

HISTORY Mystery

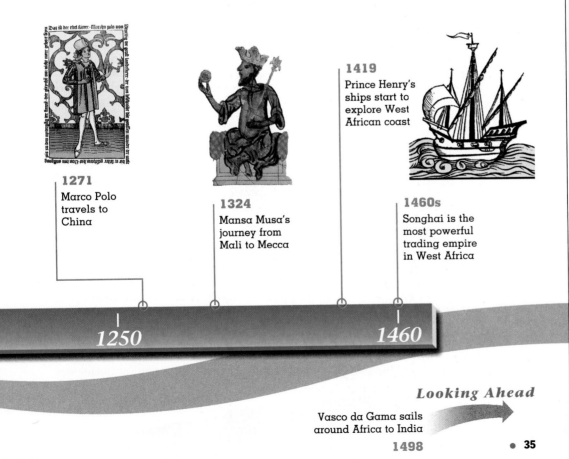

In the early 1400s China had the world's greatest sailing fleet, commanded by Admiral Zheng He. By the early 1500s few Chinese ships sailed the seas. What happened to the Chinese navy? (In Chapter 2 you will learn more about this History Mystery.)

Photo from Louise Levathes' *When China Ruled the Seas* (1994)

1271
Marco Polo travels to China

1324
Mansa Musa's journey from Mali to Mecca

1419
Prince Henry's ships start to explore West African coast

1460s
Songhai is the most powerful trading empire in West Africa

1250   *1460*

Looking Ahead
Vasco da Gama sails around Africa to India
1498

• **35**

Time Line

Marco Polo Marco Polo's account of his travels inspired European interest in trade with Asia. (p. 44)

Mansa Musa As Europeans learned of his wealth, they became interested in African trade. (p. 40)

Prince Henry of Portugal Prince Henry supported over 50 expeditions, which advanced European knowledge of geography and expanded trade. (p. 36)

Songhai By the time the Portuguese began sailing along the West African coast, Songhai had replaced Mali as the most powerful empire in the region. (p. 40)

Looking Ahead Vasco da Gama's voyage gave Portugal control of the first all-water route from Europe to Asia. It also ended Columbus's hope of getting Portugal to support his plan.

Beginning the Story

Prince Henry the Navigator

As trade expanded, Europeans wanted to trade directly with Asians instead of dealing with Arab middlemen. Prince Henry of Portugal organized expeditions to Africa to expand trade in the mid-1400s. For his planning skills, he was called "the Navigator," even though he never joined the expeditions. The voyages Henry promoted increased European knowledge of geography and navigation, led to exploration for trade routes, and eventually led Europeans to the Americas.

Setting the Stage Activity

Maps vs. Oral Directions

Divide the class into pairs, with each student choosing a nearby destination that his or her partner does not know how to get to. Partners will take turns giving directions, first orally and then by creating a map. Have the class discuss advantages of maps. Conclude by pointing out how critical cartography was to exploration.

See the Introducing the Chapter Activity, International Trade. **Take-Home Planner 1,** p. 12.

✳ **History Footnote**

During Prince Henry's time, Portugal had a royal historian named Azurara, who wrote about Henry's life and the exploratory expeditions. In his *Chronicle of the Discovery of Guinea,* Azurara stated one of Henry's goals for the expeditions: "If in these territories there should be any harbors where [sailors] could enter without peril, they could bring back merchandise at little cost, because there would be no other persons to compete with them." The *Chronicle* comes to a close in 1448 when Portugal became embroiled in a civil war. The work of Azurara provides insight into Henry's motivations and accomplishments as a sponsor of exploratory expeditions.

Beginning the Story with

Prince Henry the Navigator

O n March 4, 1394, Queen Philippa of Portugal gave birth to her third son, Prince Henry. At the time Henry was born, Europeans had little contact with Asia and Africa. They were completely isolated from North and South America. No one in Europe even suspected that these continents existed.

As Queen Philippa held her son, she could not have dreamed that he would grow up to help lead Europe out of its isolation. She might have found a clue to Henry's future, though, in his horoscope. It predicted that her son was "bound to attempt the discovery of things which were hidden from other men and secret."

The Young Conqueror

Prince Henry grew up to be a serious, deeply religious young man. He had no interest in politics. Instead, he spent his time learning about military matters and studying mathematics and astronomy. Henry was also very curious about the world beyond Europe. He read everything he could find about distant lands, trying to sort out fact from legend.

As a young man, Henry helped his father, King John I, plan a raid on the North African trading town of Ceuta (SYOOT-ah). Located on the Strait of Gibraltar, which connects the Mediterranean Sea and the Atlantic Ocean, Ceuta was a natural meeting point for African, Arab, and European traders. Both father and son agreed that Ceuta would be a rich prize indeed. As they laid their plans, Henry pleaded, "When God pleases that we arrive at Ceuta, let me be among the first to embark."

King John granted his son's wish. In 1415 Prince Henry led the way when Portuguese troops stormed and captured Ceuta. The young conqueror was

History Bookshelf

McKissack, Patricia and Fredrick. *The Royal Kingdoms of Ghana, Mali, and Songhay: Life in Medieval Africa.* Holt, 1994. In a narrative format, the authors give an accurate account of Ghana, Mali, and Songhai. It was chosen as a 1994 Notable Children's Trade Book in the Field of Social Studies.

Also of interest:

Hernandez, Xavier, and Pilar Comes. *Barmi: A Mediterranean City Through the Ages.* Houghton Mifflin, 1990.

Reid, Struan. *Exploration by Sea (The Silk and Spice Routes).* New Discovery Books, 1994.

Twist, Clint. *Marco Polo: Overland to Medieval China.* Raintree/Steck-Vaughn, 1994.

amazed by the wealth that he found there. He saw houses and shops filled with Oriental rugs, gold and silver coins, precious jewels, and sacks of cinnamon, pepper, and other spices.

The gold, Henry learned, came from West Africa. Many of the other goods came from "the Indies," as Europeans called the Asian lands of India and China and the islands off the Asian mainland. After seeing Ceuta, Henry began to dream of the wealth that would pour into Portugal if only it could trade directly with these distant lands.

The prince knew that all land routes to Africa and Asia were controlled by Arab traders, so he looked to the sea. If Portuguese traders could reach Africa and Asia by sea, they could bypass the Arabs completely.

The flags on this Portuguese map, made in 1502, show Portugal's successful efforts to find a sea route to Africa and explore its coasts.

The Navigator

Back home in Portugal, Prince Henry turned to making his dream a reality. Around 1419 he began by sending ships out to explore the west coast of Africa and establish trade for gold. The prince never joined these voyages, but because he set their course, he was nicknamed "the Navigator."

The greatest challenge facing Prince Henry was fear of the unknown. Most European sailors were deathly afraid of sailing far from familiar waters. In their minds, the Atlantic Ocean was a mysterious "Green Sea of Darkness." Henry ignored such fears. As his ships prepared to leave for Africa, he advised his captains to record everything they saw. When the ships returned, Henry listened carefully to his captains' reports and then gave new orders. "Go back," he always said. "Go back, and go still farther."

The voyages begun by Henry would eventually lead European explorers to the Americas. However, Henry did not act alone. People and events in Africa, Asia, and the rest of Europe set the stage for his voyages. This chapter gives you a picture of those peoples and events, bringing the story up to the mid-1400s.

Hands-On → HISTORY

Activity

The sailors sent out by Prince Henry had heard many tales about the "Green Sea of Darkness." There were stories of giant sea snakes that fed on ships, whirlpools strong enough to sink ships, and winds fierce enough to push ships to the ends of the earth. Imagine that you are a sailor on one of Henry's ships as it enters unexplored waters. Write a diary entry describing your greatest fear.

Discussion

Thinking Historically

1. **Why would finding a sea route to the Indies help the Portuguese in their trade with Asia?** (They would no longer have to deal with Arab traders, who acted as selling agents.)

2. **Why do you think Prince Henry never joined the voyages?** (Perhaps he could best serve his country by planning and compiling information from expeditions.)

3. **Why do you think sailors agreed to go on voyages of exploration? Explain.** (Sailors may have had a sense of adventure or needed to make a living.)

See the Chapter In-Depth Activity, Designing a Travel Brochure. **Take-Home Planner 1,** p. 13.

Teaching the Hands-On

┌ - - - - - - → HISTORY

To help students imagine sailors' fears, begin by asking what present-day travelers might fear (accidents, running out of money, becoming lost, getting robbed). Then have them imagine why Prince Henry's sailors may have felt more fear. Diary entries should reflect the anxiety of not knowing what one may encounter.

For a journal writing activity on Prince Henry, see student page 56.

Introducing the Section

Warm-Up Activity

Trading Goods

To help students understand supply and demand, have them trade "goods." Provide five types: a large supply (about 60) of one, a small supply (about 5) of another, and a moderate supply (about 30) of each of the others. Some possible items are paper clips, folders, pencils, pens, and erasers. Divide the class into groups of three, distributing the large and moderate supplies equally. Give the "rare" item to one group. After the groups negotiate, discuss how scarcity affects trade.

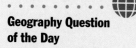

Geography Question of the Day

Ask students to identify what present-day countries Timbuktu, Gao, Bilma, Mogadishu, Mombasa, Kilwa, and Mozambique would be located in. Have them refer to the maps on p. 39 and pp. R2–R3. (Timbuktu, Gao: Mali; Bilma: Nigeria; Mogadishu: Somalia; Mombasa: Kenya; Kilwa: Tanzania; Mozambique: Mozambique.)

Section Objectives

★ Describe Africa's trade links with the Middle East and Asia.
★ Identify the ways the West African empires became wealthy.
★ Summarize the ways of life shared by West Africans in the 1400s.

Teaching Resources

Take-Home Planner 1, pp. 10–17
Chapter Resources Binder
  Study Guide, p. 9
  Reinforcement
  Skills Development, pp. 15–16
Geography Extensions
American Readings
Using Historical Documents
Transparency Activities
Chapter and Unit Tests

1. Trading Empires of Africa

Reading Guide

Section Focus Africa's links with the world in the 1400s

1. What trade links existed between Africa, the Middle East, and Asia?
2. What supported the wealthy empires of Ghana, Mali, and Songhai?
3. What ways of life did most West Africans share?

In the mid-1430s two of Prince Henry's sea captains sailing south along the coast of West Africa found footprints of men and camels in the sand. Hearing the news, Henry quickly ordered the captains to

❝go as far as you can, and try to bring news of these people. . . . To me it would be no small thing to have some man to tell me of this land!❞

As you will read in Section 3, much of Europe had been isolated from the rest of the world for hundreds of years. Thus, the continent of Africa was a land of mystery to Henry, as to most Europeans.

In fact, in the 1400s Africa was home to flourishing cultures and civilizations that had long been linked by trade to the Middle East, India, and China. Now, African peoples and African goods were to play an important role in arousing European interest in the resources of the rest of the world.

A Long History of Trade

Africans have a long history of trade, going back as far as 3100 B.C., when the great civilization of Egypt arose. Archaeologists have learned much about this trade from records, artifacts, and scenes of daily life painted on walls.

Egyptian traders sailed throughout the eastern Mediterranean Sea and the Red Sea to bring home cedar logs, silver, and horses. Following land routes south from Egypt, they found ivory, spices, copper, and cattle. For these goods, Egyptians traded gold, wheat, and papyrus, a kind of paper made from reed plants.

South of Egypt rose another ancient civilization called Kush that was a trading power by 250 B.C. The Kushites traded not only in Africa but also in Arabia, India, and China. They also learned how to use iron to make tools and weapons. Archaeologists have found heaps of ironworking waste in their capital city, Meroë. It was a great ironworking center and a crossroads for trade.

East African Trade

About A.D. 1000, trade centers began to appear in eastern Africa. The most powerful was Zimbabwe (zim-BAH-bway), which became the center of a flourishing empire in the 1400s.

Zimbabwe traders took gold, ivory, and precious stones to east coast seaports. From there, Arab and Indian ships carried the goods to Asia. The ships returned with porcelain (china), spices, cloth, and jewels from China and India.

This trade brought prosperity to East African seaports. Kilwa, the chief trading center, was one of the most beautiful cities in the world. Houses were built of stone and coral, and gardens flourished everywhere.

In the mid-1000s, Spanish-Arab geographer al-Bakri wrote about Ghana in *Book of Roads and Kingdoms*. An excerpt appears on this page. He described Ghana's capital as a city made up of two towns. In one of these lived the Muslim merchants. According to al-Bakri, this town had 12 mosques and the homes of the merchants. In the other town were the king's palace and dome-shaped homes of members of his court. In 1914, a French official identified ruins at Kumbi Salih in present-day Mauritania. Archaeologists excavated the ruins in the 1950s. They found that the site was the remains of the Ghana capital city's Muslim commercial town.

Developing the Section

Discussion

Checking Understanding

1. Why did East African seaports prosper during the 1400s? (They were shipping centers for goods coming into and leaving the East African empires on Arab and Indian ships.)

2. How did the rulers in the Sudan become wealthy? (They taxed trade.)

Stimulating Critical Thinking

3. How did the supply of goods affect trade in West Africa? (West Africans traded excess goods. Those who had excess salt traded for gold and ivory.)

Teaching the Reading Maps

Check understanding of the map by asking which kingdom or empire had the most gold in West Africa (Ashanti) and in East Africa (Mwanamutapa). **Answers to Reading Maps: 1.** Gold, ivory, slaves, spices, hides, jewels, copper, salt, and gum arabic **2.** Northern Africa because of Sahara, west central Africa because of rain forests, and eastern Africa because of mountains.

Trade in Africa 1450

Trade routes · Spices · Rain Forest · Hides · Desert · Jewels · Gold · Copper · Ivory · Salt · Slaves · Gum arabic

Reading Maps

1. What goods attracted traders to Africa?
2. In what parts of Africa is travel very difficult? Why?

Western Trading Empires

Trading empires also appeared in the Sudan, a broad belt of open country sandwiched between the Sahara Desert and the rain forests of West Africa. The most powerful were the empires of Ghana, Mali, and Songhai.

The wealth of these empires came from the gold and salt trade. Parts of West Africa had huge deposits of gold but were desperate for salt. Yet to the north, in the Sahara, salt was so common that people used blocks of it to build houses.

North African caravans crossed the Sahara Desert, carrying salt as well as sugar, grain, and cloth. Merchants traded these goods in the Sudan for gold, ivory, spices, and other products from West Africa. By taxing the trade, rulers in the Sudan became rich.

Ghana Ghana, which took control of this trade in the 400s, became the first great empire of West Africa. The Spanish-Arab geographer al-Bakri wrote of King Tenkamenin of Ghana:

❝He sits in a pavilion around which stand ten horses with gold embroidered trappings. Behind the king stand ten pages holding shields and gold-mounted swords. . . . The door of the pavilion is guarded by dogs . . . who wear collars of gold.❞

The spread of Islam Followers of a new religion called Islam joined caravans from North Africa. Islam began in Arabia in the early 600s with the Prophet Muhammad. By the mid-700s his followers, called Muslims, had conquered the Middle East, parts of Asia, North Africa, and Spain. Throughout this vast Islamic Empire, people of different cultures converted to the new faith.

Muslim traders brought their faith across the Sahara. Soon African ruling families and merchants were converting to Islam.

See the Study Guide activity in **Chapter Resources Binder**, p. 9.

No one knows when slavery began, but it was practiced for thousands of years in many societies throughout the world. Slavery existed in ancient China, India, Egypt, Greece, and Rome, as well as in the Middle East and Africa. In the Americas, the Incas, Mayas, and Aztecs of South America and Mesoamerica had slaves. So did many North American peoples.

Through Muslim traders, West African gold spread throughout the Islamic Empire and to Europe, which was running out of precious metals. Soon much of the gold used to make European and Islamic coins came from West Africa.

Mali and Songhai In the mid-1200s a new kingdom called Mali took control of the gold and salt trade. Its rulers adopted Islam and spread the faith to many people.

Mali's greatest emperor was Mansa Musa (MAHN-sah MOO-sah), a devout Muslim. Under his rule, Timbuktu, the capital, became a center of learning for students and scholars from across the Muslim world.

In 1324 Mansa Musa made a spectacular journey to Mecca, a holy city of Islam. With him he took 60,000 men, including 500 slaves. Each slave carried a bar of gold weighing about four pounds. News of the trip spread even to Europe. Europeans were so impressed with Mansa Musa's wealth that they pictured him on a map of Africa.

By the mid-1400s, when Prince Henry's ships were sailing along the West African coast, Songhai (SONG-hī) had replaced Mali as the largest and most powerful trading empire in West Africa. Within 50 years, it would control the gold and salt trade in a region larger than all of western Europe.

The Slave Trade

Along with gold, salt, and ivory, slaves were of value in trading centers like Songhai. Most African kingdoms, like those in ancient civilizations the world over, had long used slaves to do some of the labor. Prisoners of war, criminals, and people who could not

At the height of the Songhai Empire, Jenne (jeh-NAY), in present-day Mali, was an important center of trade and learning. Today, bustling trade still goes on in Jenne. In this recent photograph, people gather at a weekly market to buy and sell local products as well as products from other countries.

African oral traditions provide a rich source of folk tales, poetry, songs, and proverbs. The storyteller, usually an elderly person, used sound effects and changing voice rhythms to bring tales to life. The audience added sound effects and details, acted out parts, and sang songs. One popular type of tale, the "story without an ending," challenged listeners to create a fitting conclusion.

Some stories are very long, such as one account of the earth's creation that took a week to recite. Others might be told in a few minutes. Popular folk tales include antics of animal tricksters and escape stories. In one Benin folk tale, a cruel king orders a new palace to be built from the top down. A wise man helps the people escape this demand by informing the king that tradition requires the ruler to lay the first stone.

pay their debts were often sold into slavery. While visiting a West African city, an Arab traveler known as Leo Africanus wrote:

"There is a place where they sell countless . . . slaves on market days. A fifteen-year-old girl is worth about six ducats and a young man nearly as much; little children and aged slaves are worth about half that sum."

Around the 1100s the slave trade began to grow. More and more Muslim traders were coming into Africa, buying enslaved Africans, and selling them throughout the Islamic Empire.

Later the Portuguese and other Europeans would also find profit in the slave trade. As you will read in Chapter 6, millions of West Africans were to be taken across the Atlantic and sold as slaves. These peoples would play a vital part in creating and enriching new cultures in the Americas.

West African Life

When Prince Henry's mariners finally reached West Africa, they met a bewildering mixture of peoples and languages. Despite the differences, however, West Africans had much in common.

Most West Africans made their living by farming. Farmland was so valued that it belonged to the village, not to individuals. As a local chief explained, the land in his village belonged to "a vast family, of which many are dead, few are living, and countless members are unborn." As members of a village "family," West Africans put social harmony and the needs of the community above personal concerns.

Religion Although some West Africans had converted to Islam by the time the Portuguese arrived, most still followed their traditional religions. They believed that the world had been created by a single High God. Beneath this deity stood lesser gods who controlled daily life. These were the gods West Africans prayed to for rain, a good harvest, or a cure from disease.

West Africans believed that the dead become spirits. They treated the spirits of the dead with great respect. In return, they hoped the spirits would bless the living.

The arts Most West African art had a religious purpose. Sculptors created carved masks representing the gods. When people wore these masks at religious ceremonies, it was believed that the power of the gods flowed through them.

Dance was also an important part of West African ceremonies. People danced to the complex music of drums, which wove together many rhythms at once. They heard each rhythm as a distinct pattern and then chose one to follow with their feet.

Storytelling was another important art. West Africans used stories to teach the young about their religion and history. Many tales featured the trickster, a character who used cunning to outwit others, even the High God.

West Africans valued poetry and the art of public speaking. They recited poems to honor the gods and praise great deeds. They chanted work poems, or songs, to make hard jobs easier. Good speakers were greatly admired for their ability to inspire, teach, and entertain with well-chosen words.

Roots of African American Culture

The West Africans who were brought to the Americas as slaves were forced to give up much of their way of life. Elements of their culture, however, survived and even thrived on this side of the Atlantic.

Checking Understanding

1. What types of people were often made slaves in Africa? Why did slavery grow? (Prisoners of war, criminals, and debtors. Muslim traders expanded it.)

2. How were West African peoples different and similar? (Different peoples and languages, but most farmed and valued community over personal concerns. Most followed traditional religions, and valued dance, storytelling, and poetry.)

Stimulating Critical Thinking

3. Why do you think social harmony was important to West Africans? (Without harmony, meeting a village's basic needs would be hard.)

Section Activity

Practicing the Oral Tradition

To focus on storytelling skills and the importance of oral history, have each student write a story or poem and present it orally. It can tell of a community event, personal experience, or family tradition. It might teach a personal value. Before the presentations, discuss what skills and techniques are part of good oral storytelling. Afterwards, have students note examples of techniques used. Conclude by discussing the uses of oral history today.

The West African kingdom of Benin flourished between the 1400s and the mid-1600s in what is present-day Nigeria. The plaque of the court musicians depicts drummers. Other musicians played bells, rattles, and trumpets made of elephant tusks. The bronze bust of the queen mother shows her with a high, beaded headdress that was a symbol of her position.

Three court musicians play the drums in the court of the Oba, or king, of Benin.

The mother of the king of Benin had a great responsibility— she taught the king's heir how to rule.

These statues show messengers who traveled to Benin from the nearby city of Ife (EE-feh).

◯ **Link to Art**

Benin bronze Bronze heads made in the kingdom of Benin (beh-NEEN) in West Africa are among the finest statues ever made. In the 1400s Benin sculptors produced these statues for their kings by lost-wax casting. In this difficult process, molds were shaped from soft wax, coated with damp clay, and heated. The heat hardened the clay mold and melted out—or "lost"—the wax. Molten bronze, poured into the mold, hardened to form the statues.

Discuss Suggest some reasons why kings might have wanted the statues. What do the statues tell us about civilization in Benin?

African religious beliefs, for example, are still followed in many parts of the Americas. African rhythms can be heard in styles of American music ranging from Dixieland jazz to Delta blues and from rock and roll to reggae. Many of our most inspiring public speakers—leaders such as Martin Luther King, Jr., Marian Wright Edelman, and Jesse Jackson—have drawn on a tradition that places great value on the power of the spoken word.

★ **1. Section Review**

1. What did East Africans and Asians trade?
2. How did trade create the empires of Ghana, Mali, and Songhai?
3. **Critical Thinking** A West African chief said the land in his village belonged to "a vast family, of which many are dead, few are living, and countless members are unborn." What do you think he meant?

(Answers continued from side margin)

(b) A Muslim Arab trader might say the slave trade was an old custom, stress its profitability, and note that many rulers were willing partners.

3. Answers might note that slavery was a long-standing tradition. Students might imagine that victors in war would believe they had a right to profit. They might also imagine economic benefits of having slaves as workers and of trading them.

4. (a) One benefit is to better understand what motivated people. By seeing events through their eyes, one can also avoid snap judgments. (b) One risk is letting imagination become guesswork or fantasy. Another is being reluctant to make any judgments.

For further application, have students do the Applying Skills activity in the Chapter Survey (p. 56).

If students need to review the skill, use the Skills Development transparency and activity in the **Chapter Resources Binder**, pp. 15–16.

Skill Lab

Skill Tips

Reading history is a two-step process:
• First read to answer *who*, *what*, and *where* questions.
• Then read with imagination to answer *why* and *how* questions, putting yourself in the place of people of the past.
• Be sure your imagination is grounded in reality.

Acquiring Information
Reading History

"These [Muslims] have many horses, which they trade and take to the land of the Blacks, exchanging them with the rulers for slaves. Ten or fifteen slaves are usually given for one of these horses, according to their quality."

So wrote one of the first Portuguese travelers in West Africa in the 1400s. The Europeans soon greatly expanded the slave trade in Africa, but slavery itself was common there long before their arrival.

Question to Investigate

Why did Africans practice slavery?

Procedure

Often the most interesting questions in history are not *what*, *who*, and *where* but rather *why* and *how*. Why did people of the past act, believe, or think as they did? How did they live? Such questions are hard to answer because we cannot simply ask the people involved. Instead we have to use our imaginations as we read. To explore the Question to Investigate, read sources **A** and **B**.

❶ Look first for factual information.
a. Who were the slaves? In what places did slavery exist?
b. What kept slavery growing?

❷ Reread the sources with imagination to explore *why* and *how* questions.
a. Imagine you were an African ruler who allowed slavery. Write a paragraph explaining your views on the slave trade.
b. Imagine you were a Muslim slave trader. Write a paragraph describing why you bought slaves.

Sources to Use

A Reread "The Slave Trade" on page 40.

B "At Benin [people objected to] the enslavement of the natives of the country—of men and women, that is, who were within the protection of the Oba of Benin, a monarch whose power derived from God. By custom and by moral law, [they said,] slaves ought to be men and women captured from neighboring peoples. They ought to be 'outsiders,' 'unbelievers.' This rule was often broken."

From Basil Davidson, *Black Mother: The Years of the African Slave Trade* (Little, Brown, 1961)

❸ Historians sometimes combine factual information with interpretations. Good historians let the reader know when they are imagining. Answer the Question to Investigate by combining facts and imagination.

❹ Think about the benefits and risks in reading history imaginatively.
a. Describe one benefit.
b. Describe one risk.

Introducing the Skill Lab

The goal of this lab is to help students see the need to use their imaginations when exploring history—and to take care when doing so. Begin by asking why it helps to imagine ourselves "in the shoes" of people of the past. Students should see the need to reserve judgment initially.

Since the Question to Investigate focuses on reasons for slavery in Africa, remind students that slavery was a widespread practice throughout the world. After students complete the lab, you may wish to compare slavery in Africa with slavery in the Americas.

Skill Lab
Answers

1. (a) Slaves were to be prisoners of war, criminals, and debtors. They included men and women, children, and elderly. Slavery existed in most African kingdoms and throughout the world. (b) Muslim traders.

2. (a) An African ruler might note that enslaving prisoners and selling them was justified as a prize of victory. The ruler might also stress that slaves were outsiders and did not have the same rights as people of the kingdom.

(Answers continued in top margin)

Introducing the Section

Vocabulary

navigation (p. 46) the science of getting ships from place to place

---

Warm-Up
Activity

Inferring from a Picture

To help students focus on the nature of trade between Europe and Asia, have them make inferences about the activity shown in the picture on this page. Have them write a paragraph describing what products they think are being traded for the cloth and where they think the traders are from. (Students might note that the traders do not look Asian and might be Muslim Arabs from the Middle East. They might infer that the bags contain spices.)

Geography Question of the Day

To stress that traders traveled great distances to exchange goods, have students measure a segment of a trade route shown on the map on page 45. Suggest that they use string to trace a route and then use the scale to measure the string. They might estimate, for example, the length of the route between Bombay and Ormuz (about 1,500 miles or 2,420 km).

Section Objectives

★ Describe the trade routes between Asia and Europe and Africa.
★ Explain the impact of Asian ideas and inventions on the world.
★ Explain how China became the world's most powerful country in the 1400s.

Teaching Resources

Take-Home Planner 1, pp. 10–17
Chapter Resources Binder
  Study Guide, p. 10
  Reinforcement, pp. 13–14
  Skills Development
Geography Extensions
American Readings, p. 5
Using Historical Documents
Transparency Activities
Chapter and Unit Tests

2. The Wealth of Asia

Reading Guide

New Term navigation

Section Focus **Asia's links with the world in the 1400s**

1. How did trade goods travel across Asia and from Asia to Africa and Europe?
2. What Asian ideas and inventions had a great impact on the world?
3. What enabled China to be the most powerful country in the world in the 1400s?

One of the books that inspired Prince Henry's interest in exploration was written by an Italian traveler named Marco Polo. In 1271 the 17-year-old Polo had crossed Asia to China with his father and uncle. They returned 24 years later with a fortune in jewels.

Polo's book about their adventures, *Description of the World*, is filled with amazing stories. In one he describes a day at the court of the Great Khan, China's ruler:

"On this day the Great Khan receives gifts of more than 100,000 white horses, of great beauty and price. And on this day also there is a procession of his elephants, fully 5,000 in number. . . . Each one bears on its back two strong-boxes . . . filled with the Khan's plate [dishes of silver or gold]."

Europeans, who knew almost nothing about the civilizations of Asia, found such tales hard to believe. Still, the hope of finding lands rich in gold, silver, jewels, fine cloth, and spices drew them eastward like a magnet.

This picture shows Italian merchants trading bolts of cloth for products of Asia. It was an illustration in Marco Polo's book *Description of the World*. Completed in 1298, the book awakened European interest in Asia.

Specific Learning Disabilities
Students with orientation-related disabilities often find reading maps very difficult because of a poor sense of direction and distance. Help students reorganize the mapped information into spider web graphics. They could list each trade good and name the countries where it is produced. For

example, they might write "spices" in the middle circle of a web and write the names of Asian areas that produced them—East Indies, Philippines, China, India—in circles radiating from the center. After they prepare webs for each product, help them draw conclusions about goods the countries might trade.

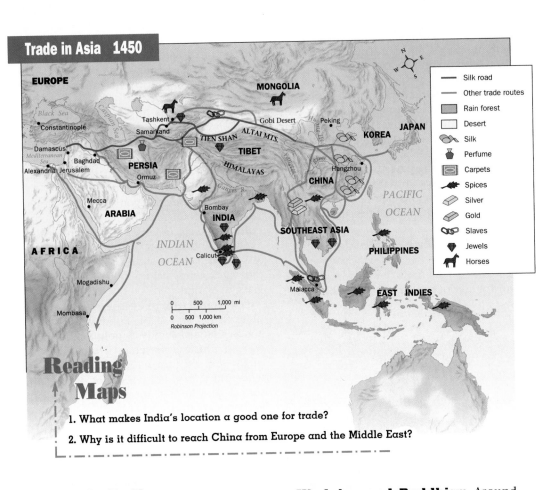

Trade in Asia 1450

Reading Maps

1. What makes India's location a good one for trade?

2. Why is it difficult to reach China from Europe and the Middle East?

Trade in India

When the Polos were traveling in Asia, they had no idea of the history that lay behind the shimmering cities and bustling trade that they saw. As early as 2500 B.C., people in cities in India had well-planned roads and water systems with drains and sewers. At about a hundred sites, archaeologists have uncovered the ruins of these large ancient cities.

Archaeologists have also found evidence of widespread trade. Soapstone seals from India, which traders used to identify property or sign contracts, have been found in the ruins of Middle Eastern cities.

Hinduism and Buddhism Around 1500 B.C., people called Aryans invaded northern India. The Aryans dominated India for the next 2,000 years, spreading their language, customs, and religious ideas. Out of those ideas came two of the world's major religions. The first, Hinduism, became the major religion of India and remains so today. The second, Buddhism, spread across China, Korea, Japan, and Southeast Asia.

India in the 1400s By the 1400s Muslim armies had conquered much of India. Under Muslim rule, trade continued to flourish. Foreign merchants came to India to buy silk and cotton cloth, spices, jewels,

Discussion

Checking Understanding

1. How did Marco Polo's book increase interest in trade with Asia? (Europeans learned of Asian riches and wanted them.)

2. What evidence indicates that India traded with Middle Eastern cities? (Soapstone seals from India in Middle Eastern cities.)

Stimulating Critical Thinking

3. Why do you think many Europeans found Marco Polo's stories hard to believe? (Most had no contact with people in Asia.)

4. Why do you think spices were valued trading goods? (Spices helped preserve foods; spices made foods taste better.)

Teaching the
↑ Reading Maps

To help students focus on the map, ask what bodies of water were crossed by the trade routes. (Pacific and Indian oceans, Persian Gulf, Red and Mediterranean seas) **Answers to Reading Maps: 1.** Midway between Arabia and China. **2.** Deserts and mountains.

See the Study Guide activity in **Chapter Resources Binder,** p. 10.

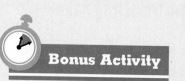
✠ Connections to Art

The picture of silk spinning on this page is a detail of a painting on a porcelain vase made during the Ming dynasty (about A.D. 1368 to 1644). The Ming dynasty was well-known for improvements in porcelain. During this dynasty, porcelain makers began using an imported cobalt that was high in iron and low in manganese to produce the blue paint used to decorate some white porcelain pieces. The imported cobalt helped give the porcelain a richer blue color than Chinese cobalt, which was high in manganese and low in iron. Painters made their designs with the cobalt paint before the porcelain was glazed. They also used other types of paint to decorate porcelain pieces after they were glazed.

perfumes, sugar, and rice. Their ships carried the wealth of India to eastern Africa and the Middle East.

Through trade, people discovered Indian ideas and inventions unknown to their own cultures. Often they adapted these to their own way of life. Indian mathematicians developed the decimal number system we use today, and it passed on to Arabs and then Europeans. Indian fairy tales, too, spread to Arabia and Europe. "Cinderella," for example, was originally an Indian story.

China, a Great Power

Northeast of India lay the largest and most powerful country in the world at that time—China. As early as 221 B.C., a strong ruler had unified China. Later rulers added to the empire until it covered a large part of the continent of Asia. Highways, canals, and a postal system linked it together.

Expanding trade As the Chinese empire expanded, so did its trade. China established trade links with India, Korea, Japan, the Middle East, and Africa.

Some Chinese trade goods began to reach Europe by about A.D. 100. Silk, bronze goods, pottery, and spices flowed west from China, as well as India, along a route known as the Silk Road. On the shores of the Mediterranean, Romans paid for these goods with glass, dyes, and gold.

Few traders traveled the entire 4,000 miles (6,400 km) of the Silk Road. Instead, goods changed hands at points along the way. A Chinese merchant, for example, might sell silk to a trader in central Asia, who sold it to a Persian dealer, who then sold it to a Roman merchant. With each exchange, the price went up.

As trade expanded, China's trade centers grew into cities. By the 1200s Hangzhou (HAN-JOW) was the world's largest city. Chinese cities had public carriages, street drains, coal for heat, and paper money—none of which were known to Europeans at that time.

New technology China also had a higher level of technology than any other civilization. Around 1050 the Chinese invented printing with movable type—some 400 years before this technology was developed in Europe.

Gunpowder was also a Chinese invention, used in fireworks as well as weapons. By the 1300s the Chinese had a cannon they could use on land and on their many warships at sea.

The Chinese made great advances in **navigation**—the science of getting ships

Silk was one of China's most prized items of trade. Here women unwind the delicate strands from silk-worm cocoons and form them into a long thread of raw silk.

Yang Min, the Chinese trader who brought the giraffe to China, had thought the giraffe was a *qilin*, a mythical animal that the Chinese considered sacred. They believed that it only appeared in prosperous and peaceful times. The Chinese made the *qilin* a symbol of goodness because of the animal's gentle nature. They described it as having the body of a deer, hooves like a horse, and one to three horns on its head. Yang Min thought its appearance was surely a sign of the emperor's greatness. To commemorate the presentation of the *qilin*, a calligrapher painted its picture on silk and wrote a poem about it, noting:

Gentle is the animal, that in all antiquity has been seen but once. The manifestation of its divine spirit rises up to heaven's abode.

As a result of Zheng He's voyages, foreign ambassadors came to China to pay tribute to the emperor. Ambassadors from Malindi on the coast of East Africa brought this giraffe.

from place to place. They invented the magnetic compass, which made it possible for ships to sail out of sight of land and still find their way home. This technology spread to Arab sailors, who passed it on to Europeans. The compass made it possible for European explorers to sail to the Americas and back.

The Chinese also developed a new kind of sailing ship called a junk. The largest junks had four decks and four to six masts, and could carry 500 sailors. Below deck were watertight compartments—not seen in European ships until much later—that helped keep the ship afloat.

By the 1300s Chinese junks were sailing trade routes that stretched from Japan to East Africa. These ships were not only reliable but also comfortable. Writing of his voyage on a four-decked junk, an Arab traveler described "cabins and saloons for merchants, . . . and garden herbs, vegetables, and ginger [growing] in wooden tubs."

The Voyages of Zheng He

In the early 1400s, when Prince Henry's sea captains were creeping down the West African coast, Chinese junks were sailing throughout the Indian Ocean. The great admiral Zheng He (JUNG HUH) assembled a fleet of more than 300 ships, with a total crew of 28,000 men, to visit other countries. The ships were part of the greatest navy in the world at that time.

Like later European voyagers, Zheng He's goal was to increase his country's wealth

Polynesian navigators More than 2,000 years before Zheng He's voyages, a seafaring people called Polynesians were sailing the Pacific. About A.D. 400 they reached the islands that today make up the state of Hawaii.

Polynesian navigators did not have maps or instruments. Instead, they used their knowledge of the sun, stars, winds, and ocean currents. They passed this knowledge from generation to generation in the form of chants.

For their journeys, the Polynesians built huge canoes with sails made of woven leaves. The canoes carried not only people but also plants and livestock—everything the Polynesians needed to survive in their new island homes.

Checking Understanding

1. How did the Chinese help make European exploration of the Americas possible? (The Chinese invented the magnetic compass that enabled Europeans to sail to the Americas and return to Europe.)

Stimulating Critical Thinking

2. Which early Chinese inventions do you think have had the greatest impact on the world? Explain. (Answers may include gunpowder because of its use in firearms and the compass because of its use by explorers.)

Teaching the

The islands of Hawaii were not inhabited when the Polynesians from the Marquesas Islands arrived. Help students locate the Marquesas Islands (8.5° south and 141° west) and Hawaiian Islands (22° north and 158° west) on the world map on pp. R2–R3. Ask: **About how far is it between these islands?** (About 2,500 miles or 4,023 km) Have students compare the Polynesian and Chinese voyagers in terms of distances traveled, navigational techniques, and provisions.

Sometimes history and fiction mix. Zheng He became a popular subject of Chinese folk tales and plays that related actual and fictional accounts of his life. Puppeteers, using carved puppets on sticks, performed a play about three kings who trap Zheng He's fleet. The admiral outwits them by luring them aboard his ship and capturing them. This and similar stories made him a hero.

For selections of Chinese poetry, see **American Readings**, p. 5.

Teaching the

⌒ Point of View

⌐ After students read about the two historians' theories, ask them to identify the inside and outside pressures mentioned. Have them consider whether there might have been more than one reason. Finally, ask why the end of the voyages was an important event.

Closing the Section

Wrap-Up Activity

Writing a Diary Entry

To focus on the wealth and technological advances of China, have students write a diary entry from the perspective of a Chinese official. In their diary entry they are to explain why they think China is superior to Europe.

Section Review
Answers

1. Definition: *navigation* (46)
2. Early links included trade for spices, jewels, silk, and gold from central Asia and China for glass, dyes, and gold from Europe.
3. Possible examples: Decimal system, fairy tales, magnetic compass, gunpowder.
4. The United States might have adapted mainly Asian ideas and values.

and power by expanding trade. Between 1405 and 1433, he sailed to places as far away as India, Arabia, East Africa, and perhaps even Australia.

Zheng He fought pirates and unfriendly rulers to make China a major power in the Indian Ocean. He traded China's prized silks and porcelains for ivory, precious stones, spices, and medicines. He also brought back firsthand knowledge of distant lands.

Then, suddenly, the voyages stopped. After 1433 China began withdrawing its navy from the open seas. "Warships, no longer sent out to sea on patrols, were anchored in ports where they rotted from neglect," wrote the historian Lo Jung-pang. In 1525 the government ordered all ocean-going ships to be destroyed and the merchants who sailed them to be arrested.

⌒ Point of View

⌐ **Why did the Chinese voyages stop?**

Why did China withdraw from the seas? Louise Levathes, author of *When China Ruled the Seas,* sees part of the answer in a power struggle at court. Some officials favored China's foreign trade. They had gained wealth and power from it. Other officials believed that China did not need foreign trade. If they could stop the trade, they could also curb their rivals' power.

According to historian Levathes, the anti-trade officials created

❝a series of government restrictions limiting boat size and civilian participation in overseas trade. If court officials could not control . . . trade activities, at least they could impede [hinder] them.❞

Historian Paul Kennedy sees the threat of invasion as a reason for ending the voyages.

❝The northern frontiers of the empire were again under some pressure from the Mongols [enemies of the Chinese]. . . . Under such circumstances, a large navy was an expensive luxury.❞

What if Zheng He had continued his voyages? According to Kennedy, his ships "might well have been able to sail around Africa and 'discover' Portugal several decades before Henry the Navigator's voyages began earnestly to push south [along the West African coast]."

Asian Roots in America

It was not until the mid-1800s that Chinese began crossing the Pacific to seek new opportunities in the Kingdom of Hawaii and the United States. In the next 150 years, people from China as well as Japan, Korea, the Philippines, India, and elsewhere in Asia came to America.

Over the years, Asian immigrants have played vital roles in building the nation's railroads, working its mines, introducing new crops and farming methods, and expanding science and technology. The diverse cultures they have brought with them have also enriched American life.

★ 2. Section Review

1. Define **navigation.**
2. What early trade links existed between Europe and Asia?
3. Give at least two examples of Asian ideas or inventions that spread to other parts of the world.
4. **Critical Thinking** How might the United States be different today if Chinese explorers had reached the Americas in the mid-1400s?

★ **Section Objectives**

★ Explain what happened to Europe after the fall of the Roman Empire.
★ Describe the impact of the Crusades on life in Europe.
★ Give reasons why Portugal led European exploration during the 1400s.

Teaching Resources

Take-Home Planner 1, pp. 10–17
Chapter Resources Binder
  Study Guide, p. 11
  Reinforcement
  Skills Development
Geography Extensions, pp. 3–4
American Readings, pp. 6–8
Using Historical Documents, pp. 13–16
Transparency Activities
Chapter and Unit Tests, pp. 9–12

Introducing the Section

Vocabulary

feudalism (p. 50) a system of government based on agreement between a lord and his vassals

colony (p. 53) settlement made by a group of people in a distant place that remains under the control of their country

3. Europe Looks Outward

Reading Guide

New Terms feudalism, colony

Section Focus Europeans' interest in new trade routes to Africa and Asia

1. What happened in Europe after the fall of the Roman Empire?
2. How did the Crusades change life in Europe?
3. Why did Portugal take the lead in exploration?

Warm-Up Activity

Imagining a Peasant's Choice

To help students imagine the impact of stories about Africa and Asia, have them imagine themselves as the peasant shown in the stained glass window on this page. If given the chance to join a voyage in search of riches in those distant lands, what would their choice be? Have them write their responses, explaining how their fears and hopes led to their choices. Conclude by discussing the pros and cons of joining such a voyage.

As the Chinese withdrew from the seas in the 1400s, trade between Asia, Africa, and the Middle East was left mostly to Arab merchants. It would not be long, though, before Europeans—like Prince Henry—began to look for ways to bite off a piece of this rich trade.

Europeans, however, were in no position to challenge the Arabs for control of their trade routes. In the 1400s Europe was still relatively weak, emerging from centuries of hard times, unrest, and isolation.

Europe's Beginnings

Like Africa, Asia, and the Americas, Europe had seen the rise and fall of civilizations. The most powerful of these—the Roman Empire—ruled most of Europe, the Middle East, and northern Africa from 27 B.C. to A.D. 476.

The Romans not only unified this entire area under one rule but also brought peace to its many different peoples. Trade moved along a system of new roads linking all parts of the empire. Roman laws applied to all people.

Fall of the Roman Empire The Roman Empire collapsed in the 400s when invaders captured its towns and cities. Europe then split into many small, warring

kingdoms. Law and order ended. Trade declined and almost disappeared. Cities everywhere shrank to towns, and towns gave way to fields.

Only manors—large estates owned by wealthy lords—survived. The lands of a manor were worked by peasants called serfs. The serfs were not free to leave the service of their lords. For their part, lords had to protect their serfs from attacks by bandits and foreign invaders.

In the 900s new invaders appeared. The most feared of all were sea raiders from

This stained-glass window shows a serf planting grain seeds by hand. The entire family took part in the production of food.

Geography Question of the Day

Have students use the map on page 51 to identify the main European seaports along the trade routes between Europe and Asia. (Genoa and Venice) Ask: **Why do you think these cities became the leading trade centers in Europe?** (Both were easily accessible to Arab ships.)

Although many people joined the Crusades for religious purposes, others wanted to gain land or promote trade. Still others joined to escape hardships. The most unusual group were tens of thousands of children.

In 1212, two waves of children from France and Germany began marching to the sea. They wanted to be transported to the Middle East where they believed they would conquer Palestine through love and kindness rather than war. This expedition ended in disaster. Many children died on their way to the European port cities and at sea. Many others were captured and enslaved. The Children's Crusade failed miserably, but it did lead to renewed interest in the conquest of Jerusalem.

Developing the Section

Teaching the

∞ Link to the Present

Have students note similarities and differences in uses of spices then and now. Ask why Europeans of the 1400s valued spices so much more than we do today. Students should note that Europeans then used spices to preserve food, not just flavor it, and also used them as medicine. Also, spices were new to most Europeans and were harder to obtain than they are today.

Section Activity

Making a Spice Chart

To help students understand why spices were valued, have them create a spice information chart. The chart should be divided into squares, each containing a sample of a spice, its name, where it is grown, its uses, and its price per ounce. Students might also identify which spices are used in their own homes and in what recipes. Conclude by discussing which spices are most common, how they are used, and where they come from.

∞ Link to the Present

The appeal of spices Why were spices a driving force in European voyages of exploration? Spices did not just make food delicious. In the days before refrigeration, spices helped keep food from spoiling—and disguised the taste once spoilage occurred. They were also used as medicines.

In time, spices native to Asia came to be grown in other places, including the West Indies and South America. Today you can find the spices Europeans once prized in every grocery store.

Scandinavia called Vikings or Northmen. The Vikings looted and burned towns and killed or sold as slaves any people they captured. Across western Europe, frightened people prayed, "From the fury of the Northmen, Good Lord, deliver us!"

Feudalism A new system of government arose as people turned to their lords for protection against invaders. This system, known as **feudalism,** was based on agreements between a lord and his vassals. A lord might be a king or a wealthy landowner. A vassal was someone who promised to serve a lord in exchange for a grant of land.

The most important service vassals owed their lords was to fight for them. Under the feudal system, a lord could quickly pull together an army of his vassals to ward off Viking raiders or other enemies.

Life became more settled under feudalism. Serfs cleared forests to make more farmland and produce more crops. The growing food supply could feed more people. Between 1050 and 1300, Europe's population tripled. Trade expanded. Villages grew into towns, and towns into cities.

At the same time, feudalism divided Europe into thousands of small territories, each ruled by its own lord. When not fighting invaders, these lords often fought among themselves.

Europe Rises Out of Feudalism

The Christian religion was the one unifying force in European life. Christianity had begun in Palestine during the Roman Empire. This faith was based on the ideas of a Jewish teacher named Jesus. Christianity spread rapidly, and by feudal times the Roman Catholic Church had become the center of religious life in western Europe.

Europe's Christians called Palestine the Holy Land because it was there that Jesus had lived and died. For centuries, devout Christians had traveled to Palestine to visit holy shrines. Then in 1070 the Seljuk Turks, who were Muslims, took control of Palestine and closed it to Christian travelers.

The Crusades Pope Urban II, the head of the Catholic Church, was outraged by the Turks' actions. In 1095 he called on Europe's lords to stop fighting among themselves and unite to free the Holy Land from the Turks.

Thousands answered the pope's call. They sewed the symbol of their faith—the Christian cross—on their clothes and called themselves crusaders, from the Latin word *crux,* which means "cross." The crusaders marched off to war under the battle cry "God wills it."

For two centuries, armies of crusaders battled the Turks for Palestine. In the end, the Europeans failed in their mission.

New trade In Palestine, however, the crusaders were introduced to a new world of exotic goods from Asia—sugar, melons, lemons, fine silk and cotton cloth, perfumes,

Kinesthetic learners often find it easier to integrate mapped information through hands-on and tactile experiences. With the maps on pages 45 and 51, students can use their fingers to trace trade routes between Asia and Europe. As they do, help them identify points at which products would be traded. You may wish to have students show this transfer of products by drawing a progression chart with arrows to show the transfer of goods from Asia to Europe. This activity will help students see why Europeans had to pay high prices for goods from Asia.

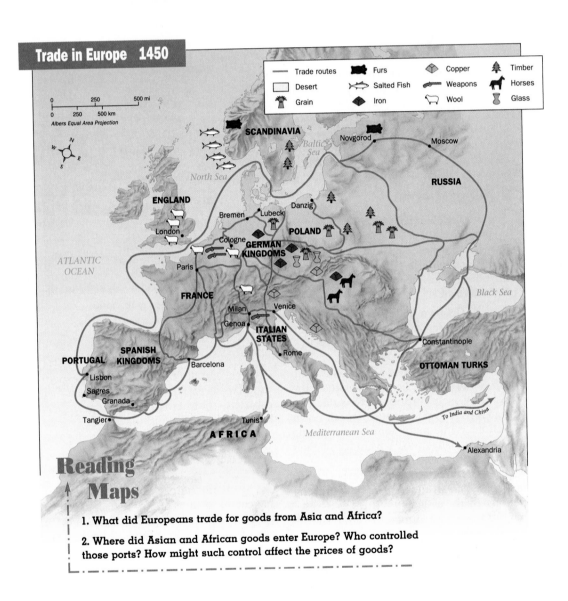

Trade in Europe 1450

Reading Maps

1. What did Europeans trade for goods from Asia and Africa?

2. Where did Asian and African goods enter Europe? Who controlled those ports? How might such control affect the prices of goods?

Discussion

Checking Understanding

1. What were good and bad effects of feudalism? (Life became more settled, which allowed Europeans to increase food production and establish towns and cities. However, feudalism fostered rivalry between lords, which often led to war.)

2. Why were prices for Middle Eastern goods so high in Europe? (Italian merchants bought goods from Arabs who bought them from Africans and Asians. The merchants at each stage took a profit.)

Stimulating Critical Thinking

3. How did the Crusades affect trade between Europe and the Middle East? (Europeans were exposed to a variety of goods, leading to increased trade.)

Teaching the
Reading Maps

To help students focus on the map, ask: **What types of regions were main sources of metals? Of farm products?** (Mountainous areas were sources of metals; plains were sources of farm products.) **Answers to Reading Maps: 1.** Grain, iron, copper, wool, timber, and weapons. **2.** Through the cities of Genoa and Venice, which were controlled by Italian merchants. Such control probably raised prices.

and spices. Europeans could not get enough of these wonderful new luxuries.

A brisk trade sprang up between Europe and the Middle East. Arab merchants sold spices, perfumes, and other goods to Italian traders from Venice and Genoa. The Italians then resold the goods at high prices to merchants in other parts of Europe.

Western European merchants resented the high prices. Some dreamed of cutting their costs by trading directly with Africa and Asia. Since Arabs controlled existing trade routes, the only hope was to find a new sea route to those distant lands. Such an undertaking, however, would need the support of a strong and ambitious ruler.

Remind students that photography was not yet invented during the 1400s, so their cover designs should not include photos. Ask them to brainstorm topics that might have been interesting to people during the 1400s. They can also examine pictures in the chapter for ideas. After choosing topics, students can briefly outline main ideas to be covered in their books and decide on descriptive titles. Display their designs and tables of contents on a bulletin board with a title such as "European Books of the Month in the Late 1400s."

Bonus Activity

Using a Compass

By magnetizing a needle and making a primitive compass, students can see how to use a compass to identify directions. Point out that a compass needle points to the magnetic north pole. Have small groups make their own compass by rubbing a needle on a magnet and taping the needle to a cork floating in a bowl of water. After the needle points to the north, have them use index cards to label the cardinal directions on the classroom walls based on the needle pointing to the magnetic north pole. Conclude by asking why the compass was an important tool for sailors.

✳ **History Footnote**

As a cultural movement, the Renaissance in Europe is known for great achievements in exploration, the arts, architecture, and science. One of the most versatile and talented achievers was Leonardo da Vinci. Trained as a painter, da Vinci also studied anatomy, botany, and earth science. He filled notebooks with detailed scientific sketches of the human body and engineering designs for inventions, including sketches for a parachute, a movable bridge, and a flying machine.

See the Study Guide activity in **Chapter Resources Binder**, p. 11. See **American Readings**, pp. 6–8.

Hands-On

------→ *HISTORY*

Designing a book The invention of movable type in Europe helped spread the ideas of the Renaissance. In 1456 Johannes Gutenberg, a German printer, published the first printed book in Europe. Because printed books were less costly than hand-copied manuscripts, the writings of Renaissance thinkers became available to many people in Europe.

Activity

① Imagine that you are a printer working in the mid-1400s. Design the cover of a book about Africa, Asia, and Europe in the 1400s. You might use symbols, designs, or illustrations in keeping with the main ideas of the book.

② Create a table of contents and write a brief introduction, summarizing the book.

A printing shop in the 1500s

The rise of nations Under feudalism, Europe's rulers were no stronger than the lords they were supposed to rule. The Crusades, however, helped to break down feudalism. While many lords were fighting in Palestine, kings took advantage of their absence to increase their power.

Gradually, a few kings were able to unify large areas under their rule, creating nations. By the early 1400s there were three nations in western Europe: England, France, and Portugal.

The rulers of these new nations envied the wealth that poured into Venice and Genoa. They saw that they could increase their wealth and power by expanding trade. Like the merchants, they wanted to find a water route to the trade of Asia and the gold of Africa.

The Renaissance Interest in finding other routes to Asia and Africa occurred at a time when Europeans were more and more curious about the world around them. They wanted to explore nature, the arts, ancient cultures, and distant lands. These new attitudes were part of the Renaissance—the rebirth—that Europeans experienced between the 1300s and the 1500s.

Portugal Leads the Way

The Renaissance, the rise of nations, merchants' dreams of new trade and sources of gold—all these forces set the stage for an era of exploration. Only leadership and know-how were missing.

Prince Henry supplied both. He had great curiosity about the world and was determined to succeed. A deeply religious man, he hoped not only to expand Portuguese power but also to spread Christianity to new lands.

Of the three nations in Europe, only Portugal was in a position to begin seeking new sea routes. France and England were locked in a war that would last until the mid-1400s. Portugal was at peace. The Portuguese were also a seafaring people.

✠ ....
Connections to Economics

In Portugal, there was some criticism of Henry's expeditions. They were costing a lot and not producing income. Then in 1441, one of Henry's caravels returned with Africans captured by the crew. These were the first enslaved people brought from West Africa to Europe. Soon Portugal was involved in a profitable slave trade, and criticism stopped.

For an example of early European printing, see **Using Historical Documents**, pp. 13–16.

A center for exploration Henry set up a center for exploration at Sagres (SAH-greesh) in southern Portugal. He brought mathematicians, geographers, and sea captains to this center to teach his crews everything they knew about navigation and maps. It was here that the Portuguese prince earned the name Henry the Navigator.

At Sagres, sailors learned how to use the magnetic compass—which Arab seamen had brought to Europe from China—to find their direction at sea. They also learned how to use an instrument called the astrolabe to determine their precise latitude, which means distance from the equator.

Henry's shipbuilders developed a new kind of European ship called the caravel. The caravel carried two kinds of sails—one square, one triangular—so that it could sail into the wind as well as with the wind. The new ship gave Henry's crews confidence to venture far from Portugal, knowing that they could turn around and come home no matter which way the wind blew.

Exploring the African coast Henry's first target was West Africa and its gold trade. To reach that goal, his ships would have to sail south, past Cape Bojador (BAHJ-uh-DOR). Time and again they turned back before rounding the cape, stopped by the widespread belief that

❝beyond this cape there is no race of men . . . and the sea [is] so shallow . . . while the currents are so terrible that no ship having once passed the cape, will ever be able to return.❞

In 1434 a ship finally rounded the cape and wiped away "the shadow of fear." From then on, Henry's explorers sailed farther and farther southward.

Along the way the Portuguese discovered the island of Madeira off the African coast. After seeing samples of the soil, Prince

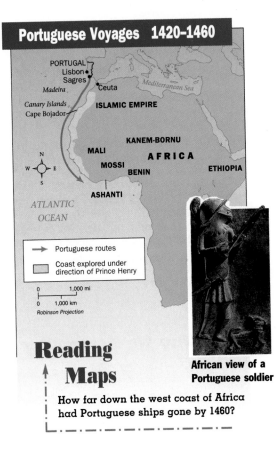

Portuguese Voyages   1420–1460

PORTUGAL
Lisbon
Sagres
Madeira
Ceuta
Mediterranean Sea
Canary Islands
Cape Bojador
ISLAMIC EMPIRE
KANEM-BORNU
MALI   **A F R I C A**
MOSSI
BENIN   **ETHIOPIA**
ASHANTI
ATLANTIC OCEAN

N
W   E
S

→ Portuguese routes

Coast explored under direction of Prince Henry

0   1,000 mi
0   1,000 km
Robinson Projection

Reading Maps

African view of a Portuguese soldier

How far down the west coast of Africa had Portuguese ships gone by 1460?

Henry established a colony on the sunny island to grow sugar cane. A **colony** is a settlement made by a group of people in a distant place that remains under the control of their home country.

West African trade In the 1440s Henry's ship captains made contact with African and Arab merchants and found a resource as valuable as gold: people to do work. In 1444 Henry's explorers brought 200 Africans home to sell as slaves.

Henry also sent enslaved Africans to his colony on Madeira to work in the cane fields. As European demand for sugar grew, so did the demand for slaves. The slave trade proved so profitable that in 1448

Closing the Section

Wrap-Up Activity

Creating Tableaux

To help students see the importance of key events in Europe, have small groups pose in tableaux, or dramatic scenes. Assign an event to each group. Ask the groups to prepare a tableau for their scene. Some possibilities: crusaders marching to war; Arab and Italian merchants; the building of a caravel; sailors using a map, compass, and astrolabe. As each group presents its scene, ask the class to identify its importance for European trade and exploration.

Section Review
Answers

1. Definitions: *feudalism* (50), *colony* (53)

2. Christianity was a unifying force, and feudalism divided Europe.

3. After the Crusades introduced Europeans to Asian goods, trade sprang up between European and Asian merchants. Because feudal lords were involved in the Crusades, monarchs took advantage of their absence to unify large areas into nations.

4. He was curious about exploring the world beyond Europe and put his curiosity into action.

To check understanding of "Why We Remember," assign Thinking Critically question 3 on student page 56.

Tips for Teaching

At-Risk Students

At-risk students working below grade level may have difficulty synthesizing chapter information and drawing conclusions about the importance of European trade interests to American history. Provide them with copies of the Chapter 2 Summary. Read and discuss the summary and the "Why We Remember" feature on this page together. Help students draw conclusions about the importance of trade by asking questions such as: Why did the Europeans begin sea explorations? What effect did the search for trade routes have on the Americas?

Henry had a trading post built on an island off the West African coast. This was the first European trading post established overseas.

The Portuguese relied on the help of African princes who had slave-dealers bring enslaved men, women, and children to the coast. There, they were traded to the Portuguese in exchange for cloth, beads, metal goods, and firearms.

The impact of Prince Henry When Henry died in 1460, his ships had not yet reached the southern tip of Africa. Nor had they found their way to Asia. The prince, however, had opened the way for such voyages. In time, others would take over where he left off and find a sea route to the wealth of Asia.

In the process, European explorers would bump into another great source of wealth—the Americas. Thousands of Europeans would stream across the Atlantic, bringing their cultures to these lands, one of which became the United States.

3. Section Review

1. Define **feudalism** and **colony**.
2. What united Europe after the fall of Rome? What divided it?
3. What effect did the Crusades have on trade? On the rise of nations?
4. **Critical Thinking** How did Prince Henry show the spirit of the Renaissance?

Why We Remember

Africa, Asia, and Europe in the 1400s

In the 1400s Africa and Asia had the resources and the trade they needed and wanted. They were not reaching out for more. In fact, China turned inward, withdrawing from exploration and trade.

Europe, however, was looking outward. Several forces pushed Europeans toward exploration. One was the appetite for gold and the luxuries introduced by the crusaders. Another was the curiosity sparked by the Renaissance. A third was that new European nations saw trade as a way to gain greater wealth and power.

Prince Henry was no explorer himself, but he did something more important. He helped conquer the greatest difficulty facing Europeans—fear of the unknown. Under his direction, the Portuguese went where no Europeans had gone before, and began replacing ancient fears with facts. The voyages inspired by Henry would eventually lead European explorers to the Americas. There the story of what would become the United States begins.

Ptolemy's ideas about geography were presented in his eight-book *Guide to Geography*. This collection contained over 20 maps, identified places by latitude and longitude, and provided instructions on how to make maps. His *Guide to Geography* had an important historical impact because explorers used it to support their idea that Europeans could reach the Indies by sailing west. In addition to being a great geographer, Ptolemy was a noted astronomer. In his 13-book treatise *The Mathematical Collection,* also called the *Almagest,* he detailed the Ptolemaic system of the universe. In the system, earth was a sphere that stood still; and the sun, moon, and other planets revolved around it. His geocentric view of the earth remained the most widely accepted idea of the universe until the mid-1500s.

Geography Lab

Comparing Historical and Modern Maps

Claudius Ptolemy (TAHL-uh-mee) was a great geographer who lived in Egypt around A.D. 150. Ptolemy did not have computers or satellites, as mapmakers do today. He relied on the word of travelers and his own calculations. Then he used his imagination to fill in the gaps.

Europeans were still using Ptolemy's maps in the mid-1400s. The diagram below compares the outline of Ptolemy's map (right) with a modern map to help you see what Europeans in the mid-1400s thought the world was like.

Ptolemy's map

Using Map Skills

1. Is the earth's surface mostly land or mostly water? What did Europeans in the mid-1400s think?

2. Which continent does Ptolemy's map show most accurately? Least accurately? Does that surprise you? Why or why not?

3. Imagine this map on a globe. If you were using such a globe, what would you say was the best route from Europe to China? Why?

4. **Hands-On Geography** Draw a map of a part of your community that you travel through often. Use memory and your imagination, not another map. When you are through, meet with four or five other students to review maps. What places could someone find by using your map? Where might they get lost?

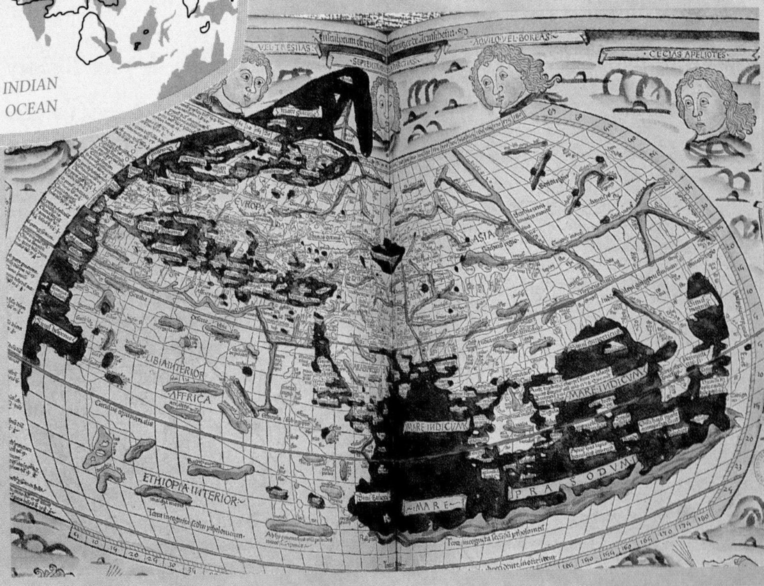

Teaching the Geography Lab

Have students trace the outlines of Ptolemy's continents on the diagram. Ask: **Did Ptolemy think the continents were larger or smaller than they actually are?** (larger) **Based on Ptolemy's map, do you think he thought the earth was round or flat?** (round) Display a world map and help students identify differences between Ptolemy's map and the world map.

Using Map Skills
Answers

1. The earth's surface is mostly water (about 70 percent), but Europeans of the 1400s thought it was mostly land.

2. Ptolemy's map shows Europe most accurately and Asia least accurately. Most students will not be surprised by the distortions because most of Asia and Africa had not been explored at the time of Ptolemy.

3. Because of the vast amount of land and the relatively little amount of water shown on the map, people are likely to conclude that a water route to China from Europe would be the shortest and best route.

4. Students' maps are likely to have the most detail in areas with which students are most familiar. Someone following the map would most likely become lost in sections with less detail.

See the activity on an historic map of Africa in **Geography Extensions,** pp. 3–4.

Survey Answers

Reviewing Vocabulary

Definitions are found on these pages: *navigation* (46), *feudalism* (50), *colony* (53).

Reviewing Main Ideas

1. Gold and salt were most important; sugar, wheat, and cloth from North Africa and ivory from West Africa were also traded.

2. Accept any three of the following: emphasis on social harmony and community needs, farming for a living, village ownership of land, belief in gods, belief that the dead become spirits, carving of masks for religious ceremonies, ceremonial dances, storytelling, and emphasis on poetry and public speaking.

3. Goods were transported over land routes, such as the Silk Road, and through sea routes on the Pacific and Indian oceans.

4. (a) The magnetic compass. (b) From Arab traders, who got it from the Chinese.

5. Because lords and their armies protected people, life became more settled. Serfs could clear more land and grow more crops, enabling the population to increase. Towns and cities developed. However, warfare was common.

6. (a) Crusaders were introduced to Asian goods while trying to conquer Palestine. European desire for these goods led to trade between Europe and the Middle East. (b) They were dissatisfied with indirect trade because of additional costs placed on goods by traders from the Middle East and European seaports.

7. England and France were at war. Only Portugal had the opportunity and leadership to direct exploration.

(Answers continued in top margin)

Thinking Critically

1. The African slave trade might have remained small. People would have been more isolated, with less access to one another's goods and ideas. If the Turks had not taken over Palestine, Europeans might not have learned about African and Asian goods. Feudalism may have lasted longer.

2. Agree: government had little use for the goods exchanged, spent too much money sponsoring voyages, and did not need contact with other cultures. Disagree: voyages provided important information about geography and other cultures and led to valuable trade.

3. Forces that led to European exploration were desire for gold and luxuries introduced by crusaders, desire to spread Christianity,

Chapter Survey ☆

Reviewing Vocabulary

Define the following terms.
1. navigation
2. feudalism
3. colony

Reviewing Main Ideas

1. What goods were the basis of trade between West African trading empires and North Africa?
2. Name three beliefs or ways of life that most West Africans shared.
3. Describe two ways that Asian goods reached other continents.
4. (a) What Chinese invention helped make European voyages of exploration in the 1400s possible? (b) How did Europeans obtain this invention?
5. How did feudalism change the way that people lived in Europe?
6. (a) How did the Crusades help to increase trade between Europe and the Middle East? (b) Were western European merchants satisfied with the trade? Explain why or why not.
7. Why was Portugal the only European nation to begin seeking new sea routes in the early 1400s?

Thinking Critically

1. Synthesis How might the history of Africa, Asia, or Europe have been changed if the Islamic Empire had *not* existed? Support your answer with examples from the text.
2. Evaluation In the late 1400s a government official in China described the expeditions of Zheng He as a waste of money—and of sailors' lives. "Although he [Zheng He] returned with wonderful, precious things, what benefit was it to the state? This was merely . . . bad government." Do you agree with the official's opinion? Explain.
3. Why We Remember: Analysis What forces pushed Europeans toward exploration in the 1400s? Which force do you think was the most important? Give supporting examples from the text.

Applying Skills

Reading history Review the information about how the Crusades began. Then use what you learned on page 43 to write an answer to this question: Why did so many Europeans fight for so long to try to capture the land of Palestine from the Seljuk Turks?

History Mystery

The Chinese navy Answer the History Mystery on page 35. How would you go about learning more about the decision of the Chinese government to get rid of the navy? How might China's history have been changed if the navy had continued to exist?

Writing in Your History Journal

1. Keys to History (a) The time line on pages 34–35 has six Keys to History. In your journal, list each key and describe why it is important to know about. (b) If you could have been present at one event on the time line, which would you choose, and why? Write your response in your journal.
2. Prince Henry the Navigator Prince Henry sent ships out to explore the west coast of Africa and advised his captains to report everything they saw. In your journal, write a dialogue between Prince Henry and one of his captains who has just returned from a voyage.

curiosity sparked by the Renaissance, and the desire of new nations for wealth and power. Opinions will vary. Some may say religion was most important because it led to the Crusades. Some may say curiosity was most important because it led to exploration. Some may point to desire for wealth and power because it led Europeans to seek most favorable trade and thus spurred exploration.

Applying Skills

Students might note that Christianity was a major unifying force in Europe at the time, and in Palestine was the Holy Land, to which Europeans wanted access. At the same time, fighting was a way of life. Students might conclude that these two factors led Europeans to try capturing Palestine.
(Answers continued in side margin)

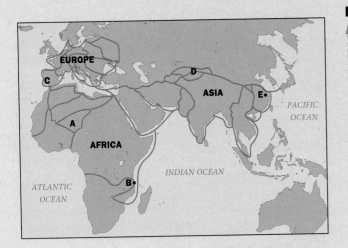

Reviewing Geography

1. For each letter on the map, write the name of a city, a trade route, a trading empire, or a nation.

2. Geographic Thinking People move from place to place for many different reasons. Sometimes people want to move; other times, they are forced to.

List at least three reasons why people moved in the 1400s. Then list at least three reasons why people move today. How are the causes of movement in the past and the present similar? How are they different?

History Mystery

Information on the Chinese navy is on p. 48. To learn more, students might read secondary sources and translations of primary sources on the topic. With the navy, China might have continued to rank high in military power, technology, and trade. It might have reached the Americas before Europeans.

Writing in Your History Journal

1. (a) Explanations should be similar to the time line notes on teacher pages 34–35. (b) Students' choices may vary. For example, they may choose Marco Polo's trip to China in order to see the riches of the Great Khan.

2. Students' dialogues may have the captain offering information, and the prince asking for more detail.

3. Advantages: little conflict, security, support from others, protection from poverty. Disadvantages: small likelihood of wealth, fewer chances to pursue individual goals, less self-reliance.

Reviewing Geography

1. (A) Songhai, (B) Kilwa, (C) Portugal, (D) Silk Road, (E) Hangzhou

2. Some reasons: trade, slavery, war, exploration, religious fervor. Some reasons today: war, natural disasters, persecution, employment, and cultural and climate preferences. Similarities: economic reasons, war. Difference: more voluntary today.

Alternative Assessment

Teacher's Take-Home Planner 1, p. 13, includes suggestions and scoring rubrics for the Alternative Assessment activity.

3. Citizenship In their daily lives, most West Africans put social harmony and the needs of the village above personal concerns. In addition, farmland belonged to the village, not to individuals. What advantages might this way of life have? What disadvantages? Write your responses in your journal.

Alternative Assessment

Teaching a class at Sagres Imagine that you are going to teach a class at Prince Henry's center for exploration at Sagres. The topic is the economy of Africa, Asia, or Europe. The prince wants you to provide explorers with as much information as possible about trade and technology. Explorers will also need to know about people's ways of life.

❶ Choose the continent you want to discuss—Africa, Asia, or Europe.

❷ Prepare an outline of what you plan to teach and make a list of the materials you need, including visual aids. For example, you may want to use a large, illustrated map of the continent.

❸ Start with the information in the chapter and do additional research as needed to provide enough background.

❹ When your planning is complete, teach the class.

Your work will be evaluated on the following criteria:
• you provide adequate information to present a picture of the continent
• you provide information that is accurate
• you present the information in clear, interesting ways

3 Voyages of Exploration
1450–1610

Chapter Planning Guide

Section	Student Text	Teacher's Edition Activities
Opener and Story pp. 58–61	**Keys to History Time Line** **History Mystery** Beginning the Story with **Christopher Columbus**	**Setting the Stage Activity** Effects of the Printing Press, p. 60
1 **The Quest for Trade Routes by Sea** pp. 62–67	**Reading Maps** Voyages of Dias and da Gama, p. 64; Voyages of Columbus 1492–1503, p. 66 **World Link** Expulsion of Jews from Spain, p. 65 **Link to Literature** *Morning Girl*, pp. 82–83	**Warm-Up Activity** Identifying Risk-Worthy Goals, p. 62 **Geography Question of the Day,** p. 62 **Section Activity** First Impressions: Writing Dialogs, p. 64 **Bonus Activity** Role-playing Dias's Crew, p. 63 **Wrap-Up Activity** Comparison Charts, p. 67
2 **Seeds of Change** pp. 68–72	**Hands-On History** Simulating the spread of smallpox, p. 69 **Point of View** How did the slave trade affect Africa?, p. 71 **Geography Lab** The Horse Comes to North America, p. 72	**Warm-Up Activity** Taking a Plant and Animal Inventory, p. 68 **Geography Question of the Day,** p. 68 **Section Activity** Cuisine and the Columbian Exchange, p. 70 **Bonus Activity** Identifying Exchanges Today, p. 70 **Wrap-Up Activity** Identifying Good and Bad Effects, p. 71
3 **The Race for Discovery** pp. 73–79	**Reading Maps** Voyage of Magellan 1519–1521, p. 74; Search for the Northwest Passage 1497–1610, p. 77 **Link to Art** Inuit man and woman with child, p. 75 **Link to the Present** Tomorrow's explorers, p. 76 **Skill Lab** Historical Research, p. 79	**Warm-Up Activity** Looking for a Northwest Passage, p. 73 **Geography Question of the Day,** p. 73 **Section Activity** Writing Ships' Logs, p. 74 **Bonus Activity** Writing Sailor Journal Entries, p. 76 **Wrap-Up Activity** Identifying Explorers' Routes, p. 78
Evaluation	✓ **Section 1 Review,** p. 67 ✓ **Section 2 Review,** p. 71 ✓ **Section 3 Review,** p. 78 ✓ **Chapter Survey,** pp. 80–81 **Alternative Assessment** Holding a debate, p. 81	✓ **Answers to Section 1 Review,** p. 67 ✓ **Answers to Section 2 Review,** p. 71 ✓ **Answers to Section 3 Review,** p. 78 ✓ **Answers to Chapter Survey,** pp. 80–81 (Alternative Assessment guidelines are in the Take-Home Planner.)

Teacher's Resource Package

 Chapter Summaries: English and Spanish, pp. 10–11

 Chapter Resources Binder
> **Study Guide** Identifying Main Ideas, p. 17
> **Reinforcement** Tracking Events, pp. 21–22

American Readings Columbus's First Voyage, pp. 9–10; Encountering the "Caribees," p. 11

 Chapter Resources Binder
> **Study Guide** Supplying Supporting Evidence, p. 18

Geography Extensions Spread of the Horse, pp. 5–6

Using Historical Documents Huejotzingo Codex, pp. 17–19

 Chapter Resources Binder
> **Study Guide** Organizing Information, p. 19
> **Skills Development** Historical Research, pp. 23–24

American Readings The Attractions of Florida, p. 12

Chapter and Unit Tests Chapter 3 Tests, Forms A and B, pp. 13–16

Take-Home Planner

Introducing the Chapter Activity Mapping the School, p. 20

Chapter In-Depth Activity Identifying the Legacy of Exchange, p. 21

Reduced Views
> **Study Guide,** p. 22
> **Reinforcement,** p. 23
> **American Readings,** p. 24
Unit 1 Answers, pp. 28–34

Reduced Views
> **Study Guide,** p. 22
> **Geography Extensions,** p. 25
> **Using Historical Documents,** p. 25
Unit 1 Answers, pp. 28–34

Reduced Views
> **Study Guide,** p. 22
> **Skills Development,** p. 23
> **American Readings,** p. 24
Unit 1 Answers, pp. 28–34

Reduced Views
> **Chapter Tests,** p. 25
Unit 1 Answers, pp. 28–34

Alternative Assessment Guidelines for scoring the Chapter Survey activity, p. 21

Additional Resources

Wall Time Line

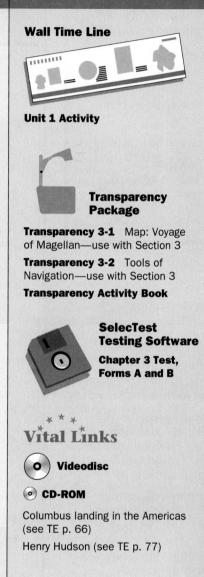

Unit 1 Activity

Transparency Package

Transparency 3-1 Map: Voyage of Magellan—use with Section 3

Transparency 3-2 Tools of Navigation—use with Section 3

Transparency Activity Book

SelecTest Testing Software

Chapter 3 Test, Forms A and B

Vital Links

⊙ **Videodisc**

⊙ **CD-ROM**

Columbus landing in the Americas (see TE p. 66)

Henry Hudson (see TE p. 77)

57B

Teaching Resources

Take-Home Planner 1
 Introducing Chapter Activity
 Chapter In-Depth Activity
 Alternative Assessment
Chapter Resources Binder
Geography Extensions
American Readings
Using Historical Documents
Transparency Activities
Wall Time Line Activities
Chapter Summaries
Chapter and Unit Tests
SelecTest Test File
Vital Links CD-ROM/Videodisc

Time Line

Keys to History

Keys to History journal writing activity is on pages 80–81 in the Chapter Survey.

Columbus reaches the Americas Columbus was the first European to have a lasting impact on the Americas. (p. 65)

Columbian Exchange begins The exchange of plants, animals, people, and diseases begun by Columbus transformed the world. (p. 68)

Looking Back The arrival of Europeans was to doom the Aztec empire and other North American cultures and civilizations.

World Link See p. 65.

Chapter Objectives

★ Explain how Europe's search for trade routes led to new discoveries.
★ Explain the Columbian Exchange.
★ Describe the voyages made to find a way around or through the Americas.

Chapter Overview
In the 1400s Europeans wanted to establish direct trade with Africa and Asia. Among the early explorers who were looking for a trade route by sea were Bartolomeu Dias, Vasco da Gama, and Christopher Columbus.

Columbus, convinced he could reach the riches of the Indies by sailing west, encountered continents unknown to Europeans. Sailing for Spain, he made four trips

1450–1610

Chapter **3**

Voyages of Exploration

Sections

Beginning the Story with Christopher Columbus

1. **The Quest for Trade Routes by Sea**
2. **Seeds of Change**
3. **The Race for Discovery**

 Keys to History

SANTA MARIA
NAO CAPITANEADA POR CRISTOBAL COLON EN EL DESCUBRIMIENTO DE AMERICA 14-92. AL NAUFRAGAR, SE SE CONSTRUYE CON SUS RESTOS EL FUERTE NAVIDAD EN LA ISLA LA ESPAÑOLA PRIMER ASENTAMIEN DE ESPAÑOLES EN EL NUEVO MUNDO.

1492
Christopher Columbus reaches the Americas
Columbus's flagship

1492
Columbian Exchange begins
Columbus took chilies back to Europe

1450   **1475**

Looking Back
Aztecs build Tenochtitlán
1345

World Link
Ferdinand and Isabella expel Jews from Spain
1492

to the Americas, but believed until his death that he had reached the Indies.

His voyages to the Americas led to the Columbian Exchange, an exchange of plants, animals, diseases, and people that would eventually affect the whole world.

In the race for discovery that followed Columbus's voyages and Magellan's circum-navigation, Spain gained control of the southern routes. England, the Netherlands, and France searched for a Northwest Passage, but to no avail. However, they gained valuable resources and made claims to land in North America.

Teaching the HISTORY Mystery

Students will find the answer on p. 67. See Chapter Survey, p. 80, for additional questions.

HISTORY Mystery

Areas of land and bodies of water are often named for explorers. It was from the voyages of Christopher Columbus that Europeans first learned of the American continents. Why are these areas of land not called North and South Columbia?

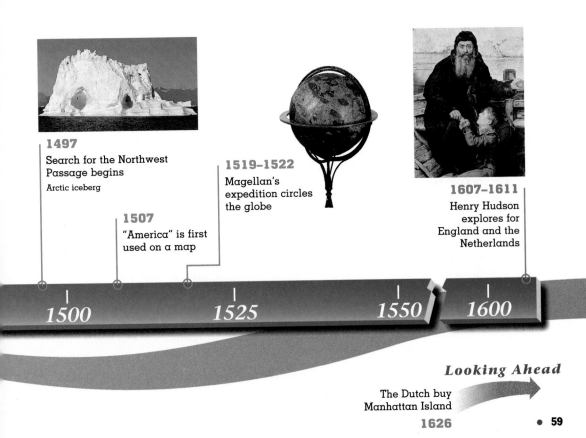

1497
Search for the Northwest Passage begins
Arctic iceberg

1507
"America" is first used on a map

1519–1522
Magellan's expedition circles the globe

1607–1611
Henry Hudson explores for England and the Netherlands

1500   1525   1550   1600

Looking Ahead
The Dutch buy Manhattan Island
1626

● **59**

Time Line

Search for the Northwest Passage begins Since Spain controlled waters off South America, her rivals looked for a northern route through the Americas to Asia. (p. 75)

"America" first used on a map The land was named after the explorer Amerigo Vespucci who, unlike Columbus, recognized that a "new world" lay between Europe and Asia. (p. 67)

Magellan's expedition circles the globe Magellan proved that Columbus was right in saying Asia could be reached from Europe by sailing west. (p. 73)

Hudson explores Although Henry Hudson failed to find a Northwest Passage, his voyages established English claims to Canada and Dutch claims in present-day New York. (p. 76)

Looking Ahead The Dutch founded the town of New Amsterdam on Manhattan Island, controlling the best natural harbor on North America's Atlantic coast.

Beginning the Story

Christopher Columbus

Students will read about how Columbus took to the sea, learned chart making, taught himself Latin and Spanish, and became an expert navigator. They will learn how someone with intelligence, courage, and imagination was influenced by and affected the world he lived in.

Setting the Stage
Activity

Effects of the Printing Press

To help students see how the printing press helped spur exploration, have them create a cause-effect chain. Point out that Gutenberg invented his press around the time Columbus was born. Beginning with the event "Printing press invented," have students make a cause-effect chain that ends with "Many Europeans want to explore Asia and Africa." After discussing their cause-effect chains, lead into the story by asking them to imagine growing up in a seaport and reading the travel stories of Marco Polo.

See the Introducing the Chapter Activity, Mapping the School. **Take-Home Planner 1**, p. 20.

✳ History Footnote

No portraits were made of Columbus during his lifetime. Fifty years after his death, when the significance of his voyages became apparent, likenesses of the Admiral were created by the hundreds. Of course, by then, no one could be certain what Columbus looked like. His son Ferdinand reported that his father "was a well-made man, of a height above the medium, with a long face, and cheekbones somewhat prominent; neither too fat nor too lean. He had an aquiline [hooked] nose, light-colored eyes, and a ruddy complexion." Many scholars believe that the portrait shown on this page most closely corresponds to written accounts.

Beginning the Story with

Christopher Columbus

August 13, 1476. For an Italian sailor named Christopher Columbus, it was a day of disaster—a day when he looked death in the face and said, "Not yet." The 25-year-old Columbus was a member of the crew aboard a trading ship sailing from Genoa, Italy, to England. On that August morning, French pirates attacked the ship off the coast of Portugal. The battle raged all day amid smoke and flames. As night fell, the battered trading vessel sank to the bottom of the sea.

Columbus would have sunk as well, had he not grabbed a long wooden oar to keep himself afloat. All through the night, he forced his tired legs to kick, rest, then kick again. Miraculously, he managed to reach the shore of Portugal, some 6 miles (10 km) away. Local people took him in and cared for him. As soon as he was well enough to travel, Columbus made his way to Lisbon, the capital of Portugal.

The Weaver's Son

Up until he arrived in Lisbon, there was nothing about Columbus that seemed to mark him for greatness. He was born in the bustling seaport of Genoa about 1451. His father, Domenico Colombo, was a weaver of wool. His mother, Susanna, came from a family of weavers. In those days a weaver's son could only dream of going to school. Instead, Columbus worked at the looms with his father.

Yet the restless boy gazed longingly at the hardworking trading ships that lined Genoa's busy docks, and at the age of 14 Columbus took to the sea. For the next few years, he divided his time between trading voyages and helping his father on shore.

History Bookshelf

Meltzer, Milton. *Columbus and the World Around Him.* Franklin Watts, 1990. Meltzer gives a fascinating and balanced view of Columbus. He tells of the European culture that shaped him, how Columbus's desire for riches drove him, and how his unshakable belief in his superiority led to the exploitation of Indians. This book has been selected as a School Library Journal Best Book of the Year, an NCTE Outstanding Nonfiction Work for Children, and a Notable Children's Trade Book in the Field of Social Studies in 1990.

Also of interest:

Dor-Ner, Zvi. *Columbus and the Age of Discovery.* William Morrow, 1991.

Wilford, John Noble. *The Mysterious History of Columbus: An Exploration of the Man, the Myth, the Legacy.* Knopf, 1991.

In Lisbon, however, Columbus's life changed forever. In 1476 Portugal was the European center of seagoing exploration and trade. Merchant ships crowded the harbor. People swarmed in and out of trading and banking houses. Christopher's younger brother Bartholomew was already in Lisbon, making detailed maps of coastlines called *charts*. Chart makers were often the first to hear the reports of voyages to foreign shores.

Working with Bartholomew, Christopher learned chart making. He also learned to speak Portuguese and taught himself to read and write both Latin and Spanish. He read every geography and travel book he could lay his hands on. One of his favorites was Marco Polo's *Description of the World*. After the excitement of Lisbon, Columbus could never return to Genoa and his father's looms.

In 1992—500 years after Columbus set sail for the Americas—Spanish authorities built this replica of his flagship, the *Santa María*.

The Merchant Seaman

In 1477, undaunted by his narrow escape from death, Columbus left chart making to go to sea once more. Trading ships took him as far north as Iceland and as far south as the Portuguese posts in West Africa. At every port he listened to stories, studied maps, and collected information. Gradually he became an expert navigator, ship's officer, and finally captain.

Columbus became convinced that ships could reach the Indies most easily by sailing westward across the Atlantic. Although most educated people of his day knew that the world was round, few believed a ship could survive such a voyage. The distance simply seemed too great. Sailors feared that far out at sea there would be no breezes to power their sailing ships. Helpless in the still air, they would perish from thirst or starvation.

Such fears did not stop Columbus. In his travels he had heard tales of boiling seas near the equator, but he had crossed the equator and seen for himself that the seas did not boil. Surely the fear that there were no breezes in the middle of the ocean would also turn out to be untrue. All he needed was a chance to show that his ideas about a route to Asia were right. Given that chance, he would find wealth beyond dreams. Given that chance, he would change the world.

Hands-On → *HISTORY*

Activity

Imagine that you are Columbus applying for a job as commander of a fleet of ships. The fleet will be going on a voyage of exploration into unknown seas. As Columbus, list the experiences you would put on your job application to convince the owner of the ships that you are qualified for command.

Discussion

Thinking Historically

1. How did Columbus's place of birth influence his choice of career? (Born in the bustling seaport of Genoa, he yearned to go to sea. At age 14 he began to sail on trading ships.)

2. How did a disaster at sea change his life? (When his ship sank, he came ashore in Portugal. In Lisbon, he developed his idea of reaching the Indies by sailing west.)

3. What qualities made it possible for Columbus to do what he did? (Persistence, curiosity, desire for knowledge.)

See the Chapter In-Depth Activity, Identifying the Legacy of Exchange. **Take-Home Planner 1,** p. 21.

Teaching the Hands-On

- - - - - - - → *HISTORY*

First ask what qualities and skills would make someone a good commander. Students might mention courage, leadership, knowledge of geography, and experience on ships. Write these suggestions on the chalkboard. In making their lists, students should review the story for evidence of how Columbus met these criteria.

For a journal writing activity on Christopher Columbus, see student page 80.

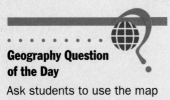

1. The Quest for Trade Routes by Sea

Reading Guide

New Terms **expedition, cape, finance**

Section Focus **How Europe's search for trade routes led to new and surprising knowledge**

1. **What is known about the people who reached the Americas before Columbus?**
2. **What did Dias and da Gama add to Europe's store of knowledge?**
3. **What did Columbus achieve, and what did he think he had achieved?**

If you had been in school 50 years ago and your teacher had asked, "Who discovered America?" you would probably have answered, "Columbus!" But was Columbus really the first? In Chapter 1 you read that Paleo-Indians crossed Beringia to the Americas thousands of years earlier. There are also many theories about non-Indian visitors to the Americas before Columbus.

For example, an Irish monk named Brendan who lived during the 500s told of a voyage to a "land of promise." His descriptions fit parts of North America. Polynesians, too, may have visited the Americas. Some scholars believe that statues on Easter Island off the coast of Chile were made long ago by voyagers from Polynesia.

Other scholars suggest that Egyptians, Romans, Africans, or Asians may have reached the Americas long ago. So far, however, no firm evidence has been found for any visitors except the Vikings—the seagoing people of Scandinavia that you read about in Chapter 2.

The Vikings

In 1963 archaeologists found the remains of one Viking settlement at L'Anse aux

Meadows, in Newfoundland. The discovery suggests that old Norse sagas—stories of heroic deeds—are indeed true.

One saga tells of Thorfinn Karlsefni, who sailed about A.D. 1010 with 250 men and women and a herd of livestock. The group settled in a place they named Vinland, or Land of the Vine. Scholars believe that L'Anse aux Meadows could be Vinland.

People the settlers called Skraelings (SKRAY-lings) came to trade skins and furs for swords and axes. The Vikings offered milk and red cloth instead. When a Skraeling tried to steal a weapon, the Vikings killed him. A fierce fight followed. The settlers decided to abandon the new land "since there would always be fear and strife . . . there on account of those who already inhabited it."

New Trade Routes

If other Europeans ever heard the Vinland saga, they thought it was just a story. Four hundred years later, they still had no idea that two great continents lay across the ocean to the west. As you read in Chapter 2, Portuguese sailors navigated by hugging the coast instead of sailing the open sea. By 1484

History Footnote

Unlike Vasco da Gama, Bartolomeu Dias received little reward and recognition from King John II for his achievement. He helped direct the building of da Gama's ships for the voyage to India but was not included on the voyage itself. When he drowned in a hurricane off the coast of Brazil in 1500, he was playing a minor role—as a pilot of just one of 13 ships in Pedro Cabral's expedition.

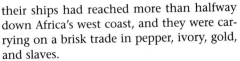

See the Study Guide activity in **Chapter Resources Binder**, p. 17.

their ships had reached more than halfway down Africa's west coast, and they were carrying on a brisk trade in pepper, ivory, gold, and slaves.

Meanwhile, King John II sent Portuguese ships further and further down the African coast. The Portuguese were drawn on by their desire to find a new route to the Indies.

Dias In 1487 Bartolomeu Dias [DEE-us] set out on an **expedition**—a journey organized for a definite purpose. King John II of Portugal had ordered him to find the tip of Africa. Dias had sailed for thousands of miles along the coast when a violent storm arose, driving his ships far out to sea. The sailors were certain they would all die.

When the storm passed, the crew discovered that they had been blown around the **cape**—a piece of land sticking into the sea—at the southern tip of Africa. Dias named it the Cape of Storms. He wanted to

sail on, but his frightened crew forced him to turn back.

When the king heard Dias's report, he felt that the wealth of the Indies was within his reach. Overjoyed, he gave a new name to the Cape of Storms. He called it the Cape of Good Hope, by which it is still known.

Columbus In 1484, before the Dias expedition, Columbus had told King John of his own plan to reach the Indies by sailing westward. He fully expected the king to **finance**—which means to supply money for—his voyage.

The king's advisors thought that Columbus's estimates of the size of the earth and its oceans were wrong. In fact, Columbus had miscalculated. He believed that Japan was about 3,000 nautical miles (5,556 km) from Portugal. Actually, it is more than 10,000 miles (18,519 km). The king turned Columbus down.

Today, re-creations of Viking longhouses stand at L'Anse aux Meadows in northern Newfoundland. Archaeologists began to study the site in the 1960s. They discovered traces of dwellings, remains of fire pits, and bits of worked iron. They also found a Norse-style weight used to spin yarn and a piece of bone.

Developing the Section

Discussion

Checking Understanding

1. What do the archaeological finds in L'Anse aux Meadows suggest? (They suggest that an old Norse saga about a group who settled in a place they named Vinland is true.)

Stimulating Critical Thinking

2. Suppose that long before Columbus European rulers had proof that two continents lay between Europe and Asia. Do you think they would have sent expeditions there? Explain. (Those who say no might explain that most European rulers were looking for sea routes to the Indies, not new lands to settle. Others might argue that many would see opportunity in settling the continent and exploring its resources.)

Bonus Activity

Role-playing Dias's Crew

To stress the challenges of a voyage into the unknown, have students role-play possible scenarios between Dias and his crew at different points in their journey. To prepare, they should review the description of the voyage. The role-play should reflect their ideas about dangers the crew faced, how Dias kept them going, and how they might have felt after months at sea.

1450–1610 Chapter 3 • **63**

63

Have students compare the explorers' routes. Ask why Dias stayed much closer to the coast. (He did not know how far it was to the southern tip.) Point out that by sailing further west, da Gama avoided coastal storms and took advantage of prevailing winds. Then ask why he at first stayed close to the eastern coast. (Waters were unfamiliar.) Have students review the text to explain why his route suddenly changed. (Arab guide showed him across the Indian Ocean.)
Answer to Reading Maps: Dias proved that there was a way around Africa, and da Gama proved Europeans could reach Asia by sailing up the east coast of Africa and across the Indian Ocean.

Section Activity

First Impressions: Writing Dialogs

To imagine how Indians and Europeans might have reacted to their first encounter, have pairs of students write dialogs. Half will involve two Indians, one who has met Europeans and one who has not. The first tells of the encounter, explaining observations and feelings in response to the other's questions. The other dialogs will be similar in format, but with two Europeans. Conclude by summarizing the observations and feelings, and discussing possible reasons for them.

✳ **History Footnote**

Portugal tried to keep its knowledge of sea routes a secret from European rivals. In the late 1400s King John II began a policy of making betrayal of such secrets punishable by death. Still, information leaked out. Sea captains passed along knowledge when they were hired by different governments. Also, sailors and merchants gossiped in ports. Meanwhile, maps were often smuggled.

The earliest surviving record of Portuguese discoveries, the Cantino chart of 1502, was smuggled to one of the Italian princes, who feared that da Gama's success in reaching India threatened Italian control of the overland spice trade with Asia.

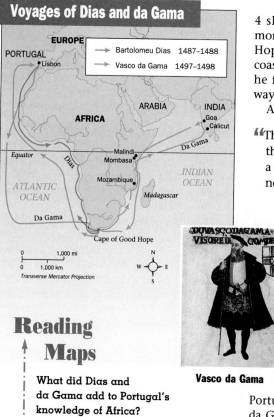

Vasco da Gama

Reading Maps

↑ What did Dias and da Gama add to Portugal's knowledge of Africa?

4 ships and a crew of 170. In only four months da Gama rounded the Cape of Good Hope. Then he made his way up the east coast of Africa, stopping now and then until he found an Arab guide to show him the way across the Indian Ocean.

A poet later described da Gama's triumph:

❝This is the story of heroes who, leaving their native Portugal behind them, opened a way to Ceylon and further, across seas no man had ever sailed before.❞

Da Gama's fleet reached India in May 1498. He filled his ships with silks, pepper, cinnamon, and other goods. By the time he got back to Lisbon in September 1499, however, he had lost half of his fleet and most of his crew, including his brother.

The rewards were great, though. The king named him Admiral of the Sea of India and gave him an income for life. Dazzled by the promise of enormous wealth, Portuguese merchants rushed to follow in da Gama's tracks, and Portugal became the center of a thriving Asia trade.

Columbus did not give up easily. The success of Dias, however, dashed his hopes of finding support in Portugal. Why would the king risk money on his plan for an Atlantic crossing when Portuguese ships were sure to reach the Indies by sailing around Africa?

The Portuguese Reach Asia

Indeed, a tough and strong-willed sea captain, Vasco da Gama, did complete the all-water route from Portugal to Asia. He sailed from Lisbon on July 8, 1497, with

Admiral of the Ocean Sea

Meanwhile, Columbus, having failed in Portugal, moved on to Spain. There he tried to persuade King Ferdinand and Queen Isabella to support him. The king and queen did not say yes, but they did not say no, either. Columbus had to wait.

One reason for the delay was that Spain was at war. Ferdinand and Isabella were fighting to unify Spain as a strong, Catholic nation. In 1492, they succeeded in driving out Spain's Muslims and forcing its Jews to convert to Christianity or flee. Then the royal couple turned their attention to Columbus's plan.

At-Risk Students

At-risk students often find it difficult to understand the use of words with multiple meanings. For example, they may not understand the meaning of *planted* in the sentence "The landing party gave a prayer of thanks, then solemnly planted Spanish banners and a cross." Review with them strategies they can use, such as reading the passage again for context clues to meaning, checking a dictionary, or asking for help. Point out that in the example sentence, *planted* means to set firmly into the ground so that something will not fall. Later they will encounter *planted* in the sense of setting up colonies.

Perhaps their recent victory filled the king and queen with pride. Perhaps they hoped for a sea route to rival the Portuguese route to the Indies. Whatever the reason, they agreed to sponsor Columbus. It was the wisest investment they ever made.

The king and queen gave Columbus two caravels—the *Niña* and the *Pinta*—and a cargo ship, the *Santa María*. On August 3, 1492, the little fleet left Spain, first sailing south to the Canary Islands, then west into the open sea. As they left the Canaries, Columbus wrote:

> "This day we completely lost sight of land, and many men sighed and wept for fear they would not see it again for a long time. I comforted them with great promises of land and riches."

Reaching the Americas As the days passed, the crew grew rebellious. Columbus soothed their fears by lying to them. He said they had gone a shorter distance each day than they really had. He did not want them to know they were so far from home. Fortunately, on October 12, 1492, they spotted land—a low island in what today is the Bahamas, in the Caribbean Sea.

Relieved to have found land at last, Columbus had himself rowed to shore. The landing party gave a prayer of thanks, then solemnly planted Spanish banners and a cross. In those days, Europeans thought that a Christian nation had a right to take over any land not ruled by a Christian. So, despite the fact that the island was inhabited, Columbus claimed it for Spain and Christianity and named it San Salvador, which means "Holy Savior."

Although San Salvador did not look at all like the Indies, Columbus was certain that he had reached Asia. He called the Taino (TĪ-nō) people who lived there *Indios*—Indians. He wrote in his diary:

> "All those that I saw were young people, for none did I see of more than thirty years of age. They are all very well-formed. . . . They believe very firmly that I, with these ships and crew, came from the sky, and in such opinion they received me at every place where I landed, after they lost their terror."

A short time later, the *Santa María* ran aground. With the *Niña* and the *Pinta* Columbus sailed back to Spain to report that he had reached Asia. He took with him several natives whom he had captured, as well as curiosities such as parrots, strange plants, and gold trinkets.

Columbus was greeted as a hero. Crowds cheered him wherever he went, and Ferdinand and Isabella rewarded him with the title Admiral of the Ocean Sea.

World Link

Expulsion of Jews from Spain

In 1492 Ferdinand and Isabella ordered Spanish Jews to convert to Christianity or leave the country. That order started a chain of events that led to an early Jewish community in what is now the United States.

Many Spanish Jews resettled in Portugal. To please Ferdinand and Isabella, Portugal also ordered Jews to convert or leave. This time many Jews went to the Netherlands, and eventually some moved on to a Dutch settlement in Brazil. When that settlement fell to the Portuguese in 1654, a small group of Spanish-Portuguese Jews found their way to another Dutch settlement in what is now New York State.

Checking Understanding

1. Why was Columbus unable to get the help he needed in Portugal? (King John's advisors thought his estimates of the size of the earth and its oceans were wrong, and Dias's success in rounding the Cape of Good Hope meant that Portugal already had a water route to India.)

2. Why did Columbus lie to his crew? (Each day he told them they had gone a shorter distance than they had so they would not be aware of how far they were from home and become more discouraged or afraid.)

Stimulating Critical Thinking

3. What do you think the Taino people thought of Columbus and his crew? (Reactions might have included surprise at their arrival, fear, and curiosity about their unusual clothes and behavior.)

For a fictional account of an Indian girl's first encounter with Europeans, see the Link to Literature on pp. 82–83.

Teaching the

World Link

Point out that the Spanish and other Europeans had the same attitude toward Indians as they had toward Jews or any group with a culture and beliefs different from their own.

Be sure students understand that this is a modern map and that in Columbus's time distances could not be figured precisely. Direct them to compare this map with the world map on pp. R2–R3 to find the modern nations.

Answers to Reading Maps:
1. Around Cuba, Haiti, and Dominican Republic on his first voyage. Around Puerto Rico, Jamaica, Haiti, Dominican Republic, and Cuba on his second voyage. Around Trinidad, Venezuela, and Dominican Republic on his third voyage. Around Panama, Costa Rica, Nicaragua, Honduras, Jamaica, and Puerto Rico on his fourth voyage.
2. Students might suggest that he thought it was the mainland because he did not sail around it to see that it was an island or because it looked like what he expected the Chinese mainland to look like.

★★★
Vital Links

Columbus landing in the Americas (Picture) Unit 1, Side 1, Search 20339

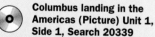

See also Unit 1 Explore CD-ROM location 185.

✠ **Connections to Civics**

The European kings and queens headed governments known as monarchies. A monarchy is a form of government in which one person—usually the son or daughter of the previous monarch—heads the nation. In the past, most monarchies were absolute. This meant that the monarch had complete control of the government. Today, many monarchies are constitutional or limited.

For accounts of Columbus's first voyage and encounters with Indians, see **American Readings,** pp. 9–11.

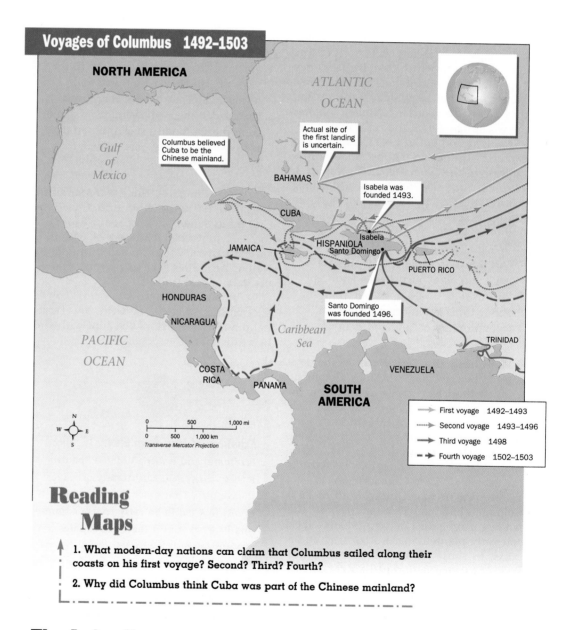

Voyages of Columbus   1492–1503

NORTH AMERICA

ATLANTIC OCEAN

Gulf of Mexico

Columbus believed Cuba to be the Chinese mainland.

Actual site of the first landing is uncertain.

BAHAMAS

Isabela was founded 1493.

CUBA

Isabela

JAMAICA

HISPANIOLA
Santo Domingo

PUERTO RICO

HONDURAS

Santo Domingo was founded 1496.

NICARAGUA

Caribbean Sea

PACIFIC OCEAN

TRINIDAD

COSTA RICA

PANAMA

VENEZUELA

SOUTH AMERICA

0   500   1,000 mi
0   500   1,000 km
Transverse Mercator Projection

→ First voyage   1492–1493
⋯ Second voyage   1493–1496
→ Third voyage   1498
– → Fourth voyage   1502–1503

Reading Maps

↑ 1. What modern-day nations can claim that Columbus sailed along their coasts on his first voyage? Second? Third? Fourth?

2. Why did Columbus think Cuba was part of the Chinese mainland?

The Later Voyages

The king and queen were eager to profit from the discoveries of their new admiral. They asked Columbus to establish a colony in the faraway land he had claimed for Spain.

Columbus sailed west again in September 1493. This time, instead of 3 small vessels, he commanded a proud fleet of 17 ships crowded with carpenters, farmers, soldiers, and missionaries. The missionaries hoped to win over the native people to the Catholic faith.

In sailing the Atlantic, navigators tried to take advantage of prevailing winds—those that usually blow from the same direction and travel long distances. Columbus traveled from northeast to southwest. In this region north of the equator, the prevailing winds flow from northeast to southwest. These "northeast trade winds" literally blew his ships to the Caribbean islands.

Sailing into the northeast trade winds made the return trip slower. In time, navigators found prevailing winds further north that flowed from west to east. Another aid in sailing from America back to Europe was the discovery of the Gulf Stream—a strong ocean current moving northeast along the Atlantic coast of North America. With the Gulf Stream and the prevailing winds, explorers had a natural set of navigational aids.

In his diary Columbus wrote about the beaches of San Salvador. He also described jewelry like the gold nose ring worn by this Cuna woman today.

The ships carried everything Columbus thought the colony would need. Columbus chose a site for Spain's first permanent colony, Isabela, on a large island that came to be called Hispaniola (HIS-puhn-YŌ-luh). Isabela was too near a swamp, however, and had little fresh water. When Columbus left Hispaniola, he gave his brother Bartholomew instructions to establish a new settlement—Santo Domingo.

Altogether, Columbus made four trips to the Americas. On his final visit in 1502 he sailed along the Central American coast. He named the area Costa Rica, meaning "Rich Coast," which showed that his hope for wealth in these lands was still alive.

Columbus returned from his voyage a discouraged man. He had proved to be a failure as governor of Hispaniola. In Spain, jealous people worked to deprive him of the honors and income Isabella and Ferdinand had promised. Until his death on May 19, 1506, however, Columbus held to the belief that he had reached the Indies.

A Land "We May Call America"

Although Columbus may have gone to his grave believing he had reached Asia, his rivals knew otherwise. One was Amerigo Vespucci (AH-meh-REE-gō ves-POOT-chee), an Italian trader. He searched nearly the full length of the South American coast, looking for a way to India. He wrote that a "new world" lay between Europe and Asia.

In 1507 German geographer Martin Waldseemüller (VAHLT-zay-MYOOL-er) published a new map. It featured a previously unknown land which, he wrote, "since Amerigo found it, we may call . . . America." Other map makers followed. Thus lands of the Western Hemisphere were named after Vespucci instead of Columbus.

However, the foothold Columbus established in the Caribbean would expand into a vast empire. By 1600, Spain would control much of North and South America, and would be one of the world's richest nations. Spain owed much of this wealth and power to the vision and determination of the Admiral of the Ocean Sea.

⭐ 1. Section Review

1. Define **expedition, cape,** and **finance.**
2. What evidence suggests that the Vikings reached North America?
3. How did the route that Dias and da Gama established help Portugal?
4. Why did Ferdinand and Isabella sponsor Columbus?
5. What areas did Columbus explore on his four expeditions?
6. **Critical Thinking** What qualities do you think people like Dias, da Gama, and Columbus must have had to lead their crews on such risky voyages?

Wrap-Up Activity

Comparison Charts
To review the European explorations, have students create charts comparing the voyages of the Vikings, Dias, da Gama, and Columbus. Chart headings should include the following: Date, Purpose, Effects. Conclude by summarizing similarities and differences.

Section Review
Answers
1. Definitions: *expedition* (63), *cape* (63), *finance* (63)
2. The remains of a Viking settlement in Newfoundland suggest that the Vikings reached North America.
3. Dias and da Gama established a sea route around Africa so that Portugal could trade directly with Asia.
4. They may have been filled with pride from a recent victory or hoped for a sea route to rival the Portuguese.
5. Columbus explored Caribbean islands and the coasts of South America and Central America. He thought he was in the Indies.
6. Answers will vary but may include courage, imagination, persistence, and leadership.

Vocabulary

infectious diseases (p. 68) illnesses passed from one person to another

plantation (p. 70) a large estate where a single crop is grown for profit

legacy (p. 71) something handed down from past generations

Taking a Plant and Animal Inventory

To prepare for studying the Columbian Exchange, have each student make a table with these headings: Fruits, Vegetables, Animals. Have them fill in examples (for animals, list those used for food, clothing, or transportation). Then have them place a check mark next to any they think is native to the Americas. After they read the section, have them add to and correct their tables.

Geography Question of the Day

Provide students with a world outline map (in **Geography Extensions**) and the following definition: "The Western Hemisphere extends from 20 degrees west longitude to 160 degrees east longitude." Have them lightly shade in that area, list the names of continents within it, and list the names of continents in the Eastern Hemisphere. (The map may also be used for the Geography Question on p. 73.)

Section Objectives

★ Explain why infectious diseases had such a terrible effect on American Indians.

★ Describe how the exchange of food plants benefited Europe.

★ Identify how the transfer of animals changed the lives of some American Indians.

Teaching Resources

Take-Home Planner 1, pp. 18–25

Chapter Resources Binder

　Study Guide, p. 18

　Reinforcement

　Skills Development

Geography Extensions, pp. 5–6

　American Readings

Using Historical Documents, pp. 17–19

　Transparency Activities

　Chapter and Unit Tests

2. Seeds of Change

Reading Guide

New Terms **infectious diseases, plantation, legacy**

Section Focus **The worldwide exchange of plants, animals, diseases, and people begun by Columbus**

1. Why did infectious diseases have such a terrible effect on American Indians?
2. How did the exchange of food plants benefit Europeans?
3. How did the transfer of animals change the lives of some American Indians?

Is popcorn one of your favorite snacks? French fries, peanut butter, chocolate, cola? All of these treats come from plants that were first raised by American Indian farmers. Not one was known outside of the Americas before the voyages of Columbus. Now they are known around the world.

The voyages of Columbus marked the beginning of a great biological and human exchange between the Eastern and Western Hemispheres. As Columbus sailed back and forth to the Americas, he carried the beginnings, or "seeds," of great changes that would affect the whole world.

Among these seeds of change were diseases, plants, and animals. Scholars call this transfer the Columbian Exchange. According to historian Alfred Crosby, the Columbian Exchange "was the most important event in human history since the end of the Ice Age."

Disease, Accidental Seed of Change

Disease was the first of the seeds of change to make itself felt in the Americas. On Columbus's first voyage, some of the Taino Indians he met caught a lung disease from his crew. Many died because they had no immunity—natural protection.

Before Columbus, the Indians had few **infectious diseases**—illnesses passed from one person to another. Thousands of years earlier their ancestors had passed through the ice and snow of Siberia and Alaska on their long trek into the Americas. The cold had killed the germs of many serious illnesses. For centuries, Indians were free of smallpox, cholera, measles, and even influenza, which is also known as the flu.

On the other hand, infectious diseases were common in the Eastern Hemisphere. For example, a disease called bubonic plague or the Black Death swept into Europe from Asia in the mid-1300s. One out of every three Europeans died.

Rapid spread of disease Columbus, and the Europeans and Africans who came after him, unknowingly carried diseases to which the Indians had no immunity. These infectious diseases spread rapidly, passing from Indian to Indian.

Wherever people met to trade, there was a chance that they were passing on diseases as well as trade goods. Racing ahead of explorers and settlers, the invisible killers often destroyed whole populations of Native Americans. Sometimes, when Europeans and Africans reached an area for the first time, they found that the Indians who once lived there had all died.

The human body has natural defenses that fight against infectious diseases caused by bacteria and viruses. One type is barriers. Unbroken skin acts as a barrier, preventing many microorganisms from entering the body. Mucus in the mouth and nose traps many, and stomach acid kills some. Another barrier is harmless bacteria that often crowd out other microorganisms.

See the Study Guide activity in **Chapter Resources Binder**, p. 18.

See the Study Guide activity in **Chapter Resources Binder**, p. 18.

In despair, one Mayan Indian described a smallpox epidemic among his people:

"Great was the stench of the dead. After our fathers and grandfathers succumbed [died], half of the people fled to the fields. The dogs and vultures devoured [ate] the bodies. . . . Your grandfathers died. . . . So it was that we became orphans, oh, my sons! So we became when we were young. . . . We were born to die!"

By the end of the 1700s, there were fewer than half—perhaps only one-tenth—as many native people in the Americas as there had been before Columbus's voyages. Disease was the main cause of this terrible destruction.

The Exchange of Plants

While the people of North and South America were dying of new diseases, foods from the Americas were causing population growth in the Eastern Hemisphere. Corn and potatoes—which grow in many climates—and other American crops greatly improved the food supply. As a result, the population of Europe and Asia increased. Africa's population grew, too, though not until the 1800s.

Hands-On *HISTORY*

Simulating the spread of smallpox Epidemics of infectious diseases have changed the course of history. For centuries, smallpox epidemics swept the Eastern Hemisphere. The germ spread easily, and there was no treatment. As many as 70 percent of the infected people died. Survivors were usually permanently scarred, and some were blinded.

The last known case of smallpox occurred in 1977. Today, smallpox exists only in a few scientific laboratories. Although scientists did not find a cure, vaccination wiped out the disease. Unfortunately, vaccination came too late for hundreds of millions of people.

Activity To see how epidemics can affect populations, estimate how quickly smallpox could spread in your school.

① Suppose that on Day 1 a single student with smallpox infects one other student. On Day 2, each of those two students infects one other student, for a total of four infected students. It goes on this way through Day 3, Day 4, and so on. How many days would it take for every student in your class to be infected?

② Then calculate how long it would take for every student in your school to be infected.

③ Show your results in a graph or an illustration.

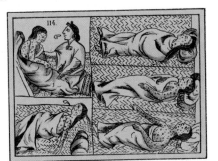

Smallpox victims, from an old Aztec book

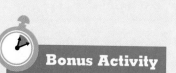
✳ **History Footnote**

During the mid-1500s English explorers brought the potato to their country and then introduced it to Scotland and Ireland. Potatoes grew easily in Ireland and soon became the chief crop and a mainstay in the Irish diet. In years when the potato crop failed, famine resulted. Later, students will learn about the devastating effects when a blight destroyed the crop in the mid-1800s.

The Columbian Exchange

From the West

Corn	Pumpkins	Cashews
Potatoes	Squashes	Petunias
Tomatoes	Pineapples	Wild rice
Chocolate	Peanuts	Peppers

From the East

Horses	Wheat	Watermelons
Cattle	Sugar	Citrus fruits
Sheep	Peaches	Daffodils
Chickens	Pears	Dandelions

Corn and potatoes Columbus was probably the first to take corn to Europe. He wrote in his diary that he had learned of "a sort of grain [the Taino] called *maiz*." In Europe today corn is known as *maize*.

Corn spread quickly into Europe, Africa, and Asia. Although northern Europeans did not eat much corn themselves, they fed it to their livestock. As a result, they had larger and healthier livestock to provide their meat and milk.

Potatoes came from high in the Andes in South America. Even today, people of the Andes grow many varieties of potatoes—large and small, white, yellow, red, blue, pink, and purple.

At first some Europeans feared that potatoes would cause disease or even death. Gradually, they realized that potatoes were easy to grow and provided more food per acre than other crops. With potatoes helping to ease hunger in northern Europe, the population of Europe grew.

Other American plants Other plants from the Americas also helped improve diets in the Eastern Hemisphere. Nigerians learned to grow sweet potatoes and corn, Italians added tomato sauce to pasta, Hungarians put paprika in goulash, Eastern European Jews enjoyed potato pancakes, and Chinese added chilies and peanuts to stir-fried vegetables.

Sugar The exchange of plants went both ways. On his second voyage, Columbus brought plants such as wheat, grapes, and sugar cane for his settlers on Hispaniola. Of these plants, sugar cane was to have the greatest impact on human history.

Hoping to earn great profits from growing sugar cane, the settlers created plantations. A **plantation** is a large estate where a single crop is grown for profit. Plantation crops require a large labor force.

The Spanish began clearing Caribbean islands of their trees to plant sugar cane. At first they forced Indians to work the plantations. As the Indians were wiped out by European diseases, the Spanish looked to Africa for workers. They were following the example of the Portuguese, who made captive Africans work plantations on Madeira and the Canary Islands.

For an Aztec pictorial record of aspects of the Columbian Exchange, see **Using Historical Documents**, pp. 17–19.

The Slave Trade

Suddenly there was a great need for labor and much money to be made in the slave trade. Arab and African traders raided villages, capturing men, women, and children to sell to Europeans as slaves.

Point of View

How did the slave trade affect Africa?

Traders, ship captains, and plantation owners saw the slave trade as a way to profit. King Nzinga Mbemba (ehn-ZING-ah ehm-BEM-bah) of the Kongo had a different view. In 1526 he wrote a letter calling on King John III of Portugal to end the trade.

❝Sir, Your Highness should know how our Kingdom is being lost in so many ways. . . . We cannot reckon how great the damage is, since merchants are taking every day our natives. . . . Our country is being completely depopulated, and Your Highness should not agree with this or accept it. . . . It is our will that in these Kingdoms there should not be any trade of slaves.❞

There is no record of King John's reply, but the enslavement of Africans went on. In the process, African societies were destroyed as millions of their people were sent to the Americas.

The Transfer of Animals

Little good came to Native Americans from the Columbian Exchange. The main exception was animals. Before Columbus, Indians had only a few useful domestic animals: dogs, ducks, turkeys, guinea pigs, and llamas. Imagine what a difference cattle, sheep, pigs, goats, and horses made in their diet, clothing, and transportation.

Of all the animals that Columbus brought to America, the Indians were most interested in horses. At first the strange creatures terrified the Indians. They called horses "sky dogs," believing they were monsters or messengers of the gods.

Because horses were an advantage in hunting and war, the Spanish tried to keep them out of Indian hands. However, many Indian tribes quickly learned to value the beauty and strength of the horse. Especially on the grasslands of North and South America, Indians made the horse an important part of their lives.

The Exchange Continues

Columbus's voyages began a huge exchange of plants, animals, and diseases between the Eastern and Western Hemispheres. They also set off a movement of peoples—Europeans, Africans, and Asians. In fact, the story of the Americas since Columbus's time is often the story of people on the move. This movement of people and of the other seeds of change continues. The Columbian Exchange is the true **legacy**—something handed down from past generations—of Christopher Columbus.

⭐ ## 2. Section Review

1. Define **infectious diseases, plantation,** and **legacy.**
2. Why did European diseases have such a severe effect on Native Americans?
3. How did American food plants affect the population of Europe? Explain.
4. How did the spread of sugar lead to a great movement of people?
5. **Critical Thinking** List two examples of the following statement: The movement of people and of the other seeds of change continues today.

Geography Lab

Begin by having students identify two main ways Indians used horses (hunting and transportation). Point out that previously the Plains Indians mainly hunted deer and elk. It was hard to hunt the large buffalo herds in the open on foot, so they tried to stampede them off cliffs. With the horse, they could easily pursue and kill buffalo. The horse also freed them from pulling sledges on foot or using dogs. They could now transport buffalo meat to their villages more easily.

Link to History
Answers

1. (a) Mainly the Great Plains and Rocky Mountains; also the Central Lowlands and the Pacific Mountains and Valleys; (b) Five of the following: Apache, Navajo, Ute, Shoshone, Crow, Cayuse, Nez Percé, Iowa, Cree, Blackfoot, Hidatsa, Mandan, Cheyenne, Sioux, Pawnee, Illinois, Osage, Kiowa, and Caddo; (c) 231 years.

2. Horses made hunting buffalo easier, and Indians may have given up farming and moved to follow the buffalo.

3. Explain that the content of the drawing and not artistic quality is important. Accept all reasonable renderings.

See the activity on the spread of the horse in **Geography Extensions,** pp. 5–6.

⁕ Geography Footnote

The top illustration shows a detail of the painting *Indians Hunting Buffalo with Bows and Lances* by frontier painter George Catlin. Catlin's paintings and drawings are considered to be among the most important studies of North American Indians because he observed their cultures while they were still intact, before they were affected by other Americans moving west.

Catlin spent his summers between 1830 and 1836 with various Indian nations. He painted in St. Louis, along the Missouri River and the upper Mississippi River, and in Texas. Many of his paintings can be seen in the Whitney Gallery of Western Art in Cody, Wyoming, and the Smithsonian Institution in Washington, D.C.

Geography Lab

The Horse Comes to North America

The horses that the Spanish introduced into the Americas greatly changed how some Indians lived. Some of the horses got loose, and soon herds of wild horses were roaming the grasslands of North America. Indians rounded up wild horses. They also captured horses from the Spanish invaders. For Indians who acquired the horse, life was never the same again. Use the map and pictures to draw conclusions about how the horse changed their lives.

Indians hunting with bows and lances

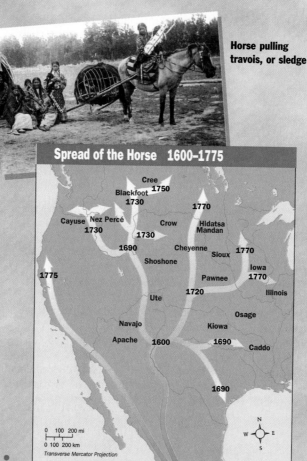

Horse pulling travois, or sledge

Spread of the Horse 1600–1775

Cree 1750
Blackfoot 1730
Cayuse 1730
Nez Percé 1730
Crow 1690
Hidatsa Mandan
Shoshone
Cheyenne
Sioux 1770
Iowa 1770
Pawnee
Illinois
Ute 1720
Osage
Navajo
Kiowa
Apache 1600
Caddo 1690
1690
1770
1775

0 100 200 mi
0 100 200 km
Transverse Mercator Projection

N S E W

Link to History

1. (a) Into what geographic regions did the horse spread? To answer, refer to the map on pages P4–P5. (b) List 5 tribes that adopted the horse. (c) The Spanish first brought horses into Mexico in 1519. How long did it take horses to spread to the northernmost point on this map?

2. When some tribes acquired the horse, they gave up farming and began to move from place to place. Using the pictures as evidence, what reasons can you think of for this change?

3. **Hands-On Geography** Plains Indians often decorated buffalo hides with picture histories of tribal life. Included were tribal "firsts," such as the first time a member of the tribe saw a horse. Draw a picture to show how a Plains Indian artist might have depicted his or her first sighting of a horse.

Section Objectives

★ Describe what Balboa and Magellan added to Europeans' knowledge.
★ Summarize the results of the search for the Northwest Passage.
★ Explain why European interest shifted from Asia to the Americas.

Teaching Resources

Take-Home Planner 1, pp. 18–25
Chapter Resources Binder
  Study Guide, p. 19
  Reinforcement
  Skills Development, pp. 23–24
Geography Extensions
American Readings, p. 12
Using Historical Documents
Transparency Activities
Chapter and Unit Tests, pp. 13–16

3. The Race for Discovery

Reading Guide

New Term strait

Section Focus **Europe's search for a way around or through the Americas**

1. **What did Balboa and Magellan add to Europeans' knowledge of the world?**
2. **What were the results of the search for the Northwest Passage?**
3. **Why did European interest begin to shift from Asia to the Americas?**

Spain and Portugal were the first to seek sea routes to Asia. Other nations, however, were determined to share the Asia trade, too. Before long, England, the Netherlands, and France were also racing to find routes.

Treaty of Tordesillas

At first, Portugal's King John II claimed the islands Columbus had found. After all, he said, they were near other Portuguese islands. To settle the dispute, Spain and Portugal agreed to the Treaty of Tordesillas (TORD-uh-SEE-yuhs) in 1494.

The treaty fixed an imaginary Line of Demarcation through the Atlantic from the North to the South Pole. Spain could claim lands west of the line. Portugal could claim lands to the east. The line guaranteed Portugal its ocean route around Africa.

The line brought Portugal good luck in 1500, when Pedro Álvares Cabral set sail from Lisbon intending to follow da Gama's route. He swung so far out into the Atlantic, however, that he landed on the coast of Brazil. He claimed the land for Portugal.

Balboa

Meanwhile, Europeans were still trying to reach the Indies by sailing west. They searched for a way around the Americas.

Little did they realize what a great ocean lay between the Americas and Asia.

The first European to see that ocean's eastern shores was Vasco Núñez de Balboa. He was seeking his fortune in Panama in 1513 when he heard Indians tell of a vast sea. With a large force of Spaniards and Indians, Balboa struggled over snake-infested marshlands, steaming rain forests, and steep mountains until he reached the sea.

Balboa called it the South Sea because he thought it lay to the south of Panama. We call it the Pacific Ocean. He plunged in and claimed the sea and all its coasts and bays for Spain. He never profited from his discovery, however. Rivals accused him of betraying the king, and he was beheaded.

Magellan

Balboa saw the Pacific, but Ferdinand Magellan was the first European to try to cross this vast ocean. No one knew what an ordeal that would be.

Magellan, a Portuguese sea captain, had made several voyages around Africa to India and the Spice Islands in present-day Indonesia. Like Columbus, he thought the world was smaller than it is. Convinced that he could find a short route to the Indies by sailing west, Magellan persuaded Charles I, the new king of Spain, to finance the trip.

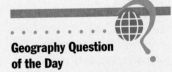

Point out that because this is a flat map made from the perspective of the North Pole, land areas are distorted. **Answer to Reading Maps:** The map shows that Magellan's crew circled the globe by sailing from Europe around South America, Asia, and Africa and then back to Europe. They first crossed the Atlantic, hugged the east coast of South America, went around its southern tip, and then crossed the Pacific through the Philippines, past Australia, around Africa, and back to Spain.

Section Activity

Writing Ships' Logs

To help students imagine a voyage, have them write entries into the captain's log of Magellan, Cabot, or Hudson. Explain that the log is a historical record that provides daily information about events during the voyage. Entries should provide information about the ship, crew, places visited, and people met. Students may wish to research further information about the explorations of the captain they choose. They might also include maps showing the route taken.

✳ **History Footnote**

Although the Spanish king approved Magellan's plan, he was cautious about investing in the voyage. He provided only five leaky, old ships with ragtag crews. He knew that even if Magellan reached the Spice Islands, there was no guarantee that Spain could claim them. It was not clear whether the islands were within the Spanish zone established by the Treaty of Tordesillas.

When the *Victoria* finally reached Spain, the sale of its cargo of cloves paid for the cost of the expedition, inspiring Spain to launch two more voyages. A 1525 expedition made it as far as the Molucca Islands in Indonesia. A voyage the following year turned back before reaching the Strait of Magellan. After 1527, Spanish attempts to cross the Pacific were made only from Mexico.

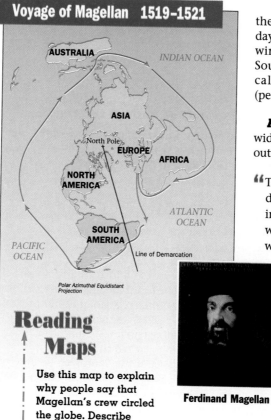

Voyage of Magellan 1519–1521

AUSTRALIA

INDIAN OCEAN

ASIA

North Pole

EUROPE

AFRICA

NORTH AMERICA

ATLANTIC OCEAN

PACIFIC OCEAN

SOUTH AMERICA

Line of Demarcation

Polar Azimuthal Equidistant Projection

Reading Maps

↑ Use this map to explain why people say that Magellan's crew circled the globe. Describe their route.

Ferdinand Magellan

The Strait of Magellan Magellan crossed the Atlantic in 1519 with 5 ships and a crew of 280 and began to look for a way around South America. That winter bad luck began to plague him. One ship wrecked. He had to stop a mutiny. Then he learned that his suppliers had given him only a third of the supplies he had paid for.

Nevertheless, in spring Magellan went on. As he reached the tip of South America, some of his crew deserted, taking one ship.

With three ships Magellan headed into a **strait**—a narrow waterway connecting larger bodies of water. This twisting 350-mile-long (563-km) passage is now called

the Strait of Magellan in his honor. For 38 days he battled rough currents and howling winds. When he finally reached Balboa's South Sea, Magellan was so struck by its calm that he renamed it the Pacific (peaceful) Ocean.

Across the Pacific The Pacific was wider than Magellan imagined. His men ran out of food. One sailor described their ordeal:

❝The biscuit we were eating no longer deserved the name of bread. It was nothing but dust and worm. The water . . . was putrid [rotten] and offensive. We were even so far reduced to eat pieces of leather, sawdust, and even mice that sold for half a ducat [a silver coin] apiece.❞

In spite of hardships, Magellan reached the Philippines in March 1521. There, after surviving the dreadful voyage, he was killed in a war between islanders.

Two ships sailed on. One sprang a leak and sank. The other, the *Victoria*, picked up a cargo of cloves in the Spice Islands. Then the Portuguese captured half its crew when it stopped for supplies.

For the 18 survivors, the terrible voyage finally ended on September 6, 1522, when they reached Spain at last. The first Europeans to circle the globe, they had proved that Columbus was right. Ships could reach Asia from Europe by sailing west, but the way was long and difficult.

The Northwest Passage

Columbus and Magellan had sailed under the Spanish flag. In other countries, too, people dreamed of Asia's treasures. Soon English, French, and Dutch ships were crossing the Atlantic. Spain's rivals hoped to

* History Footnote

John Cabot was born Giovanni Caboto in Genoa, Italy, about the same time Columbus was born. He moved to England in the 1480s. He first asked the king of Portugal and the king of Spain to finance a voyage to find a shorter route than Columbus's. Finally, the English king granted Cabot the right to "find whatsoever isles, countries, regions, or provinces" and to claim them for England.

For an English sailor's impressions of Florida, see **American Readings**, p. 12.

find a northern route, or Northwest Passage, through the Americas. They looked to the north because Spanish warships patrolled the waters off South America.

English Exploration

The first to take up the challenge was John Cabot, an Italian living in England. In 1497 he reached Newfoundland with one small ship. Like Columbus, Cabot believed he had reached Asia.

The next year Cabot returned to the Americas with five ships full of trade goods. One turned back. The others were never heard from again. Cabot lost his life, but his voyages gave England a basis for claiming land in North America.

Meanwhile, a debate raged over the best route to Asia. Several ships tried to sail

Link to Art

Inuit man and woman with child (about 1577) Martin Frobisher captured an Inuit family near Hudson Bay and brought them to London, where they died within a month. John White made this drawing of the Inuits aboard Frobisher's ship. **Discuss** Exploring parties often included an artist. What were the benefits of having someone along who could draw? Today, would an exploring party take an artist along? Explain your answer.

Checking Understanding

1. Why was the Treaty of Tordesillas drawn up? (To settle disputes between Spain and Portugal over claims to lands.)

2. Why did England, the Netherlands, and France look for a Northwest Passage? (Those countries wanted to trade in the Indies too, but the southern routes were patrolled by Spanish warships.)

Stimulating Critical Thinking

3. If you were the ruler of Spain, would you have considered Magellan's voyage mainly a success or a failure? Explain. (On the negative side, only 1 ship and 18 crew members survived. News that a westward voyage to Asia was long and hard would also have been a disappointment. On the positive side, the crew was first to circle the globe and brought a cargo of cloves and valuable knowledge for future navigators.)

Teaching the

⟋ **Link to Art**

Have students imagine themselves living in England in the 1500s and looking at these drawings for the first time. What would they conclude about the way of life of the Inuits? (That they lived in a cold environment and hunted using bows and arrows.) **Discussion Answers:** An artist could record the way plants, animals, and people looked. Today, still cameras and video cameras would make an artist unnecessary.

Teaching the

Link to the Present

Point out that computer simulations make it possible for potential pilots and space explorers to experience conditions that are very much like those they might actually encounter. Students can find out more about the space camp by writing: U.S. Space Camp, Tranquility Base, Huntsville, AL 35807.

Bonus Activity

Writing Sailor Journal Entries

To help students understand voyages from the perspective of sailors, have them write journal entries from the beginning, middle, and end of a voyage. They should imagine themselves taking part in Magellan's expedition or Hudson's voyage in 1610. Conclude by having them compare entries. Then discuss how and why a crew member's perspective might have differed from the captain's.

See the Study Guide activity in **Chapter Resources Binder**, p. 19.

Tips for Teaching

Students with Limited English

Students with limited English proficiency may be unfamiliar with many English place names. To reinforce understanding, have them label an outline map with places identified in the chapter. (See **Geography Extensions** for an outline map.) They should add phonetic pronunciations.

Link to the Present

Tomorrow's explorers Though Columbus and other explorers read the works of navigators and astronomers, they learned most of what they knew by sailing the seas. Astronauts, on the other hand, go through careful training before they explore space.

To get a taste of what astronauts learn, young people can attend one of NASA's space camps. At the Space Camp/Academy in Huntsville, Alabama, for example, campers in the seventh through ninth grades build and launch model rockets, try out space suits, and take part in simulated space missions.

northeast around Norway and Russia. Some men froze to death. Others turned back, discouraged by everlasting wind and ice.

Frobisher In 1576 English explorers again took up the quest. Martin Frobisher made three voyages looking for a Northwest Passage. One of his seamen marveled at the icebergs they saw:

❝Of what great bigness and depth some islands of ice be here, . . . islands more than half a mile [around].❞

At one point Frobisher found stones that he thought sparkled with gold. Actually, it was iron pyrite, or "fool's gold." He also thought he found a passage, but it was the body of water today called Frobisher Bay, in northern Canada. Frobisher took tons of worthless rocks back to England, but he also took back valuable information about sailing the icy Arctic waters.

Hudson Despite their failures, the English stubbornly continued the search for the Northwest Passage. Three times they sent an eager sea captain, Henry Hudson, "to discover a Passage by the North Pole to Japan and China." Blocked by fields of ice on his first voyage in 1607, he tried again the following year but met the same result.

Again in 1610, Hudson worked for the English. His ship, the *Discovery*, sailed into a huge body of water he felt sure was the Pacific. Then winter fell, and the waters turned to ice, imprisoning the ship.

The ice broke in the spring, and Hudson was eager to move on. When he refused to stop for fresh food, the crew mutinied. They cast Hudson, his son John, and some of the crew adrift to die amid chunks of ice in the bay now called Hudson Bay. A few mutineers lived to tell the tale, but they were never punished. What they knew was too valuable to future explorers.

Dutch Exploration

In 1609—the year before his final voyage—Hudson had sailed under the Dutch flag. Dutch merchants wanted a share of the Indies trade, so they hired Hudson to find the Northwest Passage. Instead, Hudson found the river that is now named for him— the Hudson River, in present-day New York. Although it proved to be another dead end, Hudson's third voyage gave the Netherlands a claim in North America.

French Exploration

France was too involved with European affairs to seek a route to Asia at first. Then King Francis I, who desperately needed money, heard about Magellan's profitable load of cloves. He thought about the opportunities he might be missing. The king decided to join the search for a way to the wealth of Asia.

Verrazano filled the gap between Spanish explorations to the south and those of the English to the north. His observations showed that the Americas were a continuous land mass. However, he believed that this land mass was a narrow strip, beyond which lay the Pacific Ocean. Actually, what he saw was the wide Pimlico Sound beyond Cape Hatteras, North Carolina.

Discussion

Checking Understanding

1. **Which explorer sailed for two different countries? What did he find?** (Hudson sailed for England and the Netherlands and explored the Hudson River and Hudson Bay.)

2. **How did Cartier establish France's gateway to North America?** (He explored the St. Lawrence River and established friendly relations with the Indians with whom he came in contact.)

Stimulating Critical Thinking

3. **Why do you think explorers persisted in their search for a Northwest Passage?** (Students might suggest that they continued looking for a passage so that they could trade directly with the Indies.)

Teaching the
↑ **Reading Maps**

Have students describe each route. **Answers to Reading Maps:**
1. (a) France (Cartier), (b) England (Hudson), (c) Netherlands (Hudson).
2. North American land mass, ice pack.

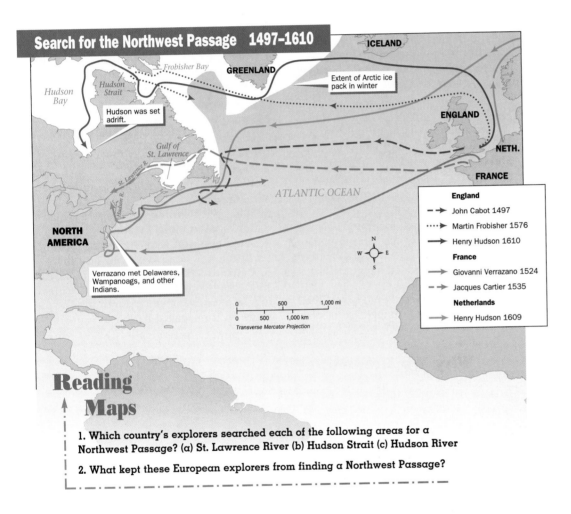

Search for the Northwest Passage   1497–1610

England
- - → John Cabot 1497
····→ Martin Frobisher 1576
——→ Henry Hudson 1610

France
——→ Giovanni Verrazano 1524
- - → Jacques Cartier 1535

Netherlands
——→ Henry Hudson 1609

Reading Maps

1. **Which country's explorers searched each of the following areas for a Northwest Passage? (a) St. Lawrence River (b) Hudson Strait (c) Hudson River**

2. **What kept these European explorers from finding a Northwest Passage?**

Verrazano In 1524 King Francis sent Giovanni Verrazano (vehr-rah-TSAH-nō), an Italian navigator, "to discover new lands" and find the passage to Asia. Verrazano landed on the coast of present-day North Carolina where, he boasted, "there appeared to us a new land never before seen by anyone, ancient or modern."

Verrazano sailed as far north as Newfoundland, landing at several places along the way. He wrote the earliest account of the east coast of North America, but he did not find the Northwest Passage.

Cartier Jacques Cartier followed Verrazano to North America. Cartier's three trips between 1534 and 1541 laid the basis for French claims. He, too, failed to find a passage to Asia, but he did explore the Gulf of St. Lawrence.

The king had told Cartier "to discover certain islands and lands where it is said a great quantity of gold and other precious things are to be found." Thus, when Cartier heard Indian tales of a land rich in gold and silver, he ventured far up the St. Lawrence River looking for it. He found no precious

★ ★ ★
Vital Links

Henry Hudson (Picture)
Unit 1, Side 1, Search
24474

See also Unit 1 Explore
CD-ROM location 221.

**Identifying
Explorers' Routes**

To review the voyages, have each student choose an explorer and draw his route on an outline map without identifying the explorer's name. Have students exchange maps and identify which explorer's route is being shown.

**Section Review
Answers**

1. Definition: *strait* (74)

2. Balboa was the first to see the Pacific Ocean, which he called the South Sea, thinking it was south of Asia. Magellan circumnavigated the globe and proved that ships could reach Asia by sailing west from Europe.

3. The Northwest Passage is a way to reach Asia by sailing west and north. The English, Dutch, and French looked for it because Spain controlled the southern routes.

4. Europeans were looking for gold and spices but found timber, furs, and fish.

5. Answers will vary. One argument in favor is the possibility of gaining great wealth. Arguments against would focus on the great dangers faced by explorers, many of whom died.

To check understanding of "Why We Remember," assign Thinking Critically question 3 on student page 80.

---

metals, but he did settle the first French colony in the Americas, near Quebec.

Cartier established friendly relations with Indians. A sailor described one meeting:

> **"**We . . . made signs to them that we wished them no harm and sent two men on shore to offer them some knives and other iron goods. . . . They sent on shore part of their people with some of their furs; and the two parties traded.**"**

Europeans still had not found a North-west Passage. Neither had they found the gold and spices they had looked so hard for. However, they had added much to Europe's geographic knowledge.

In fact, a Northwest Passage was finally discovered in 1906, although ice blocks it most of the year. Long before, however, Europeans had begun to realize that the timber, furs, and fish of North America were worth as much to them as the spices of Asia.

3. Section Review

1. Define **strait**.

2. What did Europeans learn from Balboa and Magellan?

3. What is a "Northwest Passage"? Which nations looked for it? Why?

4. What resources were Europeans looking for in the Americas? What did they find?

5. Critical Thinking If this were the 1500s, and your 15-year-old cousin wanted to join a voyage of exploration, would you argue for it or against it? Explain.

Why We Remember

Voyages of Exploration

Christopher Columbus expected to be remembered as the man who opened a westward route to Asia. Instead, he died in 1506 a nearly forgotten man. No important people came to his funeral. No one put up a statue in his honor. No one wrote the story of his life until 300 years later.

At the time of his death, Europeans were still puzzled by what Columbus had found. For centuries they had believed that the earth consisted of Europe, Asia, and Africa. Only gradually did they realize that Columbus had explored lands entirely new to them.

Today we can look back and see that Columbus did more than alter European views of the world. He began a chain of events that completely reshaped the Americas. Disease drastically reduced the Indian population of the Americas. Meanwhile, peoples from Europe and Africa, and then from all parts of the globe, streamed in. Out of this blending of the world's peoples have come new cultures and new nations, including our own.

historical narratives are also likely sources. (b) Biographies and historical narratives would likely have the most information because they have more detail than an encyclopedia. (c) Students should explain why the sources they choose are best for their questions.

For further application, have students do the Applying Skills activity in the Chapter Survey (p. 80).

If students need to review the skill, use the Skills Development transparency and activity in the **Chapter Resources Binder**, pp. 23–24.

Skill Lab

Acquiring Information
Historical Research

Henry Hudson lost his life searching for the Northwest Passage. What had he hoped to gain for himself? Why did he think he could succeed? Was he to blame for the events that led his crew to abandon him? The purpose of historical research is to try to find answers to questions like these.

Skill Tips

- When you read about history, think about what is missing that you want to know. Write these thoughts down as questions.
- Start by researching the question you think might be the easiest to answer—or the most interesting.
- Decide which source is most likely to answer your question. If necessary, go on to other sources. As you research, write down new questions that come to mind.

Question to Investigate

What questions can be raised about explorers like Henry Hudson, and where might you find the answers?

Procedure

Historians are asking questions all the time. To try to find answers, they turn to a variety of sources, including the ones described in **A** to **F**. Use the descriptions and your own knowledge about these sources to do the following:

1 Think of questions to research.
a. Two questions about Hudson are "What routes did he follow?" and "Was he a good captain?" Write two other questions about him.
b. Write two questions about another explorer mentioned in Section 3.

2 For each question, identify the source or sources most likely to have the answer.
a. What source(s) would be best for finding out what routes Hudson followed? Explain.
b. What source(s) would be best for finding information about how good a captain Hudson was? Explain.
c. For each of the four questions you wrote, tell what source(s) you would use and why.

Sources to Use

A **Encyclopedias** are sets of books with articles about a variety of topics, arranged alphabetically.

B **Biographies** tell the stories of real people's lives. An autobiography is the writer's own story.

C **Historical narratives** describe past events in story form, which may or may not be written by someone who took part in the events. This textbook includes historical narrative.

D **Historical atlases** are books of maps related to past events.

E **Government records** are facts the government has collected, often presented in a summary called a *statistical abstract*.

F **Magazines** are called *periodicals* because they are published at regular periods. Some magazines focus on the latest information historians have found.

Introducing the Skill Lab

Point out that this lab will help students direct their own research, as they think of questions to explore and select the best sources for answering them. Like historians, they may not always find the answers. However, by getting into the habit of asking their own questions, they will make their study of the past more interesting and meaningful.

Skill Lab
Answers

1. (a) Questions will vary. Some might relate to motivations, such as "Why did Hudson sail for the Dutch in 1609 after sailing for England previously?" Others might focus on relationships with the crews, such as "Did Hudson treat his sailors unfairly?" (b) The two questions should be about Cabral, Balboa, Magellan, Cabot, Frobisher, Verrazano, or Cartier. They must require research beyond the text. Some possibilities are to ask about the explorer's background, motivations, details about the voyages, his views on the voyages, and public reputation.

2. (a) Historical atlases are the most likely source because they are books of maps. Encyclopedias and
(Answers continued in top margin)

Survey Answers

Reviewing Vocabulary

Definitions may be found on the following pages: *expedition* (63), *cape* (63), *finance* (63), *infectious diseases* (68), *plantation* (70), *legacy* (71), *strait* (74).

Reviewing Main Ideas

1. After Dias found the tip of Africa, da Gama sailed around the tip, up the east coast of Africa, and across the Indian Ocean to Calicut.

2. Columbus thought he had reached the Indies; he did not, but he did explore lands the Europeans had not known existed.

3. Corn was fed to livestock, which resulted in larger, healthier livestock. Potatoes, which provide more food per acre than other foods, eased hunger in northern Europe.

4. Before the Columbian Exchange, Indians had only a few useful domestic animals. The addition of cattle, sheep, pigs, goats, and horses provided more sources of food, clothing, and transportation.

5. Magellan proved that Asia could be reached by sailing west from Europe.

6. The main obstacles they faced were the cold, wind, and ice.

7. They gained geographic knowledge; learned of resources like furs, timber, and fish; and established a basis for claims to parts of North America.

Thinking Critically

1. Examples may vary, but may include the following discoveries: Dias's of the cape at the southern tip of Africa, Columbus's of parts of the Americas, Cabral's of Brazil, Cabot's of Newfoundland, Frobisher's of Frobisher

(Answers continued in top margin)

Bay, and Hudson's of Hudson Bay.

2. Answers may include the idea that Europeans may have ignored the riches of North America while exploiting the riches of the Indies.

3. Answers will vary but should reflect the understanding that (a) Columbus thought he had found a route to Asia; (b) most Europeans in 1506 had probably not heard of Columbus; (c) Columbus changed the way Europeans viewed their world; (d) answers will vary.

Applying Skills

Students' research should reflect their ability to follow instructions and to use appropriate resources.

Chapter Survey ★

Reviewing Vocabulary

Define the following terms.
1. expedition
2. cape
3. finance
4. infectious diseases
5. plantation
6. legacy
7. strait

Reviewing Main Ideas

1. How did da Gama build on what Dias accomplished?
2. What is the difference between what Columbus thought he had achieved and what he actually did achieve?
3. How did corn and potatoes from the Americas improve the diets of Europeans?
4. Why was the transfer of European animals a good thing for some Indians?
5. What did Magellan's voyage prove?
6. What obstacles did explorers who were searching for the Northwest Passage face?
7. What did Europeans gain through their explorations of North America?

Thinking Critically

1. Application Major discoveries often come about by accident. Illustrate this idea with three examples from the chapter.
2. Synthesis Suppose John Cabot had found the Northwest Passage in 1498. How might the story of European exploration of North America have been different?
3. Why We Remember: Evaluation Tell how each person might complete a sentence beginning this way: "Columbus's chief contribution . . ." (a) Columbus (b) a European living in 1506 (c) a modern-day historian (d) you

Applying Skills

Historical research Choose a modern explorer or adventurer. Some possibilities are an astronaut, a scientist studying a remote area of the world, a mountain climber, or an undersea explorer. Write down three questions that you could research about this explorer or adventurer. Then identify what source or sources you would use to answer each question and explain why.

History Mystery

Naming places Answer the History Mystery on page 59. Did Vespucci deserve to have the Americas named after him? Why, or why not? What places in North and South America are named after Columbus?

Writing in Your History Journal

1. Keys to History (a) The time line on pages 58–59 has six Keys to History. In your journal, list each key and explain why it is important to know about it. (b) What three other events from the chapter would you add to the time line? List those events with their dates in your journal, and tell why you think each one should be a Key to History.
2. Christopher Columbus Would you rather have been Christopher Columbus or Henry the Navigator? In your journal write a paragraph that answers that question and gives your reasons. Consider the backgrounds, motives, and accomplishments of the two men.
3. Citizenship For many years some states, cities, and private groups honored Columbus with a celebration in October. In 1971 Columbus Day—the second Monday in October—became a legal holiday. Now, some Americans say Columbus Day should be a day of sorrow or remembrance. How do you

Information on page 67 explains that a German geographer named the land after Amerigo Vespucci because Vespucci first identified it as a "new world." Some students may think that Vespucci deserved the honor because of his explorations of the South American coast and his recognition that it was not Asia. Others may suggest that Columbus still deserved the honor because of the impact of his voyages on other explorers. Students might identify the city of Columbus, Ohio, and the country of Colombia.

Writing in Your History Journal

1. (a) Explanations should be similar to the time line notes on teacher pages 58–59.
(Answers continued in side margin)

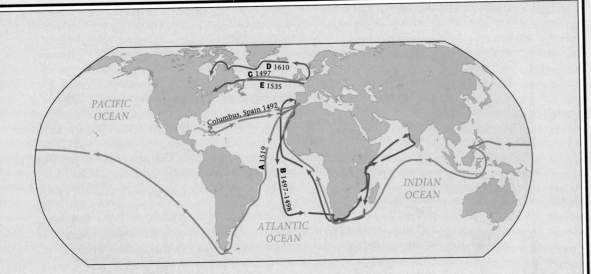

Reviewing Geography

1. For each lettered route on the map, write the name of the explorer and the country for which he was sailing.

2. **Geographic Thinking** In 1492, German geographer Martin Behaim made the first globe. It showed the earth as Europeans imagined it when Columbus first set sail. What oceans and continents were on that globe? List three vital new pieces of information map makers had to consider when they revised the globe 75 years later.

think Columbus Day should be remembered? In your journal write a letter to the editor of a newspaper in your state answering that question. Give your reasons.

Alternative Assessment

Holding a debate People generally agree that the "discovery" of the Americas by Columbus had both positive and negative results. With three other students, plan a debate on the issue: "Columbus: Hero or Villain?" Consider the question of whether the positive results of Columbus's voyages outweighed the negative, or vice versa.

❶ Divide your group into two opposing teams with two people on each team.

❷ In preparing your team's arguments, consider what you have read in this chapter, and then do additional research as needed. Be sure to think about the effects of Columbus's discovery on people and events of today, as well as the effects on people and events of the 1400s and 1500s.

❸ When you have finished preparing your arguments, hold the debate.

Your work will be evaluated on the following criteria:
• you present your arguments clearly
• you back up your arguments with facts
• your arguments are logical
• you base your arguments on reasons, not on emotions

(b) Additions should reflect an understanding of what makes an event historically important and should be accurately described and dated.

2. Answers will vary but should reflect an understanding of the roles and accomplishments of Prince Henry and Columbus.

3. Opinions will vary, but letters should reflect an understanding of a variety of positive and negative effects of the discovery.

Reviewing Geography

1. (A) Magellan, Spain; (B) da Gama, Portugal; (C) Cabot, England; (D) Hudson, England; (E) Cartier, France

2. Students should be able to see that Europe, Asia, Africa, the Atlantic Ocean and the Mediterranean were on the 1492 globe. Seventy-five years later map makers knew about the Americas and the Pacific Ocean and more about Africa's east coast and the Indian Ocean.

Alternative Assessment

Teacher's Take-Home Planner 1, p. 21, includes suggestions and scoring rubrics for the Alternative Assessment activity.

Literature Footnote

Michael Dorris shows the humanity of the Indians Columbus met by giving a touching face to two young adolescents and their family. Dorris's characters conform to Columbus's description of the Tainos (see p. 65). *Morning Girl* won the 1993 Scott O'Dell Award for Historical Fiction and was chosen as one of the School Library Journal's Best Books of the Year for 1992.

Teaching the

Link to Literature

Introduce *Morning Girl* by explaining that alternate chapters in the novel are narrated by Morning Girl and her brother Star Boy. Together they tell what it is like to grow up in a Taino community. Their community strives to coexist with the natural world, not to dominate it. This encounter with Columbus and his crew takes place in the last chapter of the book. As students read, have them look for examples of how the author has tried to look at the experience through the eyes of a young Indian girl.

Link to Literature

Morning Girl by Michael Dorris

The novel *Morning Girl* describes the life of Arawak Indians living on a Caribbean Island in the late 1400s. Author Michael Dorris, a Modoc Indian, tells the story through the eyes of 12-year-old Morning Girl and her younger brother, Star Boy. The following passage is narrated by Morning Girl.

Dawn made a glare on the ocean, so I splashed through the shallow surf and dived without looking. . . . Then, far in the distance, I heard an unfamiliar and frightening sound. It was like the panting of some giant animal, a steady, slow rhythm, dangerous and hungry. And it was coming closer.

I forgot I was still beneath the surface until I needed air. But when I broke into the sunlight, the water sparkling all around me, the noise turned out to be nothing! Only a canoe! The breathing was the dip of many paddles! It was only *people* coming to visit, and since I could see they hadn't painted themselves to appear fierce, they must be friendly or lost.

I swam closer to get a better look and had to stop myself from laughing. The strangers had wrapped every part of their bodies with colorful leaves and cotton. Some had decorated their faces with fur and wore shiny rocks on their heads. Compared to us, they were very round. . . . But really, to laugh at guests, no matter how odd, would be impolite, especially since I was the first to meet them. If I was foolish, they would think they had arrived at a foolish place. . . .

I kicked toward the canoe and called out the simplest thing. "Hello!"

One of the people heard me, and he was so startled that he stood up, made his eyes small, as fearful as I had been a moment earlier. Then he spotted me, and I waved like I've seen adults do when visitors arrive, my fingers spread to show that my hand was empty.

The man stared at me as though he'd never seen a girl before, then shouted something to his relatives. They all stopped paddling and looked in my direction.

"Hello," I tried again. "Welcome to home. My name is Morning Girl. My mother is She Wins the Race. My father is Speaks to Birds. My brother is Star Boy. We will feed you and introduce you to everyone."

All the fat people in the canoe began pointing at me and talking at once. In their excitement they almost

Arawak wooden carving

Caribbean Island settlement today

turned themselves over, and I allowed my body to sink beneath the waves for a moment in order to hide my smile. One must always treat guests with respect, . . . even when they are as brainless as gulls.

When I came up they were still watching, the way babies do: wide eyed and with their mouths uncovered. They had much to learn about how to behave.

"Bring your canoe to the beach," I shouted. . . . "I will go to the village and bring back Mother and Father for you to talk to."

Finally one of them spoke to me, but I couldn't understand anything he said. Maybe he was talking Carib or some other impossible language. But I was sure that we would find ways to get along together. It never took that much time, and acting out your thoughts with your hands could be funny. You had to guess at everything and you made mistakes, but by midday I was certain we could all be seated in a circle, eating steamed fish and giving each other presents. It would be a special day, a memorable day, a day full and new.

I was close enough to shore now for my feet to touch bottom, and quickly I made my way to dry land. . . .

"Leave your canoe right here," I suggested in my most pleasant voice. "It will not wash away, because the tide is going out. I'll be back soon with the right people."

The strangers were drifting in the surf, arguing among themselves, not even paying attention to me any longer. They seemed worried, very confused, very unsure what to do next. It was clear they hadn't traveled much before.

I hurried up the path to our house. . . . As I dodged through the trees, I hoped I hadn't done anything to make the visitors leave before I got back, before we learned their names. If they were gone, Star Boy would claim that they were just a story, just my last dream before daylight. But I didn't think that was true. I knew they were real.

Carib:
A language spoken by one group of Indian people who lived on islands in the Caribbean Sea.

A Closer Look

1. How does Morning Girl describe the strangers in the boat?

2. How do you think the strangers would have described themselves?

3. What do you learn about Arawak customs for treating guests?

From *Morning Girl* by Michael Dorris. Copyright © 1992 by Michael Dorris. Reprinted by permission of Hyperion Books for Children.

• **83**

83

Unit Survey

Making Connections
Answers

1. Answers will vary, but students should know that many would die of the infectious diseases the Europeans brought. Since many of the Indians thought the Europeans were godlike, they were open to being conquered and exploited.

2. Answers will vary, but might include such influences as music, foods, and clothing.

3. Another European probably would have discovered the Americas since so many wanted to find an ocean route to Asia.

Teaching the Unit Project

Begin by creating a class list of favorite foods and dishes. How do these dishes fit into the Food Guide Pyramid? Where do the ingredients for these dishes come from? Refer students to the list on p. 70 and to reference materials. Help students decide how much time to spend on various aspects of the project.

Evaluation Criteria

The project can be evaluated according to the criteria listed below, using a scale for each: 4 = exemplary, 3 = good, 2 = adequate, 1 = poor.

Completing the task The poster includes a complete plan for three meals using a variety of foods. The origins of all the foods are identified. The meals are balanced according to the food groups.
(Continued in top margin)

Knowing content The poster contains accurate information based on research and on a clear understanding of the Food Guide Pyramid.
Thinking critically Students show good judgment in planning the meals to fit the pyramid guidelines.
Communicating ideas The poster displays the information in a clear, attractive manner.

Thinking It Over
Answers should show an understanding of how much our foods are an intermingling of many cultures and origins. Very few menus would consist of foods with American origins only. Today even many small towns across the country have restaurants that feature cuisines of other cultures.

Unit Survey

Making Connections

Review

1. Suppose that you know nothing about history beyond what you have read in this unit. Considering what you have learned, what would you predict for the peoples of North America after Europeans arrived? Why?

2. Modern life in the United States has roots in Africa, Asia, and Europe as well as in the Americas. Give two examples of each of these influences.

3. Agree or disagree with this statement: If Columbus had not come upon the Americas, some other European would have. Give evidence for your position.

Linking History, Health, and Art

Project

Healthy Foods from Around the World

A trip to the grocery store would be very different if the Columbian Exchange had never happened. Where do the foods you eat come from? How can you build a healthy diet with foods from around the world?

Project Steps

Work alone or with a partner.

❶ Study the Food Guide Pyramid.

❷ Plan a day's meals and snacks to fit with the pyramid. Keep in mind:

• Plan for variety in each food group.
• Limit fats, oils, and sweets.
• Include some foods you have never tried. For ideas, check cookbooks or magazines.
• Include combination foods, listing main ingredients. For example, pizza: wheat crust, tomato sauce, cheese, sausage.

❸ Do research to find out what continents your foods originally came from. Start with a dictionary and an encyclopedia, then move on to books about food.

❹ Create a poster showing your food plan and origins of the various foods.

Food Guide Pyramid

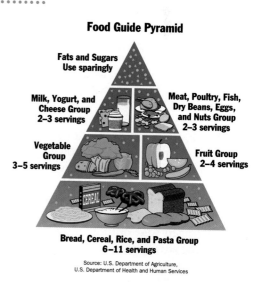

Fats and Sugars Use sparingly

Milk, Yogurt, and Cheese Group 2–3 servings

Meat, Poultry, Fish, Dry Beans, Eggs, and Nuts Group 2–3 servings

Vegetable Group 3–5 servings

Fruit Group 2–4 servings

Bread, Cereal, Rice, and Pasta Group 6–11 servings

Source: U.S. Department of Agriculture, U.S. Department of Health and Human Services

❺ Share your poster with classmates. Make a class list of continents represented.

Thinking It Over How difficult would it be to plan a healthy, varied diet if you could use only foods native to the Americas? What evidence do you see that new foods are still being brought to our country?

Objectives

★ Describe how place names change.
★ Explain how historians use historic maps.

Detail from Jansson's Magellanica map

Scholar's Tool Kit

Maps

Imagine that you are an explorer sailing from Europe in the 1500s or 1600s. You sail through waters that no European has charted. You lay eyes on lands that no European has seen before. How do you describe these places? What do you call them?

European explorers often faced these questions as they gathered information about new places. Map makers, seeking to draw what the explorers described, also faced the naming question. What did they do? They gave lands and waters names. Many of the names explorers and map makers gave are the ones we use today. Others have changed. By examining early maps, historians can trace the history of place names. That is one reason why maps are an important tool of history.

A Map Maker's Dilemma

The map shown on the next page was published in the Netherlands around 1709. That was about 200 years after Magellan's historic voyage around the world, which you read about in Chapter 3. The map shows the region at the tip of South America known today as Tierra del Fuego. When Magellan found a water route through its maze of islands, he called the sea on the western side the "Pacific" because it seemed so peaceful. Seven years earlier, though, explorer Vasco Núñez de Balboa had seen the same ocean and named it "Mar del Sur," meaning "South Sea."

Jan Jansson, the famous Dutch map maker, was obviously aware of the two names for the same body of water. He recorded both names

Introducing
How Do We Know?

Maps

Point out that for a very long time people have been making maps to record their travels and to define their world. Sailors' charts of seacoasts were in common use in the 1300s and 1400s. Columbus used them and was a map maker himself. Only one of his maps, which shows the northern part of Hispaniola, is known to still exist.

The map on the next page was made in the early 1700s and shows the southern tip of South America. Point out that by examining early maps like this one historians can learn much about the people who made them, what they knew about their world, and the history of place names.

Setting the Stage
Activity

Analyzing the Cape

To prepare for discussing the map on the next page, have students study the world map on pages R2–R3 or a modern map of South America. They should identify the physical features of the southern tip of South America, as well as which nations extend to the tip.

1. Answers may include the idea that parts of the map may be nearly accurate since so many details are shown, but others may not be accurate because methods of surveying were probably not as exact then as they are today.

2. Labeled areas are along the coast and unlabeled areas are in the interior. This suggests that explorers explored only the coastal areas.

3. Answers will vary depending on the community in which students live. Older communities are more likely to have changes than newer communities.

Bonus Activity

Creating Maps of the "Unknown"

To help students imagine some reasons for illustrating maps, have them create an "early" map of Tierra del Fuego. Point out that early maps of the Americas often included drawings reflecting fears of the unknown. Have students imagine those fears (shipwrecks, storms, hostile peoples, sea monsters) and illustrate their maps accordingly. After creating their maps at home, they can compare them in class and discuss purposes of the illustrations.

History Footnote

The crisscrossed lines on the maps on this page and the previous page are called rhumb lines. By following the compass direction of the rhumb lines, navigators were able to keep a fairly constant course.

Critical Thinking

1. Jan Jansson had never traveled to the area shown on this map. How accurate do you think the map is? Why?

Critical Thinking

2. What patterns do you notice in the areas that are labeled and not labeled on the map? How do you explain these patterns?

on this map. In the upper left-hand corner is printed "Mar Dee Zur"—Dutch for "South Sea." Below it are the Latin words "a Ferd. Magellano dictum Mare Pacifico," meaning "Pacific Ocean as named by Ferdinand Magellan." Over time, though, Pacific Ocean became the accepted name.

What's in a Name?

Although Magellan himself was killed in the Philippine Islands and his record of the voyage was lost, one of the survivors kept a diary. He was Antonio Pigafetta, an Italian who went on the expedition as a tourist and not as a crewman or officer. In his diary Pigafetta not only described the various places Magellan visited, but also recorded the

We know from Jansson's map that the name of the Pacific Ocean was still not fixed and that Magellanica was the name preferred for Tierra del Fuego as late as 1709.

names Magellan gave to those places. According to Pigafetta, Magellan named the strait at the tip of South America "Channel of All Saints." Over the years the strait received other names, but eventually became known as the Strait of Magellan.

While going through the strait, Magellan named the land on either side. The land to the north he named "Patagonia," because the people who lived there supposedly had big feet. The land to the south he named "Tierra del Fuego," or Land of Fire, because the people there lit bonfires at night. The name Patagonia stuck, but map makers labeled the southern land Magellanica in honor of Magellan, as shown on this map. Eventually, however, Tierra del Fuego became the permanent name.

Like many early maps, this one shows fanciful people and creatures as decoration. At least one creature shown here is based on fact: the penguin. Pigafetta described penguins in his diary. Interestingly, a species of penguin native to this region is named Magellanica in Magellan's honor.

Contrary to what you might think, the naming process is not over. Thanks to today's technology, explorers are at work on new frontiers, finding unnamed geographical features. These new frontiers are outer space and the ocean floor. As in the age of sail, features of these new frontiers are often named in honor of those who explore them.

? Critical Thinking

3. How has your community changed in recent years? See if you can find an old map of your area at the local library. How have names and places changed over time?

Scholar at Work

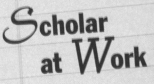

Create a map of your route from home to school. Rename certain features to honor yourself and your friends who follow the same route. Add decorative pictures to make your map more interesting. Then give your map to a classmate who does not use your route to see if he or she can follow it.

Discussion

Checking Understanding

1. **What part of South America is shown on Jansson's map?** (The southern tip.)

2. **When was this map made?** (1709)

3. **Which names are different from the ones on a present-day map?** (Magellanica is now known as Tierra del Fuego. What Jansson also labeled as the South Sea is the Pacific Ocean.)

Teaching the Scholar at Work

Suggest that students use a street map of their community to trace familiar routes. They may wish to trace the map and enhance it by including landmarks. Suggest that students provide reasons for renaming particular features. For instance, they might rename a street in honor of a friend who lives on that street.

Unit 2

Introducing the Unit

Van Bergen Overmantel

Point out that this scene is part of a painting created for display over the mantel of the Van Bergen farmhouse in New York. Explain that it shows the Van Bergen farmhouse itself. Ask: **How does this painting relate to the topic of this unit?** (The scene is an example of results of efforts of settlers—the newcomers—to tame the so-called "wilderness" and make the land their own.)

Explain that throughout this unit students will see the impact of European colonization of the Americas—not only on the land and the native peoples but also on people from Africa, most of whom were enslaved.

Teaching the

Hands-On

┌ ─ ─ ─ ─ ─ ─ ➤ HISTORY

This activity will help students imagine what life was like in colonial times. To help them brainstorm specific scrapbook items, first ask them to think about general types of things that colonists might have kept as mementos (diary notes, letters, invitations, paintings, drawings, pieces of clothing, scraps of cloth, locks of hair, pressed flowers, feathers, etc.). To expand possibilities, suggest that students think of filling a memory box, which would allow including items that are not flat (toys, crafts made from wood or clay, school items, etc.).

88

Unit Overview

By the 1540s, Spain had conquered much of Central and South America and parts of North America for "gold, God, and the glory of Spain." The king divided the empire into the viceroyalties of New Spain and Peru, and also gave favored Spaniards rights to land and Indian labor. In the 1600s the French, Dutch, and English challenged Spain's empire by planting colonies in North America.

Desire for wealth and power led England to encourage colonization of the eastern coast of North America. Between 1607 and 1732 companies, proprietors, and settlers—acting for various economic, nationalist, or religious reasons—set up 13 colonies. Different climates and terrains led to varying patterns of settlement in the New England, Middle, and Southern Colonies.

Unit 2

1500–1750

Chapters

4. **The Conquest of the Americas**

5. **Planting English Colonies**

6. **Life in the English Colonies**

Hands-On ➤ HISTORY

Activity

Assume that it is 1720 and you live on a farm like the New York farm in this painting. Imagine growing up here before electricity, cars, and cameras were invented. You keep a scrapbook of souvenirs of places, people, and events that are especially important to you. Think of at least ten items for your scrapbook.

Van Bergen Overmantel (detail)
attributed to John Heaten, 1732–1733

See the Unit 2 activity in **Wall Time Line Activities.**

Newcomers in the Americas

Checking Understanding

1. What does the painting reveal about the environment around the farm? (It is hilly and forested.)

2. How can you tell that this is a farm? (Wagon loaded with containers—perhaps milk—and the worker in the foreground.)

3. What do the farmhouse walls appear to be made of? (Students may suggest either stones or bricks—more likely bricks because of the regular shapes.)

4. How does the painting show that the farm is prosperous? (The house is well-built. The man and woman at the right, who are apparently the owners, are well dressed, as are the four children to their left. They all seem to be able to relax while others work.)

Stimulating Critical Thinking

5. What, if anything, can you conclude from observing the woman at the far left? (The fact that she carries a bucket indicates that she is a worker. There is not enough information to indicate whether she was hired or enslaved.)

6. What might have led owners to have paintings made of their farms? (Pride in having started and developed a prosperous farm.)

4 The Conquest of the Americas
1500–1700

Chapter Planning Guide

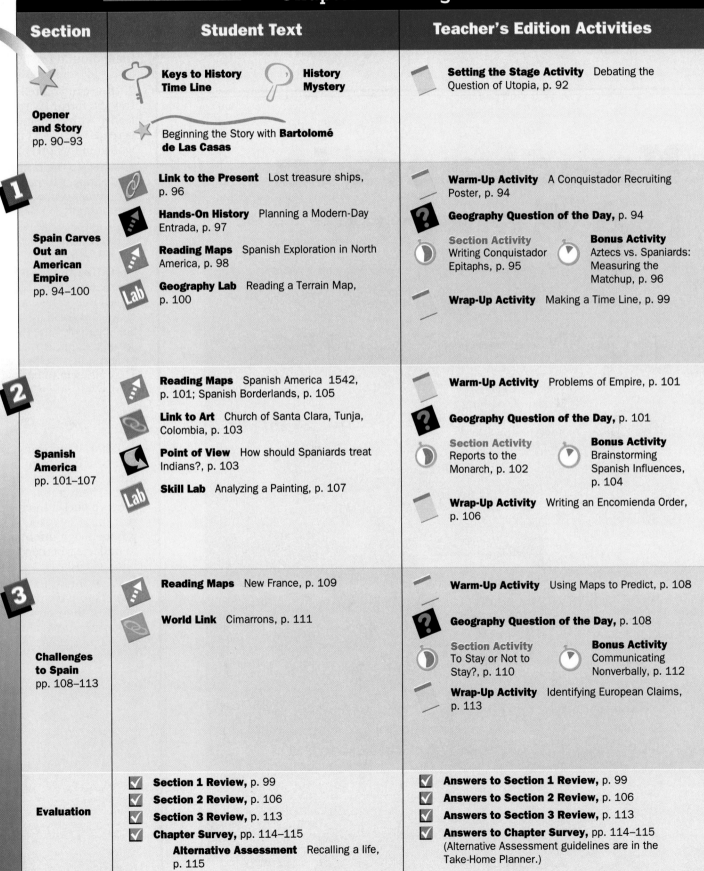

Section	Student Text	Teacher's Edition Activities
Opener and Story pp. 90–93	**Keys to History Time Line** **History Mystery** Beginning the Story with **Bartolomé de Las Casas**	**Setting the Stage Activity** Debating the Question of Utopia, p. 92
1 **Spain Carves Out an American Empire** pp. 94–100	**Link to the Present** Lost treasure ships, p. 96 **Hands-On History** Planning a Modern-Day Entrada, p. 97 **Reading Maps** Spanish Exploration in North America, p. 98 **Geography Lab** Reading a Terrain Map, p. 100	**Warm-Up Activity** A Conquistador Recruiting Poster, p. 94 **Geography Question of the Day,** p. 94 **Section Activity** Writing Conquistador Epitaphs, p. 95 **Bonus Activity** Aztecs vs. Spaniards: Measuring the Matchup, p. 96 **Wrap-Up Activity** Making a Time Line, p. 99
2 **Spanish America** pp. 101–107	**Reading Maps** Spanish America 1542, p. 101; Spanish Borderlands, p. 105 **Link to Art** Church of Santa Clara, Tunja, Colombia, p. 103 **Point of View** How should Spaniards treat Indians?, p. 103 **Skill Lab** Analyzing a Painting, p. 107	**Warm-Up Activity** Problems of Empire, p. 101 **Geography Question of the Day,** p. 101 **Section Activity** Reports to the Monarch, p. 102 **Bonus Activity** Brainstorming Spanish Influences, p. 104 **Wrap-Up Activity** Writing an Encomienda Order, p. 106
3 **Challenges to Spain** pp. 108–113	**Reading Maps** New France, p. 109 **World Link** Cimarrons, p. 111	**Warm-Up Activity** Using Maps to Predict, p. 108 **Geography Question of the Day,** p. 108 **Section Activity** To Stay or Not to Stay?, p. 110 **Bonus Activity** Communicating Nonverbally, p. 112 **Wrap-Up Activity** Identifying European Claims, p. 113
Evaluation	✓ **Section 1 Review,** p. 99 ✓ **Section 2 Review,** p. 106 ✓ **Section 3 Review,** p. 113 ✓ **Chapter Survey,** pp. 114–115 **Alternative Assessment** Recalling a life, p. 115	✓ **Answers to Section 1 Review,** p. 99 ✓ **Answers to Section 2 Review,** p. 106 ✓ **Answers to Section 3 Review,** p. 113 ✓ **Answers to Chapter Survey,** pp. 114–115 (Alternative Assessment guidelines are in the Take-Home Planner.)

Teacher's Resource Package

 Chapter Summaries: English and Spanish, pp. 12–13

 Chapter Resources Binder
Study Guide Relating Cause and Effect, p. 25
Using Historical Documents Cortés Coat of Arms, pp. 20–26
Geography Extensions Using a Terrain Map, pp. 7–8
American Readings An Aztec Account of the Conquest, p. 13

 Chapter Resources Binder
Study Guide Previewing Headings, p. 26
Skills Development Analyzing a Painting, pp. 31–32

 Chapter Resources Binder
Study Guide Organizing Information, p. 27
Reinforcement Recalling Information, pp. 29–30
American Readings The Iroquois League, p. 14; The Great River Mississippi, pp. 15–16

 Chapter and Unit Tests Chapter 4 Tests, Forms A and B, pp. 25–28

Take-Home Planner

Introducing the Chapter Activity
Spanish Influence in the United States, p. 4
Chapter In-Depth Activity Comparing Conquests, p. 4

Reduced Views
Study Guide, p. 6
Geography Extensions, p. 9
American Readings, p. 8
Using Historical Documents, p. 9
Unit 2 Answers, pp. 27–32

Reduced Views
Study Guide, p. 6
Skills Development, p. 7
Unit 2 Answers, pp. 27–32

Reduced Views
Study Guide, p. 6
Reinforcement, p. 7
American Readings, p. 8
Unit 2 Answers, pp. 27–32

Reduced Views
Chapter Tests, p. 9
Unit 2 Answers, pp. 27–32
Alternative Assessment Guidelines for scoring the Chapter Survey activity, p. 5

Additional Resources

Wall Time Line

Chapter 4 Activity

Transparency Package

Transparency 4-1 Map: Spanish Borderlands—use with Section 2
Transparency 4-2 Southwest Adobe—use with Section 2
Transparency Activity Book

SelecTest Testing Software
Chapter 4 Test, Forms A and B

★★★ Vital Links

◉ **Videodisc**

◉ **CD-ROM**

Cortés entering Mexico (see TE p. 96)

DeSoto's treatment of Indians (see TE p. 98)

American-Indian Labor (see TE p. 102)

Swedes arriving in New Netherland (see TE p. 110)

Spanish Armada (see TE p. 112)

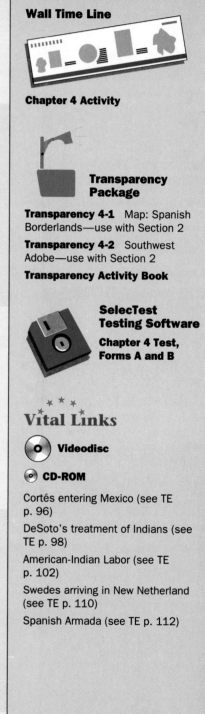

Take-Home Planner 2
  Introducing Chapter Activity
  Chapter In-Depth Activity
  Alternative Assessment
Chapter Resources Binder
Geography Extensions
American Readings
Using Historical Documents
Transparency Activities
Wall Time Line Activities
Chapter Summaries
Chapter and Unit Tests
SelecTest Test File
Vital Links CD-ROM/Videodisc

Time Line

Keys to History

Keys to History journal writing activities are on page 115 in the Chapter Survey.

Ponce de León in Florida Ponce de León led the first Spanish armed expedition into what is now the southern United States. (p. 97)

Cortés's conquest of Mexico Cortés, the first famous conquistador, laid the foundation for Spain's empire in the Americas. (p. 94)

Las Casas Las Casas was the leading Spanish protester against the mistreatment of Indians. (p. 93)

Looking Back Spain's conquest of the Americas began with Columbus's first voyage.

★ Summarize how Spain conquered the Indian civilizations and gained great wealth.
★ Describe the distinctive culture that arose in Spanish America.
★ Describe the American colonies of Spain's European rivals.

Chapter Overview

Spaniards' goals for the Americas were to win Christian converts, gain gold, and bring glory to Spain. Conquistadors Cortés and Pizarro destroyed the Aztec and Inca empires. Later explorers entered the borderlands, expanding Spain's territory in the Americas to an area larger than Europe and making Spain the world's most powerful nation.

1500–1700

Chapter 4

Sections

Beginning the Story with Bartolomé de Las Casas
1. **Spain Carves Out an American Empire**
2. **Spanish America**
3. **Challenges to Spain**

The Conquest of the Americas

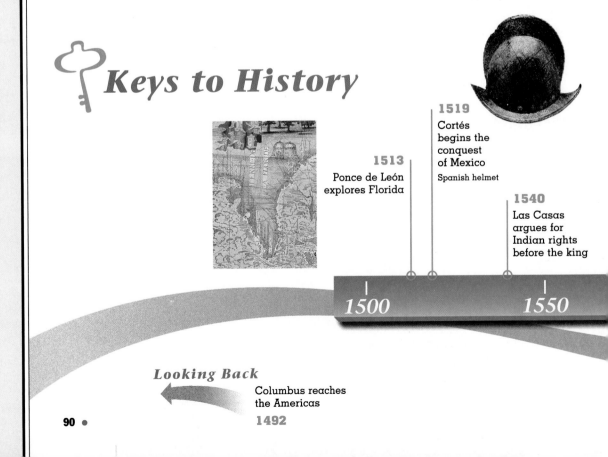

Keys to History

1513
Ponce de León explores Florida

1519
Cortés begins the conquest of Mexico
Spanish helmet

1540
Las Casas argues for Indian rights before the king

1500

1550

Looking Back
Columbus reaches the Americas
1492

With the help of Catholic missionaries, the Spanish government hoped to teach Indians Christianity and to spread the Spanish way of life. However, encounters between Spaniards, Indians, and Africans resulted in new ways of life. Although Indians were to be protected, they were often treated as slaves while Spain enriched itself by taking gold and silver from the colonies. Spain expanded settlements further north to discourage France and England from exploring the borderlands.

France built forts along the St. Lawrence and Mississippi Rivers. French settlers included traders, trappers, and missionaries. The Netherlands set up bases along the Hudson and Delaware Rivers. England's first attempts to set up colonies failed. However, its defeat of the Armada marked the rise of England and decline of Spain as a power.

Teaching the
HISTORY
Mystery

Students will find the answer on p. 96. See Chapter Survey, p. 114, for additional questions.

HISTORY *Mystery*

A huge Aztec army beat back the first Spanish attack on Tenochtitlán—a city of hundreds of thousands of people. When fewer than 600 Spanish launched a second attack, however, the city fell, and with it, the empire. How did so few conquer so many?

Time Line

Founding of St. Augustine St. Augustine is the oldest permanent European settlement in the United States. (p. 104)

Defeat of the Armada The English defeat of the Spanish Armada marked the beginning of the decline of Spain and the rise of England as a world power. (p. 112)

Champlain founds Quebec The French were interested in trade, not land, and so they were business partners with the Indians, not their conquerors. (p. 108)

La Salle explores the Mississippi The French built a chain of forts along the St. Lawrence and down the Mississippi. (p. 110)

World Link See p. 111.

Looking Ahead In the Treaty of Paris, which ended the French and Indian War, France gave up most of its lands in North America.

1565
Founding of
St. Augustine
Fort in St. Augustine

1588
Defeat of
the Spanish
Armada

1682
La Salle explores
the Mississippi

Detail from *La Salle Erecting
a Cross and Taking Possession
of the Land* by George Catlin

1608
Champlain
founds Quebec

1600   1650   1700

World Link

Drake and the Cimarrons
steal Spanish gold
1573

Looking Ahead

France gives up its lands
in North America
1763

• **91**

Bartolomé de Las Casas

Las Casas took part in the Spanish conquest of the Caribbean and was given land and captive Indians as a reward. The Indians, who mined for gold, made Las Casas a wealthy man, but the words of a priest named Antonio de Montesinos made him think about treatment of the Indians. He eventually freed his Indians and worked vigorously to change the ways Indians were treated. In recognition of his work, Spanish officials gave him the title "Protector of the Indians."

Setting the Stage Activity

Debating the Question of Utopia

To prepare students for reading about treatment of Indians, point out the Renaissance idea of a society where all were treated equally. Thomas More's 1516 book *Utopia* described such a society. (The Latin title means "nowhere.") Assign teams to debate whether people can create a truly just and equal society.

See the Introducing the Chapter Activity, Spanish Influence in the United States, **Take-Home Planner 2**, p. 4.

※ **History Footnote**

Las Casas's defense of the Indians may have been based in part on the belief that the "New World" was the Utopia that Renaissance philosophers wrote and argued about, a world where people lived in harmony and peace. The colonists, most of the clergy, and most educated people of his day opposed Las Casas. Arguments of both sides hinged on whether the Indians were seen as equals.

In 1547 Juan Ginés de Sepúlveda argued that the Spanish were right to subjugate the Indians because "these barbarians . . . are so inferior to the Spanish . . . as are children to adults."

Beginning the Story with

Bartolomé de Las Casas

Have you ever heard someone speak words so powerful, so heavy with truth, that, try as you might, you can neither ignore nor forget them? On December 11, 1511, Bartolomé de Las Casas heard such words spoken by a priest on the Caribbean island of Hispaniola. For three years he tried to push the priest's words out of his mind. Finally, though, they would change his life completely.

The Soldier-Priest

As a teenager in Seville, Spain, Bartolomé de Las Casas had seen the Indians Columbus brought from America. At the time, he thought little about these strangers from a distant shore. He went to a university, and, after completing his studies, sailed to America with dreams of making a fortune.

Las Casas served as a soldier in the Spanish conquest of the Caribbean islands. Like other Spanish soldiers, he received a large piece of land as a reward. He also received a certain number of captive Indians to till the soil and dig for ore on his new land. Las Casas had the Indians mine for gold on his estate. Their labor soon made him a wealthy man. In 1510, when he was 36, Las Casas became a Catholic priest. Still, he continued his money making.

Then, on that December day in 1511, Las Casas heard a priest named Antonio de Montesinos preach against the enslavement of Indians. The priest looked out at his well-fed flock of Spanish colonists and asked:

❝Tell me, by what right or justice do you hold these Indians in such a cruel and horrible servitude? On what authority have you waged such detestable [horrible] wars against these people who dwelt so quietly and

History Bookshelf

Marrin, Albert. *The Sea King: Sir Francis Drake and His Times*. Atheneum, 1995. In *The Sea King*, Marrin chronicles the life and times of Sir Francis Drake. An excellent navigator and commander, Drake helped England gain superiority on the sea. The narrative examines the difficulty of sea life, the horrors of the Spanish Inquisition, and the English defeat of the Spanish Armada as it reveals details of Drake's fascinating life and role in history.

Also of interest:

Burrell, Roy. *Life in the Time of Moctezuma and the Aztecs*. Raintree Steck-Vaughn, 1992.

Coulter, Tony. *Jacques Cartier, Samuel de Champlain, and the Explorers of Canada*. Chelsea House, 1993.

Marrin, Albert. *Inca and Spaniard*. Atheneum, 1989.

peacefully in their own land? . . . Why do you keep them so oppressed [crushed] and exhausted, without giving them enough to eat or curing them of the sicknesses they incur [get] from the excessive labor you give them? . . . Are you not bound to love them as you love yourselves? Don't you understand this? Don't you feel this?**"**

Montesinos's words troubled Las Casas so much that he wrote them down in his diary. Still, he refused to give up his land or the labor of the Indians, arguing that he was fair to the native people who worked his land. The next year, Las Casas helped to conquer Cuba, for which he was awarded more land and more Indian labor. For a time, the stinging questions raised by Montesinos faded from his mind.

While priests like Las Casas spoke out against Spanish abuse of Indians, they also toiled to convert them. In Indian villages priests often replaced local temples with Christian churches.

Protector of the Indians

Las Casas stayed in Cuba as a village priest. In 1514, while preparing a sermon, he came across a passage in the Bible that brought Montesinos's words back to him. By this time, Las Casas knew, more than nine-tenths of the Indians on Hispaniola had died of disease and ill-treatment. The native peoples of Cuba, he feared, were about to suffer a similar fate.

"Don't you understand this?" Las Casas remembered Montesinos asking. "Don't you feel this?" Yes, yes, he answered at last.

At that moment Las Casas suddenly saw that everything done to the Indians thus far was unjust. He knew that he would spend the rest of his life trying to right those wrongs.

Las Casas immediately gave up his lands and Indian workers. He began writing fiery protests against the mistreatment of native peoples. In 1516 he made the first of several trips to Spain to appeal for help in his cause. Spanish officials gave him the title "Protector of the Indians." In Spain and in Spanish America, his arguments set off a stormy debate over treatment of Indians. That bitter battle lasted for more than two centuries.

Hands-On ▸ *HISTORY*

Activity

Imagine you are Las Casas on your way back to Spain in 1516. Your goal is to persuade government officials to find ways to protect the native peoples of America from mistreatment by Spanish colonists. Decide what facts, figures, and arguments you might use to get their attention. Then outline a short speech using those arguments.

Discussion

Thinking Historically

1. How did Las Casas become a wealthy man? (He was given land and Indians as a reward for serving as a soldier in the Spanish conquest. He had the Indians mine gold for him.)

2. What changed his life? (He finally took to heart the words of a priest named Montesinos, who said "Tell me, by what right or justice do you hold these Indians in such a cruel and horrible servitude?")

3. What arguments do you think Las Casas's opponents used? (Students might note that others probably thought the Indians were inferior and could only benefit from working for and having contact with the Spanish.)

See the Chapter In-Depth Activity, Comparing Conquests. **Take-Home Planner 2**, p. 4.

Teaching the

Hands-On ┈┈┈┈▸ *HISTORY*

Have small groups give speeches to each other. Each group can choose the best ideas from its members and then select one person to give a speech representing the group's ideas.

For a journal writing activity on Bartolomé de Las Casas, see student page 115.

Warm-Up Activity

A Conquistador Recruiting Poster

To help students imagine why Spanish soldiers joined expeditions to the Americas, have them create a recruiting poster. After listing possible benefits (wealth, fame, land, etc.) they can design posters that would point up these advantages to attract recruits. Conclude by having students display and compare posters.

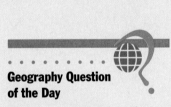

Geography Question of the Day

Have students analyze the map on page 95 to answer these questions: How is the city organized? (Temple at the center surrounded by houses and other buildings.) What might be advantages and disadvantages of building it in the middle of a lake? (Advantages: protection from attack, good supplies of water and fish, beauty of surroundings; disadvantages: possibilities of flooding, of overcrowding, and—if enough crops cannot be grown on the island—of successful siege.)

Section Objectives

★ Explain how the Spanish conquered Mexico and Peru.
★ Describe what the Spanish gained from this conquest.
★ Explain how the expeditions north of Mexico benefited Spain.

Teaching Resources

Take-Home Planner 2, pp. 2–9

Chapter Resources Binder
  Study Guide, p. 25
  Reinforcement
  Skills Development
Geography Extensions, pp. 7–8
American Readings, p. 13
Using Historical Documents, pp. 20–26
  Transparency Activities
  Chapter and Unit Tests

1. Spain Carves Out an American Empire

Reading Guide

New Term conquistadors

Section Focus How Spain conquered mighty Indian civilizations and gained great wealth and a vast empire

1. How did the Spanish conquer Mexico and Peru?
2. What did the Spanish gain from the conquest of Mexico and Peru?
3. How did expeditions into lands north of Mexico benefit Spain?

Twenty-five years after Columbus's first voyage, Spain had settlements on many Caribbean islands. Next, Spaniards eagerly looked to the mainland. They had three goals: to win converts to Christianity, to gain gold for their king and themselves, and to bring glory to Spain. Holding to those goals, they carved out an empire in the Americas.

In this Indian drawing, Malinche translates for Cortés. The curled symbols represent speech.

The Conquest of Mexico

The men who shaped Spain's empire are known as **conquistadors** (kahn-KEES-tuh-dorz), which means "conquerors." The first to earn great fame as a conquistador was Hernán Cortés, conqueror of Mexico.

Conquistadors hoped to gain wealth. They compared themselves to knights, but many put wealth above all other values. Cortés himself said, "My men and I suffer from a disease that only gold can cure!"

In fact, dreams of gold brought Cortés to Hispaniola as a young man of 19. Seven years later, like Las Casas, Cortés joined in the Spanish conquest of Cuba. For his services the government rewarded him with land, Indian workers, and a job as secretary to the governor of the Caribbean islands.

When Cortés heard rumors of a fabulous civilization in central Mexico, he saw his chance for riches. He got permission from the governor to organize an expedition.

Cortés's expedition Cortés was lucky as well as ambitious. When he reached the Mexican coast in 1519, he learned that many Indians there feared the powerful Aztecs of central Mexico. These enemies of the Aztecs, Cortés saw, could help him.

For an Aztec account of the conquest, see **American Readings**, p. 13.

As a sign of goodwill, a village chief gave Cortés an enslaved woman named Malinche (mah-LEEN-chay). She spoke Nahuatl (NAH-waht-l), which is the Aztec language, and other Indian languages. The Spaniards renamed her Doña Marina (DON-yah mah-REE-nah). She learned Spanish quickly and became Cortés's most trusted guide.

The march to Tenochtitlán When Cortés was ready to march inland, he told his men to destroy their ships. Cortés told them that they could "look for help from no one except from God, and would have to rely on their own good swords and stout hearts." They could not turn back.

Hearing about Cortés, some Aztecs thought he might be the god Quetzalcoatl (ket-SAHL-kō-AHT-l). According to tradition, Quetzalcoatl had set out to sea long ago on a raft of serpents, promising to return one day from the east. The Aztec emperor, Moctezuma (MAHK-tuh-ZOO-muh), feared that Quetzalcoatl might be returning now to claim his kingdom.

Hoping to keep Quetzalcoatl away, Moctezuma sent messengers to Cortés with gifts of gold and silver. The gifts did not have the effect Moctezuma hoped for. They made the Spaniards even more eager to reach the capital of the Aztec empire, Tenochtitlán. An Indian described the scene:

❝ When they were given these presents, the Spaniards burst into smiles; their eyes shone with pleasure. . . . They picked up the gold and fingered it like monkeys. . . . They hungered like pigs for that gold. ❞

The Spaniards' route took them through Tlaxcala (TLAHS-KAHL-uh), where icy winds blew off the mountains. The route was fortunate, though. The Tlaxcalans, enemies of the Aztecs, joined Cortés.

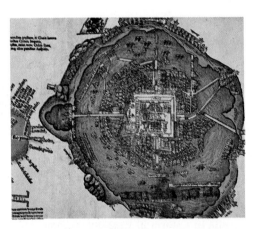

Temple Square, with its Great Temple—*el Templo Mayor*—is at the center of this old Spanish map of Tenochtitlán. Six causeways, which are roadways raised above the water, lead to the island city.

When the Spaniards saw Tenochtitlán at last, they were astonished. Houses, towers, and temples sparkled in the sun. "Some of our soldiers asked whether the things that we saw were not a dream," wrote one.

Moctezuma The emperor welcomed the Spaniards as guests. The Spaniards soon took Moctezuma prisoner, however, planning to control the empire through him. They made him send gifts to the Spanish king. The Spaniards also stumbled onto Moctezuma's hidden treasure. So great was the store of gold, silver, and jewels that it took three days to remove it.

Meanwhile, Cortés tried to convert Moctezuma to the Christian faith. Cortés warned the priests of Tenochtitlán's *Templo Mayor*, "I shall be happy to fight for my God against your gods." Then he smashed the religious figures in the temple.

The Aztecs rebelled, stoning Moctezuma to death for failing to rid them of the Spaniards. Aztecs and Spaniards clashed in a terrible battle that cost the lives of thousands. Finally, the Spanish army fled Tenochtitlán and took refuge in Tlaxcala.

Developing the Section

Discussion

Checking Understanding

1. What help did Cortés have in his effort to conquer the Aztecs? (Indian enemies of the Aztecs, the guide Malinche, and the legend of Quetzalcoatl.)

Stimulating Critical Thinking

2. "They hungered like pigs for that gold." What does this image say about what the Indian writer thought of the Spaniards? (By comparing them to pigs, the writer seems to show contempt.)

Section Activity

Writing Conquistador Epitaphs

To underscore effects of the expeditions, have small groups write epitaphs for Cortés, Pizarro, de Vaca, de Soto, and Coronado. Describe the purpose of an epitaph and provide an example. Then ask each group to write two epitaphs for each, one from the Spanish viewpoint and the other from the Indians' viewpoint. Conclude by having each group read some epitaphs aloud while members of other groups identify who is being described.

Point out that pirates, who were often supported by the governments of England and France, were a greater threat to treasure-laden Spanish ships than storms were. To defend against pirates, Spain started a fleet system: Ships carrying gold and silver were required to travel in groups and protected by warships on their way to Spain.

Bonus Activity

Aztecs vs. Spaniards: Measuring the Matchup

Have students identify advantages and disadvantages of each side in the conflict. One approach is to have them imagine themselves as Cortés making a diary entry assessing his chances of conquering the Aztecs. Another is to make a chart listing the strengths and weaknesses of each side.

✦✦✦
Vital Links

○ **Cortés entering Mexico (Picture) Unit 1, Side 1, Search 21650**

○ **See also Unit 1 Explore CD-ROM location 195.**

Students with Limited English

Spanish names and terms in this chapter provide an excellent opportunity for students whose primary language is Spanish to serve as tutors. They might provide clues to pronunciation by offering tips such as noting that *ll* in Spanish is pronounced like *y* in English.

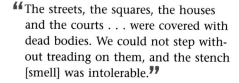

For an activity on the coat of arms granted to Cortés, see **Using Historical Documents**, pp. 20–26.

Link to the Present

Lost treasure ships Sunken treasure haunts the dreams of many an adventurer. For Melvin Fisher, that dream came true. For nine years he searched the ocean floor off the coast of Florida. Finally, in 1980 and 1985, he located the remains of the *Santa Margarita* and the *Nuestra Señora de Atocha*. The two ships, bound from Cuba to Spain, had sunk in a storm in 1622. By the time Fisher ended his search in 1986, he had salvaged cannons, muskets, and swords, as well as gold, silver, and emeralds worth millions of dollars. Even so, much of the ships' cargo still lies quietly beneath the sea.

Fall of the Aztecs In Tlaxcala Cortés reorganized his army. Then he turned toward Tenochtitlán, this time with 600 Spanish soldiers and thousands of Tlaxcalans. Cortés's army took the towns around Tenochtitlán one by one, cutting off Aztec supply lines. Then they attacked the city.

Although the Aztecs far outnumbered them, the Spanish had several advantages. They had guns and iron swords, while the Aztecs had lances and arrows tipped with stone. Spanish horses amazed the Aztecs, who had never faced such strange creatures in battle. In addition, thousands of Indians who were eager to destroy the Aztecs fought side by side with the Spanish.

Most important of all, the Spanish had a silent and deadly helper, smallpox. It killed many thousands of Aztecs, even while they were fighting to save their city. Wrote Bernal Díaz del Castillo (DEE-ahs del kahs-TEE-yō), who served with Cortés:

❝The streets, the squares, the houses and the courts . . . were covered with dead bodies. We could not step without treading on them, and the stench [smell] was intolerable.❞

On August 13, 1521, after a fierce struggle, Tenochtitlán fell. The Aztec empire ended that day. In a well-known poem, "Broken Spears," one Aztec mourned his loss:

❝Broken spears lie in the roads;
We have torn our hair in our grief.
The houses are roofless now. . . .
And the walls are splattered with gore. . . .
We have pounded our hands in despair
Against the adobe walls
For . . . our city is lost and dead.❞

The Conquest of Peru

Far to the south of Mexico lay the Inca empire of Peru. It, too, was destroyed by a conquistador with the help of smallpox.

Rumors of wealth lured Francisco Pizarro (pih-ZAR-ō) and his small army to Peru. Smallpox had arrived before him, killing thousands of Incas. Thousands more had died in Incan wars. When Pizarro arrived in 1532, the wars were over, and Atahualpa (AH-tuh-WAHL-puh) was ruler.

Pizarro had a plan to conquer Peru. He invited Atahualpa to a meeting, then kidnapped him. Pizarro said he would free Atahualpa for a room filled once with gold and twice again with silver. To save their ruler, many Incas gave up their gold and silver. Pizarro was not to be trusted, though. Once he had the treasure, he had Atahualpa killed, then quickly subdued the empire.

Tales of treasure soon drew more Spaniards to Peru. From there, expeditions went out to Ecuador, Colombia, and Chile. The land of the Incas became a stepping-stone to the rest of South America.

Accounts of the conquest of the Aztecs reveal both the Spanish and Aztec points of view. Aztec accounts and writings were collected in codices, or manuscripts. Book 12 of the Florentine Codex is a history of Cortés's conquest written in the 1550s by Aztecs for the Spanish friar Bernardino de Sahagun. Sahagun was fluent in Nahuatl, the Aztec language, and drew on the accounts of "prominent elders, well versed in all matters . . . who were present in the war when this city was conquered." The Spanish account by Bernal Díaz, *The Discovery and Conquest of Mexico,* was written decades later.

Hands-On → *HISTORY*

Planning a modern-day entrada Explorers tried to be prepared. They took foods like grain and beans, along with livestock and poultry for future slaughter. They carried items to trade with the native peoples, as well as armor, guns, and swords in case the people proved to be unfriendly. For practical reasons, they packed shovels, hoes, and pans. For symbolic reasons, they carried flags, banners, and crosses.

Activity Imagine yourself as the leader of a modern-day entrada. You plan to take 50 people into a remote area to build 10 vacation cabins. There is a paved road for the first 50 miles, but you do not know what lies beyond. Your sponsors have asked you to list the items you need for 6 months and to explain why you need them. Answer this request in a letter. Keep these tips in mind:

• If you use vehicles, they will need fuel. If you use animals, they will need food and water.

• You will be far from stores and hospitals.

• You may have to deal with a variety of weather conditions and geographic features.

Explorers unloading supplies

Wealth of the Indies The treasures of the great Indian civilizations aroused envy in everyone who heard about them. In the long run, however, it was the gold and silver mines of Mexico and South America that created the greatest wealth.

The Spanish forced Indians to dig gold and silver ore. They produced so much that it was sent to Spain in large fleets of ships. These treasure fleets made tempting targets for pirates and for private ships paid for by Spain's jealous rivals, England and France.

Into the Borderlands

In Mexico and Peru, conquistadors had found riches beyond their wildest dreams. Hoping for more, the Spanish soon began to send *entradas*—armed expeditions— northward into lands that are now northern Mexico and the southern United States. This area was known as the borderlands.

Ponce de León Juan Ponce de León (PAHN-suh day lay-ON) made the first entrada north. He had come to the Americas with Columbus and stayed to conquer Puerto Rico. Ponce de León heard of an island with much gold and a spring that gave eternal youth to anyone who drank its waters. In March 1513 he reached a land he named Florida, but Indians drove him out. He did not find gold or a "Fountain of Youth."

Cabeza de Vaca More dramatic is the story of Álvar Núñez Cabeza de Vaca (kah-BAY-sah day VAH-kah). He was an officer on an entrada led by Pánfilo de Narváez (nahr-VAH-ays). They reached Florida in 1528 and marched inland.

When Indians drove Narváez and his men back to the coast, they could not find their ships, so they set out to sea in hastily built rafts. Many of the Spaniards, including Narváez, soon drowned or died of hunger and thirst.

Checking Understanding

1. How did Pizarro conquer Peru? (He kidnapped the Inca ruler Atahualpa and held him for a ransom of gold and silver. Once he had the treasure, he killed Atahualpa and subdued the empire.)

2. What helped both Cortés and Pizarro? (They were both helped by struggles between different groups of Indians and, most importantly, by smallpox, which killed many Indians.)

Stimulating Critical Thinking

3. Why do you think the Inca and Aztec treasures did not satisfy the Spaniards? (Students might think that the Spaniards were motivated by greed or by the belief that because so many riches were readily available there must be many more riches that had not been exploited.)

Teaching the

Hands-On
→ *HISTORY*

Small groups of students can begin by brainstorming to make lists of difficulties they might encounter and possible necessary supplies. You may wish to assign categories like food, transportation, and protective equipment to separate groups. Relate the activity to any experiences students may have had when camping or going on an extended vacation.

Direct students also to notice what Indian nations are listed on the map.
Answer to Reading Maps: Ponce de León explored the Florida coast; Cortés went from Cuba to what is now Mexico City; Narváez explored Florida and the Gulf of Mexico; Cabeza de Vaca was enslaved by Indians on the Texas coast, escaped and wandered along the Rio Grande and then to Mexico City; from Florida de Soto explored the southeastern part of present-day United States; de Niza explored what is now New Mexico and Arizona; Coronado explored New Mexico and Arizona, and some of his group went as far north as present-day Kansas; Cabrillo explored the west coast of North America to what is now Oregon.

✱ **History Footnote**

Cabeza de Vaca and his companions made their way through Indian lands by posing as healers, using prayer, a bit of theater, and probably the power of suggestion to cure. Indians, in turn, gave them food, lodging, and escorts. When they met some other Spaniards, the Indian escorts could not believe they were of the same people. Cabeza de Vaca said of these other Spaniards: "We healed the sick, they killed the sound [healthy]; we came naked and barefoot, they [came] clothed, horsed and lanced; we coveted nothing but gave whatever we were given, while they robbed whomever they found."

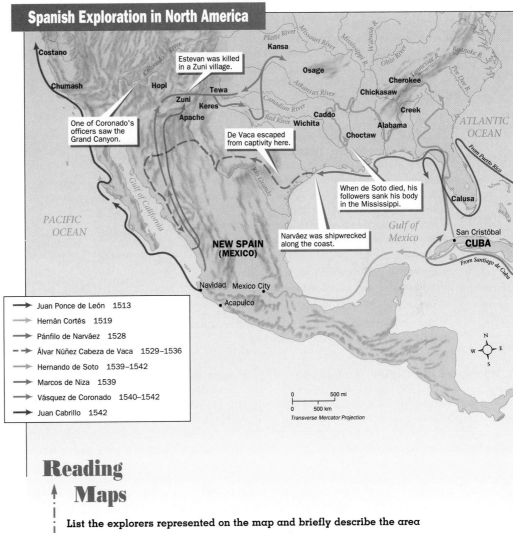

Spanish Exploration in North America

Juan Ponce de León   1513
Hernán Cortés   1519
Pánfilo de Narváez   1528
Álvar Núñez Cabeza de Vaca   1529–1536
Hernando de Soto   1539–1542
Marcos de Niza   1539
Vásquez de Coronado   1540–1542
Juan Cabrillo   1542

Reading
↑   **Maps**

List the explorers represented on the map and briefly describe the area each one explored.

Cabeza de Vaca washed up on the Texas coast, where Indians enslaved him for six years. Finally he escaped and set out for Mexico City. Along the way he joined three other castaways from the Narváez expedition—two Spaniards and an African named Estevan (eh-STAY-bahn). The wanderers arrived safely in Mexico City in April 1536.

Cabeza de Vaca had not seen treasures during his years of wandering in the borderlands, but he had heard stories about "towns of great population and great houses." His stories set off rumors of Seven Cities of Gold supposedly to be found somewhere to the north, and the rumors spurred on other explorers.

See the Study Guide activity in **Chapter Resources Binder**, p. 25.

De Soto Hernando de Soto, governor of Cuba, heard the rumors of Seven Cities. He had been with Pizarro in Peru, where he filled his purse with Inca gold. Vowing to find more treasure, he left his wife, Doña Ysabel (DŌ-nyah IZ-uh-BEL), to govern Cuba and sailed for Florida.

De Soto landed in Florida in 1539 with hundreds of soldiers, herds of pigs and horses, and packs of fierce dogs. For four years he searched the southeastern part of the present-day United States, chasing rumors of gold and looting Indian villages.

De Soto found a few pearls but no gold. Sick and depressed, he died near the Mississippi River in May 1542. After that, his troops wanted only to get to safety. The survivors—300 men and a woman—made it to Mexico in the fall of 1543.

Coronado The Mexican viceroy, or governor, had also heard Cabeza de Vaca's stories. In 1539 he sent Marcos de Niza into what is now New Mexico and Arizona to find the cities. Cabeza de Vaca's companion Estevan went along. As Estevan entered one Zuni pueblo—a village of flat-roofed stone or adobe buildings—the Indians killed him.

Watching from a distance, de Niza thought the adobe shimmering in the sun was gold. He rushed back to Mexico with the news that he had found one of the cities of gold.

In 1540 the viceroy sent Francisco Vásquez de Coronado, with de Niza as guide, to conquer the city. Coronado found only an adobe village. "Such were the curses that some hurled at [de Niza]," wrote one Spaniard, "that I pray God may protect him from them." Enraged, Coronado sent de Niza home.

Coronado's expedition stayed at the pueblo that winter, forcing the Indians to share their food. When the Indians rebelled, Coronado burned 13 villages. The Pueblo Indians would not forget the Spaniards.

Some of Coronado's men traveled as far north as present-day Kansas, but they found no golden cities. Discouraged, they returned to Mexico. Although they found no treasure, they did bring back knowledge of the land and its people. They had seen pueblos, prairies, bison, the Colorado River, the Rio Grande, and the Grand Canyon.

Cabrillo In 1542 Juan Rodríguez Cabrillo (kah-BREE-yō) led one more entrada in search of gold. His two tiny ships sailed from Mexico's Pacific shore northward as far as what is now southern Oregon. Although Cabrillo died during the voyage, his expedition explored 1,200 miles (1,931 km) of coastline and claimed it for Spain.

Spain's American Empire

Within just 50 years of Columbus's first voyage, Spain had become the richest, most powerful nation in Europe. It possessed a huge empire in the Americas, and its treasure ships brought great wealth home to Spain.

Although conquistadors did not find cities of gold and silver north of Mexico, the entradas into the borderlands expanded Spain's empire. Spain could now claim an area larger than all of Europe.

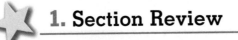

1. Section Review

1. Define **conquistadors**.
2. Give an example of how each of Spain's three goals in the Americas was carried out.
3. Why were the Spaniards able to defeat the Aztecs? The Incas?
4. What part of North America did each of these people explore: Ponce de León, Cabeza de Vaca, de Soto, Coronado?
5. Critical Thinking Spaniards in the 1500s took pride in the boldness of the conquistadors. At the same time some were disturbed by the conquistadors' treatment of the Indians. Give reasons for each view.

Closing the Section

Wrap-Up Activity

Making a Time Line
To review Spanish conquests and explorations in the Americas, have students make a time line. They should begin their time lines in 1513 and use different strips of color to represent the length of different explorations.

Section Review
Answers

1. Definition: *conquistadors* (94)

2. To spread Christianity, Cortés tried to convert Moctezuma. He also destroyed religious figures in the temple. Spaniards found gold in Tenochtitlán and Peru. By finding gold and claiming land, the conquistadors made Spain the richest, most powerful nation in Europe.

3. Spaniards had horses and superior weapons and the help of smallpox, which killed many thousands of Indians. In Mexico, they also had Indian allies.

4. Ponce de León explored Florida; Cabeza de Vaca, the southern part of Texas; de Soto, southeastern United States; and Coronado, southwestern United States.

5. Spaniards might have been proud of how the conquistadors conquered people and took land to further enrich Spain. However, some may have seen the harsh treatment of the Indians as going against Christian beliefs.

Geography Lab

Point out that modern terrain maps like the one shown here use shading and other methods to show what the earth might look like from space. The shading here suggests mountains rising above the surrounding landscape. Have students compare how the modern and Aztec maps show terrain and routes.

Using Map Skills
Answers

1. Information about terrain may indicate whether the journey will be slow and hard or fast and easy. Also, some terrain may require special planning and equipment.

2. It tells that the land was hilly or mountainous by showing hills or mountains in a side view.

3. It shows mountains north, west, and south of Tenochtitlán.

4. They are very high peaks and would thus have been hard to cross directly. Cortés may have avoided them because he saw them in the distance, or Indians may have steered him to mountain passes.

5. Routes will vary. Although they cannot avoid mountains, students should search for routes that avoid the highest and widest stretches.

See the activity on terrain maps in **Geography Extensions**, pp. 7–8.

Geography Lab

Reading a Terrain Map

Since ancient times, travelers have tried to find ways to show others where they went, how they got there, and what the **terrain**—all the physical features of an area of land—was like. People have thought of several different solutions to this problem.

The Aztec picture record on this page is one attempt to show a route and the land it went through. In the picture, Aztec traders are going out from Tenochtitlán into the surrounding countryside. The modern map of Cortés's route is another example. Compare the Aztec record and the modern map to help you understand maps that show terrain.

Merchants, from an Aztec book

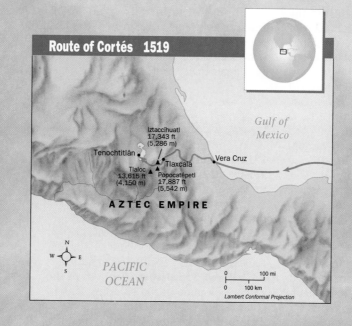

Route of Cortés 1519

Iztaccíhuatl
17,343 ft
(5,286 m)

Tenochtitlán

Tlaxcala

Vera Cruz

Gulf of Mexico

Tlaloc
13,615 ft
(4,150 m)

Popocatépetl
17,887 ft
(5,542 m)

AZTEC EMPIRE

N
W · E
S

PACIFIC OCEAN

0   100 mi
0   100 km
Lambert Conformal Projection

Using Map Skills

1. Why is it helpful to know the terrain of land you plan to travel through?

2. What does the Aztec picture record tell you about terrain near Tenochtitlán? How?

3. How does the map of Cortés's invasion route support the picture record?

4. Why did Cortés avoid the places marked on the map with triangles? How do you suppose he managed to avoid them?

5. **Hands-On Geography** Suppose you are going on a bicycle trip from Chicago to San Francisco. You want to follow the most direct route, while avoiding as many mountains as you can. Use the maps on pages R4–R5 and R6–R7 to help you plan your route. Draw your route on an outline map of the United States. Explain why the route is a good one to take.

Section Objectives

★ Explain how Spain governed its colonies.
★ Describe how Spaniards treated Native Americans.
★ Explain why Spain established settlements in the borderlands.

Teaching Resources

Take-Home Planner 2, pp. 2–9
Chapter Resources Binder
  Study Guide, p. 26
  Reinforcement
  Skills Development, pp. 31–32
Geography Extensions
American Readings
Using Historical Documents
Transparency Activities
Chapter and Unit Tests

Introducing the Section

Vocabulary

mercantilism (p. 102) an economic idea whereby a nation became strong by filling its treasury

---

Warm-Up Activity

Problems of Empire

To focus on challenges of creating an empire, have students brainstorm what would have to be done (set up a government, enforce laws, deal with cultural differences, etc.). Then have them list what specific steps would have to be taken to meet those challenges. After they read the section they can evaluate steps the Spaniards took.

2. Spanish America

Reading Guide

New Term mercantilism

Section Focus How a distinctive culture arose in Spanish America

1. How did Spain govern its colonies?
2. How did Spaniards treat Native Americans?
3. Why did Spain establish settlements in the borderlands?

By 1530 the time of the conquistadors was passing. Soldiers who had come to the Americas to conquer stayed to run plantations, ranches, and mines. Settlers arrived, and new missionaries came to bring the Catholic faith to the Indians.

To rule his American empire, in 1535 Spain's King Charles I divided it into two parts—Peru and New Spain. He appointed a viceroy to govern each part. They were to create a society like the one they had left behind in Spain.

The Church

In Spain the king was the head of the Catholic Church as well as the government. King Charles saw it as his duty to establish the Church in the Americas and convert Indians to Christianity.

To teach Indians Christianity, as well as Spanish crafts and farming methods, missionaries gathered them into villages called missions. Some Indians adopted Christianity quickly. In 1524 one missionary wrote:

"When the [missionaries] travel, the Indians come out to the roads with their children in their arms, and with their sick on their backs, . . . demanding to be baptized.**"**

Indians, however, did not want Christianity forced on them. Although missionaries often meant well, their work uprooted Indian cultures. Some Indians kept their old beliefs. Others practiced the two religions side by side.

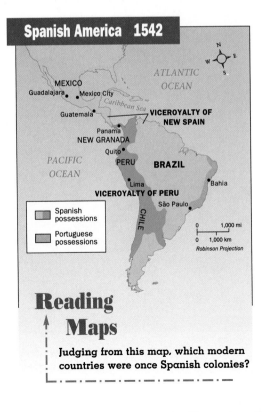

Spanish America 1542

MEXICO
Guadalajara • Mexico City
Guatemala
ATLANTIC OCEAN
Caribbean Sea
VICEROYALTY OF NEW SPAIN
Panama
NEW GRANADA
Quito •
PACIFIC OCEAN
PERU
Lima •
VICEROYALTY OF PERU
BRAZIL
• Bahia
São Paulo
CHILE

☐ Spanish possessions
☐ Portuguese possessions

0   1,000 mi
0   1,000 km
Robinson Projection

Reading Maps

Judging from this map, which modern countries were once Spanish colonies?

Geography Question of the Day

Have students examine the maps on pages R4–R7 and list names of Spanish origin. If possible, have Spanish-speaking students translate.

Teaching the Reading Maps

Ask why the map focuses on Central and South America (focus on Spanish colonies). **Answer to Reading Maps:** Labels identify Mexico, Guatemala, Panama, Peru, and Chile. Students may refer to pp. R2–R3 to list others.

As missionaries spread out, soldiers were sent to protect them and any settlers who went with them. Thus forts, called *presidios,* grew up alongside many missions.

The Laws of the Indies

The viceroys carried out orders that the king's advisors—the Council of the Indies—sent from Spain. These orders were signed *Yo el Rey,* which means "I, the King." The council organized its rules into a code called the Laws of the Indies.

The Laws of the Indies applied Spanish thinking to colonial society. For example, each city in the colonies was to be laid out like a city in Spain, with a public square, a church, a jail, and "arcades for tradesmen."

The child in this painting has a Spanish father and an Indian mother. By 1800 about a third of the people of Spanish America and Brazil had a mixed heritage.

Social classes Society in Spain was divided into social classes, from the king down to peasant farmers, with African slaves at the bottom. Following that pattern, the Laws divided the people of the colonies into social classes, too.

At the top were *peninsulares* (PEH-nihn-soo-LAHR-ays)—people born in Spain. They held the highest church and government positions. Next in importance were *creoles,* born in the Americas to Spanish parents. They might have wealth and education, but never the influence of peninsulares.

Many Spaniards who came to the colonies married Indian women. Their children, part Spanish and part Indian, belonged to the third class, called *mestizos.* They could not own land but worked on farms and ranches and at crafts in the cities.

By law, Indians and Africans were included in Spanish society. However, they were in the lowest classes and had the fewest rights and opportunities.

Throughout the colonies, Spaniards, Indians, and Africans intermarried. As a result, an entirely new group of people arose—people known today as *Latinos.*

Increasing Spain's Wealth

Charles and the kings who came after him applied a new economic idea called **mercantilism** to Spain's empire. According to this idea, a nation became strong by filling its treasury with gold and silver. It could add to its wealth by owning gold and silver mines or by selling more to other countries than it bought from them.

Colonies played an important part in Spain's mercantilism. On the one hand, they sent gold and silver to Spain. On the other hand, colonists bought manufactured goods from the home country. Strict rules forced colonists to trade only with Spanish merchants.

In Spain a gentleman, or *hidalgo,* was a man of property who did not have to work because he had others work for him. Encomiendas were a way for ordinary soldiers to rise to the level of hidalgos. When the king tried to abolish encomiendas in 1542, therefore, it is not surprising that Spaniards in America paid little attention to his orders.

∞ Link to Art

Church of Santa Clara, Tunja, Colombia This church ceiling is a blend of Spanish and Indian ideas. Spanish priests had Indians build churches like the ones in Spain. Indian artisans carved and painted the walls and ceilings, following Spanish examples. However, they were also inspired by their own traditions of colorful, complex patterns. The sun symbol is both Indian and European. Many Indians worshipped the sun as the creator of their people. In Europe the sun symbolized knowledge, as well as heaven. **Discuss** To create this ceiling, what native skills do you think Indians used?

Encomiendas Although the colonies existed for the good of Spain, the king thought it was Spain's duty to care for the Indians. The two ideas clashed in the *encomienda* (ehn-kō-mee-EHN-dah) system.

Under this system the king gave favored Spaniards a right to the labor of a certain number of Indians. For example, the king gave Cortés the services of 100,000 Indians in a 25,000-square-mile (64,750-square-km) area. Some Spaniards thought of the Indians as similar to the serfs who labored for European landowners.

⟳ Point of View

How should Spaniards treat Indians?

A person who received an encomienda was supposed to protect the Indians and teach them Christianity. In practice, however, many colonists treated Indians as slaves.

Antonio de Montesinos was the first to speak out against this treatment of Indians, and his words moved Bartolomé de Las Casas. Las Casas, in turn, inspired others to take up the cause, but he also set off a hot debate.

Discussion

Checking Understanding

1. What was the purpose of the missions? (They were villages where missionaries gathered Indians to teach Christianity and Spanish crafts and farming methods.)

2. What were the social classes in Spanish America? (*Peninsulares,* people born in Spain, were at the top. Then came *creoles,* born in the Americas of Spanish parents. *Mestizos* were of mixed Spanish and Indian blood. At the bottom were Indians and Africans.)

Stimulating Critical Thinking

3. How were missions and encomiendas similar? Different? (Both used Indian labor and were intended to protect the Indians and teach them Christianity. However, missions were organized mainly for religious purposes and encomiendas mainly for economic purposes.)

Teaching the

∞ Link to Art

Point out that Indians preserved native symbols in the churches they built. Painted on the walls are Indian princesses among Christian saints, American jungle leaves intertwined with European plants, and native instruments played by European mythological heroes. **Discussion Answers:** Indians had skills in woodcarving and painting, as well as knowledge of natural sources of paint pigments and experience in using symbols to express ideas.

The history of St. Augustine reflects the conflicting claims of various European countries in the Americas. Francis Drake sacked and burned it in 1586. In 1702 the British governor of Carolina destroyed the town but failed to take the fort, Castillo de San Marcos (shown on p. 106). Spain held control of St. Augustine until 1763, when the Spanish king gave it to the British as part of the settlement at the end of the Seven Years' War. Control reverted back to Spain at the end of the War of Independence in 1783. In 1821 Florida became part of the United States.

Teaching the

Point of View

↳ Point out that Spanish Catholics believed that theirs was the one true religion, and they wanted to bring eternal life to Indians and other "infidels." Some used as their justification for subjugating Indians this instruction from the Book of Genesis: "replenish the earth and subdue it: and have dominion [control] over . . . every living thing that moveth upon the earth." Sepúlveda never actually witnessed the treatment of the Indians, whereas Las Casas knew firsthand how they were treated.

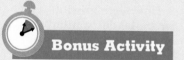

Bonus Activity

Brainstorming Spanish Influences

To explore the legacy of the Spanish empire in the Americas, have students brainstorm examples of Spanish influence on American life today. Examples should include Spanish influences in the areas of music, art, architecture, movies, and foods.

One Spanish scholar, Juan Ginés de Sepúlveda, reasoned that it was natural for some people to be slaves. Didn't Indians deserve harsh treatment, he asked, because they had been guilty of such sins as human sacrifice and idol worship? He argued:

> ❝How can we doubt that these people— so uncivilized, so barbaric, contaminated with so many impieties and obscenities [sins and immoral acts]—have been justly conquered by such an excellent, pious, and most just king? . . . [The Spanish] can destroy barbarism and educate [Indians] to a more humane and virtuous life. And if the [Indians] reject such rule, it can be imposed upon them by force of arms.❞

In 1540 Las Casas returned to Spain to put his case before the king. He used sarcasm to point out that Spaniards were failing in their duty to protect and educate Indians.

> ❝The Spaniards entered . . . like wolves, tigers, and lions which had been starving for many days, and since forty years they have done nothing else . . . than outrage, slay, afflict, torment, and destroy. In this way have they cared for [Indian] lives—and for their souls.❞

Stirred by Las Casas, King Charles I reformed the encomienda system in 1542. However, many colonists protested the reforms and ignored the limits on their rights to Indian labor. ↻

Settling the Borderlands

At first, Spain did little to encourage settlement of the areas explored by Cabeza de Vaca, de Soto, and Coronado. When rival nations began to show an interest, however, the king changed his mind. News of French or English threats encouraged him to send soldiers, settlers, and missionaries to protect the borderlands.

Foreign threats One threat to Spain's empire came from France. In 1564, a party of French Protestants built Fort Caroline in Florida. When 13 of the settlers used the colony's only boat to raid Spanish ships, the king of Spain quickly sent a cold-hearted soldier, Don Pedro Menéndez de Avilés, to drive the French out.

Nearby in Florida, Menéndez founded the colony of St. Augustine in 1565. It was too far from Spain's other settlements to prosper, but Spain held on to it for almost 300 years. St. Augustine is the oldest permanent European settlement in the United States.

Francis Drake Another threat came from the English pirate, Francis Drake. Drake sailed around the tip of South America into the Pacific, where he captured a treasure ship off the coast of Peru. He then sailed up the California coast, returning home across the Pacific in 1580. It was only the second voyage around the world.

The Spanish were convinced that Drake had found the fabled Northwest Passage from the Atlantic to the Pacific. Did this mean that England could easily attack New Spain on both the east and west coasts?

New Mexico and Arizona In 1598 Juan de Oñate (ō-NYAH-tay) led 400 settlers, including slaves and missionaries, into the area they called New Mexico. About 40,000 Indians already lived there in some 60 pueblos along the Rio Grande. At first the Pueblo people gave Oñate shelter and let the missionaries baptize converts.

In 1609 a new leader, Pedro de Peralta, laid out the city of Santa Fe, following the Laws of the Indies. By the time English Pilgrims landed at Plymouth Rock, the New Mexico colony was well established.

Tips for Teaching

Visual Learners

Visual learners will benefit from making connections between images and the text. As you discuss Spanish America ask: What places on the map are mentioned in the text? What does the map or picture tell you? What does the text tell you? How are the maps and pictures related to the text?

Discussion

Checking Understanding

1. Why did the king send soldiers, settlers, and missionaries to settle the borderlands? (To protect Spanish holdings by keeping forces of rival nations away from the borders.)

Stimulating Critical Thinking

2. The Spaniards saw Indians as "uncivilized." Might the Indians have felt the same way about the Spaniards? Explain. (Indians might have considered as uncivilized such Spanish actions as forced labor and harsh treatment of workers.)

Teaching the Reading Maps

Have students compare this map with the one on pages R4–R5 to identify names of some of the places that still exist today in the United States. Students may also recognize names of other places that are cities today but are not big enough to appear on the United States map (such as Taos and St. Augustine). **Answer to Reading Maps:** Florida, Texas, Arizona, New Mexico, and California.

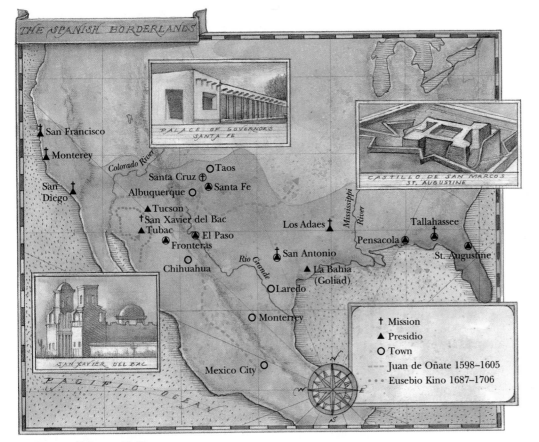

Reading Maps

Compare this map with the map of the United States today on pages R6–R7. In which states would you expect to find evidence of Spanish influence?

Unfortunately, here, as in other parts of the Americas, kindness was repaid with cruelty. The Spaniards forced Pueblo Indians to labor for them, to pay tribute, and to practice the Catholic religion. In 1680, a Tewa Indian named Popé (pō-PAY) planned a revolt. On August 10—at the same hour of the day—Tewas, Keres, Hopis, Zunis, and other tribes rose up and drove the Spanish out. Twelve years passed before the Spanish returned.

Meanwhile, in 1687 a missionary and explorer, Eusebio Kino (ay-oo-ZA-byō KEE-nō), built a chain of missions in present-day Arizona. A few hundred settlers and miners trickled in after Kino, but the Spanish population of Arizona remained small.

Texas Rumors of a French settlement sent Spanish soldiers hurrying to Texas in 1689. They found that a tiny French colony had failed. However, the Spanish leader,

Closing the Section

Writing an Encomienda Order

To review goals for the colonies, have students imagine themselves as the monarch writing an order for encomiendas. The order should outline how the encomiendas should produce wealth for Spain while at the same time help the Indians. Have them sign their orders, *"Yo el Rey."*

Section Review
Answers

1. Definition: *mercantilism* (102)

2. The king was head of the Spanish Catholic Church and supported the establishment of missions to convert the Indians. The king ruled the colonies through the Council of the Indies and established a code of laws.

3. Worry about the French entering Spanish territory prompted settlements in Texas and Florida. Missions were established in New Mexico to convert the Indians and to discourage English attacks from the west. Worry about Russians moving farther down the coast led to California settlements.

4. Answers will vary but should include the idea that the king wanted to reform the system to better protect the Indians while colonists, who depended on Indian labor for their wealth, ignored the reforms.

Connections to Art

Spanish influences can be seen today in architecture and art throughout the Southwest. A combination of Spanish and Indian influences can be seen in the work of artists and architects like Jose Clemente Orozco, Diego Rivera, Frank Romero, and Frida Kahlo. The Spanish missions of California were restored and embellished beginning in the late 1800s. Other Spanish-influenced architecture can be seen throughout the southwestern United States in buildings like Scotty's Castle in Death Valley, California, and the San Xavier del Bac Mission near Tucson, Arizona.

Between 1672 and 1687 unknown numbers of Indian laborers cut limestone blocks, hauled them, and fitted them together to make the walls of Castillo de San Marcos. This Spanish fort could shelter as many as 1,500 people. More than once its massive walls have resisted cannon fire, and the old fort still stands in St. Augustine, Florida.

Alonso de León, gave a glowing report of native people called Tejas (TAY-hahs), from an Indian word for friends: "Certainly it is a pity that people so rational should have no one to teach them [Christianity]."

Missionaries hastened to Texas, but the Tejas ordered them out. In 1718, Spanish soldiers, settlers, and priests returned and established the mission and presidio of San Antonio—again to warn the French.

California The last part of North America that Spain colonized was California. In the mid-1700s the Spanish heard about Russian fur hunters in Alaska. They worried that the Russians would move south.

Gaspar de Portolá (POR-tō-LAH), a soldier, and Junípero Serra, a missionary, led a band of Spaniards to San Diego Bay in 1769. There they built the first of a chain of 21 missions and 4 presidios that would one day link San Diego and San Francisco. As for the Russians, they did plant a settlement in California, but not until 1812.

The arc of settlements The Spanish population of the borderlands grew slowly. By the middle of the 1700s, though, Spain had scattered missions, presidios, and towns in a great arc across what is now the southern United States. The people who made their way into the region brought Spanish ways: skills in arts and architecture, the Spanish language, the Catholic religion, and ranching and mining techniques.

Today, many Americans can trace their ancestry to these settlers. In addition, the influence of Spanish culture is easy to see in buildings, place names, and ways of life in what were once New Spain's borderlands.

2. Section Review

1. Define **mercantilism**.

2. Explain the following statement and give two examples: Spanish America was closely controlled by the king of Spain.

3. Why did Spain establish missions and settlements in each of the following places: Florida, New Mexico, Texas, California?

4. Critical Thinking Compare the hopes of the Spanish kings for the encomienda system with the settlers' expectations.

3. The Spaniards treated Indians unfairly and cruelly.

4. (a) The painting is consistent with the chapter's information on Spaniards treating Indians like slaves and not protecting them. Based on the chapter, the painting appears accurate. (b) Students might suggest other paintings and written accounts from Indian and Spanish viewpoints.

For further application, have students do the Applying Skills activity in the Chapter Survey (p. 114).

If students need to review the skill, use the Skills Development transparency and activity in the **Chapter Resources Binder,** *pp. 31–32.*

Skill Lab

Skill Tips

Ask yourself:
● At first glance, what does the painting show?
● Does it try to create a mood (for example: cheerful, gloomy, calm, violent)?
● What details create that mood?
● What do the details and the mood tell me about the artist's purpose?

Acquiring Information
Analyzing a Painting

The painting below is more than 400 years old and shows a scene from Spanish America in the 1500s. For centuries artists have used paintings to express their feelings about people, places, and events. Paintings can be a valuable source of information about history. Often the ones in museums or books have captions. However, try to draw your own conclusions rather than relying on captions.

Question to Investigate

What was the relationship between the Spanish and the Indians in the 1500s?

Procedure

To use a painting as a source of information, you must ask both "what" and "why" questions. Analyze this painting to determine its basic features as you explore the Question to Investigate.

Source to Use

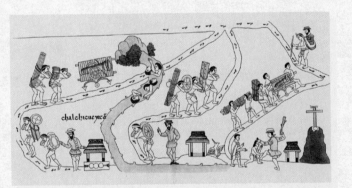

chalchicueyeca

❶ Determine *what* information the painting provides about Spanish America.
a. Identify the main image, if any.
b. Identify the smaller details.

❷ Think about possible reasons *why* the artist made the painting.
a. Did the artist try to create a certain mood? Explain your answer.
b. Was the artist trying to get the viewer to think or feel a certain way about Spanish America? Explain.

❸ Based on the painting alone, how would you answer the Question to Investigate?

❹ Evaluate how useful the painting is as a source of information.
a. In light of what you have read in the chapter, how accurate do you think this painting is? Explain.
b. What other kinds of information might you look for in order to check the accuracy of this painting?

Introducing the Skill Lab

This lab focuses on reinforcing the fact that a painting can be a source of historical information. Students should carefully observe major and minor details, letting a painting "speak for itself." You may wish to caution against drawing firm conclusions based on just one painting. Later labs will address critical thinking skills such as recognizing point of view, detecting bias, and determining credibility.

Skill Lab
Answers

1. (a) There is no single main image. (b) Spaniards are forcing Indians to carry wooden shafts, metal shields, cannons, and other objects. One Indian carries a Spaniard. Also, a Spaniard beats an Indian near a Christian cross, and bodies of dead Indians float in a river. The nature of the three structures is unclear.

2. (a) Although the Indians' facial expressions are not clear, the burdened workers, dead bodies, and the beating make the mood of the painting grim. (b) The artist seems to encourage criticism of Spaniards' treatment of Indians. Every scene shows Indians being burdened or treated brutally.

(Answers continued in top margin)

Introducing the Section

Vocabulary

persecution (p. 108) attacking, imprisoning, torturing, or killing people for their beliefs

league (p. 110) a group with a common purpose

Warm-Up Activity

Using Maps to Predict

Have students use the maps in Chapter 3 on the search for a Northwest Passage to predict which countries would challenge Spain and where those countries would establish settlements.

Geography Question of the Day

Provide students with an outline map of the world (see **Geography Extensions**). Have them shade in the areas of the Spanish empire in the Americas and New France, using the maps on pages 101 and 109 as references. Then have them compare the sizes of Spanish and French claims in the Americas, using a small paper square as a rough measuring tool. After counting approximately how many squares fit in each shaded area, they can identify which empire was larger and by approximately how much (such as one and one-fourth times).

Section Objectives

★ Explain how the Protestant Reformation affected the Americas.
★ Compare and contrast New France and New Spain.
★ Compare and contrast New Netherland and New Spain.
★ Explain why England's early colonies failed.

Teaching Resources

Take-Home Planner 2, pp. 2–9
Chapter Resources Binder
  Study Guide, p. 27
  Reinforcement, pp. 29–30
  Skills Development
Geography Extensions
American Readings, pp. 14–16
Using Historical Documents
Transparency Activities
Chapter and Unit Tests, pp. 25–28

3. Challenges to Spain

Reading Guide

New Terms persecution, league

Section Focus The American colonies of Spain's European rivals

1. How did Europe's Protestant Reformation affect the Americas?
2. In what ways did New France differ from New Spain?
3. In what ways did New Netherland differ from New Spain?
4. Why did England's early colonies fail?

During the 1500s, Spain ruled the world's largest empire. Europeans said, "When Spain moves, the world trembles." Two forces were at work, however, to change Spain's position. One force for change was that rival nations began to establish their own colonies. The other was religious rivalry.

Catholics and Protestants

For centuries the Catholic Church was the only Christian church in western Europe. Then in 1517 Martin Luther, a German monk, spoke out against what he saw as false teachings and acts within the Church. Other people, including John Calvin in Switzerland, began to protest, too. Because they were protesting, they were called Protestants, and the movement they started was called the Protestant Reformation.

Protestants and Catholics struggled for power in the name of God. Spain, France, Belgium, and most of Germany remained Catholic. Switzerland, the Netherlands, England, and the Scandinavian countries became Protestant. Catholics in Protestant countries and Protestants in Catholic countries were often victims of **persecution.** That means they were attacked, thrown in prison, tortured, or killed for their beliefs.

Europe's religious conflicts affected the Americas in two ways. First, rival nations saw colonies as a chance to spread their religion. Second, people who suffered persecution saw colonies as a means of escape.

New France

Hoping to find wealth to rival Spain's and to convert Indians to Christianity, the French explored nearly two-thirds of North America. They did not find gold or a passage to Asia. Instead, their treasure was mink, beaver, and other furs prized in Europe for fashionable clothing.

Canada French fishermen had been catching cod near Newfoundland since the early 1500s. They often stopped along shore to trade cloth, knives, and kettles for furs offered by Indians. To expand this trade, in 1608 a young French geographer, Samuel de Champlain, built a trading post atop cliffs along the St. Lawrence River. He called the place by its Indian name, *Quebec.* For the next 150 years Quebec was a base for French traders, trappers, soldiers, and missionaries.

Adventurous French trappers and traders, called *coureurs de bois* (koo-rer duh BWAH) hacked through thick woodlands, and boatmen called *voyageurs* (vwah-yah-ZHERZ)

Some French Huguenots did make it to North America. French Huguenots built Fort Caroline, mentioned on page 104, but Menéndez attacked them because they were an "evil Lutheran sect." Sparing the women and children, Menéndez and his group killed all the men at the fort. Menéndez believed that Protestants and Indians "held similar beliefs, probably satanic in origin" and reported to his king that "to chastise them in this way would serve God Our Lord, as well as Your Majesty, and we should thus be left more free from this wicked sect."

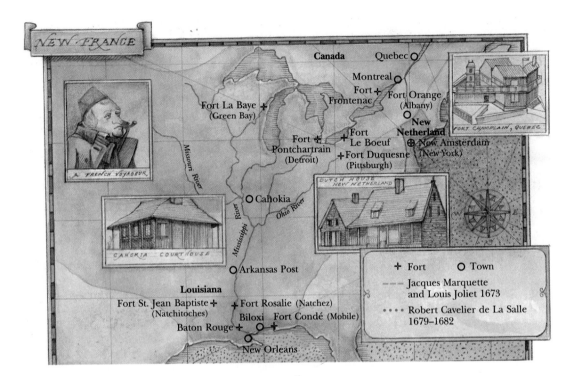

Reading Maps

↑ Compare this map with the map on page 105. In what areas do you think French and Spanish interests were most likely to conflict? Explain your reasons.

paddled along winding streams. Robed missionaries went, too, preaching to Indians. By the 1660s these woodsmen and priests had tramped all around the Great Lakes.

New France grew slowly, however. One reason was that farmers were discouraged by Canada's harsh climate and short growing season.

Another reason was that the king barred the people most willing to come—French Protestants, called *Huguenots* (HYOO-guh-NAHTS). Catholics, permitted in the colony, had little reason to leave France. So New France was left largely to those who chose to roam its forests and sail its rich coastal waters rather than settle down.

The fur trade Because the French were more interested in furs than land, they did not set out to conquer the Indians as the Spanish had done. Instead, the French and Indians became business partners.

Champlain made trade agreements with the tribes near Quebec, especially the Hurons. Huron traders took yearly trips into the forest north of the St. Lawrence. There they traded Huron farm products to other tribes for furs.

Back in Quebec, or in nearby Montreal, they exchanged the furs for European goods, which they used to buy more furs, and so on. To the south the Iroquois made similar agreements with Dutch and English traders.

Checking Understanding

1. What started the Protestant Reformation? (Luther and Calvin protested what they saw as false Catholic teachings and practices.)

2. What most interested the French in the Americas? (Trading for furs.)

Stimulating Critical Thinking

3. How did Europe's religious conflicts affect New France? (Missionaries helped explore. New France had few settlers because French Protestants were not allowed to emigrate.)

Teaching the
↑ **Reading Maps**

To help students focus on information in the map, ask what routes are shown. (Marquette and Joliet, and La Salle.)

Answer to Reading Maps: The area between western Florida and eastern Texas because France built towns and forts in the Mississippi Valley, in the middle of the arc of Spanish settlements from Florida across the Gulf of Mexico.

See the Study Guide activity in **Chapter Resources Binder**, p. 27.

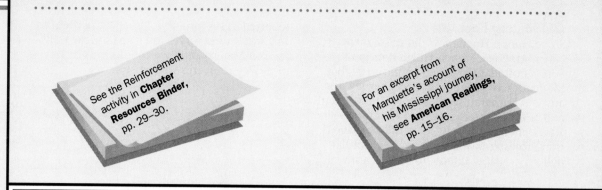
See the Reinforcement activity in **Chapter Resources Binder,** pp. 29–30.

For an excerpt from Marquette's account of his Mississippi journey, see **American Readings,** pp. 15–16.

The French government tried to force its colonists in America to farm the land. The fur trade was so profitable, however, that by 1680 one out of every three men in New France was a trapper.

The Iroquois League The Hurons were glad to have French help against the Iroquois. For years the Hurons and the Iroquois tribes—Mohawks, Oneidas, Onondagas, Cayugas, and Senecas—had fought each other. The Iroquois tribes had also feuded among themselves.

In about 1570 two men—Deganawida and Hiawatha—had a vision of what they called a "Great Peace." They convinced the Iroquois tribes to form a **league,** which is a group with a common purpose. The Iroquois League, or League of the Five Nations, ended the feuding between the tribes. It also made them stronger against their enemies.

The rivalry between the Iroquois and the Hurons grew, spurred on by competition for furs. When the Iroquois killed off the fur-bearing animals in their territory, they moved onto Huron lands. In 1649 they attacked the Hurons and scattered them into the forests. Then the Iroquois defeated one tribe after another until they had destroyed nearly all the tribes that traded with the French.

Louisiana Seeking new trading partners, the French ventured farther inland along the rivers and lakes of North America. Jacques Marquette (zhahk mar-KET), a missionary who had been working near Lake Michigan, heard about a great river to the west. He and Louis Joliet (LOO-ee JŌ-lee-ET), a coureur de bois, set out to find it. In 1673 they paddled a canoe 700 miles (1,127 km) south on the Mississippi River and then made their way back again.

Word of Marquette and Joliet's journey reached Robert Cavelier de La Salle, who was building forts and trading posts in the Great Lakes area. La Salle followed Marquette and Joliet's route, but he went all the way to the Gulf of Mexico. On April 9, 1682, he planted a French flag at the mouth of the river and claimed the Mississippi Valley for France. He named it Louisiana for King Louis XIV.

To keep other Europeans out, the French built a chain of forts and posts along the St. Lawrence and down the Mississippi. The cities of Montreal, Green Bay, Chicago, Detroit, St. Louis, Natchez, and New Orleans all began as French forts or posts.

New Netherland

Another American city, New York, owes its start to the Dutch. During the 1600s tiny Netherlands was a major trading nation. Its merchants formed the Dutch West India Company to carry out trade. Based on Henry Hudson's voyage for the Netherlands, they claimed lands along the Hudson River.

Dutch traders flocked to the area. Soon Dutch settlers formed the colony of New

In a letter to his government, Peter Jansen van Schagen of the Dutch West India Company wrote about the arrival of a Dutch ship in New Netherland and the purchase of Manhattan. The Dutch government was unimpressed because it was just one trading settlement of many they had all over the world. There is no record of what the Manhattan Indians thought of the transaction.

Netherland. Its largest community, New Amsterdam, was on an island at the mouth of the Hudson. The company wanted good relations with Indians, so it gave Governor Peter Minuit the following instructions:

> "In case there should be any Indians living on the . . . island, . . . they must not be expelled with violence or threats but be persuaded with kind words . . . or should be given something."

Obeying his orders, in 1626 Minuit bought the island from the Manhattan Indians for trade goods worth about $24. Manhattan Island is the heart of New York City today.

To encourage settlement, the company gave land to wealthy landlords called *patroons*, who were to bring in settlers. The Dutch accepted people of different religions. Among New Netherland's first settlers were Protestants fleeing persecution in Belgium.

New Sweden New Netherland soon felt competition from Sweden, which established a trading company in 1637. The next year the company hired the former Dutch governor, Peter Minuit, to lead 50 Swedish, Finnish, and Dutch settlers to the banks of the Delaware River near present-day Wilmington. The Delaware Indians were eager to trade, and the colony prospered.

The people of New Netherland looked on their neighbors in New Sweden as intruders. In 1655 a new Dutch governor, the fiery, one-legged Peter Stuyvesant, led an attack on New Sweden. Minuit's settlers gave in, and New Sweden became part of New Netherland.

English America

England mostly ignored the Americas until 1558, when Elizabeth became queen. Determined to make England powerful, she united her Protestant subjects in a fierce rivalry against Catholic Spain.

A group of English sea captains, called the Sea Dogs, had been raiding Spanish ports and ships. When the boldest Sea Dog of all, Francis Drake, seized a treasure ship—as you read in Section 2—and sailed home across the Pacific with millions of dollars worth of gold, the queen was delighted. On board his ship, the *Golden Hind*, she made him a knight.

The Spanish Armada Philip II of Spain, the son of King Charles, was furious. He demanded that Elizabeth punish Drake. When she refused, Philip assembled a mighty armada—fleet of warships—and in July 1588 sent it to crush England. One English observer described the Armada:

> "the Spanish fleet with lofty turrets like castles, [in a formation] like a half-moon, the wings thereof spreading out about the length of seven miles, . . . and the ocean groaning under the weight of them."

Cimarrons Thousands of Cimarrons—Africans who had escaped slavery on Spanish plantations—lived in the dense brush and rain forests of Spanish America. In 1573 a group of Cimarrons helped Francis Drake raid a mule train carrying treasure from Peru to Panama. According to one of Drake's men, the Cimarrons were glad to join in "to revenge the wrongs . . . the Spanish nation had done to them." Later, Africans who fled enslavement on English plantations to live in the forests of North America were called Maroons, after the Cimarrons.

Discussion

Checking Understanding

1. What part of North America did the French claim? (The area from Quebec to the Great Lakes and south along the Mississippi River to New Orleans.)

2. What part did the Netherlands claim? (The area along the Hudson River and the banks of the Delaware River.)

Stimulating Critical Thinking

3. Why do you think the French government tried to force its settlers in America to farm the land? (Students might suggest the government wanted to be able to keep rival European nations from intruding on its claims. If settlers stayed in one place and farmed, it would be easier for them to claim and hold the land.)

Teaching the

Point out that *Cimarrons* comes from the Spanish word *cimarrones*, meaning "cattle that run wild." Ask why the Spaniards might have used this term. (It reflects the fact that the Africans had escaped from plantations and that the Spaniards treated them like animals.) Ask why the Cimarrons helped the English. (To get revenge against the Spaniards who had enslaved them.) Point out that by the 1600s the Spaniards had succeeded in reducing the Cimarrons' numbers and wearing down their resistance.

Communicating Nonverbally

To underscore the difficulty of communicating across language barriers, have small groups invent hand signals that Europeans and Indians might have used with each other. Each group should select three or four messages they think would have been most important to communicate and then develop hand signals for each. Conclude by having groups demonstrate their signals for other groups to interpret.

Vital Links

Spanish Armada (Picture)
Unit 1, Side 1, Search
24456

See also Unit 1 Explore
CD-ROM location 218.

✠ **Connections to Literature**

The legend of the courtly Sir Walter Raleigh spreading his cloak over a puddle so Queen Elizabeth could cross with dry shoes is mentioned in Sir Walter Scott's novel *Kenilworth*. Raleigh himself was a poet and prose writer. Only a few of his works have survived because he circulated his poems in manuscript and did not publish them. His prose works include a sea battle narrative.

This portrait of Queen Elizabeth I celebrates the defeat of the Spanish Armada. Her hand rests atop the globe, a sign of English power. In one picture on the wall behind her, wind fills the sails of the English fleet. In the other, a storm dashes the Armada against the rocks. The war between Spain and England dragged on, however, ending officially in 1604, a year after Elizabeth's death.

Cannonballs flew as the Armada and the English fleet, led by Drake, blasted away in the waters between England and France. On the night of August 7 the English filled eight ships with gunpowder, set them afire, and launched them toward the Armada. Expecting explosions, the Armada scattered northward. Then on August 13, a mighty storm arose. It battered what remained of the Spanish fleet. Fewer than half the ships ever returned to Spain.

The defeat of the Armada marked a turning point in history. Spain had been the greatest power in Europe for nearly a century. Now, Spain declined. In the future England would control the seas and create an empire that stretched around the globe.

England's first attempts At first England's path to empire was rocky. Sir Humphrey Gilbert tried to plant a colony in Newfoundland in 1583, but he and his colonists lost their lives in a storm at sea.

Gilbert's brother, Sir Walter Raleigh, chose a site further south, on Roanoke Island off the coast of present-day North Carolina. He named his colony Virginia in honor of

Elizabeth, who was called the Virgin Queen. Unfortunately, the settlers were more interested in gold than crops. Sir Francis Drake rescued the hungry survivors in 1586.

The next year Raleigh tried again, sending settlers under the command of John White. White returned to England for supplies, leaving behind 117 settlers, including his daughter and her family.

White could not get back to Roanoke until 1590. When he arrived, all he found was an empty fort, a few tattered books, and pieces of rusty armor. On a doorpost were carved the letters C R O A T O A N. White guessed that the colonists had taken refuge with friendly Indians on nearby Croatan Island, but he never found them.

Future colonies Although the earliest English colonies failed, there were lessons to be learned from the effort. Gilbert and Raleigh had put up their own money. Now others could see that keeping a colony going might be too big an undertaking for any one man and his wallet.

People in England, however, kept dreaming of colonies in the Americas. In an

History Footnote

Queen Elizabeth I ruled England between 1558 and 1603. Her reign saw many accomplishments. Despite strife at home, she helped launch the English exploration and eventual settlement of the Americas as well as the defeat of the Spanish Armada. At home she was occupied by religious strife between Catholics and Protestants. She signed laws called the Religious Settlement of 1559 that reestablished the Church of England, founded by her father, Henry VIII. These laws enforced the use of a state-approved prayer book. The church remains the official church of Great Britain today, and the monarch is the titular head of the church.

English play written in 1605, a sea captain described the Americas of his dreams:

“Gold is more plentiful there than copper is with us. Why, Man, all their dripping pans are pure gold, and all the chains . . . are massive gold. For rubies and diamonds, they gather them by the seashore to hang on their children's coats.”

Richard Hakluyt, a minister, had another dream. English colonies, he wrote, "may stay [stop] the Spanish king . . . from flowing over all the face of . . . America."

Why We Remember

The Conquest of the Americas

Bartolomé de Las Casas returned to Spain at the age of 72. He spent his remaining 20 years writing. He filled one work, *A Very Brief Report of the Destruction of the Indies*, with sickening descriptions of cruel treatment of Indians. Las Casas may have exaggerated the number of Indians who perished as a result of the conquest. Still, no one could deny that for many native peoples, the arrival of Europeans was a disaster beyond measure. That fact alone would be reason enough to remember the conquest of the Americas.

There are other reasons why we remember this period, however. It was a time of great adventures and extraordinary accomplishments. Even today, the stories of men like Cortés, Pizarro, Cabeza de Vaca, Drake, and Champlain have the power to surprise, amaze, astonish, and appall us.

Perhaps most important, we remember the period as a time of endings and beginnings. While the old civilizations of the Americas were being destroyed, new ones were being born. From these painful beginnings would come the new peoples and nations of North and South America.

3. Section Review

1. Define **persecution** and **league**.
2. Explain two ways the Reformation spurred colony-building in the Americas.
3. Why was New France so sparsely settled?
4. What was the chief interest of the Netherlands in North America?
5. Give two reasons why England's first colonies failed.
6. **Critical Thinking** Compare the relationship between Indians and the French with the relationship between Indians and the Spanish.

Closing the Section

Wrap-Up Activity

Identifying European Claims

To review which areas in the present-day United States were claimed by the French, Dutch, and English, have students color and label an outline map (see **Geography Extensions**). Have them refer to the map and the descriptions in this section, as well as to the maps on pages R4–R7.

Section Review
Answers

1. Definitions: *persecution* (108), *league* (110)
2. Rival nations saw chances to spread their religions, and people who suffered religious persecution saw means of escape.
3. The French were more interested in trading, farmers found the territory inhospitable, and the people willing to come were barred by the king.
4. Trade.
5. They lacked backing, and settlers were more interested in finding gold than in raising crops.
6. The French were on friendly terms with the Indians they traded with, while the Spaniards forced Indians to work their plantations and mines.

To check understanding of "Why We Remember," assign Thinking Critically question 3 on student page 114.

Survey Answers

Reviewing Vocabulary

Definitions are found on these pages: *conquistadors* (94), *mercantilism* (102), *persecution* (108), *league* (110).

Reviewing Main Ideas

1. Guns and swords, horses, Indian allies, and smallpox.

2. Gold and silver mines.

3. The entradas did not produce gold or other treasure. They did produce information about the borderlands and helped Spain claim a vast empire.

4. Missionaries wanted to convert Indians and teach them the Spanish way of life. Some Indians adopted Christianity, some resisted, and others practiced both Christianity and traditional religions. Missionaries' actions often had the effect of enslaving Indians, uprooting them, and destroying their cultures.

5. Spain did little to settle the borderlands until rivals began to show interest. Examples include the French presence in Florida that resulted in founding of St. Augustine, Drake's voyage that resulted in settlements in Arizona and New Mexico, French presence in Texas that led to founding of San Antonio, and concerns about Russians that led to missions and presidios in California.

6. The French and the Dutch had good relations with some groups of Indians because the Europeans wanted to trade.

7. They learned that setting up and maintaining a colony was too large an undertaking for one person.

Thinking Critically

1. Montesinos believed Indians were human beings and should not be enslaved
(Answers continued in top margin)

114

---

or treated cruelly. Sepúlveda believed the Indians deserved to be conquered because they were uncivilized and sinful. Las Casas believed the Spanish should care for the Indians. Students might say that it would be hard to convince Sepúlveda because he truly believed his ideas; others might say he could be convinced if he could be shown that Indians were worthy human beings and that the Spaniards were treating them cruelly.

2. Letters should note Spain's great wealth as a result of its American colonies and try to convince the queen to set up colonies in North America so that England could gain wealth and prestige. The letter might also be written from the viewpoint of a spy assessing Spain's strengths and weaknesses.

3. Students may choose Peru, Mexico, Canada, or the United States. Answers would

---

Chapter Survey ★

Reviewing Vocabulary

Define the following terms.
1. conquistadors   3. persecution
2. mercantilism   4. league

Reviewing Main Ideas

1. What advantages enabled the Spanish to conquer the Aztecs?
2. What did the Spanish find in Mexico and South America that produced the greatest wealth for them?
3. In what ways were the Spanish entradas into lands north of Mexico both a failure and a success?
4. What did the Spanish missionaries want to accomplish? Describe three effects their actions had on Indians.
5. Explain the following statement: Without meaning to, Spain's rivals encouraged Spain to settle the borderlands. Give two supporting examples.
6. What kinds of relationships did the French and the Dutch establish with Indians? Why?
7. What lesson did the English learn from the failures of their first American colonies?

Thinking Critically

1. **Analysis** Reread the statements by Antonio de Montesinos, Juan Ginés de Sepúlveda, and Bartolomé de Las Casas. Based on those statements, list the basic beliefs of each man. Could Montesinos or Las Casas have persuaded Sepúlveda to change his mind? Why or why not?
2. **Synthesis** Imagine that you are one of Queen Elizabeth's advisors and are on a trip to Spain. Write a letter to the queen telling her what you see in Spain and why it makes you think that England should rush to establish colonies in North America.

3. Why We Remember: Application
Imagine a television series called *A Very Brief Report on the Creation of the Americas*. Each program will feature one present-day country. The program will be divided into three parts: (1) the old ways of life, (2) people who made a difference, (3) the new way of life. Choose one country. List two or three topics you would include in each part of a program about that country.

Applying Skills

Analyzing a Painting Read the Section Focus and Reading Guide questions on page 120. Choose a painting in that section to analyze. Answer numbers 1–3 without looking at the caption. Then read the caption and answer number 4. Keep in mind what you learned in the Skill Lab on page 107.

1. Identify the main image in the painting, if any. Identify as many smaller details as you can.
2. Describe the painting's mood. How does the artist create that mood?
3. Summarize the story that the painting tells. What do you think was the artist's purpose?
4. What similarities and differences do you find between what you have written and what the caption says?

History Mystery

Analyzing forces of destruction Answer the History Mystery on page 91. In what ways could a widespread epidemic affect a large city today? How might such an event disrupt peoples' lives? How might it affect peoples' states of mind? How would people react?

provide information about Indian ways of life before and after the arrival of Europeans, name individuals or groups who brought change, and discuss the new way of life established by colonists. Some topics might be religious traditions, music, food, clothing, and ethnic diversity.

Applying Skills

Answers depend on the paintings chosen.

For the Jamestown painting on page 123, for example, answers might be:

1. Settlers working is the main action. Ships in the background and specific activities are details.

2. Answers may vary. Students may detect a positive mood, reflecting progress in setting up a colony.

3. It portrays the building of Jamestown, *(Answers continued in side margin)*

the first permanent English colony.

4. Similarities and differences depend on students' comments.

History Mystery

The Spanish conquered the Aztecs easily because they had firearms, horses, and Indian allies, and were also aided by the smallpox epidemic. An epidemic could panic people, resulting in quarantines and disruption of daily life. Some types of disruption might be the burden on health services, the closing of libraries, and people's increased suspicion of each other.

Writing in Your History Journal

1. (a) Explanations should be similar to the time line notes on teacher pages 90–91. (b) Facts should reflect chapter information.

2. Entries should reflect chapter information and understanding of Las Casas's moral dilemma.

3. Reforms were not in their economic interests, they saw Indians as inferior, and the king could not directly control their actions.

Reviewing Geography

1. (A) New France, (B) New Netherland, (C) Viceroyalty of Peru, (D) Viceroyalty of New Spain.

2. Accept any reasonable entries. Many places in western and southwestern United States have Spanish names. French names are likely to be found in the Great Lakes and Mississippi River areas.

Alternative Assessment

Teacher's Take-Home Planner 2, p. 5, includes suggestions and scoring rubrics for the Alternative Assessment activity.

Reviewing Geography

1. The letters on the map represent European possessions in the Americas in 1650. Write the name of each possession.

2. **Geographic Thinking** Many places in the United States have Spanish or French names. List five or more places with Spanish names and five or more with French names. Use the maps on pages R4–R5 and R6–R7, an atlas, or a dictionary for help, if you need it. What patterns, if any, do you see in the locations of the names? What other evidence of Spanish or French influence might you expect to find in a place with a Spanish or French name?

Writing in Your History Journal

1. **Keys to History** (a) The time line on pages 90–91 has seven Keys to History. In your journal, describe why each one is important. (b) Choose one of the events on the time line, and imagine yourself as a news reporter on the scene. Write a list of 10 facts you plan to include in your news story.

2. **Bartolomé de Las Casas** As Las Casas, write a diary entry expressing your thoughts at the moment you decided to give up using the forced labor of Indian workers on your land.

3. **Citizenship** You have read that King Charles of Spain reformed the encomienda system to limit the colonists' rights to Indian labor. Without knowing the details of his reforms, why do you suppose the colonists paid so little attention to them? Write your response in your journal.

Alternative Assessment

Recalling a life With classmates, prepare slips of paper each with the name of one person from the chapter on it, for example, Cortés, Moctezuma, Cabeza de Vaca, de Soto, Popé, and Queen Elizabeth. Put the slips in a bag and take turns drawing out one name apiece.

Imagine that you are the person whose name you have drawn. Prepare a presentation that answers these questions: What did you do with your life? Why? How did you serve your people? What are you proud of? How do you answer your critics? The presentation may include acting out, speech, and visual aids.

Your work will be evaluated on the following criteria:

• you present the person's life accurately

• you present the person's point of view

• you make the person seem real

5 Planting English Colonies
1600–1750

Chapter Planning Guide

Section	Student Text	Teacher's Edition Activities
Opener and Story pp. 116–119	**Keys to History Time Line** **History Mystery** Beginning the Story with **Pocahontas**	**Setting the Stage Activity** Reacting to Strangers, p. 118
1 **The First English Colonies** pp. 120–127	**Reading Maps** Jamestown and Plymouth 1620, p. 122 **Link to the Present** Lost settlement found, p. 124 **Geography Lab** The Coastal Lowlands, p. 127	**Warm-Up Activity** Listing Reasons for Colonization, p. 120 **Geography Question of the Day,** p. 120 **Section Activity** Creating Colonial Laws, p. 125 **Bonus Activity** Writing an Indentured Servant Contract, p. 124 **Wrap-Up Activity** Comparing Colonies, p. 126
2 **Puritan Colonies in New England** pp. 128–132	**Point of View** Are there limits to liberty?, p. 130 **Reading Maps** New England 1660, p. 131	**Warm-Up Activity** A Puritan View of Settlement, p. 128 **Geography Question of the Day,** p. 128 **Section Activity** Deciding Whether to Emigrate, p. 129 **Bonus Activity** Williams Defending Himself, p. 130 **Wrap-Up Activity** An Indian Protest Letter, p. 132
3 **Later English Colonies** pp. 133–139	**World Link** Huguenots flee France, p. 134 **Reading Maps** The Thirteen Colonies 1760, p. 135 **Hands-On History** Advertising the colonies, p. 136 **Link to Art** *The Peaceable Kingdom,* p. 137 **Skill Lab** Analyzing Statistical Tables, p. 139	**Warm-Up Activity** Preparing a Time Line, p. 133 **Geography Question of the Day,** p. 133 **Section Activity** A Colonial Documentary, p. 134 **Bonus Activity** "Best" and "Worst" Colonies, p. 136 **Wrap-Up Activity** Writing Editorials, p. 138
Evaluation	☑ **Section 1 Review,** p. 126 ☑ **Section 2 Review,** p. 132 ☑ **Section 3 Review,** p. 138 ☑ **Chapter Survey,** pp. 140–141 **Alternative Assessment** Planning a colony, p. 141	☑ **Answers to Section 1 Review,** p. 126 ☑ **Answers to Section 2 Review,** p. 132 ☑ **Answers to Section 3 Review,** p. 138 ☑ **Answers to Chapter Survey,** pp. 140–141 (Alternative Assessment guidelines are in the Take-Home Planner.)

Teacher's Resource Package

Chapter Summaries: English and Spanish, pp. 14–15

Chapter Resources Binder
Study Guide Previewing Headings, p. 33
Geography Extensions The Coastal Lowlands, pp. 9–10
American Readings Starving Time in Virginia, p. 17; The Mayflower Compact, p. 18

Chapter Resources Binder
Study Guide Locating Supporting Information, p. 34
Reinforcement Identifying People, pp. 37–38
American Readings "A Blessed Memory," p. 19
Using Historical Documents The Fundamental Orders of Connecticut, pp. 27–31

Chapter Resources Binder
Study Guide Reading for Details, p. 35
Skills Development Analyzing Statistical Tables, pp. 39–40
American Readings Becoming an Indentured Servant, p. 20

Chapter and Unit Tests Chapter 5 Tests, Forms A and B, pp. 29–32

Take-Home Planner

Introducing the Chapter Activity
Housing in a New Land, p. 12

Chapter In-Depth Activity Making a Colonial Scene, p. 13

Reduced Views
Study Guide, p. 14
Geography Extensions, p. 17
American Readings, p. 16
Unit 2 Answers, pp. 27–32

Reduced Views
Study Guide, p. 14
Reinforcement, p. 15
American Readings, p. 16
Using Historical Documents, p. 17
Unit 2 Answers, pp. 27–32

Reduced Views
Study Guide, p. 14
Skills Development, p. 15
American Readings, p. 16
Unit 2 Answers, pp. 27–32

Reduced Views
Chapter Tests, p. 17
Unit 2 Answers, pp. 27–32
Alternative Assessment Guidelines for scoring the Chapter Survey activity, p. 13

Additional Resources

Wall Time Line

Unit 2 Activity

Transparency Package

Transparency 5-1 Jamestown—use with Section 1
Transparency 5-2 Jamestown and Plymouth—use with Section 1
Transparency Activity Book

SelecTest Testing Software

Chapter 5 Test, Forms A and B

Vital Links

 Videodisc

CD-ROM

Jamestown (see TE p. 122)

Early home life at Jamestown (see TE p. 123)

Early punishment in stockades (see TE p. 130)

William Penn and Delaware Indians (see TE p. 136)

5

Teaching Resources

Take-Home Planner 2
  Introducing Chapter Activity
  Chapter In-Depth Activity
  Alternative Assessment
Chapter Resources Binder
Geography Extensions
American Readings
Using Historical Documents
Transparency Activities
Wall Time Line Activities
Chapter Summaries
Chapter and Unit Tests
SelecTest Test File
Vital Links CD-ROM/Videodisc

Time Line

Keys to History

Keys to History journal writing activities are on page 140 in the Chapter Survey.

Jamestown The Jamestown settlers established the first permanent English colony in America. (p. 122)

House of Burgesses The Virginia House of Burgesses was the first elected legislature in the English colonies. (p. 124)

Anne Hutchinson For openly disagreeing with the teachings of Puritan leaders, Hutchinson was forced to leave Massachusetts. (p. 130)

Looking Back With the disappearance of the Roanoke settlers, the first attempts of the British to colonize North America failed.

Chapter Overview

In England, an economic revolution resulted in farmers losing their land at the same time that many people were seeking religious freedom. English settlers hoped to find relief in North America. The first permanent English settlement was Jamestown in Virginia. Here the first colonial legislature met in 1619. Puritans founded Plymouth. In the Mayflower Compact, they agreed to obey all laws passed

---

1600–1750

Chapter 5

Planting English Colonies

Sections

Beginning the Story with Pocahontas

1. **The First English Colonies**
2. **Puritan Colonies in New England**
3. **Later English Colonies**

Keys to History

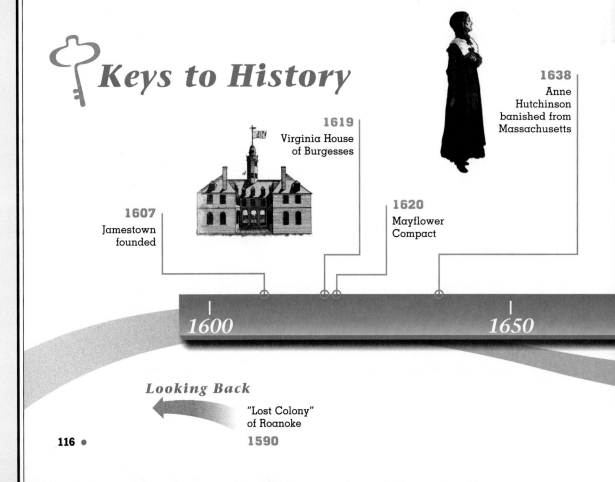

1607
Jamestown founded

1619
Virginia House of Burgesses

1620
Mayflower Compact

1638
Anne Hutchinson banished from Massachusetts

1600

1650

Looking Back
"Lost Colony" of Roanoke
1590

by the community. Plymouth later became part of Massachusetts.

The Puritans forced people who disagreed with their religious teachings to leave Massachusetts. As a result, Rhode Island and Connecticut were founded. Colonists looking for farmland settled New Hampshire and Maine. The longest and most devastating land conflict between settlers and Indians was King Philip's War.

By the 1630s, proprietors like the Calverts of Maryland were setting up colonies. Carolina was divided, with South Carolina beginning to thrive by growing rice. The English divided New Netherland into four colonies, including New York and New Jersey. William Penn colonized Pennsylvania as a religious refuge. Delaware separated from Pennsylvania in 1776. Georgia was the last English colony in North America.

Teaching the HISTORY Mystery

Students will find the solution on p. 126. See Chapter Survey, p. 140, for additional questions.

Time Line

King Philip's War Chief Metacomet led the Wampanoags in the most serious conflict between Indians and colonists. (p. 132)

Pennsylvania William Penn founded his colony as a refuge for Quakers and others persecuted for their religious beliefs. (p. 136)

Georgia James Oglethorpe founded the last English colony as a haven for debtors and as a buffer against Spanish Florida. (p. 137)

World Link See p. 134.

Looking Ahead After Spain ceded Florida to the United States, the United States held all land east of the Mississippi River.

HISTORY Mystery

After a terrible first winter at Plymouth, the Pilgrims were rescued by an English-speaking Indian. Where had the Indian come from, and how had he learned English?

1675

King Philip's War

Chief Metacomet, known as King Philip

1681

Penn plans "holy experiment" in Pennsylvania

Plate showing German settlers

1732

Georgia, the last English colony

James Oglethorpe, founder of Georgia

1700

1750

World Link

Huguenots flee France

1685

Looking Ahead

Spain gives up Florida

1819

• **117**

Beginning the Story

Pocahontas

Pocahontas was largely responsible for Jamestown's survival. She saved John Smith's life and brought colonists food. When relations between Indians and settlers deteriorated, the settlers kidnapped Pocahontas. In Jamestown, she learned about the English culture. Her marriage to colonist John Rolfe resulted in an uneasy peace between the Indians and colonists for several years.

Setting the Stage
Activity

Reacting to Strangers

To help students identify with the situation Pocahontas and her people faced, have them write about how they would react to the arrival of strangers. Divide the class into small groups and have them imagine that a gang from out of town is trying to take control of a local park. Ask them to discuss how they would react to these strangers and what the community should do. Each group should summarize their discussion in a short paragraph.

See the Introducing the Chapter Activity, Housing in a New Land. **Take-Home Planner 2,** p. 12.

✳ **History Footnote**

Pocahontas was the daughter of the leader of the Powhatan Confederacy. The confederacy was formed by her grandfather, an Algonkin chief, who migrated to the Virginia area in the 1500s. Her grandfather conquered five tribes and with his tribe organized them into the confederacy. Her father, Wahunsenacawh, took the name Powhatan after becoming the confederacy's leader. He expanded the confederacy to include about 24 additional tribes. By the early 1600s the small but powerful confederacy was made up of about 9,000 people. They lived in an area that extended from the Great Dismal Swamp in the south to the Potomac River in the north.

Beginning the Story with

Pocahontas

For two bitterly cold weeks Captain John Smith had been led from one Indian town to another. In late December 1607, the English captive was finally brought to the village of Powhatan, the powerful chief of the Indians in Virginia. As Smith entered Powhatan's longhouse, he was greeted by a shout—a salute to him as a chief of the recently arrived English colonists.

In the dim light of the longhouse, Smith saw rows of men and women "with their heads and shoulders painted red." He also saw Powhatan, a tall, impressive man draped in a fur robe. He did not notice a 12-year-old girl standing in the shadows. Her name was Pocahontas. Smith would soon owe her his life.

Helping the English Strangers

Pocahontas listened as her father, Powhatan, and his council debated the stranger's fate. Then she heard the decision: The white chief must die.

Warriors grabbed Smith, pushed his head down on a stone, and raised their clubs to strike him dead. At that instant Pocahontas darted forward and begged her father to have mercy. Smith later wrote that she "got [my] head in her arms, and laid her own upon [mine] to save [me] from death." A few days later, Smith was safely back in the English settlement of Jamestown.

To save Smith, Pocahontas had followed a custom of her people and adopted him as her brother. She may have rescued Smith out of curiosity, or perhaps she acted out of sympathy. Smith himself wrote that her "compassionate, pitiful heart . . . gave me much cause to respect her."

Adopting Smith was, for Pocahontas, a serious commitment. That winter the settlers would have starved had she not helped them. "Every once in four or five days, Pocahontas with her attendants brought . . . provision [food]," wrote Smith. "She, next under God, was . . . the instrument to preserve this colony from death, famine, and utter confusion."

History Bookshelf

Smith, Carter, ed. *The Explorers and Settlers: A Sourcebook on Colonial America*. The Millbrook Press, 1991. This overview of European exploration and colonization of North America is richly illustrated with period maps and drawings. The text offers background from the first European landings and explorations to the westward movement of the colonies. Time frames juxtapose world and colonial events.

Also of interest:

Bowen, Gary. *Stranded at Plimouth Plantation*. HarperCollins, 1994.

Fritz, Jean. *The Double Life of Pocahontas*. Putnam, 1983.

IlgenFritz, Elizabeth. *Anne Hutchinson*. Chelsea House, 1991.

From Pocahontas to Rebecca

Smith returned to England in 1609. After that, relations between Indians and the colonists began to grow tense. Fearing war, the English kidnapped Pocahontas in 1613 and held her hostage in Jamestown to prevent an attack on the settlement.

Unlike her friends and relatives who mistrusted the English, Pocahontas was fascinated by the strangers from across the sea. She took advantage of her time in Jamestown to learn the language and customs of the colonists. The settlers were especially pleased by her interest in their religion. They believed it their duty to bring the Christian faith to American Indians.

At least one colonist found the Indian hostage equally fascinating. That summer John Rolfe fell in love with Pocahontas. In a letter to the colony's governor, Thomas Dale, Rolfe asked for permission to marry her. He said he was making this request

This detail from a map of Virginia prepared by John Smith shows Powhatan and his council deciding Smith's fate.

"for the good of this plantation [Jamestown], for the honor of our country, for the glory of God, . . . and for the converting to the true knowledge of God and Jesus Christ [of] an unbelieving creature, namely Pocahontas, to whom my hearty and best thoughts are, and have [for] a long time been, so entangled."

How did Pocahontas feel about this marriage? She may have fallen in love with Rolfe. Certainly she impressed him with "her great appearance of love to me." She may also have hoped that their marriage would bring peace between the colonists and her people. It was probably for that reason that both Governor Dale and Powhatan approved the match.

Pocahontas completed her instruction in the Christian religion and was baptized as Rebecca. Within a year she and Rolfe were wed. For the next few years, colonists and Indians lived together without conflict, protected by Rebecca and John Rolfe's "married peace."

Hands-On HISTORY

Activity

In his *Generall Historie of Virginia*, John Smith wrote about his rescue by Pocahontas, but we have no account of this event from her point of view. Write the story of her decision to save the white chief as you think she might have told it.

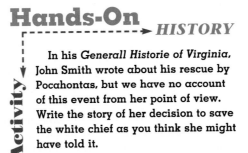

See the Chapter In-Depth Activity, Making a Colonial Scene. **Take-Home Planner 2,** p. 13.

Discussion

Thinking Historically

1. Why did Smith respect Pocahontas? (She showed him and the other colonists compassion.)

2. Do you think Pocahontas was brave for trying to save Smith? (Some students may believe she was brave to disagree with her father and the council. Others may believe that because her father was chief, she knew no harm would come to her for intervening on Smith's behalf.)

3. Why do you think Powhatan agreed to let Pocahontas marry Rolfe? (Students may suggest that he permitted the marriage to ensure peace, that Pocahontas convinced him that this is what she wanted, or that he saw Pocahontas serving as a go-between.)

Teaching the Hands-On

HISTORY

Remind students that Pocahontas was only 12 years old when she saved Smith. Suggest that they write their story as a diary entry a young girl might make. Their stories should reflect Pocahontas's feelings about the event.

For a journal writing activity on Pocahontas, see student page 141.

Vocabulary

invest (p. 120) to use your money to help a business get started or grow

joint-stock company (p. 122) a business that raised money by selling shares, called stock

exports (p. 123) goods sent out of one country to sell in another

indentured servants (p. 124) people who signed a contract agreeing to work four to seven years without pay for the person who paid their passage

representatives (p. 124) people who are chosen to speak and act in government for their fellow citizens

legislature (p. 124) a group of people chosen to make laws

royal colony (p. 125) colony in which the monarch appointed governor and advisors

Section Objectives

★ Explain why the English wanted to set up colonies.

★ Describe the changes in the Virginia Colony between 1607 and 1624.

★ Identify the Plymouth Colony's goals and the colonists' methods of achieving them.

Teaching Resources

Take-Home Planner 2, pp. 10–17

Chapter Resources Binder

Study Guide, p. 33

Reinforcement

Skills Development

Geography Extensions, pp. 9–10

American Readings, pp. 17–18

Using Historical Documents

Transparency Activities

Chapter and Unit Tests

Warm-Up
Activity

Listing Reasons for Colonization

Have small groups list two or three reasons to colonize. They can later compare their reasons with those noted in the text.

Geography Question of the Day

Have students study the maps on pages 122 and R6–R7 to identify present-day states where tribes and colonies were located, and which tribes lived in what is now Canada.

1. The First English Colonies

Reading Guide

New Terms **invest, joint-stock company, exports, indentured servants, representatives, legislature, royal colony**

Section Focus **England's colonies in Virginia and Plymouth**

1. Why did the English want to establish colonies in America?
2. How did Virginia change between 1607 and 1624?
3. What goal did Plymouth colonists have, and how did they reach it?

The dramatic story of Pocahontas, the young Indian woman who saved John Smith and married John Rolfe, took place in Virginia, the first permanent English colony in North America. Between 1607 and 1732, England was to start 13 colonies along the Atlantic coast.

What caused this great interest in colonies? Why did the English government encourage it? The answers to these questions are found in two great changes that were taking place in England. One change was economic, the other was religious.

An Economic Revolution

The changes in England's economy have been called an economic revolution. As a result of the revolution, some people gained great wealth, while others were plunged into poverty. To both the wealthy and the poor, colonies in America offered opportunity and hope.

Strange as it may seem, the revolution began with sheep. In the 1500s the demand for woolen cloth in Europe suddenly soared. To meet the demand, English landowners enclosed their farms, fencing off large areas as grazing lands for sheep. Manufacturers, in turn, spun and wove the wool into cloth, which merchants sold throughout Europe.

This trade brought great wealth to landowners, wool manufacturers, and merchants. Many of them began looking for ways to invest their new wealth. To **invest** means to use your money to help a business get started or grow, with the hope that you will earn a profit. As you will see, colonies began to look like a good investment.

The uprooted While the wool trade brought wealth to some, it caused great hardship for countless English families. For generations, farmers had rented small plots from large landowners. When landowners enclosed their fields to raise sheep, these farmers lost their farms—and their jobs.

Uprooted men, women, and children drifted from countryside to town to city, looking for work. Many were reduced to begging or stealing to survive. Is it any wonder that many of these desperate people would risk the long voyage to North America in the hope of a fresh start in colonies?

English leaders, too, saw colonies as a way to solve the problem of the growing numbers of the poor. Worried by the "swarms of idle persons," one observer noted:

"If we seek not some ways for their foreign employment, we must provide shortly more prisons and corrections for their bad conditions."

The men shown in the illustration below were the group of Catholics who plotted to blow up the Parliament building on November 5, 1605. On that day, King James I, the queen, and their oldest son would be present in Parliament. Led by Robert Catesby, the conspirators enlisted the help of Guy Fawkes, a military expert. The conspirators not only wanted revenge but also hoped that the confusion caused by the bombing would lead to a Catholic takeover of the government. After English leaders learned of the plot, they discovered Fawkes and kegs of gunpowder in the Parliament's basement. Today the English celebrate November 5 as Guy Fawkes Day, a day of thanksgiving that the plot was foiled.

This idea of sending "idle persons" to colonies fit well with the government's policy of mercantilism. England wanted to sell more to other countries than it bought. In colonies, England's poor could produce raw materials, such as lumber, that England would otherwise have to buy from foreign nations. At the same time, the colonists would buy England's manufactured goods, thus adding to the nation's wealth.

Religious Conflict

Meanwhile, conflict over religion was causing others in England to think of starting colonies. In the mid-1500s England had broken away from the Roman Catholic Church and established the Church of England. By law, all English people had to worship in this new Protestant church.

Not everyone accepted the Church of England, though. On the one hand, many English Catholics wanted to keep their old religion. Some English Protestants, on the other hand, thought the Church of England was too much like the Catholic Church. These people were called Puritans because they believed in simpler, "purer" forms of worship.

The government of England tried to force both Catholics and Puritans to accept the Church of England. According to William Bradford, who later became governor of Plymouth Colony,

❝Some [Puritans] were taken and clapped up in prison, others had their houses . . . watched night and day, and hardly escaped.❞

Both Catholics and Protestants began to think of colonies in North America as a place where they might practice their religion without interference. Thus, conflict over religion, as well as new wealth and desperate poverty, pushed England into an era of colonization.

Despite the ban on the Roman Catholic Church, many English Catholics practiced their faith in secret. Angered by anti-Catholic laws, this group of men plotted against government leaders in 1605.

Developing the Section

Discussion

Checking Understanding

1. How did the economic revolution in England help lead to colonization? (To meet increased demand for wool, landowners began enclosing their land to raise sheep rather than rent land to farmers. Colonies provided an opportunity for the uprooted farmers.)

2. How did religious conflict affect colonization? (Because the Church of England was the only state-sanctioned church, Puritans and Catholics chose to colonize so that they could practice their own religions freely.)

Stimulating Critical Thinking

3. Given the earlier experiences of the Spanish, French, and Dutch, would you have been willing to invest in colonies in the early 1600s? (Students may note that investing in a colony was risky, but it also provided an opportunity for great wealth.)

See the Study Guide activity in **Chapter Resources Binder**, p. 33.

Teaching the
↑ Reading Maps

Have students examine the map to identify the major information it provides. (The extent of English land grants; the locations of Jamestown, Virginia, Plymouth, and New England; and the locations of Indian tribes.)
Answer to Reading Maps:
The Powhatans lived in the area near Jamestown.

For John Smith's description of the "starving time" in Jamestown, see *American Readings*, p. 17.

✠ Connections to Science

The mosquitoes at Jamestown were *Anopheles* mosquitoes that carried the parasites *Plasmodia*. *Plasmodia* can cause malaria in humans. The parasites enter the human blood when a mosquito bites a person. In the human body, the *Plasmodia* multiply and cause cells to burst. The bursting of cells results in such typical symptoms as intermittent attacks of chills and fevers. The most serious form of malaria weakens the infected person after each attack. If untreated, as at Jamestown, the disease can lead to death. Malaria was just one of the causes of the high death rate among Jamestown settlers.

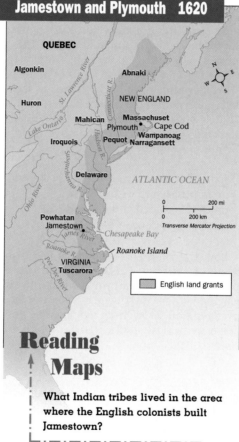

Jamestown and Plymouth 1620

QUEBEC
Algonkin
Abnaki
Huron
NEW ENGLAND
Mahican
Massachuset
Plymouth • Cape Cod
Iroquois
Wampanoag
Pequot Narragansett
Delaware
ATLANTIC OCEAN
0 _____ 200 mi
0 _____ 200 km
Transverse Mercator Projection
Powhatan
Jamestown •
James River Chesapeake Bay
Roanoke R.
Roanoke Island
VIRGINIA
Tuscarora
Pee Dee River

☐ English land grants

Reading
↑ Maps

What Indian tribes lived in the area where the English colonists built Jamestown?

Virginia, the First Colony

Merchants founded the first permanent English colony in Virginia. They hoped to find precious metals and other raw materials that England needed.

Establishing a colony was expensive and risky. Thus, the merchants organized the Virginia Company of London. It was a **joint-stock company**—a business that raised money by selling shares, called stock, to investors. The profits were to be divided among the investors according to the number of shares each had.

In a document called a charter, the king, James I, granted the Virginia Company the right to "plant," or establish, colonies in Virginia. Investors eagerly bought stock. As a result, the company was able to buy the ships and supplies it needed to launch a colony.

Building Jamestown In the spring of 1607, 105 men and boys sailed up a broad river in Chesapeake Bay. They named the river the James and their settlement Jamestown in honor of their king.

From the first, Jamestown was in trouble. Ignoring orders from the Virginia Company, the leaders located their settlement on low, swampy ground. The only drinking water was salty, and the area swarmed with mosquitoes. Disease spread rapidly.

Then, instead of planting crops, the colonists rushed off to search for gold. As Captain John Smith later wrote:

❝There was no talk, no hope, no work, but dig gold, wash gold, refine gold, load gold.❞

Too late did they learn that their gold was really fool's gold.

Hard times During the first 7 months in Jamestown, 73 colonists died of hunger and disease. The rest owed their lives to the inspired leadership of John Smith and to the friendship of Pocahontas.

After Smith took control of the colony in 1608, he forced the settlers to plant crops. He declared, "He that will not work, shall not eat." More supplies also arrived from England. So did more colonists.

A year later, Smith was burned in a gunpowder explosion and returned to England. Without him, the colony fell into disorder. As supplies ran out, people ate rats to stay alive. The winter of 1609–1610 became known as the "starving time." When spring came, only 60 of 500 colonists were still alive.

Tobacco cultivation became the mainstay of settlements in Virginia. Before long, the colonists were exporting vast quantities of tobacco to England. By 1618, they exported almost 50,000 pounds (22,680 kg). As Virginians grew more and more tobacco, they neglected to grow enough crops to feed themselves. The Virginia Company provided food supplies to the colonists in return for controlling the tobacco trade. Despite the high demand for tobacco, King James I of England hated the product. He noted that "Smoking is a custom loathsome to the eye, hateful to the nose, harmful to the brain, dangerous to the lungs." He even encouraged Parliament to ban the import of tobacco in 1621, but the members were persuaded by the Virginia Company not to do so.

Changes in Virginia

Hope for survival of the colony came from tobacco, an American "weed" that had become very popular in Europe. The soil of Virginia was ideal for growing tobacco, and in 1612 John Rolfe, husband of Pocahontas, developed a method of drying it for shipment to England.

Tobacco exports soared. **Exports** are goods sent out of one country to sell in another. The Virginia Company was pleased by the new tobacco trade. However, life in Jamestown was very hard, and few English people wanted to live there.

To stir up interest in Virginia, in 1616 the company brought Pocahontas and John Rolfe to England. Everywhere Pocahontas went, she caused a sensation. Merchants, church leaders, and even the king and queen were eager to meet her.

To attract more settlers, the Virginia Company also made several important changes in the colony. First, in 1618 the company gave colonists the right to own land. Until then, the company had owned all land in Virginia. Now people who paid their own way to the colony were granted 50 acres. They received another 50 acres for each new settler they brought with them.

Indentured servants To encourage settlers who could not afford to pay their own way to Virginia, the company allowed

Discussion

Checking Understanding

1. **Why did Smith set up a work law?** (The settlers were more interested in quick riches than in survival. Smith realized the settlers needed to meet their basic needs so that they could survive.)

2. **Why did the Virginia Company eventually allow colonists to own land?** (Because life was not easy in the colony, few people wanted to live there. The company hoped to attract settlers by giving them land.)

Stimulating Critical Thinking

3. **If you had lived in England in 1618, would the Virginia Company's offer of land convince you to go to Virginia? Why or why not?** (Students may suggest they would go if they were unemployed farmers because the offer would give them land to farm. They might not want to emigrate if they were living in comfortable circumstances or were very afraid of the voyage.)

★★★
Vital Links

Early home life at Jamestown (Picture) Unit 1, Side 1, Search 34187

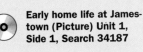

See also Unit 1 Explore CD-ROM location 286.

No one knows what Jamestown looked like in 1607 because some of the site has been washed away by the James River. This artist's view shows how the colonists might have built a protective wall around their tents and huts.

Teaching the

Link to the Present

Point out that the archaeologists unexpectedly discovered Martin's Hundred as they were working to restore the nineteenth-century plantation Carter's Grove. The discovery was significant because it gave a glimpse into the way of life of early colonists. The excavation uncovered the ground plan for a palisade fort and an outlying village as well as household and military artifacts. Ask: **What things about early colonial life do you think archaeologists would most want to know?** (Students might suggest that archaeologists may most want to know about the daily life of the colonists or about major events that affected the colonists.)

Bonus Activity

An Indentured Servant Contract

To help students imagine an indentured servant's situation, have them write a contract. The contract should state what the indentured servant and the colonist who pays the passage must do. Have students exchange and compare their contracts, discussing the pros and cons of becoming an indentured servant.

✳ **History Footnote**

Between July 30 and August 4, 1619, the general assembly of the House of Burgesses met for the first time. Included were the governor, the council, and 2 burgesses from each of 11 districts. The assembly checked qualifications of each burgess, discussed worsening Indian relations, and passed many rules, or acts. The governor could veto any act passed by the assembly, and every act needed approval of the Virginia Company to become law. As part of authorizing the assembly, the company made a promise that was to take effect after the colony's government was well established. The company stated that the orders of its own court would not be binding on the colony unless the assembly approved them. With this promise, the idea of self-government took root in the colony.

Link to the Present

Lost settlement found In 1619, 220 English colonists arrived in Virginia and built a village on Martin's Hundred, a tract of land on the James River. Three years later, the village had ceased to exist. What happened?

In the late 1970s archaeologists discovered the site of the settlement. Finding many bones in one grave told archaeologists that infectious disease had hit the village, causing many deaths at one time. Most of the settlers, however, died in the Indian attack of 1622. Archaeologists found evidence of violent death, hasty burials, and ashes from burning buildings.

There is still much to be learned about early settlements in Virginia. Today's tools of archaeology are helping in the process.

---

them to come as **indentured servants.** That is, they signed a contract called an indenture, agreeing to work four to seven years without pay for the person who paid their passage. At the end of the period, indentured servants were free. Usually they received some new clothes and perhaps money or tools to help them start supporting themselves.

It was as indentured servants that many of England's uprooted farmers came to the colonies. They were willing to set out for a new land in the hope that at the end of the contract they could find work or buy a plot of land to farm.

In 1619 the company sent 90 young women to Virginia. It hoped that settlers who married and started families would make Virginia their permanent home. Many of the women married at once. Each husband paid the cost of his wife's transportation in tobacco. The women who did not marry became indentured servants.

The House of Burgesses The year 1619 also marked the first step toward self-government in Virginia. Until then the Virginia Company had appointed the governor and his council of advisors.

Now the company allowed adult male landowners to elect **representatives**—people who are chosen to speak and act in government for their fellow citizens. This system was more like the one in England. There citizens had a voice in their government through representatives they elected to a legislature called Parliament. A **legislature** is a group of people chosen to make laws.

In Virginia the representatives, called *burgesses*, were to meet as an assembly called the House of Burgesses. The assembly, along with the governor's council, became the colony's legislature. It gave the English colonists a degree of self-government that was unheard of at that time in the Spanish and French colonies in America.

Conflict Between Colonists and Indians

Tobacco gave settlers a valuable product to sell, and new tobacco farms spread along the James River. Soon planters were expanding into the lands of neighboring Indian tribes. Conflict erupted as Indians tried to protect their lands and families.

In March 1622 Indian warriors attacked the colony, killing 347 settlers. One of them was John Rolfe, whose marriage to Pocahontas had given hope of peace between Indians and colonists. Pocahontas herself had died of smallpox in England.

The colonists struck back with such thoroughness that they broke the power of the

After Pocahontas died of smallpox, John Rolfe returned to America alone. He left his son Thomas, whom he never saw again, in the care of an uncle. Thomas Rolfe lived in England until he returned to Virginia 13 years after his father's death. There he took possession of land left to him by his father and his grandfather, Powhatan. Although he visited the Powhatan people, Thomas lived among the English and married an English woman. One of his descendants was John Randolph, a U.S. representative and senator who served during the early 1800s.

This photograph of Plymouth today gives a sense of the harshness of the Pilgrims' first winter in New England. In 4 months, 44 people died.

Virginia tribes. In one example of revenge, described by colonist Robert Bennett, 200 Indians were killed at a peace conference because the wine they drank "was sent of purpose . . . to poison them."

A royal colony The warfare left much of Jamestown in ruins and the Virginia Company in serious difficulties. In 1624 only 1,200 colonists remained, and the investors had lost nearly $5 million.

As a result, King James I took away the Virginia Company's charter. He made Virginia a **royal colony**, which means that the king appointed the governor and the council of advisors. James tried to do away with the House of Burgesses, but the Virginians insisted on having a voice in government. Like the struggling colony, the House of Burgesses clung to life.

Plymouth Colony

The colony of Virginia had been started by investors and adventurers looking for profits and gold. The people who planted the next English colony were seeking something far different—the right to worship as they wished. They became known as Pilgrims because they made their journey for religious reasons.

Earlier in this section you read about conflict between Catholics and Puritans and the Church of England. Most Puritans stayed within the church and tried to change it. The Pilgrims, however, were Puritans who decided to set up a separate church. Because they were breaking English law, they were persecuted.

A small group of Pilgrims fled to the Netherlands. There they could worship as

Closing the Section

Section Review
Answers

1. Definitions: *invest* (120), *joint-stock company* (122), *exports* (123), *indentured servants* (124), *representatives* (124), *legislature* (124), *royal colony* (125)

2. It displaced many farmers, who were willing to become colonists. Some landowners who became wealthy invested in colonies.

3. Accept two of these changes: the right to own land, indentured servants, the House of Burgesses, arrival of women. All encouraged people to become or remain colonists. House of Burgesses gave colonists a voice in government.

4. The Pilgrims were Puritans who broke away from the Church of England. They were persecuted for breaking the law that required membership in the Church of England. Other Puritans remained in the Church of England and tried to change it.

126

✳ **History Footnote**

The Pilgrims organized a government that included a governor, assistants to the governor, and a legislature. The governor and assistants were elected each year. The first governor, John Carver, died in the spring of 1621, and William Bradford was elected to replace him. Bradford served as governor for 30 out of the next 35 years. Bradford not only helped the colony survive through his strong leadership but also recorded its history in his book *Of Plymouth Plantation, 1620–1647*.

To have students read the Mayflower Compact, see **American Readings,** p. 18.

---

they wished, but they feared their children would grow up more Dutch than English.

As a result, a number of Pilgrims decided to establish their own community in North America. King James gave them permission to settle north of Jamestown as long as they did not stir up trouble.

In September 1620 about 100 voyagers set out from Plymouth, England, in a leaky, overcrowded boat named the *Mayflower*. One-third of them were Pilgrims. The others were non-Pilgrim "strangers," who planned to settle in Virginia.

The Mayflower Compact After a stormy 66-day voyage, the *Mayflower* reached the American coast at Cape Cod, in the region the English called New England. The ship had been blown far north of Virginia, where the Pilgrims had permission to settle. The laws in their charter applied only to Virginia, so the group decided they must organize their own government.

Pilgrim leaders drafted an agreement known as the Mayflower Compact, which 41 Pilgrims and "strangers" signed on board the *Mayflower*. In the compact, the signers agreed to make laws "for the general good of the colony, unto which we promise all due . . . obedience." Dated November 21, 1620, the Mayflower Compact helped establish the American tradition that government rests on the consent of the governed.

Help from Squanto The early history of Plymouth Colony is one of suffering. The site was barren. Half of the colonists sickened and died during the first year.

Like the settlers in Jamestown, who relied on Pocahontas, the Pilgrims owed their survival to an Indian. His name was Squanto, and he was a Wampanoag (WAHM-puh-NŌ-ahg) who had been to England and could speak English.

Squanto's story was not as unusual as you might think. Since the 1500s, English fish-ermen and Indians had been trading along the Atlantic coast. Some captains kidnapped the Indians to sell as slaves. Squanto was captured in 1614 and sold in Spain.

Squanto escaped to England, where he lived for several years before being sent to Newfoundland. Unhappy there, Squanto returned to England and found a ship headed for Cape Cod. When he arrived at last, in 1619, he discovered that disease had wiped out his entire village.

To the Pilgrims, Squanto must have seemed like a gift from God. He not only taught the colonists about farming but helped them establish friendly relations with neighboring tribes. Sadly, Squanto died from a disease brought to America by the people he did so much to help.

The Pilgrims' contributions Despite Squanto's help, Plymouth Colony never prospered. In 1691 it was taken over by the nearby colony of Massachusetts.

Plymouth, however, remains important in our nation's history. The Pilgrims believed that people have the right to create their own laws and to worship as they wish. Such ideas are among the building blocks of the government we have today.

⭐ 1. Section Review

1. Define **invest, joint-stock company, exports, indentured servants, representatives, legislature,** and **royal colony.**
2. How did the movement to enclose farmland affect English hopes for colonies?
3. Describe two important changes in Virginia in 1618 and 1619. How did the changes help the colony?
4. **Critical Thinking** How were the Puritans and the Pilgrims similar? How were they different?

John Smith provided an account of the land in the Chesapeake Bay area in *The General History of Virginia, New-England, and the Summer Isles,* first published in 1624. The quote here is taken from the second book of the six-book history. The author claimed he wrote the book to help make the English aware of the opportunities that colonizing offered. Smith's book was the first of many books that assessed the economic promise of the Americas for the English. Others included Daniel Denton's *Brief Description of New York,* published in 1670; William Penn's *Province of Pennsylvania,* published in 1682; and Thomas Ashe's *Carolina,* also published in 1682.

Geography Lab

The Coastal Lowlands

The explorer Giovanni Verrazano once called the Coastal Lowlands "spacious land, . . . with many beautiful fields and plains, full of the largest forests." The English later planted colonies in this fertile region that stretches from Massachusetts to Texas. The lowlands are watered by many rivers that plunge from higher ground to the north and west. The place where the higher ground drops abruptly to the plains below is known as the **Fall Line.** Use John Smith's description and the illustrations on this page to gather information about the Coastal Lowlands.

Chesapeake Bay, Maryland

John Smith on Virginia

"The land—white hilly sands, . . . and all along the shores great plenty of pines and firs. . . . Here are mountains, hills, plains, valleys, rivers, brooks, all running most pleasantly into a fair bay. . . . The more southward, the farther off from the bay are those mountains, from which fall certain brooks which [become] navigable rivers. . . . The [vegetation] of the earth in most places doth . . . prove the nature of the soil to be lusty and very rich."

Baltimore, Maryland, 1752

Developing a Mental Map

Refer to the map of regions on pages P4–P5, as well as the maps on pages R4–R5 and R6–R7 to help you answer the questions.

1. What states lie within the Coastal Lowlands?

2. Estimate the width of the lowlands.

3. What two large plains do the Coastal Lowlands include?

4. What parts of Smith's description of Virginia also apply to the places pictured on this page?

5. **Hands-On Geography** Baltimore, Maryland, is just one city that was built where a river crosses the Fall Line. Imagine that you are one of Baltimore's founders. Write a letter to a newspaper in England bragging about Baltimore's location.

Teaching the Geography Lab

Ask students to identify the general characteristics of the Coastal Lowlands after reading the introductory paragraph and examining the pictures. Ask: **What is the Fall Line?** (The place where the higher ground drops to the plains.) Have them use the map on pp. R6–R7 to locate the Chesapeake Bay and Baltimore, Maryland. Ask: **What is Baltimore's location in relation to Chesapeake Bay?** (On a river that flows into the bay.)

Developing a Mental Map
Answers

1. Maine, New Hampshire, Massachusetts, Connecticut, New York, Pennsylvania, New Jersey, Delaware, Maryland, Virginia, North Carolina, South Carolina, Georgia, Florida, Alabama, Mississippi, Louisiana, and Texas.

2. About 250 miles (400 km) at its broadest.

3. Atlantic Coastal Plain and Gulf Coastal Plain.

4. The rolling hills, nearby mountains, plains, and rivers apply to Baltimore; the plentiful coastal trees and fair bay apply to Chesapeake Bay.

5. Letters may describe river with access to sea, rolling hills, mountains, and plentiful trees.

See activity on the Coastal Lowlands in **Geography Extensions,** pp. 9–10.

Introducing the Section

Vocabulary

bicameral (p. 129) two-house

Warm-Up Activity

A Puritan View of Settlement

To help underscore the Puritan view on settling in America, ask students to imagine being a Puritan leader who is planning to set up a colony in New England. Have them write a speech explaining why they think they have a right to take Indian lands. Their speeches should include both religious and economic arguments.

Geography Question of the Day

Ask students to examine the paintings on pages 123 and 129 in order to write a paragraph summarizing the effect of colonial growth on the land and people who lived there. The paragraph should also explain whether they think each artist viewed the growth positively or negatively.

For a selection by Puritan poet Anne Bradstreet, see American Readings, p. 19.

Section Objectives

★ Describe the dream the Puritans had and how they achieved it.
★ Explain the reasons why new colonies were formed in New England.
★ Identify the causes for conflict between the Puritans and the American Indians.

Teaching Resources

Take-Home Planner 2, pp. 10–17
Chapter Resources Binder
Study Guide, p. 34
Reinforcement, pp. 37–38
Skills Development
Geography Extensions
American Readings, p. 19
Using Historical Documents, pp. 27–31
Transparency Activities
Chapter and Unit Tests

---

2. Puritan Colonies in New England

Reading Guide

New Term bicameral

Section Focus The colonies established by the English Puritans

1. What dream did the Puritans have, and how did they make it real?
2. Why were new colonies established in New England?
3. What caused conflict between Puritans and American Indians?

"Follow the counsel of Micah: to do justly, to love mercy, to walk humbly with our God. For this end, we must . . . rejoice together, mourn together, labor and suffer together, always having before our eyes . . . our common work."

So said Puritan leader John Winthrop to his followers in a sermon in 1630. On board a ship sailing to North America, Winthrop urged them to build the Christian community God wanted for his people. Such a community, Winthrop promised, would be "like a city upon a hill"—an example for all people to follow.

Massachusetts

In England, many Puritans were prosperous landowners and merchants. They had gained power in England's Parliament and were using it to try to purify the Church of England.

Faced with this threat, King Charles I set out to destroy the Puritans. He had Puritan leaders jailed, and some were even tortured. Winthrop and a group of leading Puritans decided that their only hope was to leave England and establish a colony based on Puritan ideas in America.

In 1629 a group of Puritans formed a joint-stock company, which they called the Massachusetts Bay Company. The king gave them a charter to settle on land north of Plymouth. Unlike other charters, this one did not require company stockholders to meet in England. As a result, the Puritans were able to move the company to Massachusetts and to set up the kind of colony they wanted.

Self-government was vital to the leaders of the Massachusetts Bay Company because they had a clear goal. They planned to create a community where Puritans would live together according to the true law of God as they understood it.

The Great Migration The Puritans wanted their "city upon a hill" to be an economic success as well as a model Christian community. They came well-prepared for life in a new land, bringing plenty of food, tools, livestock, and supplies. As a result, there was no "starving time," as in Jamestown, or winter of horror, as in Plymouth.

Every year ships brought new supplies and colonists. Between 1630 and 1640, in what was called the Great Migration, some 20,000 people arrived in Boston, the capital city of Massachusetts.

✠ Connections to Art
Frederick Edwin Church painted this scene, *Hooker and Company Journeying Through the Wilderness from Plymouth to Hartford in 1636,* about 200 years after Hooker left Massachusetts. Church excelled at painting landscapes and the effects of light on them, as in the setting sun in this painting. His paintings celebrate the beauty of nature. He was a student of Thomas Cole, a member of the Hudson River School, a group of painters specializing in grand landscapes.

See the Study Guide activity in Chapter Resources Binder, p. 34.

By no means were all of the new arrivals Puritans. Driven by hard times in England and hopes for a better life in America, non-Puritans also came to Massachusetts.

Representative government At first, all decisions were made by 12 stockholders of the company acting as a legislature called the General Court. They also elected the governor and his assistants. Winthrop became the first governor and served a total of 16 years.

Faced with a few leaders making all the rules, other colonists demanded a voice in government. In 1631 government leaders allowed all male members of Puritan churches to attend the General Court.

As the population grew, the General Court became too large. In 1634 church members in each town began electing deputies to represent them in the General Court. Ten years later, the General Court became a **bicameral,** or two-house, legislature, with the governor's assistants sitting in one "house" and the deputies in the other.

Dissent Leads to Expansion

Religion was closely tied to government in Massachusetts. All colonists, Puritan or not, were bound by law to live by Puritan rules. Winthrop and other colony leaders would not permit dissent.

Except for places like the Connecticut Valley, soil in New England was thin. Lured by the promise of good farmland, these followers of the Reverend Thomas Hooker traveled to Connecticut, driving their cattle before them.

1600–1750 Chapter 5 ● **129**

Developing the Section

Discussion

Checking Understanding
1. Why did the Puritan leaders decide to set up a colony in America? (Many were arrested for trying to change the Church of England. They decided to leave so that they could put their ideas into effect.)

Stimulating Critical Thinking
2. Why do you think non-Puritans were willing to live by Puritan rules? (Students may suggest they had the benefit of living in a well-organized colony or that they did not find the laws too restrictive.)

Section Activity

Deciding Whether to Emigrate
To help students understand the factors in making such a decision, have small groups imagine themselves as a group of Puritans in England. Each group should list pros or cons of moving to America. They should consider religious, social, and economic factors, as well as physical challenges of the voyage and getting settled in America. After evaluating their list, they should decide whether to emigrate. Conclude by having a member of each group report on their decision and the reasons for it.

Students with Limited English

To help students understand the Williams quote and other primary sources, explain the use of brackets and ellipses. Emphasize that brackets are used to add words or numbers not contained in the quote. In this case, brackets enclose definitions of words that may be unfamiliar and numbers that help identify points made by Williams. Ellipses indicate text is missing. A period and an ellipsis (four dots) indicate that the end of a sentence or a group of sentences have been deleted. An ellipsis without a period indicates that a word or words have been deleted within a sentence.

Teaching the

Point of View

Point out that Roger Williams believed in the right of religious choice but also supported the importance of obeying laws. Discuss his comparison of colonial laws to procedures followed on a ship. Ask: **Do rights and freedoms ever come in conflict with responsibilities?** (Students might point out that we have freedom of speech, but we cannot use that freedom to libel others.)

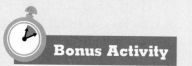

Bonus Activity

Williams Defending Himself

To underscore Williams's beliefs, have small groups write scripts for a scene in which he confronts Puritan leaders. The script should focus on an exchange of religious views between Williams and the leaders. Some groups might act out their scenes.

Vital Links

○ **Early punishment in stockades (Picture) Unit 1, Side 1, Search 38921**

○ **See also Unit 1 Explore CD-ROM location 333.**

Thus, it was not long before conflicts began. Puritans who questioned beliefs or rules were punished or driven out. Others chose to leave. In the next 50 years, 3 new colonies were formed in New England, out of range of Massachusetts control.

Rhode Island

Roger Williams was the first to break away. Williams had arrived in Massachusetts in 1631. Although he was a Puritan minister, he soon accused leaders of not following the teachings of the Bible. Then he opposed the law that everyone must go to religious services. Finally, he questioned the colonists' right to take Indian lands without paying for them.

Williams's views so angered Puritan leaders that in 1635 the General Court ordered him sent back to England. Governor Winthrop, however, worried that Williams would be arrested in England. Warned by Winthrop, Williams fled with a few of his followers. The group spent the winter with nearby Narragansett (NAYR-uh-GAN-sit) Indians.

The next year Williams bought land from the Narragansetts and established the settlement of Providence. Under his leadership, Providence and several neighboring towns formed a colony called Rhode Island. They received a charter from the king in 1644.

In his new home, Williams rejected the idea of close ties between church and government. He promised that no colonist would be punished "for any differences in opinion in matters of religion."

Point of View

Are there limits to liberty?

People of all faiths came to Rhode Island for religious freedom. Soon, however, some began to argue that they should also be free from obeying the colony's laws. Roger

Williams disagreed. In a letter written in 1655, he said that colonists could worship as they wished, but they had to obey the laws. To make his point, he used the example of passengers and a commander on a ship at sea.

❝There goes many a ship to sea with many hundred souls in one ship. . . . Papists [Catholics] and Protestants, Jews and Turks [Muslims] may be embarked in one ship. . . .

All the liberty of conscience that ever I pleaded for turns upon these two hinges—[1] that none of the Papists, Protestants, Jews, or Turks be forced to come to the ship's prayers or worship, [2] nor compelled [kept] from their own particular prayers or worship, if they practice any. . . .

[However,] I never denied that . . . the commander of this ship ought to command the ship's course, yea, and also command that justice [and] peace . . . be kept and practiced, both among the seamen and all the passengers.❞

As Americans, we treasure our liberty, but what would it be like to live without any laws?

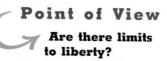

Anne Hutchinson Like Roger Williams, Anne Hutchinson also clashed with Puritan leaders in Massachusetts. The wife of a wealthy merchant and the mother of 11 children, she arrived in Boston in 1634. Strong-willed and brilliant, she attracted followers who came to weekly meetings in her home to discuss religion.

Hutchinson got in trouble when she questioned church teachings and said that God spoke to people directly instead of through church officials. Puritan leaders thought Hutchinson's views were dangerous to the colony, and they ordered her to stand trial. In the spring of 1638 the General Court banished her "as being a woman not fit for our society."

Hutchinson and her family fled to Rhode Island and later to New Netherland. In 1643 she and five of her children were killed by Indians. Governor Winthrop had taken pity on Roger Williams, but he could not forgive Anne Hutchinson. Her death, he wrote in his journal, was "a special manifestation [sign] of divine [God's] justice."

Connecticut

As early as 1633, Puritans seeking good farmland and fur trade opportunities had begun to move into the region that is today the state of Connecticut. The region also attracted the Reverend Thomas Hooker, who had disagreed with Puritan leaders about religious issues.

In 1636 Hooker led three church congregations into the Connecticut River valley, where they established farms and towns. A year later the residents organized the colony of Connecticut. For 25 years, it remained an independent colony without a charter from the king.

In 1639 representatives from the towns drew up a plan of government called the Fundamental Orders of Connecticut. Hooker's belief in government based on the will of the people became part of the Fundamental Orders. Although the plan set up a government like that of Massachusetts, the right to vote was not limited to church members.

New Hampshire and Maine

In their search for good farmland, colonists from Massachusetts also moved north, almost to the border of New France. In the region that is now New Hampshire and Maine, they built settlements and farmed and fished.

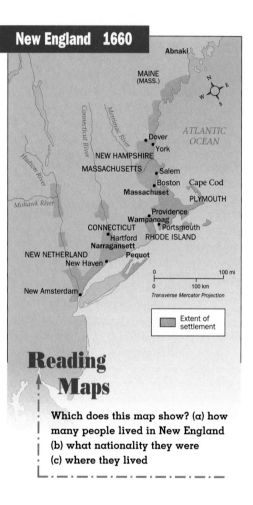

New England 1660

- Abnaki
- MAINE (MASS.)
- Connecticut River
- Merrimac River
- Hudson River
- Mohawk River
- Dover
- York
- NEW HAMPSHIRE
- MASSACHUSETTS
- Salem
- Boston
- Massachuset
- Cape Cod
- PLYMOUTH
- Providence
- Wampanoag
- CONNECTICUT
- Hartford
- Portsmouth
- RHODE ISLAND
- Narragansett
- Pequot
- NEW NETHERLAND
- New Haven
- New Amsterdam
- ATLANTIC OCEAN

0 ___ 100 mi
0 ___ 100 km
Transverse Mercator Projection

Extent of settlement

Reading Maps

Which does this map show? (a) how many people lived in New England (b) what nationality they were (c) where they lived

Massachusetts claimed that both of these areas were a part of its territory. In 1679, however, the king established a separate colony called New Hampshire. Maine would remain a part of Massachusetts until 1820.

Puritans and Indians Clash

Lured by what seemed to be unlimited empty land, the Puritans had quickly spread throughout New England. Of course, the land was not really empty. American Indians had lived and farmed and hunted there for thousands of years.

See the activity on the Fundamental Orders of Connecticut in **Using Historical Documents,** pp. 27–31.

An Indian Protest Letter

To help students understand the Indians' point of view, ask them to imagine themselves as an Indian leader who wants to avoid fighting the colonists. Have them write a protest letter to the governor of the colony outlining their grievances and asking for remedies.

Section Review Answers

1. Definition: *bicameral* (129)
2. Winthrop may have meant that the community would stand out as an example of the best type of community to emulate.
3. People settled in Rhode Island and Connecticut because they had views that differed with the laws and values of Massachusetts and because they wanted to expand their economic opportunities by acquiring farmland or taking part in the fur trade.
4. The causes were disagreements over land and the colony's requirement that Indians obey their laws. The effects were wars in which many colonists and Indians were killed, colonial towns were damaged, Indians were enslaved, and the Indian tribes lost their power.
5. Accept all opinions about the possible mission of present-day Americans. For example, many Americans work to help find a solution to homelessness.

132

✳ History Footnote

As a result of the conflict between colonists and the Pequots, known as the Pequot War, the tribe was greatly diminished. Many members were sold into slavery in Bermuda or given as slaves to Indian groups friendly to the colonists. The colonies changed all Pequot place names and prohibited use of the tribal name. Today about 200 members of the tribe survive.

See the Reinforcement activity in **Chapter Resources Binder,** pp. 37–38.

As a child, Metacomet watched the Puritans take over Indian lands and force his people to obey English laws. After he became chief, he led New England tribes in resisting the English colonists.

Although Indians like Squanto had been of vital help to them at first, most Puritans thought of Indians as savages. By contrast, they saw themselves as chosen by God. Thus they felt no guilt about taking Indian lands. In fact, when the Puritans learned that disease had killed thousands of Indians not long before their arrival, they saw it as a sign of God's helping hand.

With two groups—the Indians and the colonists—both claiming their right to the land, conflict was bound to occur. In 1637 colonists blamed the murder of two English traders on the Pequot (PEE-kwaht) Indians of Connecticut. Although the colonists lacked clear evidence that the Pequots were involved, they set fire to the Pequots' main village. Out of 500 Indians in the village, "not over eight escaped out of our hands," boasted one colonist.

King Philip's War The longest, bloodiest war between Indians and colonists in New England broke out in 1675. This time the spark was Plymouth Colony's trial and hanging of three Wampanoags for the murder of a Christian Indian. In response, Wampanoag chief Metacomet, who was called King Philip by the English, organized the New England tribes to drive out the English colonists.

The conflict, known as King Philip's War, spread from Massachusetts to Maine. By the time peace was agreed on in 1678, some 600 colonists had been killed. Half the English towns suffered damage, and 12 were completely destroyed.

The power of the New England tribes was also destroyed, however. Colonists killed about 3,000 Indians, including Metacomet. They sold his wife and child and hundreds of other Indians into slavery in the West Indies. Never again would the tribes pose a serious threat to New England.

⭐ 2. Section Review

1. Define **bicameral**.
2. John Winthrop hoped Massachusetts would be "like a city upon a hill." What did he mean?
3. Give two reasons why people settled in Rhode Island and Connecticut.
4. What were the causes and effects of conflict between the Indians and the Puritans?
5. **Critical Thinking** The Puritans came to America with a mission. Do you think Americans today have a mission? If so, what do you think it is?

Section Objectives

★ Explain how the visions of the founders affected the colonies they organized.
★ Identify the ways the English competed with the Spanish and Dutch in America.

Teaching Resources

Take-Home Planner 2, pp. 10–17
Chapter Resources Binder
　Study Guide, p. 35
　Reinforcement
　Skills Development, pp. 39–40
　Geography Extensions
American Readings, p. 20
　Using Historical Documents
　Transparency Activities
Chapter and Unit Tests, pp. 29–32

Introducing the Section

Vocabulary

proprietary colonies (p. 133) colonies organized by owners who controlled the land and appointed the governors

Warm-Up Activity

Preparing a Time Line

To help place the founding of colonies into a time frame, have students prepare a time line for the years 1600 to 1750, divided into decades. They should review the first two sections of the chapter and place the founding date and name of each colony on the time line. When they finish reading this section, they can add the colonies discussed to their time line.

Geography Question of the Day

Ask students to list two colonies or towns named after people (such as Jamestown, Virginia, New York, Maryland, Carolina), two after places in Europe (such as New Netherland and Plymouth), and one after an Indian tribe (Massachusetts or Delaware). They can refer back to sections 1 and 2, as well as to maps and subheads in section 3.

3. Later English Colonies

Reading Guide

New Term **proprietary colonies**

Section Focus **The founding of new English colonies in North America**

1. How did the hopes and plans of founders shape the colonies they started?
2. How did the English compete with the Spanish and Dutch in America?

Certain names are always connected with the founding of the English colonies. John Smith and Pocahontas saved Virginia. John Winthrop led the Puritans to Massachusetts. Roger Williams started Rhode Island.

In the 1630s wealthy "royal favorites" began to start colonies on land given them by the king. These were called **proprietary colonies** because the owners, known as proprietors, organized the colonies, controlled the land, and appointed governors.

The motives of the proprietors varied. Some sought wealth. Others wanted to help the persecuted or the poor. As a result, the proprietary colonies lured a wide variety of people from England and Europe who were looking for a fresh start in life.

Maryland

Maryland was the first successful proprietary colony. It was planned by George Calvert, Lord Baltimore, as a refuge for Catholics who, like Puritans, were being persecuted in England.

King Charles I granted land north of Virginia to his friend Calvert and named it "Marilande" for his queen, Henrietta Maria. Calvert died before the charter was issued in 1632, so the colony went to his son Cecilius.

Two years later the first colonists arrived in Maryland. From the start, Calvert allowed both Catholics and Protestants to follow their religions. Soon people from both groups were moving to Maryland, where they grew tobacco and corn.

As proprietor, Calvert had complete power to govern the colony. However, the charter required that he heed the advice of landowners. Thus, in 1635 Calvert allowed residents to elect an assembly to make laws.

Religious toleration Many settlers in Maryland were wealthy Catholics. Many more, though, were Protestant workers and indentured servants. Calvert feared the Protestants would try to prevent the Catholics from following their religion.

At Calvert's request, the Maryland assembly passed the Toleration Act of 1649. According to the act, the government would tolerate, or respect, the beliefs of both Catholics and Protestants. The act did not tolerate non-Christian religions, such as Judaism. Yet considering the strict rules in England and Massachusetts, this was a step toward greater religious freedom.

Two Carolinas

In 1663 King Charles II granted the land between Virginia and Spanish Florida to a group of eight noblemen. He hoped that having English colonists in the area would keep the Spanish from advancing any farther into North America.

Explain that France and many other European nations had state religions—usually Roman Catholicism. Protestants were discriminated against in these nations. Ask: **How did discrimination against the Huguenots help the English colonies and hurt France?** (The French lost people who made valuable contributions to their economy, and the English colonies gained them.)

Section Activity

A Colonial Documentary

To help students synthesize information about proprietary colonies, have them prepare a documentary script. Discuss the documentary as a film medium that may include narration, live action, and still photography. Divide the class into small groups, assigning each a proprietary colony. The groups should write a script for a narrator who discusses the founding and early years of the colony. They should include suggestions for visuals. If they have access to video equipment, they might produce the documentary.

✳ **History Footnote**

Peter Stuyvesant arrived in New Netherland as the colony's new director general in 1647. Through strong and often harsh leadership, he returned order to the colony. He tightened trading regulations and helped restore confidence in the Dutch West India Company. He also captured New Sweden. After his surrender of New Amsterdam, Stuyvesant went to the Netherlands to defend his decision. A few years later, he returned and lived out his life on his farm in what is now Manhattan.

See the Study Guide activity in **Chapter Resources Binder,** p. 35.

World  Link

Huguenots flee France In 1685 the French government banned the Protestant religion. Huguenots (Protestants) were ordered to educate their children in the Catholic faith, and they were not allowed to leave the country.

In spite of these laws, more than 50,000 Huguenot families fled France. Many of them settled in South Carolina, New York, and Massachusetts.

Many Huguenots were merchants and skilled craftspeople. Their loss was a blow to the industry and trade of France—and a great boon to the English colonies.

From the start, Carolina, the "land of Charles," was a divided colony. Independent farmers from Virginia moved into the northern part. Ignoring the Carolina proprietors' claim to the land, they settled down to raise tobacco, corn, and livestock.

Carolina's proprietors were more interested in the southern part of the colony, where they built the port city of Charles Town (now Charleston). Settlers came from England's West Indies islands, which had been captured from Spain. However, the proprietors had a terrible time finding ways to make the colony prosper.

Planters tried to raise crops that could not be grown in England, such as olives, grapes, and sugar cane. None did well. The colonists had better luck with cattle and hogs as well as "naval stores" for ships—tar, pitch, and turpentine, made from pine sap.

The most money was to be made from the Indian slave trade, however. Carolina traders bought Indians who had been taken prisoner in wars between local tribes. Then they shipped the captives to the West Indies to be sold as slaves. This trade caused more warfare between tribes as well as conflict between colonists and Indians.

Finally, in the 1690s Carolina found a crop well-suited to its soil and climate—rice. English planters knew nothing about growing rice, however. They depended on the knowledge and labor of enslaved Africans brought into Carolina from rice-growing areas in West Africa. By the early 1700s "Carolina gold," as rice was called, had ensured the prosperity of the colony.

The colony divides Conflict between the proprietors and the colonists led to the division of Carolina. Colonists complained that the proprietors ignored their right of self-government and failed to protect them from Spanish and Indian attacks.

In 1719 angry colonists in the southern part of the colony rebelled, and the king made South Carolina a separate royal colony. Ten years later, North Carolina also became a royal colony.

Fall of New Netherland

While Carolina was being built to stop the Spanish in the south, the English were getting rid of another competitor farther north. King Charles II thought the Dutch colonists of New Netherland had no right to settle on what he believed was English territory. The Dutch also were competing with English merchants for colonial trade.

In 1664 Charles decided to capture the Dutch colony. In August four British warships sailed into New Amsterdam's harbor. The British sent Governor Peter Stuyvesant a note demanding surrender. Stuyvesant tore up the note and called on the people of the town to fight.

They refused. They hated the harsh Stuyvesant. If anyone complained of his

Learning Disabilities

Students who have visual perception problems may have great difficulty in isolating information on detailed maps. Students will be more successful in answering the Reading Maps questions if they make their own simplified map by tracing the outline of the map onto a sheet of tracing paper. They

should draw approximate boundaries for the northernmost and southernmost English colonies and label this section "English Colonies." Then have them label the Appalachians, Spanish land, and French land. They can use their simplified maps to answer the questions.

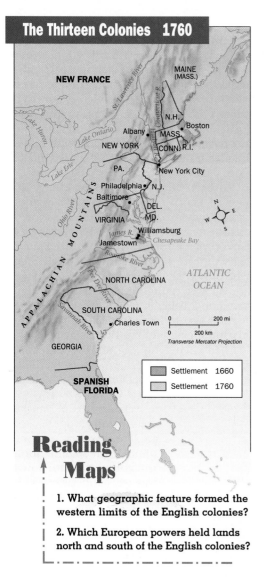

The Thirteen Colonies 1760

Reading Maps

1. What geographic feature formed the western limits of the English colonies?

2. Which European powers held lands north and south of the English colonies?

rule, he had warned, "I will make him a foot shorter, and send the pieces to Holland [the Netherlands], and let him appeal that way."

Forced to give in, Stuyvesant surrendered without a shot. Charles II noted with pleasure the capture of New Amsterdam and its new name: "A very good town, but we have got the better of it, and 'tis now called New York." By fall, England had conquered the rest of the Dutch colony.

New Jersey and New York

Charles gave New Netherland to his brother, James, Duke of York. In time, four proprietary colonies were carved out of the former Dutch colony—New Jersey, New York, Pennsylvania, and Delaware.

Soon after the conquest, James gave his lands between the Hudson and Delaware Rivers to his friends Lord John Berkeley and Sir George Carteret. They named the territory New Jersey for Carteret's home, the island of Jersey in the English Channel.

Lured by rich farmland, some Dutch, Swedes, and Finns had already settled in New Jersey. Soon Puritans began to arrive, searching for better land or greater religious freedom than New England offered.

Eager to bring in more colonists, the proprietors leased land at fair rents and permitted a representative assembly. The colony grew quickly, but conflict erupted between the colonists and the proprietors. In 1702 New Jersey became a royal colony.

New York James kept the northern part of New Netherland, which he renamed New York. Already New York City was on its way to becoming a major trading center that attracted people from many parts of the world. Most of the settlers were Dutch, but many English, Swedes, French, Portuguese, and Africans lived there as well.

The former Dutch residents praised James's fairness. He let them keep their land and practice their own religion.

English settlers, however, complained that James treated New York like a conquered country. They demanded the right to elect a legislature. James refused, arguing that it would destroy "the peace of the government." In fact, New York did not get its first elected assembly until 1683.

Discussion

Checking Understanding

1. Did the Act of Toleration grant religious freedom to all people? Explain. (No, it granted freedom of religion only to Christians, not to non-Christians.)

2. Why did Stuyvesant surrender New Amsterdam without a fight? (Colonists refused to support Stuyvesant and his harsh rule.)

Stimulating Critical Thinking

3. How might New Englanders have reacted to the English capture of New Netherland? Why? (They were probably pleased that the English gained control of New Netherland because a foreign nation would no longer hold the land south of them and they could move there and still be in English territory.)

Teaching the
Reading Maps

To help students focus on the map, ask: **How many English colonies were established in North America by 1760? What was the northernmost English colony? The southernmost?** (By 1760, the English had 13 colonies in North America. Maine, part of Massachusetts, was the northernmost, and Georgia was the southernmost.) **Answers to Reading Maps: 1.** The Appalachian Mountains **2.** France held territory to the north, and Spain held territory to the south.

Before William Penn came to Pennsylvania, he began making plans for "a greene Countrie Towne, which will never be burnt, and all-ways be wholesome." Penn did not want his city to be destroyed by the fires and plagues that he had seen in Europe. As a result, Penn's surveyor general, Thomas Holme, planned the layout of the city before building began. Holme plotted a grid extending out from a city square in the middle. This grid plan became a model for other cities. As part of the plan, streets were wider than in any other city. The two main streets were 100 feet (30.48 m) wide, and other streets were 50 feet (15.24 m) wide.

Pennsylvania

William Penn, who started the colony of Pennsylvania, was a very different sort of proprietor. Penn was destined to be rich and powerful. He was the son of a wealthy admiral and friendly with the future King Charles II and James, Duke of York.

In the mid-1660s Penn joined a new religion, the Religious Society of Friends. Members were called Quakers because they "quaked" before God.

Quaker beliefs upset religious and government leaders in England. Quakers treated everyone as equals. They saw no need for ministers and refused to pay taxes to the Church of England. They did not believe in war and refused to serve as soldiers.

As a result, Quakers were persecuted in England and also in Massachusetts. Penn himself was jailed for eight months in the Tower of London for writing a pamphlet that praised the Quaker faith.

Penn dreamed of finding a haven for Quakers in America, and his connections with the king made it come true. In 1681 he received a grant from Charles II for territory north of Maryland. He called it Pennsylvania—"Penn's Woods." Penn's father had loaned Charles money, which the king had not repaid. By repaying the debt with American land, Charles also helped his old friend.

Penn's "holy experiment" Penn viewed Pennsylvania as a "holy experiment," where Quakers and others would "shape their own laws." His Frame of Government for the colony called for a legislature to be elected by all adult men who owned property or paid taxes. The plan also allowed settlers to practice any religion based on a belief in God.

Penn also believed in dealing fairly with his Indian neighbors, the Delawares. He learned their language and bought land from them at fair prices. Pennsylvanians and Delawares lived in peace for many years.

Settlers from many countries in Europe flocked to Pennsylvania, and the population soared. Soon the colony's major town was well underway. Penn called the town Philadelphia, the Greek word for "brotherly love."

Delaware To give his colony an outlet to the sea, in 1682 Penn obtained the land called Delaware from the Duke of York. By 1704 people in Delaware had their own assembly but shared a governor with Pennsylvania. Delaware did not become a separate colony until 1776.

Hands-On
— — — — → *HISTORY*

Advertising the colonies Imagine that you work for an advertising company. You are to come up with an ad to lure settlers to one of the 13 English colonies.

Activity

1 After reading the chapter, choose a colony and the type of ad you will create, such as a brochure, poster, or jingle.

2 Decide what makes your colony special. Why should people in the 1700s move there? To answer that question, review the information in the chapter and do research if necessary.

3 Create the ad and present it to your classmates. Are they ready to sail to North America?

1609 ad for Virginia

The organizers of the colony of Georgia carefully screened people who applied to settle there. They spent months choosing the first settlers. Although they were willing to take debtors, the organizers wanted only people "of good families, and of liberal, or, at least, easy education." They also required that before being accepted as settlers, debtors had to repay their debts. The colony offered the settlers an attractive package. They would pay a settler's passage to Georgia and give land, seed, and farming tools. They also promised to support settlers until the first crops were harvested.

Discussion

Checking Understanding

1. How did Pennsylvania's religious policy differ from that of Maryland? (Pennsylvania allowed people to practice any faith that was based on the belief in God; Maryland's policy granted religious freedom only to members of Christian faiths.)

Stimulating Critical Thinking

2. Why do you think so many people from many European countries chose to settle in Pennsylvania rather than in other colonies? (Students may suggest that they chose Pennsylvania because they would have religious freedom, they would be treated equally by the Quakers, and they could participate in elections if they owned land and paid taxes.)

Teaching the

◯ **Link to Art**

Explain that Hicks's *The Peaceable Kingdom* is based on the Bible verse Isaiah 11:6 that says, in time, natural enemies in the animal world would lie down together, and children would be the leaders of all creatures. **Discussion Answer:** Students may suggest that the message of the painting is that all creatures including humans can learn to live peacefully together.

◯ Link to Art

The Peaceable Kingdom (1835) Edward Hicks, an artist and Quaker preacher, painted historical and religious scenes. In the foreground of this painting, he shows animals that are enemies on earth living in peace with children in God's kingdom. In the background, William Penn and the Delaware Indians sign a treaty. **Discuss** What do you think is the message of the painting?

Georgia

The founder of Georgia, the last of England's 13 colonies, had a dream. As a young man, James Oglethorpe had been shocked when a friend died in prison. The friend's only crime was being too poor to pay his debts. Knowing that thousands of poor men and women in England faced the same fate, Oglethorpe decided to help them get a fresh start in America.

In 1732 Oglethorpe and a group of wealthy friends got a charter from King George II to found a colony between South Carolina and Spanish Florida. The king named it Georgia after himself.

Closing the Section

Writing Editorials

To underscore effects of English expansion along the Atlantic coast, have students write editorials from different perspectives. Assign one-third to imagine themselves as authorities in England, one-third as colonists, and one-third as Indians. Invite volunteers to read their editorials to the class. Conclude by comparing viewpoints.

Section Review
Answers

1. Definition: *proprietary colonies* (133)

2. Pennsylvania and Maryland were religious refuges. Carolina was founded to discourage further Spanish occupation.

3. The English king did not believe the Dutch had any right to inhabit land claimed by England, and the Dutch were competing with the English for colonial trade. England gained four new colonies, and the Dutch lost their claim to American lands.

4. Students may say his plans helped and hurt the colony. He kept the Spanish from moving north, but his policy of limiting land holdings resulted in few people coming to Georgia.

To check understanding of "Why We Remember," assign Thinking Critically question 3 on page 140.

138

✳ History Footnote

When Oglethorpe arrived in Georgia, he promised the Indians that he would treat them fairly and justly. He kept this promise. He negotiated with the Creeks for land. They gave up almost all the land between the Savannah and Altahama rivers to Oglethorpe. The Creeks did keep a small amount of land near Savannah so that they would have a place to camp when they visited the city. To prevent traders from cheating the Indians, Oglethorpe established a schedule of prices for which goods could be bartered. For example, the Indians could acquire a blanket for one buckskin and a gun for ten buckskins.

From the start, Oglethorpe had two goals. One was to provide land where debtors could become independent farmers. The other was to serve the king by stopping the Spanish in Florida from moving north.

Oglethorpe succeeded in holding off the Spanish. He built forts and brought in English troops to protect the colony. He also had the good luck to gain the friendship of Mary Musgrove, whose mother was a Creek Indian and whose father was English. Mary Musgrove helped maintain good relations between the powerful Creeks and the English in their struggles against the Spanish.

Less successful were Oglethorpe's plans for debtors. He wanted Georgia to be a community of small farms, so he limited the size of land holdings and banned slavery. To control the colony's development, he refused to allow a representative assembly.

Under these conditions, few settlers, debtors or not, wanted to come to Georgia. The ones who did come demanded changes or moved to other colonies. As a result, Oglethorpe's rules were given up, and in 1752 Georgia became a royal colony. Only then did Georgia begin to prosper.

⭐ 3. Section Review

1. Define **proprietary colonies.**
2. Compare the reasons for establishing Maryland, Pennsylvania, and Carolina.
3. Why did England take over New Netherland, and what were the results?
4. Critical Thinking Did James Oglethorpe's plans help or hurt the colony of Georgia? Explain your answer.

Why We Remember

Planting English Colonies

If you visit Washington, D.C., and the Capitol building where Congress meets, take a moment to stand in the rotunda under the great dome. There you will see a mural showing the history of the United States. One of the earliest scenes shows Pocahontas being baptized in Jamestown.

At that moment, Powhatan's daughter could not have known what her efforts to help the English in Jamestown would lead to. In little more than a century, her people would be almost wiped out, and the number of colonies would soar. By the time Georgia was founded in 1732, the English had planted a string of 13 colonies stretching from Canada to Florida along the Atlantic coast.

Today we remember the planting of English colonies because it was, in part, from those seeds that the United States would later grow. The men and women who first came to England's colonies brought with them the religious, political, and economic ideas that would help shape the early history of the United States.

4. The data shows that between 1680 and 1750 the population of all the colonies increased greatly, and the overall population became more evenly distributed. The fastest growing colony—in terms of increase in percentage of the total population—was Pennsylvania (from 0.4% to 10.2%), followed by South Carolina and New Jersey.

For further application, have students do the Applying Skills activity in the Chapter Survey (p. 140).

If students need to review the skill, use the Skills Development transparency and activity in the Chapter Resources Binder, pp. 39–40.

Skill Lab

Skill Tips

- Arrange the information so it is logical and easy to follow.
- Make the title and the row and column headings accurate and clear.
- Look across rows and down columns for similarities, differences, increases, or decreases.

Acquiring Information
Analyzing Statistical Tables

Between 1680 and 1750 the total colonial population grew rapidly—from a mere 150,000 to almost 1,200,000. As the total population grew, some colonies went through bigger changes than others.

Question to Investigate

Between 1680 and 1750 which colonies were growing fastest?

Procedure

Exploring changes in population involves analyzing statistics—facts in the form of numbers. A **statistical table** is an orderly arrangement of such numbers in rows and columns. To answer the question, you will be creating and analyzing your own table.

❶ Arrange the data in columns and rows. Use **A** and **B** to create a statistical table titled "Population by Colony: 1680 and 1750."

❷ Compare the data by reading across the rows.
a. Compare each colony's populations in 1680 and 1750. How many went up? Down?
b. Compare each colony's percentages in 1680 and 1750. How many went up? Down?

❸ Compare the data by reading down the columns.
a. Which two colonies had the largest populations in 1680? In 1750?
b. Look at the differences in percentages—first for 1680 and then for 1750. In which year was there a greater variety? Explain.

❹ Summarize the data. Based on the data in your table, answer the Question to Investigate.

Data to Use

A

Population by Colony 1680			
Colony	Population	Percentage of Total	Rank
Connecticut	17,246	11.4%	4
Delaware	1,005	0.7%	11
Maryland	17,904	11.8%	3
Massachusetts	46,152	30.5%	1
New Hampshire	2,047	1.3%	9
New Jersey	3,400	2.2%	8
New York	9,830	6.5%	5
North Carolina	5,430	3.6%	6
Pennsylvania	680	0.4%	12
Rhode Island	3,017	2.0%	7
South Carolina	1,200	0.8%	10
Virginia	43,596	28.8%	2

B In 1750 New Hampshire's population was 27,505, or 2.3% of the total population. Figures for other colonies: Massachusetts, 188,000 (16.1%); Rhode Island, 33,226 (2.8%); Connecticut, 111,280 (9.5%); New York, 76,696 (6.6%); New Jersey, 71,393 (6.1%); Pennsylvania, 119,666 (10.2%); Delaware, 28,704 (2.5%); Maryland, 141,073 (12.1%); Virginia, 231,033 (19.7%); North Carolina, 72,984 (6.2%); South Carolina, 64,000 (5.5%); and Georgia, 5,200 (0.4%). Georgia became a colony in 1732.

Source: *Historical Statistics of the United States*

Introducing the Skill Lab

To help students compare options for arranging the data, complete step 1 as a class. With the Question to Investigate in mind, ask them to consider how best to set up a table for comparing the data. As students suggest various options for column headings, put them on the chalkboard for comparison.

Skill Lab
Answers

1. The most efficient format for identifying changes would have "Colony," "Population," and "Percentage of Total" as main column headings. Each of the last two would have two subheads—"1680" and "1750." Rank might be added, but the percentage changes are the key figures.

2. (a) All the populations went up. (b) Nine percentages went up; three went down.

3. (a) Massachusetts and Virginia. In 1680 the former was largest; in 1750, the latter. (b) There was greater variety in 1680, when more than half of the population lived in Massachusetts and Virginia. By 1750 the population had become more evenly distributed, with about a third of the population living in those two states.

(Answers continued in top margin)

Survey Answers

Reviewing Vocabulary

Definitions are found on these pages: *invest* (120), *joint-stock company* (122), *exports* (123), *indentured servants* (124), *representatives* (124), *legislature* (124), *royal colony* (125), *bicameral* (129), *proprietary colonies* (133).

Reviewing Main Ideas

1. The government wanted markets for goods, resources for use, and a way to solve the problem of England's poor.

2. Giving colonists the right to own land, allowing people without money to come to the colony as indentured servants, and establishing the House of Burgesses.

3. The Pilgrims of Plymouth sought freedom of religious worship. The settlers of Virginia wanted profit.

4. (a) Puritans founded Massachusetts as a colony where they could have religious freedom. (b) Williams founded Rhode Island after being banished from Massachusetts. (c) Hooker helped found Connecticut after disagreeing with Puritan leaders in Massachusetts.

5. They disagreed over land and observance of laws. The war left thousands dead, destroyed many towns, and decreased the power of the New England tribes.

6. The English founded the Carolinas and Georgia to stop the Spanish from moving north. New York, New Jersey, Pennsylvania, and Delaware were part of conquered New Netherland.

7. All set up havens— Maryland for Catholics, Pennsylvania for Quakers, and Georgia for debtors. Maryland and Pennsylvania were successful. Georgia did not attract many debtors because of its strict rules.

(Answers continued in top margin)

140

Thinking Critically

1. Students may suggest a number of qualities such as bravery and curiosity.

2. Maryland gave all Christians freedom of religion. Pennsylvania gave religious freedom to all people who believed in God. Rhode Island welcomed people of all faiths.

3. The English and Indians had conflicts over land that led to fighting. The Spanish subjugated many Indians and forced them into slavery and to become Christians. The French traded and formed alliances with the Indians.

Applying Skills

New York, Pennsylvania, and New Jersey have the largest percentages of the population today. This differs from 1750, when Virginia, Massachusetts, and Maryland had

Chapter Survey ★

Reviewing Vocabulary

Define the following terms.
1. invest
2. joint-stock company
3. exports
4. indentured servants
5. representatives
6. legislature
7. royal colony
8. bicameral
9. proprietary colonies

Reviewing Main Ideas

1. Why did starting colonies make sense to the English government?
2. Describe two changes the Virginia Company made to help its colony survive after the "starving time."
3. How did the people who started Plymouth Colony differ from those who started Virginia Colony?
4. What led to the founding of each of the following colonies? (a) Massachusetts (b) Rhode Island (c) Connecticut
5. What was the main reason for conflict between Puritans and Indians? Describe the situation after King Philip's War.
6. Which colonies resulted from England's competition with Spain? With the Netherlands? Explain why.
7. What general goal did the founders of Maryland, Pennsylvania, and Georgia have in common? How successful was each colony in achieving that goal?

Thinking Critically

1. Synthesis What qualities did the Jamestown colonists probably have in order to leave home and settle in a land unknown to them? Explain why you chose particular qualities.
2. Application Respect for the beliefs of non-Protestants led to greater religious freedom in the colonies. How did individual colonies contribute to this change?

3. Why We Remember: Analysis How were relations between colonists and Indians different in the English, Spanish, and French colonies?

Applying Skills

Analyzing statistical tables How does the population distribution of the 13 colonies in 1750 compare with the distribution among those states today?
1. Create a statistical table titled "Populations of Selected States in 1995." For each state, show the population, the percentage of the total population of those 13 states, and the rank. You can get population figures from the table on pages R19–R23.
2. Analyze your table. Which states have the largest percentages? What similarities and differences can you find between the data in this table and the table you made for the Skill Lab?

History Mystery

Help from an Indian Answer the History Mystery on page 117. How would you go about learning more about Squanto's life in America and Europe? How might the history of Plymouth Colony have been different if the Pilgrims had not met Squanto?

Writing in Your History Journal

1. Keys to History (a) The time line on pages 116–117 has seven Keys to History. In your journal, list each key and describe why it is important to know about. (b) In your journal, make a chart with two columns. Label one column "Causes," and the other "Effects." Choose an event on the time line and describe the causes and the effects of that event.

the largest percentages. In 1750, Georgia had the smallest population, but it ranks fifth today. Rhode Island, New Hampshire, and Delaware had small populations in 1750, and they remain relatively small today.

History Mystery

A sea captain sold Squanto as a slave in Spain. Squanto escaped to England and later returned to America. Students might find more information about Squanto in library and reference books. If they had not met Squanto, the Pilgrims may not have been able to survive.

Writing in Your History Journal

1. (a) Explanations should be similar to the time line notes on teacher pages 116–117. (b) Tables will vary but should reflect the *(Answers continued in side margin)*

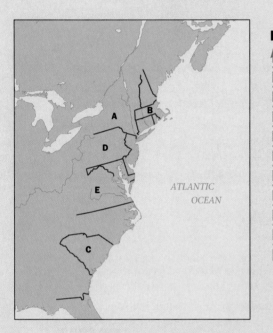

ATLANTIC
OCEAN

Reviewing Geography

1. For each letter on the map, write the name of the colony.

2. Geographic Thinking In 1699 colonists moved the capital of Virginia from Jamestown to Williamsburg, a town that had been settled in 1633. Williamsburg is about 7 miles (11 km) from Jamestown, on a high ridge between the James and York Rivers. What might be some advantages of Williamsburg's location over that of Jamestown? What might be some disadvantages?

2. Pocahontas Write the following headings in your journal: "Jamestown Colonist," "Virginia Indian." Under each heading, list at least three words that such a person might have used to describe Pocahontas. Add a third heading, your name, and list three words that you would use to describe Pocahontas. Then write a paragraph explaining any differences in these views of Pocahontas.

3. Thinking Historically How might relations between the Indians and the Puritans have been different if the Puritans had followed William Penn's beliefs and practices? Write your responses in your journal.

Alternative Assessment

Citizenship: Planning a colony
Imagine that the English king has given your class a charter to start a proprietary colony in North America. How will you organize it?

❶ With a group of three or four other proprietors, prepare a plan for the colony. Start with the information in the chapter and do additional research as needed to decide the goals of the colony and how you expect to achieve them.

❷ As you make your plan, consider these questions: What will you do to attract settlers to the colony? How will you avoid the problems that the Jamestown and Plymouth colonists had? How will you make the colony prosper? How will you govern the colony?

Your plan will be evaluated on the following criteria:
• it presents the information in clear, interesting ways
• it provides information that is realistic for the colonial period
• it provides information that takes into account the successes and failures of other colonies

multiple causes and effects of the chosen event. For example, causes of King Philip's War include land disagreements, the Puritan wish to force Indians to obey Puritan laws, and the trial and execution of Indians. Effects include the death of thousands, the destruction of towns, and the tribes' loss of power.

2. Student responses will vary but should reflect how the Indians and colonists would have viewed Pocahontas differently and how their own view would be different from a historical perspective.

3. Students may respond that the Puritans and the Indians would have lived more peacefully together with mutual respect.

Reviewing Geography

1. (A) New York,
(B) Massachusetts,
(C) South Carolina,
(D) Pennsylvania,
(E) Virginia

2. Possible advantages: Williamsburg was not built on low, swampy land subject to flooding. Soil would drain better, and there would be fewer mosquitoes. Possible disadvantages: Williamsburg was not a seaport, so people and goods would have to be carried across land to the water route.

Alternative Assessment

Teacher's Take-Home Planner 2, p. 13, includes suggestions and scoring rubrics for the Alternative Assessment activity.

6 Life in the English Colonies
1600–1750

Chapter Planning Guide

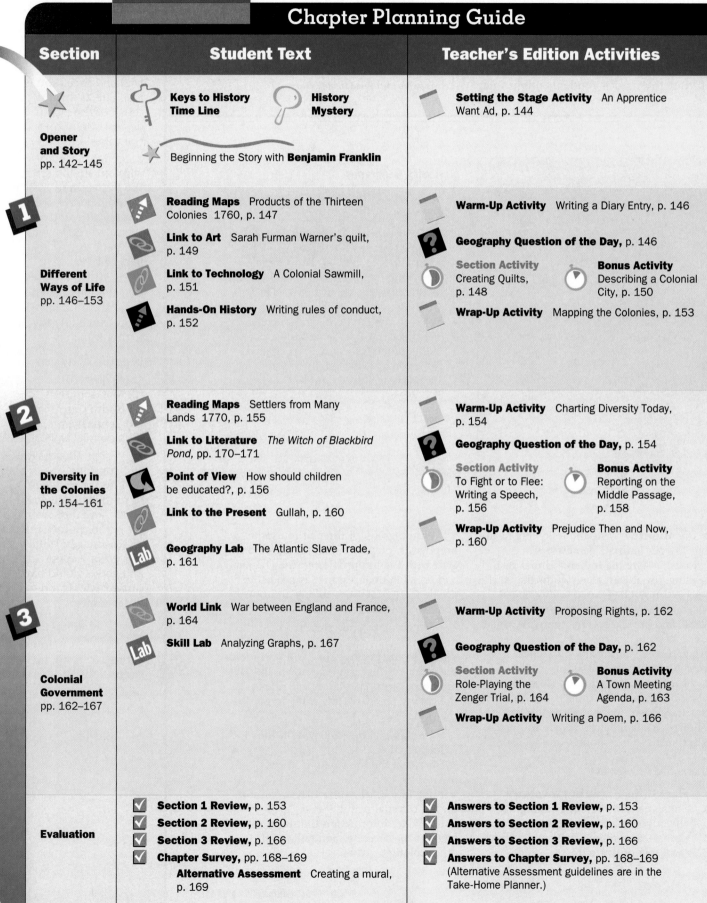

Section	Student Text	Teacher's Edition Activities
Opener and Story pp. 142–145	**Keys to History Time Line** **History Mystery** Beginning the Story with **Benjamin Franklin**	**Setting the Stage Activity** An Apprentice Want Ad, p. 144
1 **Different Ways of Life** pp. 146–153	**Reading Maps** Products of the Thirteen Colonies 1760, p. 147 **Link to Art** Sarah Furman Warner's quilt, p. 149 **Link to Technology** A Colonial Sawmill, p. 151 **Hands-On History** Writing rules of conduct, p. 152	**Warm-Up Activity** Writing a Diary Entry, p. 146 **Geography Question of the Day,** p. 146 **Section Activity** Creating Quilts, p. 148 **Bonus Activity** Describing a Colonial City, p. 150 **Wrap-Up Activity** Mapping the Colonies, p. 153
2 **Diversity in the Colonies** pp. 154–161	**Reading Maps** Settlers from Many Lands 1770, p. 155 **Link to Literature** *The Witch of Blackbird Pond*, pp. 170–171 **Point of View** How should children be educated?, p. 156 **Link to the Present** Gullah, p. 160 **Geography Lab** The Atlantic Slave Trade, p. 161	**Warm-Up Activity** Charting Diversity Today, p. 154 **Geography Question of the Day,** p. 154 **Section Activity** To Fight or to Flee: Writing a Speech, p. 156 **Bonus Activity** Reporting on the Middle Passage, p. 158 **Wrap-Up Activity** Prejudice Then and Now, p. 160
3 **Colonial Government** pp. 162–167	**World Link** War between England and France, p. 164 **Skill Lab** Analyzing Graphs, p. 167	**Warm-Up Activity** Proposing Rights, p. 162 **Geography Question of the Day,** p. 162 **Section Activity** Role-Playing the Zenger Trial, p. 164 **Bonus Activity** A Town Meeting Agenda, p. 163 **Wrap-Up Activity** Writing a Poem, p. 166
Evaluation	☑ **Section 1 Review,** p. 153 ☑ **Section 2 Review,** p. 160 ☑ **Section 3 Review,** p. 166 ☑ **Chapter Survey,** pp. 168–169 **Alternative Assessment** Creating a mural, p. 169	☑ **Answers to Section 1 Review,** p. 153 ☑ **Answers to Section 2 Review,** p. 160 ☑ **Answers to Section 3 Review,** p. 166 ☑ **Answers to Chapter Survey,** pp. 168–169 (Alternative Assessment guidelines are in the Take-Home Planner.)

Teacher's Resource Package

 Chapter Summaries: English and Spanish,
pp. 16–17

Chapter Resources Binder
Study Guide   Visual Images, p. 41

Reinforcement   Identifying Regions,
pp. 45–46
American Readings   Eliza Lucas Pinckney,
Planter, p. 21

Chapter Resources Binder
Study Guide   Reading for Details,
p. 42
Geography Extensions   The Atlantic Slave
Trade, pp. 11–12
American Readings   The Middle Passage,
pp. 22–23; Protest Against the Slave Trade,
p. 24

Chapter Resources Binder
Study Guide   Identifying Main Ideas,
p. 43
Skills Development   Analyzing
Graphs, pp. 47–48
Using Historical Documents   The Magna
Carta, pp. 32–37

Chapter and Unit Tests   Chapter 6 Tests,
Forms A and B, pp. 33–36

Take-Home Planner

Introducing the Chapter Activity
Making Workshop Signs, p. 20

Chapter In-Depth Activity   Stopping
Slavery by Never Starting It, p. 20

Reduced Views
Study Guide, p. 22
Reinforcement, p. 23
American Readings, p. 24
Unit 2 Answers, pp. 27–32

Reduced Views
Study Guide, p. 22
Geography Extensions, p. 25
American Readings, p. 24
Unit 2 Answers, pp. 27–32

Reduced Views
Study Guide, p. 22
Skills Development, p. 23
Using Historical Documents,
p. 25
Unit 2 Answers, pp. 27–32

Reduced Views
Chapter Tests, p. 25
Unit 2 Answers, pp. 27–32
Alternative Assessment   Guidelines for
scoring the Chapter Survey activity, p. 21

Additional Resources

Wall Time Line

Unit 2 Activity

**Transparency
Package**

Transparency 6-1   Colonial
Sawmill—use with Section 1
Transparency 6-2   Colonial
Home—use with Section 1
Transparency Activity Book

**SelecTest
Testing Software**
**Chapter 6 Test,
Forms A and B**

★ ★ ★
Vital Links

 Videodisc

CD-ROM

"Virginia Reel" (see TE p. 150)
Backcountry settlers (see TE
p. 152)
Voice of slave on the Middle
Passage (see TE p. 158)
"African Song" (see TE p. 159)
Zenger trial (see TE p. 165)
Salem witch trial (see TE p. 170)

6

Teaching Resources

Take-Home Planner 2
 Introducing Chapter Activity
 Chapter In-Depth Activity
 Alternative Assessment
Chapter Resources Binder
Geography Extensions
American Readings
Using Historical Documents
Transparency Activities
Wall Time Line Activities
Chapter Summaries
Chapter and Unit Tests
SelecTest Test File
Vital Links CD-ROM/Videodisc

Time Line

Keys to History

Keys to History journal writing activity is on page 169 in the Chapter Survey.

First Africans in English colonies The arrival of more than 20 Africans in Jamestown, some of whom were slaves, marked the beginning of black slavery in the English colonies. (p. 157)

First college in the English colonies The Puritans founded Harvard College to train ministers. (p. 148)

Looking Back Founded by the Spanish, St. Augustine is the oldest permanent European settlement in what is now the United States.

★ Compare different ways of life in the English colonies.
★ Discuss how diversity of people affected ways of life in the colonies.
★ Explain how colonists learned to govern themselves.

Chapter Overview
Differences in resources and in people's beliefs led to different settlement patterns in the English colonies. In New England the land, climate, and Puritan emphasis on community led most colonists to gather in towns around the harbors. Many fished and traded for a living. The rich soil of the Middle Colonies encouraged large farms, and the rivers provided transportation for trade

---

1600–1750

Chapter 6

Life in the English Colonies

Sections

Beginning the Story with Benjamin Franklin
1. **Different Ways of Life**
2. **Diversity in the Colonies**
3. **Colonial Government**

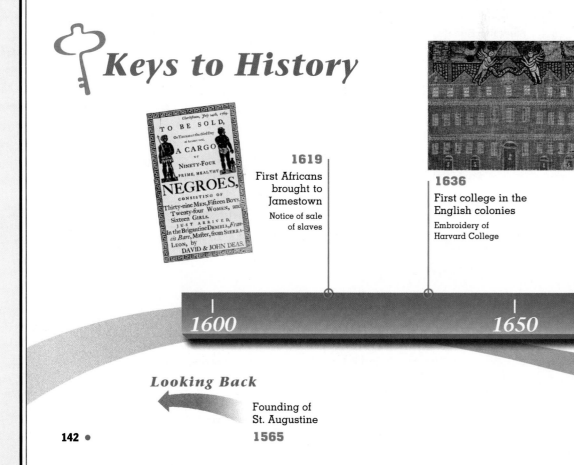

Keys to History

1619
First Africans brought to Jamestown
Notice of sale of slaves

1636
First college in the English colonies
Embroidery of Harvard College

1600

1650

Looking Back

Founding of St. Augustine
1565

and power for mills. Philadelphia and New York became major ports. On plantations in the Southern Colonies, planters grew cash crops like tobacco and rice. However, most southern settlers, like the backcountry settlers, were subsistence farmers.

Colonists from Europe brought with them their old prejudices. English settlers were intolerant of settlers from other countries. Religious prejudice was also common.

Racism was directed at American Indians, whose lands were taken, and at Africans, thousands of whom were enslaved.

The English colonists came to America with a love of liberty rooted in their past. Colonists soon became used to running their own affairs. They especially valued their right of self-government. Colonists often ignored British attempts to control trade, but Britain decided to enforce its trade laws.

Teaching the
HISTORY
Mystery

Students will find the answer on p. 159. See Chapter Survey, p. 168, for additional questions.

HISTORY
Mystery

The banjo was unknown in England and Europe, yet it was a well-known musical instrument in the English colonies. Where did the banjo come from?

1730s
Great Awakening begins
Preacher George Whitefield

1732
Ben Franklin publishes *Poor Richard's Almanac*
Picture in almanac

1735
Trial of Peter Zenger
Zenger's newspaper

1676
Bacon's Rebellion

1700

1750

World Link

War between England and France
1689

Looking Ahead

Colonists protest against the Stamp Act
1765

● **143**

Time Line

Bacon's Rebellion The revolt against Virginia's government reflected the tension between colonial governments and the backcountry settlers. (p. 153)

The Great Awakening The Great Awakening revived interest in religion throughout the colonies. (p. 155)

Poor Richard's Almanac Franklin's almanac, a compilation of advice and proverbs, became the second most popular book in the colonies. The Bible was the most popular. (p. 145)

Trial of Peter Zenger The acquittal of Peter Zenger on the charge of libel inspired colonists to speak out for freedom of the press. (p. 163)

World Link See p. 164.

Looking Ahead Protests against the Stamp Act marked the first widespread colonial opposition to British policies.

Beginning the Story

Benjamin Franklin

Running away from an apprenticeship in his brother's print shop in Boston, young Benjamin Franklin headed for Philadelphia. There he quickly found work as a printer's assistant. Before long he opened his own print shop and became a successful businessman. From his humble origins, Franklin rose to become an author, printer, inventor, scientist, politician, and statesman. He exemplified the spirit of America, where talent and hard work were recognized and rewarded.

Setting the Stage
Activity

An Apprentice Want Ad

To underscore the nature of the apprentice system, have students write an ad demanding the return of a runaway. Explain that apprenticeship was a common method of learning a trade, yet a harsh system allowing few freedoms. The ad should describe the apprentice's appearance, skills, and possible destination. Ask volunteers to read their ads.

See the Introducing the Chapter Activity, Making Workshop Signs. **Take-Home Planner 2**, p. 20.

✳ History Footnote

As a teenager, Franklin wrote a series of letters to the newspaper published by his brother James. Thinking that his brother would not print what he wrote, Franklin submitted the letters anonymously under the name "Mrs. Silence Dogood," supposedly a widow from the Boston area. Franklin named his fictitious writer after the subtitle of the book *Bonifacius: Essays to Do Good,* written by Cotton Mather, a well-known Puritan leader. The letters were well-received and widely read in Boston. They spanned a range of topics from the ridicule of hoop skirts to the criticism of the courts. Franklin wrote 14 "Silence Dogood" letters.

Beginning the Story with

Benjamin Franklin

On a Sunday morning in 1723, a 17-year-old stepped off a boat onto Philadelphia's Market Street wharf. His pockets bulged with extra socks and shirts. He was tired, dirty, hungry—and nearly broke.

The young man walked until he found a bakery. He later recalled trying to buy "biscuits such as we had in Boston." The baker did not make biscuits. "I asked for a three-penny loaf, and was told they had none such." His stomach growling, he finally asked the baker for "three-penny worth of any sort."

"He gave me, accordingly, three great puffy rolls. I was surprised at the quantity, but took it, and, having no room in my pockets, walked off with a roll under each arm, and eating the other. Thus I went up Market Street as far as Fourth Street, passing by the door of Mr. Read, my future wife's father, when she, standing at the door, saw me and thought I made, as I certainly did, a most awkward, ridiculous appearance.**"**

The embarrassed young man followed a crowd of "clean dressed people" into a Quaker meetinghouse and promptly fell asleep.

The Runaway from Boston

The sleeping teenager with crumbs on his shirt was a runaway apprentice named Benjamin Franklin. At the age of 12, Franklin had been apprenticed to his brother James, who owned a printing shop in Boston. Apprentices, like indentured servants, were bound by contracts to work for their masters for a fixed number of years. Ben's contract was for nine years. During this period, the apprentice was expected to work long hours for no pay. In exchange for

History Bookshelf

Meltzer, Milton. *Benjamin Franklin: The New American.* Franklin Watts, 1988. Without overlooking Franklin's faults and mistakes, the author presents a human portrait of a man of his times. Richly illustrated with paintings, cartoons, etchings, and drawings, the book was chosen as an American Library Association Notable Book for Children in 1988.

Also of interest:

Sherrow, Victoria. *Huskings, Quiltings, and Barn Raisings.* Walker Publishing Company, 1992.

Warner, John F. *Colonial American Home Life.* Franklin Watts, 1993.

Washburne, Carolyn Kott. *A Multicultural Portrait of Colonial Life.* Marshall Cavendish, 1994.

his brother's labor, James promised to teach Ben the printing trade.

Like many masters, James felt free to beat his apprentice when displeased with his work. Ben came to resent his brother and "the blows his passion too often urged him to bestow upon me." After five years of such treatment, Ben decided to run away.

A sympathetic sea captain smuggled Franklin to New York City. He walked and then took another boat to Philadelphia. There, Franklin quickly found work as a printer's assistant. In a few years he was able to open his own printing shop.

Business Success

To succeed, Franklin had to print something people would buy. His first big seller was a newspaper called the *Pennsylvania Gazette.* Late in 1732 the *Gazette* carried an advertisement for a new almanac written by "Richard Saunders" and printed by B. Franklin. In fact, the author and printer were one and the same, a secret kept by Franklin for many years.

Like other almanacs, *Poor Richard's Almanac* contained a calendar of the coming year along with weather predictions and planting times for crops. Between these topics, Franklin inserted wise and witty sayings. Here are three examples:

❝Work as if you were to live 100 years, pray as if you were to die tomorrow.
When the well's dry, we know the worth of water.
Three may keep a secret, if two of them are dead.❞

Poor Richard's Almanac quickly became the most popular book in the English colonies after the Bible. It made Franklin a wealthy man.

Benjamin Franklin went on to become a well-known scientist and inventor, a colonial leader, and a diplomat. It was said that only in the English colonies of North America could a penniless runaway become a success simply through talent and hard work.

The Philadelphia that Ben Franklin knew lives on today in Elfreth's Alley. The brick houses were built in the early 1700s. The street-lamps are based on a design by Franklin.

Hands-On → *HISTORY*

Imagine that you are Poor Richard. Create a calendar of the coming week, including information about class and school events. Then write a saying for each day of the week. Keep your sayings short and to the point.

Activity

Thinking Historically

1. How was Franklin like many other colonists? (He was hard-working, thrifty, practical, and self-reliant.)

2. Would it be possible for Franklin to achieve success today? (Yes: abilities and hard work would make him a success; no: lack of education would hold him back.)

3. Do you think Franklin would recommend the apprentice system? Why or why not? (Some may think he would because it helped people learn trades. Others may think he would argue that some employers took advantage of apprentices.)

See the Chapter In-Depth Activity, Stopping Slavery by Never Starting It. **Take-Home Planner 2,** p. 20.

Teaching the

Hands-On
┌ - - - - - → *HISTORY*

Emphasize that the saying should provide advice. Encourage students to relate their sayings to the events they are noting in their calendars. A saying like "to avoid delay, be prepared today" might appear for the day of a class field trip.

For a journal writing activity on Benjamin Franklin, see student page 169.

Vocabulary

subsistence farming (p. 146) raising enough food to subsist—to survive—on

literacy (p. 148) the ability to read and write

imports (p. 150) products brought in from another country to be sold

Tidewater (p. 150) low, wet area on the Atlantic coastal plain

cash crops (p. 150) crops raised to be sold for a profit

Warm-Up Activity

Writing a Diary Entry

Have students identify jobs that were needed in the colonies. Ask them to imagine that they must choose a job in which they will train as an apprentice. Have them write a diary entry identifying what kind of apprenticeship they want and why. Conclude by having students share their entries with the class.

Geography Question of the Day

Ask students to write an answer to the following question: If you were moving to the backcountry to start a farm, how would you choose a site and what would you have to do to change the site into farmland?

---

1. Different Ways of Life

Reading Guide

New Terms subsistence farming, literacy, imports, Tidewater, cash crops

Section Focus The different ways of life in the English colonies

1. How did colonists use the land and resources they found in North America?
2. What patterns of settlement did they create in different regions?
3. How did settlement patterns affect towns and schooling?

When Ben Franklin sat down to write *Poor Richard's Almanac,* he had a clear picture of his readers in mind. Most were farming folk who did **subsistence farming.** That means they raised just enough to subsist—to survive—on, with perhaps a little surplus to sell or trade.

Even so, visitors traveling through the colonies were struck by how different life was from region to region. The way the colonists lived depended in part on the land and the resources they found. In some cases it also depended on where the colonists came from and the ideas they brought with them about the kinds of societies they hoped to build.

The New England Colonies

The colonists who settled in New England found a "rocky, barren, bushy, wild-woody" land. During the last ice age, glaciers scraped across New England's hilly land, carrying off most of the soil. They dumped the rich earth into the sea, where it mounded into great banks. Ocean plants thrived on these undersea banks, as did millions of fish.

Making a living The soil the glaciers left behind is thin and rocky. The region also has only five months of warm weather

between killing frosts. In that short growing season, it was hard for colonial farmers to raise much of a surplus to sell.

Given the poor land and harsh climate, many settlers chose to make their living from the sea and the forests. Fishing grounds were rich in cod, mackerel, and halibut. New Englanders dried and salted fish and sold them to other colonies, the English West Indies, and to Europe.

From the forests came lumber for building fishing boats and merchant ships. Soon every port town had a shipyard as well as ropemakers, sailmakers, and blacksmiths. In time, New England ships carried Virginia tobacco, Carolina rice, and other colonial products to England. There the ships were loaded with manufactured goods to be sold in the colonies.

Settling in towns Unlike colonists in other regions, New Englanders settled in close-knit towns. The geography of the region encouraged this pattern of settlement. It was natural for colonists to cluster around good fishing harbors or pockets of fertile farmland.

Puritan religious beliefs also supported this settlement pattern. The Puritans hoped to build a model Christian community. In this community, people would live, work, and worship together. Each person would "watch over his neighbor's soul as his own."

Students with Limited English

Students with limited English often have difficulty identifying main ideas and distinguishing them from supporting details. Explain that the questions listed under the reading guide at the beginning of each section give clues to the main ideas presented in the section. Have students read the three questions

at the beginning of section 1. Then ask them to write each main idea in the central circle of a separate spider web. (For example, one main idea is ways in which colonists used natural resources.) As they read, students should add supporting details to each web. They can then use the webs as study guides for the section.

Developing the Section

Discussion

Checking Understanding

1. Why did many New Englanders turn to the sea and forests to earn a living? (Poor soil and harsh climate discouraged large farms, but fish were abundant and forests provided resources for shipbuilding.)

2. How did New England's geography affect settlement? (People settled near harbors and land that was good for subsistence farming.)

Stimulating Critical Thinking

3. How did fish and forests help make New England a trade center? (Fish were sold to other colonies and overseas; lumber was used to build merchant ships.)

Teaching the
↑ **Reading Maps**

Point out that numbers near the pictures correspond to those on the map. Ask: **What are the numbers for?** (To identify where the activities took place.) **What information do the pictures and map provide?** (Pictures show economic activities; the map locates them.) **Answer to Reading Maps:** Shipbuilding made New England a center of trade; large farms in the Middle Colonies harvested grain; in the Southern Colonies rice was grown; forested land in the backcountry was cleared for subsistence farms.

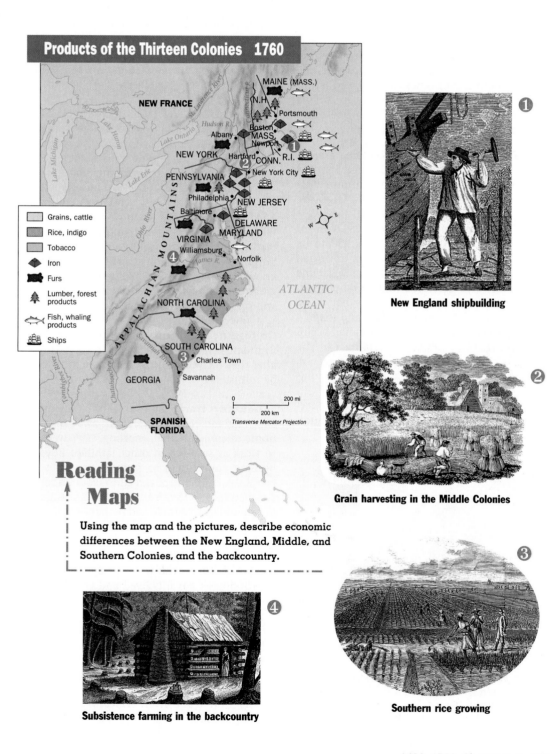

Products of the Thirteen Colonies 1760

Legend:
- Grains, cattle
- Rice, indigo
- Tobacco
- Iron
- Furs
- Lumber, forest products
- Fish, whaling products
- Ships

0   200 mi
0   200 km
Transverse Mercator Projection

New England shipbuilding ❶

Grain harvesting in the Middle Colonies ❷

Southern rice growing ❸

Subsistence farming in the backcountry ❹

Reading
↑ Maps

Using the map and the pictures, describe economic differences between the New England, Middle, and Southern Colonies, and the backcountry.

Creating Quilts

To show regional characteristics, have students work in groups to make quilts. Point out that designs often revealed much about colonial life. Assign each group a region (New England, Middle, Southern, or backcountry) and give each member a square of cloth or construction paper. After drawing regional scenes on the squares, they will sew or glue them into a quilt. Provide several books with pictures of quilts to show the rich variety of designs. Conclude by having groups examine each other's quilts to identify regional characteristics.

See the Study Guide activity in the **Chapter Resources Binder**, p. 41.

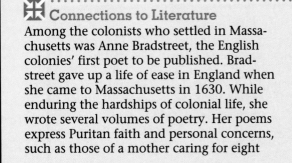

Connections to Literature

Among the colonists who settled in Massachusetts was Anne Bradstreet, the English colonies' first poet to be published. Bradstreet gave up a life of ease in England when she came to Massachusetts in 1630. While enduring the hardships of colonial life, she wrote several volumes of poetry. Her poems express Puritan faith and personal concerns, such as those of a mother caring for eight children. Bradstreet's work was not published in the colonies. As she wrote, "such despite they cast on female wits / if what I do prove well, it won't advance—They'll say 'tis stol'n or else it was by chance." But many of her poems are preserved because a relative took them to London where they were published.

Town life centered around the meetinghouse where Puritans gathered to worship. They built their homes close by, so that no one lived too far away to come to Sunday meetings. Just as important, no one could escape a neighbor's "holy watching."

Family life Daily life centered around the family, which was usually large. Families with 8 or 9 children were common. Ben Franklin's family was unusually large—he was the youngest of 17 children.

There was plenty of work for every member of the family to do. Crops had to be planted, cared for, and harvested. Cows had to be milked, and livestock fed. Vegetable gardens and orchards had to be tended. Butter, bread, cheese, and cider had to be made, as did clothing, candles, and soap.

By the age of 8, most children had begun working. Boys joined their fathers in the fields or in the family business. At age 10, Franklin was cutting wicks and filling molds in his father's candle-making shop.

Girls helped their mothers with household, barnyard, and garden tasks. In addition, wives and daughters helped with the harvesting, delivered babies, nursed the sick, and cared for the elderly.

Education The Puritans, as well as most other colonists, placed a high value on **literacy**—the ability to read and write. They wanted their children to be able to read God's word directly from the Bible.

To encourage literacy, Massachusetts led the colonies in providing schools. A law in 1647 required every town of 50 or more families to hire an instructor to teach reading and writing. Young children were taught by women at home in what were known as dame schools. Older boys attended grammar schools provided by larger towns and run by male schoolmasters.

A few young men went on to Harvard College near Boston. The Puritans had founded Harvard in 1636, only six years after they arrived, mainly to prepare men to be ministers.

Leaving home By the age of 12, many New England children were sent away from home to complete their training. Girls went to work as servants in other families. Boys became apprentices to farmers or tradespeople. An apprentice agreed to work under a skilled master for a certain period of time in order to learn a trade and perhaps reading and writing.

During these years, young people learned the skills they would need to succeed on their own. Those who were not apprenticed or working as servants lived and worked at home until they married.

After young people married, they often left their hometowns in search of better land and opportunities. As they moved, they took with them the pattern of settling in towns rather than on scattered farms. Throughout New England today, there are towns that trace their history back to Puritan founders.

Over time, small schools, paid for by local taxes, spread across New England. A single teacher would teach students, from 3-year-olds to teenagers, in a one-room schoolhouse.

As the colonies became more settled and prosperous, theater became a popular entertainment. Williamsburg, Virginia, boasted the first colonial theater in 1718, followed later by theaters in New York and Charles Town. Local actors performed, sometimes supported by traveling British actors. In 1749 the first performance by a professional British acting troupe in the colonies took place, before audiences in Virginia, New York, and Maryland. Philadelphia, however, forbade the troupe to perform, and the troupe did not even try to play in New England. New England's Puritans and Pennsylvania's Quakers opposed stage plays as improper, nonreligious entertainment. By the time of the War of Independence, however, Boston was the only major city to ban stage plays.

∞ Link to Art

Sarah Furman Warner's quilt Faced with the cold winters of North America, colonial women made quilts to keep their families warm. Using scraps of cloth, bits of worn-out clothing, and even muslin flour sacks, quilters created "paintings in fabric" that were passed down from generation to generation.

This picture shows part of a quilt that was made by Sarah Furman Warner, who probably lived in Connecticut, around 1800. **Discuss** What does this detail of the quilt show about New England life? If you were to give this detail of the quilt a title, what would it be? Why?

The Middle Colonies

From the beginning of the colonial period, the Middle Colonies attracted a great variety of settlers. Some were drawn to the area by the promise of good land. Others came for the freedom to worship as they wished in Pennsylvania.

As a result, the population of the Middle Colonies grew rapidly. Between 1680 and 1750, the number of colonists in Pennsylvania alone increased from 680 to more than 119,000.

The land The smaller Middle Colonies, New Jersey and Delaware, lay on the flat Atlantic Coastal Plain. The two larger colonies, Pennsylvania and New York, stretched from the coastal plain up to hill country known as the Piedmont. Beyond the Piedmont lay the Appalachian Mountains.

Rivers both great and small flow eastward out of the Appalachians to the Atlantic Ocean. At the eastern edge of the Piedmont, the land drops sharply. Here rivers tumble in waterfalls and rapids to the coastal plain below. For this reason, the eastern edge of the Piedmont is known as the Fall Line.

Making a living Both the coastal plain and the Piedmont offered settlers deep, rich soil. William Penn told the truth when he advertised Pennsylvania as "a good and fruitful land, in some places . . . like to our best vales [valleys] in England."

So good was the soil that the region was soon exporting wheat, barley, oats, and livestock to the Southern Colonies and the West Indies. Most farmers in the Middle Colonies spread out across the land rather than following the New England pattern of settling in towns.

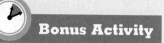

Bonus Activity

Describing a Colonial City

As students examine pictures of colonial cities they infer aspects of colonial life. Provide books and other resources that have illustrations depicting different colonial cities. The *American Heritage Pictorial Atlas of United States History* is a good source. Have groups choose a colonial city and use the pictures to write a description of what life was like there. Conclude by having groups discuss similarities and differences between cities.

★ ★ ★
Vital Links

"Virginia Reel" (Song)
Unit 1, Side 1, Search
48355, Play to 50465

See also Unit 1 Explore
CD-ROM location 386.

For excerpts from letters of Eliza Lucas Pinckney, see **American Readings,** p. 21.

✳ History Footnote

Eliza Lucas's family had moved to South Carolina in 1738 from Antigua, a West Indies British colony. They had come to claim three plantations near Charles Town that her father had inherited. Returning to Antigua a year later, her father left the plantations in the care of young Eliza, who spent three years experimenting with crops, including ginger, cotton, alfalfa, and indigo.

After successfully growing and marketing indigo, she shared her knowledge with other South Carolina planters. By 1754, South Carolina was exporting about one million pounds (454,000 kg) of indigo a year.

Some colonists used the rapidly falling water along the Fall Line to provide power to mills, ironworks, and other kinds of workshops. Visitors to the region found skilled workers making hardware, clocks, watches, locks, guns, glass, stoneware, nails, paper, rope, and cloth.

Trade in the Middle Colonies kept port towns bustling. The hub of Pennsylvania's commerce was Philadelphia. By the mid-1700s it was the largest city in the colonies. New York City, the other great center of business in the Middle Colonies, was the second largest.

Into both cities poured crops and livestock for shipment to other regions or abroad. From England came imports—books, paintings, clothing, and furniture. **Imports** are products brought in from another country to be sold. New ideas came, too. When the fork became the latest fashion for dining, wealthy city people quickly learned how to use it.

Education Like the Puritans, the Quakers wanted their children to be able to read the Bible. So did members of many other religious groups that settled in the Middle Colonies. Just how children were to be educated was left up to each family or group to decide. Some religious groups, such as the Quakers, built schools for their children. Other children were taught at home.

The Southern Colonies

The Southern Colonies covered a large area with a great variety of climates and soils. By 1750 they also had the most colonists. Life here was very different from New England and the Middle Colonies.

The land Seen from the ocean, the Southern Colonies appeared to have no solid shoreline. From Maryland to Georgia, the Atlantic Coastal Plain is laced with rivers, bays, swamps, and estuaries. The water level of all these waterways moves up and down with the daily rise and fall of the tide. For this reason, colonists called this low, wet area the **Tidewater.**

The Tidewater is well-suited for growing crops on a large scale. The soil is fertile, and rainfall is plentiful. Best of all, the growing season lasts up to eight months.

This area was not, however, a healthy place for people in colonial times. The wetlands bred a deadly combination of mosquitoes and disease. As temperatures rose each summer, so did the death rate.

As a result, life expectancy in the Southern Colonies was lower than in New England and the Middle Colonies. In one county in Virginia, nearly one-fourth of the children had lost both parents by the age of 13.

Making a living Most of the settlers in the Southern Colonies did subsistence farming. They raised grain and vegetables on small farms. A few had the help of indentured servants, but most relied on the family to work the farm.

The kind of farming for which the Southern Colonies became famous, though, was the plantation, where a single crop was grown for profit. Crops that are raised to be sold for a profit are called **cash crops.**

The tobacco of Virginia, Maryland, and North Carolina became the most profitable cash crop of the English colonies. After the 1690s, rice became an important cash crop in South Carolina and Georgia. Later, in the 1740s, 17-year-old Eliza Lucas of South Carolina produced the first successful crop of indigo, a plant used to make blue dye. It, too, became a cash crop.

Plantation life To succeed, a plantation owner needed a large tract of good land and a large work force. As you will read in the next section, finding enough workers was one of the planters' biggest problems.

Corn was a basic crop in the colonies. Nothing of the corn plant was wasted. Cattle and oxen ate its leaves. The husks became mattress stuffing, and children made dolls from its stalks. Colonists ate corn on the cob, corn puddings and stews, and cornmeal bread. Corn was fermented to make beer and whiskey and was an ingredient in a cure for toothache. The English looked down on American corn. When a London newspaper wrote that the grain was not digestible, Benjamin Franklin defended corn, writing that "Indian corn, take it for all in all, is one of the most agreeable and wholesome grains in the world . . . and that johny or hoecake, hot from the fire, is better than a Yorkshire muffin."

Link to Technology

A Colonial Sawmill

Colonial Americans relied heavily on water power to fuel industry. A mill placed at the bottom of a waterfall used the force of the falling water. Sawmills were especially common because wood was plentiful and colonists used lumber to build homes and ships and to make millions of barrels for trade and industry. Lumber was also a major colonial export.

❶ The water wheel, turned by a waterfall or stream, provided the power to operate the mill.

❷ The water wheel powered the mechanism that moved the logs through the mill.

❸ Gears attached to the water wheel moved the saw blade up and down to cut the logs as they moved past.

❹ The cut lumber—100 board feet an hour—fell into the stream at the end of the mill, to be gathered later.

Checking Understanding

1. Why did a variety of settlers find the Middle Colonies attractive? (The land was good for farming; the colonies offered religious tolerance.)

2. Why were the Middle Colonies a good place to manufacture many kinds of goods? (Rivers along the Fall Line provided power to operate mills and workshops.)

Stimulating Critical Thinking

3. What do you think was the advantage of the long growing season in the Tidewater area? (Farmers could plant and harvest more than one crop in a single season.)

Teaching the

Link to Technology

Point out that water wheels convert the energy of moving water into mechanical energy. The one shown on this page is a vertical, overshot waterwheel. Water from above the wheel falls into buckets on the waterwheel, and the weight of the water turns the wheel. The turning wheel is connected to mechanisms and gears that operate the mill. Have students use the numbered illustration and captions to describe the mill operation.

Connections to Art

By the 1700s, a number of colonists were wealthy enough to afford having formal portraits of themselves and their families painted, such as the one shown on this page. At first, most colonial painters were immigrants from Europe. Before long, however, artists born in the colonies were gaining recognition. Many began their work in the colonies and then went to England, at least for a time. There they studied and painted. Among the most famous artists born in the colonies was John Singleton Copley. According to John Adams, Copley was "the greatest master that ever was in America."

Hands-On
- - - - - - - - → *HISTORY*

Writing rules of conduct Learning good manners was an important part of a child's education in the Southern Colonies. As a boy, George Washington copied down a list of 110 "rules of civility and decent behavior in company and conversation." Here are a few examples.

"1st Every action done in company ought to be with some sign of respect to those that are present. . . .

37th In speaking to men of quality do not lean nor look them full in the face, nor approach too near them. . . .

46th Take all admonitions [advice] thankfully. . . .

110th Labor to keep alive . . . that little spark of celestial [heavenly] fire called conscience."

- - - → **Activity** If Washington were alive now, what rules of conduct would he need to learn? Write three of your own "rules of decent behavior in company and conversation" to guide him.

The Rapalje children, 1768

By the early 1700s, plantations had spread out along most Tidewater rivers. Oceangoing ships moved up and down the rivers, picking up crops and dropping off goods made in England and in other colonies. Access was so easy that few towns grew into centers of trade.

The distance between neighbors meant that plantations had to be self-sufficient— able to take care of their own needs. Like a New England town, a large plantation had its own blacksmith, miller, weaver, and butcher. People met in their homes rather than in meetinghouses.

As for education, some wealthy planters hired indentured servants or tutors from northern colleges to teach their children at home. Others provided funds for private schools. Still others sent their children to schools in England. Almost everyone else did without schooling.

The Backcountry

To the west of the Tidewater, the land slopes upward onto the Piedmont and the foothills of the Appalachians. This region of low, rolling hills stretches from Pennsylvania south to Georgia. Settlers called it the backcountry.

The land The backcountry was a hilly, densely wooded region. Its forests teemed with fish and wildlife, making it a prized Indian hunting ground. Tucked among the hills were fertile hollows and valleys with good soil.

To settlers from Scotland and Ireland the backcountry offered just what they had crossed the Atlantic to find—a kind of freedom that they called "elbowroom." For decades the Scots and Irish had lived under the rule of English landlords and soldiers.

Many settlers in the backcountry raised "woods" cattle. They were grazed in cow pens, large areas scattered throughout the backcountry. One visitor described such an area: "A Cow-Pen generally consists of a very large Cottage or House in the Woods, with about . . . one hundred acres, inclosed with high Rails and divided; a small Inclosure they keep for Corn, for the family, and the rest is the Pasture in which they keep their Calves . . . they may perhaps have a stock of four or five hundred to a thousand Head of Cattle belonging to a Cow Pen, these run as they please in the Great Woods."

At hog killing time in the fall, settlers joked that "all the hog was used but the squeal." The meat from four large hogs, salted in barrels, could keep a family fed through winter. Settlers made the fat into lard to use for cooking. They used the intestines to make sausage skins and long hair from the tail to sew buckskin clothing.

Far off in the backcountry, they were at last beyond the reach of both.

Daily life Backcountry settlers lived rough, simple lives. Families were large and close-knit. Home was usually a log cabin set in a small clearing. Wives and daughters raised small crops of corn and vegetables while husbands and sons hunted and fished. Schools were few and far between, so children were taught what they needed to know at home.

Most backcountry settlements were far from the colonial assemblies that governed them. When trouble arose between Indians and settlers who were taking their lands for farms, the settlers often felt that their government failed to protect them.

Tension boiled over in Virginia in 1676. There, a planter named Nathaniel Bacon led a group of 300 neighbors in attacking local Indian villages. Then, to show their anger at the colonial government, they burned Jamestown.

Bacon's Rebellion, as it was called, ended when Bacon died of an illness. However, relations between colonial governments and backcountry settlers would continue to be strained.

1. Section Review

1. Define **subsistence farming, literacy, imports, Tidewater,** and **cash crops.**
2. What resources were most important to the colonists' success in New England? In the Southern Colonies?
3. What attracted settlers to the Middle Colonies? To the backcountry?
4. What conditions led to the growth of colonial towns? What conditions hurt their growth?
5. Critical Thinking In which region would you have most wanted to live? Give reasons to support your answer.

Closing the Section

Section Review
Answers

1. Definitions: *subsistence farming* (146), *literacy* (148), *imports* (150), *Tidewater* (150), *cash crops* (150)
2. New England: abundant fishing grounds, good harbors, forests; Southern Colonies: fertile soil, plentiful rainfall, warm climate.
3. Middle Colonies: rich soil, religious toleration. Backcountry: freedom to live and work as one pleased.
4. New England: proximity to good harbors and emphasis on close communities of believers; Middle Colonies: trade; Southern Colonies: easy access to rivers. Large distances between settlements and isolation hurt growth of towns.
5. Students might choose New England because of community lifestyle, Middle Colonies because of trade opportunity, Southern Colonies because of self-sufficiency of plantations, or backcountry because of close-knit families.

Warm-Up Activity

Charting Diversity Today

By identifying the diversity of Americans today, students gain insight into colonial diversity. Have them prepare a diversity chart for Americans today. The chart might include columns for country of origin, language, culture, and religion. As they read this section, students can compare the diversity of populations in the colonies with the diversity of the present-day population in the United States.

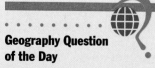

Geography Question of the Day

Direct students to the illustrations and captions on pages 147 and 157. Have them note differences in ways settlers and Indians used the land. (Settlers cleared large areas and used great quantities of the resources for trade, whereas Indians cleared very little and used only resources they needed to survive.)

Teaching Resources

Take-Home Planner 2, pp. 20–25

Chapter Resources Binder

  Study Guide, p. 42

  Reinforcement

  Skills Development

Geography Extensions, pp. 11–12

American Readings, pp. 22–24

Using Historical Documents

Transparency Activities

Chapter and Unit Tests

2. Diversity in the Colonies

Reading Guide

New Terms prejudice, revival, racism

Section Focus How the great variety of people shaped life in the colonies

1. What prejudices did settlers bring to the colonies?
2. Why did conflicts arise between colonists and American Indians?
3. What caused the enslavement of Africans to become part of colonial life?

On his first journey from Boston to Philadelphia in 1723, Ben Franklin must have been struck by the mix of people he met. Unlike mostly Puritan New England, Pennsylvania boasted many nationalities and religions. A Maryland doctor who made a tour of the colony in the 1740s wrote of dining at a tavern with

❝Scots, English, Dutch, Germans, and Irish; there were Roman Catholics, Churchmen, Presbyterians, Quakers, Newlightmen, Methodists, Seventh Day men, Moravians, Anabaptists, and one Jew.❞

Differences Among European Americans

The first settlers in the colonies were mostly English. After the 1680s, a growing number came from other parts of Europe. Each group brought with it old patterns of prejudice against people of other nationalities. A **prejudice** is a bad opinion of people based only on such factors as their religion, nationality, or appearance.

English colonists, for example, often looked down on settlers from France and other parts of Europe. Such people, with their diverse languages and customs, seemed strange to the English.

In Pennsylvania, prejudice was especially strong against settlers from a part of Germany called the Palatine. The Palatines continued to speak German and stayed apart from their English neighbors. By the 1760s Germans made up one-third of the population of Pennsylvania. A worried Ben Franklin asked:

❝Why should Pennsylvania, founded by the English, become a colony of aliens [foreigners], who will shortly become so numerous as to Germanize us?❞

In time, such prejudice softened. As people began working together to build new lives, the importance of national backgrounds faded.

Religious prejudice Religious prejudice was slower to fade. Although most colonists were Protestants, they belonged to many different sects, with different beliefs. Most sects were intolerant of people who did not share their beliefs.

When Quakers came to Virginia, for example, laws were passed to try to drive them out. Prejudice against Roman Catholics was even stronger, even in Maryland, which had been founded as a haven for Catholics. By the early 1700s, Protestants in the Maryland legislature had put limits on Catholics' freedom to worship.

✳ **History Footnote**

Throughout Europe in the 1500s and 1600s, Christians feared that there were witches who had supernatural powers from the devil. Puritans and many other colonists brought this strong fear with them to America. Although suspected witches were persecuted in other colonies, Massachusetts held the most infamous witch trials in Salem in 1692. The trials were the result of a witch hunt begun after several local girls began screaming as though tortured, making strange noises, and crawling around. Accusations and rumors led to the arrest of over 150 suspected witches. At the time, witchcraft was punishable by death, and 19 suspects were executed. Ministers helped end the witch scare, and in 1693 the suspects still in jail were released.

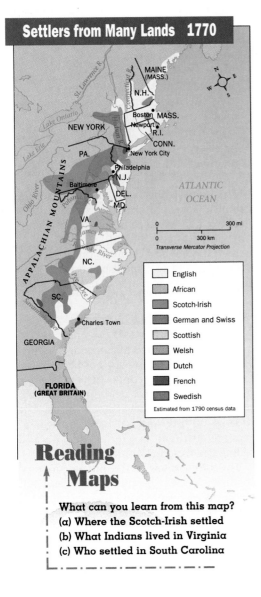

Settlers from Many Lands 1770

☐	English
▨	African
▨	Scotch-Irish
▨	German and Swiss
☐	Scottish
▨	Welsh
☐	Dutch
▨	French
▨	Swedish

Estimated from 1790 census data

Reading Maps

What can you learn from this map?
(a) Where the Scotch-Irish settled
(b) What Indians lived in Virginia
(c) Who settled in South Carolina

Jews suffered as well. Nowhere in the colonies did Jews have the right to vote or hold office. Still, they were allowed to worship and work in peace. As a result, in the mid-1700s the 1,000 or so Jews in the English colonies were probably the freest Jews on earth.

The Great Awakening

In the early years, religion played a very important part in the lives of most colonists. As time went by, however, faith faded and church membership declined. "The forms of religion were kept up," a Puritan said, but the "power of godliness" was missing. Another colonist wrote that "religion lay a-dying."

A revival of faith In the 1730s and 1740s, a **revival**—a renewed interest in religion—swept the colonies. The colonists called this renewal of faith the Great Awakening.

The flames of revival were fanned by preachers who traveled from town to town holding outdoor meetings. At these gatherings they delivered fiery "awakening sermons," urging listeners to renew their commitment to Christian faith.

The most famous preacher of the Great Awakening was an Englishman named George Whitefield. Wherever he spoke, he drew huge crowds. One day in Boston he preached to 20,000 people. His message made women tremble and men weep.

Results of the Awakening Revivals touched the hearts and souls of countless colonists. In Philadelphia, Franklin wrote:

❝From being thoughtless or indifferent about religion, it seemed as if all the world were growing religious, so that one could not walk through the town in an evening without hearing psalms sung in different families of every street.❞

The Great Awakening divided religious groups everywhere. New England was hit especially hard as church members chose sides. Some clung to old churches and teachings. Others were attracted to the revivalist message that all souls were equal before God, and all people could have a personal experience of faith.

Developing the Section

Discussion

Checking Understanding

1. What are examples of religious prejudice in the colonies? (Restrictions on Catholics in Maryland, Virginia trying to drive out Quakers, Jews not allowed to vote or hold office.)

2. What brought about the Great Awakening? (Revival meetings led by preachers.)

Stimulating Critical Thinking

3. Why do you think interest in religion had declined before the Great Awakening? (Perhaps people found strict religious rules hard to follow or were too busy trying to make a living.)

Teaching the ↑ Reading Maps

Have students identify major groups within each colony. **Answer to Reading Maps:** The map provides information about (a) and (c), but not (b).

See the Study Guide activity in the **Chapter Resources Binder,** p. 42.

For a fictional account of rumors of witchcraft in a Puritan town, see the Link to Literature on pages 170–171.

The devastating effects on American Indians of the diseases brought by Europeans continued into the 1600s. Smallpox, cholera, measles, and mumps claimed the lives of thousands and reduced many groups to remnants. Among these were the Sewee people who lived around the Santee River in South Carolina. It is estimated that the Sewee numbered around 800 in 1670.

Only 30 years later, a visitor to the area, John Lawson, found barely 50 people. Lawson noted that the Sewee suffered the same fate that "all other Nations of Indians are [observed] to partake . . . when the Europeans come."

The split between these groups led to new prejudices. At the same time, the Great Awakening showed the need for religious toleration if the colonists were to live together in peace.

Colonists and Indians in Conflict

Although some patterns of prejudice were fading, others were growing stronger. These prejudices arose from **racism**—the belief that one race of people is superior to another. The first people to suffer from racism in the English colonies were American Indians.

Early meetings Most early meetings between colonists and Indians were friendly. In Chapter 5 you read that Pocahontas and Squanto saved the first English settlers from starving. Sadly, such early friendships did not last.

Racism colored the colonists' attitude toward Indians. Sure that the English way of life was best, they at first tried to turn native peoples into English Protestants like themselves. The Indians, though, had no interest in giving up their own cultures. They were happy to trade with the colonists, but not to live like them.

Point of View
How should children be educated?

An incident in 1744 shows the different views of colonists and Indians. It took place at a meeting between Virginia officials and Iroquois leaders. As a gesture of goodwill, the officials offered to send some Iroquois youths to college and to "bring them up in the best manner."

The Iroquois thanked the officials but said no. They had already sent some of their sons to the colonists' college. When the teenagers came home,

> "they were bad runners, ignorant of every means of living in the woods, unable to bear either cold or hunger, knew neither how to build a cabin [or] take a deer, . . . [and] they were totally good for nothing."

The Iroquois then offered to educate the colonists' sons, promising to "instruct them in all we know, and to make men of them." This offer was also refused.

Both Indians and colonists preferred their own ways of life. Would it be possible for them to live together in peace?

Who Owns the Land?

The greatest source of misunderstanding was over land. Indians did not believe that land belonged to people. Instead, people belonged to the land where they farmed, hunted, fished, and gathered foods. The idea of buying and selling land was as strange to them as that of buying and selling the wind or the sky.

The colonists saw land as private property. In their view, the best use of the land was for farms and settlements. They thought it was wasteful to leave some land wild, as Indians often did. Thus they did not hesitate to take over land that Indians had been using for generations. Land, wrote Governor John Winthrop of Massachusetts, should belong "to any that could and would improve it."

To fight or flee As the colonies grew, settlers cleared and plowed more and more land, and forests disappeared. So did the animals that Indian hunters needed to feed their families. In 1642 Miantonomo, a Narragansett chief, complained:

John Rolfe described the arrival of the first Africans in North America in a letter to Sir Edwin Sandys, a member of the Virginia Company. "He [Captain Jope, a Dutch ship commander] brought not anything but 20 and odd [Africans], which the governor and cape merchant bought for victualles [food] . . . at the best and easiest rates they could." These first Africans may have been sold as bound servants or as slaves, but by the 1640s the custom of selling Africans as slaves for life was established. By the 1660s and 1670s, colonies were passing laws that reinforced slavery. In 1664, for example, Maryland passed a law declaring all Africans in the colony slaves for life.

Discussion

Checking Understanding

1. How did conflict between colonists and Indians begin? (Colonists wanted Indians to accept their way of life and they began taking over Indian lands. Indians and colonists had different ideas about how to use the land.)

2. How did the colonists' use of the land affect the Indians? (Colonists destroyed the resources that Indians depended on for shelter and food.)

Stimulating Critical Thinking

3. How did racism affect colonists' actions toward Indians? (Colonists viewed Indian cultures as inferior and thus felt justified in taking Indian lands and destroying Indian ways of life.)

American Indians, such as these fishermen and the women making maple syrup, believed in taking from nature just enough to live on. Colonists, though, saw such resources as profitable trade goods.

"Our fathers had plenty of deer, . . . fish and fowl. But these English have gotten our land. . . . Their cows and horses eat the grass, and their hogs spoil our clam banks, and we shall all be starved."

Hunger, combined with European diseases, wiped out many tribes. The rest faced a terrible choice. Should they fight the invaders or flee their ancient homelands?

Endless conflict You have read that some tribes did stand and fight, only to be destroyed. Others fled to what they hoped would be safety in the backcountry. They were not safe for long.

As colonists moved into the backcountry, new conflicts arose. Indians saw settlers as greedy invaders who stole their land and burned their villages. Settlers saw Indians as dangerous, ready to attack at any moment.

Such attitudes were to exist wherever Indians and settlers confronted each other.

African Americans

The second group to suffer from racism in the English colonies were Africans. The first Africans were brought to Virginia in 1619. Historians think that at least some of them worked as indentured servants and were later freed. A few bought land and white and black servants of their own.

By the late 1600s, however, southern planters were in need of workers. Fewer English people were coming to the colonies as indentured servants. To solve the problem, planters adopted a system that had long been used on Caribbean sugar plantations—slavery. Under this system, workers belonged to their owners for life. So did their children.

Reporting on the Middle Passage

Students gain insight into the horrors of the Atlantic slave trade by writing a news report. Tell them to imagine that they are doing an investigative report on the Middle Passage. Suggest that they describe the passage through the experiences of captured Africans. Remind them that a reporter would write a story that describes who, what, where, when, why, and how. Provide time for students to write and discuss reports.

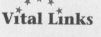
Vital Links

Voice of slave on the Middle Passage (First Person Account) Unit 1, Side 1, Search 26432, Play to 27152

See also Unit 1 Explore CD-ROM location 249.

For an excerpt from Equiano's account of the Middle Passage, see **American Readings**, pp. 22–23.

Tips for Teaching

Visual Learners

The illustrations on page 158 showing conditions on slave ships graphically reinforce the excerpt from Equiano's book. Visual learners can analyze these illustrations as you read the excerpt aloud. Have them relate what they see in the pictures to Equiano's description.

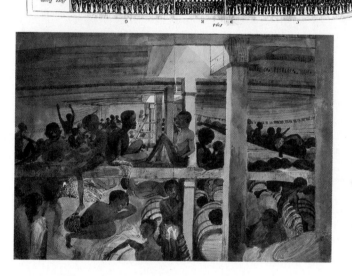

Enslaved Africans going to America were crammed so closely together in slave ships that they could barely move. After the voyage came the terror of sale. Olaudah Equiano, a victim of the slave trade, described his experiences in a book.

The Atlantic Slave Trade

When Tidewater planters began buying enslaved Africans in large numbers, the Atlantic slave trade was already a big business. Every year American and European captains sailed to West Africa. There they traded cloth, rum, and guns for Africans captured by slavers. They carried their human cargoes back across the Atlantic for sale in the Americas as slaves.

For the captured Africans, the horrors of that voyage, known as the "Middle Passage," were beyond imagining. Packed into ships, many died of disease or despair and were thrown overboard. The sharks that followed slave ships seldom went hungry. Olaudah Equiano, who was born in 1745 in present-day Nigeria, made that voyage at about the age of 10. Later he wrote:

❝The closeness of the place, . . . added to the number in the ship, which was so crowded that each had scarcely room to turn himself, almost suffocated us. . . . The shrieks of the women, and the groans of the dying, rendered the whole a scene of horror.❞

Terrified, Equiano refused to eat anything, hoping "for the last friend, Death, to relieve me." However, he was among those who survived.

Even with the high death rate, the slave trade was very profitable. Many colonial merchants earned fortunes by trading in human beings. Between the 1500s and the 1800s, at least 10 million Africans were sent into slavery in North and South America. Some historians claim the real figure was closer to 20 million.

Throughout the colonial period, there was very little opposition by white people to the practice of slavery. Quakers recorded the first known protest. In 1688, a Quaker congregation in Germantown, near Philadelphia, signed a petition stating that it was un-Christian to "bring men hither, or to rob and sell them against their will."

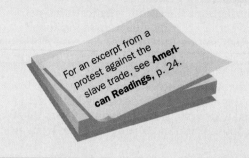

For an excerpt from a protest against the slave trade, see **American Readings**, p. 24.

Discussion

Checking Understanding

1. Why was the Middle Passage a voyage of horrors for enslaved Africans? (So many were crammed together in ships that scores died of disease, suffocation, and despair.)

2. Why did the New England and Middle Colonies have far fewer enslaved Africans than the Southern Colonies? (Farms were smaller and did not require a large labor force. Slavery was not necessary to the trade and commerce of the New England and Middle Colonies.)

Stimulating Critical Thinking

3. Why do you think music, dance, and art became important parts of the new African American culture? (Students may infer that these arts provided some relief from the horrors of slavery, as well as a common bond between people from different African cultures who spoke different languages.)

"Slave Young, Slave Long"

By the early 1700s, enslaved Africans could be found in every English colony. In the New England and Middle Colonies, though, farmers did not have plantations, which required large work forces. Thus there were never many slaves living in the northern colonies.

The slave population grew rapidly in the Southern Colonies, however. Planters in Maryland, Virginia, and North Carolina bought thousands of Africans to work their tobacco fields. South Carolina rice planters were eager to have slaves from rice-growing regions of Africa. They also used slaves to raise indigo and cattle.

Slaves faced a lifetime of unrewarded toil. Most worked as field hands, raising the cash crops that allowed their owners to live well. Others worked at skilled trades or as household servants. They began working by age 6 and continued until they died. As one old enslaved African put it, "Slave young, slave long."

A New African American Culture

On their arrival in the English colonies, some Africans rebelled by refusing to work or trying to run away. Escape in an unknown land was very difficult, though, and rebellion was severely punished.

As a result, most Africans learned to survive as best they could. They came from many different cultures, with different languages and traditions. Under the most difficult of conditions they began to create a new African American culture.

This new culture preserved much that slaves had brought with them from Africa. Their music and dances pulsed with African rhythms. Musical instruments like the banjo were African, too. African designs showed up in their weavings, wood carvings, pottery, and quilts.

African legends and stories survived, as well. Children still heard the tale of how the lion got its roar. Br'er Rabbit, the wily hero of many slave tales, was based on the African trickster Shulo the Hare.

✶ ✶ ✶
Vital Links

"African Song" (Song) Unit 1, Side 2, Search 02598, Play to 04227

See also Unit 1 Explore CD-ROM location 259.

Planters with large estates often hired overseers to supervise the work of slaves. The overseer in this picture probably got fired for doing more relaxing than overseeing. As one planter complained, "The overseer there is but a chattering fellow, promises much but does little." By the mid-1700s some large plantations no longer used overseers.

Teaching the

Have students translate the first Gullah sentence. ("If you can't behave yourselves, I'll take you straight home.") Explain that Gullah words such as *gumbo* have become part of American speech. Ask students why they think Gullah is still used today. (Perhaps to preserve a cultural tradition.)

Closing the Section

Wrap-Up Activity

Prejudice Then and Now

To compare prejudices today with those in colonial times, have students make a chart. Columns should be labeled "Racial," "Ethnic," and "Religious." Rows should have these labels: Colonial examples and Examples today. Conclude by discussing whether prejudice is less or more widespread today.

Section Review Answers

1. Definitions: *prejudice* (154), *revival* (155), *racism* (156)

2. Against other countries, races, or religions.

3. Land; Indians did not believe it could be owned, but settlers saw it as property.

4. Few indentured servants so planters bought slaves.

✳ **History Footnote**

Throughout the colonies Africans resisted slavery, usually by escaping. Many sought refuge among Indians or in Spanish Florida.

From 1733 the Spanish offered freedom to all slaves from the north. As a result, some Africans headed for St. Augustine. In September 1739 a leader named Cato gathered a group of slaves along the Stono River in South Carolina. Seizing weapons from an arsenal, they headed south. Before they were caught they had killed about 30 whites. The Stono River uprising was one of the few slave revolts that occurred from the 1600s until the Civil War.

⦿ **Link to the Present**

Gullah "If unna kyant behave unna self, I'll tek yu straight home." Can you figure out what that sentence means? It is in a language called Gullah. Developed by enslaved Africans 300 years ago, Gullah is still spoken in parts of the southeastern United States.

Enslaved Africans came from a variety of cultures, each with its own language. Brought together on plantations, they needed to communicate with both the planters and one another. In South Carolina and Georgia, especially on the Sea Islands off the coast, slaves combined African languages and English to create Gullah.

Gullah is still a living language. In 1994 the American Bible Society published part of the New Testament in Gullah. The Gullah name for the Book of Luke is "De Good Nyews Bout Jedus Christ Wa Luke Write."

Benjamin Banneker taught himself mathematics and astronomy. Later he helped plan Washington, D.C.

matician, was the son of a freed slave. He became famous for his almanacs.

Free African Americans did not have the same rights or opportunities as other colonists did, though. Few whites were willing to accept blacks as their equals.

Why did whites think blacks were less than equal? Colonist John Woolman, a Quaker, blamed the system of slavery itself. When whites heard blacks called "slaves" and saw them doing only the hardest, dirtiest work, he wrote,

❝[it] tends gradually to fix a notion in the mind that they [African Americans] are a sort of people below us in nature.❞

Woolman spoke out against slavery. Still, the racist thinking of most white colonists continues to haunt America today.

In time, most slaves adopted the Christian faith. They were drawn by its message that all people are equal in the sight of God and its promise of a better life to come after death. Here, too, African Americans blended elements of African religions with the new faith.

Free but Not Equal

Free African Americans—who had been given their freedom or who had escaped—lived throughout the colonies. Most worked as laborers or household servants. A few prospered. Benjamin Banneker, a mathe-

⭐ ## 2. Section Review

1. Define **prejudice, revival,** and **racism.**
2. What old prejudices did settlers bring with them to the English colonies?
3. What was the greatest source of conflict between colonists and American Indians? Explain why.
4. **Critical Thinking** What conditions enabled slavery to become so firmly rooted in the Southern Colonies?

Dutch shipping companies were the primary importers of slaves to Virginia until 1660. Then Britain set up an English trading company, the Royal Adventurers. Chartered to carry on the slave trade, it was reorganized in 1672 as the Royal African Company. The company was to have a monopoly in the slave trade, but the control of the slave trade was never effectively enforced.

Geography Lab

The Atlantic Slave Trade

Enslaved Africans were the key laborers on plantations in North and South America. The exact number will never be known, but at least 10 million Africans were sent into slavery in the Americas. Use the map and the table to determine some lasting effects of this huge forced movement of peoples.

The Way People Describe Themselves 1990s

	White	Black	*Mixed	Other
United States	80%	12%		8%
Haiti		95%	5%	
Jamaica		75%	13%	12%
Brazil	53%	11%	34%	3%
Nicaragua	10%	9%	77%	4%
Venezuela	20%	9%	69%	2%

*Different mixtures of black, white, and Indian ancestors
Source: Encyclopædia Britannica

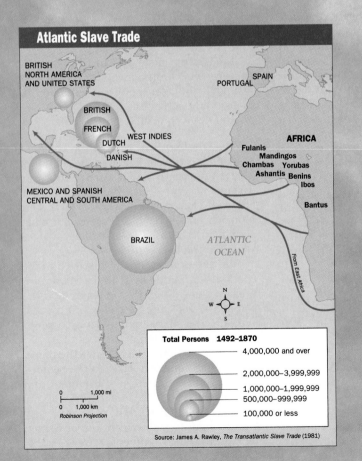

Atlantic Slave Trade

BRITISH NORTH AMERICA AND UNITED STATES

SPAIN

PORTUGAL

BRITISH

FRENCH

WEST INDIES

DUTCH

DANISH

AFRICA

Fulanis
Mandingos
Chambas   Yorubas
Ashantis   Benins
Ibos

MEXICO AND SPANISH CENTRAL AND SOUTH AMERICA

Bantus

BRAZIL

ATLANTIC OCEAN

From East Africa

N W E S

Total Persons 1492–1870

— 4,000,000 and over
— 2,000,000–3,999,999
— 1,000,000–1,999,999
— 500,000–999,999
— 100,000 or less

0   1,000 mi
0   1,000 km
Robinson Projection

Source: James A. Rawley, The Transatlantic Slave Trade (1981)

Link to History

1. From what parts of Africa were African laborers sent?

2. What countries took part in the Atlantic slave trade?

3. Where in the Western Hemisphere were the largest number of Africans sent? The smallest number?

4. On the map on pages R2–R3 locate the nations listed in the table. How do you explain the differences in the makeup of the population in the different nations?

5. **Hands-On Geography** Imagine that you are writing a book on African traditions in one country in the Western Hemisphere. List six cultural characteristics you might study to find evidence of links to Africa. Cultural characteristics include ideas, customs, skills, and arts. For example, you might compare foods eaten in the country you chose with the traditional dishes of Africa.

Teaching the Geography Lab

Have students identify the kind of information shown on the map and the table. Ask: **What is the subject of the map?** (Atlantic slave trade) **What is the subject of the table?** (People's self-identification in the 1990s) **What continents are shown on the map?** (Africa, Europe, North America, and South America) Based on the map and the table, ask them to draw some conclusions about effects of the slave trade on North and South America.

Link to History Answers

1. West and East Africa.

2. Britain, Spain, France, Netherlands, Denmark, United States, Mexico, Brazil.

3. The largest number were sent to Brazil; the smallest to the Danish West Indies.

4. Answers might include: some countries relied more heavily on African labor than others; some countries were not as vigorously colonized as others.

5. Suggest that students investigate such areas as music, dance, folklore, festivals, language.

See the activity on the Atlantic slave trade in **Geography Extensions,** pp. 11–12.

Vocabulary

tyranny (p. 162) the harsh use of power

militia (p. 163) citizens trained to fight in an emergency

libel (p. 164) print statements that damage a person's good name

Proposing Rights

Have students imagine themselves as colonists and work in groups to list rights and freedoms they want. Then compile a class list to compare later with what colonists actually had or wanted.

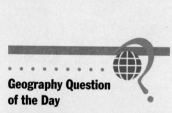

Geography Question of the Day

Have students use the world map on pages R2–R3 to identify how far it was from Britain to the colonies (about 3,000 miles, or 5,000 km). Have them identify problems in governing colonies so far away.

See **Using Historical Documents**, pp. 32–37, for an activity on the Magna Carta.

Section Objectives

★ Identify the rights and freedoms colonists valued.

★ Examine the way that colonial governments worked.

★ Describe ways that Britain tried to control colonial affairs.

Teaching Resources

Take-Home Planner 2, pp. 18–25

Chapter Resources Binder

  Study Guide, p. 43

  Reinforcement

  Skills Development, pp. 47–48

  Geography Extensions

  American Readings

  Using Historical Documents, pp. 32–37

  Transparency Activities

Chapter and Unit Tests, pp. 33–36

---

3. Colonial Government

Reading Guide

New Terms tyranny, militia, libel

Section Focus How the colonists learned to govern themselves

1. What rights and freedoms did the colonists value?
2. How did colonial governments work?
3. How did Great Britain try to control colonial affairs?

At the age of 42, Ben Franklin retired from business. For a time, he threw himself into the study of a new form of energy called electricity. This research brought him fame at home and in Europe.

In 1753 Franklin was appointed postmaster general for the colonies. The growth of the colonies had been truly astonishing. In 1650 there had been barely 50,000 colonists, most of them living in Massachusetts and Virginia. By 1750 there were more than a million colonists spread from Maine to Georgia.

In his new job Franklin traveled throughout the colonies, looking for ways to improve postal service. Along the way he met people of every background. Despite their differences, he found that most colonists had something in common: a deep attachment to their basic rights and freedoms.

A Love of Liberty

English colonists' love of liberty was rooted in their past. The English had a long history of struggling to protect their rights from the **tyranny**—the harsh use of power—of rulers.

The Magna Carta The first victory in that struggle came in 1215 when English nobles forced King John to sign the Magna Carta, or Great Charter. This agreement said that a monarch could not tax the people without consulting them. It also gave people accused of crimes the right to a trial by a jury of their peers, or equals.

This was the first time an English ruler had accepted limits on his or her power. Although the agreement was intended to protect only nobles, the rights it listed were eventually given to all English people.

The Declaration of Rights The next milestone in the struggle was the founding of Parliament in 1265. Parliament was formed of representatives from across England. They met regularly to advise their monarch on new laws and taxes. But what if their ruler refused to take their advice? Who had the last word?

That question was finally answered in the Glorious Revolution of 1688. In the revolution, Parliament forced King James II off the throne. In 1689 the new king and queen, William and Mary, signed an agreement called the Declaration of Rights.

The Declaration of Rights gave the power to make laws and levy taxes to the people's elected representatives in Parliament and no one else. It also listed the rights of all the people, including the right to trial by jury and the right to make a petition, or written request, to the government.

One right cherished by English colonists was that of habeas corpus, the Latin term meaning literally "you should have the body." It refers to the police holding a person, or body, under arrest. A writ of habeas corpus is a court document requiring that a person accused of a crime be brought promptly before a judge for a hearing. This protects a person from arbitrary arrest or long imprisonment without a court hearing. Habeas corpus originated in medieval England and was firmly embodied in English law in the Habeas Corpus Amendment Act of 1679. The right of habeas corpus is guaranteed by Article 1, section 9, of the Constitution of the United States and can only be suspended in times of war or rebellion.

The Right of Self-Government

One of the freedoms the colonists valued most was the right of self-government. In no other country on earth, not even in Great Britain,* did ordinary people have as much freedom to run their own affairs as did the colonists.

By the 1750s every colony had its own elected assembly. Like Parliament, each assembly had the power to pass laws and levy taxes. The assemblies also decided how tax money should be spent.

Colonists were also used to governing their local communities. New Englanders, for example, held town meetings to discuss such issues as how much to pay the schoolmaster or how to organize a **militia**—citizens trained to fight in an emergency. After everyone had a chance to speak, they took a vote to settle the issue.

Assemblies and governors
Besides an assembly, most colonies had governors appointed by the crown. The governor was responsible for seeing that the colony followed English laws. He had to approve any act passed by the assembly before it could become law. In theory, this meant the governor had a great deal of power.

In practice, however, assemblies found ways to get around governors. One way was to refuse to vote a salary for a governor who did not cooperate. Another way was to refuse to vote money for something a governor wanted. Franklin called this practice the "purchase of good laws." To the governors, it felt more like blackmail.

Soldiers burned Peter Zenger's newspaper that criticized the New York governor. The trial of Zenger led to one of the earliest calls for freedom of the press.

Peter Zenger and a Free Press

Many colonial governors were hardworking and honest. Some, however, were lazy or corrupt. Today we expect our free press to tell us if officials are dishonest. In colonial times, however, freedom of the

Developing the Section

Discussion

Checking Understanding

1. How did the English heritage influence the colonists? (Tradition of limiting royal power, representatives, and guaranteeing basic rights and freedoms.)

Stimulating Critical Thinking

2. Why did colonists think self-government was important? (They were far from Britain and needed to make their own decisions.)

Bonus Activity

A Town Meeting Agenda

Divide the class into groups and have each group prepare an agenda for a New England town meeting. For example, the town may need to find a new minister or hire a new school teacher. Conclude by having students share their agendas with the class and explain how they chose their agenda items.

See the Study Guide activity in the **Chapter Resources Binder,** p. 43.

*In 1707 the Kingdom of England and Wales united with the Kingdom of Scotland under one government, called Great Britain. Colonists, however, continued to speak of "England."

War between England and France

In the late 1600s a great struggle was shaping up between England and France for power in Europe as well as in North America. Between 1689 and 1748, three bitter wars engulfed Europe. People in North America were unable to stay out of them. To help pay for the wars, England needed more revenue than ever before from its American colonies.

In 1754 another war would break out. In the end it would determine which nation would win the competition for power in Europe and North America.

press did not exist in England or in the English colonies. Under English law, criticizing an official in print was dangerous.

A New York printer named Peter Zenger learned this lesson when he was thrown into jail in 1734 and held for ten months. Zenger had printed articles in his newspaper, the *Weekly Journal*, accusing New York's governor of taking bribes. He was charged with **libel**—printing statements that damage a person's good name.

When his trial began in 1735, Zenger's cause seemed hopeless. The judges had been handpicked by the governor. They chose a young, inexperienced lawyer to defend Zenger. As the defense began, however, a white-haired gentleman limped forward to address the court on Zenger's behalf. He was Andrew Hamilton, probably the ablest lawyer in the colonies.

A call for freedom of the press
Hamilton admitted that Zenger had printed the statements criticizing the governor. If those statements were false, they would indeed be libel. But the statements were true, he argued, and the truth could never be called libel. The real issue, Hamilton told the jury, was not libel, but rather the freedom to print the truth. He concluded:

"The question before the court . . . is not of small or private concern. It is not the cause of a poor printer, nor of New York alone. . . . It may in its consequence affect every free person that lives under a British government. . . . It is the best cause. It is the cause of liberty, . . . the liberty both of exposing and opposing arbitrary power [abuse of power] by speaking and writing truth."

The jury took just ten minutes to decide that Zenger was not guilty.

Although the verdict freed Zenger, it did not change English law, and therefore it did not guarantee freedom of the press in the English colonies. However, the Zenger case did inspire other colonists to continue the fight for freedom of the press and to criticize officials who abused their power.

The Navigation Acts

The one area of life that colonists did not control was trade. Beginning in 1660, Parliament passed a series of laws known as the Navigation Acts. The purpose of these acts was to control trade with the colonies in three ways.

First, all trade goods coming to and from the colonies had to be carried in English or colonial ships. This law was good for both English and colonial shipowners.

Second, the Navigation Acts listed colonial products that could be sold only in England. The list included tobacco, sugar, forest products, and furs. This control ensured the British a steady flow of colonial

By the middle of the 1600s, the colonies and Britain had developed a trading system that benefited both sides of the Atlantic. The navy protected colonial commerce, and colonial traders found a ready market for their products in England. They also had access to manufactured goods and credit. Port towns that existed largely for the exchange of international goods arose and prospered. Among the largest were Boston, Philadelphia, New York, and Charles Town. For their part, the British benefited from the colonial market for their manufactured goods, the interest they received for credit, and the income from selling colonial products on the European continent.

Discussion

Checking Understanding

1. What did England expect to gain by the Navigation Acts? (To ensure that all trade goods were carried by English or colonial ships, ensure a steady supply of colonial resources at low prices, and tax foreign goods to encourage colonists to buy English goods instead.)

2. How did the Navigation Acts help and hurt the colonists? (They helped colonial shipbuilders because goods could be carried only on colonial or English ships. However, they made it illegal for colonists to sell goods to other countries and made foreign goods more expensive in the colonies.)

Stimulating Critical Thinking

3. Do you think British leaders had a right to expect the colonies to help make Britain richer? (Some may think that since the colonists were British citizens protected by the British army and navy, the leaders could expect them to contribute to Britain's wealth. Others may argue that the colonies had grown with little help from the British government and that therefore the colonists owed little to the mother country.)

This detail from a 1739 sketch shows the importance of Charles Town (now Charleston), South Carolina, as a center of trade. It also was the port of entry for more than 40 percent of the enslaved Africans brought directly to the colonies.

products at low prices. It hurt the colonists, however. They could not sell their goods in other countries, even if the prices were higher there.

Third, any goods coming to the colonies from countries other than England had to pass through England. There they were taxed and loaded onto English or colonial ships. This law, too, helped English merchants but hurt colonists. The taxes made the foreign goods more expensive for colonists to buy than similar English goods.

For nearly 100 years, colonists accepted these trade controls with little complaint. For one thing, the laws were not often enforced. When they were, merchants got around them by smuggling goods in and out of the colonies.

Britain Prepares to Crack Down

In the 1750s, however, British leaders began paying closer attention to their American colonies. Britain still saw the colonies in terms of mercantilism. The colonies were to make the home country richer by trading only with it, and they were to obey the rules laid down by Parliament.

Instead, colonists were ignoring the Navigation Acts. To make matters worse, colonial assemblies were gaining power at the expense of their governors and acting too independently.

In a humorous verse, Benjamin Franklin compared Great Britain to a mother who

★ ★ ★
Vital Links

Zenger trial (Picture) Unit 1, Side 1, Search 39801

See also Unit 1 Explore CD-ROM location 356.

Writing a Poem

To focus on simmering resentment of British laws, have students imagine themselves as colonists writing humorous poems like Franklin's. Some topics are to describe governors as royal puppets, comment on the Zenger trial, or criticize the Navigation Acts. Ask volunteers to read their poems to the class.

Section Review
Answers

1. Definitions: *tyranny* (162), *militia* (163), *libel* (164)

2. Magna Carta, founding of Parliament, Glorious Revolution, Declaration of Rights of 1689.

3. Both could pass laws, levy taxes, and decide how to spend money.

4. To make sure the colonies did most of their buying and selling with Britain rather than with foreign countries.

5. Arguments for: public's right to know, need to hold officials accountable; arguments against: ruining reputations unnecessarily, threat to privacy.

To check understanding of "Why We Remember," assign Thinking Critically question 3 on page 168.

✠ **Connections to Economics**

Because British trade policies favored Britain and to avoid spending currency, colonists developed triangular trade routes. Some routes violated British law since they involved direct trade with other nations. One route carried colonial fish, grain, and lumber to the West Indies in exchange for sugar and molasses. These were shipped to Britain and Europe and traded for manufactured goods.

Another route took New England rum to Africa and exchanged it for slaves. Slaves were sold in the West Indies for sugar and molasses, which in turn were shipped to New England and made into rum. By the early 1700s, most slaves were taken directly from Africa to mainland colonies. Other triangular trade continued, however, bringing great profits to colonial merchants.

---

insists on treating her grown children (the colonists) like babies:

❝We have an old mother that
    peevish is grown;
She snubs us like children that
    scarce walk alone;
She forgets we're grown up and
    have sense of our own.❞

Britain, however, had other ideas. The time had come, it decided, to crack down on the colonies.

⭐ 3. Section Review

1. Define **tyranny, militia,** and **libel.**
2. What were the sources of the rights and freedoms that were important to the colonists?
3. In what ways were colonial assemblies like Parliament?
4. What was the purpose of the Navigation Acts?
5. Critical Thinking Should the press be free to print anything about anyone, as long as it prints the truth? Why or why not?

Why We Remember

Life in the English Colonies

By 1750 the English colonies were home to more than a million people. With the exception of a few individuals like Ben Franklin, most of them are long forgotten. Their legacy, however, is still very much alive.

The colonists came from a world where most people were desperately poor and would remain so. In that world, wealth and power belonged to the privileged few. Also, people looked, talked, and thought like their neighbors. Differences in language, religion, or ways of life could lead to war.

On the east coast of North America, the colonists created a different world. Here a penniless runaway could become a success through talent and hard work. Ordinary people had a greater voice in running their governments. People were freer to work, worship, and raise their children as they thought best. In this world most people found it better to tolerate differences than to fight over them. This was the world that they passed on to the future.

The colonists left another, more painful legacy as well: a pattern of racism toward people of color. This legacy led to the destruction of countless native peoples and the enslavement of millions of Africans. This legacy of prejudice is also part of our world today.

(Answers continued from side margin)
3. (a) The overall pattern in 1750 met England's goal: the colonies imported more than they exported to England. **(b)** Exceptions were colonies exporting the most farm products—particularly tobacco, which was in great demand in England and was the most profitable colonial cash crop. New England and Middle Colonies had fewer natural resources that England wanted.

For further application, have students do the Applying Skills activity in the Chapter Survey (p. 168).

If students need to review the skill, use the Skills Development transparency and activity in the Chapter Resources Binder, pp. 47–48.

Skill Lab

Acquiring Information
Analyzing Graphs

Sell more than you buy. That is what England tried to do by controlling colonial trade. In fact, trade officials in London kept track of yearly imports and exports to see whether that goal was being met. The totals for 1750—a typical year—must have brought both smiles and frowns to their faces.

Question to Investigate

How well did England meet its goal of selling more than it bought from the colonies?

Procedure

Explore the question by using data to make graphs. Look at the Skill Tips and study **A**, **B**, and **C**.

❶ Decide what graphs to make.
a. Make a graph that best shows exports and imports for each colony or area.
b. Make a graph that best shows each colony or area's percentage of total exports.

❷ Analyze the graphs.
a. Which colonies or areas exported more than they imported?
b. What percentage of the total exports came from those colonies or areas?

❸ Summarize the graphs and relate the data to what you know about history.
a. Describe the overall trade pattern.
b. How would you explain the exceptions? (Consider the products England wanted most.)

Skill Tips

- A bar graph shows amounts for different years, places, things, or people.
- A circle graph shows percentages. It shows how parts relate to the whole.
- A line graph shows changes in amounts.

Data to Use

Key:
C = The Carolinas
G = Georgia
NE = New England
NY/NJ = New York and New Jersey
P/D = Pennsylvania and Delaware
V/M = Virginia and Maryland

Data Source for **A**, **B**, and **C**: *Historical Statistics of the United States*

A

Colonial Trade with England 1750		
Colony/Area	**Exports**	**Imports**
C	191,607	133,037
G	1,942	2,125
NE	48,455	343,659
NY/NJ	35,634	267,130
P/D	28,191	217,713
V/M	508,939	349,419
Total	**814,768**	**1,313,083**

Values in British pounds

B

New England's Trade with England 1750

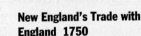

C Imports from England by Colony/Area 1750

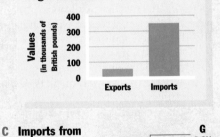

Introducing the Skill Lab

Direct students to look at the Skill Tips to review the purposes of the three main types of graphs: bar, circle, and line. Have them give examples of when each type of graph would be useful. Then point out that in this lab they will be deciding what types of graphs to make as they compare how much various colonies sold to England and bought from England.

Skill Lab
Answers

1. (a) The best graph would be an extended version of bar graph B, showing an export and import bar for each of the six colonies or regions. The title might read "Colonial Trade with England 1750," with the name of each colony or region appearing below its export and import bars. **(b)** Because the goal is to show percentages, a circle graph like C would be best, titled "Exports to England by Colony/Area 1750."
2. (a) Carolina and Virginia/ Maryland exported more than they imported. **(b)** The 2 regions had 86 percent of the total colonial exports to England.

(Answers continued in top margin)

Survey Answers

Reviewing Vocabulary

Definitions may be found on the following pages: *subsistence farming* (146), *literacy* (148), *imports* (150), *Tidewater* (150), *cash crops* (150), *prejudice* (154), *revival* (155), *racism* (156), *tyranny* (162), *militia* (163), *libel* (164).

Reviewing Main Ideas

1. (a) Building ships for fishing and trade; (b) skilled workers manufactured goods; (c) planters raised cash crops on plantations.

2. They were most likely to attend in New England because most people settled in towns, and most towns had schools. Backcountry people were least likely to attend because they lived on isolated farms.

3. (a) Against Roman Catholics, Quakers, and Jews. (b) It split religious groups and led to new prejudices.

4. Colonists viewed land as property to buy and sell; Indians believed no one could own it.

5. (a) Fewer indentured servants were coming to the colonies, and planters needed a large labor force. (b) Northern colonies had smaller farms, which did not need a large labor force.

6. They elected their assemblies and held town meetings.

7. The Navigation Acts allowed only colonial or English ships to carry goods to and from the colonies. They listed goods that could only be sold in England, and foreign goods had to pass through England and be taxed. The laws were rarely enforced, and colonists ignored them or smuggled goods.

(Answers continued in top margin)

Thinking Critically

1. The colonist lived in the Middle Colonies, where there was ample supply of falling water along the Fall Line to power mills and workshops. The Middle Colonies exported wheat, barley, oats, and livestock to the Southern Colonies and West Indies.

2. Answers will vary. Some students may argue that even without racism, settlers' ideas about the use of land would have still brought them into conflict with Indians. They could point to conflict among Europeans for lands when racism is not an issue. Students should cite evidence and examples to support their arguments.

3. Among examples are the diversity of people, which exists today in the United States; racism and prejudice, which has not been

---

Chapter Survey ★

Reviewing Vocabulary

Define the following terms.
1. subsistence farming
2. literacy
3. imports
4. Tidewater
5. cash crops
6. prejudice
7. revival
8. racism
9. tyranny
10. militia
11. libel

Reviewing Main Ideas

1. Describe one way that people made a living in each of the following regions.
(a) New England (b) the Middle Colonies (c) the Southern Colonies

2. In which region were children *most* likely to attend school? Why? In which region were children *least* likely to attend school? Why?

3. (a) What religious prejudices did most colonists have? (b) How did the Great Awakening affect religious prejudice?

4. How did colonists' attitudes about land contrast with those of Indians?

5. (a) Why did the use of indentured servants give way to the practice of buying slaves in the Southern Colonies? (b) Why were there fewer slaves in New England and the Middle Colonies?

6. How did colonists take part in governing themselves?

7. How were the Navigation Acts designed to control colonial trade? Why did the colonists accept the acts for so long?

Thinking Critically

1. Application Imagine that you found a letter written by a colonist. Part of the letter reads: "Of mills, brick kilns [ovens for baking bricks], and tile ovens, we have the necessary number. Our surplus of grain and cattle we trade to Barbados [a West Indies island] for rum, syrup, sugar, and salt." In what region do you think the colonist lived? Why?

2. Evaluation Explain why you agree or disagree with the following statement: If there had been no racism in the English colonies, colonists and American Indians would have lived in peace, and slavery would not have existed.

3. Why We Remember: Analysis A historian wrote: "In a number of ways what Americans would be for generations to come was settled in the course of those first hundred years [of English settlement]." Give three examples from the text that support this view.

Applying Skills

Analyzing graphs In the Skill Lab on page 167 you made graphs using import and export data that English trade officials collected more than 200 years ago. How much do you depend on imports? For example, how much of your clothing is imported (made in other countries)?
1. Count the items of clothing you own. Look at the labels and list the countries where the items were made.
2. Tally the number of items from each country.
3. Use your data to make a graph to answer the question: "Where does most of my clothing come from?"
4. Analyze your graph and summarize what it shows.

History Mystery

The banjo Answer the History Mystery on page 143. How would you go about learning how the banjo has changed since the 1600s? How would you find out what kinds of modern music use the banjo?

overcome; and ideas of self-government, which Americans still hold.

Applying Skills

Students might use the graphs on page 167 as a model for their own. They should see that the task requires using either a circle graph or a bar graph. Suggest that they experiment with each type to decide which format is most effective for displaying the data.

History Mystery

West Africans brought the banjo. Sources on how the banjo has changed might include reference works on African American culture. Sources on modern uses are works on music and musical instruments.

Writing in Your History Journal

1. (a) Explanations should be similar to the
(Answers continued in side margin)

time line notes on teacher pages 142–143. (b) Events will vary, but should be described from the viewpoint of a colonist.

2. Students will probably say that Franklin would agree because of his personal experience of going from being a poor apprentice to a well-respected leader.

3. Some may point out that Americans today still are very protective of their rights and freedoms. Others, however, may argue that many are only concerned about their own rights, not those of others, and that many are apathetic about politics.

Reviewing Geography

1. (A) tobacco, (B) grains and cattle, (C) rice and indigo, (D) fish and whaling products, (E) lumber and forest products

2. Land forms, water, climate, and vegetation encouraged different ways of making a living. For example, in New England plentiful forests near a coastal area encouraged people to build ships for trade. Answers to the second question will vary, but students may note that modern technology controls indoor climate. Have them cite examples for their arguments.

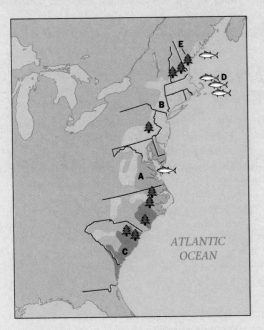

ATLANTIC
OCEAN

Reviewing Geography

1. For each letter on the map, write the colonial product or products.

2. **Geographic Thinking** One colonist wrote that the people of the New England, Middle, and Southern Colonies were "as different as their climates." How did geography influence ways of life in the regions? Do you think differences in climate are as important to people today as they were in colonial times? Explain your answer.

Alternative Assessment

Teacher's Take-Home Planner 2, p. 21, includes suggestions and scoring rubrics for the Alternative Assessment activity.

Writing in Your History Journal

1. **Keys to History** (a) The time line on pages 142–143 has six Keys to History. In your journal, list each key and describe why it is important to know about it. (b) Imagine that you are a colonist. Choose one of the events on the time line and write a letter to a friend or a relative describing the event and your reactions to it.

2. **Benjamin Franklin** English colonists boasted that North America offered plenty of opportunities for hard-working people to rise to success. Do you think Ben Franklin would have agreed with this view? In your journal, explain why or why not.

3. **Citizenship** Most people in the English colonies loved liberty and cherished the right of self-government. Do you think that Americans today share the colonists' values? Why or why not? Write your responses in your journal.

Alternative Assessment

Creating a mural With your classmates, create a mural called "Life in the English Colonies: A Story of Diversity." The mural should have three sections: the New England Colonies, the Middle Colonies, and the Southern Colonies.

❶ As a class, decide on the height and width of the whole mural. Then discuss how you will show the diversity of people in the colonies as well as the diverse ways of life.

❷ Divide into three groups to illustrate the sections of the mural. You may want to do additional research before you begin.

Your mural will be evaluated on the following criteria:

• it portrays the diverse people and ways of life in the English colonies
• it provides information that is accurate
• it presents the information in clear, inviting ways

Introduce *The Witch of Blackbird Pond* by providing information about vocabulary. For example, it was common practice for Puritans to refer to individual male community members in good stead as Goodman and to their wives as Goodwife. Point out the vocabulary terms in the margins and have students use them to paraphrase sentences that contain unfamiliar terms. Emphasize that Puritan families in the late 1600s would experience fear and shame and perhaps shunning if a family member were accused of witchcraft or of helping a witch. Because the punishment for witchcraft was death, Kit exhibited great courage by defying the accepted norms of the community and helping a person in need.

★ ★ ★
Vital Links

⊙ **Salem witch trial (Picture)**
Unit 1, Side 1, Search 39777

⊙ **See also Unit 1 Explore**
CD-ROM location 352.

✱ Literature Footnote

Elizabeth George Speare has won the prestigious Newbery Award for children's literature twice, in 1959 for *The Witch of Blackbird Pond* and in 1962 for *The Bronze Bow*. A longtime resident of New England, she uses this locale to recreate the northeastern colonial American experience. Among her other books are *Calico Captive* and *The Sign of the Beaver*.

∞ Link to Literature

The Witch of Blackbird Pond by Elizabeth George Speare

At age 16, Kit Tyler comes to live with her Uncle Matthew and Aunt Rachel in a Puritan town in colonial New England. Kit makes friends with a Quaker widow named Hannah Tupper—an isolated woman the Puritans view with suspicion. When three children die of a mysterious fever, townspeople blame Hannah, saying she must be a witch. Kit helps Hannah escape before a mob burns her hut. One morning some townspeople pay a visit to Kit's home.

deacon:
a leader in the church

constable:
policeman

contempt:
scorn

summat:
something

There were four callers, one a deacon from the church, the constable of the town, and Goodman Cruff and his wife. They were not excited this morning. They looked hard and purposeful, and Goodwife Cruff's eyes glittered toward Kit with contempt and something else she could not interpret.

"I know you don't hold with witchcraft," the constable began, "but we've summat to say as may change your mind."

"You arrested your witch?" asked Matthew with impatience.

"Not that. The town's rid of that one for good."

Matthew stared at him in alarm. "What have you done?"

"Not what you fear. We didn't lay hands on the old woman. She slipped through our trap somehow."

"And we know how!" hissed Goodwife Cruff. Kit felt a wave of fear that left her sick and dizzy.

The deacon glanced at Goodwife Cruff uneasily. "I don't quite go along with them," he said. "But I got to admit the thing looks mighty queer. We've combed the whole town this morning, ever since dawn. There's not a trace of her. Don't see how she could have got far."

"We know right enough. They'll never find her!" broke in Goodwife Cruff. "No use trying to shush me, Adam Cruff. You tell them what we saw."

Her husband cleared his throat. "I didn't rightly see it myself," he apologized. "But there's some as saw that big yeller cat of hers come arunnin' out of the house. Couple of fellers took a shot at it. But the ones as got a good look claims it had a great fat mouse in its mouth, and it never let go, even when the bullets came after it."

His wife drew a hissing breath. *"That mouse was Hannah Tupper!* 'Tis not the first time she's changed herself into a creature. They say when the moon is full—"

"Now hold on a minute, Matthew," cautioned the constable at Matthew's scornful gesture, "you can't

hornbook

⁜ Literature Footnote

In *The Witch of Blackbird Pond* Kit Tyler, an orphan from the West Indies, moves to Massachusetts to live with her Puritan aunt and uncle. She is taken into custody for helping a suspected witch disappear. Fighting against Puritan superstitions, she stands up for her beliefs. The strong plot and compelling characters highlight the witch hunts of the late 1600s.

Stimulating Critical Thinking

1. Why do you think Kit feared Goodwife Cruff? (Goodwife Cruff was sure that Kit helped Hannah and therefore Kit could be taken by the authorities.)

2. How did Matthew try to protect his niece? Could he prevent the authorities from taking Kit? (He blames himself for not controlling the actions of the girl. He could not help Kit without risking the welfare of his family.)

3. If Matthew did not believe Hannah was a witch, why do you think he still told Kit not to visit her? (He knew that if Kit visited her, Kit would come under suspicion and risk being arrested.)

A Closer Look
Answers

1. Matthew's gestures and comments indicate he was scornful of the witch hunt.

2. Goodwife Cruff is portrayed as narrow-minded, self-righteous, and unforgiving.

3. The constable and the deacon seem to be unsure about the evidence, but they are being pressured by Goodwife Cruff to take Kit into custody. Perhaps they fear that if they do not take action, they too will come under suspicion.

Trial of a suspected witch in Puritan New England

gainsay it. There's things happen we better not look at too close. The woman's gone, and I say good riddance."

gainsay: deny, speak against

"She's gone straight back to Satan!" pronounced Goodwife Cruff, *"but she's left another to do her work!"*

Kit could have laughed out loud, but a look at Goodwife Cruff sobered her. The woman's eyes were fastened on her face with a cunning triumph.

"They found summat when they searched her place. Better take a look at this, Matthew." The constable drew something shining from his pocket. It was the little silver hornbook.

"What is it?" asked Matthew.

"Looks like a sort of hornbook."

"Who ever saw a hornbook like that?" demanded Goodman Cruff. "'Tis the devil's own writing."

hornbook: a page with the alphabet, numbers, etc., mounted on a board and protected by a thin, clear sheet of horn

"Has the Lord's Prayer on it," the constable reminded him. "Look at the letters on the handle, Matthew."

Matthew took the thing in his hands reluctantly and turned it over.

"Ask *her* where it came from," jibed Goodwife Cruff, unable to keep silent.

There was a harsh gasp from Rachel. Matthew lifted his eyes from the hornbook to his niece's white face. "Can this be yours, Katherine?" he asked.

Kit's lips were stiff. "Yes sir," she answered faintly. . . .

"I don't understand this, Katherine. I forbade you—you understood it perfectly—to go to that woman's house."

"I know. But Hannah needed me, and I needed her. She wasn't a witch, Uncle Matthew. If you could have only known her—"

Matthew looked back at the constable. "I am chagrined," he said with dignity, "that I have not controlled my own household. But the girl is young and ignorant. I hold myself to blame for my laxness."

chagrined: embarrassed

laxness: carelessness

"Take no blame to yourself, Matthew." The constable rose to his feet. "I'm sorry, what with your daughter sick and all, but we've got to lock this girl up."

A Closer Look

1. What is Matthew's attitude toward the witch hunt?

2. How does the author characterize Goodwife Cruff? Give examples.

3. Do you think the constable and the deacon believe Kit is a witch? Explain.

Making Connections

Answers

1. Economic: gain wealth; religious: convert the Indians or seek religious refuge; political: gain power.

2. Many tribes of Indians, colonists from different European nations, European people born in North America, Africans, and people of mixed European-Indian or European-African descent.

3. Spanish: Catholic, complete control of colonial governments, gold and silver and ranches; English: mainly Protestant, some self-government, cash crops and raw materials.

Teaching the Unit Project

Suggest that students write the Jamestown Settlement Museum for additional information. The museum is a living-history museum with re-creations of the Jamestown Fort, a Powhatan village, and the three ships that brought the first Jamestown settlers to the colony. Students may write Jamestown Settlement, P.O. Box JF, Williamsburg, Virginia 23187.

Evaluation Criteria

The project can be evaluated according to the criteria listed below, using a scale for each:
4 = exemplary, 3 = good, 2 = adequate, 1 = poor.

Completing the task The model contains dimensions drawn to scale for the palisades. Buildings and other items are clearly labeled.
(Continued in top margin)

Knowing content The model reflects accurate information based on research.
Thinking critically Students show good judgment about what details to show based on research information. The project reflects good judgment in choosing the scale.
Communicating ideas The model displays the fort in a clear, attractive layout.

Thinking It Over

Many students may believe that because we have a wealth of video, audio, and written records, historians could compile an accurate account of our time without readjusting their thinking. Others may believe that because of the complexities of society and government, historians would have to adjust their thinking. Accept all responses supported by good reasons.

Unit Survey

Making Connections

Review

1. What reasons did Europeans have for establishing colonies in the Americas?
2. Describe the diversity of peoples living in North America (including what is now Mexico) in 1700.

3. Compare the Spanish colonies with the English colonies in terms of government, religion, and economy.

Linking History, Math, and Art

Project

Reconstructing the Jamestown Fort

As eager as they were to search for gold, the founders of Jamestown still built a wooden fort during their first month in Virginia. Historians have known this for a long time; what they have *not* known is exactly what the fort looked like—or where it was located. Prompted by the 400th anniversary of Jamestown's founding, archaeologists have renewed their efforts to find the fort. While they dig, try your hand at reconstructing the fort.

Project Steps

Work with a group.

❶ Study the information in the box, refer to the sample diagram shown here, and look at the picture on page 123.

❷ Find out more about what the fort and settlement may have looked like. In addition to library books, check recent newspaper and magazine articles for new information on Jamestown.

❸ Plan a model of the Jamestown fort.
• Calculate the approximate length of each side of the fort.
• Decide what scale you will use.
• Based on your research, decide what buildings and other items to include inside

One colonist, William Strachey, wrote that the fort was triangular, 300 by 300 by 420 feet (90 by 90 by 126 m) and close to the James River. Because the river now covers at least 100 yards (90 m) of what was shoreline, historians assume the fort is underwater. But some archaeologists think Strachey's numbers did not include the half-moon-shaped bastion at each corner of the fort, where large guns were mounted. With the bastions, each side may have been about 100 feet (30 m) longer than Strachey's figures. Thus, part of the fort may be underground, not underwater.

bastion

Scale: 1 cm = 100 ft

the fort and what size to make them. It may help to sketch as you plan.

❹ Gather your materials and begin construction. To identify buildings and other items, either make labels and attach them to the model, or make and label a drawing of the finished fort as viewed from above.

Thinking It Over Historians today must continually adjust their thinking in light of new discoveries. Do you think historians 400 years from now will have to do the same as they study our lives? Explain.

Objectives

★ Describe public records as tools used by historians.

★ Identify the kinds of information that historians can acquire from public records.

★ Explain how historians can use public records to draw conclusions about past events and people.

How Do We Know?

Warrant submitted with veteran's pension application

Scholar's Tool Kit

Public Records

As the year 1776 drew to a close, the American Revolution seemed on the brink of collapse. General George Washington confided to his cousin, "Our only dependence now is upon the speedy enlistment of a new army."

One of those who answered Washington's appeal for help was Andrew Allard. Leaving behind his young wife Zerviah and an infant son, Private Allard marched with his militia unit to join Washington in New York.

Learning About the Life of a Soldier

In writing the history of the American Revolution, scholars have a difficult time learning about the lives of ordinary people like Andrew Allard. Most Americans at the time could neither read nor write. As a result, the majority of these early Americans have been lost to history.

One place that historians look for information about Americans from times past is in the National Archives in Washington, D.C. The Archives is responsible for saving public records. These records include tax, court, and census records, military service and pension files, legal documents, treaties, and correspondence. If it were not for these records we would not know the Allard story.

After the American Revolution, Congress passed several acts giving free land and pensions to war veterans and their widows and children. When applying for pensions, veterans often sent Congress diaries,

• 173

Introducing
How Do We Know?

Public Records

One way historians learn about the events and people of the past is by studying public records. One pension file kept in the National Archives contained personal documents offered as proof that a soldier named Andrew Allard served during the War of Independence. Through the diary pages and letters in the file, historians gained valuable insight into the role an ordinary soldier played during the war. Without the public records, Allard's story may never have been known.

Setting the Stage
Activity

Analyzing Documents

To help students see how documents can reveal historical information, divide the class into groups of three or four, giving each group a different document to analyze. Documents might include birth certificates, marriage licenses, passports, diplomas, voter registration forms, and driver's license applications. The groups should list what they could learn about a person from the document they were given. Allow time for the groups to identify their document and share their lists with the class.

1. Students may respond that the Archives keeps records that provide statistical data and official documents with historical importance.

2. Answers will vary depending on students' specific interests. Some may wish to examine census data and shipboard records as part of research into their family's history. Others may wish to investigate a specific event. Accept all responses that reflect an understanding of what types of records are in the Archives.

3. Some examples of types of information are birth, marriage, and death certificates; election results; old laws; names of past government officials; and records of land use and boundaries.

Bonus Activity

Editing a Letter

By copyediting the excerpts from Allard's and Green's letters, students can analyze how written English has changed over time. Point out that the excerpts are printed just as Allard and Green wrote them. Stress that spelling, capitalization, and other mechanics of American English have been standardized since the time of the letters. Then ask students to work with partners to write copyedited versions of the excerpts.

✳ History Footnote

The National Archives, an independent federal agency, was established in 1934. It is officially called the National Archives and Records Administration. Among the many documents housed by the Archives are the original copies of the Declaration of Independence and the Constitution of the United States. These historic documents are on permanent display in the Archive's Exhibition Hall for visitors to view. The documents are protected by enclosed cases that can be lowered quickly into a fireproof and shockproof safe in case of an emergency.

❓ Critical Thinking

1. The National Archives keeps only 2 to 3 percent of the documents the government generates. How do you suppose the Archives decides what to keep?

These pages from Allard's journal tell about events in December 1776 and January 1777. What could historians learn from his account?

❓ Critical Thinking

2. Millions of ordinary citizens visit the Archives each year to research their family history or satisfy their curiosity about historic events. Suppose you were to spend an afternoon at the Archives. What subject or event would you want to research? Why?

letters, and other documents to prove that they had served in the Continental Army. These items then became a part of the public records at the National Archives.

Among the 80,000 Revolutionary War Pension Application Files is one from Private Allard's widow Zerviah. In 1844 the 88-year-old woman asked Congress for a pension based on her husband's service in the Continental Army. Fortunately for us, Andrew Allard was one of the few colonial soldiers who could write. With her application Zerviah submitted six tattered pages from his diary, a letter he wrote her, and a letter from one of his fellow soldiers.

Telling the Story

The public records in the Allard pension application file tell a touching story—one that puts a human face on the war. "Desember 16 1776 This morning i lef my Hom in Order to march for Newyork," Andrew wrote in his diary. Five days later he recorded a "verey Smart Storm of Snow" that covered the ground "tow feat deap."

From Bound Creek, Connecticut, 390 miles (624 km) from home, Private Allard sent Zerviah a letter in the winter of 1777. Although in good health, he had had a narrow escape from the British.

History Footnote

According to the National Archives, its mission is "not just to preserve America's most important documents but to promote a deeper understanding of our nation's past." The Archives achieves this mission by providing a variety of programs and public access to its records. The records are kept at its building in Washington, D.C., and in records centers and regional archives throughout the nation. The Archives also oversees the operation of nine presidential libraries and two presidential materials projects. Each presidential library keeps the papers and memorabilia of a particular president. The libraries offer research opportunities as well as programs to help provide a better understanding of individual presidents and of the presidency in general.

Discussion

"I went out a scout one day this week a Long with Lt. Willson and a Eleven more and wee all had A Chans to Come a Cross the Lite hors [British cavalry]. I being a littel Distanc from the Rest of our men had Like to have ben taken by them but thru the Goodness of God I Got to Rest of our party and wee made a stand and wee keep them Back til . . . they Retreated. . . . I Remain Your Loving Andrew Allard."

That was the last time Zerviah heard from her husband. By September 1777 Private Allard was dead—killed not by enemy bullets, but by an illness called "camp distemper."

Zerviah learned of her husband's death from Elias Green, one of Andrew's fellow soldiers. Green informed her of the "vary heavy Peas of news" in a letter written from Blandford, Massachusetts on August 25, 1777. "No Pains was wanting in takeing cair of him," Green assured her. "He had a good feather bed to Lay on, but all means was to no afect." Green sent Zerviah Andrew's diary "for his sun thit he might have it to Remember him by."

Because Zerviah applied for a pension, we now know of one soldier's small but honorable contribution to the cause of American liberty. Private Allard was not a war hero, but he served his country at a time when victory seemed impossible and when many other soldiers chose to defect or desert. Without his diary and letters, and without the National Archives files, we would never have known Private Allard's story.

? Critical Thinking

3. The National Archives is not the only place where you can find public records. Counties and cities also have records offices. What types of things might you learn about the history of your area at such an office?

Scholar at *Work*

For historians, the National Archives is like a giant family collection of memories. Every family acquires and saves documents that it may later need. Work with your family to list the kinds of documents your family saves. From these records, what story could a historian tell about your family?

Checking Understanding

1. Why do historians know little about the lives of many ordinary Americans of the 1700s? (Many people could not write, so left no written records themselves.)

2. What is the purpose of the National Archives? (To preserve public records.)

3. What documents did Zerviah Allard send with her pension application? Why? (Pages from her husband's diary, his letter to her, and a letter from a soldier telling her of his death. She wanted to prove he served in the army.)

Teaching the *Scholar* at *Work*

Brainstorm and list on the chalkboard documents families might keep, such as birth certificates, marriage licenses, deeds and leases, award certificates, diplomas, canceled checks, tax returns, health records, and job résumés. You may also wish to discuss where families might keep documents—in safety deposit boxes, a file cabinet, a desk drawer, boxes of memorabilia, scrapbooks, etc.

Introducing the Unit

The Declaration of Independence, 4 July 1776

The painting depicts the committee that drafted the Declaration presenting it to John Hancock, the president of Congress, who is seated. Committee members are (left to right) John Adams, Roger Sherman, Robert Livingston, Thomas Jefferson, and Benjamin Franklin. (The man standing to the right of the desk with his hand on the book is Charles Thomson.) Ask: **How does this painting relate to the subject of the unit?** (The Declaration stated the intent to break from British rule.)

Teaching the

Hands-On

┌ ─ ─ ─ ─ ─ ─ ─ ➤ *HISTORY*

A modern scene might be a presidential press conference, a summit meeting, or a ceremony at which the President signs a bill into law. Students should consider not only how men and women would be dressed but also what types of people would be present (camera crews, reporters with microphones and laptop computers, etc.). Follow-up discussion might focus on why such an event would be more public than the one in the painting.

Unit Overview

By 1763 Britain had defeated France in North America, becoming the major power on the continent. When Britain tried to pay off war debts by taxing the colonies, colonists protested "taxation without representation." As protests and British retaliations increased tensions, the First Continental Congress met in 1774, hoping for a peaceful solution. After colonial grievances were not resolved and fighting broke out in 1775, the Second Continental Congress declared the colonies independent in 1776. After early defeats in the war, the patriots, with the aid of France and Spain, forced Britain to recognize the independence of the United States in 1783. In 1787 the Constitutional Convention drafted a plan of government to replace the Articles of Confederation. The Constitution was ratified in 1788.

1750–1791

Unit **3**

Chapters

7. The Years of Conflict

8. The War of Independence

9. Creating the Constitution

Hands-On
- - - - - - - - - - - ➤ *HISTORY*

Activity

In this painting a group of trusted and important citizens are shown meeting to make a decision that will affect all Americans. The event took place in 1776. If you were to photograph a similar event today, how would your picture differ from this painting? For example, this picture shows men wearing ruffled shirts and breeches and writing with quill pens. In a present-day photograph how might people be dressed? How might they be taking notes? Describe your photograph, explaining the differences you would expect to see.

The Declaration of Independence, 4 July 1776 (detail)
by John Trumbull, 1786–1794

176 •

John Trumbull (1756–1843), who had served in the Continental Army as an aide to George Washington, is best known for scenes of the War of Independence. Encouraged by John Adams and Thomas Jefferson, he began in 1785 to work on a series of paintings glorifying the most famous Patriot leaders. First he made individual portraits of many of these men, painting them from life. Later he copied these portraits into larger revolutionary scenes. Several of his large paintings, including *The Declaration of Independence*, decorate the rotunda of the Capitol building. Jefferson called Trumbull's paintings "monuments of the tastes as well as the great revolutionary scenes of our country."

A New Nation Begins

1. In what ways are the people in the painting similar? (They are all well-dressed white males.)

2. What seems to be the mood of the people in the painting? How can you tell? (They seem very serious and grim. No one is smiling.)

Stimulating Critical Thinking

3. Why do you think the men look grim? (In declaring independence, they had committed treason against Britain. With their action, they were risking their lives and the lives of many other Americans.)

4. Which person, if any, do you think the artist wants you to notice the most? Explain. (Jefferson, who stands at the center and holds the document. Students may know that he did the actual writing.)

See the Unit 3 activity in **Wall Time Line Activities.**

7 The Years of Conflict
1754–1774

Chapter Planning Guide

Section	Student Text	Teacher's Edition Activities
Opener and Story pp. 178–181	**Keys to History Time Line** — **History Mystery** — Beginning the Story with **George Washington**	**Setting the Stage Activity** How Much Do You Know?, p. 180
1 **The French and Indian War** pp. 182–185	**Reading Maps** The French and Indian War 1754–1763, p. 183 — **World Link** The British in India, p. 185	**Warm-Up Activity** A Report on Fort Necessity, p. 182 — **Geography Question of the Day**, p. 182 — **Section Activity** Role-playing an Interview, p. 184 — **Bonus Activity** A Letter to Pitt, p. 184 — **Wrap-Up Activity** A French View, p. 185
2 **Growing Pains** pp. 186–193	**Reading Maps** European Claims 1750 and 1763, p. 187 — **Point of View** Did the colonies owe obedience to Britain?, p. 188 — **Link to the Present** Boycotts, p. 190 — **Link to Art** *The Bloody Massacre*, p. 191 — **Skill Lab** Primary and Secondary Sources, p. 193	**Warm-Up Activity** Colonial Hopes, p. 186 — **Geography Question of the Day**, p. 186 — **Section Activity** Franklin Appearing Before Parliament, p. 188 — **Bonus Activity** The People Speak, p. 190 — **Wrap-Up Activity** A Cause-Effect Chain, p. 192
3 **The Road to Revolution** pp. 194–199	**Hands-On History** Classifying types of protest, p. 196 — **Geography Lab** Colonial Communication, p. 199	**Warm-Up Activity** News by Mail, p. 194 — **Geography Question of the Day**, p. 194 — **Section Activity** Boston Tea Party News Reports, p. 196 — **Bonus Activity** Protest Slogans, p. 197 — **Wrap-Up Activity** Letters on the Coercive Acts, p. 198
Evaluation	☑ **Section 1 Review,** p. 185 — ☑ **Section 2 Review,** p. 192 — ☑ **Section 3 Review,** p. 198 — ☑ **Chapter Survey,** pp. 200–201 — **Alternative Assessment** Role-playing the Continental Congress, p. 201	☑ **Answers to Section 1 Review,** p. 185 — ☑ **Answers to Section 2 Review,** p. 192 — ☑ **Answers to Section 3 Review,** p. 198 — ☑ **Answers to Chapter Survey,** pp. 200–201 (Alternative Assessment guidelines are in the Take-Home Planner.)

Teacher's Resource Package

Chapter Summaries: English and Spanish, pp. 18–19

Chapter Resources Binder
Study Guide Skimming to Locate Information, p. 49
Reinforcement Determining Cause and Effect, pp. 53–54

Chapter Resources Binder
Study Guide Identifying Viewpoints, p. 50
Skills Development Primary and Secondary Sources, pp. 55–56
American Readings Franklin Faces Parliament, p. 25; Organizing Boycotts, p. 26

Chapter Resources Binder
Study Guide Summarizing Information, p. 51
Geography Extensions Colonial Communication, pp. 13–14
Using Historical Documents The Articles of Association, pp. 38–45
American Readings The Boston Tea Party, pp. 27–28

Chapter and Unit Tests Chapter 7 Tests, Forms A and B, pp. 45–48

Take-Home Planner

Introducing the Chapter Activity
What Can We Do About America?, p. 4

Chapter In-Depth Activity Protest!, p. 4

Reduced Views
Study Guide, p. 6
Reinforcement, p. 7
Unit 3 Answers, pp. 27–33

Reduced Views
Study Guide, p. 6
Skills Development, p. 7
American Readings, p. 8
Unit 3 Answers, pp. 27–33

Reduced Views
Study Guide, p. 6
Geography Extensions, p. 9
American Readings, p. 8
Using Historical Documents, p. 9
Unit 3 Answers, pp. 27–33

Reduced Views
Chapter Tests, p. 9
Unit 3 Answers, pp. 27–33

Alternative Assessment Guidelines for scoring the Chapter Survey activity, p. 5

Additional Resources

Wall Time Line

Unit 3 Activity

Transparency Package

Transparency 7-1 Paul Revere's *The Bloody Massacre*—use with Section 2
Transparency 7-2 *The Patriotick Barber of New York*—use with Section 3
Transparency Activity Book

SelecTest Testing Software
Chapter 7 Test, Forms A and B

★★★ Vital Links ★★★

 Videodisc

CD-ROM

French and Indian War (see TE p. 184)
Voice of newspaper publisher (see TE p. 189)
"Revolutionary Tea" (see TE p. 196)

Take-Home Planner 3
  Introducing Chapter Activity
  Chapter In-Depth Activity
  Alternative Assessment
Chapter Resources Binder
Geography Extensions
American Readings
Using Historical Documents
Transparency Activities
Wall Time Line Activities
Chapter Summaries
Chapter and Unit Tests
SelecTest Test File
Vital Links CD-ROM/Videodisc

Time Line

Keys to History

Keys to History journal writing activity is on page 200 in the Chapter Survey.

French and Indian War begins The war between France and Britain decided who would be the main power in North America. (p. 182)

Stamp Act The stamp tax led to the first widespread colonial protests to British policies. (p. 188)

Looking Back The Zenger trial set the precedent for freedom of the press in the American colonies.

World Link See p. 185.

Chapter Objectives

★ Explain the colonial conflict with the British and the roles Indians played in the conflict.
★ Identify what led to the colonists' growing dissatisfaction with British rule.
★ Discuss the events that led Britain and the colonists to the brink of war.

Chapter Overview
In 1754 war broke out between Britain and France over power in Europe and overseas colonies. After English colonial leaders tried but failed to unite the 13 colonies for common defense, Britain sent troops to North America. A British blockade and decisive victories in Canada forced France to give up its claims in North America in the 1763 Treaty of Paris.

1754–1774

Chapter 7

The Years of Conflict

Sections

Beginning the Story with George Washington
1. **The French and Indian War**
2. **Growing Pains**
3. **The Road to Revolution**

Keys to History

1754
French and Indian War begins
Powder horn showing battle sites

1765
Stamp Act
Teapot protesting the Stamp Act

1754 | 1763

Looking Back
Zenger freedom of press trial
1735

World Link
France surrenders most claims in India to Britain
1763

British efforts to control a larger empire angered colonists. To avoid clashes with Indians, Britain forbade settlement west of the Appalachians. To pay for colonial defense, it imposed taxes through the Sugar Act of 1764, the Stamp Act of 1765, and the Townshend Acts of 1767. Colonists protested "taxation without representation" through petitions, boycotts, and demonstrations—including the one leading to the Boston Massacre.

Colonists spread word of British threats through Committees of Correspondence. The Tea Act of 1773 led to boycotts and the Boston Tea Party. When Britain reacted by passing the "Intolerable Acts," colonial leaders met in 1774 as the First Continental Congress and called for repeal of the Intolerable Acts. Meanwhile, boycotts continued and colonists prepared for the possibility of war.

Teaching the HISTORY Mystery

Students will find information on p. 188. See Chapter Survey, p. 200, for additional questions.

HISTORY Mystery

This skull and crossbones cartoon was a protest against stamps like the one shown next to it. Why would the colonists consider a small stamp dangerous enough to label it with a skull and crossbones?

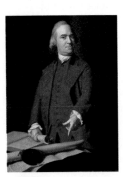

1767
Sam Adams emerges as protest leader

1770
Boston Massacre
Coffin sketches with initials of some victims

1773
Boston Tea Party
British engraving made in 1789

1774
First Continental Congress

1769   1774

Looking Ahead

Battles of Lexington and Concord
1775

Time Line

Sam Adams Skill with words made Adams a leader of colonial protest against British taxation. (p. 191)

Boston Massacre News that British soldiers had fired upon a riotous crowd of colonists was used by protest leaders to stir anti-British feeling. (p. 192)

Boston Tea Party The dumping of tea into Boston Harbor challenged British authority, leading to the Intolerable Acts. (p. 195)

First Continental Congress The meeting was an effort by the colonies to unite in response to the Intolerable Acts. (p. 196)

Looking Ahead Shots fired by British troops and colonial militias at Lexington and Concord started the War of Independence.

George Washington

Students may be surprised that as a young man Washington was a staunch supporter of Britain. Like most colonists, Washington saw himself as a British citizen with a tradition of being loyal to "king and country." He hoped for a place of honor within the empire as a British officer. As students read this story and section 1, they will see how his dream was denied. With his wounded pride, Washington can be seen as representing the growing colonial resentment of being treated unfairly by the mother country.

How Much Do You Know?

To check students' knowledge of Washington, have small groups list what comes to mind when they hear his name. They should note any images, characteristics, or stories that they recall. Make a list on the chalkboard of students' responses. Then ask students to summarize what kind of a person they think Washington was.

See the Introducing the Chapter Activity, What Can We Do About America?, **Take-Home Planner 3,** p. 4.

✱ **History Footnote**

Despite his surrender at Fort Necessity, Washington was highly regarded by colonists and was appointed as head of Virginia's militia in the backcountry, where he served until 1758. When he attended the First and Second Continental Congresses, his impressive military air made him seem to John Adams the obvious choice for commander of the Continental Army.

Beginning the Story with

George Washington

By the time he was 22, George Washington was a commander of militia fighting French soldiers in the backcountry. How did this young man who grew up on a Virginia plantation end up leading soldiers at such a young age? For Washington, it was the result of ambition.

At the age of 15 George Washington knew what he wanted in life—to be rich and respected. His problem was that he had no land. His older brother Lawrence had inherited the family plantation when their father died. First, George learned to be a surveyor. That career was a dead end, though. He would be working for the rich, not joining their ranks. There had to be a better way to reach his goals.

An Officer and a Gentleman

That better way, Washington decided, was to become an officer in the British army. As an officer and a gentleman, he would command respect and receive a handsome salary. The only problem was that most British officers believed that colonists made poor soldiers. Still, Washington had his mind set on a military career. The first step was to get some experience. In 1752, at age 20, he was made a major in the Virginia militia.

The following year, the young major got a chance to prove himself. A volunteer was needed to lead a small expedition north into French territory. Virginia's governor was alarmed by rumors that French soldiers based near Lake Erie were about to move south into the Ohio Valley, an area claimed by Virginia. If the rumors were true, the French had to be warned to stay out or risk war. Major Washington eagerly stepped forward to carry the message.

Lewis, Thomas A. *For King and Country: The Maturing of George Washington, 1748–1760.* HarperCollins, 1993. Students may enjoy reading more about the youthful George Washington at a time in his life when he was distinguished more by his ambition than by his ability. This book presents a straightforward, modern view of Washington as a man who became a national hero as a result of sheer determination and hard work.

Also of interest:

Kaminski, John P., and Jill Adair McCaughan, eds. *A Great and Good Man: George Washington in the Eyes of His Contemporaries.* Madison House, 1989.

After two months of hard travel across 1,000 miles (1,600 km) of rugged land in the dead of winter, Washington reached Fort Le Boeuf [leh BUFF] near Lake Erie. The French officers of the fort invited him to dine with them. He later wrote in his journal, "The wine, as they dosed themselves pretty plentifully with it, soon banished restraint. They told me that it was their absolute design to take possession of the Ohio." The French made no effort to hide the fleet of more than 200 canoes that would carry them into the Ohio Valley when spring came.

Washington rushed back to Virginia with the news. As a reward for completing the dangerous mission, the governor promoted him to lieutenant colonel in the militia.

Washington's first military mission, in the winter of 1753, was nearly his last. He almost froze to death crossing an ice-clogged river.

"I Heard the Bullets Whistle"

In the spring of 1754, Washington led a small militia force to the Ohio Valley. They were to protect Virginians building a fort where the Allegheny (al-uh-GAY-nee) and Monongahela (muh-NAHN-guh-HEE-luh) Rivers meet to form the Ohio River. He arrived too late. The French had already chased the Virginians away and built a fort named Fort Duquesne (doo-KAYN).

In Washington's eyes the French had committed an act of war. At that point he made one of the few mistakes of his military career. He attacked a small French force camped nearby, even though France and Britain were not at war. It was an easy victory. "I heard the bullets whistle," he wrote in a letter home, "and, believe me, there is something charming in the sound."

The French sent a large force to punish the Virginians. Washington and his men quickly built a fort that he called Fort Necessity. In the first day of fighting, the French killed a third of Washington's soldiers. Realizing that it was hopeless to hold out, Washington decided to surrender.

The French allowed the young officer and his men to return home, where Washington was welcomed as a hero. He had stood up to the French against great odds. To British army leaders, however, his surrender was more proof that colonials were not officer material.

Hands-On ▸ HISTORY

Activity

You read what Washington wrote home after his victory over the French. Write another letter home from Washington after his surrender of Fort Necessity. Describe the feelings he might have had about his own future in the military and about the ability of the colonial militia.

Discussion

Thinking Historically

1. Why did Washington choose a military career? (He was unlikely to become respected and rich as a landowner or surveyor. As a British officer, he would be respected and well paid.)

2. How can you tell that he seized opportunity rather than waiting for it to come to him? (He took steps to gain military experience and quickly volunteered for a dangerous mission to prove himself.)

See the Chapter In-Depth Activity, Protest! **Take-Home Planner 3,** p. 4.

Teaching the

Hands-On

▸ *HISTORY*

To help students imagine Washington's feelings, have them recall how they have felt after losing a contest or game. How might he have felt about losing an important battle? To help students get started, suggest beginning the letter, "Dear Family, Do you recall the letter in which I wrote you that I was charmed by the whistle of bullets? Well . . . "

For a journal writing activity on George Washington, see student page 201.

Warm-Up Activity

A Report on Fort Necessity

To help students imagine the effect of the battle at Fort Necessity, have them write reports on it to authorities in Britain. They should imagine themselves as British army leaders describing the significance of the defeat and recommending what actions should now be taken by Britain and the colonies. As they read the section, they can compare their proposals with what the British did.

Geography Question of the Day

Ask students to make a mental map of Washington's progress from Virginia to Fort Le Boeuf, back to Virginia, and then to the Ohio Valley at the head of a fighting force in 1754. Write a paragraph estimating the number of miles he had to travel.

Section Objectives

★ Identify how Indians contributed to the balance of power between the French and the British.
★ Explain the failure of the Albany Plan.
★ Explain how Britain won the French and Indian War and what the victory gained.

Teaching Resources

Take-Home Planner 3, pp. 2–9
Chapter Resources Binder
Study Guide, p. 49
Reinforcement, pp. 53–54
Skills Development
Geography Extensions
American Readings
Using Historical Documents
Transparency Activities
Chapter and Unit Tests

1. The French and Indian War

Reading Guide

New Terms allies, blockade, cede

Section Focus Why the British fought and defeated the French

1. Why were Indians involved in the conflict between the French and British?
2. Why did the colonies reject a plan for their common defense?
3. How did Britain win the French and Indian War, and what did it gain?

The battle George Washington fought at Fort Necessity in 1754 was only one of many in a long-running conflict over control of western lands and the fur trade. Since the 1600s French fur trappers and their Indian **allies**—helpers in times of trouble—had clashed with English settlers.

In 1756 the conflict became part of a wider war between France and Britain—the fourth time they had fought in less than a century. Each of the previous three wars had left little change in North America. However, this war—known in the colonies as the French and Indian War—would make Britain the main power on the continent.

Conflict in the Backcountry

Describing the conflict in North America as the "British" fighting the "French and Indians" paints too simple a picture. Only colonies that claimed western lands were eager to fight the French. Meanwhile, the colonies competed with one another in trying to settle the backcountry and expand the fur trade. Whenever the militia from one colony helped another to fight the French, it was out of self-interest.

Referring to the "French and Indians" is also misleading because not all the Indian tribes were allies of the French. The French usually had better relations with Indians

because the French wanted to trade, not take land. By favoring some tribes over others, however, they made enemies, including the powerful Iroquois League.

The Indians of each tribe looked to their own needs in deciding whether to side with the French, with the British, or with neither. Playing one side against the other, they considered what goods they could get at what price, how much respect they were given, and who seemed more powerful.

For their part, the French and British constantly competed for Indian allies. They needed Indian friends to trade with and to protect them from attacks by other Indians. Most importantly, Indian allies could help them when they fought each other.

The Albany Plan

In 1754, as the French built fort after fort in the Great Lakes region, the Iroquois began having second thoughts about being allies with the British. Britain ordered colonies from Virginia northward to send delegates to meet with the Iroquois leaders in Albany, New York. Despite attempts to convince them to help if war broke out, the Iroquois decided not to take sides.

After the Iroquois leaders left the meeting, Benjamin Franklin proposed a plan for all of the colonies to unite in defending

The map on this page can help visual learners grasp more than the movements of the British in invading Canada. Have students sketch the map area on a separate piece of paper, shading the area occupied or threatened by the French. Then suggest visualizing the general locations of the colonies. Point out that the location of French forts permitted easy collaboration with nearby Indian allies, while the English colonists often had to travel long distances to meet with potential Indian allies, such as the Iroquois. This will help students better understand the difficulty in fighting the French.

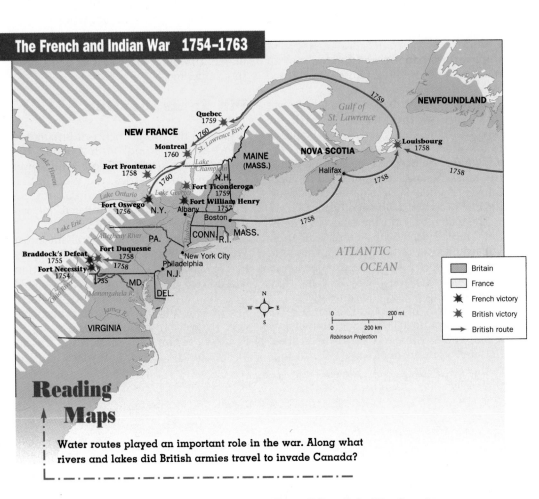

The French and Indian War 1754–1763

Reading Maps

Water routes played an important role in the war. Along what rivers and lakes did British armies travel to invade Canada?

themselves. His plan called for the colonial legislatures to send representatives to a council led by a governor appointed by the king. The council would act for all the colonies in making Indian treaties, raising an army, and building forts. To pay its expenses, it would have the power to collect taxes.

When the plan was sent to the legislatures, though, not a single one approved it. They believed that only representatives elected by the people should decide on taxes. So ended the Albany Plan, the first attempt to unite all the colonies. Clearly they were not yet willing to cooperate with one another.

Braddock's Defeat

After the failure of the Albany Plan and Washington's defeat at Fort Necessity, Virginia's governor asked Britain for help. In 1755 Britain sent 1,400 soldiers under General Edward Braddock to try to drive the French from the Ohio Valley. Virginia and nearby colonies were asked to pay for the troops' supplies and to provide militia for a march on Fort Duquesne.

As the militiamen were being organized, one officer was noticeably absent—George Washington. When he returned from Fort Necessity, Washington learned that orders

Discussion

Checking Understanding

1. Why did Britain send troops to North America? (After the failure of the Albany Plan and the defeat at Fort Necessity, Virginia's governor asked for help in driving the French out.)

Stimulating Critical Thinking

2. What other factors might have caused colonial legislatures to reject the Albany Plan? (They may have counted on Britain sending help. Some colonies may have felt less threatened by the French than others. The colonies did not trust one another.)

Teaching the Reading Maps

To help students focus on the "story" the map tells, ask them to summarize the war using the map alone. Suggest putting battles in order, identifying each as either a French or a British victory. (The French scored early victories, but the British turned the tide with a string of successes.) **Answer to Reading Maps:** St. Lawrence River, Lake Champlain, Lake Ontario, Hudson River, Allegheny River, Ohio River.

Role-playing an Interview

By role-playing an interview between Washington and British officers, students identify the pros and cons of training colonial militia. Have students imagine they are the young George Washington in an interview with British officers. In small groups, they should list reasons why the British should train more colonial officers and why the British might oppose this.

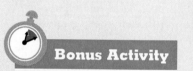

A Letter to Pitt

By writing a letter, students explain how a painting of the Battle of Quebec reflects Pitt's strategy to win the war. Have students look carefully at the illustration on page 184 and imagine that they are sending a letter to William Pitt describing the battle and explaining how the victory resulted from his strategy.

★ ★ ★
Vital Links

○ French and Indian War (Picture) Unit 1, Side 1, Search 40644

○ See also Unit 1 Explore CD-ROM location 366.

✠ **Connections to Literature**

Henry Wadsworth Longfellow's narrative poem *Evangeline,* written in 1847, tells how the French and Indian War affected a young man and woman. The couple is separated when the British remove residents of French descent from Nova Scotia, known to the French as Acadia. Evangeline searches a lifetime for her friend, only to find him many years later as he is dying.

The relocation of the Acadians was spurred by British concern about controlling the large French population in the area. In 1755 Acadians were loaded on British ships and moved to other British colonies. Many made their way south to Louisiana to be near other French-speaking people, where their descendants today are known as *Cajuns,* derived from the word *Acadians.*

from Britain had lowered the ranks of all militia officers. His pride injured, he resigned and returned home.

George's brother had died, so George was now running the plantation. Still, he missed the military. He wrote to Braddock to ask about a position. When offered only a low rank, he declined. Instead, he joined the general's staff as a volunteer. If he could impress Braddock, perhaps there was still hope of becoming a British officer.

The march to Fort Duquesne was a disaster. Ambushed by the French and their Indian allies, the British panicked. They were used to the open battlefields of Europe, where they could keep the enemy in view. They were not ready for hit-and-run warfare.

Two-thirds of Braddock's force were killed or wounded. Braddock himself was killed, and Washington narrowly escaped. He later wrote in his journal, "I had four Bullets through my Coat and two horses shot under me."

Pitt Turns the Tide

In 1756 the conflict between Britain and France spread beyond North America. The two countries fought each other for power in Europe, India, Africa, the West Indies, and on the high seas. As Britain focused on the fighting in Europe, it suffered one setback after another in North America.

The tide turned when the brilliant leader William Pitt was appointed prime minister in 1757. Boasting "I can save this nation and no one else can," Pitt launched a bold strategy. He decided that victory in North America was the key to winning the global war. He got Parliament to raise taxes in Britain to pay for a larger army, and he sent his best officers to North America.

The British won a decisive victory at Quebec in 1759. A British artist showed the landing and the battle taking place at the same time.

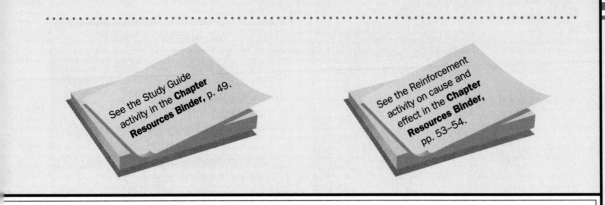

See the Study Guide activity in the **Chapter Resources Binder**, p. 49.

See the Reinforcement activity on cause and effect in the **Chapter Resources Binder**, pp. 53–54.

Teaching the

World **Link**

Have students locate India on the map on pages R2–R3. Ask how Britain could effectively fight such a widespread war. (It had a powerful navy.)

Pitt ordered a blockade of New France. A **blockade** is the shutting off of a place by ships or troops to prevent supplies from reaching it. In 1758 the British captured Louisbourg, giving them control of the Gulf of St. Lawrence. (See map on page 183.)

The blockade strangled French supply lines, leading most of France's Indian allies to make peace with the British. Lacking supplies and help from the Indians, the French abandoned Fort Duquesne, burning it to the ground. The British later built their own fort there, naming it Fort Pitt. The site today is Pittsburgh. Other victories followed rapidly, as British forces captured one French fort after another.

The British attack Quebec The British delivered their crushing blow at Quebec in 1759. Quebec guarded the St. Lawrence River, the gateway to supplying French forts in the interior. Under the cover of darkness, General James Wolfe led his troops up the cliffs and onto the Plains of Abraham outside the city. They were ready when the French awoke.

The British won the fierce battle that followed, in which both Wolfe and his brave opponent, General Louis Joseph de Montcalm (mōn-KALM), lost their lives. A year later the fall of Montreal marked the end of French power in North America.

Britain Triumphs

The war dragged on for several years. Finally, in 1763, Britain and France signed the Treaty of Paris, ending the global conflict that became known in Europe as the Seven Years' War.

The previous year France had agreed to **cede**—give up—Louisiana to Spain. In the Treaty of Paris, France now ceded Canada to Britain. French forces left North America, and France surrendered to Britain almost all her claims in India. The door had opened to

World **Link**

The British in India The Treaty of Paris in 1763 sealed Britain's triumph over France—not only in North America but also in India. France gave up most of its claims there, opening the door to almost 200 years of British control.

The British saw India as a glittering prize, with its rich trade in spices, silks, and jewels. After the American colonies broke away, India was the "jewel in the crown" of Britain's empire. Not until 1947 was it granted independence.

a vast British empire upon which, it would be said, "the sun never set."

The sun had set, though, on Washington's hope for a place of honor within that empire. After Fort Duquesne fell in 1758, he again asked to be made a British officer and was turned down. He decided to turn his back on the military. He took pride, however, in having protected what he called his "country," Virginia. He would return to his plantation there.

1. Section Review

1. Define **allies, blockade,** and **cede.**
2. What role did the Indians play in the conflict between the French and British?
3. What was the purpose of the Albany Plan and why was it rejected?
4. What were the main causes and effects of the British victory in the war?
5. Critical Thinking If the French had won, do you think they would have taken control of the 13 colonies? Explain.

Closing the Section

Wrap-Up Activity

A French View

To review the war's impact, have students imagine themselves as a French leader who has just signed the Treaty of Paris. Have them write a diary entry explaining why France lost and what effect that loss will have on North America.

Section Review
Answers

1. Definitions: *allies* (p. 182), *blockade* (p. 185), *cede* (p. 185)
2. They chose sides according to their own best interests. Indian allies helped the French most.
3. To unite colonies for defense. Legislatures did not want council to have power to tax.
4. Causes: larger army and navy, blockade; effects: French ceded territories, Britain now major power on continent.
5. Yes: French were expansionist. No: could not control large colonial population.

Vocabulary

proclamation (p. 187) official announcement

customs duties (p. 188) charges on foreign imports

revenue (p. 188) income

writs of assistance (p. 188) general search warrants

repeal (p. 189) do away with

boycott (p. 189) refuse to buy

Warm-Up Activity

Colonial Hopes

By writing a journal entry, students consider what different groups hoped to gain after the war. Ask them to imagine they are a colonial leader, an ordinary settler, a British official in America, a British soldier, or a colonial militia member. Have them write a short diary entry describing their expectations for the future. Ask volunteers to share their entries.

Geography Question of the Day

Ask students to suppose that a member of the British government was comparing the two maps on p. 187. Have them write a diary entry predicting what problems might arise from having a larger empire in North America.

Section Objectives

★ Explain why Britain and the colonies came into conflict over western lands.
★ Identify why and how colonists protested the Stamp Act.
★ Describe the effects of the Townshend Acts.

Teaching Resources

Take-Home Planner 3, pp. 2–9

Chapter Resources Binder

  Study Guide, p. 50

  Reinforcement

  Skills Development, pp. 55–56

  Geography Extensions

American Readings, pp. 25–26

  Using Historical Documents

Transparency Activities

  Chapter and Unit Tests

---

2. Growing Pains

Reading Guide

New Terms proclamation, customs duties, revenue, writs of assistance, repeal, boycott

Section Focus Why the colonists began to resent British rule

1. Why did Britain and the colonists come into conflict over western lands?
2. Why and how did the colonists protest the Stamp Act?
3. What were the effects of the Townshend Acts?

For Britain and the 13 colonies, the joy over winning the French and Indian War was short-lived. The mother country soon came into increasing conflict with her "children," as both Britain and the colonies began to feel growing pains.

For Britain the growing pains were the burdens of organizing a larger empire. How would it govern the vast territory that had been New France? How would it pay the increased cost of defending its empire? To meet these challenges, Parliament decided to take tighter control over the colonies and get more money from them.

For a long time the colonies had felt the growing pains of challenging the mother country's authority. British trade laws were rarely enforced. Colonial merchants often defied these laws by smuggling goods into the colonies. Meanwhile, colonial legislatures could usually get royal governors to cooperate with them by threatening not to pay their salaries.

Before the war, the colonies had been used to governing themselves. Now, in trying to control a wider empire, Parliament would pass laws that clashed with the colonists' desire to preserve their tradition of self-government. As the conflict worsened, many colonists would come to believe that they had more in common with one another than with Britain.

Problems in the West

Two main problems faced Britain as it tried to govern the large area that had been New France. One was how to deal with the Indian tribes who lived there. The other was whether to allow settlers to move west, turning Indian hunting grounds into farms.

Pontiac's Rebellion Britain's victory had stunned France's Indian allies. Their fears for the future deepened when they found the British to be stingy, greedy, and eager for revenge. The French had given the Indians many presents and allowed them to buy goods on credit. Not so the British, whose Indian policy was now being set by harsh officials like Lord Jeffrey Amherst.

Amherst declared that the former French allies "must be punished but not bribed." He refused to give them any gunpowder, although they depended on guns for hunting. If they starved, all the better, he believed. He even suggested sending "the Small Pox among those dissatisfied tribes."

The fear and frustration of the Great Lakes tribes erupted in 1763, in Pontiac's Rebellion. Pontiac, an Ottawa chief who was a great religious and political leader, gathered neighboring tribes to attack British forts. By July 1763 only Detroit, Fort Pitt, and Fort Niagara remained in British hands.

Connections to Economics

Mercantilism was the economic policy of Britain throughout the colonial period. Under this system the government maintained strict control of economic affairs. The aims of mercantilism included increased national wealth through strictly regulated trade, increased development of agriculture and manufacturing, a favorable trade balance, and reliable foreign trade markets for goods. For Britain, the colonies were essential to the system. They provided markets for British manufactured goods, and they were rich sources of raw materials. In turn, many colonists received benefits from British economic rule, particularly protection of the British navy for their trade ships.

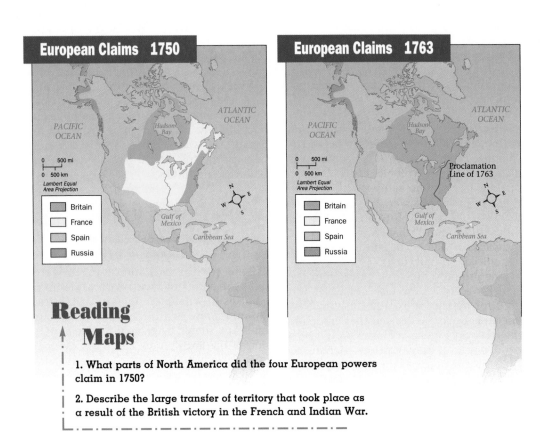

European Claims 1750

PACIFIC OCEAN

ATLANTIC OCEAN

Hudson Bay

0 500 mi
0 500 km
Lambert Equal Area Projection

Gulf of Mexico

Caribbean Sea

N W E S

- Britain
- France
- Spain
- Russia

European Claims 1763

PACIFIC OCEAN

ATLANTIC OCEAN

Hudson Bay

0 500 mi
0 500 km
Lambert Equal Area Projection

Proclamation Line of 1763

Gulf of Mexico

Caribbean Sea

N W E S

- Britain
- France
- Spain
- Russia

Reading Maps

1. What parts of North America did the four European powers claim in 1750?

2. Describe the large transfer of territory that took place as a result of the British victory in the French and Indian War.

Without their usual help from the French, the tribes could not fight for long. They finally signed peace treaties with the British. The Indians had made Amherst pay dearly, though. They had captured or killed nearly 2,000 Englishmen.

The Proclamation of 1763 Parliament had to face the question of how to prevent further conflict with the Indians. It came up with an answer in the Proclamation of 1763. This **proclamation**—which means an official announcement—said that colonists could not settle west of the Appalachians. Settlers already living there were ordered to leave. In addition, the British government would take control of the fur trade.

The law was meant to buy time until Britain could sign treaties with the Indians. Land buyers, fur traders, and settlers, however, saw things differently. Now that the French were defeated and Pontiac's Rebellion had ended, they were eager to push westward. Most ignored the proclamation.

Parliament Taxes the Colonies

To enforce the Proclamation of 1763 and protect the colonists from the Indians, Britain declared that it needed an army of 10,000 soldiers in North America. But who should pay to support them? Taxpayers in Britain were already burdened with the debt

See **American Readings,**
p. 25, for Franklin's testimony before Parliament
on the Stamp Act.

Connections to Civics

Protections in the first state constitutions, and later in the United States Constitution, grew directly out of colonists' experiences during this period. Conflicts with Britain prompted familiar elements of the Bill of Rights such as freedom of speech, protection against search and seizure, the right to due process and a jury trial, and the right of petition for redress of grievances.

See the Study Guide activity in the **Chapter Resources Binder,** p. 50.

from the French and Indian War. The new British prime minister, George Grenville, looked for a way to make the colonies pay more for their own defense.

The Sugar Act Grenville knew that Parliament had never directly taxed the colonies. The Navigation Acts had only regulated trade so the colonies would do most of their buying and selling with Britain. Colonial merchants were to pay **customs duties**—charges on foreign imports—in order to sell non-British goods. However, merchants usually avoided the duties by bribing officials or smuggling.

One product often smuggled from the French West Indies was molasses, which was used for making rum, especially in New England. Grenville decided that enforcing the duty on foreign molasses would be a good way to raise **revenue**—income. In 1764 Parliament passed the Sugar Act, which cut in half the duty on foreign molasses to encourage merchants to pay it. However, the law also gave officials new powers to crack down on smuggling.

Under the Sugar Act, customs officials could enter any building at any time, using general search warrants called **writs of assistance.** Colonists accused of smuggling would face a panel of British judges instead of a jury of their peers. Also, they would be considered guilty unless proven innocent. Many colonists saw these searches and the denial of a jury trial as threats to their rights as Englishmen.

Meanwhile, Parliament's effort to get revenue went against the colonists' belief that they could only be taxed by their own legislatures. Protests against "taxation without representation," however, came mainly from New England merchants, who were most affected by the Sugar Act.

The Stamp Act To get even more revenue to pay for the colonies' defense,

Parliament passed the Stamp Act in 1765. Now colonists had to buy special stamps to put on legal documents, dice, and playing cards. Newspapers had to be printed on special stamped paper. Though stamp taxes had already been imposed for years in Britain, this was Parliament's first attempt to force the colonies to pay any tax other than customs duties.

Point of View

Did the colonies owe obedience to Britain?

Even within Parliament there were different points of view on this question. Charles Townshend declared that the colonies were "children planted by our care" and should be grateful for the protection of the British army and navy. Colonel Isaac Barré, who had served under General Wolfe in the French and Indian War, angrily responded,

"They planted by your care? No! Your oppressions planted them in America. They fled from your tyranny to a then uncultivated and unhospitable country. . . . And believe me, remember I this day told you so, that same spirit of freedom . . . will accompany them still."

Britain would soon feel the effects of that spirit of freedom in the colonies.

Protesting the Stamp Act

Unlike the Sugar Act, the Stamp Act affected people of every colony and social class, including leaders such as lawyers, newspaper publishers, and ministers. Protestors argued that only representatives they elected should be able to tax them. Such men lived near them and understood their

The term *boycott* originated with a hated land agent in 1897 Ireland, Charles C. Boycott. This English rent collector was so hated by the Irish tenants with whom he dealt that he was ostracized by them. Their circumstances were very like those of the American colonists. The English ruling class was inclined to regard the Irish as uncivilized, and Ireland itself as a source of revenue.

See American Readings, p. 26, for letters from colonial women promoting boycotts.

Discussion

Checking Understanding

1. Why did Parliament want more money from the colonies? (To pay debts from the French and Indian War and support its army in the colonies.)

2. What effects did Britain's effort to tax the colonies have on the colonists? (Angered them because they felt their rights were being violated; colonies began to feel they might have more in common with each other than with Britain; colonists protested the taxation.)

Stimulating Critical Thinking

3. If the government imposed a stamp tax today, how would people be affected? (Prices of newspapers and fees for legal documents such as birth certificates and marriage licenses would likely go up.)

needs, unlike Parliament, which met thousands of miles across the sea. The protestors insisted that Parliament was taking their money against their will.

Concern was so widespread that nine colonies sent delegates to a meeting in New York called the Stamp Act Congress. The delegates saw the need for the colonies to put aside rivalries over land claims and trade in order to meet the common threat. Said Christopher Gadsden of South Carolina, "There ought to be no New Englanders, no New Yorkers known on the continent, but all of us Americans."

The delegates declared that British citizens could not be taxed without representation and that Parliament did not represent the colonies. They sent a petition to Parliament asking it to **repeal**—do away with—the Stamp Act and the Sugar Act.

Many colonists took matters into their own hands. Calling themselves Sons and Daughters of Liberty, they decided to **boycott**—refuse to buy—British goods. Daughters of Liberty agreed to wear homespun wool dresses rather than buy imported British cloth. Such pledges, known as nonimportation agreements, were common throughout the colonies.

Some protests turned ugly. Tax collectors complained about "Sons of Violence" who tried to pressure them by breaking windows in their houses and even threatening their lives. Boston tax collector Andrew Oliver got a grim warning when an effigy—a dummy—of him was hanged and burned. A crowd in Connecticut even started to bury a tax collector alive. Only after hearing dirt being shoveled onto the coffin lid did he agree to resign.

Britain tried to tax the colonists by requiring them to buy special stamps for all legal documents and for newspapers. Tax collectors were appointed to sell the stamps, but most colonists refused to buy them. In one form of protest, they burned stamped papers.

★ ★ ★
Vital Links

○ Voice of newspaper publisher (First Person Account) Unit 2, Side 1, Search 12614, Play to 13271

○ See also Unit 2 Explore CD-ROM location 63.

William Pitt was an ardent admirer of the colonists and understood their rapidly growing desire for liberty and independence. In a 1770 speech to Parliament he said, "I love the Americans because they love liberty, and I love them for the noble efforts they made in the last war" (the French and Indian War). In 1777, the War of Independence underway, he reaffirmed his opinion before Parliament, "If I were an American, as I am an Englishman, while a foreign troop was landed in my country, I never would lay down my arms—never—never—never! You cannot conquer America."

Repeal of the Stamp Act

Within a few short months the protests had stopped efforts to collect the stamp tax. A shocked Parliament met in 1766 to debate whether to repeal the Stamp Act. Some members argued that giving in would encourage colonists to defy Parliament. Others worried that ordering the army to enforce the Stamp Act would lead to rebellion.

Grenville insisted that Parliament had a right to impose any laws, not just those regulating trade. "Great Britain protects America; America is bound to yield obedience," he declared. "If not, tell me when the Americans were emancipated [made free]?" William Pitt angrily replied, "I desire to know when they were made slaves."

Meanwhile, British merchants had been hurt by the boycotts and begged for repeal of the Stamp Act. After a fierce debate Parliament finally voted to do so. The Sugar Act, though, remained in effect.

To save face, Parliament passed an act declaring it could make laws for the colonies "in all cases whatsoever." Colonists paid little attention to this Declaratory Act. Parliament could claim any right it wanted, as long as it did not try to act on its claim. In the meantime, colonists celebrated the repeal of the Stamp Act by ringing church bells and setting off fireworks.

The Townshend Acts

Parliament continued to struggle with the debt problem. Soon it looked again to the colonies for revenue. In 1767 Charles Townshend, now in charge of the British treasury, came up with a new plan.

Townshend knew that many colonial leaders had recognized Parliament's right to regulate trade. Therefore, he convinced Parliament to pass the Townshend Acts. These laws imposed duties on popular goods that could only be imported from Britain: paint, lead, glass, paper, and tea.

The colonists saw the Townshend duties for exactly what they were—taxes in disguise. Even worse, some of the revenue

∞ **Link to the Present**

Boycotts Would you be willing to give up eating grapes or lettuce? In the 1960s and 1970s, the United Farm Workers union, led by Cesar Chavez, urged shoppers not to buy those products. They hoped a boycott would force grape and lettuce growers to pay them better wages and provide better working conditions.

The idea behind a boycott is simple—if you make your opponents lose enough money, they will do what you want. The challenge is to get enough people to go along with the boycott. In the case of the farm workers, each boycott took more than four years before being declared a success.

Cesar Chavez

WILLIAM JACKSON,
an *IMPORTER*; at the
BRAZEN HEAD,
North Side of the TOWN-HOUSE,
and Opposite the Town-Pump, in
Corn-hill, BOSTON.

It is desired that the Sons and Daughters of *LIBERTY*, would not buy any one thing of him, for in so doing they will bring Disgrace upon themselves, and their Posterity, for ever and ever, AMEN.

Colonial boycott notice

Gifted Students

Students can benefit from examining reproductions of colonial broadsides, engravings, and political cartoons. The period leading up to the War of Independence was rich in satirical drawings. Students might earn extra credit by finding examples at the library and presenting them to the class.

Checking Understanding

1. **Why did Parliament repeal the Stamp Act?** (Colonists had violently protested, and British merchants had complained about the boycott.)

Stimulating Critical Thinking

2. **If you were a member of Parliament, would you have voted to repeal the Stamp Act? Why or why not?** (Yes: tax almost uncollectable anyway, not worth cost of enforcement and risk of rebellion; no: tax burden not heavy, take a stand now or colonists will disobey in future.)

Teaching the

∞ **Link to Art**

Have students compare the engraving with the narrative on p. 192 and sources on p. 193. In analyzing how the engraving presents one point of view, students might also consider why Crispus Attucks is not shown. (They might suggest he was omitted for racist reasons—that the death of white people would arouse more anger than the death of a black person.) **Discussion Answers:** Soldiers are shown as aggressive and the colonists as passive victims. Soldiers would object to being shown as coldblooded killers instead of frightened men. He does not show the colonists baiting or attacking them because he wants to portray the conflict as an unprovoked massacre.

∞ **Link to Art**

The Bloody Massacre (1770) Paul Revere's title for his engraving reflected his purpose: to present a one-sided view of the conflict. (See page 192.) **Discuss** Compare the way Revere portrays the soldiers and the colonists. What do you think the British soldiers might have said about the way Revere has shown them? What actions of the colonists does Revere choose not to show? Why do you think he does not show those actions?

went to pay salaries of the royal governors, who had up until then been paid by the colonial legislatures. Now the governors would be more likely to support Parliament than to speak up for the colonies.

Colonial Leaders of Protest

Several protest leaders emerged in 1767 to alert colonists that their self-government was threatened. Most notable was Samuel Adams of Boston, a master at inflaming people with symbols and words.

On one day Adams might be seen staging a rally to hang a tax collector in effigy from a "liberty pole." On another he would be writing an essay criticizing the governor, who once complained that "every dip of his pen stung like a horned snake." Adams had a motto, "Take a stand at the start," and he never let up.

More cautious but equally passionate about the colonists' rights was Sam's cousin John Adams, a lawyer. Like Samuel Adams, John had come to believe that Parliament did not represent the colonies and therefore had no right to pass any laws binding them, not even on matters of trade.

Perhaps the best speaker among the protest leaders was Patrick Henry, a member of the Virginia House of Burgesses. A back-country lawyer with a silver tongue, he could move listeners to tears. He would later become famous for declaring, "Give me liberty or give me death."

Colonial legislatures joined in the rising protest. The Massachusetts legislature urged other colonies to boycott British goods. The New York legislature refused to house British troops as required by a law called the Quartering Act. Parliament dismissed both legislatures and sent troops to Boston.

Such actions seemed to confirm what leaders like Sam Adams were warning—that Britain intended to end the colonists' tradition of self-government. George Washington, who had joined in the boycott, wrote:

❝At a time when our lordly Masters in Great Britain will be satisfied with nothing less than the [loss] of American freedom, it seems highly necessary that something should be done to . . . maintain the liberty which we had derived from our ancestors. . . . Yet arms [war] should be the last resource.❞

**A Cause-Effect
Chain**

To review events, have
students make a cause-
effect chain. It should
begin with "Britain wins
the French and Indian
War," followed by
British actions, colonial
responses, and British
reactions. Conclude by
writing a chain on the
chalkboard, asking stu-
dents to supply events.

Section Review
Answers

1. Definitions: *proclamation*
(p. 187), *customs duties*
(p. 188), *revenue* (p. 188),
writs of assistance (p. 188),
repeal (p. 189), *boycott*
(p. 189)

2. To prevent further
conflict with the Indians.
Colonists ignored it.

3. This was the first tax
imposed on the colonies
other than customs duties.
It would affect most colonists, including leaders
such as lawyers, publishers,
and ministers. Protesters felt
they should be taxed only
by elected representatives.

4. They objected to taxation
without representation.
Also, taxes would pay royal
governors' salaries, under-
cutting the power of elected
legislatures.

5. Some may argue that
widespread refusal to pay
would have left it unen-
forceable and led to repeal.
Others may say the British
would fear only violent
protest.

192

On the night following the Boston
Massacre, a meeting of more than one
thousand people was held in Boston's Old
South Meeting House to protest the killings.
The meeting, at which threats of violent
retaliation were made, lasted long into the
night. At the end the governor sent word
that the hated British troops would be
retired to their barracks, out of the public
view. The troops were eventually withdrawn
to an island in Boston harbor; it was hoped
that this would mollify Bostonians and help
avoid further incidents.

The Boston Massacre

Tensions in the colonies rose with each
passing day, and protests turned violent. On
March 5, 1770, an angry crowd taunted
nine British soldiers guarding the Boston customs building. The crowd threw whatever
they could get their hands on—sticks, snowballs, oyster shells, and ice chunks.

The frightened soldiers opened fire, killing five and wounding several more. The
first to die was Crispus Attucks, a former
slave who had become a sailor and one of
the Sons of Liberty. The British commander
and soldiers were charged with murder.

John Adams thought that the crowd had
provoked the soldiers, and he successfully
defended them in court. Sam Adams saw the
shooting as a chance to whip up anti-British
feeling. He called it "the Boston Massacre."
Paul Revere, a local silversmith, made an
engraving showing soldiers firing on
unarmed citizens. Prints of the picture were
sent throughout the colonies.

The Colonists Cool Off

On the very day of the Boston Massacre,
Parliament met to discuss the effects of the
Townshend Acts. King George III urged
restraint, not wanting to drive the colonies
to revolt. Parliament agreed and repealed
the duties except the one on tea, which
provided the most income.

Parliament assumed that the colonists
were so fond of tea that they would be willing to pay the duty. Keeping the tea duty was
also its way of saying it had the right to
impose laws. The Sugar Act also remained.

Most colonists were satisfied just to get
rid of the other Townshend duties. Despite
Sam Adams' warning that every calm day
"strengthens our opponent and weakens
us," the protests died down. For his part,
John Adams was lying low. "I shall certainly

Paul
Revere

John
Adams

Samuel
Adams

become more retired and cautious," he
wrote in his diary. "I shall certainly mind
my own farm and my own office."

Two years passed without serious incident, but Sam Adams was on the alert. He
was certain that Parliament would make
another mistake, and when it did he would
be ready. "Where there is a spark of patriotic
fire," he wrote, "we will enkindle [light] it."

★ 2. Section Review

1. Define **proclamation, customs
duties, revenue, writs of assistance,
repeal,** and **boycott.**
2. What was the purpose of the Proclamation of 1763, and how did colonists react?
3. Explain the uproar over the Stamp Act.
4. Why did the colonists oppose the
Townshend Acts?
5. Critical Thinking Do you think that
violent protests were necessary to get the
Stamp Act repealed? Explain.

(Answers continued from side margin)

3. (a) They all describe what led to the shooting. (b) No. A, C, and D place more blame on the colonists. B cites testimony against soldiers, though author's own viewpoint cannot be inferred. (c) Four excerpts are not enough to base a conclusion on. Since eyewitnesses disagreed, it is unlikely that the question can ever be answered.

For further application, have students do the Applying Skills activity in the Chapter Survey (p. 200).

If students need to review the skill, use the Skills Development transparency and activity in the Chapter Resources Binder, pp. 55–56.

Skill Lab

Thinking Critically
Primary and Secondary Sources

Was the Boston Massacre a killing of helpless, unresisting colonists? At the trial of British Captain Thomas Preston and his soldiers, some witnesses said that the colonists provoked the shooting. Others disagreed.

Question to Investigate

Who was to blame for the Boston Massacre?

Procedure

To explore the question, you will look at some primary and secondary sources. **A primary source** is an artifact or record from someone who experienced the event described. A **secondary source** is made by someone who did not experience the event described. Secondary sources, such as this textbook, are based on primary sources. Read the sources and do the following.

❶ Identify whether each source is primary or secondary. Explain how you can tell.

❷ Identify the information each source gives.
a. What people and actions does each one describe?
b. From what types of primary sources do you think the secondary sources got their information? Explain.

❸ Compare the information.
a. What do the sources have in common?
b. Do they agree with each other? Explain.
c. Do you think the Question to Investigate can ever be answered for certain? Explain.

Skill Tips

• Some examples of primary sources are autobiographies, records of oral interviews, diaries, letters, photos, films, and artifacts like tools or weapons.
• Some examples of secondary sources are biographies, history books, and encyclopedias.
• Paintings, political cartoons, and newspaper articles can be either primary or secondary sources.

Sources to Use

A "One of these people [Crispus Attucks], a stout man with a long cordwood stick, threw himself in, and made a blow at [struck] the officer. I saw the officer try to ward off the stroke. The stout man then turned around and struck the soldier's gun. He knocked his gun away and struck him over the head. This stout man cried, 'Kill the dogs. Knock them over.' This was the general cry. The people then crowded in."

From the trial testimony of Andrew, an enslaved African American

B "The prosecution attacked vigorously, parading witness after witness to the stand; . . . all of them agreed that the Captain gave the order to fire—and, equally important, that there was no provocation for it beyond name-calling and a few snowballs."

From "The Boston Massacre," by Thomas J. Fleming, *American Heritage*, December 1966

C "I asked him then . . . whether he thought they fired in self-defense or on purpose to destroy the people. He said he really thought they did fire to defend themselves; that he did not blame the man, whoever he was, who shot him."

From the testimony of Dr. John Jeffries, who treated a wounded colonist who later died

D Reread the description of the Boston Massacre on page 192.

Introducing the Skill Lab

Point out that the main reason for determining whether a source is primary or secondary is to understand how it might be useful. Primary sources are best for revealing personal reactions. Secondary sources are usually better for giving the "big picture"—including a variety of reactions, analyzing causes and effects, or providing a broader perspective. Since either type of source can include opinions and inaccurate statements of fact, students should approach both with a critical eye.

Skill Lab
Answers

1. Source A is primary, an eyewitness; B is secondary, written in 1966; C is primary, an eyewitness; D is secondary, from a textbook.

2. (a) A: conflict between Attucks and the officer; B: trial witnesses testifying that soldiers fired without cause; C: colonist's statement that soldiers fired in self-defense; D: an account that soldiers were frightened and were acquitted of murder charges. (b) B: court transcripts and eyewitness accounts of trial; D: statements by John and Sam Adams, eyewitness accounts of shooting.

(Answers continued in top margin)

Introducing the Section

Vocabulary

monopoly (p. 194) complete control

News by Mail

To see how accounts can be slanted, have students write a persuasive letter about a present-day news event or issue. They should imagine they are writing to a friend who is living in an area without television or newspapers and therefore depends solely on letters for news of events. Have some students read their letters, and discuss how easy it is to present only one side of an event or issue.

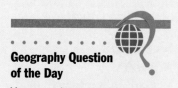

Geography Question of the Day

Have students use the map on p. 199 to estimate the distance from Boston to Charles Town. Then have them list what factors would make it difficult for news to travel quickly between those cities. (In addition to the long distance, other possible hindrances are the need to rely on horseback riders, rider fatigue, injuries to horses, poor road conditions.)

Section Objectives

★ Describe the purpose of the Committees of Correspondence.
★ Identify why and how colonists united to protest the Tea Act.
★ Discuss the purpose and results of the First Continental Congress.

Teaching Resources

Take-Home Planner 3, pp. 2–9
Chapter Resources Binder
Study Guide, p. 51
Reinforcement
Skills Development
Geography Extensions, pp. 13–14
American Readings, pp. 27–28
Using Historical Documents, pp. 38–45
Transparency Activities
Chapter and Unit Tests, pp. 45–48

3. The Road to Revolution

Reading Guide

New Term monopoly

Section Focus **What led Britain and the colonies to the brink of war**

1. Why were Committees of Correspondence formed?
2. Why and how did the colonists unite to protest the Tea Act?
3. What were the purpose and results of the First Continental Congress?

Although it repealed most of the Townshend Acts in 1770, Parliament still insisted it had complete power over the colonies. Also, warships patrolling the Atlantic coast were a reminder that Britain was willing to use force.

Committees of Correspondence

In June 1772 the calm was shattered after the *Gaspee*, a British schooner chasing smugglers, ran aground in Rhode Island. That night colonists removed the crew and burned the boat to the waterline. Rumors spread that if any of the colonists were caught they would be sent to Britain for trial, denying their right to a trial by a jury of their peers.

Four days later, Massachusetts Governor Thomas Hutchinson announced that Parliament would now pay his salary. This news reopened a simmering issue. Did Parliament or the colonial legislatures control the governors? Hutchinson had also written to friends in London suggesting that colonists' liberties should be limited for the good of the empire. When the public learned of these letters, there was an outcry of protest.

Samuel Adams made good use of these events. To him, all such British actions were part of a plot to deny the colonists their rights as Englishmen. In November 1772 he began organizing groups of letter writers known as "Committees of Correspondence" to spread news from town to town about British threats to those rights. The more outrageous the story, the better Adams liked it. Within two years all the colonies were linked by Committees of Correspondence.

Still, Sam Adams had not found an issue powerful enough to rally all the colonies around. "I wish we could arouse the continent," he wrote to a friend.

The Tea Act

In 1773 Adams got the issue he wanted when Parliament passed the Tea Act. This law gave the British East India Company a **monopoly**—complete control—of sales of British tea in the colonies. Colonial merchants thought this would put many of them out of business. They also suspected that British monopolies on other products would soon follow.

Parliament had not intended the Tea Act to be a slap in the face to the colonists. It was passed to help another part of the empire. The British East India Company was responsible for governing India, but was heavily in debt. The Tea Act would help it get back on its feet. The colonists objected

Sam Adams was neither the first nor the last to use letters to further his cause. You may wish to bring materials to class from organizations dedicated to monitoring and preserving civil rights. Amnesty International uses letter-writing campaigns to alert civil authorities to abuses, such as denial of trial by jury. It asks members to write governments asking for the release of those jailed unjustly. The strategy has been effective in raising public awareness of civil rights violations.

For a description of the Boston Tea Party, see **American Readings,** pp. 27–28.

that Parliament had no right to finance other parts of its colonial empire by running their merchants out of business.

Committees of Correspondence urged colonists to boycott East India tea. A group of 51 women in Edenton, North Carolina, for instance, agreed not to drink British tea or wear clothing from Britain until the Tea Act was repealed. The boycott was so effective that most of the company's ships returned to Britain without unloading their cargoes.

The Boston Tea Party

Massachusetts Governor Hutchinson challenged the boycott. He declared that the company ships in Boston harbor would not leave until their cargo was unloaded. The Sons of Liberty decided to do the unloading, but not in the way the governor had in mind.

Disguised as Indians, they boarded three East India Company ships on the evening of December 16, 1773. As hundreds of Bostonians cheered from the docks, the "Indians" chopped open 342 chests of tea and tossed them into the sea.

In Britain and in the colonies, most people saw the Boston Tea Party as a point of no return. John Adams declared, "This Destruction of the Tea is so bold, so daring, so firm, intrepid and inflexible, and it must have so important Consequences." King George III declared, "The Colonies must either submit [give in] or triumph."

The "Intolerable Acts"

To punish Massachusetts, Parliament passed a series of laws in 1774 called the Coercive Acts. The navy would blockade Boston harbor until the ruined tea was paid

Members of the Sons of Liberty protested the Tea Act by dumping chests of tea into Boston harbor to make "salt water tea."

Checking Understanding

1. Who organized the Committees of Correspondence and why? (Sam Adams arranged for letter writers to spread news about British threats to colonists' freedoms.)

2. Why did the Sons of Liberty stage the Boston Tea Party? (Governor Hutchinson refused to ship British East India Company tea back to Britain, despite the boycott.)

Stimulating Critical Thinking

3. John Adams praised the Boston Tea Party, but Benjamin Franklin called it an act of violent injustice. With whom do you agree? Explain. (Those who agree with Adams may note that no person was injured and no property destroyed other than the tea. Those who agree with Franklin might argue that property was destroyed nonetheless and that the ship's crew were probably violently intimidated.)

See the Study Guide activity in the **Chapter Resources Binder,** p. 51.

✳ **History Footnote**

Housing British troops with colonists was more than an inconvenience. It was a move guaranteed to inflame colonists' tempers. Prejudice among British soldiers against colonists had only worsened since the French and Indian War, and the colonists returned the dislike. If the British saw colonists as bumpkins, the colonists saw British soldiers as brutes.

See **Using Historical Documents**, pp. 38–45, for a resolution passed by the First Continental Congress.

Hands-On
→ HISTORY

Classifying types of protest Protests take many forms—some centuries-old and some new. Some methods used long ago, such as boycotts and demonstrations, are still common. Others would seem strange or cruel today. Can you imagine, for example, someone being tarred and feathered? In this activity, you will compare protests in colonial times with those today.

Activity

① Make a list titled "Colonial Protests." Give specific examples, such as "refusing to buy British tea."

② Make a list titled "Protests Today." Give specific examples.

③ Sort the examples into general types, such as "boycotts" or "destroying property." Identify each type as violent or nonviolent.

Tax collector being tarred and feathered

④ Arrange the examples in a table with four columns labeled "Type of Protest," "Violent or Nonviolent?," "Colonial Examples," and "Modern Examples."

⑤ Write a paragraph summarizing similarities and differences between protests then and now.

for. Also, a military governor would rule Massachusetts. British officials charged with crimes would be tried outside the colony. Colonists would have to house and feed British troops. Angry colonists called these laws the "Intolerable Acts."

By punishing Massachusetts, Parliament hoped to make the other colonies afraid to challenge British authority. Instead, the Coercive Acts had the opposite effect. Even though many colonists believed that destroying the tea was going too far, they saw the British reaction as a greater threat. When Boston's port was closed, merchants across America closed shops in sympathy, flags flew at half-mast, and other colonies sent donations of food and money.

Meanwhile, Parliament also passed the Quebec Act to provide government for the French people of Quebec. Quebec would be ruled by a governor with no elected legislature. Its boundaries would expand to include much of the territory between the 13 colonies and the Mississippi River. Many colonists saw the Quebec Act as a threat to the future of their self-government.

The First Continental Congress

When Virginia's legislature proposed a day of fasting and prayer for the people of Boston, the governor dissolved the legislature. The legislators then met at a nearby inn and drew up a resolution declaring that the blockade of Boston was an attack on all the colonies. They called for a Continental Congress to meet "to consult upon the present unhappy state of the colonies."

Students with Limited English

To help students integrate the information in the chart, allow those whose primary language is not English to translate the chart into their primary language and copy it into a notebook or journal. Students might also draw a time line labeled with the names and dates of the British laws.

In September 1774 delegates from all of the colonies except Georgia met in Philadelphia as the First Continental Congress. Their goal was to look for a peaceful way to resolve their conflict with Britain.

Patrick Henry urged the delegates to look beyond their own colonies and consider the interests of all. "Virginians, Pennsylvanians, New Yorkers, and New Englanders are no more," he declared. "I am not a Virginian but an American."

Politically, the Congress was split about equally into three groups: conservatives, moderates, and radicals. The conservatives opposed anything that might lead to a break with Britain. George Washington was among the moderates, who believed that Parliament had a right to regulate trade but not tax the colonies.

The radicals included John Adams and Sam Adams. They argued that Parliament had no right to impose laws on the colonies.

Steps Toward the American Revolution 1763–1774

British Law	What It Did	Colonial Reaction
Proclamation of 1763	Prohibited settlement west of the Appalachians	Protests, defiance
Sugar Act (1764)	Lowered duties on molasses, but first time duties used to collect revenue; denied jury trial to accused smugglers	Protests, petitions
Stamp Act (1765)	Required all written materials to be printed on stamped paper; first direct tax to get revenue (repealed in 1766)	Stamp Act Congress, petitions, boycotts, demonstrations
Declaratory Act (1766)	Declared Parliament's right to impose any laws on colonies	Little notice because of Stamp Act repeal
Townshend Acts (1767)	Taxed tea, lead, glass, paint, and paper; governors to be paid by Parliament (most repealed in 1770)	Boycotts, riots, demonstrations
Tea Act (1773)	Required that only East India Company may import and sell tea	Boycotts, Boston Tea Party
Coercive Acts (1774) ("Intolerable Acts")	Closed Boston port until destroyed tea paid for; suspended town meetings; appointed military governor of Massachusetts; permitted trials of government officials to be in England	Other colonies sent food and money to Massachusetts; call for Continental Congress

Source: Oxford Book of Reference on English History

Checking Understanding

1. Why did the British close Boston's port? (To punish acts of protest.)

2. What other measures were in the Coercive Acts? (Massachusetts would have a military governor; British officials charged with crimes would not be tried in the colony; colonists must house and feed British troops.)

3. How did the colonies respond to the Coercive Acts? (They banded together in sympathy with Boston. Virginia called for a Continental Congress.)

Stimulating Critical Thinking

4. What effects would closing the harbor have on life in Boston? (No travel by ship; shortage of food and equipment; failing merchant businesses; people going hungry.)

Bonus Activity

Protest Slogans

To help students imagine colonial grievances, have small groups create slogans protesting various British policies. For instance, slogans against the Quartering Act might declare "Louts out!" or "In the barracks, yes—in my home, no!" Each group should create three slogans, read them aloud to the class, and have others identify the targets of protest.

Closing
the Section

Wrap-Up Activity

Letters on the Coercive Acts

To help students imagine colonists' reactions to the Coercive Acts, have them write letters to the editor of the *Boston Bugle* on September 1, 1774, just before the meeting of the First Continental Congress. The letters should be written as if by ordinary citizens telling how the Coercive Acts affect their lives and what should be done to try to solve the problem.

Section Review
Answers

1. Definition: *monopoly* (p. 194)

2. To tell colonists of British threats to liberties.

3. The act amounted to a monopoly on tea; it affected many people since nearly everyone drank tea.

4. The delegates recommended a boycott of British goods. They were unwilling to use force unless nothing else worked.

5. It showed the colonists were willing to use violence and to destroy British property.

To check understanding of "Why We Remember," assign Thinking Critically question 3 on page 200.

✳ **History Footnote**

Joseph Galloway was a lawyer and a colonial representative from Pennsylvania to the First Continental Congress. Although he agreed that the Americans had legitimate complaints against Britain, he recognized and supported the legitimacy of British rule over the colonies. At the congress, Galloway presented a plan of union by which the colonial governments and the British government would jointly administer colonial affairs. The plan failed to pass the congress by one vote. Galloway, who had hoped for compromise, refused to participate in the Second Continental Congress and spoke out against independence.

In spite of their differences, the delegates all opposed the Coercive Acts. They approved a Declaration of Rights and Grievances, which condemned the Coercive Acts and affirmed the rights to life, liberty, and property. The declaration denied Parliament's right to tax the colonies.

The Congress recommended that every county, town, and city form committees to enforce a boycott on British goods. The overall attitude was a willingness to resist with force only if all else failed. The delegates agreed to meet again the following May if Britain did not change its policies.

War Clouds

Towns formed committees to enforce the boycott. Violators faced punishments ranging from having their names published in newspapers to being tarred and feathered.

Some colonists, though, were alarmed by such actions. One conservative accused the committees of "knocking out any Man's Brains that dares presume to speak his Mind freely about the present Contest."

In case the boycott did not work, the colonists rushed to organize militias. The colonies stood on the brink of war.

3. Section Review

1. Define **monopoly**.
2. What was the purpose of the Committees of Correspondence?
3. Why did the Tea Act anger the colonists?
4. What actions did the First Continental Congress take and why?
5. **Critical Thinking** Why might Parliament have thought that the Boston Tea Party was the most dangerous protest yet?

Why We Remember

The Years of Conflict

When George Washington was a boy growing up in Virginia, he often spoke of Britain as "home." So did most colonists. During the years of conflict, as Britain tried to tighten its control over the colonies, such feelings of loyalty began to change to resentment. Many colonists feared that the rights and liberties they had come to value were suddenly at risk.

Washington and his fellow colonists faced a clear choice. It would have been easier not to take action. That was not the choice of many brave colonists. Rich and poor, humble and proud, these Americans stood up to every attack on their freedoms. They fought back at first with boycotts and demonstrations. When peaceful measures failed, many were prepared to take up arms and fight for their rights. We live in a free country today because Washington and thousands like him refused to accept tyranny.

Improvements of colonial roads were matched by the rapid rise in the spread of news by mail. Boston's 1772 Committee of Correspondence was joined by similar organizations in more than half of the 260 towns in Massachusetts. In 1773 Virginia's House of Burgesses proposed that each colony appoint a committee of correspondence. Within a year, almost every colony had such a network in place. By the time the Coercive Acts were imposed upon Boston in 1774, the means were in place to rapidly inform the colonies of Boston's plight, thus paving the way for concerted action by the colonies. The First Continental Congress was a direct outgrowth of the committees.

Geography Lab

Colonial Communication

Surrounded by "howling wilderness," as one settler called it, the earliest colonists traveled little. When they did, they floated down rivers or picked their way along Indian footpaths. In time, some paths became horse trails, and horse trails became roads. The British government improved some roads and built others so that post riders—mail carriers on horseback—could get through.

Still, travel was difficult. So how were colonists able to share the news and the ideas that eventually brought them closer together?

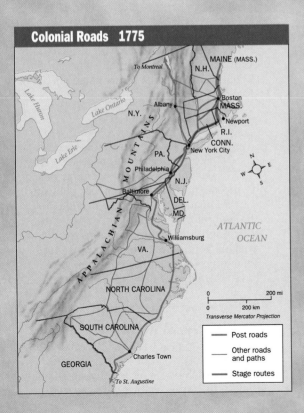

Colonial Roads 1775

Post roads
Other roads and paths
Stage routes

0   200 mi
0   200 km
Transverse Mercator Projection

Postal Milestones

1692 Royal colonial post opens. Boston–Philadelphia mail: 1 week.

1720 New York–Philadelphia mail: 3 days.

1753 Parliament appoints Benjamin Franklin postmaster. New York–Philadelphia mail: 1½ days.

1756 New York–Philadelphia by stagecoach: 3 or more days.

1758 Colonial post begins to carry newspapers.

1764 New York–Philadelphia mail: 1 day.

1771 New York–Philadelphia by stagecoach: 2 days.

1775 Continental Congress authorizes a postal service. Royal post closes.

1775 There are twice as many colonial newspapers as in 1755.

Link to History

1. Imagine that it is 1775. Someone says, "How can the colonists organize a rebellion? They can barely communicate with each other!" What is your answer?

2. Agree or disagree: Without meaning to, the British helped colonial unity. Explain.

3. **Hands-On Geography** The year is 1771. Your stagecoach line just bought new coaches to deliver passengers and packages. Prepare an advertisement to attract customers. Include information about improved routes and schedules.

Teaching the Geography Lab

Direct students' attention to passages in the chapter that support the evidence in the lab of increasing ease of communication among colonies (for instance, the discussion of Committees of Correspondence on p. 194).

Link to History
Answers

1. Students may dispute the claim by citing the system of roads shown on the map as well as improvements in means of communication in the list of postal milestones.

2. Students should note that the British helped the cause of colonial unity by establishing a postal service and improving the roads over which mail was delivered, thus making possible the rapid transmission of news and increasing the feelings of common interest among the colonists. They might also note that with each repressive act, Britain helped unite the colonists against the government.

3. The advertisement should draw on the information provided in the list of postal milestones.

See the activity on colonial communication in **Geography Extensions**, pp. 13–14.

Reviewing Vocabulary

Definitions may be found on the following pages: *allies* (p. 182), *blockade* (p. 185), *cede* (p. 185), *proclamation* (p. 187), *customs duties* (p. 188), *revenue* (p. 188), *writs of assistance* (p. 188), *repeal* (p. 189), *boycott* (p. 189), *monopoly* (p. 194).

Reviewing Main Ideas

1. At first they were British allies, but as the French grew stronger they decided to be neutral.

2. Pitt raised taxes in Britain to pay for a larger army; he sent his best officers; he set up a naval blockade of New France.

3. Britain tried to avoid conflict between colonists and Indians. Colonists generally ignored the order.

4. (a) To gain revenue to pay for the colonies' defense. (b) It required colonists to buy special stamps for documents, and newspapers could be printed only on special stamped paper. (c) That only representatives colonists elected—not Parliament—had the right to tax them.

5. They saw the duties as taxes in disguise. Also, since some of the money would be used to pay colonial governors, they feared governors would be less likely to speak up for their interests.

6. The rumor that those responsible for burning the *Gaspee* would be sent to Britain for trial, and the outcry over Governor Hutchinson's letters suggesting that colonists' liberties be limited.

7. (a) The Tea Act led to a boycott of British tea, which led to British ships being
(Answers continued in top margin)

unable to unload cargoes, which led to Hutchinson's order to unload the tea, which led to the Sons of Liberty dumping the cargo. (b) The Boston Tea Party led Parliament to pass the (c) Coercive Acts to punish the people of Massachusetts. Colonial opposition to these acts led to (d) calling for a Continental Congress to discuss the conflict between Britain and the colonies.

Thinking Critically

1. When the Albany Congress proposed that the colonies unite to defend themselves, every colonial legislature voted against it, whereas the First Continental Congress voted to enforce a boycott in every colony. The colonists had come to see British actions as threatening their liberties; this common threat united the colonies.

Chapter Survey ★

Reviewing Vocabulary

Define the following terms.

1. allies
2. blockade
3. cede
4. proclamation
5. customs duties
6. revenue
7. writs of assistance
8. repeal
9. boycott
10. monopoly

Reviewing Main Ideas

1. What role did the Iroquois play in the conflict between the French and the British in North America?

2. Explain how William Pitt's actions helped lead to Britain's victory in the French and Indian War.

3. Why did Britain order the colonists to stay east of the Appalachian Mountains in the Proclamation of 1763? How did the colonists respond?

4. Describe each of the following with regard to the Stamp Act: (a) its purpose (b) what it required colonists to do (c) what argument colonists made against it

5. Why did the colonists oppose the idea of paying the duties required by the Townshend Acts?

6. What two incidents led to the formation of Committees of Correspondence?

7. Explain how each event led to the next: (a) Tea Act (b) Boston Tea Party (c) Coercive Acts (d) First Continental Congress

Thinking Critically

1. Analysis The First Continental Congress succeeded where the Albany Congress failed. Explain how and why.

2. Synthesis Imagine that the year is 2024. Everyone in the United Colonies of America is getting ready to celebrate the 250th anniversary of the Declaration of Loyalty to the British Empire. Describe the events that led to that declaration in 1774.

How did Britain and the colonies avoid the split that had threatened them?

3. Why We Remember: Analysis Why do you think some colonists protested against the British policies but other colonists did not?

Applying Skills

Primary and secondary sources The Boston Massacre is one of the many examples of a conflict that each side blamed the other for starting. Find an example of such a conflict today. It might be an event described in a newspaper or magazine article, or a conflict between two people or groups that you know. Then do the following:

1. Identify at least three sources of information about the conflict.

2. Tell whether each source is a primary or secondary source. Explain how you can tell.

3. Tell what ways the sources agree or disagree.

History Mystery

The "fatal" stamp Answer the History Mystery on page 179. The skull and crossbones cartoon that appears next to the stamp was published by a Philadelphia newspaper to blame the stamp for "killing" the newspaper. How might the stamps hurt a newspaper? Imagine yourself as a colonist. What are some ways in which the stamps might have affected your daily life?

Writing in Your History Journal

1. Keys to History (a) The time line on pages 178–179 has six Keys to History. In your journal, describe why each one is important. (b) Discuss the events in this chapter with two adults.

2. Faced with the boycott of British tea, Parliament repealed the Tea Act as it had the Stamp Act and most of the Townshend duties, and allowed colonists to elect representatives to Parliament. In response, colonists stopped boycotts and accepted taxes levied by Parliament.

3. Students may say that some colonists had closer ties to Britain and could not be comfortable protesting laws passed by Parliament. Others may point out that colonists loyal to Britain might receive favors under British rule and would not want to lose privileges.

Applying Skills

1–3. Selections should reflect the definitions and uses of primary and secondary sources as described on page 193.
(Answers continued in side margin)

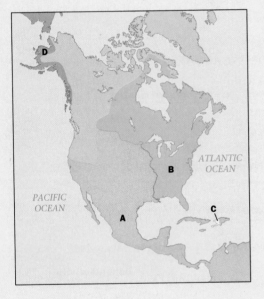

PACIFIC
OCEAN

ATLANTIC
OCEAN

Reviewing Geography

1. For each colored area marked with a letter on the map, write the letter and the name of the European country that claimed the area.

2. Geographic Thinking About 3,000 miles (4,800 km) of ocean separate London and Boston. Historians often point to this separation as a major influence on the conflict between Britain and its American colonies. What evidence do you find in the chapter to support this idea? Do you think that physical separation between government and the people must always lead to conflict? Explain your answer.

What other events do the three of you think should be on the time line? Write those events and their dates in your journal, and tell why you think each event should be added.

2. George Washington Imagine that you are a British officer in 1754. You have received a report of Washington's actions against the French in the Ohio Valley. In your journal, write your thoughts about whether he deserves to be made an officer in the British army. Give reasons to support your opinion.

3. Citizenship Imagine that you are a colonist living in 1774. Do you support the conservatives, the moderates, or the radicals? Why? Write your responses in your journal.

Alternative Assessment

Citizenship: Role-playing the Continental Congress With two other students, role-play a discussion at the First Continental Congress. One member will play the role of a conservative, another a moderate, and the third a radical.

❶ Meet as a group to decide what role each member will play.

❷ Each member will review the chapter and do other research as needed to become familiar with his or her role.

❸ Meet again as a group to plan the role play to include the following: (a) each member presents a position and summarizes reasons for it; (b) each of the other members responds to that position; and (c) the group decides on a course of action.

❹ Do the role play.

Your work will be evaluated on the following criteria:
• you reenact the events of the Congress accurately
• your group presents its position and arguments clearly
• you stay "in character" as a delegate

The War of Independence
1775–1783

Chapter Planning Guide

Section	Student Text	Teacher's Edition Activities
Opener and Story pp. 202–205	**Keys to History Time Line** **History Mystery** Beginning the Story with **Joseph Martin**	**Setting the Stage Activity** Off to War, p. 204
1 **The War Begins** pp. 206–210	**Point of View** Lexington: Who fired the first shot?, p. 207 **Link to the Present** The information superhighway, p. 207 **Link to Literature** *April Morning*, pp. 228–229 **Skill Lab** Statements of Fact and Opinions, p. 210	**Warm-Up Activity** Preparing for War, p. 206 **Geography Question of the Day,** p. 206 **Section Activity** Creating Political Cartoons, p. 208 **Bonus Activity** Dear Diary, p. 208 **Wrap-Up Activity** Charting Outcomes, p. 209
2 **The Issue of Independence** pp. 211–215	**Hands-On History** Promoting the Declaration of Independence exhibit, p. 212	**Warm-Up Activity** Message from the King, p. 211 **Geography Question of the Day,** p. 211 **Section Activity** Taking Sides, p. 212 **Bonus Activity** Letter of Commendation, p. 214 **Wrap-Up Activity** Playing *Jeopardy!*®, p. 215
3 **The War in the North** pp. 216–220	**Link to Art** *Washington Crossing the Delaware*, p. 217 **World Link** Spanish settlers in California, p. 218 **Geography Lab** Reading a War Map, p. 220	**Warm-Up Activity** Writing for Supplies, p. 216 **Geography Question of the Day,** p. 216 **Section Activity** Predicting the Victor, p. 218 **Bonus Activity** Advice for Burgoyne, p. 218 **Wrap-Up Activity** Charting Victories, p. 219
4 **The End of the War** pp. 221–225	**Reading Maps** The War in the South and West 1778–1781, p. 223; North America 1783, p. 224	**Warm-Up Activity** Note from a Spy, p. 221 **Geography Question of the Day,** p. 221 **Section Activity** Planning an Attack, p. 222 **Bonus Activity** Loyalist News Article, p. 224 **Wrap-Up Activity** Assessing a Defeat, p. 225
Evaluation	☑ **Section 1 Review,** p. 209 ☑ **Section 2 Review,** p. 215 ☑ **Section 3 Review,** p. 219 ☑ **Section 4 Review,** p. 225 ☑ **Chapter Survey,** pp. 226–227 **Alternative Assessment** Acting out opposing roles, p. 227	☑ **Answers to Section 1 Review,** p. 209 ☑ **Answers to Section 2 Review,** p. 215 ☑ **Answers to Section 3 Review,** p. 219 ☑ **Answers to Section 4 Review,** p. 225 ☑ **Answers to Chapter Survey,** pp. 226–227 (Alternative Assessment guidelines are in the Take-Home Planner.)

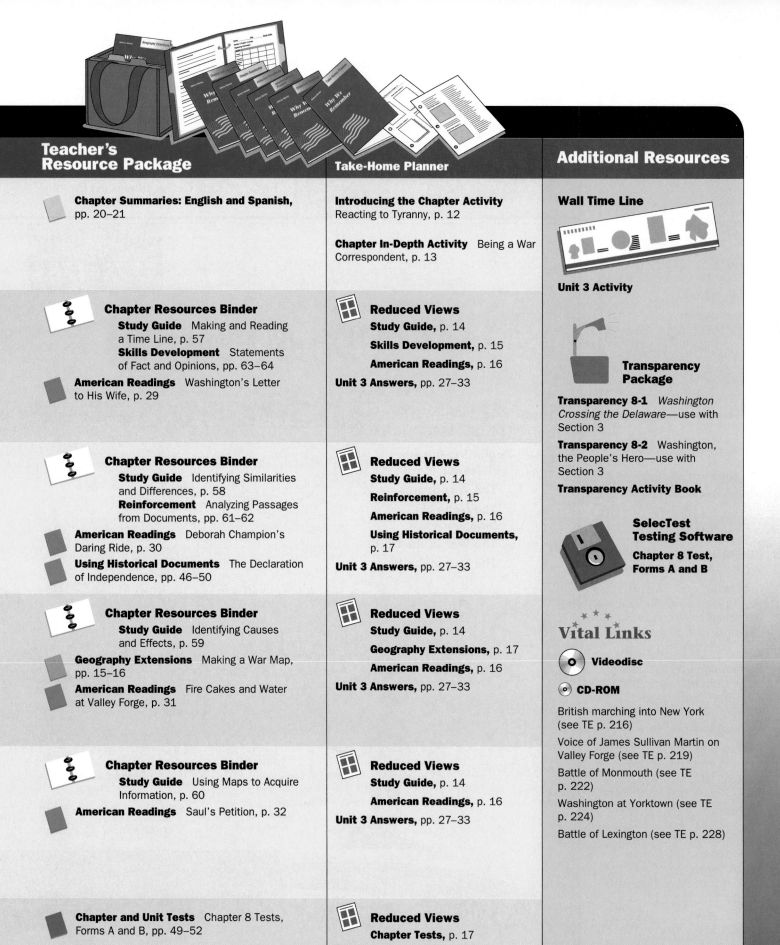

Teacher's Resource Package

Chapter Summaries: English and Spanish, pp. 20–21

Chapter Resources Binder
Study Guide Making and Reading a Time Line, p. 57
Skills Development Statements of Fact and Opinions, pp. 63–64
American Readings Washington's Letter to His Wife, p. 29

Chapter Resources Binder
Study Guide Identifying Similarities and Differences, p. 58
Reinforcement Analyzing Passages from Documents, pp. 61–62
American Readings Deborah Champion's Daring Ride, p. 30
Using Historical Documents The Declaration of Independence, pp. 46–50

Chapter Resources Binder
Study Guide Identifying Causes and Effects, p. 59
Geography Extensions Making a War Map, pp. 15–16
American Readings Fire Cakes and Water at Valley Forge, p. 31

Chapter Resources Binder
Study Guide Using Maps to Acquire Information, p. 60
American Readings Saul's Petition, p. 32

Chapter and Unit Tests Chapter 8 Tests, Forms A and B, pp. 49–52

Take-Home Planner

Introducing the Chapter Activity
Reacting to Tyranny, p. 12

Chapter In-Depth Activity Being a War Correspondent, p. 13

Reduced Views
Study Guide, p. 14
Skills Development, p. 15
American Readings, p. 16
Unit 3 Answers, pp. 27–33

Reduced Views
Study Guide, p. 14
Reinforcement, p. 15
American Readings, p. 16
Using Historical Documents, p. 17
Unit 3 Answers, pp. 27–33

Reduced Views
Study Guide, p. 14
Geography Extensions, p. 17
American Readings, p. 16
Unit 3 Answers, pp. 27–33

Reduced Views
Study Guide, p. 14
American Readings, p. 16
Unit 3 Answers, pp. 27–33

Reduced Views
Chapter Tests, p. 17
Unit 3 Answers, pp. 27–33

Alternative Assessment Guidelines for scoring the Chapter Survey activity, p. 13

Additional Resources

Wall Time Line

Unit 3 Activity

Transparency Package

Transparency 8-1 *Washington Crossing the Delaware*—use with Section 3
Transparency 8-2 Washington, the People's Hero—use with Section 3
Transparency Activity Book

SelecTest Testing Software
Chapter 8 Test, Forms A and B

Vital Links

⊙ **Videodisc**

⊙ **CD-ROM**

British marching into New York (see TE p. 216)

Voice of James Sullivan Martin on Valley Forge (see TE p. 219)

Battle of Monmouth (see TE p. 222)

Washington at Yorktown (see TE p. 224)

Battle of Lexington (see TE p. 228)

201B

Teaching Resources

Take-Home Planner 3
  Introducing Chapter Activity
  Chapter In-Depth Activity
  Alternative Assessment
Chapter Resources Binder
Geography Extensions
American Readings
Using Historical Documents
Transparency Activities
Wall Time Line Activities
Chapter Summaries
Chapter and Unit Tests
SelecTest Test File
Vital Links CD-ROM/Videodisc

Time Line

Keys to History
Keys to History journal writing activity is on page 226 in the Chapter Survey.

Lexington and Concord War broke out when shots were fired by British troops attempting to disarm the colonial militia. (p. 206)

Common Sense Thomas Paine's popular pamphlet convinced many doubtful colonists of the advantages of independence. (p. 211)

Declaration of Independence Congress commissioned Thomas Jefferson to explain the colonies' reasons for separating from Britain. (p. 212)

Looking Back Colonists protested the Intolerable Acts by dumping three shiploads of British tea into Boston's blockaded harbor.

World Link See p. 218.

202

Chapter Objectives

★ Describe how conflict with Britain led to war.
★ Identify the reasons the Continental Congress gave for declaring independence.
★ Summarize the experiences of the Continental Army from the spring of 1776 to the harsh winter of 1777–1778.
★ Explain what factors turned the tide of the war and led to victory by the colonists.

Chapter Overview

The exchange of fire at Lexington and Concord signaled the beginning of the War of Independence. The Second Continental Congress chose George Washington to be the commander in chief of the army. The British won a costly victory at Bunker Hill before abandoning Boston in 1776.

The Congress sought peace with England. However, King George III rejected the Olive

---

1775–1783

Chapter *8* The War of Independence

Sections

Beginning the Story with Joseph Martin
1. **The War Begins**
2. **The Issue of Independence**
3. **The War in the North**
4. **The End of the War**

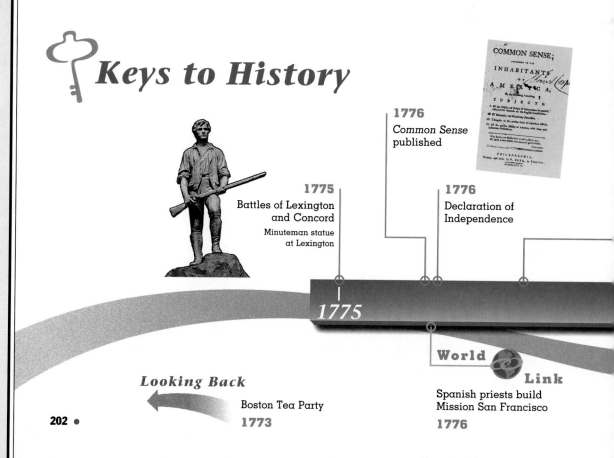

Keys to History

1776
Common Sense published

1775
Battles of Lexington and Concord
Minuteman statue at Lexington

1776
Declaration of Independence

1775

World **Link**
Spanish priests build Mission San Francisco
1776

Looking Back
Boston Tea Party
1773

Branch Petition. At this point, Thomas Paine's *Common Sense* swayed many colonists' opinions in favor of independence. Yet the Declaration of Independence divided Americans between Patriots and Loyalists.

Despite funding and supply problems, the Americans were able to defeat Hessian troops at Trenton. With the help of von Steuben, the forces were drilled into top fighting form.

Americans began winning victories as Spain and France provided help. In the south, guerrilla fighting delayed the British advance. In the west, Americans gained control of the Ohio River Valley. Surrounded at Yorktown, Cornwallis surrendered. In the 1783 Treaty of Paris, Britain recognized the United States as a new nation and ceded all its land from Florida to Canada to the Mississippi River.

Teaching the HISTORY Mystery

Students will find the answer on page 221. See Chapter Survey, page 226, for additional questions.

Time Line

Valley Forge At the low point of the war, Washington's troops endured a bitter winter of hunger, exposure, and desertion. (p. 218)

Surrender at Yorktown The Patriot defeat of Cornwallis led to the end of the war. (p. 224)

Treaty of Paris Britain recognized the United States as an independent nation and ceded its claims west to the Mississippi River. (p. 224)

Looking Ahead
Abandoning the Articles of Confederation, the representatives at the Constitutional Convention write a new Constitution in 1787.

HISTORY Mystery

General Washington's best spies in Philadelphia informed him that the British wanted their laundry returned immediately, "finished or unfinished." Why did Washington care about the British soldiers' laundry?

1777–1778
Winter at Valley Forge
General Lafayette and General Washington at Valley Forge

1781
British surrender at Yorktown

1783
Treaty of Paris recognizes American independence

1779

1783

Looking Ahead
Constitutional Convention
1787

● **203**

Joseph Martin

Joseph Martin, who joined the Continental Army at the age of 16 in 1776, wrote his memoirs in 1830. He recounted his youthful longing to join the "unbeatable" American forces and his experience as a Patriot soldier. He witnessed both the suffering at Valley Forge and the victory at Yorktown. As they see events through Martin's eyes, students can get a more personal sense of the war's impact.

Off to War

To help students understand what it was like to go off to war, ask them to imagine they are leaving home tomorrow to join the army. They will not see their friends or family for two years and are allowed to take only a small knapsack with personal belongings. Have them write a description of what they would take and why. (Students might mention photos of family and friends, favorite books or music, portable tape or CD players, and other items that would help them feel at home.)

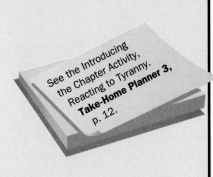

See the Introducing
the Chapter Activity,
Reacting to Tyranny.
Take-Home Planner 3,
p. 12.

❋ **History Footnote**

The state militias, from whose ranks the Continental Army got many of its troops, had a tradition of enlisting "citizen-soldiers." These were men whose primary responsibilities were to their own families and property. Such soldiers might live at home most of the time, going out to fight only in emergencies, and returning home after a few weeks or months.

Beginning the Story with

Joseph Martin

In 1830 an aging farmer in the village of Prospect, Maine, picked up his pen and began to write. His name was Joseph Martin. He was not a writer by trade or training. Still, Martin had a story he wanted to tell. The events he began to write about had taken place more than half a century earlier. Yet they were as fresh in his mind as if they had happened only yesterday.

Martin thought back to his childhood. "I lived with my parents until I was upwards of seven years old," he began. When his father lost his job, Joseph was sent to live with his grandparents on their Connecticut farm. Martin grew up hearing about the quarrels between the colonies and Britain:

Joseph Martin did not arrive in New York soon enough to see the king's statue being toppled. The lead was made into musket balls so the king's troops might have "melted majesty" fired at them.

History Bookshelf

Zall, P. M., ed. *Becoming American: Young People in the American Revolution.* Linnet Books, 1993. Students may enjoy reading about teenagers' experiences during the Revolutionary period, through diaries and letters.

Also of interest:

Asimov, Isaac. *The Birth of the United States.* Houghton Mifflin, 1974.

Davis, Burke. *Black Heroes of the American Revolution.* Harcourt Brace, 1976.

Kent, Deborah. *The American Revolution: "Give Me Liberty or Give Me Death."* Enslow Publishers, Inc., 1994.

McGovern, Ann. *The Secret Soldier: The Story of Deborah Sampson.* Four Winds Press, 1975.

> "I remember the stir in the country occasioned by the Stamp Act, but I was so young that I did not understand the meaning of it. I likewise remember the disturbances that followed the repeal of the Stamp Act, until the destruction of the tea at Boston and elsewhere. I was then thirteen or fourteen years old and began to understand something of the works going on."

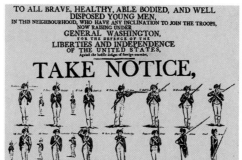

This recruiting poster shows how to fire a musket. Recruits were offered an annual wage of $60 and an opportunity for "honorable service."

On a spring day in 1775, Martin was plowing when "all of a sudden the bells fell to ringing and three guns were repeatedly fired in succession down in the village." Martin knew at once that "something more than the sound of a carriage wheel was in the wind." That something was the outbreak of fighting between the colonies and Britain.

"I was now what I had long wished to be"

In Martin's village, young men were enlisting in the militia. Each man who signed up was paid a one-dollar bonus. At 15, Martin was too young to enlist. "O, thought I, if I were but old enough to put myself forward, I would be the possessor of one dollar." He would also be out from under his grandparents' supervision.

A year later, recruiters were back in Martin's village. They were looking for volunteers to go to New York, where the British were rumored to have a force of 15,000 troops. "I did not care if there had been fifteen times fifteen thousand," wrote Martin. "I never spent a thought about numbers; the Americans were invincible [unbeatable] in my opinion."

The Connecticut teenager traded his plow for a musket and set off for New York City. "I was now what I had long wished to be," he wrote, "a soldier." For Joseph Martin, the adventure of a lifetime had begun. He would witness not only one of the darkest moments of the war—the winter at Valley Forge—but also the victory at Yorktown that led to peace. As you read this chapter, put yourself in his place. Imagine how he and other soldiers might have gone from near-despair to triumph.

Hands-On ----→ *HISTORY*

Activity

What would have convinced you to join Joseph Martin in 1776? Patriotism? Love of liberty? Bonus money? Thirst for adventure? Design your own recruiting poster aimed at persuading colonists your age to take up arms against Britain.

Warm-Up Activity

Preparing for War

To help students understand how colonists prepared for war, have them write a speech explaining what steps to take. Ask them to imagine they are each the mayor of a small Massachusetts town in 1775. They are to write a speech to deliver at a town meeting. It should summarize events leading up to the "present," and explain what precautions and preparations people should make in case of war with Britain. (These might include hiding valuables, storing food, finding weapons, etc.)

Geography Question of the Day

Post a description on the board of Massachusetts topography and climate (wooded, very rocky, many rivers and creeks, cool and dry, harsh winters). Also post the following assignment: Jot down a list of strategies an American military leader might have employed to fight the British in this terrain. (Using woods as cover to fire on British; blocking roads with stones or snow to stall mounted troops and supply wagons; destroying bridges.)

Section Objectives

★ Identify what triggered the outbreak of hostilities.
★ Describe the Second Continental Congress's response to the crisis.
★ Explain why British troops abandoned Boston in 1776.

Teaching Resources

Take-Home Planner 3, pp. 10–17
Chapter Resources Binder
  Study Guide, p. 57
  Reinforcement
  Skills Development, pp. 63–64
Geography Extensions
American Readings, p. 29
Using Historical Documents
Transparency Activities
Chapter and Unit Tests

1. The War Begins

Reading Guide

New Term minutemen

Section Focus How the conflict with Britain led to war

1. What triggered the outbreak of fighting?
2. How did the Second Continental Congress respond to the crisis?
3. Why did British troops finally leave Boston in 1776?

The conflict that turned Joseph Martin into a soldier began in Massachusetts. For months after the passage of the Intolerable Acts, the militia drilled and marched throughout New England. These volunteers called themselves **minutemen** because they were ready to fight at a minute's notice.

The governor of Massachusetts, General Thomas Gage, believed that the minutemen were preparing for war. When Gage's spies reported that guns and powder were being stored in the village of Concord, he decided to act. Gage ordered 700 British soldiers to march the 20 miles (32 km) from Boston to Concord and seize the colonists' weapons.

First Shots at Lexington

The colonists also had spies. When Gage's troops slipped out of Boston late on April 18, 1775, they were closely watched. Paul Revere and William Dawes then galloped through the countryside, spreading the word that the British were coming.

In the misty light of dawn, about 70 minutemen gathered nervously in front of the tavern in Lexington, a village on the road to Concord. Their leader, Captain John Parker, ordered, "Stand your ground. Don't fire unless fired upon! But if they mean to have a war, let it begin here."

As the British approached, the minutemen headed for cover behind a stone wall. Suddenly a shot rang out. The redcoats rushed forward, firing wildly. When the guns fell silent, eight minutemen lay dead or wounded. The British gave three cheers for victory and marched on to Concord.

In their march from Concord to Boston, the British looted and burned houses. A cartoon shows them as greedy wolves.

The example of Patriot editorializing in the cartoon on page 206 exactly captures the general population's feelings about the British soldiers. Indeed, the behavior of the British army often made Patriots of citizens who were neutral or even Loyalist. The commanders seemed unable or unwilling to put a stop to looting and arson by soldiers.

See the Study Guide activity in the **Chapter Resources Binder**, p. 57.

Point of View

Lexington: Who fired the first shot?

Each side claimed that the other fired first at Lexington. Thirty-four minutemen signed a statement swearing that

❝Whilst our backs were turned on the troops, we were fired on by them, and a number of our men were instantly killed or wounded. Not a gun was fired by any person in our company on the regulars, to our knowledge, before they fired on us, and they continued firing until we had all made our escape.❞

British Lieutenant William Sutherland saw things differently:

❝I heard Major Pitcairn's voice call out 'Soldiers, don't fire, keep your ranks, form and surround them.' Instantly some of the villains who got over the hedge fired at us which our men for the first time returned. . . . It is very unlikely that our men should have fired [first], otherwise they [might] have hurt their own officers who galloped in amongst this armed mob.❞

Which side did fire that first fateful shot? Because eyewitnesses disagree, we can never know for sure. What does seem clear is that neither side wanted the blame.

From Concord to Boston

Once in Concord, the British troops found only two or three small cannons. After a brief battle with minutemen at Concord's North Bridge, the frustrated redcoats headed back to Boston. The march was a nightmare. A British officer reported "heavy fire from all sides, from walls, fences, houses, trees,

barns." A soldier noted that "even women had firelocks [guns]."

By the time the British reached Boston, 74 had been killed and 200 wounded. American losses totaled 49 killed and 41 wounded. Riders raced through the colonies shouting the news, "The war has begun!" A Philadelphia woman wrote to a British officer she knew in Boston:

❝All ranks of men amongst us are in arms. Nothing is heard now in our streets but the trumpet and drum; and the universal cry is 'Americans, to arms!'❞

The Second Continental Congress

The fighting had broken out shortly before the Second Continental Congress was to meet in Philadelphia. When the delegates

◎ Link to the Present

The information superhighway "The British are coming!" "The war has begun!" It took three weeks for riders to reach South Carolina with news of Lexington and Concord. Today people can learn about a distant event within moments. We take television for granted, just as we do telephones and computers.

The so-called information superhighway—with its use of computer, phone, and television technology—promises new sources of instant communication. We will be sending and receiving an ever greater variety and amount of information—in a fraction of the time it took Paul Revere to saddle his horse.

▶ Discussion

Checking Understanding

1. Why were the militia called "minutemen"? (They claimed to be ready to fight at a minute's notice.)
2. Why did the British go to Concord? (They heard the militia was stockpiling weapons and intended to take them away.)

Stimulating Critical Thinking

3. Why do you think the militia confronted the British? (They expected the British to harm them and wanted to protect their homes.)

Teaching the

Point of View

Ask students to consider why there are different versions of what happened at Lexington. (Perhaps people were excited and confused. Each side wanted to picture the other as aggressor.)

For a fictional account of a 15-year-old at Lexington, see the Link to Literature on pages 228–229.

Teaching the

◎ Link to the Present

Ask what it might be like to learn about an event weeks later. Would reactions be the same as if they had learned immediately? (Might not change reaction but could change ability to respond.)

The painting reproduced on this page shows at a glance the fighting tactics of the British Army. They marched forward in long, straight rows. The soldiers, with their eyes kept rigidly to the front despite fallen comrades at their feet, continue the assault. This scene tells the viewer much about the discipline of the red-coats and illustrates how their battle dress and formation made them easy targets.

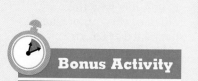

See **American Readings,** p. 29, for Washington's letter to his wife after being named commander in chief.

Creating Political Cartoons

By preparing political cartoons, students identify how colonists might have viewed the events at Lexington and Concord. Bring examples of political cartoons from newspapers or magazines to class. Discuss the cartoons as tools of commentary on events or issues. Then have pairs of students create political cartoons that might have appeared in a Massachusetts newspaper in 1776. Assign each pair a point of view—either supporting or opposing British rule. Allow pairs to write a description of their cartoon or to draw it. Remind them to use labels and captions, if necessary.

Dear Diary

To help them reflect on the experiences of an ordinary soldier, have students write diary entries dated April 20, 1775, after the encounters at Lexington and Concord. Students may write from the point of view of a minuteman or a redcoat, recounting what happened and what they thought and felt during the battle.

gathered as planned on May 10, 1775, they faced a situation far worse than they had expected. The hope that boycotts would bring a peaceful solution was gone. Now war seemed certain.

Congress had to decide who should command the New England militiamen camped around Boston. John Adams proposed creating a Continental Army with troops from all the colonies.

To lead the new army, Adams nominated a gentleman who would command the respect "of all America and unite . . . the colonies better than any other person." That gentleman was Colonel George Washington of Virginia. On June 15 Washington was unanimously elected commander in chief of the army.

The Battle of Bunker Hill

The militiamen did not wait for orders. On the night of June 16, about 1,000 of them slipped onto the Charlestown Peninsula near Boston to take control of Bunker Hill and nearby Breed's Hill. They built a fort on top of Breed's Hill to allow them to rain cannon fire on the British.

Governor Gage and his officers decided to end this threat at once. The following afternoon about 2,200 scarlet-coated British soldiers formed long rows at the base of Breed's Hill. When General William Howe gave the order to attack, the men moved slowly but steadily up the slope. "Our troops advanced with great confidence," wrote a British officer, "expecting an easy victory."

Sweating under 100 pounds of gear and hot wool uniforms, the British regroup for another attack in the Battle of Bunker Hill.

In their frontal attack on Breed's Hill, the British demonstrated their lack of respect for the colonial militias. They believed that no colonial militia could be the match of a trained fighting force. In addition, they found it hard to acknowledge that their adversaries were so determined that they would continue to fight even when they ran out of ammunition.

The British were not alone in their contempt for the fighting trim of the American militias. No less an authority than George Washington said, "Never was such a rabble dignified by the name of army." Washington's task in training his troops was a formidable one.

In their hilltop fort, the Americans swallowed their fear, determined to obey the order, "Don't fire until you see the whites of their eyes." Only when the redcoats were within 15 to 20 paces did trigger fingers tighten. The red lines were shattered by what one British officer described as "a continued sheet of fire."

The stunned redcoats fell back, regrouped, and within a half-hour attacked once more. Again the Americans stopped the advance with gunfire. The British troops fled down the hill, stumbling over fallen comrades. Howe ordered yet a third attack. This time his troops took the hill, but only because the Americans ran out of gunpowder and were forced to throw stones.

The British losses that day were staggering. More than 1,000 British troops had been killed or wounded, compared with about 400 Americans. Describing what became known as the Battle of Bunker Hill, British General Henry Clinton called it "a dear bought victory" and added that "another such would have ruined us." The battle, which proved to be the bloodiest of the war, had shown that colonists could fight and that British soldiers could be stopped.

The Invasion of Canada

While the militia clashed with British troops in Massachusetts, Congress made plans to invade Canada. If Britain lost Canada as a base to attack the colonies, it would talk peace, or so Congress hoped.

Early in 1775, soon after Lexington and Concord, troops led by Benedict Arnold and Ethan Allen captured Fort Ticonderoga, which controlled a key route into Canada. In the fall, 300 troops under Richard Montgomery attacked Montreal. The city fell without a fight, but ahead lay the fortress city of Quebec. Near Quebec, Montgomery's force was joined by 600 troops led by Arnold.

The Americans had hoped that Canadians would join their struggle. Most Canadians, however, were satisfied under British government. To them, the Americans looked like invaders.

Without Canadian help, the Americans were too weak to storm Quebec. Instead they attacked at night during a howling blizzard, hoping to catch defenders off guard. The attack was a disaster. Montgomery and about 100 of his men were killed. Arnold was wounded but escaped to Fort Ticonderoga with the survivors.

Victory in Boston

A week after Bunker Hill, Washington arrived in Boston to take command. He brought order to the ragtag group of undisciplined soldiers, but the army lacked experience. Washington dared not attack without artillery—large guns—to bombard the British. He sent men to bring cannons from Fort Ticonderoga. They loaded 59 cannons onto huge sleds and dragged them 300 miles (480 km) to Boston.

On March 4, 1776, the British awoke to an astonishing sight. The ridges overlooking the city bristled with cannons. Rather than risk another Bunker Hill, the British abandoned Boston. Many Americans hoped that the war was over. In fact, it had just begun.

1. Section Review

1. Define **minutemen.**
2. Why did the war begin?
3. What were two important decisions that the Second Continental Congress made?
4. Why did the British leave Boston?
5. Critical Thinking Why can Bunker Hill be called both a defeat and a victory for the colonists?

Closing
the Section

Wrap-Up
Activity

Charting Outcomes

To help students identify the significance of the first events of the war, have them chart the outcomes of specific events for the Americans and for the British. Small groups should prepare a three-column chart, labeling the columns "Event," "Outcome for Colonists," and "Outcome for British." Events include: shots at Lexington, British return to Boston, Battle of Bunker Hill, invasion of Canada, defense of Boston.

Section Review
Answers

1. Definition: *minutemen* (206)
2. Thomas Gage, the governor of Massachusetts, believed the colonists were preparing for war. He ordered his troops to confiscate American weapons in Concord.
3. Formed the Continental Army, appointed George Washington as commander, decided to invade Canada.
4. The Americans had occupied the heights around the city and trained artillery on the British.
5. It could be seen as a defeat because the colonists lost the hill, and as a victory because they inflicted so much damage.

If students need to review the skill, use the Skills Development transparency and activity in the Chapter Resources Binder, pp. 63–64.

2. (a) Sources A and C differ on British killed (74 and 73), British wounded (200 and 174), and Americans wounded (41 and 39). (b) Information came from different primary and secondary sources. A definitive count was never made. (c) Differences are not important because the numbers are close.

3. (a) Examples will vary. (b) Example: British judgment that colonists did not fight "properly" is based on British army's tradition of combat.

4. Without definitive records, the exact number of dead and wounded cannot be determined, but it can be said that neither side scored a clear victory.

For further application, have students do the Applying Skills activity in the Chapter Survey (p. 226).

Introducing the Skill Lab

To make sure students understand which meaning of *fact* is being used, have them explain the difference between "I have the facts" and "Get your facts straight." To make sure they can distinguish a statement of fact from an opinion, have them characterize the sentence, "The battles of Lexington and Concord occurred in 1935" (statement of fact that can be disproved), and the quote at the beginning of the lab (opinion because "cowardly" is a subjective judgment).

Once students understand the distinction between statements of fact and opinions, point out that primary and secondary sources often mix the two. Students should also recognize that historical accounts often conflict.

Skill Lab
Answers

1. (a) Some statements of fact: "274 hit home," "49 killed." Some opinions: "atrocious," "disgrace . . . the most uncivilized nation," "never engage us properly." (b) Example: number of casualties could be proved, at least in theory. (c) Example: notion of fighting "properly" is subjective.
(Answers continued in top margin)

Skill Lab

Skill Tips

- Statements of fact usually relate to "what," "when," "where," and "who" questions.
- Opinions usually relate to questions like: "Was it right or wrong?" "Was it good or bad?" "How important was it?"

Thinking Critically
Statements of Fact and Opinions

"They are raw, undisciplined, cowardly men." So sneered a British leader who saw the minutemen as no match for the redcoats. Along the road from Concord to Boston on April 19, 1775, the two sides showed signs of how they would match up.

Question to Investigate

What was the outcome of the clashes along the road from Concord to Boston?

Procedure

Descriptions of historical events often mix statements of fact with opinions. A **statement of fact** is a word, phrase, or sentence that can be either proved or disproved. An **opinion** expresses a feeling or thought that cannot be proved or disproved. Keep this difference in mind as you read sources **A** to **E.**

1 Identify the statements of fact and opinions.
a. List examples in a table with columns labeled "Source," "Statements of Fact," and "Opinions."
b. Pick one of the statements of fact and explain how it might be proved or disproved.
c. Pick one of the opinions and explain why it cannot be proved or disproved.

2 Analyze differences in the statements of fact.
a. List the differences.
b. How would you explain the differences?
c. Do the differences seem important? Explain.

3 Analyze the opinions.
a. Pick two opinions from the two primary sources.
b. For each of these opinions, explain why you think the person thought this way.

4 Do you think the Question to Investigate has one "right" answer? Explain.

Sources to Use

A "From Concord to Boston," on page 207.

B "Casualties had been remarkably light. . . . The Americans' marksmanship had been atrocious [very bad]; of upward of some 75,000 rounds fired by the rebels only 274 hit home."

From Richard Snow, *American Heritage,* April 1974

C "The total casualties on both sides were not large: the British lost 73 killed, 174 wounded, and 26 missing; the Americans, 49 killed and 39 wounded."

From John M. Blum et al., *The National Experience* (Harcourt, 1968)

D "A great number of the houses on the road were plundered . . . several were burned . . . old men peaceably in their houses were shot dead, and such scenes exhibited as would disgrace . . . the most uncivilized nation."

From a letter by Joseph Warren of the Massachusetts Assembly to the people of Britain, April 26, 1775

E "They would never engage us properly." "They did not make one gallant attempt . . . but kept under cover."

British soldiers' comments about the minutemen

2. The Issue of Independence

Reading Guide

New Terms **Patriots, Loyalists, mercenaries**

Section Focus **The debate and challenges of seeking independence**

1. What reasons did the Second Continental Congress give for declaring independence?
2. How did declaring independence divide Americans?
3. What were the strengths and weaknesses of each side in the war?

In spite of the fighting in Massachusetts and Canada, few colonists actually wanted independence from Britain. Most were still loyal British subjects. They just wanted Parliament to recognize their rights and give up its hateful policies.

The Olive Branch Petition

Many Americans pinned their hopes for peace on King George III. Once the king understood their position, they told themselves, he would convince Parliament to change its policies.

In the summer of 1775, Congress sent a petition—a written request—to George III, swearing loyalty and begging him to help end the quarrel. John Adams called this petition an "olive branch" because olive tree branches are an old symbol of peace.

The king refused to even read the Olive Branch Petition. The Battle of Bunker Hill had been the last straw. Declaring that the colonies were now in a state of rebellion, he called on Parliament to prepare for war.

Common Sense

With the rejection of the Olive Branch Petition, the colonies faced a difficult deci-

sion. They could surrender and hope that the British would show mercy. On the other hand, they could choose to fight for independence. Were the colonies ready to take such a bold step?

It was Thomas Paine, recently arrived from England, who took the horror out of the idea of separation. Early in 1776 Paine published a pamphlet titled *Common Sense*. In it he argued passionately that Americans had nothing to gain and much to lose from remaining tied to Britain:

"Everything that is right and reasonable pleads for separation. The blood of the slain, the weeping voice of nature cries, 'TIS TIME TO PART."

Paine's words electrified the colonies. Within a few months readers had snapped up more than 100,000 copies of *Common Sense*. Paine pointed out that independence would give Americans the freedom to set up their own government and trade with whomever they pleased. They could shape their own future.

Suddenly the idea of independence began to seem sensible rather than unthinkable. "I find *Common Sense* is working a powerful change in the minds of many men," observed Washington.

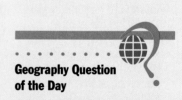

Teaching the

Hands-On ------→ *HISTORY*

Discuss promotional announcements students have seen or heard. Ask: **What was the message of the announcement? How did the announcement create interest?** Then divide the class into cooperative groups. Encourage groups to divide the work of creating the announcement into two parts: text and visuals. Each group member should be responsible for a specific task such as compiling and organizing information, writing, editing, producing visuals, and so on.

Section
Activity

Taking Sides

By debating which side to support in the war, students gain insight into the views of African Americans and Indians. Divide the class into four groups—two should prepare arguments as African Americans and two as an Indian tribal council. Assign each group a position supporting the Patriots or the British, and provide time for them to prepare their arguments. Have groups select members to take part in the debate. Students might vote on which side to support based on the arguments.

✠ Connections to Civics

In drafting the Declaration of Independence, Jefferson was strongly influenced by the ideas of British philosopher John Locke. Locke emphasized that people naturally have certain rights and duties, and among these are life and liberty. Locke believed if a government fails to protect its citizens' rights, the people have a right to change it.

See **Using Historical Documents,** pp. 46–50, for an activity on the original Declaration of Independence.

The Declaration of Independence

In the spring of 1776, Congress appointed a committee to prepare a declaration of independence. The task of writing it went to 23-year-old Thomas Jefferson, who said little but could speak brilliantly with his pen.

Jefferson's job was to explain to the world why the colonies should separate from Britain. His argument was simple but revolutionary. It began with the statement that all people have certain natural rights:

“We hold these truths to be self-evident, that all men are created equal, that they are endowed by their Creator with certain unalienable rights, that among these are life, liberty, and the pursuit of happiness.”

Hands-On ------→ *HISTORY*

Promoting the Declaration of Independence exhibit The original Declaration of Independence is preserved in a glass and bronze case at the National Archives in Washington, D.C. The case is filled with helium to protect the fragile, faded document from the air. The shatterproof glass is tinted to protect it from the light. Each night the case is lowered into a reinforced vault beneath the floor.

→**Activity** Create an announcement to encourage people to visit the exhibit. You can make a script for a TV or radio commercial, a layout for a magazine or newspaper ad, or a poster. "Sell" the exhibit to your viewer or listener by telling how the document and its ideals relate to our lives today.

**Declaration of
Independence exhibit**

People create governments, argued Jefferson, "to secure these rights." If a government fails to do so, "it is the right of the people to alter or abolish it." That is just what the Americans intended to do.

Jefferson went on to list the wrongdoings of King George III. The king had not, he wrote, allowed laws "necessary for the public good." He had taxed Americans "without our consent." Now he was "waging war against us." For these and other reasons, declared Jefferson, "these united colonies are, and of right ought to be, free and independent states."

By July 2, the declaration was ready for Congress to debate. Most delegates liked what they saw, except for a passage on slavery. Jefferson had charged the king with violating the "sacred rights of life and liberty . . . of a distant people [by] carrying them into slavery."

Almost no one in Congress supported this charge. Southern delegates worried that it might lead to demands that the slaves be freed. Even delegates who opposed slavery felt that blaming the king for slavery was unfair. The passage was struck out.

On July 4, 1776, Congress approved the final version. In doing so they promised to support the cause of independence with "our lives, our fortunes, and our sacred honor." John Hancock, president of Congress, signed the document with a flourish.

By approving the Declaration, the delegates showed great bravery. If the new "free and independent states" failed to win the war, these leaders could be hanged for

✠ **Connections to Geography**

Before the War of Independence, the Iroquois dominated the enormous area bounded by the Kennebec River in Maine, the Ottawa River in Canada, the Illinois River, and the Tennessee River. Since the Iroquois wanted to protect this territory, they felt they had a strong stake in the outcome of the war. The sophisticated, tightly knit Iroquois Confederacy had been founded on principles of neutrality and cooperation among the different peoples scattered throughout these lands. The war caused this neutrality to fail, as fighting broke out between the different tribes of the Confederacy.

treason. Benjamin Franklin joked that "we must all hang together, or most assuredly we shall all hang separately."

Patriots and Loyalists

Not everyone in the colonies supported the Declaration. Only about a third of Americans called themselves **Patriots**—strong supporters of independence. Another third were **Loyalists**—colonists who did not want independence. They saw themselves as law-abiding people, faithful to king and country. The last third did not want to risk their lives or their property by taking sides in the struggle.

Disagreements over independence pitted neighbor against neighbor, friend against friend. One of John Adams's closest friends was a Loyalist. Ending that friendship, wrote Adams, was "the sharpest thorn on which I ever set my foot." Even families were divided. Franklin's son William was a Loyalist, much to his father's distress.

African Americans and the war
For African Americans, the Declaration of Independence raised hard questions. If "all men are created equal," how could there be slaves? Would independence mean that African Americans who were slaves would be freed? Should African Americans join the Patriots in the hope that a society based on equal rights would end slavery?

Many African Americans did join the Patriot cause. Black minutemen fought at Lexington and Concord. When the British stormed up Breed's Hill, they were fired on by black as well as white Patriots.

When Washington first took command, however, he did not let African Americans join the army. He feared it would encourage slaves to leave their owners. The British, on the other hand, promised to free any slaves of Patriots if they escaped. Thousands of slaves answered the call.

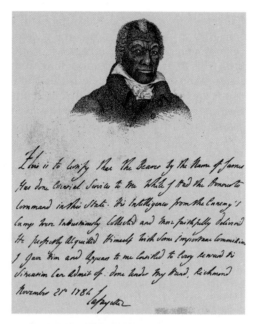

Patriot spy James Armistead received this letter of praise from General Lafayette for his reports on British troop movements in Virginia.

A shortage of white volunteers soon forced Washington to enlist black soldiers. Some 5,000 African Americans fought on the Patriot side.

Indians and the war The conflict divided not only white Americans and black Americans but also Indians. Most Indians remained neutral or sided with the British, who they hoped would defend them against land-hungry colonists. However, some helped the Patriots.

Within the Iroquois Confederacy, most of the Senecas, Cayugas, Onondagas, and Mohawks sided with the British, but most of the Oneidas and Tuscaroras helped the Patriots. The war divided many Indian families as well. One Oneida warrior, for instance, was captured by his brother, a British supporter, who then handed him over to the Senecas to be killed.

See the Study Guide activity in the **Chapter Resources Binder**, p. 58.

Discussion

Checking Understanding

1. What reason does the Declaration give for the colonies separating from Britain? (Britain failed to protect colonists' rights.)

2. Why did some colonists disagree? (Loyalists saw themselves as British subjects.)

Stimulating Critical Thinking

3. What do you think the words "all men are created equal" meant to the Congress members? (All white men able to vote were created equal.)

4. How do you interpret the words "all men are created equal"? (Everyone has equal rights.)

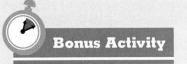
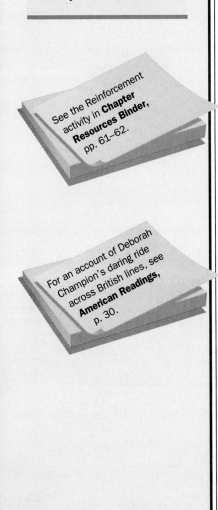

See the Reinforcement activity in **Chapter Resources Binder,** pp. 61–62.

For an account of Deborah Champion's daring ride across British lines, see **American Readings,** p. 30.

In the end, the war would bring neither Indians nor African Americans the rewards they sought. Even those Indians who sided with the Patriots would soon find their lands taken by settlers. Meanwhile, thousands of the slaves who had joined the Continental Army were returned to their masters after the war.

British Strengths and Weaknesses

In preparing for war, Britain was confident of its strength. It had a well-trained army that would soon be joined by 30,000 **mercenaries**—soldiers who fight for money. These mercenaries were called Hessians because most of them came from Hesse–Cassel, a part of Germany.

Surely the redcoats and Hessians would crush the Continental Army. Meanwhile, the mighty British navy would rule the sea, landing troops and supplies anywhere along the coast.

Still, the British faced huge problems. One was the distance between Britain and America. Sending troops and supplies across 3,000 miles (4,800 km) of ocean was slow and costly. A second problem was that the colonists were fighting a defensive war to protect their own land. The British could not stamp out the rebellion by simply capturing a few cities. They would have to break the Patriots' will to fight.

American Weaknesses and Strengths

The Patriots had their own weaknesses. One was lack of money. Having refused to give Congress the power to tax, the 13 newly independent states squabbled over

This fortified house at Johnstown, New York, was a site of frequent meetings between British troops and their Indian allies.

Another Patriot strength was in weaponry. The firearm issued to the British soldier was a highly inaccurate musket with a smooth bore (inner surface of the barrel). The British usually stood in lines and fired all at the same time to increase their chances of hitting the enemy. Patriot troops increasingly made use of an American invention, the flintlock. With a grooved (rifled) barrel, this weapon was much more accurate. This made it possible for Americans to abandon fighting in ranks and firing together; they could now take cover and fire at their leisure, picking off the enemy one by one.

how much each should pay for the war effort. As a result, the army was constantly short of weapons, clothing, and food.

The army also lacked experienced soldiers. Frustrated by low pay and eager to return to their farms and workshops, many enlisted for only six months or a year. Just when they were learning to be soldiers, they picked up their muskets and went home.

The army did slowly improve in discipline, skills, and confidence, largely because of great leadership. George Washington inspired the respect of his soldiers. Their faith in him held the army together. Patriot leadership also shone on the seas. Though the Continental Navy had just a few ships, daring captains like John Paul Jones scored stunning victories.

What most kept the Patriot cause alive, though, was the dedication of ordinary people who gave their lives and property to gain independence. These people were the soldiers, like Joseph Martin, who kept re-enlisting. They were the seamen on the privateers—privately owned ships that attacked enemy ships and ports. They were the Patriots at home. Haym Salomon, for instance, gave his fortune to Congress to help pay for the war effort.

Women and the war Women helped the war effort by keeping farms and workshops going and working as camp cooks and nurses. An artillery officer's wife named Mary Ludwig Hays often carried water to thirsty troops during battles. This act of courage and kindness earned her the nickname "Molly Pitcher." A few women, like Deborah Sampson, even dressed as men and joined the army.

The Patriots' strength was not in numbers but in the dedication and leadership of those who remained faithful through the darkest days of the war. Without them the struggle would soon have been lost.

Many Patriot women knew how to use muskets to defend their homes. Deborah Sampson (above) enlisted in the army disguised as a man.

⭐ 2. Section Review

1. Define **Patriots, Loyalists,** and **mercenaries.**
2. According to the Declaration of Independence, why was it necessary to break away from Britain?
3. Why did the idea of independence divide Americans?
4. Name two British strengths and two weaknesses. Name two American strengths and two weaknesses.
5. Critical Thinking Explain what you think the Declaration's rights to "life, liberty, and the pursuit of happiness" mean to Americans today.

Closing the Section

Wrap-Up Activity

Playing Jeopardy!®
To review the section, have students work in groups to write answers to which other students are to supply the questions. Give each group a category (Declaration of Independence, Patriots, Indians, Women, etc.) and have them write two answers and questions. For example: answer—The nickname of Patriot Mary Ludwig Hays; question—What is Molly Pitcher? Have groups challenge each other to provide questions.

Section Review Answers

1. Definitions: *Patriots* (213), *Loyalists* (213), *mercenaries* (214)

2. King violated colonists' rights as British citizens, so obligations toward Britain were dissolved.

3. Some supported independence, while others remained loyal; others neutral to avoid risking lives or property.

4. British strengths: trained army, mercenaries, navy, money from Britain; weaknesses: having to ship troops and supplies long distances, Americans fighting defensive war. American strengths: improving skills and confidence, leadership, dedication; weaknesses: lack of money, inexperienced.

5. Answers should recognize importance of rights to individuals.

---

3. The War in the North

Reading Guide

New Term profiteers

Section Focus How the Continental Army survived the darkest days of the war

1. What was the British plan for winning the war?
2. Why was the Battle of Saratoga a turning point in the war?

After the British fled Boston in March 1776, Washington knew that they would try to take New York City. A victory there would give them an excellent harbor and a good location for launching attacks on Boston and Philadelphia.

Washington rushed the Continental Army to New York, where Joseph Martin joined their ranks. Hoping to "snuff a little gunpowder," he had enlisted two days after the signing of the Declaration.

The British Capture New York

By the time Joseph Martin joined the army, it had swelled to about 23,000 soldiers. Even so, the Americans were outnumbered by the 32,000 British and Hessian troops camped on nearby Staten Island. When the two forces met in late summer, the British drove Martin and his fellow Patriots out of New York and chased them across New Jersey. As the weather turned cold and hopes faded, soldiers deserted.

When Washington reached safety in Pennsylvania that fall, he had only 3,000 soldiers. Most of these soldiers had agreed to fight just until the end of December. Unless more troops could be found soon, Washington wrote, "I think the game will be pretty well up."

Victory in New Jersey

On December 23, 1776, Washington gathered what was left of his troops to listen to a reading from Thomas Paine's new pamphlet, *The Crisis:*

"These are the times that try men's souls: The summer soldier and the sunshine patriot will, in this crisis, shrink from the service of their country; but he that stands it NOW, deserves the love and thanks of man and woman. Tyranny, like hell, is not easily conquered; yet . . . the harder the conflict, the more glorious the triumph."

The words inspired the war-weary soldiers. Still, Washington desperately needed a victory to bolster the spirits of the tiny army. He revealed a bold plan to attack Hessian troops camped for the winter in Trenton, New Jersey.

On the night of December 25, while the Hessians celebrated Christmas in cozy Trenton houses, Washington's army was leaving Pennsylvania and crossing the ice-choked Delaware River in small boats. From their landing point in New Jersey, the troops marched silently toward Trenton. A violent snowstorm chilled them to the bone, and ice cut through their flimsy footwear. When

Thomas Paine, who had such success with *Common Sense,* was the son of a Quaker corset maker from England. He decided to seek his fortune in America after meeting Benjamin Franklin in London. In 1774 he arrived in Philadelphia with letters of introduction from Franklin. He shared the strong humanitarian values of the Quakers. He rejected the idea of inherited wealth or power for only a privileged few, in favor of government by and for the benefit of ordinary people. Paine wrote *The Crisis* for the express purpose of bolstering the morale of discouraged Patriots and Washington's troops at Valley Forge.

Developing the Section

Discussion

Checking Understanding

1. Why did the British want to capture New York City? (Location perfect for attacking Boston and Philadelphia, good harbor.)
2. What was the result of the victory at Trenton? (Thousands joined army.)

Stimulating Critical Thinking

3. How would you define a "sunshine patriot"? (Person who is loyal only when times are good and no sacrifice is required.)

Teaching the

⌇ **Link to Art**

Ask how Leutze portrays the heroism of the soldiers and Washington's leadership. **Discussion Answers:** Reflected the Patriots' courage and determination. The critic's opinion may have been based on the idea that the painting instilled patriotism and signaled the resolve of the American people.

See the Study Guide activity in the **Chapter Resources Binder**, p. 59.

⌇ **Link to Art**

Washington Crossing the Delaware (1851) This painting, by the German-born American artist Emanuel Leutze, caused a sensation when first shown in New York City. Newspapers reported that "crowds throng to see it." One paper called it "the most majestic, and most effective painting ever exhibited in America." **Discuss** Why do you think this painting was so popular? Why do you think an art critic in 1851 said that it "should be viewed and studied by every American"?

dawn broke, the Americans' route could be traced by a trail of bloody footprints.

The Hessians were caught completely by surprise and quickly surrendered. Not one American was killed in the attack. Usually Washington kept his feelings under tight control, but not now. "This is a glorious day for our country!" he cried.

So it was. As news of the victory at Trenton spread, thousands of volunteers joined the Continental Army. The Patriots' cause was still alive.

Britain's Victory Plan

In early 1777 the British General John Burgoyne came up with what seemed a sure-fire plan to end the war. He would lead an army south from Canada into New York to capture the upper Hudson River Valley. Lieutenant Colonel Barry St. Leger would lead a flanking army from the west. At the same time General Howe would lead troops upriver from New York City to conquer the lower Hudson River Valley.

Gifted Students
Gifted students benefit from exploring topics in more detail. Suggest that students research further into Washington's daring decision to attack Trenton in midwinter, the "Winter of Despair" at Valley Forge, or von Steuben's contribution to the war effort. Encourage them to be creative in preparing written reports in formats such as news articles, plays, or poems. For example, students might write a television documentary script that details the conditions the troops at Valley Forge faced and the effects those conditions can have on military personnel. They might organize a student-led seminar in which they share their work.

Teaching the

World · Link

Ask: **Why might Spain have thought this was a good time to establish settlements in California?** (With rebellion, British were not likely to have time or resources to press western claims.)

Section Activity

Predicting the Victor

Have small groups predict who would win the war based on the outcome of each battle discussed in the section: New York, Trenton, and Saratoga. Each group should weigh the importance of each battle and choose a representative to explain its conclusions.

Bonus Activity

Advice for Burgoyne

Help students infer the reaction of Indians to Burgoyne's plan by having them write an argument against a land route. Imagine that they are one of the Iroquois warriors fighting on the side of Burgoyne. They should draft a short persuasive speech to convince him to change his plan for taking an overland route.

World · Link

Spanish settlers in California While Britain fought to keep its colonies, on the other side of the continent Spain continued to claim more land. Father Junípero Serra had been sent north from New Spain with an expedition of priests and soldiers to occupy California.

Reaching San Diego Bay in 1769, Serra used Indians to build Mission San Diego. In 1776 Mission San Francisco was founded. By 1823 Serra and other priests had founded 21 missions in California.

The three armies were to meet at Albany. By controlling the valley, the British could choke off the flow of men and supplies from New England. Officials in London had approved Burgoyne's plan. They had also given Howe permission to attack Philadelphia. They expected him to defeat the Patriot forces quickly and be ready in time to help Burgoyne.

Burgoyne began his invasion of New York in late June. He left Canada with 8,000 troops and several hundred Indian warriors. (See the map on page 220.) On reaching Lake Champlain, he loaded his army onto boats and sailed south to Fort Ticonderoga. The fort fell without a fight on July 6, 1777.

Burgoyne's mistake Burgoyne could have sailed south on Lake George to the upper Hudson River. Instead, he made a fateful decision to take a shortcut across 23 miles (32 km) of rugged, roadless land.

On a map it looked like a short walk, but Burgoyne had more than 600 wagons with him. Thirty held his personal baggage. (Even on a march "Gentleman Johnny" ate off silver plates.) His troops spent weeks hacking a road through tangled forests and soggy swamps. By the time they staggered out, the Americans were ready.

The Battle of Saratoga

Burgoyne fought his way to Saratoga on the Hudson River. There his battered army was caught in a trap. Militiamen directed by Polish engineer Thaddeus Kosciusko (kosh-CHOOSH-kah) had built well-fortified defenses above the river.

Burgoyne looked for help, but in vain. Howe was busy playing hide-and-seek with Washington's forces around Philadelphia. St. Leger had been forced to turn back after attacking Fort Stanwix. Without help from either the west or south, Burgoyne admitted defeat on October 17, 1777.

Historians have called the victory at Saratoga a turning point. Up to this point, the American cause had looked hopeless. Even Britain's traditional enemies, France and Spain, had refused to get involved. Now, however, the Americans did not look like losers. They had taken on one of the finest fighting forces in the world and had won.

Early in 1778 the United States and France signed a treaty of alliance. France sent money and soldiers. French warships began attacking British ships in American waters. The following year Spain entered the war against Britain. The American cause no longer looked hopeless.

Winter at Valley Forge

The war was far from won, however. While Burgoyne was going down to defeat in New York, Howe had taken Philadelphia. During the fall Washington tried but failed to recapture the city. When the weather turned cold, he moved his army to winter quarters at Valley Forge, Pennsylvania.

The British had long criticized new words Americans used as corruption of the king's English. Thomas Jefferson coined the word *belittle*. Londoners criticized its use severely at the time. Yet Jefferson noted that there were many differences between the colonies and England—"differences . . . of soil, climate, culture, productions, laws, religion, and government." He went on to say that creating new words would give strength to the language and help people express new ideas.

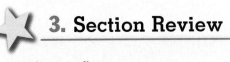 See **American Readings,** p. 31, for an account of conditions at Valley Forge.

★ ★ ★
Vital Links

Voice of James Sullivan Martin on Valley Forge (First Person Account) Unit 2, Side 1, Search 16600, Play to 17343

See also Unit 2 Explore CD-ROM location 86.

These cabins were built in Valley Forge National Historical Park to recall the Continental Army's bitter "Winter of Despair" in 1777–1778. During that winter, about one quarter of the 10,000 soldiers there died from cold, starvation, and smallpox.

That winter at Valley Forge was memorable for its misery. For Thanksgiving, wrote Joseph Martin, the troops received "half a gill [four tablespoons] of rice and a tablespoon of vinegar." He added:

"The army was now not only starved but naked. The greatest part were not only shirtless and barefoot, but destitute of [lacking] all other clothing, especially blankets. Hungry, barefoot, and clothed in rags, many soldiers deserted."

Men went hungry because local farmers preferred selling food to the British, who paid in gold coin, not the paper money issued by Congress. The men were half-naked because merchants in Boston had raised their prices for uniforms and blankets.

Wherever General Washington turned in his search for supplies, he met wartime **profiteers**—people who demanded unfair profits for their goods. It made his blood boil. "No punishment," he wrote, "is too great for the man who can build his greatness upon his country's ruin."

Help from von Steuben Despite its misery, the army survived. Washington put Baron Friedrich von Steuben in charge of training. Newly arrived from the German region of Prussia, von Steuben knew little English, but his ear-splitting curses helped take the men's minds off their growling stomachs. Martin described the Prussian's training as "continual drill."

Von Steuben's methods worked wonders. "The army grows stronger every day," wrote one officer. "There is a spirit of discipline among the troops that is better than numbers." Meanwhile, an unbreakable bond had grown between Washington and the soldiers who survived that winter.

Spring brought new life and hope to the troops at Valley Forge. The army had endured. The Patriots had won new allies. Now could they drive the British off American soil? That was the question that Washington still had to answer.

★ 3. Section Review

1. Define **profiteers**.
2. How did the British plan to win the war?
3. Why was the Battle of Saratoga important?
4. **Critical Thinking** Von Steuben noted that American soldiers often questioned orders. What might explain this attitude?

Closing the Section

Wrap-Up Activity

Charting Victories

Have students create a chart identifying the gains and losses of the Americans and British between the years 1776 and 1778. Have them enter the name of each battle, who won, and why. Students might keep their charts and add the names of later battles as they continue reading.

Section Review Answers

1. Definition: *profiteers* (p. 219)
2. By joining their forces in the Hudson River Valley and defeating Washington.
3. Showed British not unbeatable, encouraged Spain and France to help.
4. Perhaps soldiers felt that as Americans they had a right to question authority, that the spirit of independence extended to the army.

The map on this page is a Transverse Mercator projection. The projection is named after the sixteenth century geographer, Gerardus Mercator, who created it. In a Mercator projection, the longitude lines are equally spaced, and the parallel lines are spaced farther apart as distance from the equator increases. The projection is not practical for world maps because of the distortion in scale, which results in distortions of area. Greenland, for example, looks larger than South America in the Mercator projection, whereas in fact South America is larger.

Teaching the
Geography Lab

To help students integrate the information on the map, have them place the names and dates of battles on a time line. In this way they can gain a sense of how long it took an army to march from one location to another. This in turn might help them understand the fatigue shown by the soldiers in the painting.

Using Map Skills
Answers

1. The bold lines represent the routes of the British and American armies; the arrows indicate the direction of movement; the splashes indicate either American or British military victories.

2. The British, at New York City, on August 27, 1776.

3. It would be better to have a map that shows paved roads and the historical route.

4. The map shows who won and lost which battles over the course of two years; the painting shows what it must have been like for soldiers to march long distances during that time.

5. Student summaries should list the battles shown on the map for the year 1777 and include something about the circumstances of each battle. Students preparing visual aids might do a simple enlargement of the map area on this page and mark the locations of the relevant battles.

See the activity in Geography Extensions, pp. 15–16.

Geography Lab

Reading a War Map

In July 1776 a great fleet carrying the largest army the British had ever sent overseas—32,000 troops—sailed into New York harbor. The map and painting on this page provide information about what happened over the next year and a half of fighting. What can you learn about the American War of Independence from the map? In what way does the painting expand upon the story that the map tells?

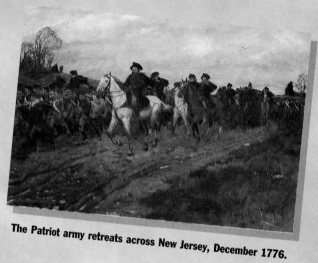

The Patriot army retreats across New Jersey, December 1776.

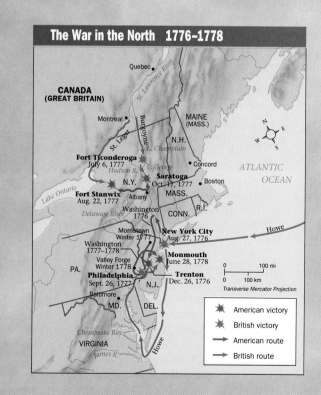

The War in the North 1776–1778

Quebec

CANADA (GREAT BRITAIN)

Montreal

St. Lawrence River

Burgoyne

St. Leger

MAINE (MASS.)

N.H.

L. Champlain

Fort Ticonderoga
July 6, 1777

Hudson R.

• Concord

ATLANTIC OCEAN

Lake Ontario

Fort Stanwix
Aug. 22, 1777

N.Y.

Saratoga
Oct. 17, 1777

Albany

• Boston

MASS.

Washington 1776

Delaware River

CONN.

R.I.

Morristown
Winter 1777

New York City
Aug. 27, 1776

Howe

Washington 1777–1778

Valley Forge
Winter 1778

Monmouth
June 28, 1778

PA.

Philadelphia
Sept. 26, 1777

N.J.

Trenton
Dec. 26, 1776

0   100 mi
0   100 km
Transverse Mercator Projection

Baltimore •

MD.   DEL.

Chesapeake Bay

VIRGINIA

James R.

Howe

★ American victory
✷ British victory
→ American route
→ British route

Using Map Skills

Study the map. Then use the map and the painting to understand events of 1776 and 1777.

1. What do the bold lines on the map represent? The arrows? The splashes of color?

2. Which side won the earliest battle shown on the map?

3. If you wanted to follow Washington's exact route from New York to Trenton today by car, could you do it using this map? Why or why not?

4. Compare the map and the picture. What do you learn about the American War of Independence from each?

5. **Hands-On Geography** You are an aide to General Washington. The Continental Congress wants a report on the events of 1777. Washington asks you to prepare a short summary of troop movements and important battles. Prepare a presentation for Congress, including any visual aids you think will help.

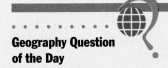
4. The End of the War

Reading Guide

New Term guerrillas

Section Focus How Americans won their war of independence

1. How was the war fought in the southern states and across the Appalachians?
2. How did the Americans finally defeat the British?
3. What did the new United States gain from the treaty ending the war?

In the spring of 1778, Washington received a message from his best spies in Philadelphia, the washerwomen. Their British customers had suddenly ordered all laundry to be returned at once, "finished or unfinished."

To Washington, this news could mean only one thing. The British were about to abandon Philadelphia. General Henry Clinton, who had replaced Howe, had heard that the French fleet was heading for North America. He decided to move his troops back to defend New York City. Now it would be Washington's turn to chase an army across New Jersey.

The Battle of Monmouth

Washington caught up with the British near the town of Monmouth and attacked. His second-in-command, General Charles Lee, took charge of leading the assault on the enemy's rear guard. Lee started forward with no real battle plan. When British reinforcements arrived, he ordered a retreat. Joseph Martin reported what happened next:

"In a few minutes the Commander-in-Chief . . . crossed the road just where we were sitting. I heard him ask our officers, 'by whose order the troops were retreating,' and being answered, 'by General Lee's.' He said something, but . . . he was too far off for me to hear it distinctly. Those that were nearer to him said that his words were 'd—n him.' Whether he did thus express himself or not I do not know. It was certainly very unlike him, but he seemed at the instant to be in a great passion.**"**

Washington angrily charged forward to halt the retreat. By the end of the day, it was the British who were pulling back. That night the British slipped back into New York City. Washington camped his troops near the city and wrote in his journal:

"It is not a little pleasing . . . that after two years maneuvering . . . both armies are brought back to the very point they set out from.**"**

The Patriots had held their own against the British, which was a victory in itself.

The War Moves South

Having failed in the northern states, the British moved the war south. In 1780 Clinton led a force that took Charles Town, the major southern port. This was the worst defeat suffered by the Patriots in the war. Clinton returned to New York, leaving General Charles Cornwallis in control of South Carolina.

Section Activity

Planning an Attack

To help students understand battle strategies, have them plan an attack on the British at Yorktown. Divide the class into small groups and designate members as either American or French commanders. Before reading about the outcome at Yorktown, the group members should prepare a plan of attack. Explain that they should include troop movements, sources of provisions, and time frames in their plan. Have each group provide a short oral report on its strategy.

See the Study Guide activity in the **Chapter Resources Binder,** p. 60.

★★★
Vital Links

Battle of Monmouth (Picture) Unit 2, Side 1, Search 17377

See also Unit 2 Explore CD-ROM location 92.

Connections to Language Arts

The term *guerrilla* is a diminutive of the Spanish word for war, *guerra.* It literally means "little war." The first known use of the term *guerrilla* was during the Napoleonic Peninsular War, which lasted from 1808 to 1814. The British hero Lord Wellington used the term in dispatches in 1809.

For a postwar petition for freedom from a slave who was a Patriot spy, see **American Readings,** p. 32.

The Patriot cause was kept alive by guerrilla fighters like Francis Marion, the famous "Swamp Fox." **Guerrillas** are soldiers who are not part of the regular army and who make hit-and-run attacks. Marion's guerrillas repeatedly attacked the British, then faded like ghosts into the tidewater swamps.

In 1780 Washington sent his best commander, General Nathanael Greene, south to slow the British advance. To avoid losing his small army in large battles, Greene led the British on an exhausting chase through the backcountry. Greene summed up his strategy in these words: "We fight, get beat, rise, and fight again."

The strategy worked. In 1781 General Cornwallis announced that he was "quite tired of marching about the country." He decided to move his army north to a sleepy tobacco port in Virginia called Yorktown.

Victory in the West

Small Patriot forces also made their mark fighting the British in the west. In 1777 a young Virginian named George Rogers Clark headed west across the Appalachian Mountains. Clark's mission was as large as his ambition. He planned to drive the British out of the Ohio River Valley and the Great Lakes region.

Clark could find only 200 backcountry Patriots to join his mission impossible. Still he pressed on, writing to a friend that "great things have been effected by a few men well conducted [led]." Clark and his small force did do great things. Sailing down the Ohio River on flatboats, they captured one British fort after another. By 1779 the Americans had seized control of the Ohio River Valley.

Francis Marion, known as the "Swamp Fox," led his band of guerrillas on daring raids in the Carolinas. They terrorized Loyalist militia and kept the British busy protecting supply lines.

During the progress of Cornwallis's troops through the South, and especially during his slow retreat to Yorktown, ordinary civilians frequently fled before the British arrived in their towns. They wanted to avoid being robbed, beaten, or worse at the hands of British soldiers. Sixteen-year-old Betsy Ambler, daughter of Virginia's treasurer, wrote to a friend about her family's sudden exodus from Richmond, leaving home, friends, and belongings: "My father seemed to think we hadn't a moment to lose—such terror and confusion you have no idea of—governor, council, everybody scampering."

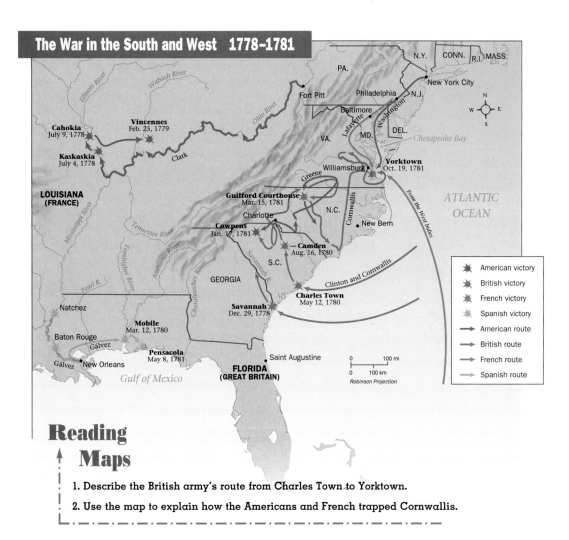

The War in the South and West 1778-1781

Reading Maps

1. Describe the British army's route from Charles Town to Yorktown.

2. Use the map to explain how the Americans and French trapped Cornwallis.

Help from Spain Clark was helped during his campaign by Bernardo de Gálvez, the governor of Spanish Louisiana. Gálvez sent Clark gunpowder and supplies from his base in New Orleans.

When Spain finally declared war on Britain in 1779, Gálvez could do more than send aid. He quickly pulled together a force of soldiers from Spain, Mexico, and the Caribbean. With his troops Gálvez drove the British from their forts along the Mississippi River.

In 1781 Gálvez organized a much larger army and attacked a British base in Pensacola, Florida. There he trapped 2,500 British soldiers, troops who would no longer be able to come to the aid of Cornwallis in Virginia.

Between them, Clark and Gálvez had broken Britain's hold on the vast region between the 13 states and the Mississippi River. When the time came to talk peace, their success meant that this area would become part of the United States, not Canada.

Checking Understanding

1. **What makes guerrillas different from regular army soldiers?** (They are not necessarily part of a regular army or militia; they make hit-and-run attacks on the enemy rather than fighting big battles.)

2. **How did Bernardo de Gálvez help the Americans?** (He sent supplies and soldiers to help in the fight against the British.)

Stimulating Critical Thinking

3. **Do you think George Washington would have agreed with George Rogers Clark when he said, "Great things have been effected by a few men well conducted"?** (Yes: good leadership was the key to the success of Patriot troops; no: lack of supplies can sink even a well-led army.)

Teaching the Reading Maps

Suggest that students prepare a chart with three columns listing the battles that American, French, and Spanish forces fought with the British and the outcomes of each. **Answers to Reading Maps: 1.** Northwest to Cowpens or to Camden and then to Cowpens, northeast to Guilford Courthouse, southeast to the North Carolina coast, and north to Yorktown. **2.** American and French troops marched south and surrounded Yorktown from the land, while ships sailed north to Yorktown.

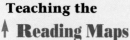
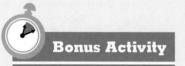

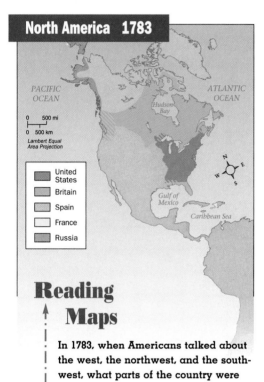

Reading Maps

In 1783, when Americans talked about the west, the northwest, and the southwest, what parts of the country were they talking about?

Victory at Yorktown

By the summer of 1781, Cornwallis was comfortably settled on the shores of the Chesapeake Bay. He knew that as long as the Royal Navy controlled the seas, British ships could keep his army supplied. He could always get his soldiers out by sea, though he was sure that would not be necessary.

Cornwallis would not have felt so confident if he had known what France was up to. Since entering the war in 1778, the French had sent 5,000 soldiers to America. In 1781, they decided to send 3,000 more in 28 warships.

Washington decided it was time to lay a trap. American and French troops under the Marquis de Lafayette and Baron von Steuben moved south from New York to Virginia. There they surrounded Yorktown by land. Meanwhile, French warships brought Washington's troops south from Baltimore, arriving just in time to seal off the entrance to Chesapeake Bay. Cornwallis was now cut off from the British fleet.

The trap was sprung on October 7, 1781. Joseph Martin was watching when a rising flag signaled the American and French artillery to open fire on Yorktown. He wrote:

❝About noon the much-wished-for signal went up. I confess I felt a secret pride swell in my heart when I saw the "star-spangled banner" waving majestically in the very faces of our . . . adversaries [enemies]. . . . A simultaneous discharge of all the guns followed.❞

The pounding of exploding cannonballs and rockets went on for days, Martin wrote, until "most of the guns in the enemy's works were silenced." On October 19, 1781, Cornwallis surrendered.

The next morning, 8,000 British troops left Yorktown to lay down their arms. They marched slowly to the tune of "The World Turned Upside Down." Martin wrote that "it was a noble sight to us, and the more so, as it seemed to promise a speedy conclusion to the contest."

The Treaty of Paris

That promise came true. As a result of the American victory at Yorktown, Britain began peace talks with its former colonies. Early in 1783, the United States and Britain signed a peace treaty in Paris.

In the Treaty of Paris, Britain recognized the United States as an independent nation. It also agreed to cede to the new nation all lands between the Atlantic Coast and the Mississippi River, from Florida to Canada.

James Armistead, pictured on page 213, played a role in closing the trap at Yorktown. For a time, Lafayette's forces were the only American troops outside Yorktown, and he soon received word from Washington to hold Cornwallis's troops there at all costs. Lafayette, concerned that the British troops might escape before the larger forces could arrive, needed information about Cornwallis's plans. Armistead, who had been posing in the British camp as a runaway slave and convert to the British cause, was able to provide Lafayette with information about British maneuvers. After the surrender at Yorktown, Lafayette presented Armistead with his testimonial letter. Armistead subsequently changed his name to James Armistead Lafayette.

The United States, in turn, agreed to return property taken from Loyalists during the war. It also promised to allow British merchants to collect debts owed to them by Americans. Eight years had passed since Joseph Martin heard the bells that marked the beginning of war. Now the War of Independence was finally over.

Not all Americans were pleased with the peace terms. Despite promises of fair treatment, more than 27,000 Loyalists, both white and black, gave up their homes to resettle in Canada. They feared for their lives if they stayed, and for good reason. During the war Loyalists had often been badly treated by their neighbors.

Still, for most Americans, the end of the war was a time for rejoicing. They had won the freedom to shape their own future.

Looking ahead, George Washington was awed by the responsibility that came with that freedom. "With our fate," he wrote at war's end, "will the destiny of unborn millions be involved."

⭐ 4. Section Review

1. Define **guerrillas**.
2. How could General Greene lose his battles but still "win" his struggle against the British?
3. How did the American victory at Saratoga make Yorktown possible?
4. Critical Thinking What effect did the victories of Clark and Gálvez have on British peace terms in the Treaty of Paris?

Why We Remember

The War of Independence

Joseph Martin died in 1850 at the age of 90. His tombstone bears the words "A Soldier of the Revolution." Today we still remember Martin and his fellow soldiers for their heroism and sacrifice. They risked everything, even life itself, to fight for freedom. For their service, they got little but thanks. "I never received any pay worth the name while I belonged to the army," recalled Martin.

We remember their War of Independence because it gave birth to the United States of America as a free nation. It also won for the new nation vast lands into which its people would soon expand.

The war left other results as well. For Indians who had sided with Britain, the result would soon prove tragic. Without British protection, they would not be able to stop settlers from moving into their homelands. For African Americans, the effects of the war were mixed. Some had won their freedom fighting for independence. Many others, though, remained slaves.

Even so, Americans today remember the War of Independence as a glorious beginning. A new nation had been born based on new ideas.

Wrap-Up Activity

Assessing a Defeat
To help students understand why Yorktown was decisive, have them imagine themselves as British generals evaluating the military situation after the defeat. Have them make lists of reasons for and against continuing the war, followed by explanations of the decision to seek peace.

Section Review
Answers

1. Definition: *guerrillas* (222)
2. By harrying the British around the countryside, he slowed their advance and hastened the time when the British would settle in Yorktown.
3. Saratoga showed the French and Spanish that they could help the Patriots and hope to win against the British. Yorktown could not have been surrounded and taken without the help of these allies.
4. Because Clark drove the British from forts in the Ohio River Valley while Gálvez cleared them from forts along the Mississippi, Britain ceded the land west of the Appalachians.

To check understanding of "Why We Remember," assign Thinking Critically question 3 on student page 226.

Reviewing Vocabulary

Definitions are found on these pages: *minutemen* (206), *Patriots* (213), *Loyalists* (213), *mercenaries* (214), *profiteers* (219), *guerrillas* (222).

Reviewing Main Ideas

1. Governor Gage sent the soldiers to search for and confiscate stockpiled weapons from the militias; shots were fired and the War of Independence began.

2. To protect their rights; when a government no longer protects those rights, the people are entitled to dissolve the government.

3. They lacked disciplined and experienced soldiers and funds to support the army; strengths were dedicated supporters and good leadership.

4. Burgoyne's plan was to unite the British forces and control the Hudson River Valley so that American forces in New England could not be supplied; it failed because the forces under the command of St. Leger and Howe never arrived to join him, and he allowed the Americans too much time to prepare for his coming.

5. Saratoga showed potential allies that the American side could win the war with their help.

6. George Rogers Clark's small band of fighters drove the British out of the Ohio River Valley, and Spanish allies drove the British from the Mississippi River Valley.

7. American and French forces converged on Yorktown by land and sea and surrounded it, cutting off any possibility of Cornwallis's escape. They then shelled the town until Cornwallis surrendered.

(Answers continued in top margin)

Thinking Critically

1. It called for the establishment of a Continental army and appointed George Washington to command it, but it also composed and sent the Olive Branch Petition swearing loyalty to England and asking George III to help prevent war.

2. Students who agree may point out the crucial help from France and Spain; those who disagree may say that the war would have been won eventually as American forces chased the British and wore them down.

3. Accept work that is consistent with Martin's views and character as revealed in the text.

Applying Skills

1–3. Identifications of facts and opinions

Chapter Survey ★

Reviewing Vocabulary

Define the following terms.
1. minutemen
2. Patriots
3. Loyalists
4. mercenaries
5. profiteers
6. guerrillas

Reviewing Main Ideas

1. Why were British soldiers from Boston sent to Concord in April 1775? What happened as a result?
2. According to the Declaration of Independence, why do people create governments? When do people have the right to alter or abolish their government?
3. What did the Patriots lack at the beginning of the war? What were the strengths of the Patriots?
4. What did General Burgoyne's plan for winning the war involve? Why did the plan fail?
5. How did the victory at Saratoga help the American cause?
6. How was Britain's hold on the region between the 13 states and the Mississippi River broken?
7. Describe the trap that led to the British surrender at Yorktown.

Thinking Critically

1. **Synthesis** How did the Second Continental Congress show that it wanted peace but was ready for war in the summer of 1775?
2. **Evaluation** Agree or disagree with this statement: "If the Americans had fought the War of Independence by themselves, they would have lost." Explain why you think as you do.
3. **Why We Remember: Synthesis** Create an imaginary conversation between Joseph Martin and a friend who tries to convince him not to enlist.

Applying Skills

Statements of fact and opinions Read an editorial in a newspaper or magazine about the effects of a recent battle somewhere in the world.
1. Make a chart with the headings "Statements of Fact" and "Opinions."
2. Under the headings, write down the examples of each fact and opinion that you find in the editorial.
3. Exchange charts with a partner. Do you agree with each other's choices for each column? If you cannot agree on the choices, explain why.

History Mystery

British uniforms Answer the History Mystery on page 203. Now imagine yourself as a Patriot living in a city occupied by the British. What considerations would you have to weigh in deciding whether to spy on the British? As a spy, how might you gather information about the British?

Writing in Your History Journal

1. **Keys to History** (a) The time line on pages 202–203 has six Keys to History. In your journal, describe why each one is important to know about. (b) Choose any two events on the time line. Write an explanation of how the two events are related.

2. **Joseph Martin** An epitaph is a short statement in memory of a person who has died. It is usually put on the person's gravestone. In the past, epitaphs often began with the words "Here lies [person's name], who . . ." and went on to tell why the person would be mourned and remembered. In your journal, write an epitaph for Joseph Martin.

in students' charts should be consistent with the newspaper account they choose.

History Mystery

The information about return of laundry indicated to Washington that the British had been suddenly ordered to leave Philadelphia. Accept any reasonable answers: some students might say that they would consider the possibility they might be caught and hanged as a spy; others may feel they would be in good position to gather information about the British. Some ways to gather information might be eavesdropping on Loyalists' conversations, loitering near British camps to observe troop movements, and finding out from merchants and farmers about supplies requested by British troops.
(Answers continued in side margin)

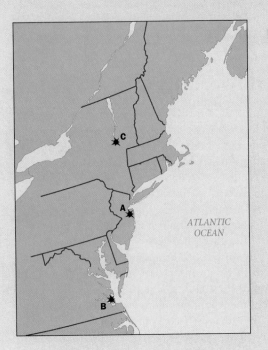

ATLANTIC OCEAN

Reviewing Geography

1. The letters on the map represent three major battles in the War of Independence. Write the name of each.

2. Geographic Thinking In Europe in the 1700s, battles were fought face to face in open fields, with soldiers moving forward and firing in tight, orderly groups. American warfare turned out to be quite different. How did the Americans make successful use of their environment to win the War of Independence? Why do you suppose the British and Hessian soldiers did not do the same?

3. Citizenship George Washington accepted the position of commander in chief of the Continental Army on the condition that he receive no salary. He asked only for reimbursement for his expenses. Why do you suppose that he refused to accept any pay? Write your response in your journal.

Alternative Assessment

Acting out opposing roles With a partner, prepare and present a play consisting of conversations between a Patriot and a Loyalist during the War of Independence.

❶ Choose the two characters that you will role play. They can be men or women, members of the same family or neighbors, northerners or southerners, white or black or Indian.

❷ Pick four scenes, in chronological order. For example, Scene 1 might occur after Lexington and Concord, Scene 2 after the Declaration of Independence, Scene 3 after Saratoga, and Scene 4 after Yorktown.

❸ Create conversations for each scene. Be sure they include descriptions of events as well as opinions of the events and the people involved in them.

Your work will be evaluated on the following criteria:
• you describe the four historical events accurately
• you describe the events in the correct chronological order
• you describe experiences and express opinions that real Patriots and Loyalists might have held
• you hold your audience's interest with a lively presentation

1. (a) Explanations should be similar to the time line notes on teacher pages 202–203. (b) Accept accurate additions that reflect understanding of the events.

2. Epitaphs should reflect an understanding of Martin's contributions to the war.

3. Students may note that Washington seems to have been a man of good character and strong will; others may suggest that he was wealthy anyway. They may also note he might have suspected his men would not be paid regularly and wanted to be sure he did not get anything that they did not.

Reviewing Geography

1. (A) Monmouth, (B) Yorktown, (C) Saratoga

2. Americans often used natural and constructed features in their environment as cover for troop movements. Examples are the American militia on the road to Lexington and Concord and American guerrillas in the South. Students might speculate that tradition kept British and Hessian soldiers from doing the same.

Alternative Assessment

Teacher's Take-Home Planner 3, p. 13, includes suggestions and scoring rubrics for the Alternative Assessment activity.

The excerpt is a first-person narrative from the point of view of a teenager who takes part in the fighting at Lexington. Let students know that although the account is fictional—unlike Joseph Martin's memoir—a fictional account can be effective in helping the reader to explore the feelings people might have had at a battle like Lexington, and allows the central character to narrate events as they happen rather than in long retrospect, as in a memoir.

★ ★ ★
Vital Links

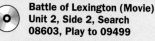

🔘 **Battle of Lexington (Movie)**
Unit 2, Side 2, Search 08603, Play to 09499

◉ See also Unit 2 Explore CD-ROM location 228.

✳ **Literature Footnote**

You may wish to suggest that students find and read *April Morning*, which follows the fortunes of Adam Cooper after Lexington and Concord. Students who enjoyed this piece might also enjoy *Johnny Tremain*, by Esther Forbes, in which a young apprentice in Boston joins Paul Revere and other notable revolutionaries to oppose the British. In *My Brother Sam Is Dead*, by James Lincoln Collier, the Meeker family lives in a Loyalist town, though the family is trying not to choose sides. Their neutrality is destroyed and their family threatened when one son joins the Patriots.

◎ Link to Literature

April Morning by Howard Fast

The year is 1775. The day is April 19. On this misty morning 15-year-old Adam Cooper finds himself holding a musket and standing on Lexington Green with his father and their neighbors. The British are coming, and the confrontation to follow will change Adam's life and the course of history.

I looked at the men and boys around me, and their faces were gray and drawn and old in the predawn. The whole eastern sky was gray now; we were a part of it; and the gray lay in dew upon the grass of the common. My belly was queasy, but out of fatigue not out of fear; and I told myself that the British would not come. Had we made fools of ourselves? How did the men feel, standing here in the lines on the common, with every manner of weapon, bird guns, muskets, matchlocks, rifles, and even an old blunderbuss that Ephraim Drake insisted was the best weapon ever invented. . . .

And then, after all the waiting, all the climax and the anticlimax of the long night, the British came and dawn came. Men who were talking dropped their voices to whispers, and then the whispers stopped, and in the distance, through the morning mist, we heard the beat of the British drums. It began as a rustle. Then it was the sound of a boy running through the reeds of a dry swamp. Then it was my own sound as I ran along a picket fence with a stick, and how did I come to be here, grown, with a gun in my wet hands? Fear began. I felt it prickle on my spine. I felt it like a weight in my belly. I felt it like a sickness around my heart, and its accompaniment was the steady, increasing roll of the redcoat drums. . . .

First, there were three officers on horseback. Then two flag-bearers carrying the British colors. Then a corps of eight drums. Then rank after rank of redcoats, stretching back on the road and into the curtain of mist, and emerging from the mist constantly, so that they appeared to be an endless force and an endless number. . . .

And the redcoats did not quicken their pace or slow it, but marched up the road with the same even pace, up to the edge of the common; and when they were there, one of the officers held up his arm—and

Continental Army musket

the drums stopped and the soldiers stopped. . . .

The three officers sat on their horses, studying us. The morning air was cold and clean and sharp, and I could see their faces and the faces of the redcoat soldiers behind them, the black bands of their knapsacks, the glitter of their buckles. Their coats were red as fire, but their light trousers were stained and dirty from the march.

Then, one of the officers sang out to them, "Fix bayonets!" and all down the line, the bayonets sparkled in the morning sun, and we heard the ring of metal against metal as they were clamped onto the guns.

One of the officers spurred his horse, and holding it at hard check, cantered onto the common with great style, rode past us and back in a circle to the others. He was smiling, but his smile was a sneer. . . .

Then another British officer—I discovered afterward that he was Major Pitcairn—called out orders: "Columns right!" and then, "By the left flank," and "Drums to the rear!" The drummers stood still and beat their drums, and the redcoats marched past them smartly, wheeling and parading across the common, while the three mounted officers spurred over the grass at a sharp canter, straight across our front and then back, reining in their prancing horses to face us. Meanwhile, the redcoats marched onto the common, the first company wheeling to face us when it was past our front of thirty-three men, the second company repeating the exercise, until they made a wall of red coats across the common, with no more than thirty or forty paces separating us. Even so close, they were unreal; only their guns were real, and their glittering bayonets too—and suddenly, I realized, and I believed that everyone else around me realized, that this was not to be an exercise or a parade or an argument, but something undreamed of and unimagined.

Militiaman Amos Doolittle showed his view of what happened on Lexington Green in his 1775 drawing.

bayonet:
a short sword attached to the barrel of a rifle

canter:
moderate gallop

A Closer Look

1. What details does the author use to contrast the men and boys on the Green with the British soldiers?

2. How does Adam view himself as he takes part in the confrontation?

3. What does Adam mean when he calls the confrontation "something undreamed of and unimagined"?

From *April Morning* by Howard Fast. Copyright © 1961 and renewed 1989 by Howard Fast. Reprinted by permission of Crown Publishers, Inc.

• **229**

Stimulating Critical Thinking

1. How does the author make the redcoats seem frightening? (He describes them as though they were a huge machine by using repetitive language. They come "rank after rank," as "an endless force, and an endless number.")

2. Does the author hint who will fire the first shot? (Students may say he hints that the British will. They line up in a threatening way and perhaps the "undreamed of and unimagined" thing will be that they fire. Others may feel that since the colonists have been waiting all night, they have intended to fight. Some may feel there is insufficient evidence in the passage.)

A Closer Look
Answers

1. Fast describes the colonists as a small, motley group standing gray and cold in the wet dawn, while the numerous British troops gleam with spit and polish, marching confidently, identically armed and dressed. Fast suggests that the colonists' feelings might be as varied as their weapons, while the British seem to have one will.

2. He sees himself as only recently a child, thrust into battle, and cannot understand how he got there.

3. Answers may vary. Students may suggest that no one imagined the British would open fire; some may feel that Adam never believed the fight would take place.

9 Creating the Constitution
1776–1791

Chapter Planning Guide

Section	Student Text	Teacher's Edition Activities
Opener and Story pp. 230–233	**Keys to History Time Line**　**History Mystery**　Beginning the Story with **James Madison**	**Setting the Stage Activity** Drawing a Caricature, p. 232
1 **The Nation's Shaky Start** pp. 234–240	**Reading Maps** The United States 1790, p. 235　**Link to Technology** Minting a Coin, p. 237　**World Link** The China trade, p. 238　**Geography Lab** The Central Lowlands, p. 240	**Warm-Up Activity** Views on National Government, p. 234　**Geography Question of the Day,** p. 234　**Section Activity** A Confusion of Currency, p. 238　**Bonus Activity** Advertising the Northwest Territory, p. 236　**Wrap-Up Activity** Writing a Persuasive Letter, p. 239
2 **The Constitutional Convention** pp. 241–245	**Link to Art** Signing the Constitution, p. 243	**Warm-Up Activity** Convention Rules, p. 241　**Geography Question of the Day,** p. 241　**Section Activity** A Convention Report, p. 242　**Bonus Activity** Interviewing a Delegate, p. 244　**Wrap-Up Activity** Preparing a Slogan, p. 245
3 **The Struggle for Ratification** pp. 246–249	**Point of View** Should the Constitution be ratified?, p. 247　**Link to the Present** The 27th Amendment, p. 248　**Skill Lab** Point of View, p. 249	**Warm-Up Activity** A Patrick Henry Diary Entry, p. 246　**Geography Question of the Day,** p. 246　**Section Activity** Federalist–Anti-Federalist Dialogue, p. 247　**Wrap-Up Activity** "Out of Many, One," p. 248
4 **An Enduring Framework** pp. 250–253	**Hands-On History** Proposing an amendment, p. 251	**Warm-Up Activity** An Amendment Time Line, p. 250　**Geography Question of the Day,** p. 250　**Section Activity** Surveying Adults, p. 252　**Bonus Activity** Class Constitutions, p. 252　**Wrap-Up Activity** Expressing Opinion, p. 253
Evaluation	☑ **Section 1 Review,** p. 239　☑ **Section 2 Review,** p. 245　☑ **Section 3 Review,** p. 248　☑ **Section 4 Review,** p. 253　☑ **Chapter Survey,** pp. 254–255　**Alternative Assessment** Creating a Constitution exhibit, p. 255	☑ **Answers to Section 1 Review,** p. 239　☑ **Answers to Section 2 Review,** p. 245　☑ **Answers to Section 3 Review,** p. 248　☑ **Answers to Section 4 Review,** p. 253　☑ **Answers to Chapter Survey,** pp. 254–255　(Alternative Assessment guidelines are in the Take-Home Planner.)

Teacher's Resource Package

Chapter Summaries: English and Spanish, pp. 22–23

Chapter Resources Binder
Study Guide Previewing Headings, p. 65
Geography Extensions The Central Lowlands, pp. 17–18
American Readings Views of Shays' Rebellion, p. 33

Chapter Resources Binder
Study Guide Reading for Details, p. 66
American Readings Delegates to the Constitutional Convention, p. 34; Letters from the Convention, pp. 35–36
Using Historical Documents The United States Constitution, pp. 51–55

Chapter Resources Binder
Study Guide Skimming for Information, p. 67
Skills Development Point of View, pp. 71–72

Chapter Resources Binder
Study Guide Identifying Main Ideas, p. 68
Reinforcement Using a Graphic Organizer, pp. 69–70

Chapter and Unit Tests Chapter 9 Tests, Forms A and B, pp. 53–56

Take-Home Planner

Introducing the Chapter Activity Dividing the Powers of Government, p. 20
Chapter In-Depth Activity Creating a Compromise, p. 21

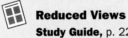
Reduced Views
Study Guide, p. 22
Reinforcement, p. 23
Geography Extensions, p. 25
American Readings, p. 24
Unit 3 Answers, pp. 27–33

Reduced Views
Study Guide, p. 22
American Readings, p. 24
Using Historical Documents, p. 25
Unit 3 Answers, pp. 27–33

Reduced Views
Study Guide, p. 22
Skills Development, p. 23
Unit 3 Answers, pp. 27–33

Reduced Views
Study Guide, p. 22
Reinforcement, p. 23
Unit 3 Answers, pp. 27–33

Reduced Views
Chapter Tests, p. 25
Unit 3 Answers, pp. 27–33
Alternative Assessment Guidelines for scoring the Chapter Survey activity, p. 21

Additional Resources

Wall Time Line

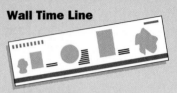

Unit 3 Activity

Transparency Package

Transparency 9-1 The Great Seal—use with Section 1
Transparency 9-2 Signing the Constitution—use with Section 2
Transparency Activity Book

SelecTest Testing Software
Chapter 9 Test, Forms A and B

Vital Links

Videodisc

CD-ROM

Virginia currency (see TE p. 236)
Voice of Benjamin Franklin (see TE p. 244)

229B

9

Teaching Resources

Take-Home Planner 3
  Introducing Chapter Activity
  Chapter In-Depth Activity
  Alternative Assessment
Chapter Resources Binder
Geography Extensions
American Readings
Using Historical Documents
Transparency Activities
Wall Time Line Activities
Chapter Summaries
Chapter and Unit Tests
SelecTest Test File
Vital Links CD-ROM/Videodisc

Time Line

Keys to History

Keys to History journal writing activity is on page 254 in the Chapter Survey.

State constitutions By writing constitutions the 13 former colonies declared themselves independent republics. (p. 234)

Articles of Confederation The Articles were the first plan of government for the new nation, a loose alliance of independent states. (p. 234)

Looking Back By sending delegates to the First Continental Congress, the colonies had recognized the need to act together for their common interest.

World Link See p. 238.

Chapter Objectives

★ Describe the problems the new nation faced.
★ Explain how the Constitutional Convention drafted a plan for government.
★ Describe how the Constitution became the law.
★ Summarize the ideas that have made the Constitution endure.

Chapter Overview

The independent states created constitutions giving most power to elected legislatures. The Articles of Confederation gave Congress authority to direct the army and deal with foreign nations.

Congress passed laws on settling western regions but had no power to tax states or settle arguments between states over trade and boundaries. Weaknesses of the confederation

1776–1791

Chapter 9

Creating the Constitution

Sections

Beginning the Story with James Madison
1. **The Nation's Shaky Start**
2. **The Constitutional Convention**
3. **The Struggle for Ratification**
4. **An Enduring Framework**

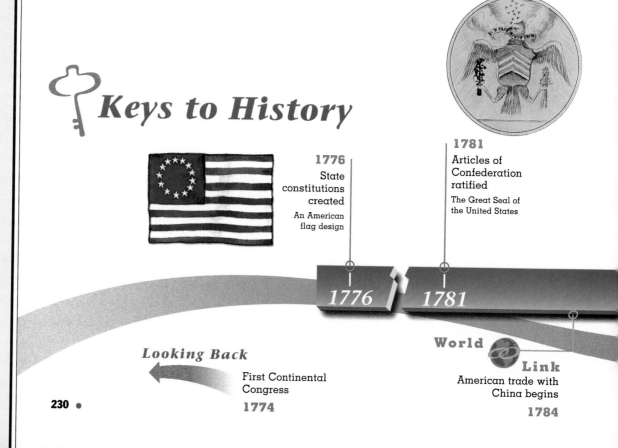

Keys to History

1776
State constitutions created

An American flag design

1781
Articles of Confederation ratified

The Great Seal of the United States

1776   *1781*

Looking Back
First Continental Congress
1774

World Link
American trade with China begins
1784

spurred states to send delegates to a Constitutional Convention, where compromise yielded a new plan for a strong national government.

During state debates over ratification, anti-Federalists warned the Constitution would give the federal government too much power. The Federalist promise to add a Bill of Rights helped win ratification.

To help the government adjust to changing times, the Constitution provides a flexible framework of general principles and allows amendments. Three principles limit the federal government's power. Federalism divides power between the states and federal government. Separation of powers divides federal power between the executive, legislative, and judicial branches. Checks and balances provide ways for each branch to limit the power of the other two.

Teaching the
HISTORY
Mystery

Students will find the answer on p. 245. See Chapter Survey, p. 254, for questions related to the History Mystery.

Time Line

Shays' Rebellion The revolt of Massachusetts farmers spurred states to send delegates to the Constitutional Convention. (p. 238)

Northwest Ordinance With this law, Congress planned how to divide the territory into states. (p. 236)

Constitutional Convention The delegates drafted a plan for a strong national government. (p. 241)

Constitution ratified When New Hampshire became the ninth state to ratify, the new plan of government was officially approved. (p. 248)

Bill of Rights The first ten amendments to the Constitution safeguard individual freedoms. (p. 248)

Looking Ahead Differing views of how much power the Constitution gives the federal government led to the forming of the Federalist and Republican parties.

HISTORY *Mystery*

This is part of a piece of furniture known as the "Rising Sun Chair." The chair has been preserved for over 200 years. What has made it famous?

1787
Shays' Rebellion
Daniel Shays

1787
Constitutional Convention
Inkstand used for signing the Constitution

1788
Constitution ratified
Banner celebrating ratification

1787
Northwest Ordinance

1791
Bill of Rights ratified

1786

1791

Looking Ahead
Federalist and Republican parties formed
1792

● **231**

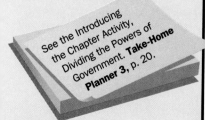

✳ History Footnote

Madison met Jefferson while serving in Virginia's legislature. Their lifelong friendship saw both become President. In many ways they were similar, coming from the same social class, growing up in the same part of Virginia, and sharing many beliefs about the role of government. Neither was outgoing, and so both were often considered aloof.

Beginning the Story with

James Madison

If the young James Madison pictured here were to walk into your classroom today, you would not be impressed. Madison was a small, pale, and sickly boy with a thin, weak voice. He was also painfully shy.

Madison was born in 1751 and was raised on a plantation in Virginia. All his life he was plagued by fevers. He also suffered from seizures in which his entire body would stiffen for several moments. His doctor said these attacks were a form of epilepsy, a disorder of the nervous system. Young James called the seizures his "falling sickness."

The Young Scholar

One thing that was neither small nor sickly about Madison was his mind. By the time he was 11, Madison had read every one of the 85 books in his father's library. When Madison ran out of books to read at home, his father sent him to school in a neighboring county. James was a good student, quickly learning French, Latin, and Greek so that he could read books written in those languages. He also studied history, geography, astronomy, algebra, and geometry.

At the age of 18, Madison entered Princeton College in New Jersey. He threw himself into his studies, working hard enough to finish a three-year course of studies in two years. He also found time to join in student pranks such as setting off firecrackers in a newcomer's bed.

After graduating from Princeton, Madison suffered a mental collapse. It is true that he had been studying hard and getting by on very little sleep. Still, he was suffering from more than exhaustion. Most likely, the young scholar was depressed because he did not know what he wanted to do with his life.

Madison was quite sure that he did not want to be a planter like his father, who depended on slaves to work his land. While at Princeton Madison had come to hate slavery. He had to find another career. But what?

History Bookshelf

Anderson, Joan. *1787*. Harcourt Brace, 1987. Combining fact and fiction, *1787* dramatizes the story of the writing of the Constitution. Seen through the eyes of an assistant to Madison, the story relates what happened in Philadelphia during that summer. This book was chosen as a 1987 Notable Children's Trade Book in the Field of Social Studies.

Also of interest:

Fritz, Jean. *The Great Little Madison*. Putnam, 1989.

Kelly, Regina Z. *James Madison: Statesman and President*. Marshall Cavendish, 1991.

Meltzer, Milton. *The Bill of Rights: How We Got It and What It Means*. Thomas Y. Crowell, 1990.

His voice was too weak for him to be a minister. Who would want to listen to him preach? He found the study of law depressingly "coarse and dry." That left running for public office. In a letter to a friend, however, Madison had declared, "I do not meddle in politics."

In this dark mood, Madison became convinced that he was destined to die young. Not that it mattered much to him anyway. In a letter to a friend he said that he was "too dull and infirm [sickly] now to look out for any extraordinary things in this world." He could not have been more wrong.

A North-West Prospect of Nassau Hall (detail) by Reverend Jonathan Fisher, 1807

Madison and about 100 other students studied, dined, and slept in Princeton College's Nassau Hall.

"Meddling in Politics"

It was "meddling in politics" that pulled Madison out of his depression. As the colonies moved toward a showdown with Britain, he was swept up in the struggle. In 1774 the young man joined the local Orange County Committee of Safety to help prepare Virginia for war. Two years later he was elected to represent his county at a state convention. There he voted to throw Virginia's support behind the Declaration of Independence.

In 1780 Virginia sent Madison to Philadelphia as a delegate to the Continental Congress. At 29, he was the youngest member of Congress, and the smallest—"No bigger than a half piece of soap," said one delegate. He was also the shyest. After inviting Madison to a party, one delegate's wife described him as "a gloomy stiff creature . . . with nothing engaging or even bearable about his manners."

During his first six months in Congress, Madison did not so much as open his mouth. When he finally did manage to speak, his voice was so weak that other members had to strain their ears in order to hear him. The delegates to Congress quickly learned, however, that when the young man from Virginia spoke, he was worth listening to. James Madison may not have known it yet, but he had found his career at last.

Hands-On → HISTORY

Activity

Make a chart of school subjects that compares what Madison studied with what you, your parents, and your grandparents studied. Gather information from your parents and grandparents through interviews, including information about what their United States history courses were like. Use your chart to identify what has changed and what has stayed the same.

Thinking Historically

1. What careers did Madison reject? Why? (Planter, because of slavery; minister, voice too weak; lawyer, law "coarse and dry.")

2. What characteristics made him an unlikely politician? (Shy, soft-spoken, not very engaging.)

3. Could he be a successful politician today? Explain. (Anyone shy and unimposing would have a hard time in the age of television.)

See the Chapter In-Depth Activity, Creating a Compromise. **Take-Home Planner 3,** p. 21.

Teaching the

Hands-On
------- → HISTORY

If possible, display older textbooks for students to compare with their current ones. Suggest that when they do the interviews they share what they have learned in their courses so that parents and grandparents can tell how their own courses differed. Students should ask in what grades their parents and grandparents studied various subjects.

For a journal writing activity on James Madison, see student page 255.

Introducing the Section

Vocabulary

constitution (p. 234) a plan of government

republic (p. 234) a government run by elected representatives of the people

bill of rights (p. 234) a list of rights and freedoms guaranteed to the people

confederation (p. 234) an alliance of independent states

depression (p. 238) a long, sharp decline in economic activity

Section Objectives

★ Describe the kind of government created under the Articles of Confederation.

★ Explain the problems that led to calls for a convention.

Teaching Resources

Take-Home Planner 3, pp. 18–25
Chapter Resources Binder
  Study Guide, p. 65
  Reinforcement
  Skills Development
Geography Extensions, pp. 17–18
American Readings, p. 33
Using Historical Documents
Transparency Activities
Chapter and Unit Tests

1. The Nation's Shaky Start

Reading Guide

New Terms constitution, republic, bill of rights, confederation, depression

Section Focus The problems the new nation faced after independence

1. What kind of government did the Articles of Confederation create?
2. What problems led to calls for a convention to revise the Articles?

When the War of Independence ended, no one was happier than James Madison. He had doubts, though, about whether the 13 former colonies could create a new nation. During the war they had squabbled over land, trade, and the question of how much power to give the Continental Congress.

New State Governments

After declaring themselves "free and independent states" in 1776, each state had quickly created a **constitution**—a plan of government. In effect, each became a separate **republic,** a government run by elected representatives of the people.

These new states were determined to prevent the tyranny they had accused Britain of imposing. State constitutions gave most of the power to legislatures elected by the people. Officials once appointed by the king—governors and judges—were now elected for a limited term. Most state constitutions included a **bill of rights,** a list of rights and freedoms guaranteed to the people.

Articles of Confederation

As the war raged on, the state governments had seen the need for a central authority to direct the army and deal with foreign nations. Yet the states feared giving Congress too much power. A strong national government might trample the very rights they were fighting for.

In 1777 Congress proposed a plan to create a **confederation**—an alliance of independent states. This plan, called the Articles of Confederation, was finally approved by all of the states in 1781. Under the Articles each state would have one vote in Congress. Major decisions had to be approved by 9 of the 13 states.

The Articles gave Congress the right to raise an army and navy, control foreign affairs, coin money, and set up a postal system. However, Congress was not allowed to regulate trade or to tax. The states were fearful of handing those powers over to a central government.

Both during and after the war, Congress had to beg for money to carry out its policies. All too often, states ignored these humble requests. The result, said Madison, was that Congress was about as effective at uniting the states as "a rope of sand."

Settling Western Lands

Congress did manage to decide how to develop the western lands that Britain ceded to the United States after the war. Even before the War of Independence, pathfinders like Daniel Boone had begun leading small groups of settlers across the

Warm-Up Activity

Views on National Government

To help students predict what type of national government the states might accept, have small groups imagine themselves as state legislators shortly after the Declaration of Independence. Assign each group a state and have them discuss whether a national government is needed and, if so, what powers it should or should not have. After groups list ideas, have them share conclusions.

Geography Question of the Day

Have students look at the map on p. 235 to identify which states could expand westward (New York, Pennsylvania, Virginia, North and South Carolina, Georgia) and explain why the others could not.

Connections to Math

Surveying is the technique used to mark the boundaries of townships, sections, half-sections, and so forth. Parallax, the difference in direction of an object when seen from two positions, is used for measuring the distance to an object. Surveyors must know geometry and trigonometry because they use angles and triangles in making measurements.

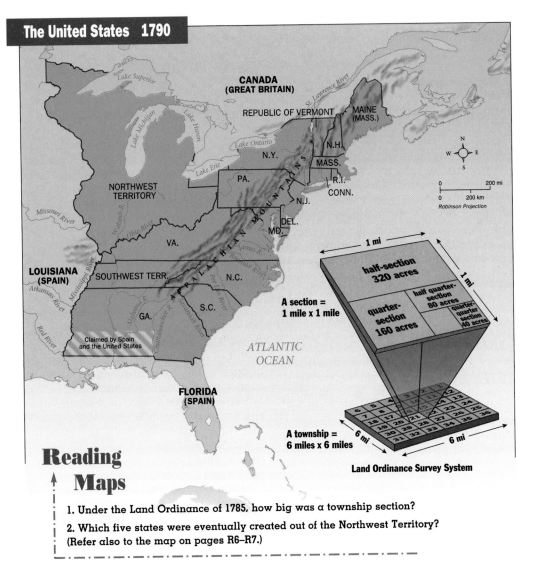

The United States 1790

Land Ordinance Survey System

A section = 1 mile x 1 mile

A township = 6 miles x 6 miles

half-section 320 acres

quarter-section 160 acres

half quarter-section 80 acres

quarter-quarter section 40 acres

Reading Maps

1. Under the Land Ordinance of 1785, how big was a township section?

2. Which five states were eventually created out of the Northwest Territory? (Refer also to the map on pages R6–R7.)

Developing the Section

Discussion

Checking Understanding

1. **What rights did Congress have under the Articles?** (To raise an army and a navy, handle foreign affairs, coin money, and set up a postal system.)

2. **What rights was it denied?** (To regulate trade or tax.)

Stimulating Critical Thinking

3. **What problems might have occurred because Congress could not tax?** (Answers may vary, but students should understand that governments need money for various reasons.)

Teaching the Reading Maps

Have students note which states on the map look different from how they look today (Virginia, Georgia). **Answers to Reading Maps: 1.** one square mile **2.** Ohio, Indiana, Illinois, Wisconsin, Michigan

See the Study Guide activity in the **Chapter Resources Binder**, p. 65.

Appalachians. After the war, this trickle of settlers turned into a flood.

There was no orderly way of dividing up and selling western lands. Settlers simply claimed land they liked. To mark a claim, they might cut their initials into trees along its boundaries. Imagine the confusion that arose. Where did one settler's claim end and another's begin?

To end such confusion, Congress passed the Land Ordinance of 1785. This law divided the western land "purchased of the Indian inhabitants" into areas called townships. Each township was 6 miles (10 km) square, with 36 sections (see map on this page). Four sections were set aside for use by the national government. Income from another section would support public schools. Money from

Bonus Activity

Advertising the Northwest Territory

By creating a promotional brochure, students infer conditions that would appeal to potential settlers of the Northwest Territory. Have small groups imagine they own a company that wants to encourage settlement in the Northwest Territory. Each group should write and illustrate a brochure designed to entice new settlers. Brochures should emphasize the wonders of the new land, the plan for settling it, and the importance of getting enough settlers so the territory can become a state.

★ ★ ★
Vital Links

Virginia currency (Picture) Unit 2, Side 1, Search 13667

See also Unit 2 Explore CD-ROM location 71.

✳ History Footnote

A group of New England speculators formed the Ohio Company to buy land and send settlers to the Northwest Territory. Delegates elected by potential investors made decisions for the company, which was organized in Boston. They raised capital by selling shares for $1,000 each. They sold 250 shares in one year and contracted to buy from Congress 750,000 acres in what is now southeastern Ohio. A party of 47 surveyors, carpenters, boat builders, blacksmiths, and laborers went to establish a town where the Ohio and the Muskingum rivers joined. They arrived there on April 7, 1788 and founded Marietta, Ohio, the first town in the Northwest Territory.

the sale of the other sections would help the government pay the war debt.

The Northwest Ordinance Surveyors began mapping townships in the Northwest Territory—the area north of the Ohio River, west of Pennsylvania, and east of the Mississippi. By 1787 the job was far enough along to begin selling sections, but how would the newly settled areas be governed?

Congress answered that question in the Northwest Ordinance of 1787. This law called for dividing the Northwest Territory into three, four, or five smaller territories.

Once settlers arrived in a territory, Congress would appoint a governor. As soon as there were 5,000 adult males, they could elect a legislature. When its population reached 60,000, a territory could apply to Congress to become a state, equal to the older states in every way.

The Northwest Ordinance was designed to ensure that democracy moved west. It included a bill of rights, made slavery illegal in the territories, stated that "good faith shall always be observed towards the Indians," and declared that "schools and the means of education shall forever be encouraged." Thomas Jefferson saw the western lands becoming "an Empire for Liberty."

Disputes with Britain and Spain

Congress was less successful in dealing with other nations. Britain refused to give up forts in the Northwest Territory, despite promises to do so in the Treaty of Paris. The British argued that Americans had broken the treaty by not paying debts owed to British merchants. Congress had no power either to force the British out or to make Americans live up to the treaty terms.

Spain, meanwhile, challenged American claims to the land between the Ohio River and Spanish Florida. In 1784 Spain closed the Mississippi River to American shippers to discourage settlers from moving into this region. Now settlers west of the rugged Appalachians had no good way to ship their crops to distant markets in the east.

These disputes showed the country's weakness in dealing with other nations. After the war the army had been disbanded, and Congress had no funds to create a new army. The new nation could not back up its protests with force. This sad state of affairs led Congressman Alexander Hamilton to grumble that the government was "fit for neither war nor peace."

Quarrels Among the States

Britain and Spain felt free to ignore American demands because they thought that the United States would not be united for long. Even before the war ended, the states were quarreling among themselves. Peace only seemed to make matters worse.

Many arguments were over trade. After the war some states began taxing goods from other states. New York, for example, taxed cabbage from New Jersey and firewood from Connecticut. Merchants complained, but Congress could do nothing to help.

States also quarreled over boundaries. In one conflict, Maryland and Virginia almost went to war because both claimed the Potomac River where it ran between them. Many Europeans believed such quarrels would tear the United States apart. Then Britain and Spain would be ready to pick up the pieces.

Money Troubles

The not-so-United States also had money troubles. Congress had little gold and silver to make into coins. Faced with a money shortage, the states began printing their own

Link to Technology

Minting a Coin

Today Americans agree on a common form of money—coins and bills made by the United States government. In the years after the War of Independence, though, there was no one system. State governments as well as private individuals printed bills and made coins by a process known as **minting**. The illustrations show a coin minting process used at the time of the War of Independence.

(A) Spanish dollar, or "Piece of Eight," one of the most common coins in colonial America; (B) Pine Tree Shilling, one of the first coins minted in America, introduced in 1652; (C) Fugio Cent, the first official United States coin, introduced in 1787

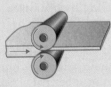

① The cast metal is rolled several times to even out its thickness.

② A machine called a blanking press punches out the coin shapes, called *blanks*.

③ The blank is stamped with its design, and a *reeding plate* forms the ridged edge.

A Coin Today

These words appear on all U.S. coins.

The official motto of the United States: Latin for "out of many, one"

Today an artist draws a large portrait, which is then reduced and engraved on a coin mold called a *die*.

Indicates the location of the mint where the coin was made ("D" for Denver)

Coins were first *reeded* on the edge to keep people from cutting off chunks of valuable metal.

1776–1791 Chapter 9 • **237**

Teaching the

World  **Link**

Help students see the connection between a weak Congress under the Articles and the problems of the trading merchants. Ask how the government might have dealt with Britain's ban of American trade to the West Indies if it had been stronger.

For Jefferson's and Abigail Adams's views on Shays' Rebellion, see **American Readings,** p. 33.

✠ Connections to Literature

One ballad of the time characterized Shays' Rebellion as an evil act, associating him with the devil and with Pluto, the god of the underworld:

> My name is Shays; in former days
> In Pelham I did dwell, Sir.
> But now I'm forced to leave this place
> Because I did rebel, Sir.

> Within the State I lived of late,
> By Satan's foul invention,
> In Pluto's cause against the laws
> I raised an insurrection.

After Shays fled from Pelham, Massachusetts, to Vermont, he was convicted and sentenced to death in absentia. Massachusetts granted him a pardon in 1788.

World  **Link**

The China trade Squabbles over currency and taxes were not the only problems facing American merchants. After Britain banned American trade with the British West Indies in 1783, these merchants had to scramble to find new overseas markets.

One possibility was China. As a first step, some merchants outfitted a ship called the *Empress of China.* It sailed from New York in 1784 with a cargo of rum, furs, and ginseng, a medicinal herb. The ship returned loaded with tea, silk, and porcelain. Gradually China became an important partner in trade.

Foreign ships in a Chinese port

currency. Before long, a dozen different kinds of paper bills were floating from state to state.

Americans came to see the bills as being nearly worthless. Some states passed laws requiring creditors—people who lent money—to accept paper money as payment for debts. The result was the odd sight of creditors fleeing debtors to avoid having to accept payment in what they saw as worthless paper, or "rag money." A single national currency would have helped end such confusion, but Congress lacked the power to stop states from printing money.

Shays' Rebellion

By the mid 1780s the country was in the grip of a **depression,** a long, sharp decline in economic activity. Farmers in western Massachusetts were especially hard hit by falling crop prices. Many did not earn enough to pay their debts and state taxes. Judges ordered them to sell their livestock or land to pay off the debts.

The desperate farmers asked the state legislature to allow them to pay debts with their crops instead of money. When the legislature refused, they took matters into their own hands. Led by Daniel Shays, a hero of Bunker Hill, they protested in front of courthouses, waving their muskets. The angry mobs struck fear into the hearts of even the toughest judges, forcing many of the courts to close.

Early in 1787 Shays and his followers marched on the national arsenal at Springfield. They were planning to seize the weapons stored there. Since Congress had no army to defend the arsenal, Massachusetts had to send the state militia to restore order. The troops crushed the uprising and arrested Shays.

To many Americans, Shays' Rebellion was yet another sign that the nation could not hold together. A worried Madison wrote to a friend that:

❝No money is paid to the public treasury; no respect is paid to the federal authority [Congress]. . . . It is not possible that a government can last long under these circumstances.❞

The Call for a Convention

In September 1786, a few months before Shays' Rebellion, delegates from five states had met in Annapolis, Maryland, in order to discuss trade problems. Madison was one of

Although Shays' Rebellion alarmed many Americans, Jefferson had a different view, expressed in a letter to Madison:

> I hold it then that a little rebellion now and then is a good thing, and as necessary in the political world as storms in the physical. Unsuccessful rebellions, indeed, generally establish the encroachments on the rights of the people who have produced them. An observation of this truth should render honest republican governors so mild in their punishment of rebellions as not to discourage them too much. It is a medicine necessary for the sound health of government.

When Daniel Shays led his band of angry farmers into Springfield, Massachusetts, in January 1787, they were met by state militia. The troops fired to protect the federal arsenal. As a present-day marker bears witness, by the end of February Shays' Rebellion had been completely crushed.

the leaders at this meeting. The Annapolis Convention ended with a call for a meeting of delegates from all 13 states in Philadelphia in May 1787 to consider "the situation of the United States."

The shock of Shays' Rebellion spurred every state but Rhode Island to agree to send delegates. Congress suspected that the delegates might seek to scrap the current plan of government. Therefore, it declared that the meeting should be "for the sole and express purpose of revising the Articles of Confederation."

Dumping the Articles of Confederation, however, was exactly what Madison had in mind. A year earlier he had written Thomas Jefferson, then the American ambassador to France, asking Jefferson to send him any books that "may throw light on . . . confederacies which have existed." The books arrived by the hundreds.

Madison threw himself into the study of governments, both ancient and modern.

The lesson of the past, he found, was always the same: federations with weak central governments would soon be torn apart by quarrels and disputes. Had Americans learned that lesson well enough? Were they ready to create a stronger government?

★ 1. Section Review

1. Define **constitution, republic, bill of rights, confederation,** and **depression.**

2. How did fear of tyranny affect the creation of the state constitutions and the Articles of Confederation?

3. What were the main weaknesses of the new government under the Articles of Confederation?

4. Critical Thinking Do you think Shays and his followers had a good reason to rebel against the government? Why or why not?

In this Geography Lab, students study a photograph, a personal account, and maps to help them understand the appeal of the Northwest Territory to settlers. Ask: **What does the photo show? What part of Smith's statement relates to it?** (A Central Lowlands farm. "Soil is amazingly rich, . . . as level as a bowling plain, and vastly extensive.")

Developing a Mental Map
Answers

1. New York, Pennsylvania, Ohio, Indiana, Michigan, Wisconsin, Illinois, Minnesota, Iowa, Missouri, Texas, Oklahoma, Kansas, Nebraska, South Dakota, North Dakota.

2. From sea level to 2000 feet (610 m).

3. Photo shows flat land. Smith describes land "as level as a bowling plain" but also notes that there are hills.

4. Yes. Smith describes soil that is "amazingly rich," land that is "amazingly fertile." The photograph shows rich farmland.

5. Answers should reflect an understanding of the richness of the land as Smith described it, as well as the security of remaining at home.

See the activity on The Central Lowlands in **Geography Extensions,** pp. 17–18.

✳ Geography Footnote

The northern parts of the Central Lowlands and the Great Lakes were formed during the ice age when ice sheets covered large regions of land. As the ice spread out, it pushed rocks and soil ahead of it. As the ice retreated, it left soil, silt, gravel, and rocks. It also formed lakes and drainage channels. The ice age leveled most of the surface of the Central Lowlands. Loess, or silt deposited by the wind, covers much of the southern part of the Central Lowlands. The loess is what provides the rich soil that farmers in the area rely on.

Geography Lab

Midwest corn and dairy farm

The Central Lowlands

Free of British rule, restless Americans sought land and opportunity west of the Appalachians. Many headed for the Northwest Territory, most of which lay in the geographic region now known as the Central Lowlands.

Throughout much of the territory, settlers had to chop down trees to clear land for farms. However, in some places there were meadows, and settlers who traveled to the western edge of the territory found themselves on a vast prairie, surrounded by tall grasses as far as they could see.

James Smith, a Virginian who explored the area in the 1790s, praised the land. What pictures of the Central Lowlands come to mind as you read his statement?

James Smith's Statement

"Bordering on the rivers, the land exceeds description. Suffice it to say that the soil is amazingly rich, ... as level as a bowling plain, and vastly extensive. . . . [Away from the rivers] the land is still amazingly fertile, covered with a heavy growth of timber, such as white and red oak, hickory, ash, beech, sugar tree [sugar maple], walnut, buckeye, etc. . . . As to mountains, there are properly speaking none; there are, however, high hills from which a beautiful view of the adjoining [neighboring] country presents itself. . . . [W]hite clover and blue-grass grow spontaneously wherever the land is cleared. . . . A country so famous for grass must of course be excellent for all kinds of stock. Here I saw the finest beef and mutton [cattle and sheep] that I ever saw, fed on grass. Hogs also increase and fatten in the woods in a most surprising manner."

Developing a Mental Map

Refer to the map of geographic regions on pages P4–P5 and the maps on pages R4–R5 and R6–R7 to answer the questions.

1. What states lie partly or completely within the Central Lowlands?

2. Most of the Central Lowlands region falls within one elevation range. What is that range?

3. The Central Lowlands are sometimes described as "flat to gently rolling." What evidence of that do you find on this page?

4. One early writer called the Central Lowlands "The Garden of the World." Would James Smith agree? How does the picture on this page support that description?

5. **Hands-On Geography** With a partner, imagine that you are members of a farming family in Maryland in 1788. You are trying to decide whether to move to the Northwest Territory or stay put. Carry on a conversation in which you give arguments for and against the move.

Teaching Resources

Take-Home Planner 3, pp. 18–25

Chapter Resources Binder

  Study Guide, p. 66

  Reinforcement

  Skills Development

  Geography Extensions

American Readings, pp. 34–36

Using Historical Documents, pp. 51–55

Transparency Activities

Chapter and Unit Tests

Introducing the Section

Vocabulary

legislative branch (p. 242) the branch of government that makes the laws

executive branch (p. 242) the branch of government that carries out the laws

judicial branch (p. 242) a system of courts to interpret the laws

ratify (p. 245) approve

2. The Constitutional Convention

Reading Guide

New Terms legislative branch, executive branch, judicial branch, ratify

Section Focus How the Constitutional Convention drafted a new plan of government

1. Who attended the Constitutional Convention?
2. How did the new plan of government differ from the Articles of Confederation?
3. What compromises did the delegates reach to produce the constitution?

Philadelphia was already hot and humid when delegates to the convention began drifting into the city. None of them knew it yet, but they would be there all summer.

A Profile of the Delegates

All of the 55 delegates were white males, and almost all were well-educated and wealthy. About a third owned slaves. There were half a dozen planters and almost three dozen lawyers. The convention delegates were the nation's ablest political leaders. Many had been leading Patriots and had helped draw up state constitutions. Thomas Jefferson, who was still in France, called them "an assembly of demi-gods."

James Madison was the best-prepared of the delegates. Despite his weak voice, he would address the convention more than 200 times in the weeks ahead. His influence was so great that later he would be called the Father of the Constitution.

When not speaking, Madison took notes. Sitting near the front of the room so that he would miss nothing, he wrote down almost every word in his own shorthand. At night he rewrote his notes in longhand. Today Madison's notes cover more than 600 printed pages. From this record we know what went on at the convention day by day.

Getting Started

On May 25 the convention began. For the next four months the east room of the Pennsylvania State House would be the center of the delegates' lives. When they arrived each morning, the east room was cool and inviting. By noon it was an oven. Despite the hot weather, the windows had to be locked for secrecy and for protection from insects.

The delegates' first action was to elect George Washington president of the convention. No man was more admired or respected. Washington's presence would keep the convention from flying apart in its worst moments.

Next the delegates agreed on a set of rules. Each could speak twice on a subject, and no one was to whisper, pass notes, or read while others spoke. Each state had one vote, and decisions would be by majority vote of the states present.

The most important rule was secrecy. No one was to say anything to anyone about what went on in their discussions. The delegates wanted to feel free to state their opinions and even change their minds later on. The rule of secrecy was taken very seriously. During that long summer, not a single word about the convention debates appeared in any newspaper.

Warm-Up Activity

Convention Rules

To help students imagine the problems of conducting the Constitutional Convention, have small groups create lists of rules for the meetings. In brainstorming rules, they should keep in mind what they already know about conflicts between the states. They should also consider what they already know about rules of conduct for meetings, at the theater, in debates, and so forth.

Geography Question of the Day

Explain that it was hot and humid in Philadelphia in the summer of 1787. Have students describe how hot, humid weather affects people and list steps that might be taken to function in such an environment.

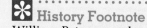
William Paterson, who proposed the New Jersey Plan, was born in Ireland. He served his state as a member of the state constitutional convention in 1776, a state senator in 1789 and 1790, and governor from 1790 to 1793. He also served as a Supreme Court Justice from 1793 until his death in 1806. The city of Paterson, New Jersey, is named after him.

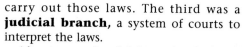
For firsthand descriptions of some convention delegates, see **American Readings,** p. 34.

See the Study Guide activity in the **Chapter Resources Binder,** p. 66.

Developing the Section

Section Activity

A Convention Report

To help students understand the issues and compromises, have them imagine that television was available during the 1780s and that they are commentators doing a wrap-up report on the convention. Beginning with short background statements on the delegates and setting, they should proceed to a concise summary of major features of the Constitution, explaining how compromise was a key factor. The report should be understandable to the average citizen. Reports can be prepared individually or in groups, with members of reporter panels covering different topics (powers given to Congress, powers denied to Congress, the presidency, etc.).

The Virginia Plan and the New Jersey Plan

By May 29 the stage was set for debate, and the Virginia delegates wasted no time. Thanks largely to Madison's ideas and research, they already had a plan. The Articles of Confederation, they said, were beyond mending and should be scrapped. A national government—one with real authority—should replace the loose alliance of independent states.

Under the Virginia Plan, the government would have three parts, or branches. The first was a bicameral **legislative branch,** which would make the laws. The second was an **executive branch,** which would carry out those laws. The third was a **judicial branch,** a system of courts to interpret the laws.

After two weeks of debate, the delegates agreed on the need for a new national government with three branches. They wanted most of the power to rest with the legislative branch, just as it did in each state. The question of how to elect members of Congress, therefore, was critical. It would rock the convention for more than a month.

The Virginia Plan proposed that members of Congress be directly elected by the voters, rather than by the state legislatures. The number of members representing each state would be based on that state's population. States that had a larger number of people would have more representatives.

Delegates from small states hated the Virginia Plan because they feared that the large states would always be able to outvote them. They came up with a plan of their own, which William Paterson of New Jersey presented on June 15.

Under the New Jersey Plan, Congress would have just one house, and each state would have one vote. Representatives to Congress would be elected by the state legislatures.

Madison argued that the New Jersey Plan would leave too much power in the hands of each state. He said it would do little to cure the problems the nation had faced under the Articles of Confederation. After much debate, the majority agreed and voted to reject the small states' plan.

This illustration captures a Philadelphia street scene around the time of the Constitutional Convention. A church steeple rises on the left.

History Footnote

One piece of evidence of Washington's imposing presence at the convention was his reaction upon being informed that a delegate had left notes in the hall outside the meeting room. Another delegate brought the notes to Washington, who pocketed them until the day's meeting was about to end. Then, in his sternest voice, he lectured the delegates on the importance of secrecy.

He ended by saying, "I know not whose paper it is, but here it is, let him who owns it take it." He flung the notes on his desk and walked out of the room. The guilty party, however, was unwilling to risk Washington's displeasure, and the notes were never claimed. Instead, they lay on the desk for days.

Link to Art

Signing the Constitution (1940) This famous painting by Howard Chandler Christy (1873–1952) is on display in the Capitol building, Washington, D.C. **Discuss** What impression of the delegates do you get and why? Now compare this painting with the one on page 217. How are they similar?

The Great Compromise

The debate over representation in Congress did not end with that vote. It grew more bitter day by day. Small states insisted that if they were not given a fair share of power, they would quit the convention. When the delegates' tempers seemed to be at the breaking point, Benjamin Franklin proposed beginning each day's session with a prayer asking for wisdom. As the meetings moved into July, the convention seemed close to collapse.

A committee led by Roger Sherman tried to break the deadlock. It proposed that Congress have a House of Representatives and a Senate. In the House the number of members from a state would be based on its population and elected directly by voters. In the Senate each state would have two senators elected by its legislature.

Neither side liked this plan. Madison opposed it for two weeks but finally agreed that it was better to compromise than to fail. Because the plan saved the convention, it is known as the Great Compromise.

1776–1791 Chapter 9 • **243**

Discussion

Checking Understanding

1. What was the difference between the Virginia and New Jersey plans? Which states did each plan appeal to and why? (Virginia: two houses, members elected by voters, number based on state population. New Jersey: one house, elected by legislatures, one vote per state. Virginia: states with large populations—gave them more power in Congress; New Jersey: small states—gave them equal vote.)

2. What was the Great Compromise? (Merged ideas from the two plans, with House based on state population and each state having equal vote in Senate.)

Stimulating Critical Thinking

3. Were the delegates right to keep the debates secret? (Yes: factions might have pressured or threatened delegates, making it hard to carefully debate complex issues. No: in a republic, debate should be open—earns public trust.)

Teaching the

Link to Art

Ask students whom they can identify in the painting. (Washington towers over the other delegates. Franklin sits in the forefront with Madison on his left.) **Discussion Answers:** Delegates appear dignified and rich, reflected in poses and clothing. Both paintings give Washington prominence, with a firm, heroic stance.

243

During the convenion one debate on state versus national power was over whether there should be a national army, and if so, how large it should be. Delegates weighed the need for protection against foreign invasion against the possibility that the national government would use the army to force the states to do its will, thus threatening state sovereignty. One delegate argued for limiting the size of the national army to 3,000 soldiers, so that it would be no larger than the combined forces of all the state militias. When Washington heard this proposal, he sarcastically remarked that he saw no problem with it—as long as the Constitution made it illegal for an enemy to attack the United States with more than 3,000 soldiers!

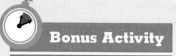

The Three-Fifths Compromise

The delegates still had to decide how many members each state would have in the House. The southern states wanted slaves to count as part of a state's population. Northern delegates objected. Their states had few slaves. Besides, they said, slaves were treated as property, not as citizens.

Still, the northern delegates knew that without southern support a new plan of government could not be approved. They finally agreed to count a slave as three-fifths of a person when determining a state's population. This settlement became known as the Three-Fifths Compromise.

A page of a draft of the Constitution has notes by Virginia's George Mason. He suggested that the President take an oath to obey the Constitution.

Compromises on Trade

Northerners and southerners also disagreed on trade issues. Most northerners wanted Congress to control trade between the states and with other countries. A national trade policy would protect their industries against foreign competition.

Southerners worried that Congress might tax their exports, such as rice and tobacco. Some also feared that the slave trade would be outlawed. In fact, ten states had already passed laws against bringing in Africans to be sold as slaves.

Many delegates, including slave owners like Madison and Washington, were urging a national ban on the slave trade. Delegates from North and South Carolina and Georgia were determined to protect it. One warned that "the true question at present is whether the southern states shall or shall not be parties to the Union."

Again, a compromise saved the convention. The northerners agreed that Congress could not end the slave trade for 20 years, until 1808. Nor could it tax exports. In exchange, the southern delegates agreed that Congress could control most other trade.

Electing the President

During that steamy summer, the delegates struggled over how to choose the President. Could ordinary voters be trusted to make a wise choice? On the other hand, could a President who was elected by Congress feel free to act independently?

After some 60 votes, the delegates agreed to create a special body called the Electoral College. Every four years each state would choose as many electors as it had members in the House and Senate. The electors would vote for a President and Vice-President. If the Electoral College could not reach agreement, the House of Representatives would choose.

In 1787 Benjamin Franklin was an old man of 81. His hands shook and he suffered from gout. In a speech that another delegate read for him because he could not stand up, he expressed his wish "that every member of the Convention . . . would with me on this occasion doubt a little of his own infallibility, and . . . put his name to this instrument."

For letters from some convention delegates, see **American Readings,** pp. 35–36.

The outlines of states on the chart's left side reflect their status in 1781, when Vermont was a separate republic. Massachusetts governed Maine (indicated by a connecting line). The outlines on the right side reflect their status in 1791, after Vermont joined the Union.

Closing the Section

Wrap-Up Activity

Preparing a Slogan

To underscore strengths of the Constitution, have students imagine "marketing" it in 1787. Ask them to prepare a slogan that stresses a benefit of the Constitution over the Articles. Refer them to the chart on this page.

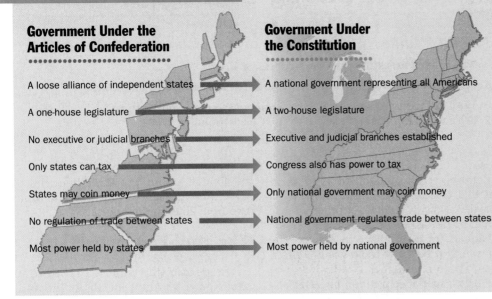

From the Articles to the Constitution

Government Under the Articles of Confederation

A loose alliance of independent states

A one-house legislature

No executive or judicial branches

Only states can tax

States may coin money

No regulation of trade between states

Most power held by states

Government Under the Constitution

A national government representing all Americans

A two-house legislature

Executive and judicial branches established

Congress also has power to tax

Only national government may coin money

National government regulates trade between states

Most power held by national government

Signing the Constitution

By summer's end, the hard work was nearly over. A final question, though, remained. Who should **ratify**—approve—the new plan of government—the people or the state legislatures?

The majority of delegates agreed that the Constitution would be ratified by the people. As Madison put it, the people were "the fountain of all power" and therefore should have the final say. Also, the delegates knew that the state legislatures probably would have rejected the new plan because it would weaken their power.

On September 17, 1787, the delegates gathered to sign the final document. Madison recorded Franklin's confident thoughts on the convention's accomplishment:

❝Doct. Franklin, looking towards the President's chair, at the back of which a rising sun happened to be painted . . .

'I have,' said he, 'often in the course of the session . . . looked at that [sun] behind the President without being able to tell whether it was rising or setting: But now, at length, I have the happiness to know that it is a rising and not a setting sun.'❞

The elderly printer saw a new day dawning for the young United States.

⭐ 2. Section Review

1. Define **legislative branch, executive branch, judicial branch,** and **ratify.**
2. How did the Constitution make the national government stronger?
3. In what sense was the Constitution a "creature of compromise"?
4. Critical Thinking How representative of "the people" was the Constitutional Convention? Explain your conclusion.

Section Review Answers

1. Definitions:
legislative branch (p. 242),
executive branch (p. 242),
judicial branch (p. 242),
ratify (p. 245)

2. Gave Congress power to tax, coin money, regulate interstate trade.

3. Reflects compromises between states—northern and southern, large and small.

4. Not representative—all wealthy, white males.

Introducing the Section

Vocabulary

amendments (p. 248)
changes to the Constitution

due process of law (p. 248)
following legal steps in a court of law

3. The Struggle for Ratification

Reading Guide

New Terms amendments, due process of law

Section Focus How the Constitution became the law of the land

1. Why did many Americans fear and oppose the new Constitution?
2. Why was a bill of rights added to the Constitution in 1791?

In October 1787, Madison wrote to Jefferson that creating the Constitution was "a miracle." Now, it seemed, another miracle would be needed to get it ratified.

Nine states would have to approve the Constitution before it could go into effect. The decision on whether to ratify was to be made by a special convention in each state. Delegates to these conventions were to be elected by the voters. Many of those delegates would be suspicious of a plan for a strong national government.

The Federalists

Supporters of ratification called themselves Federalists. They wanted to assure Americans that the Constitution would create a more effective national government, not an all-powerful one. Madison threw himself into the fight. With the help of Alexander Hamilton and John Jay, he wrote a series of newspaper articles telling how the new plan would work. These articles were later collected and published in book form as *The Federalist*.

The writers explained how the Constitution would unite the quarreling states into a single strong republic. This government would not threaten liberties because its powers were limited. The states would make most decisions affecting people's lives. Also, the writers argued, power would be divided among the three branches of government. Each would keep the other two from abusing their powers.

The Anti-Federalists

The people who opposed ratification were known as Anti-Federalists. The Anti-Federalists did not have an effective strategy for swaying public opinion. At the ratifying conventions, however, they spoke strongly of fears that the national government would have too much power over the states.

Patrick Henry warned that the Constitution "squints toward monarchy" in giving the President command of an army and navy. Anti-Federalists also warned that federal courts would swallow up state courts, and Congress would burden the people with new taxes. They complained that there was no bill of rights. Most of all, they feared that a powerful national government might bring a tyranny as bad as the British rule they had freed themselves from.

The Massachusetts Debate

Despite Anti-Federalist fears, ratification moved along smoothly at first. By early 1788, Delaware, Pennsylvania, New Jersey, Georgia, and Connecticut had all ratified. At the Massachusetts convention, however, memories of Shays' Rebellion were still

James Madison, Alexander Hamilton, and John Jay wrote 85 letters to newspapers in order to influence ratification, especially in New York. All but eight were published in the *Independent Journal,* a semi-weekly New York newspaper, under the name of "Publius." While Madison typically gets credited for the project, Hamilton actually wrote 51 of the essays. Madison wrote 29, while John Jay wrote 5. The essays were later collected and published in book form as *The Federalist.* They are still quoted regularly by the United States Supreme Court to show how the Constitution was understood by the people who helped to write it.

fresh. Many farmers who had fought alongside Shays were suspicious of a more powerful government.

(Point of View

Should the Constitution be ratified?

During the Massachusetts convention, an old farmer named Amos Singletry warned:

❝These lawyers and men of learning, and moneyed men that talk so finely . . . They expect to be the managers of this Constitution, and get all the power and all the money into their own hands. And then they will swallow up us little fellows.❞

Jonathan Smith, another delegate who was also a farmer, disagreed:

❝I have lived in a part of the country where I have known the worth of good government by the want [lack] of it. There was a black cloud [Shays' Rebellion] that rose in the east last winter and spread over the west. . . . When I saw this Constitution, I found that it was a cure for these disorders. . . . I don't think worse of the Constitution because lawyers, and moneyed men, are fond of it. . . . These lawyers, these moneyed men, these men of learning, are all embarked on the same cause with us, and we must swim or sink together.❞

Smith's words, however, did little to calm Anti-Federalist fears.

The Federalists looked to the only person who might tip the balance in their direction. That person was the state's proud governor, John Hancock. He had stayed away, in part because his feet were swollen from an attack of gout. More important, he did not want to commit himself until he saw how the delegates were leaning.

The desperate Federalists promised to support Hancock for Vice-President if the Constitution were ratified. Taking the bait, he had himself carried into the convention, his swollen feet wrapped in bandages. His support and the Federalists' promise to add a bill of rights turned the tide. The vote was close, 187 to 168, but Massachusetts became the sixth state to ratify.

Three days before the ratification vote in New York, the Federalists held a parade in New York City. A float honoring Constitutional Convention delegate Alexander Hamilton led the parade.

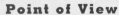

Explain that it took over 200 years for the salary amendment to be ratified. Ask: **Why do you think it took so long to ratify this amendment?**

Closing the Section

Wrap-Up Activity

"Out of Many, One"
Ask students to explain the meaning of our national motto, "E pluribus unum," and have them find the words on coins and a dollar bill. Then ask them to write a description of what the motto meant when first adopted in 1782, how that meaning changed when the Constitution was ratified, and what the motto means to us today.

Section Review
Answers

1. Definitions: *amendments* (p. 248), *due process of law* (p. 248)
2. President should not control army and navy, federal courts would swallow up state courts, Congress would overtax people, and there was no bill of rights.
3. Helped sway the vote in Massachusetts and other states.
4. Shays' Rebellion took place in Massachusetts and reflected the fears of a powerful government.

248

✳ **History Footnote**
The need for a bill of rights was by no means self-evident at the time. In fact, some feared including one because it might prove too limiting or might imply that any right not included did not exist. Madison said,

My own opinion has always been in favor of a bill of rights; provided it be so framed as not to imply powers not meant to be included in the enumeration. At the same time I have never thought the omission a material defect, nor been anxious to supply it even by subsequent amendment, for any other reason than that it is anxiously desired—by others.

∞ **Link to the Present**

The 27th Amendment The framers never expected an amendment to take over 200 years to be ratified. But it happened. In 1789 James Madison proposed that if Congress voted to change its salaries, the change should not go into effect until after an election for the House of Representatives. Voters could then reelect or reject members who approved a pay raise for themselves.

After only six states ratified it between 1789 and 1792, the amendment was almost forgotten. Congress had set no deadline, though, and in 1978 a new wave of ratifications began. By 1992, three-fourths of the states had ratified it, and the Constitution had gained a 27th amendment.

Ratification at Last

In June 1788 the Constitution was officially approved when the ninth state, New Hampshire, voted to ratify. The new government would stand little chance of survival, though, without approval by the four remaining states, which had about 40 percent of the total population.

The promise of a bill of rights finally turned the tide. Virginia ratified by the narrow vote of 89 to 79. In New York the margin was 3 votes, 30 to 27.

By late 1788, every state but one had ratified. Rhode Island remained out of the new union until 1790. Meanwhile, elections were held for the first Congress. The Electoral College also met and elected George Washington President and John Adams Vice-President.

The Bill of Rights

In 1789 Representative James Madison urged Congress to fulfill the Federalists' promise to add a bill of rights. He then put forward a list of 12 **amendments,** which are changes to the Constitution.

Under the Constitution, three-fourths of the states must ratify an amendment before it can become law. The states rejected the first two amendments. One would have limited the size of Congress, and the other would have limited when members of Congress could raise their salaries. Both were considered unnecessary. By 1791, the states had approved the other ten, which together form the Bill of Rights.

The Bill of Rights guarantees our most cherished freedoms, such as the freedoms of speech, the press, assembly, and worship. It provides legal rights such as trial by jury. It also prohibits the government from taking away "life, liberty, or property" without **due process of law,** which means following legal steps in a court of law. The full text of the Bill of Rights is on pages R59–R62.

When Madison first proposed the Bill of Rights, some people called them useless "paper barriers" against abuses of power. These protections, though, have proved far stronger than Madison had hoped.

⭐ ## 3. Section Review

1. Define **amendments** and **due process of law.**
2. What arguments did Anti-Federalists make against the Constitution?
3. Why did the promise to add a bill of rights help win ratification?
4. **Critical Thinking** The Federalists saw the debate in Massachusetts as a key test of whether the Constitution would be ratified. Why do you think they felt this way?

(Answers continued from side margin)
the decision directly limits rights of students like her. (b) B might agree because as a school administrator he is concerned with maintaining discipline and authority. D might agree because he bears overall responsibility for the school.

3. Sources A and C would likely favor few, if any, limits because they stress preserving rights. B and D would subordinate those freedoms to the goal of educating students.

4. Opinions will vary. Students might be most likely to agree with a fellow student. Answers should reflect awareness of how backgrounds influence opinions.

For further application, have students do the Applying Skills activity in the Chapter Survey (p. 254).

If students need to review the skill, use the Skills Development transparency and activity in the **Chapter Resources Binder**, pp. 71–72.

Skill Lab

Thinking Critically
Point of View

How does the First Amendment apply to students? In 1969 the Supreme Court declared, "It can hardly be argued that either students or teachers shed their constitutional rights to freedom of speech or expression at the schoolhouse gate." But in a 1988 case the Court ruled that schools can censor student publications if an educational purpose is served. People bring a variety of beliefs and values to this continuing debate.

Skill Tips

Ask yourself:
• What do I know about the person's background (age, culture, social position, beliefs)?
• What does the person seem to think is important or not?
• How might the person's background affect how he or she feels?
• Who might feel differently? Why?

Question to Investigate

How much freedom should writers and editors of student newspapers have?

Procedure

Different people often see and report the same thing differently. Therefore, historians and others who want to understand history must first understand **point of view**—the background or position from which a person observes something. Study the Skill Tips. Then read the sources and answer the following questions.

❶ Compare the opinions.
a. Which ones agree with the 1988 Supreme Court decision? Why?
b. Which ones disagree? Why?

❷ Ask yourself how personal backgrounds might affect the opinions.
a. Put yourself in the shoes of one of the persons who disagrees with the decision. Why might that person feel this way?
b. Put yourself in the shoes of one of the persons who agrees with the decision. Why might that person feel this way?

❸ The Question to Investigate asks for an opinion. What answer do you think each person would give? Explain.

❹ Which person do you agree with the most? The least? How do you think your own background affects your opinion?

Sources to Use

A "This [1988 Supreme Court] decision cuts the First Amendment legs off the student press."

Paul McMasters, professional journalist

B "The authority of boards of education would have been threatened if this [1988 Supreme Court] case had been lost."

Francis Huss, school superintendent

C "We are human beings, we have rights—they must not be ignored."

Priscilla Marco, student journalist

D "First Amendment rights and censorship have nothing whatsoever to do with putting out a student newspaper. It's a matter of teaching students to write well and responsibly."

Dr. Howard Hurwitz, school principal

Introducing the Skill Lab

Discuss the different meanings of the term *point of view*, noting that it can be used to mean "opinion" but that in this Skill Lab it refers to a person's standpoint or background. Tell students that a point of view is like a pair of binoculars or a telescope, serving as a lens through which a person sees the world. It can clarify some aspects of what is observed and distort others. It can lead a person to focus on certain aspects of an issue or event and to ignore or pay less attention to others.

Skill Lab
Answers

1. (a) Source B agrees because he thinks that the authority of school boards would have been threatened if no limits were placed on school newspapers. D agrees with the Court that the school must consider the educational effect of school newspapers. (b) Source A disagrees, seeing the decision as a basic threat to freedom of the press. C disagrees, seeing the decision as a threat to basic human rights.

2. (a) Source A might disagree because restricting freedom of the press threatens his career as a journalist. C might disagree because

(Answers continued in top margin)

![star graphic]

Introducing the Section

Vocabulary

federalism (p. 251) the division of power between the states and the national government

separation of powers (p. 252) the division of government power among legislative, executive, and judicial branches

checks and balances (p. 252) system by which each branch of government can check the power of the other two

Warm-Up Activity

An Amendment Time Line

By drawing a time line identifying the years in which each amendment to the Constitution was passed, students can note the general stability and endurance of the Constitution. Have students draw a time line divided into decades beginning with the 1790s and write each amendment in the appropriate place on the time line. Help students analyze the time line and draw conclusions about the Constitution's stability.

Geography Question of the Day

Provide students with an unlabeled map of the United States and ask them to label it, showing which states sent delegates to the original Congress and which states were added as time went on.

Section Objectives

★ Describe how the Constitution has met the needs of changing times.

★ Explain how power is divided between the federal and state governments and among the three federal branches.

★ Describe how the system of checks and balances works.

Teaching Resources

Take-Home Planner 3, pp. 18–25

Chapter Resources Binder

  Study Guide, p. 68

  Reinforcement, pp. 69–70

  Skills Development

Geography Extensions

American Readings

Using Historical Documents

Transparency Activities

Chapter and Unit Tests, pp. 53–56

4. An Enduring Framework

Reading Guide

New Terms federalism, separation of powers, checks and balances

Section Focus The ideas that have made the Constitution an enduring framework of government

1. How has the Constitution been able to meet the needs of changing times?
2. How is power divided between the federal and state governments and among the three branches of the federal government?
3. How does the system of checks and balances work?

You will find the full text of the Constitution on pages R34–R73.

When the Constitutional Convention ended, a woman asked its oldest delegate, "What kind of government have you given us, Dr. Franklin?" Replied Franklin, "A Republic, Madame, if you can keep it." A republic is a government run by representatives elected by the people. It is based on the idea of popular sovereignty—letting the people rule.

Like many Americans, Franklin was not at all sure that such a government could last. Madison hoped it would "still be around when the nation's population neared 200 million." Yet even he had his doubts. In fact, the United States has survived more than 200 years of growth and change. No other nation on earth has had such an enduring framework of government.

Federalism

Powers of National Government	Shared Powers	Powers of State Governments
• Maintain army and navy	• Enforce laws	• Conduct elections
• Declare war	• Establish courts	• Establish schools
• Coin money	• Borrow money	• Regulate businesses within the state
• Regulate trade between states and with foreign nations	• Protect the health and safety of the people	• Establish local governments
• Make all laws necessary for carrying out delegated powers	• Build roads	• Regulate marriages
	• Collect taxes	• Assume other powers not given to the national government or denied to the states

Tips for Teaching

Students with Limited English
Students may lack the knowledge to analyze the Venn diagram on page 250 and the flow chart on page 252. Explain their structures and purposes. You may wish to draw an empty Venn diagram and have students help write entries. Using self-stick notes to cover portions of the flow chart may help students identify checks

and balances. For example, place notes over all entries except those between the executive and legislative branches. Then explain how these two branches check each other. Move the notes and discuss the checks between the executive and judicial branches, and so on.

Hands-On *HISTORY*

Proposing an amendment More than 10,000 ideas for amendments to the Constitution have been proposed. Very few have even made it past Congress. Even when Congress approves an amendment, ratification is far from assured. The failure of the Equal Rights Amendment (ERA) is an example.

Any citizen or group of citizens may propose an amendment. One recent proposal is to allow prayer in public schools. Another is to require the federal government to balance its budget. The test for these and other ideas is whether they can gain widespread support.

ERA demonstration

Activity Test your idea for an amendment.

❶ Write the amendment.

❷ Explain why you think it could be ratified.

❸ Read your proposal to 12 people old enough to vote. Ask if each would support it and why.

❹ If fewer than 9 supported it, explain how you would reword it to gain more support.

A Flexible Plan

The men who framed, or wrote, the Constitution knew that they could not imagine every problem that might arise. Therefore, they made the government flexible enough to adapt to new situations.

One way the Constitution is flexible is that it can be amended. The framers purposely made the amendment process difficult, though, so that people would have to think carefully about making changes. Thousands of proposals for amendments have been brought before Congress, but only 27 have been approved.

The framers also provided flexibility by stating the purposes and powers of the government in broad terms instead of going into detail. For example, the Constitution says that one of the purposes of the government is "to establish justice." Just how to do that is left up to Congress.

Likewise, the Constitution gives Congress the power "to make all laws which shall be

necessary and proper" to carry out the purposes of government. This broad power is sometimes called the "elastic clause" because it can be stretched to fit changing needs over time.

While giving the government elbowroom to carry out its duties, the Constitution also limits the government's powers. Woven throughout the document are three main principles that keep the government from becoming too powerful. These principles are federalism, separation of powers, and checks and balances.

A Federal System

The division of power between the states and the national government is known as **federalism.** Madison believed that the national government had to have more power than the states if the nation were to survive. He also knew that most people felt a deep loyalty to their states and would not support a plan that stripped state governments of

Developing the Section

Discussion

Checking Understanding

1. In what ways is our Constitution flexible? (It can be amended, and principles are stated in broad terms.)

Stimulating Critical Thinking

2. The Constitution is designed to provide a government that is "by the people, for the people." Do you think that it has been successful? (Students might note that women and minorities have had to fight for equal rights or opportunities.)

Teaching the Hands-On *HISTORY*

Remind students that most proposed amendments today have time limits in which they must be ratified. Ask: **Why do you think time limits have been imposed? Should they have been imposed?** Suggest that students learn more about an amendment that has been proposed recently, researching the arguments for and against the amendment.

See the Study Guide activity in the **Chapter Resources Binder,** p. 68.

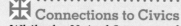

Connections to Civics

While the United States may be the oldest republic still in existence today, it is not the longest enduring or the first. Rome was declared a republic in 509 B.C., after defeating the Etruscans. While its government was vastly different from ours, the ideas for our three-branch system are loosely based on the Roman Republic. The word *senate* comes from the Roman council of 300 senators, who acted as an advisory body to the chief executive. The Roman Republic, which lasted for almost 400 years, ended in 27 B.C. when Augustus declared himself emperor.

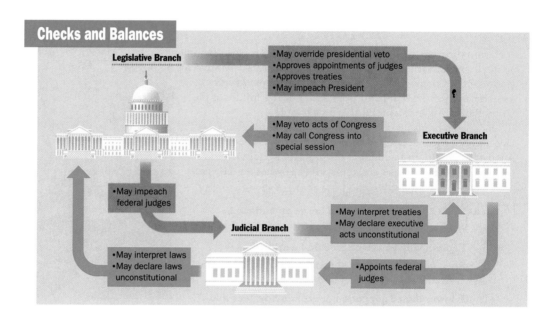

Checks and Balances

Legislative Branch
- May override presidential veto
- Approves appointments of judges
- Approves treaties
- May impeach President

Executive Branch
- May veto acts of Congress
- May call Congress into special session

Judicial Branch
- May impeach federal judges
- May interpret treaties
- May declare executive acts unconstitutional
- May interpret laws
- May declare laws unconstitutional
- Appoints federal judges

their power. The solution was to create a federal system that divides power between the state and national levels.

Some powers belong only to the national, or federal, government, such as powers to declare war or coin money. All federal powers are listed in the Constitution. Other powers are shared by the federal and state governments, such as the powers to levy taxes and set up court systems.

Some powers belong to the states alone. Only the states can set up public school systems. Marriage and divorce laws are made by state legislatures, not by Congress. Most criminal laws are state laws. Such laws may differ from state to state, depending on local needs, attitudes, and conditions.

Separation of Powers

The division of government power among legislative, executive, and judicial branches is called **separation of powers.** Only Congress makes the laws, only the executive branch enforces them, and only the courts have the final say in interpreting them. As a result, no one branch of government can become too powerful.

The principle of separation of powers was first proposed in 1748 by the Baron de Montesquieu, a well-known French philosopher. The idea was familiar to most Americans in 1787 and was already included in several state constitutions.

Montesquieu argued that if the same person or group had all the power to make, enforce, and judge the laws, the result was likely to be tyranny. If these powers were separated, then one branch could act as a brake on the other two if they began to misuse their powers.

Checks and Balances

The system by which each branch of government can check—limit—the power of the other two is called **checks and balances.** The President, for example, can check the lawmaking power of Congress by vetoing—refusing to approve—a law he thinks unwise or unfair. Congress can check

History Footnote
The power of the Supreme Court to declare acts of Congress unconstitutional was established in 1803 in the *Marbury* v. *Madison* case. President John Adams had appointed William Marbury justice of the peace of the District of Columbia but failed to deliver the signed document before the end of his term. Madison, the new secretary of state, refused to deliver the commission, and Marbury sued him in the Supreme Court. Chief Justice John Marshall declared that the act giving Marbury the right to sue in the Supreme Court was in violation of Article 3 of the Constitution, which states that only cases involving states and foreign ambassadors can be brought before the Supreme Court. Marshall's decision established the precedent of judicial review.

the President's veto power by overriding a veto with a two-thirds vote of both houses. The Supreme Court can check both the President and Congress by declaring their actions unconstitutional, that is, in violation of the Constitution.

The system of checks and balances was designed to control government power. As Madison wrote in *The Federalist*:

❝If men were angels, no government would be necessary. If angels were to govern men, . . . [no] controls on government would be necessary. . . . You must first enable the government to control the governed; and in the next place, oblige [force] it to control itself.❞

Because the Constitution has provided a flexible framework for controlling both the people who govern and the people who are being governed, it has served the American people long and well.

4. Section Review

1. Define **federalism, separation of powers,** and **checks and balances.**
2. What makes the Constitution flexible?
3. Why did the framers provide for separation of powers and for checks and balances?
4. Critical Thinking What do you think are some advantages and disadvantages of a federal system?

Why We Remember

Creating the Constitution

Despite his prediction that he would die young, James Madison lived to the ripe old age of 85. During his life, he hid away his notes on the Constitutional Convention. They were not published until after his death in 1836. Only then did Americans learn what a close call the creation of the Constitution had been and how often the convention had been held together by "no more than the strength of a hair."

Today we study and remember the creation of the Constitution for two reasons. First, as citizens we need to understand how our government works. To do this, it helps to know a bit about the hopes, fears, and beliefs of the people who created the framework for the federal government.

Second, we remember the framing of the Constitution because it is a written plan of self-government by the people. For thousands of years, nations had been built by the strong and ruled by force. In 1787 Americans set out to test the idea that a nation could be built on the consent of the people. That their experiment succeeded at all is remarkable. That it succeeded so well is truly amazing.

Closing the Section

Wrap-Up Activity

Expressing Opinion

Students determine what aspect of the Constitution is most important to them as they express opinions about the Constitution. Have students write a brief opinion statement expressing what aspect of the Constitution—federalism, separation of powers, or checks and balances—is most important to them, and why.

Section Review
Answers

1. Definitions: *federalism* (p. 251), *separation of powers* (p. 252), *checks and balances* (p. 252)

2. It can be amended, and gives Congress the power to make necessary laws.

3. To control government power and prevent tyranny.

4. Advantages: distributes power, which makes abuse less likely, allows some local control of government; disadvantages: lines of authority may not be clear; conflicting policies of state and national governments, differing laws in different states.

To check understanding of "Why We Remember," assign Thinking Critically question 3 on student page 254.

Reviewing Vocabulary

Definitions are found
on these pages:
constitution (p. 234),
republic (p. 234),
bill of rights (p. 234),
confederation (p. 234),
depression (p. 238),
legislative branch (p. 242),
executive branch (p. 242),
judicial branch (p. 242),
ratify (p. 245),
amendments (p. 248),
due process of law (p. 248),
federalism (p. 251),
separation of powers (p. 252),
checks and balances (p. 252).

Reviewing Main Ideas

1. Congress had the right
to raise an army and a navy,
control foreign affairs, coin
money, and set up a postal
system. It could not raise
taxes or regulate trade,
which meant that it did
not have enough money,
and could not settle states'
disputes.

2. The Virginia Plan gave
the national government
real authority as opposed
to the lack of authority of
the loose alliance of states
set up by the Articles.

3. Answers will vary.
Students should show an
understanding of the Great
Compromise, the Three-
Fifths Compromise, or
the compromise on trade.

4. They feared the national
government would have
too much power.

5. They agreed so that
Massachusetts would ratify.

6. The Constitution can
be amended, and principles
and powers of government
are stated in broad terms.

7. Government power is
divided among the legislative, executive, and judicial
branches, and each branch
can check the power of the
other two.

(Answers continued in top margin)

Thinking Critically

1. Agree: students may cite evidence such
as that states taxed goods from other states,
states printed their own money, and states
quarreled over boundaries. Disagree: they
may state that Congress could raise an army
and a navy, coin money, and set up a postal
system. It also developed a plan for managing western lands.

2. Answers are likely to show an understanding of how publicity might have
affected delegates' ability to compromise,
or how publicity may have led delegates
to form decisions based on public reaction
to the proceedings.

3. In a world full of governments that ruled
by force, the delegates to the Constitutional
Convention created a framework for a

Chapter Survey ★

Reviewing Vocabulary

Define the following terms.

1. constitution
2. republic
3. bill of rights
4. confederation
5. depression
6. legislative branch
7. executive branch
8. judicial branch
9. ratify
10. amendments
11. due process of law
12. federalism
13. separation of powers
14. checks and balances

Reviewing Main Ideas

1. What powers did Congress have under
the Articles of Confederation? What powers
did it lack? List two results of Congress's
lack of power.
2. How did the Virginia Plan differ from
the Articles of Confederation?
3. Describe one of the compromises that
the delegates made at the Constitutional
Convention.
4. What did Anti-Federalists fear would
happen under the new Constitution?
5. Why did the Federalists promise to add
a bill of rights to the Constitution?
6. Describe one way in which the
Constitution makes the government
flexible enough to adapt to new situations.
7. How did the framers try to ensure that
no one branch of the federal government
could become too powerful?

Thinking Critically

1. **Application** Agree or disagree with
this statement: Under the Articles of Confederation, the United States was really
13 nations. Support your answer with
evidence from the chapter.
2. **Synthesis** Suppose delegates to the
Constitutional Convention had leaked
information about their discussions to
newspaper writers. What might have
happened as a result?
3. **Why We Remember: Analysis** In
what way was the Constitution an experiment? Why do you think this experiment
was important?

Applying Skills

Point of view Write about a recent
freedom of speech issue or situation that
several people you know reacted to or
described in different ways. Then, recalling
what you learned about point of view in
the Skill Lab on page 249, write responses
to the following questions:
1. How do these people's points of view,
or backgrounds, differ?
2. How might these differences have
affected their reactions or descriptions?

History Mystery

The "Rising Sun Chair"
Answer the History Mystery on
page 231. Why do you think this
chair became an important symbol of
the Constitutional Convention? Do you
think that symbol is as meaningful today
as it was to Franklin and others of his
time? Explain.

Writing in Your History Journal

1. Keys to History
a. The time line on pages 230–231
has seven Keys to History. In your
journal, describe why each one is
important to know about.
b. Choose one of the events on the time
line. Imagine yourself as someone who
was alive when the event occurred. Write
a diary entry as that person, describing
your reactions to the event.

government whose power was limited by the people. The experiment was important because it offered the chance for people to have a government that worked in their interests, rather than one in whose interests the people worked.

Applying Skills

Students should be able to state why they think people feel as they do based on differences in their backgrounds or points of view.

History Mystery

Franklin's speech summarizing the convention made the "Rising Sun Chair" famous. Students should understand that a rising sun is a symbol for new beginnings. They should be able to cite reasons whether the symbol is relevant today.

(Answers continued in side margin)

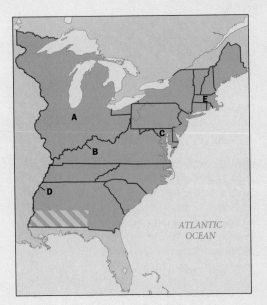

ATLANTIC OCEAN

Reviewing Geography

1. The letters on the map represent a territory, two rivers, and two states. Write the name of each.

2. Geographic Thinking The survey system used in the Northwest Territory was later used in states and territories across the nation. Look at the map on pages R6–R7. Compare the boundaries of states west of the Appalachian Mountains—especially those west of the Mississippi River—with those of eastern states. What main difference do you see, and how do you account for it? Describe the way in which fields, roads, and communities are laid out where you live, and try to account for that.

2. James Madison In your journal, write a brief description of a plot for a movie about Madison titled *The Comeback Kid*. Your plot should begin with Madison's experiences as a young boy and end with his involvement as a delegate to the Constitutional Convention.

3. Citizenship Read the Bill of Rights on pages R59–R62. Which of the rights in the first ten amendments is most important to you? Why? Write your responses in your journal.

Alternative Assessment

Creating a Constitution exhibit With a partner or a small group, create an exhibit about the Constitution for fifth grade students. Your exhibit should tell and show the following:
• what led to the call for a Constitutional Convention
• what happened during the Constitutional Convention

• what the main features of the Constitution are
• how the Constitution affects the lives of Americans today

Your exhibit might include posters, flowcharts, drawings, audiotapes, and pictures and articles you have copied or cut out of newspapers and magazines.

Start with the information that is presented in this chapter and then do additional research as needed. You might interview some relatives, neighbors, and friends about what the Constitution means to them.

Your work will be evaluated on the following criteria:
• it covers a variety of topics related to the Constitution
• it presents accurate information about the Constitution
• it presents the information in ways that are understandable and motivating to younger students

Writing in Your History Journal

1. (a) Explanations should be similar to the time line notes on teacher pages 230–231. (b) Students' diary entries should show an understanding of the chapter's main ideas.

2. Students should be able to show how Madison overcame sickness and depression to become a major contributor as a delegate to the convention.

3. Students should be able to show how the right they choose relates to their own lives in specific ways.

Reviewing Geography

1. (A) Northwest Territory, (B) Ohio River, (C) Maryland, (D) Mississippi River, (E) Massachusetts

2. Students may note that the boundaries of the western states are straighter than those of eastern states. The survey system established by the Land Ordinance may account for this regularity. Students' communities may or may not be laid out in the grid system established by the Land Ordinance, depending on where they live.

Alternative Assessment

Teacher's Take-Home Planner 3, p. 21, includes suggestions and scoring rubrics for the Alternative Assessment activity.

Unit Survey

Making Connections

Answers

1. The colonies came into conflict over settling the backcountry and expanding the fur trade. They overcame these conflicts and began to work together in response to repression by Britain. The lasting effect was that colonists began to support one another to work for common interests.

2. Adams meant the colonists had already decided on and begun working for independence from British rule long before the war. Loyalists may have disagreed because of their allegiance to Britain.

3. Although answers may vary, students may identify the refusal of all states to support the Albany Plan, the adoption of the Articles of Confederation, and the Anti-Federalist opposition to the ratification of the Constitution.

Teaching the

Unit Project

Remind students to use what they know about creating rhythm in poetry or to use the tune of a song they already know when writing their lyrics. Students may want to write a chorus first. Some possibilities for tunes are "Old MacDonald Had a Farm," "Home on the Range," "This Land is Your Land," and "Battle Hymn of the Republic."

Evaluation Criteria

The project can be evaluated according to the criteria listed below, using a scale for each: 4 = exemplary, 3 = good, 2 = adequate, 1 = poor. *(Continued in top margin)*

Completing the task The song is planned carefully and taught to classmates.

Knowing content The song contains accurate information about the topic.

Thinking critically Students show good judgment in tailoring the lyrics to achieve the effect.

Communicating ideas The song's purpose is clearly expressed in the lyrics.

Thinking It Over
Students may cite strong rhythm and meaningful lyrics as qualities that set songs apart. Opinions about how Patriots or Loyalists might react to the song would depend in part on the position students take in their song.

Unit Survey

Making Connections

Review

1. What caused conflicts between the colonies? What forces and events drove the colonies to work together? Did those forces and events have a lasting effect on the conflicts between the colonies? Explain.
2. In 1818 John Adams said, "The Revolution was effected [achieved] before the war commenced [began]. The Revolution was in the minds and hearts of the people." What do you think Adams meant? Who might have disagreed with him and why?
3. "From the beginning of the French and Indian War through ratification of the Constitution, many Americans resisted the creation of a strong central government." Support that statement with three specific examples from the unit.

Linking History, Language Arts, and Music

Project

Creating a Patriotic Song

First, then, throw aside your topknots of pride,
Wear none but your own country linen,
Of Economy boast, let your pride be the most,
To show clothes of your own make and spinning.

Those are the lyrics to part of a song that the Daughters of Liberty sang during the boycott of British goods. Throughout the revolutionary period, Americans wrote and sang songs to protest British rule, to rally their spirits, and to honor the memory of important events. Imagine yourself as part of a colonial songwriting team. You and your partner want to create a song that supports the Patriot cause.

Project Steps

Work with a partner to complete the following steps.

❶ Plan to write a song (a) to protest a British action against the colonies, (b) to rally the Continental Army's spirits when things look grim during the war, or (c) to

honor the memory of a major event of the period. Choose the specific topic or event for your song.

❷ Decide what to do about a tune for your song. You may write the tune yourself or use a tune from either an existing modern song or a historical one like "Yankee Doodle."

❸ Write the lyrics for the song. Keep the specific purpose of the song in mind; also remember that you are writing for the Patriots. Make sure the lyrics and the tune work together.

❹ Teach the song to your classmates. Hand out copies of the song, or write it on the board or on a transparency for display. You might first sing the song or play a tape of yourselves singing it.

Thinking It Over Songs can have strong effects on our emotions. What qualities set a powerful song apart from a song that fails to move us? How might the Patriots have felt when they heard your song? How might the Loyalists have felt?

Objectives

★ Compare and contrast Charles Bird King's painting with Inman's copy.

★ Describe the kind of information historians find in paintings, lithographs, and photographs.

★ Compare and contrast the kinds of information from pictures with the information contained in descriptions and other types of text.

How Do We Know?

Young Omahaw, War Eagle, Little Missouri, and Pawnees, (1821), by Charles Bird King

Scholar's Tool Kit

Pictures

Imagine walking down the dusty, unpaved streets of Washington, D.C., in the early 1800s and coming upon groups of Indians, some in buckskins and some in suits and ties. Indian leaders often visited Washington to meet with government officials. In November 1821 a delegation of Plains Indians—Pawnees, Omahas, Kansas, Otos, and Missouris—arrived. Officials showed them the sights and gave them friendship medals bearing the likeness of President James Monroe.

One official was particularly eager to meet the visitors. He was Thomas McKenney, superintendent of Indian trade, and later the head of the Bureau of Indian Affairs. Because McKenney believed that settlers were destroying the Indians' ways of life, he was trying to preserve information about them. He collected clothing, weapons, samples of medicines, and other objects Indians used.

"Perfect Likenesses"

McKenney also wanted a record of how the Indians looked and dressed. In the days before photography, drawings and paintings were the usual way to record how people looked. So McKenney persuaded the delegates to have their portraits painted. He asked artist Charles Bird King to make "perfect likenesses," showing not only the faces of his subjects, but also their clothing and the way they wore their hair. King made many paintings of the Plains delegation. He sent a portrait home with each delegate and McKenney kept eight to hang in his office. These were the first of many paintings McKenney would collect.

Introducing
How Do We Know?

Pictures

In this Scholar's Tool Kit students learn how pictures are an important source of historical information. The examples are paintings by Charles Bird King of Plains Indians who came to Washington, D.C., in the early 1800s, and the lithographs that were made from them. Students will read how lithographs are made and how they helped spread information more widely in the 1800s.

Setting the Stage
Activity

Making "Perfect Likenesses"

To underscore the importance of visual records, have students draw and describe classroom objects. Divide the class into groups of three. Give one student five minutes to make a drawing of something in the classroom, such as another student, a plant, a desk, or someone's shoe. As the drawing is made, have another student write a description of the same thing. Then have the third student make a copy of the first student's drawing. Discuss as a class how the two drawings differ and what kinds of information the descriptions and the drawings contain. Ask what someone could learn from the drawing that they could not learn from the description.

1. Students should see that Inman's copy is not a perfect likeness and may argue that since King's painting was done from life it could be trusted more.

2. Answers may vary, but students may see that a lithograph would give information about an Indian's dress and objects he is wearing that makes them easier to picture than information from a description would.

3. King's portraits reflect the fact that the Indians are handsome, proud, and dignified. The fact that King's goal was to create "perfect likenesses" makes it likely that the paintings are reliable sources.

✳ **History Footnote**
Henry Inman was one of the founders of the National Academy of Design. Among the portraits he painted were those of Chief Justice John Marshall, President Martin Van Buren, naturalist John James Audubon, author Nathaniel Hawthorne, nurse Clara Barton, and poet William Wordsworth. Inman also worked with lithography.

❓ Critical Thinking

1. Compare the portrait with the lithograph. Do you think the lithograph is a "perfect likeness"? Which would you trust more?

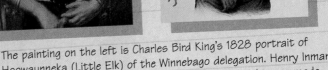

The painting on the left is Charles Bird King's 1828 portrait of Hoowaunneka (Little Elk) of the Winnebago delegation. Henry Inman painted a copy, from which the lithograph on the right was made.

McKenney thought of the paintings as tools for future historians. He also saw them as a way to get rich. McKenney knew that people all over the world were curious about American Indians. His idea was to publish copies of the paintings in books and sell the books here and in Europe.

Luckily for McKenney, a new printing method called *lithography* had come to the United States from Europe in 1818. Pictures made by this process are called *lithographs*. Lithography was quicker and cheaper than older methods of printing pictures. Now even ordinary people could afford prints of paintings, drawings, and maps.

The German inventor of lithography based the process on the fact that grease and water do not mix. First he drew a picture on a stone with a greasy crayon. Then he spread water on the stone. The water dampened the stone but not the crayon lines. Next he smeared greasy ink on the stone. The ink did not stick to the damp parts of the stone, but it did stick to the crayon. Finally the lithographer pressed heavy paper onto the stone. The picture printed on the paper. Because the printer could use only one color of ink at a time, the print was usually black. Someone would then paint the colors on it by hand.

❓ Critical Thinking

2. If you were trying to find out about one of the Indians who visited Washington, what kind of information could you gain from a lithograph that you might not gain from a written description?

To make lithographs of Charles Bird King's paintings, McKenney hired another artist, Henry Inman, to copy the paintings. Next, a lithograph artist copied each of Inman's copies onto a stone.

Lithography provided a pictorial record of American life during the 1800s. The partnership firm of Nathaniel Currier and James Ives produced thousands of lithographs. Many of the lithographs were hand-colored by women working in a production line. Each woman applied a separate color to a print. Currier and Ives lithographs were extremely popular throughout the United States. Historians now use prints of their lithographs as pictorial evidence of everyday American customs, manners, and sports as well as important historical events of the middle and late 1800s.

When the 20 volumes of the *History of the Indian Tribes of North America* were published between 1834 and 1844, they included hand-colored lithographs of 120 Indians. McKenney advertised the pictures as "perfect likenesses."

A Lasting Record

Meanwhile, many of the original paintings were sent to the Smithsonian Institution, where, tragically, a fire destroyed most of them in 1865. Whether or not McKenney's lithographs are perfect likenesses, historians are lucky they exist. Inman's copies and McKenney's lithographs are now the only portraits we have of some of the most famous Indians who lived in the early 1800s.

Historians and anthropologists use the lithographs as a valuable source of information. A historian might want to see, for example, which Indians were awarded medals. An anthropologist might compare the clothing worn by members of different tribes.

In the mid-1800s, photography began to take the place of lithography as a way of copying works of art. For example, the pictures of paintings you see in this book are photographs of the paintings. Like lithographs, photographs give us information about people, places, events, and works of art we would not otherwise see. Images captured today in photographs, as well as on film and videotape, will be data for historians in the future.

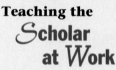

Critical Thinking

3. An artist's point of view affects how he or she portrays a subject. What attitudes did King express? Are King's paintings a reliable source of information?

Scholar at Work

As a class, choose a building, person, or event in your community. Work with a partner to draw a detailed picture of the subject. Then display the class's pictures. With your partner, imagine that you are historians 100 years from now. What questions would you ask yourselves about the pictures? Write a brief report explaining what you might learn. What other sources of information might you check?

Discussion

Checking Understanding

1. How is a lithograph made? (A drawing is made on a stone with a greasy crayon. The stone is dampened and covered with ink, which sticks to the crayoned picture. Then heavy paper is pressed on the stone, and the inked picture is printed on the paper.)

2. What happened to most of Charles Bird King's paintings of Indians? (They were destroyed in a fire at the Smithsonian Institution in 1865.)

3. How do we know about these destroyed paintings? (Copies were made of them, and lithographs were made of the copies and published in Thomas McKenney's book *History of the Indian Tribes of North America*.)

Teaching the Scholar at Work

Give students photographs, news descriptions, and any other reports available about the building, person, or event the class chooses. You might pair more competent artists with less competent ones or have groups of students work on the detailed pictures together.

Introducing the Unit

A View of New Orleans Taken from the Plantation of Marigny, November, 1803

This painting celebrates the acquisition of New Orleans with the Louisiana Purchase of 1803. That landmark event doubled the size of the United States and ushered in an era of westward expansion and economic development.

Throughout the unit, students will explore ways in which the political leaders and citizens of the emerging United States laid a foundation for growth, defining the direction the nation would take for generations to come.

Teaching the
Hands-On → HISTORY

Brainstorm with students to create a list of characteristics of the community pictured. Modes of transportation, buildings, clothing, and natural resources may all be clues to economic opportunities. Have students work in small groups to plan their businesses. Plans may include sketches as well as written descriptions of the businesses and students' reasons for selecting them. When plans are complete, have a "town meeting." Invite each group to present ideas to the community to elicit support. Ask students to combine the best ideas from each group.

Unit Overview

Washington and Adams were faced with organizing a new government, while avoiding conflicts abroad and at home. Though disagreements led to the birth of parties, the election of 1800 proved the nation's ability to solve differences peaceably.

Internal and international strife continued under Jefferson and Madison. The Supreme Court established judicial review with the *Marbury* v. *Madison* case. The United States went to war with Britain in the War of 1812.

The early 1800s saw the growth of industry and expansion of transportation links. The United States announced the Monroe Doctrine in the hope of protecting American interests in the Western Hemisphere. The Missouri Compromise tried to resolve differences about slavery as the nation expanded.

1789–1824

Unit 4

Chapters

10. **The First Years of the Republic**

11. **The Jefferson Era**

12. **The Confident Years**

Hands-On → HISTORY

Activity

At the left of this view of New Orleans in 1803, you can see the Mississippi River. Suppose that it is 1803 and you want to start a business. You have just inherited the piece of land in the foreground—the one with the three cows in it. Examine the whole scene for clues to economic opportunities in the city, then decide what business to put on your land. Draw a plan for your business and write a statement explaining why you expect it to be successful.

A View of New Orleans Taken from the Plantation of Marigny, November, 1803 (detail)
by Boqueto de Woieseri

✳ History Footnote

French artist John L. Boqueta de Woieseri arrived in New Orleans in May 1803, the month the Louisiana Purchase agreement was signed. His painting, the first known view of New Orleans as an American city, reflects a mood of prosperity and expansion. He eventually published a set of aquatint engravings of six cities, titled *A View of the First Cities of the United States.*

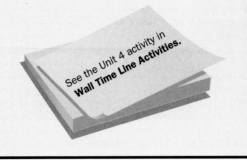

See the Unit 4 activity in **Wall Time Line Activities.**

The Early Years

☆EVERY☆   ☆THING☆   ☆PROSPERS☆

Discussion

Checking Understanding

1. What elements in the painting show that it depicts an earlier time? (Horse-drawn carriages, ships with sails, style of dress, and a contrast with the size of New Orleans today.)

2. What does the bird represent? (The United States)

Stimulating Critical Thinking

3. How would this painting be different if it had been painted by an Indian at that time? (Might focus on the loss of land to settlers or the effect of development on natural resources.)

For an in-depth unit project on "inventions that built America," see **Unit Interdisciplinary Projects,** pp. 19–28.

10 The First Years of the Republic
1789–1801

Chapter Planning Guide

Section	Student Text	Teacher's Edition Activities
Opener and Story pp. 262–265	**Keys to History Time Line** **History Mystery** Beginning the Story with **Abigail Adams**	**Setting the Stage Activity** Examining Attitudes Toward Women, p. 264
1 The First Difficult Years pp. 266–271	**Link to Art** The Federal style, p. 268 **Geography Lab** Reading a Population Density Map, p. 271	**Warm-Up Activity** Defining Government's Role, p. 266 **Geography Question of the Day,** p. 266 **Section Activity** Editorial Cartoons, p. 267 **Bonus Activity** Tariff Posters, p. 269 **Wrap-Up Activity** Role-Playing, p. 270
2 Conflicts at Home and Abroad pp. 272–278	**World Link** Kamehameha unifies Hawaii, p. 275 **Reading Maps** Western Settlement 1795, p. 277	**Warm-Up Activity** Negotiating Conflict, p. 272 **Geography Question of the Day,** p. 272 **Section Activity** Planning a Newscast, p. 276 **Bonus Activity** Expressing Point of View in Art, p. 274 **Wrap-Up Activity** Writing a Diary, p. 278
3 The Birth of Political Parties pp. 279–285	**Link to the Present** New Columbia?, p. 282 **Point of View** Are there limits to freedom of the press?, p. 282 **Hands-On History** Designing political party symbols, p. 283 **Skill Lab** Cause and Effect, p. 285	**Warm-Up Activity** Describing Today's Political Parties, p. 279 **Geography Question of the Day,** p. 279 **Section Activity** Taking a Poll, p. 280 **Bonus Activity** Writing a Speech, p. 282 **Wrap-Up Activity** Writing a Slogan, p. 284
Evaluation	☑ **Section 1 Review,** p. 270 ☑ **Section 2 Review,** p. 278 ☑ **Section 3 Review,** p. 284 ☑ **Chapter Survey,** pp. 286–287 **Alternative Assessment** Campaigning for President, p. 287	☑ **Answers to Section 1 Review,** p. 270 ☑ **Answers to Section 2 Review,** p. 278 ☑ **Answers to Section 3 Review,** p. 284 ☑ **Answers to Chapter Survey,** pp. 286–287 (Alternative Assessment guidelines are in the Take-Home Planner.)

Teacher's Resource Package

Chapter Summaries: English and Spanish, pp. 24–25

Chapter Resources Binder
  Study Guide Using Questions to Guide Reading, p. 73
Geography Extensions Population Density, pp. 19–20
Using Historical Documents The Residence Act of 1790, pp. 56–60

Chapter Resources Binder
  Study Guide Supplying Supporting Evidence, p. 74
  Reinforcement Distinguishing Relationships, pp. 77–78
American Readings Moses Austin Travels to the Mississippi, pp. 37–38

Chapter Resources Binder
  Study Guide Previewing Headings, p. 75
  Skills Development Cause and Effect, pp. 79–80
American Readings Hamilton and Jefferson: "Opposite Sides of a Penny," p. 39; Abigail Adams Describes the White House, p. 40

Chapter and Unit Tests Chapter 10 Tests, Forms A and B, pp. 65–68

Take-Home Planner

Introducing the Chapter Activity
The First President's First Speech, p. 4

Chapter In-Depth Activity Role-Playing the Debt Debate, p. 4

Reduced Views
  Study Guide, p. 6
  Geography Extensions, p. 9
  Using Historical Documents, p. 9
Unit 4 Answers, pp. 28–34

Reduced Views
  Study Guide, p. 6
  Reinforcement, p. 7
  American Readings, p. 8
Unit 4 Answers, pp. 28–34

Reduced Views
  Study Guide, p. 6
  Skills Development, p. 7
  American Readings, p. 8
Unit 4 Answers, pp. 28–34

Reduced Views
  Chapter Tests, p. 9
Unit 4 Answers, pp. 28–34

Alternative Assessment Guidelines for scoring the Chapter Survey activity, p. 5

Additional Resources

Wall Time Line

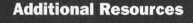

Unit 4 Activity

Transparency Package

Transparency 10-1 Map: United States Population Density 1790—use with Section 1

Transparency 10-2 Schedule of the 1790 Census—use with Section 1

Transparency Activity Book

SelecTest Testing Software

Chapter 10 Test, Forms A and B

★ ★ ★
Vital Links

 Videodisc

CD-ROM

Benjamin Banneker's almanac (see TE p. 269)

Whiskey Rebellion (see TE p. 274)

Time Line

Keys to History

Keys to History journal writing activities are on page 286 in the Chapter Survey.

Washington becomes first President Washington faced the challenge of turning the Constitution into a real government. (p. 266)

French Revolution begins Some Americans saw this as a victory for democracy, while others feared its violence. (p. 272)

First political parties formed Although not foreseen by the Constitution's framers, political parties formed around different ideas. (p. 279)

Looking Back The Constitution became the law of the land and the backbone of American government.

Chapter Objectives

★ Identify the challenges of creating a new government for a new nation.
★ Describe Washington's struggles to keep the nation out of war at home and abroad.
★ Explain the rise of political parties and their impact on American politics.

Chapter Overview

Following his inauguration, Washington worked with Congress to create the executive and judicial branches of the new government. Congress agreed to raise funds through tariffs, pay off the federal debt, and assume states' debts. Establishment of a national bank prompted debate between two cabinet members: Jefferson opposed the bank and Hamilton favored it.

1789–1801

Chapter 10

The First Years of the Republic

Sections

Beginning the Story with Abigail Adams
1. **The First Difficult Years**
2. **Conflicts at Home and Abroad**
3. **The Birth of Political Parties**

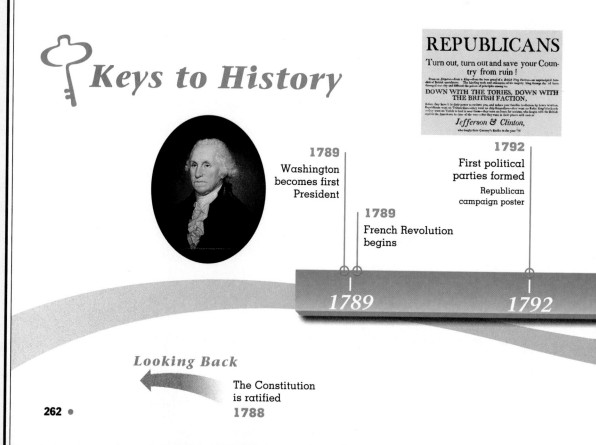

Keys to History

REPUBLICANS
Turn out, turn out and save your Country from ruin !

DOWN WITH THE TORIES, DOWN WITH THE BRITISH FACTION,

Jefferson & Clinton,

1789
Washington becomes first President

1789
French Revolution begins

1792
First political parties formed
Republican campaign poster

1789

1792

Looking Back

The Constitution is ratified
1788

In his second term, Washington struggled to keep the United States out of war, proclaiming neutrality during the French Revolution and in the war between France and Britain. Jay's Treaty and Pinckney's Treaty were peaceful attempts to solve other problems. On the domestic front, troops put down the Whiskey Rebellion (a tax revolt) and defeated an alliance of Ohio Valley Indians at the Battle of Fallen Timbers.

By 1796, political parties were firmly established. Federalists, led by Alexander Hamilton, favored a strong national government. Republicans, led by Jefferson, favored the power of individual states. Another source of debate was Federalist support of the Alien and Sedition Acts. The election of 1800 was a victory for Jefferson and a sign that the new government allowed for peaceful transfer of power.

Teaching the HISTORY Mystery

Students will find the answer on p. 269. See Chapter Survey, p. 286, for additional questions.

Time Line

Whiskey Rebellion To show that federal laws must be obeyed, President Washington himself led troops to put down this tax rebellion. (p. 273)

Washington's Farewell Address Washington warned against party rivalry and advised against foreign alliances. (p. 278)

Alien and Sedition Acts Republicans charged that these laws, allowing the President to jail or deport suspicious aliens and banning anti-government writing and speech, violated the First Amendment. (p. 281)

Nation's capital moves to Washington, D.C. Although still unfinished, Washington, D.C., became the official home of the federal government. (p. 282)

World Link See p. 275.

Looking Ahead
The Louisiana Purchase would usher in an era of westward expansion and development.

HISTORY Mystery

One evening at dinner, three people sat down and struck a deal that led to the building of one of the great cities of the world. Who were these people, and what was the deal?

1794
Whiskey Rebellion
Farmers tar and feather a tax collector

1796
Washington's
Farewell Address

1798
Alien and
Sedition Acts
Cartoon of battle
in Congress

1800
Nation's capital moves to
Washington, D.C.

Detail of design for
Capitol building

1795   *1798*   *1801*

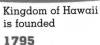

World Link
Kingdom of Hawaii
is founded
1795

Looking Ahead
The Louisiana
Purchase
1803

● **263**

America's early years were times of change, as a new nation took shape. Abigail Adams is in many ways a symbol of this transitional time. Challenging the traditional role of women, she was independent, well-read, and witty, not afraid to express her opinion to her husband. John respected her advice. In fact, some critics called her "Mrs. President." In spite of detractors, Abigail's strong voice put her at the heart of this pivotal period.

✳ History Footnote

John and Abigail Adams exchanged hundreds of letters throughout their lives together. Although John's public demeanor was quite serious, the letters reveal an affectionate spirit; he addresses his wife-to-be as "Miss Adorable," and confides in her his most private observations. Abigail's letters, in turn, are filled with keen commentaries on events both political and personal.

In a preface to a collection of his grandparents' letters, Charles Francis Adams remarked: "Statesmen and Generals rarely say all they think or feel. . . . We look for the workings of the heart. . . . The solitary meditation, the confidential whisper to a friend, never meant to reach the ear of the multitude, the secret wishes, not blazoned forth to catch applause, the fluctuations between fear and hope."

Beginning the Story with

Abigail Adams

When a young lawyer named John Adams first met 15-year-old Abigail Smith in 1759, he was not impressed. He wrote in his diary that Abigail and her sisters were "not fond, not frank, not candid."

The Smith girls would probably have agreed. As daughters of a Puritan minister, they had learned to control their emotions. They could not openly express "joy or grief, love, or any other passion."

Adams did admit that the girls had "wits." Abigail and her sisters had been taught reading and writing along with the "womanly arts" of housekeeping and sewing. The schooling of most New England girls stopped there. Reverend Smith was determined, however, that his daughters would be educated. After learning to read, Abigail began reading the books in her father's library and soon came to share his passion for knowledge.

"Partner of all my joys and sorrows"

Two years later, John Adams met Abigail Smith again. This time he saw her differently. Not only did Abigail appear attractive and gracious, she was also bright, witty, and remarkably well-read. He later wrote in his diary:

❝Tender feelings, sensible, friendly. Not a disagreeable word or action. Prudent, modest, delicate, soft, sensible, obliging, active.❞

They were the words of a man falling in love.

Abigail was equally attracted to John Adams. Why? Certainly not because of his looks. John was a short, lumpy man. And certainly not for his money. John was not rich, and as a colonial lawyer he was unlikely to become so. He did, however, have a brilliant mind and was passionate about books, ideas, and politics. When her mind met his, sparks flew.

History Bookshelf

Raymond Bial. *Frontier Home*. Houghton Mifflin, 1993. Through text and photos of artifacts, this book describes what daily life was like for settlers in the late 1700s and the 1800s.

Also of interest:

Ashabranner, Melissa, and Brent Ashabranner. *Counting America: The Story of the United States Census*. Putnam, 1989.

Conley, Kevin. *Benjamin Banneker: Scientist and Mathematician*. Chelsea House, 1989.

Faber, Doris, and Harold Faber. *The Birth of a Nation*. Charles Scribner's Sons, 1989.

Hilton, Suzanne. *A Capital Capital City: 1790–1814*. Macmillan, 1992.

Stefoff, Rebecca. *John Adams: 2nd President of the United States*. Garrett, 1988.

Yates, Elizabeth. *Amos Fortune, Free Man*. Dutton, 1950.

Still, Abigail was cautious about giving away her heart. At that time, a wife was expected to obey her husband, not think for herself. Abigail knew that she would die in such a marriage. She longed for someone who would treat her as an equal, as well as love her. "Alas," she wrote, such men were as scarce as "justice, honesty, prudence, and many other virtues."

Abigail found that rare man in John Adams. While he teased Abigail about her "unladylike habit of reading, writing and thinking," he loved her sense of independence. She was very pleased when he asked her to be "the dear partner of all my joys and sorrows." On October 25, 1764, they were married.

Abigail and John Adams spent the first 20 years of their marriage in this house in Quincy (formerly Braintree), Massachusetts. Abigail ran the farm during John's long absences.

Wife and "Widow"

So began a remarkable partnership. The couple spent their first years together on a farm near Boston, where John became a leader in the rebellion against British rule. During this time Abigail gave birth to five children.

In 1774 Massachusetts sent John Adams to the Continental Congress in Philadelphia. Abigail and the children remained on the farm. At first, they expected that John would be away a few weeks. The weeks soon stretched into months. When Congress chose Adams to represent the United States in France during the Revolutionary War, months lengthened into years.

During her years of "widowhood" Abigail raised the children and managed the family's finances. She found that she had a good head for business, ordering glassware and rugs from Europe and selling them to local housewives. Abigail also kept in touch with John's political friends, and knew as much about politics in America as any man.

Abigail and the children finally joined John in France in 1784. They moved to England a year later when John was appointed ambassador to Great Britain. By 1788 the couple was eager to come home. With a constitution soon to be approved, John looked forward to a role in the new government. Abigail had hoped that he was done with politics so that she could return "to our own little farm, feeding my poultry and improving my garden." Retirement, however, would have to wait.

Hands-On → HISTORY

Activity

Drawing from the story above and the chapter to follow, make a time line of Abigail's life. Choose at least five events to place on the time line. Some examples might be when Abigail first meets John, and when she moves to France. Next to the year for each event, write down Abigail's age at the time.

Chapter 10 • **265**

Discussion

Thinking Historically

1. How was the view of women in Abigail Adams's time different from today? (Women were not encouraged to read or learn more than was needed to run a household.)

2. In what ways was Abigail Adams an unusual women of her time? (Well-read, managed family finances, politically informed.)

3. What does John Adams's treatment of Abigail tell you about him as a person? (His respect for her showed open-mindedness.)

See the Chapter In-Depth Activity, Role-Playing the Debt Debate. **Take-Home Planner 4,** p. 4.

Teaching the Hands-On → HISTORY

Have students refer to the time line on pages 262–263 as a model. Some may wish to illustrate their time lines. Conclude by asking them to compare the stages of Abigail's life—such as marriage or having children—with those of a contemporary woman they know.

For a journal writing activity on Abigail Adams, see student page 287.

Vocabulary

inauguration (p. 266) ceremony that installs a new President

cabinet (p. 267) executive department heads

tariffs (p. 267) taxes on imports

bond (p. 269) a promise to repay a loan plus interest

speculators (p. 269) people who risk buying, hoping to profit if the price rises

constitutional (p. 270) permitted by the Constitution

strict construction (p. 270) view that federal government has power to do only what is written in the Constitution

loose construction (p. 270) view that federal government has broader powers than those listed in the Constitution

Warm-Up
Activity

Defining Government's Role

Have groups list functions and services the federal government should provide. Compare lists and discuss how different ideas about its role might affect its structure.

Geography Question of the Day

Based on the painting on pages 260–261, ask students to make two lists: how city growth affected the environment, and how the environment affected people.

Teaching Resources

Take-Home Planner 4, pp. 2–9

Chapter Resources Binder

  Study Guide, p. 73

  Reinforcement

  Skills Development

Geography Extensions, pp. 19–20

American Readings

Using Historical Documents, pp. 56–60

Transparency Activities

Chapter and Unit Tests

1. The First Difficult Years

Reading Guide

New Terms **inauguration, cabinet, tariffs, bond, speculators, constitutional, strict construction, loose construction**

Section Focus **The challenges of creating a new government for a new nation**

1. How were the new executive and judicial branches organized?
2. How did the new government deal with its financial problems?
3. What issues divided Hamilton and Jefferson?

John and Abigail Adams returned from England before the nation's first election. As expected, Washington was elected President and Adams Vice-President. John headed for New York, the capital, where America's experiment in democracy was to begin.

Launching the New Government

On April 30, 1789, George Washington was sworn in as President. A cheering crowd witnessed his **inauguration,** the ceremony that installs a new President.

Washington did not share the crowd's enthusiasm. In a nation of 13 quarreling states, he knew it would be difficult to turn the Constitution into a real government. Washington's hands shook during his inaugural address as he spoke of the "experiment" entrusted to Americans. With them rested the future of liberty.

A divided Congress Washington had reason to feel uneasy about his new job. He headed a government with no money and a deeply divided Congress.

There were two main groups in Congress. One was eager to build a strong national government that would discourage rebel-

lions and invasions and solve the nation's financial problems. Alexander Hamilton led this group, known as the Federalists. Thomas Jefferson guided the second group, the Republicans. They wanted to protect the rights of states by keeping the central government weak.

The title debate John Adams learned how divided Congress was when he asked it to create a title for the President. Adams pointed out that European rulers had titles like "Your Majesty." Many in Congress objected that a President was not a king. The debate fizzled out when Washington made clear that he was content to be known simply as "Mr. President."

Setting Up the Executive Branch

Next, Congress created three executive departments: a State Department to carry on relations with other nations, a Department of War to defend the country, and a Treasury Department to handle the government's money. In addition, an Attorney General would serve as the President's legal advisor and a Postmaster General would run the postal system.

At-Risk Students

Students with histories of academic difficulties may be intimidated by textbooks. Newspapers are one supplementary item you can use for motivation. Allowing students to select news items that relate to course content—as suggested in the Section Activity—gives them control over their learning, helps them see the relevance of school, and allows them an opportunity to be "class experts" on a topic. Students may need some initial guidance in recognizing different types of articles and in applying comprehension strategies. Integrating newspapers can be a way to give all students, including those at risk, a lifelong literacy tool.

President Washington (far right) is pictured with his first cabinet: Henry Knox, Thomas Jefferson, and Alexander Hamilton (left to right). Today, the President's cabinet has grown to 14 members.

Washington chose Jefferson as his Secretary of State and Hamilton as Secretary of Treasury. He made Henry Knox Secretary of War. At first, Washington met with his department heads alone. Later, he found it useful to meet with them as a group. Together, the executive department heads became known as the President's **cabinet.** The cabinet would advise the President and help carry out the nation's laws.

Organizing the Federal Courts

The Constitution called for Congress to plan a federal court system headed by a Supreme Court. This time, Congress fought over what kind of judicial branch to create. The Federalists, favoring a strong federal government, called for a court system with broad powers. The Republicans, favoring the powers of the states, preferred no courts other than the Supreme Court.

In 1789 Congress passed the Judiciary Act. It created a national court system with three levels, as shown below. District courts, one in each state, would try cases involving federal laws. Cases from district courts could be appealed to circuit courts and finally to the Supreme Court.

Federalists were pleased with this plan and with Washington's appointment of John Jay as the first Chief Justice of the Supreme Court. Republicans called the new court system "monstrous."

Federal Court System 1789

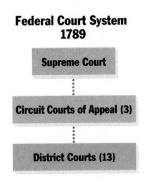

Supreme Court

Circuit Courts of Appeal (3)

District Courts (13)

Funding the New Government

The greatest problem facing the new government was money. The treasury had no money to pay government salaries or to begin paying off the nation's debts.

Congress agreed to raise funds through **tariffs,** which are taxes on imports. They could not, however, agree on which imports to tax. Southerners called for a tariff on molasses brought from the West Indies. New Englanders, who imported molasses to make rum, objected to this plan. When someone called for a tariff on slaves, it was the southerners' turn to say no, never!

Pennsylvania proposed a tariff on iron products to protect its iron industry from

Discussion

Checking Understanding

1. What did the two conflicting groups in Congress believe? (Federalists: strong national government; Republicans: protect rights of states.)

2. What executive departments were created first? (State, War, Treasury)

Stimulating Critical Thinking

3. Do you agree with the Federalists or the Republicans? Explain. (Answers should reflect understanding of party differences.)

Section Activity

Editorial Cartoons

Ask students to bring to class editorial cartoons or newspaper articles that describe a current political issue. Help them identify issues that divided Congress in the early days as well as today, such as taxes or states' rights. Ask them to choose one issue, either from the section or from the recent news, and express their views in an editorial cartoon.

See the Study Guide activity in **Chapter Resources Binder,** p. 73.

Ask students to examine the photo of Monticello and describe how the building looks and how it makes them feel. Point out that the Federal style represents the hoped-for calm and order of the new nation. This classical style, with its smooth, clean design, represented the new spirit of democracy and marked a clean break with the ornate, ostentatious style of the palaces of European monarchs. Ask students how the appearance of buildings can affect people's attitudes about an institution. Use your school or another building as an example. **Discussion Answers:** Students' examples should reflect an understanding of the basic features of the style.

For an activity on the law establishing Washington, D.C., as the capital, see **Using Historical Documents**, pp. 56–60.

✠ ⋯ **Connections to Economics**

Government bonds reached unprecedented popularity when the Treasury issued a series of bonds to help finance the nation's efforts in World War I. Between 1917 and 1919, Americans bought approximately $21 billion worth of "Liberty Bonds" and "Victory Bonds." To sell these bonds, Liberty loan committees approached the public directly, making presentations in theaters, movie houses, hotels, and restaurants. Banks helped in the effort by lending money to individuals, at an interest rate equal to the rate of return on the bonds, to enable them to purchase bonds and participate in the drive.

∞ **Link to Art**

The Federal style Architecture is the art of designing and constructing buildings. In the early years of the United States, architects looked to Greece and Rome, the birthplaces of democracy, for inspiration. Elements of this architecture, known as the Federal style, included such Greek forms as columns, gently sloping roofs, and smooth stone walls. Domes, a feature that the Romans loved and perfected, were often used as well. Pictured here is Monticello, the home Jefferson designed for himself in Virginia. Other examples include many of the government buildings in Washington, D.C. **Discuss** What kind of buildings in your area have Federal style features?

competition. Southerners did not want to pay more for imported nails and hinges.

In 1792 Congress finally passed a weak tariff bill. Having watched the endless quarreling, Abigail Adams wrote, "I firmly believe if I live ten years longer, I shall see a division between the northern and southern states." Abigail's fears were not unfounded. A split would indeed take place, but not for another 70 years.

Paying the Nation's Debts

The fight over tariffs was a warm-up for the battle over paying the nation's debts. The federal and state governments had borrowed large sums of money from American citizens and foreign banks to wage the revolution. Now their reputation was on the line. If they did not repay the loans, who would take the new nation seriously?

Benjamin Banneker, a self-taught son of slaves, was highly regarded for his work in mathematics and astronomy, demonstrated in the success of his almanacs. Almanacs were essential then, for they included tables charting the phases of the moon, the times of sunrise and sunset, and other information useful to farmers, navigators, and others in a time when clocks were scarce. Banneker sent a copy of his first almanac to Thomas Jefferson, asking the Secretary of State for help in improving the situation of African Americans. Jefferson responded to Banneker and sent his almanacs to European scientists, where they were much-admired. Later, abolitionists promoted Banneker's work as proof that prejudice based on skin color was without merit.

In 1790 Hamilton presented Congress with a two-part plan for paying off these debts. The first plan dealt with the federal debt, the second with the states' debts.

The federal debt During the war Congress had issued bonds to patriots and foreign banks that lent it money. A **bond** is a piece of paper given in exchange for money. The bond is a promise to repay the loan plus interest by a certain date.

After the war, Congress had no funds to pay off its bonds. People desperate for money sold their bonds to speculators for less than their original value. **Speculators** take a risk on buying something, hoping to make money if the price for it rises.

The speculators were gambling that the government would one day repay its bonds at full value. Hamilton's plan proposed to do just that. Critics said that the plan would reward speculators, which was unfair to patriots who had helped pay for the war for independence.

The states' debts The second part of Hamilton's debt plan called for the federal government to pay off the states' debts. Northern states had large debts and favored the plan. Most southern states opposed it. They had paid their debts. Why should they help states that had not done the same?

Neither side would budge. Finally, a frustrated Hamilton appealed to Jefferson. After listening to Hamilton's concern about the debt, Jefferson agreed to arrange a dinner meeting to discuss the issue.

At dinner Hamilton offered to make a deal with Madison and Jefferson. The men knew that northerners and southerners were at odds over the location of the nation's permanent capital. Hamilton, a northerner, promised to support a southern capital city on the Potomac River if Jefferson and Madison agreed to get southern support for the debt plan.

Both northern and southern states accepted the deal. Hamilton's debt plan became law.

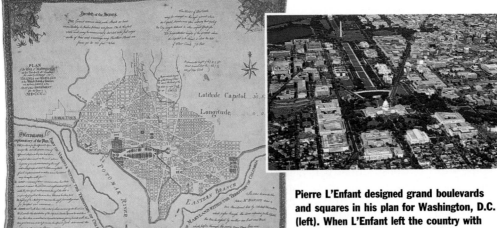

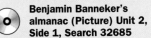

Pierre L'Enfant designed grand boulevards and squares in his plan for Washington, D.C. (left). When L'Enfant left the country with his plans, African American scientist Benjamin Banneker recreated them entirely from memory. Above is a view of the capital today.

Closing the Section

Role-Playing

Have small groups plan and role-play an interview with President Washington, reflecting on his first term in office and his second victory in 1792. One member should play Washington, with the others asking questions. Topics might include challenges of organizing a new government, budget problems, and ongoing arguments between Hamilton and Jefferson that forced Washington to run for a second term in spite of his desire to retire.

Section Review
Answers

1. Definitions: *inauguration* (266), *cabinet* (267), *tariffs* (267), *bond* (269), *speculators* (269), *constitutional* (270), *strict construction* (270), *loose construction* (270)

2. Americans objected to this obvious reminder of the English monarchs.

3. The federal government would repay government bonds at their full value and assume the states' debts.

4. Accept any examples that show an understanding of the issue. For instance a New Englander would oppose a tariff on molasses, needed to make rum.

✠ **Connections to Civics**

Neither the Federalists nor the Republicans claimed universal suffrage as a goal. Federalists in particular wanted to protect the voice of the propertied class. At that time most states limited the vote to adult white males with property. New Jersey's constitution did not specifically exclude women from voting, so until it was changed in 1807, some women did vote.

Amendments to the Constitution eventually forced all states to adopt universal adult suffrage. Women won the right to vote with the 19th Amendment in 1920. Though the 15th Amendment of 1870 stated the right to vote could not be denied based on race, some states continued to use poll taxes and literacy tests to exclude black voters. Poll taxes were finally outlawed in 1964 by the 24th Amendment.

Establishing a National Bank

Hamilton next asked Congress to set up a national bank. This bank would keep tax funds safe, issue paper money that people could trust, and make loans. Hamilton's proposal had strong opponents. They raised two questions: Who would benefit from the bank, and was it **constitutional**—permitted by the Constitution?

Hamilton's view Hamilton was a northern city lawyer. He believed that the nation's future was in manufacturing and trade. A national bank would make loans to businesses to build factories and ships. As business expanded, Hamilton argued, the nation would prosper and all would benefit.

Hamilton saw loans to farmers as wasteful. He thought the nation already depended too much on farming.

Jefferson's view Jefferson was a southern planter. He believed that the country's future lay with its honest, free-thinking, independent farmers. A national bank, he argued, would help only bankers and merchants. The government should deposit its money in small local banks that would help the common people, rather than making a few city folk even richer.

Strict versus loose construction Jefferson also believed that a national bank was unconstitutional. He called for **strict construction,** the view that the government has the power to do only what is written in the Constitution. If it is not in the Constitution, he said, then Congress cannot do it. The Constitution means exactly what it says. Any other view would give Congress "a boundless field of power."

Hamilton, in contrast, favored **loose construction,** the view that the federal government has broader powers than those listed in the Constitution. He argued that the "elastic clause" allows the government to do what is needed to carry out its functions. One of the government's duties is to uphold the value of money. A national bank would fulfill that duty.

In the end, Congress voted for the bank. Yet to this day, Americans disagree on how to interpret the Constitution.

The Election of 1792

By 1792 Washington was ready to retire. Endless bickering in Congress had left him weary of political life. He told Madison that he would rather "go to his farm, take his spade in hand and work for his bread, than remain in his present situation."

Because of the growing rift between Hamilton and Jefferson, both men convinced Washington to run for a second term. He was the only leader, they said, who was able to stand above the quarrels and keep the new government from flying apart.

That fall, Washington was re-elected President and Adams Vice-President. Both men knew that the national experiment in government by the people had just begun. Difficult times still lay ahead.

1. Section Review

1. Define the terms **inauguration, cabinet, tariffs, bond, speculators, constitutional, strict construction,** and **loose construction.**

2. Why did some people oppose the title "Your Majesty" for the President?

3. What were the two parts of Hamilton's solution to the debt problem?

4. Critical Thinking Imagine that as a member of Congress you voted against the tariff of 1792. Where might you come from and why did you vote no?

Census takers in 1790 were true pioneers, often traveling in remote areas without the aid of maps, for the fee of $1 for every 150 persons counted. All enumerators, hired by U.S. marshals, were on their own, with no possibility of verifying information collected.

There are other differences between the census of 1790 and today's censuses. The records were publicly posted then; today, the records are strictly confidential. Also, not everyone was counted. American Indians were excluded, and, in a compromise between northern and southern states, black slaves were only counted as "three-fifths" of a person. On March 3, 1792, the nation's first census was complete, showing a total population of 3,893,635.

Geography Lab

Reading a Population Density Map

A Philadelphia street scene in 1790

The first United States census began on August 2, 1790. Counting the population was not easy. Most Americans lived in rural areas, where census takers had to walk or ride over poor roads—or no roads at all. In addition, many people did not understand why the government wanted to know about them. Some hid, others refused to answer questions, and a few even attacked the census takers.

This map is based on the first census. It shows **population density**—the average number of people in a certain-sized area. On this map, the colors stand for the average number of people in a square mile.

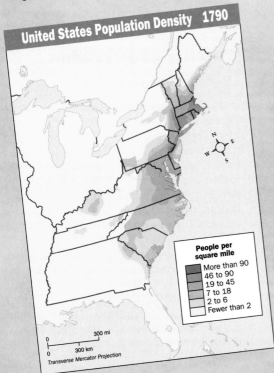

United States Population Density 1790

People per square mile
More than 90
46 to 90
19 to 45
7 to 18
2 to 6
Fewer than 2

300 mi
300 km
Transverse Mercator Projection

Using Map Skills

Study the map. Then answer the questions. Refer to the maps on pages R4–R5 and R6–R7, if necessary.

1. What was the range of population densities in Pennsylvania?

2. Starting at the Atlantic Coast and moving inland, describe Virginia in terms of its population density.

3. Find the spots where the population density was 90 and over. What cities are at those spots?

4. How does the map support the claim that the Appalachians slowed down but did not stop Americans moving westward?

5. **Hands-On Geography** Imagine that one morning you wake up somewhere in the United States—200 years ago. Of all the places on the map, where would you want to wake up? To help you decide, with a partner make a chart listing advantages and disadvantages of living in high, medium, and low population density areas in 1790.

Teaching the Geography Lab

Explain that the Constitution requires that a census be completed every ten years. Census figures determine the number of representatives each state has in the House of Representatives.

Discuss the features of the map. Ask students to consider the advantages of a thematic map like this one over, for example, a table of population figures. Discuss what other kinds of information might be appropriately presented on a thematic map.

Using Map Skills
Answers

1. From under 2 persons per square mile to more than 90.

2. The state is most densely populated along the coast, with 19–45 people per square mile, and becomes less populated moving westward, down to 2–6 people per square mile.

3. Boston, Philadelphia.

4. Population pockets west of the mountains indicate some people did cross them.

5. Responses should show an understanding of the map and provide thoughtful reasons.

See the activity on population density in **Geography Extensions,** pp. 19–20.

Section Objectives

★ Explain how the French Revolution divided America.
★ Identify the basis for Washington's foreign policy.
★ Describe how Washington dealt with tax rebels and Indian lands beyond the Appalachians.

Teaching Resources

Take-Home Planner 4, pp. 2–9
Chapter Resources Binder
  Study Guide, p. 74
  Reinforcement, pp. 77–78
  Skills Development
Geography Extensions
American Readings, pp. 37–38
Using Historical Documents
Transparency Activities
Chapter and Unit Tests

Warm-Up Activity

Negotiating Conflict

Ask students to imagine walking home from school and encountering two other students fighting. Ask for volunteers to describe how they might react to the situation, such as continuing home, trying to stop the fight, or getting involved in the fight on behalf of one of the students. Discuss the risks of each action. Tell students that nations sometimes face similar decisions.

Geography Question of the Day

Ask students to write a paragraph describing some of the major geographical features and natural resources in your area and suggest reasons your area might have been attractive to settlers.

2. Conflicts at Home and Abroad

Reading Guide

New Terms neutral, excise tax, impressed

Section Focus Washington's struggles to keep the nation out of war

1. How did the French Revolution divide Americans?
2. What was the basis of Washington's foreign policy?
3. How did Washington deal with tax rebels and Indian lands beyond the Appalachians?

Weary of political life, Abigail Adams decided to remain in Massachusetts during John's second term as Vice-President. John, missing Abigail, wondered if "some fault unknown has brought upon me such punishments, to be separated both when we were too young and when we are too old." He especially missed her advice as the nation debated the drama unfolding in France.

The French Revolution

In 1789 the people of France had risen up against their king. The leaders of this revolution promised a democracy. Three years later, France became a republic and declared "a war of all peoples against all kings."

At first, these events thrilled many Americans. Jefferson and his followers were inspired to call themselves Republicans because of the French uprising. They saw it as part of a great crusade for democracy and "the liberty of the whole earth" that had begun with the American Revolution.

In time, however, news from France caused Americans to think again. Riots broke out in Paris as the poor turned against the rich. Mobs cheered as the new government chopped off the heads of 17,000 wealthy French men and women. In 1793, during the "Reign of Terror," a radical group beheaded the king. France, they declared, would never have a king again.

Hamilton and his Federalist followers were horrified by the bloodshed in France. Many of them were wealthy themselves, and they began to wonder if the common people in America had too much power. "Behold France," warned a Federalist, "an open hell . . . in which we see . . . perhaps our own future."

Washington Proclaims Neutrality

By 1793 France was at war with most of Europe and Great Britain. The conflict posed a problem for the United States. During the American Revolution, the Americans and French had made a treaty promising to help each other in wartime. Without French support, Americans might not have won their independence. Now, Jefferson and the Republicans thought the United States had a duty to help France.

Hamilton and the Federalists argued that aiding France would mean war with Britain. That would be a disaster. The government depended on the income it received from tariffs on British imports. If the United States sided with anyone, Hamilton argued, it should be with the British.

History Footnote
In 1789 a deputy of the French National Assembly, Dr. Joseph Ignace Guillotin, proposed a new method of capital punishment, one that was seen as more humane, quick, and dignified, and that delivered to all criminals the equal treatment promised by the Declaration of the Rights of Man. The result was the guillotine, a device that decapitated with the clean stroke of a blade.

The guillotine delivered the "equal treatment" it promised. It was first used in April 1792, to execute a man who had committed a violent robbery. The next year, 20,000 watched as Louis XVI suffered the same fate. Before he died, he proclaimed his innocence and announced: "I pardon those who have brought about my death and I pray that the blood you are about to shed may never be required of France."

Washington listened, but knew the nation was not ready for war. He chose to remain **neutral,** which means not taking either side in a conflict. In April 1793, the President issued a Proclamation of Neutrality. It warned Americans "to avoid all acts" that might help any warring nation.

The Genêt Affair That same month, a minister from the French government arrived in South Carolina. Edmond Genêt [zheh-NAY] liked to be called "Citizen" Genêt to show he was a man of the people.

As he made his way north, Citizen Genêt was greeted by cheering crowds. His popularity quickly went to his head. In his speeches he attacked "Old Washington" and the Proclamation of Neutrality. Genêt urged Americans to join France in war against Britain, and encouraged American seamen to attack British ships.

Jefferson admired France but could not stomach Genêt's actions. Calling the minister "indecent toward the President," Jefferson agreed to ask France to call Genêt home. When the French replaced Genêt, the threat to neutrality faded.

Problems West of the Appalachians

With Genêt replaced, Washington could breathe easier. He had steered the nation away from war. At home, however, he faced two major challenges in the Ohio Valley.

The Whiskey Rebellion In 1791 Congress had put an **excise tax**—a tax on the production or sale of a certain product— on whiskey. Backcountry farmers, from Georgia to Pennsylvania, hated this tax.

Opponents of the French Revolution were beheaded in public. Some Americans were shocked by this brutal turn of events in France.

See the Study Guide activity in **Chapter Resources Binder**, p. 74.

Discussion

Checking Understanding

1. Why did Jefferson believe the U.S. should help France? (France helped the United States gain independence.)

2. Why was Genêt asked to leave the U.S.? (He attacked Washington's policy and reputation, and urged Americans to join war against Britain.)

Stimulating Critical Thinking

3. Compare the French and American Revolutions. (French Revolution was struggle for power within one country, took ideals of democracy to more radical conclusions than Americans did, and embraced missionary zeal to spread revolution. American Revolution was a democratic struggle that included a fight for independence.)

4. Was Washington right in keeping the United States out of the war? (Yes: young nation needed to focus on domestic problems. No: moral obligation to help France, which helped U.S. gain independence.)

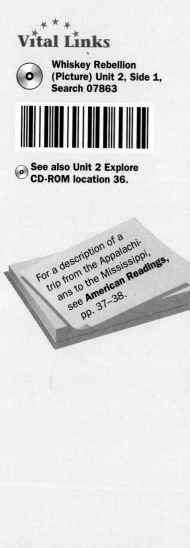

Bonus Activity

Expressing Point of View in Art

After reading about and discussing the Battle of Fallen Timbers, ask students to illustrate the event from the point of view of either General Wayne or Little Turtle. Compare the completed illustrations, asking students why they chose to include the details they did. Discuss how perspective affects how an event is depicted, both in pictures and in words.

★ ★ ★
Vital Links

Whiskey Rebellion (Picture) Unit 2, Side 1, Search 07863

See also Unit 2 Explore CD-ROM location 36.

For a description of the Appalachians to the Mississippi, trip from the see **American Readings**, pp. 37–38.

✠ **Connections to Art**

The events of the early years of the republic were recorded by painters in the neoclassical tradition, artists who believed that great art should be based on important subjects such as historical events.

One of the most famous painters of that time was Charles Willson Peale. As a soldier, Peale recorded on canvas events of the War of Independence and later painted portraits of the leading Patriot figures, including a rare sitting with Washington in 1795. Peale taught his 11 children to paint, and his daughter Sarah Miriam Peale is often cited as the first female professional American artist.

Abigail Adams visited Peale's studio in 1776 and wrote to John that "I wish I had Leisure, and Tranquility of Mind to amuse myself with these Elegant, and ingenious Arts of Painting."

The only time a President has led troops into battle is when George Washington did so to put down the Whiskey Rebellion.

Whiskey, distilled from grain, was often used to buy goods when cash was scarce. Backcountry farmers protested loudly to Congress against the whiskey tax.

After hearing these protests, Congress lowered the excise tax in 1794. Most farmers began to pay up. In western Pennsylvania, however, tax rebels known as "Whiskey Boys" terrorized farmers who paid the hated tax. Tax collectors in the area were tarred and feathered and burned with hot irons.

Hamilton urged Washington to stamp out the Whiskey Rebellion before it became another Shays' Rebellion. In the summer of 1794, commander in chief Washington led an army of 13,000 soldiers across the mountains. In the face of this force, the rebels vanished into the woods.

To Jefferson and the Republicans, sending an army to arrest a few tax dodgers seemed silly. Hamilton and Washington, however, believed they had done what was needed to make sure that federal law was "the supreme law of the land."

Conflicts over Indian lands At the same time, Washington faced a second problem in the Ohio country. Alarmed by land-hungry settlers, Indian tribes there had formed a loose confederacy to protect their homelands. They declared the Ohio River to be the border between their lands to the north and the United States to the south.

The United States government, however, ignored the boundary. It allowed settlers to cross the Ohio River into Indian lands and cut down the forests for farms. Led by Little Turtle of the Miamis and Blue Jacket of the Shawnees, the Indians raided these settlements, burning houses and fields.

Little Turtle, chief of the Miamis, led the confederation of Shawnee, Miami, Potawatomi, and Chippewa tribes in the Northwest Territory. After General Wayne's arrival at Fort Recovery, Little Turtle counseled his allies: "The Americans are now led by a chief who never sleeps. . . . There is something that whispers to me it would be prudent to listen to offers of peace." Little Turtle's suggestion was rejected, and he was replaced by Turkey Foot who, with Blue Jacket, led the confederacy to defeat at the hands of General Wayne. Wayne and his troops dealt a crippling blow. In addition to the lives lost in battle, they burned Indian villages and 5,000 acres of crops.

President Washington refused to talk with the Indians. Instead, he sent two armies north of the Ohio River to defend the settlers. In 1791 the Indians crushed the armies in the biggest defeat that Indians ever dealt the United States. More than 900 soldiers were killed or wounded. The Indians felt unbeatable.

Washington gave command of the next army to General "Mad Anthony" Wayne. He was nicknamed "Mad Anthony" because of his reckless conduct in battles. Wayne spent almost two years training his soldiers.

The Battle of Fallen Timbers As the battle neared, the Indians hoped to surprise Wayne's men at a place called Fallen Timbers. Wayne took so long to reach it, however, that many Indians had returned to their villages. The result was an easy victory for Wayne in August 1794.

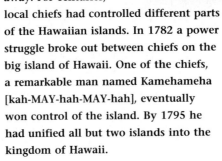

World Link

Kamehameha unifies Hawaii As the United States struggled through its early years, another new nation was born thousands of miles away. For centuries, local chiefs had controlled different parts of the Hawaiian islands. In 1782 a power struggle broke out between chiefs on the big island of Hawaii. One of the chiefs, a remarkable man named Kamehameha [kah-MAY-hah-MAY-hah], eventually won control of the island. By 1795 he had unified all but two islands into the kingdom of Hawaii.

Wayne's troops had made deadly use of their bayonets. An Ottawa Indian said:

"We could not stand against the sharp ends of their guns. . . . Our moccasins trickled blood in the sand, and the water was red in the river."

The defeat at Fallen Timbers crushed the spirit of the Indians in the Northwest. They had little choice but to accept the 1795 Treaty of Greenville. With it, they lost much of Ohio and Indiana to the settlers. The Indians were forced to retreat even further into the North American continent.

Conflict with Britain

Many Americans blamed Britain for the troubles in the Ohio Valley. The British had kept their forts there after the American

Little Turtle (above) and other Indian leaders signed the Treaty of Greenville in 1795 after their defeat at the Battle of Fallen Timbers.

Discussion

Checking Understanding

1. How did Republicans and Federalists view Washington's actions in the Whiskey Rebellion? (Federalists thought it was important to uphold federal law; Republicans thought it was unnecessary.)

2. What was the result of the Treaty of Greenville? (The Indians lost most of Ohio and Indiana and had to move further west.)

Stimulating Critical Thinking

3. If you were Washington, how would you have handled the conflict between Indians and settlers? (Encourage students to share a variety of solutions, including ones avoiding conflict.)

Teaching the

World Link

Have students locate the islands on the world map on pages R2–R3. Discuss how governing a group of islands might be different from governing a single body of land. Ask: **How was Hawaii's unification different from the unification of the 13 states?** (Islands were unified after a power struggle; 13 former colonies unified because of shared opposition to Britain.)

Students with Limited English

Students with limited English may have trouble organizing and synthesizing information. Graphic organizers can be very beneficial to students having trouble understanding the content of this section. For example help students construct a flow chart showing the sequence of events that led to the Battle of Fallen Timbers or Jay's Treaty and Pinckney's Treaty. Some students may enjoy working together to draw a series of pictures to represent the events described here as well. These and other types of visual tools may prove less intimidating than the written text and will help students focus on the most important points.

Planning a Newscast

Have small groups of students plan and deliver newscasts, selecting and reporting on two or three events from the section they feel are most important. Students may choose to role-play interviews as a part of their presentations. If possible, audiotape or videotape the newscasts. After each group has made its presentation, discuss some of the differences among them. Ask students how they decided what was especially important and how to best present each piece of information.

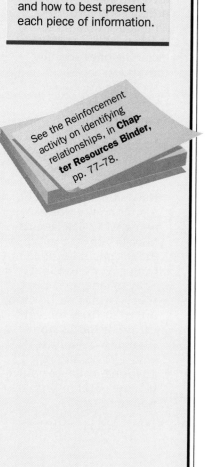

See the Reinforcement activity on identifying relationships, in **Chapter Resources Binder,** pp. 77–78.

Jay's Treaty angered most Americans. Here a crowd burns an effigy of John Jay.

Revolution. Now they were letting Canadian fur traders use them to do business with the Indians. Settlers suspected, though, that the forts were more than trading posts. They accused Britain of supplying the Indians with weapons to resist the settlers.

Troubles at sea Americans had a second reason for being angry with Britain. France and Britain were at war in 1794. American merchants believed that as long as the United States remained neutral in the war, their ships should be free to trade with both nations. Britain and France did not share this view. They attacked American ships heading for each other's ports.

Since Britain had the larger navy, it did more damage, seizing hundreds of American ships. The sailors on these vessels were **impressed**—forced to work on British war-

ships—or thrown into foul prisons. Americans were outraged by such treatment.

In 1794 Congress urged Washington to find a peaceful way out of the conflict. Just in case, however, Congress also voted to raise an army and build a navy.

Jay's Treaty

Washington sent Chief Justice John Jay to London to persuade the British to stop attacking American ships and sailors. He was also to ask the British to give up their forts in the Northwest.

Jay's Treaty, the result of his trip, was both a success and a failure. The British agreed to give up their forts. They refused, however, to halt attacks against American ships trading with France. Nor would the British stop impressing American seamen. John Adams knew that the treaty would be unpopular. "I am very much afraid of this Treaty!" he wrote to Abigail.

The American response As Adams had feared, Jay's Treaty stirred up a storm of protest. In Boston an angry mob burned a British ship. When Alexander Hamilton spoke in favor of the treaty, New Yorkers pelted him with rocks.

Republican newspapers heaped insults on both Washington and Jay. The papers called the President a "hypocrite," and accused Jay of selling out his country. One paper wrote:

❝John Jay, ah! the arch traitor—
seize him, drown him, hang him,
burn him, flay him alive!❞

Such attacks sickened Abigail Adams. She wrote angrily of the "orators and printers" who had opened the "floodgates of scurrility [nastiness] and abuse upon the President and Mr. Jay." Despite the uproar, the Senate approved Jay's Treaty. For all of its faults, the treaty did keep the United States out of war.

Connections to Science

As American cities became more densely populated, their residents were faced with the challenges of controlling communicable diseases. Philadelphia, the nation's largest city, with a population of approximately 43,000, was ravaged in 1793 by yellow fever, now known to be spread by mosquitoes. The epidemic caused the nation's government to temporarily halt operations as many fled the city. By the time a frost ended the epidemic, more than 5,000 people had died of the fever.

Also during that time, British physician Edward Jenner developed a vaccination to combat another communicable disease: smallpox. Smallpox was officially declared eradicated throughout the world in 1977.

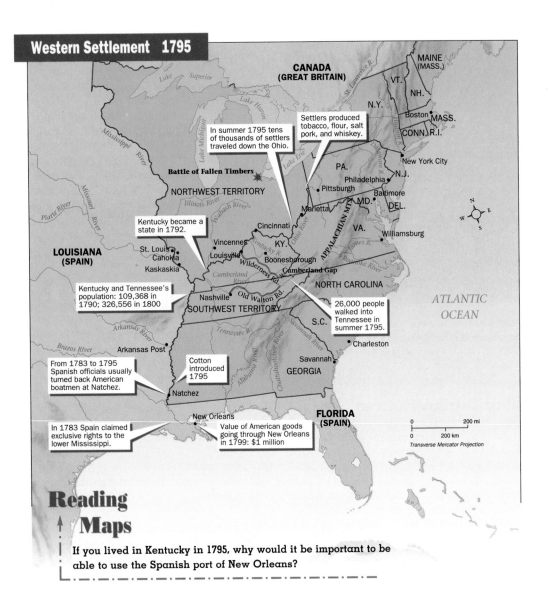

Western Settlement 1795

In summer 1795 tens of thousands of settlers traveled down the Ohio.

Settlers produced tobacco, flour, salt pork, and whiskey.

Battle of Fallen Timbers

Kentucky became a state in 1792.

Kentucky and Tennessee's population: 109,368 in 1790; 326,556 in 1800

26,000 people walked into Tennessee in summer 1795.

From 1783 to 1795 Spanish officials usually turned back American boatmen at Natchez.

Cotton introduced 1795

In 1783 Spain claimed exclusive rights to the lower Mississippi.

Value of American goods going through New Orleans in 1799: $1 million

0   200 mi
0   200 km
Transverse Mercator Projection

Reading Maps

If you lived in Kentucky in 1795, why would it be important to be able to use the Spanish port of New Orleans?

Pinckney's Treaty

Jay's Treaty served another purpose. It helped Thomas Pinckney make a deal with Spain. Pinckney had gone to Spain to settle boundary disputes and to gain the right of Americans to send goods through New Orleans. Afraid that Jay's Treaty might lead to an alliance between the United States and Britain, Spain cooperated with Pinckney.

Pinckney's Treaty of 1795 was good news to western farmers. It gave Americans use of the Mississippi and the port of New Orleans for shipping goods. Spain also gave up its claim to a large chunk of territory north of Florida. Americans welcomed the new treaty.

Checking Understanding

1. What were two reasons Americans were angry with the British in 1794? (They thought the British were using their forts to supply Indians with weapons; British were attacking American ships and taking sailors.)

2. How did Jay's Treaty help Thomas Pinckney? (Spain agreed to Pinckney's Treaty because of fears that Jay's Treaty would lead to an alliance between the U.S. and Britain.)

Stimulating Critical Thinking

3. Compare American newspaper attacks on John Jay with press treatment of politicians today. (Today's press is also free to criticize public officials; press today would not print violent threats.)

Teaching the Reading Maps

Have students identify the main types of information presented on the map (growth and movement of population, type and value of goods produced). Ask how a map showing current information would differ. **Answer to Reading Maps:** It would be easier to ship goods via the nearby Mississippi than carry them over mountains.

Writing a Diary

To help students reflect on the events of the early years of America, have them write diary entries for President Washington. The entries could include what he feels were his accomplishments as President, what were the "best" and "worst" times for him and the country, and his thoughts on the future of the country he helped build.

Section Review
Answers

1. Definitions: *neutral* (273), *excise tax* (273), *impressed* (276)

2. The Federalists were frightened by the violence and worried the people of America might threaten their leaders as well.

3. He issued a Proclamation of Neutrality, stating America should avoid helping warring nations, and he asked Jay and Pinckney to negotiate treaties to peacefully settle disputes with Britain and Spain.

4. Support: Jay's Treaty stopped British support of Indians and Pinckney's Treaty gave Americans more territory and a way to ship their goods; oppose: Jay's Treaty did not stop British attacks on boats, which hurt trade.

✳ History Footnote

Home at Mount Vernon at last, Washington did not have long to enjoy the peaceful retirement he had anticipated. On December 14, 1799, he died at age 67 after a brief and sudden illness. He was given a military funeral and buried in the family tomb at Mount Vernon. For months after his death, thousands of Americans continued to wear mourning clothes.

Politics sometimes turned violent, such as when Republican Matthew Lyon and Federalist Roger Griswold attacked each other in Congress.

Washington Retires

As Washington's second term came to a close, the President announced that he would not run again. As with his cabinet meetings, Washington set a model for future Presidents to follow. No President would serve more than two terms until President Franklin Roosevelt was elected to third and fourth terms in the 1940s.

The Farewell Address Before leaving office in 1796, Washington prepared an address to his "Friends and Fellow Citizens." He reminded Americans of all that united them, despite their diversity:

❝With slight shades of difference, you have the same religion, manners, habits, and political principles. You have in a common cause fought and triumphed together.❞

Washington then warned of two threats to the nation. The first was the fighting between Federalists and Republicans over such issues as the national bank and foreign alliances. Such conflicts, he said, arise from strong "passions," and could tear the nation apart.

Second, Washington warned Americans not to risk their "peace and prosperity" by getting involved in European power struggles. "It is our true policy," he said, "to steer clear of permanent alliances with any portion of the foreign world."

Washington's Farewell Address is one of the most famous speeches in American history. His advice to avoid foreign alliances guided American foreign policy for nearly 150 years.

Washington's accomplishments The President retired amid cheers from Federalists. Despite some criticism from Republicans, Washington could take pride in what he had accomplished.

The new government was up and running. The nation was on a sound financial footing. Settlers were moving westward so rapidly that two new states had already joined the Union—Kentucky in 1792 and Tennessee in 1796. Most of all, Washington had steered his government safely through difficult, quarrelsome times. He left the nation united and at peace.

⭐ 2. Section Review

1. Define **neutral, excise tax,** and **impressed.**
2. How did the Federalists view the French Revolution?
3. Describe two ways that Washington tried to steer clear of foreign conflicts.
4. **Critical Thinking** If you were a western farmer, would you have supported or opposed the Jay and Pinckney treaties? Explain your reasons.

★ Identify issues dividing Federalists and Republicans in 1796.

★ Describe the Alien and Sedition Acts and summarize the arguments for and against them.

★ Explain the importance of the election of 1800.

Teaching Resources

Take-Home Planner 4, pp. 2–9

Chapter Resources Binder

  Study Guide, p. 75

  Reinforcement

  Skills Development, pp. 79–80

  Geography Extensions

  American Readings, pp. 39–40

  Using Historical Documents

  Transparency Activities

Chapter and Unit Tests, pp. 65–68

Introducing the Section

Vocabulary

political parties (p. 279) organized groups of people with similar ideas about government

aliens (p. 281) foreigners who are not yet citizens of the nation in which they live

sedition (p. 281) action that might cause people to rebel against the government

nullify (p. 282) declare that a certain law will not be enforced

states' rights (p. 282) the idea that states may nullify federal laws

3. The Birth of Political Parties

Reading Guide

New Terms political parties, aliens, sedition, nullify, states' rights

Section Focus The rise of political parties and their impact on American politics

1. What issues and ideas divided the Federalists and Republicans in 1796?
2. What were the Alien and Sedition Acts? Why were they approved? Why were they opposed?
3. What made the election of 1800 a turning point for the country?

When John Adams heard that Washington was planning to retire, he wrote to Abigail that "either we must enter upon ardours [labors] more trying than any ever yet experienced; or retire . . . for life." Abigail replied that were it left to her, "I should immediately say retire."

The Federalists and Republicans did not wait for John and Abigail to decide their future. With Washington's announcement, both groups began organizing for the next presidential election in 1796.

Political Parties Develop

The framers of the Constitution had expected that the most able leader in the nation would be chosen President. They did not imagine the rise of **political parties**—organized groups of people with similar ideas about government. By the early 1790s, however, two political parties were fighting for control of the nation's government. The party with the most votes could control both Congress and the presidency.

The Republicans In 1796 the Republican Party backed Thomas Jefferson for President. Jefferson favored the power of individual states over the federal government in most matters. His message was that

the new national government, under the Federalists, had grown too large.

The Republicans also attacked Federalist plans for the economy (see the chart on the next page) as helping the wealthy few rather than the common people. Such talk appealed to farmers and working people, particularly in southern and western states.

The Federalists Unlike the Republicans, the Federalists believed in a strong government that would protect trade and help business. It would also guard against foreign attacks. These ideas appealed to businesspeople and merchants.

Alexander Hamilton, the leader of the Federalists, distrusted the common folk who "are turbulent and changing; they seldom judge or determine [what is] right." He longed to be President, but his economic ideas had made him too many enemies. Instead, the Federalists backed John Adams.

The Election of 1796

When the vote came in, Adams had won the presidency by just three electoral votes. Jefferson came in second, which made him Vice-President. The nation was in a difficult situation. Its top two leaders belonged to different political parties.

Developing the Section

Section Activity

Taking a Poll

Have students work in groups to plan and carry out polls to determine the percentage of people today who would agree with the Federalists or the Republicans. Guide them in working together to devise lists of questions based on the chart on this page, such as, "Do you think the government should be run by wealthy people or by average people?" They should decide what questions are irrelevant today, such as "pro-British" vs. "pro-French." They should also consider what to do if people give "Federalist" responses to some questions and "Republican" responses to others. Finally, they should plan how they will carry out the polls and tabulate and present results.

See the Study Guide activity in **Chapter Resources Binder**, p. 75.

✱ **History Footnote**

Abigail Adams's outspoken nature won her many critics, but she would not be silenced. In an often-quoted letter to her husband John in 1776, she urged him and the other founders to "remember the ladies, and be more generous and favorable to them than your ancestors. Do not put such unlimited power into the hands of the husbands. Remember all men would be tyrants if they could. If particular care and attention is not paid to the ladies we are determined to foment a rebellion, and will not hold ourselves bound by any laws in which we have no voice or representation." Abigail herself never led anything like the rebellion she described, and it would be almost 150 years before women even gained the right to vote. But as her critics showed, expressing her views was in itself a bold step.

The First Political Parties

Federalists	Republicans
Leaders Alexander Hamilton John Adams	**Leaders** Thomas Jefferson James Madison
Regions strongest in northern towns and coastal south	**Regions** strongest in northern farming areas and southern and western backcountry
Hamilton	Jefferson
Beliefs rule by wealthy, educated people	**Beliefs** rule by the common people
strong national government	weak national government
loose construction of the Constitution	strict construction of the Constitution
limits on states' rights	protection of states' rights
laws to help businesspeople	laws to help farmers
high tariffs to protect manufacturers in the United States	low tariffs to keep goods cheap for farmers
powerful national bank	no national bank
pro-British	pro-French

At first, President Adams tried to work with Jefferson. Political differences, however, could ruin old friendships. Jefferson himself wrote sadly that "men who have been intimate [close] all their lives cross the streets to avoid meeting, and turn their heads another way."

Unable to work with Jefferson, Adams turned to Abigail for advice. One senator complained that "the President would not dare make a nomination" without his wife's approval. Abigail responded tartly that even "if a woman does not hold the reins of government, I see no reason for her not judging how they are conducted."

Trouble with France

As the war between France and Britain dragged on and on, Adams found it hard to continue a policy of neutrality. French leaders, seeing Jay's Treaty between the United States and Britain as a threat, had increased attacks on American ships.

The XYZ Affair Adams sent three diplomats to France to seek an end to the attacks. Upon arrival, they were met by three secret agents of the French government. The agents—known as Mr. X, Mr. Y, and Mr. Z—demanded a tribute, or bribe, of

Connections to Literature

While Abigail Adams was criticized for expressing her opinion privately to her husband, a British writer, Mary Wollstonecraft, gained widespread notice for her 1792 work, *A Vindication of the Rights of Woman*. Wollstonecraft's *Vindication* described the injustices suffered by women and criticized society's role in forcing women to assume a subordinate role. Throughout her life, Wollstonecraft was a voice for women's rights, and for the rights of men and women of the working class. She died in 1797, shortly after the birth of a daughter who was to become Mary Wollstonecraft Shelley, the author of *Frankenstein, or the Modern Prometheus*.

$250,000 before any peace talks began. The American delegates refused to pay.

The XYZ Affair enraged Americans. The Federalists, who distrusted France, prepared for war. Their slogan was "Millions for defense, but not one cent for tribute."

The "half war" The United States, too weak to risk all-out war, instead fought an undeclared war, a "half war," by capturing more than 80 French ships. In 1800 Adams again sent envoys to a French government now led by Napoleon Bonaparte. Napoleon agreed to end the 1778 alliance between the United States and France. In exchange, Adams dropped demands that France pay for ships it had seized.

With this agreement Adams lost the support of anti-French Federalists—support he would need to win a second term as President. Even so, Adams believed he had done what was right. He later wrote:

❝I desire no other inscription over my gravestone than: 'Here lies John Adams, who took upon himself the responsibility of the peace with France in the year 1800.'❞

Alien and Sedition Acts

During the "half war," some Federalists spread wild rumors that French spies were plotting to burn down churches, free slaves, and chop off heads in every town square. Meanwhile, Republican papers criticized the Federalists, describing the President as "bald, blind, crippled, toothless Adams."

Fearful of these harsh attacks, and of rumors about spies, the Federalists passed the Alien and Sedition Acts in 1798. **Aliens** are foreigners who are not yet citizens of the nation in which they live. The Alien Acts gave the President power to jail or deport aliens if they were troublesome or suspected to be spies. The Alien Acts frightened some foreigners into leaving the country.

Sedition is action that might cause people to rebel against the government. The Sedition Act banned writing or speech that stirred up hatred against Congress or the President. Republicans believed that this act was mostly a Federalist attempt to silence them. In fact, several Republican newspaper editors were arrested under this law. A few were convicted and fined.

What role should a President's wife play? Like Abigail Adams (left), Nancy Reagan (middle) and Hillary Clinton (right) have been criticized for advising their husbands.

Discussion

Checking Understanding

1. Why did the Republicans have support in rural areas? (Republicans saw the nation in the future as one of independent farmers and supported laws to help farmers, such as low tariffs to keep goods cheap.)

2. What led to the Alien and Sedition Acts? (The "half war" with France increased fear of French spies; Adams's actions drew harsh attacks in the Republican press.)

Stimulating Critical Thinking

3. Do you think the American diplomats should have paid Mr. X, Mr. Y, and Mr. Z? Explain. (No: cannot ensure they would fulfill their promise; no nation should have to pay to have peace talks. Yes: government should have done all it could to avoid war.)

4. Do you think a President's spouse should be able to advise the President on policy? Explain. (Yes: President has other non-elected advisors, and spouse might understand and communicate best with President. No: close personal relationship might give spouse too much influence as a non-elected advisor.)

For a poetic comparison of Hamilton and Jefferson, see **American Readings**, p. 39.

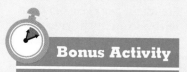
Remind students that the delegates at the Constitutional Convention decided that the capital should be located in a district to give the federal government complete sovereignty over the site and to avoid favoritism among states. Discuss arguments for and against statehood. For example, since D.C. residents pay federal income tax, perhaps they deserve to have voting representatives in Congress. Statehood may also give residents power to address problems affecting their city. Opponents may say that the federal government should not have to share control of its capital with a state.

Teaching the

Point of View

Help students articulate views in support of and in opposition to Allen's speech. Ask them to compare the debate with the same debate today.

⏱ Bonus Activity

Writing a Speech

To personalize freedoms, have students write and deliver speeches in which they express their views on limiting the freedom of the press today.

Abigail Adams's journey from Massachusetts to Washington, D.C., was not an easy one, requiring travel over more than 500 miles of often muddy, undeveloped roads. On her way to join her husband, Abigail and her companions became lost in the woods south of Baltimore, until finally a passerby was able to direct them to the capital. "We have, indeed, come into a new country" Abigail wrote a friend, complaining of the rustic surroundings and the large, unfinished, ill-heated house.

John Adams, however, was pleased with their new home. He wrote Abigail: "I pray heaven to bestow the best blessings on this house, and on all that shall hereafter inhabit it. May none but honest and wise men ever rule under this roof!"

Link to the Present

New Columbia? From the start, the residents of Washington, D.C., have been second-class citizens. They live in a city without a state. This means they have no senators. Their delegate to the House of Representatives can make speeches but cannot vote. As a result, Washingtonians have no voice in making the nation's laws. Furthermore, although they elect a mayor and city council, Congress can overturn any city council decision.

For years Washingtonians have demanded statehood for the District of Columbia. In 1993 the House voted down a bill that would have created the state of New Columbia. Statehood supporters, however, vow to continue their fight.

Point of View
Are there limits to freedom of the press?

Republicans denounced the Sedition Act. They said it violated the First Amendment, which protects freedom of speech and of the press. John Allen, a Federalist congressman, defended the act in a speech to the House. He read an attack on Adams that was full of lies, then asked:

❝Because the Constitution guarantees . . . freedom of the press, am I at liberty to falsely call you a murderer, an atheist [a nonbeliever in God]? . . . Freedom of the press was never understood to give the right of publishing falsehood and slanders [lies], nor of inciting [calling for] sedition.❞

How would you answer Representative Allen? Would you put limits on freedom of the press? Why or why not?

The Virginia and Kentucky Resolutions

The Alien and Sedition Acts created a crisis for the young republic. Jefferson and Madison, fearful of tyranny by the federal government, turned to the states to protect people's freedoms. The two men drew up resolutions—statements—opposing these acts. The Virginia and Kentucky state legislatures approved their resolutions.

Both resolutions charged that the Alien and Sedition Acts were unconstitutional. The Kentucky Resolution also said that if an act of Congress violates the Constitution, states have the right to nullify it. To **nullify** means to declare that a certain law will not be enforced. The idea that states may nullify federal laws became known as the **states' rights** theory.

Abigail Adams wondered how the nation could remain united if states chose to obey some laws of Congress and to nullify others. In the end, no other state adopted the Virginia and Kentucky Resolutions. The states' rights theory, however, would be debated many times in the years ahead.

The New Capital

While controversy raged over the Alien and Sedition Acts, the government moved to its new capital, Washington, D.C. (see plan, page 269). Life was not easy in the unfinished capital. Rain turned its unpaved roads into impassable swamps. When Abigail Adams arrived, she found a few buildings "scattered over a space of ten miles, and trees and stumps in plenty."

One of those buildings was the "President's House." The First Lady described it as

According to political writer William Safire, Thomas Nast's 1874 cartoon that led to widespread use of the elephant and donkey symbols was inspired by two events. First, the *New York Herald* had scared voters by accusing President Ulysses S. Grant of "Caesarism," depicting him with a crown on his head—a reference to seeking a third term. The second event was a hoax: the *Herald* falsely reported that zoo animals had escaped and were stalking Central Park. Safire states that Nast combined the events in a cartoon, showing "an ass (symbolizing the *Herald*) wearing a lion's skin (the scary prospect of Caesarism) frightening away the other animals in the forest (Central Park)." One of the animals was an elephant, representing the Republican vote that the threat of Caesarism frightened away.

Hands-On *HISTORY*

Designing political party symbols A donkey and an elephant—almost everyone recognizes them as the symbols of today's Democratic and Republican parties. The Democrats' donkey first appeared in the 1820s. It was later made famous by Thomas Nast, a political cartoonist, who also invented the Republican elephant in an 1874 cartoon.

Imagine that you are a political cartoonist in 1800 and you need to design a symbol for both the Federalist and Republican parties. They should be kept simple, and should not favor any one party.

Democratic donkey

Republican elephant

➤ Activity

① Review the information about the Federalists and Republicans, especially the chart on page 280.

② Draw sketches or write descriptions of symbols you might use.

③ When you have decided which two symbols work best, do a final sketch or description of each.

④ Show or describe your symbols to your classmates. Explain why you chose them.

Discussion

Checking Understanding

1. What did critics say was unconstitutional about the Sedition Act? (Violated First Amendment protections of freedom of speech and press.)

2. What is one reason Adams lost his bid for a second term? (Many in his party objected to his 1800 agreement with France.)

Stimulating Critical Thinking

3. Should states be able to nullify a federal law? Explain. (Yes: should not enforce a law they consider unconstitutional; check on federal power. No: nation should abide by decisions of elected Congress; confusing if states do not follow same laws.)

4. Compare the campaign of 1800 with campaigns today. (Compare kinds of attacks and discuss television's impact.)

Teaching the Hands-On *HISTORY*

Symbols may suggest which groups of people the party favors, such as a farmer's pitchfork or scholar's cap, or focus on a party belief. Conclude by asking why party symbols are useful.

For Abigail Adams's description of the White House, see *American Readings*, p. 40.

a place where "not one room or chamber is finished." She used the East Room for hanging laundry, as it was unfit for anything else. As the 1800 election approached, John and Abigail Adams tried to adjust to life in the new capital.

Election of 1800

In the election of 1800 John Adams ran for a second term. He campaigned on his achievements as President. Many people in his own Federalist party, however, objected to his agreement with France. They were not eager to see him re-elected.

The Republicans backed Jefferson for President and Aaron Burr for Vice-President. Jefferson portrayed himself as the defender of freedom and states' rights. He wanted to shrink the government by getting rid of the army and reducing the navy. He also opposed alliances with any nation.

The campaign was run as much on insults as on issues. Republicans attacked Adams as a tyrant who wanted to turn the presidency into a monarchy so that he could be king, followed by his children as well. Federalists labeled Jefferson an atheist who, if elected, would "destroy religion."

Who is President? When the votes were counted in early 1801, it was clear that Adams had lost. But to whom? To Jefferson or to Burr?

Each elector cast two votes for President. The candidate with the most votes was to become President, the second-place candidate Vice-President. In 1800 each Republican elector cast one vote for Jefferson and one vote for Burr. The result was a tie. In a presidential election, the House of Representatives breaks such a tie.

Although Jefferson was the Republican choice for President, the Federalists wanted to embarrass him. They voted for Burr. For 6 days and 35 ballots the tie continued. At last, Hamilton broke the tie by throwing his support to Jefferson. Of the two candidates,

Writing a Slogan

To help students synthesize information, have them work in groups to write a slogan describing the period 1796–1800. Encourage them to consider major events. To get them started, provide an example of a slogan, such as "the era of peaceful conflict."

Section Review
Answers

1. Definitions: *political parties* (279), *aliens* (281), *sedition* (281), *nullify* (282), *states' rights* (282)

2. Federalists: northern towns and coastal south because these areas had many business people and manufacturers who benefited from Federalist policies; Republicans: farming areas because they supported laws to help farmers.

3. Fears of French spies, Republican press attacks on Federalists.

4. Agree: In both cases, people were not allowed to say what they believed and could be punished for speaking out against the government; disagree: Unlike British rulers, American leaders were elected, and voters who disagreed with them could vote against them in the next election.

To check understanding of "Why We Remember," assign Thinking Critically question 3 on student page 286.

284

✳ **History Footnote**

As time passed, even the deep rift between John Adams and Thomas Jefferson healed. A mutual friend, Dr. Benjamin Rush, encouraged the two to communicate with one another again. By 1812 the former rivals had begun corresponding, discussing and debating in their letters a variety of scientific and religious questions and contemporary events. The two maintained their renewed friendship until their deaths. On the fiftieth anniversary of the signing of the Declaration of Independence, July 4, 1826, a dying John Adams spoke his last words: "Jefferson still survives." He did not know that on that very day, Jefferson, too, had died.

---

he told his fellow Federalists, Jefferson is "by far not so dangerous a man."

In 1804 the Twelfth Amendment was added to the Constitution to prevent such a tie again. Electors now vote separately for the President and Vice-President.

A peaceful change The 1800 election was a victory for the Republicans and for peaceful change. In most countries at the time, power changed hands through war or revolution. Here, power had passed peacefully from one party to another without bloodshed.

3. Section Review

1. Define **political parties, aliens, sedition, nullify,** and **states' rights.**
2. What areas of the country favored the Federalists? the Republicans? Explain why.
3. What fears motivated the Federalists to pass the Alien and Sedition Acts?
4. Critical Thinking Republicans thought the Alien and Sedition Acts were as bad as British rule before the Revolution. Why do you agree or disagree?

Why We Remember

The First Years of the Republic

For John and Abigail Adams the 1800 election was a painful defeat. For all of their married lives, they had put serving their country above their own happiness. Being rejected by the voters hurt. Abigail and John hurried home to their farm in Quincy, Massachusetts, as soon as they could leave the capital. Abigail died in Massachusetts on October 28, 1818.

The republic's early years were filled with conflicts and quarrels. Abigail herself had grown disgusted with the new politics. The "abuse and scandal," she wrote, were "enough to ruin . . . the best people in the world." Still, Americans had learned important lessons. They found that writing a constitution was only the first step; turning that piece of paper into a real government was a huge challenge. Doing so in the face of intense disagreements over what the Constitution meant was an even greater challenge—and remains so today.

Finally, Americans learned that it was far better to fight for their beliefs with political parties and votes than with armies and bullets. Elections like the one in 1800 may seem nasty, but they allow the opposition to be heard and they give Americans clear choices between candidates and ideas. Once voters have made that choice, power can pass peacefully from one group to another.

3. (a) Sources agree that the Sedition Act targeted Republicans and led to arrests of some Republican editors. (b) Source B stresses that the Sedition Act was an attempt to crush free speech. Source C downplays this threat, stressing that few people were affected or intimidated.

For further application, have students do the Applying Skills activity in the Chapter Survey (p. 286).

If students need to review the skill, use the Skills Development transparency and activity in the **Chapter Resources Binder,** *pp. 79–80.*

Skill Lab

Thinking Critically
Cause and Effect

Imagine being arrested for criticizing the President. That is exactly what happened to Representative Matthew Lyon of Vermont in 1798. After Lyon mocked John Adams and attacked his administration's policy toward France, he was fined $1,000 and thrown in jail for violating the Sedition Act.

Question to Investigate

What were some causes and effects of the Sedition Act?

Procedure

A cause is something that brings about an event, which is the effect. An **immediate cause** directly brings about an event. A **long-range cause** takes months or even years to bring about an event. An **immediate effect** occurs right away. A **long-range effect** occurs months or even years later. Read sources **A** to **C** to explore the causes and effects of the Sedition Act.

1 Identify causes and effects.
a. State two causes of the act.
b. State two effects of the act.

2 Distinguish between immediate and long-range causes or effects.
a. State an immediate effect of the act.
b. State a long-range effect of the act.

3 Compare descriptions of causes and effects in the different sources.
a. State one way in which the sources agree.
b. How do **B** and **C** differ on the seriousness of the act's effects?

Skill Tips

● Words like *reason, purpose,* and *design* signal causes. Words like *reaction, result,* and *outcome* signal effects.

● Any event may be both a cause and an effect, and may have more than one cause and one effect.

● Different authors have different opinions about causes and effects.

Sources to Use

A Reread pages 281–282.

B "Many outspoken Jeffersonian [newspaper] editors were indicted [charged] under the Sedition Act, and ten were brought to trial. All of them were convicted, often by packed [biased] juries swayed by prejudiced Federalist judges. . . . This attempt by the Federalists to crush free speech and silence the opposition party, high-handed as it was, undoubtedly made many converts for the Jeffersonians."

From Thomas A. Bailey and David M. Kennedy, *The American Pageant* (Heath, 1991)

C "Every defendant was a Republican, every judge and almost every juror a Federalist. . . . All this was labeled by the Jeffersonians, 'The Federalist Reign of Terror.' Looked at in the perspective of history, it was nothing of the sort. . . . Nobody was drowned, hanged, or tortured, nobody went before a firing squad. A few scurrilous [abusive] journalists were silenced, a few received terms in jail. . . . Nobody was prevented from voting against the Federalists in the next elections, state or national. . . . [In] the congressional elections of 1800, the Republicans obtained emphatic majorities in House and Senate. Thus, in 1801 the Federalists went out of power in every branch of government except the judiciary."

From Samuel Eliot Morison et al., *Growth of the American Republic* (Oxford Univ., 1980)

Introducing the Skill Lab

Point out that identifying causes and effects is not simple, and stress that events typically have multiple causes and effects. To help students see the difference between immediate and long-range causes, provide examples for an event, such as a student receiving an outstanding-student award: immediate cause—final grade point average, long-range cause —months of studying; immediate effect—present from parents, long-range effect—college scholarship.

Skill Lab
Answers

1. (a) Examples of causes: Republican press criticism, rumors of spies, Federalist desire to silence critics.
(b) Examples of effects: arrests, convictions, and jailing or fining of some Republican editors; protests of Sedition Act; Kentucky and Virginia Resolutions; increased support for Republicans; Republican victory in 1800.

2. (a) Some immediate effects: arrests, convictions, jail terms or fines, Republican protests, Kentucky and Virginia Resolutions.
(b) Some long-range effects: increased support for Republicans, Republican victory in 1800.

(Answers continued in top margin)

Survey Answers

Reviewing Vocabulary

Definitions are found on these pages: *inauguration* (266), *cabinet* (267), *tariffs* (267), *bond* (269), *speculators* (269), *constitutional* (270), *strict construction* (270), *loose construction* (270), *neutral* (273), *excise tax* (273), *impressed* (276), *political parties* (279), *aliens* (281), *sedition* (281), *nullify* (282), *states' rights* (282).

Reviewing Main Ideas

1. Executive: State, War, and Treasury departments; Attorney General; Postmaster General. Judicial: federal system with 13 district courts, 3 circuit courts, and Supreme Court.

2. Money; levied tariffs, enacted plan to pay debts, established national bank.

3. Jefferson favored strict construction: if a power is not specifically stated in the Constitution, the federal government cannot claim it. Hamilton favored loose construction: Constitution gives federal government power to do what it needs to carry out its duties.

4. Washington issued a Proclamation of Neutrality and sent Jay to persuade Britain to stop attacking American ships. He knew the U.S. was not strong enough to fight a war.

5. Whiskey Rebellion, conflicts with Indians over land. Washington sent an army to deal with each.

6. Federalists: strong national government, limit states' rights, tariffs to protect manufacturers. Republicans: weak national government, strong states, low tariffs so goods would be cheap for farmers.

7. France saw Jay's Treaty as a threat and increased attacks on U.S. ships.
(Answers continued in top margin)

286

French agents demanded a bribe before beginning peace talks. The U.S. waged a "half war," capturing French ships. Fear of French spies and of newspaper attacks led to Alien and Sedition Acts. Virginia and Kentucky approved resolutions opposing the acts.

Thinking Critically

1. Jay's Treaty: removed British from Ohio Valley, making area safer for settlers; kept U.S. out of the war between France and Britain; led to Pinckney's Treaty. Pinckney's Treaty: gave U.S. more territory; gave Americans right to use Mississippi River and port of New Orleans for shipping goods; encouraged settlement west of Appalachians.

2. Agree: nation lacked money and military power to fight a war, had to deal with domestic problems first. Disagree: U.S. owed loyalty to either France or Britain.

Chapter Survey ★

Reviewing Vocabulary

Define the following terms.
1. inauguration
2. cabinet
3. tariffs
4. bond
5. speculators
6. constitutional
7. strict construction
8. loose construction
9. neutral
10. excise tax
11. impressed
12. political parties
13. aliens
14. sedition
15. nullify
16. states' rights

Reviewing Main Ideas

1. Describe the executive and judicial branches as Congress first organized them.
2. What was the greatest problem facing the new government, and how did Congress solve it?
3. Describe how Jefferson and Hamilton differed in their interpretations of the Constitution.
4. How did Washington respond to the war between France and Britain? Why did he respond as he did?
5. What two challenges arose west of the Appalachian Mountains during Washington's presidency? How did Washington deal with them?
6. How did Federalists and Republicans differ in their views on each of the following? (a) strength of the national government (b) states' rights (c) tariffs
7. Explain how each event led to the next. (a) Jay's Treaty (b) XYZ Affair (c) "half war" (d) Alien and Sedition Acts (e) Virginia and Kentucky Resolutions

Thinking Critically

1. **Analysis** How did Jay's Treaty and Pinckney's Treaty affect the new nation's growth and security?
2. **Application** Agree or disagree with this statement: Washington's foreign policy was the best one for that period in our history. Explain why you agree or disagree, and support your answer with evidence from the chapter.
3. **Why We Remember: Evaluation** Jefferson supported the idea of political parties, but Washington feared that they might be more harmful than useful to the nation. Do you agree with Jefferson or Washington? Explain your answer.

Applying Skills

Cause and effect Think of a recent effort to censor something, such as the effort to reduce violence on television. Then do the following:
1. Identify the causes. Explain how they led to that effort to censor.
2. Identify the effects. Explain how they resulted from that effort to censor.
3. Make a flowchart to summarize these causes and effects. As you did in the Skill Lab on page 285, identify which ones are immediate and which are long-range.

History Mystery

The nation's capital Answer the History Mystery on page 263. How would you go about finding out who these people are and what deal they made with each other? What problems were the three people trying to solve? If such a deal had not been struck, what location would you have chosen for the nation's capital and why?

Writing in Your History Journal

1. **Keys to History** (a) The time line on pages 262–263 has seven Keys to History. In your journal, describe why each one is important to know about. (b) What other events

3. Agree with Washington: parties encourage divisiveness and discourage cooperation. Agree with Jefferson: political disagreements are inevitable; parties make it possible for individuals to express their opinions; parties act as watchdogs over one another.

Applying Skills

Students' flowcharts should reflect an understanding of the definitions under "Procedure" on page 285, as well as the understanding that an event may have multiple causes and/or effects, both immediate and long-range.

History Mystery

The answer can be found on page 269. Suggestions for a new capital city should include reasons based on geographical, political, or other factors.
(Answers continued in side margin)

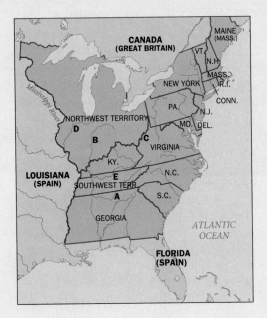

Reviewing Geography

1. Each letter on the map represents a river that empties into either the Mississippi or the Ohio. Write the name of each river.

2. Geographic Thinking Look at the maps on pages R4–R5 and R6–R7. From those maps alone, could you guess that the site of the nation's capital was a compromise between northern and southern interests? Explain. What else does the capital site tell you about what was important to people in 1790? If the nation's leaders had known how the United States would eventually expand, might they have chosen a different site? Why or why not?

from the chapter would you add to the time line? Write those events and their dates in your journal and tell why you think each event should be added.

2. Abigail Adams Abigail was attacked, at times, for giving her husband advice about political matters. How do you think she felt about such criticism? In your journal write a conversation Abigail might have had with a close friend about it.

3. Thinking Historically If you had been alive in 1800, which of the two political parties—Federalist or Republican—would you have favored? Why? What ideas do you like in both parties? Write your responses in your journal.

Alternative Assessment

Citizenship: Campaigning for President With several other students, reenact the presidential election campaign of 1800. First, divide into two groups representing the

Federalist and Republican parties. Within your group, assign someone to be the candidate: John Adams or Thomas Jefferson. Other group members will be campaign aides.

Think of your class as voters. You want to win their support for your candidate. To do so, you might create campaign posters and cartoons, write news articles supporting the candidate, and write a speech that your candidate can deliver to the voters. Keep an eye on what the other party does in the campaign, and help the voters be aware that your candidate is the better one.

Your work will be evaluated on the following criteria:
• you make a strong effort to get your candidate elected
• your campaign activities and materials reflect the issues facing the parties and candidates in 1800 and their positions
• your campaign activities and materials are appealing and persuasive

Writing in Your History Journal

1. (a) Explanations should be similar to the time line notes on teacher pages 262–263. (b) Accept accurate additions that show an understanding of what makes an event historically important.

2. Conversations should reflect her sense of independence and her knowledge of politics.

3. Responses should reflect an understanding of differences between the parties.

Reviewing Geography

1. (A) Tennessee River, (B) Wabash River, (C) Ohio River, (D) Illinois River, (E) Cumberland River

2. Site appears to be a compromise because it is in the middle of the coast. The location on the Potomac River, near the ocean, shows importance of water transportation. Location also reflects the fact that most Americans still lived near coastal areas. If they had foreseen future expansion, they might have built the capital farther west; the rugged backcountry and lack of modern transportation may have stopped them.

Alternative Assessment

Teacher's Take-Home Planner 4, p. 5, includes suggestions and scoring rubrics for the Alternative Assessment activity.

11 The Jefferson Era
1801–1815

Chapter Planning Guide

Section	Student Text	Teacher's Edition Activities
Opener and Story pp. 288–291	**Keys to History Time Line** / **History Mystery** / Beginning the Story with **Tecumseh**	**Setting the Stage Activity** Mapping Conflicting Claims, p. 290
1 **The New Republican President** pp. 292–299	**Point of View** Did the Court attack the President's power?, p. 294 / **Reading Maps** The Louisiana Purchase, p. 295 / **World Link** Haiti breaks free, p. 296 / **Hands-On History** Designing a peace medal, p. 297 / **Link to Art** *Landscape with a Lake,* p. 298 / **Geography Lab** The Rocky Mountains, p. 299 / **Link to Literature** *The Journals of Lewis and Clark,* pp. 312–313	**Warm-Up Activity** Letter to Europe, p. 292 / **Geography Question of the Day,** p. 292 / **Section Activity** Election Posters, p. 296 **Bonus Activity** Jefferson's Journal, p. 294 / **Wrap-Up Activity** Five Clues, p. 298
2 **Troubles at Sea** pp. 300–302	**Link to the Present** Sea piracy today, p. 300 / **Reading Maps** The Barbary States, p. 301	**Warm-Up Activity** Writing Captains' Logs, p. 300 / **Geography Question of the Day,** p. 300 / **Section Activity** Advising on the Embargo, p. 301 / **Wrap-Up Activity** Writing a Press Release, p. 302
3 **The War of 1812** pp. 303–309	**Reading Maps** The War of 1812, p. 306 / **Skill Lab** Detecting Bias, p. 309	**Warm-Up Activity** Using Charts to Predict, p. 303 / **Geography Question of the Day,** p. 303 / **Section Activity** Writing an Eyewitness Account, p. 304 **Bonus Activity** Writing a Dialogue, p. 306 / **Wrap-Up Activity** Making a Cause-Effect Chart, p. 308
Evaluation	☑ **Section 1 Review,** p. 298 / ☑ **Section 2 Review,** p. 302 / ☑ **Section 3 Review,** p. 308 / ☑ **Chapter Survey,** pp. 310–311 **Alternative Assessment** Creating a front page, p. 311	☑ **Answers to Section 1 Review,** p. 298 / ☑ **Answers to Section 2 Review,** p. 302 / ☑ **Answers to Section 3 Review,** p. 308 / ☑ **Answers to Chapter Survey,** pp. 310–311 (Alternative Assessment guidelines are in the Take-Home Planner.)

Teacher's Resource Package

 Chapter Summaries: English and Spanish, pp. 26–27

 Chapter Resources Binder
Study Guide Completing a Graphic Organizer, p. 81
Geography Extensions The Rocky Mountains, pp. 21–22
American Readings Napoleon Gives Up Louisiana, p. 41; Pike Is Captured by the Spanish, p. 42
Using Historical Documents Quaker Antislavery Petition, pp. 61–65

 Chapter Resources Binder
Study Guide Sequencing, p. 82

Reinforcement Analyzing a Primary Source, pp. 85–86
American Readings Kidnapping on the Ocean, p. 43

Chapter Resources Binder
Study Guide Previewing Headings, p. 83
Skills Development Detecting Bias, pp. 87–88
American Readings "The Star-Spangled Banner," p. 44

Chapter and Unit Tests Chapter 11 Tests, Forms A and B, pp. 69–72

Take-Home Planner

Introducing the Chapter Activity Exploring Other Worlds, p. 12

Chapter In-Depth Activity Storytelling: Meeting a Great Person, p. 12

Reduced Views
Study Guide, p. 14
Geography Extensions, p. 17
American Readings, p. 16
Using Historical Documents, p. 17
Unit 4 Answers, pp. 28–34

Reduced Views
Study Guide, p. 14
Reinforcement, p. 15
American Readings, p. 16
Unit 4 Answers, pp. 28–34

Reduced Views
Study Guide, p. 14
Skills Development, p. 15
American Readings, p. 16
Unit 4 Answers, pp. 28–34

Reduced Views
Chapter Tests, p. 17
Unit 4 Answers, pp. 28–34

Alternative Assessment Guidelines for scoring the Chapter Survey activity, p. 13

Additional Resources

Wall Time Line

Unit 4 Activity

Transparency Package

Transparency 11-1 Map: The Louisiana Purchase—use with Section 1
Transparency 11-2 Mandan Buffalo Robe—use with Section 1
Transparency Activity Book

SelecTest Testing Software
Chapter 11 Test, Forms A and B

Vital Links

Videodisc

CD-ROM

Nez Percé with Lewis and Clark (see TE p. 296)

Battle of Tippecanoe (see TE p. 304)

Tecumseh saving prisoners (see TE p. 305)

"The Star-Spangled Banner" (see TE p. 307)

11

Teaching Resources

Take-Home Planner 4
  Introducing Chapter Activity
  Chapter In-Depth Activity
  Alternative Assessment
Chapter Resources Binder
Geography Extensions
American Readings
Using Historical Documents
Transparency Activities
Wall Time Line Activities
Chapter Summaries
Chapter and Unit Tests
SelecTest Test File
Vital Links CD-ROM/Videodisc

Time Line

Keys to History

Keys to History journal writing activity is on page 310 in the Chapter Survey.

Marbury v. Madison
In this important decision, the Supreme Court and Chief Justice Marshall established the right of the Court to determine whether laws are constitutional or not. (p. 293)

Louisiana Purchase The Louisiana Purchase doubled the size of the United States and added 200,000 inhabitants. (p. 294)

Lewis and Clark Lewis and Clark explored beyond the Louisiana Territory westward to the Pacific Ocean. (p. 296)

Looking Back With his Farewell Address, Washington advised the citizens that he would not be a candidate for a third presidential term.

World Link See p. 296.

Chapter Objectives

★ Explain how President Jefferson put his Republican ideas to work as President.
★ Describe how the United States responded to threats to trade.
★ Summarize how the United States fought the War of 1812.

Chapter Overview

Although Jefferson attempted to govern by his Republican ideals, many things happened during his terms that led him to put his views aside. The Supreme Court established the policy of judicial review. The Louisiana Purchase, which doubled the size of the U.S., tested Jefferson's ideals because the Constitution has no provisions for buying land. Lewis and Clark came back with

1801–1815

Chapter 11
The Jefferson Era

Sections

Beginning the Story with Tecumseh
1. **The New Republican President**
2. **Troubles at Sea**
3. **The War of 1812**

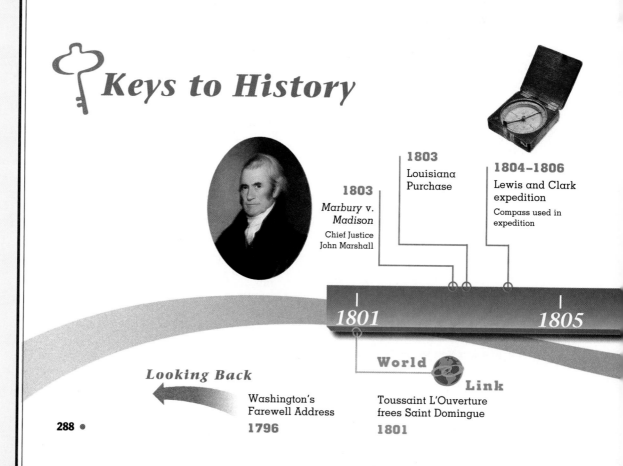

🔑 Keys to History

1803
Marbury v. Madison
Chief Justice John Marshall

1803
Louisiana Purchase

1804–1806
Lewis and Clark expedition
Compass used in expedition

1801

1805

Looking Back
Washington's Farewell Address
1796

World Link
Toussaint L'Ouverture frees Saint Domingue
1801

a treasure trove of information about the wonders of the land just purchased.

Increasing trade problems eventually led to a war with Britain. American ships and sailors were faced with British impressment and threat of British seizure of American ships headed for France and French seizure of ships headed for Britain. Jefferson's embargo plan did little to relieve the situation.

When problems with Indians in the Indiana Territory were linked to British support of the Indians, Americans cried for war. The United States won some major victories against Britain in the War of 1812. They succeeded in standing up to the most powerful nation in the world and gained a new sense of nationalism.

Students will find the answer on p. 307. See Chapter Survey, p. 310, for additional questions.

HISTORY *Mystery*

The greatest American victory in the War of 1812 was in a battle that need not have been fought. What was the battle, and why was it unnecessary?

1811

Tecumseh's forces meet Harrison's troops at the Battle of Tippecanoe

1812–1815

War of 1812

An American sailor

1814

Francis Scott Key writes "The Star-Spangled Banner"

Flag that inspired Key

1815

Battle of New Orleans

1810   1815

Looking Ahead

Monroe Doctrine is issued

1823

• **289**

Time Line

Tippecanoe While Tecumseh was away, his forces attacked, but failed to defeat, army troops camped near the Tippecanoe River. (p. 304)

War of 1812 Victories over Britain in the war gave Americans a new sense of national pride. (p. 303)

"The Star-Spangled Banner" Inspired by the American flag still waving over a besieged Fort McHenry, Francis Scott Key wrote the poem that would become the national anthem. (p. 307)

The Battle of New Orleans Andrew Jackson became a popular hero after this victory in the War of 1812. (p. 307)

Looking Ahead The Monroe Doctrine warned Europe not to interfere with new American nations.

Beginning the Story

Tecumseh

As settlers moved west of the Appalachians, the Shawnee chief Tecumseh worked to organize the Indian tribes for common defense. His efforts gave the Indians a unity of purpose and also led to greater strife between the Americans and the British, who supported Indian resistance.

Setting the Stage Activity

Mapping Conflicting Claims

To help students see which tribes were threatened by western settlement in the early 1800s, have them fill in an outline map (from **Geography Extensions**). Referring to maps on pages 29 and 277, they should label the region between the Appalachians and the Mississippi with the following: Indian homelands, states added by 1805 (Kentucky, Tennessee, Ohio), the Northwest Territory, the Wilderness Road, and the Old Walton Road.

See the Introducing the Chapter Activity, Exploring Other Worlds. **Take-Home Planner 4**, p. 12.

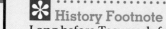

History Footnote

Long before Tecumseh formed his confederation, other Indians west of the Appalachians had tried to band together to preserve their ways of life and keep settlers from taking their lands. In the mid-1700s, Pontiac, an Ottawa chief, formed an alliance with Indians of the Ohio Valley, but they were defeated in Pontiac's War in 1763. The Delawares, Shawnees, Wyandots, and other Indians of the Ohio Valley were defeated in 1774. Chief Little Turtle formed the Miami confederation of Shawnees, Chippewas, Potowatomis, and other Indians in 1790 and enjoyed some success before the Battle of Fallen Timbers dealt the final blow to that alliance. Tecumseh had a larger vision, and in his effort to unite Indians he visited almost every group east of the Mississippi River.

Beginning the Story with

Tecumseh

When the Shawnee chief Tecumseh [tuh-KUM-suh] was born in present-day Ohio in 1768, his people still followed their traditional way of life. They lived in small villages throughout the Ohio Valley. In the summer, while the men hunted, the women planted crops and gathered the gifts of the forest. It was a good life, so good that whites taken prisoner by the Shawnees often preferred to stay with them, even after being "rescued" by other whites.

In the 1770s settlers from the east began crossing the mountains into the Indians' lands. By 1774, some 10,000 settlers lived in Kentucky alone. That same year, Tecumseh's father was killed in a bloody clash between the Shawnees and the settlers. While still a child, Tecumseh also lost two brothers and countless friends and relatives in battles with settlers. Three times he experienced the terror of having his village attacked and burned by white raiders.

As Tecumseh watched the flames devour his home, he saw more than a village being destroyed. The settlers threatened the very existence of the Shawnees and their way of life. Tecumseh's horrifying experiences as a child drove him, as a man, to unite the tribes of the Ohio country into a great coalition against the settlers' advance.

The Young Tecumseh

Tecumseh's Shawnee name was *nila ni tekamthi msi-pessi*, which meant the Man Who Waits, the Crouching Panther, or the Shooting Star. His people had named him well. As the boy grew to manhood, he would be all of these and more. Unable to pronounce the name, settlers called him Tecumseh.

In 1794 Tecumseh fought with the Miami chief Little Turtle against American soldiers at the Battle of Fallen Timbers. Sometime after this defeat,

History Bookshelf

Bohner, Charles. *Bold Journey.* Houghton Mifflin, 1987. A fictional character, 18-year-old Hugh McNeal, joins the expedition of Lewis and Clark. Through his eyes, Lewis and Clark and their adventures come alive. *Bold Journey* was a Young Adults' Choice book of 1987.
Also of interest:
Bober, Natalie S. *Thomas Jefferson, Man on a Mountain.* Atheneum, 1988.
Elting, John Robert. *Amateurs to Arms! A Military History of the War of 1812.* Algonquin Books, 1991.
Lacy, Dan Mabry. *The Lewis and Clark Expedition.* A Focus Book, 1974.
Meltzer, Milton. *Thomas Jefferson.* Franklin Watts, 1991.

Discussion

Thinking Historically

1. What were Tecumseh's experiences while growing up with settlers? (His father, two brothers, and many friends and relatives were killed in battles with settlers. Three times his village was attacked and burned.)

2. Why do you think he chose not to marry Rebecca Galloway? (The fate of his people and their way of life were probably more important to him than any feelings he had for her.)

3. What traits made him such an effective leader? (He was a powerful speaker with great strength and a purpose.)

Shawnees originally farmed and hunted along the Cumberland River in present-day Kentucky. Settlers forced them north of the Ohio River by the end of the 1700s. Even there they would not find security from the flood of settlers.

he befriended a white woman named Rebecca Galloway, the daughter of Ohio farmers. She taught him about Shakespeare, the Bible, and American history. Rebecca would have married Tecumseh if he had agreed to give up the Indian way of life, but he refused. Instead, he devoted the rest of his life to driving the settlers from his homeland.

See the Chapter In-Depth Activity, Storytelling: Meeting a Great Person. **Take-Home Planner 4,** p. 12.

The "Shooting Star" Unites His People

"Where today are the Narrangansetts, the Mohawks, the Pocanets, and many other once powerful tribes of our people? They have vanished before . . . the white man, as snow before a summer sun." So spoke Tecumseh as he rallied his people. By 1805, Tecumseh the Shooting Star was in constant motion, visiting tribes from the Great Lakes to Florida. At each stop his message was the same: By themselves, America's native peoples could not survive against the white man. They must either stop fighting among themselves and unite against the settlers, or lose everything. To his Creek Indian friends Tecumseh declared:

"Burn their dwellings. Destroy their [live] stock. The red people own the country . . . [make] war now. War forever. War upon the living. War upon the dead. Dig up their corpses [bodies] from the grave. Our country must give no rest to a white man's bones.**"**

Among Indians, Tecumseh inspired hope, pride, and unity of purpose. As his fame spread, even his enemies came to admire him. Tecumseh's message fired the hearts of Indians from Canada to the Gulf of Mexico and cast a long shadow on the events that would lead to the War of 1812.

Teaching the Hands-On ---▶ HISTORY

To help students think about their role as interviewer, suggest that they look at interviews in newspapers or magazines and note the kinds of questions asked. Ask them to consider how the point of view of a modern reporter who travels back in time might differ from that of a reporter who lived in the early 1800s.

Hands-On ▶ HISTORY

Activity

Imagine that you are a newspaper reporter in the United States today. Going back in time, you visit Tecumseh in his village of Prophetstown for a newspaper interview. Write a short article describing Tecumseh's view of the settlers, and what he wants to do as an Indian leader and why.

For a journal writing activity on Tecumseh, see student page 310.

★

**Introducing
the Section**

Vocabulary

judicial review (p. 293) the
power to decide whether an act
of Congress is constitutional

Letter to Europe

To help students review
differences between
Republicans and Federal-
ists, have them write letters outlining the ideas of
both parties. Tell them to
imagine that they are citizens of the United States
in 1800 who are writing
to relatives in Europe.
The letters should explain
the differences in Federalist and Republican ideas.
They should also suggest
how things might change
now that a Republican
is President. Have them
refer to the chart on page
280 if necessary.

**Geography Question
of the Day**

To review the size of the
nation when Jefferson took
office, have students shade in
an outline map of the United
States as of 1801. Have them
label the names of states and
territories.

Section Objectives

★ Describe how the Supreme Court established its power of judicial review.
★ Explain how Jefferson doubled the size of
the country.
★ Identify the first Americans to explore the
vast new territory of Louisiana.

1. The New Republican President

Reading Guide

New Term **judicial review**

Section Focus **How Jefferson put his Republican ideas to work as President**

1. How did the Supreme Court establish its power of judicial review?
2. How did President Jefferson double the size of the United States?
3. Who were the first Americans to explore the vast new territory of Louisiana?

In 1801 Thomas Jefferson became the first
President to take the oath of office in
Washington, D.C. Jefferson's inauguration
fit his Republican beliefs that government
should be kept small and simple.

Washington and Adams had traveled to
their inaugurations in fancy carriages.
Jefferson, however, walked from his rooming
house to the Capitol building. His simple
suit, wrote one reporter, "was, as usual, that
of a plain citizen."

In his inaugural address, Jefferson tried to
heal the wounds left by the election and
offer hope for the future:

❝Let us, then, fellow citizens, unite with
one heart and one mind. . . . We are all
Republicans, we are all Federalists.**❞**

Republican Ideas
Put to Work

As President, Jefferson tried to live by his
words and put Republican ideas about
government to work. To keep the government small, he cut the number of federal
officials and the size of the army and navy.
To protect people's liberties, he let the Alien
and Sedition Acts expire. Jefferson also
convinced Congress to end the hated excise
tax on whiskey.

On the other hand, the new President did
not try to undo Federalist economic policies.
His government continued to pay off the
national debt and allowed the Bank of the
United States to function.

At the President's House, Jefferson the
Republican ended many of the customs of
Presidents Washington and Adams. Guests
now shook hands with the President, instead
of bowing before him. Formal receptions
were replaced with informal dinners at a
round table, so that no person appeared
superior to anyone else. Jefferson hired a
French chef, however, and served fine wines.

A New Role for the Court

With Jefferson's election, Republicans
controlled both Congress and the presidency. Thanks to John Adams, however,
Federalists dominated the third branch of
government, the judicial branch.

During his last weeks in office, Adams
had taken several steps to keep the judicial
branch in Federalist hands. One was to
choose John Marshall to be Chief Justice of
the Supreme Court. Although Marshall was
a cousin of Thomas Jefferson, and a fellow
Virginian, he despised Jefferson's Republican
ideas. Marshall's firm will and sharp mind
were to make him a worthy opponent for
Jefferson's strong personality.

⊞ **Connections to Science**

Jefferson invented a new type of plow and clock (see pictures below). These and other clever devices, such as a swivel chair, can be seen at his home, Monticello. More important, perhaps, Jefferson supported other American inventors. He corresponded with and aided Oliver Evans, one of the pioneers of the high-pressure steam engine. He also influenced Eli Whitney with stories of an inventive French merchant named Honoré Blanc, who developed a system of interchangeable parts for gun-making. Whitney was the leader in a movement to design and use standardized parts in manufactured items in the United States. Jefferson, while serving as Secretary of State before he became President, was in charge of signing patents.

Checking Understanding

1. As President, what steps did Jefferson take to put Republican ideas into practice? (To keep government small, reduced number of federal officials and size of military; let Alien and Sedition Acts expire; ended whiskey tax; followed simpler customs when entertaining.)

2. Which branches of the central government were controlled by the Republicans? By the Federalists? (Republicans: legislative and executive; Federalists: judicial.)

Stimulating Critical Thinking

3. Why do you think Jefferson continued the Federalist policy of paying the nation's debts? Explain. (Opinions will vary, but students may suggest that he recognized it was important to maintain the government's credibility.)

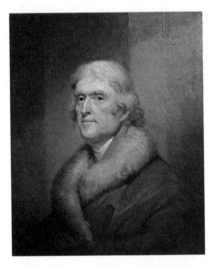
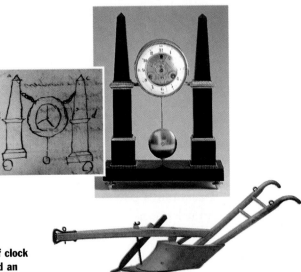

As an inventor, Jefferson designed a new type of clock and plow. He was also a musician, a farmer, and an architect, and he spoke many languages.

See the Study Guide activity in **Chapter Resources Binder**, p. 81.

Midnight judges Adams had also pushed the Judiciary Act of 1801 through Congress. This act created more positions for judges, which Adams rushed to fill. Indeed, the night before Jefferson's inauguration, Adams stayed up late signing commissions—orders—appointing loyal Federalists to these new judgeships.

Marbury v. Madison Soon after taking office, Jefferson noticed that a stack of commissions for new judges had not been delivered. Without receiving a commission, a person could not act as a judge. Calling the Federalist commissions "an outrage," Jefferson told Secretary of State James Madison not to deliver them.

One man who did not receive his commission was William Marbury. Marbury turned to the Supreme Court for help. The Judiciary Act of 1789 gave the Supreme Court the power to force federal officials to perform their duties. Therefore, Marbury argued, the Court could order Madison to give him his commission.

In 1803 the Supreme Court looked at the case of *Marbury* v. *Madison*. (The v. stands for versus, or against.) The outcome of the case forever changed the relationship of the three branches of government.

In his decision, Chief Justice Marshall agreed that the Judiciary Act of 1789 had given the Supreme Court the power to force federal officials to do their jobs. However, Marshall and the Court ruled that the Judiciary Act of 1789 was unconstitutional because the Constitution did not grant such power to the Court. Therefore, the Supreme Court could not force Madison to give Marbury his commission.

Judicial review John Marshall's decision in *Marbury* v. *Madison* was important because it established the power of judicial review for the Supreme Court. **Judicial review** is the power to decide whether or not an act of Congress is constitutional. Just as the President could veto acts passed by Congress, now the Supreme Court could rule them unconstitutional.

A Quaker petition antici-
pates the conflict over
westward expansion
of slavery. See **Using
Historical Documents,**
pp. 61–65.

For some of Napoleon's
statements about
Louisiana, see **American
Readings,** p. 41.

In the decision, Marshall wrote that it was the "duty" of the Court "to say what the law is." This case was a new development in American democracy. It put the Supreme Court on an equal footing with Congress and the President. Instead of power resting with just two branches of the federal government, a third branch now shared federal power.

Point of View
Did the Court attack the President's power?

Republican newspapers saw the ruling in *Marbury* v. *Madison* as an attack on the President's role as the only one who could veto laws. The *Independent Chronicle* wrote:

> The attempt of the Supreme Court . . . to control the Executive . . . seems to be no less than a commencement [beginning] of war between the . . . departments [branches]. The Court must be defeated.

The historian James McGregor Burns, writing in 1982, disagreed. This case, he believed, established a new role for the Supreme Court.

> Republicans had missed the point. The court had not invaded the executive [the President]. . . . What the Chief Justice had done was far more important. Marshall, in voiding an act of Congress signed by the President . . . was creating the great precedent of judicial invalidation [repeal] of congressional action.

The Supreme Court's new power stunned the Republicans. The Federalists, on the other hand, welcomed the Court's decision. Why do you think the two parties reacted so differently?

The Louisiana Purchase

Meanwhile, the United States was growing rapidly. West of the Appalachians, new territories were being organized. Even farther west, across the Mississippi River, lay vast lands little known by Europeans. This immense region, called Louisiana, was first claimed by France. It was given to Spain after the French and Indian War.

In 1800 the French ruler Napoleon Bonaparte bullied Spain into giving Louisiana back to France. Napoleon planned to settle Louisiana with farmers who would raise food for France's Caribbean sugar colonies.

Napoleon's dreams frightened Americans living west of the Appalachians. Under Pinckney's Treaty with Spain, they had freely used the Mississippi River and the port of New Orleans to ship their crops to market. What if Napoleon closed New Orleans to American goods? It would be a disaster for western farmers.

An unexpected bargain In 1803 Jefferson sent James Monroe to France. His mission was to persuade Napoleon to sell New Orleans to the United States.

While Monroe was crossing the Atlantic, Napoleon changed his plans for Louisiana. A few months earlier, enslaved people in the Caribbean colony of Saint Domingue [sahn doh-MING] successfully rebelled against French rule. Having lost his most valuable sugar colony, Napoleon no longer needed to turn Louisiana into a breadbasket for Saint Domingue (later renamed Haiti).

On the brink of war with Great Britain, Napoleon also knew that he did not have a navy to protect French lands in North America. Rather than lose Louisiana to Britain, why not sell it to the Americans? Monroe accepted Napoleon's offer. On April 30, 1803, he signed a treaty with France in which the United States agreed to buy Louisiana for about $15 million.

Connections to Geography

Napoleon conquered almost all of Europe, but one might say that geography kept him from achieving world domination. Though a brilliant military strategist, he could not conquer Britain, his greatest enemy, because it was accessible only by sea and was defended by a superior navy. Although he wanted to hold on to Louisiana, he could not afford to send troops to defend the territory while trying to conquer Europe at the same time. Finally, Napoleon failed to conquer Russia, defeated by the country's vastness and its terrible winter climate. He lost more than 500,000 of the 600,000 troops who marched into Russia with him.

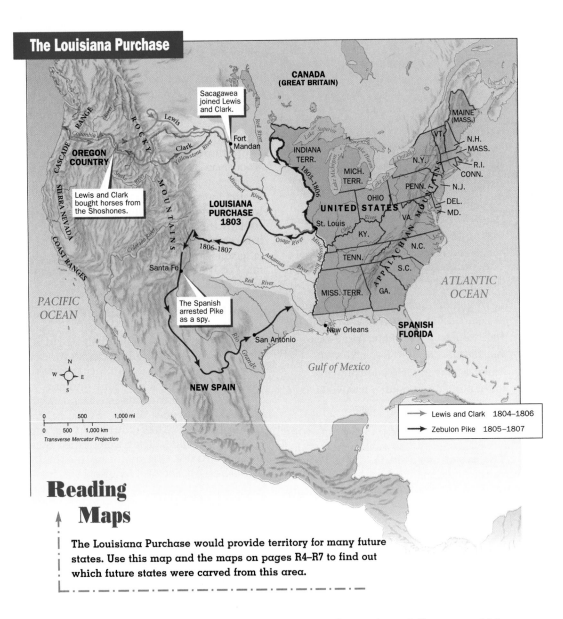

The Louisiana Purchase

Sacagawea joined Lewis and Clark.

Fort Mandan

Lewis and Clark bought horses from the Shoshones.

OREGON COUNTRY

LOUISIANA PURCHASE 1803

1806–1807

Santa Fe

The Spanish arrested Pike as a spy.

San Antonio

NEW SPAIN

PACIFIC OCEAN

CANADA (GREAT BRITAIN)

MAINE (MASS.)
VT
N.H.
MASS.
INDIANA TERR.
N.Y.
R.I.
CONN.
MICH. TERR.
PENN.
N.J.
OHIO
UNITED STATES
DEL.
MD.
VA.
St. Louis
KY.
N.C.
TENN.
S.C.
MISS. TERR.
GA.

ATLANTIC OCEAN

New Orleans

SPANISH FLORIDA

Gulf of Mexico

| | Lewis and Clark 1804–1806 |
| | Zebulon Pike 1805–1807 |

0   500   1,000 mi
0   500   1,000 km
Transverse Mercator Projection

Reading Maps

The Louisiana Purchase would provide territory for many future states. Use this map and the maps on pages R4–R7 to find out which future states were carved from this area.

Jefferson's dilemma Jefferson was thrilled with Monroe's success. Still, the purchase of Louisiana created a problem for him. As a Republican, he stood for strict construction of the Constitution. The Constitution did not mention the purchase of foreign lands as one of the government's powers. To approve the purchase, Jefferson would have to go against his Republican ideals.

A constitutional amendment would solve the problem, but Jefferson knew that an amendment could not be adopted quickly enough. He put aside his doubts and asked the Senate to approve the purchase.

Discussion

Checking Understanding

1. Why did Jefferson think it was important to purchase New Orleans? (Mississippi River, which empties into the Gulf at New Orleans, was important to western farmers for getting crops to market.)

2. What may have prompted Napoleon to offer the Louisiana region to the United States? (He had intended to use it to grow crops to support his sugar colony. When he lost that colony to rebellion, he may have felt Louisiana was not worth defending.)

Stimulating Critical Thinking

3. How might the United States be different today without the Louisiana Purchase? (Far less land, perhaps unfriendly neighbor to west, no access to Pacific, even more focused on Europe.)

Teaching the Reading Maps

Have students add to an outline map the date each state in the Louisiana Territory entered the Union. They can refer to pages R19–R23. (Louisiana 1812, Missouri 1821, Arkansas 1836, Iowa 1846, Minnesota 1858, Kansas 1861, Nebraska 1867, North and South Dakota and Montana 1889, Wyoming 1890, Oklahoma 1907.)

The lives of the Plains Indians revolved around the horse and the buffalo. Horses, which they acquired from the Spaniards in the late 1600s, changed the Indians' way of life. Some nations, like the Cheyenne, became hunters and gave up farming. Horses made it easier to follow and hunt buffalo.

Indians made use of every part of the buffalo. They ate the meat and used the hide for moccasins, shields, tepee coverings, and clothing. Bones were made into knives and jewelry. Even the horns and hooves were used. Horns were made into vessels to hold gunpowder, and hooves were made into bowls and spoons. The pioneers who followed Lewis and Clark into the West killed and drove away the buffalo, forever changing and finally destroying the Plains Indians' ways of life.

Teaching the

World  Link

First have students locate Haiti on a world map (pages R2–R3). After they read the feature, ask them to consider how the American and French revolutions might have influenced the revolt. Point out that France outlawed slavery in 1793, but that Napoleon tried to reestablish it in Haiti in 1802.

Section **Activity**

Election Posters

To highlight issues during Jefferson's first term, have small groups each create two 1804 election posters, one supporting Jefferson and one criticizing him. They should consider how his decisions might be portrayed as harmful or helpful, domestically or in foreign affairs. Key decisions are reducing the size of government and military, continuing the Federalist debt and bank policies, and the Louisiana Purchase.

★ ★ ★
Vital Links

🔘 **Nez Percé with Lewis and Clark (Movie) Unit 2, Side 2, Search 01585, Play to 02611**

🔘 See also Unit 2 Explore CD-ROM location 284.

World  Link

Haiti breaks free
Toussaint L'Ouverture [too-SAHN loo-vehr-TYOOR] was born into slavery in the French Caribbean colony of Saint Domingue (now Haiti). Self-educated, he led a slave revolt that began in 1791. By 1801 his army had conquered the entire island of Hispaniola.

The next year Napoleon sent 20,000 French soldiers to retake the colony. Toussaint was captured and sent to prison in France, but his followers fought on. By 1803 Napoleon knew that Saint Domingue and his dream of a French North America were lost. He sold Louisiana to the United States just a few weeks after Toussaint died in prison.

The purchase debate To many Americans, the Louisiana Purchase looked like the bargain of the century. The new territory would double the size of the United States at the low price of three cents an acre. Even so, there was opposition.

The size of the new territory bothered people who believed that it would make the United States too large to govern. Others fussed about the cost. "We are to give money of which we have too little," wrote a Boston critic, "for land of which we already have too much."

The Senate finally approved the treaty late in 1803. The Louisiana Purchase doubled the size of the United States, and added 200,000 Native American, French, and Spanish inhabitants.

Lewis and Clark

Louisiana was now American territory, but no one knew just how large it was, or what treasures it contained. To find out, Jefferson asked his 27-year-old secretary, Meriwether Lewis, to lead an expedition. Lewis chose William Clark, an experienced woodsman and soldier, as co-leader.

Jefferson gave Lewis and Clark instructions for the journey. They were to explore rivers for a route to the Pacific, open trade with Indians they met, and, most of all, collect information. "Objects worthy of notice," Jefferson wrote, "will be the soil and face [terrain] of the country, the animals, . . . the winds prevailing at different seasons."

Up the Missouri In May 1804, Lewis and Clark's expedition left St. Louis by boat and headed up the Missouri River. About 30 men joined them, including Clark's African American slave, York. By summer they were deep into the land of the Plains Indians.

The expedition wintered in a Mandan village in what is now North Dakota. In the spring of 1805, they continued up the Missouri in canoes. They were joined by a guide, Toussaint Charbonneau [too-SAHN shar-bah-NOH], and his 17-year-old Shoshone wife, Sacagawea [SAK-uh-juh-WEE-uh]. Sacagawea had been kidnapped as a child and taken far from her mountain homeland. She would serve as an interpreter.

On to the Pacific Late that summer they reached Shoshone country in the foothills of the Rockies. One day, Lewis wrote:

❝ [Sacagawea began] to dance and show every mark of the most extravagant joy. . . . A woman [Sacagawea's sister] made her way through the crowd toward Sacagawea, and recognizing each other, they embraced with the most tender affection. ❞

Sacagawea served as more than just an interpreter on the Lewis and Clark expedition. She expanded the company's diet of meat, bread, and flour pudding to include roots, wild onions, and berries. These foods supplied vitamins that helped keep the explorers healthy. Her presence signaled to Indians they encountered that this was a friendly expedition. In one instance, she saved much of the medicine, seeds, trade goods, and journals when the expedition's supply canoe almost capsized. She did all this while caring for her infant son, who was just 2 months old when the journey started.

Hands-On → HISTORY

Designing a peace medal On their journey to the Pacific, Lewis and Clark carried peace medals from President Jefferson to give as offerings of friendship to Indians that they met. President Washington had begun the tradition of giving out medals in the United States, and it continued for 100 years.

President Clinton revived the tradition in 1994 when he invited Indian leaders from across the nation to a meeting at the White House. There he gave Jefferson peace medals to his guests. One side of the medal features an image of Jefferson, whom Clinton admires very much. On the other is a handshake of peace.

Jefferson peace medal

Activity Imagine that you are to explore a region where you will encounter people who are unknown in the United States.

① Design a medal to give to these people in friendship. What would you put on the front of your medal? On the back?

② Draw the design on a surface large enough for the entire class to see.

③ When you present your design to the class, explain the images that you chose for the medal.

Sacagawea also recognized the Shoshone chief as her brother, Cameahwait [kah-MAY-eh-wayt]. She persuaded him to guide the expedition across the rugged Rocky Mountains before early snows blocked the passes. They struggled over range after range of mountains, finally reaching the great Columbia River "and the object of all our labors," the Pacific Ocean.

The expedition spent its second winter camped near the ocean, in dismal conditions. Almost constant rain rotted their clothes and spoiled their food. When spring came, they recrossed the Rockies and Great Plains. Arriving in St. Louis on September 23, 1806, Lewis wrote to President Jefferson:

"It is with pleasure that I announce to you the safe arrival of myself and party at twelve o'clock today at this place [St. Louis] with our papers and baggage. In obedience to our orders, we have penetrated the continent of North America to the Pacific Ocean."

Lewis and Clark had done even more than "penetrate the continent." They had exceeded President Jefferson's wildest expectations. Their "papers and baggage" contained a treasure trove of priceless information about the newly purchased lands that would soon beckon Americans westward.

Pike's Expedition

While Lewis and Clark were on their way home in 1806, another expedition set out from St. Louis to explore a different part of the Louisiana Purchase. This one was led by an adventurous army officer and explorer named Zebulon Pike.

Pike and his party pushed west across the Kansas plains along the Osage and Arkansas Rivers. Upon reaching the Colorado Rockies, Pike caught sight of the "Grand Peak," now named Pikes Peak.

As winter closed in, Pike and his men became lost and wandered south into present-day New Mexico. There, Spanish soldiers arrested them as spies and took them deep into Mexico. Pike's party was held captive until the spring of 1807.

Discussion

Checking Understanding

1. What were the purposes of the Lewis and Clark expedition? (To find a route to the Pacific, trade with Indians, and collect information about the land and animals.)

2. How long did their expedition take? (2 years and 5 months)

Stimulating Critical Thinking

3. What could have caused the Lewis and Clark expedition to fail? (Indians might have been hostile, the winters harsh, the Rockies too hard to cross, and some of their party might have been struck by illness.)

Teaching the Hands-On → HISTORY

Students may design medals that depict people, places, ideas, or events. Suggest that they think in terms of images that are simple, direct, and understandable regardless of the language spoken by their intended audience.

For more excerpts from the journals of Lewis and Clark, see the Link to Literature feature on pages 312–313.

For Pike's report of his encounter with Spanish soldiers, see **American Readings**, p. 42.

Point out that Washington Allston was one of the first Americans to paint in the Romantic tradition of the 1800s. Romantic painters emphasized emotion and imagination over rational thought. **Discussion Answer:** Students may think that he intended to depict nature as beautiful and awe-inspiring rather than dangerous.

Closing the Section

Wrap-Up Activity

Five Clues

Have students work in pairs to write five clues about a person, place, event, issue, or concept discussed in the section. Clues should be progressively more informative. Each pair can then challenge other pairs to identify the topics with as few clues as possible. They can keep score by totaling the number of clues needed to identify each pair's topic.

Section Review Answers

1. Definition: *judicial review* (293)

2. Gain access to the Gulf, double nation's size.

3. The United States might not have acquired the Louisiana Territory and might still only have land east of the Mississippi.

✳ **History Footnote**

There was much controversy surrounding Zebulon Pike's mission. The Spaniards believed him to be an American spy and wrote a strongly worded protest to the American government. After the United States denied that it used spies for any purpose, Spain cut off diplomatic relations. Pike's mission was ordered by his friend General Wilkinson, the governor of the upper Louisiana Territory. When Pike returned from Mexico, where he was held captive, Wilkinson was unmasked as a double agent for Spain and a dangerous traitor to the United States. Many suspicions were raised about Pike's mission. Had Pike gotten lost as he said, or did he go into Spanish territory on purpose? Though he was later acquitted of any wrongdoing, many still wondered about the true nature of his mission.

⚬ **Link to Art**

Landscape with a Lake (1804) During Jefferson's presidency, American painting entered the Romantic period. Romantic artists celebrated the beauty of nature. Their work reflected feelings of hope and nationalism as Americans expanded into new lands. During his painting career, Washington Allston developed a "love for the wild and marvellous." In this painting, he contrasts the majesty of nature with the tiny human figure. **Discuss** Do you think the artist intended to depict nature as friendly or dangerous? Explain your answer.

On his return home, Pike wrote a popular book about his journey. In it he praised the Spanish settlers in New Mexico for their "heaven-like qualities of hospitality and kindness." Pike also described the sea of grass that covered much of the whole region, calling it a desert. Later, mapmakers would label the Great Plains as desert. For the next half century, settlers would avoid this region.

1. Section Review

1. Define **judicial review**.

2. What reasons did the United States have for purchasing Louisiana?

3. Critical Thinking How might a map of the United States look different today if all Presidents had followed a strict construction of the Constitution?

Before Lewis and Clark crossed the Rockies, few white people who had penetrated this barrier kept records of their journeys. Spaniards had made tentative advances into the southern fringes, and Alexander Mackenzie had crossed the Rockies in 1793, but far to the north in Canada. Lewis and Clark did not linger, searching for a quick way through the mountains.

Geography Lab

The Rocky Mountains

When Lewis and Clark set out on their journey, they did not know how rugged the Rocky Mountain region would be. After struggling across the Bitterroot Range of the Rockies, Clark wrote, "I have been wet and as cold . . . as I ever was in my life." Another member of the party described the Bitterroots as "the most terrible mountains I ever beheld."

Rugged. Terrible. Majestic. These words describe the Rockies. What other words come to your mind as you study this page?

Grand Tetons, Wyoming (above). Mountain goat (left). San Juan Mountains, southern Colorado (below).

Developing a Mental Map

Refer to the maps on pages P4–P5 and R4–R7.

1. Through what states do the Rockies extend? Where is the highest peak? Between what two states does the Bitterroot Range lie?

2. What region lies east of the Rocky Mountains? Looking at the picture on the lower left side, compare the two regions.

3. The Rocky Mountain region is one of the least populated in the United States. It is also a major tourist destination. How do you explain these facts?

4. **Hands-On Geography**
Write a travel plan for a week-long vacation in the Rockies. You may want to do some research. Consider these questions: What season of the year will you go, and why? What parks will you visit? What sights do you expect to see? What activities do you expect to enjoy?

Teaching the Geography Lab

To give students a better understanding of the region, help them contrast the Rockies and the Appalachians. Rockies extend father—3,000 miles (4,080 km) vs. 1,500 miles (2,400 km)—and are taller. Tallest Appalachian peak is 6,684 feet (2,037 m). Colorado alone has more than 40 peaks higher than 14,000 feet (4,267 m). Point out that the Continental Divide runs through the Rockies (rivers west of it flow toward Pacific; east, toward Atlantic).

Developing a Mental Map
Answers

1. Alaska, Washington, Idaho, Montana, Wyoming, Colorado, Utah, New Mexico; Mt. Elbert, 14,433 feet (4,400 m); Idaho and Montana.

2. Great Plains—flat region of grasses, wildflowers, and few trees; contrasts with rugged, barren mountain peaks.

3. Scenery and wildlife attract tourists, but weather and rugged terrain make life difficult.

4. Answers will vary. Choices of times depend on activity choices.

See the activity on the Rocky Mountains in **Geography Extensions,** pp. 21–22.

Introducing the Section

Vocabulary

embargo (p. 302) complete halt in trade

Warm-Up Activity

Writing Captains' Logs

To help students identify dangers faced by sailors, have them imagine being captain of a ship in the early 1800s. They should write entries into captains' logs about an obstacle they encountered, such as a storm or pirates, and how they handled it.

Geography Question of the Day

To help students identify possible shipping routes, give them outline maps of the U.S. and Europe that include rivers. Tell them that they are farmers in the Midwest who want to get their goods to markets in Italy. Have them trace the most direct water routes for their goods.

Teaching the

Link to the Present

Ask students what they know about piracy today. If necessary, point out that it may include the stealing of ideas, inventions, or products, particularly those protected by copyright or patents.

Section Objectives

★ Explain how the United States dealt with pirates from the Barbary States.
★ Describe how Britain and France treated American ships and sailors.
★ Describe what Jefferson did to try to protect American trade and how effective it was.

Teaching Resources

Take-Home Planner 4, pp. 10–17
Chapter Resources Binder
  Study Guide, p. 82
  Reinforcement, pp. 85–86
  Skills Development
Geography Extensions
American Readings, p. 43
Using Historical Documents
Transparency Activities
Chapter and Unit Tests

2. Troubles at Sea

Reading Guide

New Term embargo

Section Focus How the United States responded to threats to American trade from other nations

1. How did the United States deal with pirates from the Barbary States?
2. How did Britain and France treat American ships and sailors?
3. How did Jefferson try to protect American trade? How effective was his policy?

In 1804 Jefferson won re-election for President by overwhelming his opponent, the Federalist Charles Pinckney. Although the election went smoothly, trouble lay ahead. Threats to American trade forced Jefferson, like the nation's first two Presidents, to turn his attention away from home.

The Barbary Pirates Strike

For years, pirates from the four Barbary States of North Africa—Morocco, Algiers, Tunis, and Tripoli—had seized American ships in the Mediterranean Sea. Presidents Washington and Adams had quietly paid tribute money to these states in exchange for protection against pirate raids.

In 1801 the ruler of Tripoli demanded still more tribute money. Jefferson refused to pay up, and the Barbary pirates once again plundered American ships. Jefferson sent the small American navy to the Mediterranean. It was too weak, however, to end the pirate attacks. Only in 1815 did a rebuilt navy join a European fleet to destroy the pirate bases.

Other Threats to Trade

Pirates were not the only threat to American trade. During Jefferson's presidency, France and Britain were almost continuously

at war. In 1803 Jefferson declared the United States neutral, as Washington had done before him. As the war dragged on, however, Jefferson found it more and more difficult to maintain neutrality.

Link to the Present

Sea piracy today The end of the Barbary pirates was not the end of piracy. Today's sea pirates capture booty worth as much as $250 million every year. Pirate attacks can take place almost anywhere, though most occur off the coasts of South and Southeast Asia. Ships in the waters off Singapore are favorite targets.

Some raids involve a few men armed with knives and swords. They board a ship and take whatever cash and valuables they can carry off. Other attacks involve large, well-organized groups. Such pirates might use radar and automatic weapons in their plan to steal a ship's entire cargo—anything from coffee to videocassette recorders. Some pirates have stolen entire ships!

See the Study Guide activity in **Chapter Resources Binder**, p. 82.

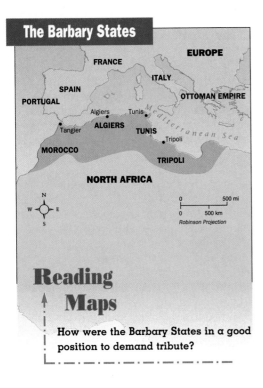

The Barbary States

Reading Maps

How were the Barbary States in a good position to demand tribute?

In 1806 Britain clamped a blockade around French-controlled ports in Europe. Napoleon struck back, ordering a blockade of Britain. Both nations seized American ships heading for the other's ports.

Worse yet, British sea captains began searching ships along the American coast, looking for deserters—sailors who leave ship without permission. Any sailor who appeared to be English could be impressed, even if he was an American citizen. Jefferson complained that "England has become a den of pirates and France has become a den of thieves."

The *Chesapeake–Leopard* Affair

Britain's policy of impressment angered Americans. Their anger turned to rage with the *Chesapeake–Leopard* affair.

In 1807 the *Leopard,* a British warship, stopped the *Chesapeake,* an American naval ship, off the Virginia coast. Captain James Barron of the *Chesapeake* invited a British officer aboard to exchange mail. Once on board, the officer declared that he would search the ship for deserters. "Sir!" Barron replied hotly, "This is a national vessel of the United States." No one, he declared, would search his ship.

In reply, the *Leopard* opened fire on the *Chesapeake,* killing or wounding 21 American sailors. When the *Chesapeake* surrendered, the British found only one deserter aboard. They promptly hanged him.

Jefferson's Embargo

As the battered *Chesapeake* limped into port, Americans came down with a severe case of war fever. Not since the battle at Lexington during the War for Independence, had Jefferson seen the people so ready for war. The British had, he wrote, "given us cause for war

In 1803 a young naval officer, Stephen Decatur (lower right), led an attack against the Barbary pirates of Tripoli.

Closing the Section

Wrap-Up Activity

Writing a Press Release

To help students see why Jefferson did not run for a third term, have them write a press release explaining his possible reasons. Their reasons should be based on what they know about Jefferson and his first and second terms. They might include references to obstacles he ran into that led him to put his political ideals aside.

Section Review
Answers

1. Definition: *embargo* (302)
2. Barbary States wanted tribute in exchange for protection against pirates. Jefferson refused to pay.
3. The British opened fire when the *Chesapeake*'s captain would not let them search his ship for deserters. The British killed or wounded 21 Americans.
4. He tried an embargo, which hurt Americans more than it did the British and French. Suggestions may include more negotiations. Students should show awareness that the embargo, Non-Intercourse Act, and threats to cut off trade failed.

For John Adams's protest against impressment, see **American Readings**, p. 43.

In the early 1800s ships that carried cargo and passengers started regularly scheduled crossings between the United States and Europe. Before that, ships had waited for a full cargo and favorable weather before setting sail. Competition between companies offering regularly scheduled trips was so fierce that captains sailed their ships day and night in all kinds of weather to make the crossing in the shortest time possible—three to four weeks going east with the help of westerly winds and five to six weeks traveling west. The advent of regularly scheduled trips probably made piracy easier and more profitable than it had been before.

This cartoon opposing the embargo shows the turtle Ograbme ("embargo" backwards) snapping at an American trying to trade with Britain.

before. . . . But now they have touched a chord which vibrates in every heart."

Still, Jefferson dreaded going to war. Knowing his navy was weak, he proposed an **embargo**—a complete halt in trade—with other nations. Under the Embargo Act of 1807, no ships could leave American ports and no foreign ships could enter them. Jefferson hoped that the embargo would prove so painful to France and Britain that they would stop attacking American ships.

Instead, Americans suffered more from the embargo than Europeans did. Thousands of sailors lost their jobs. Only soup kitchens set up in port cities kept them from starving. Merchants, meanwhile, watched helplessly as their ships rotted away at deserted docks.

As the embargo continued, many seamen survived by smuggling goods into the country. New Englanders opposed the "Dambargo," and even talked of forming their own nation. Jefferson snapped back:

❝New England commerce has kept us in hot water from the commencement [beginning] of our government, and is now engaging us in war.❞

The Embargo Fails

In the presidential election of 1808, opposition to the embargo was an issue. Thomas Jefferson, looking forward to shaking off "the shackles of power," decided against a third term as President. He threw his support behind James Madison, who won easily.

In 1809, just days before the end of his term, Jefferson ended the embargo and signed the Non-Intercourse, or non-trade, Act. Now Americans could trade with any nation except Britain and France. As soon as those powers would stop seizing American ships and men, the United States would reopen trade with them.

Like the embargo, the Non-Intercourse Act was a failure. When American ships returned to sea, French and British warships seized them once again. In 1810 a frustrated Congress tried a new policy. Americans could trade with both France and Britain until one of the powers stopped seizing American ships. The United States would then cut off trade with the other.

When this policy also failed, a growing number of Americans saw war as unavoidable. The question was: War with France or war with Britain?

★ 2. Section Review

1. Define **embargo**.
2. What did the Barbary States want from the United States? How did Jefferson respond to their demand?
3. What happened to the *Chesapeake* that so outraged Americans?
4. **Critical Thinking** Briefly explain Jefferson's policy toward Britain and France. Describe a different way that the United States might have responded. What might the results have been?

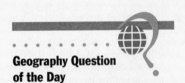

Section Objectives

★ Explain why the United States declared war on Britain in 1812.
★ Describe the impact of the war on the Indians of the Ohio country.
★ Describe the final effect of the war on the United States.

Teaching Resources
Take-Home Planner 4, pp. 10–17
Chapter Resources Binder
Study Guide, p. 83
Reinforcement
Skills Development, pp. 87–88
Geography Extensions
American Readings, p. 44
Using Historical Documents
Transparency Activities
Chapter and Unit Tests, pp. 69–72

3. The War of 1812

Reading Guide

New Term nationalism

Section Focus **How the United States fought its second war with Britain**

1. Why did the United States declare war against Britain in 1812?
2. What was the impact of the war on the Indians of the Ohio country?
3. What was the final effect of the war on the United States?

Two events pushed the United States toward war with Britain. First, in 1810 Napoleon declared that France would end its attacks on American ships. Without waiting to see if France would keep its promise, President Madison cut off trade with Britain. However the British continued to seize American ships. Madison began to think that war was the only way to make Britain respect American rights.

Tecumseh and the Prophet

Even before President Madison stopped trade with Britain, developments in the Indiana Territory had increased tensions with Britain. There, Tecumseh was moving forward with his dream of an Indian confederacy that would stop the spread of settlers. Tecumseh's brother played an important role in pursuing this dream.

As a young man, the brother had been a loud, drunken troublemaker. Then, one day in the spring of 1805, he fell into a deep sleep. Upon awakening, he reported that he had died and visited the Great Spirit in paradise. He returned to life with a message from the Great Spirit: Indians must reject the ways of white people if they wanted to enter paradise after death.

The Shawnees called Tecumseh's brother Tenskwatawa [ten-SKWAH-tah-wah], or "Open Door." In their eyes, he had opened the door to paradise. To others, he was known as the Prophet.

Together, Tecumseh and the Prophet were a powerful team. They spoke of Indian unity, urged tribes not to surrender any more land, and warned them against drinking alcohol. Wherever the two went, Indians listened.

Prophetstown Followers of Tecumseh and the Prophet built Prophetstown, their capital, on the Tippecanoe River in the present-day state of Indiana. As Prophetstown and the Indian alliance grew, so did the worries of settlers.

William Henry Harrison, the governor of the Indiana Territory, had warned that Tecumseh was "one of those uncommon

The Prophet urged Indians to follow their traditional way of life and avoid contact with settlers. Only then, he claimed, would they have the will to stop the settlers.

Introducing the Section

Vocabulary

nationalism (p. 308) pride in one's country

Warm-Up Activity

Using Charts to Predict

To help students make predictions, have them draw up charts identifying reasons for going to war with either Britain or France. Have them review section 2 if necessary. They then use their charts to predict which country, if either, the war would be with.

Geography Question of the Day

Give students a list of some important towns and cities of the United States in 1812, such as Boston, New York, Philadelphia, Norfolk (VA), Charleston (SC), New Orleans, and St. Louis. Have them locate the cities on a map and draw conclusions about why these cities may have been important. (They are all important port cities on rivers or the ocean.)

Writing an Eyewitness Account

To help students understand the impact of events on individuals, have them work in pairs to write first-person accounts of events. They can imagine being present at one of the major events described in the section. A newspaper has asked them to write stories of their eyewitness accounts. Assign each pair an event, such as the Battle of Tippecanoe, Perry's victory on Lake Erie, the Battle of Thames, the Battle of Horseshoe Bend, the burning of Washington, the attack on Fort McHenry, or the Battle of New Orleans. After researching more about the event, they should write their accounts in a way that gives the reader a sense of what it was like to be there.

★ ★ ★
Vital Links

Battle of Tippecanoe (Picture) Unit 2, Side 1, Search 49844

◉ **See also Unit 2 Explore CD-ROM location 287.**

✳ **History Footnote**

Harrison's rout of the Indians at the Battle of Tippecanoe earned him the nickname "Tippecanoe." He ran for President in 1836 and lost. When he ran with John Tyler in 1840, his campaign slogan was "Tippecanoe and Tyler, Too." Advisors recommended that he say "not one single word about his principles or creed." Running on his reputation as a military hero, he won.

See the Study Guide activity in **Chapter Resources Binder**, p. 83.

Indian forces and United States soldiers battled in the forests near the Tippecanoe River. In 1811 President Madison had ordered Governor Harrison to strike at the Indians living in the area.

geniuses [who] . . . produce revolutions." President Jefferson had dreaded a conflict with the Indians. He urged Harrison to avoid war. "Our system is to live in perpetual [lasting] peace with the Indians," he declared.

The Battle of Tippecanoe

Governor Harrison continued to watch the growth of Prophetstown with alarm. In the fall of 1811, while Tecumseh was away visiting southern tribes, Harrison marched more than 1,000 soldiers to Prophetstown. His plan was to attack the Indians living there with "bayonets and buckshot," and then burn the village.

The Shawnee Prophet made plans of his own. He promised the outnumbered Indians that his magic would make the white soldiers powerless. As a cold rain began to fall just before sunrise on November 7, the Indians made a surprise charge into Harrison's army camp on the Tippecanoe River. When they failed to gain an easy victory, though, they lost hope and deserted Prophetstown.

Harrison could hardly believe his luck, since the Indians had lost no more lives than had his army. He burned Prophetstown down to the ground.

Harrison's victory did not prevent the outbreak of an Indian war. Instead, it scattered Tecumseh's followers, who took revenge on isolated settlements across the Indiana Territory. Settlers fled the area.

Westerners blamed the British for their troubles. Harrison agreed. In the ashes of Prophetstown he had found British-made weapons. Harrison wrote that "the Indians on this frontier have been completely armed and equipped from the British [in Canada]." To make the area safe for settlers, the British must be forced out of Canada.

War Is Declared

By 1812 war fever was rising among southern and western Republicans. They were so eager for battle that Federalists called them "War Hawks." The War Hawks disliked the British for their mistreatment of American sailors and for supporting Indian resistance to settlers in the Indiana Territory. Southern War Hawks hoped to seize Florida from Britain's ally, Spain.

Surprisingly, support for war was weakest in New England, which had suffered most from attacks on ships. The embargo had taught New England merchants that some trade with Britain was better than none.

In June 1812 the War Hawks persuaded Congress to declare war on Britain. That same month Britain agreed to stop attacking American ships. The news did not reach

Oliver Perry's younger brother, Matthew, was also a great naval officer. Unlike Oliver, who sailed and fought only in the United States, Matthew was responsible for many victories overseas. For instance, in 1843 he commanded the African Squadron, which helped destroy the slave trade. His most significant accomplishment was the opening of trade with Japan. In 1854, after impressing the Japanese with a show of force, he arranged a treaty that protected American sailors and property in Japanese waters. The treaty changed American and European foreign policy toward Japan and changed the domestic situation in Japan itself.

Washington, D.C., for weeks, however. By then, it was too late. The United States and Britain were at war.

The Invasion of Canada

The United States was not prepared for war. The army had only 7,000 untested soldiers, the navy only 16 ships. Nor were Americans united behind the war. Northern Federalists opposed it. In the election of 1812, Madison won a second term only by carrying the southern and western states.

The War Hawks, however, were confident that conquering Canada was "a mere matter of marching." Half a million Canadians would be no match for 8 million Americans. Besides, they said, Canadians would welcome Americans as liberators.

Rather than welcoming the Americans, however, Canadians united to push back the invaders. Tecumseh's followers joined the Canadians in this effort. Americans tried to invade Canada three times in 1812. Each attempt ended in failure.

Oliver Perry's victory The following year, Americans scored two victories in the Northwest. The first occurred on the Great Lakes, where Captain Oliver Perry had assembled a makeshift fleet of ten vessels. He then requested of his commander:

When the British nearly destroyed Oliver Perry's ship, his men rowed him to another, from which he continued the battle.

1801–1815 Chapter 11 • **305**

Checking Understanding

1. Why were the War Hawks so anxious to declare war on Britain? (They disliked the British mistreatment of American sailors and their support of Indian resistance to settlers in the Indiana territory.)

2. Why did the War Hawks believe that conquering Canada would be easy? (They thought Canadians would welcome them as liberators, and Americans outnumbered Canadians.)

Stimulating Critical Thinking

3. The War of 1812 has been called "the Second War of Independence." In what ways, if any, is this description appropriate? (Answers will vary, but students should note that before the war Britain had much influence over American trade and was affecting U.S. relations with Indians.)

★ ★ ★
Vital Links

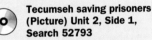

Tecumseh saving prisoners (Picture) Unit 2, Side 1, Search 52793

See also Unit 2 Explore CD-ROM location 305.

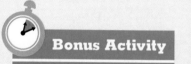
✳ **History Footnote**

In the early 1800s newspaper reporters referred to the White House as the President's House. During the second half of the century, Executive Mansion was the generally accepted newspaper term. As early as 1809, Henry Dearborn, Jefferson's Secretary of War, called it the White House. Daniel Webster mentioned the White House in a letter to a friend in 1813. The French minister, reporting to Talleyrand about the British invasion of Washington, said he "found [the British] General Ross in the White House, where he was collecting furniture . . . preparing to set it on fire." The term may have been used as early as 1798 when the first coat of whitewash was put on the building. President Theodore Roosevelt made the White House the official term in 1901.

"Give me men, sir, and I will gain both for you and myself honor and glory on this lake [Erie], or perish in the attempt."

In September 1813, Perry's navy destroyed a British fleet on Lake Erie. In what is now a famous phrase, Perry reported: "We have met the enemy, and they are ours!" Perry soon controlled the Great Lakes and sent the British into retreat.

Tecumseh dies Perry's success on the Great Lakes encouraged William Henry Harrison to invade Canada with 4,500 soldiers. On October 5, 1813, they met a combined British and Indian force at the Thames [temz] River north of Lake Erie.

The Battle of the Thames ended in a victory for the United States. However, it was a disaster for the Indians of the region. Tecumseh was killed, and with him died the dream of a united Indian people. A few weeks later, the Indians of the Ohio country signed a peace treaty with Harrison.

Farther south, Indians suffered another defeat. In March 1814 American troops and Cherokees led by General Andrew Jackson crushed a Creek force at Horseshoe Bend in present-day Alabama. The Creeks were forced to give up large parts of Georgia and Alabama. The Indians' struggle to save their land and way of life seemed hopeless.

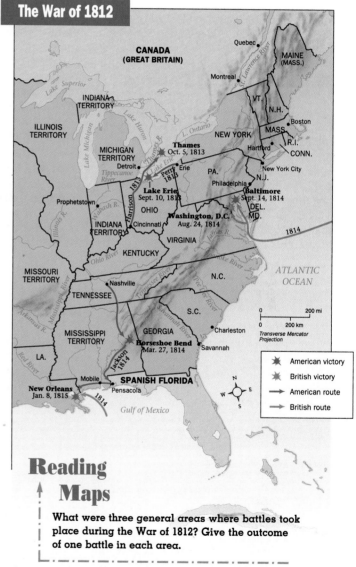

Reading Maps

What were three general areas where battles took place during the War of 1812? Give the outcome of one battle in each area.

Britain Strikes Back

In August 1814, the British decided to bring the war to American soil by marching on Washington, D.C. When they reached the nation's capital, they set it on fire. Washington burned as the President and

There is some evidence that Key wrote his poem to be sung to the tune of the old English drinking song "Anacreon in Heaven." The song was popular in that day, and the meter and verse form of "The Star-Spangled Banner" are similar to that of the drinking song. As soon as Key reached Baltimore after the battle, he had handbill copies of his verse printed and distributed. The song became very popular in and around Baltimore, where it was sung by military personnel encamped there. The song did not achieve national prominence until the Civil War. The U.S. Army started using it in 1895.

the United States government fled to Virginia. The British then enjoyed a splendid dinner at the President's House. After finishing their meal, they set fire to the house as well.

"The Star-Spangled Banner" Next, the British attacked nearby Baltimore, a vital port city on Chesapeake Bay. Fort McHenry guarded the entrance to Baltimore's harbor. On September 13, 1814, British warships bombed the fort all day and night. Exploding rockets cast a red glare over the harbor.

Through the night, Francis Scott Key, an American lawyer, watched the bombardment from a ship in the harbor. As dawn broke, he was thrilled to see a tattered American flag still waving above the fort. Key captured his feelings in a poem called the "The Defense of Fort McHenry." Later set to music as "The Star-Spangled Banner," it was adopted as the national anthem in 1931.

The Hartford Convention

Despite Britain's failure to take Baltimore, American hopes seemed dim in late 1814. Britain was sending more troops to North America. The federal government had no money, and the capital was burned to the ground. A visitor found President Madison looking "miserable." Congressman Daniel Webster predicted that "if peace does not come this winter, the government will die of its own weakness."

In December, New England Federalists met in Hartford, Connecticut, to discuss their opposition to President Madison and the war with the British. The Federalists proposed seven amendments to the Constitution that would give New England a stronger voice in Congress.

When delegates from the Hartford Convention arrived in Washington, though, no one paid attention to them. Instead, people were celebrating the Battle of New Orleans and the Treaty of Ghent.

The Battle of New Orleans

While Federalists were meeting in Hartford, 5,300 experienced British troops had been preparing to attack a fortified New Orleans. The city was defended by General Andrew Jackson and a "backwoods rabble" of untrained troops, free African Americans, Indians, and a few pirates.

Some people objected to Jackson's decision to arm the 200 free African Americans—it might encourage slaves to revolt. Nonsense, replied Jackson, "the free men of color would make excellent soldiers." He insisted they be treated the same as his other troops.

On January 8, 1815, the British launched a grand assault against Jackson's army. The Americans greeted them with a storm of gunfire. The battle turned into a slaughter. At least 2,000 British were killed or wounded, while only 8 Americans died. After just half an hour, the British surrendered. One soldier described the battleground as "a sea of blood."

When news of this stunning victory reached Washington, D.C., Andrew Jackson became a national hero. The gloom that had hung over the nation for the previous few months lifted.

A New Feeling of Pride

Soon the nation received even more good news. A peace treaty had been signed two weeks before Jackson's troops defeated the British at New Orleans. Thus, the Battle of New Orleans had been unnecessary.

The Treaty of Ghent ended the war, but it did not deal with British seizure of American ships. John Quincy Adams, the American negotiator, said the agreement "settled nothing." Still, Americans were pleased to have peace, even without victory.

▶ **Discussion**

Checking Understanding

1. Which battles of the War of 1812 did the United States win? (Lake Erie, Thames, New Orleans, Horseshoe Bend, Baltimore)

2. How did the British bring the war to American soil? (By attacking Washington, D.C.)

Stimulating Critical Thinking

3. Suppose that news of the peace treaty had come early enough to prevent the Battle of New Orleans. What do you think would have been the effect on the nation? (Perhaps there would be less of a sense of national pride. For despite naval victories and the victory at the battle of the Thames, the United States would not have achieved a victory over a large force of experienced British troops.)

★ ★ ★
Vital Links

"The Star-Spangled Banner" (Song) Unit 2, Side 1, Search 00431, Play to 02988

See also Unit 2 Explore CD-ROM location 10.

For the text of "The Star-Spangled Banner," see **American Readings**, p. 44.

Closing the Section

Wrap-Up Activity

Making a Cause-Effect Chart

To help students understand the War of 1812, have pairs create cause-effect charts. They should show relationships among the Indians, the British, and Americans; the effect of the war on Americans' feelings about their country; and the effect of Tecumseh's death.

Section Review
Answers

1. Definition: *nationalism* (308)

2. War Hawks disliked the British for mistreating American sailors and supporting Indian resistance. Southern War Hawks wanted to seize Florida.

3. Tecumseh was killed in the Battle of the Thames in Canada, and his dream of uniting Indians failed.

4. Answers may vary, but students should see that Indians lost their hope of uniting and thus their hunting grounds in Indiana Territory. The war settled little between Britain and the U.S., but led to a new sense of nationalism.

To check understanding of "Why We Remember," assign Thinking Critically question 3 on student page 310.

To help students understand a section of a chapter, teach them Chamot's note-taking system, called the "T-list." Have them draw a large T on notebook paper. On the left side of the T, they write the main ideas or section objectives. On the right side of the T, opposite each main idea, they write details from the section that support each main idea or objective. Alternatively, prepare such notes yourself and give them to students before they begin reading a section as a study guide. For some sections, you may want to give students a T-list with the left side filled in and have them add details on the right side as they read.

Peace brought with it a new spirit of **nationalism**—a strong feeling of pride in one's country. Americans were proud that their young nation had stood up against the most powerful nation in the world. Never again would Great Britain threaten the United States.

"The people," wrote Treasury Secretary Albert Gallatin, "are more American. They feel and act more as a nation." For many, this new feeling of national pride was victory enough.

3. Section Review

1. Define **nationalism**.
2. Why did the War Hawks want war with Great Britain?
3. What effect did the war in Canada have on Tecumseh's dream for the Indians?
4. Critical Thinking The War of 1812 involved the Americans, British, and American Indians. Who do you think lost the most? Who gained the most? Explain.

Why We Remember

The Jefferson Era

Between 1801 and 1817, the United States was led by two founders of the Republican Party, Thomas Jefferson and James Madison. For many people in the United States, the Jefferson era was a time of growth and national pride. For Indians, however, it was a time first of hope and then of defeat.

During this time, Jefferson and the Republicans tried to put their political ideas into practice. The task was not easy. They believed in strict construction of the Constitution, but they put that belief aside to buy Louisiana. They supported states' rights, yet they paid little attention to the needs of the New England states during the embargo and the War of 1812.

Looking back on this era, historians describe it as an exciting time of expansion and exploration. The Louisiana Purchase doubled the size of the young nation. Lewis and Clark, as well as Pike, began exploration of that vast region. At the same time, a flood of settlers poured into the Ohio and Mississippi Valleys.

Indians remember the Jefferson era differently. Settlers were an unwelcome threat to their homeland and way of life. In response to this danger, Tecumseh became a great Indian leader and his brother, Tenskwatawa, a prophet. For a time they brought hope to many Indians that they could live as they had always done. With the defeat at Tippecanoe and the death of Tecumseh, that hope gave way to despair. In the future, although Indians in other regions would resist expansion by settlers, no leader would again try to unite Indians from Canada to Florida.

(Answers continued from side margin)
way. He focuses on the effect of the fires in dramatically lighting the night sky. The government buildings have no special meaning to him.

3. (a) In calling it a house, Smith reflects the American rejection of monarchy. In calling it a palace, Glieg reflects the British tradition of monarchy. He is used to the head of the government living in a palace. (b) As a patriotic American, she sees the buildings as symbols of the young nation.

4. Students could read more excerpts from the Smith and Bayard accounts. They could also research other American, British, and perhaps French accounts.

For further application, have students do the Applying Skills activity in the Chapter Survey (p. 310).

If students need to review the skill, use the Skills Development transparency and activity in the **Chapter Resources Binder,** pp. 87–88.

Skill Lab

Thinking Critically
Detecting Bias

Americans were shocked when the British burned Washington, D.C., in 1814. Never before or since has an enemy invaded our nation's capital. As you might expect, American and British observers at the time viewed the event quite differently.

Question to Investigate

How did different people react to the burning of the nation's capital?

Procedure

To explore the question, read sources **A** and **B**. Look for evidence of **bias,** a one-sided or slanted view. Bias is related to point of view (see page 249). A person's general background can lead to a one-sided view on a topic. Study the Skill Tips and then do the following.

❶ Identify clues to bias in the sources.
a. List words and phrases from source **A** that reflect bias.
b. List words and phrases from source **B** that reflect bias.

❷ Describe the bias of each writer.
a. Describe the bias in source **A.**
b. Describe the bias in source **B.**

❸ Consider how point of view might contribute to the bias of each writer.
a. Why do you think **A** refers to the President's "house," while **B** calls it a "palace"?
b. Why do you think the Capitol building and the President's House might mean so much to the writer of source **A**?

❹ Tell what else you might do to answer the Question to Investigate.

Skill Tips

To detect bias, look for:
• "loaded"—emotionally charged—words
• exaggerations
• opinions stated as if they were obvious truths
• focus on only one side of an issue
• what the person does *not* say

Sources to Use

A "Those beautiful pillars in [the] Representatives' Hall were cracked and broken. The roof, that noble dome, lay in ashes.

In the President's House, not an inch but its cracked and blackened walls remained. That scene, when I last visited it, was so splendid! It was crowded with the great, the ambitious, and patriotic heroes. Now it was nothing but ashes.

Was it these ashes, now crushed underfoot, which once had the power to inflate pride? . . . Who would have thought that this mass, so magnificent, should in the space of a few hours be thus destroyed?"

From a letter by Margaret Bayard Smith, a resident of Washington, D.C.

B "You can conceive nothing finer than the sight. . . . The sky was brilliantly illumined by the different [fires]; and a dark red light was thrown upon the road, sufficient to permit each man to view his comrade's face. . . . Of the senate-house, the President's palace, the barracks, the dockyard, &c. [etc.] nothing could be seen, except heaps of smoking ruins; and even the bridge, a noble structure upwards of a mile in length, was almost wholly demolished."

From an account by George R. Glieg, a British officer who took part in the invasion

• 309

Introducing the Skill Lab

Distinguish bias (a particular slanted view on a specific topic) from point of view (a person's general background). A person's general point of view may or may not lead to a bias on a specific topic. Point out that a bias can be either positive or negative, and that it can affect a description of a historical event or person, sometimes leading to serious misunderstandings. The term *prejudice* refers to any bias that becomes a firm and unreasonable judgment about someone or something.

Skill Lab
Answers

1. (a) Beautiful, noble, splendid, great, ambitious, patriotic heroes, power to inflate pride, magnificent. (b) Nothing finer, brilliantly illumined, comrade's face, palace, noble.

2. (a) American Margaret Bayard Smith describes the destruction in the capital in a negative way. She focuses on contrasting the present appearance of the buildings with their beautiful original appearance. She sees the change as a tragedy because the buildings were a source of pride to her. (b) British officer George Glieg sees the destruction in a positive

(Answers continued in top margin)

7. (a) Indians' hopes were dashed by American victories in the battles at Thames and Horseshoe Bend. (b) Created new spirit of nationalism.

Thinking Critically

1. *Marbury* v. *Madison* strengthened principles of separation of powers and checks and balances by putting the Court on an equal footing with the other branches and giving

it a kind of veto power.

2. Students who feel that he was successful may cite allowing the Alien and Sedition Acts to expire, efforts to keep federal government small, Louisiana Purchase, and success in keeping country out of war. Students who feel he was not may cite problems that neutrality caused, failure of Embargo and Non-Intercourse acts, and frugality that kept the nation from industrializing more quickly

Chapter Survey

Reviewing Vocabulary

Define the following terms.
1. judicial review   3. nationalism
2. embargo

Reviewing Main Ideas

1. What is judicial review? In what case did the Supreme Court establish its power of judicial review?
2. Why did Napoleon want to sell Louisiana? Why did Jefferson want to buy it?
3. What was the main goal of the Lewis and Clark expedition? How did the expedition meet Jefferson's expectations?
4. What happened to American ships when they tried to sail to British or French ports in 1806 and 1807? Why did the British search American ships along the American coast?
5. Explain the purpose of the Embargo Act, and why it was not effective.
6. Why did the United States go to war with Britain rather than with France?
7. How did the War of 1812 affect each of the following? (a) Indians' hopes for their future (b) white Americans' feelings toward their country

Thinking Critically

1. **Analysis** How did *Marbury* v. *Madison* strengthen the constitutional principle of checks and balances?
2. **Evaluation** Choose at least three events during Jefferson's presidency. Do you see these events as failures or successes for Jefferson? Explain.
3. **Why We Remember: Analysis** Explain the following statement: The Jefferson era was a time of new opportunities for settlers, and lost opportunities for the Ohio Valley Indians. Give examples for both groups of people.

Applying Skills

Detecting bias The accounts you read on page 309 showed two different ways of looking at the burning of Washington, D.C. Think of a recent news event involving a conflict between nations or people. Find at least two articles that describe the event and that contain evidence of bias.
1. List the clues to bias that you found in each article.
2. Summarize each writer's bias.
3. Explain how each writer's background might contribute to his or her bias.

History Mystery

The unnecessary battle Answer the History Mystery on page 289. How could you find out how news traveled at that time? How might such news travel today? What role did poor communications play at the beginning of the war?

Writing in Your History Journal

1. **Keys to History** (a) The time line on pages 288–289 has seven Keys to History. In your journal, describe why each is important to know. (b) Choose three other events or people in the chapter that you would like to add to the time line and explain why.
2. **Tecumseh** The Prophet led the Indians into battle at Tippecanoe River. Tecumseh himself was not there. In your journal write what Tecumseh's thoughts might have been when he received the news about the battle.
3. **Citizenship** Imagine that you are Thomas Jefferson in the year 1808. Write a letter to James Madison explaining why you have decided

and meeting challenges from Britain and France.

3. Opportunities for settlers included land in the Ohio and Mississippi Valleys. Lost opportunities for Indians included failure of Tecumseh's attempt to form an alliance to stop settlers.

Applying Skills

Answers should reflect an understanding of bias and clues to bias, as well as of the relationship between point of view and bias.

History Mystery

Information on the Battle of New Orleans is found on page 307. To learn how news traveled then, students could research the history of communications. Methods today include phone, fax, radio, television, computers, and satellites. Early in the war, news *(Answers continued in side margin)*

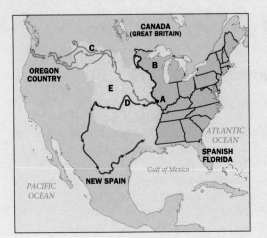

Reviewing Geography

1. The letters on the map represent two territories, two expeditions, and the starting place of the expeditions. Write the name of each.

2. Geographic Thinking Before the Louisiana Purchase, Jefferson wrote to a friend, "There is on the globe a single spot, the possessor of which is our natural and habitual enemy. It is New Orleans." Study the map on page 277. Why was New Orleans vital as a port? What alternatives would western farmers have had if Napoleon had closed New Orleans or if the British had taken it in the War of 1812? How adequate would those alternatives have been? What do Jefferson's words tell you about the importance of the West in the early 1800s?

---

not to run for President again and why you think he should run.

Alternative Assessment

Creating a front page It is June 1812, and Congress has just declared war on Britain. With several classmates, create the front page for tomorrow's edition of the newspaper.

First, decide where the paper is published: the North, South, or West. Then make a plan for the front page by following these guidelines:
• Every item on the page should relate to the declaration of war.
• There should be one major article plus sidebars. Sidebars are shorter articles that further explain some part of the information in the main article and are printed alongside it. One sidebar might be "Events

That Led to Declaration of War." Another might be "Local Reaction to the War."
• Your publisher wants you to include an editorial stating the publisher's opinion of the declaration of war.

When your planning is complete, write the articles and headlines and prepare some illustrations that will make the front page more interesting. For illustrations, include at least one picture, one cartoon, and one map. Lay out the front page on a large sheet of paper or poster board. Put it on the bulletin board so others can read it.

Your front page will be evaluated on the following criteria:
• it provides in-depth information about the causes of the War of 1812
• it reflects regional attitudes of the time
• it is snappy, creative, and grabs the attention of readers

---

that the British agreed to stop attacking ships reached Washington weeks after war was declared.

Writing in Your History Journal

1. (a) Explanations should be similar to the time line notes on teacher pages 288–289. (b) Entries will vary, but should show understanding of effects of an event.

2. Answers will vary, but should show Tecumseh's concern for the safety of his people and his disappointment in having his followers scattered.

3. Accept responses that reflect an understanding of why Jefferson wanted to retire and of his admiration of Madison. Answers may draw on information about both men from previous chapters.

Reviewing Geography

1. (A) St. Louis, (B) Indiana Territory, (C) Lewis and Clark expedition, (D) Pike's expedition, (E) Louisiana Territory.

2. New Orleans was the outlet port that served the entire Mississippi River. Western farmers would have to ship their goods up the Mississippi and overland to the Great Lakes and then overland again to reach the St. Lawrence River. This would be time-consuming and costly. In stressing New Orleans' importance, Jefferson implied that the western lands to which it was a gateway were important to the United States.

Alternative Assessment

Teacher's Take-Home Planner 4, p. 13, includes suggestions and scoring rubrics for the Alternative Assessment activity.

Teaching the

Link to Literature

Tell students that Lewis and Clark made a remarkable team. Each had talents that complemented the other's. Lewis was somewhat of a loner, while Clark was affable and outgoing. Lewis was better trained in the sciences of that time, but Clark was a brilliant natural geographer and a master of wilderness survival. Both were brave, decisive, and intelligent leaders. Most important, they worked together well.

✳ Literature Footnote

The eight volumes of the journals of Lewis and Clark and other members of the expedition, *Original Journals of the Lewis and Clark Expedition, 1804–1806,* were edited by Reuben Gold Thwaites and published by Dodd, Mead & Co. from 1904–1905. Bernard De Voto edited an admirable condensed version of the journals, which was published by Houghton Mifflin in 1953.

Link to Literature

The Journals of Lewis and Clark

As explorers, part of Lewis and Clark's job was to keep a record of their journey. Whenever they had a spare moment—usually at night by the campfire—the tired explorers opened their leather-bound notebooks, took out their quill pens and bottle of ink, and wrote down what they saw and did that day. When reading these passages, remember that Lewis and Clark were soldiers, not scholars. Their spelling, punctuation, and use of words look strange to us today. Still, their diaries are treasures of history.

Lewis

Saturday April 13th 1805. We found a number of carcases of the Buffaloe lying along shore, which had been drowned by falling through the ice in winter. We saw also many tracks of the white bear of enormous size, along the river shore and about the carcases of the Buffaloe, on which I presume they feed. We have not as yet seen one of these anamals, tho' their tracks are so abundant and recent. The men as well as ourselves are anxious to meet with some of these bear. The Indians [tell] of the strength and **ferocity** of this animal, which they never dare to attack but in parties of six eight or ten persons; and are even then frequently defeated with the loss of one or more of thier party.

ferocity:
fierceness

Sunday August 11th 1805. I was overjoyed at the sight of this stranger [a Shoshone Indian]. . . . I mad[e] him the signal of friendship known to the Indians of the Rocky mountains and those of the Missouri, which is by holding the **mantle** or robe in your hands at two corners then th[r]owing [it] up in the air higher than the head bringing it to the earth as if in the act of spreading it, thus repeating three times. . . . He did not remain untill I got nearer than about 100 paces when he suddonly turned his ho[r]se about, gave him the whip leaped the creek and disapeared in the willow brush in an instant and with him vanished all my hopes of obtaining horses for the preasent.

mantle:
cape

Tuesday August 20th 1805. I can discover that these people are by no means friendly to the Spaniards. Their complaint is, that the Spaniards will not let them have fire arms and amunition. . . . Their bloodthirsty neighbours to the east of them, being in possession of fire arms, hunt them up and murder them without rispect to sex or age and **plunder** them of their horses on all occasions. They told me that to avoid their

plunder:
to rob by force

✳ Literature Footnote

Students might enjoy perusing *American Odyssey: The Journey of Lewis and Clark,* Ingvard Henry Eide, editor and photographer (Rand McNally & Co., 1969). This book combines selected journal entries of Lewis and Clark and other members of the expedition with black and white photographs that capture the wonder of the sights the party encountered on their journey.

This page from William Clark's journal shows his detailed description of an evergreen shrub.

enemies . . . they were obliged to remain in the interior of these mountains . . . sometimes living for weeks without meat and only a little fish roots and berries. But this, added Câmeahwait, with his ferce eyes and lank jaws grown meager for the want of food, would not be the case if we had guns. We could then live in the country of buffaloe and eat as our enimies do and not be compelled to hide ourselves in these mountains and live on roots and berries as the bear do.

meager: thin

compelled: forced

Clark

Wednesday [Sunday] Septr. 15th 1805. Several horses sliped and roled down steep hills which hurt them verry much. The one which carried my desk & small trunk turned over & roled down a mountain for 40 yards & lodged against a tree, broke the desk the horse escaped and appeared but little hurt. When we arrived at the top, we could find no water and concluded to camp and make use of the snow we found on the top to make our supe.

Wed 17th Sept 1806. At 11 A.M. we met a Captin McClellin assending in a large boat. This gentleman was somewhat astonished to see us return and appeared rejoiced to meet us. We found him a man of information and from whome we received a partial account of the political state of our country. We were makeing enquires and exchangeing answers untill near midnight. This gentleman informed us that we had been long since given [up] by the people of the U S generaly and almost forgotton. The president of the U. States had yet hopes of us.

A Closer Look

1. What were some of the challenges and dangers Lewis and Clark faced?

2. What seems to be the attitude of the explorers toward the new things they are seeing? What words give you these clues?

3. What did the explorers learn about what some Indians thought of the Spanish? Why might this be useful to Americans?

From *Original Journals of the Lewis and Clark Expedition, 1804–1806,* edited by Reuben Gold Thwaites. New York: Arno Press, 1969.

● 313

Stimulating Critical Thinking

1. What do you think Lewis thought of Câmeahwait and other Indians he encountered? (Students may note that he seemed to have some sympathy for Câmeahwait's plight and called the Indians' neighbors "bloodthirsty." They might also note that many whites felt superior to Indians.)

2. Do you think Lewis and Clark found the encounters with wild animals frightening? (Students may note that Lewis reports seeing the bear tracks rather matter-of-factly, though the description Indians gave him must have been frightening. They may also note that the expedition depended on wild animals for food.)

A Closer Look Answers

1. Wild animals, unfriendly Indians, rough terrain, accidents that endangered horses and equipment.

2. Lewis seems impressed. He notes the enormous size of bear tracks and the eagerness to see a bear. He remarks on Câmeahwait's fierce eyes. Clark's excerpts have a more matter-of-fact tone, reflecting no emotion.

3. That some Indians "are by no means friendly to the Spaniards," knowledge that might be used in negotiations to gain Florida.

12 The Confident Years
1816–1830

Chapter Planning Guide

Section	Student Text	Teacher's Edition Activities
Opener and Story pp. 314–317	**Keys to History Time Line** / **History Mystery** / Beginning the Story with **The Mill Girls**	**Setting the Stage Activity** To Work Full-Time?, p. 316
1 **A Revolution in Industry** pp. 318–321	**Link to the Present** Women in the work force, p. 320	**Warm-Up Activity** Thinking About Machines, p. 318 **Geography Question of the Day,** p. 318 **Section Activity** Using Mass Production, p. 319 **Bonus Activity** Drawing an Invention, p. 320 **Wrap-Up Activity** Starting a Mill, p. 321
2 **New Forms of Transportation** pp. 322–327	**Reading Maps** Roads and Canals 1830–1850, p. 323 **Link to Technology** The Canal Lock, pp. 324–325 **Geography Lab** Steamboats and Westward Expansion, p. 327	**Warm-Up Activity** Transportation Then and Now, p. 322 **Geography Question of the Day,** p. 322 **Section Activity** Creating Transportation Ads, p. 324 **Bonus Activity** Debating the Canal, p. 325 **Wrap-Up Activity** Making a Transportation Chart, p. 326
3 **A Bold Foreign Policy** pp. 328–331	**Link to Art** *The War of Independence*, p. 329 **Reading Maps** The Western Hemisphere 1825, p. 330 **World Link** Russia claims much of Pacific Northwest, p. 331	**Warm-Up Activity** Reasons to Be Bold?, p. 328 **Geography Question of the Day,** p. 328 **Section Activity** Painting a Mural, p. 330 **Wrap-Up Activity** Portraying Leaders, p. 331
4 **Strains on National Unity** pp. 332–337	**Reading Maps** The Missouri Compromise 1820, p. 334 **Hands-On History** Making compromises, p. 335 **Point of View** Was the Missouri Compromise good for the nation?, p. 335 **Skill Lab** Generalizations, p. 337	**Warm-Up Activity** Understanding the Panic, p. 332 **Geography Question of the Day,** p. 332 **Section Activity** Mapping Sectional Differences, p. 334 **Bonus Activity** Creating a Political Cartoon, p. 333 **Wrap-Up Activity** A Missouri Compromise Graphic, p. 336
Evaluation	☑ **Section 1 Review,** p. 321 ☑ **Section 2 Review,** p. 326 ☑ **Section 3 Review,** p. 331 ☑ **Section 4 Review,** p. 336 ☑ **Chapter Survey,** pp. 338–339 **Alternative Assessment** Writing about current events, p. 339	☑ **Answers to Section 1 Review,** p. 321 ☑ **Answers to Section 2 Review,** p. 326 ☑ **Answers to Section 3 Review,** p. 331 ☑ **Answers to Section 4 Review,** p. 336 ☑ **Answers to Chapter Survey,** pp. 338–339 (Alternative Assessment guidelines are in the Take-Home Planner.)

Teacher's Resource Package

Chapter Summaries: English and Spanish, pp. 28–29

Chapter Resources Binder
> **Study Guide** Completing a Graphic Organizer, p. 89
> **Reinforcement** Summarizing Information, pp. 93–94

American Readings In the Mill, p. 45

Using Historical Documents The Cotton Gin Patent, pp. 66–69

Chapter Resources Binder
> **Study Guide** Analyzing Problems and Solutions, p. 90

Geography Extensions Steamboats on the Mississippi, pp. 23–24

American Readings Hazards on the Erie Canal, p. 46; Travels by Boat, Stage, Railroad, and Canal, pp. 47–48

Chapter Resources Binder
> **Study Guide** Writing an Outline, p. 91

Chapter Resources Binder
> **Study Guide** Completing a Graphic Organizer, p. 92
> **Skills Development** Using Generalizations, pp. 95–96

Chapter and Unit Tests Chapter 12 Tests, Forms A and B, pp. 73–76

Take-Home Planner

Introducing the Chapter Activity Technology and History, p. 20

Chapter In-Depth Activity Writing a Travel Journal, p. 20

Reduced Views
> **Study Guide,** p. 22
> **Reinforcement,** p. 23
> **American Readings,** p. 24
> **Using Historical Documents,** p. 25

Unit 4 Answers, pp. 28–34

Reduced Views
> **Study Guide,** p. 22
> **Geography Extensions,** p. 25
> **American Readings,** p. 24

Unit 4 Answers, pp. 28–34

Reduced Views
> **Study Guide,** p. 22

Unit 4 Answers, pp. 28–34

Reduced Views
> **Study Guide,** p. 22
> **Skills Development,** p. 23

Unit 4 Answers, pp. 28–34

Reduced Views
> **Chapter Tests,** p. 25

Unit 4 Answers, pp. 28–34

Alternative Assessment Guidelines for scoring the Chapter Survey activity, p. 21

Additional Resources

Wall Time Line

Unit 4 Activity

Transparency Package

Transparency 12-1 Map: Roads and Canals—use with Section 2

Transparency 12-2 Dangers of Travel—use with Section 2

Transparency Activity Book

SelecTest Testing Software
Chapter 12 Test, Forms A and B

Vital Links

⊙ **Videodisc**

⊙ **CD-ROM**

Water Mills (see TE p. 320)
"The Erie Canal" (see TE p. 324)

12

Teaching Resources

Take-Home Planner 4
  Introducing Chapter Activity
  Chapter In-Depth Activity
  Alternative Assessment
Chapter Resources Binder
Geography Extensions
American Readings
Using Historical Documents
Transparency Activities
Wall Time Line Activities
Chapter Summaries
Chapter and Unit Tests
SelecTest Test File
Vital Links CD-ROM/Videodisc

Time Line

Keys to History

Keys to History journal writing activity is on page 338 in the Chapter Survey.

Samuel Slater builds the first American spinning mill The spinning jenny began the Industrial Revolution—the shift of the production of goods from hand tools to machines and from homes to factories. (p. 318)

Eli Whitney's cotton gin The cotton gin made cotton a profitable cash crop in the South. It increased the demand for slave labor and led southerners to move west seeking more cotton land. (p. 319)

Looking Back In 1787 Congress banned slavery in the Northwest Territory.

314

★ Identify new technology that began to change the way Americans lived.
★ Describe new transportation that linked the nation together.
★ Explain the new directions in foreign policy set by James Monroe and John Quincy Adams.
★ Identify the events that tested Americans' spirit of unity after the War of 1812.

Chapter Overview
The construction of the first spinning mill in the United States by Samuel Slater in 1790 and of Francis Cabot Lowell's cotton mill in 1815 started the Industrial Revolution in the United States. Eli Whitney invented the cotton gin in 1793, setting the stage for the prosperous cotton kingdom. The federal government encouraged industry with the founding of the Bank of

1816–1830

Chapter 12

The Confident Years

Sections

Beginning the Story with the Mill Girls
1. **A Revolution in Industry**
2. **New Forms of Transportation**
3. **A Bold Foreign Policy**
4. **Strains on National Unity**

 *Keys to History*

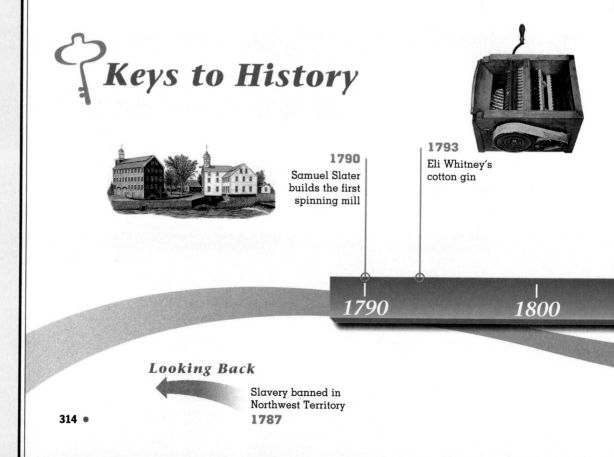

1790
Samuel Slater builds the first spinning mill

1793
Eli Whitney's cotton gin

1790   *1800*

Looking Back

Slavery banned in Northwest Territory
1787

314 ●

the United States and the second protective tariff.

A transportation revolution enabled the nation's new industries to prosper. Advances included the paved National Road and invention of the steamboat and the railroad. The Erie Canal provided an all-water route from New York City to the Great Lakes.

New directions in foreign policy during James Monroe's presidency included settling territorial issues with Britain and gaining control of Florida from Spain. The Monroe Doctrine declared the Americas closed to future European colonization.

The Era of Good Feelings of Monroe's presidency was dampened by the financial panic of 1819. The sense of national unity gave way to growing sectionalism, resulting from the conflict over expansion of slavery. The Missouri Compromise of 1820 temporarily put this conflict to rest.

HISTORY Mystery

In 1830 hundreds of Americans gathered to watch a race between two trains. Why did the train that lost the race turn out to be the real winner?

1807
First voyage of the *Clermont*

1817–1825
Era of Good Feelings

1820
Missouri Compromise
Congress permits expansion of slavery

1823
Monroe Doctrine
President James Monroe

1825
Opening of the Erie Canal

1810   *1820*   *1830*

World Link
Russia claims much of Pacific Northwest
1821

Looking Ahead
Strike by Lowell millworkers
1836

● **315**

Teaching the
HISTORY
Mystery

Students will find the answer on p. 326. See Chapter Survey, p. 338, for additional information and questions.

Time Line

First voyage of the *Clermont* Robert H. Fulton's steamboat revolutionized river travel. (p. 322)

Era of Good Feelings This term was used to describe James Monroe's presidency, referring to the sense of national unity following the War of 1812. (p. 332)

Missouri Compromise As sectional tensions increased over the issue of expanding slavery, Congress compromised by agreeing that Missouri would join the Union as a slave state and Maine as a free state, and by banning slavery north of latitude 36° 30′. (p. 334)

Monroe Doctrine President Monroe warned European countries against interfering with the nations in Latin America. (p. 331)

Erie Canal The canal created an all-water route from New York City to the Great Lakes, providing an inexpensive means of trade and travel. (p. 324)

World Link See p. 331.

Looking Ahead The strike by Lowell millworkers in 1836 reflected dissatisfaction with wages and working conditions.

The Mill Girls

The first cotton mill opened in Massachusetts in 1815. Mill owners advertised for farm girls to work in the mills. The young women lived in boarding houses and worked long hours. Some, however, appreciated their independence and opportunities to pursue education and culture.

To Work Full-Time?

To help students understand pros and cons of becoming factory workers, have them do a paired writing activity. They imagine having a choice between going to school, as they do now, and taking a full-time job, such as in a store, restaurant, or factory. Have one student in each pair write a letter describing two advantages of full-time work. The other replies in a letter pointing out its disadvantages and the advantages of staying in school. The pair exchanges one more set of letters responding to each other and adding arguments. Allot about four minutes for each letter. With the class, discuss major pros and cons.

See the Introducing the Chapter Activity, Technology and History. **Take-Home Planner 4,** p. 20.

❋ **History Footnote**

In their avid reading, the Lowell mill girls mainly patronized lending libraries, which dispensed novels for a subscription rate of about six cents a week. Reading was so popular among the young women that one factory sign read "No Reading in the Mills." One factory supervisor was said to have taken a drawerful of Bibles from his workers. The girls evaded the rule by putting pages from books on walls and loom frames. One mill girl wrote, "As well forbid us Yankee girls to breathe as read; we cannot help it."

The girls' literary leanings are reflected in *The Lowell Offering,* a factory magazine published during the 1840s. Contributors often wrote of the everyday life of mill workers.

Beginning the Story with

The Mill Girls

When the mill girls, as they were called, felt overworked, underpaid, or just plain homesick, they sang:

❝Oh, isn't it a pity that such a pretty girl as I
Should be sent to the factory to pine away and die?❞

Going to work in the cotton mills of New England was hardly a death sentence, though. Most young women worked for only three or four years before returning home or leaving to get married.

The Lure of Millwork

The opportunity for women to become millworkers came about when a group of businessmen called the Boston Associates opened the first of many cotton mills in Massachusetts in 1815. They offered to pay New England farm girls up to three dollars a week. This pay was six times what a woman working as a teacher or a servant might make. The Boston Associates knew, though, that men would demand twice as much money for the same jobs.

To convince farm families to let their daughters live and work away from home, the mill owners built boarding houses and assured nervous parents that their daughters would live under the watchful eyes of "respectable women." They also promised to make "every provision for religious worship."

"Another Pay Day"

Most young women found working in the mills both an adventure and a trial. Few had ever been away from home before. Many liked the independence of living in a boarding house—even with six boarders in a room, sleeping three

History Bookshelf

Weisman, Joanne B. *Lowell Mill Girls: Life in the Factory.* Discovery Enterprises Ltd., 1991. The experiences of New England farm girls who became mill girls are reflected in their own accounts.

Also of interest:

Nirgiotis, Nicholas. *Erie Canal: Gateway to the West.* Watts, 1993.

Wormser, Richard. *The Iron Horse: How the Railroads Changed America.* Walker & Co., 1993.

Discussion

Thinking Historically

1. Why do you think parents allowed or encouraged daughters to work in mills? (They would not have to support them. The girls could make money and participate in cultural activities. There was less opportunity in staying on the family farm.)

2. What were disadvantages of factory work? (Girls were separated from families. Factory work was more regimented.)

3. What were advantages of factory work? (The girls were independent, earned money, and had cultural opportunities.)

See the Chapter In-Depth Activity, Writing a Travel Journal. **Take-Home Planner 4,** p. 20.

In mills owned by the Boston Associates, raw cotton was spun into thread. Then the thread was woven into cloth on power looms. This picture shows mill girls operating the machines that wound the thread onto huge bobbins, or spools, for weaving.

to a bed. One girl wrote home bragging, "I don't even have my bed to make. Quite a lady, to be sure."

Compared to farm chores, millwork was not hard. The hours, however, were long. Harriet Farley described her workday:

"We go in at five o'clock; at seven we come out to breakfast; at half-past seven we return to our work, and stay until half-past twelve. At one . . . we return to our work, and stay until seven at night. Then the evening is all our own."

Millwork also offered young women a chance to exchange the isolation of farm life for city life. During their evenings, many mill girls in Lowell, Massachusetts, took classes, went to concerts, and read books from the library. Some even wrote and published their own magazine, the *Lowell Offering.*

Then as now, though, the best day was payday. Being paid for their work was a new experience for most young women. So was having money of their own. A New Hampshire mill girl wrote to her sister:

"Since I have wrote you, another pay day has come around. I earned 14 dollars and a half, nine and a half dollars beside my board [payment for a room and meals]. . . . I like it well as ever and Sarah don't I feel independent of everyone! The thought that I am living on no one is a happy one indeed to me."

The mill girls were not the only Americans to face new experiences in the years after the War of 1812. New technology and the growth of industry were changing the way Americans lived.

Hands-On *HISTORY*

Activity

Imagine that you are a 15-year-old living on a New England farm in 1817. You and your parents have seen an ad seeking young women to work in a cotton mill. Create a dialogue between you and your parents about whether you should take a job as a millworker.

Teaching the Hands-On *HISTORY*

Before students begin writing dialogues, encourage them to consider different possibilities. One possibility might be parents encouraging a reluctant daughter to go to work. Alternatively, the daughter might be adventurous and independent, and the parents might be cautious or fearful.

For a journal writing activity on the mill girls, see student page 339.

Introducing the Section

Vocabulary

Industrial Revolution (p. 319) the shift of production from hand tools to machines and from homes to factories

mass production (p. 320) using machines to make large quantities of goods faster and cheaper than they could be made by hand

protective tariff (p. 321) a tax placed on imported goods

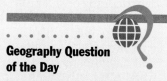

Warm-Up Activity

Thinking About Machines

To help students understand the enormous changes that machines can cause, have them list several machines that make work easier at home, such as dishwashers or computers. They should write a short explanation of the work the machines do and how they save time and effort as compared to older ways of doing the work.

Geography Question of the Day

Have students look at the pictures on pages 318–319 and at the Link to Technology on page 151 and write a paragraph explaining what geographic features they would look for if they were planning to build a mill in the 1800s. They should then explain whether they would need the same features today.

Section Objectives

★ Describe how the Industrial Revolution changed the way goods were produced.

★ Explain why the invention of the cotton gin was important to southern farmers.

★ Explain how the federal government helped American business grow.

Teaching Resources

Take-Home Planner 4, pp. 18–25

Chapter Resources Binder

   Study Guide, p. 89

   Reinforcement, pp. 93–94

   Skills Development

Geography Extensions

American Readings, p. 45

Using Historical Documents, pp. 66–69

Transparency Activities

Chapter and Unit Tests

---

1. A Revolution in Industry

Reading Guide

New Terms Industrial Revolution, mass production, protective tariff

Section Focus New technology that began to change the way Americans lived

1. How did the Industrial Revolution change the way goods were produced?
2. Why was the invention of the cotton gin important to southern farmers?
3. How did the federal government help American business grow?

Few of the young women who first went to work in the cotton mills knew it, but their work was helping bring to reality the dreams of three enterprising men. The first was a mechanic with an amazing memory. The second was a tinkerer who loved inventing things. The third was a merchant blessed with both brains and money. These three men were creating a revolution in industry in the United States.

Slater's Spinning Mill

The mechanic—Samuel Slater—came to the United States from England in 1789. At that time, almost all of the goods Americans needed were made by hand, either at home or in small workshops.

This way of producing goods had existed in England, too, until the mid-1700s. Then English mechanics invented the spinning

The Blackstone River supplied the power for Samuel Slater's first spinning mill. Slater hired families, including children as young as 8, to turn cotton into thread. Weavers working at home wove the thread into cloth.

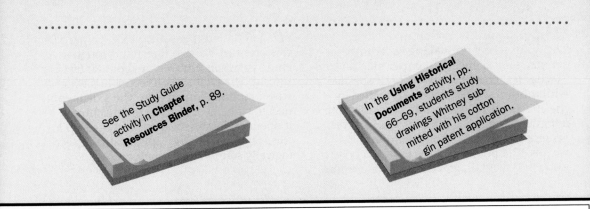

See the Study Guide activity in **Chapter Resources Binder**, p. 89.

In the **Using Historical Documents** activity, pp. 66–69, students study drawings Whitney submitted with his cotton gin patent application.

Checking Understanding

1. What marked the beginning of the Industrial Revolution in the United States? (Samuel Slater's construction of the first spinning mill.)

Stimulating Critical Thinking

2. How do you think family life was affected by the use of families, children, and farm girls as mill workers? (Way of life changed from rural to urban; working children accepted responsibility at an early age.)

Section Activity

Using Mass Production

To show differences between producing goods in small workshops and in factories, have students make a product in two different ways. Half of them will work individually, performing all production steps. Ask the other half to use "mass production," with each student performing one step. Have the class compare methods. Students might suggest a product, or have them make a paper clock, with a round face, cut-out numbers pasted on the face, and hands attached with a brad.

Two machines were vital in cotton production. Cotton gins, like these in the picture, removed the seeds. Then huge presses packed the ginned cotton into bales for easier transport to market.

jenny, a machine that could spin wool or cotton fiber into thread. The new machine was powered by water turning a water wheel. For this reason, spinning mills, or factories, were built beside fast-flowing rivers.

The spinning jenny began a revolution in the way goods were produced. This shift of production from hand tools to machines and from homes to factories is known as the **Industrial Revolution.**

The first American mill The British wanted to keep the spinning jenny their secret. They would not allow drawings of the machines, or people who used the machines, to leave the country.

Samuel Slater got around this restriction by memorizing every detail of a spinning jenny. Then he sailed to the United States disguised as a farm worker. Once there, Slater teamed up with merchant Moses Brown to turn his memories into machines. In 1790 they built the nation's first spinning mill at Pawtucket, Rhode Island. The Industrial Revolution in the United States had begun.

Whitney's Cotton Gin

By 1815 Slater had helped to build 20 spinning mills. As the number of mills multiplied, so did the demand for cotton. Finding enough cotton could have been a problem had it not been for a Massachusetts inventor named Eli Whitney.

In 1792 Whitney traveled to Georgia. At that time, southerners were facing hard times. Prices for their cash crops—tobacco, rice, and indigo—were so low that it hardly paid to plant them. As they planted less, their demand for slave labor declined. It seemed that slavery might soon die out.

While visiting a plantation, Whitney saw slaves picking seeds out of raw cotton. It was such slow work, planters said, that they could not make a profit growing cotton. As Whitney later recalled:

> All agreed that if a machine could be invented that would clean the cotton with expedition [speed], it would be a great thing . . . to the country.

In 1793 Whitney invented just such a machine. His cotton engine, known as a "gin," cleaned 50 times as much cotton in a day as a worker could by hand. Planters now had what they wanted most—a profitable cash crop.

The cotton kingdom Cotton production soared, and with it a renewed demand for slaves to do the work. Soon ambitious southerners were moving westward, looking for new land to plant in cotton. They took their slaves west with them or bought slaves from traders. Instead of dying out, slavery became an important part of what became known as the "cotton kingdom."

Bonus Activity

Drawing an Invention

Provide a book that illustrates the spinning jenny, cotton mill, cotton gin, steamboat, or steam locomotive. Have students make their own drawings of the invention, writing a paragraph that tells how it works.

★ ★ ★
Vital Links

◉ **Water Mills (Movie)**
Unit 2, Side 2, Search
02616, Play to 03338

◉ See also Unit 2 Explore
CD-ROM location 174.

For a description of conditions at the Lowell mills, see **American Readings**, p. 45.

⊞ **Connections to Science**

The water wheel uses falling water to generate mechanical energy to power machinery. Mechanical energy is the energy associated with motion. Water power is provided by the effects of gravity on water flowing from a higher place to a lower place, as in a river, waterfall, or dam. A cubic foot of water weighs 62.4 pounds. At the base of a body of water 100 feet tall, gravity creates a pressure of 6,240 pounds per square foot. To harness this pressure, water is directed through a chute in which it travels at about 80 feet per second. The chute is connected to a water wheel mounted on an axle. The axle is connected by belts or gears to the machinery it operates. Because water is not used up in this creation of energy, it is a valuable, ecologically sound energy source.

⌇ **Link to the Present**

Women in the work force Ever since New England mills hired their first mill girls, large numbers of American women have been seeking jobs for pay. Today, about 60 percent of all American women work outside the home, many in jobs once held only by men. Almost half of the nation's accountants and bus drivers are now women. So are nearly 20 percent of doctors and lawyers.

Yet on average, modern women still earn only 72¢ for every dollar earned by men. The pay gap will probably not close until jobs traditionally held by women, such as nurse, secretary, and food server, pay as much as jobs for men with the same level of training.

Lowell's Cotton Mill

In 1810 a Boston merchant named Francis Cabot Lowell went to England for a vacation. There he took a close look at a new English invention, the power loom. This machine wove thread into cloth much faster than any hand weaver could.

Lowell returned to Boston with the loom's design in his head. In 1815 he and his partners, the Boston Associates, opened a cotton mill on the Merrimack River in Waltham, Massachusetts. It was the first American mill that did both spinning and weaving under one roof. As one observer said, the mill

❝took your bale of cotton in at one end and gave out yards of cloth at the other, after goodness knows what digestive process.❞

Lowell needed more than new technology to succeed. He also needed a steady supply of workers. He solved this problem by hiring young women from the New England countryside. Many were happy to become mill girls, trading unpaid farm work for a job with real wages.

Lowell died in 1817, but the success of his mill convinced the Boston Associates to expand. Soon they opened a second and larger cotton mill in a new town they called Lowell. By 1855 there were 52 cotton mills on the Merrimack River, all patterned after the cotton mill that Francis Cabot Lowell had opened in 1815.

Mass Production

The cotton gin was not the only contribution Eli Whitney made to the Industrial Revolution. He was also a pioneer in **mass production**—using machines to make large quantities of goods faster and cheaper than they could be made by hand.

In 1798 Whitney opened a factory to make muskets for the United States Army. Before that time, muskets had been made by skilled gunsmiths who painstakingly shaped and fitted together the parts. Whitney's machines turned out interchangeable parts. For example, every trigger was exactly the same and could be used in any musket.

In his factory each worker had just one or two simple tasks to do. Thus Whitney could hire less-skilled workers who could produce muskets faster and at lower cost. Workers could take little pride in such jobs, though. The work was boring and required little training or skill.

Whitney's methods were widely copied by other businesses. Slowly but surely, crafting products by hand at home gave way to mass production in factories. In time, factories would produce everything from clocks and clothing to shoes and shovels.

✳ History Footnote

In 1819, in the case of *McCulloch* v. *Maryland,* the Supreme Court upheld the right of Congress to create a national bank. As cashier of the Baltimore branch of the Bank of the United States, James McCulloch refused to pay a Maryland state tax on the Bank. After upholding Congress's right to create a national bank, the Court declared the state tax unconstitutional in interfering with an instrument of the federal government. Chief Justice John Marshall stated that federal powers prevail in any conflict between state and federal governments, saying that the American people "did not design to make their government dependent on the states."

The city of Lowell, Massachusetts, grew up around the water-driven cotton mills on the Merrimack River. Today the mills have been restored in a part of the city that the United States government has made into a national historic park.

The American System

Pleased with the rise of new industries, President Madison called on Congress to help American business grow and compete in the world. In response, Representatives Henry Clay and John C. Calhoun shaped a package of bills they called the American System. There was something in the package, they promised, to meet the needs of every section of the country.

A new national bank The first part of the American System was the creation of a new national bank. The charter for the first bank had ended in 1811 and was not renewed. In 1816 Congress set up a new Bank of the United States with a 20-year charter. This part of the package appealed mostly to northern businesspeople, who wanted bank loans for building industries and merchant ships.

A protective tariff The second part of the American System was a **protective tariff**—a tax placed on imported goods. The tariff would protect American manufacturers. By making imported goods more expensive, it would encourage people to buy American-made goods.

Southerners, who had little manufacturing to protect, opposed the tariff. Still, after a heated debate, Congress passed the nation's first protective tariff in 1816.

Internal improvements The American System also included a bill to fund an improved transportation system—called "internal improvements." In introducing this bill, Calhoun called on Congress to unite the growing nation. "Let us bind the republic together," he said, "with a perfect system of roads and canals."

Congress passed the internal improvements bill, but President Madison vetoed it. He felt the Constitution needed to be amended to give Congress the power to act in this area. Even without federal funds, though, the United States was beginning a transportation revolution.

⭐ 1. Section Review

1. Define **Industrial Revolution, mass production,** and **protective tariff.**
2. Compare the way that goods were made before and after the Industrial Revolution.
3. What did Congress do to encourage Americans to buy American-made goods?
4. Critical Thinking What was the relationship between the cotton gin and the cotton kingdom?

Closing the Section

Wrap-Up Activity

Starting a Mill

To help students recognize what was involved in starting a cotton mill, have small groups pretend they are businesspeople in 1820. Have them discuss and list their major needs: location, equipment, raw materials, workers. Encourage them to recognize the importance of readily available sources of energy and labor, and of good transportation to bring cotton and workers to the factory.

Section Review
Answers

1. Definitions: *Industrial Revolution* (319), *mass production* (320), *protective tariff* (321)
2. Before: goods manufactured by hand at home or in small workshops; after: more goods produced in factories with machines. Students may also note interchangeable parts and division of labor.
3. Protective tariff.
4. Cotton gin made it easier and cheaper to remove cotton seeds, enabling southern farmers to make a profit from growing cotton. As a result cotton production soared, demand for slaves increased, and farmers moved west looking for new cotton land.

See the Study Guide
activity in **Chapter
Resources Binder**, p. 90.

2. New Forms of Transportation

Reading Guide

Section Focus **New transportation that linked the nation together**

1. How did new roads and riverboats improve transportation?
2. What triggered canal building in the 1820s?
3. How did the railroad era in the United States begin?

For many mill girls, the adventure of leaving home to go to work began with the journey to Lowell, Massachusetts. If they made the trip by sled in winter, snow made bumpy roads fairly smooth. Winter travelers, however, faced the risk of being stranded midway through their journey by a sudden thaw.

Those who traveled in warmer seasons faced other hazards. In dry weather, the roads were dusty and deeply rutted. Girls traveling to Lowell by stagecoach arrived shaken and covered with grime. When it rained, they were lucky to arrive at all. Wet weather turned unpaved roads into swamps in which a horse could sink up to its belly.

The National Road

In fact, in the early 1800s good roads were hard to find anywhere in the United States. The few that existed were usually turnpikes—roads built by private companies that charged travelers a fee known as a toll.

In 1806 Congress had voted funds to build a road across the Appalachian Mountains. The purpose of this highway was to tie the new western states to the rest of the country. By 1818 the National Road stretched from Baltimore to the town of Wheeling on the Ohio River.

Compared with most roads, the National Road was a joy to travel. It was paved with layers of crushed rock and gravel. Stone bridges spanned streams along its route. It

was still dotted with tree stumps, but according to one report they had been "rounded and trimmed so as to present no serious obstacles to carriages." So many people used the National Road that one traveler observed:

❝Old America seems to be breaking up and moving westward. We are seldom out of sight, as we travel on this grand track, towards the Ohio, of family groups before and behind us.❞

As popular as the National Road was, though, Madison's veto of internal improvements (see page 321) meant that there would be no other roads like it for some time.

Rivers and Steamboats

Since colonial times, Americans had used their rivers as highways. Traveling by water was faster and cheaper than by land, at least when floating downstream. Moving upstream against a swift current was another matter.

River travel was revolutionized by an inventor named Robert Fulton. In 1807 Fulton connected a steam engine to two huge paddle wheels mounted on a raft. He named his new steam-powered riverboat the *Clermont*. Onlookers called it "Fulton's Folly."

Fulton tested his odd-looking "furnace on a raft" on the Hudson River. When he fired up the engine, it showered him with sparks and soot. Then, to almost everyone's

Robert Fulton is generally credited with the invention of the steamboat. However, another American, John Fitch, had run a steamboat for an entire summer in 1790. Unfortunately, Fitch was ahead of his time: he did not have qualified mechanics to assist him with his steamboat designs, and the public, not ready for the huge changes that steamboat travel would create, scorned his invention. Fulton was able to incorporate the technology developed by Fitch and others into a commercially successful steamboat. He was also a good salesman and had many influential friends. Fulton studied Fitch's plans and diagrams and was accused of stealing the invention. He replied, "Every artist, who invents a new and useful machine, must choose it of known parts of other machines."

Developing the Section

Discussion

Checking Understanding

1. What were advantages and disadvantages of water travel? (Faster and cheaper, but technology not developed to allow travel upstream against current.)

Stimulating Critical Thinking

2. Should the Congress have continued to pay for roads? Explain. (Yes: good roads important for nation's economy and sense of national unity; no: Constitution did not grant power to build roads; should be funded by businesses.)

Teaching the Reading Maps

Have students identify the major roads (National, Catskill Turnpike, Coastal, Great Valley, Wilderness, Nashville, Fall Line, Unicoi, Natchez Trace) and major canals (Erie, Chenango, Pennsylvania, Ohio and Erie, Miami and Ohio, Wabash and Erie). **Answers to Reading Maps:** Miami and Ohio Canal north to Toledo; overland through Marietta and north to Baltimore or Philadelphia; north on the Miami and Ohio Canal, northeast on Lake Erie, east on Erie Canal to Albany, and south by land to New York. Routes using canals would be faster and cheaper.

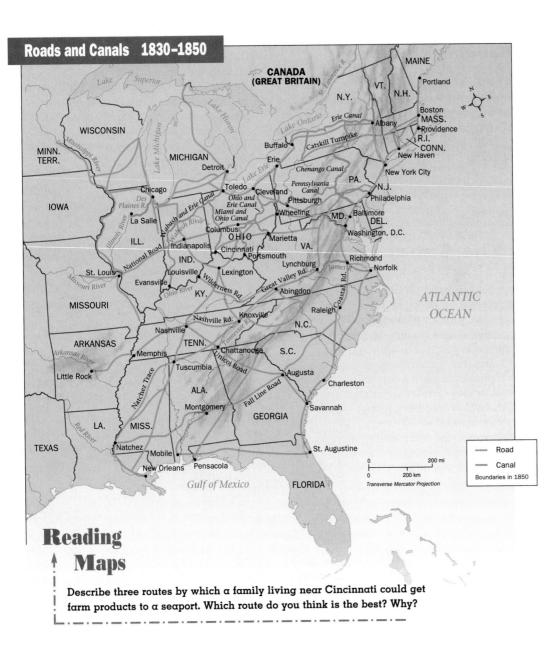

Roads and Canals 1830–1850

Reading Maps

Describe three routes by which a family living near Cincinnati could get farm products to a seaport. Which route do you think is the best? Why?

amazement, the *Clermont* began to move. Before long, it was chugging up the Hudson at almost 5 miles (8 km) per hour.

Fulton wrote of that momentous day, "I overtook many boats and passed them as if they had been at anchor. The power of the steamboat is now fully proved." By the 1820s smoke-belching steamboats were hauling passengers and freight up and down eastern and western rivers and across the Great Lakes.

Make sure that students understand the definition of *canal:* an artificial river or stream cut into the earth. On the Erie Canal a broad towpath was built alongside the canal. Teams of horses or mules walked on the towpaths attached to towlines that pulled boats through the canal.

Section Activity

Creating Transportation Ads

Have students create newspaper ads for newly built roads, steamboats, canals, or railroads. Assign one type to each student and have them imagine "selling" that type in the 1820s. They must decide what their audiences' interests are. For example they might advertise the railroad as a fast, comfortable passenger service. Encourage imaginative slogans and illustrations to stress that the technology is "new" and "modern."

★ ★ ★
Vital Links

"The Erie Canal" (Song) Unit 2, Side 1, Search 25357, Play to 27575

See also Unit 2 Explore CD-ROM location 169.

✳ History Footnote

To build the Erie Canal, workers had to cut down trees and remove stumps and roots without machinery. Using horses and mules they cleared the way for the canal and its towpath. One challenging area was a swamp known as the Montezuma Marshes, which was full of malaria-carrying mosquitoes. One observer said that the insects "fell upon the diggers in hordes" and "the men came in with eyes swollen almost shut and hands so poisoned they could hardly wield tools." Over 1,000 workers became ill with malaria, and many died. Mud from the swampy area refilled the channels almost as soon as they were dug out. As they dug, the workers had to reinforce the channel sides with dry earth. Finally, a young engineer found a special limestone in the area that effectively sealed the canal's walls.

Building Canals

"Rivers are ungovernable things," Ben Franklin once wrote. "Canals are quiet and always manageable." Canals had two advantages over rivers and roads. First, they could be built where rivers did not run. Second, one mule pulling a canal boat could haul as much freight as 50 horses or mules could on the best of roads.

In 1817 the New York governor, DeWitt Clinton, convinced his state legislature to provide funds to dig a canal 40 feet (12 m) wide to link the Hudson River and Lake Erie. It would cut through about 360 miles (580 km) of wilderness.

∞ Link to Technology

The Canal Lock

Canals allowed boats to move through what otherwise would have been impassable waterfalls, rapids, or shallows, opening up the interior of the United States to shipping and trading. Sending freight by boat was much faster and less expensive than by wagon. For example, to send a ton of freight 360 miles (580 km) overland in 1825 would have cost $100 and taken 20 days. By canal, the same load would have cost only $10, and taken just 8 days.

Upstream water level

Upstream gates closed

Securing post

Valves open

Upstream gates closed

Downstream gates open

Downstream water level

Connections to Music

Both the canals and the railroads gave birth to folk songs. The sights and sounds of a steam locomotive roaring through the countryside led to such lyrics as "You can hear the whistle blow a hundred miles." Another folk song, "Low Bridge, Everybody Down," referred to the low bridges built over the Erie Canal. People on the decks of boats were in danger of being hurt or even killed as the boats went under these bridges. The song echoes the warning of:

> Low bridge, everybody down.
> Low bridge, for we're coming to a town.
> And you'll always know your neighbor,
> You'll always know your pal,
> If you've ever navigated
> On the Erie Canal!

When finished in 1825, the Erie Canal created an all-water route from New York City to the Great Lakes. For the first time farmers in the Old Northwest had a good way to ship their crops to eastern cities.

The Erie Canal was an instant success. It cut the cost and time of hauling freight from Lake Erie to New York City. It also provided an inexpensive way for people to move into present-day Michigan. Canal traffic was so heavy that "Clinton's Big Ditch" paid for itself in just nine years.

The success of the Erie Canal spurred other canal projects. Within a few years all kinds of goods were moving from town to town on a growing network of canals.

How a Boat Moves Upstream Through a Lock

1. The water in the lock is lowered to the downstream level by draining water from the downstream end. The boat enters the lock.

2. Once the gates are closed behind the boat, the boat is fastened to securing posts and valves open on the upstream end. The water level in the lock rises to the upstream level.

3. The upstream gates are opened, and the boat passes out of the lock.

The process is reversed for a boat traveling downstream.

Checking Understanding

1. What advantages did canals have over rivers and roads? (They could be built where rivers did not run. One mule pulling a canal boat could haul as much freight as 50 horses or mules on a good road.)

2. What two areas were connected by the Erie Canal? (New York City and the Great Lakes)

Stimulating Critical Thinking

3. Jefferson thought Clinton's canal plan was "madness." Why do you think he and many others felt this way? (It would be costly and difficult. People often object to new plans, not seeing the need for them.)

 **Bonus Activity**

Debating the Canal

To help students see pros and cons of the Erie Canal, have small groups debate the issue. Half the students in each group will cite reasons that the canal is a good idea. The other half, acting as citizens opposed to the project, state their reasons.

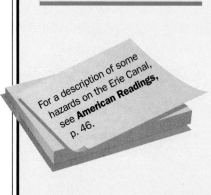

For a description of some hazards on the Erie Canal, see **American Readings,** p. 46.

Closing the Section

Making a Transportation Chart

To help students summarize forms of transportation discussed in the section, have them fill in a chart with columns headed "roads," "steamboats," "canals," and "railroads." Ask them to suggest topics for the left-hand side of the chart, such as advantages and locations.

Section Review
Answers

1. The inability of boats to go upstream had limited the usefulness of river travel even though it was faster and cheaper than land travel. Steamboats increased river travel because they could go upstream.

2. The Erie Canal provided western farmers with a good way to ship crops to eastern cities at low cost.

3. Rail lines could go wherever freight needed to go, were cheaper to build than canals, and did not freeze in winter.

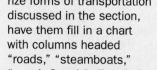

For Frances Kemble's comparison of different types of transportation, see **American Readings,** pp. 47–48.

Tips for Teaching

Visual Learners

Create a graphic organizer to help students comprehend types of transportation. For example, draw four squares, for roads, steamboats, canals, and railroads. Show students how to fill in the first square:

Form of Transportation: roads
Why: To make travel by horse and carriage faster and smoother
Who: Congress voted funds
What: National Road
When: 1818
Where: From Baltimore to Wheeling

Have students complete a similar organizer for the other three types. Ask volunteers to write their responses on the board.

In this sketch, excited passengers cheer the moment when *Tom Thumb* overtook and passed the horse-drawn car. Although the steam engine did not win, it showed the potential of steam power over horse power.

Travel on Rails

It turned out, however, that the future of transportation lay not on water but on rails. Like canals, rails could go where rivers did not run. Laying rails was far cheaper than digging canals, though, and rails did not freeze up in wintertime.

The first railroads used horses to pull a train of wagons on rails over short distances. Then in 1827 a group of Baltimore business leaders decided to build a much longer railroad across the Appalachians to the Ohio Valley. They hoped a railroad would bring western business to Baltimore.

The owners of the Baltimore and Ohio Railroad planned to use horses to pull the trains over the mountains. Mechanic Peter Cooper, however, had a better idea.

Tom Thumb In 1830 Cooper mounted a small steam engine on a wagon to create an "iron horse." The engine, called *Tom Thumb,* reached the amazing speed of 18 miles (29 km) an hour, three times the top speed of a horse-drawn train.

Local stagecoach companies did not want to compete with steam engines. They organized a race to prove that a horse could outrun any "teakettle on a truck."

Hundreds of onlookers gathered outside Baltimore to watch the race. The horse got off to a faster start. *Tom Thumb* gained speed slowly, but soon, according to one witness, "the race was neck and neck, nose and nose—then the engine passed the horse." Sudenly, the engine began to wheeze, and the horse galloped to victory.

Still, Cooper was the real winner that day. He had proved that steam engines could move faster than horses and haul heavier loads. Within months of *Tom Thumb*'s defeat, steam railroad companies had begun laying track in several states. The railroad era in the United States had begun.

2. Section Review

1. Why did the invention of the steamboat increase river travel?

2. What made the Erie Canal so useful to western farmers?

3. Critical Thinking Many people predicted that railroads would be the fastest and least expensive way to move goods throughout the nation. Give three facts they could have used to support that prediction.

Robert Fulton and John Fitch had built steamboats that could navigate rivers in the East. Western rivers, however, offered new challenges to steamboat builders. First, western waters moved much more swiftly. Second, the water was cluttered with half-submerged trees, called snags, that threatened to wreck boats.

Geography Lab

Steamboats and Westward Expansion

In September 1811 the steamboat *New Orleans* set out from Pittsburgh with a crew of 12 and 3 passengers—Nicholas Roosevelt, his wife, and the family dog. They steamed down the Ohio River and then the Mississippi. The boat survived rapids, an earthquake, and an Indian attack before reaching New Orleans in January 1812. It was the first steamboat on western waters.

Other steamboats followed, bringing people west. In 1835 a St. Louis newspaper reported, "Every steamboat that arrives at our wharves is crowded with passengers. . . . Many of these remain with us."

Steamboats in the West

Year	Number of boats
1817	17
1820	69
1830	187
1840	536
1850	740
1860	735

Source: Louis C. Hunter, *Steamboats on the Western Rivers*

Population 1810–1860

Year	St. Louis	New Orleans
1810	—*	17,242
1820	—*	27,176
1830	4,977	46,082
1840	16,469	102,193
1850	77,860	116,375
1860	160,773	168,675

*No figures available before 1830

Source: John L. Andriot, *Population Abstract of the United States*

Herman Melville's Trip on the Mississippi

Herman Melville wrote this description of his fellow steamboat passengers: "[There were] natives of all sorts, and foreigners; men of business and men of pleasure; parlor men and backwoodsmen; farm-hunters and fame-hunters, heiress-hunters, gold-hunters, buffalo-hunters. . . . Fine ladies in slippers, and moccasined [Indian women]; northern speculators and eastern philosophers; English, Irish, German, Scotch, Danes; Santa Fe traders in striped blankets . . . [and] Mississippi cotton planters; Quakers in full drab, . . . slaves . . . and young Spanish creoles."

Link to History

Use the quotations and tables to draw conclusions about how steamboat travel affected westward expansion.

1. Name three types of people who were traveling west with Melville. Speculate about where they were headed, and why.

2. How did St. Louis and New Orleans change between 1810 and 1860? What is the connection between that change and the change in steamboats?

3. Write a sentence summarizing how steamboats affected westward expansion.

4. **Hands-On Geography** Imagine that you are a Boston newspaper reporter in 1830. You have just completed a steamboat trip from New Orleans to St. Louis. Write a short article describing what you have seen.

Teaching the Geography Lab

Have students read the quotation at the end of the introduction. Ask: **How do the tables support this statement from a St. Louis newspaper?** (The statement says many steamboat passengers remained in the city. Between 1830 and 1840 there was a dramatic increase in both the number of western steamboats and the population of St. Louis.)

Link to History
Answers

1. Businesspeople, pleasure seekers, hunters, farmers, people looking for wealthy spouses, wealthy men and women, Indians, investors, Quakers, slaves. People were going west to seek fortune, adventure, or a spouse.

2. Both cities grew immensely between 1810 and 1860. The growth was directly connected to the increase in the number of steamboats, which made travel to the cities easier.

3. Steamboats made westward settlement easier.

4. Articles will vary but should include descriptions of many different kinds of people who went west seeking their fortunes.

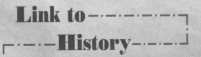

See the activity on steamboats in **Geography Extensions**, pp. 23–24.

3. A Bold Foreign Policy

Reading Guide

New Term immigration

Section Focus The new directions in foreign policy set by James Monroe and John Quincy Adams

1. How did the United States improve its relations with Great Britain?
2. How did Florida become part of the United States?
3. What was the purpose of the Monroe Doctrine?

The tradition of Republican Presidents from Virginia continued in 1816 with the election of James Monroe. Compared with Jefferson and Madison, Monroe was not a great leader or thinker, but he was admired for his long service to the party. Fortunately, he was wise enough to appoint the best people he could find to his cabinet.

Monroe's most brilliant choice was John Quincy Adams to be Secretary of State. The son of John and Abigail Adams, John Quincy had served as the nation's ambassador to four European countries. He had also helped to negotiate the peace treaty ending the War of 1812. As Secretary of State, Adams shaped a bold foreign policy that would guide the United States in world affairs for the century to come.

Agreement with Britain

The first goal of Adams's foreign policy was to make a lasting peace with Britain. Adams knew that the Treaty of Ghent had not settled the disputes that led to the War of 1812 (see page 307). He was determined to build a new relationship with Britain based on cooperation, not conflict.

Adams improved relations with Britain by settling old boundary issues. In a treaty known as the Convention of 1818, the border between Canada and the Louisiana Purchase was fixed at the 49th parallel (see the map on page 330). The United States and Britain also agreed to share Oregon Country in the Pacific Northwest.

Canadian suspicions Despite this agreement, Canadians remained suspicious of the United States. In 1775 and again in 1812, Americans had invaded Canada. No treaty could ease Canadians' deep distrust of their southern neighbor.

After the War of 1812, the British government encouraged immigration to Canada. **Immigration** is the movement of people from one country to make their home in another. Settlers poured into Canada from England, Scotland, and Ireland.

Immigrants from the United States were not so welcome. Americans moving to certain areas in Canada could not buy land until they had lived there for seven years. Still, some Americans did settle in Canada, especially African Americans fleeing slavery and prejudice in the United States.

Takeover of Florida

The second goal of Adams's policy was to acquire the Spanish colony of Florida. Over the years, Spain's hold on Florida had grown weak. When farmers in Georgia complained

✳️ **History Footnote**
Father Hidalgo made his speech calling for Mexican independence in the town of Dolores, which is now known as Dolores Hidalgo. The speech is remembered as *Grito de Dolores*—"Cry of Dolores." The anniversary of that speech, September 16, is celebrated throughout Mexico to honor independence. On that day, leaders read the speech to crowds of celebrants.

See the Study Guide activity in **Chapter Resources Binder**, p. 91.

Link to Art

The War of Independence Since the time of the Mayas, Mexican artists have been creating murals, or wall paintings, to tell the history of their people. The scene at right is part of a huge mural in the National Museum of History in Mexico City. Painted by Juan O'Gorman in 1960 and 1961, the mural tells the story of the Mexican War of Independence. In this detail Father Miguel Hidalgo (center) calls for revolt against Spanish rule.

Discuss What words would you use to describe the people in the mural? Based on this scene, why do you think murals are called "the people's art"?

about raids by Seminole Indians and escaped slaves who lived with the Seminoles in Florida, Spain could do little to halt the attacks. In 1818 Monroe called on Andrew Jackson—the hero of the Battle of New Orleans—to stop the raids.

General Jackson marched 3,000 troops into Florida to track down the raiders. Once there, he pursued the Seminoles, destroyed their villages, and executed two chiefs. He also went beyond his orders and seized two Spanish military posts. Spain protested and demanded that Jackson be punished for disobeying orders.

Adams-Onís Treaty Instead, Adams sent Spain this message: Get control of Florida or get out. Spain, faced with problems in its Latin American colonies, decided to get out. In the 1819 Adams-Onís Treaty, Spain ceded Florida to the United States and gave up its claim on Oregon Country.

New Latin American Nations

Meanwhile, revolution was sweeping Latin America. Colonists from Mexico to Argentina fought to throw off Spanish rule. Spain wanted Adams to promise not to recognize the independence of its rebelling colonies. Adams refused to make that promise.

Mexico wins independence In Mexico the drive for independence was inspired by a priest named Miguel Hidalgo (mee-GEL ee-DAHL-gō). In 1810 the priest cried out to his people, "My children, when will you recover lands stolen from your ancestors 300 years ago by the hated Spaniards?"

Hidalgo was put to death by the Spanish, but his speech touched off a revolution that lasted ten long years. In 1821 Mexico won its independence. Three years later, it became a republic with an elected president.

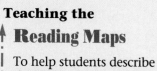

Teaching the
↑ Reading Maps

To help students describe the United States boundaries in 1825, have them refer to the maps on pages R4–R7. **Answers to Reading Maps: 1.** Bounded on the north by Canada and on the west by the Rockies and Mexico. **2.** Mexico, British Honduras, United Provinces of Central America, Haiti, Santo Domingo, Greater Colombia, Brazil, Peru, Bolivia, Paraguay, Argentina, Chile.

Section Activity

Painting a Mural

Have students work in small groups to paint different parts of a mural illustrating some events in this chapter. Some subjects include the Industrial Revolution, new forms of transportation, Jackson's invasion of Florida, or the liberation of Latin America from Spanish rule. Have each group decide on a specific event or period they will illustrate. Attach a long sheet of butcher paper to a classroom wall and have each group paint a portion. Students in each group may divide up tasks, with some doing research and some drawing or painting.

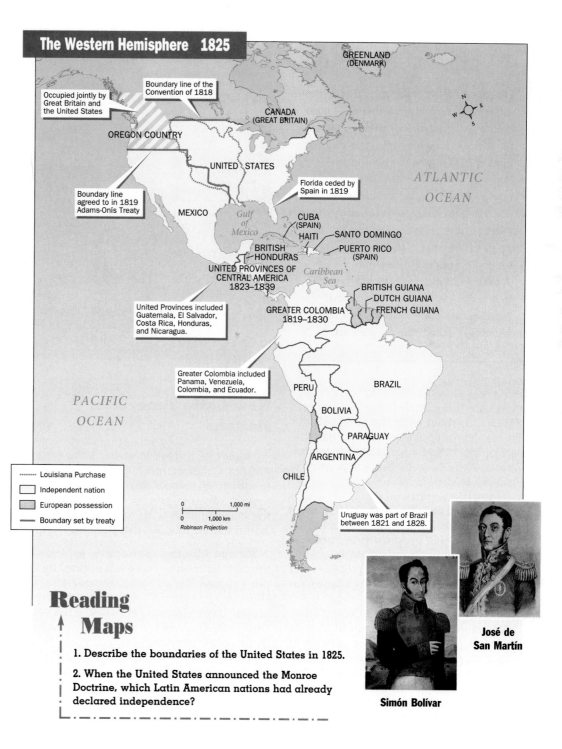

The Western Hemisphere 1825

GREENLAND (DENMARK)

Occupied jointly by Great Britain and the United States

Boundary line of the Convention of 1818

CANADA (GREAT BRITAIN)

OREGON COUNTRY

UNITED STATES

ATLANTIC OCEAN

Boundary line agreed to in 1819 Adams-Onís Treaty

MEXICO

Gulf of Mexico

Florida ceded by Spain in 1819

CUBA (SPAIN)

HAITI — SANTO DOMINGO

BRITISH HONDURAS

PUERTO RICO (SPAIN)

UNITED PROVINCES OF CENTRAL AMERICA 1823–1839

Caribbean Sea

United Provinces included Guatemala, El Salvador, Costa Rica, Honduras, and Nicaragua.

GREATER COLOMBIA 1819–1830

BRITISH GUIANA
DUTCH GUIANA
FRENCH GUIANA

Greater Colombia included Panama, Venezuela, Colombia, and Ecuador.

PERU

BRAZIL

PACIFIC OCEAN

BOLIVIA

PARAGUAY

ARGENTINA

CHILE

- - - - - Louisiana Purchase

☐ Independent nation

☐ European possession

— Boundary set by treaty

0   1,000 mi
0   1,000 km
Robinson Projection

Uruguay was part of Brazil between 1821 and 1828.

José de San Martín

Simón Bolívar

Reading
↑ Maps

1. Describe the boundaries of the United States in 1825.

2. When the United States announced the Monroe Doctrine, which Latin American nations had already declared independence?

Monroe often sought the advice of Jefferson and Madison. Both favored accepting Britain's offer to send a joint warning against interfering in the Western Hemisphere. Monroe finally agreed with John Quincy Adams that a joint agreement would not prevent British interference. The Monroe Doctrine, though, attracted little notice in Europe, where it was considered empty bluster.

Teaching the

World  Link

To help students understand why Russia was seen as a threat, have them locate the Bering Strait, Alaska, Oregon Country, and Fort Ross on maps.

World  Link

Russia claims much of Pacific Northwest

Startling news reached Secretary of State John Quincy Adams in 1821. Russia had claimed a stretch of the Pacific Northwest from the Bering Strait south to Oregon Country—land already claimed by both the United States and Britain.

Since 1741 a colony of Russians in Alaska had been trading with the Indians for furs. In 1812 they moved south into Spanish California, where they established a trading post called Fort Ross, north of San Francisco.

Angered by Russia's new claim, Adams warned that "the American continents are no longer subjects for *any* new European colonial establishments." In 1824 Russia canceled its claim on Oregon Country.

Independence for South America

Two great leaders freed South America from Spanish rule. In 1810 General Simón Bolívar (see-MON bō-LEE-vahr), a Venezuelan, launched a revolution in northern South America. By 1819 Bolívar had liberated Venezuela, Colombia, Panama, Ecuador, and part of Peru.

An Argentine general, José de San Martín (hō-SAY day SAHN-mahr-TEEN), led the struggle for independence in southern South America. After freeing Argentina, Uruguay, and Paraguay, San Martín drove Spain out of Chile.

The liberation of South America from Spanish rule was completed in 1824. That year Bolívar's forces defeated a Spanish army in Peru, and the last Spanish troops left South America.

The Monroe Doctrine

Both the United States and Great Britain supported the Latin American revolutions. The monarchs of Europe did not. They were alarmed by the spread of democracy. Some, especially the rulers of France and Russia, began to talk of helping Spain recover its lost colonies.

In 1823 Britain asked the United States to join it in sending a message to Spain, France, and Russia. The message would warn them to leave Latin America alone. Adams, however, argued that the United States should speak for itself. President Monroe agreed. He asked Adams to draft an American statement on the subject.

In 1823 President Monroe issued that statement, which became known as the Monroe Doctrine. The Americas, he said, were closed to "future colonization by any European powers." He warned Europe not to interfere with the new nations of Latin America "for the purpose of oppressing them, or controlling . . . their destiny." In return, he promised, the United States would stay out of Europe's affairs.

Most people in the United States liked Monroe's message that the Americas were for Americans. In the years ahead, the Monroe Doctrine would remain a pillar of the nation's foreign policy.

⭐ 3. Section Review

1. Define **immigration.**
2. What agreement did the United States and Britain make about Oregon Country?
3. How did the United States solve the problems between Georgia and the Spanish colony of Florida?
4. Critical Thinking How did events in Latin America and in Europe lead to the Monroe Doctrine?

Closing the Section

Wrap-Up Activity

Portraying Leaders

Have each student prepare a one-minute, first-person talk describing accomplishments of one of the following: Monroe, Adams, Jackson, Hidalgo, Bolívar, or San Martín. Have volunteers give their talks and answer questions from classmates.

Section Review
Answers

1. Definition: *immigration* (328)
2. To share Oregon Country.
3. Jackson stopped Seminole raids into Georgia. Adams got Spain to cede Florida.
4. France and Russia talked of helping Spain regain colonies lost as a result of revolution.

332

---

4. Strains on National Unity

Reading Guide

New Terms financial panic, sectionalism

Section Focus The events that tested Americans' spirit of unity after the War of 1812

1. Why was there an "era of good feelings" after the War of 1812?
2. What led to the Panic of 1819?
3. How did the issue of statehood for Missouri threaten national unity?

At his first inauguration in 1817, President Monroe spoke not as a Republican or a Virginian. He spoke as an American filled with pride in his country, saying:

❝If we look to the history of other nations, we find no example of a growth so rapid, so gigantic, of a people so prosperous and happy. . . . How near our government has approached to perfection.❞

The Era of Good Feelings

After taking office, the Republican Monroe toured New England, the stronghold of the Federalist Party. Even there, however, Americans had turned away from the Federalists for failing to support the War of 1812. Wherever Monroe went, he was greeted by thousands of people lining the streets to cheer him. One newspaper reported:

❝The visit of the President seems to have wholly allayed [calmed] the storms of party. People now meet in the same room who, a short while since, would scarcely pass along the same street.❞

So many New Englanders turned out to greet Monroe that a Boston newspaper reported the beginning of "the era of good feelings."

These good feelings were to assure Monroe of easy re-election in 1820. By then, however, new problems were arising to threaten national unity.

The Panic of 1819

The good feelings were sorely tested when the nation was hit by a financial panic in 1819. A **financial panic** is widespread fear caused by a sudden downturn in prices or change in property values.

After the War of 1812, prices for American farm products in Europe had risen sharply. Happy farmers rushed out to buy more land on which to plant cash crops. As a result, land prices soared.

State banks fueled the boom by loaning money to almost anyone who needed cash to buy land. The Bank of the United States, too, loaned large sums to land buyers. For a time, everyone seemed to be making money in land deals.

Boom to bust The boom went bust in 1819 when crop prices overseas dropped like a stone. Cotton, which had soared to 33¢ a pound, fell to 14¢. Suddenly, many farmers could not pay their debts. They risked being sent to debtors' prisons, where they would remain until friends or relatives paid the debts.

Samuel Morse, the inventor of the telegraph, was a noted American painter. He painted the huge picture shown on this page, *The Old House of Representatives*, in 1822. Morse planned to take this painting and others on a moneymaking tour around the United States. To attract attention, he included a portrait of the Pawnee chief Petalesharro, who was in Washington when Morse was working on the painting. It is likely, though not certain, that Petalesharro actually visited the House of Representatives. Petalesharro became a celebrity on his visit to Washington because of his eagle feather war bonnet, the first of its kind to be seen in the East. Morse's painting was not so celebrated—so few people paid to see it that he turned to inventing to make a living.

Developing the Section

Discussion

Checking Understanding

1. What caused the Panic of 1819? (When crop prices were high, farmers took out loans to buy more land. When prices fell suddenly in 1819, farmers could not pay debts.)

2. How did the Bank of the United States worsen the financial situation? (It took over the property of people who could not pay their debts.)

Stimulating Critical Thinking

3. Who do you think was most to blame for the Panic of 1819? (Answers might be the state banks for lending money too freely; the national bank for taking property of debtors; the farmers themselves for being overly optimistic in borrowing money.)

In the Monroe era—as today—Congress often met in the evening. This painting shows a debate that took place in the Capitol, newly rebuilt after being burned in the War of 1812. Pawnee chief Petalesharro, a visitor to Washington, watches from an upper gallery.

In the next three years, the panic spread from farms to towns and cities. Many shops and factories failed, and thousands of workers lost their jobs. Citizens of a hard-hit Pennsylvania town sent a petition to Congress asking for help. They reported:

❝The larger part of the people . . . can hardly obtain the very necessaries [essentials] of life. . . . Debts are unpaid, creditors dissatisfied, and the jails full of honest but unfortunate persons whose wives and children have thereby become a burden on the township.❞

The Bank of the United States made a bad situation worse by taking over the property of borrowers who could not pay their debts. Thousands of people lost their farms, homes, and businesses to the bank. As a result, wrote one observer, "the bank was saved and the people were ruined."

The Expansion of Slavery

An even heavier blow to the Era of Good Feelings fell when controversy over slavery flared up in Congress. The issue was whether to permit slavery to expand into the new states that were being formed out of the Louisiana Purchase.

The Northwest Ordinance of 1787 had set out the steps for forming new states (see page 236). It had also banned slavery in the Northwest Territory. Thus, the new states of Ohio, Indiana, and Illinois were "free states"—states where slavery was not permitted. New states south of the Northwest Territory—Kentucky, Tennessee, Louisiana, Mississippi, and Alabama—allowed slavery.

Bonus Activity

Creating a Political Cartoon

To help students focus on important events, have them draw and caption a political cartoon. Let each choose a topic: the Era of Good Feelings, the Panic of 1819, the Bank's taking over of debtors' property, Senate rejection of the Tallmadge Amendment, or the Missouri Compromise. You might have students bring in current political cartoons to analyze before creating their own.

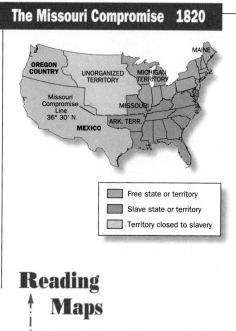

The Missouri Compromise 1820

MAINE

OREGON COUNTRY

UNORGANIZED TERRITORY

MICHIGAN TERRITORY

Missouri Compromise Line 36° 30' N

MISSOURI

ARK. TERR.

MEXICO

- Free state or territory
- Slave state or territory
- Territory closed to slavery

Reading
↑ Maps

After the Missouri Compromise, how many senators were there from slave states and how many from free states?

Early in 1819 Missouri Territory—part of the Louisiana Purchase—asked to join the Union as a "slave state." By then, every state north of Delaware had taken action to end slavery. Part of Missouri lay as far north as many of these free states.

The Tallmadge Amendment Northerners in Congress wanted to keep slavery from spreading. Many thought slavery was wrong. In addition, they feared that representatives from new slave states would increase the power of the southern states in the House and the Senate. Senator Rufus King of New York put the matter bluntly:

❝If slavery be permitted in Missouri, . . . what hope can be entertained [kept] that it will ever be prohibited in any of the new states that will be formed in the immense region west of the Mississippi?❞

Thus, when the bill to make Missouri a state came before Congress in February 1819, northerners reacted quickly. Representative James Tallmadge of New York introduced an amendment to the bill that called for an end to slavery in Missouri.

Southerners in Congress greeted the Tallmadge Amendment with a roar of protest. What constitutional power, they asked, did Congress have to decide whether a state should be slave or free? That choice belonged to the people of each state. Besides, if Congress were allowed to meddle with slavery in Missouri, might it not try to abolish slavery elsewhere?

The Tallmadge Amendment was approved by the House of Representatives. There the North, with its greater population, had a majority. In the Senate, however, the North and the South had the same number of votes, and southerners blocked the amendment. Congress was deadlocked and would remain so for more than a year.

The growth of sectionalism As the debate over expanding slavery raged on, it became increasingly bitter. The good feelings and sense of national unity that had come out of the War of 1812 soon gave way to sectionalism. **Sectionalism** is devotion to the interests of one's own section over those of the nation as a whole.

The Missouri Compromise

Sectional differences on the Missouri question ran so deep in Congress that they worried Henry Clay, the Speaker of the House. "The words *civil war* and *disunion* are uttered almost without emotion," Clay reported. Under his guidance, Congress reached a compromise in March 1820.

Despite Henry Clay's charm and eloquence, he never succeeded in being elected President, despite five attempts. "I had rather be right than be President," he said during one controversy. Clay was known for his devotion to principle as well as for "the uncontrolled expression of violent feelings" during his speeches to Congress. His first speech on the Missouri question was a riveting four-hour performance. He foresaw that the argument over the expansion of slavery was potentially disastrous for the Union, and he fought desperately, using eloquence, cajoling, and threats, to solve it with a compromise. An appropriate quotation from one of Clay's speeches marks his grave: "I know no North—no South—no East—no West."

Hands-On → *HISTORY*

Making compromises Henry Clay's "mode of speaking is very forcible. He fixes the attention by his earnest and emphatic [strong] tones and gestures." So said a member of the House of Representatives in 1820. Clay's success in settling disputes in Congress earned him the name the Great Compromiser.

Henry Clay

➤ Activity

❶ Try being a Great Compromiser. Choose a problem or dispute at the school, local, state, or national level that you think needs settling.

❷ Find out as much as you can about the problem. Interview family members, friends, or neighbors. Read newspaper or magazine articles and listen to television or radio broadcasts.

❸ Write a description of the problem, the solutions proposed, and a compromise that all sides might agree to accept. Keep in mind that in a compromise each side gives up part of what it wants.

❹ Describe the compromise to your classmates. Will it work? What do they think?

The Missouri Compromise allowed Missouri into the Union as a slave state. At the same time, Maine, which had recently asked to join the Union, entered as a free state. In this way the balance between slave and free states in the Senate was preserved at 12 states each.

The compromise also drew a line across the Louisiana Purchase at latitude 36° 30'. North of that line, slavery was forever banned, except in Missouri. South of that line, slavery was permitted.

Although it passed, the compromise pleased few people. In the North, members of Congress who had voted for it were accused of selling out. In the South, the new ban on slavery was deeply resented.

The compromise especially alarmed former President Thomas Jefferson. He wrote to a friend that "this momentous question, like a firebell in the night, awakened and filled me with terror."

⤻ Point of View

Was the Missouri Compromise good for the nation?

Secretary of State John Quincy Adams had very mixed feelings about the Missouri Compromise. Adams hated slavery. In his eyes it was "the great and foul stain" on the United States. Even so, he decided not to speak out against Clay's compromise and advised President Monroe to approve it.

Although Adams wanted to abolish slavery, he believed that the Constitution did not give that power to the federal government. "The abolition of slavery where it is already established," he wrote, "must be left entirely to the people of the state itself." The compromise seemed to be the best that could be passed under the circumstances.

In the privacy of his diary, however, Adams revealed his inner conflict over the wisdom of remaining silent:

Discussion

Checking Understanding

1. What did the Tallmadge Amendment call for? (An end to slavery in Missouri.)

Stimulating Critical Thinking

2. Were northern members of Congress selling out in supporting the Missouri Compromise? Explain. (Yes: should have stood up for convictions; no: better for each side to have partial victory than to risk destroying the Union.)

Teaching the

Hands-On → *HISTORY*

Ask students for examples of compromises they have made with families and friends. Then ask for less personal examples, as on local or national issues, such as smokers' vs. nonsmokers' rights, legalization of gambling, and gun control.

Teaching the

⤻ **Point of View**

Have students state two main reasons why Adams supported the compromise. (He thought the Constitution did not give the federal government power to abolish slavery and that taking a hard line would put the Union "at hazard.") Ask what the last sentence of his statement meant. (Perhaps the Union was not worth preserving at the cost of allowing slavery.)

Closing the Section

Section Review Answers

1. Definitions: *financial panic* (332), *sectionalism* (334)

2. People had turned away from the Federalists, so there was a sense of political unity.

3. Farmers were hardest hit because they had borrowed money for land; when cotton prices dropped they could not repay loans.

4. The threat to national unity caused by sectionalism. New problem: few satisfied by compromise, southern resentment of new ban on slavery.

5. Opinions will vary. Students should consider growing political competition in Congress between northern and southern states, the expansion of the cotton kingdom and of slavery, and the growing all-or-nothing nature of the slavery issue.

To check understanding of "Why We Remember," assign Thinking Critically question 3 on student page 338.

"I have favored this Missouri Compromise . . . from extreme unwillingness to put the Union at hazard [risk]. But perhaps it would have been a wiser as well as a bolder course to have persisted in the [no-slavery] restriction upon Missouri. . . . If the Union must be dissolved, slavery is precisely the question upon which it ought to break."

The conflict over slavery had been settled for now, but Adams feared that sectionalism would continue to strain national unity. In fact, the debate over slavery in Missouri was just the beginning of a struggle that was to lead to a tragic civil war.

4. Section Review

1. Define **financial panic** and **sectionalism**.
2. What led to an "era of good feelings" after the War of 1812?
3. Who was hardest hit by the Panic of 1819 and why?
4. When Congress approved the Missouri Compromise in 1820, what problem did it solve? What problem did the Missouri Compromise cause?
5. **Critical Thinking** Do you think that the growth of sectionalism in 1819 could have been avoided? Give evidence from the text to support your answer.

Why We Remember

The Confident Years

The Missouri Compromise put the slavery question aside, at least for a time. With that issue behind them, most Americans quickly regained their sense of confidence in the nation's future. Everywhere they saw signs of progress and growth.

Despite the setbacks of the Panic of 1819, the nation's economy was soon growing again. Southern cotton production rose every year. In the Old Northwest, forests gave way to a landscape of farms. In the Northeast, mills and factories sprouted beside every river, and young women left farms to become mill girls. New forms of transportation carried goods made in those factories to more Americans every year.

During these confident years, President Monroe issued the nation's first bold statement of foreign policy. The Monroe Doctrine asserted that the United States would not accept European interference in American affairs—not in North America, Central America, or South America. By its very boldness, the doctrine told the world that the United States was becoming a strong, confident nation.

(Answers continued from side margin)

p. 332: "The good feelings were sorely tested . . . by . . . panic in 1819"; p. 333: "In the next three years, the panic spread . . ."; "An even heavier blow . . . fell when controversy over slavery flared up . . ."; p. 334: "The good feelings . . . soon gave way to sectionalism." Examples from source B: ". . . second term was a time of quite bad feelings"; ". . . sectionalism was on the increase"; ". . . factional disputes began to break out." (c) The label applies well to the first two years of Monroe's presidency, but feelings of national unity and prosperity soon declined.

3. Example: A Time of Short-lived Nationalism and Growing Sectionalism.

For further application, have students do the Applying Skills activity in the Chapter Survey (p. 338).

If students need to review the skill, use the Skills Development transparency and activity in the **Chapter Resources Binder,** pp. 95–96.

Skill Lab

Thinking Critically

Generalizations

Columbian Exchange. Half War. Industrial Revolution. Labels like these have been used to describe time periods or events of the past. An accurate label can be a helpful tool when we try to understand the past. An inaccurate label, however, can lead to misunderstandings about history.

Skill Tips

• To identify a generalization, look for a sentence or phrase that sums up specific points.

• To evaluate a generalization, ask yourself, "Which are stronger—the examples or the exceptions?"

• When you make a generalization, it is usually more accurate to use words like *most, many, usually, often,* and *generally.*

Question to Investigate

Is the label *Era of Good Feelings* a good description of James Monroe's presidency?

Procedure

A label like *Era of Good Feelings* is an example of a **generalization,** a broad statement that is meant to sum up the specific characteristics of something. A generalization can be a phrase or a sentence. To determine how accurate a generalization is, you need to check how well it is supported by specific examples. Explore the Question to Investigate by doing the following.

❶ Identify who or what the generalization is about.
a. Write a sentence explaining what the generalization *Era of Good Feelings* means.
b. What time period does it refer to? Who was feeling good about what?

❷ Evaluate the generalization.
a. List examples from sources **A** and **B** that support the generalization.
b. List examples from sources **A** and **B** that are exceptions to the generalization.
c. In your mind, weigh the examples against the exceptions and answer the Question to Investigate.

❸ Write your own generalization about Monroe's presidency. Explain why you think it is accurate.

Sources to Use

A Reread Section 4 (pages 332–336).

B "Although Monroe's personal popularity during his first term had brought glowing references to his administration as an 'era of good feelings,' his second term was a time of quite bad feelings. True, the President was still well liked, and party politics had virtually disappeared—almost everyone professed [claimed] to be a Republican. But sectionalism was on the increase. And with everybody in the same party, factional disputes [disagreements within the party] began to break out."

From Margaret L. Coit et al., *The Growing Years* (Time Inc.: 1963)

Exceptions:

1.
2.

Examples:

1.
2.

Introducing the Skill Lab

Discuss how historical generalizations can be useful. (They provide a way to remember main characteristics of periods, events, and people.) Ask why they can be misleading. (In trying to understand the past, people may be tempted to jump to easy conclusions, ignoring contradictory evidence.)

Skill Lab
Answers

1. (a) It refers to James Monroe's presidency, a period during which there was a general sense of national unity and lack of political party rivalry. (b) 1817–1825. Most Americans supported Monroe and felt good about the lack of party rivalry.

2. (a) Examples from source A, p. 332: "Wherever Monroe went, he was greeted by thousands of people lining the streets to cheer him"; "The visit of the President . . . wholly allayed the storms of party"; "These good feelings were to assure Monroe of easy re-election in 1820." Examples from source B: ". . . Monroe's personal popularity during his first term had brought glowing references to . . . an 'era of good feelings'"; ". . . still well liked, and party politics had virtually disappeared. . . ."
(b) Examples from source A,
(Answers continued in top margin)

for northern mills; no: slavery expanded.

2. Monroe Doctrine gave impression of confidence and strength. Missouri Compromise shows disunity.

3. Industrial Revolution, improvements in transportation, great increase in cotton production. More northerners working in factories and more southerners increasing slave holdings and moving west.

Applying Skills

Answers should reflect understanding of the definition of generalization, as discussed on p. 337. Supporting examples should be specific and concrete.

History Mystery

Steam-powered train proved it could move faster than horses and haul heavier loads.

Survey Answers

Reviewing Vocabulary

Definitions are found on these pages: *Industrial Revolution* (319), *mass production* (320), *protective tariff* (321), *immigration* (328), *financial panic* (332), *sectionalism* (334).

Reviewing Main Ideas

1. Slater brought the spinning jenny to the United States, beginning the shift to machines and to factories. Whitney invented the cotton gin, and pioneered interchangeable parts. Lowell opened the first American cotton mill.

2. (a) To help American business grow and compete in the world. (b) National bank, protective tariff.

3. (a) Faster and cheaper, especially with steamboat. (b) Could be built where rivers did not go. (c) Cheaper, did not freeze.

4. Settled the issue of the border with Canada, agreed to share Oregon Country, got Spain to cede Florida.

5. (a) To tell European powers to leave Latin American nations alone and give up further colonization in the Americas. (b) Revolutions in Latin America and talk among European nations of helping Spain regain its colonies.

6. Took over property of debtors; many lost farms, homes, and businesses.

7. (a) Missouri entered the Union as slave state and Maine as free state. Slavery was banned in the Louisiana Purchase territory north of latitude 36° 30'. (b) Northern members of Congress were accused of selling out. Southerners were not happy about the new ban on slavery.

Thinking Critically

1. Yes: profitable cash crop for South and raw material
(Answers continued in top margin)

Chapter Survey

Reviewing Vocabulary

Define the following terms.
1. Industrial Revolution 4. immigration
2. mass production 5. financial panic
3. protective tariff 6. sectionalism

Reviewing Main Ideas

1. Describe how Samuel Slater, Eli Whitney, and Francis Cabot Lowell contributed to the Industrial Revolution.

2. (a) What was the goal of the American System? (b) Which parts of the system were put into practice?

3. What were the advantages of using (a) rivers instead of roads? (b) canals instead of rivers? (c) railroads instead of canals?

4. How did Secretary of State Adams achieve his goals of lasting peace with Britain and the takeover of the Spanish colony of Florida?

5. (a) What was the purpose of the Monroe Doctrine? (b) What events led President Monroe to issue the doctrine?

6. How did the Bank of the United States help to make the Panic of 1819 worse?

7. (a) What were the main provisions of the Missouri Compromise? (b) Were northerners and southerners satisfied with the compromise? Explain.

Thinking Critically

1. Evaluation Southern farmers believed that the invention of a machine to clean cotton quickly would be a "great thing . . . to the country." Do you think that the invention of the cotton gin was a "great thing"? Explain why or why not.

2. Analysis What impression of the United States might Europeans get as a result of the Monroe Doctrine? As a result of the Missouri Compromise?

3. Why We Remember: Analysis The period around 1815 has been called one of the major turning points in the history of the United States. What major economic changes were taking place at this time? How did these changes affect Americans?

Applying Skills

Generalizations Think about your school experiences over the years and focus on a period of time that stands out in your mind.

1. Write a generalization about that period. It can be a phrase such as "Fifth Grade: The Time of Troubles," or a sentence such as "Seventh grade was an easy year."

2. List at least two examples that support your generalization.

3. List any exceptions to your generalization.

4. Explain why your generalization is accurate. Note how the supporting examples outweigh any exceptions.

History Mystery

The train race Answer the History Mystery on page 315. Not all Americans welcomed the railroads. One critic said, "The railroad . . . is the Devil's own invention, compounded of fire, smoke, soot, and dirt, spreading its infernal poison throughout the fair countryside." What would you say in reply to this criticism? What advantages did railroads have?

Writing in Your History Journal

1. Keys to History (a) The time line on pages 314–315 has seven Keys to History. In your journal, describe why each one is important to know about. (b) Imagine that you are a foreign visitor traveling in the United

Answers might include that pollution was minor trade-off for fast, efficient transportation. Advantages: could go where rivers did not run, cheaper than canals, did not freeze.

Writing in Your History Journal

1. (a) Explanations should be similar to the time line notes on teacher pages 314–315. (b) Events should show relevance beyond U.S., such as Monroe Doctrine.

2. Students who choose millwork may cite earning money, living away from home, meeting new people, taking classes, and attending concerts. Students who choose farm work may cite remaining close to families, working outdoors, not having a rigid work schedule, and privacy.

3. They feared the Union would be destroyed over the slavery issue. Some may think that *(Answers continued in side margin)*

taking a moral stand was more important than preserving the Union; others, that it was more important to preserve the Union and hope slavery would die out on its own.

Reviewing Geography

1. (A) Spain ceded Florida in the 1819 Adams-Onís Treaty. (B) In the Convention of 1818, the border was fixed at the 49th parallel. (C) In the Adams-Onís Treaty, Spain also gave up its claim on Oregon Country. Russia canceled its claim in 1824. (D) In the Convention of 1818, the U.S. and Britain agreed to share Oregon Country.

2. Examples of changing the environment might include clearing forests; planting crops like cotton; building roads, canals, railroads, and mills. Examples of adapting: using sleds in winter; paving roads with layers of crushed rock and gravel; building stone bridges; traveling downriver.

Alternative Assessment

Teacher's Take-Home Planner 4, p. 21, includes suggestions and scoring rubrics for the Alternative Assessment activity.

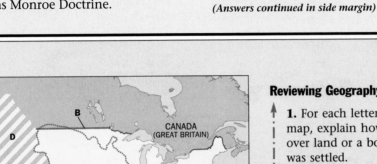

Reviewing Geography

1. For each letter on the map, explain how a dispute over land or a boundary was settled.

2. **Geographic Thinking** In the early 1800s Americans viewed the environment as "a challenge requiring action." Give three examples of how Americans faced that challenge and changed the environment to meet their needs. Then give two examples of how Americans had to adapt to the environment.

States in 1830. Which events on the time line would you be most interested in and why? Write your response in your journal.

2. **The Mill Girls** Would you have preferred to work in a New England mill or on the family farm? In your journal, explain your reasons. Consider such issues as pay, living and working conditions, and personal freedom.

3. **Citizenship** The Missouri Compromise filled Thomas Jefferson with terror. John Quincy Adams thought it was "a title page to a great tragic volume." What did both leaders fear? Should northerners have continued to oppose the compromise? Why? Write your responses in your journal.

Alternative Assessment

Writing about current events With a partner, carry on a correspondence about three events between 1816 and 1830.

❶ You and your partner each choose a person you want to be—a cotton planter

in Georgia, a mill owner in Rhode Island, a farmer in Indiana, or a riverboat captain on the Hudson River or Mississippi River.

❷ In a letter to your partner, describe your reaction to one of the following events: creation of the new Bank of the United States, passage of the first protective tariff, the Panic of 1819, the Missouri Compromise, the Monroe Doctrine, the opening of the Erie Canal. Your partner reads and replies to your letter, describing his or her reaction to the event.

❸ Next, your partner chooses one of the events above and writes to you about it, and you reply.

❹ Decide which partner will write a letter about the third event, and which will reply.

Your work will be evaluated on the following criteria:
• you describe historical events accurately
• the ideas you express are reasonable
• your letters are imaginative and interesting

Knowing content The invention demonstrates a new idea that meets a need.

Thinking critically The invention demonstrates imaginative thinking. The scale drawing or model includes details that serve a purpose and could be constructed.

Communicating ideas The presentation is clear and informative.

Thinking It Over

Answers might include that often people are not psychologically ready for inventions that will change their lives. Inventions are still rejected today. For example it has taken many years for some people to accept computers in everyday life. An invention of lasting value fills a need and is made of easy-to-obtain materials.

Making Connections

Answers

1. Washington tried to remain neutral or to negotiate with Britain. Jefferson tried to use trade laws to force Britain to stop illegal acts, whereas Madison went to war. Under Monroe, the U.S. negotiated with Britain on the border with Canada.

2. By 1830 the United States included Florida and the Louisiana Territory. It had canals, a national road, and railroads.

3. Northerners and southerners disagreed about Hamilton's program, including paying the national debt during Washington's administration. Northerners were in favor of payment; southerners were not.

Teaching the

Unit Project

Help students brainstorm ideas for inventions. Have them name some simple inventions that fulfill important needs, such as the paper clip or the safety pin. Encourage them to think of new ideas that fill a real need, no matter how simple. They might focus on the needs of a particular group, such as small children or senior citizens.

Evaluation Criteria

The project can be evaluated according to the criteria listed below, using a scale for each: 4 = exemplary, 3 = good, 2 = adequate, 1 = poor.

Completing the task Sketches and notes indicate a plan. A scale drawing or model shows details. An explanation tells how it meets a need.
(Continued in top margin)

Unit Survey

Review

Making Connections

1. Compare the way Presidents Washington, Jefferson, Madison, and Monroe handled relations with Britain.

2. Physically, the United States was very different in 1830 than it had been only 40 years before. Describe three differences.

3. Support the following: Conflict between the North and the South over the Missouri question was not new; its roots went back at least as far as Washington's presidency.

Project

Linking History, Technology, and Art

Inventing a New Gadget

"Build a better mousetrap and the world will beat a path to your door." That old saying reflects the hopes and dreams of inventors throughout time.

The ideas of inventors like Eli Whitney, Robert Fulton, and Peter Cooper have changed the lives of people and nations. Other ideas never get off the ground. Protective goggles for chickens and a parachute cap to wear when jumping from a burning building are two examples. Yet the inventors were serious about wanting to improve people's—not to mention chickens'—lives. What invention can you come up with to make life better?

Project Steps

Work on your own or with a partner.

❶ Decide what task you would like to do faster or more easily. It might be anything from combing the cat to watering the plants or taking out the trash. How could a new invention help you do it?

❷ Design the invention. What materials will it be made of? How will they be put together? How will it work? Make sketches and jot down descriptions as you plan.

❸ Make a scale drawing or model. In a model, you can substitute materials if necessary. For example, you can use aluminum foil for steel.

❹ Write an explanation to go with your drawing or model. Include why you think your invention is useful.

❺ Share your invention with your classmates. Do they agree that it is an idea whose time has come?

Thinking It Over Many inventions that eventually changed history were scorned as crazy at first. Why do you suppose that happened? Do you think it still happens today? What qualities does an invention of lasting value have?

Objectives

★ Describe the tools and methods used by oral historians.

★ Identify the kinds of information that historians can acquire from oral history.

★ Explain how historians can use oral history and archaeology to draw conclusions about past cultures.

How Do We Know?

Dr. Theresa Singleton of the Smithsonian Institution

Scholar's Tool Kit
Oral History

How do historians know about the lives of African Americans on southern plantations before the Civil War? Since most were slaves and not allowed to read or write, they left few written records. Yet historians working today have been able to piece together much of this history. An important tool in their research is **oral history**—historical data in the form of personal recollections or stories passed on by word of mouth.

Theresa Singleton, an anthropologist and archaeologist, uses oral history to gather information about this period. "I want to know how these African Americans spent their daily lives," she says. "How did they build their homes? How did they prepare their food? How did they craft their household equipment and personal possessions?" Most of all, she says, she wants to know how their African heritage lived on.

Using the Tools of History

How does Dr. Singleton use oral history now, nearly 150 years after slaves in the South were freed? After slavery was abolished, scholars and other interested people interviewed former slaves to learn as much as they could about life under slavery. These stories were written down, and some were published as slave narratives. Even though the stories are now in written form, we refer to them as oral history because they are in the words of the people who told them. Dr. Singleton studies these stories to learn how African Americans spent their daily lives.

● **341**

★

Introducing
How Do We Know?

Oral History

Ask students to tell what they think is meant by oral history. Explain that it is personal recollections or stories passed on by word of mouth. Point out that it can help us find out about an event or period that was not written about extensively or for which eyewitness accounts are crucial.

In this feature, students learn how oral history and archaeological evidence have increased our knowledge about daily lives of enslaved African Americans on southern plantations before the Civil War. Slaves were not allowed to read or write, so there are few written records. However, historians interviewed former slaves and published their stories. Scholars today can study these narratives, along with artifacts from slaves' living areas.

Setting the Stage
Activity

Creating Interview Questions

To help students see the importance of oral history, have them imagine being an historian who interviewed a former slave. Have them write five questions they would have asked to find out more about his or her daily life. Have volunteers read their questions, discussing why each one would be helpful.

341

Critical Thinking
Answers

1. Since slaves were not allowed to read or write, they did not leave written records. Personal narratives by slaves, as opposed to stories by slave owners or others, are crucial in finding out how slaves lived. Other areas of research might include societies with no written language, events not well-documented in writing, or daily life in any society.

2. Answers might include: Was the person in a good position to observe what he or she is relating? What is the time lapse between the event and the account? How does the person's manner of speaking reflect his or her experiences? Does the person have a bias that should be considered when interpreting the story?

3. Paintings and photographs, accounts by plantation owners or visitors from the North and Europe, and novels or plays of the time would be useful for providing details and views on life under slavery.

Bonus Activity

Identifying Artifacts

To show how artifacts and the stories behind them can contribute to history, challenge students to identify artifacts of their daily lives that would be found if their closets were excavated a century from now. Have them write interpretations that historians might make. Then have them write a brief explanation they would give orally to the historians.

✳ History Footnote

The first interviews of former slaves began at Fisk University in Tennessee in 1927, when a graduate student in anthropology compiled narratives of 100 people. A larger oral history project was sponsored by the Federal Writers' Project of the Works Progress Administration between 1936 and 1938.

Federal workers who conducted the interviews were told not to influence their subjects' point of view and to take down their words as exactly as possible. They asked questions about everyday conditions of life under slavery, experiences during the Civil War and Reconstruction, and later family and personal life. Some sample questions were "How did slaves carry news from one plantation to another?" and "What medicine did the slaves use for sickness?"

❓ Critical Thinking

1. Why is oral history an especially useful tool in studying what life was like for slaves? For what other areas of research would oral history be valuable?

❓ Critical Thinking

2. What questions about the source might you ask yourself when listening to or reading an oral history?

Dr. Singleton also uses a second tool of history—archaeology—to give her a more complete picture. Her team excavates areas where slaves once lived. They find pieces of pottery, broken glass, food bones, and tools in the ground where houses once stood. This evidence can confirm and add to what Dr. Singleton learns from oral history.

What Scholars Have Learned

By studying oral history and archaeological evidence, Dr. Singleton and her colleagues have learned a great deal about African American life. "Despite the oppressive and inhuman conditions of slavery," she declares, "enslaved Africans and their descendants were able to nurture and sustain a few aspects of their African heritage."

For example, broken pieces of pottery found at sites of slave quarters seem to show a connection to African traditions. "The use of this pottery," says Singleton, "suggests that enslaved African Americans prepared their food to suit their own tastes according to African cuisines. Slaves liked to eat gumbos and pilafs, which they prepared in a single pot. These tasty dishes are today popular meals in the South and represent a legacy of African-introduced cooking practices."

Also commonly found are colored glass beads, especially blue ones. Oral history helped Dr. Singleton understand. In the words of former slave Mollie Dawson, "Most all the young girls had what we called a charm string. They was a lot prettier than these strings we buys at the store now. This charm string was supposed to bring good luck to the owner of it."

Especially rich sources of information are the root cellars, or storage pits, that slaves sometimes dug under the floors of their houses. Archaeologists have found tools, locks, nails, buttons, glass, pottery, and discarded food bones in these pits.

The pits were intended for storage, but they were also excellent places to hide things. Slaves hid tools, food, guns, and other things they took from their owners or were forbidden to own. The practice of hiding food is confirmed by oral history. Said former slave Charles

At least five of the women in this 1862 photograph are wearing beaded necklaces like the ones Mollie Dawson described.

? **Critical Thinking**

3. Dr. Singleton uses both oral history and archaeology in her research. What other tools of history might a scholar use to piece together the story of what slave life was like? How might those tools be useful?

Grandy, "I got so hungry I stealed chickens off the roost. . . . We would cook the chicken at night, eat him, and burn the feathers. We always had a trap in the floor to hide these chickens in."

Scholars like Dr. Singleton are learning many things about slave life not known from written sources. "For example, the frequency with which lead pencils, slates, eye glasses, and gun parts turn up at archaeological sites," she says, "suggests that more slaves had access to fire-arms and possessed literacy [reading] and number skills than previously thought from the study of written records alone."

As the study of oral history and archaeological sites continues, scholars like Dr. Singleton are likely to continue to shed new light on African American history. Their findings will become a part of the history that a new generation of scholars will study.

Scholar at Work

Collecting oral history is something you can do now. Ask a member of your family to tell you a true story about his or her life. You may use a tape recorder or take notes to capture the details of this oral history. Be prepared to tell the story to your class. What might the story tell someone in the future about what life was like at the time?

• 343

> **Discussion**

Checking Understanding

1. What does Dr. Singleton want to find out about African Americans on southern plantations before the Civil War? (Daily lives and how their African heritage lived on.)

2. How were oral histories of the slaves gathered? (Historians interviewed former slaves and wrote down their recollections.)

3. What tool besides oral history has helped historians learn about life under slavery? (Archaeology— collecting items from the ground where slave quarters once stood.)

4. What items did slaves hide? (Tools, food, guns.)

5. What new information about slaves has Dr. Singleton learned? (Slaves had more access to guns and better literacy and math skills than previously thought.)

Teaching the
Scholar at Work

Encourage students to focus on an interesting event or period when they interview a family member. Topics might include the Vietnam or Gulf Wars, American space exploration, and the assassination of President Kennedy. Students might also ask an older person about a specific area of everyday life during his or her childhood, such as transportation, toys, entertainment, or school.

Unit 5

Introducing the Unit

Westward the Course of Empire Takes Its Way

This painting depicts a group of pioneers making their way across rough terrain, looking toward a vast expanse of seemingly uninhabited land. Leutze's mural, which covers a wall of the Capitol building, expresses the mood of this era of exploration, expansion, and westward growth. Throughout this unit, students will discover how the nation continued to expand and change both geographically and politically.

Teaching the

Hands-On

- - - - - - - ▶ *HISTORY*

To help students plan their cartoon strips, discuss reasons why people at that time might have chosen to travel westward, such as a desire for adventure or opportunity. Students should select one of the pioneers depicted by Leutze for their discussion, trying to imagine what feelings that person might express. As you discuss the finished products, ask them to identify visual details from the painting that helped them decide whether or not they would make the journey.

Unit Overview

Jackson and the Democrats gave common people a greater voice in politics. He tried to help farmers and small businesses by supporting the Indian Removal Act and opposing the national bank. He took a firm stand against nullification.

Texas gained independence from Mexico. Many Americans moved to Oregon, Utah, and California.

Industry expanded in the Northeast, the Midwest flourished through farming and trade, and the South relied on plantations. Slave revolts, unionization, and an anti-immigrant movement marked the mid-1800s.

Reformers sought to improve education, politics, hospitals, and prisons. Temperance, religious, abolition, and women's rights movements gained support. The mid-1800s saw a flowering of literature and art.

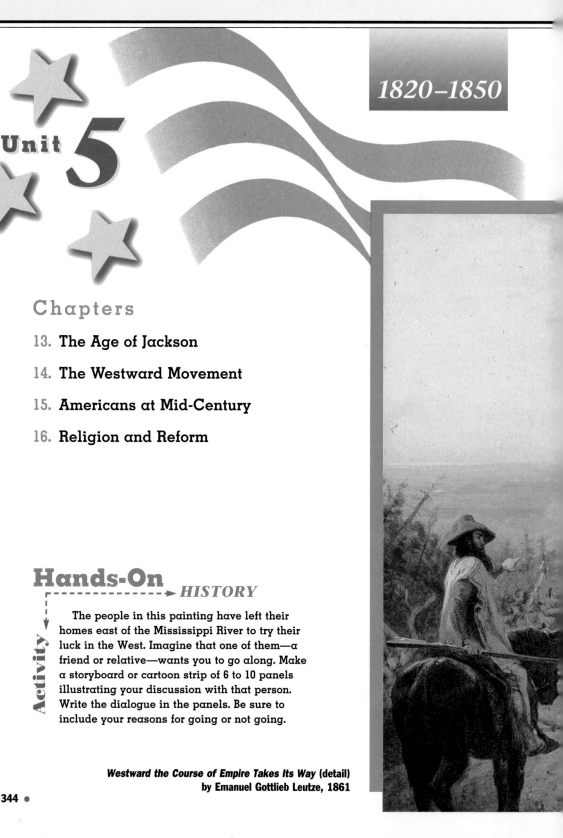

Unit 5

1820–1850

Chapters

13. **The Age of Jackson**

14. **The Westward Movement**

15. **Americans at Mid-Century**

16. **Religion and Reform**

Hands-On
- - - - - - - - ▶ *HISTORY*

Activity

The people in this painting have left their homes east of the Mississippi River to try their luck in the West. Imagine that one of them—a friend or relative—wants you to go along. Make a storyboard or cartoon strip of 6 to 10 panels illustrating your discussion with that person. Write the dialogue in the panels. Be sure to include your reasons for going or not going.

Westward the Course of Empire Takes Its Way (detail)
by Emanuel Gottlieb Leutze, 1861

* History Footnote

Emanuel Leutze concentrated on American history subjects, including his famous *Washington Crossing the Delaware*. The detail below is from a 20 by 30 foot mural that the federal government commissioned for the Capitol building. In preparation, he made the difficult journey to the Rocky Mountains to observe the landscape and traveled to Germany to study fresco painting.

See the Unit 5 activity in **Wall Time Line Activities.**

Expansion and Reform

Discussion

Checking Understanding

1. What are the people in the painting doing? (Traveling westward)

2. What modes of transportation are they using? (Covered wagons, horses, on foot)

Stimulating Critical Thinking

3. What feelings do you think the artist was trying to evoke? (The painting shows both the difficulty of the journey and the hopefulness.)

4. How do you think an American Indian living at that time would view this painting? (An Indian would probably see the pioneers, with their guns, as a threat.)

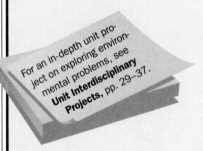

For an in-depth unit project on exploring environmental problems, see **Unit Interdisciplinary Projects,** pp. 29–37.

Chapter Planning Guide

Section	Student Text	Teacher's Edition Activities

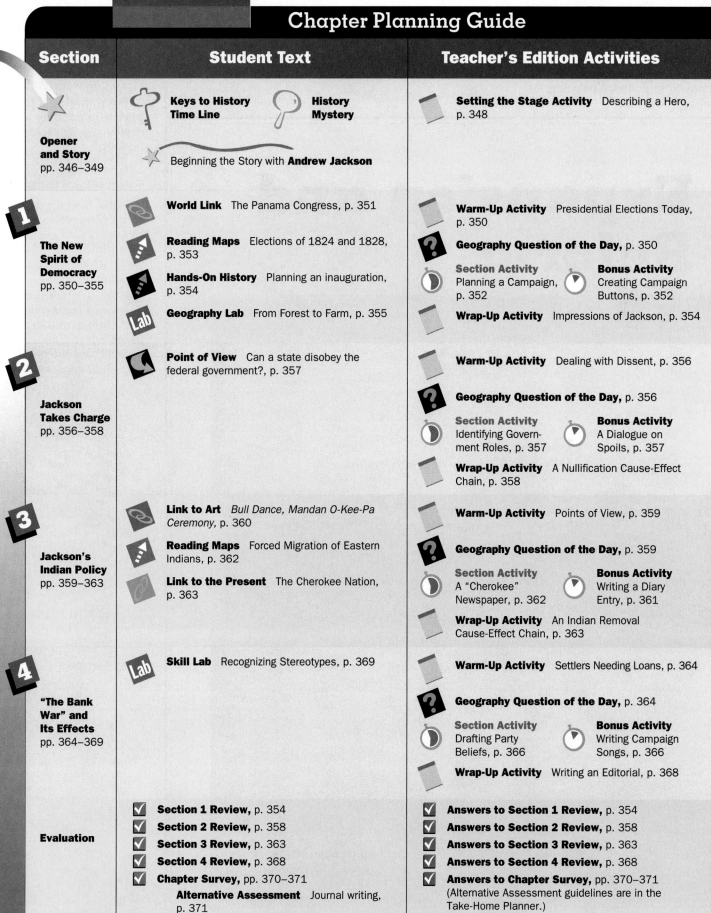

Opener and Story pp. 346–349

Keys to History Time Line

History Mystery

Beginning the Story with **Andrew Jackson**

Setting the Stage Activity Describing a Hero, p. 348

---

1 **The New Spirit of Democracy** pp. 350–355

World Link The Panama Congress, p. 351

Reading Maps Elections of 1824 and 1828, p. 353

Hands-On History Planning an inauguration, p. 354

Geography Lab From Forest to Farm, p. 355

Warm-Up Activity Presidential Elections Today, p. 350

Geography Question of the Day, p. 350

Section Activity Planning a Campaign, p. 352

Bonus Activity Creating Campaign Buttons, p. 352

Wrap-Up Activity Impressions of Jackson, p. 354

---

2 **Jackson Takes Charge** pp. 356–358

Point of View Can a state disobey the federal government?, p. 357

Warm-Up Activity Dealing with Dissent, p. 356

Geography Question of the Day, p. 356

Section Activity Identifying Government Roles, p. 357

Bonus Activity A Dialogue on Spoils, p. 357

Wrap-Up Activity A Nullification Cause-Effect Chain, p. 358

---

3 **Jackson's Indian Policy** pp. 359–363

Link to Art *Bull Dance, Mandan O-Kee-Pa Ceremony*, p. 360

Reading Maps Forced Migration of Eastern Indians, p. 362

Link to the Present The Cherokee Nation, p. 363

Warm-Up Activity Points of View, p. 359

Geography Question of the Day, p. 359

Section Activity A "Cherokee" Newspaper, p. 362

Bonus Activity Writing a Diary Entry, p. 361

Wrap-Up Activity An Indian Removal Cause-Effect Chain, p. 363

---

4 **"The Bank War" and Its Effects** pp. 364–369

Skill Lab Recognizing Stereotypes, p. 369

Warm-Up Activity Settlers Needing Loans, p. 364

Geography Question of the Day, p. 364

Section Activity Drafting Party Beliefs, p. 366

Bonus Activity Writing Campaign Songs, p. 366

Wrap-Up Activity Writing an Editorial, p. 368

Evaluation

☑ **Section 1 Review,** p. 354
☑ **Section 2 Review,** p. 358
☑ **Section 3 Review,** p. 363
☑ **Section 4 Review,** p. 368
☑ **Chapter Survey,** pp. 370–371
Alternative Assessment Journal writing, p. 371

☑ **Answers to Section 1 Review,** p. 354
☑ **Answers to Section 2 Review,** p. 358
☑ **Answers to Section 3 Review,** p. 363
☑ **Answers to Section 4 Review,** p. 368
☑ **Answers to Chapter Survey,** pp. 370–371
(Alternative Assessment guidelines are in the Take-Home Planner.)

Teacher's Resource Package

Take-Home Planner

Additional Resources

Chapter Summaries: English and Spanish, pp. 30–31

Introducing the Chapter Activity Wish Lists for the Federal Government, p. 4

Chapter In-Depth Activity Battle with the Bank, p. 4

Wall Time Line

Unit 5 Activity

Chapter Resources Binder
Study Guide Completing an Identity Table, p. 97
Geography Extensions A Settler's Guide, pp. 25–26
American Readings A Day for the People, p. 49

Reduced Views
Study Guide, p. 6
Geography Extensions, p. 9
American Readings, p. 8
Unit 5 Answers, pp. 36–44

Transparency Package

Transparency 13-1 Catlin's *Bull Dance, Mandan O-Kee-Pa Ceremony*—use with Section 3

Transparency 13-2 Catlin's *Comanche Village*—use with Section 3

Transparency Activity Book

Chapter Resources Binder
Study Guide Using a Graphic Organizer, p. 98
Reinforcement Identifying Viewpoints, pp. 101–102

Reduced Views
Study Guide, p. 6
Reinforcement, p. 7
Unit 5 Answers, pp. 36–44

SelecTest Testing Software
Chapter 13 Test, Forms A and B

Chapter Resources Binder
Study Guide Identifying Main Ideas, p. 99
American Readings Reaction to Removal, p. 50; On the Trail of Tears, pp. 51–52
Using Historical Documents Letter from Andrew Jackson to Secretary of War Eaton, pp. 70–75

Reduced Views
Study Guide, p. 6
American Readings, p. 8
Using Historical Documents, p. 9
Unit 5 Answers, pp. 36–44

★ ★ ★
Vital Links

Videodisc

CD-ROM

Andrew Jackson (see TE p. 352)

President Jackson's Kitchen Cabinet (see TE p. 358)

Voice of Corn Tassel (see TE p. 359)

Seminoles in canoes (see TE p. 362)

Chapter Resources Binder
Study Guide Completing a Chart, p. 100
Skills Development Recognizing Stereotypes, pp. 103–104

Reduced Views
Study Guide, p. 6
Skills Development, p. 7
Unit 5 Answers, pp. 36–44

Chapter and Unit Tests Chapter 13 Tests, Forms A and B, pp. 87–90

Reduced Views
Chapter Tests, p. 9
Unit 5 Answers, pp. 36–44

Alternative Assessment Guidelines for scoring the Chapter Survey activity, p. 5

13

Teaching Resources

Take-Home Planner 5
  Introducing Chapter Activity
  Chapter In-Depth Activity
  Alternative Assessment
Chapter Resources Binder
Geography Extensions
American Readings
Using Historical Documents
Transparency Activities
Wall Time Line Activities
Chapter Summaries
Chapter and Unit Tests
SelecTest Test File
Vital Links CD-ROM/Videodisc

Time Line

Keys to History

Keys to History journal writing activities are on page 370 in the Chapter Survey.

John Quincy Adams elected President Adams's belief in a strong national government was in conflict with growing sectionalism. (p. 350)

Tariff of Abominations South Carolina leaders threatened to secede in response to the tariff, prompting a crisis for the Union. (pp. 356–358)

Andrew Jackson elected President His election was seen as a victory for the common people. (p. 353)

Looking Back General Andrew Jackson became a hero by leading American troops to victory against the British.

World Link See p. 351.

346

Chapter Objectives

★ Explain how Andrew Jackson became President.
★ Describe Jackson's response to a threat to the Union.
★ Describe the Indian Removal Act and its effects.
★ Summarize the causes and effects of Jackson's "war" with the Bank of the United States.

Chapter Overview

After a disappointing loss in the election of 1824, Jackson's supporters unified under the name of the Democratic Party. Their victory in 1828, in which twice as many votes were cast as in 1824, was seen as a triumph of the common people. Jacksonian Democracy was born.

One of Jackson's first challenges was prompted by the Tariff of 1828, which

---

1824–1840

Chapter 13

The Age of Jackson

Sections

Beginning the Story with Andrew Jackson
1. **The New Spirit of Democracy**
2. **Jackson Takes Charge**
3. **Jackson's Indian Policy**
4. **"The Bank War" and Its Effects**

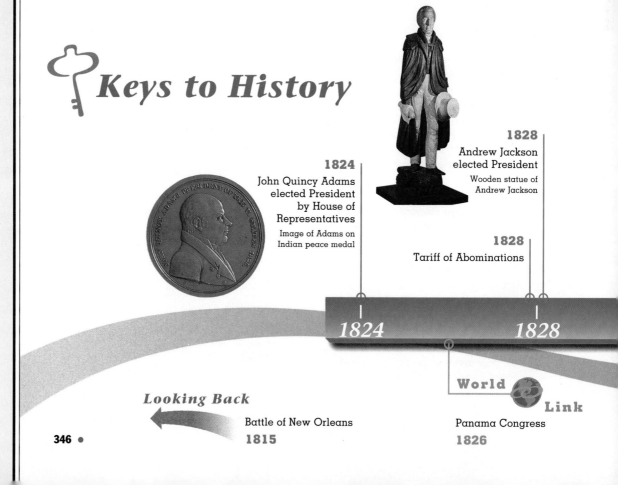

Keys to History

1824
John Quincy Adams
elected President
by House of
Representatives
Image of Adams on
Indian peace medal

1828
Andrew Jackson
elected President
Wooden statue of
Andrew Jackson

1828
Tariff of Abominations

1824   **1828**

Looking Back
Battle of New Orleans
1815

World Link
Panama Congress
1826

346 •

southerners called the "Tariff of Abominations." South Carolina threatened to secede if forced to honor the tariff. Jackson had the tariff lowered but denied that states had the right to nullify a federal law. His firm stand helped hold the Union together.

Jackson also was faced with conflicts between settlers and Indians. At his urging, Congress passed the Indian Removal Act. One result of this policy was the Trail of Tears, in which 4,000 Cherokees died while being forced out of Georgia by U.S. troops.

Honoring his promise to defend the common people, Jackson moved to destroy the Bank of the United States, which he said benefited only the wealthy. This "bank war" prompted the rise of the Whig Party. Economic troubles paved the way for the Whigs to finally win the presidency in 1840.

HISTORY *Mystery*

In 1838 many residents of homes like this were forced to leave their communities. Who were these people, and why were they driven away?

1830
Webster-Hayne debates
Daniel Webster (left) and Robert Hayne

1830
Indian Removal Act

1838
The Trail of Tears
Detail of *The Endless Trail* by Jerome Tiger

1840
"Tippecanoe and Tyler, too!"
An election campaign souvenir: a miniature log cabin

1832 *1836* *1840*

Looking Ahead

Republican Party formed
1854 • **347**

Teaching the HISTORY *Mystery*

Students will find further information on pp. 361–363. See Chapter Survey, p. 370, for additional information and questions.

Time Line

Webster-Hayne debates In one of the most dramatic debates in Senate history, these senators disagreed on whether or not states could nullify a federal law. (p. 357)

Indian Removal Act This act led to treaties that forced eastern Indians to move to land west of the Mississippi. (p. 361)

The Trail of Tears As many as 4,000 Cherokees died on the journey between Georgia and what is now Oklahoma, forced out of their homes by the Georgia militia. (p. 362)

"Tippecanoe and Tyler, too!" With campaign slogans like this, Whigs rallied popular support in their 1840 campaign for the presidency. (pp. 366–367)

Looking Ahead Split by the slavery issue, the Whig party dissolved and the Republicans, with the support of abolitionists, emerged.

Beginning the Story

Andrew Jackson

As the United States entered an era of westward growth and expansion, it was only appropriate that Andrew Jackson would emerge as a leader. Jackson had western origins, a record of bravery and military triumph, and a commanding personality befitting a hero of a nation. Jacksonian Democracy, as his style of politics was called, for the first time challenged the power of the elite and wealthy and changed the face of American politics.

Setting the Stage
Activity

Describing a Hero

To prepare students for reading about Andrew Jackson—a hero to many in his time—have them consider what qualities they think a hero should possess. Have them create a word web, with the word *hero* in the center and identifying traits around it. Have students compare their word webs. As they read about Jackson, have them consider whether he would fit their definition of a hero today.

See the Introducing the Chapter Activity, Wish Lists for the Federal Government. **Take- Home Planner 5,** p. 4.

✳ History Footnote

A ferocious temper got Jackson involved in a number of duels. In 1806 Charles Dickinson, a Nashville lawyer who was considered to be the best pistol shot in Tennessee, insulted Jackson's wife and called him a coward. Jackson challenged Dickinson to a duel.

As expected, Dickinson got off the first shot. The bullet struck Jackson in the chest. Although seriously wounded, he slowly raised his pistol, took careful aim, and fired. Dickinson fell, mortally wounded.

By then Jackson's boots had filled with blood, and he was near death himself. Dickinson's bullet had struck so close to his heart that doctors could not remove it. When a friend later asked how he could shoot with such a grave wound, the fiery Jackson snapped, "I should have hit him if he had shot me through the brain!"

Beginning the Story with

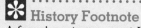

Andrew Jackson

Have you ever taken a close look at the portrait on a $20 bill? It is the long, thin face of Andrew Jackson, our seventh President. He looks every bit a President, very calm and dignified. Now look again, especially at the eyes. They were his most striking feature. When Jackson felt strongly about something, his eyes blazed. At such moments he could inspire love, respect, and even terror.

A Rough Childhood

The man behind those eyes was born to poor Scotch-Irish parents in the Carolina backcountry. Jackson never knew his father, who died before the boy was born. His mother dreamed of her son becoming a minister. Jackson, however, was not cut out for the church. He loved sports more than school-work. There was also something reckless about him. Jackson would pick a fight at the drop of a hat and, as a friend said, "he'd drop the hat himself."

Jackson's childhood was cut short by the War of Independence. At the age of 13 he joined the local militia and was captured by British troops. One day an officer ordered Jackson to clean the officer's boots. "Sir," the boy replied with stubborn pride, "I am a prisoner of war and demand to be treated as such." The outraged officer responded with a slash of his sword, gashing Jackson's head and cutting his hand to the bone. Jackson carried those scars, and a hatred of the British, to his grave.

Worse was yet to come. The British released Jackson just as a smallpox epidemic hit the Carolinas. The boy barely survived the disease. "When it left me I was a skeleton," he remembered, "not quite six feet tall and a little over six inches thick." His mother was not so lucky. "When tidings of her death reached me," Jackson recalled, "I at first could not believe it. When I finally realized the truth, I felt utterly alone."

History Bookshelf

Hirschfelder, Arlene B., and Beverly R. Singer, eds. *Rising Voices: Writings of Young Native Americans.* Scribner's, 1992. In this collection of poems and essays, young Native Americans share views on their families, culture, and history. It was a School Library Journal "Best Book of the Year" in 1992.

Also of interest:

Hoyt-Goldsmith, Diane. *Cherokee Summer.* Holiday House, 1993.

Klausner, Janet. *Sequoyah's Gift.* Harper-Collins, 1993.

Sandak, Cass R. *The Jacksons.* Crestwood House, 1992.

After joining the militia at the age of 13 during the War of Independence, Jackson was captured by the British. When he refused to polish a British officer's boots, the officer slashed him with a sword.

Backcountry Lawyer

With peace came fresh opportunities for young Americans with ambition. Jackson decided to become a lawyer, even though he had few qualifications. He disliked reading and had never mastered spelling. His speech and writing often showed poor grammar, though he could at times be persuasive.

At the age of 20, Jackson moved to Salisbury, North Carolina, to work in a law office. He soon made a reputation as "the most roaring, rollicking, game-cocking, horse-racing, card-playing, mischievous fellow" to hit that town. The wonder is that he learned any law at all.

A year later, Jackson crossed the Appalachians to practice law in Nashville, Tennessee. In 1788, Nashville was just a tiny cluster of rough log cabins and tents overlooking the Cumberland River. Still, there was plenty of business for a backcountry lawyer. Jackson built a thriving practice, earning enough money to buy land and slaves and to set himself up as a planter.

"Old Hickory"

Jackson wore a number of hats before he became President. He served as a United States senator and as a judge on the Tennessee Supreme Court. It was as a military hero, though, that he won the hearts of Americans everywhere. He led a crushing defeat of the Creek Indians in Alabama. He followed that triumph with his surprising victory over the British in the Battle of New Orleans during the War of 1812. Then he drove the Spanish from Florida.

By 1820 Jackson was the most famous man in the United States and the nation's first real hero since George Washington. He seemed so tough—like hickorywood—that his soldiers called him "Old Hickory." It was the perfect nickname.

Hands-On → HISTORY

Activity

Imagine yourself as one of Jackson's supporters in his campaign to become a United States senator. Opponents are saying that Jackson is not worthy to be a senator because he is not well educated. Write an editorial arguing that his background and personal characteristics qualify him to serve his nation in the Senate.

Discussion

Thinking Historically

1. How would you describe Jackson's childhood? (It was difficult, marred by poverty, war, the death of his parents, and a near-fatal bout with smallpox.)

2. Compare Jackson's preparation for a law career with that of a lawyer today. (Unlike in Jackson's time, today one must complete college and law school and pass a bar exam to practice law.)

3. "Old Hickory" was one nickname for Jackson. What would be another appropriate nickname? (Nicknames, such as "Fiery Eyes" or "Fighting Andy," might reflect fierce temper, rowdiness, or courage.)

See the Chapter In-Depth Activity, Battle with the Bank. **Take-Home Planner 5**, p. 4.

Teaching the Hands-On

- - - - - - → HISTORY

As a prewriting activity, have students work in pairs to list Jackson's relevant experiences and characteristics, identifying why each is important. For example, they might list "stood up to British officer as a boy," noting that it shows willingness to fight for beliefs.

For a journal writing activity on Andrew Jackson, see student page 371.

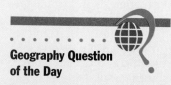
1. The New Spirit of Democracy

Reading Guide

New Terms caucus, suffrage, mudslinging

Section Focus How Andrew Jackson became President

1. How did the Democratic Party get its start?
2. Why did many Americans cheer the election of 1828 as a victory for democracy?

George Washington, a war hero, had made an outstanding President. Andrew Jackson's friends thought he would do equally well, and they encouraged him to run.

In many ways, though, Jackson did not fit the mold. All of the previous Presidents had been polished, well-educated men who had been born into wealthy families. Although Jackson was now a successful plantation owner, he was a rough-cut, self-made man from the ranks of the "common people"—small farmers and tradespeople.

The Election of 1824

The election of 1824 marked a turning point in American politics. Traditionally, a political party chose a single candidate at a **caucus,** a private meeting of party leaders. As the election approached, a caucus nominated William Crawford of Georgia to be the Republican candidate. However, sectionalism was now dividing the party. Other Republican candidates from other sections of the country challenged Crawford.

One leading rival was John Quincy Adams, who had strong support from the manufacturing and shipping interests of the Northeast. Jackson of Tennessee and Henry Clay of Kentucky were the two other main candidates. Both looked to western farmers for support. Crawford, meanwhile, appealed to the plantation owners of the South.

When the election was over, no one was a clear winner. Jackson had more popular and electoral votes, but he did not have a majority in the Electoral College. In such situations, the House of Representatives must choose from among the three leading candidates. Clay had come in fourth, so he was out of the running. He urged his backers in the House to support Adams. As a result, Adams became President.

As President, Adams named Clay to be his Secretary of State. The arrangement made sense because Clay and Adams both supported the American System and a strong national government. Jackson's followers, though, accused Adams and Clay of making "a corrupt bargain." They promised to get revenge in the next election.

The Adams Presidency

In fact, Adams was an honest, patriotic leader. He had a grand vision for the nation. The national government would support economic growth by building roads and canals while also promoting "the elegant arts, the advancement of literature, and the progress of the sciences."

The President's hope for a stronger, more active national government, however, was out of step with the growing sectionalism of the times. Southerners feared that his proposals would have a high price tag, to be paid

Influenced in part by the American and French Revolutions, Simón Bolívar became known as *El Libertador*—the Liberator—after leading an army of volunteers to free Venezuela from Spanish rule in 1813. The struggle for independence in the region had many setbacks, as King Ferdinand of Spain sent troops to punish revolutionaries. Bolívar persevered and emerged as president of Gran Colombia (Venezuela, Colombia, and Ecuador). Bolívar hoped for a union of all of the Spanish-speaking nations of South America, but his plan was never realized. The Panama Congress was a failure, and conflicts within Gran Colombia and between Bolívar and leaders of the other South American nations escalated. In 1828, the former hero was forced from power. He died two years later of tuberculosis.

John Quincy Adams, a man of patriotism and firm principles, believed in a strong national government.

by higher tariffs. They also suspected that a stronger government might try to do away with slavery.

Meanwhile, Adams offended westerners by supporting the Bank of the United States. Many westerners had lost farms and homes to the Bank during the Panic of 1819 (see page 332).

The President's policy of trying to protect Indian lands was unpopular with both southerners and westerners. When he wanted to send troops to protect the lands of the Creek Indians in Georgia, for instance, Congress refused to support him. It was clear that he would face an uphill campaign for re-election in 1828.

A New Democratic Party

Right after Jackson lost in 1824, his supporters began looking ahead to the election of 1828. Their campaign was masterminded by Martin Van Buren, a stout, red-haired Senator from New York who was nicknamed the "Red Fox" and the "Little Magician."

Van Buren was well aware that there would be thousands of new voters casting ballots in 1828, and most would be common people. In the West, the newly admitted states had granted **suffrage**—the right to vote—to most white men over the age of 21, even if they did not own property. Pressured by reformers in eastern cities, most other states followed the West's lead.

Many decades would pass before women, Indians, and most African Americans were granted the right to vote. Still, democracy was on the march.

The method of electing the President had become more democratic, too. By 1828, presidential electors in all but two states were chosen directly by the voters rather than by the state legislatures.

Van Buren saw that the time was ripe for a new party. He and other Jackson backers adopted the name Democratic Party and called themselves Jacksonian Democrats. Their candidate, they claimed, would speak for "the people"—average Americans, rather than the wealthy and privileged.

World Link

The Panama Congress John Quincy Adams had a vision of a United States powerful enough to stand up to the nations of Europe. Simón Bolívar—"the Liberator" of South America—had a similar goal for Latin America.

As a first step toward a stronger Latin America, Bolívar called for a congress of Latin American nations to take place in Panama City in 1826. Against his wishes, the United States was also invited. Adams, however, feared being drawn into an agreement to protect Latin America. He need not have worried, for only four nations sent delegates. The congress did set the stage, though, for later cooperation among Latin American nations to achieve common goals.

 **Connections to Civics**

By the presidential election of 1840, voter participation reached a high of 80 percent, and remained over 70 percent until 1900. Participation in this century has been low, however, with turnout rarely exceeding 60 percent for presidential elections. Local elections yield even lower turnouts.

Most democracies in the world have a far higher turnout, with many European nations boasting participation of over 80 percent in national elections. While many factors influence participation, some blame our system of requiring individuals to register prior to the election, a practice initiated around 1900 to ensure that people only vote once. In most other democracies, the government registers voters automatically.

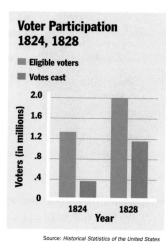

Voter Participation 1824, 1828

Source: Historical Statistics of the United States

Artist George Caleb Bingham often painted scenes that expressed the spirit of expanding democracy. In *Stump Speaking*, a candidate addresses a crowd of voters in the countryside. Behind him sits a rival taking notes.

Meanwhile, Adams and his followers had chosen a new name for their party. They now called themselves National Republicans to reflect their belief in a strong national government.

The Election of 1828

As the election of 1828 approached, Democrats and National Republicans both hoped for support from every section of the country. Therefore, they avoided taking stands on sectional issues like slavery. They focused instead on the personal backgrounds of Adams and Jackson.

Republicans sneered that Jackson was crude and uneducated. Jackson himself admitted he was a poor speller, joking that he could not respect someone who spelled a word only one way. Republicans also tried to label him as a gambler and a brawler. They even called him a murderer because he had fought a number of duels.

Democrats portrayed Adams as out of touch with the common people. Adams himself admitted, "I am a man of reserved, cold, and forbidding manners." Even an admirer of Adams said that he was "hard as a piece of granite and cold as a lump of ice."

The election marked the beginning of modern politics with all its hoopla. Democrats organized huge parades, rallies, and barbecues, where neighbors gathered to cheer for "Old Hickory." Afterward supporters went home waving hickory sticks and chanting campaign slogans like, "Adams can write, but Jackson can fight."

With both sides avoiding the issues, the contest was marked by **mudslinging**—wild charges and lies about the candidates. Democrats falsely charged Adams with using taxpayers' money to buy gambling tables for the White House. Republicans unfairly accused Jackson of knowingly marrying his wife Rachel before the divorce from her first husband became final.

Learning Disabled Students

One way to help students with learning disabilities is through cooperative grouping. Cooperative groups provide an opportunity for students to hear several explanations of a concept from peers in a setting that may be less embarrassing than in a class discussion. In addition to educational benefits, placing students in mixed-ability groups has been shown to foster greater acceptance of academic and physical differences.

When using cooperative grouping, judge groups both on their collective product and the performance of each individual. This will encourage active participation of all members.

When the mudslinging was over, Jackson had won a solid victory: 647,000 votes for him and 508,000 for Adams. The electoral vote was 178 to 83. Jackson and his vice-presidential running mate, John C. Calhoun of South Carolina, carried all sections of the country except New England.

The election of 1828 has often been viewed as a western and southern victory because much of Jackson's support came from those sections of the country. "Old Hickory" could not have won, though, without the votes of many eastern factory workers and other daily wage earners.

With the increase in the number of eligible voters, more than twice as many ballots were cast in 1828 as in 1824. Ordinary people across the country had voted, and Jackson was their choice. More than anything, it was a victory for control of government by the common people—an idea that became known as Jacksonian Democracy.

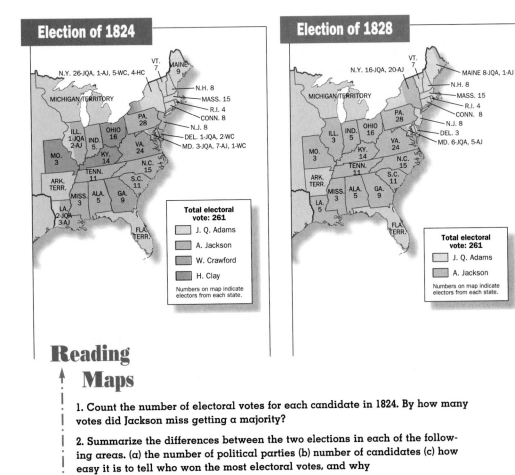

Reading Maps

1. Count the number of electoral votes for each candidate in 1824. By how many votes did Jackson miss getting a majority?

2. Summarize the differences between the two elections in each of the following areas. (a) the number of political parties (b) number of candidates (c) how easy it is to tell who won the most electoral votes, and why

See **American Readings,** p. 49, for an account of Jackson's inaugural celebration.

History Footnote

Soon after his inauguration, Jackson ordered massive improvements to the White House, grown threadbare during the frugal John Quincy Adams presidency. He ordered chandeliers, rich new carpeting, upholstery, drapes, and sterling silver, crystal, and china, totaling over $50,000 during his two terms.

One newspaper reporter defended such spending by arguing that Jackson was showing that he wanted the company of the common people by creating a comfortable place for them to visit. This, the reporter wrote, was in contrast to Adams, whose guests were forced to stand in a mansion full of "cobwebs, a few old chairs, lumbering benches and broken glass." Jackson's critics saw his spending in a different light. For them, it was another example of the arrogant "King Andrew."

Hands-On
- - - - - - → *HISTORY*

Planning an inauguration The celebration that followed Andrew Jackson's inauguration was anything but well planned. It did send a message to the nation, though. By making "common people" guests at the White House, Jackson was signaling that he would use his power to open up opportunities for average Americans.

A crowd at the White House after Jackson's inauguration

Activity

Since Jackson's time, inaugural celebrations have been carefully planned to reflect the President's beliefs and goals for the nation. Imagine that you have been elected President and are planning your celebration.

❶ State your two or three main goals for the nation.

❷ For each goal, make a list of events—such as parades, parties, and concerts. Explain how each one represents your goal.

❸ Make a schedule, with times and places.

Jackson's Inauguration

On Inauguration Day, thousands filled the streets of Washington to welcome their hero. Senator Daniel Webster commented:

❝I never saw such a crowd here before. People have come five hundred miles to see General Jackson, and they really seem to think that the country has been rescued from some dreadful danger.❞

Jackson gave a dignified inaugural address. What followed has become an Inauguration Day legend. Jackson was "nearly pressed to death" by admirers crowding into the White House to wish him well. He had to sneak out a back door and hide in a nearby hotel.

Meanwhile, the rowdy guests smashed crystal and china and ruined rugs with their muddy boots. Only after waiters moved the food and drink outside did people leave— some by climbing out the windows.

One witness described the scene as "the reign of King Mob." Socialite Margaret Bayard Smith wrote:

❝Ladies fainted, men were seen with bloody noses, and such a scene of confusion took place as is impossible to describe. . . . But it was the People's day, and the People's President, and the People would rule.❞

1. Section Review

1. Define **caucus, suffrage,** and **mudslinging.**
2. Who organized the Democratic Party and why?
3. What was Jacksonian Democracy?
4. Critical Thinking What dangers do you think wealthy Americans saw in the idea of "letting the people rule"?

✳ Geography Footnote
In 1800, the ratio of rural to urban dwellers
was 15 to 1; by 1850, it was 5 to 1. Between
1820 and 1850, the number of cities with a
population of over 8,000 quadrupled. In that
same period, the largest eastern cities experienced a boom in population, in spite of massive westward movement. Boston increased
from 42,000 to 137,000; New York grew from
123,000 to 515,000.

Geography Lab

From Forest to Farm

Once, much of eastern North
America was densely forested. Because
early settlers found no European-style
farms and towns, they thought of the land
as empty. They plunged into the forest, axes
in hand, to create farms. Historian David
Lowenthal describes the settlers' attitude toward
land: "Empty, it must be filled; unfinished, it
must be completed; wild, it must be tamed."

These pictures, made around 1850, show
changes in a farm in western New York over
a period of years.

A

B

C

Link to History

1. According to Lowenthal,
what did settlers hope to do?

2. Describe the changes in this
New York farm the way the
family who owned the farm
might have described them.

3. What might someone who
had been a trapper in the
northeastern woodlands since
about 1800 have said about the
changes, and why?

4. Imagine that you are looking
at a picture showing this same
New York area today. List
three changes you would
probably find between picture
C and that area today.

5. **Hands-On Geography**
People often disagree about
how to use land. Write two
different captions for this set
of scenes as if the captions
were written by different
people with opposing views
on clearing land.

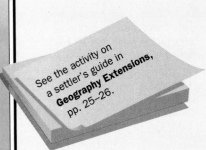

See the activity on
a settler's guide in
Geography Extensions,
pp. 25–26.

Warm-Up Activity

Dealing with Dissent

To lead up to the topic of nullification, have students imagine that the school has instituted a new dress code and some students refuse to comply. Have them write a letter recommending what the administration should do in response. Conclude by discussing and comparing possible responses and their effects.

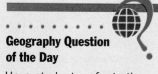

Geography Question of the Day

Have students refer to the land use map on page R9. Ask them to compare two regions and identify how geographical differences might affect each region's priorities. For example, they may note that the Midwest (largely cropland) may emphasize policies that benefit farmers, whereas the urban Northeast may focus on improving conditions in cities.

Section Objectives

★ Explain why the nullification issue arose again.
★ Identify the steps Jackson took to pre-serve the Union.

Teaching Resources

Take-Home Planner 5, pp. 2–9
Chapter Resources Binder
  Study Guide, p. 98
  Reinforcement, pp. 101–102
  Skills Development
  Geography Extensions
  American Readings
  Using Historical Documents
  Transparency Activities
  Chapter and Unit Tests

2. Jackson Takes Charge

Reading Guide

New Terms spoils system, secede, sovereignty

Section Focus Jackson's response to a threat to the Union

1. Why did the issue of nullification arise again?
2. What steps did Jackson take to preserve the Union?

Jackson handled the presidency as he handled everything else in life—he took firm control. Unlike earlier Presidents, he rarely met with his cabinet. He was more likely to seek advice from trusted friends, who were said to meet in the White House kitchen. The so-called "Kitchen Cabinet" actually had little influence. Final decisions were Jackson's alone.

As defender of the common people, Jackson set out to change the national government. It was too powerful, he said, and favored the rich. He vowed that he would reduce it "to that simple machine which the Constitution created."

The Spoils System

One practice Jackson considered unfair was giving government workers lifetime jobs. He said they should be forced to "go back to making a living as other people do." When a new President replaced workers with new appointees, he argued, it made democracy stronger by giving more people a chance to serve.

Critics replied that workers should be chosen for their ability rather than for their loyalty to the President's political party. They called the practice of rewarding political supporters with jobs the **spoils system.** The term came from the saying "to the victor belong the spoils [prizes]."

Jackson's enemies exaggerated the number of Republicans he replaced. Of 10,000 workers, only about 900 lost their jobs. Jackson did replace more workers than any previous President, however, starting a trend that later Presidents were glad to follow.

Still, Jackson put patriotism above party loyalty. One worker who had been replaced confronted him and said:

❝Sir, I have been removed as postmaster from Albany but there is something I wish to show you. I want you to see my wounds, sir, received while defending my country from the British . . . and my thanks is removal from my office, the only position I have to sustain me in my old age.❞

"Button your jacket," Jackson replied. "You are still postmaster."

A "Tariff of Abominations"

Jackson's patriotism and leadership were soon challenged by an issue that threatened to break up the Union. The crisis had begun when Congress passed the Tariff of 1828.

New England manufacturers welcomed the tariff. Now they could raise prices and still outsell imported products. However, southern planters resented having to pay more for manufactured goods.

Connections to Civics

The spoils system remained in place until corruption and an increasing need for skilled civil servants led to reform. In 1871 President Grant appointed the first U.S. Civil Service Commission, and in 1883 the Pendleton Act created the civil service system. Most federal and many state or local employees are now hired on the basis of competitive examinations. The civil service has expanded steadily since Jackson's time. Currently, there are about three million civilian federal employees.

See the Study Guide activity in **Chapter Resources Binder**, p. 98, and the Reinforcement activity, pp. 101–102.

In South Carolina, state leaders demanded that the government reduce the Tariff of 1828, which they called the "Tariff of Abominations." If not, they threatened that their state would **secede**—break away from the United States.

Into the conflict stepped Vice-President John C. Calhoun. He realized that his chance to be President would be destroyed if his home state seceded. Looking for a solution, he argued that a state could nullify, or reject, a federal law it considered unconstitutional. Nullification had been proposed before (see page 282). This time, however, the idea seemed to strike at the heart of the union.

Point of View

Can a state disobey the federal government?

In 1830 two of the most gifted speakers in the Senate—Robert Hayne of South Carolina and Daniel Webster of Massachusetts—debated this question.

Hayne argued that the states had created the Constitution and therefore still had **sovereignty**—the power to control their affairs. Any state legislature, he said, could nullify a federal law to protect its citizens' liberties. Hayne declared:

"The very life of our system is the independence of the states. I am opposed, therefore, in any shape, to all unnecessary extension of the power or the influence . . . of the Union over the states.**"**

Webster responded that the national government gets its authority directly from the people, not the state legislatures:

"It is the people's Constitution, the people's government, made for the people, made by the people, and answerable to the people.**"**

This cartoon protests that the Tariff of 1828 placed a burden on southern planters in order to help northern manufacturers get rich.

Webster argued that the Constitution allows only the Supreme Court to declare a law unconstitutional. He warned that if each state could reject federal laws, the nation would be torn apart. He closed with a ringing appeal for "Liberty and Union, now and forever, one and inseparable."

The Nullification Crisis

Everyone was anxious to know whether Jackson would agree that a state could refuse to obey a federal law. The answer came at a dinner on April 13, 1830, honoring Thomas Jefferson's birthday. All the leading Democrats were there.

At the dinner, southerners made a series of toasts to states' rights. Jackson rose, looked directly at Calhoun, and proposed his own toast: "Our Union—it must be preserved." Calhoun skillfully countered with: "The Union, next to our liberty, most dear."

Jackson's toast revealed he was not as strong a supporter of states' rights as southerners had hoped. As a southern planter, though, he understood objections to the tariff. In 1832 he got Congress to lower it.

Teaching the
Point of View

Work with students to make a chart on the board listing arguments for and against nullification. As they identify arguments for each side, ask them to consider what each side feared.

Section Activity

Identifying Government Roles

To help students distinguish federal, state, and local roles, have them clip articles or take notes on television broadcasts describing actions taken by each level of government. Have small groups share their findings and discuss what they think Hayne and Webster would think about the roles each level is currently playing.

Bonus Activity

A Dialogue on Spoils

To help students analyze differing points of view on the spoils system, have them write a dialogue between the former postmaster quoted on page 356 and the person hired to replace him. Ask them to consider what each would say about Jackson's policy on hiring.

Closing the Section

Section Review
Answers

1. Definitions: *spoils system* (356), *secede* (357), *sovereignty* (357)

2. For: states created Constitution and retained sovereignty; states have right to protect citizens' liberties. Against: only Supreme Court can declare a law unconstitutional; nullification would tear nation apart.

3. He got Congress to pass Force Bill, giving power to use armed forces to collect tariff. He urged a compromise tariff.

4. Yes: issue so clearly divided the North and South, and southerners saw livelihood threatened. No: civil war unlikely since no other states threatened secession.

Though the debate over slavery was still largely absent from the political arena, by the 1830s antislavery organizations in the North had grown rapidly. In 1835 the American Anti-Slavery Society (AAS) embarked on a postal campaign, flooding the South with abolitionist literature and causing an angry response among slaveholders. As a result, a law excluding mailing of antislavery literature was supported by Jackson and nearly passed in Congress. Though the bill failed, local postmasters succeeded in practically eliminating further antislavery mailing campaigns. (Students will read about the movements to end slavery in Chapter 16, pages 440–445.)

In a dramatic Senate debate, Daniel Webster attacked the view that a state could nullify, or reject, a federal law. At the far left sits John C. Calhoun, who had proposed the idea of nullification.

South Carolina leaders refused to accept the new, lower tariff. They spoke of preparing for war if the national government tried to collect the tariff by force. Jackson reacted swiftly to their threat, warning that "disunion by armed force is treason." He told one South Carolina congressman:

> They can talk and write resolutions and print threats to their hearts' content. But if one drop of blood be shed there in defiance of the laws of the United States, I will hang the first man of them I can get my hands on to the first tree I can find.

In 1833 Jackson got Congress to pass the "Force Bill," which gave him power to use the army and navy, if needed, to collect the tariff. In public, though, he controlled his temper to avoid adding fuel to the fire.

A combination of events finally ended the nullification crisis. First, no other state threatened to secede. Meanwhile, Jackson urged Congress to pass a compromise tariff. He signed the Force Bill and the tariff on the same day. South Carolina accepted the tariff. Jackson had played a major role in holding the Union together.

★ 2. Section Review

1. Define **spoils system, secede,** and **sovereignty.**
2. What were some arguments for and against nullification?
3. How did Jackson respond to South Carolina's threat to secede?
4. **Critical Thinking** Could a civil war have broken out over the tariff? Explain.

Section Objectives

★ Explain why Jackson supported the removal of Indians from their lands.

★ Describe how the eastern Indian tribes reacted to the forced removal.

Teaching Resources

Take-Home Planner 5, pp. 2–9

Chapter Resources Binder

  Study Guide, p. 99

  Reinforcement

  Skills Development

  Geography Extensions

American Readings, pp. 50–52

Using Historical Documents, pp. 70–75

Transparency Activities

Chapter and Unit Tests

Introducing the Section

Warm-Up Activity

Points of View

To help students compare differing viewpoints, have them look at the painting on pages 344–345 from both the Indian and settler perspectives. For each perspective, have them write a title for the painting and an explanation for that title.

3. Jackson's Indian Policy

Reading Guide

Section Focus The Indian Removal Act and its effects

1. Why did Jackson support forcing Indians to move off their lands?
2. How did the eastern Indian tribes react to forced removal?

When Andrew Jackson became President, very few Indians—only about 125,000—still lived east of the Mississippi River. Disease, war, and enslavement had greatly reduced their numbers. Meanwhile, the nation's population had grown to nearly 13 million. Indian lands east of the Mississippi were more and more in demand.

Ever since the Louisiana Purchase in 1803, the federal government had been encouraging Indians to sell their lands and move west of the Mississippi. As President, one of Jackson's major goals was to speed up this removal of the Indians.

The Roots of Jackson's Policy

Jackson's goal was shaped by his earlier experiences fighting against the Creeks and Seminoles. He respected his opponents, who called him "Big Knife." When he became President, however, the wars over Indian lands east of the Mississippi had mostly ended. Jackson believed that the settlers now had a right to those lands.

As a politician, Jackson saw that removing Indians from their homelands would open up opportunities for many southern and western farmers and small businessmen—the people who had voted for him. He would make sure that nothing stood in their way—neither the Indians nor the federal government.

At the same time, though, Jackson argued that removing the Indians was the best way to protect them. In letters to the tribes, he warned that if they stayed in their homelands they would be destroyed by settlers:

❝Where you now are, you and my white children are too near to each other to live in harmony and peace. Your game is gone, and many of your people will not work and till the earth. . . . The land beyond the Mississippi belongs to the President and no one else, and he will give it to you forever.❞

This offer, however, did not appeal to most of the eastern Indians. They wanted to remain in their homelands.

Indians in the Southeast

The majority of eastern Indians were members of five southeastern tribes—the Cherokees, Creeks, Chickasaws, Choctaws, and Seminoles. Hoping to be allowed to keep their lands, many had taken up farming and adapted to white culture. Some even had large plantations and owned slaves.

Many learned to read and write English. A Cherokee named Sequoyah [sih-KWOY-uh] also invented a system for writing the Cherokee language. The Cherokees had their own newspaper and a constitution modeled after the United States Constitution.

Geography Question of the Day

Have students use the map on page 362 to list at least ten eastern tribes that were forced to move west. Next to each tribe's name, they should identify in what present-day state its original homeland was located.

Vital Links

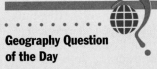

Voice of Corn Tassel (First Person Account) Unit 2, Side 1, Search 50723, Play to 51564

See also Unit 2 Explore CD-ROM location 290.

Developing the Section

Teaching the

⚭ Link to Art

Tell students that the ceremony, according to Catlin's records, had three purposes: to celebrate the end of an ancient flood, to make the buffalo herds fertile, and to provide a chance for young men to show off their endurance. Also explain that the head-dresses and other costumes were worn as a part of the ceremony and did not rep-resent everyday dress of the Mandans. **Discussion Answers:** Some possible observations are that buf-falo played a key role in their lives; they lived near one another in relatively large communities; danc-ing and music were a part of their celebrations; and they built large, round shelters.

See the Study Guide activity in **Chapter Resources Binder**, p. 99.

In **Using Historical Documents**, pp. 70–75, students analyze a letter from Jackson regarding Indian policy.

✠ **Connections to Art**

Though George Catlin failed to achieve his goal of building his own museum, 450 of his original paintings finally found a home in the Smithsonian Institution in 1879. Catlin's paintings and writings were a contribution to subsequent artists and historians, a dedi-cated attempt to represent Indians accurately and sensitively. He wrote: "I love [this] peo-ple who always made me welcome to the best they had . . . who are honest without laws, who have no jails or no poorhouse . . . a people who have never raised a hand against me, or stole my property . . . who have never fought a battle with white men except on their own ground . . . a people who live and keep what is their own without lock and key . . . and oh! how I love a people who don't live for the love of money."

⚭ **Link to Art**

Bull Dance, Mandan O-Kee-Pa Ceremony (1832) This painting by George Catlin shows a ceremony of the Mandan tribe of the northern Plains. Between 1830 and 1836 Catlin created a series of paintings to arouse public sympathy for Indians and preserve a visual record of their fast-vanishing ways of life. In 1837 a smallpox epidemic killed almost all of the Mandan tribe. **Discuss** What does the painting reveal about the Mandan way of life?

The people whom white settlers called "the Five Civilized Tribes" would have been content to live peacefully with their neigh-bors, but that was not to be. Planters wanted the tribes' rich lands because cotton farming had exhausted the soil on their own plan-tations. They demanded that the federal government remove the Indians.

Planters in Georgia, which was home to the Cherokees and the Creeks, pointed to an

Settlers' hunger for more farmland was prompted in part by technological advances that made it possible for farmers to handle larger amounts of land. Eli Whitney's cotton gin had been improved and made widely available since its 1792 invention. Other inventions contributed to westward expansion. In 1838, John Deere perfected his design for a steel plow capable of turning the hard prairie soil. In that same period, Cyrus McCormick patented his extremely successful mechanical reaper, greatly reducing the amount of labor needed to cut wheat from the fields.

agreement made with the federal government back in 1802. Georgia had given up its claim to a large area of western land. In return, the federal government had agreed to remove the Indians as soon as treaties could be negotiated.

By 1828, the federal government still had not acted, so Georgia declared that Cherokee lands belonged to the state. The Cherokees, faced with losing their lands, appealed to the federal government for protection.

Jackson Versus the Court

In his annual message before the Congress in December 1829, Jackson declared his support for Georgia. He said that a state had a right to control lands within its borders, and that Indians living there must obey the state's laws. His view was shared by most members of Congress.

Reformers in New England, church groups, and especially missionaries who lived with the Cherokees all protested that the Cherokees had a right to keep their land. When Congress and the President ignored their protests, the Cherokees and their allies appealed to the Supreme Court.

The Court, under Chief Justice John Marshall, ruled that the Cherokees should be able to keep their lands because of an early treaty with the federal government. Such a treaty with an Indian tribe, the Court declared, was an agreement between two nations and therefore could not be overruled by a state.

The Court's decision proved to be a hollow victory. Georgia officials ignored it, and Jackson refused to enforce it. He thought that treating Indian tribes as nations was senseless. Also, he believed that his oath as President bound him to obey the Constitution as *he*, not the Court, interpreted it. He is reported to have said, "Well, John Marshall has made his decision, now let him enforce it."

The Indian Removal Act

In May 1830, at Jackson's urging, Congress passed the Indian Removal Act. The act allowed the President to make treaties with eastern tribes to exchange their lands for land west of the Mississippi.

The removal treaties were supposed to be voluntary. In fact, though, federal agents got tribal leaders to sign the treaties by misleading them. Indians were also threatened by armed settlers who had already begun to occupy their lands.

The government agreed to pay the Indians for any property they left behind. It promised to protect them in their new lands and give them food and clothing for one year. Despite these promises, the removals rarely went smoothly. They turned out to be poorly planned and caused much suffering.

Indian Resistance

Indian removal is a tragic chapter in American history. Most of the tribes accepted their fate with little or no resistance. They signed the treaties, packed belongings, and moved to the barren lands set aside across the Mississippi. A few tribes, though, strongly resisted removal.

The Black Hawk War Black Hawk, a leader of the Sauk and Fox Indians of the Wisconsin Territory, challenged a removal treaty. When the government forced most of the Sauk and Fox across the Mississippi to Iowa Territory in 1831, Black Hawk refused to stay in Iowa. Instead, he returned the next year to tribal lands in Illinois, even though settlers now lived there.

Tempers flared and shots were fired. The result is known as the Black Hawk War, although it was more like a massacre. Most of Black Hawk's followers were killed as they tried to escape by crossing the Mississippi. He was captured and sent to prison.

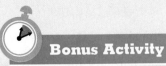

See *American Readings*, p. 50, for Indian protests against removal.

The *Cherokee Phoenix,* the first Indian newspaper published in the United States, made its debut in 1828, published in both the Cherokee and English languages. Its first editorial outlined its goals, "hoping for that happy period when all the Indian tribes of America shall rise, Phoenix-like, from the ashes." *Phoenix* editorials critical of Jackson's policies were reprinted in newspapers nationwide and in Europe. In 1834 the Georgia militia stormed the *Phoenix* office and confiscated the press.

For an account of the Trail of Tears, see **American Readings,** pp. 51–52.

For an account of the Trail of Tears, see **American Readings,** pp. 51–52.

Section Activity

A "Cherokee" Newspaper

Have small groups imagine being Cherokee journalists. Groups should identify the year in which they are writing (1830 to 1838) and use the information in this section to develop articles, editorials, drawings or cartoons, and any other features. For example, an 1830 newspaper might include a story describing the Indian Removal Act, an editorial urging resistance, and a cartoon depicting Jackson unfavorably.

Teaching the Reading Maps

Students might use a string to trace the path and measure it against the scale.

Answer to Reading Maps: Seminoles: 900 miles (1,440 km); Cherokees, Ottowas: 800 miles (1,280 km); Miamis, Shawnees: 700 miles (1,120 km); Creeks, Potawatomis, Iowas, Sauks, Foxes: 600 miles (960 km); Kickapoos, Choctaws: 300 miles (480 km).

Vital Links

Seminoles in canoes (Picture) Unit 2, Side 1, Search 51616

See also Unit 2 Explore CD-ROM location 299.

The Trail of Tears Most Cherokees refused to leave their homes. In 1838, two years after Jackson left the presidency, the Georgia militia was ordered to force them out. Soldiers brutally rounded up 17,000 Cherokees and marched them to Indian Territory, which is today Oklahoma.

As many as 4,000 Cherokees died along the way. The tribe remembers this terrible journey as "The Trail Where They Cried." History books call it "The Trail of Tears." Many years later, a Georgia soldier who participated in the dreadful removal of the Cherokees said:

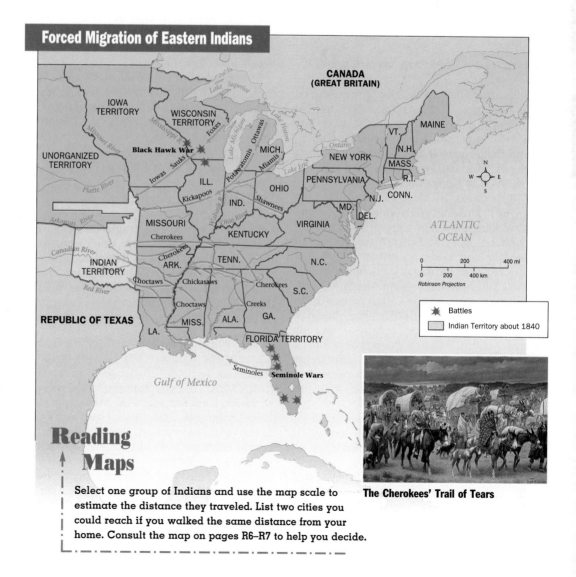

Forced Migration of Eastern Indians

The Cherokees' Trail of Tears

Reading Maps

Select one group of Indians and use the map scale to estimate the distance they traveled. List two cities you could reach if you walked the same distance from your home. Consult the map on pages R6–R7 to help you decide.

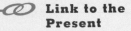

✳ **History Footnote**

From 1985 to 1994, Wilma Mankiller was principal chief of the Cherokee Nation and the first woman to lead a major Native American tribe. The Cherokee Nation is the second largest in the U.S. (after the Navajos), with a worldwide membership of over 140,000.

Mankiller has dedicated herself to improving life for the Cherokees while preserving cultural values and traditions. In her autobiography she writes: "If I am to be remembered, I want it to be because I am fortunate enough to have become my tribe's first female chief. But I also want to be remembered for emphasizing the fact that we have indigenous solutions to our problems. Cherokee values, especially those of helping one another and of our interconnections with the land, can be used to address contemporary issues."

Teaching the

⌒⌒ **Link to the Present**

Ask students to consider why the Cherokees and other Indian nations sought to govern themselves (tribal pride; best knowledge of own needs and problems; ancestors did not agree to become part of United States).

"I fought through the Civil War and have seen men shot to pieces and slaughtered by the thousands, but the Cherokee removal was the cruelest work I ever knew."

The Seminole War The Indians who fought most strongly against removal were the Seminoles of Florida. They were helped by former African American slaves who had escaped from plantations in Georgia and Alabama.

Beginning in 1835 the Seminoles and their allies waged fierce guerrilla campaigns against the United States Army. The Seminole chief, Osceola [os-ee-Ō-lah], was captured in 1837 while flying a flag of truce, but the Seminoles fought on. The long struggle that is known as the Seminole War did not end until 1842. It was the most costly Indian war that the United States ever fought.

A number of Seminoles eventually were sent to Indian Territory. However, many hid in the Florida swamps and never surrendered. Their descendants remain in Florida to this day.

Seminole chief Osceola died in prison only a few days after George Catlin finished painting this portrait in 1837.

⌒⌒ **Link to the Present**

The Cherokee Nation Exhausted, sick, and starving, the last Cherokees staggered into Indian Territory in early 1839. In their suffering and sorrow, it would have been easy to give up. Instead, they rebuilt their lives by starting schools, farms, ranches, and mines.

Events that led to Oklahoma statehood in 1907, however, almost destroyed the Cherokees. The federal government took away much of their land and officially dissolved their nation. Forced to depend on the federal government for financial support, many Cherokees lived in poverty and despair.

The 1970s brought renewed hope, as Congress gave Indian nations the authority to govern themselves. Under the leadership of strong chiefs like Wilma Mankiller, the Cherokees built roads and water systems, set up health-care clinics, and organized job-training programs. As they did after the Trail of Tears, the Cherokees have rebuilt their nation as well as their faith in themselves.

⭐ **3. Section Review**

1. Why did Jackson support efforts to remove the eastern Indian tribes from their homelands?
2. What were different ways in which eastern tribes responded to the government's policy of removal?
3. Critical Thinking How do you think Jackson should be judged for his Indian policy? Explain.

Closing the Section

Wrap-Up Activity

An Indian Removal Cause-Effect Chain

Have students work in pairs to make a cause-effect chain, beginning with the Indian Removal Act. Effects might include the Black Hawk War, the Trail of Tears, and the Seminole War. Below each item on the chain, students should briefly describe its importance.

Section Review Answers

1. To open up opportunities for settlers who had voted for him. He claimed removal was best way to protect Indians.

2. Cherokees appealed to the Court, and many refused to leave; Seminoles, Sauks and Foxes fought wars.

3. Some may see policy as unjust and inconsistent with his support of "common people." Others may say removal was necessary to protect Indians in face of westward expansion.

Settlers Needing Loans

To emphasize the importance of loans to settlers, have students do a role-play. Appoint one pair as bankers, giving them five certificates, each worth $300. Divide the rest of the class into six or more families of settlers. Have each meet with the bankers to request a $300 loan for land purchase. The bankers decide how the money is distributed. Discuss how the bankers decided who should get the money and what might be the effects of not getting a loan.

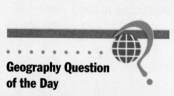

Geography Question of the Day

Have students write a paragraph describing the area in which they live as they imagine it looked before people settled there.

Section Objectives

★ Identify reasons for Jackson's opposition to the Bank of the United States.
★ Describe the formation of the Whig Party.
★ Explain why the Democrats lost the election of 1840.

Teaching Resources

Take-Home Planner 5, pp. 2–9
Chapter Resources Binder
  Study Guide, p. 100
  Reinforcement
  Skills Development, pp. 103–104
  Geography Extensions
  American Readings
  Using Historical Documents
  Transparency Activities
Chapter and Unit Tests, pp. 87–90

4. "The Bank War" and Its Effects

Reading Guide

Section Focus **The causes and effects of Jackson's "war" with the Bank of the United States**

1. Why was Jackson an enemy of the Bank of the United States?
2. What led to the forming of the Whig Party?
3. Why did the Democrats lose the election of 1840?

Jackson took his strongest stand as defender of the common people in fighting a "war" with the Bank of the United States. The Bank was a private corporation chartered by Congress in 1816. The national government owned one-fifth of the stock and kept all of its deposits there.

In Jackson's eyes, the Bank was a "monster"—a monopoly created to make "rich men . . . richer by act of Congress." To him, the main villain was the Bank's wealthy president, Nicholas Biddle.

The Power of the Bank

Biddle was one of the most powerful men in the country. He owned much of the Bank's stock, appointed its officials, set interest rates, and decided who got loans. He saw it as his duty to make sure the Bank's currency was "good as gold." Therefore, he insisted on keeping a reserve of 50 percent—50¢ worth of gold and silver coins for every paper dollar the bank loaned out.

State banks loaned money more freely, usually keeping only a 25 percent reserve. In western territories, most independent "wildcat banks" kept no reserve. In short, paper money issued by the Bank of the United States was the most dependable. Sometimes Biddle tried to force small banks to be more cautious by refusing to accept their paper money at branches of the Bank.

Poor southerners and westerners who needed to borrow money to buy land hated Biddle's policy toward small banks. Jackson shared their bitterness. He believed the Bank was trying to keep wealth in the hands of a few and deny opportunity to the many. Jackson made no secret of the fact that when the Bank's charter came up for renewal in 1836, he would oppose it.

Clay Forces the Issue

Biddle was not worried—he had powerful friends. Among them was Henry Clay, who planned to run for President in 1832. Clay made the Bank a major issue in his campaign. He asked Biddle to apply for early renewal of the charter. Clay figured that if Jackson signed the bill, he would offend voters in the South and West. If he vetoed it, he would offend the Northeast.

The plan worked to a point. In the summer of 1832, Congress agreed to recharter the Bank. When the bill came to him, Jackson lay sick in bed in the White House. He told his close friend Martin Van Buren that the bill was a personal attack. "The Bank, Mr. Van Buren, is trying to kill me," he said, "but I will kill it."

True to his word, Jackson vetoed the Bank bill. He explained that the Bank gave unjust advantages to the wealthy at the expense of "humble members of society—the farmers,

Bank loans were critical to westward expansion at that time, making it possible for settlers to purchase public lands. After the Land Act of 1800, public lots were sold for $2 an acre. The economic crisis of 1819 prompted a lowering of the price to $1.25 an acre.

Throughout the 1800s there was a growing movement in support of giving land free to settlers in recognition of the value of their improvements to the territory. In 1832, Jackson stated that "the public lands should cease as soon as practicable to be a source of revenue." The homestead movement finally won its cause with the Homestead Act of 1862, a law that provided millions of acres of public land practically free of charge to settlers willing to live on and make improvements to the land.

mechanics, and laborers." His arguments were so effective that friends of the Bank in Congress were unable to override the veto.

Clay was wrong about the effect of the veto on the 1832 election. Voters cared less about the Bank than he and Biddle had thought. Jackson easily won re-election, crushing Clay by a margin of 219 to 49 electoral votes. Van Buren became the new Vice-President.

Jackson was not content simply to let the Bank die a natural death. Instead of waiting until the Bank's charter expired in 1836, he moved to destroy it immediately. "I have it chained," Jackson gloated. "Now the monster must perish."

He ordered the government to take all federal money out of the Bank and put it in state banks. His enemies called them his "pet banks," charging that the state banks selected for holding federal money were those run by loyal Democrats.

The Rise of the Whig Party

One result of the "bank war" was the rise of a new political party. The National Republicans, the party of John Quincy Adams and Henry Clay, joined forces with many states' rights supporters, bankers, and Democrats unhappy with Jackson. They formed the Whig Party.

This cartoon shows Andrew Jackson in the middle of a nightmare. He drags Henry Clay behind him as he attacks the "monster" Bank of the United States.

See the Study Guide activity in **Chapter Resources Binder,** p. 100.

Since Harrison, seven other Presidents have died in office: Zachary Taylor, Abraham Lincoln, James Garfield, William McKinley, Warren Harding, Franklin Roosevelt, and John F. Kennedy. Only Richard Nixon has resigned.

In 1947, Congress established the line of succession that is used today: Vice-President, Speaker of the House of Representatives, president pro tempore of the Senate, and Secretary of State, followed by the remaining cabinet members in the order in which their executive departments were created.

The Whigs took their name from the Whig Party in England, which stood for limiting the king's powers. They said the United States now had its own tyrant. They mockingly called President Jackson "King Andrew the First."

The election of 1836 The Whigs agreed on only one thing—their hatred of Jackson and his policies. Otherwise the party was very disorganized and lacked a statement of political beliefs. In the election of 1836, the Whigs were not strong enough to defeat the Democratic candidate, Van Buren.

Van Buren had won after promising to follow in Jackson's footsteps. In fact, many people saw his election as Old Hickory's third presidential victory. Voters had shown they still loved Jackson by electing his handpicked successor.

The Panic of 1837

Two months after Van Buren took office, the country slipped into the worst economic depression it had ever known—the Panic of 1837. Van Buren was blamed for it, but in fact Jackson's economic policies were part of the cause.

During the last years of Jackson's presidency, state banks had been freely lending paper money to people who made quick profits by buying and selling public lands. Jackson had worried that land prices would rise too quickly. In 1836 he had ordered that only gold or silver coins, known as specie, could be used to buy public lands.

The order, called the Specie Circular, slowed land sales but also weakened the banks. Panicked customers brought their paper money into banks, demanding gold and silver coins in return. If the President did not trust paper money, they thought, why should they?

Meanwhile, a financial crisis in Britain led British bankers to demand that American banks repay their loans. The British also stopped buying cotton, so cotton and land prices tumbled. Many banks failed and unemployment rose. The depression continued throughout Van Buren's term.

"Tippecanoe and Tyler, Too!"

As the election of 1840 approached, the Whigs smelled victory. They were confident that voters would blame "Martin Van Ruin" for the depression. They picked a candidate—William Henry Harrison of Ohio—who would appeal to common people in every section of the country. To attract southern votes, they nominated John Tyler of Virginia for Vice-President.

Like Jackson, Harrison had been a general who became famous as a military hero. He was the victor at the Battle of Tippecanoe in 1811. Also, like Jackson, he had risen from poverty to wealth by his own effort.

Instead of taking a stand on issues, each party criticized the other's candidate. One Democrat poked fun at the 68-year-old Harrison's age, saying he should just sit in a log cabin and drink cider the rest of his days. The joke backfired, as Whigs contrasted their "log cabin" candidate with the rich-looking Martin Van Buren. Calling Harrison a true representative of the common people, they said Van Buren's table was set with the finest golden plates.

In what became known as the "log cabin campaign," Whigs held huge rallies to entertain voters. They shouted "Tippecanoe and Tyler, Too!" and sang songs from the *Log Cabin Songbook*. Calling Harrison "Old Tip" and Van Buren "Matt," one song declared:

"Old Tip, he wears a homespun shirt,
  He has no ruffled shirt, wirt, wirt.
But Matt, he has the golden plate,
  And he's a little squirt, wirt, wirt."

At Risk Students

Adult family members can help bridge the gap between the material presented and students' own lives. For example, in Section 1 students can talk with them about their own experiences in voting, discovering why they think voting is important or what factors might make voting difficult. In Section 4, students may find out about the process of applying for a bank loan today, and in preparation for the Section Activity, they may discuss with their families what issues are important to them and their communities. Throughout the year, look for ways that families can play a role in enriching students' learning.

In their 1840 campaign, the Whigs distributed many items—songsheets, pamphlets, handkerchiefs, and even hairbrushes—promoting William Henry Harrison as the "log cabin candidate."

The campaign was filled with monkey business that has never since been equaled. Whigs rolled huge balls covered with campaign slogans from town to town and state to state. As the supporters of "Tip and Ty" pushed the balls, they sang:

> Tippecanoe and Tyler, too.
> And with them we'll beat little
> Van, Van, Van.
> Oh! Van is a used-up man.

The Democrats were amazed. One veteran of the 1828 campaign moaned, "We have taught them to conquer us!" The Whigs gained control of Congress, and Harrison defeated Van Buren by an electoral vote of 234 to 60. The popular vote was much closer. Harrison won by 150,000 votes out of the 2.4 million cast.

Harrison had little opportunity to enjoy his victory, though. He caught a severe cold on Inauguration Day and died of pneumonia a month later.

"His Accidency"

John Tyler was now President. For the first time, a Vice-President had reached the highest office because of a President's death. Some people began referring to Tyler as "His Accidency."

The Whigs planned an ambitious program and expected Tyler to approve it. They wanted to set up another Bank of the United States and to spend more federal money on canals and roads. They were also in favor of a higher tariff.

Tyler, who was a strong believer in states' rights, would have none of this. Although he had left the Democratic Party because of Jackson's stand on nullification, at heart he was still a Democrat. He opposed his new party on almost every issue. He vetoed bills in support of a national bank, tariffs, and internal improvements.

As a result, angry Whig leaders kicked Tyler out of the party. They refused to nominate him for re-election in 1844.

Discussion

Checking Understanding

1. **Why did the Whigs refer to Jackson as "King Andrew the First"?** (They thought he acted like a tyrannical monarch.)

2. **What were some causes of the Panic of 1837?** (Specie Circular weakened state banks, and customers panicked over value of paper money; British bankers demanded loans be repaid; British stopped buying cotton, causing cotton and land prices to fall.)

Stimulating Critical Thinking

3. **What do you think are good and bad effects of campaign rallies?** (Good: help get citizens involved, provide information on issues. Bad: oversimplify issues, trivialize elections with circus atmosphere.)

4. **Was it right for Tyler to oppose the Whigs after he got into office? Explain.** (Yes: had a right to think for himself. No: elected as Whig so should have supported party.)

Writing an Editorial

To review events leading to the rise of the Whig Party and the Democrats' loss, have students write editorials from the point of view of a writer in 1840. Editorials should identify the most important events of Jackson's second term and Van Buren's presidency, and present the writer's opinion of both Presidents' performances.

Section Review

Answers

1. He thought the Bank benefited the rich and denied opportunity to the poor.

2. The "bank war" prompted those unhappy with Jackson—including National Republicans, states' rights supporters, and bankers—to unite to challenge him.

3. Voters blamed Democrats for the depression, and the Whigs ran an aggressive campaign to win voters.

4. With growing sectionalism, issues such as slavery, tariffs, and states' rights were divisive and were sure to alienate some voters. The Whigs were only united in their opposition to the Democrats and did not really have particular stands on issues.

To check understanding of "Why We Remember," assign Thinking Critically question 3 on student page 371.

Jackson watched these events with keen interest. Politics was one of the few pleasures left to the old warrior, now in ill health at the Hermitage, his estate near Nashville. When Harrison won the election of 1840, Jackson had said he hoped to live long enough to see another Democrat as President. In a way, his wish came true with Tyler.

When Tyler recommended that Congress add Texas to the Union, Jackson was overjoyed. A strong nationalist to the end, he exclaimed: "All is safe at last!"

4. Section Review

1. Why did Andrew Jackson oppose the Bank of the United States?
2. Why was the Whig Party formed?
3. Why did the Democrats lose the election of 1840?
4. Critical Thinking Why do you think that serious issues received little attention in the political campaigns leading up to the election of 1840?

Why We Remember

The Age of Jackson

When Old Hickory died in the spring of 1845 at the age of 78, the nation went into mourning. All across the country there were solemn services marking the passing of a remarkable leader.

The Age of Jackson was over, but Jackson's legacy lived on. One of his gifts to the future was the Democratic Party. It is our oldest political party.

Jackson changed American politics forever. In the past, politics had been for the wealthy and powerful. Jackson and his Democrats brought common folk into politics for the first time by making campaigns more exciting.

Jackson also changed the role of the President. Until he took office, most Presidents had seen their duty as running the executive branch and carrying out the will of Congress. Jackson, however, believed the President's job was to represent the will of the people in national affairs. He was the first President to veto acts of Congress that, in his view, did not do what the people wanted done. He would not be the last.

Finally, Jackson gave new meaning to the American Dream. Presidents before him had all been well born and well educated. Jackson was neither. When a woman who knew him as a young man heard he was running for President, she exclaimed:

"What! Jackson up for President? JACKSON? ANDREW Jackson? The Jackson that used to live in Salisbury? . . . Well, if Andrew Jackson can be President, anybody can!**"**

(Answers continued from side margin)
3. (a) Kinglike: refusal to enforce Court decision in favor of Cherokees, veto of Bank bill, removal of federal money from the Bank. Not Kinglike: retaining postmaster of Albany, urging Congress to seek a compromise to nullification crisis. (b) Answers will vary. Students may say that some people portrayed Jackson as a king because they thought he acted like a tyrant regarding such issues as the Bank, and that such a stereotype, while not completely accurate, had some basis in truth.

For further application, have students do the Applying Skills activity in the Chapter Survey (p. 370).

If students need to review the skill, use the Skills Development transparency and activity in the **Chapter Resources Binder,** pp. 103–104.

Skill Lab

Skill Tips

Some clues to stereotypes:
- exaggerated statements or pictures
- overly negative or overly positive statements or pictures
- generalizations that are too broad (often containing words like *all*, *every*, or *none*)

Thinking Critically
Recognizing Stereotypes

In the presidential campaign of 1828, Democrats sneered that John Quincy Adams was an aristocrat like his father, John Adams. "King John the Second," they called him. Little did Jackson's supporters dream that Jackson himself would be labeled "King Andrew" during his presidency.

Question to Investigate

Was it fair of Andrew Jackson's critics to accuse him of acting like a king?

Procedure

"King Andrew" is an example of a **stereotype**—an oversimplified image of a person, group, or idea. Stereotypes can be expressed in statements or pictures. They can be negative or positive. Either way, you need to recognize them in order to judge people and events fairly. Study the political cartoon, which appeared during Jackson's second term.

❶ Identify the stereotype.
a. List features of the cartoon that fit clues in the Skill Tips.
b. Explain whether the stereotype is positive or negative.

❷ Identify who might have created the stereotype and why.
a. Did the cartoonist support or oppose Jackson? Explain.
b. Why do you think the cartoon was created? Explain, using details from the cartoon.

❸ Evaluate how well the stereotype fits.
a. List examples of Jackson's actions under two headings: *Kinglike* and *Not Kinglike*.
b. Answer the Question to Investigate.

Source to Use

KING ANDREW THE FIRST.

Introducing the Skill Lab

Point out that a stereotype is a generalization (see page 337) formed by many people, and that stereotypes may be applied to a variety of subjects, such as a person, group, belief, or lifestyle. By forming a stereotype, people are trying to fit the subject into a mold. To make sure students understand the concept, ask them to describe a stereotype that many adults might have of a "typical teenager."

Skill Lab
Answers

1. (a) Picture of Jackson in kingly outfit and labels "King Andrew the First" and "Born to Command" are exaggerations. (b) Since the nation was a democracy and Jackson's supporters had called Adams a king, portraying Jackson as a king was meant as an insult. Therefore, the stereotype is negative.

2. (a) Since the cartoon provides a negative stereotype, the cartoonist was likely an opponent, possibly a Whig. (b) The cartoonist seems to be protesting and perhaps warning the public about what he thinks is Jackson's misuse of power. He shows Jackson using the veto in a tyrannical way, stepping on the Bank bill and the Constitution itself.

(Answers continued in top margin)

Chapter Survey

Reviewing Vocabulary

Define the following terms.
1. caucus
2. suffrage
3. mudslinging
4. spoils system
5. secede
6. sovereignty

Reviewing Main Ideas

1. How did the candidates and campaigns during the election of 1828 differ from those during the election of 1824?
2. What events led to the nullification crisis of 1832?
3. How did Jackson respond to South Carolina's actions and why?
4. Explain why Jackson favored the removal of eastern Indians from their homelands.
5. Describe how each of the following tribes resisted removal and what happened as a result. (a) Sauk and Fox (b) Seminoles (c) Cherokees
6. Why did Jackson see the Bank as a threat to common people?
7. What were the political and economic effects of Jackson's "war" with the Bank?

Thinking Critically

1. Application Mudslinging occurs today, just as it did in the elections of Jackson's time. Give two examples from recent political campaigns. Why do you think mudslinging has been so common? How do you think it affects our democracy?
2. Analysis Find evidence from the chapter to support the following statement: Andrew Jackson can be called a bundle of contradictions.
3. Why We Remember: Evaluation How did Jackson give new meaning to the American Dream? Do you think his election was good for the future of American democracy? Explain.

Applying Skills

Recognizing stereotypes Recalling what you learned about stereotypes on page 369, find a recent political cartoon that presents a stereotype of a government official or candidate. Then write responses to these questions:
1. Describe the stereotype. Explain whether it is positive or negative.
2. Why do you think the cartoonist created the stereotype?
3. Based on what you know about the official or candidate, how well do you think the stereotype fits? Explain.

History Mystery

A Georgia plantation Answer the History Mystery on page 347. The two-story brick mansion shown in the photo was built in 1804 and is now a state historic site. The owner of this mansion had 800 acres of farmland, 42 cabins, 6 barns, a mill, a trading post, and more than 1,000 peach trees. Recall why this person and others like him decided to live in houses like this and to farm the land. Considering their reasons, why do you think they might have been surprised and angry at being told they had to leave?

Writing in Your History Journal

1. Keys to History (a) The time line on pages 346–347 has seven Keys to History. In your journal, describe why each one is important to know about. (b) Decide on a category of additional events for the time line, such as *Economic Events* or *Events Related to Indian Removal*. Write the appropriate events and their dates in your journal, along with why you think the events should be added.

Answers should reflect understanding of the characteristics of a stereotype (p. 369). If students do not know enough about the subject to evaluate the fairness, suggest they research the person's actions and beliefs.

Many Cherokees lived in homes like the one shown on p. 347. They had taken up farming and adapted to white American culture in the hope of remaining on their land. They were shocked to learn they would be forced from their land so that white settlers could have it. They are likely to have been angry because they did everything they
(Answers continued in side margin)

could to show that they would live peaceably within the mainstream under the federal government's own rules.

Writing in Your History Journal

1. (a) Explanations should be similar to the time line notes on teacher pages 346–347. (b) Events will vary.

2. Explanations should include reasons. Some may believe he would not succeed because he lacked academic skills. Others may say he would because he stood up for his beliefs.

3. Responses should reflect understanding of candidates' views and personalities. Some may say a candidate like Adams would not be favored because he supported a strong national government and did not have an attractive personality. Others may say Jackson would not be favored because he lacked education and would make the executive branch too strong.

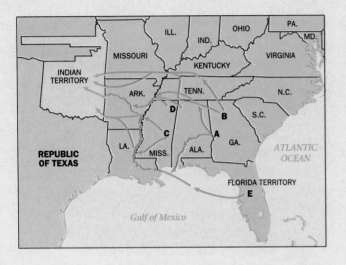

Reviewing Geography

1. Each letter on the map represents one of the tribes forced to move west of the Mississippi in the early 1800s. Write each letter and the name of the tribe.

2. Geographic Thinking In Jackson's time people thought of the United States as having three distinct sections, or regions. What were those three sections? Where were they? How did they differ? Do people today think of the United States as having those same three sections? Explain.

Reviewing Geography

1. (A) Creeks, (B) Cherokees, (C) Choctaws, (D) Chickasaws, (E) Seminoles

2. North (manufacturing and shipping states in Northeast), South (plantation states east of Appalachians: Virginia, Carolinas, Georgia), West (west of Appalachians). Disagreements over tariffs, banks, slavery, and treatment of Indians. Students may point to newer divisions, such as urban versus rural.

Alternative Assessment

Teacher's Take-Home Planner 5, p. 5, includes suggestions and scoring rubrics for the Alternative Assessment activity.

2. Andrew Jackson Imagine that you went to grade school with Andrew Jackson. Would you vote for him as the classmate "Most Likely to Succeed" or the one "Least Likely to Succeed"? Explain in your journal. If necessary, review the information on page 348.

3. Citizenship Imagine two modern presidential candidates, one with a personality and views like John Quincy Adams and another with a personality and views like Andrew Jackson. Which candidate do you think would be more likely to be elected President today? Why? Write your response in your journal.

Alternative Assessment

Journal writing Imagine that you lived during "The Age of Jackson" and were writing journal notes on events and issues of your day.

❶ Decide what kind of person you are: your gender, the section of the country where you live, your type of job, and your social background.

❷ Write one or more journal entries on each of the following topics, describing the topics and also your thoughts and reactions to them.
• The election of 1828
• The Webster-Hayne debates
• Jackson's Indian policy
• The "bank war"
• The election of 1840

Your work will be evaluated on the following criteria
• you are careful to base your descriptions on historical facts
• your reactions to the topics reflect the likely viewpoint of the type of person you represent
• your journal entries are interesting and creative

14 The Westward Movement
1820–1850

Chapter Planning Guide

Section	Student Text	Teacher's Edition Activities
Opener and Story pp. 372–375	**Keys to History Time Line** · **History Mystery** Beginning the Story with **John and Jessie Frémont**	**Setting the Stage Activity** Expedition Notes, p. 374
1 Trappers and Traders Blaze the Way pp. 376–379	**Link to Art** *The Trapper's Bride*, p. 378 **Link to the Present** Santa Fe then and now, p. 379	**Warm-Up Activity** Comparing Maps, p. 376 **Geography Question of the Day,** p. 376 **Section Activity** Setting Up a Trading Company, p. 377 · **Bonus Activity** Writing a Tall Tale, p. 378 **Wrap-Up Activity** Designing a Newspaper Ad, p. 379
2 The Republic of Texas pp. 380–384	**Point of View** Why did Texans declare their independence?, p. 383 **Reading Maps** The Texas War for Independence, p. 384	**Warm-Up Activity** Writing About Moving, p. 380 **Geography Question of the Day,** p. 380 **Section Activity** Viewpoints on the Alamo, p. 382 · **Bonus Activity** Writing an Editorial, p. 382 **Wrap-Up Activity** A Sam Houston Speech, p. 384
3 Trails West pp. 385–392	**Reading Maps** Trails to the West, p. 387 **Hands-On History** Making decisions on the trail, p. 388 **Skill Lab** Determining Credibility, p. 392	**Warm-Up Activity** Planning a Trip, p. 385 **Geography Question of the Day,** p. 385 **Section Activity** Hardships Then and Now, p. 390 · **Bonus Activity** A Menu for the Oregon Trail, p. 386 **Wrap-Up Activity** Making a Time Line, p. 391
4 Manifest Destiny Triumphs pp. 393–399	**Reading Maps** The Mexican-American War 1846–1848, p. 395; The United States 1853, p. 396 **World Link** "Golden Mountain," p. 397 **Geography Lab** Basins and Ranges, p. 399	**Warm-Up Activity** Discussing Manifest Destiny, p. 393 **Geography Question of the Day,** p. 393 **Section Activity** Reporting on the War, p. 394 · **Bonus Activity** Tourist Attractions, p. 396 **Wrap-Up Activity** Mapping the Nation's Growth, p. 398
Evaluation	✓ **Section 1 Review,** p. 379 ✓ **Section 2 Review,** p. 384 ✓ **Section 3 Review,** p. 391 ✓ **Section 4 Review,** p. 398 ✓ **Chapter Survey,** pp. 400–401 　**Alternative Assessment** Planning a western, p. 401	✓ **Answers to Section 1 Review,** p. 379 ✓ **Answers to Section 2 Review,** p. 384 ✓ **Answers to Section 3 Review,** p. 391 ✓ **Answers to Section 4 Review,** p. 398 ✓ **Answers to Chapter Survey,** pp. 400–401 (Alternative Assessment guidelines are in the Take-Home Planner.)

Teacher's Resource Package

Chapter Summaries: English and Spanish, pp. 32–33

Chapter Resources Binder
Study Guide Identifying People and Places, p. 105
American Readings The Life of a Mountain Man, pp. 53–54

Chapter Resources Binder
Study Guide Completing a Time Line, p. 106
Reinforcement Analyzing a Primary Source, pp. 109–110

Chapter Resources Binder
Study Guide Telling *Who, What, When,* and *Where,* p. 107
Skills Development Determining Credibility, pp. 111–112
American Readings Women's Journeys Westward, pp. 55–56
Using Historical Documents Frémont Maps of the Oregon Trail, pp. 76–80

Chapter Resources Binder
Study Guide Identifying Main Ideas and Supporting Details, p. 108
Geography Extensions The Great Basin, pp. 27–28

Chapter and Unit Tests Chapter 14 Tests, Forms A and B, pp. 91–94

Take-Home Planner

Introducing the Chapter Activity Brainstorming Facts About the West, p. 12

Chapter In-Depth Activity Planning a Trip Westward, p. 13

Reduced Views
Study Guide, p. 14
American Readings, p. 16
Unit 5 Answers, pp. 36–44

Reduced Views
Study Guide, p. 14
Reinforcement, p. 15
Unit 5 Answers, pp. 36–44

Reduced Views
Study Guide, p. 14
Skills Development, p. 15
American Readings, p. 16
Using Historical Documents, p. 17
Unit 5 Answers, pp. 36–44

Reduced Views
Study Guide, p. 14
Geography Extensions, p. 17
Unit 5 Answers, pp. 36–44

Reduced Views
Chapter Tests, p. 17
Unit 5 Answers, pp. 36–44

Alternative Assessment Guidelines for scoring the Chapter Survey activity, p. 13

Additional Resources

Wall Time Line

Unit 5 Activity

Transparency Package

Transparency 14-1 Rancho San Miguelito, California—use with Section 4

Transparency 14-2 Illustrations from the Mexican-American Boundary Survey—use with Section 4

Transparency Activity Book

SelecTest Testing Software
Chapter 14 Test, Forms A and B

★ ★ ★
Vital Links

◉ **Videodisc**

◎ **CD-ROM**

James Beckwourth (see TE p. 378)

Voice of José María Sánchez (see TE p. 381)

Battle of the Alamo (see TE p. 383)

"Cielito Lindo" (see TE p. 386)

Wagon Train (see TE p. 388)

Joseph Smith preaching (see TE p. 390)

Mexican-American War (see TE p. 396)

Teaching Resources

Take-Home Planner 5
  Introducing Chapter Activity
  Chapter In-Depth Activity
  Alternative Assessment
Chapter Resources Binder
Geography Extensions
American Readings
Using Historical Documents
Transparency Activities
Wall Time Line Activities
Chapter Summaries
Chapter and Unit Tests
SelecTest Test File
Vital Links CD-ROM/Videodisc

Time Line

Keys to History

Keys to History journal writing activity is on page 400 in the Chapter Survey.

Becknell on the Santa Fe Trail The Santa Fe Trail opened the Southwest to American traders and settlers. (p. 379)

First fur trappers' rendezvous The rendezvous gave trappers a market for their furs and a place to buy necessities. (p. 378)

Looking Back The Lewis and Clark Expedition explored the Louisiana Purchase and the Pacific Northwest.

Chapter Objectives

★ Describe the events that drew Americans' attention to the West.
★ Summarize how Texas became an independent nation.
★ Describe how Americans began to settle the Far West.
★ Summarize the final steps to achieving Manifest Destiny.

Chapter Overview
Expansionists believed that prosperity depended on growth, and that the nation's manifest destiny was to expand to the Pacific. Mountain men trapped furs and later guided travelers across the mountains. Traders on the Santa Fe Trail urged other Americans to move to the Southwest.
  Americans settled in Texas to grow cotton, and when Mexico banned American

1820–1850

Chapter 14

Sections

Beginning the Story with John and Jessie Frémont
1. **Trappers and Traders Blaze the Way**
2. **The Republic of Texas**
3. **Trails West**
4. **Manifest Destiny Triumphs**

The Westward Movement

Keys to History

1821
William Becknell blazes the Santa Fe Trail
American merchants sight Santa Fe

1823
First fur trappers' rendezvous
Painting of a mountain man

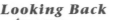

1820   *1830*

Looking Back

Lewis and Clark Expedition
1804–1806

immigration, they fought for and won independence from Mexico. Congress refused to annex Texas because northerners were opposed to admitting another slave state.

Americans struggled over the Oregon and California trails because they had heard that the Pacific Coast had rich soil and a good climate. Mormons went to Utah to avoid persecution. Indians and Mexicans at first welcomed the Americans, but many later grew to resent their presence.

During Polk's administration, Congress agreed to the British proposal to divide Oregon at the 49th parallel. In the Southwest the United States angered Mexico by claiming the Rio Grande as its border. Friction with Mexico led to war. At the war's end, the United States had gained a huge territory. After the gold rush California joined the Union in 1850.

HISTORY *Mystery*

For many years the words "Great American Desert" appeared on maps of North America. Yet this desert does not actually exist. What part of the United States was once known as the "Great American Desert," and why?

1835–1836

"Remember the Alamo" becomes Texas rallying cry

Stamp honoring the battle of the Alamo

1836

Whitmans lead first families on the Oregon Trail

Monument to women pioneers

1846–1848

War with Mexico

Treaty of Guadalupe Hidalgo, ending the war

1849

Height of California gold rush

1840

1850

World Link

Wars between Britain and China
1839–1860

Looking Ahead

First transcontinental railroad completed
1869

• 373

Teaching the HISTORY *Mystery*

Students will find the answer on p. 385. See Chapter Survey, p. 400, for additional questions.

Time Line

The Alamo "Remember the Alamo" was the rallying cry of Texans fighting for independence from Mexico. (p. 383)

Whitmans in Oregon Following the Whitmans, thousands of settlers moved west on the Oregon Trail. (p. 386)

War with Mexico The Mexican Cession, gained as a result of the war with Mexico, marked the final triumph of Manifest Destiny. The United States now stretched from sea to sea. (pp. 394–397)

California gold rush When word of the discovery of gold in California got out, prospectors from around the world rushed in. (pp. 397–398)

World Link See p. 397.

Looking Ahead Movement of goods and people between West and East became much easier with the completion of the first transcontinental railroad.

Beginning the Story

John and Jessie Frémont

Army officer John Frémont married young Jessie Benton—daughter of the powerful expansionist Senator Thomas Hart Benton—in 1841. Soon after, he took charge of an army expedition to survey a route from the Mississippi River to the Rocky Mountains. Jessie used his expedition notes to write the official report, which became a bestseller. Frémont's successive trips and the books Jessie helped write about them excited easterners' interest in the beauty and bounty of the West and served as guidebooks for travelers. Frémont became known as "The Pathfinder."

Setting the Stage
Activity

Expedition Notes

To help students understand the importance of keeping good records on an expedition, have them make journal notes describing their own neighborhood to newcomers. Their notes should include maps and information on finding food, transportation, and a place to stay.

See the Introducing the Chapter Activity, Brainstorming Facts About the West. **Take-Home Planner 5**, p. 12.

★ **History Footnote**

John and Jessie's fortunes rose and fell during their life together. Frémont's fourth expedition, searching for a railroad route through the Rockies, was unsuccessful. Land that the Frémonts bought in California did make them wealthy. In 1856, John Frémont became the first Republican candidate for President, running under the slogan, "Free Speech, Free Press, Free Soil, Free Men, Frémont, and Victory!" During the Civil War, he commanded the Western Department of the Union army. He was transferred to Virginia when he tried to seize the land of Confederate supporters in Missouri and free their slaves. The Frémonts had lost their fortune by the mid-1870s, and Jessie supported them by writing children's stories and reminiscences. John died in 1890 and Jessie in 1902.

Beginning the Story with

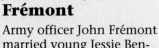

John and Jessie Frémont

When John C. Frémont (FREE-mont)—a dashing, charming, and intensely ambitious army officer—first visited the Washington home of Missouri Senator Thomas Hart Benton, the two men found they shared a passionate interest in expanding the nation westward. As much as the senator and his wife liked Frémont, however, neither had thought of him as a husband for their 16-year-old daughter Jessie.

At age 27, Frémont seemed too old for Jessie. His family background was also questionable. Frémont's mother had left her husband to live with a penniless French artist. Frémont had managed to get a good education, but he had been expelled from college his senior year for cutting classes. He just was not what they had in mind for a son-in-law.

Their daughter Jessie—a talented, bold, headstrong young woman—had different ideas. When Jessie looked at John Frémont, she saw her future. John and Jessie were married in a secret ceremony in 1841, when Jessie was just 17. A month later, her parents gave their blessing.

Exploring the West

Soon after the wedding, Frémont took charge of an army expedition to survey a route from the Mississippi River to the Rocky Mountains. With him went a German map maker named Charles Preuss, a fur trapper and guide named Kit Carson, and Jessie's 12-year-old brother Randolph. Senator Benton sent his son to prove that western travel was safe even for children.

Traveling west across the plains, Frémont and Preuss made detailed observations of landscapes, plants, and animals. With this information they would later produce the most accurate maps yet made of the region. As the

History Bookshelf

McClung, Robert M. *Hugh Glass, Mountain Man.* Morrow, 1990. In this biographical novel based on historical accounts, the author tells about the exploits of a legendary mountain man in the West. *Hugh Glass* was chosen as a Notable Children's Trade Book in the Field of Social Studies in 1990.

Also of interest:

Levy, Joann. *They Saw the Elephant: Women in the California Gold Rush.* Archon Books, 1990.

Kloss, Doris. *Sarah Winnemucca.* Dillon, 1981.

Nardo, Don. *The Mexican-American War.* Lucent Books, 1991.

Yee, Paul. *Tales from the Gold Mountain: Stories of the Chinese in the New World.* Macmillan, 1990.

expedition neared the Rocky Mountains, someone warned Frémont that the Cheyennes and Sioux would attack anyone who crossed into their hunting grounds. Frémont responded with his own warning:

> **"**We are few, and you are many, and may kill us all. . . . Do you think that our great chief [the President] will let his soldiers die and forget to cover their graves? Before the snows melt again, his warriors will sweep away your villages.**"**

The Indians let the expedition pass unharmed. When Frémont finally reached the crest of the Rockies, he climbed the tallest peak he could find and unfurled an American flag. When he returned home weeks later, he draped this same flag over Jessie, who lay in bed resting after the birth of their first child. "This flag was raised over the highest peak of the Rocky Mountains," he announced dramatically. "I have brought it to you."

This scene from one of Frémont's reports shows members of his party in the Sierra Nevada. They are stamping out a spot in the snow to make a campsite.

The Pathfinder

Frémont also brought Jessie his expedition notes, which she helped turn into an official report. In fact, although John's name was on the report, Jessie actually wrote much of it. "The horseback life, the sleep in the open air," she later explained, "had unfitted Mr. Frémont for the indoor work of writing." Luckily for him, his wife had a way with words. Thanks to her skillful pen, the report became a bestseller.

During the next few years Frémont led more expeditions west. After each journey, Jessie helped him write books that excited readers in the East about the beauty and bounty of the West. Frémont's widely read books helped to inspire a great westward migration. They also served as guides for would-be settlers, providing them with information about routes, campsites, rivers, wildlife, and weather. Little wonder that Frémont became known to his adoring public as "The Pathfinder."

Hands-On → *HISTORY*

Activity

Imagine that the Frémonts have hired you to paint a portrait of each of them. They have decided what to wear. Now you must think of special objects—for example, a pen or a map—to put in each portrait to help viewers understand John and Jessie Frémont. For each portrait list three such objects and suggest an appropriate background. Then make sketches for the portraits.

Discussion

Thinking Historically

1. Why did the Bentons think Frémont was less than suitable as a husband for their daughter? (He was too old, his family background was questionable, and he had been expelled from college.)

2. How did Jessie help further John's career? (She helped fashion his expedition notes into best-selling books.)

3. What contributions did they make to the settling of the West? (John, through his expeditions, and Jessie, through her writings, made the West more familiar, a place where people could imagine themselves living.)

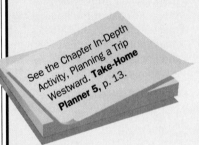

See the Chapter In-Depth Activity, Planning a Trip Westward. **Take-Home Planner 5,** p. 13.

Teaching the

Hands-On

---→ *HISTORY*

In making their lists of objects and their sketches of the backgrounds of the portraits, students should consider John's and Jessie's unique experiences and contributions. For example, since Jessie's contributions were connected with her writing, the background for her portrait might be bookshelves or a writing desk.

For a journal writing activity on John and Jessie Frémont, see student page 401.

Comparing Maps

To help students focus on the West, have them compare a map of the United States just after the Louisiana Purchase with a map today. Ask them to identify differences between the two maps, as well as what the United States might have gained from owning the land west of the Louisiana Purchase. Students might note that access to the Pacific would provide a waterway to Asia.

Geography Question of the Day

Have students write a brief description about the allure and dangers of the West for the mountain men and other early explorers. Suggest that they use the map of the Geographic Regions of the United States on pages P4–P5, the map of the Louisiana Purchase on page 295, and what they learned about the Lewis and Clark Expedition in Chapter 11.

Section Objectives

★ Explain Manifest Destiny.
★ Describe how the activities of mountain men and Santa Fe traders created enthusiasm for the Far West.

Teaching Resources

Take-Home Planner 5, pp. 10–17

Chapter Resources Binder

  Study Guide, p. 105
    Reinforcement
    Skills Development
  Geography Extensions
  American Readings, pp. 53–54
  Using Historical Documents
  Transparency Activities
  Chapter and Unit Tests

1. Trappers and Traders Blaze the Way

Reading Guide

New Term expansionists

Section Focus Events that drew Americans' attention to the West

1. What was Manifest Destiny?
2. How did the activities of mountain men and Santa Fe traders create enthusiasm for the Far West?

In the early 1800s, when an American talked about "the West," he or she probably meant the Old Northwest or the Old Southwest. These were the lands between the Appalachians and the Mississippi River.

Already, however, a few American explorers and adventurers were moving beyond the Mississippi, into the Louisiana Territory and farther. Better transportation—especially the steamboat—encouraged some. Hard times pushed others west in search of fresh opportunities.

When these Americans talked about "the West," they meant the land just west of the Mississippi River. The land that lay far across the continent from the Atlantic Coast became known as "the Far West."

Gradually many different kinds of people drifted into the West—Americans, Germans, French, and others. They were trappers, farmers, adventurers, and people who simply wanted to get away from everyone else. Some were heroes and some were villains. In the West they met the Indians and the Mexicans who already lived there.

The story of the West is a story of possibilities and of danger. Most of all, it is the story of the meeting of many different peoples. From this meeting, new ways of life would emerge.

Manifest Destiny

John C. Frémont, his wife Jessie, and her father, Thomas Hart Benton, were eager **expansionists**—people who believe that their country's prosperity depends on enlarging its territory. They dreamed of a United States with borders stretching from coast to coast. Jessie called it "a grand plan."

In 1845 John O'Sullivan, the editor of a New York newspaper, gave the grand plan a name. He called it Manifest Destiny. In an editorial he declared that God had given the United States a "manifest destiny to overspread the continent."

Manifest means obvious, or clear. Destiny means fate. Supporters of Manifest Destiny believed that God had blessed their country. It was clear to them that Americans had the right, even the duty, to expand their way of life and their government westward until the United States reached across the continent to the Pacific Ocean.

Some people argued that by expanding the nation to the Pacific Coast, Americans could fulfill the dreams of Christopher Columbus. According to these expansionists, the United States would become the route to Asia that Europeans had searched for so long. Thomas Hart Benton urged:

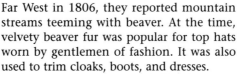

Connections to Science

Beavers may have been hunted more than any other animal in North America from the 1600s through the 1800s. Fur trading was so heavy in the 1800s that beavers had been almost hunted to extinction by the late 1800s. Canada and the United States eventually passed laws to protect them. Today beavers can be hunted only at designated times of the year. A beaver has short underfur and long guard hairs. The underfur traps air, which keeps the beaver warm, even in the coldest lakes and rivers.

See the Study Guide activity in **Chapter Resources Binder,** p. 105.

> " Let us vindicate [set right] the glory of Columbus by realizing his divine idea of arriving in the east [Asia] by going to the west."

Of course, most of the land west of the United States in the 1840s belonged to Mexico. The rest was part of Oregon Country, which the United States shared with England. The claims of other nations did not stop the dreams of expansionists, though. Neither did the fact that many Indians already occupied the land.

Mountain Men

American enthusiasm for the Far West began with the stories of Lewis and Clark and the trappers and traders who followed them. When Lewis and Clark returned from the Far West in 1806, they reported mountain streams teeming with beaver. At the time, velvety beaver fur was popular for top hats worn by gentlemen of fashion. It was also used to trim cloaks, boots, and dresses.

The year after Lewis and Clark's return, Manuel Lisa, a Spanish American trader from St. Louis, ventured up the Missouri River to the Yellowstone River. Where the Little Bighorn River meets the Yellowstone, he built Fort Manuel. From there he sent trappers into the Rocky Mountains.

Other fur companies followed Lisa. These companies hired restless young men willing to risk their lives in the western mountains for an annual salary of $200. The trappers were known as mountain men.

Mountain men worked alone or in small groups. Their lives were often lonely, usually dangerous, and always hard. Many of them earned colorful reputations. For example,

This picture of two mountain men at work looks quite peaceful. In fact, trapping was dangerous. Some hazards that trappers might face were drowning, bad falls, gunshots, rattlesnakes, bears, and infections.

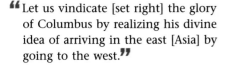

Manuel Lisa

Jim Beckwourth

Developing the Section

Discussion

Checking Understanding

1. Who coined the term *Manifest Destiny*? Where? (John O'Sullivan, in an 1845 New York newspaper editorial.)

2. Who were the mountain men? (Men who went into the Rocky Mountains to trap beaver.)

Stimulating Critical Thinking

3. How might the idea of Manifest Destiny have influenced treatment of Indians? (If settlers thought they had a God-given duty to expand westward, they might have assumed the right to displace Indians.)

4. What might have been some arguments against expansion? (Avoid conflict with Indians and with other nations that claimed the lands; lands hard to reach.)

Section Activity

Setting Up a Trading Company

To help students understand the lives of fur trappers, have small groups plan their own fur-trading companies. Each plan should describe what types of land the trappers will cross, supplies and skills needed, how they will interact with Indians, and how they will get the furs to market. Each group should decide on an appropriate name for their company.

1820–1850 Chapter 14 • **377**

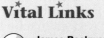
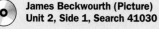
William Henry Ashley introduced cost-cutting innovations in the fur-trading business so he could compete with more established groups such as Hudson's Bay Company. His first innovation was to eliminate the permanent fort. He took his trappers into the mountains in brigades to trap in the fall and spring, and returned with them to St. Louis in the summer. He cut expenses further by establishing the rendezvous system, which led to "free trappers," trappers not employed by Ashley or by any other fur-trading companies.

For a description of the life of mountain men, see **American Readings,** pp. 53–54.

Hugh Glass lived to tell about his hand-to-paw fight with a grizzly bear. Jim Beckwourth, son of a Virginia slave, became a chief of the Crow Indians.

In fact, many trappers owed their mountaineering skills and knowledge of trails to Indians. Often they lived and worked side by side with Indians and married Indian women. American writer Washington Irving once observed:

> **❝**You cannot pay a free trapper a greater compliment than to persuade him you have mistaken him for an Indian.**❞**

The rendezvous Each summer between 1823 and 1837, trappers met at a prearranged spot for a large gathering known as the rendezvous (RAHN-day-VOO). Indian traders and trappers were welcomed, too. Here they met supply wagons sent from St. Louis by the fur companies.

The rendezvous was a grand fair where trappers sold furs and bought necessities and luxuries for the next year, such as ammunition, traps, axes, sugar, and coffee. It was also a time for games, gossip, and gambling. By the end of a rendezvous, more than one mountain man found he had gambled away all the money he had earned from his furs that year.

Western guides The time when mountain men roamed the West was short. By 1840 the beaver were almost extinct from over-hunting, and beaver hats had gone out of style.

By then, though, the mountain men had learned much about the landscape of the West. Like Kit Carson, Frémont's guide, other mountain men took jobs as guides and interpreters. Government exploration parties and settlers heading west depended on mountain men to show them the way.

Link to Art

The Trapper's Bride (1850) The wedding in this painting took place in 1837. That was the year William Stewart, a Scottish adventurer, invited artist Alfred Jacob Miller to the Rockies. During the summer rendezvous of hundreds of trappers and thousands of Shoshones, Crows, Nez Percés, and other Indians, Miller sketched the people around him.

Back home in New Orleans, he used his sketches as models for paintings that showed friendly relations between trappers and Indians. **Discuss** How does the painting indicate that mountain men and Indians saw each other as equals?

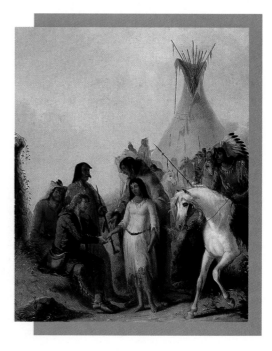

History Footnote

Santa Fe, the capital of New Mexico, was founded by Don Pedro de Peralta in 1610 on the site of an ancient Indian pueblo. The name *Santa Fe* means "Holy Faith." In the 1600s Santa Fe was a center of Franciscan missionary work and Spanish exploration of the surrounding area. The Palace of the Governors was built by Peralta in 1610 and was continuously occupied by Spanish, Mexican, and United States governors until 1909. It was restored as a museum in 1914. From the 1920s to the present, Santa Fe has been a magnet for writers, artists, and musicians.

Teaching the

Link to the Present

After students read about the importance of Santa Fe's efforts to preserve its past, ask what aspects of the past have been preserved in their area.

Link to the Present

Santa Fe then and now The people of Santa Fe have taken great care to preserve their past. If American, Mexican, and Indian traders of the 1800s could come back to the city today, they would find much that looked familiar.

Laws in Santa Fe require new buildings to be built in the traditional adobe style. Along the north side of the plaza—where the Santa Fe Trail ended—the Palace of the Governors is kept looking much as it did when the Spanish built it nearly 400 years ago. In the shadows of the palace's covered walkway, Indians spread out silver and turquoise jewelry and other wares for sale, just as in the past. And artists of Spanish descent still sell wood-carvings and weavings at the yearly Spanish Market.

Santa Fe Traders

Santa Fe traders also played a big part in drawing people west. In 1800 Santa Fe was a distant outpost of the Spanish empire. Mexico City, the capital of Mexico, lay more than 1,500 miles (2,413 km) to the south over difficult mountain roads. Santa Fe had almost 4,000 citizens and a rich supply of silver and furs, but lacked manufactured goods such as cloth, cooking utensils, and tools.

As early as 1804 an enterprising merchant from Illinois went to Santa Fe hoping to open up trade. Suspecting the merchant of spying, Spanish authorities arrested him. The situation changed dramatically, however, when Mexico won its independence from Spain in 1821 (see page 329). After that, Mexico opened its northern borders to foreign traders.

In that same year William Becknell, a Missouri trader, reached Santa Fe with a train of pack mules loaded with goods. He made such a large profit that he returned the following year with wagons.

Becknell became known as the Father of the Santa Fe Trail. The route he blazed stretched across nearly 800 miles (1,287 km) of wide prairies and scorching deserts between Independence, Missouri, and Santa Fe. Other traders rushed to use the new route. One outfit went to Santa Fe with merchandise worth $35,000 and returned with silver and furs worth $190,000.

The stories of the Santa Fe traders—like those of the mountain men—encouraged Americans to think about moving west, even beyond the boundaries of the United States. The traders proved that wagon trains were a practical and safe means of crossing the plains. They also brought back word that the borders of Mexico were weakly guarded. They led immigrants to believe that they could move into Texas, New Mexico, and California with little risk.

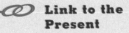

1. Section Review

1. Define **expansionists.**
2. For Americans, how did the meaning of the expression "the West" change between 1800 and 1820?
3. What was one argument in favor of Manifest Destiny?
4. How did the mountain men and the Santa Fe traders each make it easier for Americans to think about moving west?
5. **Critical Thinking** Write three questions that you would ask a mountain man in 1840 if you were thinking about moving from an eastern city to an area west of the Rockies.

Closing the Section

Wrap-Up Activity

Designing a Newspaper Ad

Have students design a newspaper ad extolling virtues of the newly acquired lands. The ad should try to persuade people to move there. It might also suggest hiring a mountain guide or trading in Santa Fe.

Section Review Answers

1. Definition: *expansionists* (376)
2. West changed from meaning the area between the Appalachians and the Mississippi to the area west of the Mississippi.
3. Answers may include: God intended Americans to expand; would fulfill dream of a route to Asia.
4. Mountain men were guides; traders proved wagon trains were practical and safe and that Mexico's borders were weakly defended.
5. Some possibilities: What is the best place to make a home? What supplies would I need? What dangers might I face?

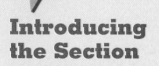

Introducing the Section

Vocabulary

annex (p. 384) to take territory and add it to one's own country

Writing About Moving

To underscore the personal issues involved in westward expansion, have students imagine that their family is moving to a new state. Ask them to write a letter to a friend or draw a picture that addresses the following questions: What things might you look forward to? What things might you miss about your old home? What things would you be glad to leave behind?

Geography Question of the Day

To help students focus on the importance of Texas to the United States today, provide them with a map of Texas that shows its economic products. Have them write a few sentences explaining the importance of these goods to the rest of the United States.

Section Objectives

★ Summarize why Americans wanted to settle in Texas and why Mexico let them.
★ Explain why Mexico banned American immigration to Texas in 1830.
★ Explain why the United States rejected annexing Texas in 1836.

Teaching Resources

Take-Home Planner 5, pp. 10–17
Chapter Resources Binder
  Study Guide, p. 106
  Reinforcement, pp. 109–110
  Skills Development
Geography Extensions
American Readings
Using Historical Documents
Transparency Activities
Chapter and Unit Tests

2. The Republic of Texas

Reading Guide

New Term annex

Section Focus How Texas became an independent nation

1. Why did Americans want to settle in Texas, and why did Mexico let them?
2. Why did Mexico ban American immigration to Texas in 1830?
3. What caused the United States to reject Texas annexation in 1836?

Trappers and traders were not the only Americans interested in Mexican land. Southern farmers began to hear of Texas, an ideal place to grow cotton. However, Texas belonged to the King of Spain, and he had ruled it off limits for Americans.

Austin's Dream

In 1820 Missouri banker Moses Austin went to San Antonio, capital of Spanish Texas, and asked authorities to grant him land in Texas. He planned to sell it to American settlers at a profit. Spanish authorities approved. In return, he promised to bring in 300 families who would swear loyalty to Spain. They would defend the area against illegal American immigrants.

In 1821, as Austin prepared to launch his community, he fell gravely ill. On his deathbed he asked his son Stephen to carry on his dream. Although Stephen had hoped to become a lawyer, he felt he could not say no. He appealed to Spanish authorities, who gave him permission to carry on in his father's place. Later, Stephen recalled:

❝ I bid an everlasting farewell to my native country, and adopted this [Mexico], and in so doing I determined to fulfill rigidly all the duties and obligations of a Mexican citizen.**❞**

Approval from Mexico

Stephen Austin brought the first group of settlers to land lying between the Brazos and Colorado Rivers in 1821. He named the area San Felipe de Austin. Thus began what would become the state of Texas.

Soon Austin learned that Mexico had won its independence. Would the new government allow the Americans to stay? Austin set out on the 1,200-mile (1,931-km) journey to Mexico City to talk to officials.

Austin ended up staying in Mexico City for more than a year. He learned to speak Spanish. Then he quietly presented his case. He promised to fill the land with respectable people who would defend it against Apaches, Comanches, and American bandits and horse thieves.

In April 1823 the Mexican authorities approved the colony, with certain conditions. Every settler had to become a Mexican citizen and abide by Mexican laws. Every settler also had to promise to become a Roman Catholic. Austin agreed.

Settling Texas

Austin's colony prospered. By 1830 it had as many as 20,000 people. Some were from other parts of Mexico, but most were Americans. They included hundreds of

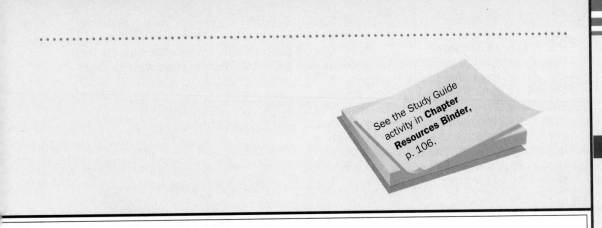

See the Study Guide activity in **Chapter Resources Binder**, p. 106.

farmers from the South looking for good cotton land. The population also included African Americans, both free and enslaved.

Pleased by the success of Austin's colony, Mexico granted land to other Americans. The new settlers, however, did not always become Roman Catholics and abide by Mexican laws, as they had promised.

The rapid growth of American settlements alarmed Mexican authorities. In 1828 a Mexican general reported that Americans in Texas outnumbered Mexicans ten to one. "Either the government occupies Texas now," he wrote, "or it is lost forever."

In 1830, fearful that the settlers might seize Texas, the Mexican government banned American immigration. The government also outlawed the slave trade, put customs duties on goods from the United States, and sent troops to enforce the new laws.

The Quarrel with Mexico

Texans did not like the government's actions. They especially resented it when Mexico combined Texas with another state, Coahuila (kō-uh-WEE-luh), and moved its capital to a city 500 miles (805 km) away. To make matters worse, Texas got only one seat in the Coahuila-Texas legislature.

In 1833 Texans learned that an army officer named Antonio López de Santa Anna had taken over Mexico's government. They signed petitions asking the new government to change the immigration law. They also asked that Texas be made a separate Mexican state so they could run their own affairs.

Stephen Austin carried the petitions to Mexico City. There he got the government to lift the immigration ban. He also heard that Santa Anna could not be trusted. Worried,

San Antonio was already a century old in the 1830s when Americans began to quarrel with Mexico. Across the main plaza you can see the clock above the old town hall, the center of power in Spanish Texas.

Discussion

Checking Understanding

1. How did the first American settlement in Texas begin? (Stephen Austin, who had an agreement with the Spanish government, brought 300 families to the area between the Brazos and Colorado Rivers.)

2. When Mexico won independence from Spain, what conditions did it set for American settlers in Texas? (They had to become Mexican citizens, abide by Mexican laws, and promise to become Roman Catholic.)

Stimulating Critical Thinking

3. What reasons might Spain and, later, Mexico, have had for letting Americans settle in Texas? (Settlers could be taxed and would help defend the land against Indians and illegal American immigrants.)

★ ★ ★
Vital Links

Voice of José María Sánchez (First Person Account) Unit 3, Side 1, Search 42623, Play to 43207

See also Unit 3 Explore CD-ROM location 275.

Section Activity

Viewpoints on the Alamo

To focus on the clash between Texans and Mexican authorities, have students form two groups. One group will imagine they are the defenders of the Alamo. The other will imagine being soldiers in Santa Anna's army. Each group should discuss and prepare to report on the battle of the Alamo from their perspective. The Texans should include the hopelessness of their plight, their anger at being attacked, and their desire for independence. The Mexicans should speak of the need to stop rebellion and their anger at the ungrateful Americans, whom they had allowed to settle in their country. Both sides should be descriptive and emotional. Have pairs of students role-play their parts.

Bonus Activity

Writing an Editorial

To point up differences in opinion among Texans fighting Santa Anna, have students write editorials for an American newspaper in Texas in 1836. Some should support the position of demanding better representation in the Mexican government. Others should support seeking independence from Mexico.

❋ **History Footnote**

Born in Virginia, Sam Houston ran away from home at 15 to live for almost three years with Cherokees. Later he joined Andrew Jackson's army to fight the Creeks. Severely wounded in battle, he resigned from the army, studied law, and was elected to various political posts in Tennessee. In 1823 he was elected to the House of Representatives and served four years. Elected governor of Tennessee, he resigned after his wife left him. He then moved to Texas to trade with Indians.

The Reinforcement activity focuses on a letter from the Alamo. **Chapter Resources Binder,** pp. 109–110.

Austin wrote a letter urging Texans to form their own government. "The fate of Texas depends upon itself," he wrote.

When Santa Anna's officials found out about the letter, they thought Austin was plotting to tear Texas away from Mexico. They had Austin arrested and held in prison in Mexico City for nearly two years.

The Texas Revolution

In 1835 Santa Anna took total control of the Mexican government. Wherever Mexicans rebelled, Santa Anna ordered the army to put them down. Texans learned that Santa Anna was sending troops to Texas.

In November Texans held a convention in San Felipe. At first, they could not agree on whether they were loyal Mexicans fighting for statehood or rebels fighting for independence. In any case, they chose an ex-governor of Tennessee, Sam Houston, to command their volunteer army. Houston was a powerful leader.

Meanwhile, Texas volunteers in San Antonio surrounded the Alamo, a former mission occupied by a small Mexican army. The Texans let the Mexican troops go when they promised not to fight Texans again.

The Alamo Then word came that Santa Anna's army was marching on San Antonio. One of the American volunteers, Jim Bowie, declared that saving Texas meant saving San Antonio first. He wrote:

❝[Commander] Neill and myself have come to the solemn resolution that we will rather die in these ditches than give it [San Antonio] up to the enemy.❞

Americans, together with Mexicans who opposed Santa Anna, gathered at the Alamo. On February 23 Santa Anna demanded unconditional surrender. Two days later Captain Juan Seguin slipped out of the Alamo with a desperate plea from Lieutenant Colonel William Travis:

❝It will be impossible for us to keep them out much longer. If they overpower us, we fall a sacrifice at the shrine of our country. . . . Give me help, oh my Country!❞

The Alamo was first a mission, then a fort. Today the Lone Star flag flies over the restored building in memory of those who fought for Texas independence.

Santa Anna's magnetic personality led him to power in Mexico 11 times as president-dictator in the 1800s. In fact, he actually fought for the Spanish when Mexicans first struggled for independence in 1810. In 1821 he switched sides to join Agustín de Iturbide, who won independence for Mexico and declared himself emperor. Santa Anna expected favors that were not forthcoming, so he in turn drove Iturbide from power. He seized control of the government in 1834 and abolished the federal constitution, but lost his power when Texas declared independence. He regained the presidency from 1841 to 1844 but then fled to Jamaica when liberal forces rebelled. He became president again in 1853 but was overthrown and exiled two years later. Santa Anna died in poverty in 1876.

No help came. On March 6 Santa Anna's troops captured the Alamo, killing its more than 180 defenders. Among the dead was Davy Crockett, a former congressman from Tennessee. A few women and children survived the terrible ordeal.

Santa Anna ordered 18-year-old Susannah Dickerson, an Alamo survivor whose husband had just been slain, to ride out and spread word of the Texans' defeat. He hoped that news of the bloodshed at the Alamo would stop further rebellion. Instead, "Remember the Alamo!" became a rallying cry that inspired Texans to fight on.

⟲ Point of View
Why did Texans declare their independence?

In 1836, in a town called Washington-on-the-Brazos, Texans wrote a declaration of independence. In their view, they were not declaring war on Mexico, but on Santa Anna's government.

❝Now, the good people of Texas . . . do solemnly declare:

1st. That they have taken up arms in defense of their Rights and Liberties, . . . and in defense of the . . . Constitution of Mexico.

2nd. That Texas is no longer, morally or civilly, bound by the compact of Union; yet . . . they [Texans] offer their support and assistance to such of the Mexicans . . . as will take up arms against their military despotism [Santa Anna's tyranny].

3rd. That they do not acknowledge that the present authorities of [Mexico] have the right to govern . . . Texas.

4th. That they will not cease to carry on war against the . . . authorities whilst their troops are within . . . Texas.

5th. That they hold it be their right . . . to establish an independent Government; but they will continue faithful to the Mexican Government so long as that nation is governed by the Constitution.❞

Santa Anna viewed the rebellion differently. In a speech to Mexican troops, he claimed that American settlers had planned all along to fill Texas with Americans and then take it away from Mexico:

❝Forgetting what they owe to the supreme government of the nation which so generously admitted them to its bosom, gave them fertile lands to cultivate, and allowed them all the means to live in comfort and abundance—they have risen . . . , under the pretense of sustaining a system [supporting the old government] which an immense majority of Mexicans have asked to have changed, thus concealing their criminal purpose of dismembering [tearing apart] the . . . Republic [Mexico].❞

It was too late for either side to listen to the other, however. The day the Texans finished writing their Declaration of Independence was the same day Travis wrote his plea for help. By the time the delegates received the message, Travis and the others were dead. ⟲

Independence

Santa Anna's troops marched across Texas, burning towns as they went. After his victory at Goliad, Santa Anna ordered all prisoners shot. The Texas rallying cry became, "Remember the Alamo! Remember Goliad!"

Sam Houston had a clever idea. He let everyone think that he and his troops were retreating. Santa Anna followed Houston

Checking Understanding

1. What became rallying cries for Texans and why? ("Remember the Alamo," to gain revenge for killing of Alamo's defenders; "Remember Goliad," because Santa Anna ordered all prisoners killed.)

Stimulating Critical Thinking

2. How might the United States have been affected if Texas had remained part of Mexico? (Students might note importance of Texas oil, beef, and cotton to our country's economy.)

Teaching the
⟲ Point of View

⟲ Ask students to identify statements indicating the declaration writers were opposed to Santa Anna, not the Mexican constitution. (1st, in defense of constitution; 2nd, offer support against Santa Anna; 5th, continue faithful to Mexican government.) Ask how Santa Anna appealed to his troops' emotions. (He made Americans seem ungrateful, hinted that they were plotting to destroy Mexico.)

★★★
Vital Links

💿 **Battle of the Alamo (Picture) Unit 3, Side 1, Search 41690**

💿 See also Unit 3 Explore CD-ROM location 273.

Gifted Students

A strength of gifted students is the ability to recognize the influence of point of view on the way an event is described. You can help your gifted students hone this critical-thinking skill by having them read a book or see a film about the Texas Revolution. Ask them to analyze the point of view of the book or film.

Is it pro-American or pro-Mexican? Are characters considered good or bad on the basis of their loyalties? How might the story differ if it were presented from a different point of view? Encourage students to write critical analyses. Conclude by helping them recognize that stories can be colored by the viewpoint of the writer.

Teaching the Reading Maps

To help students see why Texans lost the Alamo and Goliad but won San Jacinto, have them note that the first two were closer to Mexico and therefore less defendable. **Answers to Reading Maps: 1.** Northeast to San Antonio; east through San Felipe. 2. San Jacinto.

Closing the Section

Wrap-Up Activity

A Sam Houston Speech

Have students pretend they are Sam Houston writing his inaugural address as President of Texas. The speech should review what led to the war, express pride in victory and disappointment at not being annexed, and recognize feelings of Mexicans living in an independent Texas.

Section Review Answers

1. Definition: *annex* (384)

2. To grow cotton.

3. To protect land against Indians and illegal immigrants. Later, Mexico feared settlers would seize Texas.

4. Feared it would lead to war; northerners did not want another slave state.

5. Some events: the Alamo, Santa Anna's defeat, and problems facing the Mexican Congress.

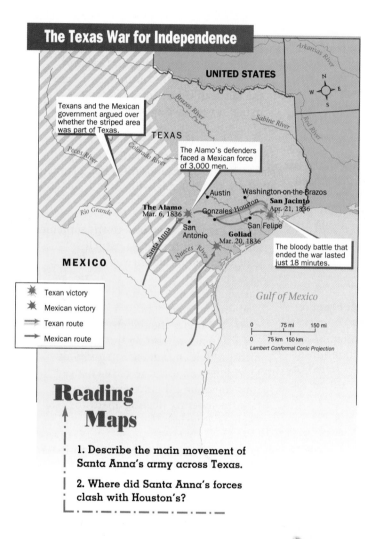

The Texas War for Independence

Texans and the Mexican government argued over whether the striped area was part of Texas.

The Alamo's defenders faced a Mexican force of 3,000 men.

UNITED STATES

TEXAS

Austin • Washington-on-the-Brazos
The Alamo • San Jacinto
Mar. 6, 1836 • Gonzales Houston • Apr. 21, 1836
San • San Felipe
Antonio • Goliad
Mar. 20, 1836

MEXICO

The bloody battle that ended the war lasted just 18 minutes.

Gulf of Mexico

✹ Texan victory
✳ Mexican victory
→ Texan route
→ Mexican route

0   75 mi   150 mi
0   75 km 150 km
Lambert Conformal Conic Projection

Reading Maps

1. Describe the main movement of Santa Anna's army across Texas.

2. Where did Santa Anna's forces clash with Houston's?

Lone Star Republic

Meanwhile, Texans ratified a constitution and elected Sam Houston President. Because most Texans had come from the South, their constitution made slavery legal. Texans expected the United States to recognize Texas as an independent nation, then **annex** it, which means to take territory and add it on to a country.

Southerners welcomed the idea of annexation. It would mean another slave state in the Union. Northerners opposed it for the same reason. Many people on both sides feared that annexation would lead to war with Mexico. As a result, Congress recognized Texas as a nation but did not annex it.

Texas—also known as the Lone Star Republic because of the single star on its flag—was independent for nearly ten years. In that time the Texas question remained a controversial issue in United States politics.

deep into Texas. On April 21, 1836, Houston's forces turned suddenly and trapped Santa Anna's troops at the San Jacinto River. To gain his freedom, Santa Anna ordered all his armies to leave Texas immediately. The Texans released him several months later.

The Mexican Congress was furious with Santa Anna. They refused to recognize that Texans had won. Other urgent problems, however, kept them from sending a new army to retake Texas.

2. Section Review

1. Define **annex**.

2. Explain why Americans settled in Texas.

3. Why did Mexico encourage Americans at first, then ban American immigration?

4. Why did the United States government decide against annexing Texas in 1836?

5. **Critical Thinking** Choose three events and explain how each one helped lead to Texas's independence.

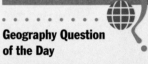

3. Trails West

Reading Guide

Section Focus How Americans began to settle the Far West

1. What drew American settlers to California and Oregon?
2. What was life like on the Oregon Trail?
3. Why did the Mormons go west?
4. What did Indians and Mexicans think of the rush of settlers?

While Texans were fighting for independence, other Americans were looking for lands to settle even farther west. They eagerly listened to the stories told by explorers, trappers, and traders.

Early reports had been discouraging. In the 1820s Major Stephen Long had explored the plains from the Mississippi River to the Rockies. Because he saw few trees and very little water, he made the mistake of thinking that the plains could never become good farmland. He called a large area that is now part of Kansas and Colorado the "Great American Desert."

More appealing were the stories that trappers and traders told of the Far West. Although California and Oregon Country were not part of the United States, by the 1830s Americans were eyeing them with great interest.

Huge cattle ranches sprawled across Mexican California. Cowboys called *vaqueros*—like those racing down this dusty road—were expert riders.

1820–1850 Chapter 14 ● **385**

A Menu for the Oregon Trail

To help students understand the rigorous life on the trail, have them plan a weekly menu for a family moving to Oregon. You may wish to have the class brainstorm the types of food people could carry or find, and the meals they could prepare on the trail.

Vital Links

"Cielito Lindo" (Song)
Unit 2, Side 1, Search
41048, Play to 43504

See also Unit 2 Explore
CD-ROM location 272.

See the Study Guide activity in **Chapter Resources Binder**, p. 107.

✳ **History Footnote**

Chief Winnemucca, a Paiute, led one of Frémont's expeditions over the Sierra Nevada into California. There he served as an army scout for Frémont during the war with Mexico. When Chief Winnemucca returned to his people's homeland in the Great Basin in what is now western Nevada, he convinced 30 Paiute families to go with him to California, where he believed they would have a better life. The families worked as ranch hands and maids in California, but they grew homesick, and Chief Winnemucca led them back to their homeland. His granddaughter, Sarah, later became a spokesperson for Indian rights.

California

As you read in Chapter 1, California was home to many Indian tribes. The first Europeans to arrive were the Spanish. Between 1769 and 1823 Spanish missionaries established a chain of 21 missions along the California coast from San Diego to Sonoma, north of San Francisco.

When Mexico became independent, California was part of the new nation. Communication was slow, though, between the faraway government in Mexico City and the small population of *Californios,* the descendants of the Spanish settlers. Over time, Californios began to think of themselves as separate from Mexico.

The first Americans to reach California came by sea. In the 1820s they sailed along the coast buying cow hides to be used for making shoes and animal fat for candles.

The California Trail

In 1833 fur trader Benjamin Bonneville hired mountain man Joseph Reddeford Walker to find a practical overland route to California. With 40 men Joe Walker left the Green River in the Rocky Mountains, crossed the Great Basin, and climbed to the crest of the Sierra Nevada. Walker's route into California became known as the California Trail.

Californians greeted Walker and his party warmly. Mexican cattle ranchers entertained Walker's party with barbecues and displays of roping and riding.

Like Texas, California was sparsely settled. Mexican authorities in California offered Walker land if he would bring in reliable settlers. Walker turned down the offer, but six of his men stayed in California.

Back in the United States, Walker told about the rich soil, warm sun, and good times to be found in California. One of his men, Zenas Leonard, expressed the same eagerness as other expansionists:

"Our government . . . should assert her claim by taking possession of the whole territory as soon as possible—for we have good reason to suppose that the territory west of the mountain [Rockies] will some day be equally as important to [the] nation as that on the east."

The Oregon Trail

The California Trail branched off from an earlier route that fur traders and trappers had made by following Indian trails west. Later known as the Oregon Trail, that route stretched from Independence, Missouri, west across 2,000 miles (3,219 km) of prairies, mountains, and deserts.

The Oregon Trail ended in Oregon Country. (See the map on page 387.) In 1818 the United States and England had agreed to occupy the region jointly. At that time, the only British and American citizens in the area were a few fur traders.

Then Christian missionaries became interested in Oregon. In 1836 Marcus and Narcissa Whitman started west on the Oregon Trail with Eliza and Henry Spalding. Marcus had already scouted the trail. Now, the Whitmans wanted to prove that women—indeed, entire families with their wagons—could travel to Oregon.

The Whitmans' main goal was to convert the Cayuse Indians to Christianity, so they built a mission in eastern Oregon. They are best remembered, though, because their glowing reports of Oregon's climate and soil attracted settlers by the thousands.

What started as a trickle became a flood. By 1840 only 13 people had followed the Whitmans to Oregon. In spring 1843 almost 1,000 people left Missouri and headed west.

Frémont's surveys In 1842, to encourage even more Americans to go west, the United States government sent John C. Frémont to survey the Oregon Trail. Frémont

Connections to Economics

One of the factors that led to the great migration westward was the economic panic of 1837 and the severe depression that resulted. The panic was in part a result of Andrew Jackson's financial policies. In 1832, Jackson issued a "Specie Circular" forbidding the Treasury to accept anything but gold and silver as payment for public lands (see page 366). Then he and the Congress decided to give surplus Treasury funds to the states. These policies had their effect during the Van Buren presidency: bank failures, factory closings, and thousands of people thrown out of work. Many of these people decided to start a new life out west.

Trails to the West

Reading Maps

Select one trail. Describe landforms you would expect to meet as you traveled westward on that trail. Refer to the map on pages R4–R5 for additional information.

Checking Understanding

1. **Why did the *Californios* think of themselves as separate from Mexico?** (Communication with the distant government in Mexico City was very slow.)

2. **What were the Whitmans' goals?** (To convert Cayuse Indians to Christianity and prove that women and families could move to Oregon.)

Stimulating Critical Thinking

3. **Why did the number of people moving to Oregon increase so rapidly in 1843?** (Students might attribute the growth to the glowing reports by Frémont and the Whitmans, Frémont's maps, and the urge to fulfill expansionist dreams.)

Teaching the
↑ **Reading Maps**

Before students answer the questions, review types of landforms (plains, hills, mountains, plateaus, etc.). **Answer to Reading Maps:** Answers will vary, depending upon the route chosen. The Oregon Trail, for instance, would pass through the Great Plains, Black Hills, Rocky Mountains, Columbia Plateau, and Cascade Range.

See **Using Historical Documents**, pp. 76–80, for an activity on Frémont's map of the Oregon Trail.

✠ **Connections to Science**

Cholera is an infectious disease caused by bacteria that attack the intestines and cause extreme dehydration and eventually shock and death. To prevent the disease from spreading, persons with the disease must be isolated, and strict sanitary measures must be followed—water and cooking utensils must be sterilized, food carefully cooked, and hands washed frequently. These steps were, of course, difficult on the trails west, and cholera epidemics were common during the peak years when many thousands of emigrants crowded the trails. Today people traveling to areas where cholera might be a problem can receive a vaccine that gives them partial protection.

Hands-On *HISTORY*

┌ - - - - - - →

Making decisions on the trail Thousands of pioneers made the westward journey in sturdy covered wagons called *prairie schooners*. A family might cram 2,000 pounds of possessions into their 4-foot by 12-foot wagon. Not everything survived the journey, however. When the trail became too rough, people often had to abandon furniture and other items.

└ - - - → **Activity**

❶ With a partner, imagine you are on the Oregon Trail in 1850. Your possessions include a rifle, ammunition, bedding, hatchet, flour, iron stove, tin dishes, clothing, washbowl, dried beef, hoe, coffee, violin, plow, shovel, clock, china dishes, chest of drawers, coffeepot, and rocking chair. Write each item on an index card or slip of paper.

❷ In addition, on each of six cards write a hazard you might meet on the trail. For example: "You come to the flooded Platte River. Lighten your load before crossing."

❸ Take turns: One person draws a hazard card and reads it aloud. The other person chooses two items to throw out.

❹ When you have finished, look at the items that remain. Compare your results with those of other teams. What team made the best choices? Explain.

followed up the first survey with two other trips, one of them with Joe Walker as guide.

The government published the reports Frémont wrote with his wife, Jessie, and a detailed map of the trail. The map showed river crossings, pastures, and hazards. It was printed in seven large sections that could be read easily, even in bouncing wagons.

Life on the Trail

Thanks in part to Frémont's work, hopeful immigrants gathered in Independence, Missouri, each spring, bound for Oregon and California. They organized into wagon trains—lines of wagons traveling together. Each train chose a captain—often a former mountain man—who was expected to know the route and make key decisions.

Life on the trail quickly fell into a routine. Everyone had to be up and about before sunrise. Women and girls prepared breakfast. Men and boys yoked the oxen. As the sun rose, the wagon train got under way. By evening on a good day, the train might have traveled 15 miles (24 km).

Timing was vital, however. Wagon trains had to leave Independence by May to get across the mountains before winter. Travelers caught in the Rockies or Sierra Nevada when snow fell faced disaster. In 1846 a group of 87 people bound for California—the Donner party—was trapped by early winter storms in the Sierra. Only 45 of them survived starvation and the freezing snows.

Snow was just one danger. Wagons broke down, and horses and oxen died. Travelers also faced snakebites, stampedes, raging rivers, and grassland fires. They killed each other in robberies and arguments.

Still, most deaths were caused by disease, especially cholera. In 1852 Ezra Meeker met

Connections to Literature

In the latter half of the 1800s, the exploits of people on the trails west were recounted in sensational and melodramatic dime novels. Beadle and Adams published E. L. Wheeler's popular series of tales about Deadwood Dick. Out of the dime-novel tradition grew the western. The most popular writer of westerns was Zane Grey, who wrote more than 50 best-selling novels, the sales of which totaled more than 40 million copies. Grey wrote his first novel in 1904. His enormously popular *Riders of the Purple Sage,* considered by some critics to be the best western ever written, shows authentic details about life in the West.

11 wagons returning east, all driven by women. Cholera had killed every man in the wagon train. That same year a woman pioneer noted in her diary that she had seen 21 freshly dug graves in 18 miles.

The mighty highway In spite of danger and death, the Oregon Trail became a mighty highway, in some places a mile wide where wagons moved along side by side. Because so many horses, oxen, and other livestock traveled with the trains, simply finding grass to feed the animals was a major chore. Pierre de Smet, a Catholic missionary, described the situation in 1851:

❝ This noble highway . . . is as smooth as a barn floor swept by the winds, and not a blade of grass can shoot up on it on account of continued passing.❞

The lead wagons of one train were sometimes only a few yards behind the last wagons of the train in front of them. Imagine what it must have been like to be part of a procession such as the one James Wilkins described in his diary on June 13, 1850:

❝ [I] find many companies continually in sight. In fact it is one continued stream. As far as we can see, both in front and near the horizon is dotted with white wagon covers of emigrants, like a string of beads.❞

Four days after Wilkins wrote these words, 6,034 people passed Fort Laramie, Wyoming, an all-time record for one day on the Oregon Trail. Between 1840 and 1860 more than 250,000 people trooped over the trail. In some places their wagon wheels carved deep ruts in the earth that can still be seen today.

The Mormons

Oregon and California were not the only destinations of the overland trails. Members of the Church of Jesus Christ of Latter-day Saints, more commonly known as Mormons, made their way to Utah.

Joseph Smith founded the church in New York in the 1820s. However, some of the Mormons' neighbors thought their beliefs were dangerously different. For example,

In this painting, westward-bound pioneers are seeking the advice of an experienced mountain man. The earliest immigrants knew little about the geography of the land that lay ahead of them after they left Missouri. Often all they knew was that they were heading for the setting sun.

Discussion

Checking Understanding

1. What dangers did people face on the trails? (Early winter, broken wagons, livestock dying, snake bites, stampedes, raging rivers, grassland fires, disease.)

2. Why did the Oregon Trail become known as the Mighty Highway? (Wagon trains, sometimes a mile wide, came one right behind the other.)

Stimulating Critical Thinking

3. If you had lived in the 1840s, why might you have decided to travel west on one of the emigrant trails? (Answers will vary but may include tales of fertile land, Frémont's maps, hard times at home, religious persecution of Mormons.)

For women's accounts of life on the trail, see **American Readings,** pp. 55–56.

✳ **History Footnote**

Although movies and literature have made much of Indian attacks on the trails west, probably no more than a thousand people were killed in clashes between Indians and emigrants. Many Indians were friendly, trading with caravans and acting as guides. There are monuments on the trails to slain emigrants, but none to slain Indians, who were sometimes shot for target practice.

Mormons at first shared all property, and some Mormons believed that a man could have more than one wife.

Smith and his followers moved several times to find a place where they could practice their religion in peace. They founded Nauvoo, Illinois, to be a model Mormon community. Instead, in 1844 mobs angered by Mormon beliefs killed Joseph Smith and threatened other Mormons.

After Smith's death, Brigham Young became head of the church. He and other leaders studied Frémont's report on the West, then chose an isolated valley near the Great Salt Lake to be the Mormons' next home.

Making the desert bloom Moving large numbers of people from Illinois to Utah was a challenge. Some Mormons came from even farther away—Germany, England, and Scandinavia. Following a route that paralleled the Oregon Trail, the first 148 settlers arrived at Salt Lake in July 1847. Within ten years their number had swelled to more than 20,000.

After a year of near-starvation, the colony started to prosper. Thanks to hard work and a well-planned irrigation system, green fields sprouted out of the arid landscape.

Indians in the Far West

What about the people who already occupied the Far West? Spaniards and their Mexican descendants had been there for more than 100 years. Indians had lived in

In the 1850s these Mormon converts from Europe walked 1,300 miles (2,092 km) from Iowa to Utah, pulling their belongings in hand carts.

In her attempts to help her people, Sarah Winnemucca became famous in her day. Newspapers carried stories and pictures of "Princess Winnemucca," and she and her father visited Washington, D.C., in 1880, where they met with President Hayes and Secretary of the Interior Carl Schurz. Sarah gave a series of lectures about the Paiutes throughout the East. She told her audiences that the Paiutes did not want charity but wanted a place where they could live in peace. Sarah wrote about her life and her people in *Life Among the Paiutes,* which was published in 1884. She died of tuberculosis in 1891.

Sarah Winnemucca spoke five languages, including Spanish and English. She became a valued interpreter, scout, and teacher, and spoke out for the rights of the Paiute people.

the region for many centuries. What did they make of the newcomers?

Some Indians were alarmed. Sarah Winnemucca, a member of the Paiute tribe, described what happened when the first wagon train came into Nevada in the late 1840s.

❝What a fright we all got one morning to hear that white people were coming. Our mothers buried me and my cousin. They placed sage bushes over our faces to keep the sun from burning them and there we were left all day. They told us if we heard any noises not to cry out, for if we did the white people would surely kill us and eat us.❞

Still, many Indians found it in their interest to trade with settlers. In addition, some Indians earned money by helping wagon trains. For example, members of the Kansa tribe ferried wagons across the Platte River for a fee.

However, misunderstandings occurred, and conflicts broke out. The Whitmans' mission and school among the Cayuse Indians was the site of the first major violence between Indians and American settlers in the Far West.

The Cayuses had welcomed the mission at first. Then Cayuse children caught measles from a white visitor. The disease spread, killing half the tribe. The grieving survivors attacked the mission, killing the Whitmans and ten others. In return, settlers attacked Indians, even some who had had nothing to do with the raid. Indians and settlers in the West began to distrust one another.

Americans in California

By the end of 1845 roughly 800 Americans had settled among the 7,500 Mexicans and 72,000 Indians in California. At first, Mexican Californians welcomed the Americans.

However, when John C. Frémont's third expedition reached California in 1845, his party of 60 or so well-armed men worried the Mexican authorities. Having heard how Texas had slipped from Mexico's grasp, they ordered Frémont to leave California.

The next year some Californios met to discuss how to make the area strong and prosperous. One suggested an alliance with the leading naval power, Britain. Another favored France. Then voices spoke up for joining the United States. "With the United States," said one, "California will grow strong and flourish." Meanwhile, the idea that California's future lay with the United States was growing among American expansionists, too.

⭐ 3. Section Review

1. How did Americans first became interested in settling in California? In Oregon?
2. Describe three dangerous situations that could arise on the Oregon Trail.
3. Why did the Mormons settle in Utah?
4. Critical Thinking Imagine that you were a *Californio* at the 1846 meeting about California's future. What is one argument you might have heard against joining the United States?

Closing the Section

Wrap-Up Activity

Making a Time Line
To reinforce understanding of events surrounding the great emigration to the Far West, have small groups make time lines. On their time lines they should note the people and events mentioned in the section, beginning with Joe Walker in 1833 and concluding with Frémont in California.

Section Review
Answers

1. California: tales of traders and trappers. Oregon: Frémont's reports and maps, the Whitmans' successful trip.
2. Answers may include getting stuck in the mountains during winter, stampedes, disease, and grassland fires.
3. They were forced out of other communities by people who opposed their religious beliefs.
4. Answers might include the idea that the *Californios* wanted independence or feared being overwhelmed by Americans, as happened in Texas.

392

On the other hand, he was not writing for the public, so might be more likely to tell the truth.

3. (a) Similarities: Carson and Godey crept up and fired on Indians. Differences: Frémont saying they gave a war shout vs. Preuss saying they did not; Frémont saying they charged fearlessly vs. no mention of this by Preuss; Frémont not saying that Carson shot

an Indian in the back vs. Preuss saying he did. (b) Encyclopedias, Carson biographies, historians' descriptions, accounts by Carson.

For further application, have students do the Applying Skills activity in the Chapter Survey (p. 400).

If students need to review the skill, use the Skills Development transparency and activity in the **Chapter Resources Binder,** pp. 111–112.

Introducing the Skill Lab

Discuss why it is important not to simply accept a source at face value without first questioning its qualifications. Before students examine sources A and B, have them analyze the Carson biography excerpt, keeping the Skill Tips in mind. (Such a glowing description is a sign of possible exaggeration. A biographer might tend to portray Carson in an overly positive way to enhance the legend.)

Skill Lab
Answers

1. (a) Probably from Carson and/or Godey. (b) Since Frémont and Preuss did not actually witness the event, and because Carson and/or Godey might not have related it accurately, their accounts may not be entirely accurate.

2. (a) Frémont believed in Manifest Destiny at the expense of Indians and so might be biased in favor of Carson and Godey. Also, the expedition reports might be slanted because they were written for government officials and the public. They would not be likely to depict a hero like Carson as cowardly or sneaky. (b) As a foreigner, Preuss might be less inclined to approve of attacks on Indians, so might be biased against Carson and Godey.

(Answers continued in top margin)

Skill Lab

Thinking Critically
Determining Credibility

"[He] is one of the most extraordinary men of the present era. His fame . . . is far surpassed by . . . personal traits of courage, coolness, fidelity [loyalty], kindness, honor, and friendship." So ran one biography of Kit Carson, whose widely reported adventures made him a larger-than-life hero.

Question to Investigate

Was Kit Carson a brave man or a coward?

Procedure

Read these two accounts of an event that occurred during one of John Frémont's expeditions, when Carson and another man chased Indians who had stolen horses. To get at the truth, try to determine the **credibility,** or believability, of each source.

❶ Consider how the writer got the information.
a. How did Frémont and Preuss probably learn of the encounter with the Indians?
b. What effect might the source of information have on the accuracy of their accounts?

❷ Consider the writer's point of view and purpose.
a. Recall what you know about Frémont. How might his point of view and purpose affect his accuracy?
b. Preuss was a foreign visitor who kept a diary. How might these factors affect his accuracy?

❸ Compare the sources.
a. List similarities and differences in the accounts.
b. Suggest where you might find more information in order to answer the Question to Investigate.

Skill Tips

When you read a source, ask yourself:
● How did the writer get his or her information?
● What else do I know about the writer, such as point of view and purpose for writing?
● Is there any reason to think the writer might exaggerate, leave out important facts, or otherwise fail to tell the truth?
● What other sources might I compare with this one?

Sources to Use

A "[Kit Carson and Alex Godey] . . . proceeded quietly and had got within thirty or forty yards of their object, when a movement among the horses discovered them to the Indians; giving the war shout, they [Carson and Godey] instantly charged into the camp, regardless of the number [of Indians] which the four lodges would imply. The Indians received them with a flight of arrows . . . ; our men fired their rifles upon a steady aim and rushed in. Two Indians were stretched on the ground, fatally pierced with bullets. . . ."

From *Report of the Exploring Expedition to the Rocky Mountains* by John C. Frémont (University Microfilms, 1966)

B "Yesterday we stopped here to give Godey and Kit a chance to pursue the horsethieves. . . . Are these whites not much worse than the Indians? . . . These two heroes . . . shot the Indians [by] creeping up on them from behind. . . . The Indians are braver in a similar situation. Before they shoot, they raise a yelling war whoop. Kit and Alex sneaked, like cats, as close as possible. Kit shot an Indian in the back."

From *Exploring with Frémont* by Charles Preuss (University of Oklahoma Press, 1958). Preuss was the German map maker who accompanied Frémont.

★ Explain why the United States went to war with Mexico.
★ List President Polk's goals in the war.
★ Summarize the treaty of Guadalupe Hidalgo.
★ Describe how the discovery of gold changed California.

Teaching Resources

Take-Home Planner 5, pp. 10–17
Chapter Resources Binder
  Study Guide, p. 108
  Reinforcement
  Skills Development
Geography Extensions, pp. 27–28
American Readings
Using Historical Documents
Transparency Activities
Chapter and Unit Tests, pp. 91–94

Introducing the Section

Warm-Up Activity

Discussing Manifest Destiny

To prepare for studying effects of Manifest Destiny, organize a panel discussion. First divide the class into small groups. Half the groups will support Manifest Destiny; the other half will oppose it. Have the groups predict benefits of Manifest Destiny for the nation, its effect on people already living in the West, and its effect on U.S. foreign policy. Have a member of each group serve on the discussion panel. Panel members should take turns presenting ideas and responding to other members.

4. Manifest Destiny Triumphs

Reading Guide

Section Focus Final steps to achieving Manifest Destiny

1. Why did the United States go to war with Mexico?
2. What were President Polk's goals in the war?
3. What is the Treaty of Guadalupe Hidalgo?
4. How did the discovery of gold change California?

In the mid-1840s Americans were scattered throughout the Far West and in Texas. As more and more Americans made the West their home, the idea grew that the area should belong to the United States.

By 1844 Manifest Destiny was becoming a powerful force in American politics. One delegate to a New Jersey political convention pledged, "We will give him [any young American] Oregon for his summer shade and the region of Texas as his winter pasture."

Annexing Texas and Oregon

The Democrats' candidate for President in 1844 was James K. Polk of Tennessee. Polk was a strong believer in Manifest Destiny.

President John Tyler, a Whig, also supported the idea of Manifest Destiny and planned to annex Texas if he won re-election. However, the majority of Whigs were strongly antislavery and opposed admitting

This painting became famous in the 1800s because it expressed the feelings of many Americans about Manifest Destiny. In it the spirit of Manifest Destiny is leading settlers west, stringing telegraph wires as she goes. How does the artist show his biases about American settlement of the West?

Geography Question of the Day

To help students understand why it would be easy for the Americans to gain the land west of the Appalachians, have them list the countries that owned Louisiana (France), Texas and California (Mexico), and Oregon (Britain shared it). Have them estimate the distance of these territories from the countries that owned them. Ask them to identify what factors other than distance may have made the territories difficult to defend.

1820–1850 Chapter 14 • **393**

Reporting on the War

To explore arguments for and against declaring war on Mexico, have pairs imagine that they are American army officers who have just heard of the attack in April 1846. Assign half the pairs to write a report to the President advising that the United States declare war. The other pairs will write a letter advising against war. The reports should include evidence and show historical imagination—the ability to imagine what an officer of that period might think. After the reports are finished, have the class share them and decide which arguments are most effective.

See the Study Guide activity in **Chapter Resources Binder**, p. 108.

✳ History Footnote

Many Mexicans, including President José Joaquín Herrera, had practical reasons for wanting to avoid war with the United States. Mexican officials had warned the United States that if it annexed Texas, Mexico would have to declare war. But when Texas was annexed, many people in Mexico argued for a negotiated settlement. They saw a war with the United States as potentially disastrous.

The morale of the troops was low because the treasury had run out of money to pay them. While Mexico had a larger army, the United States had a population twice the size of Mexico's, and could easily recruit more soldiers. The United States also had a navy and many cannon factories. Mexico had no navy and only a few cannon factories.

Texas as a slave state. Rather than nominate Tyler for a second term, the Whigs chose Henry Clay as their candidate.

Polk's victory in the election showed that the voters were in an expansionist mood. Congress quickly annexed Texas, which became a state in December 1845.

"Fifty-four Forty or Fight!" Once in office, Polk turned his attention to Oregon. In the past the United States had offered to divide Oregon Country with Britain at the 49th parallel of latitude.

Britain had refused. Now, however, Polk and the Democrats were demanding all of Oregon—54° 40´ north latitude. They rallied behind the slogan, "Fifty-four Forty or Fight!"

In 1846 the British said they were ready to divide Oregon at the 49th parallel. They also pledged to stay out of disputes between the United States and Mexico. Polk put the question to the Senate, which accepted the 49th parallel as the Oregon boundary.

War with Mexico

Meanwhile, Mexican officials were enraged over the annexation of Texas. They became even angrier when the United States claimed the Rio Grande as its boundary with Mexico. Mexicans placed the Texas boundary at the Nueces River, north of the Rio Grande.

Hostilities begin In late April 1846, Mexican troops fired at an American patrol along the Rio Grande, killing or wounding 16 soldiers. Mexico claimed that the patrol was in its territory. Polk, however, charged:

❝Mexico has passed the boundary of the United States, has invaded our territory and shed American blood upon the American soil.❞

He asked Congress to declare war.

Some Americans were against the war. For example, Abraham Lincoln, then a congressman from Illinois, believed the American soldiers had actually been on Mexican soil. An American colonel in Texas privately agreed. He wrote in his diary:

❝It looks as if the government sent a small force on purpose to bring on a war, so as to have a pretext [excuse] for taking California and as much of this country as it chooses. . . . My heart is not in this business.❞

Congress voted, however, eagerly for war: 40 votes to 2 in the Senate and 173 to 14 in the House. On May 12, 1846, the United States declared war on Mexico.

The first campaign Polk's first goal was to drive the Mexicans away from the Rio Grande. General Zachary Taylor led troops into northern Mexico and captured the fort at Monterrey in September.

In February 1847 General Santa Anna attacked Taylor at Buena Vista in a mountain pass near Monterrey. For two days more than 15,000 Mexicans tried to dislodge a smaller American army from the rocky heights. Instead, Taylor forced Santa Anna to retreat, which ended the fighting in northern Mexico.

New Mexico Polk's second goal was to occupy New Mexico and California. New Mexicans had mixed feelings about the United States. Like Texans, they were a long way from Mexico City. Their closest trade ties were north, along the Santa Fe Trail. In August 1846 General Stephen Watts Kearny captured Santa Fe without a shot. Although some New Mexicans opposed him over the next few months, Kearny kept control.

California John C. Frémont was in California when war broke out. Without authority, he encouraged Americans, as well

Zachary Taylor received his first military commission from Thomas Jefferson in 1808. Taylor defended Fort Harrison in the Indiana Territory during the War of 1812 and defeated the Seminole Indians in 1837. He was appointed commander of the second department of the western division of the army in 1841. In contrast to his rival, Winfield Scott, known as "Old Fuss and

Feathers" because of his love of fancy military dress, Zachary Taylor was known by his troops as "Old Rough and Ready" because he dressed in dirty, backwoods clothes. Scott liked strict discipline, while Taylor liked to fraternize with his troops. Both men wanted to be President. Taylor was elected in 1849 but died a little more than a year later. Scott ran in 1852 but was defeated by Franklin Pierce.

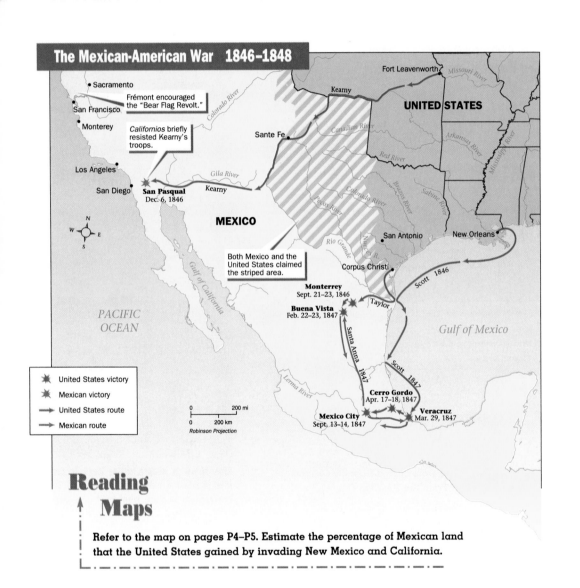

The Mexican-American War 1846–1848

Frémont encouraged the "Bear Flag Revolt."

Californios briefly resisted Kearny's troops.

Both Mexico and the United States claimed the striped area.

San Pasqual
Dec. 6, 1846

Monterrey
Sept. 21–23, 1846

Buena Vista
Feb. 22–23, 1847

Cerro Gordo
Apr. 17–18, 1847

Veracruz
Mar. 29, 1847

Mexico City
Sept. 13–14, 1847

* United States victory
* Mexican victory
→ United States route
→ Mexican route

Reading Maps

Refer to the map on pages P4–P5. Estimate the percentage of Mexican land that the United States gained by invading New Mexico and California.

as some Mexican citizens, to declare independence and establish the Bear Flag Republic.

United States naval vessels arrived in San Francisco and Monterey Bays in July. Bear Flaggers joined the naval forces led by Admiral Robert Stockton, and by August they took Santa Barbara, Los Angeles, and San Diego. While Kearny was in Santa Fe, Americans were gaining control in California.

Like the people of New Mexico, Californians were divided. Some resisted. Others quietly agreed to American rule because they thought it would make California more prosperous.

Kearny arrived in December. Due to a mix-up over their orders, he and Stockton had a dispute over who had the highest authority in California. Frémont sided with Stockton.

Discussion

Checking Understanding

1. What did the slogan "Fifty-four Forty or Fight" mean? (Some Americans wanted all of Oregon up to the 54° 40' north latitude and would go to war with Britain to get it.)

2. How did the war with Mexico begin? (Mexican soldiers fired at an American patrol unit along the Rio Grande, killing or wounding 16 soldiers.)

Stimulating Critical Thinking

3. If you were a Mexican in the 1840s, how might you have reacted to the idea of Manifest Destiny? (Might argue that Mexico rightfully owned lands that had been New Spain. Might criticize the notion that the U.S. should fulfill Columbus's dream, arguing that if any country in the Americas could claim Columbus's legacy, it would be Mexico, since Mexico took over lands from Spain.)

Teaching the Reading Maps

It will help students to answer the questions if you have them research the size of Mexico today, as well as the size of the area covered by present-day California, Utah, Nevada, Arizona, and New Mexico. **Answer to Reading Maps:** More than two-thirds.

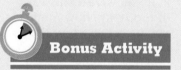

Teaching the
Reading Maps

Have students compare the map of the territories with a political map of the United States today (pages R6–R7), using the rivers on the territorial map as landmarks. **Answers to Reading Maps:** Oregon, Washington, and Idaho were carved from the Oregon Territory. California, Utah, Nevada, Arizona, and New Mexico were carved from the Mexican Cession.

Bonus Activity

Tourist Attractions

To underscore the impact of Mexican culture, have students identify present-day cities in areas that were part of the Texas Annexation and Mexican Cession, such as San Antonio, Santa Fe, San Francisco, San Diego, and Monterey. For each city, assign a small group to identify and describe at least one historical landmark from its Mexican past.

★★★
Vital Links

Mexican-American War (Picture) Unit 3, Side 1, Search 49450

See also Unit 3 Explore location 396.

396

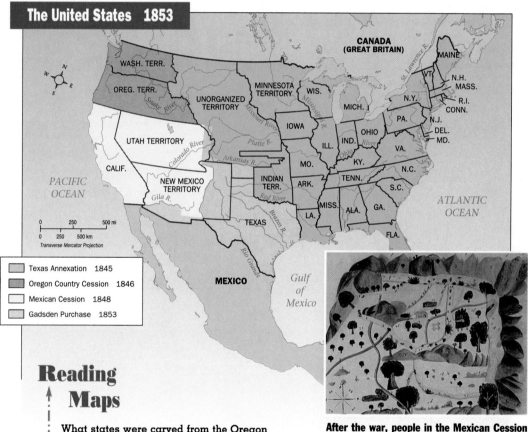

The United States 1853

Texas Annexation 1845
Oregon Country Cession 1846
Mexican Cession 1848
Gadsden Purchase 1853

Reading Maps

What states were carved from the Oregon Territory? From the Mexican Cession?

After the war, people in the Mexican Cession filed illustrated maps with the United States government to show what land they owned.

Even after Kearny won out, Frémont defied him. Kearny had Frémont arrested. A military court convicted Frémont of disobedience and conduct unbecoming an officer. Frémont's military career was over. Still, in the eyes of many, he remained a hero.

The final campaign Polk's final goal was Mexico's surrender. General Winfield Scott landed at Veracruz, where Cortés had landed centuries before. At nearby Cerro Gordo, Scott won a decisive victory. Like Cortés, Scott marched toward Mexico City, which he captured in September 1847.

The Treaty of Guadalupe Hidalgo

The Treaty of Guadalupe Hidalgo, signed in February 1848, marked the final triumph of Manifest Destiny. Mexico had to give up more than 500,000 square miles (1,295,000 square km). In return for this land, known as the Mexican Cession, the United States paid $15 million.

Almost 70,000 Mexicans lived in the Mexican Cession. These people became Americans overnight. Although the treaty guaranteed

396 ● *Chapter 14 1820–1850*

James Gadsden, a Yale graduate, was a businessperson before he joined the army and took part in the War of 1812 and the Seminole Wars. He later served for a number of years as the president of the South Carolina Railroad. In that position, he actively worked to unite small southern railroads and connect them to a transcontinental line. Although his efforts failed, he received support from his friend Jefferson Davis. In 1853, Davis, then the Secretary of War, encouraged the President to appoint Gadsden as Minister to Mexico. In the Senate, many northerners objected to the Gadsden Purchase. They feared that slavery would be introduced to a new territory. The treaty was finally approved despite the opposition.

Checking Understanding

1. What did the Treaty of Guadalupe Hidalgo guarantee? (Mexico would give up 500,000 square miles of territory; in return, U.S. would pay $15 million.)

2. What was the Gadsden Purchase? (For $10 million, James Gadsden purchased from Mexico a strip of land south of the Mexican Cession, on which the U.S. hoped to build a railroad.)

Stimulating Critical Thinking

3. If you had been a Mexican citizen living in the Mexican Cession, why might you have stayed? Why might you have moved to Mexico? (Those who stayed might feel more attached to their land and jobs than to a faraway government. Those who left might resent U.S. for starting war and fear prejudice against their nationality and Catholic religion.)

them citizenship and property rights, some Mexican Americans lost their land. Many, feeling like foreigners in their own homeland, emigrated to Mexico.

Most Mexican Americans remained, hoping to carve out a future in the United States. Today, Mexican traditions of religion, language, and architecture flourish in Mexican Cession lands—now the American Southwest.

The Gadsden Purchase In 1853 the United States acquired still more land from Mexico. James Gadsden, the United States Minister to Mexico, negotiated the $10 million purchase of a strip of land south of the Mexican Cession. The United States wanted to build a railroad, and this land was the only part of the West that was relatively flat.

California Gold Rush

As part of Mexico, California had had a tiny population. With the discovery of gold, however, the world rushed in.

Gold was first discovered on land belonging to John Sutter. A Swiss by birth, Sutter

World Link

"Golden Mountain" The Chinese who came to California to find a fortune in gold called the land *Gam Saan*—"The Golden Mountain." Many Chinese were fleeing hard times. Between 1839 and 1860 China lost two wars to Britain. Meanwhile, a bloody civil war was raging in China. Economic conditions were harsh, too, and overcrowded farmlands made poverty worse.

Most of the Chinese who came were men. Hoping to return with bags of gold, they left their families behind. Like other miners, however, few Chinese actually struck it rich. About half returned to China. When the gold rush was over, however, thousands found other work and made California their home.

Teaching the

World Link

Ask students to recall other groups of immigrants they have read about in earlier chapters and compare reasons for immigrating and experiences in this country.

Word of the California gold rush was greeted in China with great excitement. Young men dreamed of possibilities, not only of being gold miners like the men in this photo, but also farmers and merchants. Often they borrowed money for the trip at high interest rates to be paid back from profits they expected to make in America. Between 1850 and 1900 more than 300,000 Chinese came to the United States.

Closing the Section

Wrap-Up Activity

Mapping the Nation's Growth

To review the immense growth of the United States in the mid-1800s, have students draw a map of the United States in 1853. Ask them to compare it to a map of the nation in 1825 (such as the one on page 330) and estimate by what percent the nation had grown (about 33 percent).

Section Review
Answers

1. Many people were eager to go to war with Mexico so that the U.S. could take California and New Mexico and fulfill its Manifest Destiny.

2. To drive Mexicans away from the Rio Grande, occupy New Mexico and California, and gain Mexico's surrender.

3. The U.S. gained 500,000 square miles, including California, Utah, and New Mexico territories.

4. Answers will vary, but students might note that remaining a part of Mexico would allow them to keep their traditions and customs, while becoming a part of the U.S. might improve the economy.

To check understanding of "Why We Remember," assign Thinking Critically question 3 on student page 400.

---

had come to California in 1839 and built a trading post where Sacramento is today. On January 24, 1848, one of his workers scooped up a handful of sand from the American River. In it were flakes of gold.

The news spread like wildfire. American, French, Hawaiian, Australian, Irish, German, Chinese, Italian, and Mexican prospectors rushed to California. African Americans came, too. Some were slaves, but most were free. By 1852 California had the wealthiest black population of any state.

Among the luckiest of Californians were the Frémonts. They had bought a ranch in California. To their delight, they found gold on their land and became multimillionaires.

In 1849, at the height of the rush, as many as 80,000 gold-seeking "forty-niners" poured in. Although few made fortunes, many stayed to farm or start businesses. A year later, California became the 31st state.

4. Section Review

1. Explain how the idea of Manifest Destiny contributed to war with Mexico.
2. Summarize Polk's goals in the war.
3. What did the United States gain from the Treaty of Guadalupe Hidalgo?
4. **Critical Thinking** List the main points in an argument between two California neighbors in 1846. One wants California to remain part of Mexico. The other favors an American takeover.

Why We Remember

The Westward Movement

When John Frémont and Thomas Hart Benton first met, the idea of the United States reaching to the Pacific seemed a dream. By 1850, that dream had become a reality. Looking back on her husband's role in the settlement of the West, Jessie Frémont wrote, "From the ashes of his campfires have sprung cities."

Between 1845 and 1850 the nation grew in area by about a third. It also became more diverse. The new territories were home to Indians, Mexicans, and a sprinkling of Europeans and Americans. Once gold was discovered in California, treasure seekers from around the world added to the mix of peoples.

As a result, Americans' view of their place in the world began to change. They had long thought of the United States as part of the European world. They had looked to Europe for ideas, technology, and trade. Now the nation shared borders with Latin America and looked across the Pacific toward Asia. For many Americans today, ties with Latin America and Asia are as important as ties with Europe. This change has been, perhaps, the most unexpected result of America's reach westward.

Geography Footnote

The Humboldt Sink that Delos Ashley wrote of so disparagingly was the home of the Paiute Indians, Sarah Winnemucca's people. Their name, Paiute, comes from two words meaning "water this way." They were hunter-gatherers and spent their lives around the Humboldt, Carson, and Walker river sinks in what is now western Nevada. When they visited a sink in early spring they gathered birds' eggs and tender shoots of squaw cabbage and cattail for food. They made baskets, mats, clothing, boats, and shelters called wickiups from the rushes that grew in the marsh. They fished, netted ducks, and hunted squirrels and rabbits. The settlers brought cholera and their horses and cattle stripped the area of growing things and used up the scant water supply, thus changing the Paiutes' way of life forever.

Geography Lab

Basins and Ranges

In the mid-1800s Americans were beginning to travel across the Basin and Range region. Susan Magoffin set out from Missouri with her husband, a Santa Fe trader, in 1847. In New Mexico they trekked through a basin called *Jornada del Muerto*, Spanish for "Dead Man's Journey." In 1849 Delos Ashley crossed Nevada by way of the Humboldt Sink. A sink is a low place where a river flows into a lake. What mental picture of the Basins and Ranges do their travel diaries give you?

Amargosa Valley, Nevada

Developing a Mental Map

Refer to the maps on pages P4–P5, R4–R5, and R6–R7.

1. What mountains border the Basin and Range region?

2. The region includes what states? What major cities?

3. On what points do Ashley and Magoffin agree? In what ways does the photograph confirm their diaries?

4. **Hands-On Geography** As a traveler to the West in 1850, write a letter to someone in the East. Describe the difficulties you faced crossing the Basin and Range region.

Delos Ashley's Diary

Tues., July 17. Very warm—sand roads. Toilsome as hell.

Wednes., July 18. Sand!!! Hot!!! Grass parched & dry.

Thurs., July 19. Camped 10 P.M. No grass (wheugh!!!).

Fri., July 20. 10 o'clock. Hot!!! No halt at noon. Camped 6 o'clock P.M. Grass 3 miles. Spring at slough [a low, muddy area].

Sat., July 21. Stayed at slough.

Sun., July 22. From slough to h barrenness).

Susan Magoffin's Diary

Monday 1st. . . . We are almost at the mouth of the Jornada (the long journey without water) have been traveling slowly the roads being exceedingly heavy, with two or three severe hills; . . . all the teams [were] doubled and were then just able to get over.

Friday 5th. . . . The wind blew high all the evening and the dust considerable. . . . "The dead man's lake," "Laguna del muerto" is some six ms. from where we are camped on the road. Travelers generally stop here and send off their animals to water at this spring quite a long distance too, but tis quite necessary as we shall not find water again till we strike the River [Rio Grande] forty miles ahead.

Monday 8th. . . . Camped on a high bluff about two miles from the water, and sent the stock down to it. . . . I have been bold enough to climb up and down these beautiful and rugged cliffs both yesterday and today, but I shall be more careful hereafter, as it is really dangerous.

Teaching the Geography Lab

To focus on general characteristics of the Basin and Range region, ask students to contrast this region with the farm country of the Midwest.

Developing a Mental Map
Answers

1. Rockies and Sierra Nevada.

2. Nevada; parts of Oregon, Utah, California, Arizona, and New Mexico. Major cities are Phoenix and Salt Lake City.

3. They agree that travel is difficult and there is little water. The area in the photograph looks dry.

4. Letters should show an understanding of the difficulties of finding water and the discomfort caused by sand and winds.

See activity on the Basin and Range region in **Geography Extensions**, pp. 27–28.

• **399**

399

Reviewing Vocabulary

Definitions are found on these pages: *expansionists* (376), *annex* (384).

Reviewing Main Ideas

1. (a) John Frémont led expeditions to survey and map the Oregon Trail and other trails west. (b) Jessie Frémont's reports of her husband's expeditions fired the imaginations of potential settlers. (c) John O'Sullivan wrote an editorial in which he said it was the manifest destiny of the United States to "overspread the continent." (d) Manuel Lisa sent trappers into the Rocky Mountains. (e) William Becknell was the father of the Santa Fe Trail.

2. (a) Southern farmers heard the land in Texas was good for growing cotton. (b) They hoped Americans would defend the area against bandits, horse thieves, and hostile Indians. (c) They were afraid the American settlers would seize Texas.

3. American settlers were upset when the Mexican government passed laws they did not like and combined Texas with another state. Mexicans were upset when Austin urged Texans to form their own government.

4. (a) Easterners were attracted to the rich soil and good climate. (b) The Mormons chose an isolated valley near the Great Salt Lake where they hoped to practice their beliefs without interference.

5. At first Mexicans and Indians welcomed the settlers, but both came to see them as intruders.

6. (a) Mexico was angry that the United States had annexed Texas. (b) Mexican troops fired at an American patrol along the Rio Grande.

(Answers continued in top margin)

400

---

7. In the Treaty of Guadalupe Hidalgo, Mexico ceded more than 500,000 square miles to the United States. The discovery of gold in California attracted as many as 80,000 people.

Thinking Critically

1. Examples might include trappers who went for beavers, Becknell and others who wanted to trade goods, farmers who wanted

good land, Christian missionaries who wanted to convert Indians, and Mormons who wanted to practice their religion freely.

2. Texans saw themselves as defending their rights and liberties, like the Patriots in 1776. The situations differed in that the Texans declared they were rebelling against the leaders of Mexico's government, not against Mexico itself. The War of Independence was

---

Chapter Survey ★

Reviewing Vocabulary

Define the following terms.
1. expansionists
2. annex

Reviewing Main Ideas

1. Describe the role each person played in westward expansion. (a) John C. Frémont (b) Jessie Frémont (c) John O'Sullivan (d) Manuel Lisa (e) William Becknell
2. (a) Why were many southern farmers eager to move to the Mexican state of Texas? (b) Why was Mexico agreeable to American settlement at first? (c) Why did Mexico finally ban American immigration?
3. Texas was once part of a Mexican state. Explain the disagreements that led to its becoming an independent republic.
4. (a) Why were easterners attracted to Oregon and California in the mid-1840s? (b) What was it about Utah that attracted Mormons in the same period?
5. How did the reactions of Indians and Mexicans to American settlers in the Far West change over time?
6. (a) Why was the Mexican government angry at the United States in early 1846? (b) What event triggered war between the two countries?
7. Two events of early 1848 changed the West in major ways. What were those events, and what impact did each have?

Thinking Critically

1. Application Support the following statement with three examples from the chapter: There were as many reasons for going west as there were people who did so.
2. Analysis Only about half a century separated the Texas Revolution from the American Revolution. What evidence is there that Texans of 1836 viewed their

situation as similar to the colonists' in 1776? How did the two situations differ?
3. Why We Remember: Synthesis Imagine a parent who was born in 1805 and a son or daughter who was born in 1833. Each one turned 20 years old in what year? How would each one have described the size of the United States, its boundaries, and its place in the world in those years?

Applying Skills

Credibility In their writings, John Frémont and Charles Preuss presented conflicted portrayals of Kit Carson. Likewise, modern-day writers offer different portrayals of people in the news.
1. Look through newspapers or magazines to find an article that describes a news maker in very positive or very negative terms. Write a short summary of the article.
2. Recalling what you learned about determining credibility on page 392, write a paragraph that tells:
• whether you think the article is a credible source
• why you think as you do
• how you might find information to support your opinion

History Mystery

Great American Desert Answer the History Mystery on page 373. What is a desert? Why would simply calling an area "desert" discourage people from settling there?

Writing in Your History Journal

1. Keys to History (a) The time line on pages 372–373 has six Keys to History. In your journal, explain why it is important to know about

fought for complete separation from Britain.

3. In 1825 the country had doubled in size because of the Louisiana Purchase but still looked toward Europe for culture and other values. By 1853 it had increased in size again, this time by a third, and the population had become more diverse. It spanned to the Pacific and had important ties with Latin America and Asia.

Applying Skills

Answers should reflect an understanding of what *credible* means and of clues to credibility. Answers should also show understanding of the relationship between credibility and the source.

History Mystery

Information on why the region was known *(Answers continued in side margin)*

as the "Great American Desert" is on page 385. Answers may include that since maps were the only thing people had to rely on, they would not have been interested in desert land since they did not see how they could make a living on it.

Writing in Your History Journal

1. (a) Explanations should be similar to the time line notes on teacher pages 372–373. (b) Entries will vary, but should show an understanding of the effects of an event.

2. Answers will vary but should be descriptive of and show an understanding of what is appealing about that state. For example, in Oregon, the climate is mild and the state has abundant forests.

3. Answers will vary, but should show an understanding of the effects of the policy. Those in favor may agree that the United States should span from coast to coast; those who want to halt the policy of Manifest Destiny might argue that the land belongs to other nations.

Reviewing Geography

1. (A) Mormon, (B) Oregon, (C) Old Spanish, (D) Santa Fe, (E) California, (F) Gila River

2. In both cases, the people migrating wanted to start a new life, were seeking religious freedom, or were seeking their fortune.

Alternative Assessment

Teacher's Take-Home Planner 5, p. 13, includes suggestions and scoring rubrics for the Alternative Assessment activity.

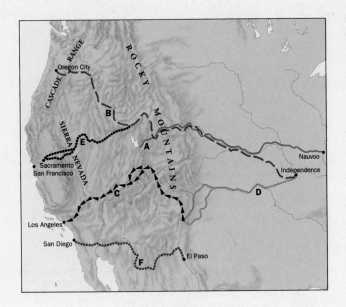

Reviewing Geography

1. Each letter on the map represents a trail to the West. Name each trail.

2. Geographic Thinking Some people have compared the huge westward migration that began in the 1840s with the migration to the English colonies in America during the 1600s and 1700s. How were the two migrations similar?

each one. (b) If you could have been at one event on the time line, which would you choose, and why? Write your response in your journal.

2. John and Jessie Frémont Imagine that it is 1842, and the federal government has hired you to encourage people to move to the Far West. In your journal, write an ad focusing on one present-day state in the Far West. Keep in mind how successful Jessie Frémont's writing was, and make your ad descriptive and appealing.

3. Citizenship Many different people had an influence on the government's policy of Manifest Destiny. Imagine that you are able to go back in time and affect the course of history. Would you try to influence the government to halt or to carry out Manifest Destiny? Explain your reasons.

Alternative Assessment

Planning a western Today, movie westerns are quite different from the ones

your parents and grandparents saw. Today's moviemakers usually try to portray events and people more realistically.

Imagine that you are a movie director. With a partner, write a plan for a short western film. Include a summary of the plot, a descriptive list of characters, brief descriptions for each of the movie's six scenes, and a script for one of the scenes.

Keep these guidelines in mind:
• Characters must be from at least two groups in this chapter, for example, American settlers, Indian trappers, Mexican ranchers, Chinese miners.
• At least one character must be a real person you read about in this chapter.
• The story must include at least one event you read about in this chapter.

Your plan will be evaluated on the following criteria:
• it describes the movie thoroughly
• it shows knowledge of historical people and events and of different points of view
• it is imaginative

15 Americans at Mid-Century
1830–1850

Chapter Planning Guide

Section	Student Text	Teacher's Edition Activities
Opener and Story pp. 402–405	**Keys to History Time Line** **History Mystery** Beginning the Story with **Frederick Douglass**	**Setting the Stage Activity** The Power of Reading, p. 404
1 **Life in the North and the South** pp. 406–413	**Reading Maps** Products of the North and South Mid-1800s, p. 407; Railroads 1850, 1860, p. 410 **Link to Technology** The Telegraph, p. 408 **Geography Lab** Reading Climate Maps, p. 413	**Warm-Up Activity** Differences at a Glance, p. 406 **Geography Question of the Day,** p. 406 **Section Activity** A North-South Dialogue, p. 410 **Bonus Activity** Using Morse Code, p. 408 **Wrap-Up Activity** Writing Want Ads, p. 412
2 **African American Life** pp. 414–418	**Link to Art** Harriet Powers's Bible quilt, p. 415 **Hands-On History** Analyzing how you use space, p. 416 **Link to the Present** Buxton reunions, p. 417 **Link to Literature** *Nightjohn*, pp. 426–427	**Warm-Up Activity** The Importance of Families, p. 414 **Geography Question of the Day,** p. 414 **Section Activity** To Revolt or Not?, p. 416 **Bonus Activity** Letters on Slavery, p. 417 **Wrap-Up Activity** A Persuasive Speech, p. 418
3 **Workers and Immigrants** pp. 419–423	**World Link** The Great Famine in Ireland, p. 421 **Point of View** Who is a true American?, p. 421 **Skill Lab** Identifying Evidence, p. 423	**Warm-Up Activity** Working Conditions, p. 419 **Geography Question of the Day,** p. 419 **Section Activity** A Strike Vote, p. 420 **Bonus Activity** Nativism Then and Now, p. 420 **Wrap-Up Activity** Making a Collage, p. 422
Evaluation	☑ **Section 1 Review,** p. 412 ☑ **Section 2 Review,** p. 418 ☑ **Section 3 Review,** p. 422 ☑ **Chapter Survey,** pp. 424–425 **Alternative Assessment** Planning a time capsule, p. 425	☑ **Answers to Section 1 Review,** p. 412 ☑ **Answers to Section 2 Review,** p. 418 ☑ **Answers to Section 3 Review,** p. 422 ☑ **Answers to Chapter Survey,** pp. 424–425 (Alternative Assessment guidelines are in the Take-Home Planner.)

Teacher's Resource Package

 Chapter Summaries: English and Spanish, pp. 34–35

 Chapter Resources Binder
Study Guide Using Questions to Guide Reading, p. 113
Geography Extensions Reading Climate Maps, pp. 29–30
American Readings A Young Whaler, pp. 57–58; A North Carolina Plantation, p. 59

 Chapter Resources Binder
Study Guide Reading for Details, p. 114
Reinforcement Organizing Information, pp. 117–118
American Readings Picking Cotton, p. 60

 Chapter Resources Binder
Study Guide Using a Graphic Organizer, p. 115
Skills Development Identifying Evidence, pp. 119–120
Using Historical Documents The Manifest of the *Acadian*, May 14, 1847, pp. 81–84

Chapter and Unit Tests Chapter 15 Tests, Forms A and B, pp. 95–98

Take-Home Planner

Introducing the Chapter Activity Creating Parallel Time Lines, p. 20

Chapter In-Depth Activity Exchanging Letters Between North and South, p. 21

Reduced Views
Study Guide, p. 22
Geography Extensions, p. 25
American Readings, p. 24
Unit 5 Answers, pp. 36–44

Reduced Views
Study Guide, p. 22
Reinforcement, p. 23
American Readings, p. 24
Unit 5 Answers, pp. 36–44

Reduced Views
Study Guide, p. 22
Skills Development, p. 23
Using Historical Documents, p. 25
Unit 5 Answers, pp. 36–44

Reduced Views
Chapter Tests, p. 25
Unit 5 Answers, pp. 36–44
Alternative Assessment Guidelines for scoring the Chapter Survey activity, p. 21

Additional Resources

Wall Time Line

Unit 5 Activity

 **Transparency Package**

Transparency 15-1 Chicago in 1856—use with Section 1
Transparency 15-2 Growth of Chicago—use with Section 1
Transparency Activity Book

 SelecTest Testing Software
Chapter 15 Test, Forms A and B

★★★ Vital Links

Videodisc

CD-ROM

Samuel Morse (see TE p. 409)
McCormick reaper (see TE p. 410)
Plantation (see TE p. 411)
Nat Turner (see TE p. 416)
Anti-Irish riot (see TE p. 420)

15

Teaching Resources

Take-Home Planner 5
   Introducing Chapter Activity
   Chapter In-Depth Activity
   Alternative Assessment
Chapter Resources Binder
Geography Extensions
American Readings
Using Historical Documents
Transparency Activities
Wall Time Line Activities
Chapter Summaries
Chapter and Unit Tests
SelecTest Test File
Vital Links CD-ROM/Videodisc

Time Line

Keys to History

Keys to History journal writing activity is on page 424 in the Chapter Survey.

Nat Turner's Revolt Slaves' resistance to slavery sometimes took the form of open revolt. The revolt led by Nat Turner was so bloody that southern states passed stricter slave codes. (p. 417)

McCormick reaper invented Cyrus McCormick revolutionized grain harvesting in the United States by creating a machine that could cut as much grain in a day as three workers could. (p. 410)

Workers strike Faced with longer hours and wage cuts, workers organized unions and went on strike to try to improve their working conditions. (p. 419)

Looking Back Eli Whitney's invention of the cotton gin turned cotton into the South's most important cash crop.

402

Chapter Objectives

★ Compare the economies of the North and South.
★ Describe what life was like for enslaved and free African Americans.
★ Identify the obstacles faced by workers and immigrants.

Chapter Overview
By the mid-1800s, the economy of the Northeast was diverse, with whaling, trade, and mass production of goods. Factory towns grew into cities. In the Midwest, the McCormick reaper turned wheat production into a big business. New cities emerged as centers of water or railroad transportation, linking the Northeast and Midwest. The South's cotton-based economy relied

1830–1850

Chapter 15

Americans at Mid-Century

Sections

Beginning the Story with Frederick Douglass

1. **Life in the North and the South**
2. **African American Life**
3. **Workers and Immigrants**

Keys to History

1831
Nat Turner's Revolt
Painting of execution of Nat Turner

1831
McCormick reaper invented

1835–1836
Workers protest wages and hours in 140 strikes

1830

Looking Back

Whitney invents cotton gin
1793

on slave labor, with little industrialization.

Enslaved African Americans had no rights, and family members were often separated. Despite this, slaves created families that struggled to stay together. They resisted slavery in subtle ways, such as by breaking tools. Some escaped or rebelled. Slave owners, in turn, became more harsh. Even free black Americans were denied the rights and opportunities of white Americans.

As industry grew in the North, the increase in skilled workers and use of machines caused wages to fall. In response, skilled workers formed trade unions, but strikes in the 1830s met little success. Meanwhile, thousands of immigrants, mainly Irish Catholics, were willing to accept low wages. Resentment and fear among many native-born Americans led to anti-Catholic riots and the forming of the Know-Nothing Party.

HISTORY *Mystery*

From New England ponds came a product much in demand in the Caribbean, India, and other tropical lands. What was that product and why was it popular?

1840s
Clipper ships speed overseas trade

1844
Samuel F. B. Morse demonstrates the telegraph
Early telegraph key

1846
Elias Howe invents sewing machine

1849
Know-Nothing Party formed
Know-Nothing election poster

1840

1850

World Link
The Great Famine in Ireland
1845

Looking Ahead
Uncle Tom's Cabin is published
1852

• **403**

Teaching the HISTORY *Mystery*

Students will find the answer on page 406. See Chapter Survey, page 424, for additional questions.

Time Line

Clipper ships American clipper ships transported goods in such record time that they took over much of the China trade. (p. 407)

Morse's telegraph Samuel F. B. Morse's invention of the telegraph gave birth to a new communications industry. (p. 409)

Howe's sewing machine The sewing machine, invented by Elias Howe, made possible mass production of clothing. (p. 408)

Know-Nothing Party Suspicious of new immigrants, some native-born Americans formed the Know-Nothing Party, which supported only white, Protestant, native-born candidates for office. (p. 421)

World Link See page 421.

Looking Ahead The descriptions of the plight of slaves in *Uncle Tom's Cabin,* written by Harriet Beecher Stowe, turned thousands of people against slavery.

Beginning the Story

Frederick Douglass

In 1845 Frederick Douglass wrote *Narrative of the Life of Frederick Douglass* to prove that he had been a slave. Some people simply refused to believe that a man so articulate and intelligent could have been a slave. As Douglass noted, "They said I did not talk like a slave, look like a slave, nor act like a slave." Douglass played a leading role in the struggle to abolish slavery and gain equality for African Americans. His willingness to battle for his convictions continues to inspire Americans.

See the Introducing the Chapter Activity, Creating Parallel Time Lines. **Take-Home Planner 5,** p. 20.

※ **History Footnote**

After Frederick Douglass escaped to the North, he was considered a fugitive slave. To avoid possible capture and reenslavement, he traveled in 1845 to Britain and Ireland. He spent two years there, speaking to audiences about slavery. Douglass used the money that he earned from speaking to buy his freedom when he returned to the United States.

Beginning the Story with

Frederick Douglass

Although he was barely 16, Frederick Augustus Washington Bailey was headed for trouble. To begin with, he had learned to read. Even more troubling, Frederick had organized a Sunday school to teach children how to read the Bible. What was so wrong? Frederick was in trouble because he was a slave, and slaves were not allowed to learn to read nor to meet with other slaves. Slave owners feared that such activities would lead slaves to escape or organize rebellions.

Indeed, Frederick's owner decided his slave's independent spirit had to be broken. In 1834 he sent Frederick to a professional slave breaker named Edward Covey.

"Broken in Body, Soul, and Spirit"

Covey was an expert at turning strong-minded African Americans into obedient slaves. His method, Frederick soon learned, consisted of equal parts of violence, fear, and overwork.

Frederick had not been on Covey's farm for a week before he received his first flogging. The lash left his body covered with bloody welts. After that he was beaten so often that "aching bones and a sore back were my constant companions."

Covey's ability to instill fear in slaves was as effective as the lash. They never knew when Covey was watching them. Frederick recalled:

❝He had the faculty of making us feel that he was always present. . . . I was prepared to expect him at any moment. . . . He would creep and crawl in ditches and gullies; hide behind stumps and bushes, and practice so much the cunning of the serpent, that Bill Smith [another slave] and I—between ourselves—never called him by any other name than 'the snake.'❞

History Bookshelf

Hamilton, Virginia. *Many Thousand Gone: African Americans from Slavery to Freedom.* Knopf, 1993. In an interesting, lively style, the author describes the lives of Frederick Douglass, Harriet Tubman, and other well-known African Americans. Virginia Hamilton has received the Regina Award for lifetime achievement in children's literature.

Also of interest:

Lester, Julius. *To Be a Slave.* Dial Books, 1968.

Meltzer, Milton, ed. *Black Americans: A History in Their Own Words.* HarperCollins, 1984.

Walter, Mildred Pitts. *Mississippi Challenge.* Macmillan, 1992.

Discussion

Thinking Historically

1. Why did slave owners consider a slave who could read a threat? (They feared that reading would lead slaves to escape or to organize revolts.)

2. Why did Frederick Douglass feel "broken in body, soul, and spirit" when sent to the slave breaker? (The slave breaker used violence, fear, and overwork to destroy Douglass's independence.)

3. Why do you think he changed his name after escaping to the North? (To avoid detection and capture.)

See the Chapter In-Depth Activity, Exchanging Letters Between North and South. **Take-Home Planner 5,** p. 21.

Breakup of families was a constant threat to enslaved African Americans. Frederick Douglass's mother was hired out to another planter, and he saw her only four or five times. Slaves sold at auctions like the one in this picture were often separated from family members and friends forever.

The last part of Covey's method, Frederick wrote, was to work his slaves beyond endurance:

> **"**It was never too hot or too cold; it could never rain, blow, hail, or snow too hard for us to work in the field. . . . The longest days were too short for him, and the shortest nights too long for him. I was somewhat unmanageable when I first went there, but a few months of this discipline tamed me. . . . I was broken in body, soul, and spirit.**"**

"The Turning Point in My Life"

Frederick finally "reached the point at which I was *not afraid to die.*" The next time Covey started to beat him, the young man threw his abuser to the ground. Master and slave fought for two hours before Covey gave up. For Frederick, this battle was "the turning point in my life as a slave." He wrote of that moment:

> **"**I felt as I never felt before. . . . My long-crushed spirit rose, cowardice departed, bold defiance took its place; and I now resolved that, however long I might remain a slave in form, the day had passed when I could be a slave in fact. I did not hesitate to let it be known of me, that the white man who expected to succeed in whipping, must also succeed in killing me.**"**

In 1838 Frederick Augustus Washington Bailey escaped from slavery and became a free man in fact, as well as in spirit. He settled in Massachusetts where he took the name by which we know him today: Frederick Douglass.

Teaching the

Hands-On
- - - - - - → HISTORY

To help students create scenes, ask them to list the people in the story. Then have them describe what took place between each person and Douglass.

For a journal writing activity on Frederick Douglass, see student page 424.

Hands-On ▸ HISTORY

Activity

Imagine that you are writing the script for a movie about the young Frederick Douglass. Based on the story above, create a list of scenes to show on film. Give a brief description of the importance of each scene.

Warm-Up
Activity

**Differences
at a Glance**

To preview the economic
differences between
regions, have students
create a graphic organizer,
beginning with two small
circles labeled North and
South. After they scan the
headings, maps, and pic-
tures, have them draw
lines radiating from the
circles and write words or
phrases describing each
region's economy. Remind
them that the Midwest is
part of the North.

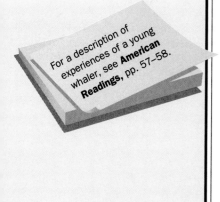

**Geography Question
of the Day**

Tell students that about half
of all cotton grown in the
South was exported to Britain.
Ask them to write a response
to this question: What did
Britain's need to import cotton reveal about its climate
and soil?

For a description of
experiences of a young
whaler, see **American
Readings**, pp. 57–58.

Section Objectives

★ Identify the major economic activities
in the Northeast.
★ Explain how the Midwest became the
nation's breadbasket.
★ Describe the ways in which growing
cotton shaped life in the South.

Teaching Resources

Take-Home Planner 5, pp. 18–25
Chapter Resources Binder
  Study Guide, p. 113
  Reinforcement
  Skills Development
Geography Extensions, pp. 29–30
American Readings, pp. 57–59
Using Historical Documents
Transparency Activities
Chapter and Unit Tests

1. Life in the North and the South

Reading Guide

Section Focus **Differences between the economies of the North and
the South in the mid-1800s**

1. What were the major economic activities in the Northeast?
2. How did the Old Northwest become the nation's breadbasket?
3. How did cotton growing shape life in the South?

When Frederick Douglass first escaped to
the North in 1838, he thought the people
there must be very poor. After all, none of
them owned slaves. "Regarding slavery as the
basis of wealth," he later wrote, "I fancied
that no people could become very wealthy
without slavery."

It was a natural mistake for someone raised
in the South. There, owning slaves was a sign
of wealth. In the free states of the North,
however, wealth was measured in different
terms. These differences shaped how people
worked and lived in the mid-1800s.

The Industrial Northeast

Frederick Douglass realized his mistake
soon after settling in the port town of New
Bedford, Massachusetts. There he was surprised to find

❝the very laboring population of
New Bedford living in better houses,
more elegantly furnished . . . than a
majority of the slaveholders on the
Eastern Shore of Maryland.❞

How, he wondered, could such people live
so well?

Whaling On his first visit to the water-
front, Douglass began to unravel the mystery
of New Bedford's wealth. There he saw "full-

rigged ships of finest model, ready to start on
whaling voyages."

New Englanders had long made a good
living from fishing. By the mid-1800s whaling had also become a profitable business
for enterprising seamen. Whale oil was in
demand because it burned cleanly in lamps.
Other parts of whales were used to manufacture everything from buggy whips to
women's corsets.

Whalers sailed the world's oceans on
voyages lasting three or four years. They
often stopped in the Hawaiian Islands for
supplies and repairs. By 1850 Honolulu was
a major whaling port.

Trade Douglass saw that trade, too, was
a source of wealth in the Northeast. New
Bedford's docks were lined "by large granite-
fronted warehouses, crowded with the good
things of this world."

By the mid-1800s American merchant
ships were trading around the world, even in
such distant lands as Russia, India, and
China. New commerce developed after 1854.
In that year Commodore Matthew Perry
opened American trade with Japan.

One of the most successful trade items was
ice. Blocks of ice cut from frozen New England ponds in winter were packed in sawdust
and shipped to customers in the Caribbean
and India. In those hot lands, ice was an
almost unknown luxury. By the 1850s ice

Designed and built in the United States, clipper ships featured streamlined hulls and three masts to support exceptionally large sails. Names of famous clipper ships, such as *Flying Cloud* and *Lightning,* reflect the speed for which they were known.

Checking Understanding

1. Explain whether the following statement is accurate: Both northerners and southerners made a good living from whaling. (No; whaling was a major economic activity only in the North, in New England.)

Stimulating Critical Thinking

2. Do you think that ice was a dependable trade item, always available for export? (No, slight changes in temperature could prevent the formation or preservation of ice.)

Teaching the
↑ **Reading Maps**

Ask how the map shows that the North was more industrialized than the South. (Names of manufacturing cities and symbols for iron and textile production are clustered in the North.) **Answer to Reading Maps:** Economic activity in the North was more varied than in the South. Northerners raised cattle, fished, and developed more industry. Agriculture was more diversified in the North.

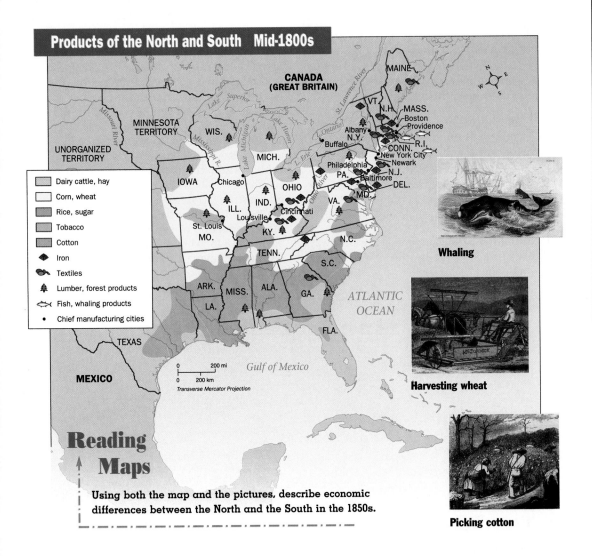

Products of the North and South   Mid-1800s

Dairy cattle, hay
Corn, wheat
Rice, sugar
Tobacco
Cotton
◆ Iron
🐚 Textiles
🌲 Lumber, forest products
🐟 Fish, whaling products
• Chief manufacturing cities

Whaling

Harvesting wheat

Picking cotton

Reading Maps

Using both the map and the pictures, describe economic differences between the North and the South in the 1850s.

See the Study Guide activity in **Chapter Resources Binder,** p. 113.

was the nation's second leading export after cotton in the number of tons shipped.

Clipper ships American cargoes fairly flew to their destinations on the clipper ships developed in the 1840s. Long and narrow, with huge sails, these ships were built "to go at a good clip." They set speed records between ports in the United States, Europe, and Asia. For example, in 1849 the clipper *Sea Witch* sailed from Hong Kong to New York in 74 days—a journey that previously had taken 6 months.

By the 1850s American clipper ships had taken over much of the China trade. During the California gold rush, clippers carried freight and passengers from New York to San Francisco in record time.

Within two decades, however, the day of the clipper ship was almost over. New ships powered by steam could carry more cargo and did not have to depend on the wind.

Using Morse Code

To help students understand Morse code, have small groups code a message, either a phrase or a short sentence. Give them a copy of Morse code, available in most encyclopedias, and provide a code for a sample message, such as "job well done." Have groups exchange and decipher each other's messages. If time permits, use a flashlight to transmit a message for students to decipher.

Teaching the

Link to Technology

As students examine the map, remind them that the telegraph enabled people to communicate over thousands of miles in minutes. Suggest that they draw lines to compare the length of time required for different means of communication. This visual aid will help them focus on the impact of the telegraph.

Tips for Teaching

At-Risk Students

To help students understand quotations, suggest that they first ask two questions about a quotation's basic meaning: Who is talking? and What is he or she talking about? In the quotation on this page, for instance, Frederick Douglass talks about how in the North ships were unloaded faster and with fewer workers than in the South. Next, have students ask themselves, What does this quotation have to do with the information it appears with? For example, Douglass's statement provides an example of how northerners were better at inventing ways to do work more efficiently.

Industry and invention On the New Bedford docks, Douglass discovered another key to the Northeast's wealth. Watching men unload a ship, he observed

"industry without bustle. . . . Everything went on as smoothly as the works of a well-adjusted machine. . . . In a southern port, twenty or thirty hands would have been employed to do what five or six did here, with the aid of a single ox."

Northerners, Douglass decided, were always inventing smarter and faster ways to get work done.

By the mid-1800s the production methods pioneered by Francis Lowell and Eli Whitney in New England had spread throughout the Northeast. More and more of the goods people used every day were produced in mills and factories by workers using machines.

At the same time, inventors were busy creating new products and industries. The rubber industry was built on Charles Goodyear's 1839 discovery of how to make rubber strong. Dozens of new products, from fire hoses to rubber bands, were the result. Mass production of clothing became possible after 1846, when Elias Howe invented a sewing machine that could make 250 stitches a minute.

Link to Technology

Receiving register punches the message onto a paper tape in a matter of minutes.

Pony Express from St. Joseph to Sacramento: 10 to 12 days

Sacramento

San Francisco

The Telegraph

The invention of the telegraph in 1844 brought a new era of rapid communication to the United States. The first telegraph line to cross the country was completed in 1861. Now people could communicate over thousands of miles in a matter of minutes, rather than days or months. As you read the labels on the map, imagine how this invention might have changed people's lives.

Covered wagon from St. Louis to Sacramento: 2 months

Samuel F. B. Morse created a system of dots, dashes, and spaces to send messages by wire. The system came to be known as Morse code, or American Morse. Various combinations of dots and dashes represent the letters a–z and numbers 1–9. A dot is made by briefly holding down the telegraph key. For a short dash, the key is held down twice as long. A long dash is equal to four dots.

The invention of the telegraph by Samuel F. B. Morse gave birth to a new communications industry. Before Morse successfully demonstrated the telegraph in 1844, messages could travel only as fast as the fastest horse or ship. Four years later telegraph wires were speeding messages to people and businesses in almost every state east of the Mississippi.

Cities grow up around industry

This burst of industry and invention greatly increased the number of factories. Factories, in turn, attracted workers, many of whom came from farms. Factory owners also found a source of low-cost labor in the immigrants entering the United States in search of opportunity.

As a result, cities began to grow up around industry in the Northeast. For example, in the 1820s Lowell, Massachusetts, was a small farming village. Two decades later it had become an industrial city of 30,000 people built around busy textile mills.

With all of this enterprise and industry, life moved at a fast pace in the Northeast. There were always people on the go, sailing to distant ports, starting new businesses, and inventing new products. In their restless activity, northerners were pioneering a new pattern of life—a pattern set by the clock, the factory bell, and the rhythms of machines.

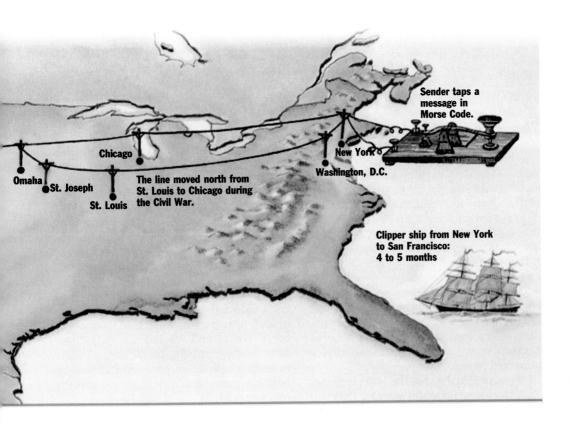

Sender taps a message in Morse Code.

New York

Chicago

The line moved north from St. Louis to Chicago during the Civil War.

Omaha

St. Joseph

St. Louis

Washington, D.C.

Clipper ship from New York to San Francisco: 4 to 5 months

Discussion

Checking Understanding

1. **What did Charles Goodyear and Elias Howe have in common?** (Both were inventors whose inventions created new industries.)

2. **What caused the farming village of Lowell to grow into an industrial city?** (The establishment of textile mills in Lowell attracted workers to the village.)

Stimulating Critical Thinking

3. **How do you think the telegraph changed people's lives?** (Reduced time it took to hear about critical political and economic events; provided a means of quick communication between separated family members.)

* * *

Vital Links

Samuel Morse (Picture) Unit 3, Side 1, Search 21801

See also Unit 3 Explore CD-ROM location 86.

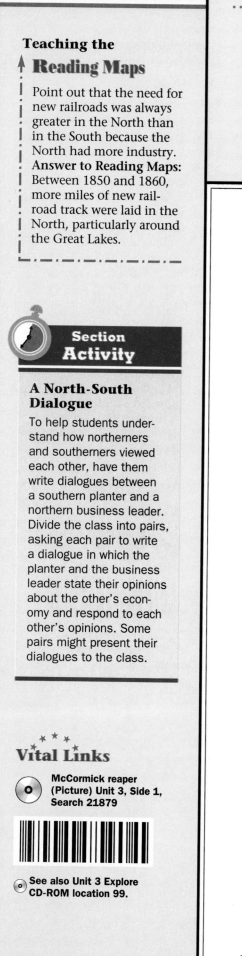

Teaching the
↑ Reading Maps

Point out that the need for new railroads was always greater in the North than in the South because the North had more industry. **Answer to Reading Maps:** Between 1850 and 1860, more miles of new railroad track were laid in the North, particularly around the Great Lakes.

Section Activity

A North-South Dialogue

To help students understand how northerners and southerners viewed each other, have them write dialogues between a southern planter and a northern business leader. Divide the class into pairs, asking each pair to write a dialogue in which the planter and the business leader state their opinions about the other's economy and respond to each other's opinions. Some pairs might present their dialogues to the class.

★★★
Vital Links

McCormick reaper (Picture) Unit 3, Side 1, Search 21879

See also Unit 3 Explore CD-ROM location 99.

410

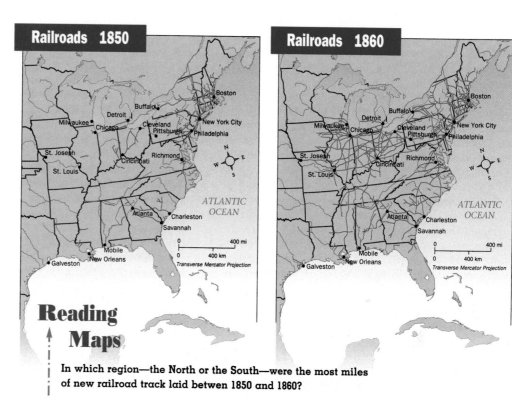

Railroads 1850

Milwaukee • Detroit • Buffalo • Boston
Chicago • Cleveland • New York City
St. Joseph • Pittsburgh • Philadelphia
St. Louis • Cincinnati • Richmond
Atlanta • Charleston
Savannah
Mobile • New Orleans
Galveston

ATLANTIC OCEAN

N W E S

0   400 mi
0   400 km
Transverse Mercator Projection

Railroads 1860

Milwaukee • Detroit • Buffalo • Boston
Chicago • Cleveland • New York City
St. Joseph • Pittsburgh • Philadelphia
St. Louis • Cincinnati • Richmond
Atlanta • Charleston
Savannah
Mobile • New Orleans
Galveston

ATLANTIC OCEAN

N W E S

0   400 mi
0   400 km
Transverse Mercator Projection

↑ Reading Maps

In which region—the North or the South—were the most miles of new railroad track laid between 1850 and 1860?

The Agricultural Midwest

In the Midwest, as the Old Northwest came to be called, most people still followed a pattern of life based on the rising and setting of the sun and the rhythm of the seasons. Farmers there cultivated some of the richest soil on earth. The grain and cattle raised on that fertile ground brought wealth to the region.

The McCormick reaper The farmers who settled in the Midwest used tools that had changed little in centuries. Then, in the mid-1800s a Virginia farmer named Cyrus McCormick invented a machine that revolutionized farming there.

McCormick knew that the harvest season was a cruel time for wheat farmers. They had only a few days to bring in their crop before the ripe grain fell to the ground. To get the job done in time, they hired crews of reapers to cut the grain by hand.

McCormick spent years developing a machine that would do the back-breaking work of the harvest crew. He was assisted by Joe Anderson, one of the McCormick family's slaves. The result in 1831 was a horse-drawn harvesting machine that cut as much grain in a day as three workers.

McCormick continued to test his machine and improve it. Finally, in 1842 he began to manufacture the reaper. To help farmers pay for it, McCormick created the installment plan. Under this plan, he allowed a farmer to make a cash down payment followed by monthly payments with interest until the cost was paid off.

McCormick's reaper was just one of the labor-saving farm machines invented in the 1830s. In 1835 brothers Hiram and John Pitts patented a combined threshing machine and fanning mill. A revolving cylinder knocked kernels of grain off stalks, and a fan blew away the chaff. In 1837 John Deere introduced a steel plow that cut a clean furrow in thick soil, unlike earlier cast iron and wood plows.

Looking for more customers, McCormick built a reaper factory in Chicago, Illinois. In 1848 he sold 500 reapers. By 1850 he had sold 4,000 more. A new age of mechanized farming had begun.

Transportation links Chicago, home of McCormick's reaper factory, was one of many new cities in the Midwest. Some, such as Cincinnati and St. Louis, grew up beside the Ohio and Mississippi Rivers. Other cities, like Chicago and Detroit, sprouted on the shores of the Great Lakes.

Transportation was the key to the growth of these cities. Crops flowed into them for shipment to northeastern cities. The boats and trains that carried crops east returned to the Midwest bringing factory goods. They also brought new settlers. By 1850 half of all Americans lived west of the Appalachians.

At mid-century railroads were just beginning to compete with riverboats and canals in the Midwest. Ten years later, the region was crisscrossed by rail lines. Railroads bound the Northeast and the Midwest so closely together that southerners viewed the two regions as one—the North.

The Cotton-Growing South

By mid-century the South was a vast cotton-growing region. As you read in Chapter 12, the invention of the cotton gin in 1793 turned cotton into the South's most important cash crop. Cotton planters put their money into land and slaves. By 1850 they had pushed the cotton kingdom west beyond the Mississippi, into Texas.

As more land was planted in cotton, production skyrocketed. By 1850 southerners were producing more than 2 million bales a year. They exported about 75 percent of it, mainly to Britain, making cotton the nation's leading export. The remaining 25 percent went to New England mills. No wonder white southerners boasted that "cotton is king."

Chicago became a center of both water and railroad transportation. A visitor in 1855 observed that Chicago "fairly smokes and roars with business."

Checking Understanding

1. How did transportation lead to the growth of new cities in the Midwest? (They were centers for shipping crops to the East and factory goods to the Midwest.)

2. Why did people in the South tend to view the Midwest and the Northeast as one region? (They were seen as one region because railroads linked them together very closely.)

Stimulating Critical Thinking

3. What made Chicago an ideal place for Cyrus McCormick to build his reaper factory? (Chicago was close to wheat farmland and was a center of both water and rail transportation.)

4. What is the connection between Howe's invention of the sewing machine in 1846 and the skyrocketing production of cotton? (The sewing machine made possible the mass production of clothing, which increased demand for cotton.)

***

Vital Links

Plantation (Picture)
Unit 3, Side 1,
Search 32787

See also Unit 3 Explore
CD-ROM location 164.

Writing Want Ads

To review the varied economic activities in the North, have students create want ads for Boston and Chicago newspapers. For each newspaper, they should identify three job opportunities, describing each in a way to "sell" it to the reader. Some possibilities are whaler, sailor on a clipper ship, iron-factory worker, sewing machine operator, railroad worker, farmhand, or telegraph operator.

Section Review
Answers

1. Two of the following: fishing, whaling, ice exporting, trade with China, iron mills, rubber industry, clothing industry, inventing new products.

2. The rich soil and the McCormick reaper.

3. As a result of the invention of the cotton gin and Britain's need for cotton, cotton became the South's most important cash crop.

4. Answers will vary. Students should consider that such machines would decrease planters' need for slave labor.

✳ **History Footnote**

In 1857 Hinton Helper published *The Impending Crisis of the South*. In it he argued that the system of slavery hindered development of trade and manufacturing, and kept non-slaveholding white southerners poor. He even proposed an 11-point program to end slavery. The book caused such a commotion in the South that Helper was forced to move to the North.

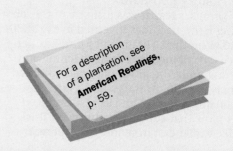
For a description of a plantation, see *American Readings*, p. 59.

This 1840 painting shows wealthy southern planters and their families gathering for the excitement of horse racing at the Oakland Race Course in Louisville, Kentucky. Families like these, though relatively few in number, were the political and social leaders of the South.

The spread of slavery The growth of the cotton kingdom caused a great demand for slave labor. Congress banned the Atlantic slave trade in 1808, so no new slaves could legally be brought into the country. Instead, slave traders traveled throughout the southeastern states buying up slaves to sell in the new southwestern cotton lands.

The demand for slave labor caused prices to soar so high that only wealthy planters could continue to buy slaves. In 1850 there were about 347,000 slaveholding families in the South. Only one-third of those families owned more than ten slaves.

About three-fourths of white southerners owned no slaves at all. Many of these people lived on small farms, grew their own food, and tended a few acres of cotton or tobacco as cash crops. Eager to "move up" in society, ambitious small farmers saved to buy land and slaves of their own.

Aware of the money to be made from cotton, southerners continued to put their money in land and slaves rather than in factories and railroads. As a result, the South remained the less industrialized section of the country. Compared to the North, the South had relatively few factories, canals, or railroads. Hinton Helper, a South Carolina writer, complained:

❝We are compelled to go to the North for almost every article . . . from matches, shoe-pegs, and paintings to cotton mills, steamships, and statuary.❞

Still, most southern planters showed little interest in the technology that was changing life in the North.

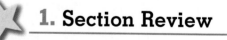

⭐ 1. Section Review

1. Describe at least two important economic activities in the Northeast.
2. What enabled people in the Midwest to be productive farmers?
3. Why was more and more land in the South planted in cotton after 1793?
4. Critical Thinking If machinery to cultivate and pick cotton had been developed in the mid-1800s, what effects might it have had on the southern economy and way of life?

Geography Footnote

Climate is the prevailing, or average, weather of a place over a long period of time. Temperature and precipitation determine climate. Latitude, elevation, and ocean currents affect temperature. Prevailing winds and mountain ranges affect precipitation. Places near the equator are generally warmer than those in higher latitudes. Temperatures are lower at high altitudes, and warm and cold ocean currents can affect temperatures of coastal areas. The air absorbs most moisture from warm parts of the oceans. The wettest places are those where winds blow inland from the ocean, and the moisture falls as precipitation. Mountain ranges can act as barriers to prevailing winds, and therefore their leeward sides may get little precipitation.

Geography Lab

Reading Climate Maps

"King Cotton" came to rule over the South largely because of the climate there. What kind of climate do you think is best for growing cotton—warm or cool, wet or dry? One way to find out is to look at climate maps.

You may have seen weather maps on TV or in the newspaper. Climate maps are similar. The lines on such maps, called **isolines**, mark off areas that are the same in some way. For example, the area between two isolines on a map that shows **precipitation**—moisture from rain and snow—will receive a similar amount of precipitation.

Cotton field, Mississippi

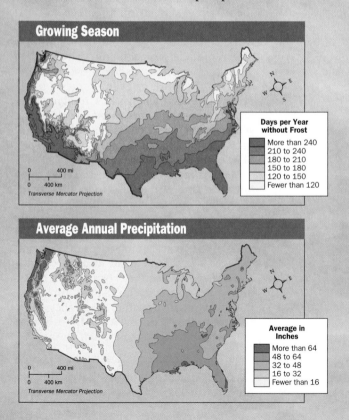

Using Map Skills

Refer to the maps on pages 407 and R6–R7 to answer the questions.

1. Name 4 states with areas that receive at least 64 inches of precipitation each year. What 5 states have areas that receive 16 inches or less each year?

2. Name 6 states that have growing seasons longer than 240 days. What 6 states have growing seasons shorter than 120 days each year?

3. What is the least amount of moisture and the minimum growing season needed for an area to be part of the "Cotton Kingdom"? Refer to the maps on this page and on page 407.

4. **Hands-On Geography** Imagine that you can move to any state in the United States. What state would you choose and how would the climate, including the precipitation, influence your decision?

● **413**

Teaching the Geography Lab

To help students understand that climate maps tell conditions needed for a particular crop to grow, refer them to the map on page 407. Have them identify states that grow cotton (Ala., Ark., Fla., Ga., La., Miss., N.C., S.C., and Tex.). To help them use the climate maps, ask which map tells whether the climate is warm or cool (top) and whether the climate is dry or wet (bottom).

Using Map Skills Answers

1. Parts of the West and South—Wash., Ore., Calif., La., Miss., Ala., Fla., and Ga.—receive at least 64 inches of rain. Parts of the West—Calif., Nev., Ariz., Utah, Or., Wash., Idaho, N. Mex., Colo., and Wyo.—receive very little rain.

2. Southern states—Ala., Fla., Ga., La., Miss., N.C., S.C., and Tex.—have growing seasons longer than 240 days. Parts of several northern and mountain states—Colo., Idaho, Utah, Mont., N. Dak., Wyo., Nev., Ore., Wash., Minn., Mich., Wis., Me., Vt., and N.H.—have growing seasons shorter than 120 days.

3. No less than 48 inches of moisture and a growing season of at least 210 days without frost.

4. Answers will depend on climate preferences.

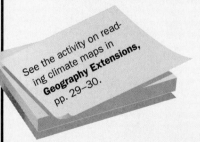

See the activity on reading climate maps in Geography Extensions, pp. 29–30.

2. African American Life

Reading Guide

New Terms slave codes, discrimination

Section Focus African American life in the South and the North

1. What were the living conditions of enslaved African Americans?
2. How did African Americans resist slavery?
3. What problems did free African Americans face?

One day in 1841, at a meeting of the Massachusetts Antislavery Society, Frederick Douglass was asked to tell his experiences as a slave. Having never spoken in public before, Douglass was so nervous he "trembled in every limb."

Still, he gave such a moving speech that he was named a lecturer for the society. In the next 14 years he traveled throughout the North speaking against slavery. He became one of the greatest public speakers in American history.

Life Under Slavery

In 1850 there were more than 3 million enslaved African Americans in the United States. By law they were property, not human beings. They could be bought and sold, and even passed down in wills. Slaves had none of the rights that free people often took for granted. As Douglass told his listeners:

❝In law, the slave has no wife,
  no children, no country, no home.
  He can own nothing, possess nothing,
  acquire nothing.❞

Living conditions Seven out of eight enslaved African Americans worked on plantations. Most were field hands who toiled from dawn to dark tending cotton, tobacco,

rice, or sugar cane. Even after dark there was still water to carry, wood to split, pigs to feed, and corn to shuck.

Not all enslaved African Americans worked in the fields. Some were skilled carpenters, blacksmiths, or mechanics. Others worked in the master's house as cooks, butlers, maids, or nursemaids. In addition to their regular work, some also served the slave community as preachers, nurses, or midwives.

On small plantations, owners personally directed the work or even worked in the fields alongside their slaves. On large plantations, many owners hired overseers to supervise the work. Overseers were paid to "care for nothing but to make a large crop." They often drove slaves mercilessly.

Many owners viewed their slaves as they did their land, something to be used hard and "worn out, not improved." They spent as little money as possible on the care of their work force.

Enslaved African Americans often lived crowded together in small wooden cabins. The owner gave them weekly rations of cornmeal and pork or bacon. Slaves improved their diets with vegetables when they were allowed to have gardens. A few times a year they received a new set of rough clothes.

The importance of families Under these difficult conditions, enslaved African Americans did their best to create families

Harriet Powers's quilt of Bible stories combines American style with traditional techniques from Dahomey in West Africa. The photo below shows 7 of the 11 panels, and 2 of the 3 rows, of her quilt. At the top left are Adam and Eve with the serpent. The top center panel shows Adam and Eve with Cain. The top right panel shows Satan. The lower row shows (left to right) Cain killing Abel; Cain in the land of Nod surrounded by bears, leopards, and other animals; Jacob's ladder; and John the Baptist baptizing Christ, with the Holy Spirit above. The bottom row, not shown, has four panels depicting Christ's crucifixion, Judas and the 30 pieces of silver, the Last Supper, and Jesus with Mary and Joseph.

∞ Link to Art

Harriet Powers's Bible quilt After finishing evening chores, enslaved African American women often worked late into the night making quilts. Using techniques from West Africa, they created quilts that told stories with bold shapes and bright colors. This picture shows part of a quilt made by Harriet Powers, who was born into slavery in Georgia in 1837. Stitched in the early 1880s, the quilt shows Bible stories. **Discuss** Compare this quilt with the quilt on page 149. How are they similar? How are they different?

and care for each other. Despite the threat of separation, they married, often using African ceremonies, and raised children.

Slaves struggled to keep their families together and to reunite separated family members. After Samuel Johnston gained his freedom in 1811, he worked for five years to earn enough money to buy his wife and children. In 1815 the Virginia legislature refused to free his children. For the next 22 years, Johnston tried without success to bring his family together.

Resistance to Slavery

Although they had no rights, enslaved African Americans had plenty of will and wits. Harriet Jacobs used hers when she escaped in 1835. She hid in an attic for seven years before she could make her way north. Later she wrote:

❝My master had power and law on his side; I had a determined will. There is might [power] in each.❞

Checking Understanding

1. How did slaves improve the quality of their lives? (They raised vegetables to improve their diets. Some served the slave community as preachers, nurses, and midwives. They struggled to keep families together.)

Stimulating Critical Thinking

2. Why might the Virginia legislature have refused to help Samuel Johnson reunite his family? (Representatives of slave owners would not have wanted to strengthen African American families. They may have feared that the family would become a source of strength or lead slaves to believe they were equal to whites.)

Teaching the

∞ Link to Art

Ask why enslaved African American women might have devoted so much time and energy to make quilts. (Source of beauty, source of artistic pride, way to express beliefs, way to take their minds off of suffering under slavery.) **Discussion Answers:** Both quilts tell a story. The quilt on page 149 uses one picture to tell a story, and the quilt on page 415 uses several.

See the Study Guide activity in **Chapter Resources Binder,** p. 114.

Section Activity

To Revolt or Not?

To focus on causes and risks of slave revolts, have students imagine themselves as slaves deciding whether to rebel. Provide the following scenario: "Your spouse and children have been sold to another planter, and you will probably never see them again. You have received severe beatings. You have recently heard rumors of a slave revolt being organized. Will you join it?" Have students work in small groups to discuss the pros and cons of joining the revolt. Conclude by asking groups to share their ideas.

Teaching the Hands-On
HISTORY

Some students might not have access to a private or semiprivate space outside the home. To help them complete the activity, ask them to think of a special place that makes them feel comfortable whenever they are in it. Ideally, it should be a place in which they can be alone.

★ ★ ★
Vital Links

🔘 **Nat Turner (Picture)**
Unit 3, Side 1,
Search 37458

🔘 See also Unit 3 Explore
CD-ROM location 205.

✱ **History Footnote**
Nat Turner believed that God had called him to lead enslaved African Americans to freedom. His plan to capture Jerusalem, Virginia, had symbolic significance because of the importance of the original city of Jerusalem. Though unsuccessful, his revolt gave hope that one day slavery would end. Many African Americans began counting time from what they called "Old Nat's War."

For a fictional account about one slave teaching another to read, see the Link to Literature feature on pp. 426–427.

For a firsthand description of conditions under slavery, see **American Readings**, p. 60.

Hands-On
HISTORY

Analyzing how you use space Many enslaved African Americans spent what little free time they had in the yards outside their cabins. There they cooked, raised vegetables for themselves, and gathered to socialize. Such patterns of using yards and gardens, some of which may have begun in Africa, are still found in the rural South.

Activity

① Whether it is a garden, a yard, a porch, or a balcony, many people have some private or semiprivate space outside the home. What space do you have?

② Study the photograph, and the diagram based on it, on the right. Then make a diagram of your space. Add a key.

③ Write a paragraph describing where the space is and how you use it.

④ Share your diagram and description with classmates.

🔘 Cook pot
🔘 Open fire
🔘 Rain barrel
▨ Vegetable garden
🌳 Shade tree
▨ Swept area

An African American yard in North Carolina, 1914

Throughout the South, enslaved African Americans resisted slavery by striking back, escaping, and organizing revolts.

Striking back Slaves became experts at secretly striking back at their masters. Field hands "accidentally" broke their tools or destroyed crops. House servants "liberated" food from the master's kitchen.

Slaves also pretended to be stupid, clumsy, sick, or insane to avoid work. "The only weapon of self-defense I could use successfully," recalled an enslaved African American named Henry Bibb, "was that of deception."

Striking back could turn deadly. So many slaves set fire to their masters' homes that the American Fire Insurance Company refused to insure property in the South.

Escaping to freedom Many slaves resisted slavery by escaping to freedom. The risks of escaping, though, were enormous. Most slaves knew little about the world beyond their plantation. Once missed, they were hunted by "slave catchers." If caught, escapees were severely punished. As Frederick Douglass planned his escape, he was filled with doubts:

❝I was making a leap in the dark. . . . It was like going to war without weapons—ten chances of defeat to one of victory.❞

Despite the dangers, thousands of slaves took the risk. Every year about 1,000 slaves fled to the North, Canada, or Mexico. Some walked to freedom, following the North Star by night. Some escaped by boat or train, using forged identity cards and clever disguises. A few slaves had themselves shipped north in boxes and coffins.

Although slaves were carefully watched so that revolt was nearly impossible, three major plots took place in the 1800s. A plan by Gabriel Prosser in 1800 involved seizing the Richmond arsenal and killing all whites in the city except Quakers and Methodists. A storm that washed out roads to Richmond foiled the plan. Denmark Vesey, who bought his freedom from slavery, plotted with others in the early 1820s to attack Charleston. However, the plotters were betrayed and later executed. After Nat Turner's revolt, which involved almost 80 slaves, Turner was captured and executed.

Slave revolts For slaves who stayed home, resistance sometimes took the form of open revolt. As early as 1739, slaves killed more than 20 whites in the Stono Uprising in South Carolina.

Fear of revolts haunted white southerners. A visitor noted:

❝I have known times here when not a single planter had a calm night's rest. They never lie down to sleep without . . . loaded pistols at their sides.❞

One of the bloodiest revolts erupted in Virginia in 1831. Nat Turner, a slave and a preacher, rose up to "slay my enemies with their own weapons." Before the two-day reign of terror ended, Turner and his followers had killed nearly 60 white men, women, and children.

Stricter slave codes Nat Turner's revolt chilled white southerners. In response, southern states passed stricter **slave codes**—laws that tightened owners' control over slaves. The new codes barred slaves from leaving their plantations without permission. They could not meet in large groups without a white person present. It was now illegal to teach a slave to read.

State after state passed new laws making it more difficult for slaves to gain freedom. They also passed laws that limited the rights of free African Americans.

Free African Americans

Of the more than 3.5 million African Americans living in the United States at mid-century, nearly 500,000 were free. Some had gained freedom when northern states banned slavery. Others escaped or were freed by southern owners. Still others, who were allowed to earn money, bought their own freedom.

∞ Link to the Present

Buxton reunions Some escaped slaves settled in new African American communities in the North. One such community was Buxton in Ontario, Canada.

Buxton grew out of the dream of William King, an Irish-born minister who wanted to help African American refugees settle in Canada. In 1849 King organized a joint-stock company to buy land near Lake Erie and sell plots to African Americans. By 1861 the thriving town had 2,000 residents.

Although many Buxton residents returned to the United States to fight in the Civil War, descendants of some of the original settlers still live there. Each year they have a reunion during the Labor Day weekend. People come from as far away as Louisiana and California to honor freedom-loving African Americans who built a successful community in Canada.

About half of the free African Americans lived in the South, half in the North. Most of them worked as laborers, craftspeople, household servants, seamstresses, or washerwomen. A few started their own businesses and some became quite wealthy.

No matter where they lived, free African Americans suffered from **discrimination**—the unfair treatment of a group of people compared with another group. Because of discrimination, free black Americans did not have the same rights and opportunities as white Americans.

In the South White southerners saw free African Americans as a dangerous influence.

1830–1850 Chapter 15 ● **417**

▶ Discussion

Checking Understanding

1. About how many slaves escaped each year, and where did they go? (Each year about 1,000 slaves escaped to the North, to Canada, or to Mexico.)

Stimulating Critical Thinking

2. Why do you think slaves were successful in striking back by pretending to be stupid, clumsy, or insane? (They took advantage of the racist view of white slave owners and overseers that black people were inferior.)

Teaching the

∞ Link to the Present

Have students locate the Canadian side of Lake Erie on the map on pages R6–R7. Explore why residents of Buxton might have returned to fight in the Civil War.

⏱ Bonus Activity

Letters on Slavery

To help students understand life under slavery, have them write letters from the viewpoint of a white northerner traveling in the South or of an escaped slave living in the North. Students who choose the first viewpoint should imagine writing to a friend in the North about conditions under slavery. Those who choose the second should imagine writing to a former master.

African American churches first came into existence in the North. Among the first African American churches to form was the African Methodist Episcopal Church, formally organized in Philadelphia in 1816. Another was the African Methodist Episcopal Zion Church, organized in New York City in 1821. Many African American churches were safe havens for former slaves who had escaped.

See the Reinforcement activity in **Chapter Resources Binder,** pp. 117–118.

Closing the Section

A Persuasive Speech

To review conditions under slavery, have students imagine helping Frederick Douglass educate people in the North about the evils of slavery. They should write short speeches describing the physical and emotional hardships imposed by slavery. Conclude by asking volunteers to read their speeches.

Section Review
Answers

1. Definitions: *slave codes* (417), *discrimination* (417)
2. Family members comforted and cared for each other and eased the pain of forced separation.
3. Answers may include striking back by breaking tools, taking food, avoiding work, setting fires, escaping, or revolting.
4. Those in the South, unlike those in the North, were regarded as a threat and were not allowed to own guns or travel freely. They also faced severe punishment for minor crimes. In both regions they did not have the same rights or opportunities as whites, facing discrimination in churches, public facilities, and political institutions.

Mary and John Jones of Chicago were both born free. They helped escaped slaves reach freedom in Canada. John Jones also led the fight against Illinois laws that banned free African Americans from voting or testifying in court.

"The superior condition of the free persons of color," complained a group of slave owners, "excites discontent among our slaves."

As a result, free African Americans in the South were not allowed to own guns or watchdogs. Nor could they travel freely. They were severely punished for even the most minor crimes. Such harsh treatment led Douglass to declare that "no colored man is really free in a slaveholding state."

In the North Even in the North, equality was little more than a dream for African Americans. A white New Yorker named Gerrit Smith observed in the 1840s:

❝Even the noblest black is denied that which is free to the vilest [worst] white. The omnibus, the [railroad] car, the ballot-box, the jury box, the halls of legislation, the army, the public lands, the school, the church, the lecture room, the [restaurant] table are all . . . denied to him.❞

Frederick Douglass learned about northern racism when he tried to join the Elm Street Church in New Bedford:

❝I was not allowed a seat in the body of the house . . . on account of my color. . . .

I tried all the other churches in New Bedford with the same result.❞

Faced with discrimination, free African Americans turned to their own communities for hope and pride. As early as the 1780s, they began forming their own Christian churches, which became centers of African American life in northern cities.

Meanwhile, free African Americans worked to gain rights for themselves and for those still enslaved. They sent petitions to Congress and state legislatures demanding equal treatment. They raised money to help escaped slaves and planned boycotts of slave-made goods. Through their efforts, they exerted a steady pressure for change.

2. Section Review

1. Define the terms **slave codes** and **discrimination.**
2. How did close family ties help slaves deal with the harshness of slavery?
3. Give two examples of ways that slaves resisted their owners' control.
4. **Critical Thinking** Compare the life of free African Americans in the North and the South. What was different? The same?

Section Objectives

★ Describe how work changed in the United States as the nation became more industrialized.
★ Explain why workers formed trade unions.
★ Identify the problems faced by immigrants in the mid-1800s.

Teaching Resources

Take-Home Planner 5, pp. 18–25
Chapter Resources Binder
   Study Guide, p. 115
   Reinforcement
   Skills Development, pp. 119–120
  Geography Extensions
  American Readings
  Using Historical Documents, pp. 81–84
  Transparency Activities
  Chapter and Unit Tests, pp. 95–98

3. Workers and Immigrants

Reading Guide

New Terms trade union, strike, nativism, nativists

Section Focus The struggle of workers and immigrants to make better lives for themselves

1. How did work change as the nation became more industrialized?
2. Why did workers form trade unions?
3. What problems did immigrants face in the mid-1800s?

After escaping to freedom in 1838, Frederick Douglass worked at a number of jobs. As he later recalled, he "sawed wood—dug cellars—shoveled coal—swept chimneys—helped to load and unload vessels—worked in Ricketson's candle works—in Richmond's brass foundry and elsewhere."

As a wage earner, Douglass worried about whether he could support himself and his family. It was a problem faced by a growing number of workers in the North.

The New Wage Earners

Since colonial times, the United States had been a good land for wage earners, especially those with skills, such as printers or carpenters. Skilled workers were well paid because there were so few of them. Most worked for wages only until they had saved enough to buy farms or start businesses.

By the early 1800s, however, working for wages began to be a way of life for many people, not a temporary condition. There were now plenty of skilled workers, too, so wages began to drop.

Also, in the new mills and factories, jobs once done by skilled workers were taken over by unskilled workers running machines. These new wage earners—many of the women and children—were paid far less than the skilled workers they replaced.

Forming Trade Unions

Faced with falling wages, skilled workers began to form trade unions. A **trade union** is a group of people who try to improve wages and working conditions in their trade, or craft. By 1810 most of the nation's larger cities had unions of printers, shoemakers, carpenters, and painters.

Philadelphia's union of shoemakers called the first organized strike in 1799 to protest pay cuts. In a **strike,** employees refuse to work, hoping to force their employer to meet their demands. After ten weeks, however, hunger drove the striking shoemakers back to work at the lower wages.

Other efforts by the early trade unions to protect workers' wages were more successful. However, in the hard times following the Panic of 1819 (see pages 332–333), thousands of workers lost both their jobs and their faith in unions.

Protesting wages and hours The economy improved in the 1830s, but wages and hours did not. As a result, labor organizations revived. In 1835 and 1836 alone, workers organized 140 strikes to protest wage cuts and longer work hours. "Ten hours . . . is as much as an employer ought to receive, or require, for a day's work," angry workers declared.

Introducing the Section

Vocabulary

trade union (p. 419) group of people who try to improve wages and working conditions in their trade

strike (p. 419) refusal to work in hope of forcing the employer to meet demands

nativism (p. 421) belief that immigrants threaten traditional American culture and institutions

nativists (p. 421) people who hold the belief of nativism

Warm-Up Activity

Working Conditions

To focus on the concept of working conditions, have small groups examine a newspaper for work-related articles. Students should identify working conditions mentioned in the articles as acceptable or unacceptable. Conclude by asking volunteers to identify working conditions they consider unacceptable and to explain why.

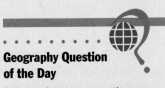

Geography Question of the Day

Ask students to use the map on page 407 to predict where new immigrants might settle and why. (Often in major port and manufacturing centers because of availability of work.)

Many of the strikes took place in factories and mills. By the 1830s millworkers were forced to labor up to 13 hours a day, 6 days a week. In 1836 more than 1,500 women workers in Lowell walked out to protest pay cuts. Eleven-year-old Harriet Hanson was one of the strikers. She later recalled:

> "When the girls in my room stood irresolute, uncertain what to do . . . I, who began to think they would not go out, after all their talk, became impatient, and started on ahead. . . . As I looked back at that long line that followed me, I was more proud than I have ever been since."

The strike failed. Within a month, the strikers had run out of money. Some straggled back to work. The leaders of the strike, including Harriet, were fired.

In fact, going on strike was a risky business at that time. Strikes were illegal—and so were unions. Workers involved in them could be fined and arrested. It was not until the 1842 court decision in *Commonwealth* v. *Hunt* that unions and strikes were declared legal.

Newcomers to America

By the 1840s many mill and factory workers were being replaced by immigrants. In the 50 years between 1776 and 1825, only 1 million immigrants had entered the country. In the 10 years between 1845 and 1854, close to 3 million newcomers arrived.

The majority of these immigrants came from northern Europe, mainly Ireland,

On the overcrowded ships that brought them to America, Irish immigrants suffered from hunger and disease. As many as 20 percent of them died during the trip.

In the 1820s about 129,000 immigrants arrived in the United States, which had a population of about 12.9 million by 1830. Immigrants from the 1820s made up about 1 percent of the nation's population. In the 1850s about 2.8 million immigrants arrived. The U.S. population in 1860 was about 31.4 million. Immigrants from the 1850s made up about 9 percent of the 1860 population. For every immigrant who arrived in the 1820s, about 22 immigrants came in the 1850s.

Germany, England, Scotland, and Scandinavia. Some moved to the Midwest in search of farmland. More settled in the Northeast where they found work in factories or building canals and railroads.

The arrival of so many newcomers in a short time caused fear and resentment among many native-born Americans. For one thing, the immigrants were willing to accept low wages for factory and construction jobs. When employers then lowered wages for everyone, angry American-born workers blamed the immigrants.

Differences in culture also raised suspicions among native-born Americans. Most of them were descended from English Protestants. They feared the effect that people with different languages, traditions, and religions would have on what they saw as the American way of life.

Nativism The belief that immigrants threaten traditional American culture and institutions is called **nativism.** People who hold that belief are known as **nativists.**

Nativists were especially hostile to Roman Catholic immigrants—mostly Irish and German. In eastern cities, bloody anti-Catholic riots broke out.

The Know-Nothings Hoping to keep immigrants from gaining political power, nativists formed secret societies and promised never to vote for an immigrant or Catholic. In 1849 one society, the Order of the Star-Spangled Banner, became a political party. It was nicknamed the "Know-Nothing Party" because its members answered any questions about the party by saying, "I know nothing."

The Know-Nothings supported only white, Protestant, native-born candidates. The appeal of their nativist message was felt in elections in 1854 and 1855. Voters from Massachusetts to California sent more than 75 Know-Nothings to Congress.

World Link

The Great Famine in Ireland Chances are, you have never thought of the potato as a powerful force in history. Yet potatoes—or the lack of them—set off a huge wave of Irish immigration to the United States in the mid-1800s.

Almost as soon as the potato reached Europe from South America in the 1500s, Europeans became dependent on it. The potato was both nutritious and easy to grow. In Ireland, people grew almost nothing else.

Then, beginning in 1845, a plant disease called a blight destroyed Ireland's potato crop. Famine set in. Before the blight ended, a million Irish people had died of starvation or disease. Another million had fled to the United States.

Point of View

Who is a true American?

In 1854 the Know-Nothings visited Abraham Lincoln, an Illinois lawyer, and offered to support him if he ran for the Senate. Lincoln declined their offer. In a letter to a friend, he revealed his reason:

❝As a nation, we began by declaring *'all men are created equal.'* We now practically read it 'all men are created equal, *except Negroes.'* When the Know-Nothings get control, it will read 'all men are created equal, except Negroes, *and foreigners, and Catholics.'* ❞

In Lincoln's view, it was wrong to discriminate against people simply because they

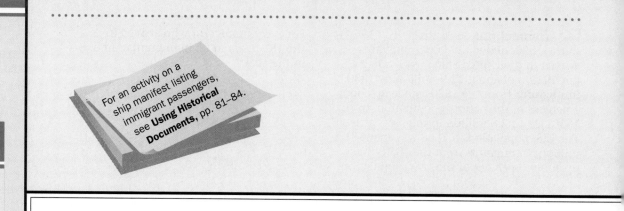

For an activity on a ship manifest listing immigrant passengers, see **Using Historical Documents**, pp. 81–84.

Closing the Section

Section Review
Answers

1. Definitions: *trade union* (419), *strike* (419), *nativism* (421), *nativists* (421)

2. Working for wages became a way of life rather than a temporary condition. Wages dropped because of the increase in skilled and unskilled workers.

3. To increase wages and decrease working hours. A person could be fined or jailed for belonging to a union or striking.

4. Native-born workers blamed the new influx of immigrants for the decline in wages and feared that their languages and customs threatened "American" culture.

5. Both faced discrimination and were not considered true Americans. Unlike the new immigrants, though, free African Americans were not seen as a threat to take jobs from native-born white northerners.

To check understanding of "Why We Remember," assign Thinking Critically question 3 on student page 424.

had been born elsewhere or were Catholics. He told the Know-Nothings that the Indians are the true native Americans. "We pushed them from their homes, and now turn upon others not fortunate enough to come over as early as our forefathers."

As Lincoln hoped, the Know-Nothing Party soon faded away, but nativism has continued to appeal to some Americans. When the economy slows down and jobs are scarce, immigrants are often accused of taking jobs away from native-born workers. They are also viewed with suspicion and even hostility depending on their race, their religion, and the country from which they come.

3. Section Review

1. Define the terms **trade union, strike, nativism,** and **nativists.**
2. How did working for wages change in the early 1800s?
3. What were the goals of the trade unions of the 1830s? Why was it dangerous to be a union member at that time?
4. What fears led some Americans to become nativists?
5. **Critical Thinking** Compare attitudes in the North toward immigrants and free African Americans. How were attitudes similar? How were they different?

Why We Remember

Americans at Mid-Century

In 1855 Frederick Douglass wrote a book about his life titled *My Bondage and My Freedom.* In it he described the misery of slavery in the South and the injustices of racism in the North. Still, he wrote, despite "the ten thousand discouragements" facing African Americans, "progress is yet possible."

The belief that we can make life better by our own efforts was widely shared by mid-century Americans. It led people to start new businesses. It encouraged inventors to create new technologies. It sent farmers and planters west to clear new land. It inspired enslaved African Americans to seek freedom and workers to organize for decent wages. And it lured immigrants from lands where progress seemed a dim hope.

Even as Douglass was writing those words, however, a gap was widening between the North and the South. While the North saw progress in terms of industry and transportation, the South committed itself ever more firmly to the system of plantations based on slavery. Increasingly, the economic interests of the two sections were coming into conflict. Increasingly, too, opposition to slavery was driving a wedge between them. The progress on which Douglass pinned his hopes would have to contend with the realities of sectional conflict.

wages in perspective, they might want information about a seamstress's typical living expenses and the working conditions and wages in other occupations for both men and women. (b) The writer would say that women were treated unfairly. Students will probably say that the evidence from the letter makes them believe that women who worked in their homes and in workshops in the 1800s were indeed treated unfairly, because they worked very long hours for very low wages, and sometimes for none at all.

For further application, have students do the Applying Skills activity in the Chapter Survey (p. 424).

If students need to review the skill, use the Skills Development transparency and activity in the **Chapter Resources Binder**, pp. 119–120.

Skill Lab

Thinking Critically
Identifying Evidence

Skill Tips

- A claim may be stated directly, or it may be implied—suggested. Read carefully.
- General types of evidence that might support a claim include statistics, names, dates, events, and descriptions.
- To evaluate how well the evidence supports a claim, ask yourself: Is the evidence specific? Is it clear? Is there enough of it? What else would I ask the writer if I could?

Not all wage earners of the early and middle 1800s worked in large mills or factories. Many, especially women, worked at home or in small workshops. In 1828 Matthew Carey, a businessman, called attention to the hardships of their lives:

"I have known a lady to expend 100 dollars on a party; pay 30 or 40 dollars for a bonnet, and 50 for a shawl; and yet make a hard bargain with a seamstress or washer-woman, who had to work at her needle or at the washing tub for 13 or 14 hours a day to make a bare livelihood for herself and a numerous family of small children."

Question to Investigate

Were women who worked at home or in workshops in the 1800s treated fairly?

Procedure

Explore the Question to Investigate by reading the letter on this page. It was written by a seamstress. Like many descriptions of historical situations and events, the letter includes a claim and supporting evidence. A **claim** is something that someone says is true. **Evidence** is information—facts, not opinions—given to support the claim. Read the source and do the following.

❶ Identify the claim being made. Decide what the letter writer is trying to prove, and state that claim in a sentence.

❷ Identify the evidence that supports the claim. List specific facts that the letter writer uses to support her claim.

❸ Evaluate the evidence.
a. Answer the questions in the last point under Skill Tips.
b. How would the letter writer answer the Question to Investigate? How would you? Explain.

Source to Use

"Only think of a poor woman, confined to her seat fifteen hours out of twenty-four to make a pair of . . . pantaloons, for which she receives only twenty-five cents. And indeed, many of them [seamstresses] are not able to make a pair in much less than two days. . . .

Only think of twelve and a half cents for making a shirt, that takes a woman a whole day, if she attends to any other work in her family. . . . How shall she clothe her poor children, or even feed them at this rate? Yet there are many poor women of my acquaintance that are placed in the disheartening [discouraging] situation I have mentioned; and many of them are widows, with a number of children. And the tailors scold us when we bring . . . the work, and some of them say the work is done ill [poorly], and then take out half the price, or give us nothing if they [choose] . . . and God help us, we have to submit to the injustice."

From a seamstress's letter that appeared in *Mechanics Free Press*, December 18, 1830

Introducing the Skill Lab

Point out that any claim is only as valid, or sound, as the evidence that supports it. If necessary, have students review the difference between statements of fact and opinions, as discussed in the Skill Lab on page 210. Before students analyze the letter, discuss the Matthew Carey quote, asking them to identify evidence of unfair treatment of seamstresses.

Skill Lab
Answers

1. Students' sentences should be similar to the following: The writer claims that seamstresses like her are treated unjustly by being paid too little for the work they do.

2. Specific statements of fact include: ". . . fifteen hours out of twenty-four to make a pair . . . ," ". . . receives only twenty-five cents . . . ," ". . . twelve and a half cents for making a shirt, that takes a woman a whole day . . . ," ". . . take out half the price, or give us nothing . . ." Students should recognize that the references to the "disheartening" situation and to the "injustice" are not evidence, because they are opinions.

3. (a) Students will probably say that the evidence is both specific and clear. To put the

(Answers continued in top margin)

Reviewing Vocabulary

Definitions may be found
on the following pages:
slave codes (417), *discrimination* (417), *trade union* (419),
strike (419), *nativism* (421),
nativists (421).

Reviewing Main Ideas

1. (a) The economy of the
Northeast was more diverse,
including whaling, trading,
and manufacturing. The economy of the Midwest was agricultural. (b) The two regions
were linked by railroads.

2. (a) The South's economy
revolved around the cotton
crop. Tobacco, rice, and
sugar cane were also grown.
(b) Only about one-fourth
of white southerners owned
slaves. Of those, about two-
thirds owned fewer than 10.
Three-fourths of white southerners—small farmers who
grew their own food and had
few cash crops—did not own
slaves.

3. Slave owners would rou-
tinely work their slaves
beyond endurance, providing
them with minimal clothing,
food, and shelter.

4. Enslaved African Americans resisted slavery by striking back at their masters in
subtle ways, such as by breaking tools or feigning inability
to work, and by escaping to
freedom or revolting.

5. (a) Free African Americans
in the South were suspected
and feared as a potential dis-
ruptive force. They were
therefore denied the right to
travel freely or own guns,
and were punished severely
for minor crimes. (b) They
were discriminated against;
for example, they were not
allowed to attend the same
churches as whites.

6. Factory workers went on
strike to protest low wages
and long work days.

(Answers continued in top margin)

7. The immigrants' languages, customs, and
religions were different. Native-born workers also resented them for accepting low
wages.

Thinking Critically

1. It is accurate because the people supported themselves in a number of ways.
They fished, traded, worked in factories,
and farmed. The South's economy might

be labeled as single-product because it
revolved around the cotton crop.

2. Answers may vary. Because the North and
the South had very different economies, their
positions on issues, such as protective tariffs
and the spread of slavery, were different.

3. Examples include the efforts of enslaved
African Americans to strike back, escape, and
revolt; the efforts of free African Americans

Chapter Survey ⭐

Reviewing Vocabulary

Define the following terms.
1. slave codes
2. discrimination
3. trade union
4. strike
5. nativism
6. nativists

Reviewing Main Ideas

1. (a) How did economic activities in the
Northeast and Midwest differ? (b) What
tied these two regions together?
2. (a) Describe the economy of the South.
(b) Who owned slaves? Who did not?
3. How did most slave owners try to get
the greatest benefit from their slaves?
4. Describe three ways that enslaved
African Americans resisted slavery.
5. (a) Why did Frederick Douglass say that
"no colored man is really free in a slaveholding state"? (b) What problems did free
African Americans face in the North?
6. Why did some factory workers in the
North go on strike in the 1830s?
7. Why were some native-born Americans
suspicious of the immigrants who came to
the United States in the mid-1800s?

Thinking Critically

1. Analysis The economy of the North
in the mid-1800s can be described as a
diversified, or varied, economy. Why do
you think this description is accurate?
What label would you use to describe the
economy of the South? Why?
2. Synthesis Predict how economic
differences between the North and the
South might contribute to conflict
between the two regions.
3. Why We Remember: Application
Frederick Douglass believed that "if there
is no struggle there is no progress." Give
three supporting examples from the text
or your own observations.

Applying Skills

Identifying evidence In the Skill Lab
on page 423 you investigated claims of
unfair working conditions by a seamstress
more than 150 years ago.
1. Find a recent claim of unfair working
conditions. It may involve someone you
know or a situation you have read about.
2. Identify the claim being made.
3. Identify the evidence that supports
the claim.
4. Explain how the evidence supports the
claim. Note if the evidence is specific and
clear and if there is enough of it. What
else would you ask if you could?

History Mystery

A popular product Answer the
History Mystery on page 403.
What invention would destroy
demand for this product? Explain.

Writing in Your History Journal

1. Keys to History (a) The time
line on pages 402–403 has seven
Keys to History. In your journal,
describe why each one is important to
know about. (b) Imagine that you are
going to teach fifth-grade students about the
events on the time line. Choose one event.
In your journal, state what you would say
about the causes and effects of the event to
help younger students understand it.
2. Frederick Douglass It is 1841. Yesterday, you attended the meeting of the
Massachusetts Antislavery Society where
Frederick Douglass first spoke about his life
as a slave. In your journal, write a letter to
Douglass giving your personal reactions to
at least two specific comments he made.
You can get ideas about what he might
have said from the quotations in the text.

to receive equal treatment; the efforts of workers to protect themselves by forming unions; the efforts of immigrants to better their lives by coming to the United States.

Applying Skills

To help students identify a claim of unfair working conditions and evidence supporting that claim, have them draw a circle around the claim and a square around each piece of evidence that supports it. They might want to number the pieces of evidence.

History Mystery

The product was ice. It was popular because it could not be found in tropical lands. The forerunner of the modern refrigerator eventually destroyed the demand for natural ice.

(Answers continued in side margin)

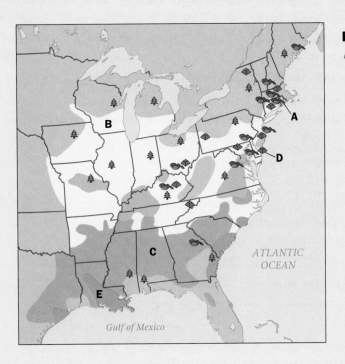

ATLANTIC OCEAN

Gulf of Mexico

Reviewing Geography

1. For each letter on the map, write the name of the product or products identified.

2. Geographic Thinking Your library probably has books that rate the states according to how desirable they are to live in. Imagine that you are writing a guide to the states in 1850. Choose one state and review information in the text, including the maps and the Geography Lab.

Write a brief description of the climate and economic opportunities that might make this state one of the best places to live.

Writing in Your History Journal

1. (a) Explanations should be similar to the time line notes on teacher pages 402–403. (b) If necessary, students may review the text in order to describe the event.

2. Refer students to Douglass's comments about the slave breaker (p. 404), overwork (p. 405), fighting the slave breaker (p. 405), living conditions in the North (p. 406), northern efficiency (p. 408), slave poverty (p. 414), escaping (p. 416), and northern racism (p. 418). Students' reactions will vary.

3. Answers will vary. Some possibilities are organizing a boycott of the streetcar company or filing a lawsuit against it.

Reviewing Geography

1. (A) textiles, (B) corn and wheat, (C) cotton, (D) iron, (E) rice and sugar.

2. Students might choose a northeastern state because of job opportunities, a southern state because of the climate and farming opportunities, or a midwestern state because of its rich soil for farming.

Alternative Assessment

Teacher's Take-Home Planner 5, page 21, includes suggestions and scoring rubrics for the Alternative Assessment activity.

3. Citizenship In the early 1860s Charlotte L. Brown, a free African American, boarded a streetcar in San Francisco, in the free state of California. As she later wrote, the conductor informed her that "colored persons were not allowed to ride" and ordered her to get out. Charlotte refused, telling the conductor that she "had a right to ride, it was a public conveyance [vehicle]." Finally, he forced her out of the car. What would you have done in this situation? Why? Write your thoughts in your journal.

Alternative Assessment

Planning a time capsule Imagine that you live in 1850 in the North or the South. The people of your town have decided to bury a time capsule in the town square.

They want to help future generations understand their past. The capsule will contain items that reflect the events, issues, and people of the years 1830 to 1850. You are on the committee to collect items for the time capsule.

With the other committee members, make a list of 15 items to include in the capsule. The items can be objects, documents, or pictures. Write a description of each item and explain why it was chosen to represent life in the mid-1800s.

Your work will be evaluated on the following criteria:
• the items you choose are appropriate for the time period and region
• the items you choose reflect major aspects of life in the mid-1800s
• you explain clearly how each item relates to the time period and region

Remind students that African American children were also forced into slavery. Stress the importance of young people like Sarny telling their stories. As students read from *Nightjohn,* point out that Sarny is the narrator and that her words do not appear in quotation marks. Suggest that they reread Sarny's words, imagining the sound of her voice. Encourage them to think of the message of Sarny's words as they read.

✳ **Literature Footnote**

Gary Paulsen's *Nightjohn* is historical fiction set in the pre–Civil War South. The story effectively shows that the ability to read and write is bound up with human dignity and independence. It also demonstrates the risks slaves took when they tried to become educated. Published in 1993, *Nightjohn* was chosen as an American Library Association Notable Book for Children in 1994.

⊗ Link to Literature

Nightjohn by Gary Paulsen

Gary Paulsen's novel, *Nightjohn,* is told from the point of view of Sarny, a 12-year-old slave. On the plantation where she lives she meets a man named John. One night, John quietly begins to teach Sarny to read and write. In the following scene, Sarny's mammy catches John teaching Sarny the letter *B.*

"What in the *hell* are you doing? Don't you know what they do to her if they find her trying to read? We already got one girl tore to pieces by the whip and the dogs. We don't need two. . . . Child, they'll cut your thumbs off if you learn to read. They'll whip you until your back looks knitted— until it looks like his back." She pointed to John, big old finger. "Is that how you got whipped?"

He shook his head. "I ran."

"And got caught."

"Not the first time."

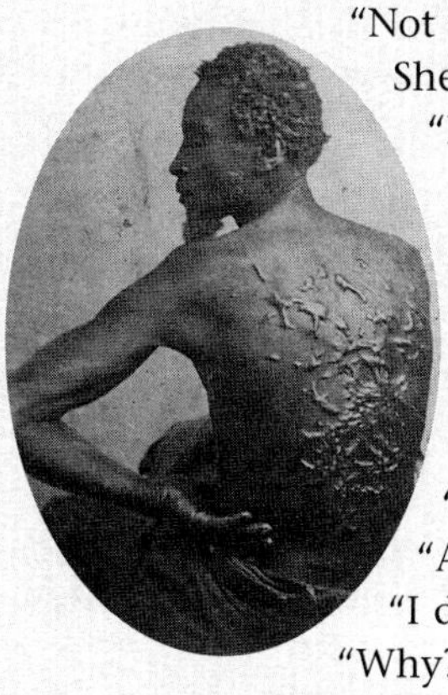

She waited. I waited.

"First time I got clean away. I went north, all the way. I was free." I'd never heard such a thing. We couldn't even talk about being free. And here was a man said he had been free by running north. I thought, How can that be?

"You ran and got away?" mammy asked.

"I did."

"You ran until you were clean away?"

"I did."

"And you came *back?*"

"I did."

"Why?"

He sighed and it sounded like his voice, like his laugh. Low and way off thunder. It made me think he was going to promise something, the way thunder promises rain. "For this."

"What you mean—this?"

"To teach reading."

quarters: lodging place for slaves

It's never quiet in the quarters. During the day the young ones run and scrabble and fight or cry and they's always a gaggle of them. At night everybody be sleeping. But not quiet. Alice, she's quiet. But they's some of them to cry. New workers who are just old enough to be working in the fields cry sometimes in their sleep. They hurt and their hands bleed and pain them from new blisters that break and break again. Old workers cry because they're old and getting to the end and have old pain. Same pain,

* Literature Footnote

Gary Paulsen, known for his meticulous research and historical accuracy, is the author of three Newbery Honor books, *The Winter Room, Hatchet,* and *Dogsong.* The National Council of Teachers of English has chosen Paulsen as one of the world's most important writers for young adults.

young and old. Some snore. Others just breathe loud.

It's a long building and dark except for the light coming in the door and the small windows, but it's never quiet. Not even at night.

Now it seemed quiet. Mammy she looked down at John. Didn't say nothing for a long time. Just looked.

I had to think to hear the breathing, night sounds.

Slave quarters were often large buildings that housed several families.

Finally mammy talks. Her voice is soft. "You came back to teach reading?"

John nodded. "That's half of it."

"What's the other half?"

"Writing." He smiled. "Course, I wasn't going to get caught. I had in mind moving, moving around. Teaching a little here, a little there. Going to do hidey-schools. But I got slow and they got fast and some crackers caught me in the woods. They were hunting bear, but the dogs came on me instead and I took to a tree and they got me."

Another long quiet. Way off, down by the river, I heard the sound of a nightbird. Singing for day. Soon the sun would come.

"Why does it matter?" Mammy leaned against the wall. She had one hand on the logs, one on her cheek. Tired. "Why do that to these young ones? To Sarny here. If they learn to read—"

"And write."

"And write, it's just grief for them. Longtime grief. They find what they don't have, can't have. It ain't good to know that. It eats at you then—to know it and not have it."

"They have to be able to write," John said. Voice pushing. He stood and reached out one hand with long fingers and touched mammy on the forehead. It was almost like he be kissing her with his fingers. Soft. Touch like black cotton in the dark. "They have to read and write. We all have to read and write so we can write about this—what they doing to us. It has to be written."

Mammy she turned and went back to her mat on the floor. Moving quiet, not looking back. She settled next to the young ones and John he turned to me and he say:

"Next is *C.*"

hidey-schools: secret schools

crackers: scornful term for poor whites

A Closer Look

1. What is mammy's reaction to Sarny learning to read? Why?

2. What does the author's description of the quarters tell you about the lives of those who live there?

3. How does mammy's attitude change as she and John talk? Why do you think this change occurs?

From *Nightjohn* by Gary Paulsen. Copyright © 1993 by Gary Paulsen. Used by permission of Delacorte Press, a division of Bantam Doubleday Publishing Group, Inc.

● 427

Discussion

Stimulating Critical Thinking

1. Why did John risk his life to teach people to read and write? (John taught his people to read and write to empower them. According to John, reading and writing would enable them to record their experiences as slaves so that others might learn about their suffering.)

2. Do you agree with Mammy's opinion about teaching young slaves to read and write? Why or why not? (Some students may disagree because reading and writing would help the children have different experiences and brighten their lives. Others may agree because it would let the children know how miserable their situation was.)

3. Sarny said, "Way off, down by the river, I heard the sound of a nightbird. Singing for day. Soon the sun would come." Is there a connection between these words and the title *Nightjohn*? (John, or Night-john, would sing by teaching people to read and write. The coming sun would be knowledge and freedom, which one day would belong to all African Americans.)

A Closer Look

Answers

1. Mammy becomes upset after finding out that Sarny is learning to read. Mammy knows what slave owners do to slaves who can read.

2. The description of the quarters reveals that they led pain-filled lives and were denied basic dignity.

3. As Mammy and John talk, she becomes less combative. Mammy changes her mind after John says that reading and writing will help them tell about their lives.

16 Religion and Reform
1820–1850

Chapter Planning Guide

Section	Student Text	Teacher's Edition Activities
Opener and Story pp. 428–431	**Keys to History Time Line** **History Mystery** Beginning the Story with **Sojourner Truth**	**Setting the Stage Activity** What's in a Name?, p. 430
1 Revival and Reform pp. 432–439	**Hands-On History** Speaking to persuade, p. 435 **Link to the Present** The environmental movement, p. 436 **Geography Lab** The First Big City Park, p. 439	**Warm-Up Activity** Analyzing Reform, p. 432 **Geography Question of the Day,** p. 432 **Section Activity** Organizing a Reform, p. 434 **Bonus Activity** Preparing a Lesson, p. 434 **Wrap-Up Activity** A Concept Web, p. 438
2 Movements to End Slavery pp. 440–446	**World Link** Britain abolishes slavery, p. 442 **Reading Maps** The Underground Railroad, p. 444 **Skill Lab** Historical Interpretations, p. 446	**Warm-Up Activity** Writing About Freedoms, p. 440 **Geography Question of the Day,** p. 440 **Section Activity** An Antislavery Paper, p. 441 **Bonus Activity** Listening to "Amazing Grace," p. 442 **Wrap-Up Activity** Who-What-Why Charts, p. 445
3 Working for Women's Rights pp. 447–451	**Point of View** What did women think about the vote?, p. 450	**Warm-Up Activity** Newspaper Search, p. 447 **Geography Question of the Day,** p. 447 **Section Activity** Adopting a List of Grievances, p. 450 **Bonus Activity** Letter to the Editor, p. 448 **Wrap-Up Activity** Making a Placard, p. 451
4 American Voices pp. 452–455	**Link to Art** *Blue Hole, Little Miami River,* p. 454	**Warm-Up Activity** Poetry Reading, p. 452 **Geography Question of the Day,** p. 452 **Section Activity** Writing a Poem, p. 453 **Bonus Activity** A Landscape Sketch, p. 454 **Wrap-Up Activity** A Literary Time Line, p. 455
Evaluation	☑ **Section 1 Review,** p. 438 ☑ **Section 2 Review,** p. 445 ☑ **Section 3 Review,** p. 451 ☑ **Section 4 Review,** p. 455 ☑ **Chapter Survey,** pp. 456–457 **Alternative Assessment** Working for reform, p. 457	☑ **Answers to Section 1 Review,** p. 438 ☑ **Answers to Section 2 Review,** p. 445 ☑ **Answers to Section 3 Review,** p. 451 ☑ **Answers to Section 4 Review,** p. 455 ☑ **Answers to Chapter Survey,** pp. 456–457 (Alternative Assessment guidelines are in the Take-Home Planner.)

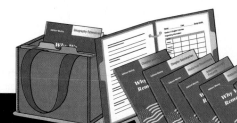

Teacher's Resource Package

Chapter Summaries: English and Spanish, pp. 36–37

Chapter Resources Binder
Study Guide Using Visual Images to Preview, p. 121
Geography Extensions Planning Parks, pp. 31–32

Chapter Resources Binder
Study Guide Identifying Roles, p. 122

Skills Development Historical Interpretations, pp. 127–128
American Readings Safe House, p. 61

Chapter Resources Binder
Study Guide Webbing, p. 123

Reinforcement Analyzing Women's Rights, pp. 125–126
American Readings A Girls' School, pp. 62–63; We Need Education, p. 64
Using Historical Documents *A Petition for Universal Suffrage* and *The Nonsense of it,* pp. 85–90

Chapter Resources Binder
Study Guide Relating Authors and Themes, p. 124

Chapter and Unit Tests Chapter 16 Tests, Forms A and B, pp. 99–102

Take-Home Planner

Introducing the Chapter Activity Calling for Reform, p. 28

Chapter In-Depth Activity Bringing an End to Slavery, p. 28

Reduced Views
Study Guide, p. 30
Geography Extensions, p. 33
Unit 5 Answers, pp. 36–44

Reduced Views
Study Guide, p. 30
Skills Development, p. 31
American Readings, p. 32
Unit 5 Answers, pp. 36–44

Reduced Views
Study Guide, p. 30
Reinforcement, p. 31
American Readings, p. 32
Using Historical Documents, p. 33
Unit 5 Answers, pp. 36–44

Reduced Views
Study Guide, p. 30
Unit 5 Answers, pp. 36–44

Reduced Views
Chapter Tests, p. 33
Unit 5 Answers, pp. 36–44
Alternative Assessment Guidelines for scoring the Chapter Survey activity, p. 29

Additional Resources

Wall Time Line

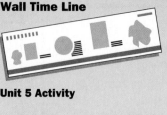

Unit 5 Activity

Transparency Package

Transparency 16-1 Winslow Homer's *The Country School*—use with Section 1
Transparency 16-2 One-Room School—use with Section 1
Transparency Activity Book

SelecTest Testing Software
Chapter 16 Test, Forms A and B

★ ★ ★
Vital Links

 Videodisc

CD-ROM

Free public schools (see TE p. 435)
Dorothea Dix (see TE p. 436)
Freedom's Journal (see TE p. 442)
Voice of Harriet Tubman (see TE p. 443)
"Follow the Drinking Gourd" (see TE p. 444)
Elizabeth Blackwell (see TE p. 448)
Voice of Elizabeth Cady Stanton (see TE p. 449)

Teaching Resources

Take-Home Planner 5
 Introducing Chapter Activity
 Chapter In-Depth Activity
 Alternative Assessment
Chapter Resources Binder
Geography Extensions
American Readings
Using Historical Documents
Transparency Activities
Wall Time Line Activities
Chapter Summaries
Chapter and Unit Tests
SelecTest Test File
Vital Links CD-ROM/Videodisc

Time Line

Keys to History

Keys to History Journal writing activity is on page 456 in the Chapter Survey.

Second Great Awakening
The religious revivals of the early 1800s encouraged people to improve their personal lives and help others through social reform. (p. 432)

Horace Mann Horace Mann led the movement to expand and improve public education, arguing that democracy required educated citizens. (p. 434)

Looking Back Although the slave trade was banned in 1808, ownership and sale of slaves in the United States continued.

Chapter Objectives

★ Identify the religious revivals and reform movements that swept the nation.
★ Describe how the movement to end slavery gained strength in the early 1800s.
★ Summarize the struggle for women's rights in the early 1800s.
★ Describe the flowering of American literature and art.

Chapter Overview

The religious revival known as the Second Great Awakening gave birth to a new spirit of social reform. People worked to improve public education, help the disabled, reform prisons, fight alcohol abuse, and create utopias.

One of the great reform causes of the age was the movement to end slavery. Free African Americans were among the first to work for abolition. Abolitionists, black and

---

1820–1850

Chapter 16

Religion and Reform

Sections

Beginning the Story with Sojourner Truth
1. **Revival and Reform**
2. **Movements to End Slavery**
3. **Working for Women's Rights**
4. **American Voices**

Keys to History

Early 1800s
Second Great Awakening sweeps the nation
Carving of Henry Ward Beecher, a revival preacher

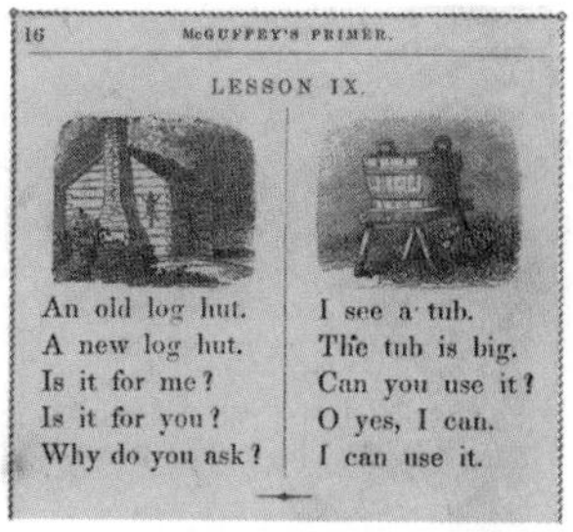

1830s
Horace Mann urges spread of public schools
McGuffey reader, an early schoolbook

16 McGUFFEY'S PRIMER.
LESSON IX.

An old log hut.
A new log hut.
Is it for me?
Is it for you?
Why do you ask?

I see a tub.
The tub is big.
Can you use it?
O yes, I can.
I can use it.

1820

1830

Looking Back
Slave trade banned in the United States
1808

white, published books and newspapers, gave speeches, and participated in the Underground Railroad.

The antislavery movement inspired women to seek their own rights. Women in the early 1800s began to gain access to education and the professions. At the Seneca Falls Convention of 1848 they demanded full rights, including the right to vote.

Many important American writers and painters came to the public's attention in this period. Unlike earlier artists, they celebrated being uniquely American. Some were influenced by the transcendental philosophy of Emerson and Thoreau.

Teaching the HISTORY Mystery

Students will find the answer on p. 448. See Chapter Survey, p. 456, for additional information and questions.

HISTORY Mystery

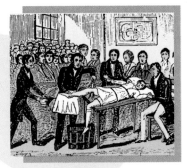

Dr. Blackwell graduated at the top of the class of 1849 from the medical school of Geneva College. Yet years earlier this brilliant student had been turned down by nearly a dozen schools. Why was Blackwell rejected?

Time Line

American Anti-Slavery Society Founded by the outspoken William Lloyd Garrison, the society called for the immediate abolition of slavery. (p. 441)

Narrative of the Life of Frederick Douglass Douglass's autobiography became popular reading and helped to fuel the antislavery movement. (p. 442)

Seneca Falls Convention This meeting marked the beginning of the women's movement in the United States. (pp. 449–450)

The Underground Railroad Harriet Tubman was one conductor on the Underground Railroad, a network of people who helped escaping slaves reach freedom. (p. 443)

World Link See p. 442.

Looking Ahead Slavery was finally ended by the Thirteenth Amendment to the Constitution.

1833
American Anti-Slavery Society established
William Lloyd Garrison

1845
Frederick Douglass publishes *Narrative of the Life of Frederick Douglass*

1848
Seneca Falls Convention on women's rights

1850s
Harriet Tubman makes heroic journeys as part of the Underground Railroad

1840

1850

 World Link

Britain abolishes slavery
1833

Looking Ahead

13th Amendment ends slavery
1865

● **429**

Sojourner Truth

Sojourner Truth was born into slavery and died in freedom. She represents in her extraordinary life the themes of religion and reform. Her deep faith gave her strength to battle injustice and oppression, and gave her hope that life could be made better. She worked in the antislavery and women's rights movements. Sojourner Truth represented the very best in the reform movement—a deep knowledge of injustice coupled with selflessness and dedication to others.

Setting the Stage
Activity

What's in a Name?

To help students appreciate Sojourner Truth's character, have them focus on her name. Ask what kind of person they think would take that name. Suggest that they look up the meanings of *sojourner* and *truth* in the dictionary. Based on the definitions, have them describe in writing what a woman by this name might be like.

See the Introducing the Chapter Activity, Calling for Reform. **Take-Home Planner 5,** p. 28.

History Footnote

Just before the excerpt from her speech quoted on this page, Sojourner Truth said:

> Well, children, where there is so much racket there must be something out of kilter. I think that 'twixt the Negroes of the South and the women of the North, all talking about rights, the white men will be in a fix pretty soon.

In the same speech, she said:

> Then that little man in black there [a clergyman], he says women can't have as much rights as men, cause Christ wasn't a woman! Where did your Christ come from? Where did your Christ come from? From God and a woman! Man had nothing to do with him.

Beginning the Story with

Sojourner Truth

Sojourner Truth had heard enough. She had come to this church in Akron, Ohio, to discuss the rights of women. And what had she heard instead? One minister after another explaining why women were too weak in mind and body to do much of anything except raise children.

Her patience worn out, she rose from her seat to reply. The idea of an African American woman, especially a former slave, making a public speech shocked some members of the audience. "No! No!" they shouted. "Don't let her speak!"

"Ain't I a Woman?"

Quite unafraid, the tall woman walked to the pulpit and began to speak. "The poor men seem to be all in confusion," she began with a laugh.

> **"**The man over there says women need to be helped into carriages and lifted over ditches and over puddles, and have the best places everywhere. Nobody helps me into carriages or over puddles, or gives me the best place—and ain't I a woman? Look at my arm! I have plowed and planted and gathered into barns, and no man could head [outdo] me—and ain't I a woman? I could work as much and eat as much as a man—when I could get it—and bear the lash as well! And ain't I a woman? I have borne thirteen children, and seen most of 'em sold into slavery, and when I cried out with my mother's grief, none but Jesus heard me—and ain't I a woman?**"**

As usual, Sojourner Truth had gone straight to the heart of the matter and spoken the truth. At the same time, she had charmed her listeners. "This unlearned African woman has a magnetic power over an audience [that is] perfectly astounding," observed an admirer. As Sojourner Truth put it, "I cannot read a book, but I can read people."

History Bookshelf

Botkin, B. A., ed. *Lay My Burden Down: A Folk History of Slavery.* University of Georgia Press, 1989. Botkin was an editor with the Federal Writers' Project in the 1930s. Under his direction, thousands of pages of interviews with former slaves were collected. A selection of these interviews is included in this fascinating book.

Also of interest:

Lanker, Brian. *I Dream a World: Portraits of Black Women Who Changed America.* Stewart, Tabori, and Chang, 1989.

Riley, Dorothy Winbush, ed. *My Soul Looks Back, 'Less I Forget: A Collection of Quotations by People of Color.* HarperCollins, 1993.

"I'll Keep You Scratching"

Sojourner Truth's legal name was Isabella ("Belle") Van Wagener. She was born in New York around 1797. Growing up in slavery, she had seen all of her 12 brothers and sisters sold by her master, a wealthy Dutch landowner. She herself was sold twice before the age of 14. One of her owners boasted that Belle was "better to me than a *man*—for she will do a good family's washing in the night, and be ready in the morning to go into the field where she will do as much raking and binding as my best hands."

In a time with no television or radio, public speaking on issues was a common way to raise public awareness and support.

New York ended slavery for adults in 1827. By that time Belle had borne several children. On gaining her freedom, she learned that her youngest son Peter was still enslaved, despite his master's promise to free him. Belle took the daring step of suing for his freedom in a state court. She won. Then, taking her two youngest children, she moved to New York City and began a new life.

Belle was a strongly spiritual person who felt very close to God. She composed hymns and memorized much of the Bible. In 1843, at nearly the age of 50, Belle came to believe that God was calling her to be a traveling minister. She changed her name to Sojourner Truth and began traveling through the northern states. She preached in churches, at open-air gatherings called camp meetings, and on city streets, telling all who would listen about God's goodness and the brotherhood of all his children.

As a speaker, Sojourner Truth was absolutely fearless. Her confidence rested in her belief that God was with her and that she was doing the Lord's work. She became active in the antislavery and women's rights movements and was a popular speaker for these causes. Her faith, as well as a ready wit, helped protect her from hecklers and their insults. In one debate a lawyer dismissed her, saying, "Old woman, do you suppose people care what you say? Why, I don't care any more for your talk than I do for the bite of a flea."

"Maybe not," Truth replied with a laugh. "But Lord willing, I'll keep you scratching."

Hands-On HISTORY

Activity

Like Sojourner Truth, some public speakers today talk of "reading people." For example, politicians try to read an audience to judge whether they have support. On the left side of a sheet of paper, list three or more clues a speaker might look for in reading people. On the right, suggest what messages the clues might give the speaker. Be prepared to demonstrate the clues and their meanings.

Discussion

Thinking Historically

1. **What was the source of Sojourner Truth's strength, both as a speaker and as a person?** (Deep religious faith.)

2. **What were some of the life experiences that sharpened her sense of injustice?** (She was born into slavery, and saw her brothers, sisters, and children sold.)

3. **What are some examples of injustices today that require reform?** (Some possibilities: economic injustice, racism, environmental concerns.)

See the Chapter In-Depth Activity, Bringing an End to Slavery. **Take-Home Planner 5,** p. 28.

Teaching the Hands-On HISTORY

If students have difficulty beginning their lists, suggest that they think about body language. For example, if members of the audience are fidgeting, yawning, or whispering, the speaker is probably losing the audience. On the other hand, if people are sitting up straight and looking directly at the speaker, he or she probably has their attention. Ask volunteers to demonstrate the clues and ask the class to interpret their meaning.

For a journal writing activity on Sojourner Truth, see student page 457.

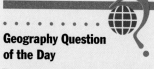
★

1. Revival and Reform

Reading Guide

New Terms social reform, temperance, utopias

Section Focus The religious revivals and reform movements that swept the nation

1. What was the Second Great Awakening?
2. What movements for social reform arose in the first half of the 1800s?
3. How did utopias show a longing for a better society?

Religious faith was the main influence on Sojourner Truth's life. Nothing mattered more than doing the things God called her to do—fighting for justice and building harmony among people. Her religious motives were typical of people of her time who sought to make society better. The early 1800s was a period of religious revivals known as the Second Great Awakening.

The Second Great Awakening

The rapid spread of the Second Great Awakening caused church membership to boom. The message of the revival was the message of evangelical Christianity—that people should turn from evil, or repent, and receive God's love and forgiveness. For people new to the Christian faith, this experience was known as conversion. The message was a democratic one: conversion was equally open to everyone.

Camp meetings One way that revival spread was through camp meetings—large outdoor gatherings that lasted several days. Families traveled for miles to attend. People slept in tents, wagons, or shelters made of tree branches and ate meals together in the open air. Often Baptist, Methodist, and Presbyterian ministers sang and preached in different parts of the camp at the same time.

The largest of all camp meetings took place at Cane Ridge, Kentucky, in August 1801. It lasted six days and attracted more than 10,000 excited people. The shouting and singing could be heard for miles. James Finley, a famous preacher, claimed:

❝The noise was like the roar of Niagara [Falls]. The vast sea of human beings seemed to be agitated as if by a storm. I counted seven ministers all preaching at once, some on stumps, others in wagons.**❞**

Circuit riders The revival message was welcomed in the West. To reach people in these sparsely populated areas, traveling ministers called circuit riders rode horseback over regular routes known as circuits. They preached sermons and tended to the spiritual needs of people too isolated and too poor to support a full-time minister.

The person credited with pioneering the circuit rider ministry was the Methodist bishop Francis Asbury. He was a circuit rider for 45 years. Because of the zeal of Asbury and his fellow preachers, the Methodists had the largest following of any Protestant church in America by the 1840s.

Although it had its beginnings in 1787, the African Methodist Episcopal Church was officially organized in 1816. Richard Allen, one of its founders, was ordained a minister in 1799 and designated a bishop in 1816. Today the African Methodist Episcopal Church has well over two million members and is active in missionary work, particularly in Africa and the West Indies.

Preachers at camp meetings felt that God's message was for everyone. They urged their listeners to turn away from bad habits, and many people did change. "Drunkards, profane swearers, liars, quarrelsome persons, etc., are remarkably reformed," reported one preacher.

African American churches The Methodists had a separate branch for African American members. It began in 1787 when church officials in Philadelphia told three free African Americans they could not sit with white members. Insulted, Richard Allen and Absalom Jones organized their own church, the Mother Bethel African Methodist Episcopal (AME) Church. AME churches are still active today.

In addition to the AME Church, which continued to spread, African Americans formed other churches in the North. African Americans could not form churches in the South until after the Civil War because laws prevented them from assembling.

When Isabella Van Wagener moved to New York City in 1829, she joined the AME Church. She was active in the church for 15 years before setting off on her traveling ministry as Sojourner Truth.

Revivals and Reform

A major outcome of the Second Great Awakening was a new spirit of **social reform**—the effort to make society better and more fair for everyone. People who converted to evangelical Christianity felt moved to improve their personal lives and also to help others. Such men and women believed that they could and should work to correct the evils in society.

Religious revivals, combined with the democratic spirit of the Age of Jackson, produced in Americans a deeper belief in equality. Caught up in religious and democratic fervor, many Americans believed that it would be simple to lift the curtains of ignorance by improving public education throughout the nation. They also turned their energies toward freeing those who were physically or mentally enslaved.

Preparing a Lesson

To experience the challenges of teaching in a one-room school, have small groups prepare reading lessons that would be taught to young children, and math lessons that older students would work on at the same time. Students might prepare a math worksheet for the older children and identify the book and vocabulary to be taught to the younger children.

Organizing a Reform

To help students recognize what goes into a successful reform movement, have small groups plan reform campaigns. Each group should identify a social problem in the school or community and propose a solution. Have them outline a campaign to inform the public about the problem, overcome opposition to reform, and win support for their proposed solution. The campaign might include speeches, editorials, posters, and cartoons. After each group has presented its campaign, have the class discuss which one might be most effective and why.

✠ Connections to Art

Winslow Homer (1836–1910) was an American painter who began his career as a magazine illustrator. Although he is probably best known today for his evocative seascapes, he painted many other aspects of the American scene, including the painting on this page. The composition of this canvas, with the balance and harmony achieved by the placement of figures and positioning of the windows, conveys the peacefulness and order of the one-room country school. Idealized though this depiction might be, it suggests an orderly world in which education could proceed undisturbed.

Before the early 1800s, most teachers were men. As reformers pushed for schools to train women teachers, more women took up teaching. This Winslow Homer painting shows a one-room country school.

Improving Public Education

The drive to improve public education was probably the most successful social reform effort before the Civil War. The ideal of public education for all children fit with the ideals of Jacksonian democracy—equality and the importance of the common person. Educating all citizens would make them better able to take part in democratic government. Christian reformers also valued education. They wanted every American to be able to read the Bible.

Except in New England, most Americans in the early 1800s saw education as the responsibility of parents. School attendance was not required. In the South and the Middle Atlantic regions, most schools were run either by religious groups or by schoolmasters paid directly by parents. The few public schools that existed were thought of as being for poor children and were seen as inferior to private schools.

Education reformers faced two major problems. They had to convince public officials and voters that public schools—supported by tax dollars—were important. They also had to ensure that the schools were open to all children equally.

Horace Mann In the 1830s Horace Mann led the effort to provide education for all children. Known as the "Father of American Public Schools," Mann believed that only educated citizens could make a democracy work. He urged that school be required for all children. He also pushed for special schools to train teachers.

Mann's reports on education won him wide respect. Some of his views stirred argument, though. For example, Mann opposed whipping and other physical punishment in school. Critics called him unpatriotic and impractical. They believed that children were

History Footnote

The father of a young deaf girl helped send Thomas Gallaudet to Europe to study methods for teaching the deaf. In France he learned the signing method of communication. Returning to Hartford, Connecticut, he founded the first school for the hearing disabled in the United States, in 1817. His two sons followed in his footsteps. Thomas founded a church for the deaf in New York City. Edward was the president of the Columbia Institution for the Deaf and Dumb in Washington, D.C. This school was later renamed Gallaudet University in honor of his father.

Hands-On → *HISTORY*

Speaking to persuade Speech can be a powerful tool. Reformers like Sojourner Truth knew that power. A good speech, well delivered, can move an audience to laughter or tears, persuade them to change their beliefs or to join a cause, and leave them with words and ideas they never forget.

Activity Remember the qualities Sojourner Truth had as you write and deliver a speech. Your goal is to persuade your classmates to join you in working for a cause.

① Choose a cause that people your age can do something about.

② Decide what action you will ask the audience to take. This is the main point of your speech.

③ Do any research needed to make your speech more interesting and persuasive.

④ Write your speech. The introduction should catch your listeners' attention. The main part should describe the importance of your cause. The conclusion should state what you want your listeners to do.

⑤ Rehearse your speech in front of a family member or friend. Ask for ideas to improve the content and delivery.

Martin Luther King, Jr., an outstanding speaker

naturally bad and only stern handling could make them useful citizens.

Thanks to reformers' efforts, the American public school system began to grow. State funds for education doubled, the quality of public schools improved, and the school year was extended to a minimum of six months. Three schools opened to train teachers.

By the 1860s, public high schools were still rare, but the number of elementary schools had greatly increased. Most northern states offered elementary education for all white children. Free black children attended separate—and inferior—schools.

Help for the Disabled

Dedicated reformers also sought to improve opportunities for disabled persons. Scores of inspired men and women devoted their lives to helping the deaf, the blind, and the mentally ill.

Schools for the deaf and the blind In 1817 Thomas Hopkins Gallaudet opened a school in Connecticut for the education of deaf students. Gallaudet's success in teaching his students to read and write, to read lips, and to communicate by hand signs brought him worldwide fame. Soon similar schools were set up elsewhere.

Samuel Gridley Howe of Massachusetts achieved similar success with blind students. At the famous Perkins Institution, Howe taught his students to read using braille—an alphabet of raised codes. He also taught them skills that would help them get jobs and lead independent lives.

The mentally ill No reformer accomplished more than Dorothea Lynde Dix, who worked with the mentally ill. A deeply religious Boston school teacher, Dix found her life's calling after teaching a Sunday school class for women at a jail. What she saw shocked her. Locked up in small, dark, unheated cells at the rear of the prison were several mentally ill women who had not committed any crime.

435

Discussion

Checking Understanding

1. What were some of Horace Mann's ideas for educational reform? (School required for all children, teacher training, no physical punishment.)

2. Who were some reformers who helped the disabled? (Gallaudet opened a school for the deaf, and Howe, for the blind. Dix helped the mentally ill.)

Stimulating Critical Thinking

3. Do you agree with Horace Mann that only educated citizens can make a democracy work? (Yes: voters need to make informed, intelligent decisions on issues. No: democracy should be based simply on the will of the people; level of education is irrelevant.)

Teaching the Hands-On → *HISTORY*

To provide a model of a powerful persuasive speech, read aloud the excerpt from Sojourner Truth's speech on page 430, or read an excerpt from a more contemporary example, such as Martin Luther King's "I Have a Dream" speech.

★★★ Vital Links

Free public schools (Picture) Unit 3, Side 1, Search 21723

See also Unit 3 Explore CD-ROM location 73.

Have students note similarities between the environmental movement of our day and the reform movements of the early 1800s. Students should note that both then and now there were committed people who pointed out the need for reform. Frequently such individuals met with initial skepticism. After working long and hard for their causes, they sometimes had the satisfaction of seeing their ideas accepted into the mainstream of opinion.

❋ **History Footnote**

Dorothea Dix was one of the most extraordinary reformers in American history. The photograph of her on this page was taken around 1849. Her face seems to reflect the strength of her character. Her speech before the Massachusetts state legislature is a classic of persuasive rhetoric. Dix concluded it by saying:

Men of Massachusetts, I beg, I implore, I demand pity and protection for these of my suffering, outraged sex. Become the benefactors of your race, the just guardians of the solemn rights you hold in trust. Raise up the fallen, succor the desolate, restore the outcast, defend the helpless, and for your eternal and great reward receive the benediction, "Well done, good and faithful servants, become rulers over many things!"

@ **Link to the
Present**

The environmental movement

"Rarely has a movement in so short a time gained such popular support, had such legislative and regulatory impact, produced so many active organizations, or become so embedded in a culture."

The author of those words was describing today's environmental movement. With roots in the 1800s, the movement itself began in the 1960s. In 1970 the government set up the Environmental Protection Agency, and activists held the first Earth Day.

Today, hundreds of groups work to preserve nature, conserve resources, and reduce pollution. They hold demonstrations and bring lawsuits against polluters. They also work to get government to pass laws protecting the environment.

Millions of individuals also do their part. They recycle, reduce their use of resources, and choose products that do minimum damage to the environment. Still, much work remains to be done. Americans will continue to strive for a cleaner, healthier planet.

The sight spurred Dix to make a two-year study of all of the jails and poorhouses in Massachusetts. Dix saw the same inhumane conditions wherever she went. In 1843 she presented her report before the state legislature:

"I tell what I have seen. . . . Insane persons confined . . . in cages, closets, cellars, stalls, pens! Chained, naked, beaten with rods, and lashed into obedience."

After getting Massachusetts to set up a hospital for the mentally ill, Dix took her cause nationwide. By 1860, as many as 15 states and Canada had separate hospitals for the mentally ill. Few reformers could claim such immediate and widespread success.

Prison Reform

Dorothea Dix was also a leader in prison reform. Prisons in her day were poorly organized. Most had large rooms with all the prisoners, including women and children, kept together. Some of these prisoners had committed violent crimes, while others were guilty only of being in debt.

Thanks to Dix and others, new prisons separated men and women and gave prisoners useful work to do. Reformers pushed for special schools for juvenile criminals and "houses of correction" for people who had committed minor crimes. These measures separated youths and petty criminals from the influence of hardened criminals.

In addition to improving conditions in prisons, reformers worked to end cruel punishment. They fought against the use of flogging, branding, and mutilation. As a result, many states outlawed such punishments.

Prison reformers won a major victory in getting rid of prisons for people whose only crime was not being able to pay their debts. As many as half of the people in these jails in the early 1800s owed less than $50. Some owed only a few pennies. How could people ever pay off even these small debts if they were in prison? By the mid-1830s debtor prisons were a thing of the past.

Dorothea Dix

The images below are from a series showing effects of drinking. The caption for the upper one reads: "James Latimer brings the bottle out for the first time; Mr. Latimer first induces his wife to 'Take a drop!'" The caption for the lower reads: "Quarrels between Mr. and Mrs. Latimer, and brutal violence between them, were the natural consequences of the too frequent use of the bottle."

Anti–alcohol abuse campaigns continued throughout the 1800s. A Women's Temperance Crusade swept through 23 states in 1873. In the crusade, women prayed and sang hymns in saloons. From the Temperance Crusade, the National Women's Christian Temperance Union (WCTU) developed in 1874. The WCTU still exists, and emphasizes the importance of educating children about the effects of alcohol and other drug abuse.

Discussion

Checking Understanding

1. What were some results of the prison-reform movement? (Men and women separated; prisoners given useful work; reform schools for juveniles; separation of minors from hardened criminals.)

2. What were some problems that reformers blamed on alcohol? (Crime, poverty, mental illness, domestic violence.)

3. What were some beliefs and characteristics of the Shakers? (They believed in the equality of all; were well organized, generous, and hard working; shared possessions in common; and did not marry.)

Stimulating Critical Thinking

4. Which of the movements mentioned on pages 436 and 437 do you think was most successful? Give reasons to support your opinion. (Answers will vary. Some students might argue that prison reform has been the most successful since the reformers managed to achieve most of the goals they set for themselves, whereas alcohol abuse continues to be a problem in our society, and there are no examples of utopias today.)

Temperance Movement

Many reformers blamed crime, poverty, and even mental illness on drunkenness. The use and abuse of alcohol was common in the early 1800s. People drank at weddings, funerals, political rallies, and even on the job. As more and more people experienced religious revival, alcohol abuse became a major concern of reform-minded preachers and church members. They began to speak out against "Demon Rum."

At first the enemies of alcohol called for **temperance**—moderation in drinking habits. Their crusade became known as the temperance movement. During the 1830s some crusaders began to demand that people not drink at all. They pushed for laws banning the sale of alcohol. The first state to pass such a law was Maine in 1846. Although a dozen other states passed similar laws, many Americans protested, and most states later repealed the bans.

Utopias

As reformers sought to create the perfect society, some people decided to form groups to achieve their goal in small communities. The communities they formed were known as **utopias,** meaning perfect societies. More than a hundred utopias sprang up between 1800 and 1900.

The Shakers Some utopias were religious communities of people who wanted to live out their faith among others with the same beliefs. You read about the Mormons in Chapter 14. Another religious community was the United Society of Believers, better known as the Shakers.

Founded by "Mother Ann" Lee, the Shakers believed in the equality of all people. They worshiped together and expressed their religious feelings in song and dance. The

Temperance crusaders published pamphlets to warn against the effects of drinking. These drawings show the change in a family from the parents' first drink to their complete ruin as violent alcoholics.

name "Shaker" came from one form of worship dance.

The Shakers were well organized, generous, and hard working. They shared all their possessions in common. At the society's peak in the 1840s, it had about 6,000 members. It then went into a slow and steady decline, in part because its members were not allowed to marry and thus had no children to carry on the community. A handful of believers kept the faith until well into the 1900s.

Oneida Another community based on religious ideas was the Oneida Community organized by John Noyes in 1848. Its main goal was perfection in every activity. Members believed in release from illness and sin through faith in God. Since Noyes considered marriage between one man and one woman to be "selfish love," he invented a

A Concept Web

Have students develop a concept web to organize information about important reform movements of this period. In a central circle they should write the phrase "Reform Movements." In circles radiating from the center they should name the specific movements, and in circles extending from these, identify leaders and accomplishments of the movements.

Section Review
Answers

1. Definitions: *social reform* (433), *temperance* (437), *utopias* (437)

2. People who converted to evangelical Christianity wanted to improve their own lives and help others. They worked to correct evils in society.

3. Examples will vary. Some possibilities: public education—help all citizens take part in democracy; help for disabled—improve opportunities for deaf, blind, and mentally ill; prison reform—eliminate unfair punishment; temperance—attempt to remove a cause of crime and poverty; utopias—attempt to create perfect societies.

4. Fairness, compassion, unselfishness. Community might be organized so each member takes turns doing different tasks.

✠ **Connections to Literature**

Brook Farm, based on cooperative living, was founded with the goal of uniting intellectual growth and manual labor. Nathaniel Hawthorne was a member of Brook Farm for only a short time. Despite his initial enthusiasm for the idea, Hawthorne soon found that communal living was not for him. Ten years after he left Brook Farm, he wrote *The Blithedale Romance* (1852), a novel about a utopian community. The novel's narrator, Miles Coverdale, coldly observes community members. Through the narrative, Hawthorne reveals shortcomings of utopian ideas, including the inability of utopian dreamers to come to grips with the realities of human nature.

Noted for their simple way of life, the Shakers made a style of furniture still admired today. The drawing above shows a form of Shaker worship dance.

system in which all members of the community were married to each other.

Although Oneida thrived economically, its marriage practices caused public protest. In 1879 the community reorganized as a business company. The Oneida company still makes manufactured goods and is known for its silverware.

New Harmony and Brook Farm
Other utopian communities were based on nonreligious ideals. In 1825 Robert Owen, who owned mills in Scotland, founded New Harmony in Indiana. Owen's ideal was a community with good working conditions, in which members shared all property.

For a short time, New Harmony appeared to be a brilliant success. However, most of the people who came there wanted more individual freedom. The community split up after only three years.

The members of Brook Farm, founded in 1841 near Boston, included some of America's most brilliant thinkers, such as Ralph Waldo Emerson, John Greenleaf Whittier, and Nathaniel Hawthorne. Members shared possessions, divided work equally, and set aside time for social and literary activities. "Our . . . aim is nothing less than Heaven on Earth," one member declared.

Brook Farm survived for a time because of an excellent school that attracted paying students from outside the community. Yet the community had more thinkers than workers, and after a few years it could not make enough money to stay afloat. In 1847 the farm had to be sold to pay bills.

 1. Section Review

1. Define **social reform, temperance,** and **utopias.**
2. How did the Second Great Awakening spur the impulse toward reform?
3. Choose two reform movements and explain how they showed reformers' urges to create a more fair society.
4. **Critical Thinking** Imagine that you are starting a utopian community. What ideals would be important to you? How would you organize your community to meet your goals?

Frederick Law Olmsted (1822–1903) designed parks in many American cities. Among his most famous, in addition to Central Park, are Prospect Park in Brooklyn, Belle Isle Park in Detroit, and Jackson Park in Chicago—designed as the location for the 1893 Columbian Exposition. Olmsted also created landscapes for Stanford University and the Vanderbilt estate in North Carolina.

Geography Lab

The First Big City Park

How could America's crowded cities be made more livable? One answer, Frederick Law Olmsted believed, was to bring nature into the city. Olmsted designed the nation's first large urban park— Central Park in New York City. The park looked so natural that visitors could not believe it was deliberately planned.

Use the quotations and picture to understand Olmsted's reasons for the park.

Central Park around 1865

Statements by Frederick Law Olmsted

"It is a scientific fact that the occasional contemplation [observation] of natural scenes . . . is favorable to the health and vigor of men and especially to the health and vigor of their intellect."

"My notion is that whatever grounds a great city may need for other public purposes, for parades, for athletic sports, for fireworks, for museums of art or science, it also needs a large ground scientifically and artistically prepared to provide such a poetic and tranquilizing [calming] influence on its people as comes through a pleasant contemplation of natural scenery."

"[Central Park has] a distinctly harmonizing and refining influence . . . favorable to courtesy, self-control, and temperance."

Link to History

1. **What did Olmsted think were the benefits of observing nature?**

2. **How did Central Park reflect Olmsted's ideas?**

3. **Today, Central Park includes an open-air theater, a zoo, an art museum, playgrounds, and facilities for baseball, tennis, volleyball, handball, and miniature golf. What might Olmsted think of modern-day Central Park?**

4. **Hands-On Geography** Develop a proposal for improving a park in your community. Include "before" and "after" drawings or maps to show the park as it is now and as it would look after your ideas were put into practice.

See the activity on parks in **Geography Extensions**, pp. 31–32.

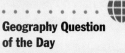
Section Objectives

★ Explain how free African Americans worked to end slavery.
★ Describe the effects that revivals and reform movements had on antislavery efforts.
★ Identify who objected to abolition and why.

2. Movements to End Slavery

Reading Guide

New Terms emancipation, abolition

Section Focus **How the movement to end slavery gained strength in the early 1800s**

1. How did free African Americans work to end slavery?
2. What effects did revivals and reform movements have on antislavery efforts?
3. Who objected to abolition and why?

Sojourner Truth's best-known reform work was her effort to end slavery. Indeed, in the great swell of reform movements of the early to mid-1800s, the antislavery movement came to overshadow all others. How could people even dream of a perfect world, many reformers asked, when millions in America were enslaved?

Early Efforts

Some opposition to slavery had existed since the first Africans arrived in the early 1600s. The steady pressure for change by African Americans, combined with Quaker calls for **emancipation**—freeing of slaves— made slow progress. By 1804 the seven states from Pennsylvania north had promised to free their slaves.

Free African Americans in the North worked hard against slavery in the South. They organized antislavery societies and mutual-aid associations to help each other and to shelter, clothe, and feed African Americans who escaped slavery.

African Americans also took political action. In 1800 James Forten, a wealthy Philadelphia businessman, presented a petition to Congress calling for emancipation. Out of 86 congressmen, only 1 sided with Forten's cause. Still, for the rest of his life Forten worked to end slavery.

Colonization

One idea popular with early supporters of emancipation was to settle freed slaves in Africa. In 1815 Paul Cuffe, a wealthy free African American, transported 38 volunteers to West Africa. There, he believed, freed slaves would have more opportunity than in the United States, where racism was strong. Cuffe intended to send groups each year, but he died before finishing his plans.

Liberia The American Colonization Society, founded in 1817, urged slaveowners to free their slaves and send them to Africa. It obtained land in West Africa and named it Liberia, from the Latin word for freedom. The Society had support from southerners who feared that if freed slaves stayed in the South, they might stir up rebellion.

Volunteers began moving to Liberia in 1821, but the colonization plan never took root. Most African Americans saw the United States as their home, not Africa. Also, the few who did go faced poverty and disease in the new colony. No more than 15,000 people moved to Liberia before the Civil War.

Northerners soon saw that colonization would not work. James Forten crusaded against colonization. He believed that slaves should be freed and educated to take their place as equals in American society.

✳ **History Footnote**

Theodore Dwight Weld was a social reformer and preacher. Weld preached the antislavery message, lobbied in Washington, and wrote books. He brought into the movement Arthur and Lewis Tappan, who later provided financial support for the American Anti-Slavery Society. Weld helped train "The Seventy"—members of the Anti-Slavery Society who spread the message of abolition throughout the North. Weld married Angelina Grimké (see student page 442). Weld's *American Slavery as It Is,* published in 1839, helped inspire Harriet Beecher Stowe's novel *Uncle Tom's Cabin,* and had a great influence on the development of the abolition movement.

James Forten and his granddaughter Charlotte worked for African American rights.

Reformers Join the Cause

In the 1820s a strong antislavery movement began. Revival leaders called on Christians to denounce slavery as evil. The democratic spirit of the time caused people to see that slavery did not fit the American values of liberty and equality. People called for **abolition**—putting an end to slavery.

Antislavery newspapers began to pop up in the North and the Midwest. Benjamin Lundy began *Genius of Universal Emancipation* in Ohio in 1821. In 1827 Samuel Cornish and John Russwurm started *Freedom's Journal,* the first African American newspaper. Such papers increased the number of people calling for abolition.

Revivalist ministers also won people to the cause. One of the most influential was Theodore Dwight Weld, a student at Lane Theological Seminary in Cincinnati. He was so fired up with antislavery fever that the school forced him to leave. Weld and his followers moved to Oberlin College, which became a center of the antislavery movement.

The American Anti-Slavery Society

While some abolitionists believed that slavery should be ended gradually, by the 1830s others had grown impatient. These abolitionists now demanded that slavery be abolished everywhere immediately.

William Lloyd Garrison Perhaps the most famous white abolitionist was William Lloyd Garrison of Boston. Garrison had worked on Lundy's newspaper but considered him too timid. On New Year's Day, 1831, Garrison began publishing his own paper, *The Liberator*. In fiery language he demanded an immediate end to slavery:

❝I am in earnest—I will not equivocate [be vague]—I will not excuse—I will not retreat a single inch—AND I WILL BE HEARD.❞

The Liberator masthead

Checking Understanding

1. What were some ideas for ending slavery? (Gradual emancipation, colonies in Africa, immediate abolition.)

2. Why did the movement to end slavery gain strength after 1820? (Religious convictions, commitment to democratic ideals, antislavery newspapers.)

Stimulating Critical Thinking

3. If you were an abolitionist in the 1820s, would you have favored a gradual end to slavery or an immediate end? Why? (Gradual: too big a change to be made quickly; would arouse less opposition. Immediate: too serious an injustice to allow to continue.)

Section Activity

An Antislavery Paper

To underscore the importance of antislavery newspapers, have cooperative groups prepare front pages for one. The pages should each include the paper's name, headlines, an antislavery article, a news story, and a political cartoon. Groups might use a computer to design and lay out their page. Display the pages for the class to discuss.

1820–1850 Chapter 16 • **441**

Teaching the

World  **Link**

Point out that the fight against slavery in the British Empire had been a long one. Slavery was declared illegal in Britain in 1772, but slavery and the slave trade continued in the British colonies until the Emancipation Act of 1833.

Bonus Activity

Listening to "Amazing Grace"

Play a recording of "Amazing Grace." Point out that this famous hymn was written by the English preacher John Newton, a former slave trader who experienced a religious conversion. Have students listen carefully to the words (or provide them with a copy) and pick out lines that refer directly to Newton's experience as a slave trader. (Some examples: "That saved a wretch like me," "I once was lost, but now I'm found," "Thro' many dangers, toils and snares, I have already come.")

★ ★ ★
Vital Links

Freedom's Journal (Picture) Unit 3, Side 1, Search 37434

See also Unit 3 Explore CD-ROM location 201.

See the Study Guide activity in **Chapter Resources Binder,** p. 122.

World  **Link**

Britain abolishes slavery Petitions to abolish slavery were so heavy that the men carrying them into Parliament staggered under the weight. British antislavery activists were demanding immediate abolition throughout the British Empire.

They got part of what they wanted in the Emancipation Act of 1833. Slavery in British colonies such as Jamaica was abolished—but not right away. Only slaves under age 6 gained immediate freedom. The rest had to stay with their owners as unpaid apprentices for several years.

In the United States, news of Britain's action fueled the flame of the abolitionist movement. While William Lloyd Garrison was disgusted by how gradual the British act was, abolitionists in general took hope in their cause.

In 1833 Garrison, along with two wealthy New York silk merchants, Arthur and Lewis Tappan, formed the American Anti-Slavery Society. Soon the society grew to 200,000 members, black and white, male and female.

In time, the society would split apart. Some members thought the only hope of ending slavery was to do it gradually, not all at once. Some feared that letting women and African Americans give speeches and play leadership roles would turn many Americans against the antislavery cause.

The Grimké sisters Among the women who played important roles in the American Anti-Slavery Society were Sarah and Angelina Grimké. Daughters of a wealthy South Carolina slaveholder, the Grimké

sisters had turned against slavery after becoming Quakers.

The sisters moved north to work for abolition. They began publishing antislavery pamphlets and making speeches, at first in homes and then in public. In 1838 Angelina appeared before the Massachusetts legislature to present an antislavery petition signed by 20,000 women.

African American Leaders

African American leaders welcomed the formation of the American Anti-Slavery Society. They thought it would help them spread the message about the evils of slavery. James Forten cheered *The Liberator* and said that Garrison's work had "roused up a spirit in our young people."

Meanwhile, African Americans continued their own long fight for abolition. From lecturing to writing to political action, African Americans worked tirelessly for the cause.

Frederick Douglass The best-known African American abolitionist was Frederick Douglass, whom you read about in Chapter 15. In addition to being a brilliant lecturer, Douglass was an effective writer. In 1845 he published an autobiography, *Narrative of the Life of Frederick Douglass,* which became popular reading among abolitionists.

Douglass wrote for *The Liberator*, but in 1847 he started his own paper, *North Star.* He made it clear that African Americans must lead the fight against slavery:

❝No one else can fight [the battle] for us. . . . Our relations to the [white] Anti-Slavery movement must be and are changed. Instead of depending upon it we must lead it.❞

Sojourner Truth No less effective as an abolitionist was Sojourner Truth. She may have lacked the education of Douglass,

Harriet Tubman was known as the "Moses of her people" because she led many—including her own parents—to freedom from slavery. Tubman was born into slavery in Maryland and worked as a maid and field hand. After escaping to Philadelphia in 1849 with the help of the Underground Railroad, she began her career of leading others to freedom. During the Civil War, she worked as a cook, nurse, and guide for the Union. After the Civil War she set up schools for freedmen in North Carolina. Later she lived in Auburn, New York, where she provided shelter for needy and elderly African Americans.

but she made up for it with her humor and clever comments. When they spoke at the same events, she would often poke fun at Douglass, and he once grumbled that she "seemed to feel it her duty to trip me up in my speeches."

On her travels through the North and West, Truth drew large crowds wherever she spoke. In 1850 a fellow abolitionist wrote the story of her life, *Narrative of Sojourner Truth,* and Truth supported herself by selling copies of the book at antislavery gatherings.

The use of force Some African Americans called for force as the only way to throw off slavery. In 1829 David Walker published a pamphlet titled *Appeal to the Colored Citizens of the World.* He urged slaves to fight for their freedom. His message terrified southerners, who offered rewards for his arrest or death. In 1830 Walker was found dead near his Boston shop.

Henry Highland Garnet, a newspaper editor, also urged slaves to resist, using force if necessary. In an 1843 speech, Garnet compared slave resistance to the American Revolution:

❝Let it no longer be a debatable question, whether it is better to choose LIBERTY or DEATH! Let your motto be RESISTANCE! RESISTANCE! RESISTANCE!— No oppressed people have ever secured their liberty without resistance.❞

Underground Railroad

Perhaps the most dramatic part of the antislavery movement was the Underground Railroad. This "railroad" had nothing to do with trains. It was a secret network of people who would shelter and feed escaping slaves along their way to freedom. Thousands of African Americans used this network.

"Conductors," many of them former slaves, risked their freedom and their lives to help slaves escape. One of the most famous conductors was Harriet Tubman, who had escaped alone as a young woman. Tubman guided more than 300 slaves north to freedom. In her 19 trips into the South, she never lost a "passenger."

In northern states free blacks and sympathetic whites directed escaping slaves to secret hiding places in homes or barns. These "stations" of the Underground Railroad were places to sleep and get food and clothes before continuing. Chased by dogs and slave catchers, escaping slaves would

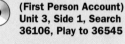

❝I appear before the immense assembly this evening as a thief and a robber. I stole this head, these limbs, this body from my master, and ran off with them.❞

Frederick Douglass, from a speech to an antislavery audience in 1842

Leading abolitionists of the time were black and white, male and female, as shown in this rare daguerreotype. Frederick Douglass is seated at the right end of the table.

Checking Understanding

1. Who were the major African American abolitionists? (Frederick Douglass was a brilliant lecturer and writer, Sojourner Truth was a gifted speaker, David Walker published a pamphlet urging slaves to fight for their freedom, and Henry Highland Garnet was a newspaper editor and speaker.)

2. What was the Underground Railroad? (A secret network of people who helped slaves escape to freedom.)

Stimulating Critical Thinking

3. Do you think that the use of violence to gain liberty is justified? Why or why not? (Yes: since violent force is often used to deny people liberty, such force may be necessary to free them; no: violence always leads to more violence and is never justified.)

★ ★ ★ Vital Links

Voice of Harriet Tubman (First Person Account) Unit 3, Side 1, Search 36106, Play to 36545

See also Unit 3 Explore CD-ROM location 192.

To help students interpret the map, ask why some arrows are wider than others (to indicate a greater number of slaves escaping along those routes). Ask which route was most heavily traveled (from Louisiana to Canada) and least heavily traveled (from Georgia and Florida to Cuba and the Bahamas). **Answer to Reading Maps:** Canada, the Northeast, the Bahamas, Cuba, and Mexico. Most escaped to Canada.

★ ★ ★
Vital Links

◉ "Follow the Drinking Gourd" (Song) Unit 3, Side 2, Search 00001, Play to 02041

◉ See also Unit 3 Explore CD-ROM location 190.

*For a description of risks taken by Underground Railroad conductors, see **American Readings**, p. 61.*

Tips for Teaching

Kinesthetic Learners
Kinesthetic learners often find it easier to understand maps through tactile experiences. Give them tracing paper and have them trace the map below, labeling states, countries, and routes. They can refer to pages R6–R7. Then, following routes with their fingers, they can name states through which the routes ran.

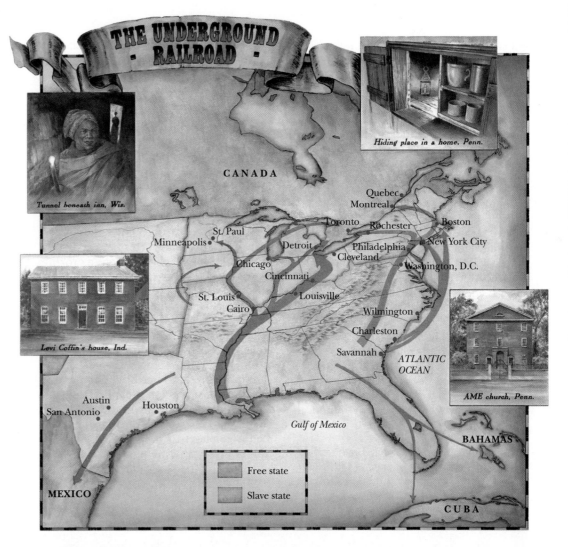

THE UNDERGROUND RAILROAD

Hiding place in a home. Penn.

Tunnel beneath inn, Wis.

Levi Coffin's house, Ind.

AME church, Penn.

CANADA

Quebec
Montreal
Toronto   Rochester   Boston
St. Paul   Detroit   Philadelphia   New York City
Minneapolis   Cleveland   Washington, D.C.
Chicago
Cincinnati
St. Louis   Louisville
Cairo
Wilmington
Charleston
Savannah   ATLANTIC OCEAN

Austin
San Antonio   Houston

Gulf of Mexico

MEXICO

BAHAMAS

CUBA

☐ Free state
☐ Slave state

Reading Maps

↑ Judging by the map, where did African Americans who were escaping slavery hope to find freedom?

often sleep by day and travel by night, following the North Star.

No one knows the actual number of slaves who used the Underground Railroad because everything about it was kept secret. Some historians estimate that as many as 100,000 African Americans used it to escape from the South.

Violent opposition to abolition was not uncommon in the early 1800s. Elijah Lovejoy had been harassed repeatedly before he lost his life trying to protect his press from destruction. In fact, anti-abolitionists had twice thrown his press into the Mississippi River. Anti-abolitionists also torched the new meeting house of the Philadelphia Female Anti-Slavery Society in May 1838.

This 1837 anti-abolitionist riot took place the night Elijah Lovejoy was killed. With five bullets in his body, Lovejoy died defending his press.

Opposition to Abolitionism

The determined efforts of abolitionists, both black and white, alarmed and even enraged some whites. In 1835 a mob destroyed Garrison's press and dragged him through the streets of Boston. Two years later a mob in Illinois killed Elijah Lovejoy, another antislavery newspaper editor.

Anti-abolitionists had several reasons for opposing an end to slavery. Obviously slaveholders—and even some southerners who did not have slaves—objected to abolition. They saw it as a threat to their way of life.

In the North, some of the violence was planned by businessmen, merchants, and bankers. They depended on southern agriculture—worked by slaves—for the raw materials their businesses needed. At the same time, northern factory workers feared that they would lose their jobs to freed slaves.

The "gag rule" In Congress, opponents of abolition became alarmed as the antislavery movement gained strength. Abolitionists were flooding Congress with petitions to outlaw slavery and the slave trade in Washington, D.C. In 1836 southern congressmen managed to pass a "gag rule" barring debate on antislavery petitions in the House of Representatives.

Former President John Quincy Adams was a representative at the time. He was not an abolitionist, but he was furious about the gag rule. To him, it violated the Bill of Rights guarantee of freedom of speech and the right of petition. It took Adams eight years, but in 1844 he finally convinced the House to repeal the obnoxious gag rule.

In spite of opposition, the abolition movement grew stronger and its message more urgent. You will see in the next chapter that the issue of slavery became linked to westward expansion, as Americans argued over whether to allow slavery in new territories and states. Even people who wanted to ignore the issue would no longer be able to, as the conflict over slavery widened the split between North and South.

2. Section Review

1. Define **emancipation** and **abolition.**
2. Choose three of the following and explain how each fought slavery: James Forten, Paul Cuffe, Samuel Cornish and John Russwurm, Frederick Douglass, Sojourner Truth, David Walker, Henry Highland Garnet, Harriet Tubman.
3. What reasons did people have for opposing abolition?
4. Critical Thinking What reasons did reformers have for opposing slavery? Why do you think slavery became the foremost issue in the United States during this time?

Closing the Section

Wrap-Up Activity

Who-What-Why Charts

To review efforts to support and oppose abolition, have pairs create charts titled "Efforts to End Slavery" and "Efforts to Preserve Slavery." Under the headings "Who," "What," and "Why," they should identify individuals and groups, what they did, and their reasons. (Note that students may not be able to complete the "What" or "Why" entries for every person or group.)

Section Review
Answers

1. Definitions: *emancipation* (440), *abolition* (441)

2. Forten petitioned Congress for emancipation; Cuffe settled freed slaves in Africa; Cornish and Russwurm started first African American newspaper; Douglass lectured and published newspaper; Truth spoke against slavery; Walker published pamphlet urging slaves to fight; Garnet was a newspaper editor; Tubman led slaves to freedom.

3. Abolition was seen as a threat to southern way of life, northern businesses depended on cheap southern products, and northern factory workers feared losing jobs.

4. Religious beliefs or belief that slavery violated democratic principles. Reasons why slavery issue was foremost will vary, perhaps that sectional conflict was already growing over tariffs and that many saw slavery as society's greatest evil.

3. (a) Some possibilities: "How were Garrison's accomplishments crucial?" "What is the difference between a moral and a political issue?" "What do you mean by the need to speak 'violently'?" (b) Those who say yes might agree that people need to be shocked out of long-held assumptions. Others may disagree, saying that many people react stubbornly when their assumptions are strongly attacked. (c) Additional information might include other historians' interpretations and primary sources on how people reacted to Garrison.

For further application, have students do the Applying Skills activity in the Chapter Survey (p. 456).

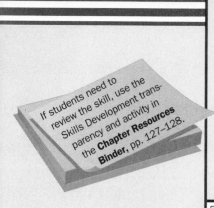

If students need to review the skill, use the Skills Development transparency and activity in the **Chapter Resources Binder**, pp. 127–128.

Introducing the Skill Lab

Discuss why it is important to interpret the past. (Need to form judgments in order to learn from the past.) Before students analyze the source, review if necessary the definitions of *statement of fact* and *opinion* (p. 210) and *claim* and *evidence* (p. 423).

Skill Lab
Answers

1. (a) Statements should be similar to the following: The historian is saying that Garrison was an effective antislavery leader whose methods were necessary.

(b) This historian would answer "No," implied by his positive view of Garrison.

2. (a) Statements of fact: ". . . led the fight to make slavery a moral rather than a political issue"; ". . . slavery could no longer be postponed or dismissed as a Southern problem"; "An ally of Garrison's and a frequent critic . . ."; ". . . she called him a 'remarkably pure-minded man . . . calmness.'"

(b) Opinions: ". . . of crucial importance"; ". . . missed the point"; ". . . *must* speak violently"; ". . . has to shatter . . . defenses, penetrate ears. . . . Shock and trauma are his necessary and inevitable weapons"; ". . . one of the best evaluations."

(Answers continued in top margin)

446

Skill Lab

Thinking Critically
Historical Interpretations

"An agreement with hell" is what abolitionist William Lloyd Garrison called the Constitution because it allowed slavery. Garrison once burned a copy of it in protest. Such words and actions led most white southerners—and many white northerners—to call him extreme. Even some who shared Garrison's hatred of slavery thought he was hurting their cause.

Question to Investigate

Did William Lloyd Garrison do the antislavery movement more harm than good?

Procedure

Historians disagree about Garrison's effect on the antislavery movement. Writing about history involves interpreting the past. In a **historical interpretation**, a historian offers an opinion about an event or person. This opinion is usually supported both by statements of fact and by other opinions. The source on this page is one historian's interpretation of Garrison's role.

❶ Identify the interpretation.
a. State the historian's opinion.
b. How do you think this historian would answer the Question to Investigate? Explain.

❷ Identify how the interpretation is supported.
a. List the statements of fact.
b. List the opinions.

❸ Evaluate how *well* the interpretation is supported.
a. State two questions you would ask this historian about his view of Garrison.
b. Has this historian persuaded you that his interpretation makes sense? Explain.
c. What is some information you would need in order to further explore the Question to Investigate?

Skill Tips

A historian is interpreting the past when he or she:
• makes claims about people or events
• gives opinions about whether something or someone was important, right, or good
• stresses one side of an issue

Source to Use

"Garrison had accomplishments of crucial importance to his credit. He had led the fight to make slavery a moral rather than a political issue. . . . The issue of slavery could no longer be postponed or dismissed as a Southern problem. Historians who have been . . . critical of Garrison for his fanaticism and rigidity have missed the point. The first voice to speak out . . . against a social injustice that the rest of society has come to take largely for granted *must* speak violently. . . . He has to shatter carefully constructed defenses, penetrate ears tuned out to his message. . . . Shock and trauma are his necessary and inevitable [unavoidable] weapons. . . .

An ally of Garrison's and a frequent critic [of him], Lydia Maria Child, made one of the best evaluations of the abolitionist leader when she called him a 'remarkably pure-minded man, whose only fault is that he cannot be moderate on a subject which it is exceedingly difficult for an honest mind to examine with calmness.'"

From Page Smith, *The Nation Comes of Age*, Vol. 4 (McGraw-Hill, 1981)

★ Explain how the antislavery movement spurred women to seek their rights.
★ Identify the progress women made in education and the professions.
★ List some important women active in the women's rights movement, and their accomplishments.

Teaching Resources

Take-Home Planner 5, pp. 26–33
Chapter Resources Binder
  Study Guide, p. 123
  Reinforcement, pp. 125–126
  Skills Development
Geography Extensions
American Readings, pp. 62–64
Using Historical Documents, pp. 85–90
Transparency Activities
Chapter and Unit Tests

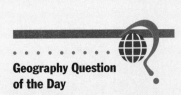

Introducing the Section

Warm-Up Activity

Newspaper Search
To introduce the topic of women's rights, have groups search recent newspapers and magazines for articles about women. Have each group identify roles that women are playing in the story, such as member of a jury, judge, politician, doctor, or parent. Ask each group to write a paragraph identifying the women and roles in their articles and telling why they think women would or would not have been playing those roles in the early 1800s.

Geography Question of the Day

Have students skim the first two sections of the chapter to identify where reformers lived and worked (mostly in the Northeast and Midwest). Tell students that the women's rights movement began during this period, too. Ask them to write a paragraph predicting where in the country that movement might have been strongest and explaining their reasons. (Northeast, which was also center of abolition movement.)

3. Working for Women's Rights

Reading Guide

Section Focus The struggle for women's rights in the early 1800s

1. How did the antislavery movement spur women to seek their rights?
2. What progress did women make in education and the professions?
3. Who were some important women active in the women's rights movement, and what did they accomplish?

The antislavery movement marked the first time that American women had played a major political role. As they fought to free slaves, however, women saw more clearly their own lack of freedom. Angelina Grimké pointed out:

❝We cannot push abolitionism forward with all our might until we take up the stumbling block out of the road. . . . What then can woman do for the slave, when she herself is under the feet of man and shamed into silence?❞

Women in the Early 1800s

The Grimkés' belief that men and women were equal was rare at that time. At the start of the 1800s, American women—especially married women—were second-class citizens with few rights. A wife's property and any money she earned belonged to her husband. Some state laws allowed husbands to beat their wives "with a reasonable instrument." No woman in America could vote, sit on a jury, or hold public office.

Before the 1830s no college or university in the United States accepted female students. Men commonly believed that the effort to learn subjects like mathematics and science would cause women to suffer nervous breakdowns. The few girls who advanced beyond elementary school attended girls' schools that prepared them to be good wives and mothers.

Progress in Education

One of the first areas that women sought to reform was education. Of the many women who crusaded for better schooling for young women, two of the most famous were Emma Hart Willard and Mary Lyon.

Women struggled for the right to an education. This daguerreotype was taken in about 1850 in a Boston school for girls.

448

✳ History Footnote

Philo Stewart, a missionary to the Choctaws, and John Jay Shipherd, a Presbyterian minister, founded the Oberlin Collegiate Institute, later called Oberlin College, in 1833. Its purpose was to educate ministers and schoolteachers for the West. Stewart and Shipherd named the school in honor of Johann Friedrich Oberlin, a minister who worked tirelessly for the poor in France. Before the school began allowing women to earn a degree, it did offer a "ladies' course," allowing women to take classes in drawing and French as well as philosophy, literature, and natural sciences. By 1838, women were able to take part in the degree program.

A woman's outfit typical of the 1850s included a whale-boned bodice, tight corset, and several petticoats. In 1851 Amelia Bloomer shocked the public with her comfortable short skirt and full "pants," which people called bloomers.

When Elizabeth Cady Stanton's embarrassed son asked her not to come to his school in bloomers, she replied:

"Now suppose you and I were taking a long walk in the fields and I had on three long petticoats. Then suppose a bull should take after us. Why, you, with your arms and legs free, could run like a shot, but I, alas! should fall. . . . Then you in your agony, when you saw the bull gaining on me, would say, 'Oh! how I wish mother could use her legs as I can!' Now why do you wish me to wear what is uncomfortable, inconvenient, and many times dangerous?"

In 1819 Willard urged the Pennsylvania state legislature to support a program to train women to be teachers. The legislature said no, but that did not stop Willard. In 1821 she opened the first high school for girls, Troy Female Seminary, in Troy, New York. The school taught girls such traditionally "male" subjects as mathematics, history, geography, and physics.

Mary Lyon dreamed of starting a college for women. In 1837 she opened Mount Holyoke Female Seminary with 80 students, aged 17 and older. Instruction at Mount Holyoke was equal to that at men's colleges. Still, it was not until 1888—40 years after Lyon died—that the school was officially recognized as a college.

In 1833 Oberlin College became the first men's college to admit women. The Ohio college made two reforms at one time by opening its doors to both women and African Americans in 1833.

Women in Professions

Women who wanted to enter professions had a hard time breaking through the education barriers. Yet as doors began to open to them, women sought training in medicine, law, the ministry, journalism, and education.

One determined woman was Elizabeth Blackwell, the first woman to earn a medical diploma in the United States. When she applied to medical school, the administrators expected her to fail. Instead, she graduated first in her class in 1849. She went on to start a nursing school and a hospital for women and children in New York City.

Women also sought training in the ministry. Revivals had already given them leadership roles in churches. Elizabeth Blackwell's sister-in-law, Antoinette Brown Blackwell, was the first woman to study at Oberlin's theological school and became the first ordained woman minister.

In 1840, the same year that the World Anti-Slavery Convention was held, Elizabeth Cady married Henry Brewster Stanton, a well-known abolitionist. Their wedding ceremony was a bit unusual because Cady insisted that the word *obey* be omitted from the traditional marriage vow—"to love, honor, and obey"—that women took. Throughout her marriage, she worked as a social reformer as well as wife and mother. The daguerreotype on this page shows Stanton with her baby daughter Harriet in 1856. Stanton worked to promote women's rights for more than 40 years. Together with Susan B. Anthony, she led the women's rights movement and cofounded the National Woman Suffrage Association.

Women Organize

The successes of women in education and the professions were milestones, but many doors were still closed to them. Reform-minded women realized that only with an organized movement for women's rights could they make real progress.

Elizabeth Cady Stanton

The question of women's rights surfaced in a dramatic way at the 1840 World Anti-Slavery Convention in London. Eight American women journeyed across the Atlantic, only to be told they could not take part because they were women. They had to sit behind a curtain, hidden from view. William Lloyd Garrison, one abolitionist who supported women's rights, sat with them in silent protest.

Shocked by their experience in London, Elizabeth Cady Stanton and Lucretia Mott decided to take matters into their own hands. Stanton and Mott realized that as long as the law did not protect women's rights, they could never achieve their goals as reformers. The two women agreed to organize the first-ever convention on women's rights.

The Seneca Falls Convention Mott, Stanton, and 3 other women called the convention for July 1848 in Seneca Falls, New York. Some 300 people, including 40 men, showed up.

To attract attention to their cause, Stanton drafted a "Declaration of Sentiments" cleverly based on the Declaration of Independence. She changed "all men are created equal" to "all men *and women* are created equal" and substituted the word "man" for "King George." Of 18 grievances in the Declaration, the last one summed up the general feeling about man's treatment of woman:

❝ He has endeavored, in every way that he could, to destroy her confidence in her own powers, to lessen her self-respect, and to make her willing to lead a dependent and abject [degraded] life. ❞

The attendees spent two days discussing the Declaration and its resolutions. They debated and voted for resolutions demanding equality in property rights, education, work, and church activities.

When Lucretia Mott spoke out against slavery, she was often the target of angry mobs.

Discussion

Checking Understanding

1. What were some of Elizabeth Blackwell's accomplishments? (First woman to earn a medical degree in the United States; started a nursing school and a hospital for women and children in New York City.)

2. What was the purpose of the Seneca Falls Convention? (To attract attention to the cause of women's rights through a Declaration of Sentiments based on the Declaration of Independence.)

Stimulating Critical Thinking

3. Why do you think that women encountered fierce resistance when arguing for their rights? (Answers might include: some people saw women's rights advocates as challenging traditional values of marriage and the family; some thought women did not need rights because men would protect them.)

★ ★ ★
Vital Links

Voice of Elizabeth Cady Stanton (First Person Account) Unit 3, Side 1, Search 41201, Play to 41390

See also Unit 3 Explore CD-ROM location 249.

The Susan B. Anthony dollar (below) was the first American coin to depict a historical woman, rather than a mythological or symbolic one. An eagle appears on the reverse side. Since the Anthony dollar is about the size of a quarter, the dollar's edge was flattened in several places to distinguish it. However, the coin was not well received by the public and is seldom found in circulation.

For a description of a girls' school and a plea for women's education, see **American Readings**, pp. 62–64.

Adopting a List of Grievances

To help students understand challenges faced by organizers of the Seneca Falls Convention, have them draw up and vote on a list of grievances. Divide the class into groups and ask each group to identify a contemporary situation—personal, local, or national—in which they think people's rights are being denied. (Some possibilities: parental rules, a school policy, evicting the homeless from a park.) Have each group discuss, agree on, and draft a list of four grievances modeled on those in the Declaration of Sentiments. Ask each group to present its grievances to the class to be voted on. You may wish to have students volunteer to explain reasons why they voted for or against certain grievances.

Teaching the

⤷ Point of View

Emphasize that even strong supporters of women's rights disagreed about a woman's right to vote. Discuss why allowing women to vote was so controversial.

For an activity on a woman suffrage petition and pamphlet, see **Using Historical Documents**, pp. 85–90.

Stanton asked that women be given the full rights of citizens—including the right to vote. The idea of woman suffrage was so radical at the time that even Lucretia Mott warned Stanton, "Why, Lizzie, [you] will make us ridiculous! We must go slowly." Still, with the help of Frederick Douglass, who attended the convention, the resolution on the vote passed by a slim margin.

Most historians view the convention as the beginning of the women's movement in the United States. At the time, however, newspapers and magazines scorned and ridiculed the convention, causing a number of women to withdraw their support. The issue of suffrage raised a storm of protest, and many of those who had signed the Declaration of Sentiments later asked to have their names removed.

Campaigning for Rights

Despite the ridicule, Stanton and other women leaders pressed forward. In 1851 the movement gained an important new member in Susan B. Anthony. Already active in the temperance and antislavery efforts, she took on women's rights, making woman suffrage her most important goal.

Anthony and Stanton formed a close team. Stanton was a strong writer and Anthony a gifted organizer and campaigner. Stanton would write fiery speeches that Anthony would travel to deliver in town after town. As Henry Stanton remarked to his wife, "You stir up Susan and she stirs up the world."

The Susan B. Anthony dollar, minted from 1979 to 1981, was the first United States coin to picture a woman (other than a symbolic type).

Another campaigner for women's rights was Lucy Stone. In 1847 Stone became the first Massachusetts woman to earn a college degree. When she married Henry Blackwell (Elizabeth Blackwell's brother), she became the first American woman to keep her maiden name. Women who did so later became known as "Lucy Stoners."

An excellent speaker, Stone had been a lecturer for the American Anti-Slavery Society before she began speaking out for women's rights. She stood up to heckling and even rioting crowds, often at great risk. She refused to pay taxes, since without the vote "women suffer taxation, and yet have no representation."

As you read earlier, Sojourner Truth began by speaking out about her religious beliefs and slavery, and ended up speaking out for women's rights as well. She delivered her famous "Ain't I a Woman?" speech at a women's convention in 1851. She also took up the cause of woman suffrage, and Elizabeth Cady Stanton and others often asked her to speak at suffrage gatherings.

Women's rights were slow in coming, and the female crusaders lost many battles. They did succeed in convincing some states to allow married women to own property and to grant women the right to keep their own wages. The demand for suffrage, however, made little progress during this period.

⤷ Point of View

What did women think about the vote?

The women and men at Seneca Falls were some of the most forward looking of their time when it came to the issue of women's rights. Still, the resolution on the vote roused heated debate even among these reformers.

Some women feared that the issue of the vote—because it was so outrageous to most people—would keep them from winning

✠ Connections to Civics

The Nineteenth Amendment guarantees women the right to vote in state and national elections. The woman suffrage amendment was first introduced in Congress in 1878 and was reintroduced every year until Congress finally approved it in 1919. After three-fourths of the states ratified the suffrage amendment, it became part of the Constitution in 1920.

See the Reinforcement activity on analyzing women's rights, in **Chapter Resources Binder**, pp. 125–126.

In 1860 women shoe-makers marched for fair pay. Today, women continue to demand equal opportunities.

other rights. Others believed that women had enough say in government by use of petitions. As one woman said:

❝Women do not need the ballot to accomplish their ends. If they are really in earnest they can secure whatever they are willing to work for in the way of . . . legislation [through petition].❞

Another common view of a woman's role was that she should influence government by influencing her sons who would vote. A woman who opposed suffrage wrote:

❝Patriotism for a woman does not begin at the ballot box. It begins when she takes pains to instruct her young son

concerning the dignity and sacredness of the ballot. . . . Women who [train] the voters will eventually hold more power than if voting themselves.❞

Yet in the minds of Elizabeth Cady Stanton and Susan B. Anthony, women would only have equality when they had the vote. Referring to the Constitution, Anthony said:

❝It is downright mockery to talk to women of their enjoyment of the 'blessings of liberty' while they are denied the only means of securing them provided by this democratic-republican government—the ballot.❞

Neither Stanton nor Anthony would live to see the day when all women in the United States would have the ballot. Yet what they started would be fulfilled some 70 years later in the Nineteenth Amendment to the Constitution.

⭐ 3. Section Review

1. Why did women involved in the anti-slavery movement also become interested in women's rights?
2. What educational opportunities were open to women at the start of the 1800s? What actions did women take to overcome their lack of opportunity?
3. Imagine that you are a woman in the mid-1800s. Choose three of the following and write a journal entry telling how each inspires you: Emma Hart Willard, Mary Lyon, Elizabeth Blackwell, Antoinette Brown Blackwell, Elizabeth Cady Stanton, Lucy Stone, Sojourner Truth.
4. Critical Thinking The Seneca Falls Convention passed a number of resolutions on women's rights. Why do you think suffrage seemed so different from other rights?

Closing the Section

Wrap-Up Activity

Making a Placard

To review issues in the women's rights movement, have small groups make placards that people attending a women's rights rally in 1848 might have displayed. Ask each group to decide what cause it wishes to support or oppose and then design and make its placard. Display the finished placards in the room.

Section Review
Answers

1. As they fought to free slaves, women recognized their own lack of freedom.
2. Before the 1830s some girls attended schools that trained them to be wives and mothers, but no college in the United States accepted women. Emma Willard and Mary Lyon opened colleges for women.
3. Answers will vary, but the journal entry should include the accomplishment of the subject and explain why it is inspiring.
4. Answers will vary but may include: Suffrage threatened the traditional political process; once they had the vote, women would have the power to bring about many other reforms.

Warm-Up Activity

Poetry Reading

To acquaint students with the works of some of the authors discussed in this section, organize a poetry reading. Have volunteers choose poems by Dickinson, Whitman, Longfellow, and Poe to read aloud to the class.

Geography Question of the Day

Write the phrase "American places" on the chalkboard. Ask students to imagine being an American writer in the early 1800s who wants to write a story that is set in a distinctly American place. Have them list several places and tell why each would be considered uniquely American. (Some examples: backcountry log cabin, New England whaling town, southern cotton plantation.)

Section Objectives

★ Identify some of the great American writers of the period.
★ Explain how these writers expressed American subjects and themes.
★ Describe the Hudson River School and what made its style American.

Teaching Resources

Take-Home Planner 5, pp. 26–33
Chapter Resources Binder
  Study Guide, p. 124
  Reinforcement
  Skills Development
  Geography Extensions
  American Readings
  Using Historical Documents
  Transparency Activities
Chapter and Unit Tests, pp. 99–102

4. American Voices

Reading Guide

Section Focus **The flowering of American literature and art**

1. Who were some of the great American writers of the period?
2. How did these writers express American subjects and themes?
3. What was the Hudson River School and what made its style American?

The early to mid-1800s saw a flowering of intellectual and creative life in the United States. While earlier American writers and painters had looked to Europe for examples and inspiration, a new generation of creative voices celebrated being uniquely American.

American Stories

American writers began to break free of European traditions in the stories they told. They focused instead on subjects and themes of American life.

Irving and Cooper Two of the earliest writers to focus on American subjects were Washington Irving and James Fenimore Cooper. Irving wrote the humorous short stories "Rip Van Winkle" and "The Legend of Sleepy Hollow." In "Rip Van Winkle" (1820) Irving explored the theme of progress in the tale of a man who falls asleep for 20 years and wakes to find his world changed.

Cooper wrote tales of the American backcountry during colonial times, idealizing relations between whites and Indians. His hero was Natty Bumppo, a frontiersman featured in such classics as *The Last of the Mohicans* (1826) and *The Deerslayer* (1841).

Hawthorne and Melville Later storytellers included novelists Nathaniel Hawthorne and Herman Melville. Hawthorne lived in Salem, Massachusetts, the center of famous witchcraft trials. He often set his works in 1600s Puritan New England. His two best-known works, *The Scarlet Letter* (1850) and *The House of the Seven Gables* (1851), focus on the themes of sin and human frailty.

Melville drew on his experiences at sea and living on South Pacific islands for the material in his novels. No one has outdone the realistic depiction of whaling in *Moby-Dick* (1851), considered Melville's greatest work. The spine-tingling adventure tells of an obsessed sea captain who destroys himself and his crew in pursuit of a white whale. Captain Ahab remains one of the most memorable characters in American fiction.

African American narrative This period also saw publication of works in the African American narrative tradition. Such works as Frederick Douglass's *Narrative of the Life of Frederick Douglass* (1845), the *Narrative of Sojourner Truth* (1850), and Harriet Jacobs's *Incidents in the Life of a Slave Girl* (1861) became immensely popular.

American Poetry

American poetry also flourished during these years. American poets, diverse in their styles, reached new heights of literary genius.

Henry Wadsworth Longfellow Perhaps the most popular poet of the time was Henry Wadsworth Longfellow. Many of his

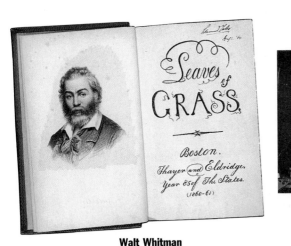

Walt Whitman

Herman Melville

Emily Dickinson

Nathaniel Hawthorne

poems celebrate events in American history. Even today people recognize the opening lines from his poem, "Paul Revere's Ride" (1863): "Listen, my children, and you shall hear / of the midnight ride of Paul Revere. . . ."

Longfellow wrote with a reformer's spirit. He opposed slavery and in 1842 published *Poems on Slavery* voicing his views. In *The Song of Hiawatha* (1855), he sought to show the humanity of Indians, often viewed as savages by white Americans of the time.

Walt Whitman Another reform-minded poet was Walt Whitman. Whitman loved democracy and once wrote that "the United States themselves are essentially the greatest poem." He wrote about common people, and often would ride on ferries and stagecoaches just to talk with ordinary Americans. He began to write his masterpiece, *Leaves of Grass*, in 1848, and continued to add to it for the rest of his life.

Edgar Allan Poe Poet, short-story writer, and critic Edgar Allan Poe did not share Whitman's optimism. He believed

that people could not improve society by their efforts. His works often explore the dark side of human nature. Though called the father of mystery and detective fiction, Poe is best known for his tales of terror and his poems, such as "The Raven."

Emily Dickinson Today considered one of the greatest American poets, Emily Dickinson was unknown in her own time. The shy and reclusive Dickinson once asked in a poem, "I'm nobody! Who are you? / Are you—Nobody too?" Only 7 of the 1,775 poems Dickinson composed were published during her lifetime, and some of those were published anonymously.

Transcendentalists

Many writers of the time were influenced by a philosophy called transcendentalism. Transcendentalists believed that people find truth within themselves, not just through experience and observation. Simply put, they believed they could "transcend," or rise

See the Study Guide activity in **Chapter Resources Binder,** p. 124.

∞ Link to Art

Landscape with Rainbow (1859) While American literature was blossoming, so was American art. The Hudson River School, a group of artists named for the area that first inspired them, wanted Americans to develop a deeper appreciation of the vast American wilderness. The painting above is by Robert S. Duncanson, an African American painter of the Hudson River School. **Discuss** From the painting, how do you think the artist views the relationship between man and nature?

above, the limits of the human mind. They emphasized self-reliance and individuality.

Transcendentalists met frequently as a discussion group in Concord, Massachusetts, beginning in 1836. The leading American transcendentalists included Ralph Waldo Emerson, Henry David Thoreau, Bronson Alcott, and Margaret Fuller. Many were committed to reform movements of the time. Transcendentalists also formed the utopian Brook Farm, which you read about earlier.

Ralph Waldo Emerson The leader of the American transcendentalists was Ralph Waldo Emerson, an essayist, poet, and public speaker. He urged people to discover strength within themselves rather than borrow ideas from others.

In tune with the democratic ideals of the time, Emerson believed in the equality of all people. Though he rejected organized religion, he shared with revivalists the belief that all people should work to improve themselves.

Henry David Thoreau's most influential work was the essay "Civil Disobedience." In it he explains that he refused to pay a poll tax because the money was to be used to support the war with Mexico. The essay eloquently defends the right of an individual to disobey the law in matters of conscience, but also recognizes the obligation to pay the penalty. For Thoreau, that penalty was a day in the Concord jail. It is said that when Emerson visited Thoreau in jail, he asked, "Henry, why are you here?" Thoreau replied, "Waldo, why are you not here?"

Thoreau's essay was to have a profound impact on twentieth-century reformers, notably Mahatma Gandhi and Martin Luther King, Jr. Both of them advocated nonviolent resistance to any authority they considered unjust.

Henry David Thoreau Among those Emerson touched was Henry David Thoreau. Thoreau, also a gifted writer and poet, shared Emerson's zeal for reform. He opposed slavery and participated in the Underground Railroad. He valued individualism, especially in deciding right and wrong. He wrote:

❝If a man does not keep pace with his companion perhaps it is because he hears a different drummer. Let him step to the music he hears.❞

Thoreau took the message of self-reliance to an extreme. He built a cabin at Walden on Emerson's property and then described his attempt at simple living in his most famous work, *Walden* (1854).

4. Section Review

1. Name three American writers of the period and give some characteristics of their work.
2. What were some of the main beliefs of the transcendentalists? How did these beliefs affect their lives?
3. Critical Thinking In what ways did the works of American writers and painters of the early to mid-1800s express a uniquely American style?

Why We Remember

Religion and Reform

"I have been 40 years a slave and 40 years free," remarked Sojourner Truth late in life, "and would be here 40 years more to have equal rights for all."

Looking back, Truth could see what reformers had accomplished. Armed with strong religious faith and democratic ideals, they had attacked a number of social problems. Reformers had made progress in improving public education, prisons, and the treatment of the mentally ill. Abolitionists had shined a spotlight on the issue of slavery. Women had begun to speak up for their rights. Still, in Sojourner Truth's eyes, there was much more to be done.

What Sojourner Truth and other reformers could not see was that they had done more than improve society in their time. They had helped shape the American ideal that ordinary people should work to help others.

That belief has endured. Americans today are among the most generous people on earth when it comes to giving their time and money to good causes. Some causes, such as improving the environment or ending world hunger, might surprise Sojourner Truth and her fellow reformers. What would not surprise them is that so many Americans still care about improving their communities, helping the less fortunate, and fighting for equality for all.

1820–1850 Chapter 16 ● **455**

Survey Answers

Reviewing Vocabulary

Definitions are found on these pages: *social reform* (433), *temperance* (437), *utopias* (437), *emancipation* (440), *abolition* (441).

Reviewing Main Ideas

1. Camp meetings, circuit riders, and the AME Church.
2. Public education: state funds doubled, school quality improved, school year lengthened, salaries increased, teacher training schools opened, number of schools increased. Help for disabled: schools for deaf and blind students, hospitals for mentally ill. Prison reform: men separated from women, juveniles separated from others, debtor prisons eliminated, cruel punishment outlawed. Temperance: some states banned sale of alcohol.
3. Possibilities: Forten petitioned for emancipation; Cuffe sent freed slaves to Africa; Lundy published newspaper; Weld helped start antislavery movement at Oberlin; Garrison published newspaper and formed antislavery society; Grimkés published pamphlets and made speeches; Douglass lectured and wrote against slavery; Truth gave speeches; Tubman helped slaves escape to freedom.
4. Some businessmen depended on southern agriculture. Some factory workers feared losing jobs to ex-slaves.
5. (a) Wife's property and money belonged to husband; no woman could vote or sit on jury; educational opportunities limited. (b) Some states allowed women to own property and keep wages; educational opportunities improved. (c) Woman suffrage.
6. Possibilities: Willard and
(Answers continued in top margin)

456

Lyon opened schools; Elizabeth Blackwell was first American woman to earn a medical diploma; Antoinette Brown Blackwell was first woman to become ordained minister; Stanton and Mott fought for rights and helped organize the Seneca Falls Convention; Anthony made speeches; Stone was first Massachusetts woman to earn college degree; Truth made speeches.

7. (a) Cooper wrote about relations between Indians and colonial settlers. (b) Hawthorne wrote about Puritan New England. (c) Longfellow wrote about events in American history. (d) Whitman wrote poetry about the common people.

Thinking Critically

1. The quote describes them well because they took unpopular stands. Examples from

Chapter Survey

Reviewing Vocabulary

Define the following terms.
1. social reform
2. temperance
3. utopias
4. emancipation
5. abolition

Reviewing Main Ideas

1. How did the message of the Second Great Awakening spread?
2. Describe the progress made by one of the following reform movements: public education, help for the disabled, prison reform, or temperance.
3. Name four people who fought against slavery, and tell what each person did for the antislavery cause.
4. What were two economic reasons behind opposition to abolitionism in the North?
5. (a) In what ways were women's rights limited in the early 1800s? (b) What progress had been made by the middle 1800s? (c) What goal would not be achieved for many years?
6. Name three people who worked to expand women's rights and opportunities, and tell what each person did for the cause.
7. Describe how each writer focused on American subjects or themes: (a) James Fenimore Cooper (b) Nathaniel Hawthorne (c) Henry Wadsworth Longfellow (d) Walt Whitman

Thinking Critically

1. Application How well does the quote by Henry David Thoreau on page 455 describe the reformers of the early and mid-1800s? Support your answer with examples from the chapter.
2. Synthesis Choose a reformer from the chapter and imagine that he or she could observe life in our country today. What might his or her reaction be? Why?

3. Why We Remember: Analysis What two basic beliefs drove reformers in the 1800s? How do they compare with the beliefs that drive modern-day Americans to work for improvements? Give examples.

Applying Skills

Historical interpretations Outspoken, controversial figures like William Lloyd Garrison are part of our past—and our present. Think of such a person in the news today. Write descriptions of the person that reflect two different ways the person might be viewed by historians of the future. Make sure your descriptions include:
• an interpretation
• support for the interpretation, in the form of facts and opinions

History Mystery

Medicine in the 1800s Answer the History Mystery on page 429. Elizabeth Blackwell had been turned down by every medical school in Philadelphia and New York City, as well as by Harvard, Yale, and Bowdoin. After she entered Geneva College she learned that she was only admitted there because administrators and students thought her application was a prank by a rival school. Why do you think they expected her to fail?

Writing in Your History Journal

1. Keys to History (a) The time line on pages 428–429 has six Keys to History. In your journal, describe why each one is important. (b) Choose a key event and imagine yourself as a television reporter assigned to cover it. In your journal, write what you will say about the event on tonight's broadcast.

the chapter may include any people who followed consciences and fought for improved public education, opportunities for disabled, prison reform, temperance, abolition, or women's rights.

2. Answers will vary depending on reformer. Answers should reflect beliefs and goals of the reformer as stated in the chapter, as well as knowledge of relevant current events.

3. Students should mention religious beliefs and democratic ideals. Both beliefs continue to influence modern reform movements, such as efforts to promote equal work opportunity or to deal with homelessness.

Applying Skills

Answers should reflect understanding of what a historical interpretation is and how it can be supported with facts and opinions.

(Answers continued in side margin)

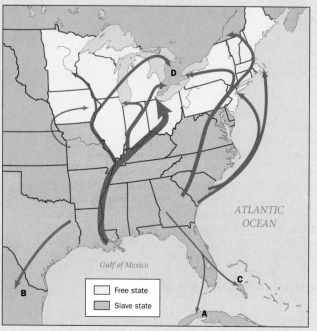

Reviewing Geography

1. The letters on the map represent foreign places to which slaves escaped. Write the name of each.

2. Geographic Thinking The people who traveled the Underground Railroad used natural features like caves and forests to hide and travel safely. Use this map and the one on pages R6–R7 to write about natural features and the railroad routes. Consider, for example, why no route went from Louisiana to Cuba, or why the route from Georgia did not branch into Indiana or Ohio.

2. Sojourner Truth In your journal, reflect on how Sojourner Truth was representative of the people of her time. You might want to think about each section of this chapter and how Sojourner Truth fits in.

⭐ **3. Citizenship** As in many reform movements, supporters of abolition and women's rights held a range of views, from conservative to radical. Does a wide range of views benefit or hurt a reform movement? Why? Write your response in your journal.

Alternative Assessment

Working for reform Work with a group. Imagine that your group has been hired by the leaders of one of the reform movements of the 1800s. Your task is to develop a campaign to advance the reformers' cause.

❶ Choose the reform movement.

❷ Brainstorm a list of campaign tactics. For example, your list might include hanging posters in public places, giving speeches, and submitting petitions to Congress.

❸ For each tactic, name the result you hope to achieve, such as changing the law or swaying public opinion.

❹ When you have finished your list, choose two tactics and share them with the class in a concrete way. For example, you might make and display posters and write a petition to hand out for signatures.

Your work will be evaluated on the following criteria:
• you make a strong effort for the cause
• you accurately reflect the beliefs and goals of reformers of the period
• your campaign activities and materials are appealing and persuasive

History Mystery

Blackwell had been turned down by nearly a dozen schools because she was a woman. They thought she would be unable to learn mathematics and science.

Writing in Your History Journal

1. (a) Explanations should be similar to the time line notes on teacher pages 428–429. (b) Scripts should reflect the chapter information and describe the scene in a lively, interesting way.

2. Answers may vary but should show an understanding of Sojourner Truth's positions on abolition and women's rights.

3. Some may feel that reform movements require radicals to push conservatives and moderates to action. Others may think extremes of radicalism or conservatism destroy unity and weaken the cause.

Reviewing Geography

1. (A) Cuba, (B) Mexico, (C) Bahamas, (D) Canada.

2. Paragraphs should include some of the following points: the reason for no Louisiana-Cuba route was the Gulf of Mexico; the route north from Georgia skirted the eastern edge of the Appalachians and probably did not branch northwest because mountains would be hard to cross.

Alternative Assessment

Teacher's Take-Home Planner 5, page 29, includes suggestions and scoring rubrics for the Alternative Assessment activity.

Making Connections

Answers

1. Answers may note that journeys along the Oregon Trail were voluntary, whereas the Indians were forced to move and the slaves were fleeing cruelty and injustice.

2. Answers will vary, but students may mention territorial growth, increase in population, improvements in transportation, results of reform movements, and development of the arts.

3. Students may mention the spirit of reform, the idea of a national destiny, the expansion of democracy to ordinary people, and the development of American literature and art.

Teaching the

Unit Project

Work with students to create a chart showing the characteristics of historical fiction. For example: portrays life in the past; includes imaginary characters, events, dialogue; integrates real people, places, events. Emphasize that historical fiction mixes the real and the imaginary. If a story is set in the Jacksonian era, it will include events from that period and may include Jackson and other historical characters as well as characters created by the author.

Evaluation Criteria

The project can be evaluated according to the criteria listed below, using a scale for each: 4 = exemplary, 3 = good, 2 = adequate, 1 = poor.

Completing the task The story contains interesting characters, setting, plot, and
(Continued in top margin)

---

background information. The story is of a reasonable length.

Knowing content The story contains accurate historical details and portrayals of historical figures.

Thinking critically Students synthesize historical detail and background information in the story.

Communicating ideas The story blends the historical and fictional convincingly.

Thinking It Over
Answers will vary, since some people prefer fiction and others nonfiction. Some students may argue that nonfiction can be just a recitation of facts, dates, and names that is difficult to absorb, while historical fiction makes history easier to absorb. Others may feel that it is difficult to distinguish between fact and fiction in historical fiction.

Unit Survey

Making Connections

Review

1. Compare and contrast the journeys made along the Trail of Tears, the Oregon Trail, and the Underground Railroad. Consider such factors as who made each journey, why they did so, and the hardships they encountered.
2. Suppose an American traveled to Europe in 1820 and did not return for 30 years.

What three changes do you think he or she would find most striking?
3. What do you think is the most important legacy that Americans who lived between 1820 and 1850 passed on to us? Explain your opinion.

Linking History, Art, and Language Arts

Project

Writing and Illustrating Historical Fiction

Have you heard the term *historical fiction*? These stories are called *fiction* because they contain some imaginary features, such as characters, events, or dialogue. They are called *historical* because they portray life as it was in the past and may include real people and places as well as imaginary ones. Try your hand at creating a piece of historical fiction.

Project Steps

Work on your own to write and illustrate your story.

❶ Choose an interesting main character. The character can be real or imaginary, male or female, and of any age—as long as he or she lived in America between 1820 and 1850. Look through the unit to get ideas. Here are a few possibilities:
• a Seminole in hiding in Florida
• the young woman forced to spread the news of the defeat at the Alamo
• the employee of John Sutter who discovered gold
• a slave escaping to freedom

• an immigrant from China, Ireland, or elsewhere
• a teenager on a farm that is a station of the Underground Railroad

❷ Decide who your other characters will be, where and when the story will take place, and what the story's plot will be.

❸ Gather background information. You may want to look through some nonfiction books for realistic historical details to include.

❹ Write the story. Do a first draft to get your thoughts on paper quickly. Then read and revise as many times as necessary to add interest, improve sentence and paragraph flow, and correct any errors in grammar, punctuation, or spelling. Keep your story under 3,500 words.

❺ Draw a cover for your story.

❻ Share your story with classmates by reading it aloud or passing it around.

Thinking It Over How do you think historical fiction compares with nonfiction as a way to learn about history? Explain your opinion.

Objectives

★ Understand what memoirs are.
★ Identify the kinds of information that historians can acquire from memoirs.
★ Understand the limitations of memoirs as a tool of history.

Charles Henry Veil

How Do We Know?

Scholar's Tool Kit
Memoirs

The Battle of Gettysburg, fought in July 1863, was one of the bloodiest battles of the American Civil War. Few battles in history caused more casualties. As many as 51,000 Confederate and Union soldiers failed to answer roll call after the three days of fighting.

A Crucial Moment

At a crucial moment early in the battle, Confederate forces were rushing through a cornfield to capture a key hill. Scrambling up the other side was a Union regiment. From atop his horse at the crest of the hill, Major General John Fulton Reynolds of the Union army watched as the two forces swept toward each other. With him were staff officers and his 21-year-old orderly, Private Charles Henry Veil.

As the Union infantry crested the hill, Confederate musket fire knocked down the first line of soldiers. Those behind them stopped and fell back in confusion. Anxious to prevent a terrible defeat, General Reynolds turned in his saddle and tried to rally the Union men.

"Forward!" he shouted. "Forward men! Drive these fellows out of there! Forward! For God's sake, forward!"

At that moment Reynolds slumped over and fell from his horse. A Confederate sharpshooter more than 200 yards (180 m) away had just made the shot of a lifetime. General Reynolds was the highest-ranking officer of the Union army killed during the Civil War.

Introducing
How Do We Know?

Memoirs

Explain that a memoir is a form of autobiographical writing that presents recollections of significant events. It differs from autobiography in that it is less private and introspective and may focus on events and people other than the writer.

Ask why a historian might read memoirs about an event (to learn details from an eyewitness, to expand knowledge of an event by collecting different points of view). Point out that memoirs are not always completely reliable. Veil's, written many years after the Battle of Gettysburg, differs in important details from the account of the event in a letter he wrote soon after the battle. Ask students to speculate why Veil changed his story.

By reading about Veil's memoir and letter, students will better understand the importance of eyewitness accounts and of historians critically examining such accounts and cross-checking them with other evidence.

Setting the Stage
Activity

Writing a Memoir

To prepare students to read about a memoir, have them write a brief account of an event they witnessed or took part in. Have them choose an event and describe what they saw and heard. Encourage them to include their reactions to the event.

1. Since the Battle of Gettysburg is often regarded as the turning point of the Civil War, it is important to have an accurate account of the battle and its effects.

2. Knowing the writer's identity and role in the situation helps the reader interpret the writer's point of view and evaluate the reliability of the account.

3. The accuracy of Veil's memoirs might be checked by reading other eyewitness accounts as well as historians' descriptions. By comparing several sources, students can piece together a more accurate account of what really happened.

Bonus Activity

Comparing Accounts

To help students see how easily information can be distorted as it is told and retold, have them play a game of "telephone." Write a brief account of an event on a piece of paper. Read it in a whisper to one student. Have that student repeat it word for word to another, and so on. When the final student has received the message, ask that student to tell the class what the message was. Then read the original message. Discuss how and why the message changed.

✳ History Footnote

John Fulton Reynolds graduated from West Point in 1841 and saw action in the Mexican-American War. He was promoted twice during that war. In 1860 he became the commandant of cadets at West Point. Shortly after the outbreak of the Civil War, he served with distinction in a number of posts. In 1862 Reynolds became the commander of the First Corps of the Army of the Potomac. He was killed on July 1, 1863, the first day of the Battle of Gettysburg. To commemorate Reynolds and the battle, the state of Pennsylvania erected a monument on the spot where he fell.

Sketch of the death of Union General John Reynolds near Gettysburg

? Critical Thinking

1. Why do you think historians care about knowing the accurate story of the Battle of Gettysburg?

That story is certain. What happened afterwards is not so certain. What we know is based largely on the testimony of Private Veil.

Veil Tells His Story

For Veil, the death of General Reynolds was such an important episode that he told and retold the story many times. He also described the event at length in his memoirs, which he wrote some 30 years later. **Memoirs** are a person's written remembrances of the events of his or her life.

Memoirs are key historical documents, but sometimes they pose dilemmas for historians. This was true in Veil's case. In a letter to a friend dated April 7, 1864—only months after the event—Veil wrote:

? Critical Thinking

2. When reading someone's memoirs, what information would you like to have about the person? Why?

"When the General fell, the only persons who were with him was Captain Mitchell & Baird and myself. When he fell we sprang from our horses. . . . We were under the impression that he was only stunned, this was all done at a glance. I caught the Gen[era]l under the arms while each of the Capt[ain]s took hold of his legs, and we commenced to carry him out of the woods. . . ."

Yet in his memoirs, written some 30 years after the event, Veil claimed that he was the only witness at the critical moment when General Reynolds was killed. Here is how Veil told the story then:

"General Reynolds fell upon his face, his arms outstretched toward the enemy. I at once sprang from my horse and ran to his side, gave one glance at his body and seeing no wound or blood, turned his body upon its back. . . . My next impression was to save him from falling into the hands of the enemy. Not having any assistance, not

⊞ **Connections to Literature**

Michael Shaara's superb novel about Gettysburg, *The Killer Angels,* published in 1974, describes the shooting and death of General Reynolds. This novel has been praised by several historians, including James M. McPherson and Stephen B. Oates, and by Ken Burns, maker of the television documentary *The Civil War. The Killer Angels* was also the basis for the movie *Gettysburg.*

one of our men being near, I picked him up by taking hold under his arms and commenced pulling him backward toward our line. As I did so, the Confederates yelled 'Drop him! Drop him!' But I kept on backing off as fast as I could and finally got over the brow of the rise, where I found some men and where we were out of range of the enemy's fire."

? **Critical Thinking**

3. Veil's memoirs are now published in book form. If you read the memoirs, how might you go about checking the accuracy of his accounts?

How Do Historians Know?

As time passed, Veil obviously enlarged his role in the event. He made himself more of a hero than he really was, failing to mention those who helped him take the body off the battlefield.

Certainly, Veil had no need to add to the facts. His role in saving the general's body from the enemy was widely known, and he was well rewarded—even by President Lincoln himself. The change in Veil's story could have been deliberate, or he could simply have forgotten. As people age, their memories sometimes fade or they have "selective memory"—remembering only the facts they want to remember.

Accounts of an event are more likely to be accurate when written closer in time to the event. In Veil's case, he gave a more believable account in his April 1864 letter. Because memories can be unreliable, scholars seek evidence from several sources in addition to memoirs. They go over all the descriptions of the event to figure out the facts. In this way, a scholar is like a detective. New discoveries of memoirs and other sources continue to affect the story we call history.

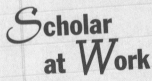 **Scholar at Work**

Anyone can write memoirs. Think of an important event that happened in your life. Write your memory of the event, telling the story with as many details as possible.

When your memoir is finished, share it with someone else—a parent, brother, sister, or friend—who was also a part of the event. Ask the person to point out any difference in his or her recollections. Working together, try to construct the most accurate story you can.

• 461

⚑ **Discussion**

Checking Understanding

1. What important event did Private Charles Henry Veil witness? (He witnessed the shooting of the highest-ranking officer of the Union army killed during the Civil War.)

2. What two accounts did Veil write of this event? (He wrote a letter describing the event and another account of the event in his memoirs.)

3. How do Veil's two accounts differ? (In his memoir, Veil enlarges his role in the event, neglecting to mention the others who helped him remove the body from the battlefield, whom he described in his letter.)

4. What does this suggest about the reliability of sources? (It suggests that memoirs can be unreliable, and historians must seek evidence from more than one source.)

Teaching the *Scholar at Work*

When you assign the activity, encourage students to list the differences between their versions and those of the others who took part in the events. When all students have completed their accounts, have them share the major differences they found. Can the class discover any pattern or make any generalizations about causes of the differences?

Introducing the Unit

Battle of Shiloh— April 6th, 1862

This lithograph depicts one of the bloodiest battles of the Civil War, which left nearly 3,500 dead and over 20,000 wounded. More Americans died in this two-day battle than in the War of Independence, the War of 1812, and the war with Mexico combined.

Throughout this unit, students will explore the divisions that erupted into the devastating Civil War, and how, through Reconstruction, those rifts in the nation began to heal.

Teaching the

Hands-On

┌ ─ ─ ─ ─ ─ ─ ▶ *HISTORY*

Have students work in pairs or small groups to discuss the painting and identify details to include in their telegrams. Students should notice the casualties and great amount of physical destruction that has already occurred, as well as the ongoing violence. Ask students to imagine what sounds they might hear from the horses, the weapons, and from the fighters themselves.

Unit Overview

As the nation expanded westward, the conflict over slavery grew. The Compromise of 1850 brought only temporary relief. In April, 1861, the Civil War began.

With the Emancipation Proclamation, the war became a struggle for freedom as well as for preserving the Union. The year 1863 marked a turning point, as Lee was turned back at Gettysburg and Grant took command of the Union army. The South surrendered in 1865.

Reconstruction saw passage of the Thirteenth, Fourteenth, and Fifteenth Amendments. However by 1877 white southerners had regained control of state governments, disenfranchised blacks, and created systems of rigid segregation. African American responses included migrating north, self-help, and open disobedience of Jim Crow laws.

1850–1905

Unit **6**

Chapters

17. **The Gathering Storm**

18. **The Civil War**

19. **Reconstruction**

Hands-On

─ ─ ─ ─ ─ ─ ─ ─ ▶ *HISTORY*

Activity

In the 1860s there was no radio, television, or Internet. People got their news mainly from newspapers. Imagine that it is 1862 and you are a journalist for a daily paper. You have just arrived at the Battle of Shiloh, in Tennessee, where both sides in the Civil War are suffering heavy losses. Send a telegram to your editor describing the sights and sounds of the battlefield.

Battle of Shiloh—April 6th, 1862 (detail)
published by the McCormick Harvesting Machine Co.,
Chicago, 1885

The Battle of Shiloh bears the name of a church located near the battle site. *Shiloh* is a Hebrew word meaning "place of peace." In the painting, Grant and the Union army are shown at the right. The sunken road in the center became known as the "Hornet's Nest," as Union soldiers fired shots from the thickets along the road, confronting repeated Confederate attacks. Though Grant's troops drove back the Confederate forces, heavy losses made the victory a hollow one.

This lithograph, which documents a pivotal battle, served another purpose. McCormick Harvesting Machine Co. included on the print a caption: "The Machines Come Victoriously Out Of Every Contest, And Without A Scratch." Prominently placed in the shed in the lower left, surviving the destruction around it, is a McCormick reaper.

Civil War and Reconstruction

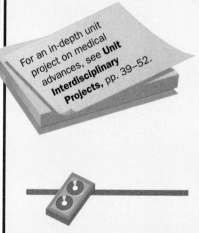
For an in-depth unit project on medical advances, see **Unit Interdisciplinary Projects**, pp. 39–52.

The Unit 6 episode of the *Why We Remember* video series focuses on Clara Barton.

Discussion

Checking Understanding

1. What details suggest this is not a modern battle? (All men are on foot or on horseback; uniforms and guns are old-fashioned; no planes, tanks, or other motorized vehicles.)

Stimulating Critical Thinking

2. What do you think it felt like to be a soldier in this battle? (Students may suggest feelings of fear or confusion.)

3. Why do you think the artist chose to depict a vast number of soldiers, rather than just General Grant? (Accept reasonable responses. For example, the artist may have wanted to give a sense of the many who suffer in war, not just its heroes.)

463

17 The Gathering Storm
1846–1861

Chapter Planning Guide

Section	Student Text	Teacher's Edition Activities
Opener and Story pp. 464–467	**Keys to History Time Line** **History Mystery** ★ Beginning the Story with **Abraham Lincoln**	**Setting the Stage Activity** Describing a Future President, p. 466
1 **Efforts to Save the Union** pp. 468–471		**Warm-Up Activity** Anticipating Issues, p. 468 **Geography Question of the Day,** p. 468 **Section Activity** Exploring the Art of Compromise, p. 470 **Bonus Activity** Protesting the Compromise of 1850, p. 470 **Wrap-Up Activity** Making a Venn Diagram, p. 471
2 **The Failure of Compromise** pp. 472–477	**Reading Maps** The Spread of Slavery, p. 474 **Hands-On History** Creating an advertisement for Kansas, p. 475 **Lab** **Skill Lab** Asking Historical Questions, p. 477	**Warm-Up Activity** The Impact of Media, p. 472 **Geography Question of the Day,** p. 472 **Section Activity** Headlines on "Bleeding Kansas," p. 474 **Bonus Activity** An *Uncle Tom's Cabin* Ad, p. 473 **Wrap-Up Activity** Briefing Buchanan, p. 476
3 **On the Brink of War** pp. 478–485	**Link to the Present** Election campaigns today, p. 480 **Link to Art** *John Brown Going to His Hanging,* p. 481 **Reading Maps** Election of 1860, p. 482 **Point of View** Is secession ever justifiable?, p. 482 **World Link** Freedom for Russian serfs, p. 483 **Lab** **Geography Lab** The Appalachian Mountains, p. 485	**Warm-Up Activity** Alternatives to Secession, p. 478 **Geography Question of the Day,** p. 478 **Section Activity** Arguing a Court Case, p. 479 **Bonus Activity** Descriptions of Fort Sumter, p. 482 **Wrap-Up Activity** Writing a News Release, p. 484
Evaluation	✓ **Section 1 Review,** p. 471 ✓ **Section 2 Review,** p. 476 ✓ **Section 3 Review,** p. 484 ✓ **Chapter Survey,** pp. 486–487 **Alternative Assessment** Covering the 1860 election on TV, p. 487	✓ **Answers to Section 1 Review,** p. 471 ✓ **Answers to Section 2 Review,** p. 476 ✓ **Answers to Section 3 Review,** p. 484 ✓ **Answers to Chapter Survey,** pp. 486–487 (Alternative Assessment guidelines are in the Take-Home Planner.)

Teacher's Resource Package

Chapter Summaries: English and Spanish, pp. 38–39

Chapter Resources Binder
Study Guide Identifying Viewpoints, p. 129
Reinforcement Interpreting Election Results, pp. 133–134
Using Historical Documents The Compromise of 1850, pp. 91–95

Chapter Resources Binder
Study Guide Using a Time Line, p. 130

Skills Development Asking Historical Questions, pp. 135–136

Chapter Resources Binder
Study Guide Identifying Causes and Effects, p. 131
Geography Extensions Describing the Mountains, pp. 33–34
American Readings Lincoln on Slavery, pp. 65–66; Fort Sumter Under Attack, pp. 67–68

Chapter and Unit Tests Chapter 17 Tests, Forms A and B, pp. 111–114

Take-Home Planner

Introducing the Chapter Activity Arguing Against Slavery, p. 4

Chapter In-Depth Activity Examining the Republican Platform, p. 4

Reduced Views
Study Guide, p. 6
Reinforcement, p. 7
Using Historical Documents, p. 9
Unit 6 Answers, pp. 28–34

Reduced Views
Study Guide, p. 6
Skills Development, p. 7
Unit 6 Answers, pp. 28–34

Reduced Views
Study Guide, p. 6
Geography Extensions, p. 9
American Readings, p. 8
Unit 6 Answers, pp. 28–34

Reduced Views
Chapter Tests, p. 9
Unit 6 Answers, pp. 28–34
Alternative Assessment Guidelines for scoring the Chapter Survey activity, p. 5

Additional Resources

Wall Time Line

Unit 6 Activity

Transparency Package

Transparency 17-1 Map: The Spread of Slavery—use with Section 2

Transparency 17-2 *Dividing the National Map*—use with Section 3

Transparency Activity Book

SelecTest Testing Software
Chapter 17 Test, Forms A and B

★★★ Vital Links

O Videodisc

◎ CD-ROM

Slave auction (see TE p. 469)

Uncle Tom's Cabin poster (see TE p. 473)

Senator attack (see TE p. 475)

Dred and Harriet Scott (see TE p. 478)

Lincoln-Douglas debates (see TE p. 480)

John Brown (see TE p. 481)

Unit 6 Videotape Clara Barton: Eyewitness to the Civil War

Teaching Resources

Take-Home Planner 6
  Introducing Chapter Activity
  Chapter In-Depth Activity
  Alternative Assessment
Chapter Resources Binder
Geography Extensions
American Readings
Using Historical Documents
Transparency Activities
Wall Time Line Activities
Chapter Summaries
Chapter and Unit Tests
SelecTest Test File
Vital Links CD-ROM/Videodisc

Time Line

Keys to History

Keys to History journal writing activities are on page 486 in the Chapter Survey.

Compromise of 1850 This compromise between proslavery and antislavery forces provided temporary relief to an unraveling Union. (p. 470)

Uncle Tom's Cabin Stowe's depiction of the brutality of slave life revitalized abolitionists' cause. (p. 472)

Republican Party formed Former Whigs and Democrats formed this party committed to antislavery issues. (p. 476)

Looking Back This compromise, in which Missouri was admitted as a slave state and slavery was prohibited in the rest of the Louisiana Purchase north of 36° 30', only temporarily answered the slavery question.

Chapter Objectives

★ Describe how the conflict over slavery revived as the nation expanded westward.
★ Identify events in the 1850s that continued to divide the North and South.
★ Identify causes of the final break between North and South.

Chapter Overview

As the nation expanded, southerners and northerners had to confront the issue of slavery in the territories. The Compromise of 1850 temporarily calmed the Union. Proslavery forces were given a stronger Fugitive Slave Law and the possibility of new slave states. For slavery foes, California was admitted as a free state, and the slave trade was abolished in Washington, D.C.

1846–1861

Chapter 17

The Gathering Storm

Sections

Beginning the Story with Abraham Lincoln
1. **Efforts to Save the Union**
2. **The Failure of Compromise**
3. **On the Brink of War**

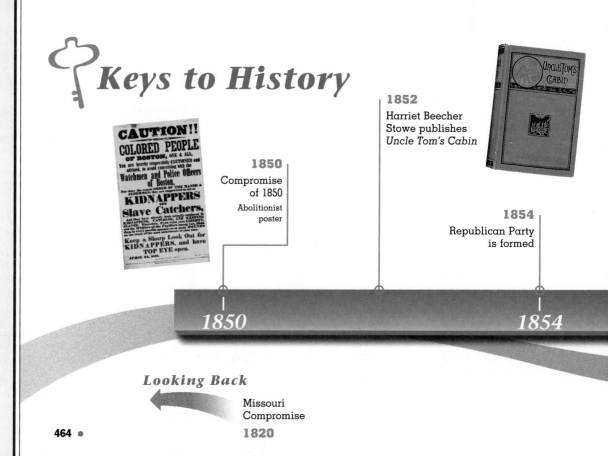

Keys to History

1850 Compromise of 1850 Abolitionist poster

1852 Harriet Beecher Stowe publishes *Uncle Tom's Cabin*

1854 Republican Party is formed

1850

1854

Looking Back
Missouri Compromise
1820

The Compromise of 1850 proved temporary as two key events gave northerners a closer look at slavery: the Fugitive Slave Law brought slave owners north to brutally kidnap escaped slaves, and the novel *Uncle Tom's Cabin* depicted the brutality of slavery. The slavery debate erupted in violence; "Bleeding Kansas" foreshadowed the Civil War. In 1854, former Democratic and Whig party members formed the Republican Party, dedicated to antislavery issues.

In the Dred Scott decision, the Supreme Court ruled that territories were open to slavery, ensuring that the issue dominated the 1860 election. A raid on Harpers Ferry by slavery opponent John Brown further convinced the public that the issue could no longer be ignored. Abraham Lincoln became the first Republican President and leader of a threatened Union: in 1861, the Civil War began.

Teaching the *HISTORY Mystery*

Students will find further information on pp. 474–475. See Chapter Survey, p. 486, for additional questions.

HISTORY *Mystery*

In 1855 fewer than 3,000 voters lived in this territory. However, more than 6,000 people voted there in the March election that year. What was the territory, and how could so many people turn out on election day?

1854–1856
"Bleeding Kansas"

1857
Dred Scott decision

1859
John Brown leads raid on Harpers Ferry

1861
Confederate forces seize Fort Sumter—Civil War begins
Confederate flag

1857

1861

World Link
Russian serfs are freed by Czar Alexander II
1861

Looking Ahead
Civil War ends
1865

• **465**

Time Line

"Bleeding Kansas" Violence between proslavery and antislavery forces erupted in a year-long battle. (p. 474)

Dred Scott decision In denying this slave's petition for freedom, the Supreme Court ruled that African Americans were not citizens and slavery could not be banned in any territory. (p. 478)

John Brown's raid on Harpers Ferry Brown and his followers seized a federal arsenal as part of their antislavery campaign. Brown was hanged for treason, drawing more attention to the antislavery cause. (p. 480)

Civil War begins Southern states seceded after Lincoln's election, and the new Confederate States of America took Fort Sumter by force, beginning the Civil War. (p. 483)

World Link See p. 483.

Looking Ahead With the surrender of Confederate leaders, the Civil War drew to a close and restoration of the Union began.

Beginning the Story

Abraham Lincoln

Abraham Lincoln's humble early years gave little hint of the almost mythical stature he was to achieve. Largely self-educated, Lincoln became known for his love of reading, his honesty and devotion to justice, and his sense of humor. It is perhaps these very human qualities that made him a leader capable of believing in the equality promised in the Declaration of Independence, and of helping the nation to live up to that promise.

Ralph Waldo Emerson described Lincoln as a man who

> . . . was at home and welcome with the humblest, and had a spirit and a practical vein in the times of terror that commanded the admiration of the wisest. His heart was as great as the world, but there was no room in it to hold the memory of a wrong.

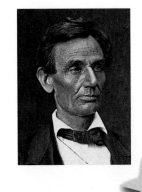

Beginning the Story with

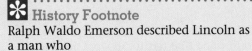

Abraham Lincoln

More than a century ago, the great Russian writer Leo Tolstoy visited his country's wild Caucasus Mountains. There, in the south of Russia, he met the chief of a mountain tribe. After listening to Tolstoy for a time, the chief said to him:

❝But you have not told us a syllable about the greatest general and greatest ruler of the world. We want to know something about him. He was a hero. He spoke with a voice of thunder, he laughed at the sunrise and his deeds were strong as the rock. . . . He was so great that he even forgave the crimes of his greatest enemies. . . . His name was Lincoln and the country in which he lived is called America. . . . Tell us of that man.❞

The Frontier Scholar

Perhaps no one at birth seemed so unlikely a candidate for greatness as Abraham Lincoln. He was born in Kentucky in 1809. His parents, Nancy and Thomas Lincoln, were frontier farmers who lived in a crudely built log cabin and barely knew how to read or write. Searching for a better life, Thomas moved his young family to Indiana, where Abe's mother died when Abe was just 9. The family later moved to Illinois. Bad luck and poverty, however, seemed to follow Thomas Lincoln wherever he went.

Living on the frontier, young Abe had very little education. All in all, he figured that his schooling "did not amount to a year." It was enough, however, to excite a craving for knowledge. Abe read everything he could lay his hands on. "My best friend," he said, "is the man who'll get me a book I ain't read." A cousin recalled, "Abe made books tell him more than they told other people."

History Bookshelf

Myers, Walter Dean. *Now Is Your Time: The African-American Struggle for Freedom.* HarperCollins, 1991. The author uses first-hand accounts and historical photographs and documents to weave the story of African Americans from the beginnings of slavery through the civil rights era. In 1992 he received the Coretta Scott King Award for *Now Is Your Time.*

Also of interest:

Fisher, Leonard Everett. *Tracks Across America: The Story of the American Railroad 1825–1900.* Holiday House, 1992.

Scott, John Anthony, and Robert Alan Scott. *John Brown of Harpers Ferry.* Facts on File, 1988.

"The Rail Splitter"

By the age of 17, Abe Lincoln had grown into a lanky giant well over 6 feet tall. He was amazingly strong and could handle an ax as well as any man. His skill at splitting logs into fence rails would earn him the nickname "The Rail Splitter." Still, Abe disliked physical labor:

❝My father taught me work, but not to love it. I never did like to work, and I don't deny it. I'd rather read, tell stories, crack jokes, talk, laugh—anything but work.❞

Lincoln tried a number of jobs, from running a store to surveying. As a shopkeeper, he earned a reputation for honesty that stuck with him for life. Stories were told of "Honest Abe" walking 6 miles to return a few cents to a woman who was overcharged for her goods. He finally found his career in the law, where he was paid for doing what he most loved—talking to people. Concerned more with gaining justice for his clients than with making money, Abe charged fees that fellow lawyers thought were laughably low.

Lincoln's concern for justice was matched by his sense of humor, as revealed in the following story. One day, Lincoln said, he and a judge were talking about trading horses. They finally agreed to make a trade at nine o'clock the next morning. Neither man was to see the other's horse before that hour. The following morning the judge arrived leading a pathetic-looking creature not much bigger than a dog. A few minutes later, Lincoln appeared carrying a wooden sawhorse. Looking at the judge's puny horse, Lincoln said, "Well, Judge, this is the first time I ever got the worst of a horse trade."

During the stormy 1850s, Lincoln's sense of justice drew him into politics. At moments of frustration and even failure, his sense of humor saved him from despair. "I laugh," he once said, "because if I didn't I would weep." As Honest Abe became a national leader, he would need all the joy and comfort that laughter could bring.

As a young man, Abe Lincoln lived an active life. He split logs for fence rails, worked on a river flatboat on two trips to New Orleans, and fought in the Black Hawk War.

Hands-On → HISTORY

Activity

Abe Lincoln loved to tell stories about his life in a down-to-earth way, spiced with humor. Think about some gift you received or something that happened to you that was funny or embarrassing. It could involve your family, perhaps, or a sports event. Then write or tell the story. Remember that you may be President someday and may use this story to help people get to know you.

See the Chapter In-Depth Activity, Examining the Republican Platform. **Take-Home Planner 6,** p. 4.

Discussion

Thinking Historically

1. **What qualities did young Lincoln show that may have helped him become a leader?** (Craving for knowledge, honesty, concern for justice, sense of humor.)

2. **How does Lincoln's background compare with those of most previous Presidents?** (Most Presidents had more formal education and came from wealthy families.)

3. **Is a sense of humor an important quality for a President? Why or why not?** (Yes: humor helps in communicating with different kinds of people and in dealing with the stress of the presidency. No: it is a President's job to handle serious situations, and a sense of humor is irrelevant.)

Teaching the Hands-On ┈┈→ *HISTORY*

If students are having difficulty thinking of a topic, remind them that the story does not have to be about a major event: describing a small act of kindness toward a classmate or sibling, for example, would be appropriate.

For a journal writing activity on Abraham Lincoln, see student page 486.

Introducing the Section

Vocabulary

popular sovereignty (p. 468)
the right of voters to decide
an issue for themselves

Warm-Up Activity

Anticipating Issues

To help students see
how westward expansion
affected the slavery debate,
have them role-play discussions between proslavery
and antislavery forces.
Divide the class into small
groups, with group mem-
bers evenly divided on both
sides of the issue. Pose the
question, Should slavery be
permitted in the new territories? Ask groups to debate
the issue and brainstorm
ideas for resolving the conflict. Conclude by having
groups share their ideas.

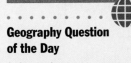

**Geography Question
of the Day**

Ask students to create a two-
column chart listing which
states were free states and
which were slave states as
of 1848. Have them refer
first to the Missouri Compromise map on page 334.
Then have them refer to the
list on pages R19–R23 to
add the six states admitted
between 1822 and 1848.

Section Objectives

★ Identify how southerners and northerners
differed over the issue of slavery in the
territories.

★ Describe the events that led to the Compromise of 1850.

★ Explain how the Compromise of 1850
dealt with the issue of slavery.

Teaching Resources

Take-Home Planner 6, pp. 2–9

Chapter Resources Binder

  Study Guide, p. 129

  Reinforcement, pp. 133–134

  Skills Development

Geography Extensions

American Readings

Using Historical Documents, pp. 91–95

Transparency Activities

Chapter and Unit Tests

1. Efforts to Save the Union

Reading Guide

New Term **popular sovereignty**

Section Focus **Conflict over slavery revives as the United States
expands westward**

1. How did southerners and northerners differ over the issue of slavery
in the territories?
2. What events led to the Compromise of 1850?
3. How did the Compromise of 1850 deal with the issue of slavery?

Abraham Lincoln entered politics during a
time of increasing tension between the North
and the South. The tension centered around
the question of slavery. As the antislavery
cause in the North grew in strength, proslavery southerners responded with equal force.

Attempts by the North and South to reach
a middle ground did not solve the basic question: Do some people have the right to
enslave others? A compromise would ease
tensions only until a new crisis arose. In the
1850s the debate over slavery also brought
into the open disagreements over states'
rights—the idea that states can overrule federal laws—and secession.

Moderates and Radicals

In both North and South, people were
divided over slavery. Northern moderates
accepted slavery where it existed, but did not
want it introduced into new states and territories. Northern radicals demanded an end
to slavery everywhere in the United States.

Before the 1830s southern moderates
viewed slavery as a necessary evil that would
gradually give way to freedom for enslaved
people. Southern radicals, however, insisted
on the right to extend slavery into all new
territories.

Slavery in the West

The slavery controversy came to center
stage during the war with Mexico. In 1846
Congressman David Wilmot, a radical northerner, proposed that slavery be prohibited in
all territory acquired from Mexico. Southern
radicals fought back by demanding that
slavery be permitted in all new territories.

To settle the conflict, some moderates from
both regions suggested extending the Missouri
Compromise line to the Pacific. Other moderates proposed giving voters in each territory
popular sovereignty—the right to decide
for themselves whether to allow slavery. To
many people, popular sovereignty seemed
the best way to end the debate over slavery in
the territories.

The debate did not end, however. Although
Wilmot's proposal was defeated in Congress,
it exposed hostile feelings between the regions
that continued to boil.

Balance of power An ongoing cause
of tension was the balance of power in the
Senate. As long as there were the same number of free states and slave states, neither
North nor South could win a vote on laws
related to slavery.

In 1848 slave and free states were, in fact,
equal in number. However, Minnesota and

History Footnote

The antislavery Democrats led by Van Buren were called "barn burners." The term came from the story of the Dutch farmer who burned down his barn to get rid of the rats. Van Buren's followers were willing to burn down the barn—the Democratic Party—by forming their own Free Soil political party. They refused to put up with the rats—proslavery Democrats.

See the Reinforcement activity in **Chapter Resources Binder,** pp. 133–134.

Oregon, where residents opposed slavery, had applied for statehood. To avoid upsetting the balance of power, Congress put off admitting them to the Union.

The Election of 1848

During the 1848 presidential campaign both Democrats and Whigs avoided the topic of slavery. The Democrats chose a northern moderate, Senator Lewis Cass, as their candidate. The Whigs turned to General Zachary Taylor, a hero of the War with Mexico.

Angry that the two major parties were ignoring the slavery issue, antislavery forces formed the Free Soil Party. With former President Martin Van Buren as their candi-date, the Free Soilers won enough northern votes away from the Democrats to throw the election to Taylor and the Whigs. The Free Soilers' success showed that the conflict over slavery in the territories was not over.

California and Popular Sovereignty

In 1849 the issue of slavery demanded fresh attention when California voters adopted a constitution banning slavery in their territory. President Taylor, who favored popular sovereignty, supported their decision and called for California statehood. People in present-day New Mexico and Utah also wanted their areas to become free states.

MURDER !!! help— neighbors help. **O** my poor Wife and Children.

CENTRAL AMERIC
CUBA
KANSAS
DEMOCRATIC PLATFORM

FORCING SLAVERY DOWN THE THROAT OF A FREESOILER

As this cartoon shows, Free Soilers feared that popular sovereignty would force the slave system down their throats.

Developing the Section

Discussion

Checking Understanding

1. How were northern and southern moderates similar? (Both were willing to accept slavery to some extent.)

2. Why was the Free Soil Party formed? (It was formed by antislavery forces who were angry that the Democrats and Whigs were avoiding the slavery issue.)

Stimulating Critical Thinking

3. Some moderates believed that slavery would eventually die out. Do you agree? Why or why not? (Yes: with increasing use of farm machines, slave labor would become less and less practical. No: southern economy had relied on slave labor too long to change; southern radicals were determined to preserve and spread slavery.)

★ ★ ★

Vital Links

Slave auction (Picture)
Unit 3, Side 1, Search 32895

See also Unit 3 Explore CD-ROM location 182.

See the Study Guide activity in **Chapter Resources Binder,** p. 129.

469

To help students understand the challenge of compromise, have them select a current controversial issue, such as welfare reform, prayer in schools, or the death penalty. Divide the class into small groups and provide time to discuss the topic. Within each group, members should state their opinions and provide supporting reasons. Then the group should try to arrive at a compromise acceptable to all members. Conclude by having each group report on the results, discussing why it was difficult to reach a compromise.

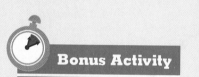

Bonus Activity

Protesting the Compromise of 1850

To underscore that the compromise did not settle the slavery issue, have students imagine themselves as either radical antislavery or proslavery protestors in 1850. Have them either write a letter to their senator or draw a cartoon criticizing the Compromise of 1850. Conclude by asking volunteers to share their protests.

✳ History Footnote

Daniel Webster was a known opponent of slavery. In his personal life, he supported the cause of freed slaves and donated money to help them buy freedom for their families. Yet in his political life, he valued moderation above all else. In a speech supporting the Compromise of 1850 he noted, "In all such disputes, there will sometimes be found men with whom everything is absolute; absolutely wrong, or absolutely right." Webster refused to take an absolute stand against slavery. For his willingness to compromise, he was seen by northern radicals as a traitor.

Taylor's action launched one of the greatest debates in the Senate's history. This time, the argument went beyond the issue of slavery. It called into question the very future of the United States.

The Compromise of 1850

Two generations met on the Senate floor to debate the issue of slavery in the territories. Henry Clay, Daniel Webster, and John C. Calhoun represented the older generation. Among those who would lead the Senate in the future were Jefferson Davis, Stephen A. Douglas, and William H. Seward.

Clay Henry Clay, with a reputation for settling disagreements, led the Senate session. The "Great Compromiser" had pre- vented a showdown between the North and South in 1820 when he pushed through the Missouri Compromise. Many senators hoped that he could do it again.

Now 73 years old and in ill health, Clay fashioned a plan for dealing with the two main issues: slavery in the West and the return of escaped slaves. He called for admitting California as a free state, but not restricting slavery in the other territories gained from Mexico. He also proposed a more aggressive fugitive slave law.

Calhoun John C. Calhoun, a southerner, rejected Clay's plan. It would not guarantee the right to slavery in the territories, he claimed. He also demanded an even tougher fugitive slave law. Treat the South fairly, he warned the Senate, or the South would secede.

In his final role as the Great Compromiser, Henry Clay (center) tried to persuade the Senate to vote for the Compromise of 1850.

For an activity on analyzing the original text of the Compromise of 1850, see **Using Historical Documents**, pp. 91–95.

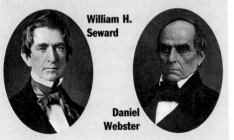

Henry Clay

John C. Calhoun

COMPROMISE OF 1850

Provisions favoring proslavery forces

• New Mexico and Utah to become territories. The slavery question to be decided by popular sovereignty.
• The new Fugitive Slave Law to require the return of escaped slaves, even slaves who had reached the North.
• Slavery still legal in Washington, D.C.

Provisions favoring antislavery forces

• California to be admitted to the Union as a free state.
• The slave trade to be abolished in Washington, D.C.

William H. Seward

Daniel Webster

Weakened by throat cancer, Calhoun had another Senator read his speech:

"How can the Union be saved? She [the South] has no compromise to offer. If you are unwilling [to meet our demands] we should part in peace."

Webster Daniel Webster, a northern moderate, pleaded for the nation's unity:

"I wish to speak today, not as a Massachusetts man, nor as a northern man, but as an American. I speak today for the preservation of the Union."

Webster's plea fell on deaf ears as northern radicals took on southern radicals. William H. Seward saw compromise over slavery as "radically wrong." Representative Horace Mann believed that the world would view the United States "with disgust" for allowing slavery.

Agreement at last Events took a sudden twist when President Taylor—a staunch opponent of compromise—fell ill from cholera and died on July 9, 1850. The new President, Millard Fillmore, came out firmly for Clay's compromise. By this time Congress knew that voters in both the North and the South favored compromise. As a result, it passed the Compromise of 1850 (see chart to the left and map on page 474).

With the passage of the Compromise of 1850, President Fillmore claimed that the nation had found "the final settlement" that would end the arguments over slavery. In fact the nation did settle into a prosperous peace for the next few years. However, Fillmore had spoken too quickly. The crisis over slavery was far from ended.

1. Section Review

1. Define **popular sovereignty.**
2. Explain the positions of northern radicals and moderates on the issue of slavery.
3. What problem did President Taylor confront and how did he handle it?
4. **Critical Thinking** As a southern radical, how would you have voted on each measure in the 1850 Compromise and why?

Closing the Section

Wrap-Up Activity

Making a Venn Diagram

To review the different views on slavery, have students create a Venn diagram with two intersecting circles representing pro- and antislavery views. Where the circles overlap, they should place moderate views, such as, "accept slavery where it exists." Northern and southern radical views should be placed in the other two areas.

Section Review
Answers

1. Definition: *popular sovereignty* (468)
2. Northern radicals demanded an end to slavery everywhere in the U.S.; moderates accepted slavery where it existed, but did not want it in new territories.
3. By voting in 1849 to ban slavery, Californians brought renewed attention to the issue, which was ignored by major parties in the 1848 election. Since Taylor supported popular sovereignty, he called for California statehood.
4. A southern radical would probably support the new Fugitive Slave Law and continuation of slavery in Washington, D.C., and would oppose the other measures because they would curb slavery's expansion.

Warm-Up Activity

The Impact of Media

To prepare for reading about *Uncle Tom's Cabin*, have students find current examples of how media brings attention to problems. Have the class select a problem such as drug abuse, gang violence, or poverty. Then ask them to identify ways that have been used recently to make the public more aware of the problem, such as specific movies, television shows, books, stories, billboards, and songs. Conclude by discussing which ways seem most effective and why.

Geography Question of the Day

Tell students they are to decide where 5,000 miles of railroad track are to be laid in the U.S. Have them trace on an outline map (from **Geography Extensions**) their ideas for routes, taking into consideration population density and terrain as indicated on the maps on pages R8 and R11.

Section Objectives

★ Explain how the Fugitive Slave Law and *Uncle Tom's Cabin* affected the slavery debate.

★ Describe how the Kansas-Nebraska Act increased tensions between the North and the South.

★ Explain why the Republican Party formed and describe its impact at that time.

Teaching Resources

Take-Home Planner 6, pp. 2–9

Chapter Resources Binder

Study Guide, p. 130

Reinforcement

Skills Development, pp. 135–136

Geography Extensions

American Readings

Using Historical Documents

Transparency Activities

Chapter and Unit Tests

2. The Failure of Compromise

Reading Guide

New Terms transcontinental railroad, platform

Section Focus Events in the 1850s continue to divide the North and South

1. How did the Fugitive Slave Law and *Uncle Tom's Cabin* affect the slavery debate?
2. How did the Kansas-Nebraska Act increase tensions between the North and the South?
3. Why did the new Republican Party form and what was its impact at the time?

The Compromise of 1850 brought only temporary relief to the nation. Americans were still deeply divided over slavery and states' rights, and it was not long before conflicts broke out again.

Three events shattered the calm. They were the enforcement of the new Fugitive Slave Law, the publication of the antislavery novel *Uncle Tom's Cabin,* and a violent struggle over slavery in Kansas. This time, efforts at compromise would fail.

The Fugitive Slave Law

Most northerners despised the Fugitive Slave Law of 1850. The law denied escaped slaves the right to have a jury trial and to testify in court on their own behalf. Anyone who helped a slave escape could be fined $1,000 and jailed for six months. Slave catchers received $10 for every African American they kidnapped in the North and brought to a slave owner in the South.

Before the new law, slavery had existed far from where most northerners lived. Now they had a firsthand look, as slave hunters came north, seeking escaped slaves. Almost 200 African Americans, even some free blacks who were not escaped slaves, were captured and sent to the South.

Northerners reacted against the kidnappings to the point of violence. A Pennsylvania mob killed a kidnapper. Frederick Douglass, himself an escaped slave, declared that "the only way to make the Fugitive Slave Law a dead letter [law] is to make half a dozen dead kidnappers."

The Fugitive Slave Law drove a deeper wedge between the North and the South. Southerners were outraged at northern resistance to it. They accused the North of breaking the Compromise of 1850. Northerners, on the other hand, were shocked by the cruelty of the law. It caused many of them to become more radical in their views of slavery.

Uncle Tom's Cabin

Northern outrage over the Fugitive Slave Law was mild, though, compared to the storm that arose when Harriet Beecher Stowe published *Uncle Tom's Cabin* in 1852. In this dramatic tale a religious and loyal old slave named Uncle Tom is beaten to death by orders of Simon Legree, one of the most hated villains in American literature.

Have you ever read a book that changed your way of thinking? Stowe's goal was to write such a book. By depicting the brutality

Connections to Literature

In addition to depicting the physical brutality suffered by the slaves, Stowe attempted in her work to show readers the emotional misery that results from families being separated by slaveholders. In a letter written soon after the publication of *Uncle Tom's Cabin,* she recounted her own heartache at the death of one of her seven children: "It was at his dying bed and at his grave that I learned what a poor slave mother may feel when her child is torn away from her." It is by this common thread of humanity that Stowe, in concluding remarks added to the novel, urged all women to take a stand against slavery. "I beseech you, pity those mothers that are constantly made childless by the American slave-trade!"

---

of slave life on a plantation, she wanted to awaken Americans to the evil in their midst.

Stowe succeeded beyond her wildest dreams. Within a year the book was a bestseller, outsold only by the Bible. As a play it shocked audiences around the world. People who read or saw *Uncle Tom's Cabin* could no longer close their eyes to slavery.

Many southerners, however, claimed that the story was full of lies. They feared that it would strengthen the influence of antislavery radicals in the North.

The Election of 1852

In the election of 1852, the Democrats nominated Franklin Pierce, who had promised to enforce the Compromise of 1850—including the Fugitive Slave Law. The Whig candidate, General Winfield Scott, took no stand on the compromise.

Pierce won almost every state. His landslide victory proved that despite the angry feelings caused by the Fugitive Slave Law and *Uncle Tom's Cabin,* most Americans still clung to the hope that the issue of slavery had been settled.

The Kansas-Nebraska Act

As it turned out, the 1852 election marked only a brief pause in the sectional conflict over slavery. The struggle started again when Senator Stephen Douglas of Illinois introduced a bill to be known as the Kansas-Nebraska Act.

A new railroad Douglas proposed that the nation build a **transcontinental railroad**—a rail line across the continent, linking east and west. He wanted it to begin at Chicago, in his home state of Illinois, and run to California. This transcontinental railroad would only succeed, Douglas thought, if the land west of the Mississippi was organized into territories.

Meanwhile, railroad boosters in the South wanted a southern route to California and the Pacific. They advised that their route would have several advantages. It would be much easier to lay tracks across the flat terrain of this route. In addition, the land needed for such a rail line—the Gadsden Purchase—had already been obtained from Mexico in 1853 (see map on page 396).

The cruelty and terror of slave life is captured by this poster for *Uncle Tom's Cabin.* Harriet Beecher Stowe (above) mistakenly feared that her future bestseller would be a failure.

To illustrate contrasting views of the Kansas conflict, have students create headlines for pro-slavery and antislavery newspapers. Divide the class into small groups, with half of them role-playing antislavery newspaper staffs and the other half proslavery newspaper staffs. Each group then plans a layout with headlines reflecting its bias, in choice of both words and topics emphasized. Possible topics include the Kansas-Nebraska Act, the election, laws passed by the proslavery legislature, the antislavery legislature, the attack on Lawrence, Brown's attack, and the killing of Brown's son. Conclude by having groups compare headlines and discuss how they reflect bias.

Teaching the Reading Maps

Point out the map key, ensuring that students understand how the four statuses differ. **Answer to Reading Maps:** Oregon Territory: closed to slavery by Compromise of 1850. Kansas Territory: closed to slavery in 1820 and 1850; in 1854 became open to slavery by popular sovereignty. Texas: by 1850 it had become a slave state.

* **History Footnote**

The development of the railroad during the 1800s was pivotal to the economic development of the U.S. By 1860, the nation had more miles of railroad track than the rest of the world combined, making shipping freight by rail far more practical and affordable than by the former leading means of transportation, the steamboat. The railroad had a direct impact on urban growth, as well. Chicago, easily accessible by rail, saw its population nearly quadruple during the 1850s. With trains traveling at roughly 30 miles an hour, the trip from New York to Chicago was reduced from three weeks to just two days. The transcontinental railroad was finally authorized by Congress in 1862 and completed in 1869.

The Spread of Slavery

The Missouri Compromise   1820

MAINE
OREGON COUNTRY
UNORGANIZED TERRITORY
MICHIGAN TERRITORY
Missouri Compromise Line 36° 30' N
MISSOURI
ARK. TERR.
MEXICO

The Compromise of 1850

OREGON TERRITORY
UNORGANIZED TERRITORY
MINN. TERR.
UTAH TERRITORY
CALIF. 1850
NEW MEXICO TERRITORY
INDIAN TERR.

The Kansas-Nebraska Act   1854

WASH. TERR.
OREGON TERRITORY
NEBRASKA TERRITORY
MINN. TERR.
UTAH TERRITORY
KANSAS TERR.
NEW MEXICO TERRITORY
INDIAN TERR.

- ☐ Free state or territory
- ☐ Slave state or territory
- ☐ Territory closed to slavery
- ☐ Slavery permitted by popular sovereignty

Reading Maps

How did Congress change the status of slavery in the Oregon Territory, Kansas Territory, and Texas in 1820, 1850, and 1854?

Kansas and Nebraska To win southern support for his northern route, Douglas called for popular sovereignty in lands to be organized as the Kansas and Nebraska territories (see map on this page).

Southerners supported the popular sovereignty idea because it allowed for the possibility of additional slave states. Northerners, however, were angry that the Kansas-Nebraska Act would overturn the Missouri Compromise of 1820, which barred slavery from that area.

What had begun as a proposal for a transcontinental railroad quickly turned into another crisis over slavery in the territories. Northern objections to Douglas's bill were loud and hostile. Still, with the support of southern congressmen and President Franklin Pierce, a Democrat, the Kansas-Nebraska bill became law in May 1854.

"Bleeding Kansas"

Douglas thought that the tempers that had flared during the Kansas-Nebraska debate would soon cool. Instead, the fight moved beyond the Senate floor to Kansas itself. The question of slavery there was to be decided by whichever side had the most voters. Senator William H. Seward of New York laid down the challenge:

❝Gentlemen of the Slave States, we will engage in competition for the virgin soil of Kansas, and God give victory to the side which is . . . right.❞

Antislavery settlers from the North raced to Kansas. They were met by proslavery settlers from the South, particularly from Missouri. Each group hoped to gain control of the territory in the upcoming election.

Two Kansas governments On election day in March 1855, nearly 5,000 Missouri residents crossed into Kansas. Their illegal votes gave the victory to proslavery candidates. The new legislature quickly passed laws protecting slavery in Kansas.

Outraged antislavery settlers in Kansas refused to accept the proslavery legislature. They elected their own legislature and set up their own government.

John Brown in Kansas With sides now sharply drawn, Kansas became a dress rehearsal for the Civil War. In May 1856 a proslavery army of "Border Ruffians" from Missouri marched into the antislavery town of Lawrence and set it on fire.

The "sack of Lawrence" inspired an abolitionist named John Brown to seek revenge. Lean, strong, and "straight . . . as a mountain pine," Brown led four of his sons and several others to a proslavery settlement. There they murdered five men by splitting open their heads with swords. In retaliation, proslavery forces killed one of Brown's sons. Brown did not back down. He vowed:

❝I have only a short time to live [and] only one death to die, and I will die fighting for this cause.❞

These brutal deaths touched off a year-long war in Kansas. Two hundred lives were lost and many homes were burned before federal troops finally restored order to "Bleeding Kansas" in late 1856.

Violence in the Senate The violence in Kansas spilled over into the halls of Congress. In a speech in May of 1856, Charles Sumner, an abolitionist senator from Massachusetts, attacked slaveholders for the "crime [committed] against Kansas."

Three days later, Representative Preston Brooks of South Carolina broke his cane over Sumner's head while Sumner was seated at his desk. Brooks was furious that Sumner had insulted Brooks's uncle in the speech. Sumner, severely injured, did not return to the Senate for more than two years.

Hands-On ▻ HISTORY

Creating an advertisement for Kansas Has your family ever used a travel agent? Present-day travel agencies help people arrange vacation trips. In the 1850s, agencies in the North served another purpose: to help antislavery settlers move to the Kansas Territory so that it would become a free state.

▻ **Activity** Imagine you are an agent working for a northern antislavery organization in 1854. Create an advertisement encouraging people to move to Kansas.

① Design and write a full-page advertisement that appeals to your readers' feelings about slavery, and to their dislike for the opposing side. You will also want to highlight the attraction of Kansas itself: good soil and plenty of open land.

② What illustrations might you use?

③ Share your finished ad with your classmates. Do they find it persuasive? Why or why not?

Poster promoting Kansas

Gifted Students

Gifted students benefit from exploring issues or topics in greater depth. Provide opportunities for independent projects or more elaborate treatments of activity suggestions. For instance, in addition to the Bonus Activity on creating an ad for *Uncle Tom's Cabin*, they might read the novel and write a review.

Closing the Section

Wrap-Up Activity

Briefing Buchanan

To review the events of the 1850s that further divided the Union, have pairs of students role-play a briefing between the newly elected President Buchanan and an advisor. The advisor should summarize factors that have increased tensions between the North and the South, identifying which are the major threats to national unity.

Section Review
Answers

1. Definitions: *transcontinental railroad* (473), *platform* (476)

2. It allowed for the possibility of additional slave states.

3. Northerners who opposed the spread of slavery wanted a party that would commit itself to antislavery issues.

4. Accept reasonable responses. For example, students may think seeing a slave kidnapper in person may have been more powerful than reading a work of fiction, while others may find the story of Uncle Tom more moving.

See the Study Guide activity in **Chapter Resources Binder**, p. 130.

SOUTHERN CHIVALRY — ARGUMENT versus CLUB'S.

Senator Sumner was praised by fellow New Englanders for his speech attacking slaveholders. Preston Brooks, a southern member of Congress, detested the speech, however. He is shown here beating Sumner on the Senate floor.

A New Republican Party

Meanwhile, northerners who opposed the spread of slavery had grown impatient with the Democratic and Whig parties. They wanted a party that would commit itself to antislavery issues. In 1854 such a party was formed. It was named the Republican Party, after the party founded by Jefferson.

The Republican Party **platform**—a statement of a political party's beliefs—took stands against the Kansas-Nebraska Act and the Fugitive Slave Law. Running on that platform, Republican candidates swept the 1854 elections in the North, especially in the Midwest. Soon, northern Whigs and Democrats were joining the new party, adding to its strength. As a result, the Democrats' main base of power shifted to the South.

The Election of 1856 The Republicans first attempted to gain the presidency in 1856. They selected John C. Frémont, western explorer and opponent of slavery, as their candidate. He campaigned with the slogan, "Free Soil, Free Speech, and Frémont." Abraham Lincoln, who had joined the Republicans, narrowly missed being nominated for Vice-President.

The Democrats were expected to nominate Stephen A. Douglas. However, they knew that the Kansas-Nebraska Act had made him unpopular with northern voters. Instead, the Democrats chose James Buchanan. He had been serving overseas as minister to England, and thus he had not taken a stand in the Kansas-Nebraska debate.

Although Frémont took 11 of the 16 free states, Buchanan won the election by carrying the southern states and 5 of the free states. As people became more alarmed that the nation might break apart, it remained to be seen if President Buchanan could hold the country together.

2. Section Review

1. Define **transcontinental railroad** and **platform**.

2. Why did southerners support the Kansas-Nebraska Act?

3. Why was the Republican Party founded?

4. Critical Thinking As a northerner, which would have affected your feelings about slavery more: the Fugitive Slave Law or *Uncle Tom's Cabin*? Explain why.

treated this way? Were other plantations similar? What was the purpose in writing? For Source B: Did the writer get information from slaves or masters? Might his point of view lead to proslavery bias? What is the evidence that women needed protection from husbands? For Source C: Were Legree and Tom based on real people? Where did the author get information on them? Are they stereotypes?

4. (a) Answers depend on questions. (b) Some possibilities: historians' descriptions, accounts by former slaves, anti- or proslavery writings or pictures.

For further application, have students do the Applying Skills activity in the Chapter Survey (p. 486).

If students need to review the skill, use the Skills Development transparency and activity in the **Chapter Resources Binder**, pp. 135–136.

Skill Lab

Using Information
Asking Historical Questions

Its promoters called it "The Greatest Book of the Age." It ranked second only to the Bible as a bestseller. *Uncle Tom's Cabin* awakened northerners to the cruelties of slavery—and enraged proslavery southerners. In essays, speeches, and even poems, southerners defended slavery as being good for both master and slave.

Question to Investigate

How were slaves treated?

Procedure

Imagine that you are a historian studying how slaves were treated. As you read the following sources, direct your research by asking historical questions.

❶ Write a sentence stating your goal.

❷ Identify the information.
a. Read sources **A** through **C** carefully.
b. Make a column for each source. List what each source says about the treatment of slaves.

❸ Identify questions to ask.
a. Read the Skill Tips for examples.
b. List three questions about each source.

❹ Decide how to get the answers.
a. Write the answers you know.
b. Name three ways you might get more information.

Is this source believable?

Skill Tips

Ask yourself questions like these:
* Is this a statement of fact, opinion, or fiction?
* Is this a credible source?
* How might the author's background affect what he or she wrote?
* Are the claims supported by enough evidence?
* Are there signs of bias, overgeneralizations, or stereotypes?

Sources to Use

A Reread Frederick Douglass's statements on pages 404–405.

B "The negro slaves of the South are the happiest and, in some sense, the freest people in the world. . . . The women do little hard work, and are protected from the despotism [cruelty] of their husbands by their masters. The negro men and stout boys work, on the average, in good weather, not more than nine hours a day."

From an 1857 essay by the Virginia lawyer George Fitzhugh

C "'And now,' said Legree, 'come here, you Tom. . . . take this yer gal and flog her; ye've seen enough on't to know how.'

'I beg Mas'r's pardon,' said Tom, '. . . It's what I an't used to—never did—and can't do, no way possible.'

'Ye'll larn a pretty smart chance of things ye never did know before I've done with ye!' said Legree, taking up a cowhide and striking Tom a heavy blow across the cheek, and following up the infliction by a shower of blows. 'There!' he said, 'now will ye tell me ye can't do it?'

'Yes Mas'r,' said Tom, putting up his hand to wipe the blood that trickled down his face. 'I'm willin' to work night and day, and work while there's breath in me; but this yer thing I can't feel it right to do; and Mas'r, I *never* shall do it—*never!*'"

From Harriet Beecher Stowe's 1852 novel, *Uncle Tom's Cabin*

Introducing the Skill Lab

Point out that the goal is to find the truth, and that students will use skills applied in earlier labs. Direct attention to the Skill Tips, reviewing the meaning of fact, opinion, credibility, point of view, evidence, bias, generalization, and stereotype. Ask how each Skills Tips question is relevant to finding truth. Have students suggest specific questions similar to each one. (For example, on credibility: "Where did the writer get information?") Show how skills connect to each other. (For example, detecting bias may raise questions about point of view.)

Skill Lab
Answers

1. Goal should be realistically limited to the task, such as: I want to compare how these sources describe treatment of slaves.

2. Source A: beaten so often "aching bones" were constant; "never too hot or too cold" to force work; "broken in body, soul, and spirit." Source B: happiest, freest people; women do little hard work, protected by masters; men and boys work no more than nine hours a day. Source C: slaves ordered to flog others; flogged often.

3. Some questions for Source A: Were all the slaves
(Answers continued in top margin)

Alternatives
to Secession

To focus attention on the secession issue, ask students to imagine that residents in your state today oppose a particular federal law. Have small groups brainstorm ideas for actions they might take, such as trying their case in court, rallying support of voters throughout the nation to oppose the law, or even moving to another country. Discuss the potential effects of each action.

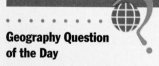

Geography Question
of the Day

Ask students to review the maps on page 474 and to write a paragraph giving a northern radical's view of the good and bad points of the changing status of slavery in the growing nation.

★ ★ ★
Vital Links

Dred and Harriet Scott (Picture) Unit 3, Side 1, Search 32799

○ **See also Unit 3 Explore CD-ROM location 166.**

Section Objectives

★ Describe how Dred Scott and the Lincoln-Douglas debates kept the slavery issue alive.

★ Explain how John Brown's raid and the 1860 election doomed hopes for compromise.

★ Describe the South's response to Abraham Lincoln's election.

Teaching Resources

Take-Home Planner 6, pp. 2–9

Chapter Resources Binder

Study Guide, p. 131

Reinforcement

Skills Development

Geography Extensions, pp. 33–34

American Readings, pp. 65–68

Using Historical Documents

Transparency Activities

Chapter and Unit Tests, pp. 111–114

★

3. On the Brink of War

Reading Guide

Section Focus **The causes of the final break between North and South**

1. How did Dred Scott and the Lincoln-Douglas debates keep the slavery issue alive?
2. How did John Brown's raid and the 1860 election doom hopes for compromise?
3. What was the South's response to Abraham Lincoln's election?

The 1856 election had avoided an all-out fight over the slavery question. However, whether it bubbled below the surface or exploded into open debate, slavery was an issue that would not go away.

James Buchanan had been President only two days when yet another crisis rocked the nation. On March 7, 1857, the Supreme Court announced its decision in the case of *Dred Scott* v. *Sandford.*

Dred Scott Decision

Dred Scott had been the slave of a Missouri surgeon, who had taken him to Illinois and the Wisconsin Territory. They lived there for several years before returning to Missouri. In 1846 Scott claimed in court that the years he had lived on free northern soil had made him a free man. The jury ruled in his favor, but the Missouri Supreme Court overruled the decision.

Soon after the Court ruled that Dred Scott must remain a slave, Scott finally gained his freedom from a new owner. He died just a year later.

Scott took his case to the United States Supreme Court. In *Dred Scott* v. *Sandford,* the Court ruled against Scott by a vote of 7 to 2. In the first place, the justices said, Scott did not have a right to a trial. African Americans—enslaved or free—were not citizens, and thus could not bring suits in federal court.

The Court also ruled that the Missouri Compromise was unconstitutional, and slavery could not be banned in any territory. Slaves were property, they reasoned, and the Fifth Amendment guaranteed the right to property. Slaveowners had the right to take slaves into any territory. Living in a free territory had not made Scott a free man.

Southern radicals praised the decision. Now all territories were open to slavery. Northerners were shocked. They accused the South of plotting with the Supreme Court and the new President to expand slavery. Buchanan had, in fact, encouraged the justices to rule in the South's favor. Instead of putting to rest the question of slavery in the territories, the Dred Scott decision only added fuel to the fire.

Lincoln-Douglas Campaign

Unhappy with the President's support of proslavery interests, Republicans wanted to "overthrow" the Democrats. In 1858 Abraham Lincoln agreed to help. He would run against Democrat Stephen A. Douglas, who was seeking re-election to the Senate from Illinois.

Innovations in technology had a huge impact on the spread of information, giving voters more information than was previously possible. Samuel Morse's telegraph allowed for rapid transmittal of information. In 1848, several major newspapers formed the Associated Press to coordinate and share the expense of dispatches via telegraph. At the same time, advances in printing and papermaking, and the expansion of the rail system, made newspapers more affordable and widely available than ever before. Americans across the country could buy a newspaper and read the current news for one or two cents a copy.

Stephen A. Douglas Douglas felt up to the challenge. He was a short, sturdy man, whom admirers called the "Little Giant." Douglas had a strong, deep voice and a brilliant mind. Although his support for the Kansas-Nebraska Act had damaged his reputation in the North, he still hoped to become President in 1860.

Abraham Lincoln Illinois Republicans believed that Lincoln, a small-town lawyer in Springfield, had the best chance of defeating Stephen Douglas. Lincoln opposed the expansion of slavery into new territories, but he was not known as a northern radical. He had been a powerful speaker at the 1856 Republican convention. Douglas himself remarked:

❝I shall have my hands full.
He [Lincoln] is the strong man
of his party . . . the best speaker . . .
in the West.❞

Still, the tall, gangly Lincoln seemed awkward beside the polished Douglas. Lincoln had a quick wit, but his voice sometimes squeaked and he used pronunciations like "git" for "get" and "thar" for "there."

Lincoln-Douglas Debates

Lincoln's strategy was to follow Douglas on the campaign trail. Douglas would arrive in a town in his private railroad car. He brought along a brass cannon to announce his arrival and to draw a large crowd. Riding as an ordinary passenger on the same train, Lincoln would address the crowd after Douglas had finished his speech.

Douglas supporters made fun of Lincoln, saying he could not attract crowds of his own. Lincoln responded by challenging Douglas to a series of debates.

Douglas accepted the challenge. He thought such debates would draw national attention

Lincoln and Douglas tried to win votes in their 1858 debates. Presidential candidates Bill Clinton, George Bush, and Ross Perot continued the tradition in their 1992 debates.

Help students compile a list on the chalkboard of words and phrases describing the current President's ideas, background, appearance, and performance. Ask them to identify where this information might have come from, such as newspaper or television reports, or talking with family and friends. Accept reasonable responses in comparing Lincoln with the current President and assessing Lincoln's chances of being elected today.

★ ★ ★
Vital Links

Lincoln-Douglas debates (Picture) Unit 3, Side 1, Search 16801

See also Unit 3 Explore CD-ROM location 33.

See the Study Guide activity in **Chapter Resources Binder,** p. 131.

✱ **History Footnote**

Stephen Douglas's views on popular sovereignty earned him enemies in both the North and the South. Their criticism was sometimes expressed by burning him in effigy. After angry northerners protested his introduction of the Kansas-Nebraska Act, Douglas commented, "I could travel from Boston to Chicago by the light of my own effigies."

For excerpts from Lincoln's statements on slavery, see **American Readings,** pp. 65–66.

Link to the Present

Election campaigns today In Lincoln's day, candidates traveled to picnics, rallies, and other gatherings to make speeches and hold debates. Modern-day candidates also travel widely and talk to as many voters as they can, but there are important differences.

Only a few thousand could see and hear the Lincoln-Douglas debates. Now television brings campaign speeches and debates into millions of homes. Yet critics claim that candidates today emphasize "sound bites"—short statements that people will easily remember—instead of solid information explaining their views.

Critics also complain that today's candidates work harder at looking attractive than at trying to address the nation's problems. Abe Lincoln was awkward and far from handsome, and he spoke in a high, squeaky voice. Do you think he could be elected today?

and boost his chances to become President. The two men met seven times in seven different Illinois towns.

In the debates, Lincoln appealed to antislavery voters by attacking Douglas's stand on slavery. Douglas did not care, Lincoln claimed, "whether slavery was voted down or voted up."

The Freeport Doctrine In the town of Freeport, Lincoln challenged Douglas to declare his position on slavery in the territories now that the Dred Scott decision had made it legal. Douglas was in a tight spot. His answer came to be called the Freeport Doctrine.

In the Freeport Doctrine, Douglas admitted that it was now legal for an owner to bring a slave into any territory. However, he said, a legislature could refuse to pass laws protecting slavery in their territory. Without such laws, slavery could not be enforced.

The result of the debates The seven debates were the highlight of a hard-fought campaign. Lincoln and Douglas spoke to crowds almost daily for four months. In the days before microphones, public speakers had to shout to be heard. By election day Douglas's throat was so sore he could barely talk.

Although Douglas narrowly defeated Lincoln, the election had broader results. The Freeport Doctrine turned many southern Democrats against Douglas, and would hurt his chances of becoming President in 1860. Lincoln, on the other hand, emerged as a national figure. His skill at challenging Douglas put the presidency within his reach.

Raid at Harpers Ferry

An event that terrified the South occurred on October 16, 1859. John Brown, the abolitionist from Kansas, appeared at Harpers Ferry, Virginia. With 21 followers he seized a federal arsenal there. He planned to give the guns to escaped slaves who in turn were to ignite a slave revolt across the South.

The plan had no hope of success. Brown never freed any slaves. Colonel Robert E. Lee led a force of marines who captured Brown and killed ten of his men, including two of his sons. Virginia authorities quickly convicted Brown of treason and of trying to start a rebellion. He was hanged six weeks later.

John Brown met his death with a dignity that made him a hero and "a new saint" for the antislavery cause. Brown also struck fear through the South. Would there be such raids in the future? Southerners were now convinced that the North would stop at nothing to destroy slavery.

480

Connections to Music

During the Civil War, Union soldiers composed and sang verses to a song called "John Brown's Body." One verse said:

> His sacrifice we share! Our sword will
>   victory crown! . . .
> For freedom and the right remember
>   old John Brown!
> His soul is marching on.

African American soldiers added their own verses to the John Brown song. Referring to white southerners, they sang:

> They will have to bow their foreheads
>   to their colored kith and kin,
> They will have to give us house-room
>   or the roof will tumble in!
> As we go marching on.

Link to Art

John Brown Going to His Hanging (1942) Most artists go to art school to develop their talent at painting. African American artist Horace Pippin did not. Instead, he taught himself. Pippin (1888–1946) painted many subjects, including landscapes, people, and historical scenes. In this painting, John Brown rides his coffin to the gallows. **Discuss** What is the mood in this scene? How does the artist use color and shapes to express the mood?

The Election of 1860

The presidential election of 1860 drove a final wedge between North and South. The Democratic Party split. Northern Democrats nominated Stephen A. Douglas and came out for popular sovereignty in the territories. Southern Democrats picked John C. Breckinridge, who supported slavery in all territories.

481

Discussion

Checking Understanding

1. What did Douglas state in the Freeport Doctrine? (It was legal for an owner to bring a slave into any territory, but a legislature did not have to pass laws to protect slavery.)

2. Why did John Brown raid Harpers Ferry? (To arm escaped slaves for a revolt.)

Stimulating Critical Thinking

3. Was John Brown a hero? (Yes: lost life for noble cause. No: killed innocent people and did not free any slaves.)

4. What else could John Brown have done to support abolition? (Perhaps nonviolent means such as distributing antislavery pamphlets, writing a book, or making speeches.)

Teaching the

Link to Art

Tell students that Pippin's mother, who claimed to have been at the hanging, is shown in the lower right corner, facing the viewer. **Discussion Answers:** The dark colors and bold images present a somber mood. Also, the perspective places the viewer in back of a faceless crowd.

★ ★ ★ Vital Links

John Brown (Picture) Unit 3, Side 1, Search 37422

See also Unit 3 Explore CD-ROM location 199.

While Lincoln campaigned for President in 1860, his appearance caught the attention of 11-year-old Grace Bedell. Grace wrote Lincoln a letter, advising him that his chances of winning the election would be improved if he were to "grow whiskers." It was said that Lincoln, a devoted father, had a great fondness for children. A week later, Grace received a kind letter from Lincoln; later that month Lincoln was photographed with the beginnings of a beard.

In February of 1861, the newly elected President stopped at the train station of Grace's hometown of Westfield, New York, and asked if his young correspondent was in the crowd. She nervously stepped forward. As she later recalled, "It seemed to me as the President stooped to kiss me that he looked very kind, yes, and sad."

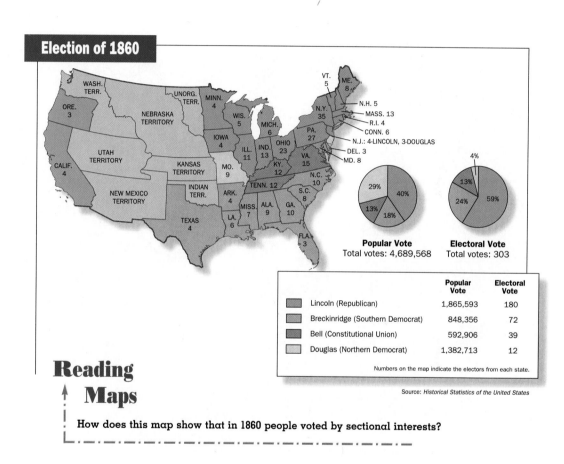

Election of 1860

	Popular Vote	Electoral Vote
Lincoln (Republican)	1,865,593	180
Breckinridge (Southern Democrat)	848,356	72
Bell (Constitutional Union)	592,906	39
Douglas (Northern Democrat)	1,382,713	12

Numbers on the map indicate the electors from each state.

Popular Vote Total votes: 4,689,568

Electoral Vote Total votes: 303

Source: *Historical Statistics of the United States*

Reading
↑ Maps

How does this map show that in 1860 people voted by sectional interests?

In a Chicago meeting hall packed with his supporters, Lincoln won the Republican nomination. The party did not call for the abolition of slavery. Rather, with Lincoln, it viewed slavery as "an evil not to be extended, but to be tolerated."

A fourth candidate, John Bell of Tennessee, was nominated by the Constitutional Union Party. This new party avoided the issue of slavery and supported the Union.

Lincoln's victory Although he won only 40 percent of the popular vote, Lincoln received a majority of the electoral votes. Thanks to the split in the Democratic Party, Abraham Lincoln was elected as the first Republican President.

The South Secedes

As Lincoln had predicted in 1858, "a house divided against itself cannot stand." Within weeks of his election, South Carolina left the Union. Alabama, Mississippi, Georgia, Florida, Louisiana, and Texas soon followed. Together they formed the Confederate States of America, with Jefferson Davis as their President.

(Point of View
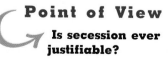
↪ Is secession ever justifiable?

Many northerners agreed with Lincoln that "no state . . . can lawfully get out of the Union." Most southerners, however, believed

At-Risk Students

To help students who are poor readers, focus first on understanding the "big picture." One way to do this is to provide opportunities to restate main ideas of the text in their own words, ideally with a partner or small group. Having a broader context will help them remember more specific details, such as dates and events.

that secession was justified. The Declaration of Independence, they pointed out, stated that people have the right to throw off an unjust government. Edmund Ruffin, a Virginia planter, declared:

> "Slaveholding states . . . [must proclaim] another declaration of independence [from the United States]. We, the children of those [founding] fathers . . . have submitted to oppression and wrong incalculably [far] greater than ever England inflicted."

Can a state ever legally secede from the nation? Under what conditions?

The Northern Response

At first few northerners took secession seriously. Some thought the South simply needed time to cool off. Others urged compromise again. Some abolitionists were happy to see the South go its separate way. Buchanan, still President in the months before Lincoln took office, hoped that Congress would reach a compromise. He did nothing, however, to help achieve one.

Lincoln's inaugural address Before his inauguration, Lincoln avoided making any statements. When he took office on March 4, 1861, though, he made his positions clear. He believed he had no legal right to interfere with slavery "in the States where it exists." However, he expressed his determination to hold the Union together:

> "The Union of these States is perpetual. . . . No state . . . can lawfully get out of the Union. . . . I therefore consider that . . . the Union is unbroken."

Lincoln would oppose all attempts at secession, but believed that there was no

need for "bloodshed or violence." He concluded with the plea: "We are not enemies but friends. We must not be enemies."

The Outbreak of War

Southern radicals ignored Lincoln's plea. While the new President organized his government, Confederate leaders prepared for war. The first test came at Fort Sumter, in the harbor at Charleston, South Carolina.

Fort Sumter Fort Sumter—a federal fort—was running short of supplies. Trying to avoid armed conflict, Lincoln announced that while he would be sending food to the fort, he would send no soldiers.

Freedom for Russian serfs In 1861 the slavery issue in the United States was coming to a crisis. In that same year 22 million Russian serfs gained their freedom with the stroke of a pen when Czar Alexander II signed the Emancipation Act.

Serfs were peasants who farmed pieces of land owned by lords. They gave part of their crop to the lord for rent and did many jobs for the lord as well. Unlike slaves in the United States, who had been forcibly brought from Africa, serfs were Russians like their lords. Like the slaves, though, they worked hard, lived in poverty, and were not allowed to move.

Under the Emancipation Act, Russian serfs could buy land, but few could find the money to pay for it. Most former serfs remained poor and discontented.

Discussion

Checking Understanding

1. **What was Lincoln's view on slavery?** (It was an evil not to be extended, but to be tolerated; he felt he had no right to interfere with slavery where it existed.)

Stimulating Critical Thinking

2. **Do you think it is fair to compare the secession to the Declaration of Independence? Why or why not?** (Yes: southern states, like the 13 colonies, were victims of abuse of government power. No: unlike the colonies, which were not represented in Parliament, southern states had representation in the national government; they should have abided by majority rule in Congress.)

Teaching the

Ask students to compare the conditions of serfs and slaves. (Both worked for landowners, lived in poverty, and were not allowed to move. However, serfs were treated as people, not property.)

✳ **History Footnote**

In an 1858 speech at Edwardsville, Illinois, Lincoln asked:

> What constitutes the bulwark of our own liberty and independence? It is not our frowning battlements, our bristling sea coasts, the guns of our war steamers. . . . Our defense is in the preservation of the spirit which prizes liberty as the heritage of all men, in all lands, everywhere.

For a southerner's description of the firing on Fort Sumter, see **American Readings,** pp. 67–68.

Closing the Section

Wrap-Up Activity

Writing a News Release

To review the section, have students write short news releases summarizing events that led to the outbreak of the Civil War. Have them compare their releases with a partner's.

Section Review Answers

1. The Court declared that African Americans did not have a right to a trial, and that no state or territory could ban slavery.

2. Lincoln followed Douglas on the campaign trail and challenged him to debates; he also forced Douglas to declare his position on slavery. The strategy worked, for even though he lost the race, he became a national figure and caused Douglas to lose some popular support. This helped Lincoln win the presidency.

3. He died fighting for his beliefs and drew attention to the cause of abolition.

4. Those who would vote against secession might focus on his statement that he would not interfere with slavery where it existed. Those who would vote for secession might focus on his view that slavery should not be extended.

To check understanding of "Why We Remember," assign Thinking Critically question 3 on student page 486.

Fort Sumter guarded one of the South's most important seaports. Thus, Confederate President Davis decided that the fort must not remain in Union hands. Confederate forces demanded that Major Robert Anderson, the commander of Fort Sumter, surrender immediately. Anderson refused.

Early in the morning of April 12, 1861, Confederate cannons opened fire. The fort withstood an intense artillery attack for over 30 hours. Anderson finally surrendered on April 13, 1861. He ordered a 50-gun salute to the United States flag as the Confederate army took the fort. The Civil War had begun.

⭐ 3. Section Review

1. Why did the Supreme Court deny Dred Scott his freedom?

2. What were Lincoln's two strategies in challenging Douglas for the Senate? Did they work?

3. Why was John Brown a hero to the abolitionist cause?

4. Critical Thinking As a southerner, would you still have voted for secession if you had first heard Lincoln's inaugural address? Why or why not?

Why We Remember

⭐ The Gathering Storm

When Abraham Lincoln learned that he had been elected President in 1860, he said to reporters, "Well, boys, your troubles are over. Mine have just begun." As the dark clouds of secession rolled across the South, it became clear how serious those troubles would be. The survival of the United States, and the fate of 4 million enslaved people, rested in Lincoln's hands.

The stormy 1850s were a turning point for the nation. Again and again Congress tried to find a lasting compromise on slavery in the territories. Yet each compromise created new problems. Lincoln understood why. Slavery was not only a political problem, it was also a deeply moral issue. As he wrote in a letter to a friend, "If slavery is not wrong, nothing is wrong."

American democracy is based on the ideal that "all men are created equal." After his election, Lincoln declared his unshakeable belief in that ideal:

❝That sentiment [ideal of equality] in the Declaration of Independence . . . gave liberty not only to the people of this country, but hope to all the world. . . . I would rather be assassinated on this spot than surrender it.❞

As the gathering storm broke over Fort Sumter, the nation would finally decide whether or not to live and die by that simple but powerful ideal.

The Appalachian National Scenic Trail, covering 14 states from Mount Katahdin in Maine to Mount Oglethorpe in northern Georgia, is the longest marked, continuous footpath in the world. Benton MacKaye, a Massachusetts forester and author, proposed the idea for the trail in an article published in 1921. It was completed in 1937.

Wooden signposts and white paint markings on trees and rocks lead the way for hikers making the journey. The trail passes through some state and national parks, but is mainly on private property, by consent of the owners. In normal conditions, a hiker can complete the trail in about four months.

Geography Lab

The Appalachian Mountains

In the isolated valleys that twist and turn through the Appalachian Mountains, the issues that divided the North and South seemed far away. Most people who lived in the hollows and thick forests of the southern Appalachians—less rugged than the Rockies—did not own slaves. Farmers there did not want to secede from the Union. The photograph and readings that follow will help you form an image of the region.

The southern Appalachian Mountains

From James Paulding's Letters

"[W]e first caught a view of the distant undulating [wavy-looking] mountain, whose fading blue outline could hardly be distinguished from the blue sky. Between us and the mountain was spread a wide landscape—shade softening into shade . . . as blended the whole into a . . . harmony. Over all was spread that rich purple hue [color]."

From a Novel by William Simms

"Let the traveler . . . look down upon the scene below. Around us, the hills gather in groups on every side. . . . The axe has not yet deprived them of a single tree, and they rise up, covered with the honored growth of a thousand summers. . . . The leaves cover the rugged limbs which sustain them, with so much ease and grace, as if for the first time they were so green and glossy. . . . The wild flowers begin to flaunt [show off] their blue and crimson draperies [curtains] about us. . . . In the winding hollows of these hills, beginning at our feet, you see the first signs of as lovely a little hamlet [village] as ever promised peace to the weary and the discontent."

From *Charlemont* by William Simms

Developing a ¬ Mental Map

Refer to pages R4–R5 and R6–R7.

1. In what states do the Appalachian Mountains lie?

2. What are the highest peaks in the Appalachians and the Rocky Mountains? How do they compare?

3. How does the photograph of the Appalachians resemble the descriptions by Paulding and Simms?

4. **Hands-On Geography** Imagine that you have just completed a hike along the Appalachian Trail—a 2,000-mile footpath from Maine to Georgia. To show your friends and family what it was like to be in the Appalachians, create a diary with pictures. Write a list of topics, and a list of types of photographs, to include in the diary. You may need to look at some additional books before you begin.

Teaching the Geography Lab

To focus students' attention on the characteristics of mountains, ask volunteers who have visited or lived in the mountains to share their experiences. Encourage students to think about how the mountain landscape might affect people's way of life. For example, travel may be more difficult, making individuals more isolated.

Developing a Mental Map
Answers

1. Maine, New Hampshire, Vermont, Massachusetts, Rhode Island, Connecticut, New York, New Jersey, Pennsylvania, Ohio, Maryland, West Virginia, Virginia, Kentucky, North Carolina, Tennessee, Georgia, Alabama, and a small portion of South Carolina and Mississippi.

2. Appalachians: Mt. Mitchell, 6,684 feet (2,037 meters). Rockies: Mt. Elbert, 14,433 feet (4,400 meters), almost 8,000 feet higher than the highest Appalachian peak.

3. Possible answers: abundant trees and other vegetation, wavy-looking appearance.

4. Diaries might include descriptions of the mountains, feelings evoked by the landscape, details about length and difficulty of the journey, and descriptions of people encountered.

See the activity on the Appalachians in *Geography Extensions*, pp. 33–34.

Survey Answers

Reviewing Vocabulary

Definitions are found on these pages: *popular sovereignty* (468), *transcontinental railroad* (473), *platform* (476).

Reviewing Main Ideas

1. Northern radicals wanted to prohibit slavery in the new territories, and southern radicals wanted to permit it. Moderates suggested extending the Missouri Compromise line to the Pacific Ocean or giving voters the right to decide whether to allow slavery.

2. California would be admitted as a free state; New Mexico and Utah would become territories in which the question of slavery would be decided by voters; the Fugitive Slave Law required the return of escaped slaves; the slave trade would be abolished in Washington, D.C., though slavery would remain legal there. Congress passed the Compromise because the President and most voters favored it.

3. Northerners were shocked as they watched kidnappers return African Americans to slavery, and some reacted violently. Southerners were angered by this reaction.

4. The Kansas-Nebraska Act created the Kansas and Nebraska territories, allowing voters there to decide the issue of slavery. Antislavery and proslavery settlers raced to Kansas to vote. Tensions erupted when a proslavery army set afire the antislavery town of Lawrence. Seeking revenge, John Brown and his followers killed five proslavery men, and proslavery forces retaliated. This touched off a war in which about 200 died.

5. (a) Antislavery issues. (b) In 1854, the Republicans defeated many Democrats in the North and the Democrats'
(Answers continued in top margin)

main power base shifted to the South. The Whigs went into decline, with northerners switching to the Republicans and the Know-Nothings, and southerners shifting to the Democrats.

6. The Court said that the Missouri Compromise, which had banned slavery in certain territories, was unconstitutional. This ruling opened slavery to all the territories.

7. (a) As a result of his debates with Douglas during the 1858 campaign for the Senate. (b) The Democratic Party was split between northern and southern Democrats. (c) Seven states seceded from the Union.

Thinking Critically

1. Answers may vary, depending on how much weight students give each provision.

2. Students should understand that the Bill

Chapter Survey

Reviewing Vocabulary

Define the following terms.
1. popular sovereignty
2. transcontinental railroad
3. platform

Reviewing Main Ideas

1. What did the various groups of radicals and moderates want to do about slavery in territory acquired from Mexico?
2. What were the terms of the Compromise of 1850, and why did Congress pass it?
3. How did the Fugitive Slave Law increase the sectional conflict between the North and the South?
4. Describe how each event led to the next. (a) Kansas-Nebraska Act (b) settlers' race to Kansas (c) sack of Lawrence (d) "Bleeding Kansas"
5. (a) What was the focus of the Republican Party platform? (b) What happened to the Democratic and Whig parties as the Republicans gained support in the 1850s?
6. How did the Supreme Court's decision in *Dred Scott* v. *Sandford* affect the issue of slavery in the territories?
7. (a) How did Abraham Lincoln become a national figure? (b) Why did he win the election of 1860? (c) What was the South's immediate response to the election?

Thinking Critically

1. Evaluation Did the Compromise of 1850 favor the North, the South, or neither? Explain your answer.
2. Application Abolitionists attacked the Supreme Court for basing its Dred Scott decision on the Fifth Amendment in the Bill of Rights. Why would they be furious about such reasoning?

3. Why We Remember: Synthesis Could the conflict between North and South have been resolved peacefully after Lincoln's election? If yes, describe a solution that might have worked. If no, explain why war was unavoidable.

Applying Skills

Asking historical questions Slavery is rare in today's world, but other violations of human rights—such as torture of prisoners—still occur. Imagine that you are a reporter. You are to interview someone who claims to have witnessed a human rights violation in another country. Write a list of five questions to ask the person. For each question, write a sentence that tells why you would ask it. Keep in mind what you learned on page 477.

History Mystery

Kansas elections Answer the history mystery on page 465. How would you find out why more people voted in the election than lived in the territory? Why did so many people vote in the election and how might you have prevented them from voting?

Writing in Your History Journal

1. Keys to History (a) The time line on pages 464–465 has seven Keys to History. In your journal, describe why each one is important to know about.
(b) Choose one of the events on the time line. Write a paragraph in your journal that describes how the course of history might have been different if that event had not taken place.
2. Abraham Lincoln Imagine that you are Leo Tolstoy trying to reply to the

of Rights is designed to protect individual liberties, yet the Court used it to deny Scott his freedom.

3. Students who think war could have been avoided may suggest a new compromise, such as dividing western lands equally between free and slave territories. Those who think war was unavoidable may cite the repeated failures at finding a lasting compromise.

Applying Skills

Answers should reflect understanding of the Procedures and Skill Tips outlined on page 477.

History Mystery

Information on the election can be found on pages 474–475. Students may suggest examining the issues surrounding the election
(Answers continued in side margin)

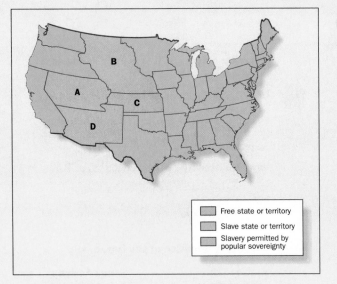

Free state or territory

Slave state or territory

Slavery permitted by popular sovereignty

Reviewing Geography

1. Each letter on the map represents a territory as it existed after the Kansas-Nebraska Act. Write the name of each.

2. Geographic Thinking Look at the map on page 474. President Fillmore believed that the 1850 Compromise ended arguments over slavery in the territories. What territory did he ignore in his conclusion? Why was a decision not reached on the question of slavery there? How might this area be organized in a way that would appeal to both South and North?

to determine the reason for the increase. Implementing stricter voter registration guidelines would help prevent fraud.

Writing in Your History Journal

1. (a) Explanations should be similar to the time line notes on teacher pages 464–465. (b) Accept responses that reflect understanding of the effects of the event.

2. Accept any answers that reflect the characterization of Lincoln in this chapter and that students can support.

3. Accept answers that students can support. Students should consider Brown's actions in Kansas and at Harpers Ferry. He was similar to terrorists today in that he used violent protest as a way to draw attention to his cause.

Reviewing Geography

1. (A) Utah Territory
(B) Nebraska Territory
(C) Kansas Territory
(D) New Mexico Territory

2. There was still a huge area of unorganized land within the nation's boundaries. As long as the potential existed for new states, the slavery issue would not be resolved. Students may suggest that a decision was not reached because by postponing it Fillmore could avoid controversy. This land might have been simply divided in half to try to satisfy both sides.

Alternative Assessment

Teacher's Take-Home Planner 6, page 5, includes suggestions and scoring rubrics for the Alternative Assessment activity.

mountain chief's request for information about Abraham Lincoln (see page 466). In your journal, write down three things about Lincoln that you believe are most important for the chief to know. Include a specific example from Lincoln's life to support each point.

3. Thinking Historically A terrorist uses violence to advance a political cause. Would you call John Brown a terrorist or a hero? Explain why. How would you compare him with terrorists today? Write your response in your journal.

Alternative Assessment

Citizenship: Covering the 1860 election on TV If television had existed in 1860, what might coverage of the presidential election have been like? With several classmates, act out an

election-night broadcast as a television network might do.

In your broadcast:

❶ Give a live report from the campaign headquarters of the candidates.

❷ Interview two voters, one from the South and one from the North. Ask them who they think will win and what the result could mean for the nation.

❸ After each live report and interview, give an election update on how many votes each candidate is receiving.

❹ Include an election map, pictures, or some other visuals in your broadcast.

Your broadcast will be evaluated on the following criteria:

• it clearly presents the issues, the candidates, and the results of the 1860 election
• it resembles a television news show
• it is interesting to your audience

18 The Civil War
1861–1865

Chapter Planning Guide

Section	Student Text	Teacher's Edition Activities
Opener and Story pp. 488–491	**Keys to History Time Line** — **History Mystery** — Beginning the Story with **Clara Barton**	**Setting the Stage Activity** A Help-Wanted Ad, p. 490
1 **Preparing for War** pp. 492–497	**Reading Maps** The Union and the Confederacy, p. 493 — **Link to Art** *Sounding Reveille*, p. 496 — **Point of View** Should the Union have refused to enlist African Americans?, p. 497	**Warm-Up Activity** Off to War: Dialogues at Home, p. 492 — **Geography Question of the Day**, p. 492 — **Section Activity** Border State Stump Speeches, p. 494 — **Bonus Activity** Enlistment Posters, p. 496 — **Wrap-Up Activity** Writing Editorials, p. 497
2 **The First Two Years of War** pp. 498–503	**Link to Literature** *Bull Run*, pp. 520–521 — **Reading Maps** The Civil War 1861–1862, p. 501 — **Link to Technology** The Camera, p. 502	**Warm-Up Activity** War Then and Now, p. 498 — **Geography Question of the Day**, p. 498 — **Section Activity** War Dispatches, p. 500 — **Bonus Activity** A Soldier's Letter Home, p. 502 — **Wrap-Up Activity** A Battle Chart, p. 503
3 **The War Effort at Home** pp. 504–510	**Link to the Present** The American Red Cross, p. 506 — **World Link** Britain stays neutral in Civil War, p. 508 — **Skill Lab** Making a Hypothesis, p. 510	**Warm-Up Activity** Lincoln's Diary, p. 504 — **Geography Question of the Day**, p. 504 — **Section Activity** Newspaper Articles, p. 506 — **Bonus Activity** Creating a Lincoln Collage, p. 508 — **Wrap-Up Activity** War Problems: A Venn Diagram, p. 509
4 **From War to Peace** pp. 511–517	**Reading Maps** The Civil War 1863–1865, p. 513 — **Hands-On History** Commemorating the Civil War, p. 514 — **Geography Lab** Reading a Grid Map, p. 517	**Warm-Up Activity** A Military Report Card, p. 511 — **Geography Question of the Day**, p. 511 — **Section Activity** Interviewing Lee and Grant, p. 512 — **Bonus Activity** Writing Song Lyrics, p. 514 — **Wrap-Up Activity** Making a Time Line, p. 516
Evaluation	☑ **Section 1 Review**, p. 497 — ☑ **Section 2 Review**, p. 503 — ☑ **Section 3 Review**, p. 509 — ☑ **Section 4 Review**, p. 516 — ☑ **Chapter Survey**, pp. 518–519 — **Alternative Assessment** Writing a play, p. 519	☑ **Answers to Section 1 Review**, p. 497 — ☑ **Answers to Section 2 Review**, p. 503 — ☑ **Answers to Section 3 Review**, p. 509 — ☑ **Answers to Section 4 Review**, p. 516 — ☑ **Answers to Chapter Survey**, pp. 518–519 (Alternative Assessment guidelines are in the Take-Home Planner.)

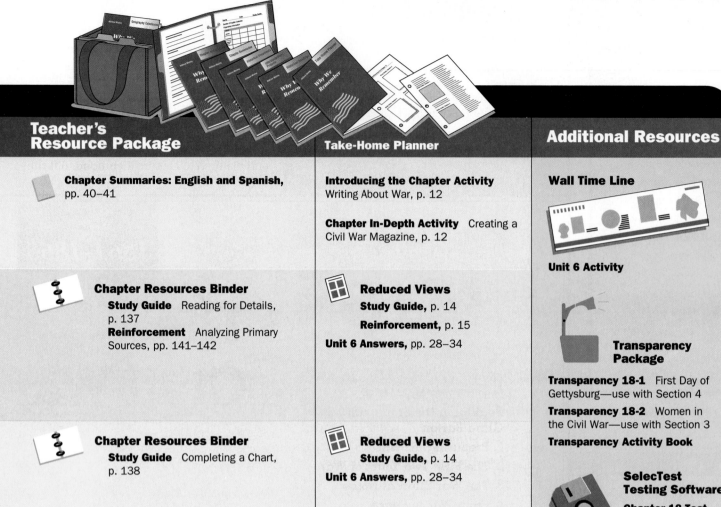

Teacher's Resource Package

Chapter Summaries: English and Spanish, pp. 40–41

Chapter Resources Binder
Study Guide Reading for Details, p. 137
Reinforcement Analyzing Primary Sources, pp. 141–142

Chapter Resources Binder
Study Guide Completing a Chart, p. 138

Chapter Resources Binder
Study Guide Completing an Outline, p. 139
Skills Development Making a Hypothesis, pp. 143–144
American Readings Celebrating Emancipation, p. 69
Using Historical Documents The Emancipation Proclamation, pp. 96–103

Chapter Resources Binder
Study Guide Completing a Graphic Organizer, p. 140
Geography Extensions Reading a Grid Map, pp. 35–36
American Readings The Gettysburg Address, p. 70; The Siege of Vicksburg, p. 71; Lee Surrenders at Appomattox, p. 72

Chapter and Unit Tests Chapter 18 Tests, Forms A and B, pp. 115–118

Take-Home Planner

Introducing the Chapter Activity Writing About War, p. 12

Chapter In-Depth Activity Creating a Civil War Magazine, p. 12

Reduced Views
Study Guide, p. 14
Reinforcement, p. 15
Unit 6 Answers, pp. 28–34

Reduced Views
Study Guide, p. 14
Unit 6 Answers, pp. 28–34

Reduced Views
Study Guide, p. 14
Skills Development, p. 15
American Readings, p. 16
Using Historical Documents, p. 17
Unit 6 Answers, pp. 28–34

Reduced Views
Study Guide, p. 14
Geography Extensions, p. 17
American Readings, p. 16
Unit 6 Answers, pp. 28–34

Reduced Views
Chapter Tests, p. 17
Unit 6 Answers, pp. 28–34

Alternative Assessment Guidelines for scoring the Chapter Survey activity, p. 13

Additional Resources

Wall Time Line

Unit 6 Activity

Transparency Package

Transparency 18-1 First Day of Gettysburg—use with Section 4
Transparency 18-2 Women in the Civil War—use with Section 3
Transparency Activity Book

SelecTest Testing Software
Chapter 18 Test, Forms A and B

✦✦✦ Vital Links

● **Videodisc**

◉ **CD-ROM**

Irish regiment (see TE p. 494)
Lincoln on McClellan (see TE p. 500)
Battle of Antietam (see TE p. 503)
African American soldiers (see TE p. 504)
Voice of nurse Kate Cummings (see TE p. 507)
War refugees (see TE p. 509)
Voice of Major Sullivan Ballou (see TE p. 512)
Gettysburg Address (see TE p. 513)
"The Battle Hymn of the Republic" (see TE p. 514)
Atlanta (see TE p. 515)

Unit 6 Videotape Clara Barton: Eyewitness to the Civil War

Teaching Resources

Take-Home Planner 6
  Introducing Chapter Activity
  Chapter In-Depth Activity
  Alternative Assessment
Chapter Resources Binder
Geography Extensions
American Readings
Using Historical Documents
Transparency Activities
Wall Time Line Activities
Chapter Summaries
Chapter and Unit Tests
SelecTest Test File
Vital Links CD-ROM/Videodisc

Time Line

Keys to History

Keys to History journal writing activities are on page 518 in the Chapter Survey.

First Battle of Bull Run The Union loss shocked northerners into realizing that the war would not be quickly won. (p. 498)

Monitor* vs. *Merrimac In this battle between the first two ironclad steamships, neither side claimed victory, dashing the Confederates' hopes of breaking the Union blockade of Norfolk, Virginia. (p. 499)

Battle of Antietam This was a turning point in the war, destroying a third of Lee's army and ruining the South's hopes of European aid. (p. 503)

Looking Back Lincoln's election led seven states in the South to secede from the Union and form the Confederacy.

World Link See p. 508.

488

Chapter Objectives

★ Describe the resources of the Union and the Confederacy.
★ Explain the failure of either army to win a victory that would end the war.
★ Describe the Civil War's effect on northerners and southerners at home.
★ Describe the Union victories that finally ended the war.

Chapter Overview
After Fort Sumter, four Border States joined the seven Confederate states. Lincoln acted to keep the other four Border States in the Union. The North had an economic advantage in the war, but the Confederacy had great military leaders, such as Robert E. Lee.

To bring the Confederate states back into the Union, Lincoln ordered a naval blockade and planned to capture Richmond. But the

1861–1865

Chapter **18**

The Civil War

Sections

Beginning the Story with Clara Barton
1. **Preparing for War**
2. **The First Two Years of War**
3. **The War Effort at Home**
4. **From War to Peace**

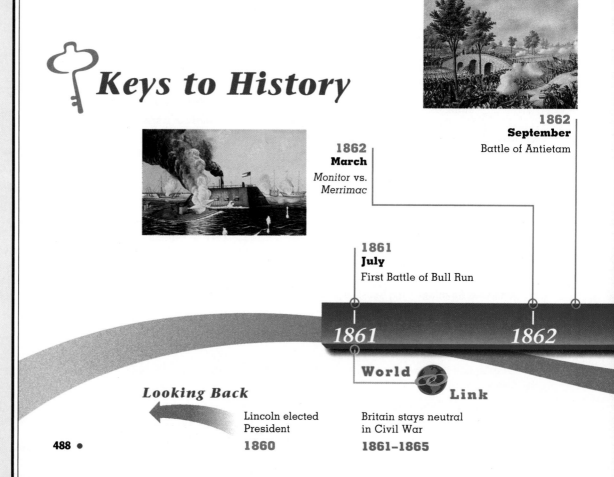

Keys to History

1862
March
Monitor vs. *Merrimac*

1862
September
Battle of Antietam

1861
July
First Battle of Bull Run

1861   *1862*

World Link

Looking Back

Lincoln elected President
1860

Britain stays neutral in Civil War
1861–1865

South won the first battle, at Bull Run. After several battles, neither side had a clear advantage. The Union realized there would be no quick victory.

In 1863 Lincoln signed the Emancipation Proclamation, and about 186,000 African Americans joined the Union army. Women helped the war effort as nurses and factory workers. However, Union citizens were protesting the draft and the income tax, while southerners were suffering from a poor economy.

In 1863 Lee's troops invaded the Union at Gettysburg; the battle resulted in a Union victory but huge losses for both sides. Grant then took Vicksburg, giving the Union control of the Mississippi. Meanwhile, Sherman waged total war through Georgia and South Carolina. On April 9, 1865, after the fall of Richmond, Lee surrendered at Appomattox Court House.

HISTORY Mystery

Although Lyons Wakeman enlisted in the Union army, family members kept this fact secret and hid the letters they received. Who was Lyons Wakeman, and what knowledge was the family hiding?

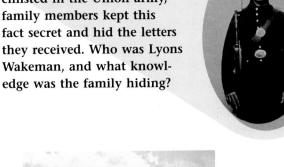

1863
January
Lincoln issues Emancipation Proclamation
Forever Free, statue of mother and children

1863
July
Battles of Gettysburg and Vicksburg
First day of Battle of Gettysburg

1864
September
Sherman's forces seize Atlanta

1865
April
Lee surrenders to Grant at Appomattox Court House

1863   *1864*   *1865*

Looking Ahead

14th Amendment guarantees equality
1868

● **489**

Teaching the
HISTORY Mystery

Students will find the answer on p. 496. See Chapter Survey, p. 518, for additional questions.

Time Line

Emancipation Proclamation The plan freeing all slaves in the Confederate states changed the war into a fight for freedom as well as for the Union. (p. 504)

Battles of Gettysburg and Vicksburg The Confederate loss at Gettysburg turned the war into a defensive war on southern soil. The southern loss at Vicksburg led to Union control of the entire Mississippi River. (pp. 511–514)

Sherman in Atlanta This Union use of total war raised spirits in the North and ensured Lincoln's re-election. (p. 515)

Lee surrenders to Grant The bloodiest war in the history of the nation ended, having cost more than 620,000 lives. (p. 516)

Looking Ahead The 14th Amendment, ratified in 1868, guaranteed equality to all men.

Beginning the Story

Clara Barton

Clara Barton overcame childhood shyness and fears to become a courageous nurse of injured Union soldiers during the Civil War. Known as "the angel of the battlefield," she followed the army from battle to battle and treated the men right on the battlefields. She showed determination in personally obtaining needed supplies. Clara Barton went on to found the American Red Cross. Her courage shines through the horrifying carnage of the Civil War.

Setting the Stage
Activity

A Help-Wanted Ad

To help students consider the contributions made by both women and men during the Civil War, have them write help-wanted ads that might have been published around the beginning of the war in 1861. Have half the class write ads asking for soldiers. Tell them to describe specifically the kind of person needed to fight the war. Have the other half advertise for jobs that could be done by women or young girls or boys. Ask several students to read their completed ads.

See the Introducing the Chapter Activity, Writing About War. **Take-Home Planner 6**, p. 12.

History Footnote

Recorded in Clara Barton's journal and memoirs are some of her amazing war experiences. She took three women with her to the Second Battle of Bull Run. The four women stayed up all night baking bread, serving soup, distributing shirts, and writing down names of wounded men. On most other trips to the battlefield, she was not allowed to take female helpers. At Chantilly she slept in a tent sitting up because the floor was filled with rainwater. She brought linen bandages to a field hospital where doctors had been dressing wounds in corn husks. When a general who did not recognize her offered protection as she made her way through wounded soldiers at Fredericksburg, she replied, "Thank you very much, but I believe I'm the best protected woman in the United States."

Beginning the Story with

Clara Barton

On September 17, 1862, Confederate and Union troops clashed in a fierce battle along Antietam (an-TEET-uhm) Creek in western Maryland. As the bullets whizzed past and the cannon balls crashed, a lone woman appeared on the battlefield. Her face darkened by gun smoke, she moved from one wounded soldier to another. To some she gave a little food and water. To others she applied bandages. Once she dug a bullet out of flesh with her pocketknife.

All through that long day the bodies piled up. At times the woman had to stop and wring the blood from her skirt to keep moving. She was so close to the raging battle that as she bent over one man a bullet clipped her sleeve and killed him. Later, after darkness fell and the pitiful cries of the wounded replaced the din of combat, she continued to help the injured and dying.

The woman helping wounded soldiers on that day of death was Clara Barton. Later generations would remember her as the founder of the American Red Cross. To the Union troops at the Battle of Antietam, she was simply "the lady" or, as a grateful army doctor put it, "the angel of the battlefield."

"I Remember Nothing But Fear"

As a young child, this fearless angel of mercy had been anything but bold. Born on Christmas Day in 1821 in Massachusetts, the youngest of five children, Clara never felt comfortable with herself. She thought she was too short and too fat. She preferred studying "boys' subjects," such as mathematics and science, to such "womanly" tasks as cooking and sewing.

Clara was also painfully shy. To help overcome her self-doubts, her parents encouraged her to excel at sports and horseback riding. Doing exciting things helped Clara hide her inner fears. So did helping others. Their praise made her feel better about herself. Nonetheless, looking back on her childhood, Clara said, "I remember nothing but fear."

History Bookshelf

Stevens, Bryna. *Frank Thompson: Her Civil War Story*. Macmillan, 1992. Using the name Frank Thompson, Emma Edmonds disguised herself as a man and served in the Union army as a nurse, mail carrier, and spy.

Also of interest:

Archer, Jules. *A House Divided: The Lives of Ulysses S. Grant and Robert E. Lee*. Scholastic, 1995.

Chang, Ina. *A Separate Battle: Women and the Civil War*. Lodestar, 1991.

Freedman, Russell. *Lincoln: A Photobiography*. Clarion, 1991.

Keith, Harold. *Rifles for Watie*. Crowell, 1957.

Mettger, Zak. *Till Victory Is Won: Black Soldiers in the Civil War*. Lodestar, 1994.

Clara Barton wanted to "go to the rescue of the men who fell." She treated them right on the battlefield rather than in hospitals behind the lines. This picture shows wounded Union soldiers in a field near Fredericksburg, Virginia.

"Between the Bullet and the Battlefield"

Clara Barton's self-doubts followed her into adulthood. She did not, however, let them keep her from standing up for herself. Once she quit a teaching job because the school board hired a man to do the same work at a higher salary. "I may sometimes be willing to teach for nothing," she declared, "but if paid at all, I shall never do a man's work for less than a man's pay."

Clara also stood her ground when she took a job as a clerk in the United States Patent Office in 1854. As one of the first women hired by the federal government, she was resented by the male clerks. They called her names, blew cigar smoke in her face, and spit tobacco juice at her feet. Their insults, she told a friend, made "about as much impression upon me as a sling shot would upon the hide of a shark."

It was as a volunteer nurse in the Civil War that Clara completely overcame her childhood fears. When the war began, neither side was prepared to care for wounded soldiers. Countless men died for lack of medical treatment. This waste of lives infuriated Clara, and she began to collect medical supplies to care for the wounded herself. In spite of the disapproval of Union officers, she followed the army into battle after battle. Her place, she said, was "anywhere between the bullet and the battlefield."

Clara's courage in battle amazed all who knew her, and perhaps even herself. In the face of death and suffering, her old fears faded away. "I may be compelled to face danger," she once told an audience, "but never *fear* it. While our soldiers can stand and *fight,* I can stand and feed and nurse them."

Hands-On → HISTORY

Activity

War correspondents traveled with the Union and Confederate armies to gather news for their papers. Imagine that you are a war correspondent with the Union army. Write a report of an interview with Clara Barton after the Battle of Antietam. Include at least three questions and her answers.

Discussion

Thinking Historically

1. **What attitudes do you see in Clara Barton's life before the Civil War that help explain her actions during the war?** (She liked "boys' subjects," she pursued active hobbies, she liked to help people, and she rebelled against sexist job and pay policies.)

2. **What character traits do you see in Clara Barton?** (She was courageous, independent, and persevering.)

3. **What do you learn about the nature of the war from Clara Barton's story?** (It was brutal, with many casualties. Medical treatment was often primitive, and supplies were scarce.)

See the Chapter In-Depth Activity, Creating a Civil War Magazine. **Take-Home Planner 6,** p. 12.

Teaching the Hands-On → *HISTORY*

To help students brainstorm questions, have them think about what people living during the Civil War would want to know about life on the battlefield. They should include some questions about Clara Barton's personal feelings, and some about what she witnessed on the battlefield.

For a journal writing activity on Clara Barton, see student page 518.

Introducing the Section

Vocabulary

habeas corpus (p. 492) a right that protects people from being held in prison unlawfully

martial law (p. 492) rule by the army instead of by the usual government officials

Off to War: Dialogues at Home

To help students imagine different reactions to the war, have small groups create dialogues between parents and children. Assign each group a different scenario: a southern planter urging his reluctant son to enlist; a northern abolitionist urging her reluctant daughter to volunteer as a nurse; a poor southern farm woman trying to dissuade her son from enlisting; a recent immigrant in the North trying to dissuade his daughter from volunteering as a nurse. Conclude by having groups share their dialogues and summarize reasons for and against joining the war effort.

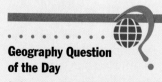

Geography Question of the Day

Ask students to refer to the map on page 493 and list the Union and Confederate states when the war began.

Section Objectives

★ Identify the slave states that did not join the Confederacy.

★ Explain why volunteers rushed to join the Union and Confederate armies.

★ List the advantages each side had as the war began.

1. Preparing for War

Reading Guide

New Terms habeas corpus, martial law

Section Focus The resources of the Union and the Confederacy

1. Which slave states did not join the Confederacy?
2. Why did volunteers rush to join the Union and Confederate armies?
3. What advantages did each side have as the war began?

The Confederate attack on Fort Sumter on April 12, 1861, plunged the nation into civil war. In Washington, D.C., Clara Barton witnessed the confusion and fear. Rumors spread wildly. The city was torn between supporters of the Union and of the Confederacy. In the Patent Office, where Clara worked, some people openly supported the Confederate cause.

Clara was a staunch Republican. In this crisis, she looked to President Lincoln to take action against "those who have dared to raise the hand of rebellion." Lincoln responded quickly and firmly. On April 15 he called for 75,000 volunteers for 90 days to put down the rebellion in the 7 Confederate states.

Taking Sides in the War

Lincoln's action had a powerful effect on the eight slave states of the Upper South. These "Border States" had not yet decided whether to join the Confederacy or stay in the Union. After Lincoln's call for volunteers, Virginia, Arkansas, North Carolina, and Tennessee seceded from the Union. Richmond, Virginia, became the capital of the Confederacy.

People in the mountainous western part of Virginia, however, remained loyal to the Union. They broke away to form the new state of West Virginia, which joined the Union in 1863.

Slave states in the Union Of the other four Border States, Delaware voted unanimously to stay in the Union. Maryland, Kentucky, and Missouri, though, were deeply divided. Lincoln knew he had to keep Maryland in the Union because the state surrounded Washington, D.C., on three sides.

When a pro-Confederate mob attacked Union soldiers traveling through Maryland on their way to Washington, Lincoln sent troops to keep order. He had pro-Confederate leaders arrested. Then he used his constitutional power to suspend the right of **habeas corpus,** which protects people from being held in prison unlawfully. Maryland stayed in the Union.

At first, Kentucky tried to stay neutral. However, when fighting broke out between pro-Confederate and pro-Union groups, Kentucky sided with the Union.

In Missouri, Union and Confederate supporters fought each other fiercely. Lincoln kept Missouri in the Union by putting the state under martial law. **Martial law** is rule by the army instead of by the usual government officials.

The war brought special anguish to people in the Border States. Brothers, cousins, and even fathers and sons fought on different sides. Clifton Prentiss of Maryland fought for

See the Study Guide activity in **Chapter Resources Binder**, p. 137.

Developing the Section

Discussion

Checking Understanding

1. How was the new state of West Virginia formed? (After Virginia joined the Confederacy, people in the western part remained loyal to the Union and formed a new state.)

Stimulating Critical Thinking

2. Was Lincoln right to suspend habeas corpus and declare martial law? Why or why not? (Yes: in wartime President should have power to take steps to save nation. No: violates democratic principles.)

Teaching the
↑ **Reading Maps**

To help students visualize the division of the nation, have them refer to the map as you point out that South Carolina's secession was quickly followed by Mississippi, Florida, Alabama, Georgia, Louisiana, and Texas. After war was declared, Virginia, Arkansas, Tennessee, and North Carolina seceded. West Virginia, Delaware, Maryland, Kentucky, and Missouri stayed with the Union, as did states and most territories of the West. **Answer to Reading Maps:** Virginia, Arkansas, North Carolina, Tennessee.

The Union and the Confederacy

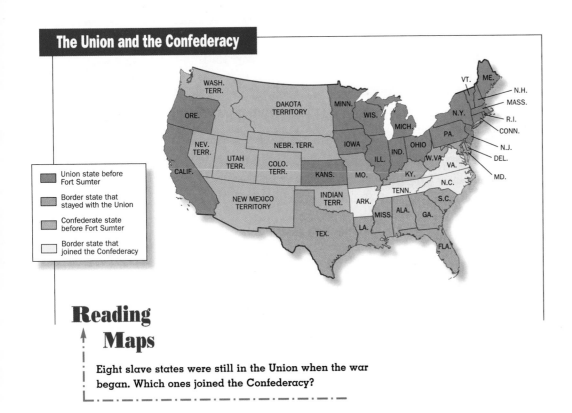

Union state before Fort Sumter

Border state that stayed with the Union

Confederate state before Fort Sumter

Border state that joined the Confederacy

Reading
↑ Maps

Eight slave states were still in the Union when the war began. Which ones joined the Confederacy?

the Union while his brother, William, was in the Confederate army. In 1865 the two brothers finally met again on their deathbeds in a hospital in Washington, D.C.

Far West states and territories Most of the states and territories of the Far West were loyal to the Union from the beginning. Early in the war, however, Union and Confederate forces struggled for control of the huge New Mexico Territory.

Texas, a Confederate state, feared a Union invasion from New Mexico, so it sent troops into the territory in 1861. They defeated the main Union forces and captured Tucson, Albuquerque, and Santa Fe.

Their victory was short-lived, though. In March 1862 Union volunteers from Colorado and New Mexico smashed a Confederate force at Glorieta Pass. The Confederates retreated to Texas, their hopes of conquering the Southwest shattered.

The Confederates had more success winning the support of the Cherokees, Creeks, Choctaws, Chickasaws, and Seminoles. Now living in Indian Territory, these southern tribes had been resettled in the West under the Indian removal policy of President Andrew Jackson (see pages 359–363). Many owned slaves and leaned strongly to the South's cause.

All five tribes signed alliances with the Confederacy. In return for their support, they received the right to send delegates to the Confederate Congress. About 15,000 Indian soldiers fought in the Confederate army.

At least 3,000 Indians fought for the North, including 135 Oneida volunteers from Wisconsin. Ely S. Parker, a New York Seneca, served as Ulysses S. Grant's military secretary.

Border State Stump Speeches

To focus on issues facing citizens at the outbreak of the Civil War, have pairs of students imagine they are representatives of the North or South traveling through the Border States. Assign half the pairs to write speeches to persuade the citizens to secede, while the other pairs write speeches to convince the states to remain in the Union. Speeches should include a mixture of moral, political, and economic reasons. They should include both rational and emotional appeals. Conclude by asking volunteers to read their speeches and having the class compare arguments.

★ ★ ★
Vital Links

Irish regiment (Picture) Unit 3, Side 1, Search 28862

See also Unit 3 Explore CD-ROM location 142.

Students With Limited English

Visuals are helpful for providing clues to meaning. Discuss the graph on page 494. For example, have a student define the word *population*. Then ask: What percentages of the population lived in the North and in the South? How is a greater population an advantage in a war? Ask similar questions for each entry on the graph.

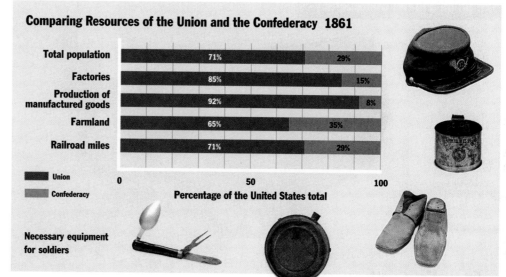

Comparing Resources of the Union and the Confederacy 1861

	Union	Confederacy
Total population	71%	29%
Factories	85%	15%
Production of manufactured goods	92%	8%
Farmland	65%	35%
Railroad miles	71%	29%

Percentage of the United States total

Necessary equipment for soldiers

Source: *Encyclopædia Britannica*

Resources for Waging War

In the spring of 1861 most people expected a short war. Northerners felt sure they would defeat the South in a few battles. Southerners were equally optimistic. An Alabamian predicted peace by 1862 because "we are going to kill the last Yankee [northerner] before that time. . . . I think I can whip 25 myself." In fact, each side had advantages it was counting on to bring it victory.

Economic strengths Northerners were confident of their greater economic strength. The Union had almost twice as much farmland as the Confederacy and would be better able to feed its armies as well as the people at home.

The graph above shows that 85 percent of the nation's factories were in the North. These factories produced almost all of the nation's manufactured goods, including guns, cloth, boots, and shoes.

The Union also had 71 percent of the nation's railroad lines, which would be essen-tial for moving troops and supplies. The Union had a navy, too, and nearly all the nation's shipbuilding took place in the North. The Confederacy had few shipyards and no navy.

Finally, the Union had more than twice as many people as the Confederacy. This greater population made little difference at first, when the two armies were fairly equal in size. Later, however, having twice as many men available to fight would turn out to be a great advantage to the Union.

Military strengths In one area the Confederacy clearly had the edge at the start of the war—it had the nation's best military leaders. One of them was Robert E. Lee of Virginia, who had graduated from the United States Military Academy at West Point and served in the Mexican-American War. During that war, Lee had been described by General Winfield Scott as "the very best soldier that I ever saw in the field."

Lee had opposed secession. When Virginia joined the Confederacy, however, everything

In 1857 Robert E. Lee inherited a large Virginia estate, including slaves, from his father-in-law. His father-in-law's will provided for the freedom of his slaves. As a lieutenant colonel in Texas in 1855, Lee had been aware of the conflict between abolitionists and slave owners throughout the country. He wrote to his wife, "In this enlightened age, there are few, I believe, but what will acknowledge that slavery as an institution is a moral and political evil in any Country." With war looming in 1860, he said, "If the slaves of the South were mine, I would surrender them all without a struggle to avert this war." In 1862 he released the slaves on his plantation.

changed. "I must side either with or against my section," he told a friend. With a heavy heart, Lee declined President Lincoln's offer of command of the Union army. "I cannot raise my hand against my birthplace, my home, my children," he explained.

Raising Armies

Expecting a short, glorious war, volunteers rushed to enlist. Southerners, who were called Johnny Rebs (for rebels), were determined to defend their homes, their loved ones, and the South's way of life from an invading Union army. One southerner wrote, "Our men *must* prevail [win] in combat, or lose their property, country, freedom, everything."

Northerners, called Billy Yanks or Yankees, fought to preserve the Union. Ted Upson of Indiana joined the army when he was barely 16. He told his father: "This Union your ancestors and mine helped to make must be saved from destruction."

Interest in having an adventure or earning a paycheck also led young men to join the army. Benjamin F. Chase joined the 5th Volunteer Infantry of New Hampshire to see the country and help his parents, who had 11 children to support. "i don't buy eny of the foolish stuff," he assured his parents when sending money home. "You may think i do but i certain don't."

Like many recruits in 1861, Chase was delighted with his new experiences and confident of a brief war. "What a good ride we shall have going south," he boasted in one of his first letters home. Even after three months in uniform, he was still enthusiastic. On January 8, 1862, he wrote:

" All of the boys in our tent are very well indeed and enjoying their health first rate. i hant been a mite home sick sense we ben out hear and have not ben a mite sick ether. Mother don't worrough a bout me a mite for i think we shall be home before long.
"

Like many recruits, these soldiers posed for portraits before marching off to war: (left) Johnny Clem, 11-year-old Union drummer, 22d Michigan Regiment; (center) unidentified Union soldier from New York; (right) Confederate Private Edwin Jennison, 2d Louisiana Cavalry.

For selections from Lee's letters, see the Reinforcement activity in **Chapter Resources Binder**, pp. 141–142.

Discussion

Checking Understanding

1. What were the North's strengths when the war began? The South's? (The North had more farmland, factories, railroad lines, and population. The South had the best military leaders.)

2. What were northerners fighting for? What were southerners fighting for? (Northerners were fighting to preserve the Union. Southerners were fighting to defend their homes and way of life.)

Stimulating Critical Thinking

3. Robert E. Lee decided not to lead the Union army. Do you agree with his decision? Why or why not? (Yes: loyalty to family and home come before loyalty to the nation. No: Lee had been trained as an officer in the United States Army and should have remained loyal to that commitment; loyalty to the nation should be more important than loyalty to one's state, otherwise there is no basis for having a nation.)

✳ History Footnote

Several women served as spies in the war. Harriet Tubman knew many secret routes on the Underground Railroad, and she recruited other former slaves to find Confederate camps and report them to Union officers. She and the others were able to give information about the location of Confederate explosives to Colonel James Montgomery in South Carolina during a Union gunboat raid in 1863.

Another Union spy, Elizabeth Van Lew, lived in a mansion in Richmond. She provided hiding places in her home for Union soldiers who had escaped from Confederate prisons.

Rose O'Neal Greenhow was a society hostess in Washington, D.C., who spied for the South. She learned of the Union's planned attack on Manassas in 1861 and sent coded information to General Beauregard, who won an important victory at Manassas.

Link to Art

Sounding Reveille (1865) Almost every family North and South had someone in uniform. People at home were desperate for news of their loved ones. "Special artists" helped satisfy that demand. Hired by illustrated newspapers, special artists went to battlefields and camps to sketch what they saw. The most gifted of these artists was Winslow Homer, who worked for *Harper's Weekly* newspaper. In this painting of a Union camp by Homer, a bugler and two drummers sound reveille, a signal to wake the soldiers each morning. **Discuss** In what ways does this painting show the everyday life of soldiers?

Although the Union and the Confederacy had rules banning boys from enlisting, many managed to join. Historians estimate that between 10 and 20 percent of all soldiers—250,000 to 420,000—were 16 years old or younger. John Mather Sloan of the 9th Texas was only 13 when he lost a leg in battle. He claimed his only regret was that "I shall not soon be able to get at the enemy."

Women soldiers Hundreds of women, too, fought for the cause. Their exact number will never be known, for they had to change their names and disguise themselves as men. Rosetta Wakeman, who joined the 153d Regiment New York State Volunteers, called herself "Lyons Wakeman" and wore men's clothing. Some women even wore fake mustaches or charcoal "whiskers."

Many African Americans were disappointed that they were not allowed to serve in the war. However, they were convinced that they would be invited to join eventually, so they actively drilled and prepared for battle. Some light-skinned African Americans became Union soldiers by pretending they were white. Others helped in any way they could, by cooking for the army, acting as servants for officers, or performing manual labor. Women did laundry, sewed, and served as nurses. In the South, African Americans served as guides and spies for the Union. Escaped slaves who sought refuge in Union camps were sometimes returned to owners who came for them, according to the government's official policy. However, some officers allowed the escaped slaves to stay and render support services.

Many of the women who enlisted were patriotic or adventurous. Some joined to be with husbands, boyfriends, or brothers. At the Battle of Antietam, Clara Barton tended a soldier, shot in the neck, whose real name turned out to be Mary Galloway. Later she helped to reunite Mary and her wounded boyfriend. After the war, Mary and her husband named their first daughter Clara, after Clara Barton.

⤷ **Point of View**

Should the Union have refused to enlist African Americans?

From the moment the war began, free African Americans flocked to recruiting centers in the North. During the first two years of war, though, the Union refused to enlist African Americans.

Lincoln's reasons for the ban were political. He feared that the slave states still in the Union would view the enlistment of black soldiers as a threat to slavery. Using African American soldiers, he argued, might drive the Border States, especially Kentucky, out of the Union and into the Confederacy. He wrote to a friend:

❝I think to lose Kentucky is nearly the same as to lose the whole game. [With] Kentucky gone, we cannot hold Missouri, nor, as I think, Maryland. These [states] all against us, and the job on our hands is too large for us. We would as well consent to separation at once, including the surrender of this capital.❞

Many white northerners thought that African Americans had no right to fight in the war. When a group of African Americans asked to form a regiment, Governor David Todd of Ohio refused, saying:

❝Do you know that this is a white man's government; that the white men are able to defend and protect it; and that to enlist a Negro soldier would be to drive every white man out of the service?❞

Frederick Douglass was outraged by such racist talk. He urged the government to focus on the goal of winning the war. He said:

❝Why does the government reject the Negro? Is he not a man? Can he not wield a sword, fire a gun, march and countermarch, and obey orders like any other? . . . Men in earnest don't fight with one hand, when they might fight with two, and a man drowning would not refuse to be saved even by a colored hand.❞

At the start of the war, most northerners were too confident of victory to listen to Douglass's advice. Only later, as the war turned long and bloody, would the Union decide to fight with two hands instead of one.

⭐ 1. Section Review

1. Define the terms **habeas corpus** and **martial law.**

2. Why did Maryland, Kentucky, and Missouri decide to stay in the Union during the Civil War?

3. Give at least three reasons why volunteers rushed to join the Union and the Confederate armies.

4. Critical Thinking A Confederate said, "The longer we have them [northerners] to fight, the more difficult they will be to defeat." What do you think the Confederate meant? Explain why you agree or disagree with this view.

Introducing the Section

Vocabulary

casualties (p. 500) soldiers killed, wounded, captured, or missing

War Then and Now

To help visualize how battles were fought during the Civil War, have students make a chart with the headings "War today" and "War in 1861." Have them list weapons and methods used today, such as planes, submarines, bombs, missiles, tanks, and automatic weapons. Then have them list the Civil War counterparts, such as horses, wooden and ironclad ships, rifles, swords, and cannons.

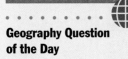

Geography Question of the Day

Ask students to suppose that the main map on page 501 was the only information they had on the war. Have them write paragraphs explaining what they could conclude about the war based on that map alone. (Confederate states were apparently on the defensive since almost all the battles were fought on their territory. Union had much stronger navy, as evident in blockade. Blockade also indicates foreign trade by sea was important to Confederacy. Control of the Mississippi also seems important because several battles were fought there.)

Section Objectives

★ Describe the Union and Confederate strategies for winning the war.
★ Explain why these strategies failed to end the war quickly.

Teaching Resources

Take-Home Planner 6, pp. 10–17
Chapter Resources Binder
  Study Guide, p. 138
    Reinforcement
    Skills Development
  Geography Extensions
  American Readings
  Using Historical Documents
  Transparency Activities
  Chapter and Unit Tests

2. The First Two Years of War

Reading Guide

New Term casualties

Section Focus **The failure of either army to win a victory that would end the war**

1. What were the Union and Confederate strategies for winning the war?
2. Why did these strategies fail to end the war quickly?

From the first, many people in both the Union and the Confederacy believed that the war would be a short one. No one, in 1861, could imagine that it would drag on for four long, bloody years.

Strategies for Victory

In Washington and Richmond, Presidents Lincoln and Davis planned their strategies. Davis's goal was to defend the Confederacy against invasion. "All we ask," he declared, "is to be left alone."

To achieve their goal, the Confederates would just push back invading Union forces. They hoped to make the war so costly that the North would give up. In this struggle, the Confederates expected help from Britain and other nations that needed the South's cotton.

Lincoln's goal was to bring the Confederate states back into the Union. His first strategy was to prevent supplies from reaching the Confederacy. He took the first step on April 19, 1861, when he ordered a naval blockade of southern seaports (see map, page 501). In a second step a year later, he ordered Union troops to take control of the Mississippi River.

Lincoln's second strategy was to capture Richmond, the Confederate capital, which was only 100 miles (160 km) from Washing-

ton. There had not been time to train an army, but northerners were anxious to end the war quickly. "On to Richmond!" they urged, and Lincoln agreed.

First Battle of Bull Run

Lincoln sent General Irvin McDowell with 30,000 soldiers into northern Virginia. Their orders were to crush the Confederate forces at the town of Manassas and then move on to Richmond.

At Manassas, McDowell found General Pierre G. T. Beauregard and a Confederate force of 21,000 in the hills above Bull Run,* a small stream. Certain of a Union victory, congressmen, reporters, and curious Washingtonians drove the 26 miles (42 km) to enjoy a picnic and watch the battle.

On the morning of July 21, 1861, the Union troops attacked, and the Confederate line began to crumble. Thomas J. Jackson and his brigade of Virginians, however, stood firm. "There is Jackson, standing like a stone wall! Rally around the Virginians!" yelled a Confederate officer.

The bravery of Stonewall Jackson—as he was called from then on—stopped the Union advance. Now the Confederates rushed forward. The Union soldiers retreated in panic. Some even stole horses and carriages from the onlookers.

---

*Union forces usually named a battle for the natural feature nearest the fighting, such as a stream or hill. The Confederates named the battle for a nearby town. Thus, the Battle of Bull Run was known in the South as the Battle of Manassas.

In terms of weapons and military tactics, the Civil War straddled two eras. It was the last of the traditional wars that featured massed columns of infantry, horse cavalry, swords, single-shot rifles, front-loaded cannons, and wooden ships. At the same time, it was the first of the modern wars because it saw the introduction of metallic cartridges, breech-loaded rifles and cannons, rapid-fire machine guns, ironclad warships, the telegraph, railroads, and other hallmarks of mechanized warfare. According to James McPherson in *The Battle Cry of Freedom*, "the old-fashioned cavalry charge against infantry . . . became obsolete in the face of rifles that could knock down horses long before their riders got within saber or pistol range."

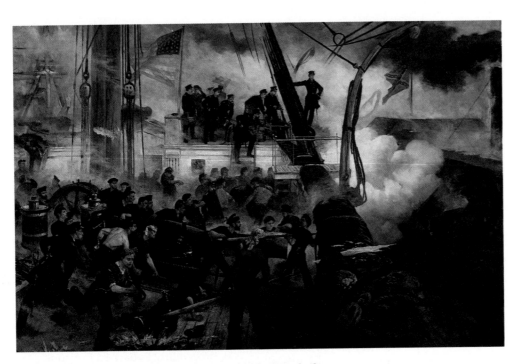

In 1864 a Union fleet led by Admiral David G. Farragut, shown in the ship's rigging, captured the Confederate port at Mobile Bay, Alabama.

The First Battle of Bull Run shocked northerners into realizing that the war would not be quickly won. Lincoln immediately called for a million volunteers to serve in the army for three years. At the same time, the easy victory gave southerners a false sense of confidence. Maybe, they thought, 1 rebel could whip 25 Yankees after all.

The War at Sea

President Lincoln had more success with his strategy of blockading southern seaports. The blockade crippled the South's ability to trade its cotton in Europe for the supplies needed to support its war effort.

In a desperate attempt to break the blockade of Norfolk, Virginia, the Confederates developed an "ironclad" warship. They covered a wooden steamship—the *Merrimac*—with iron plates and attached a large iron beak to its prow to ram and sink the ships blockading Norfolk's harbor.

Renamed the *Virginia*, the ironclad sank two Union ships and ran another aground. However, the Union, too, had built an ironclad, the *Monitor*. On March 9, 1862, the two ships battled for hours, with neither able to claim victory. The battle dashed Confederate hopes of breaking the Norfolk Harbor blockade.

Confederate sea raiders In an effort to hurt northern sea trade, the Confederacy had several warships built in England. These ships, including the *Florida* and the *Alabama*, destroyed 250 northern merchant ships. However, the loss had little effect on the Union's ability to wage the war.

Developing the Section

Discussion

Checking Understanding

1. How would a successful naval blockade by the Union help defeat the Confederacy? (It would keep the South from sending its cotton to Europe in exchange for war supplies.)

2. How did the First Battle of Bull Run change the northerners' attitude toward the war? (The Confederate victory made northerners realize the war would not be quickly won.)

Stimulating Critical Thinking

3. Why do you think the Confederates' destruction of 250 northern merchant ships had little effect on the Union's ability to wage war? (The North had plentiful resources and was not depending on trade with Europe to win the war.)

See the Study Guide activity in **Chapter Resources Binder**, p. 138.

For a fictional account of the First Battle of Bull Run, see the Link to Literature feature on pp. 520–521.

History Footnote

In August 1864, 63-year-old Admiral Farragut led his fleet past three defending Confederate forts to close Mobile, Alabama, the last remaining major southern port on the Gulf of Mexico. Farragut had himself lashed to his ship's rigging so that he would not fall to his death if wounded while commanding the battle. The Confederates had scattered mines across the channel. One mine blew up a Union ship, bottling up the whole fleet under the guns of a fort guarding the entrance to Mobile Bay. Farragut refused to retreat, and shouted what became a famous battle cry: "Damn the torpedoes! Full speed ahead." He took his ship through the minefield safely, followed by the rest of the fleet, and defeated the rebel fleet.

The Fight for the Mississippi

President Lincoln gave the task of gaining control of the Mississippi River to General Ulysses S. Grant. Grant was one of many officers who had left the army after the Mexican-American War. He quickly rejoined with the outbreak of the Civil War.

Grant proved to be an able leader. In February 1862 he captured Fort Henry and Fort Donelson. These two Confederate posts guarded the upper approaches to the Mississippi River at the Tennessee border. Grant showed his fierce determination to win by refusing to discuss terms for the Confederate surrender at Donelson. After that, U. S. Grant was sometimes known as "Unconditional Surrender" Grant.

The Battle of Shiloh With the surrender of Donelson, Confederate troops retreated south. Grant and his army followed. On April 6 the Confederates surprised them near a church named Shiloh. By the end of the day, Grant's forces were close to defeat.

Some Union officers advised retreat. "Retreat? No!" Grant replied. "I propose to attack at daylight and whip them." The next day, Grant did just that, driving the Confederates farther south.

The Battle of Shiloh gave the Union control of much of Kentucky and Tennessee. Now Union forces advanced to Memphis, Tennessee, taking the city in early June.

Farragut Meanwhile, Captain David G. Farragut led a fleet up the Mississippi River. On April 29, 1862, New Orleans surrendered. Baton Rouge, Louisiana, fell a few weeks later.

The next target was the well-defended town of Vicksburg, which was vital to Union success. Lincoln declared, "Vicksburg is the key. The war can never be brought to a close until the key is in our pocket."

Farragut was unable to take Vicksburg, and the Union's Mississippi strategy stalled. It was to be more than a year before Grant could finally capture that important Confederate stronghold.

Campaign to Seize Richmond

In the East, Lincoln now renewed the effort to capture Richmond. To command the new Army of the Potomac he chose General George B. McClellan.

McClellan took months training his raw recruits. At last, in March 1862 he landed 100,000 men on the Virginia Peninsula and advanced slowly toward Richmond. Confederate troops under General Joseph E. Johnston were waiting. They stopped the Union army at the Battle of Seven Pines on May 31 and June 1.

At this point, Robert E. Lee took over command of the Army of Northern Virginia from the wounded Johnston. In late June Lee launched a series of attacks against the Union army that drove them off the peninsula (see map, page 501).

Second Battle of Bull Run Before the Union forces could regroup, Lee surprised them on August 29 in a second battle at Bull Run. **Casualties**—soldiers killed, wounded, captured, or missing—were enormous. Clara Barton was horrified by the casualties. "The men were brot down from the [battle]field and laid on the ground beside the train . . . 'till they covered acres," she wrote. One Union soldier later recalled:

❝Long rows of wounded men were lying around. . . . The surgeons were cutting off arms, feet, hands, limbs of all kinds. As an arm or leg was cut off, it was thrown out an open window. It was an awful sight.❞

History Footnote

The Battle of Shiloh (see also pp. 462–463) was devastating to both sides, with about 20,000 killed and wounded. During the battle, General Grant rested under a tree because he was suffering from a leg wound received a few days earlier. He finally went to a makeshift field hospital, but he said that the sight of wounded and suffering men there "was more unendurable than encountering the enemy's fire, and I returned to my tree in the rain." The Confederates' fierce resistance ended Grant's hopes for a quick victory on the Mississippi, and made him realize that the entire South, and not just its army, would have to be defeated. "I gave up all idea of saving the Union except by complete conquest," he said.

(see also pp. 462–463)

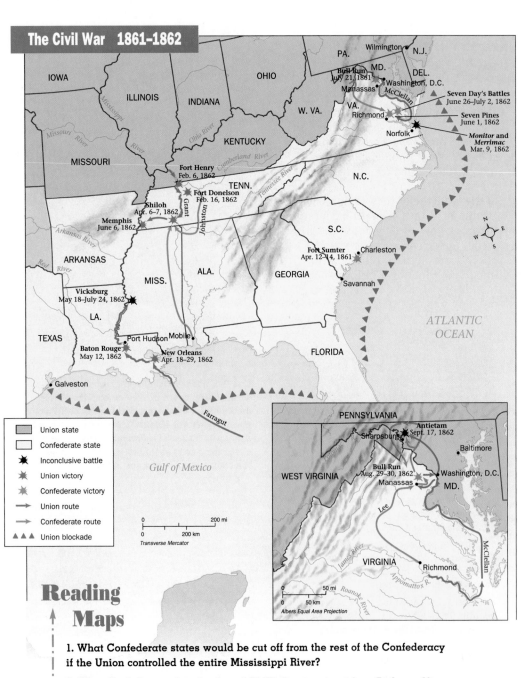

The Civil War 1861–1862

Reading Maps

1. What Confederate states would be cut off from the rest of the Confederacy if the Union controlled the entire Mississippi River?

2. What Confederate victories forced McClellan to retreat from Richmond? What route did Confederate forces under Lee take to invade the Union?

Discussion

Checking Understanding

1. What qualities made Grant an effective general? (He was fiercely determined, insisting on complete and unconditional surrender at Fort Donelson. He was persevering, refusing to retreat.)

2. Why was the capture of Vicksburg so important to the Union? (It was a well-defended town on the Mississippi; Union needed it, along with New Orleans and Baton Rouge, to control the river.)

Stimulating Critical Thinking

3. What do you think caused the terrible medical conditions described by Barton? (Both sides unprepared for enormous casualties; not enough trained medical personnel or equipment; medical techniques relatively primitive.)

Teaching the Reading Maps

To help students focus on the map, ask them to identify the two main geographic areas where Union forces were attacking the Confederates (Mississippi River and Richmond).

Answers to Reading Maps: 1. Arkansas, Texas, and Louisiana. **2.** The Battle of Seven Pines and the Seven Day's Battles. Confederate forces went from Richmond north to Manassas and then north to Antietam in Maryland.

The first war photographs were taken in the war with Mexico, from 1846 to 1848. A portable darkroom was needed for battlefield photography, which consisted of a horse-drawn wagon with a hooded canopy that allowed no light to enter. Inside the wagon were built-in containers for chemicals, and compartments for cameras, lenses, and other equipment. Mathew Brady went to the First Battle of Bull Run in a wagon such as this, along with a newspaper reporter and a sketch artist. While attempting to take photographs of soldiers and civilians fleeing the battle site, Brady got caught up in the turmoil. His wagon was overturned, and his equipment was ruined. Although he was able to save some of the exposed glass plates, no Bull Run photographs by Brady have been found.

Teaching the

Link to Technology

Point out that many of the photographs taken during the war were of the dead lying on the battlefield. Ask students how they think the extensive photographs taken and published affected people's perceptions of the war. (People were able to see fully the horrors of war as they never had before unless they had been on a battlefield; they would probably be more active in trying to put an end to the war.)

Bonus Activity

A Soldier's Letter Home

Ask students to imagine being participants in one of the Civil War battles described in this section. Have them choose a specific battle and review the facts about it. Then have them write letters home describing the sights, sounds, and feelings of the battle from the perspective of either a Union or a Confederate soldier. They should include their views on the war's prospects. Conclude by having volunteers read their letters aloud to compare perspectives.

Link to Technology

The Camera

A major development in technology around the time of the Civil War greatly changed the way we view past events. This development was the camera. While photographic technology had existed for many years, the early 1860s marked the beginning of the wide use of such technology. For the first time, even people far from the front lines could glimpse the grisly scenes of war. As a scholar's tool, photographs provide historians an important window to history—both the history of major events and of ordinary people.

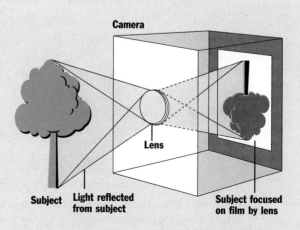

Civil War photographers would rush to the battle scene, set up cameras, then develop the photos on the spot. Perhaps the most famous Civil War photographer was Mathew Brady, who is pictured above with his portable darkroom. The top picture shows the type of photo that made Brady famous. His 1860 camera is pictured at left.

1 A shutter opens quickly, allowing light reflected from the subject to pass through the lens and expose the film.

2 The film is coated with light-sensitive silver crystals. When the reflected light touches them, they turn dark. This process is called *exposure*.

3 Where the subject is dark, it reflects very little light. Where it is bright, it reflects more light. The exposure makes a reverse image, or *negative*, on the film.

4 When the film is developed, the image becomes fixed, and a positive image can be printed—the photograph.

Camera

Lens

Subject

Light reflected from subject

Subject focused on film by lens

Vital Links

Battle of Antietam (Movie)
Unit 3, Side 1, Search
28868, Play to 29319

See also Unit 3 Explore
CD-ROM location 147.

Antietam was the first Civil War battlefield to be photographed before the dead had been buried. Arriving soon after the battle ended, photographer Alexander Gardner took this photo of Confederate dead. Photographs like this captured the horror of war for Americans.

The Battle of Antietam

With the Union forces in chaos, Lee boldly crossed into Maryland in September 1862. He hoped a successful invasion of the North would encourage Britain and France to give aid to the Confederacy.

With a little luck, Lee's gamble might have worked. However, a copy of his orders fell into Union hands, and McClellan learned the exact position of Lee's forces.

On September 17 the two armies clashed at Antietam Creek. It was to be the bloodiest day of the war, but neither side could claim victory. Lee slipped back into Virginia. McClellan, ignoring Lincoln's orders, did not pursue him.

Close to 5,000 soldiers died at Antietam, and 18,500 were wounded. One soldier who survived was Benjamin Chase. His letter home was filled with sadness and fear for the future:

"i was so lucky to get out of it alive. i thought to myself if thear mothers could only see . . . [their dead sons] they would be crasy."

Chase prayed for the "happy day" when he could talk to his mother again. "When will that day come?" he wondered. "i cant tell that, . . . perhaps never."

The Battle of Antietam was a turning point in the war. The battle ended Lee's invasion of the North, destroyed a third of his army, and shattered Confederate hopes of getting aid from abroad.

As 1862 drew to a close, neither side held a clear advantage over the other. Lee's failure at Antietam, however, gave President Lincoln the chance to take a bold step that would change the course of the war.

2. Section Review

1. Define **casualties**.
2. What was the basic goal of the Confederacy? The Union?
3. What brought Union advances to a standstill in 1862?
4. Critical Thinking How might the outcome of the war have been different if Lee had won a decisive victory at the Battle of Antietam?

Closing the Section

Wrap-Up Activity

A Battle Chart
To summarize the first two years of the war, have students create a chart of the major battles and campaigns. The chart should include the name, date, strategic importance, and result of each.

Section Review Answers

1. Definition: *casualties* (500)
2. The Confederacy wanted to defend the South against the Union's invasion. The Union wanted to bring the Confederate states back into the Union.
3. The Union's failure to take Vicksburg stalled the strategy to control the Mississippi River in 1862.
4. Answers might include that Lee's army would have continued the invasion of the North and received aid from Europe. With this help, the Confederates might have ultimately defeated the Union.

★ Describe the effect of the Emancipation Proclamation.
★ Explain how women contributed to the war effort.
★ Identify the challenges Lincoln and Davis faced as wartime leaders.

Introducing the Section

Vocabulary

draft (p. 508) a system that requires men to serve in the military

income tax (p. 509) a tax on money people earn from work or investments

Warm-Up Activity

Lincoln's Diary

Have students imagine that they are President Lincoln writing a diary entry following the Battle of Antietam. The entries should express what hopes and fears Lincoln might have felt upon reviewing the events of the first two years of the war.

Geography Question of the Day

Ask students to make a chart of the geographic advantages and disadvantages of the Union and the Confederacy. They should consider such factors as agriculture, transportation, and use of resources.

Vital Links

African American soldiers (Picture) Unit 3, Side 1, Search 28748

See also Unit 3 Explore CD-ROM location 123.

3. The War Effort at Home

Reading Guide

New Terms draft, income tax

Section Focus The Civil War's effect on northerners and southerners at home

1. What was the effect of the Emancipation Proclamation?
2. How did women contribute to the war effort?
3. What challenges did Lincoln and Davis face as wartime leaders?

From the start of the Civil War, President Lincoln had resisted pleas to abolish slavery. Although Lincoln personally hated slavery, the purpose of the war, he said, "*is* to save the Union, and is *not* either to save or to destroy slavery."

As hopes for peace dimmed, however, Lincoln changed his mind. He came to see that emancipation—freeing all slaves—was "essential to the preservation of the Union."

Moving Toward Emancipation

Several factors led Lincoln to favor emancipation. One was that it made sense from a military point of view. The Confederacy was using enslaved African Americans to build fortifications, haul supplies, and grow crops. If Lincoln freed the slaves, the Confederates would lose a vital source of labor—and the Union would gain one.

In fact, since the war began, thousands of enslaved African Americans had sought freedom by fleeing to join Union forces invading the South. Union commanders paid the escaped slaves to work as cooks, carpenters, guides, and drivers. Some commanders also accepted escaped African Americans as soldiers, forming regiments in South Carolina and Louisiana.

A second reason for emancipation was to keep European nations from helping the Confederacy. Slavery had long been abolished in Europe. Lincoln believed that emancipation would win public support for the Union in those countries.

A third factor in Lincoln's decision was pressure from abolitionists. More and more people were coming to believe that it was time to settle the slavery issue once and for all. "This rebellion has its source . . . in slavery," a Republican told the House of Representatives. Defeating the South would be useless "if slavery shall be spared to canker [infect] the heart of the nation anew."

The Emancipation Proclamation

By the summer of 1862, Lincoln's emancipation plan was ready. The President decided not to announce it, though, until Union forces had won a victory. He did not want it to seem like an act of desperation.

When the Union army turned back Lee's troops at Antietam, Lincoln saw his chance. On September 22, 1862, he issued a warning to the Confederate states: Unless they returned to the Union by January 1, 1863, he would free their slaves. The Confederacy ignored the warning.

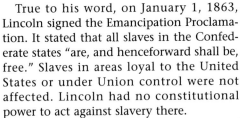

For an activity on analyzing the text of the Emancipation Proclamation, see **Using Historical Documents**, pp. 96–103.

True to his word, on January 1, 1863, Lincoln signed the Emancipation Proclamation. It stated that all slaves in the Confederate states "are, and henceforward shall be, free." Slaves in areas loyal to the United States or under Union control were not affected. Lincoln had no constitutional power to act against slavery there.

The Emancipation Proclamation changed the war into a struggle for freedom as well as for the Union. It turned the Union army into a liberating army wherever it went in the South. It won European approval for the Union cause. It was also a giant step toward abolishing all slavery. Lincoln believed that it was the "one thing that will make people remember I ever lived."

African American Troops

After the Emancipation Proclamation, African Americans could join the Union army as soldiers. About 186,000 African Americans, most of them former slaves, enlisted to fight for the Union and for their own freedom. Another 30,000 joined the navy, which had been accepting black sailors since 1861.

Even though they were risking their lives, African American soldiers were discriminated against. They were assigned to all-black regiments commanded by white officers. Most were given more than their share of digging trenches and building fortifications and bridges.

This picture shows the 54th Massachusetts Infantry leading an assault on Fort Wagner, South Carolina. Although the attack failed, the 54th fought courageously, suffering almost 50 percent casualties.

Developing the Section

Discussion

Checking Understanding

1. Why did Lincoln finally favor emancipation? (He wanted to prevent Confederacy from using slaves to help military effort, to keep European nations from supporting Confederacy, and to respond to increasing pressure from abolitionists.)

2. How were African American soldiers discriminated against? (They were placed in segregated regiments led by white officers, and were often assigned an unfair share of physical labor.)

Stimulating Critical Thinking

3. Should the Emancipation Proclamation be the main thing Lincoln is remembered for? Why or why not? (Yes: made the Union cause a fight against slavery also; in effect, Union was now committed to abolishing slavery if it won the war. No: major accomplishment was saving the Union; proclamation was a strategy to win the war rather than a moral stand, and did not itself free any slaves.)

For Charlotte Forten's account of a celebration of emancipation, see **American Readings**, p. 69.

Have students name some specific examples of how the American Red Cross has provided assistance. Explain that although the Red Cross is highly respected today, Clara Barton had a hard time persuading the United States to join the international organization in 1881. She had learned of the International Red Cross in 1869 when she was informed by its president that the United States had refused three times to join the organization. Lobbying in Washington in 1877, she learned that the United States' refusal to join was part of its policy of isolating itself from Europe. Barton finally convinced President Garfield in 1881 that the Red Cross could help people in times of peace, such as during natural disasters, as well as during international wars.

Section Activity

Newspaper Articles

To explore aspects of the war effort at home, have groups imagine they are newspaper staffs in the North and South. Have them create front pages containing articles reflecting their regional biases. Topics include the Emancipation Proclamation, the 54th Massachusetts Regiment, opposition at home, the war's effect on the economy, and contributions of women to the war effort. Conclude by having groups compare articles.

506

The Fort Wagner attack inspired commemorations, like these excerpts from "The Old Flag Never Touched the Ground":

"The Old Flag never touched the ground!"
'twas thus brave Carney spoke—
A Negro soldier: words renowned, that
Honor will invoke
Upon the records of the Race whose
heroes many are,

Records that Time cannot efface, and
Hate can never mar.
Those words were stamped with Carney's
blood upon our Country's scroll,
And though dislike, deep as a flood
against his Race may roll,
It cannot dim, nor wash away, its
crimson-written fame
Which History wrote on Wagner's day
without a tinge of shame.

Link to the Present

The American Red Cross A hurricane pounds a Florida town. Floods destroy homes and farms in Iowa. An earthquake tumbles buildings in California. Wherever disaster strikes, the American Red Cross is there to help the victims.

While in Switzerland in 1869, Clara Barton learned of the International Committee of the Red Cross, a group of volunteers who aided wounded soldiers. Impressed by its work, she founded the American branch of the Red Cross in 1881.

Barton soon expanded Red Cross activities to include disaster relief. Today the Red Cross also collects and distributes blood and teaches first aid. Most workers are volunteers, and programs are funded by private—not government—contributions.

At first, African American troops were paid as laborers, not soldiers, and all received the same pay no matter what their rank. To protest such unequal treatment, many soldiers refused to accept any pay at all. In a letter to President Lincoln, Corporal James Henry Gooding of the 54th Massachusetts Infantry asked:

❝The main question is, are we soldiers, or are we laborers? . . . We have done a soldier's duty. Why can't we have a soldier's pay?❞

In 1864 Congress finally granted black soldiers equal pay, including all back pay.

Some northerners doubted that African Americans would make good soldiers. Such doubts were quickly put to rest in battle.

For example, in a suicidal attack on Fort Wagner, South Carolina, in 1863, the 54th Massachusetts Infantry lost its commander, most of its officers, and almost half of its troops. Although terribly wounded, Sergeant William Carney carried the regiment's flags to safety. He was the first of 20 African American soldiers to win the Congressional Medal of Honor.

New Challenges for Women

Until the Civil War, women had few choices of jobs outside the home other than teacher, factory worker, or house servant. With thousands of men fighting in the war, though, women took over family farms and businesses. They also had the chance to tackle jobs usually closed to them.

Women worked in mints making coins and in offices copying documents, as Clara Barton did in the Patent Office. Women also worked in arsenals making ammunition. This was a dangerous business. After 21 women were killed in an explosion in Washington, D.C., President Lincoln led the funeral procession to Congressional Cemetery. There the victims, mostly Irish immigrants, were buried in a common grave.

Setting up hospitals When the war began, there were almost no large military hospitals. Medical officers scrambled to convert barns, tobacco warehouses, schools, and even large boats into hospitals.

Conditions in most hospitals were terrible. They lacked ways to treat water and sewage to prevent the spread of disease. In fact, twice as many soldiers died of disease as of combat wounds. Mary Boykin Chesnut described her visit to a hospital in Richmond:

❝I can never again shut out of view the sights I saw of human misery. . . . Long rows of ill men on cots. Ill of typhoid fever, of every human ailment.❞

At the time of the Civil War, doctors had not discovered the importance of using antiseptic conditions to prevent infection. Not until 1865 did Joseph Lister, a British surgeon and professor, realize that infection was caused by microorganisms, which were present not only in the air but also on a surgeon's hands and instruments. Even minor wounds to soldiers' arms and legs could result in amputation, because of the threat of infection. Sanitary conditions in camps and prisons were horrendous. Food and water were often contaminated, leading to outbreaks of dysentery and diarrhea. Malaria, pneumonia, bronchitis, scurvy, and measles were also rampant. Twice as many soldiers died from disease as were killed in combat.

Women played many roles in the war. Women workers prepared cartridges for Union guns at the arsenal in Watertown, Massachusetts. Alice Buckner of Virginia tried—without success—to smuggle medicine in her petticoat to the Confederates. Captain Sally Tompkins founded one of the best small hospitals for soldiers in the South.

Many women took wounded soldiers into their homes. Sally L. Tompkins set up a hospital in a Richmond house where she treated more than 1,300 patients. Jefferson Davis rewarded her services by appointing her a captain of cavalry.

Nursing the wounded Many noted women reformers threw themselves into the effort to nurse the wounded. Dorothea Dix, who had reformed mental hospitals, worked with Dr. Elizabeth Blackwell to set up a training program for female nurses. Dix's rules were so strict that she became known as "Dragon Dix."

Clara Barton felt "cramped" in hospitals. She preferred being on the battlefield. There she treated wounded soldiers, some of whom had gone for days without food or water.

Harriet Tubman also helped tend the wounded, working with Clara Barton in the Sea Islands off the coast of South Carolina.

Sojourner Truth worked in Union hospitals and in camps for escaped slaves. She also recruited black soldiers for the Union army. Two were her sons.

Opposition at Home

Not everyone was as patriotic and eager to serve as the brave women working in the arsenals and hospitals of the Union and the Confederacy. As the war dragged on and hopes for a quick victory faded, Presidents Davis and Lincoln both faced growing opposition at home.

States' rights A serious problem for Davis was lack of cooperation by the states in the Confederacy. Holding fast to the idea of states' rights, they resisted paying taxes and cooperating on military matters. At one point, Georgia even threatened to secede from the Confederacy.

Checking Understanding

1. What job opportunities outside the home were open to women before the Civil War? (Teacher, factory worker, house servant.)

2. How did the war open up some opportunities for African Americans and women? (Because of the growing need for soldiers, African American men were finally allowed to join the Union army and were eventually given equal pay. Meanwhile, many women had to take over family farms and businesses, and some worked at government jobs traditionally denied to them.)

Stimulating Critical Thinking

3. If you were a reformer in the early 1860s, why might you be cautious in hoping for equal rights for women and African Americans? (A reformer might suspect that the changing roles for these two groups were more a result of wartime necessity than of any basic change in the attitudes of white men.)

★ ★ ★
Vital Links

Voice of nurse Kate Cummings (First Person Account) Unit 3, Side 1, Search 26195, Play to 26465

See also Unit 3 Explore CD-ROM location 113.

1861–1865 Chapter 18 • **507**

The Copperheads objected to Lincoln's policies on the draft, military arrests, African Americans in the military, and emancipation. On all these issues, Lincoln stood firm. He supported the jailing of those who obstructed the draft, and by the summer of 1863 more than 13,000 of these objectors had been imprisoned. When Lincoln was criticized for jailing a prominent Ohio Democrat for denouncing the draft, he said, "Must I shoot a simple-minded soldier boy who deserts while I must not touch a hair of the wily agitator who induces him to desert?" In response to calls to revoke the emancipation policy, Lincoln replied, "I am a slow walker, but I never walk backward."

World Link

Britain stays neutral in Civil War

"No power dares . . . to make war on cotton. Cotton is king." So said Senator James Hammond of South Carolina in 1859. When the Civil War broke out, southern leaders expected British support. They thought Britain would want to protect the supply of cotton flowing to its textile mills.

What went wrong? Between 1860 and 1862, bad weather ruined Europe's grain crops while Union farmers were having record harvests. Britain needed northern grain more than southern cotton.

Meanwhile, in 1861 British mills had a surplus of cotton. By the time it ran out, they had found new sources of cotton in India and Egypt. Thus, Britain could afford to stay neutral in the Civil War.

Copperheads For his part, Lincoln led a Union that was far from united. Many northern Democrats were more interested in restoring peace than in saving the Union or ending slavery. Republicans called these Democrats "Copperheads," after the poisonous snake.

The draft The hottest issue faced by both the Union and the Confederacy was the **draft**—a system that requires men to serve in the military. At first both armies had more than enough volunteers. As casualties mounted, though, enlistments dropped.

In 1862 the Confederacy passed the first draft law in United States history. With a few exceptions, all white men aged 18 to 35 could be called for military service for 3 years. A draftee could avoid serving by paying for a substitute to take his place. Anyone who owned 20 slaves or more was excused from the draft. Angry southerners protested that it was "a rich man's war and a poor man's fight."

Soon the Union had to resort to the draft as well. Its draft act applied to all men aged 20 to 45. As in the South, a draftee could pay for a substitute. The Union's draft act was passed only 2 months after the Emancipation Proclamation. Copperheads accused the government of forcing white workers to fight to free the slaves, who would then compete for their jobs after the war.

When the first draft was held in July 1863, riots broke out. The worst was in New York City. There a mob, mostly Irish Americans, went on a 4-day rampage, burning draft offices and lynching African Americans. At least 105 people were killed.

Years of war aged President Lincoln, as this 1865 portrait shows, but he never doubted his war aims.

See the Study Guide activity in **Chapter Resources Binder,** p. 139.

★ ★ ★
Vital Links

○ War refugees from the South (Picture) Unit 3, Side 1, Search 28802

◉ See also Unit 3 Explore CD-ROM location 132.

Economic Strains of the War

The war placed a great strain on the economies of both sides. To pay for the Union war effort, Congress passed the nation's first **income tax**—a tax on money people earn from work or investments. The Union also raised millions of dollars through the sale of war bonds. People who bought bonds were, in effect, lending money to the government.

Unable to raise enough money to pay their bills, both governments printed money. Union notes were called "greenbacks" because of their color. Since paper money was not backed by gold or silver, it lost value during the war. Between 1862 and 1865, the value of a one-dollar Union note dropped to half that amount in gold. A similar Confederate note was worth about two cents.

Getting supplies The Union economy was up to the challenge of supplying both troops and people at home during the war. Aided by the McCormick reaper, farmers produced large crops of wheat and corn. Labor-saving machines enabled factories to keep soldiers well clothed and armed.

The Confederacy, however, suffered increasingly from shortages. Its economy, based largely on cotton and with few industries, was ill-suited to supporting a war effort.

Early in the war, southerners had made a serious mistake. They stopped shipping cotton abroad, hoping to force Britain to aid the Confederacy. The plan backfired. As you have seen, Britain did not help the South—and the South lost an important source of income.

Meanwhile the Union blockade made it increasingly difficult for the Confederacy to import supplies. After southern victories, desperate Confederate soldiers stripped dead and wounded Union soldiers of their weapons, shoes, and even uniforms.

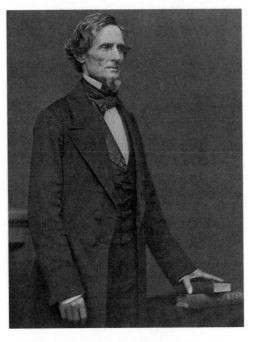

President Davis had the heavy responsibility of organizing a new nation and guiding it in war.

The Union's naval blockade was working. It was strangling the southern economy and, with it, the Confederate war effort. As a Confederate officer later admitted, the blockade "shut the Confederacy out from the world, deprived it of supplies, [and] weakened its military and naval strength."

★ 3. Section Review

1. Define **draft** and **income tax.**
2. Why did Lincoln wait to issue the Emancipation Proclamation?
3. Describe at least two contributions made by women to the war effort.
4. Critical Thinking How might public opposition in the Union and the Confederacy have weakened the war effort?

If students need to review the skill, use the Skills Development transparency and activity in the **Chapter Resources Binder**, pp. 143–144.

source B suggests that Lincoln wanted the North to have a stronger moral cause, and Source C suggests that he wanted to hurt the South as much as possible and to open up extensive recruitment of black soldiers into the Union army.

3. (a) As the sources indicate, Lincoln probably had several reasons, and therefore no one hypothesis completely explains his action.

Students might give more weight to hypotheses mentioned by more than one source, such as Lincoln's desire to weaken the South. **(b)** Accept any reasonable ideas for further research—for example, studying Lincoln's own words on the subject.

For further application, have students do the Applying Skills activity in the Chapter Survey (p. 518).

Introducing the Skill Lab

Begin by asking students why they think it might be important for a historian to make hypotheses (to help understand why events happened as they did, and perhaps to learn lessons from those events that can be applied to the present). Point out that after forming a hypothesis there is always a danger that a historian will look only at evidence that seems to support that theory, and ignore contrary evidence. A good historian will revise his or her hypothesis if necessary to fit the facts.

Skill Lab
Answers

1. Students' notes should reflect an ability to extract preliminary hypothesis ideas from the sources. For example, notes for source B might include the following possible reasons for issuing the proclamation: to encourage slaves to leave plantations, and to give the North a stronger moral cause.

2. (a) Lincoln wanted to weaken the South by depriving it of slave labor. He also wanted to cut off European support for the South. In addition, he was responding to pressure from abolitionists. **(b)** Sources B and C suggest the hypotheses mentioned in A. In addition,

(Answers continued in top margin)

Skill Lab

Using Information
Making a Hypothesis

"All persons held as slaves within any [rebellious] state . . . shall be . . . forever free." With those words, Abraham Lincoln ensured his place in history as the "Great Emancipator." Historians have long disagreed, however, about Lincoln's reasons—and timing—for the Emancipation Proclamation.

Question to Investigate

Why did President Lincoln issue the Emancipation Proclamation?

Procedure

Any answer to that question is a **hypothesis**—a theory to explain the event. Part of a historian's job is to develop hypotheses for events and situations. Then each hypothesis must be tested against available information.

1 Gather information.
a. Read sources **A**, **B**, and **C**.
b. As you read, take notes on possible reasons for the proclamation.

2 Develop several hypotheses.
a. Write the hypotheses suggested by source **A**.
b. Write two more hypotheses that sources **B** and **C** suggest to you.

3 Test each hypothesis.
a. From what you know, does each hypothesis give an adequate explanation for why Lincoln issued the proclamation? Is one hypothesis more valid? Explain.
b. What can you do to test how reasonable each hypothesis is?

Skill Tips

Keep in mind:
● To qualify as a hypothesis, a theory must be able to be tested.
● There may be more than one reasonable hypothesis to explain an event.
● Even the best hypothesis may need to be tested again if new information is available.

Sources to Use

A Reread pages 504–505.

B "Thousands of jubilant [joyful] slaves, learning of the proclamation, flocked to the invading Union armies, stripping already rundown plantations of their work force. . . . The North now had much the stronger moral cause. In addition to preserving the Union, it had committed itself to freeing the slaves."

From Thomas A. Bailey and David M. Kennedy, *The American Pageant* (D.C. Heath: 1991)

C "Three developments caused Lincoln to change his mind [and to abolish slavery]. First, the bloody fighting made many northerners want to hurt the South as much as possible. Abolishing slavery would help do that. Second, slavery helped the southern war effort. Slaves helped to build military fortifications, and they produced food. Third, slavery was a crucial issue on the Union's diplomatic front with Britain. Britain's leaders would not support a war whose aim was to keep the United States together. However, British public opinion would back a war against slavery. . . . The Emancipation Proclamation also encouraged the recruitment of black soldiers into the Union army. . . . All told, nearly 300,000 blacks served in the Union army."

From Winthrop D. Jordan et al., *The Americans* (McDougal, Littell: 1991)

Section Objectives

★ Explain why the Battles of Gettysburg and Vicksburg were turning points in the war.
★ Describe Grant's strategy for winning the war.
★ List the events that led to Lee's surrender at Appomattox.

Teaching Resources

Take-Home Planner 6, pp. 10–17
Chapter Resources Binder
  Study Guide, p. 140
    Reinforcement
    Skills Development
Geography Extensions, pp. 35–36
American Readings, pp. 70–72
Using Historical Documents
Transparency Activities
Chapter and Unit Tests, pp. 115–118

4. From War to Peace

Reading Guide

New Term total war

Section Focus **Union victories that finally ended the war**

1. Why were the Battles of Gettysburg and Vicksburg turning points in the war?
2. What was Grant's strategy for winning the war?
3. What events led to Lee's surrender at Appomattox?

The year 1862 ended in despair for the Union. The war effort in Virginia and on the Mississippi had stalled. Many northerners began to speak openly about letting the Confederacy have its independence. President Lincoln kept his sights on his goal—to win the war. He knew, however, that he needed a general he could count on to "fight battles and win victories."

Two Confederate Victories

After the Battle of Antietam, Lincoln fired General McClellan for refusing to attack Lee's retreating army. He gave command to General Ambrose E. Burnside. In December 1862 Lee soundly defeated Burnside's forces at Fredericksburg, Virginia. Benjamin Chase died that day. He was only 18 years old.

Next Lincoln turned to General Joseph Hooker. Lee stopped Hooker, too—at Chancellorsville, Virginia, in May 1863. Lee's victory was clouded, however, by the death of Stonewall Jackson. "I know not how to replace him," confessed Lee.

After Chancellorsville, Lee decided to invade the Union again. He thought that another victory, this time on northern soil, would prove to northerners and Europeans that the Confederacy could win the war. His invasion might also draw Union troops away from Vicksburg on the Mississippi.

The Battle of Gettysburg

In June 1863 Lee led his confident troops across Maryland and into Pennsylvania. On July 1 Confederate soldiers met Union soldiers in the little town of Gettysburg. General George C. Meade, the new commander of the Army of the Potomac, had been following Lee's forces. He rushed his army to Gettysburg and forced Lee to take a stand.

The greatest loss to the South at Chancellorsville was the death of Stonewall Jackson, Lee's "right arm." Jackson was accidentally shot by his own men.

Warm-Up Activity

A Military Report Card

To review the status of the war at the end of 1862, have students work in pairs to grade the performance of each side's military forces. They should write reports assessing the outcomes of the First Battle of Bull Run, the war at sea, the fight for the Mississippi, the Richmond campaign, and the Battle of Antietam. They should conclude the reports by assigning each side a letter grade for its military performance, explaining how they arrived at the grades.

Geography Question of the Day

Have students refer to the large map on page 513 to identify which states Sherman's troops marched across, and explain how it is apparent from the map that his campaign was successful. (Sherman marched through Georgia, South Carolina, and North Carolina. His path was not interrupted by Confederate victories and resulted in Union victories in Atlanta, Savannah, and Columbia.)

Interviewing
Lee and Grant

To analyze why the North won the war, have students imagine interviewing the two commanding generals following Appomattox. Have them work in small groups, assigning half the groups to write a Lee interview script and half to write a Grant interview script. Each script should include questions regarding military strategy and key victories and defeats, with answers they think the general would be likely to give. Conclude by discussing what each general might see as the key factors determining the war's outcome.

For the Gettysburg Address, see **American Readings**, p. 70.

Vital Links

Voice of Major Sullivan Ballou (First Person Account) Unit 3, Side 1, Search 26469, Play to 27413

⊙ **See also Unit 3 Explore CD-ROM location 114.**

512

✳ History Footnote

Although the Gettysburg Address is remembered as one of the great speeches in American history, its initial reception was less than enthusiastic. Lincoln had intended to use the occasion to discuss the meaning of the war as a whole, but his speech was not completed when he set out for Gettysburg. He did not finish writing it until the morning of the ceremony. The crowd of 15,000 grew restless as Edward Everett, a famous orator, preceded Lincoln and spoke for two hours. Lincoln's speech, consisting of 270 words, lasted for two minutes. His address was so unexpectedly short that a photographer who had planned to record the event was still adjusting his camera when Lincoln finished. Many people were disappointed in the speech, including many listeners, opposition newspapers, and Lincoln himself.

On the first day of the Battle of Gettysburg, Confederate troops attacked Union lines. Union forces, though, had more troops, greater firepower, and a strong defensive position on high ground.

For two days Union and Confederate forces fought furiously. Finally, on July 3, Lee risked everything on an infantry charge led by General George E. Pickett. About 15,000 Confederates hurled themselves at the center of the Union line on Cemetery Ridge. Pickett's Charge was a disaster. Half of his men were struck by Union fire as they rushed uphill. More fell in hand-to-hand combat when they reached the ridge.

The Battle of Gettysburg was a turning point in the war. On July 4 Lee, who had lost a third of his army, retreated to Virginia. From this point on, he would be fighting a defensive war on southern soil.

The Gettysburg Address The casualties at Gettysburg were staggering—23,000 for the Union and 28,000 for the Confederates. The bloodshed was so appalling that a national cemetery was created for the soldiers who died there. At the dedication ceremony on November 19, 1863, President Lincoln delivered a brief speech.

The Gettysburg Address is one of the most eloquent statements of American democracy. In it Lincoln vowed:

❝We here highly resolve that these dead shall not have died in vain; that this nation, under God, shall have a new birth of freedom; and that government of the people, by the people, for the people shall not perish from the earth.❞

Victory on the Mississippi

The Union victory at Gettysburg was quickly followed by good news from the Mississippi. After failing to storm the hilltop stronghold of Vicksburg, General Grant had surrounded it while Union gunboats bombarded it. The starving citizens held out for

After the Battle of Gettysburg, Lee blamed himself for the disastrous assault to the center of the Union line by General Pickett's troops. Most of Pickett's men were Virginians like Lee himself. In addition to the 7,500 soldiers cut down, all thirteen colonels in the division and all three brigade commanders were killed or injured. Lee realized that his gamble in taking the offensive on northern soil had failed miserably. He said to Pickett later, "Upon my shoulders rests the blame. The men and officers of your command have written the name of Virginia as high today as it has ever been written before." He said to another man, "It is I who have lost this fight and you must help me out of it the best way you can."

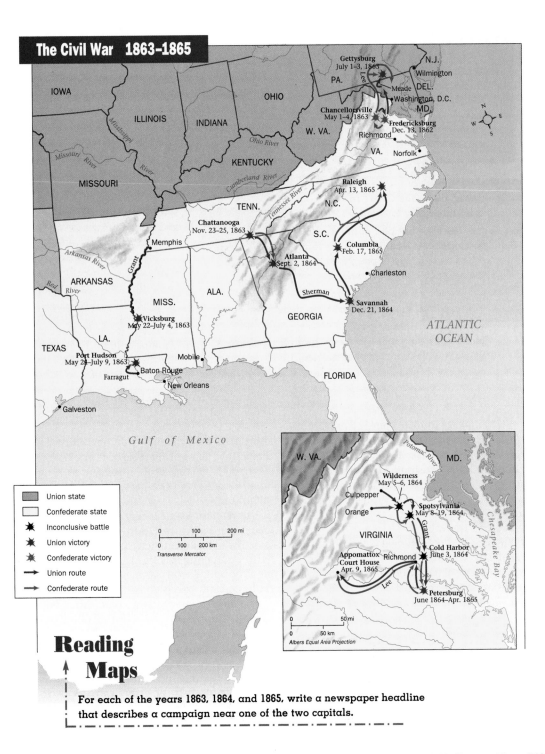

The Civil War 1863–1865

Legend:
- Union state
- Confederate state
- ✳ Inconclusive battle
- ✳ Union victory
- ✳ Confederate victory
- → Union route
- → Confederate route

0   100   200 mi
0   100   200 km
Transverse Mercator

Albers Equal Area Projection
0   50 mi
0   50 km

Reading Maps

For each of the years 1863, 1864, and 1865, write a newspaper headline that describes a campaign near one of the two capitals.

Discussion

Checking Understanding

1. Why were Union troops victorious at the Battle of Gettysburg? (They had more soldiers, greater firepower, and a good defensive position on a hill.)

Stimulating Critical Thinking

2. Why do you think the Gettysburg Address is so celebrated? (It states America's democratic philosophy in a simple, straightforward, graceful style. Its dignified manner fit the occasion. It honors people who died to save the nation.)

Teaching the
↑ Reading Maps

To help students focus on the maps, ask: **Which battles were fought near Washington, D.C.?** (Gettysburg, Wilderness, Spotsylvania, Chancellorsville, Fredericksburg) **Which were fought near Richmond?** (Cold Harbor, Petersburg) **Answer to Reading Maps:** Some possible headlines: 1863—Jackson Dies in Confederate Victory at Chancellorsville; 1864—Grant Persists in Spotsylvania; 1865—Union Batters Rebel Defenses at Petersburg.

✳ ✳ ✳
Vital Links

Gettysburg Address (First Person Account) Unit 3, Side 1, Search 25295, Play to 26191

◉ See also Unit 3 Explore CD-ROM location 112.

514

Hands-On
- - - - - → *HISTORY*

Commemorating the Civil War Since the guns fell silent more than 130 years ago, Americans have continued to remember the Civil War. In paintings, monuments, and books, as well as in movies and television dramas, we have commemorated the people and events of that dramatic period in the nation's history.

→ **Activity** You may never write a book or create a television drama about the Civil War, but you can plan a way to commemorate it.

① Decide what part of the war to commemorate. It might be an event, a person or group of people, or a theme, such as life at home.

② Decide what form to create—for example, a plaque, monument, play, pageant, or story.

③ Put your plan on paper. For example, draw a picture of a statue or write a program for a pageant. Share it with your classmates.

War monument

almost seven weeks, living in caves and eating rats, cats, dogs, and mules.

Vicksburg finally surrendered on July 4, 1863—another turning point in the war. Port Hudson, the last Confederate stronghold on the Mississippi, gave up five days later. Union forces now controlled the entire river. Lincoln was thrilled. "Grant is my man," he exclaimed, "and I am his for the rest of the war."

President Lincoln named Grant commander of all western forces. Grant responded by capturing Chattanooga, a key railroad center in Tennessee, in November 1863.

Total War

At last, Lincoln had found a general who could win battles. In March 1864 he gave Grant command of all Union forces.

The new commander had a common-sense way of looking at war. He wrote:

"The art of war is simple enough. Find out where your enemy is. Get at him as soon as you can. Strike at him as hard as you can and as often as you can, and keep moving on."

Grant believed in **total war**—war against armies and also against a people's resources and will to fight.

Now Grant mapped out a strategy to end the war. He would lead the Army of the Potomac against Lee and capture Richmond. Meanwhile, he ordered General William Tecumseh Sherman to invade Georgia and take Atlanta.

The battle for Richmond On May 4, 1864, Grant invaded northern Virginia with 120,000 troops. They clashed with Lee's army of 61,000 in the Wilderness, a dense forest. In 2 days of fighting, Grant's troops suffered 18,000 casualties. Instead of turning back, though, Grant pressed on toward Richmond.

The two armies next met at Spotsylvania Court House. Again Grant suffered heavy losses but would not retreat. "I propose to fight it out along this line if it takes all summer," he said. The two armies clashed at Cold Harbor, again with high casualties.

In a month, Grant's army had lost 50,000 soldiers, compared with about 30,000 Confederate losses. The greater population of the North meant that Grant could get more troops. Lee, however, could not replace his losses. By the time the Confederate Congress decided to use African American troops in March 1865, it would be too late to make a difference.

Atlanta was a major target of Union forces for several reasons. It had become an important symbol of the Confederacy, equal only to Richmond. It was one of the South's most important manufacturing centers, and it was an important railroad link to the Carolinas and Virginia. However, the state capital of South Carolina, Columbia, also received harsh treatment by Sherman's troops. Many northerners considered South Carolina especially at fault in the war since the first shot had been fired at Fort Sumter. Sherman telegraphed Lincoln, "The truth is the whole army is burning with an insatiable desire to wreak vengeance upon South Carolina."

Lee moved on to defend Petersburg, an important rail center 20 miles (32 km) from Richmond. If Petersburg fell, the Confederates could not hold Richmond.

The capture of Atlanta Meanwhile, Sherman moved toward Atlanta. The Confederates made Union forces pay for every advance, but by mid-July of 1864 Sherman had surrounded Atlanta.

The Confederates hoped to hold out until the Union's presidential election. They thought that war-weary northerners would reject Lincoln and elect General George McClellan, who called for an end to the war. However, on September 2, 1864, Atlanta fell. News of Sherman's victory raised spirits in the North and ensured Lincoln's reelection.

Sherman now put into effect Grant's idea of total war. To break the South's will to continue fighting, his troops burned Atlanta. Then they marched almost unopposed across Georgia. Along the way they torched barns and houses and destroyed railroad tracks, crops, and livestock.

In December Sherman reached the sea at Savannah. Then, leaving destruction in his wake, he marched north through South Carolina and into North Carolina. From there he drove on toward Richmond.

Lee Surrenders

For nine months Grant's forces battered Lee's defenses at Petersburg, the gateway to Richmond. They finally broke through on April 1, 1865. Two days later, Union troops marched into Richmond.

Lee fled with 30,000 soldiers. Grant followed. At this point, other Union forces

This painting commemorates the end of the Civil War. General Lee (left) signs the agreement surrendering his army to General Grant (right).

Discussion

Checking Understanding

1. In what way was Grant a solution to one of Lincoln's ongoing problems? (He was a successful general after many ineffective ones.)

2. How did Sherman put Grant's ideas about war into effect? (He waged total war—against the people's resources and will to fight— as he invaded Georgia and took Atlanta. His troops burned houses, barns, and factories; destroyed railroad tracks; and ruined crops and livestock.)

Stimulating Critical Thinking

3. What role do you think Sherman's march through Georgia played in Lee's surrender? (Answers might include that it was an important part of the northern victory because it warned of the ongoing destruction if war continued.)

★ ★ ★
Vital Links

Atlanta (Picture) Unit 3, Side 1, Search 38977

See also Unit 3 Explore CD-ROM location 212.

For a southerner's account of the siege of Vicksburg, see **American Readings,** p. 71.

Closing the Section

Wrap-Up Activity

Making a Time Line

To review the section, have students work in groups to create a detailed time line for the years 1863–1865. Each key event for the period should include the date and a sentence identifying it and stating its importance.

Section Review
Answers

1. Definition: *total war* (514)
2. The Battle of Gettysburg forced Lee to begin fighting a defensive war on southern soil. After the Battle of Vicksburg, Union forces controlled the entire Mississippi River.
3. Grant had more troops and so was able to surround Lee's armies in Richmond.
4. No: farms and cities were devastated and caused economic ruin for innocent citizens. Yes: it helped to put an end to the war and save the Union.

To check understanding of "Why We Remember," assign Thinking Critically question 3 on student page 518.

✳ History Footnote

After the war, Clara Barton spent more than two years helping thousands of families frantically seek missing relatives. Such searches were difficult because few soldiers carried identification. Sometimes before battle, a soldier might pin a slip of paper with his name to his uniform so he could be identified. Benjamin Chase etched his name on a coin, a forerunner of military dog tags.

For Grant's account of the surrender at Appomattox, see **American Readings**, p. 72.

---

cut off Lee's escape route. Outnumbered and surrounded, Lee decided that further fighting would be useless.

On April 9, 1865, Lee surrendered at Appomattox Court House. Grant gave generous terms. Lee's troops could go home if they promised to fight no more. All soldiers could keep their own horses. Grant also provided food for Lee's starving soldiers. In the next few days, all Confederate forces followed Lee's lead. The last general to surrender was Stand Watie of the Cherokee Nation. On May 10, Jefferson Davis was captured.

Costs of war The bloodiest war in the history of the nation had finally ended. The Union had been saved, but at the horrifying cost of more than 620,000 Union and Confederate dead.

Almost every family on both sides had lost a friend or loved one. Benjamin Chase's mother never overcame the shock of his death. Daniel and Rebecca Hite of Virginia had watched five sons go off to war. Only two came home. Clara Barton set up a "missing persons" office to help thousands of families searching for missing relatives.

For President Lincoln, the end of the war was the happiest day of his life. "Thank God I have lived to see this," he said. "I have been dreaming a horrid nightmare for four years, and now the nightmare is over."

★ 4. Section Review

1. Define **total war**.
2. Why were the Battles of Gettysburg and Vicksburg turning points in the war?
3. What Union advantage helped Grant defeat Lee in 1865?
4. **Critical Thinking** Do you think Sherman should have used total war in Georgia and the Carolinas? Give reasons for your answer.

Why We Remember

The Civil War

The Civil War, wrote the *New York Times* after the guns fell silent, "leaves us a different people forever." Nowhere was this truth easier to see than in the longstanding issue of slavery. The Union's victory in the war destroyed the system of slavery and paved the way to freedom for 4 million African Americans. Many of them had helped win that freedom on the battlefield. To Clara Barton, each one was a "soldier of freedom."

The Civil War also changed how Americans viewed their country. Before the war, most Americans thought of the United States as a loose union of separate states. When talking of their country, they said, "The United States *are*." Afterward, people in both the North and the South saw the country as a single nation and began to say, "The United States *is*."

Geography Footnote

Many sites of Civil War battles are now part of the National Park system. Some, such as Gettysburg, Fredericksburg and Spotsylvania, and Shiloh are national military parks. Others, such as Antietam, Manassas, and Petersburg, are national battlefields; and others, such as Appomattox Court House, are national historical parks. All are run by the National Park Service, which is a bureau of the United States Department of the Interior. The sites have been restored to look as much as possible as they did during the Civil War, and they include relics such as cannons and other weapons.

Geography Lab

Reading a Grid Map

Each year close to 1.5 million people visit the Gettysburg National Military Park in Pennsylvania. There they can trace the events of the battle by car or on foot.

The map shows the site of the Battle of Gettysburg. As with road maps, this map has a grid of intersecting lines. Note that the spaces between horizontal lines are labeled with letters, while the spaces between vertical lines are labeled with numbers. Thus, the squares in the grid can be referred to as A-1, A-2, and so on. The labeled grid makes it easy to find sites and describe their location on the map.

Gettysburg National Cemetery, Pennsylvania

Using Map Skills

1. Confederates approached Gettysburg on a road that passes through grid locations A-1, A-2, and B-2. What is the name of the road?

2. A Union line curled around what two hills in C-3 and C-4?

3. Confederate troops lined Seminary Ridge. From there Pickett's men charged Union troops atop Cemetery Ridge. To keep their sense of direction, they focused on a clump of trees. Give its grid location.

4. President Lincoln delivered his address where Soldier's Monument is today. Give its grid location.

5. Hands-On Geography
Use the map to plan a tour of the Gettysburg battle site. Begin at the Visitor's Center and end at McPherson's Barn, with five stops in between. Imagine a path through the park. Write instructions for the tour, using grid locations and compass directions to describe the route and the stopping points along it.

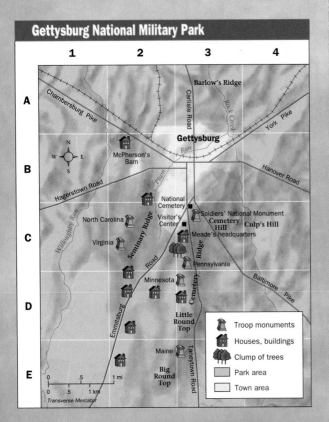

Gettysburg National Military Park

Key:
- Troop monuments
- Houses, buildings
- Clump of trees
- Park area
- Town area

Teaching the Geography Lab

To help students read the grid map, ask them to point to the area within A-3 and name the road indicated there (Carlisle Road). Have them look at the key and tell what kind of structure is located in E-3 (a troop monument). Point out that on a road map, names of streets and buildings are alphabetized next to the map with locations indicated by grid area (A-1,B-2, etc.). Suggest that students bring in road maps and practice locating streets.

Using Map Skills
Answers

1. Chambersburg Pike
2. Cemetery Hill and Culp's Hill
3. C-2, C-3
4. C-3
5. Tour instructions will vary but may include going east to Culp's Hill in C-3, south to Cemetery Hill in C-3, south to Little Round Top in D-3, north to the Minnesota Troop Monument in D-3, and northwest to Seminary Ridge in C-3.

See the activity on reading grid maps in **Geography Extensions,** pp. 35–36.

• 517

517

Survey Answers

Reviewing Vocabulary

Definitions are found on these pages: *habeas corpus* (492), *martial law* (492), *casualties* (500), *draft* (508), *income tax* (509), *total war* (514).

Reviewing Main Ideas

1. (a) the Union (b) the Union (c) the Confederacy (d) the Union (e) the Union

2. Davis planned to push back invading forces, making the war so costly that the Union would give up. Lincoln planned to blockade seaports, gain control of the Mississippi River, and capture Richmond.

3. Lincoln had mixed success. His blockade prevented importation of supplies. On the Mississippi, Union troops captured many key sites, but they failed to gain complete control of the river. They also failed to capture Richmond.

4. (a) The proclamation freed all slaves in the Confederate states, but slaves in areas loyal to the Union were not freed. (b) The war became, in part, a struggle to abolish slavery; the Union gained European support; African American soldiers bolstered the Union army.

5. Lincoln's problems included opposition from Copperheads, resistance to the draft, and raising money. Davis's problems included lack of cooperation from states, opposition to the draft, raising money, and getting supplies. Each faced the problem of a loss of value of paper money.

6. The Union victory at Gettysburg: Lee's forces were too weak to invade the North again, and European nations did not help the South. The Confederate surrender of Vicksburg led to the surrender of Port Hudson. The Union controlled the entire Mississippi River.

(Answers continued in top margin)

---

7. Grant's army broke through Lee's lines at Petersburg. Lee fled but was quickly surrounded and decided to surrender.

Thinking Critically

1. As a result of the Battle of Saratoga, France became a U.S. ally, and Spain entered the war against Britain. Their support helped make victory possible. Antietam was a turning point in the Civil War. It weakened Lee's army and hurt Confederate hopes of European aid.

2. Answers may include that he wanted to reunite the nation as quickly and as peacefully as possible. Students' opinions on terms will vary.

3. Lincoln was referring to abolishing slavery. The Emancipation Proclamation was the first step.

Chapter Survey

Reviewing Vocabulary

Define the following terms.

1. habeas corpus
2. martial law
3. casualties
4. draft
5. income tax
6. total war

Reviewing Main Ideas

1. When the Civil War began, which side had the advantage in the following areas? (a) farmland (b) factories (c) military leadership (d) population (e) transportation

2. How did President Davis plan to win the war? How did President Lincoln?

3. By the end of 1862, how successful had Lincoln been in achieving his war goal? Give supporting examples.

4. (a) What were the provisions of the Emancipation Proclamation? (b) How did the proclamation affect the war?

5. What were two problems faced at home by President Lincoln? By President Davis?

6. Describe two events that took place in the first week of July 1863 that changed the course of the war.

7. What led Lee to surrender his Army of Northern Virginia in April 1865?

Thinking Critically

1. Analysis The Battle of Saratoga was a turning point in the American War of Independence. The Battle of Antietam was a turning point in the Civil War. Compare the results of the two battles.

2. Synthesis Why do you think Grant's terms of surrender at Appomattox were so generous? If you had been in his place, what terms would you have offered? Why?

3. Why We Remember: Analysis In the Gettysburg Address, President Lincoln vowed that "this nation, under God, shall have a new birth of freedom." What do you think he meant?

Applying Skills

Making a hypothesis When Lincoln issued the Emancipation Proclamation, he was using a power of the presidency. A presidential proclamation—also called an executive order—does not require any action by Congress.

Look in newspapers and magazines to find a recent example of an executive order. Then use what you learned on page 510 to do the following:

1. Create three hypotheses to explain why the President issued the executive order.

2. Test each hypothesis against the information available to you.

3. List your hypotheses and tell which of them best explains the President's action. If you cannot choose one, explain why not. What might you do next?

History Mystery

An army recruit Answer the History Mystery on page 489. Where might you find information about Lyons Wakeman's experiences? Where would you look for evidence that Wakeman was, in fact, a soldier?

Writing in Your History Journal

1. Keys to History (a) The time line on pages 488–489 has seven Keys to History. In your journal, list each key and describe why it is important to know about. (b) Imagine that you are a reporter or "special artist" covering the Civil War. If you could cover only one event on the time line, which one would you choose? In your journal, explain the reasons for your decision.

2. Clara Barton During the Civil War, thousands of women felt the same urge to help as Clara Barton had. Imagine that

Applying Skills

Answers should show a knowledge of the definition of *hypothesis* and an understanding of the steps involved in hypothesizing. Those steps can be found in the Procedure and Skill Tips sections on page 510.

History Mystery

Information is found on page 496. Students should note the National Archives as a source of information on Lyons Wakeman.

Writing in Your History Journal

1. (a) Explanations should be similar to the time line notes on teacher pages 488–489.
(b) Choices should be supported by reasons that tell why the event is important or particularly interesting.
(Answers continued in side margin)

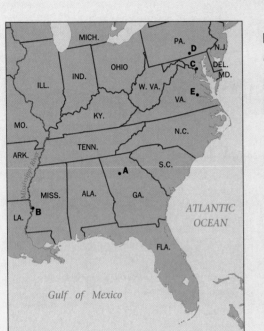

Reviewing Geography

↑ **1.** For each letter on the map, write the name of a town or city that was important during the Civil War.

2. Geographic Thinking One of the major Union strategies was to capture Richmond, which was only 100 miles (160 km) from Washington, D.C. As a result, many battles took place on Virginia soil.

   The Confederate capital was originally at Montgomery, Alabama (see the map on pages R6–R7). Imagine that Montgomery had remained the Confederate capital. How do you think Union strategy might have changed? How might it have remained the same?

you are living then. Choose a role for yourself—man or woman, old or young. Describe what you would like to do to help in the war effort.

3. Citizenship Today, the growth of cities is threatening the sites of many famous Civil War battlefields, including Gettysburg and Petersburg. Imagine that you own property on the site of Gettysburg. A developer has offered to buy your land and plans to build a factory. In your journal, write your thoughts about the offer.

Alternative Assessment

Writing a play Divided loyalties, especially in the Border States, led brothers, cousins, and fathers and sons to fight on different sides in the Civil War. With several classmates, write a one-act play about the reunion of a divided family after the war.

❶ Decide who the family members are, where they live, what they did before the war, and what role they played on which side in the war.

❷ As part of the play, have each person describe an event in which he or she took part. It might be a battle, an aspect of the war effort at home, or Lee's surrender. Use the information in the text and do additional research as needed to provide background.

❸ When your play is complete, present it to the class.

   Your work will be evaluated on the following criteria:
• you describe historical events and attitudes accurately
• you include both Union and Confederate views in the dialogue
• you present the characters and action in believable ways

2. Answers might include being a soldier, a nurse, or a factory worker; setting up hospitals; and helping escaped slaves.

3. Accept reasonable answers. If students feel the government should take the responsibility for protecting Civil War battlefields, encourage them to think about how to raise the necessary funds. They might mention the desire to preserve the environment or to promote racial or cultural pride as possible reasons.

Reviewing Geography

1. (A) Atlanta, (B) Vicksburg, (C) Washington, D.C., (D) Gettysburg, (E) Appomattox Court House

2. Students should consider Montgomery's location and the need to divide forces to fight in different arenas. The Union might attack Alabama from the Gulf of Mexico or move forces down the Mississippi and across the state of Mississippi. The strategy of having a blockade and controlling the Mississippi would remain the same. Fighting in Virginia would also continue.

Alternative Assessment

Teacher's Take-Home Planner 6, page 13, includes suggestions and scoring rubrics for the Alternative Assessment activity.

Remind students of the First Battle of Bull Run, to which onlookers from Washington traveled to observe the first battle of the Civil War. Point out that the civilians had no idea how serious the battle would be or how long the war would last. Encourage students to look for contrasts between the onlookers' expectations and what happens in reality as they read. Have them look for details that express this contrast, such as the contrast of the linen tablecloths and the eventual carnage of the battle.

✳ Literature Footnote

Paul Fleischman's novel is told by 16 different characters. All the characters are fictional, except one: Union General Irvin McDowell. However, the novel realistically presents officers' points of view. Confederate Colonel Oliver Brattle contemplates "what shells do to living flesh" as those around him look with excitement toward the battle. General McDowell reveals nervousness about commanding an army of 30,000. The soldiers reveal how pride and excitement turn to horror after they see the devastation of their first battle. With a wide array of characters, including an 11-year-old boy who wants to play the fife in the Confederate army and a young Minnesota girl who watches her brother go off to battle, the novel is suited to readers' theater performances.

∞ **Link to Literature**

Bull Run by Paul Fleischman

Bull Run, the first battle of the Civil War, took place 26 miles (42 km) outside of Washington, D.C. In his novel, *Bull Run,* author Paul Fleischman creates "eyewitnesses" who tell a vivid story of the battle—a doctor, an enslaved woman, a photographer, two soldiers, and Edmund Upwing, an African American carriage driver. In the following passage, Upwing tells of driving two congressmen and their wives to watch the Union army crush the Rebels. Like the scores of other picnickers who come to watch the "fun," Upwing's passengers experience the shock of their lives.

Morning

nags:
worn-out horses

daft:
foolish

'Twas dark as Hell's cellar when we left for Washington. I'd thought they would sleep, but they chattered like sparrows. I caught a good deal of it, as usual. Cabmen dull witted as their nags? Don't be daft! They know more of Washington than the President. Though whenever a question is put to me, I ignore it until it's asked a fourth time, that my passengers mightn't suspect I have ears.

There were plenty of other spectators heading south. The shooting commenced as we neared Centreville. We passed through the village and found a fine grassy spot on a hill overlooking Bull Run. Every last horse and buggy for hire in Washington seemed to be there. Linen tablecloths were spread out and people of quality spread out upon 'em. My passengers were in a merry mood—all but one of the men who let out that McDowell had been given command for no better reason than that he'd come from Ohio, whose governor had Lincoln's ear and had whispered "McDowell" in it constantly. 'Tis a fact. I feigned deafness, but took the precaution of noting our fastest route of retreat.

feigned:
pretended

Afternoon

teamsters:
wagon drivers who hauled goods

The shout went 'round, "The Rebels are upon us!" The words struck the picnickers like a storm, sent them shrieking into their coaches, and sent every coach bolting toward the road. My riders commanded that I put on all speed. Every driver heard the same demand. The road was narrow and choked with coaches. This mass of wheels and whips blocked the soldiers, who seemed even more eager than we to be gone. They were furious with us. How their teamsters swore! Those on foot rushed around us like an April torrent. They were bloody, dusty, and wild-eyed as wolves. "The Black Horse Cavalry is coming!" one bellowed. The air rang with rumors of hidden batteries, heartless horsemen, rivers

***
Literature Footnote

Historical fiction such as Paul Fleischman's *Bull Run* portrays the facts about a historical event, adding fictional characters and details that remain true to the event's character. He realistically portrays the doubts soldiers had before entering into battle. *Bull Run* won the 1994 Scott O'Dell Award for Historical Fiction.

This sketch of the chaos as Union forces fled Bull Run appeared in a British newspaper, the *Illustrated London News*. Illustrated newspapers sent out "special artists" to cover events of the war.

red with blood, and visions worthy of the Book of Revelation. One frantic soldier cut a horse free from a wagon's team and took off bareback. Another fugitive tried to unseat me. I drove him off with my whip. 'Tis a fact. Then there came a terrific boom. Women screamed. A Rebel shell had fallen on the road. The caravan halted. The way was blocked by a tangle of overturned wagons. The soldiers scattered or froze in fear. Men fled their buggies. A second shell struck. Then a young officer galloped up, leaped down, and dragged the vehicles away. His courage was acclaimed. We jerked forward afresh. My sharp ear learned that the man's name was Custer. All predicted that he was destined for great deeds.

Book of Revelation: the last book of the Bible, which tells about the end of the world

Night

Rain came on during the night. It soaked the men, turned the roads to muck, and added more misery to the retreat. It was past midnight when we reached Washington. . . . How my passengers railed against the soldiers! And their know-nothing officers, and the profiteers, and the press, and the generals, and the President. I learned later that week that Jeff Davis and Beauregard were pulled to pieces the same way for not pressing on toward Washington. A few days after the battle, Lincoln sent McDowell packing. This raised spirits some, but not everyone's. I heard that Horace Greeley himself, the most powerful editor in the land—who'd first told Lincoln to let the South secede, then insisted that Richmond be taken—now had sent Lincoln a letter stating that the Rebels couldn't be beaten! The winds blew fickle about the President, but he had his feet on the ground. I'm proud to say he ignored the letter.

fickle: changeable in loyalty

A Closer Look

1. How does the author's portrayal of Upwing and his passengers help paint a picture of the scene?

2. Do you think Upwing shares his passengers' expectation that the Union will win quickly? Explain.

3. How does Upwing view public opinion about the war?

• **521**

Discussion

Stimulating Critical Thinking

1. If you had been a soldier at the battle, how do you think you would have felt? (Frightened and confused because it was the first battle; annoyed or angry because civilians were making soldiers' jobs more hazardous.)

2. How do you think the event described in the selection shows what the next four years will be like? (The chaos and destruction foreshadow the shocking devastation of the entire war.)

A Closer Look
Answers

1. Upwing is a sensible narrator who gives an accurate picture of the scene. The description shows the public's attitudes toward the war and explains why the battle was so chaotic: they are foolish and do not view the event seriously.

2. Upwing seems to have a clearer understanding of the seriousness of the event as a whole, and he supports Lincoln in standing firm in his fight against the Confederates.

3. Upwing seems to recognize that everyone has opinions about the war based on personal interests and that few people understand the real issues. He seems to discount public opinion.

19 Reconstruction
1865–1905

Chapter Planning Guide

Section	Student Text	Teacher's Edition Activities
Opener and Story pp. 522–525	**Keys to History Time Line** **History Mystery** Beginning the Story with **Susie King Taylor**	**Setting the Stage Activity** Freedom Strategies, p. 524
1 **Rebuilding the Union** pp. 526–531	**Link to the Present** Juneteenth, p. 529	**Warm-Up Activity** Postwar Hopes, p. 526 **Geography Question of the Day,** p. 526 **Section Activity** Deciding as Freedmen, p. 528 **Bonus Activity** Anti-Johnson Protest Signs, p. 530 **Wrap-Up Activity** Comparing Reconstruction Plans, p. 531
2 **The South Under Reconstruction** pp. 532–537	**Hands-On History** Getting out the vote, p. 533 **Skill Lab** Making Decisions, p. 537	**Warm-Up Activity** Factors Affecting Elections, p. 532 **Geography Question of the Day,** p. 532 **Section Activity** Planning a Political Cartoon, p. 534 **Bonus Activity** Reconstruction Headlines, p. 535 **Wrap-Up Activity** Time to End Reconstruction?, p. 536
3 **The Legacy of Reconstruction** pp. 538–545	**Reading Maps** African Americans in Congress 1876, 1896, p. 540 **Link to Art** *Aspects of Negro Life: From Slavery Through Reconstruction,* p. 541 **Point of View** Were Jim Crow laws to be taken seriously?, p. 541 **World Link** Europeans divide up Africa, p. 542 **Geography Lab** The Civil War and Southern Agriculture, p. 545	**Warm-Up Activity** Postwar Problems, p. 538 **Geography Question of the Day,** p. 538 **Section Activity** A Postwar Collage, p. 540 **Bonus Activity** A Letter to a Former Master, p. 543 **Wrap-Up Activity** Steps Forward and Backward, p. 544
Evaluation	☑ **Section 1 Review,** p. 531 ☑ **Section 2 Review,** p. 536 ☑ **Section 3 Review,** p. 544 ☑ **Chapter Survey,** pp. 546–547 **Alternative Assessment** Improving on Reconstruction, p. 547	☑ **Answers to Section 1 Review,** p. 531 ☑ **Answers to Section 2 Review,** p. 536 ☑ **Answers to Section 3 Review,** p. 544 ☑ **Answers to Chapter Survey,** pp. 546–547 (Alternative Assessment guidelines are in the Take-Home Planner.)

Teacher's Resource Package

Chapter Summaries: English and Spanish, pp. 42–43

Chapter Resources Binder
    Study Guide Reading for Details, p. 145
    Reinforcement Making a Graphic Organizer, pp. 149–150
American Readings "O Captain! My Captain!," p. 73
Using Historical Documents Amnesty Oath of Robert E. Lee, pp. 104–107

Chapter Resources Binder
    Study Guide Identifying Main Ideas, p. 146
    Skills Development Making Decisions, pp. 151–152
American Readings The War-Torn South, pp. 74–75

Chapter Resources Binder
    Study Guide Using Visual Images to Preview, p. 147
Geography Extensions Rich States and Poor States 1860 vs. 1880, pp. 37–38
American Readings A Letter to a Former Master, p. 76

Chapter and Unit Tests Chapter 19 Tests, Forms A and B, pp. 119–122

Take-Home Planner

Introducing the Chapter Activity Understanding Freedom, p. 20

Chapter In-Depth Activity Writing Historical Fiction, p. 20

Reduced Views
    Study Guide, p. 22
    Reinforcement, p. 23
    American Readings, p. 24
    Using Historical Documents, p. 25
Unit 6 Answers, pp. 28–34

Reduced Views
    Study Guide, p. 22
    Skills Development, p. 23
    American Readings, p. 24
Unit 6 Answers, pp. 28–34

Reduced Views
    Study Guide, p. 22
    Geography Extensions, p. 25
    American Readings, p. 24
Unit 6 Answers, pp. 28–34

Reduced Views
    Chapter Tests, p. 25
Unit 6 Answers, pp. 28–34
Alternative Assessment Guidelines for scoring the Chapter Survey activity, p. 21

Additional Resources

Wall Time Line

Unit 6 Activity

Transparency Package

Transparency 19-1 Aaron Douglas's mural *Aspects of Negro Life: From Slavery through Reconstruction*—use with Section 3
Transparency 19-2 Building African American Communities—use with Section 3
Transparency Activity Book

SelecTest Testing Software
Chapter 19 Test, Forms A and B

Vital Links

🔘 **Videodisc**

◎ **CD-ROM**

Freedman's shop (see TE p. 528)
Freedmen's Bureau (see TE p. 530)
Hiram Revels (see TE p. 534)
Farm family (see TE p. 539)
Segregated jury (see TE p. 542)
Howard University (see TE p. 543)

Unit 6 Videotape Clara Barton: Eyewitness to the Civil War

Teaching Resources

Take-Home Planner 6
  Introducing Chapter Activity
  Chapter In-Depth Activity
  Alternative Assessment
Chapter Resources Binder
Geography Extensions
American Readings
Using Historical Documents
Transparency Activities
Wall Time Line Activities
Chapter Summaries
Chapter and Unit Tests
SelecTest Test File
Vital Links CD-ROM/Videodisc

Time Line

Keys to History

Keys to History journal writing activities are on page 546 in the Chapter Survey.

Lincoln's assassination Lincoln's death meant that Reconstruction would take place without his experience and wisdom. (p. 526)

Johnson's impeachment The conflict between President Johnson and Congress over Reconstruction led to the only impeachment of a President in U.S. history. (p. 531)

14th Amendment The 14th Amendment was ratified in an effort to ensure that African Americans would have equal rights. (p. 530)

Looking Back With the secession of the southern states and the firing on Fort Sumter, the Civil War began.

522

Chapter Objectives

★ Explain the views of Reconstruction held by the President and Congress.
★ Describe what Radical Reconstruction was and how it ended.
★ Identify how the return of power to southern Democrats affected black southerners.

Chapter Overview

After Lincoln's death the task of Reconstruction fell to Andrew Johnson. Republicans in Congress objected that his plan did not give blacks voting rights and allowed white Democrats to control southern states, passing restrictive black codes. After gaining control of Congress in 1866, Republicans passed their own plan: to rejoin the Union, southern states would have to allow black men to

1865–1905

Chapter 19

Reconstruction

Sections

Beginning the Story with Susie King Taylor
1. **Rebuilding the Union**
2. **The South Under Reconstruction**
3. **The Legacy of Reconstruction**

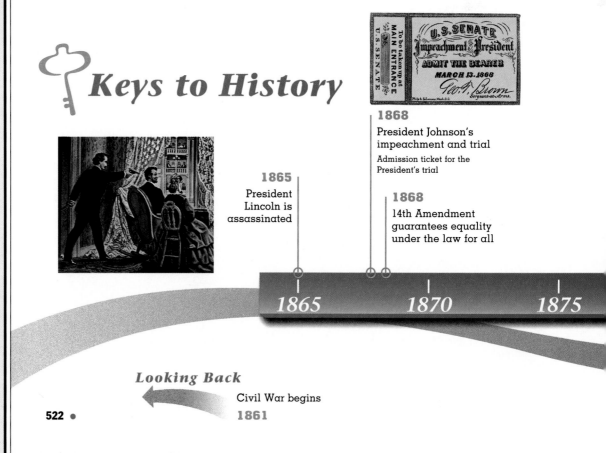

Keys to History

1868
President Johnson's impeachment and trial
Admission ticket for the President's trial

1865
President Lincoln is assassinated

1868
14th Amendment guarantees equality under the law for all

1865   *1870*   *1875*

Looking Back
Civil War begins
1861

522 ●

vote, elect new governments, and ratify the Fourteenth Amendment.

Under Radical Reconstruction, many black voters were registered, the Fourteenth and Fifteenth Amendments were ratified, and efforts were made to improve roads and schools. However, Ku Klux Klan terrorism and opposition to increased taxes helped white Democrats regain control of most southern states by 1876. Reconstruction ended in 1877.

Despite the goal of an industrialized "New South," most southerners remained poor farmers. Meanwhile, state governments reversed effects of Reconstruction by passing Jim Crow segregation laws and poll taxes to undermine the Fourteenth and Fifteenth Amendments. Some blacks migrated north, but most remained. Some hoped equality would come through education, while others stressed protesting discrimination.

HISTORY *Mystery*

More than 130,000 African Americans could vote in Louisiana in 1896. Four years later Louisiana had only 5,000 African American voters. What happened to all the other voters?

1877
Reconstruction ends
Federal troops leave the South

1880s
Jim Crow laws
An African American being evicted from a train car

1896
Plessy v. Ferguson

1905
W. E. B. Du Bois helps launch the Niagara Movement

1880 1895 1900 1905

World Link
European powers divide up Africa
1884–1885

Looking Ahead
World War I begins
1914

● 523

Teaching the HISTORY *Mystery*

Students will find the answer on pp. 539–540. See Chapter Survey, p. 546, for an additional question.

Time Line

Reconstruction ends
Following Hayes's election, Reconstruction ended and southern whites elected conservative Democratic governments. (p. 536)

Jim Crow laws These segregation laws were passed by white-controlled southern state governments as part of their effort to undo effects of Reconstruction. (p. 540)

Plessy* v. *Ferguson This landmark Supreme Court decision, with its "separate but equal" standard, made segregation legal for more than half a century, until the Court reversed it in 1954. (p. 542)

Launch of Niagara Movement African Americans responded to discrimination by forming several self-help and activist organizations, including the Niagara Movement, which led to the founding of the National Association for the Advancement of Colored People (NAACP). (p. 543)

World Link See p. 542.

Looking Ahead The reintegration of the South was shown when the entire nation faced the external threat of World War I as a united country.

Beginning the Story

Susie King Taylor

Born into slavery in Georgia, Susie King Taylor was a teenager when the Civil War began. Her experiences during and after the war were like those of many other African Americans in the South. She represents the hope with which former slaves greeted the end of the war and their new status as freedmen. Her life also reflects the subsequent struggle to try to make that hope a reality in the face of resistance from many white southerners.

Setting the Stage
Activity

Freedom Strategies

To focus on challenges of moving from slavery to freedom, divide the class into small groups and ask them to imagine that they are freed slaves at the end of the Civil War. Have each group write a strategy for the best way to survive and improve their situations. Conclude by discussing the proposed strategies and how practical they are.

See the Introducing the Chapter Activity, Understanding Freedom. **Take-**
Home Planner 6, p. 20.

Whitelaw Reid, a reporter who traveled throughout the South after the war, visited freedmen settlements on the Sea Islands. Though whites had told him that "the poor, shiftless creatures will never be able to support themselves," what he saw proved otherwise. By 1865 the Sea Island farmers had built a bank, churches, and schools. Teachers there told Reid that they saw no difference "in the facility with which these students and ordinary white children . . . learn to read." Reid left certain that "the question about [former] slaves being self-supporting is a question no longer."

Beginning the Story with

Susie King Taylor

Susie King Taylor wrote about her fellow African Americans during the Civil War, "Oh, how those people prayed for freedom!" Indeed, for the 4 million enslaved people in the United States, the meaning of the war was bound up in that one precious word—freedom. It was dangerous, though, to speak that word aloud. Susie, who was 13 years old and living in Savannah, Georgia, when the war began, remembered when her grandmother went to a church meeting one night. The people gathered at this meeting fervently sang an old hymn that spoke of their longing for freedom. "Yes," they said, "we shall all be free when the Lord shall appear."

At that moment the police burst in and arrested the churchgoers, accusing them of plotting to escape from slavery. The police claimed that when the slaves sang about being free "when the Lord shall appear," they really meant that they would be set free when the Yankees appeared. Although it was the last such meeting that Susie's grandmother attended, she never forgot that night. Susie, too, did not forget her grandmother's story. From that time forward she dreamed of meeting the Yankees herself.

Freedom on the Sea Islands

Susie's chance came in 1862 when Union ships bombarded Fort Pulaski at the entrance to Savannah's harbor. After Union troops captured the fort, General David Hunter promised freedom to all slaves in the area who could escape and reach the Union-controlled Sea Islands off the Georgia coast. Susie later wrote:

❝Two days after the taking of Fort Pulaski, my uncle took his family of seven and myself to St. Catherine Island. We landed under the protection of the Union fleet, and remained there two weeks. . . . At last, to my unbounded joy, I saw the 'Yankee.'❞

History Bookshelf

Gaines, Ernest J., *The Autobiography of Miss Jane Pittman*. Dial Press, 1971. Gaines's novel explores the experiences of Miss Pittman's life from Reconstruction to the civil rights movement of the 1960s. The novel helps put the Reconstruction era into perspective for students.

Also of interest:

Foner, Eric and Olivia Mahoney, *America's Reconstruction: People and Politics After the Civil War*. HarperCollins, 1995.

Hurmence, Belinda, *Tancy*. Clarion, 1984.

Mettger, Zak, *Reconstruction: America After the Civil War*. Lodestar, 1994.

Myers, Walter Dean, *The Glory Field*. Scholastic, 1994.

On the Sea Islands, Susie met an escaped slave named Edward King. They fell in love and were soon married. Edward King enlisted with other former slaves to form the Union army's first African American regiment, the 33rd U.S. Colored Troops. Susie King joined her new husband, serving as a nurse and laundress in the regiment. Having learned how to read and write as a child, Susie was also in great demand as a teacher. She later wrote of her war years:

African Americans, freed from slavery, are shown here in front of their log cabin after the Civil War. Susie King Taylor lived in a similar home along the coast of Georgia.

❝I taught a great many of the comrades in Company E to read and write, when they were off duty. Nearly all were anxious to learn. . . . I gave my services willingly . . . without receiving a dollar.❞

"Every prospect before you is full of hope"

After the war ended, Commander C. T. Trowbridge disbanded the African American regiment to which Susie's husband belonged. In the commander's final message to the troops, he asked them

❝to harbor no feelings of hatred toward your former masters. . . . The church, the school-house, and the right forever to be free are now secured to you, and every prospect [chance for success] before you is full of hope and encouragement. The nation guarantees you full protection and justice.❞

Susie and Edward King returned to Savannah full of hope. "A new life was before us now," Susie wrote, "all the old life left behind." Still, they could not help but wonder what that new life would hold. Most of all, they wondered how white southerners would now treat their former slaves.

For decades, most white southerners claimed that blacks were an inferior people. With slavery swept away, would whites change their often racist views? Or would the end of slavery be just the first stage of a long struggle for equality?

Hands-On ·····➤ HISTORY

Activity

In the story above, you have read several quotes from Susie King Taylor's own detailed account of her life. Imagine that you are Susie and that you want to write three more entries in your diary. Choose three events in Susie's life from the story you just read and from the chapter to follow. Write what Susie might have felt and thought at these three different moments in her life.

See the Chapter In-Depth Activity, Writing Historical Fiction. **Take-Home Planner 6**, p. 20.

Discussion

Thinking Historically

1. Why was learning to read and write so important to African Americans? (It was the main tool for bettering themselves economically and being independent of former masters.)

2. If you were in Trowbridge's regiment, what might you have thought upon hearing "the nation guarantees you full protection and justice"? (There might be a strong desire to believe this promise, but knowledge that racism was deeply rooted might temper that hope.)

Teaching the Hands-On

➤ HISTORY

Point out that some events suggested are the church meeting, going off to war with her husband, and hearing of Trowbridge's statement. Later events include running a school (p. 528), the effect of black codes on her husband (p. 529), becoming a household servant (p. 538), and moving to Boston (p. 543).

For a journal writing activity on Susie King Taylor, see student page 546.

Introducing the Section

Vocabulary

freedmen (p. 526) former slaves

Reconstruction (p. 529) bringing Confederate states back into the Union

black codes (p. 529) laws that set limits on the rights and opportunities of African Americans

impeach (p. 531) to accuse of wrongdoing and bring to trial

Warm-Up Activity

Postwar Hopes

To focus on hopes following the Civil War, have students imagine that they are either a former Union soldier, a Confederate soldier, or a slave. Ask them to each write a short paragraph identifying who they are and what their expectations are for the future.

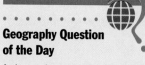

Geography Question of the Day

Ask students to identify the 11 states that had made up the Confederacy. Have them note which state was geographically different in 1865 than it had been in 1861 and explain why. (Virginia; West Virginia had seceded from eastern Virginia in 1861.)

Section Objectives

★ Identify the challenges white and black southerners faced after the Civil War.

★ Describe how President Johnson's plan for Reconstruction affected southerners.

★ Explain why Congress and Johnson fought for control of Reconstruction policy.

Teaching Resources

Take-Home Planner 6, pp. 18–25

Chapter Resources Binder

  Study Guide, p. 145

  Reinforcement, pp. 149–150

  Skills Development

Geography Extensions

American Readings, p. 73

Using Historical Documents, pp. 104–107

Transparency Activities

Chapter and Unit Tests

---

1. Rebuilding the Union

Reading Guide

New Terms freedmen, Reconstruction, black codes, impeach

Section Focus The President and Congress differ over the reconstruction of the South

1. What challenges did white and black southerners face after the Civil War?
2. What effect did President Johnson's Reconstruction plan have on southerners?
3. Why did Congress fight Johnson for control of Reconstruction policy?

Susie and Edward King were not the only people thinking about the future as the war ended. The entire nation longed for peace. But what kind of peace? A peace that would punish the South for starting the war, or one that would help rebuild the southern states? In his second inaugural address in 1865, President Lincoln spoke of a healing peace:

❝With malice [ill will] toward none, with charity for all, with firmness in the right as God gives us to see the right, let us . . . bind up the nation's wounds . . . [and] do all which may achieve and cherish a just and lasting peace.❞

Lincoln Is Assassinated

The country would never know how Lincoln might have achieved such a "just and lasting peace." On April 14, 1865, only days after the war ended, the President was shot while watching a play at Ford's Theater in Washington, D.C. When Lincoln died the following morning, Andrew Johnson was sworn in as the new President.

Lincoln had been assassinated by John Wilkes Booth, an actor and southerner who sought revenge against Lincoln and the North. Soldiers tracked Booth to a barn in Virginia where he was fatally shot.

The North reacted with sorrow to Lincoln's death. Never before had so many people "shed tears for the death of one they had never seen," wrote poet James Russell Lowell. However, sorrow soon turned to rage. Northerners blamed the South both for the war and for Lincoln's death. From across the North came the cry: "The South must be punished!"

The Defeated South

Northerners did not realize how much the South had already suffered. In addition to the staggering loss of human life, the southern economy had been destroyed. Wherever armies had marched, they had left behind smoking cities, ruined farms, and deserted plantations.

Confederate money was now worthless. Planters, without slaves, did not know how to go on. "There is nothing else I know anything about," said one, "except managing a plantation." With their society shattered, many white southerners found it hard to see a future for themselves.

The Freedmen

Black southerners, on the other hand, were overjoyed by the arrival of peace. For these former slaves, now called **freedmen**

History Footnote

John Wilkes Booth had been plotting the President's murder for about a month—since attending Lincoln's second inauguration. Booth, a southern sympathizer and white supremacist, was convinced that Lincoln was trying to make himself dictator. Booth did not appear in the English comedy *Our American Cousin* that the Lincolns went to see, but friends told him Lincoln would attend the performance. After shooting Lincoln, Booth leaped to the stage, breaking his leg in the fall. Lincoln, shot in the head, never regained consciousness. He was taken across the street to a boarding house, where he died at 7:00 A.M. the next day. Booth was on the run for ten days before being trapped in a Virginia barn and shot by a soldier.

(a term that applied to both women and men), peace meant freedom.

The Emancipation Proclamation had abolished slavery in the Confederate states. In 1865 the Thirteenth Amendment freed slaves everywhere in the nation. Until the last day of their lives, freedmen would remember that precious moment when the "freedom sun shone out." Houston Holloway recalled that when he was freed:

❝I felt like a bird out of a cage. Amen. Amen. Amen. I could hardly ask to feel any better than I did that day.❞

The dilemma of freedom Freedom appeared to open up a new world for former slaves. In the past, a husband and wife could be sold to different owners, never to see each other again. Freedom now meant that marriage could last "until death do us part."

It also meant that African Americans could be paid for their work and could choose how to spend their money.

Freedmen now had the freedom to move, but to where? Some took to the road in a painful search for family members sold away during slavery. Others moved to towns and cities. Susie and Edward King went to Savannah after the war. There they joined a community of freedmen struggling to build new lives.

Wherever they lived, though, most freedmen faced huge problems. Few knew much about the world beyond the plantation. Frederick Douglass described the freedman's desperate situation:

❝He had neither money, property, nor friends. . . . He was turned loose, naked, hungry, and destitute [poor] to the open sky.❞

After the Civil War, the streets and buildings of Richmond, Virginia, lay in ruins. Many southern cities suffered similar destruction.

Developing the Section

Discussion

Checking Understanding

1. **What were the rights that freedom brought to the former slaves?** (To live where they wanted, to stay with spouses and families, to be paid for work.)

2. **What was the most important problem that they faced?** (Without money or land, newly freed slaves were responsible for their own economic survival and well-being.)

Stimulating Critical Thinking

3. **Based on the excerpt on p. 526 from Lincoln's second inaugural address, do you think he would have required equal rights for African Americans? Why or why not?** (Yes: his reference to "firmness in the right" and a "just and lasting peace" indicate he would insist on equal rights. No: the tone of his speech indicates he did not want to punish former Confederates. Giving equality and political power to African Americans would be seen by former Confederates as a punishment.)

See **American Readings,** p. 73, for Walt Whitman's "O Captain! My Captain!"

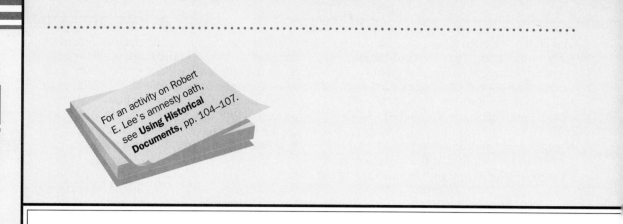
For an activity on Robert E. Lee's amnesty oath, see **Using Historical Documents**, pp. 104–107.

Section
Activity

Deciding as Freedmen

To help students understand the situation facing freedmen, have them imagine being former slaves discussing whether to stay in the South or move to the North. Divide the class into groups, with each group listing pros and cons of staying or leaving. They should consider factors such as family and community life, work opportunities, housing, and climate. Conclude by discussing the pros and cons as a class.

★ ★ ★
Vital Links

Freedman's shop (Picture) Unit 3, Side 1, Search 39043

See also Unit 3 Explore CD-ROM location 223.

See the Study Guide activity in **Chapter Resources Binder**, p. 145.

It did not take long for the 4 million freedmen to realize that their freedom was very limited. Most were unable to read or write, and had no land or money. Some were even driven from the only home they knew. One angry planter told his former slaves as he pushed them off his land, "The Yankee freed you. Now let the Yankee feed you."

The Freedmen's Bureau

Shortly before the war ended, Congress established the Freedmen's Bureau. This government agency was to give food and medical care to both blacks and whites in the South. Above all else, however, newly freed slaves wanted land and an education. The Bureau tried to provide both.

Schools and land The Freedmen's Bureau worked with educated former slaves and northern churches and charities to open up more than 4,300 schools in the South. Susie King, for example, ran a school for black children in Savannah. The educator and author Booker T. Washington later described the hunger for learning as "a whole race trying to go to school."

Freedmen were also desperate to get land of their own to farm. Congressman Thaddeus Stevens proposed breaking up the South's plantations and giving every freedman "forty acres and a mule." He argued:

The federal government helped African Americans build thousands of schools like this one in the years following the Civil War. Before the war, it had been illegal to teach slaves how to read.

Andrew Johnson was as much a self-made man as Abraham Lincoln. His family was poor, and he worked as a young man as a tailor. He did not learn to read and write until after he was married, when his wife taught him. He worked his way up in politics, serving in both houses of Congress and as governor of Tennessee. A lifelong Democrat, he was the only U.S. senator from the South to remain loyal to the United States. As a reward, Lincoln named him military governor of the parts of Tennessee occupied by Union forces from 1862. The Republicans chose him to run with Lincoln in 1864 in order to attract Democratic support.

Discussion

Checking Understanding

1. What were the purposes of the Freedmen's Bureau? (To provide food and medical care to both blacks and whites; to give freedmen education and land.)

2. Why did Republicans in Congress criticize President Johnson's Reconstruction plan? (They believed that African Americans should have been given the right to vote.)

Stimulating Critical Thinking

3. Should Congress have taken plantation land from owners and divided it among freedmen? (Yes: would help make up for slavery; best way to help ensure that freedmen could make a living. No: would violate constitutional protection of property; would anger owners, resulting in more resistance to Reconstruction.)

Teaching the
∞ Link to the Present

Point out that Juneteenth is celebrated by African Americans throughout the state of Texas. In 1980, June 19 became an official state holiday. Interest in it has grown in the last 20 years. Juneteenth is the most well-known of freedom celebrations, but African Americans in other states and localities celebrate emancipation on different dates. Students might find out if your state or locality has such a celebration.

❝We have turned . . . loose 4 million slaves without a . . . cent in their pockets. . . . This Congress is bound to provide for them until they can take care of themselves.❞

Congress, however, refused to take plantations from their owners. Doing so, most congressmen believed, would violate the Constitution's protection of property. As a result, few black southerners were able to obtain land.

Johnson's Plan for the South

After Lincoln's assassination, the task of **Reconstruction**—bringing Confederate states back into the Union—fell to President Johnson. A former Democrat from Tennessee, he favored an easy and smooth return to the Union for the southern states.

In May 1865 Johnson announced his Reconstruction plan. Each southern state could rejoin the Union once it had:

- written a new state constitution
- elected a new government
- repealed its act of secession
- canceled its war debts
- ratified the Thirteenth Amendment, which outlawed slavery in the United States (see page 527)

Republicans in Congress asked the new President to add one more requirement to his list. They wanted freedmen to be guaranteed the right to vote. Johnson ignored their request. "White men alone," he said, "must manage the South."

The First Effort at Reconstruction

By the fall of 1865, every southern state had rejoined the Union under President Johnson's plan. Not surprisingly, leaders of

∞ Link to the Present

Juneteenth On June 19, 1865, the Civil War had been over for more than two months. The Emancipation Proclamation had been law for more than two years. But until Union soldiers landed in Galveston on that day, slaves in Texas had no idea they were free. Their owners had not told them.

Juneteenth is the name given to the day when the last slaves discovered they were free. From Houston to San Francisco, people now celebrate Juneteenth with parades, concerts, and barbecues. It is a way to look back on the struggle and remember that slavery did not end overnight.

the new state governments were often the same men who had held power in the South before the Civil War.

The black codes Once in office, these leaders did their best to bring back the way of life of the old South. They passed laws called **black codes** that set limits on the rights and opportunities of African Americans. Black codes also helped planters find workers to replace their freed slaves. An African American without a job could be arrested and sent to work for a planter.

In fact, the codes barred African Americans from any jobs but farm work and unskilled labor. As a result, Susie King's husband, Edward, could not continue to work as a carpenter after the war. The only job he could find was unloading boats in Savannah's harbor.

The black codes did give certain rights to freedmen: the right to marry, own property, work for wages, and sue in court. Other

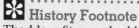

History Footnote

Thaddeus Stevens had long supported equal rights for African Americans, arguing that "there can be no state rights against human rights." Stevens declared, "I am for Negro suffrage in every rebel state. If it be just, it should not be denied; if it be necessary, it should be adopted; if it be punishment to traitors, they deserve it."

basic rights, such as serving on juries and owning weapons, were denied in most southern states. No southern states allowed freedmen the right to vote.

Black codes also barred black children from attending the new public schools in the South. According to a Louisiana lawmaker, it made no sense to use public money to educate "any but the superior race of man—the white race."

Johnson vs. Congress

As 1865 came to a close, President Johnson announced that Reconstruction was over. The former Confederate states were once again part of the Union.

Northerners and black southerners were stunned. What Johnson called Reconstruction, critics said, was "no reconstruction at all." They were outraged that the same southern men who had led the nation into its bloodiest war were now back in power. Worse yet, they feared that the black codes in the South would bring back the horrors of slavery in all but name.

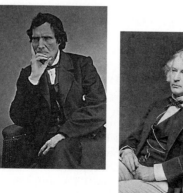

Representative Thaddeus Stevens (left) and Senator Charles Sumner (right) introduced many bills in Congress meant to protect the rights of African Americans.

Radical Republicans A group of Republicans in Congress, called Radicals, demanded that the southern states meet stricter requirements for coming back into the Union. In contrast to Johnson's plan, they insisted on full and equal rights for freedmen—a revolutionary idea in both the North and the South in 1865.

Early in 1866 the Radical Republicans, led by Representative Thaddeus Stevens of Pennsylvania and Senator Charles Sumner of Massachusetts, pushed two bills through Congress. One bill extended the life of the Freedmen's Bureau and gave it power to build more schools. A second bill, the Civil Rights Act, declared that freedmen were full citizens with the same rights as white citizens. Johnson vetoed both bills.

The Radical Republicans fought back. They persuaded Congress to act against the President's wishes. For the first time in the nation's history, a two-thirds majority in Congress voted to override a President's vetoes. Both the Freedmen's Bureau Act and the Civil Rights Act became law.

The Fourteenth Amendment Worried that the Supreme Court might overturn the Civil Rights Act, Republicans put the protections of the act into a Fourteenth Amendment. The proposed amendment gave all people born in the United States, including African Americans, the right to "equal protection of the laws." No state could deprive a citizen of "life, liberty, or property without due process of law."

Johnson opposed the amendment. In 1866 congressional elections were to be held. Johnson took his case to the people by touring northern cities and urging voters to elect Democrats. Wherever he spoke, however, he ended up in shouting matches with hecklers. The tour was a disaster. Republicans won control of both houses of Congress. They, not the President, now controlled Reconstruction.

In 1875 Johnson returned to the capital as a senator from Tennessee. When he entered the Senate chamber, there was at first an embarrassed silence. Then other senators came up to shake his hand. Later, a friend visited him at his hotel and commented that his lodgings were not as spacious as those he had had in the White House. "No," said Johnson, "but they are more comfortable."

This sketch shows an African American election judge and voters in Washington, D.C., in 1867.

Radical Reconstruction

In 1867 the Radical Republicans passed their own Reconstruction Act. State governments in the South were declared illegal. The region, except Tennessee, was divided into five districts under the control of the army.

To rejoin the Union, each state would have to do the following:

- adopt a constitution guaranteeing all male citizens, black and white, the right to vote
- elect a new government
- ratify the Fourteenth Amendment

No white southerners who had served as Confederate soldiers or officials could vote on the new state constitutions.

Radical Republicans had hoped for more. They wanted to divide up plantations into small farms for black and white southerners and build enough schools for every child in the South. However, these ideas were rejected by the full Congress.

To keep Johnson from stopping the new Reconstruction plan, Congress passed two laws to reduce his power. The Command of the Army Act limited the President's power over the army. The Tenure of Office Act barred Johnson from firing certain federal officials, including those who supported Congress instead of him, without Senate approval.

The Impeachment of Johnson

President Johnson believed both laws were unconstitutional. In February 1868 he fired Secretary of War Edwin Stanton. The House promptly voted to **impeach**—to accuse of wrongdoing and bring to trial— the President. It charged him with violating the Tenure of Office Act.

The President's lawyers argued that the Tenure of Office Act was unconstitutional. His only "crime," they said, had been to disagree with Congress. A two-thirds vote by the Senate was needed to remove him from office. Seven Republicans joined the Senate's Democrats in voting "not guilty." The President escaped removal from office by just one vote. He finished his term, but his power was broken.

⭐ 1. Section Review

1. Define **freedmen, Reconstruction, black codes,** and **impeach.**
2. How did the Freedmen's Bureau try to help former slaves start a new life?
3. Why did Congress overturn President Johnson's Reconstruction plan?
4. Critical Thinking As an African American, explain why you might have been disappointed by President Johnson's Reconstruction plan.

Closing the Section

Wrap-Up Activity

Comparing Reconstruction Plans

To review differences between the Reconstruction plans of President Johnson and Congress, have students grade each plan from the perspective of African Americans. Working in pairs, they should create two-column charts listing characteristics of each plan. After placing a plus or minus next to each characteristic, they should assign each plan a letter grade, explaining how they evaluated the characteristics.

Section Review
Answers

1. Definitions: *freedmen* (526), *Reconstruction* (529), *black codes* (529), *impeach* (531)
2. The Freedmen's Bureau provided food and medical care, set up schools, and tried—but failed—to give land to freedmen.
3. Northern Republicans in Congress thought Johnson was too lenient on the former Confederates in allowing them to control state governments and pass black codes.
4. Students might suggest disappointment that they still did not have equal rights, that they could not vote, and that Johnson declared the end of Reconstruction though restrictive black codes were still in effect.

★ Describe the new groups of voters in the South and how Congress protected them.
★ Identify the accomplishments of the Reconstruction governments.
★ Explain how the Democratic Party was able to regain control of the South.

Introducing the Section

Vocabulary

scalawags (p. 532) white southerners considered traitors or scoundrels for joining the Republicans

carpetbaggers (p. 533) northerners who moved south after the war, voting as Republicans and seeking opportunities

corruption (p. 535) using public office for illegal purposes

Warm-Up Activity

Factors Affecting Elections

Ask students to imagine that the class will be voting on the following proposal: Homework will be collected from odd-numbered rows three days a week, but from even rows only two days. Have them identify factors affecting whether it would pass. Then ask them to predict how different groups in the South might try to win elections.

Geography Question of the Day

Write the following claim on the chalkboard: "The states farthest south were the last to reenter the Union." Ask students to write paragraphs explaining whether the claim is valid. They should refer to the chart on p. 534 and map on pp. R6–R7. (Invalid: in both 1868 and 1870 a mixture of states in the middle and deep South were readmitted.)

Teaching Resources

Take-Home Planner 6, pp. 18–25
Chapter Resources Binder
  Study Guide, p. 146
  Reinforcement
  Skills Development, pp. 151–152
Geography Extensions
American Readings, pp. 74–75
Using Historical Documents
Transparency Activities
Chapter and Unit Tests

2. The South Under Reconstruction

Reading Guide

New Terms scalawags, carpetbaggers, corruption

Section Focus Radical Reconstruction in the South and why it ended

1. Who were the new voters in the South and how did Congress protect them?
2. What did the southern Reconstruction governments accomplish?
3. How was the Democratic Party able to regain control of the South?

Radical Republicans had clear goals for Reconstruction in the South. With the slave system now dead, they believed they had a rare opportunity to shape "a more perfect Union." They wanted to build a new society based on the equality of all citizens.

The key to equality, Radical Republicans argued, was the right to vote. African Americans could use the ballot to protect their rights. Therefore, ensuring voting rights was central to the Republicans' bold new Reconstruction plan.

The South's New Voters

Under the Reconstruction Act, the army returned to the South in 1867. Its first job was to register voters. Three groups of men registered to vote: African Americans, white southerners who could swear that they had opposed the war, and northerners now living in the South. The law barred from voting anyone who had fought against, or otherwise been disloyal to, the Union.

Freedmen African Americans made up the largest group of new voters. Most joined the Republicans, whom they saw as their protectors. As with new white voters in Andrew Jackson's time, many blacks had no experience in politics. Yet they knew what they

wanted. An Alabama convention of freedmen declared:

"We claim exactly the same rights . . . as are enjoyed by white men—we ask for nothing more and will be content with nothing less."

"Scalawags" The army also registered a sizable group of white southerners who swore they had not supported the Confederacy. Some were small farmers who lived in the pro-Union hill areas and had never voted before. Others were southern businessmen who lived in the towns.

A large number of the new white voters joined the Republicans, too. They saw the southern Democrats as the party of wealthy planters, while the Republicans were the party of opportunity and equality.

The South's planters were shocked that they had lost control of the political system. To them, white southerners who joined the party of Lincoln and emancipation were traitors to the South. They scorned such people, calling them **"scalawags,"** or scoundrels.

"Carpetbaggers" The last group of new voters were northerners who had moved south after the war. Some were teachers, ministers, or Freedmen's Bureau agents. Others

In the election of 1868, Grant won the electoral vote by a large margin of 214 to 80, but he got only 52.7 percent of the popular vote. The Democrat, Horatio Seymour, took Louisiana and Georgia, but Grant won Tennessee, North Carolina, South Carolina, Florida, Alabama, and Arkansas, thanks to the African American vote. Mississippi, Virginia, and Texas could not vote because they had not been readmitted to the Union. Without the black vote, Grant would have had a minority in the popular vote even though he still would have won the electoral vote.

Developing the Section

Discussion

Checking Understanding

1. How were scalawags and carpetbaggers similar? (Both voted Republican and were scorned by white southern Democrats.) **Different?** (Scalawags were native southerners. Carpetbaggers were northerners who had moved south.)

2. How did Grant win the 1868 election? (The army registered many African Americans, scalawags, and carpetbaggers as Republican voters in the South.)

Stimulating Critical Thinking

3. In what ways do you think criticisms of carpetbaggers might have been fair? In what ways might they have been unfair? (Fair: some businessmen took advantage of poor southerners. Unfair: most teachers, ministers, and Freedmen's Bureau agents were probably not motivated by personal gain.)

Hands-On *HISTORY*

Getting out the vote Did you know that voter turnout in the United States today is much lower than in most democracies? Only about half of all possible voters actually vote. Those who fail to vote may think their votes do not matter. However, voting does matter. For example, African Americans, voting for the first time, helped President Grant win the 1868 election.

➡ **Activity** Create a presentation that will persuade people in your community to vote.

❶ First, choose the best way to convince people in your area to vote. You might make posters and brochures to display at a mall, or produce a commercial for radio or television.

❷ Next, plan your presentation. If you have a registration table, make an attention-getting sign and a brochure explaining why voting counts. If you do a radio or television commercial, write one or make an audio or video tape of one.

❸ Show your sign and brochure to the class. If you have a commercial, act it out or play it on audio or video tape for the class.

Young people work to get out the vote.

Teaching the Hands-On *HISTORY*

Point out that "get out the vote" campaigns often appeal to voters' self-interest. Signs and brochures should focus on how voting can benefit the target audience, perhaps by referring to issues that directly affect their lives.

were businessmen or former Union soldiers looking for new opportunities. Most of them also registered as Republicans.

Yankee-hating southerners called these newcomers **"carpetbaggers,"** after a type of travel handbag. They saw carpetbaggers, often unfairly, as fortune hunters who had come south "to fatten on our misfortunes."

Grant Elected President

The army registered about 635,000 white voters and 735,000 black voters across the South in time for the 1868 election. That year the Republicans nominated Union war hero Ulysses S. Grant. He supported the Republicans' Reconstruction experiment.

The Democrats chose Horatio Seymour, the former governor of New York, as their candidate. Seymour wanted to return power in the South to its traditional leaders—white Democrats.

Grant won the election with the help of an estimated 500,000 African Americans who cast their first votes for the Republican candidate. The Republican Party learned a valuable lesson from the 1868 election—African Americans could contribute heavily to its election victories.

The Fifteenth Amendment Shortly after Grant's election, Congress passed the Fifteenth Amendment guaranteeing former slaves the right to vote. It states that a citizen's right to vote "shall not be denied . . . on account of race, color, or previous condition of servitude." At the time, the right of women to vote was not advanced.

Radical Republicans supported the amendment for two reasons. First, they wanted to make sure that African Americans would retain their right to vote even if the Democrats someday regained power in the South.

Second, many northern states at the time still barred African Americans from voting.

Reconstruction Begins and Ends

State	Readmitted to the Union	Reconstruction government falls
Tennessee	1866	1869
Alabama	1868	1874
Arkansas	1868	1874
Florida	1868	1877
Louisiana	1868	1877
North Carolina	1868	1870
South Carolina	1868	1877
Georgia	1870	1871
Mississippi	1870	1875
Texas	1870	1873
Virginia	1870	1870

Radical Republicans wanted voting rights granted to all men throughout the country. "We will have no peace," wrote one, "until this right is made national."

The Reconstruction Governments

Meanwhile, southern Reconstruction was under way. The first task was to rebuild state governments. Delegates were elected to constitutional conventions in each state. Many were African Americans—mostly educated men such as preachers and teachers.

New constitutions The conventions wrote the most forward-looking state constitutions in the nation. These constitutions outlawed racial discrimination and guaranteed the right to vote to every adult male, regardless of race. They also called for public schools that would be, according to Georgia's constitution, "forever free to all the children of the state."

With the new constitutions ratified, elections were held to fill state offices. To no one's surprise, but to the disgust of the South's traditional leaders, a majority of those elected were Republicans. The new southern legislatures quickly passed the Fourteenth and Fifteenth Amendments.

By 1870 all the former Confederate states had met the requirements of Congress for coming back into the Union. Reconstruction seemed complete, and federal troops withdrew from the South.

African American office-holders The South's new Reconstruction governments included a number of African American officials. In South Carolina, blacks made up a majority of the legislature for two years, and Jonathan J. Wright served for six years on the state supreme court.

Sixteen African Americans served in Congress as well. Of these, 14 men served as representatives in the House, while Mississippi sent Hiram R. Revels and Blanche K. Bruce to the Senate. The conduct of these new legislators impressed Maine's Representative James G. Blaine, who observed:

❝The colored men who took their seats in both the Senate and House . . . [were] earnest, ambitious men, whose public conduct . . . would be honorable to any race.❞

First organized in 1866, the Ku Klux Klan was officially disbanded in 1869, but many of its members went underground and created other organizations under a variety of names throughout the South. Congress responded by enacting the Ku Klux Klan Act in 1871, giving the President wide powers to combat violence designed to disrupt elections. The name Ku Klux Klan was revived in 1915 when a new national organization was formed in Atlanta. The new organization did not limit its intimidation to African Americans but also targeted Jews, Catholics, and immigrants. It reached its height, with over three million members, in the 1920s but was disbanded in 1944. A third Klan was formed in 1946 to combat the post–World War II demand for civil rights by African Americans. It still exists.

Most whites in the South detested the Reconstruction governments. They resented having had these governments "forced" on them by the much-hated Yankees. Even more they resented seeing former slaves holding public office and talking about equality.

Despite such resentment, Reconstruction governments set to work rebuilding roads and bridges and expanding the South's railroads. They built badly needed schools, as well as hospitals, orphanages, and prisons. Of course, such projects were expensive. To pay for them, the states had to raise taxes.

Pictured above are the seven African Americans who served in Congress in 1872. Twenty years later there was only one African American member of Congress.

Return to "White Man's Rule"

To win support and return their states to "white man's rule," Democrats blamed Republicans for the higher taxes. They also accused them of **corruption**—using public office for illegal purposes. While some officials did line their pockets with tax money, most were honest and capable. Still, as taxes increased, so did resentment of white and black Republican officeholders.

White terrorism Certain whites were willing to use any means necessary to stop blacks from voting and thus return the South to its traditional leaders. They formed secret organizations, such as the White League and the Ku Klux Klan, to terrorize African Americans. The White League declared that "this should be a white man's government, [and] as far as our efforts go, it shall be."

Wearing long, hooded robes, Ku Klux Klan members spread terror by night. They thundered across the countryside on horse-back, warning both black and white Republicans not to vote.

The Klan burned down the homes of Republicans who ignored their threats. African Americans were often beaten and murdered. To combat Klan terrorism Congress passed the Enforcement Acts in 1870 and 1871. These laws directed President Grant to send federal troops back into the most violent areas to protect black voters. Witnesses, however, feared the Klan's revenge and refused to testify. Few terrorists were convicted.

Democrats back in power In 1872 the Amnesty Act forgave former Confederates and gave them back the right to vote. By then, white Republicans were returning to the Democratic Party. The Democrats began to win elections in state after state.

By 1876 Democrats had regained control of all but three southern states. Republicans clung to power in South Carolina, Louisiana, and Florida, but only with the help of federal troops.

1865–1905 Chapter 19 • **535**

**Time to End
Reconstruction?**

To review effects of Reconstruction, have students
imagine themselves writ-
ing letters to the editor
during the election of
1876. Assign half to write
letters arguing for an end
to Reconstruction and the
other half to write letters
arguing against ending it.
Each letter should include
at least three reasons.
Ask some students to
read their letters aloud.
Conclude by summarizing
arguments.

Section Review
Answers

1. Definitions: *scalawags*
(532), *carpetbaggers* (533),
corruption (535)

2. African Americans, white
southerners who had not
fought for the Confederacy,
and northerners who moved
to the South could vote.
Those who had supported the
Confederacy could not vote.

3. In 1876 Republicans
agreed to return control to
white southerners in return
for enough electoral votes
to make Rutherford B. Hayes
President.

4. The federal government
might have made Klan mem-
bership a federal crime, sent
marshals to protect witnesses,
and moved trials of Klansmen
to communities where the
Klan would not have support
and where witnesses would
be less afraid to testify.

✠ **Connections to Civics**

Samuel Tilden was one of three candidates
(Andrew Jackson in 1824 and Grover Cleveland in 1888 were the others) who lost the
White House even though they received the
most popular votes. Tilden got 4.3 million
votes to Hayes's 4 million. Tilden needed
185 electoral votes to win, but he got 184.
The votes in three southern states that still
had Republican administrations—South

Carolina, Louisiana, and Florida—were overturned, although it appeared that Tilden had
a majority in all three. One Oregon vote was
disputed on a technicality. The entire dispute
was referred to an electoral commission of
seven Republicans, seven Democrats, and
one independent. Shortly before it was to
meet, the independent quit and was replaced
by a Republican. The commission decided
8–7 in favor of Hayes.

Klan members disguised themselves with hoods
and robes. These men posed in a professional
photography studio in 1868.

The End of Reconstruction

While white terrorism was increasing and
Republican power weakening in the South,
the North was losing interest in the task of
Reconstruction. The Civil War had been over
for a decade. It was time, many northerners
argued, to "let the South alone."

The disputed 1876 election In 1876
Americans went to the polls to vote for a
new President. The Democrats had nominated Governor Samuel J. Tilden of New
York. Rutherford B. Hayes from Ohio headed
the Republican ticket. Hayes knew that
most voters were tired of thinking about
Reconstruction, the Klan, and "the everlasting Negro question." In his campaign he
had said little about these issues.

When the election returns came in, Hayes
was 20 electoral votes short of victory, but
20 electoral votes from 4 states remained in
dispute. The Republican-controlled Congress
awarded all the disputed electoral votes to
Hayes. The Democrats cried foul and threatened to block his inauguration. As Inauguration Day drew near, the nation was without
a new President.

The Compromise of 1877 At the last
moment, the two parties worked out a compromise. The Democrats agreed to accept
Hayes as President. In return, Hayes agreed
to give the southern states the right to control their own affairs.

True to his word, President Hayes removed
all federal troops from the South. With the
army gone, Democrats quickly gained control of the last three southern states. "This is
a white man's country," boasted Senator
Ben Tillman of South Carolina, "and white
men must govern it."

While white southerners cheered the end
of Reconstruction, African Americans feared
what the future might hold. Henry Adams,
a Louisiana freedman, observed sadly:

❝The whole South—every state in the
South . . . has got into the hands of the
very men that held us as slaves.❞

2. Section Review

1. Define **scalawags, carpetbaggers,
and corruption.**

2. Under the Republican Reconstruction
plan, who could vote in the South and
who could not?

3. How did white southern Democrats
regain control of state government?

4. Critical Thinking Describe at least
two more actions that the government or
citizens might have taken to stop the rise
of the Klan in the South.

war. Possible good results of Congress's plan: blacks will have legal protection as they strive to improve their conditions; blacks will have power to elect officials who represent their interests. Possible bad results: white southerners may be uncooperative; disruption may result from having inexperienced people govern.

4. Accept any decision in line with the stated goal and reflecting careful consideration of possible outcomes.

For further application, have students do the Applying Skills activity in the Chapter Survey (p. 546).

If students need to review the skill, use the Skills Development transparency and activity in the **Chapter Resources Binder**, pp. 151–152.

Skill Lab

Using Information
Making Decisions

If President Lincoln had not been assassinated on April 14, 1865, he might have gone down in history as "the Great Reconstructor" as well as "the Great Emancipator." Instead, the question of how to rebuild the Confederate states was left to a new President and to a Congress opposed to that new President's ideas.

Question to Investigate

What was the best way to rebuild the South?

Procedure

Although historical events may seem inevitable to us, many have resulted from deliberate decisions that people have made. Imagine that you are a member of Congress after the Civil War. You must decide whether to support the President's Reconstruction plan or one offered by the Radical Republicans.

1 Identify the problem and your goal.
a. State the problem to be solved.
b. State your goal—what you hope to achieve.

2 Identify the options.
a. Read source **A**.
b. Summarize the two plans.

3 Evaluate each option.
a. Read sources **B** and **C**.
b. List the possible good and bad results of each plan.

4 Choose one option and explain why you chose it.

Skill Tips

Keep in mind:
● When making decisions people often have several options, some better than others. However, there is almost never a perfect solution.
● People base decisions partly on the available facts and partly on their biases, or slanted views.

Sources to Use

A Reread the two plans on pages 529–531.

B "Let us go down to Louisiana. . . . We find the Negro downtrodden. Men are imprisoned for speaking their opinions about Negro suffrage. The worst features of the slave laws are revived. The Rebels . . . are rapidly pushing their state back to the terror and gloom of the [pre-Civil War] period. They know full well that if we [northerners] leave the Negro in their hands . . . they will have little trouble in perpetuating [continuing] a system more degrading than slavery."

From Horace Greeley, *New York Daily Tribune*, November 15, 1865

C "I think if the whole regulation of Negroes, or freedmen, were left to the people of the communities in which they live, it will be administered for the best interest of the negroes as well as of the whites. I think there is a kindly feeling [by white southerners] towards the freedmen. . . . I think there is a willingness to give them every right except the right of suffrage. . . . They will eventually be endowed with that right. It is only a question of time; but it will be necessary to prepare for it by slow and regular means, as the white race was prepared. . . . It would be disastrous to give the right of suffrage now."

By James D. B. De Bow, editor of the New Orleans-based *De Bow's Review* from 1846 to 1867

Option 1
+

Option 2
+

—

Introducing the Skill Lab

Point out to students that in making their decision they need to place themselves in the shoes of a member of Congress in 1865. There is no right answer. They should not rely on hindsight but instead consider the information available at the time. In gathering information from sources B and C, they should consider the possibility of bias.

Skill Lab
Answers

1. (a) "The South needs to be rebuilt." (b) Goals will vary. Some possibilities: "To bring the South back into the Union with as little disruption as possible." "To bring the South back into the Union with equality for all its people guaranteed."

2. Summaries should reflect the plans' main points. The main difference is that Johnson's did not mention legal equality or voting rights for freedmen.

3. Some possible good results of Johnson's plan: South governed by experienced leaders; less disruption if South moves slowly toward equal rights. Possible bad results: without legal protection or the right to vote, blacks will be powerless; South may return to political and economic system like the one before the

(Answers continued in top margin)

Introducing the Section

Vocabulary

tenant farmers (p. 539) farmers who pay rent for the use of land on which they grow crops

sharecropping (p. 539) system in which tenants give part of crop as rent

poll tax (p. 540) fee for voting

grandfather clause (p. 540) clause in a voting law saying it did not apply to a man whose father or grandfather could have voted before January 1, 1867

segregation (p. 540) forced separation of races in public places

Jim Crow laws (p. 540) segregation laws

Warm-Up Activity

Postwar Problems

To identify challenges facing the South, have pairs make lists of postwar recovery tasks. They should consider such factors as physical effects on southern farms and cities, conditions of refugees, and the need for jobs. Conclude by compiling a "to do" list on the chalkboard.

Geography Question of the Day

To illustrate how tenant farming and the end of slavery changed southern plantations, have students draw layouts before and after the war. They should label buildings and divisions of land. (Before: large, undivided field area, clustered slave quarters. After: small plots, sharecropper cabins.)

Section Objectives

★ Explain why the South remained mostly rural and poor after Reconstruction.
★ Describe how the rights and conditions of black southerners changed after Reconstruction.
★ Identify ways in which African Americans responded to segregation and violence.

Teaching Resources

Take-Home Planner 6, pp. 18–25

Chapter Resources Binder

  Study Guide, p. 147

  Reinforcement

  Skills Development

Geography Extensions, pp. 37–38

American Readings, p. 76

  Using Historical Documents

  Transparency Activities

Chapter and Unit Tests, pp. 119–122

3. The Legacy of Reconstruction

Reading Guide

New Terms tenant farmers, sharecropping, poll tax, grandfather clause, segregation, Jim Crow laws

Section Focus The return to power of southern Democrats and its impact on the lives of black southerners

1. Why did the South remain mostly rural and poor after Reconstruction?
2. What happened to the rights and conditions of black southerners after Reconstruction?
3. In what ways did African Americans respond to segregation and violence?

As Reconstruction ended, southern leaders vowed to build a "New South" that would hum with industry. Under the slogan "Bring the cotton mills to the cotton," they expanded the region's textile industries by nine times between 1880 and 1900. Meanwhile, Birmingham, Alabama, became a major iron-making center.

In 1886 Georgia newspaper editor Henry Grady bragged:

"We [the South] have . . . put business above politics. We have challenged your spinners in Massachusetts and your iron-makers in Pennsylvania.**"**

Despite Grady's boasts, industry in the South did not develop as he had hoped. In the decades following the war, the North would emerge as an industrial giant. Most southerners—both black and white—would remain trapped, however, in a region that was mostly rural and poor.

Life in the "New South"

The South was still staggering from the effects of the Civil War when Reconstruction ended. The average income of southern-

ers was just 40 percent that of northerners. Many whites had lost everything in the conflict—homes, farms, and businesses. Rebuilding crushed lives would be slow work.

Freedmen under freedom For most freedmen, poverty was the unwelcome companion of freedom. They began their new lives, as Frederick Douglass noted, "empty-handed, without money . . . without a foot of land on which to stand."

For Susie King, the struggle to survive was made more difficult by her husband Edward's death. Unable to support herself and her baby on the tiny salary of a teacher, she was forced to find other work. Despite her education, the only job she could get was as a household servant.

Other freedmen also supported themselves as best they could on the pitiful wages they earned. Virginia tobacco workers reported:

"It is impossible to feed ourselves and family—starvation is certain unless a change is brought about.**"**

Tenant farming Once-wealthy planters also faced hard times. With little cash to pay workers, planters had to divide their land into small plots, which they rented to tenant

See the Study Guide activity in **Chapter Resources Binder,** p. 147.

farmers. **Tenant farmers** pay rent for the use of land on which they grow crops. Rather than pay cash, some tenant farmers paid a part—or share—of their crop as rent. This system is known as **sharecropping.**

To landless southerners—both black and white—tenant farming looked promising at first. They hoped to save enough money to buy the land. First, though, they had to borrow money to buy seeds and tools.

Had crop prices been high after the war, these farmers might have been able to repay their loans. Instead, prices fell. By 1900 two-thirds of southern farmers found themselves buried in debts and trapped in the tenant-farming, sharecropping system.

Education in the "New South"

During Reconstruction, many African Americans pinned their hopes for a better future on education. Reconstruction governments responded by opening thousands of public schools in the South.

However, when white southern Democrats regained control of their states, they cut spending on education. "Free schools are not a necessity," explained the governor of Virginia, "they are a luxury . . . to be paid for, like any other luxury, by the people who wish their benefits."

Many southern schools closed down for lack of funds. Others charged fees. By the 1880s, less than 60 percent of white children and 49 percent of black children still attended school in the "New South."

Reversing Reconstruction

Free public education was not the only Reconstruction program that the new southern leaders ended. They also found ways to rob African Americans of what remained of their political power. Freedmen still voted in the South, but white election officials refused to count their votes. A black voter in Georgia observed:

❝ We are in a majority here, but . . . there's a hole gets in the bottom of the boxes some way and lets out our votes.**❞**

New voting laws Still not satisfied, southern whites passed laws in the 1890s that made it even harder for African Americans

Sharecroppers who could not read relied on the landowner to keep records of how much money they owed. Even when harvests were good, they were often told that they owed more to the landowner than they had the year before.

Discussion

Checking Understanding

1. Why did most southerners become tenant farmers, and why did they remain poor? (They could not afford to buy land. Low crop prices left them unable to pay off their debts.)

Stimulating Critical Thinking

2. How was life in the "New South" much like life in the old South? (Despite some growth in industry, the region remained mostly rural and poor. Reconstruction efforts to provide free schools and guarantee voting rights to blacks were reversed by post-Reconstruction governments.)

3. Why do you think most of the South remained rural and poor? (Lack of money to finance industries, competition from established northern industries, difficulty of changing traditional economy by retraining work force.)

★ ★ ★ Vital Links

Farm family (Picture) Unit 3, Side 1, Search 39019

See also Unit 3 Explore CD-ROM location 219.

Ask students to compare
the numbers of African
American representatives
and senators in 1876. (6
representatives, 1 senator)
How might they explain
the difference? (More difficult to get statewide support for a black candidate.)
Answers to Reading Maps:
There were 6 in 1876, but
only 1 in 1896. During
Radical Reconstruction,
African Americans were a
powerful voting bloc, but
later restrictions denied
suffrage to most of them.

Section
Activity

A Postwar Collage

To give an overview of life
in the South, have small
groups create layouts for
collages. The goal is to
compare life during and
after Reconstruction.
Each group should decide
which topics to show,
sizes of images in relation
to each other, labels
needed, and how best to
arrange images to high-
light differences or similarities. For example, an
image of a long line of
African American voters
might be juxtaposed with
an image of one person
being denied suffrage
because of a poll tax.
Images of poor white
and black tenant farmers
might be positioned to
show that their economic
condition was the same
during and after Recon-
struction. Conclude by
having groups present
and explain layouts.

⊞ **Connections to Literature**
Some white southern writers protested the
treatment of African Americans. For instance,
George Washington Cable of New Orleans
wrote *Silent South,* one of the strongest indict-
ments of southern racial policies. Lewis H.
Blair of Richmond wrote *The Prosperity of the
South Dependent Upon the Elevation of the Negro,*
an attack on the notion of black inferiority.

---

to vote. All citizens now had to pay a **poll
tax**—a fee for voting. The tax was set high
to make voting, like schooling, a luxury that
very few black southerners could afford.

Some southern states also made potential
voters pass a literacy test to prove that they
could read. A person who failed the test
could not vote.

Lawmakers claimed that these laws did
not violate the right to vote, since they
applied to white voters, too. Whites, though,
were protected by a **grandfather clause**
in the laws after 1898. This clause said that
voting laws did not apply to a man whose
father or grandfather could have voted
before January 1, 1867. Before that day, of
course, only whites had been able to vote.

African Americans appealed to the Supreme
Court in 1898 to protect their right to vote
under the Fifteenth Amendment. To their
shock, the Court ruled against them. The
Court accepted the argument that the voting
laws were constitutional because they applied
equally to blacks and whites.

Jim Crow Laws

During Reconstruction most southern
state governments had outlawed **segregation**—the forced separation of races in
public places. Once back in power, however,
white southern Democrats began to pass
segregation laws that whites called **Jim
Crow laws.** Whites used the term Jim Crow

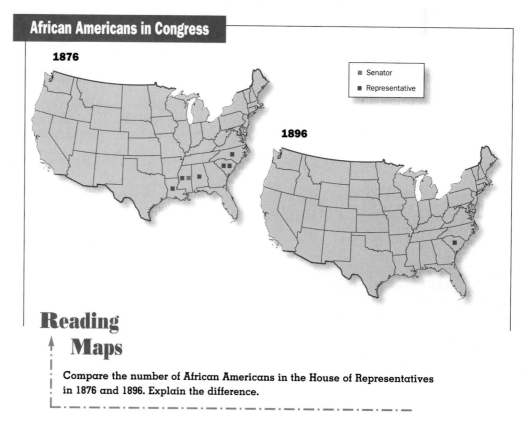

African Americans in Congress

1876

■ Senator
■ Representative

1896

Reading
↑ **Maps**

**Compare the number of African Americans in the House of Representatives
in 1876 and 1896. Explain the difference.**

Students with Limited English
Students with limited English often benefit from relating a graphic representation
to ideas in the text. Using Aaron Douglas's mural, have them identify images
representing events described in the text.
For instance, ask what the dancing and
broken chains represent, why the soldiers
leave, and why the left side is darker.

Link to Art

Aspects of Negro Life: From Slavery through Reconstruction (1934)
In Aaron Douglas's striking mural, the story unfolds from right to left. On
the right side the Emancipation Proclamation is read in 1863. In response
to the news, an enslaved man has broken his chains. The center section pays
tribute to black leaders in the South from 1867 to 1876. On the left side
black figures fall and the sky darkens as the Ku Klux Klan terrorizes black
people after the 1870s. **Discuss** What symbols does Douglas use in "telling"
the story? How does he use light and color to enhance the story?

to refer to blacks in an insulting way. In the
1880s one state after another drew a "color
line" between blacks and whites.

Point of View

Were Jim Crow laws to be taken seriously?

Most whites in the South welcomed Jim
Crow laws. The brave editor of the *News and
Courier* in Charleston, South Carolina, was
an exception. To convince his readers that
segregation was unjust, he tried poking fun
at Jim Crow laws. He wrote an article
drawing what he thought was an extreme
picture of where Jim Crow laws might lead:

"If there must be Jim Crow cars on
railroads, there should be Jim Crow
cars on the street railways . . . on all
passenger boats. . . . Jim Crow waiting
saloons [rooms]. . . . Jim Crow eating
houses. . . . Jim Crow sections of the
jury box, and a . . . Jim Crow Bible
for colored witnesses to kiss."

What seemed absurd to the editor was
not so ridiculous to other white southerners, and it turned out to be a tragedy for
African Americans. In the years to come,
nearly all of the editor's ideas actually
became law as segregation tightened its
grip on the South.

1865–1905 Chapter 19 • **541**

Discussion

Checking Understanding

1. How were many blacks prevented from voting?
(Poll taxes and literacy tests, both declared legal by the Supreme Court.)

Stimulating Critical Thinking

2. What effects do you think segregation had on blacks? (Increased hatred of whites; made them feel inferior; denied equal oppor-tunities and services.) **On whites?** (Reinforced preju-dices because segregation resulted in fewer opportuni-ties for people to understand each other.)

Teaching the
Link to Art

Ask students to explain whether the overall mood is hopeful or gloomy. (Gloomy: the hopeful beginnings give way to terrorism.) **Discussion Answers:** Some symbols: cotton, broken chains, trumpet. Concentric cir-cles act like a spotlight to focus on sections of the mural. The left side is darker to represent bleak-ness at the end of Recon-struction. Silhouettes make human figures stand out as representations.

Teaching the
Point of View

Ask students why they think the article had the opposite effect of what was intended. (Most whites welcomed Jim Crow, so any step to achieve segregation seemed reasonable to them.)

✳ **History Footnote**
In addition to Liberia and Ethiopia, there was one other independent black-ruled nation in the world at the end of the nineteenth century. Haiti won its independence from France in a long struggle from 1791 to 1804, making it the second oldest independent republic in the western hemisphere, and the oldest black republic in the world. The United States is the oldest independent republic in the hemisphere. Because of southern objections to having a black ambassador in Washington, the United States did not establish diplomatic relations with Haiti until 1862.

Teaching the

World  **Link**

Point out that Europeans saw Africa as a key source of raw materials for industry and that the race for colonies was part of a competition between European nations for political and economic power. They were able to colonize most of Africa because of advantages in weaponry and because many African societies had been weakened by the slave trade. Nonetheless, many Africans resisted colonial rule. Ask students to consider how European nations might have tried to justify their colonization of Africa. (Belief in white superiority and in a mission to "civilize" non-white peoples.)

World  **Link**

Europeans divide up Africa In 1884 European nations were racing frantically to acquire more colonies. That year the European powers met in Berlin, Germany, to carve up Africa. Soon the continent was under European control. Only Ethiopia and Liberia escaped colonization.

Ethiopia remained an independent kingdom after it defeated an invading Italian army in 1896. Liberia, founded as a home for freed American slaves in 1821, had been a republic since 1847. Whenever Europeans threatened to take over Liberia, the United States would speak up and the Europeans would back down.

Plessy v. Ferguson Many Americans believed that Jim Crow laws violated the Fourteenth Amendment's guarantee of "equal protection of the laws." When Homer Plessy was arrested for riding in a "whites-only" railroad car in Louisiana, he appealed his case to the Supreme Court.

In 1896 the Supreme Court handed down its decision in *Plessy* v. *Ferguson.* It ruled that segregation laws did not violate the Fourteenth Amendment. Facilities for both races could be separate as long as they were roughly equal.

Only one justice, John Marshall Harlan, disagreed. "Our Constitution is color blind," he wrote. He also warned that Jim Crow laws were deeply destructive. "What can more certainly arouse race hate," he asked, than these laws?

The Supreme Court's support for segregation in *Plessy* v. *Ferguson* led to a flood of new Jim Crow laws. Despite the "separate but equal" rule, though, schools and parks for whites were always better than those set aside for blacks.

The color line drawn between black and white southerners was to remain firmly in place for decades. In fact, segregation was the law of the South until 1954, when the Supreme Court finally ruled in *Brown* v. *Board of Education* that racial segregation is unconstitutional.

Responses to Segregation

As the noose of segregation tightened in the South, African Americans responded in a variety of ways. Some bravely disobeyed segregation laws. Others left the South for new homes in the North and West. Still others looked for ways to work together to improve opportunities and protect the rights of African Americans.

Open disobedience Some African Americans refused to obey Jim Crow laws. To do so, however, was dangerous. Almost 3,000 black southerners were lynched—killed by mobs—between 1892 and 1903. Most were lynched because they refused to accept segregation and "white rule."

Jim Crow laws kept blacks and whites separated for many years. This photo of a public fountain was taken in 1950 in North Carolina.

Migration Rather than put up with segregation and violence, many thousands of African Americans left the South. Some moved to the North. Susie King, for example, moved to Boston with her son. There she met and married her second husband, Russell Taylor.

Some freedmen headed west. Benjamin "Pap" Singleton organized the "Exodus of 1879"—a migration of black southerners to Kansas. Within two years close to 40,000 African Americans had moved to Kansas. Life on the plains had its hardships, but as one "Exoduster" put it, "We had rather suffer and be free."

In 1878 a group of 200 freedmen decided that "the colored man had no home in America." They chartered a ship and sailed to Liberia, a West African nation founded by freed American slaves in the 1820s. Still, few African Americans chose to leave the United States. "We are not Africans now," wrote one, "but colored Americans, and are entitled to American citizenship."

Self-help The majority of black southerners remained in the South where they had the support of their families, churches, and a close-knit community. Believing that their best hope lay in education, they built many schools and colleges. By 1900 more than 1.5 million African American children were attending school. In the South's 29 black colleges, students were preparing to become teachers, lawyers, and doctors.

Two approaches to change No African American believed more strongly in the power of education and self-help than the educator Booker T. Washington. In 1881 he founded the Tuskegee Institute in Alabama to teach practical skills such as farming and carpentry. Washington urged his students to worry less about the injustice of segregation and racial violence, and more about getting education and jobs.

Other African Americans disagreed. They were led by another outspoken black educator, William E. B. Du Bois [doo-BOYS] of Atlanta University. Unlike the more cautious Washington, Du Bois urged blacks to stand up against discrimination and demand equality. Black southerners needed leaders who would demand equal opportunities, Du Bois argued, or many jobs would remain out of their reach.

In 1905 Du Bois met with other African American reformers to form a national organization called the Niagara Movement. Five years later, this movement gave birth to the National Association for the Advancement of Colored People (NAACP).

A teacher and his students work in a laboratory at the Tuskegee Institute in 1903. The college continues to serve African Americans, with over 3,000 students enrolled today.

**Steps Forward
and Backward**

To summarize the failure
of Reconstruction, have
students create charts
with 2 columns and
3 rows. Column heads:
"How promoted," "How
prevented." Row heads:
"Political equality,"
"Economic opportunity,"
"Social equality." Stu-
dents should fill in one
example for each square,
such as "free schools"
to promote economic
opportunity. Conclude by
having volunteers fill in a
chart on the chalkboard.

**Section Review
Answers**

1. Definitions: *tenant farmers*
(539), *sharecropping* (539),
poll tax (540), *grandfather
clause* (540), *segregation* (540),
Jim Crow laws (540)

2. By imposing poll taxes and
literacy tests.

3. Washington urged a focus
on getting education and
jobs rather than protesting
discrimination. Du Bois said
no progress could come
unless blacks demanded
equal rights.

4. Answers may include leaving the South, working to get
an education and skilled job,
and contesting unfair laws
politically. Students should
consider what was feasible
after Reconstruction.

*To check understanding of
"Why We Remember," assign
Thinking Critically question
3 on student page 546.*

544

✱ **History Footnote**
In public, Booker T. Washington supported
accommodation in order to "cement the
friendship of the races and bring about
hearty cooperation between them." In light
of the reversal of Reconstruction, Washington believed that this was the only policy
that could be really effective. In private, however, he worked to stop racial discrimination.
For example, he raised funds to challenge
cases in the federal courts against disenfran-
chisement and Jim Crow laws, and he argued
against discrimination in the allocation of
funds to white and black schools.

The Failure of Reconstruction

Du Bois could not know how long and difficult the struggle would be. In the decades
that followed Reconstruction, white southerners had erected cruel barriers of segregation to strip African Americans of their rights
and opportunities.

During the same period, most white southerners, too, had failed to prosper. Only many
years later would opportunity and equality
finally come to the South.

⭐ 3. Section Review

1. Define **tenant farmers, sharecropping, poll tax, grandfather clause,
segregation,** and **Jim Crow laws.**
2. Explain how the right to vote was
denied to black southerners.
3. How did Booker T. Washington's ideas
for bettering African American lives differ
from those of William E. B. Du Bois?
4. Critical Thinking As a black southerner, how would you have responded to
Jim Crow laws, and why?

Why We Remember

Reconstruction

In 1898 Susie King Taylor returned to the South after many years in
Boston. On that journey she rode in Jim Crow railroad cars, and heard
stories about African Americans being beaten and murdered. "Each morning
you can hear of some Negro being lynched," a porter told her. "We have no
rights here." Taylor was outraged. "Was the [Civil] war in vain?" she asked.
"Has it brought freedom, in the full sense of the word, or has it not made
our condition hopeless?"

Looking back at Reconstruction, it is easy to understand and even share
Taylor's bitterness. After the Civil War, the world had seemed full of hope to
Taylor and her fellow freedmen. With support from the Republican Congress
until 1876, the South's Reconstruction governments had built schools and
granted voting rights to help make African Americans full and equal citizens.

Still, racism proved stronger than Congress's laws. The chance to breathe new
life into the nation's ideals of freedom and equality was lost. These ideals were
not, however, forgotten. The belief that all people deserve the same opportunities and rights was kept alive by black families, churches, and schools. Even in
the worst moments, Taylor believed that some day blacks and whites would live
as equal citizens in America. "I know I shall not live to see the day," she wrote,
"but it will come." This faith that the nation could overcome racism and live up
to its ideals would be Reconstruction's most hopeful legacy.

In 1860 there were about two million farms in the United States, with fewer than 1 percent of them in the West. Therefore, the West is not included in the graphs below. However, during the 1870s alone, some 170 million acres of western farmland were added. Growth was so rapid that by 1890 the Superintendent of the Census wrote, "there can hardly be said to be a frontier line."

Geography Lab

The Civil War and Southern Agriculture

Visitors to the South at the end of the Civil War described it as "almost a desert." The farmland was a ruin of burned buildings, trampled crops, and dead livestock. Use the photo and the tables to understand some of the war's effects on southern agriculture.

Union troops dig into the hillside of a plantation.

Amount of Farmland

Amount (in millions of acres)

1850   1860   1870   1880

Years

Source: Historical Statistics of the United States

Total Value of Farms

Value (in millions of dollars)

1850   1860   1870   1880

Years

Source: Historical Statistics of the United States

Link to — History

1. How did farm values change between 1850 and 1880 in the Northeast and North Central regions?

2. How did the value and amount of farmland in the South change between 1860 and 1870? Give at least three reasons for the change.

3. From 1850 to 1880 which region had the largest increase in the amount of farmland?

4. **Hands-On Geography** Imagine that you and your family must turn the land shown in the photo back into productive farmland. You have very little cash. Create a three-step plan to restore your farmland. Explain the plan and the reasons that you chose this plan.

Survey Answers

Reviewing Vocabulary

Definitions are found on these pages: *freedmen* (526), *Reconstruction* (529), *black codes* (529), *impeach* (531), *scalawags* (532), *carpetbaggers* (533), *corruption* (535), *tenant farmers* (539), *sharecropping* (539), *poll tax* (540), *grandfather clause* (540), *segregation* (540), *Jim Crow laws* (540).

Reviewing Main Ideas

1. Their lives were very difficult and insecure because they did not have the education, land, or money to take full advantage of their freedom and rights.

2. (a) They believed Johnson had been too lenient, and the black codes were oppressing African Americans. (b) Congress passed the Freedmen's Bureau Act and the Civil Rights Act, overriding the President's veto. After the election of 1866 gave the Republicans control of Congress, they passed their own Reconstruction Act. When Johnson tried to stop their plan, they broke his power by nearly removing him from office.

3. (a) African Americans, carpetbaggers, and scalawags. (b) Set up schools for former slaves and began the process of giving African Americans full civil rights.

4. Departure of federal troops from the South, election of Democratic state governments, and the Compromise of 1877.

5. Planters could not afford to pay wages for labor, so they rented plots of land to tenant farmers. Some tenants could not afford to rent the land, so they paid a share of their crop as rent. Most were unable to earn enough to buy land or repay loans for seeds and tools. Low crop prices left them trapped in debt.

(Answers continued in top margin)

546

6. Jim Crow laws, laws limiting public education, and poll taxes.

7. Some left the South for other parts of the country; some tried to educate themselves and improve skills. Some also fought unjust laws.

Thinking Critically

1. White southerners resented the changed position of former slaves and wanted to regain economic and political power. Northerners may have realized how hard it was going to be for African Americans to get the skills and resources they needed, and that white southerners were being alienated.

2. Answers will vary. Some might share Washington's view that it was more productive to accept the power structure as it was and to try to work within it. Others might agree with Du Bois that unjust laws should be contested.

Chapter Survey

Reviewing Vocabulary

Define the following terms.

1. freedmen
2. Reconstruction
3. black codes
4. impeach
5. scalawags
6. carpetbaggers
7. corruption
8. tenant farmers
9. sharecropping
10. poll tax
11. grandfather clause
12. segregation
13. Jim Crow laws

Reviewing Main Ideas

1. What was life like for freedmen immediately after the Civil War?
2. (a) Why did the Radical Republicans want to take control of Reconstruction? (b) How did they get that control?
3. (a) Who were the South's new voters and officeholders? (b) What did the Reconstruction governments accomplish?
4. Describe the events that led to the return of "white man's rule" in the South.
5. Why did southern farmers turn to sharecropping, and what were the results?
6. What were three ways that southern Democrats reversed the gains that African Americans made during Reconstruction?
7. How did African Americans respond to their treatment after Reconstruction?

Thinking Critically

1. **Analysis** Most white southerners resented Reconstruction, while many white northerners gave up on it. Why did the two groups take these positions?
2. **Evaluation** If you had been an African American in the South in the late 1800s, how might you have responded to the rising tide of segregation? Why?
3. **Why We Remember: Synthesis** Susie King Taylor once asked, "Was the [Civil] war in vain?" How would you have responded at the time, and today?

Applying Skills

Making decisions The specific problems that people face today are different from those faced by people in the United States after the Civil War. However, the basic need to solve problems by making decisions has never changed. Think about a problem you need to solve in your own life. It does not have to be a big problem, but its solution should require careful thought. Use what you learned on page 537 to decide on the best solution to the problem. Then write the following:
• a description of the problem
• steps you took in making the decision
• why you made the decision you did

History Mystery

Voting in the South Answer the History Mystery on page 523. How might such a decline in voting by African Americans after 1896 have been prevented?

Writing in Your History Journal

1. **Keys to History** (a) The time line on pages 522–523 has seven Keys to History. In your journal, describe why each one is important to know about. (b) What three events from the chapter would you add to the time line? Write those events and their dates in your journal, and tell why you think each event should be added.
2. **Susie King Taylor** People often "vote with their feet" rather than stay in a difficult or dangerous situation. In your journal, describe the times when Taylor did this. Then write responses to the following questions: What do her choices tell you about Taylor as a person? Did she make the right choice in each case? Why or why not?

3. Answers may vary, but students will probably see Taylor's bitterness as understandable in light of the dashed hopes. Nevertheless, the war did destroy slavery and open the possibility of equality. Today, most would probably still argue that the war was not in vain because the end of slavery was the necessary first step toward equal rights.

Applying Skills

Answers should reflect an understanding of the steps listed on student page 537, as well as ability to make a final choice in line with the goal to be achieved.

History Mystery

Information on voting is found on pages 539–540. Poll taxes and literacy tests
(Answers continued in side margin)

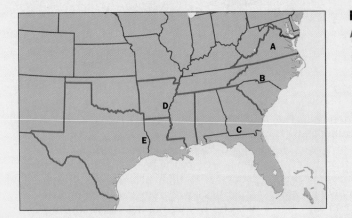

Reviewing Geography

1. Each letter on the map represents one of five military districts in which former Confederate states, except Tennessee, were divided. After each letter, write the name of the state or states in the district.

2. Geographic Thinking In looking back at Chapters 17 and 19, what factors determined the organization and use of farmland in the South before and after the Civil War? Give at least three reasons why these changes occurred.

3. Thinking Historically Reread the editor's opinions in the Point of View on page 541 and review the Supreme Court's decision in *Plessy* v. *Ferguson* on page 542. In your journal, write down the thoughts and ideas that you would want to express to the editor and to all southerners about Jim Crow laws and the Court's decision.

Alternative Assessment

Citizenship: Improving on Reconstruction Imagine that a few days from now, you will travel back through time to the Washington, D.C., of 1867. There, you will present to the members of Congress a "new and improved" Reconstruction plan. The purpose of your plan is to answer the critics of Johnson's 1865 plan while preventing the problems that you have learned will result if the Radical Republicans have their way.

Work with a partner to develop the Reconstruction plan and present it to Congress (your classmates).

In your presentation:

❶ Explain what roles former Confederate soldiers, officials, and supporters will play.

❷ Tell what rights freedmen will gain.

❸ Explain how those rights will be protected under your plan.

❹ Describe what will be done to improve the lives of all southerners.

❺ Tell what the federal government will do to make your Reconstruction a success.

❻ Include the costs of your Reconstruction and how they will be paid.

Your presentation will be evaluated on the following criteria:
• it shows a knowledge of Reconstruction
• it offers creative yet practical solutions to the challenges of the historical period
• it is clear and convincing

1865–1905 Chapter 19 • **547**

disqualified most African Americans from voting. The decline might have been prevented if the Supreme Court had declared these voting restrictions unconstitutional.

Writing in Your History Journal

1. (a) Explanations should be similar to the time line notes on teacher pages 522–523. (b) Accept additions that are accurately described and dated and that reflect an understanding of what makes an event historically important.

2. Students should mention the times when Taylor fled to the Sea Islands, returned to Savannah, and moved to Boston. In saying whether these were good choices, they should discuss her options. Answers should reflect that she was a brave person who took risks.

3. Editorials should show an understanding that the editor opposed Jim Crow laws. Notes might agree that all people deserve equal rights.

Reviewing Geography

1. (A) Virginia; (B) North Carolina, South Carolina; (C) Alabama, Georgia, Florida; (D) Arkansas, Mississippi; (E) Texas, Louisiana.

2. The major factor was the change in labor systems—from slavery to tenant farming and sharecropping. Other factors included destruction of property during the war, lack of capital for rebuilding and improvements, depletion of land from overfarming, opening up of lands in the West, and loss of markets.

Alternative Assessment

Teacher's Take-Home Planner 6, p. 21, includes suggestions and scoring rubrics for the Alternative Assessment activity.

Unit Survey

Making Connections
Answers

1. Students might suggest compromise and negotiation as alternatives. They might choose key events such as the Dred Scott decision, firing on Fort Sumter, Gettysburg, or the assassination of Lincoln, and consider effects if these events ended differently.

2. White southerners based their stand on the principle of self-determination, just as the colonists claimed the right to determine whether they wanted to be part of the British Empire. They ignored that slavery was based on oppression. Northerners may have stressed that the states had chosen to be part of the country and were obliged to remain part of it.

3. Legislative branch more powerful during 1850s and Reconstruction; executive branch stronger during the war. Easier to lead a war effort with strong President. Personalities and skills of Presidents affected which branch was stronger.

Teaching the Unit Project

Have students determine whether their state was directly involved. Suggest that they read the text and encyclopedias for background and also examine state and local history books.

Evaluation Criteria

The project can be evaluated according to the criteria listed below, using a scale for each: 4 = exemplary, 3 = good, 2 = adequate, 1 = poor.
(Continued in top margin)

Completing the task The map is well executed and accurate. Accompanying materials are relevant.

Knowing content Map presents a clear theme or fact about the state's role.

Thinking critically The materials are appropriate to the message illustrated.

Communicating ideas Map an aspect of the state's involvement.

Thinking It Over
Students' responses may show an interest in the fact that the war was between Americans, with some family members taking different sides, and that it was one of the first wars to have detailed photographs depicting it. Students may be fascinated by a particular battle, military strategy, or war-related document.

Unit Survey

Making Connections

Review

1. From 1850 to 1876, the nation struggled over the issues of slavery, secession, and Reconstruction. Could these issues have been solved in any other way than they were? Use examples to explain your answer.

2. What similarities do you suppose Southerners saw between secession and the American Revolution? What differences might Northerners have seen?

3. Although the Constitution balances the powers of the legislative and executive branches, at different times one or the other has been stronger. Which branch was stronger during the 1850s? During the Civil War? During Reconstruction? Why do you think these shifts occurred?

Linking History, Geography, and Art

Project

Your State in the Civil War

Did armies clash on the soil of your state between 1861 and 1865? Or was your state less directly involved in the war that split our nation? Even if your state was not yet a state, it was somehow affected by the Civil War. Find out how. Present what you learn in a pictorial map.

Project Steps

Work with a group.

❶ Choose one or two topics on which to focus. Here are some possibilities:
• battles that were fought in your state
• production of food, weapons, or other supplies in your state
• military or political leaders who came from your state
• citizens of your state who went to war
• contributions to the war effort by various organizations in your state
• effects of fighting, blockades, etc.

❷ Gather information about your topics. Start with this book. Then check your school or local library or the local historical society. Some students' families might have information—even photographs, letters, or other items to copy.

❸ Draw a large map of your state as it existed during the Civil War. Draw the map to scale, and include cities, land and water features, and any war-related features, such as battle sites or supply routes. Display the map on the bulletin board.

❹ Prepare pictorial or descriptive items and arrange them around the state map. Here are some possibilities:
• graphs
• drawings, paintings, or photographs
• letters or diary entries
• newspaper or magazine headlines, articles, or political cartoons
• descriptions of the events or the effects of the war

If an item relates to a specific place, use pushpins and yarn to connect the item to the correct spot on the map.

Thinking It Over How would you explain the fascination that the Civil War has for modern-day Americans? What aspect of the war do you find most interesting? Why?

Tips for Teaching

The Epilogue

You may teach the Epilogue by reading and discussing the decade pages with the class or by having students work in small groups to prepare presentations on the various decades in a Decades Review program. For suggestions for the Decades Review, see the Epilogue Activity notes in the right margin, below.

Epilogue

Continuing the Story

1860s to 1990s

A teacher reads to her class in 1900

Students debate each other in a 1995 classroom

After Reconstruction the passions that had driven the United States into a bloody civil war began to cool. The country, however, would soon be changed by forces beyond the dreams of anyone who had lived through that terrible conflict and its troubled outcome. The following pages give you an overview of those years as they unfolded decade by decade.

The story continues in 1865 as the Civil War came to a close. Your great-great-grandparents were most likely born during the years after the war. As you look back at that 25-year period, take note of the people, events, and trends that shaped American life when your great-great-grandparents were children.

Moving forward through time, try to imagine how your own family fits into the nation's past. When did your family come to this country, and from where? What changes have your grandparents and parents seen during their lifetimes? How has your childhood differed from theirs?

When you come to the present, take some time to look ahead into the future. No one knows what changes the next decades will bring. It is certain, however, that you will play a role in shaping the nation's future.

Introducing the Epilogue

Continuing the Story

The Epilogue helps students link the history they have been studying in this book to the modern history of the United States. Pages 550–561 give a decade-by-decade overview of main events, developments, and images from 1865 to the present. On each page students also see a photograph of a family of that period. On pages 562–564 they learn how futurists use trend analysis to predict the future. Then they apply their learning to predict what the years ahead may bring for them.

Epilogue Activity

Presenting a Decades Review

To gain more insight into American history since Reconstruction, have small groups focus on specific decades in depth. Assign a group to each of the 12 "decade" pages (page 550 covers 25 years). Each group presents its decade during a Decades Review program. Using the information on the page, as well as results of research, members of each group prepare a presentation that gives an overview of the decade and identifies key people, events, and ideas, explaining why each is important to remember. Encourage groups to enliven presentations with pictures, skits, and music.

Epilogue • **549**

Continuing the Story

■ 1865 to 1889

Discussion

Checking Understanding

1. What were some effects of the expansion of the rail system? (More settlers moved west, the Indian way of life was threatened, and the buffalo were destroyed.)

2. What happened at Little Bighorn in 1876? (Sitting Bull defeated Custer.)

Decade Activity

1865 to 1889

Students presenting this period should:

• Make an expanded time line with at least 15 entries.

• Write a description or act out how one event on the time line affected the people in the family photograph on the page.

• Prepare a presentation that will make the decade memorable to classmates. The presentation should include the expansion of the rail system; the increase in settlers moving west; and the conflicts between settlers and Indians.

• Show how the decade compares with the decades before and after.

History Bookshelf

Granfield, Linda. *Cowboy: An Album.* Ticknor and Fields, 1993. What was life like for a cowboy in the American West? Through archival photos, illustrations, and engaging text, Granfield gives the history of the American cowboy, a description of life on the trail, and an overview of media depictions of a romantic American tradition.

Also of interest:

Brown, Dee. Adapted by Amy Ehrlich. *Wounded Knee.* Holt, 1974.

Conrad, Pam. *Prairie Visions: The Life and Times of Solomon Butler.* HarperCollins, 1991.

Walker, Paul Robert. *Great Figures of the Wild West.* Facts on File, 1992.

A Nebraska family near their sod house in 1886

1867 First cattle drive over the Chisholm Trail

1867 United States buys Alaska

1876 Alexander Graham Bell invents the telephone

1882 Rockefeller forms Standard Oil Trust

1882 Chinese Exclusion Act

1886 American Federation of Labor organizes

1865 to 1889

Settling the American West

When the Civil War ended in 1865, vast expanses of the western United States were still untouched by settlement. By 1889, however, the western landscape was dotted with new farms, ranches, towns, mines, and logging camps. During that period railroads crisscrossed the western plains and mountains with ribbons of steel. As settlers followed the rails west, the Native American way of life on the Great Plains was swept away. So were the great herds of buffalo on which the Indians had depended.

1869

A golden spike at Promontory Point in Utah completed the first transcontinental railroad.

1876

Sitting Bull led Indians to victory over General Custer's troops at the Little Bighorn River.

1870s

Nat Love led cattle drives on the Plains before working for the railroads.

📚 **History Bookshelf**

Levinson, Nancy Smiler. *Turn of the Century: America One Hundred Years Ago.* Lodestar, 1992. In this fascinating book, the author explores the social and political movements and technological advances that ushered the United States into the 20th century. By doing so, she helps the reader gain perspective as the next century approaches.

Also of interest:

Marrin, Albert. *The Spanish-American War.* Atheneum, 1991.

Roosevelt, Theodore. *Autobiography of Theodore Roosevelt.* Da Capo Press, 1985.

A well-to-do family in their San Antonio, Texas, home

1890 to 1899

The Rise of Industry and Expansion Overseas

1890 Sioux Indians massacred at Wounded Knee

1890 Sherman Antitrust Act to reform big business

1893 Oklahoma land rush

1898 Congress passes law prohibiting annexation of Cuba

1898 Spanish-American War

By the 1890s the United States had become a major industrial power. Cities grew rapidly as people left their farms to find work in factories and mills. Long hours and miserable working conditions led to strikes and violence as workers formed unions to fight for better lives. At the same time, the United States began to expand into the Pacific and the Caribbean. The Hawaiian Islands were annexed in 1898. That same year, the United States went to war with Spain and soon won control of the Philippines, Cuba, and Puerto Rico.

1892

The Homestead Strike was marked by violence between the union and Carnegie Steel Company.

1890s

Steel production, in mills like this one, skyrocketed by the end of the nineteenth century.

1898

When the *Maine* exploded in Havana harbor, the United States used it as an excuse to declare war on Spain.

Continuing the Story

■ 1890 to 1899

Discussion

Checking Understanding

1. **How did industrialization affect people's lives?** (People left farms and moved to urban areas, often having to work long hours in miserable conditions.)

2. **What was the result of the Spanish-American War?** (The U.S. won control of the Philippines, Cuba, and Puerto Rico.)

Decade Activity

1890 to 1899

Students presenting this decade should:

• Make an expanded time line with at least 15 entries.

• Write a description or act out how one event on the time line affected the people in the family photograph on the page.

• Prepare a presentation that will make the decade memorable to classmates. The presentation should include some causes and effects of the rise of the U.S. as an industrial power; the Spanish-American War; and the expansion of the U.S. into the Pacific and the Caribbean.

• Show how the decade compares with the decades before and after.

Checking Understanding

1. Name two events in this decade that affected the history of transportation. (The world's first airplane flight by the Wright brothers; the beginning of the Panama Canal.)

2. What were the goals of the Progressives? (Cleaning up city slums, ending child labor, preserving the nation's wilderness areas as national parks.)

Decade Activity

1900 to 1909

Students presenting this decade should:

• Make an expanded time line with at least 15 entries.

• Write a description or act out how one event on the time line affected the people in the family photograph on the page.

• Prepare a presentation that will make the decade memorable to classmates. The presentation should include difficulties faced by children and immigrants in urban areas; the goals and impact of the Progressives; and the Wright brothers' historic flight.

• Show how the decade compares with the decades before and after.

History Bookshelf

Freedman, Russell. *Kids at Work: Lewis Hine and the Crusade Against Child Labor.* Clarion, 1994. Freedman tells the life story of Lewis Hine, a teacher and photographer whose shocking photographs of children working in harsh conditions helped propel the movement to abolish child labor. Several of Hine's photographs are included in the book.

Also of interest:

Freedman, Russell. *The Wright Brothers.* Holiday House, 1991.

Jacobs, William Jay. *Ellis Island.* Scribner's, 1990.

Mitchard, Jacquelyn. *Jane Addams.* Gareth Stevens, 1991.

An Italian immigrant family at supper in their tenement home

1900 to 1909

1901 Theodore Roosevelt becomes President after McKinley is assassinated

1904 Construction of the Panama Canal begins

1906 Publication of *The Jungle* exposes abuses in the meatpacking industry

1906 Pure Food and Drug Act

1909 National Association for the Advancement of Colored People (NAACP) forms

The Progressive Era

Millions of immigrants flooded into the United States in the first decade of the twentieth century. Most newcomers began their lives here in wretched city slums. Still they came, believing in the dream that life could—and would—be better for their children. That same dream inspired a new generation of reformers called Progressives. They called on government to clean up city slums, end child labor, and preserve the nation's wilderness areas as national parks. Largely ignored by the Progressives, African Americans formed their own organizations to fight racism.

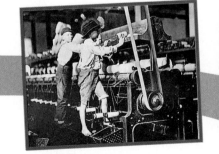

1900s

Children worked in dangerous factory conditions until child labor laws put a stop to such practices. These boys labored at a Georgia cotton mill.

1903

The naturalist John Muir (right) urged President Theodore Roosevelt (left) to preserve the nation's wilderness.

1903

The world's first airplane flight by the Wright brothers ushered in a new era of faster communication.

📚 History Bookshelf

Lawrence, Jacob. *The Great Migration.* The Museum of Modern Art/HarperCollins, 1992. In 1941 Jacob Lawrence completed a series of 60 paintings chronicling the northern migration of African Americans. Lawrence's series, reproduced in this book, is an unforgettable collection of images depicting both difficulties and triumphs.

Also of interest:

Bosco, Peter. *World War I.* Facts on File, 1991.

Hoobler, Dorothy, and Thomas Hoobler. *The Trenches.* Putnam's, 1978.

Sullivan, George. *The Day the Women Got the Vote: A Photo History of the Women's Rights Movement.* Scholastic, 1994.

Continuing the Story
■ 1910 to 1919

Discussion

Checking Understanding

1. What is the woman in the lower left photograph doing? (Marching in a parade demanding the right to vote.)

2. Why did many business-people want the U.S. to stay neutral in World War I? (They wanted to trade with all the warring parties.)

Decade Activity

1910 to 1919

Students presenting this decade should:

• Make an expanded time line with at least 15 entries.

• Write a description or act out how one event on the time line affected the people in the family photograph on the page.

• Prepare a presentation that will make the decade memorable to classmates. The presentation should include the woman suffrage movement; African American migration north; and U.S. entry into World War I.

• Show how the decade compares with the decades before and after.

A family photo taken shortly before World War I

1913 16th Amendment permits federal income tax

1913 Federal Reserve Act establishes a new banking system

1915 First federal law to regulate child labor

1917 United States enters World War I

1918 World War I ends

1910 to 1919

The First World War

When war broke out in Europe in 1914, few Americans thought it would affect their lives. Women were struggling for the right to vote. African Americans, longing for better lives, had begun a great migration from southern farms to northern cities. Businesspeople wanted the United States to stay neutral so they could continue trading with the warring powers. By 1917, however, the nation was drawn into the first global war. Young men, perhaps even your own great-grandfather, marched into battle hoping that this bloody contest would be "the war to end all wars." Sadly, that was not to be the case.

1910s

Women marched proudly in suffrage parades demanding the right to vote.

1918

This army recruitment poster encouraged men to help fight the war in Europe.

I WANT YOU FOR U.S. ARMY
NEAREST RECRUITING STATION

1914–1918

The trench warfare of World War I caused tremendous loss of life. In the Battle of the Somme, over 1 million soldiers were killed or wounded.

Epilogue ● **553**

Checking Understanding

1. Why did many Americans think of the 1920s as good times? (Women gained the right to vote; business boomed and wages rose; sports, radio, movies, jazz, and cars made life more exciting.)

2. What ended the positive national mood of the 1920s? (The Stock Market Crash of 1929.)

Decade Activity

1920 to 1929

Students presenting this decade should:

• Make an expanded time line with at least 15 entries.

• Write a description or act out how one event on the time line affected the people in the family photograph on the page.

• Prepare a presentation that will make the decade memorable to classmates. The presentation should include the passage of the Nineteenth Amendment; an accurate depiction of the "Roaring Twenties" (including the growing economy and the increase in entertainment options); and the Stock Market Crash of 1929.

• Show how the decade compares with the decades before and after.

History Bookshelf

Blocksma, Mary. *Ticket to the Twenties: A Time Traveler's Guide.* Little, Brown, 1993. In this lighthearted but informative book, students will learn what their lives might have been like in the 1920s. They will be introduced to fads, slang, popular entertainment and culture, innovations in medicine and travel, and much more.

Also of interest:

Collier, James Lincoln. *Duke Ellington.* Macmillan, 1991.

McKissack, Patricia, and Fredrick McKissack, Jr. *Black Diamond: The Story of the Negro Baseball Leagues.* Scholastic, 1994.

Randolph, Blythe. *Charles Lindbergh.* Franklin Watts, 1990.

A New York City family that supported the "Back to Africa" movement in the 1920s

1920 Prohibition Amendment ban on the sale of alcohol takes effect

1920 19th Amendment gives women the right to vote

1924 Immigration Act sets up quotas based on national origins

1925 Scopes trial tests a ban on teaching the theory of evolution

1927 Lindbergh makes the first solo flight across the Atlantic

1920 to 1929

The Twenties

For millions of Americans, the 1920s were good times. Business boomed and wages rose. The new radio, movie, and sports industries made life more interesting and exciting. Some people could even afford to buy cars. The Roaring Twenties were also a time of social change. The nation tried—and failed—to end the drinking of alcoholic beverages. Having gained the right to vote in 1920, many women now demanded the freedom to live as they chose. Then, in 1929 the boom went bust as the stock market crashed, banks ran out of money, and factories closed their doors.

1923
King Oliver's Jazz Band entertained Chicagoans during the Twenties.

1926
A magazine celebrated the new sense of freedom enjoyed by people in the 1920s.

1929
The stock market crash brought the high life of the Twenties to an abrupt end.

History Bookshelf

Turner, Robyn Montana. *Dorothea Lange.* Little, Brown, 1994. Turner provides a lively account of a woman whose photographs of migrant farm workers and the urban poor helped to shape the nation's understanding of the hardships faced in the Depression era. Many of Lange's most powerful photographs are included in this volume.

Also of interest:

Freedman, Russell. *Eleanor Roosevelt: A Life of Discovery.* Clarion, 1993.

Greenfield, Eloise, and Lessie Jones Little. *Childtimes.* HarperTrophy, 1979.

Stewart, Gail B. *The New Deal.* New Discovery, 1993.

Continuing the Story

■ 1930 to 1939

Discussion

Checking Understanding

1. **What was life like during the Great Depression?** (Many people lost their jobs and their homes, and had to struggle to feed their families.)

2. **What did President Roosevelt hope to accomplish with the New Deal?** (Help the needy, including sponsoring government projects to provide jobs for the unemployed.)

A family of migrant workers in California during the Great Depression

1930 to 1939

The Depression and New Deal

1933 Nearly one-third of U.S. workers are unemployed

1933 Franklin Roosevelt begins the New Deal to combat the Depression

1934 Hitler takes power in Germany

1935 Social Security Act

1939 World War II begins in Europe

The United States plunged into the Great Depression in the 1930s, as did the entire world. For your grandparents, they were probably hard times indeed. Across the nation, businesses and banks failed. Millions of people lost their jobs and their homes. As Americans grew impatient, they turned to the government for hope. President Franklin Roosevelt responded to the spreading sense of gloom by promising Americans a "new deal." His New Deal programs helped many needy people survive. These programs also gave vast new powers to the federal government.

Decade Activity

1930 to 1939

Students presenting this decade should:

• Make an expanded time line with at least 15 entries.

• Write a description or act out how one event on the time line affected the people in the family photograph on the page.

• Prepare a presentation that will make the decade memorable to classmates. The presentation should include conditions during the Great Depression; major programs and effects of the New Deal; the rise of Hitler; and the beginning of World War II.

• Show how the decade compares with the decades before and after.

1933

People waiting in line for food were a common sight during the Great Depression.

1937

A mural depicts men building a huge dam in the western United States. Such government projects provided many jobs for the unemployed.

1930s

President Franklin Roosevelt and his wife, Eleanor, assured Americans that a better future was not far away.

Checking Understanding

1. **What caused the entry of the United States into World War II?** (The Japanese bombing of Pearl Harbor.)

2. **Why did so many women like the one pictured on the time line enter the work force in the 1940s?** (Men were fighting in World War II, and women worked to maintain wartime production.)

Decade Activity

1940 to 1949

Students presenting this decade should:

• Make an expanded time line with at least 15 entries.

• Write a description or act out how one event on the time line affected the people in the family photograph on the page.

• Prepare a presentation that will make the decade memorable to classmates. The presentation should include the bombing of Pearl Harbor and U.S. entry into World War II; women joining the work force during the war; Japanese American internment; the atomic bomb; and early causes and events of the Cold War.

• Show how the decade compares with the decades before and after.

History Bookshelf

Colman, Penny. *Rosie the Riveter.* Crown, 1995. Colman tells the story of the nation's unsung heroines, the millions of women who joined the industrial work force during World War II. Through photographs and interviews, Colman lets the women tell their own stories of how this era changed their lives.

Also of interest:

Aaseng, Nathan. *Navajo Code Talkers.* Walker and Co., 1992.

Mauldin, Bill. *Bill Mauldin's Army: Bill Mauldin's Greatest World War II Cartoons.* Presidio Press, 1983.

Stanley, Jerry. *I Am An American: A True Story of Japanese Internment.* Crown, 1994.

A family gathering to honor its members serving as soldiers in World War II

1941 United States enters World War II

1944 D-Day: Allies invade France

1945 World War II ends

1945 United Nations formed

1947 Marshall Plan aids a devastated Europe

1949 Western countries form the NATO alliance for common defense

1940 to 1949

World War II

Only 20 years after the First World War ended, the world was once again at war. For Americans, World War II began when Japanese aircraft bombed Pearl Harbor in a surprise attack on December 7, 1941. The United States soon found itself fighting in both Europe and the Pacific. The war ended in 1945 after American planes dropped two terrifying atomic bombs on the Japanese cities of Hiroshima and Nagasaki. After the war, Americans looked forward to a long peace. Instead, they soon found themselves locked in a "Cold War" with the Soviet Union and the Communist world.

1942
Japanese American families, forced from their homes, spent the war living in internment camps.

1940s
Over 6 million women joined the work force at home to maintain wartime production.

1945
After a bloody battle between American and Japanese troops, marines finally raised the flag over the Pacific island of Iwo Jima.

![History Bookshelf] **History Bookshelf**

Levine, Ellen. *Freedom's Children*. Putnam's, 1993. Through the words of 30 African Americans who were teenagers and children during the 1950s and 1960s, Levine presents a picture of life in the segregated South and the protest movements that forever changed the face of American history.

Also of interest:

Bernstein, Leonard et al. *West Side Story*. Random House.

McGowen, Tom. *The Korean War*. Franklin Watts, 1992.

Parks, Rosa. *Rosa Parks: My Story*. Dial, 1992.

Rosset, Lisa. *James Baldwin*. Chelsea House, 1989.

A family enjoying their first television set in the 1950s

1950 to 1959

1950–1953 Korean War

1951 President Truman removes MacArthur as commander of U.S. forces in Korea

1954 In *Brown* v. *Board of Education* the Supreme Court rules school segregation unconstitutional

1956 Congress approves interstate highway system

1957 Space Age begins when the Soviet Union launches Sputnik

The Post-War Boom

In the Fifties millions of Americans were busy getting married, having babies, and moving to the suburbs. Your parents may have been born during these "baby boom" years. Baby boomers were the first Americans to grow up with a television in the living room, a car in the garage, and rock and roll music on the radio. These years also saw the birth of the modern Civil Rights movement. Slowly but surely, blacks and whites tore down the walls of segregation that had long blocked African Americans from opportunities.

1957

Angry crowds did not stop Elizabeth Eckford from attending a previously all-white Arkansas high school.

1950s

Millions of city dwellers, seeking new houses and more space, moved to the suburbs.

1950s

When the Cold War strained relations with the Soviet Union, the United States government began testing a hydrogen bomb.

Epilogue • **557**

Continuing the Story

▪ 1950 to 1959

Discussion

Checking Understanding

1. What made the baby boom generation different from earlier generations? (Many families chose to move to the suburbs; they had available to them luxuries such as television sets and cars.)

2. What was the decision made in *Brown* v. *Board of Education*? (The Supreme Court ruled that school segregation was unconstitutional.)

Decade Activity

1950 to 1959

Students presenting this decade should:

• Make an expanded time line with at least 15 entries.

• Write a description or act out how one event on the time line affected the people in the family photograph on the page.

• Prepare a presentation that will make the decade memorable to classmates. The presentation should include the events in the Civil Rights movement, including school desegregation; the way of life of the baby boom generation; the Korean War; and the Cold War.

• Show how the decade compares with the decades before and after.

Continuing the Story

■ 1960 to 1969

Discussion

Checking Understanding

1. What were causes of optimism during the 1960s? (Nation's wealth and power; election of President Kennedy; Civil Rights movement; moon landing.)

2. What events caused division and unrest in the U.S. in the 1960s? (Vietnam War protests; assassinations of President Kennedy and Martin Luther King, Jr.; Cold War.)

Decade Activity

1960 to 1969

Students presenting this decade should:

• Make an expanded time line with at least 15 entries.

• Write a description or act out how one event on the time line affected the people in the family photograph on the page.

• Prepare a presentation that will make the decade memorable to classmates. The presentation should include events in the Cold War; events in the Civil Rights movement, including the march from Selma to Montgomery; the assassinations of John F. Kennedy, Robert F. Kennedy, and Martin Luther King, Jr.; the Vietnam War and protests; and the first person on the moon.

• Show how the decade compares with the decades before and after.

History Bookshelf

Duncan, Alice Faye. *The National Civil Rights Museum Celebrates Everyday People.* Bridge-Water Books, 1995. Photos of exhibits in the National Civil Rights Museum in Memphis help illuminate the story of the Civil Rights movement and the courageous battles of its many heroes, both famous and unnamed.

Also of interest:

Devaney, John. *The Vietnam War.* Franklin Watts, 1992.

Haskins, James. *The March on Washington.* HarperCollins, 1993.

Randall, Marta. *John F. Kennedy.* Chelsea House, 1988.

A young New Mexico family that chose a more carefree lifestyle in the 1960s

1961	Berlin Wall heightens Cold War tensions
1962	Cuban missile crisis
1963	President Kennedy is assassinated
1964	Civil Rights Act
1965	Major demonstrations against Vietnam War
1968	Martin Luther King, Jr., and Robert F. Kennedy are assassinated

1960 to 1969

A Nation Divided

Americans began the decade filled with hope. They lived in the wealthiest, most powerful nation on earth and their young President, John F. Kennedy, was admired worldwide. The Civil Rights movement, meanwhile, grew more powerful and successful. On November 22, 1963, however, Kennedy was killed by an assassin's bullet. Hope turned to sorrow and then to rage as the nation was drawn into the Vietnam War. Antiwar passions and protests tore the country apart—dividing families, friends, and communities. The decade closed tragically with the murder of civil rights leader Martin Luther King, Jr.

1965

African Americans marched in Alabama, demanding the same rights that other Americans had always enjoyed.

1960s

Vietnamese fled the fires and bombing in Saigon as the Vietnam War dragged on.

1969

On July 20th the United States landed the first person on the moon.

History Bookshelf

Rodriguez, Consuelo. *Cesar Chavez.* Chelsea House, 1991. In this biography, Rodriguez relates the life and experiences of the Mexican American labor activist who led migrant farm workers in their nonviolent struggle for better working conditions. His efforts led to the first bill of rights for farm workers, signed in California in 1975.

Also of interest:

Hoff, Mark. *Gloria Steinem.* Millbrook Press, 1991.

Hoobler, Dorothy, and Thomas Hoobler. *An Album of the Seventies.* Watts, 1981.

Takaki, Ronald T. *Strangers at the Gate Again: Asian American Immigration After 1965.* Chelsea House, 1995.

Discussion

Checking Understanding

1. What protest groups and movements gained importance in the 1970s? (Environmental groups; labor groups; groups struggling for equal treatment of women, Native Americans, Hispanic Americans, and disabled Americans.)

2. Why was the marine in the photograph removing the portrait of President Nixon? (Nixon had resigned from office.)

Decade Activity

1970 to 1979

Students presenting this decade should:

• Make an expanded time line with at least 15 entries.

• Write a description or act out how one event on the time line affected the people in the family photograph on the page.

• Prepare a presentation that will make the decade memorable to classmates. The presentation should include movements and protests led by labor and environmental groups, women, and members of ethnic groups; the end of the Vietnam War; and Watergate and the resignation of Richard Nixon.

• Show how the decade compares with the decades before and after.

A family of farm laborers in front of their temporary home

1970 First Earth Day calls attention to environmental issues

1970 Grape growers recognize United Farm Workers union

1972 President Nixon opens relations with China

1975 Vietnam War ends

1979 Iranians seize American hostages in Teheran

1970 to 1979

Movements and Protests

The Vietnam War ended in defeat for the United States. When President Richard Nixon brought the last troops home in 1973, the antiwar movement disbanded. By then, however, other protest movements had developed. The National Organization for Women fought for equal rights for women. Native Americans, Latinos, disabled Americans, and other groups, too, organized to draw attention to their struggles for equal treatment. Meanwhile, concerns about threats to the environment grew into a movement to protect and clean up the nation's land, air, and water.

1974

A marine removes a portrait of President Nixon, the first President to resign from office.

1970s

Women, inspired by the feminist movement, took to the streets to demand equal rights.

1970s

American Indian protesters in Washington, D.C., proud of their way of life, called for the return of native lands.

📚 History Bookshelf

White, Ryan. *Ryan White: My Own Story.* Dial, 1991. Ryan White's story of his experiences as a young person with AIDS helped put a human face on the epidemic. The book also includes easily accessible facts about the illness.

Also of interest:

Epler, Doris M. *The Berlin Wall: How It Rose and Why It Fell.* Millbrook Press, 1992.

Schouweiler, Tom. *The Exxon-Valdez Oil Spill.* Lucent, 1991.

Stefoff, Rebecca. *George Bush.* Garrett, 1980.

Tames, Richard. *The 1980s.* Facts on File, 1990.

Discussion

Checking Understanding

1. How did the views and actions of President Reagan compare with those of President Roosevelt and his New Deal? (Roosevelt increased powers of the federal government, especially to help the poor and unemployed; Reagan emphasized self-reliance and limiting the role of government.)

2. What are the people in the lower left photo celebrating? (The end of a divided Berlin and the collapse of the Soviet Union and its empire.)

Decade Activity

1980 to 1989

Students presenting this decade should:

• Make an expanded time line with at least 15 entries.

• Write a description or act out how one event on the time line affected the people in the family photograph on the page.

• Prepare a presentation that will make the decade memorable to classmates. The presentation should include Reagan and the conservative move away from government programs, the end of the Cold War, and the appointment of Sandra Day O'Connor to the Supreme Court.

• Show how the decade compares with the decades before and after.

A family using a new personal computer in their home offfice.

1981   AIDS virus is identified

1984   First woman Supreme Court justice

1986   Iran-Contra scandal unfolds

1987   Intermediate-range Nuclear Forces (INF) Treaty

1989   Communist government in the Soviet Union collapses

1980 to 1989

The Conservative Revolution

After two decades of movements and protests, Americans turned inward during the 1980s. Wary of trying to change society, many baby boomers, now adults, concentrated more on their jobs, families, and leisure time. Emphasizing patriotism and self-reliance, President Ronald Reagan wanted government to retreat from involvement in the economy. At the same time, he increased government spending on Cold War weapons. As the decade came to a close and the Soviet Union and its empire fell apart, such spending no longer seemed necessary. After more than four decades, the Cold War was finally over.

1989

As the Cold War ended, the citizens of East Berlin and West Berlin danced on the wall that had once divided them.

1984

Both Ronald Reagan (right) and George Bush (left) served as President during the 1980s.

1989

Emergency crews tried to keep 11 million gallons of oil from destroying the Alaskan coast after a tanker spilled its load.

History Bookshelf

Reef, Catherine. *Colin Powell.* Holt/Twenty-First Century Books, 1993. In this biography of a contemporary American military hero, Reef traces the life and career of the first African American to be appointed Chair of the Joint Chiefs of Staff. Also included is an account of Powell's role in planning strategies for the Gulf War.

Also of interest:

Ashabranner, Brent. *Into a Strange Land: Unaccompanied Refugee Youth in America.* Dodd, Mead, 1987.

Landau, Elaine. *Bill Clinton.* Franklin Watts, 1993.

Lewis, Barbara. *Kids With Courage: True Stories About Young People Making a Difference.* Free Spirit, 1992.

A Vietnamese family studying English together in their new home in Texas

1991 Persian Gulf War

1992 U.S. troops join U.N. forces in Somalia

1992 A record number of women and African Americans are elected to Congress

1992 Earth Summit is held in Rio de Janeiro

1993 North American Free Trade Agreement (NAFTA) is approved

1990 to the Present

Your Time, Your Story

The 1990s are your time. In many ways growing up today is different than it was for your parents. Changing immigration patterns are making American society more diverse than it was a generation ago. More children are being raised in single-parent homes now than when your parents were young. While your parents' generation was the first to grow up with television, yours is the first to grow up with personal computers. Looking ahead, it is difficult to predict just how America's story will unfold. For you and your friends, however, that story is just beginning.

1992

In a new role overseas, American troops landed in Somalia to help put an end to starvation there.

1990s

Computers have revolutionized the way people communicate at home, school, and work.

1995

For the first time in 40 years, the United States had a Democratic President and a Republican-controlled Congress.

Continuing the Story

- 1990 to the Present

Discussion

Checking Understanding

1. How does American society in the 1990s differ from previous decades? (More diversity, wider access to personal computers, and more single-parent families.)

2. What were two major changes in Congress in the 1990s? (A record number of women and African Americans were elected; the Republicans gained control.)

Decade Activity

1990 to the Present

Students presenting this decade should:

• Make an expanded time line with at least 15 entries.

• Write a description or act out how one event on the time line affected the people in the family photograph on the page.

• Prepare a presentation that will make the decade memorable to classmates. The presentation should include the U.S. role in foreign conflicts; the spread of personal computers; changes in telecommunications; changes in Congress; and the increasing diversity of American society. Presentations may also include current events of interest to students.

• Show how the decade compares with the decades before and after.

Point out that futurists, unlike fiction writers, make their predictions on the basis of trends derived from careful analysis of information and statistics.

Making a Prediction

Ask students to make predictions about an event or development that they think will take place before they are 30 years old. Ideas might include advances in technology affecting transportation, communication, medicine, or everyday life. Students may share their ideas with the class in written or oral form. Some may wish to include visual presentations.

Discussion

Stimulating Critical Thinking

1. Which parts of the Scenario do you think would be possible with today's technology? (Some answers: a bed that checks blood pressure, a shower that sprays suds, heat jets, automatic lights and heat, televised classes.)

2. What would be the advantages and disadvantages of a "teleclass"? (Advantage: learning more in a shorter time without outside distractions; disadvantage: not being able to interact with other students and teachers.)

Into the Future

The objectives for teaching the three pages entitled "Into the Future" are to:
• Make students aware of how futurists predict the future by studying the past.
• Engage students in writing scenarios about their own futures.

"Into the Future" can be effectively taught by having the class read and discuss pages 562–563 and then do the activity described on student page 564, individually or in small groups. The activity can be used as an alternative assessment. Evaluation criteria and a scoring rubric are provided on page 564.

Into the Future

How old will you be in the year 2025?

Waking Up in 2025: A Scenario

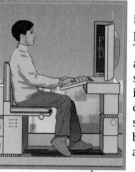

It is November 28, 2025: You wake up at 7 A.M. and your biometric bed checks your vital signs. "The old blood pressure is a little high this morning, my friend," the bed warns in a soothing tone. You step into the shower, and the showerhead automatically adjusts from your father-in-law's 6-foot, 4-inch, 240-pound frame to your slimmer body; the spray is rousingly forceful. You listen as the shower room's personal information system reports on the overnight stock activity from Tokyo.

As the shower douses you with antibacterial suds, you ask the information system for a quick personality assessment from the psychotherapeutic expert system you just installed. "Hey, relax! Try to image a sun-drenched beach," you're advised. "You'll be able to handle that marketing presentation much better." You smile, thinking about the fun you had on your last vacation in Hawaii as the shower's heat jets blast you dry. The robotic closet-valet brings out your color-coordinated, temperature-sensitive business suit, and you quickly dress. As you leave your bedroom, you sense the temperature going down behind you and the lights turning off automatically.

You peek into the kids' room to make sure they've transmitted their homework to school and have gotten dressed for their teleclass, which they "attend" for three hours in your home's media room during what used to be a long Thanksgiving holiday.

You are now ready to face an average workday in the 21st century.

From John Mahaffie and Andy Hines, *The Futurist*, Nov/Dec 1994. Reproduced with permission from *The Futurist*, published by the World Future Society, 7910 Woodmont Ave., Ste. 450, Bethesda, MD 20814.

The story above is called a **scenario.** A scenario is an imaginary account of happenings in the future. Scenarios are written by **futurists**—people who try to imagine what the future will be like. Futurists look at information from the past and the present. From that information they make predictions about what might happen in years to come and then draw up a scenario based on their predictions.

History Footnote

An early English futurist was Thomas Robert Malthus. In 1798 Malthus published a controversial pamphlet predicting that at its current rate of growth, the population of Britain would soon outstrip food production, resulting in mass misery and starvation. However, as Paul Kennedy points out in his book *Preparing for the Twenty-First Century*, Malthus's predictions did not prove accurate. He failed to foresee the effects of emigration, agricultural improvements, and the Industrial Revolution, which enabled Britain to support an expanding population with an improving standard of living.

Nevertheless, the race between population growth and food production continues to challenge futurists today as they attempt to gather data and analyze variables in an effort to predict the future.

Predicting the Future

To make a prediction, a futurist must first detect **trends**—patterns revealed, over time, by certain facts. In 1982, for example, there were three million computers in American homes. Just six years later the number of home computers had increased to over 22 million. To note such an increase in computer use is to discover a trend.

To make predictions about the future of education, a futurist might look at how many students graduate from high school and how that number has changed over the past 100 years. In observing the trend, the futurist would try to predict whether more or fewer students will finish high school in the future.

Predictions on this page were made by futurists trying to detect trends. They based these predictions on past and present facts.

Population Predictions

- The population of the United States is expected to rise from 260 million in 1994 to 390 million in 2050.
- The number of people belonging to all minority groups will be one-half of the nation's population in 2050.
- By 2010, for the first time, more people in the United States will be over 55 years of age than under 18 years of age.
- People will continue to move to southern and western states. For example, the population of California is expected to shoot up to 42 million in 2010 from its 1995 population of 32 million, while New York's population of 18 million is expected to remain the same.

Predictions About Work

- People working in service industries, such as teachers, doctors, and office workers, will increase in number.
- Factory workers in manufacturing industries will decline in number.
- New technologies will allow many people to work at home.
- More people will be **entrepreneurs,** people who start their own businesses.
- There will be 200,000 more lawyers by 2005, but 650,000 more waitresses and waiters.

Predictions About Education

- Use of **information appliances** (see below) will focus education on the individual. Classmates will study different topics at the same time. One might watch a video on volcanoes, another work on math problems, and still others create art on a computer.
- Students will learn in a variety of settings, from home to school to a museum. Schoolwork will be telecommunicated—sent by computer—between students and teachers.

Technology Predictions

- **Smart technologies** are computer chips that carry out instructions that they are given. They can adjust the temperature inside cars or regulate the darkness of toast. Smart technologies will be installed in more and more homes, schools, and workplaces.
- People will rely on **information appliances**—picture phones, computers, and faxes among them—to teleshop, televote, and telelearn. These appliances allow individuals to communicate through telephone lines.

Teaching the
Creating a Scenario for 2025

This activity is appropriate for individual students, or for pairs or small groups of students. To help them generate and organize ideas for their scenarios, have each student create a web. In the center they should put the name of their character. Radiating from the web should be details about the character's life, such as "interacts with teacher via computer." Once students have a wealth of ideas from which to choose, they can focus on doing research and bringing the best ideas together in a cohesive presentation.

Evaluation Criteria

The project can be evaluated according to the criteria listed below, using a scale for each:
4 = exemplary, 3 = good,
2 = adequate, 1 = poor.

Completing the task The scenario focuses on one day in the life of a 14-year-old in the year 2025. It provides at least ten details about his or her life inside and outside of the home.

Knowing content The scenario reflects an understanding of events and movements in the decades leading up to the present.

Thinking critically The student shows reasonable judgment in making predictions based on data and historical precedent.

Communicating ideas The student presents the scenario in a clear and engaging format.

Science fiction writers make their livings imagining what the future might hold. British writer H. G. Wells is considered by many to be the father of modern science fiction. Trained as a biologist, Wells turned to writing after an accident disabled him at age 21. Wells had hopes for the peaceful applications of scientific discoveries, and some of his novels reflect that hope. Others, however, such as *When the Sleeper Wakes: A Story of Years to Come* (1899), dramatize the potential dangers of technology.

In 1938 the American dramatist Orson Welles broadcast a radio play based on Wells's *The War of the Worlds*. The program was so convincing that it caused a nationwide panic among the many listeners who mistook it for a news report.

Creating a Scenario for 2025

Imagine you have been hired as a futurist. Your job is to create a scenario—an imaginary account—of life in 2025. The scenario should present one day in the life of an average 14-year-old American student. She or he will be your main character. Follow the steps below to meet this challenge.

❶ First, create the main character of the scenario in your mind. Imagine what one day in her or his life would be like. Think about the technologies that would be available. How would your character interact with people—parents, brothers and sisters, classmates, and teachers, among others? In your scenario describe the main character's life within the home and outside the home. Be sure to explain what schools will be like for young people in 2025.

❷ Like any futurist, research your scenario by reviewing the trends of various topics you plan to include in your story. You can trace the changes in work done by Americans, for example, by reviewing the decade projects completed by you and your classmates. Consider the current state of each topic, such as work, at this time in our history.

❸ Present your scenario as a video or an illustrated story on posterboards. Use both facts and fantasies in creating the script or captions, and in drawing the illustrations, for your presentation.

Remember that an effective scenario is a prediction that is based on trends. What trends will you base your scenario on? Be prepared to explain them.

Reference Center

Atlas   **R2**

   The World: Political   R2
   United States: Physical   R4
   United States: Political   R6
   Natural Vegetation of the United States   R8
   Land Use in the United States   R9
   Territorial Growth of the United States   R10
   Population Density in
     the United States Today   R11

Gazetteer   **R12**

The States   **R19**

The Presidents   **R24**

Key Events in United States History   **R30**

The Declaration of Independence   **R32**

Constitution Handbook   **R34**

   Introducing the Constitution Handbook   R35
   The Preamble to the Constitution   R36
   Articles of the Constitution   R37
   Amendments to the Constitution   R59

Glossary   **R74**

Index   **R80**

Acknowledgments   R102

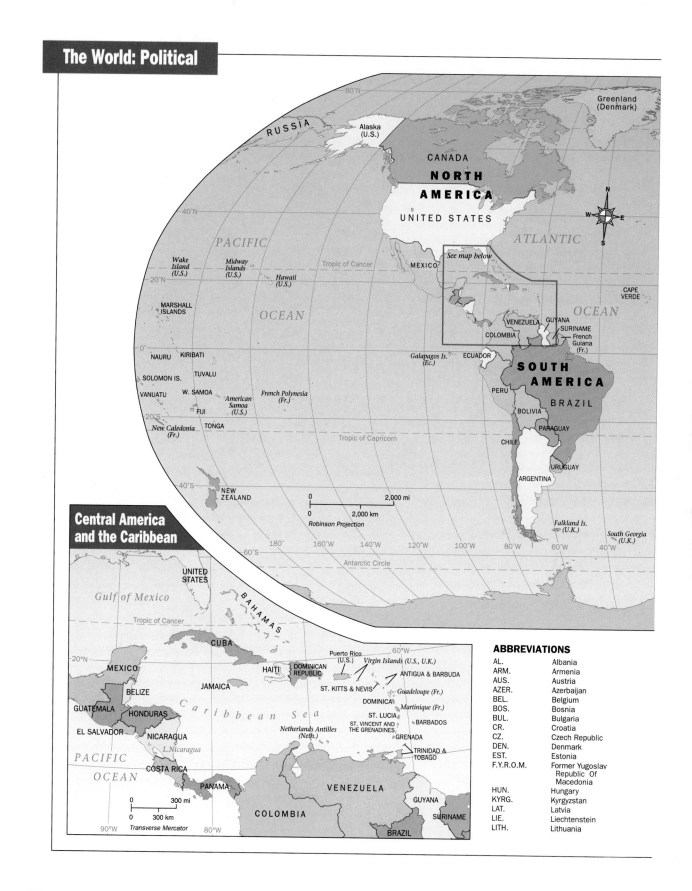

The World: Political

RUSSIA

Greenland
(Denmark)

Alaska
(U.S.)

CANADA

**NORTH
AMERICA**

UNITED STATES

40°N

PACIFIC

Wake
Island
(U.S.)

Midway
Islands
(U.S.)

Hawaii
(U.S.)

20°N

Tropic of Cancer

MEXICO

See map below

ATLANTIC

MARSHALL
ISLANDS

OCEAN

CAPE
VERDE

OCEAN

0°

NAURU KIRIBATI

Galapagos Is.
(Ec.)

ECUADOR

VENEZUELA GUYANA
SURINAME
French
Guiana
(Fr.)

COLOMBIA

SOUTH
AMERICA

SOLOMON IS.

TUVALU

VANUATU

W. SAMOA

American
Samoa
(U.S.)

French Polynesia
(Fr.)

PERU

BRAZIL

20°S

FIJI

BOLIVIA

New Caledonia
(Fr.)

TONGA

Tropic of Capricorn

PARAGUAY

CHILE

40°S

NEW
ZEALAND

0   2,000 mi

0   2,000 km

Robinson Projection

URUGUAY

ARGENTINA

Falkland Is.
(U.K.)

South Georgia
(U.K.)

180°   160°W   140°W   120°W   100°W   80°W   60°W   40°W

60°S

Antarctic Circle

Central America and the Caribbean

UNITED
STATES

Gulf of Mexico

BAHAMAS

Tropic of Cancer

CUBA

Puerto Rico
(U.S.)

60°W

Virgin Islands (U.S., U.K.)

20°N

MEXICO

HAITI

DOMINICAN
REPUBLIC

ANTIGUA & BARBUDA

JAMAICA

ST. KITTS & NEVIS

Guadeloupe (Fr.)

BELIZE

Caribbean   Sea

DOMINICA

Martinique (Fr.)

GUATEMALA

HONDURAS

ST. LUCIA

BARBADOS

EL SALVADOR

NICARAGUA

Netherlands Antilles
(Neth.)

ST. VINCENT AND
THE GRENADINES

GRENADA

L.Nicaragua

TRINIDAD &
TOBAGO

PACIFIC

COSTA RICA

OCEAN

PANAMA

VENEZUELA

GUYANA

0   300 mi

0   300 km

COLOMBIA

SURINAME

90°W   Transverse Mercator   80°W

BRAZIL

ABBREVIATIONS

AL.	Albania
ARM.	Armenia
AUS.	Austria
AZER.	Azerbaijan
BEL.	Belgium
BOS.	Bosnia
BUL.	Bulgaria
CR.	Croatia
CZ.	Czech Republic
DEN.	Denmark
EST.	Estonia
F.Y.R.O.M.	Former Yugoslav Republic Of Macedonia
HUN.	Hungary
KYRG.	Kyrgyzstan
LAT.	Latvia
LIE.	Liechtenstein
LITH.	Lithuania

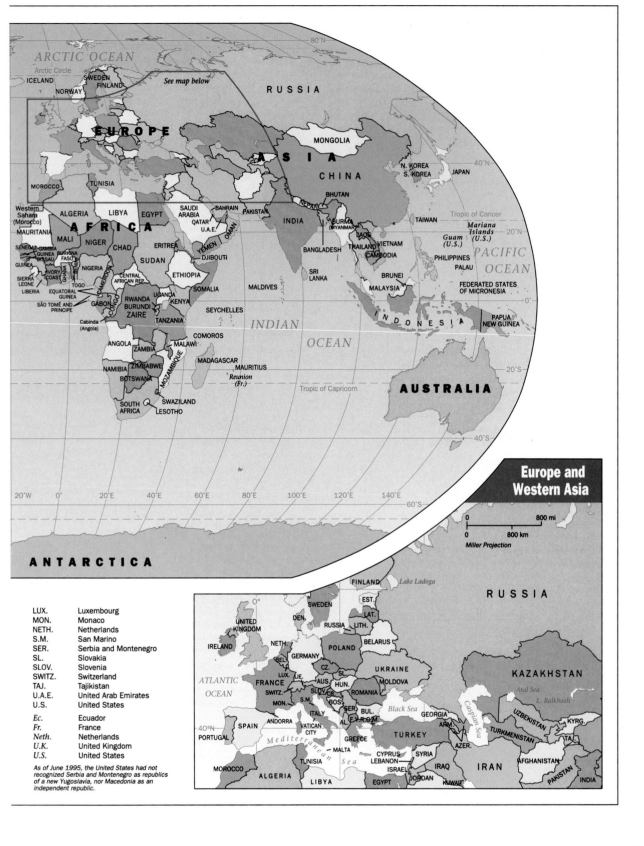

ARCTIC OCEAN

Arctic Circle

ICELAND
SWEDEN
FINLAND
NORWAY

See map below

80°N

RUSSIA

EUROPE

ASIA

MONGOLIA

40°N

CHINA

N. KOREA
S. KOREA
JAPAN

TUNISIA

MOROCCO

BHUTAN

Western
Sahara
(Morocco)

ALGERIA   LIBYA   EGYPT

AFRICA

SAUDI
ARABIA
BAHRAIN
QATAR
U.A.E.

PAKISTAN

NEPAL

INDIA

BURMA
(MYANMAR)

TAIWAN

Tropic of Cancer

Mariana
Islands
(U.S.)

20°N

MAURITANIA

MALI
NIGER
CHAD

SENEGAL GAMBIA
GUINEA
BISSAU
GUINEA
SIERRA
LEONE
LIBERIA
IVORY
COAST
GHANA
TOGO
BENIN
BURKINA
FASO
NIGERIA
CAMEROON
EQUATORIAL
GUINEA
SÃO TOMÉ AND
PRINCIPE
GABON
CONGO
Cabinda
(Angola)

CENTRAL
AFRICAN REP.

ERITREA

YEMEN

DJIBOUTI

OMAN

SUDAN

ETHIOPIA

SOMALIA

UGANDA
RWANDA
BURUNDI
ZAIRE
KENYA

TANZANIA

MALDIVES

SRI
LANKA

BANGLADESH

THAILAND
LAOS
VIETNAM
CAMBODIA

PHILIPPINES

BRUNEI

MALAYSIA

PALAU

FEDERATED STATES
OF MICRONESIA

PACIFIC
OCEAN

0°

INDONESIA

PAPUA
NEW GUINEA

SEYCHELLES

INDIAN

OCEAN

ANGOLA
ZAMBIA
MALAWI
NAMIBIA
ZIMBABWE
BOTSWANA
MOZAMBIQUE
MADAGASCAR

COMOROS

MAURITIUS
Reunion
(Fr.)

20°S

Tropic of Capricorn

AUSTRALIA

SOUTH
AFRICA
SWAZILAND
LESOTHO

40°S

20°W   0°   20°E   40°E   60°E   80°E   100°E   120°E   140°E

60°S

ANTARCTICA

LUX.	Luxembourg
MON.	Monaco
NETH.	Netherlands
S.M.	San Marino
SER.	Serbia and Montenegro
SL.	Slovakia
SLOV.	Slovenia
SWITZ.	Switzerland
TAJ.	Tajikistan
U.A.E.	United Arab Emirates
U.S.	United States
Ec.	Ecuador
Fr.	France
Neth.	Netherlands
U.K.	United Kingdom
U.S.	United States

*As of June 1995, the United States had not
recognized Serbia and Montenegro as republics
of a new Yugoslavia, nor Macedonia as an
independent republic.*

FINLAND   *Lake Ladoga*

0°

SWEDEN   EST.

DEN.   RUSSIA   LAT.
LITH.

UNITED
KINGDOM

RUSSIA

IRELAND

NETH.   BELARUS

GERMANY   POLAND

BEL.

LUX.   UKRAINE
LIE.
CZ.
SL.
FRANCE   AUS.   HUN.   MOLDOVA
SWITZ.   SLOV.   CR.
MON.   S.M.   BOS.   ROMANIA
ITALY   SER.   BUL.
AL.   F.Y.R.O.M.

KAZAKHSTAN

Aral Sea

L. Balkhash

ATLANTIC
OCEAN

40°N

SPAIN

ANDORRA

VATICAN
CITY

Black Sea

GEORGIA

Caspian Sea

UZBEKISTAN

KYRG.

ARM.
AZER.
TURKMENISTAN

TAJ.

PORTUGAL

Mediterranean

MALTA

GREECE

TURKEY

IRAN

MOROCCO

TUNISIA

Sea

CYPRUS
LEBANON
ISRAEL

SYRIA

AFGHANISTAN

PAKISTAN

ALGERIA

LIBYA

EGYPT

JORDAN
IRAQ
KUWAIT

INDIA

Atlas ● **R3**

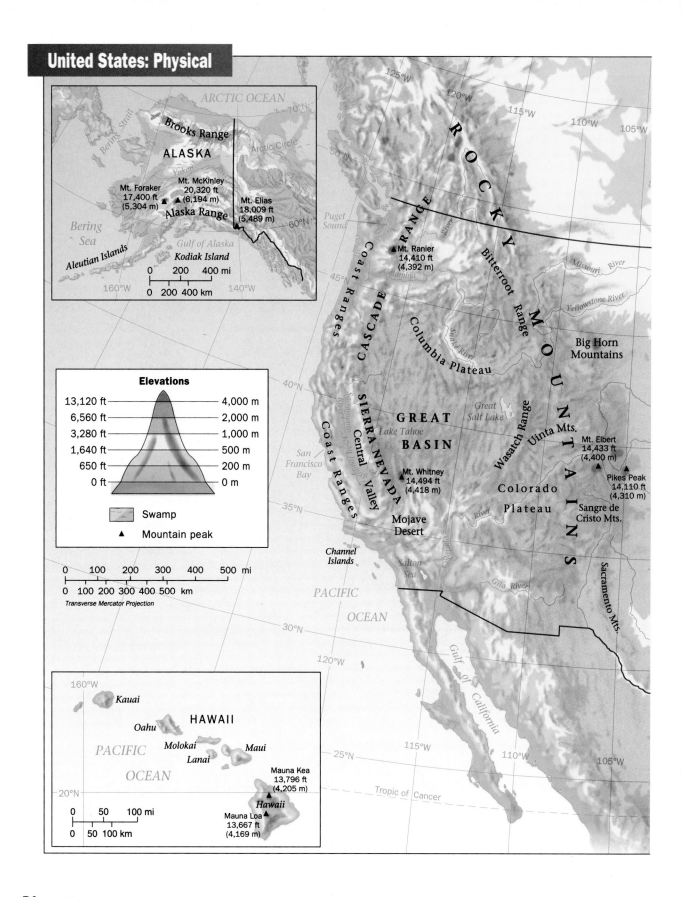

United States: Physical

ALASKA

ARCTIC OCEAN

Bering Strait

Brooks Range

Arctic Circle

Yukon

Mt. Foraker
17,400 ft
(5,304 m)

Mt. McKinley
20,320 ft
(6,194 m)

Alaska Range

Mt. Elias
18,009 ft
(5,489 m)

Bering Sea

Gulf of Alaska

Aleutian Islands

Kodiak Island

| 0 | 200 | 400 mi |
| 0 | 200 400 | km |

Elevations

13,120 ft		4,000 m
6,560 ft		2,000 m
3,280 ft		1,000 m
1,640 ft		500 m
650 ft		200 m
0 ft		0 m

Swamp

▲ Mountain peak

| 0 | 100 | 200 | 300 | 400 | 500 mi |
| 0 | 100 200 300 400 500 | km |

Transverse Mercator Projection

HAWAII

Kauai

Oahu

Molokai

Lanai

Maui

PACIFIC OCEAN

Mauna Kea
13,796 ft
(4,205 m)

Hawaii

Mauna Loa
13,667 ft
(4,169 m)

| 0 | 50 | 100 mi |
| 0 | 50 100 | km |

ROCKY RANGE

ROCKY MOUNTAINS

Coast Ranges

CASCADE RANGE

Mt. Ranier
14,410 ft
(4,392 m)

Puget Sound

Columbia River

Columbia Plateau

Snake River

Bitterroot Range

Missouri River

Yellowstone River

Big Horn Mountains

SIERRA NEVADA

Sacramento River

GREAT BASIN

Great Salt Lake

Lake Tahoe

Wasatch Range

Uinta Mts.

Mt. Elbert
14,433 ft
(4,400 m)

Mt. Whitney
14,494 ft
(4,418 m)

Central Valley

Coast Ranges

San Francisco Bay

Pikes Peak
14,110 ft
(4,310 m)

Colorado Plateau

Sangre de Cristo Mts.

Mojave Desert

Colorado River

Channel Islands

Salton Sea

Gila River

Sacramento Mts.

PACIFIC OCEAN

Gulf of California

Tropic of Cancer

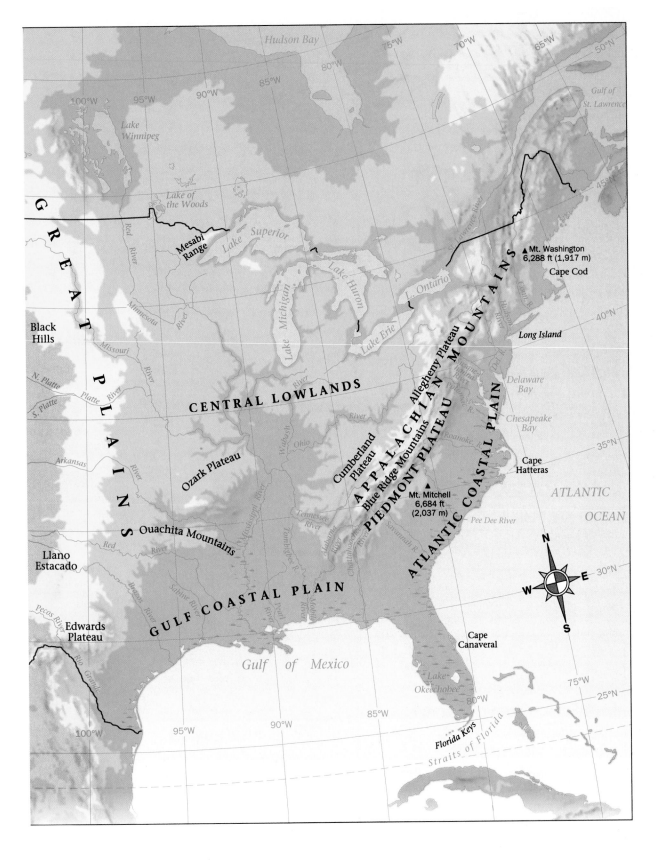

Hudson Bay

Gulf of
St. Lawrence

Lake
Winnipeg

Lake
of the Woods

Mesabi
Range

Lake Superior

Red River

Lake Huron

Lake Michigan

L. Ontario

Lawrence River

Conn. R.

▲ Mt. Washington
6,288 ft (1,917 m)

Cape Cod

Black
Hills

Minnesota River

Missouri River

N. Platte

S. Platte

Platte River

Arkansas

Lake Erie

Hudson R.

Long Island

Delaware
Bay

CENTRAL LOWLANDS

River

Wabush

Ohio

Delaware River

Susquehanna River

Potomac R.

Chesapeake
Bay

GREAT PLAINS

Ozark Plateau

Cumberland
Plateau

Allegheny Plateau

APPALACHIAN MOUNTAINS

Blue Ridge Mountains

PIEDMONT PLATEAU

Roanoke R.

35°N

Cape
Hatteras

Ouachita Mountains

Mississippi River

Tennessee River

Mt. Mitchell
6,684 ft
(2,037 m)

Savannah River

ATLANTIC COASTAL PLAIN

Pee Dee River

ATLANTIC
OCEAN

Red River

Llano
Estacado

Tombigbee R.

Alabama R.

Chattahoochee R.

30°N

Pecos River

Edwards
Plateau

Sabine River

Brazos River

Pearl River

Mobile R.

GULF COASTAL PLAIN

N
W E
S

Rio Grande

Cape
Canaveral

Gulf of Mexico

Lake
Okeechobee

75°W

25°N

80°W

Florida Keys

Straits of Florida

100°W

95°W

90°W

85°W

United States: Political

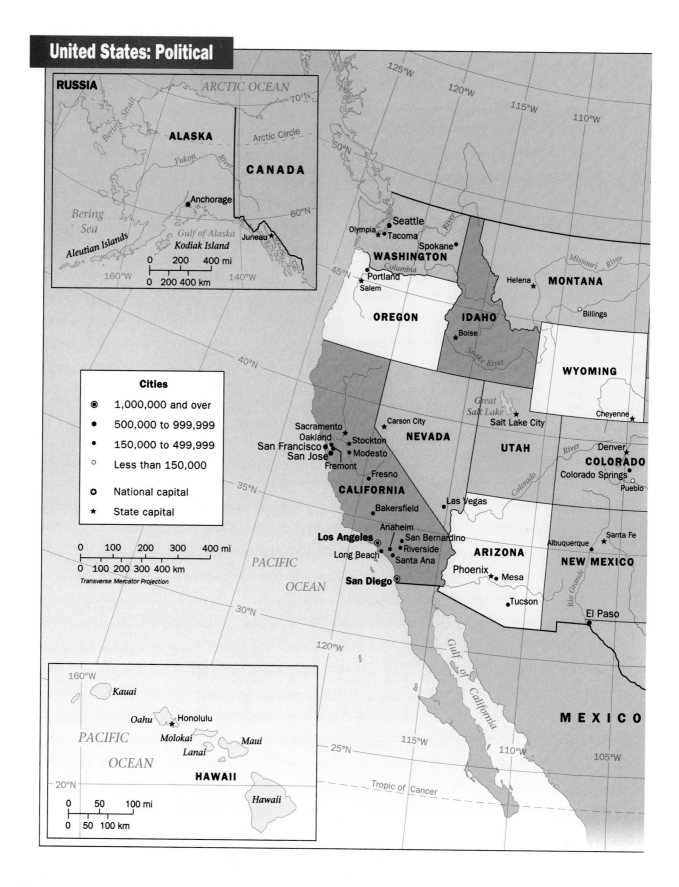

RUSSIA

ARCTIC OCEAN

70°N

ALASKA

Arctic Circle

Bering Strait

Yukon River

CANADA

60°N

● Anchorage

Bering Sea

Gulf of Alaska

Juneau ★

Aleutian Islands

Kodiak Island

| 0 | 200 | 400 mi |
| 0 | 200 400 km | |

160°W   140°W

Cities

◉ 1,000,000 and over

● 500,000 to 999,999

● 150,000 to 499,999

○ Less than 150,000

✪ National capital

★ State capital

| 0 | 100 | 200 | 300 | 400 mi |
| 0 | 100 200 300 400 km | | | |

Transverse Mercator Projection

PACIFIC

OCEAN

125°W   120°W   115°W   110°W

50°N

Seattle
Olympia ★ Tacoma
Spokane ●

WASHINGTON

Columbia River

● Portland
Salem

45°N

OREGON

IDAHO

● Boise ★

Snake River

Helena ★ **MONTANA**

○ Billings

WYOMING

40°N

Great Salt Lake ★

Carson City ★   Salt Lake City ★

Cheyenne ★

Sacramento ★
Oakland ● ● Stockton
San Francisco ● ● Modesto
San Jose ●
Fremont ●

NEVADA

UTAH

Colorado River

Denver ◉

COLORADO

Colorado Springs ●
Pueblo ●

● Fresno

35°N

CALIFORNIA

● Bakersfield

Las Vegas ●

Albuquerque ●

Santa Fe ★

Anaheim ●
Los Angeles ◉ ● San Bernardino
Long Beach ● ● Riverside
Santa Ana ●

ARIZONA

NEW MEXICO

Phoenix ★ ● Mesa

Rio Grande

San Diego ◉

● Tucson

El Paso ●

30°N

120°W

Gulf of California

M E X I C O

160°W

Kauai

PACIFIC

Oahu ● Honolulu
★
Molokai   Maui
Lanai

OCEAN

HAWAII

20°N

Hawaii

| 0 | 50 | 100 mi |
| 0 | 50 100 km | |

115°W   110°W   105°W

25°N

Tropic of Cancer

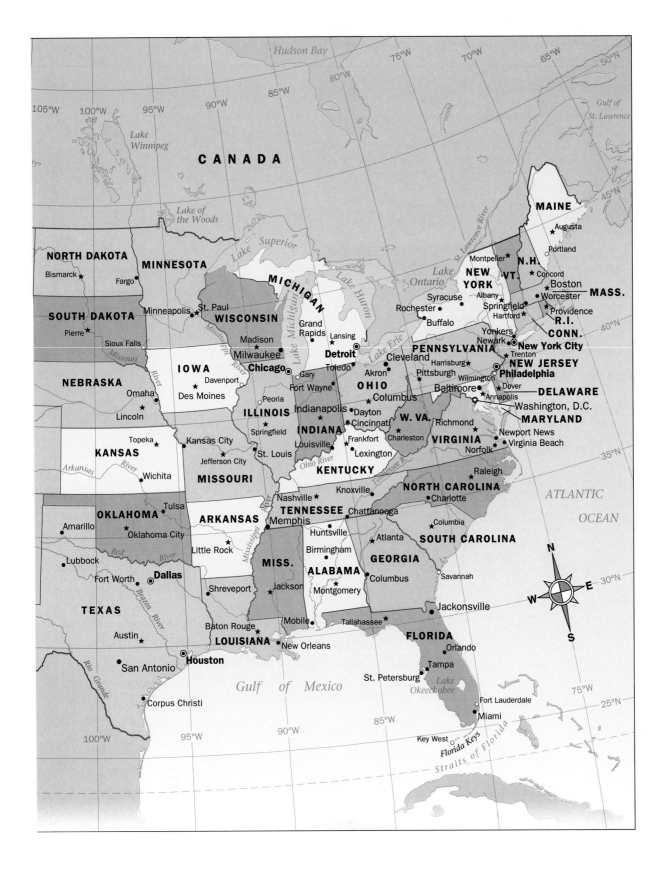

Hudson Bay

Gulf of
St. Lawrence

CANADA

Lake
Winnipeg

Lake of
the Woods

Lake Superior

MAINE
Augusta
Portland
Montpelier N.H.
NORTH DAKOTA
MINNESOTA
Bismarck
Fargo
VT. Concord
Boston
MASS.
NEW
YORK
Lake
Ontario
Albany
Worcester
Syracuse
Springfield
Providence
SOUTH DAKOTA
WISCONSIN
St. Paul
Rochester
Hartford
R.I.
Pierre
Minneapolis
Buffalo
CONN.
Madison
Grand
Rapids
Lansing
Yonkers
New York City
Sioux Falls
Milwaukee
PENNSYLVANIA
Newark
IOWA
Chicago
Detroit
Cleveland
Trenton
NEW JERSEY
NEBRASKA
Gary
Toledo
Akron
Harrisburg
Philadelphia
Davenport
Fort Wayne
Pittsburgh
Wilmington
Dover
Omaha
Des Moines
OHIO
Columbus
Baltimore
DELAWARE
Peoria
Annapolis
Lincoln
ILLINOIS
Indianapolis
Dayton
Washington, D.C.
Topeka
INDIANA
Cincinnati
W. VA.
Richmond
MARYLAND
Springfield
Kansas City
Frankfort
Charleston
Newport News
KANSAS
Louisville
VIRGINIA
Virginia Beach
Jefferson City
St. Louis
Lexington
Norfolk
Wichita
MISSOURI
KENTUCKY
Raleigh
Nashville
Knoxville
NORTH CAROLINA
Tulsa
Charlotte
OKLAHOMA
ARKANSAS
TENNESSEE
Chattanooga
Amarillo
Memphis
Columbia
Oklahoma City
Huntsville
Atlanta
SOUTH CAROLINA
Little Rock
Birmingham
Lubbock
MISS.
ALABAMA
GEORGIA
Fort Worth
Dallas
Jackson
Montgomery
Columbus
Savannah
Shreveport
TEXAS
Jacksonville
Baton Rouge
Mobile
Tallahassee
Austin
LOUISIANA
New Orleans
FLORIDA
San Antonio
Houston
Orlando
Gulf of Mexico
Tampa
St. Petersburg
Lake
Okeechobee
Corpus Christi
Fort Lauderdale
Miami
Key West
Florida Keys
Straits of Florida

ATLANTIC
OCEAN

Natural Vegetation of the United States

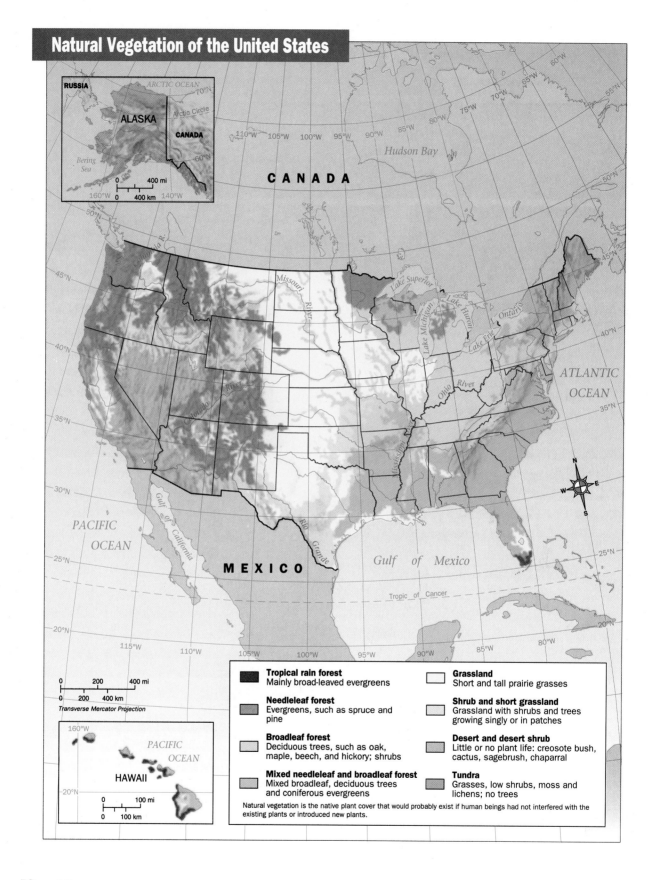

RUSSIA
ARCTIC OCEAN
ALASKA
CANADA
Bering Sea
0 400 mi
0 400 km

CANADA

Hudson Bay

Lake Superior
Lake Michigan
Lake Huron
Lake Ontario
Lake Erie

ATLANTIC OCEAN

Missouri River

Ohio River

Mississippi

PACIFIC OCEAN

Gulf of California

Colorado R.

Nevada River

MEXICO

Rio Grande

Gulf of Mexico

Tropic of Cancer

0 200 400 mi
0 200 400 km
Transverse Mercator Projection

160°W
PACIFIC OCEAN
HAWAII
20°N
0 100 mi
0 100 km

Tropical rain forest
Mainly broad-leaved evergreens

Needleleaf forest
Evergreens, such as spruce and pine

Broadleaf forest
Deciduous trees, such as oak, maple, beech, and hickory; shrubs

Mixed needleleaf and broadleaf forest
Mixed broadleaf, deciduous trees and coniferous evergreens

Grassland
Short and tall prairie grasses

Shrub and short grassland
Grassland with shrubs and trees growing singly or in patches

Desert and desert shrub
Little or no plant life: creosote bush, cactus, sagebrush, chaparral

Tundra
Grasses, low shrubs, moss and lichens; no trees

Natural vegetation is the native plant cover that would probably exist if human beings had not interfered with the existing plants or introduced new plants.

Land Use in the United States

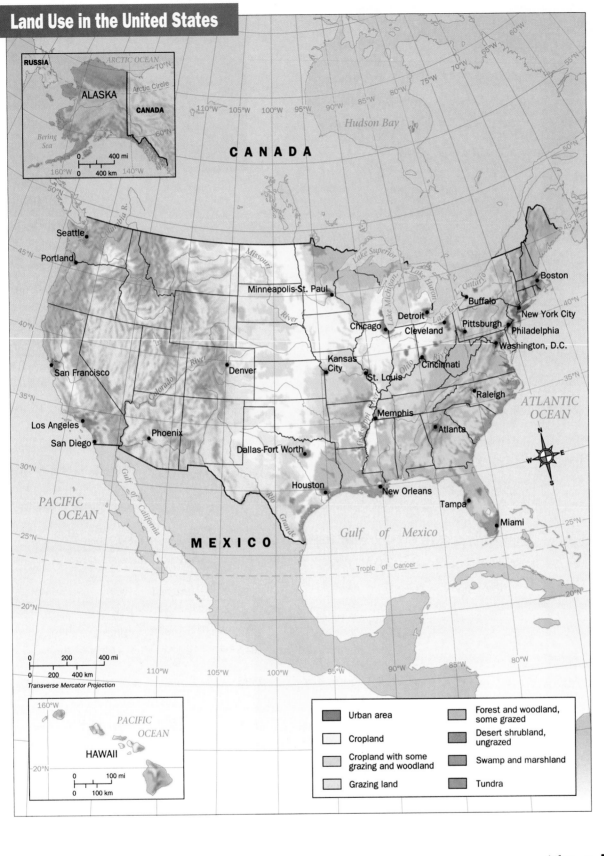

RUSSIA

ARCTIC OCEAN

70°N

ALASKA

Arctic Circle

CANADA

Bering Sea

60°N

0 400 mi

0 400 km

160°W 140°W

CANADA

Hudson Bay

110°W 105°W 100°W 95°W 90°W 85°W 80°W 75°W 70°W 65°W 60°W

50°N

Seattle

Portland

Columbia R.

Missouri

Lake Superior

Lake Michigan

Lake Huron

Lake Erie

L. Ontario

Boston

Buffalo

45°N

Minneapolis-St. Paul

River

Detroit

New York City

40°N

Chicago

Cleveland

Pittsburgh

Philadelphia

San Francisco

Colorado

River

Denver

Kansas City

St. Louis

Cincinnati

Ohio River

Washington, D.C.

35°N

Mississippi River

Raleigh

ATLANTIC OCEAN

Los Angeles

Phoenix

Memphis

Atlanta

San Diego

Dallas-Fort Worth

N

W   E

S

PACIFIC OCEAN

Gulf of California

Rio Grande

Houston

New Orleans

Tampa

30°N

25°N

MEXICO

Gulf of Mexico

Miami

20°N

Tropic of Cancer

20°N

0 200 400 mi

0 200 400 km

Transverse Mercator Projection

110°W 105°W 100°W 95°W 90°W 85°W 80°W

HAWAII

160°W

PACIFIC OCEAN

20°N

0 100 mi

0 100 km

	Urban area		Forest and woodland, some grazed
	Cropland		Desert shrubland, ungrazed
	Cropland with some grazing and woodland		Swamp and marshland
	Grazing land		Tundra

Atlas • **R9**

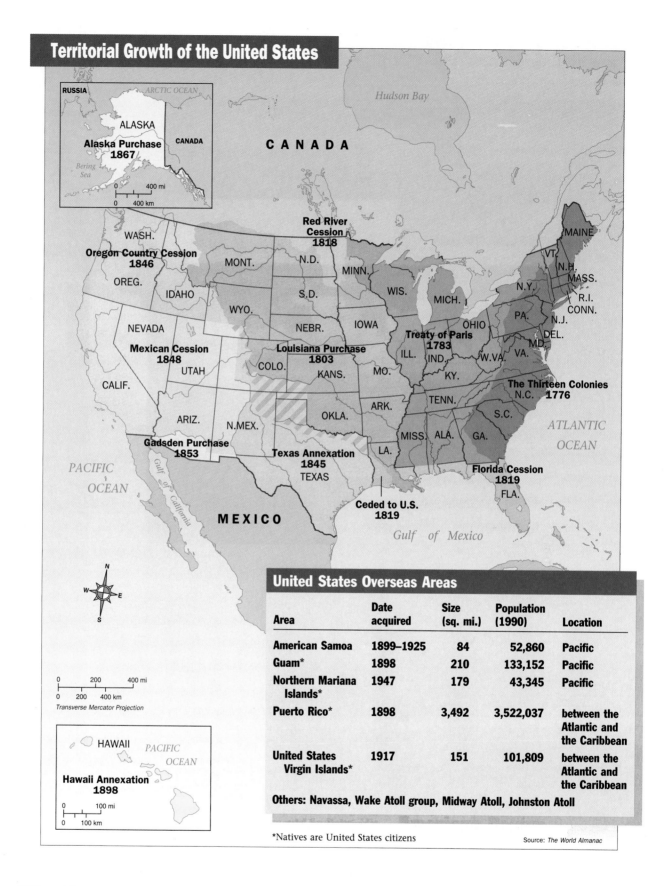

Territorial Growth of the United States

RUSSIA
ARCTIC OCEAN
ALASKA
Alaska Purchase 1867
CANADA
Bering Sea
0   400 mi
0   400 km

CANADA

Hudson Bay

WASH.
Oregon Country Cession 1846
OREG.
IDAHO
MONT.
N.D.
Red River Cession 1818
MINN.
S.D.
WIS.
MICH.
MAINE
VT.
N.H.
MASS.
N.Y.
R.I.
CONN.
PA.
N.J.
NEVADA
WYO.
NEBR.
IOWA
OHIO
Treaty of Paris 1783
DEL.
MD.
Mexican Cession 1848
UTAH
COLO.
KANS.
MO.
ILL.
IND.
W.VA.
VA.
CALIF.
KY.
The Thirteen Colonies 1776
N.C.
ARIZ.
N.MEX.
OKLA.
ARK.
TENN.
S.C.
Gadsden Purchase 1853
Texas Annexation 1845
TEXAS
MISS.
ALA.
GA.
LA.
ATLANTIC OCEAN
PACIFIC OCEAN
Gulf of California
Ceded to U.S. 1819
Florida Cession 1819
FLA.
MEXICO
Gulf of Mexico

N W E S

0   200   400 mi
0   200   400 km
Transverse Mercator Projection

HAWAII
PACIFIC OCEAN
Hawaii Annexation 1898
0   100 mi
0   100 km

United States Overseas Areas

Area	Date acquired	Size (sq. mi.)	Population (1990)	Location
American Samoa	1899–1925	84	52,860	Pacific
Guam*	1898	210	133,152	Pacific
Northern Mariana Islands*	1947	179	43,345	Pacific
Puerto Rico*	1898	3,492	3,522,037	between the Atlantic and the Caribbean
United States Virgin Islands*	1917	151	101,809	between the Atlantic and the Caribbean

Others: Navassa, Wake Atoll group, Midway Atoll, Johnston Atoll

*Natives are United States citizens

Source: *The World Almanac*

Population Density in the United States Today

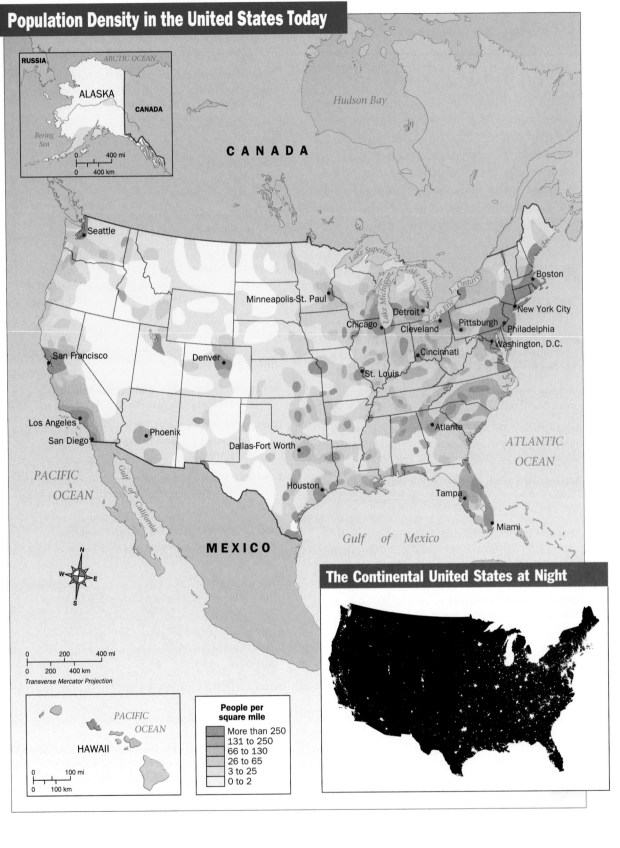

RUSSIA

ARCTIC OCEAN

ALASKA

CANADA

Bering Sea

0   400 mi

0   400 km

Hudson Bay

C A N A D A

Seattle

Lake Superior

Lake Michigan

Lake Huron

L. Ontario

Lake Erie

Minneapolis-St. Paul

Boston

Detroit

New York City

Chicago

Cleveland

Pittsburgh

Philadelphia

Washington, D.C.

San Francisco

Denver

Cincinnati

St. Louis

ATLANTIC OCEAN

Los Angeles

Phoenix

San Diego

Dallas-Fort Worth

Atlanta

PACIFIC OCEAN

Gulf of California

Houston

Tampa

Miami

MEXICO

Gulf of Mexico

N
W   E
S

0   200   400 mi

0   200   400 km

Transverse Mercator Projection

PACIFIC OCEAN

HAWAII

0   100 mi

0   100 km

People per square mile

More than 250
131 to 250
66 to 130
26 to 65
3 to 25
0 to 2

The Continental United States at Night

Gazetteer

A gazetteer is a geographical dictionary. It lists geographic features and places where major events have occurred. Each entry includes a brief description of the place.

Entries with specific locations—cities, battlefields, and other sites—have locations given according to latitude and longitude. At the end of the entry is a number that refers to the text page on which the first significant mention of the entry appears. The number that follows the letter *m* refers to the page where the place is shown on a map.

A

Alabama southern state; part of the Confederacy during the Civil War (page 306, *m323*)

Alamo (29°N 98°W) former mission in San Antonio where Texans resisted Mexican troops in 1836 (page 382, *m384*)

Alaska state located in the far northwest of North America (page 331, *mR6*)

Annapolis (39°N 77°W) site of Annapolis Convention in 1786; capital of the United States from 1783 to 1784 (page 238, *mR7*)

Antietam Creek (39°N 78°W) site where Confederate invasion of the North was stopped in 1862 (page 503, *m501*)

Appalachian Highlands elevated region in eastern North America stretching from Canada to Alabama; it includes the Appalachian Mountains (page *mP5*)

Appalachian Mountains mountain range in the Appalachian Highlands region of the eastern United States (page 485, *m155*)

Appomattox Court House (37°N 79°W) Virginia town where Lee's surrender to Grant ended the Civil War in 1865 (page 516, *m513*)

Arizona southwestern state; once part of New Spain and Mexico (page 21, *mR6*)

Arkansas southern state; once part of the Confederacy (page 492, *m323*)

Arkansas River Zebulon Pike followed this river in his 1806 exploration of the West (page 297, *m98*)

Atlanta (34°N 84°W) capital of Georgia; burned in 1864 by Union forces (page 515, *m513*)

Atlantic Coastal Plain coastal lowlands of the eastern United States; the plain grows wider in the South (page 149, *mR5*)

B

Backcountry in colonial times, a region of low, wooded hills extending from Pennsylvania to Georgia (page 152)

Baltimore (39°N 77°W) site of Fort McHenry; located at the upper end of Chesapeake Bay (page 127, *m135*)

Barbary States four North African states that raided American ships in the early 1800s; states included Morocco, Algiers, Tunis, and Tripoli (page 300, *m301*)

Basins and Ranges region in the western United States consisting of highland basins and mountains (page 399, *mP4*)

Beringia land bridge that linked Asia and North America during the last Ice Age (page 10, *m11*)

Bering Strait waterway between North America and Asia where a land bridge once existed (page 11, *mR4*)

Boston (42°N 71°W) capital of Massachusetts; center of colonial resistance to British rule (page 128, *m131*)

Brazil South American nation colonized by Portugal in the 1500s; it gained independence in 1822 (page 73, *m101*)

Breed's Hill (42°N 71°W) site near Boston where the Battle of Bunker Hill took place in 1775 (page 208)

Bull Run (39°N 77°W) site of two Civil War battles in northern Virginia; also called Manassas (page 498, *m501*)

Bunker Hill, *see* **Breed's Hill**

C

Cahokia (39°N 90°W) at one time the largest Indian town in what is now the United States; located in present-day Illinois (page 23, *m109*)

California Far West state gained by the United States from Mexico in 1848 (page 28, *m396*)

California Trail overland route stretching from Wyoming to California and established in 1833 (page 386, *m387*)

Canada nation bordering the United States to the north; originally settled by both the French and English (page 209, *m220*)

Canadian Shield lowland region that lies in north central United States (page *mP5*)

Central Lowlands region of flat to gently rolling land that lies to the west of the Appalachians (page 240, *mP5*)

Chancellorsville (38°N 77°W) town in Virginia; site of Confederate victory in 1863 (page 511, *m513*)

Charleston (33°N 80°W) port city in South Carolina; site of Fort Sumter where the Civil War began (page 134, *m277*)

Chesapeake Bay large bay surrounded by the states of Virginia, Maryland, and Delaware (page 122, *m122*)

Chicago (42°N 87°W) third largest city in the United States; major railroad and shipping center in the 1800s (page 110, *m323*)

China once a large empire in east Asia, now the most populous nation in the world (page 46, *m45*)

Cincinnati (39°N 85°W) major city in Ohio; developed as a port on the Ohio River in the early 1800s (page 411, *m407*)

Clovis (34°N 103°W) 10,000-year-old prehistoric site in present-day New Mexico (page 11, *m11*)

Coastal Lowlands coastal plain that stretches from Massachusetts to Texas along the Atlantic coast and Gulf of Mexico (page 127, *mP5*)

Colorado western state located in both the Rocky Mountain and Great Plains regions (page 20, *mR6*)

Colorado River river that flows from the Colorado Rockies to the Gulf of California (page 99, *m295*)

Columbia River explored by Lewis and Clark in 1805, this river separates Oregon and Washington (page 297, *m98*)

Concord (43°N 71°W) village near Boston and early battle site in the American Revolution (page 206)

Connecticut New England state; first settled by the English in 1636 (page 131, *m131*)

Cuba Caribbean island nation directly south of Florida (page 93, *m66*)

Cumberland Gap (37°N 84°W) pass in the Appalachian Mountains by which settlers moved into Tennessee (page *m277*)

Cuzco (14°S 72°W) center of Inca Empire in the Andes Mountains (page 17, *m16*)

D

Delaware Atlantic Coastal Plain state; first state to approve the United States Constitution (page 136, *m122*)

Delaware River river that flows into Delaware Bay and the Atlantic Ocean (page 111, *m220*)

Detroit (42°N 83°W) founded as a French fort; now the largest city in Michigan (page 110, *m323*)

District of Columbia, *see* **Washington, D.C.**

E

England southern part of the island of Great Britain (page 52, *m51*)

Erie Canal waterway built in 1825 to link New York City and the Great Lakes (page 325, *m323*)

F

Fallen Timbers (41°N 83°W) battle site at which U.S. troops defeated a force of Ohio Valley Indians in 1794 (page 275, *m277*)

Fall Line edge of the Piedmont in eastern United States where rivers tumble to the Atlantic Coastal Plain below (page 149)

Florida southern state; explored by Ponce de León in 1513 (page 97, *m323*)

Folsom (37°N 104°W) 10,000-year-old New Mexico site where prehistoric stone tools have been found (page 11, *m11*)

Fort Duquesne (40°N 80°W) French fort built on the site of present-day Pittsburgh (page 181, *m109*)

Fort Laramie (42°N 104°W) fort located along the Oregon Trail in present-day Wyoming (page 389, *m387*)

Fort McHenry (39°N 76°W) fort in Baltimore harbor; inspired Francis Scott Key's poem that later became "The Star-Spangled Banner" (page 307)

Fort Necessity (40°N 80°W) Pennsylvania fort built by Washington's troops in 1754 (page 181, *m183*)

Fort Sumter (33°N 80°W) fort guarding the harbor of Charleston, South Carolina, where the Civil War broke out (page 483, *m501*)

Fort Ticonderoga (44°N 73°W) British fort on Lake Champlain raided by American troops in 1775 (page 209, *m183*)

Fredericksburg (38°N 77°W) Virginia town; site of Lee's victory over Union troops in 1862 (pages 511, *m513*)

France nation in western Europe that first colonized Canada (page 52, *m51*)

G

Gadsden Purchase portion of present-day Arizona and New Mexico; purchased from Mexico in 1853 (page 397, *m396*)

Georgia southern state; founded by James Oglethorpe in 1732 (page 137, *m135*)

Gettysburg (40°N 77°W) Pennsylvania battle site where Lee was defeated and Lincoln made his Gettysburg Address in 1863 (page 511, *m513*)

Great Basin, *see* **Basins and Ranges**

Great Britain island nation established in 1707 and consisting of England, Wales, and Scotland (page 163)

Great Lakes Lakes Ontario, Erie, Huron, Michigan, and Superior; five large freshwater lakes on the border between the United States and Canada (page 22)

Great Plains region of grasslands east of the Rocky Mountains and west of the Mississippi River (page *mP4*)

Gulf of Mexico body of water that lies to the south of the United States (page 22, *m16*)

H

Haiti at one time a French Caribbean colony; gained its independence after an 1801 revolt (page 296, *m330*)

Harpers Ferry (39°N 78°W) West Virginia town where John Brown raided a federal arsenal in 1859 (page 480)

Hartford (42°N 73°W) Connecticut capital where New England Federalists met and demanded an end to the War of 1812 (page 307, *m131*)

Hawaii Pacific Ocean state made up of 8 major islands; originally a kingdom established by 1795 (page 275, *mR6*)

Hispaniola Caribbean island where Columbus served as governor; now includes nations of Haiti and the Dominican Republic (page 67, *m66*)

Horseshoe Bend (33°N 86°W) Alabama site where Creeks battled Andrew Jackson's troops in 1814 (page 306, *m306*)

Hudson Bay large bay in northern Canada discovered by Henry Hudson in 1610 (page 76, *m77*)

Hudson River largest river in New York state; explored by Henry Hudson for the Dutch in 1609 (page 76, *m122*)

I

Idaho northwestern state; acquired by the United States as part of the Oregon Country (page *mR6*)

Illinois state in the Central Lowlands region; originally settled as part of the Northwest Territory (page 23, *m323*)

Independence (39°N 94°W) town in Missouri where the Oregon Trail began (page 386, *m387*)

India Asian nation; goal of European traders in the 1400s and 1500s (page 45, *m45*)

Indiana Central Lowlands state; originally a part of the Northwest Territory (page 275, *m323*)

Indian Territory land in present-day Oklahoma; set aside by the United States government for forced resettlement of eastern Indian tribes (page 362, *m362*)

Interior Highlands hilly region in Missouri, Arkansas, and Oklahoma; also called the Ozark Mountains (page *mP5*)

Iowa Central Lowlands state; originally part of the Louisiana Purchase (page 390, *m323*)

J

James River river in Virginia that flows into Chesapeake Bay (page 122, *m122*)

Jamestown (37°N 77°W) Virginia site where first English settlement in North America was founded in 1607 (page 122, *m122*)

K

Kansas Great Plains state; earlier a territory where proslavery and antislavery forces battled in the 1850s (page 474, *m474*)

Kentucky state in the Central Lowlands and Appalachians; birthplace of Abraham Lincoln (page 278, *m277*)

L

Lake Champlain lake situated between Vermont and New York; site of battles during the War of Independence and the War of 1812 (page 218, *m220*)

Lake Erie one of the Great Lakes; scene of battles during the War of 1812 (page 306, *m183*)

L'Anse aux Meadows (51°N 55°W) site of Viking settlement on the Newfoundland coast around A.D. 1010 (page 62)

Lawrence (39°N 95°W) antislavery town in Kansas; set on fire by proslavery residents from Missouri in 1856 (page 475)

Lexington (42°N 71°W) village near Boston where the War of Independence began in 1775 (page 206)

Liberia West African nation founded by former American slaves in 1821 and eventually established as a republic (page 440, *mR3*)

Louisiana southern state; originally a French and Spanish colony (page 110, *m306*)

Louisiana Purchase land bought by the United States from France in 1803 that stretched from the Mississippi River to the Rocky Mountains (page 294, *m295*)

Lowell (41°N 83°W) Massachusetts city; early site of the Industrial Revolution in the United States (page 320)

M

Maine New England state; originally part of Massachusetts (page 131, *m131*)

Manassas, *see* **Bull Run**

Manhattan (41°N 74°W) island settled by the Dutch as New Amsterdam; now the heart of New York City (page 111)

Maryland Atlantic coastal state; first of the English colonies to tolerate Catholic settlers (page 133, *m135*)

Massachusetts New England state; site of first battles between the Patriots and the British in the War of Independence (page 128, *m131*)

Mexican Cession territory gained by the United States following the War with Mexico in 1848 (page 396, *m396*)

Mexico originally a center of Indian civilizations; now a nation that borders the United States to the south (page 14, *m98*)

Mexico City (19°N 99°W) capital of Mexico; site of Aztec city of Tenochtitlán (page 15, *m98*)

Michigan Central Lowlands state; originally part of the Northwest Territory (page 325, *m323*)

Minnesota state located in the Central Lowlands and Canadian Shield regions (page 468, *m493*)

Mississippi southern state; part of the Confederacy during the Civil War (page 534, *m323*)

Mississippi River longest river in the United States (page 23, *m98*)

Missouri Central Lowlands state; admitted as a slave state in 1820 (page 334, *m323*)

Missouri River tributary of the Mississippi River and second longest river in the United States (page 296, *m98*)

Monmouth (40°N 74°W) New Jersey town where Patriots battled retreating British troops (page 221, *m220*)

Montana western state; originally part of the Oregon Country and the Louisiana Purchase (page *mR6*)

Montreal (46°N 74°W) city in Canada; originally settled by the French (page 110, *m109*)

N

National Road first road built across the Appalachian Mountains (page 322, *m323*)

Nauvoo (41°N 91°W) Illinois town founded by Mormon settlers in the 1840s (page 390, *m387*)

Nebraska Great Plains state; part of the Louisiana Purchase (page 474, *mR7*)

Netherlands European nation; important trading power in the 1600s (page 76, *m77*)

Nevada western state; gained by the United States from Mexico in 1848 (page 399, *mR6*)

New England region in northeastern United States; named by English colonists for their homeland (page 126, *m122*)

Newfoundland province in eastern Canada; briefly settled by Vikings in A.D. 1000s (page 62)

New France land that was claimed by France in the 1700s, it stretched from Quebec to Louisiana (page 108, *m135*)

New Hampshire New England state; one of the original 13 states (page 131, *m131*)

New Jersey Atlantic coastal state; first settled by the Dutch and Swedes (page 135, *m135*)

New Mexico southwestern state; settled by the Spanish in 1598 (page 104, *mR6*)

New Netherland Dutch colony along the Hudson River in the 1600s (page 110, *m109*)

New Orleans (30°N 90°W) city founded by the French near the mouth of the Mississippi River (page 110, *m109*)

New Spain northern half of Spain's empire in the Western Hemisphere (page 101, *m98*)

New Sweden colony established by Swedes in Delaware and New Jersey (page 111)

New York Atlantic coastal state; settled by the Dutch in the 1600s (page 135, *m135*)

New York City (41°N 74°W) largest city in the United States; founded by the Dutch as New Amsterdam (page 110, *m135*)

North Carolina Atlantic coastal state; one of the original 13 states (page 134, *m135*)

North Dakota northern Great Plains state; location where Lewis and Clark spent their first winter (page 296, *mR7*)

Northwest Territory territory in the early 1800s; bounded by the Ohio River, the Mississippi River, and the Appalachians (page 236, *m235*)

O

Ohio Central Lowlands state; once part of the Northwest Territory (page 275, *m295*)

Ohio River river that flows from Pittsburgh to the Mississippi River (page 181, *m98*)

Ohio Valley region drained by the Ohio River (page 183)

Oklahoma southern Plains state; originally called the Indian Territory (page 362, *mR7*)

Old Northwest, *see* **Northwest Territory**

Oregon Pacific northwest state; first settled in the 1840s (page 394, *m493*)

Oregon Country area in northwest United States; at one time also claimed by Spain, Britain, and Russia (page 328, *m295*)

Oregon Trail 2,000-mile route from Independence, Missouri, to Oregon Country (page 386, *m387*)

P

Pacific Mountains and Valleys region of the United States that lies along the Pacific coast (page *mP4*)

Panama nation in Central America; crossed by Balboa in 1513 (page 73, *m66*)

Pennsylvania eastern state; founded as a colony by William Penn in 1681 (page 136, *m135*)

Peru South American nation; center of Inca Empire in the 1400s and 1500s (page 96, *m101*)

Petersburg (37°N 77°W) city in Virginia; besieged by Grant's troops for nine months until Lee's troops fled in 1865 (page 515, *m513*)

Philadelphia (40°N 75°W) Pennsylvania city; capital of the United States from 1790 to 1800 (page 136, *m135*)

Piedmont hill country in the southeast United States; it lies upland from the Atlantic Coastal Plain (page 149, *mR5*)

Pittsburgh (40°N 80°W) city in western Pennsylvania where the Ohio River begins (page 185, *m277*)

Plymouth (42°N 71°W) site of first English settlement in Massachusetts in 1620 (page 126, *m122*)

Portugal west European nation; first to begin large-scale overseas exploration in the 1400s (page 52, *m51*)

Potomac River river dividing Maryland and Virginia on which Washington, D.C., is located (page 236, *m513*)

Prophetstown (41°N 90°W) center of Tecumseh's Indian alliance in 1811; located in present-day Indiana (page 303, *m306*)

Puerto Rico Caribbean island and United States commonwealth (page *m66*)

Q

Quebec (47°N 71°W) capital of the Canadian province of Quebec; originally the capital of New France (page 108, *m109*)

R

Rhode Island New England state; founded as a colony welcoming people of all religions (page 130, *m131*)

Richmond (38°N 77°W) city in Virginia; capital of the Confederacy during most of the Civil War (page 492, *m323*)

Rio Grande river that forms part of the boundary between Mexico and the United States (page 104, *m98*)

Rocky Mountains high mountain range in western North America; reached by Lewis and Clark in 1805 (page 299, *mP4*)

Russia nation that stretches from eastern Europe to Asia (page 331, *m51*)

S

St. Augustine (30°N 81°W) city in Florida founded by the Spanish in 1565; oldest continuous European settlement in the United States (page 104, *m105*)

Saint Domingue, *see* **Haiti**

St. Lawrence River river that connects the Great Lakes and the Atlantic Ocean (page *m77*)

St. Louis (39°N 90°W) Missouri city from which Lewis and Clark set off to explore the West (page 296, *m277*)

San Antonio (29°N 98°W) southern Texas city; site of the Alamo (page 106, *m105*)

San Francisco (38°N 122°W) northern outpost of New Spain; now a major city in California (page 106, *m105*)

San Jacinto River Texan forces defeated a Mexican army along this river resulting in Texan independence (page 384, *m384*)

Santa Fe (36°N 106°W) present-day capital of New Mexico; established by the Spanish in 1609 (page 104, *m105*)

Santa Fe Trail 800-mile-long trail from Independence, Missouri, to Santa Fe, New Mexico (page 379, *m387*)

Saratoga (43°N 74°W) city in New York; site of American victory in 1777 that marked a turning point in the American Revolution (page 218, *m220*)

Shiloh (35°N 88°W) site of Union victory in Tennessee in 1862 (page 506, *m501*)

Sierra Nevada high mountain range in California and Nevada (page 386, *m295*)

South Carolina southern state; first settled by English from the West Indies (page 134, *m135*)

South Dakota northern Great Plains state; part of the Louisiana Purchase (page *mR7*)

Spain European nation; controlled vast empire in the Americas for 300 years (page 64, *m161*)

Spanish borderlands area of New Spain that occupied present-day northern Mexico and southern United States (page 97, *m105*)

Strait of Magellan (53°N 70°W) waterway at southern tip of South America (page 74)

T

Tennessee southern state; first settled in the 1790s (page 278, *m295*)

Tenochtitlán (19°N 99°W) capital of Aztec empire; now Mexico City (page 16, *m100*)

Texas southern state; part of Mexico until 1836 (page 105, *m323*)

Tippecanoe River river in Indiana where American troops defeated Tecumseh's forces in 1811 (page 304, *m306*)

Trenton (40°N 75°W) capital of New Jersey; site where Washington's army attacked Hessian troops in 1776 (page 216, *m220*)

U

United Kingdom established in 1801 when Ireland was united with Great Britain (page *mR3*)

Utah western state; first settled by Mormons (page 389, *mR6*)

V

Valley Forge (40°N 75°W) winter camp for Washington's troops in Pennsylvania from 1777 to 1778 (page 218, *m220*)

Veracruz (19°N 96°W) Mexican port from which United States troops advanced on Mexico City in 1847 (page 396, *m395*)

Vermont New England state located in the Appalachian Highlands (page *m235*)

Vinland (51°N 55°W) site of Viking settlement along the Newfoundland coast (page 62)

Vicksburg (32°N 91°W) city in Mississippi; site of Union victory in 1863 that secured control of the Mississippi River for the North (page 514, *m501*)

Virginia southern state; site of first permanent English colony in North America (page 122, *m122*)

W

Washington state in northwestern United States; once part of Oregon Country (page *mR6*)

Washington, D.C. (39°N 77°W) United States capital; established on banks of the Potomac River in 1800 (page 282, *m306*)

Western Plateaus region of plateaus and mountains in the western United States; it includes the Colorado and Columbia Plateaus (page 24, *mP4*)

West Indies Caribbean islands colonized by European powers in the 1500s and 1600s (page 134, *m161*)

West Virginia Appalachian Highland state; formed by pro-Union residents of Virginia during the Civil War (page 492, *m493*)

Wisconsin Central Lowlands state; originally part of the Northwest Territory (page *m323*)

Wyoming western state; located in the Rocky Mountain and Great Plains regions (page 299, *mR6*)

Y

Yorktown (37°N 76°W) small Virginia port; site of British surrender to the Americans in 1781 that ended the War of Independence (page 222, *m223*)

The States

Note: Population figures are 1995 estimates.

Alabama
Admitted: 1819
Capital: Montgomery
Population: 4,274,000
Area: 50,750 sq mi
    (131,443 sq km)
"Yellowhammer State"

Alaska
Admitted: 1959
Capital: Juneau
Population: 634,000
Area: 570,374 sq mi
    (1,477,269 sq km)
"The Last Frontier"

Arizona
Admitted: 1912
Capital: Phoenix
Population: 4,072,000
Area: 113,642 sq mi
    (294,333 sq km)
"Grand Canyon State"

Arkansas
Admitted: 1836
Capital: Little Rock
Population: 2,468,000
Area: 52,075 sq mi
    (134,874 sq km)
"Land of Opportunity"

California
Admitted: 1850
Capital: Sacramento
Population: 32,398,000
Area: 155,973 sq mi
    (403,970 sq km)
"Golden State"

Colorado
Admitted: 1876
Capital: Denver
Population: 3,710,000
Area: 103,729 sq mi
    (268,658 sq km)
"Centennial State"

Connecticut
Admitted: 1788
Capital: Hartford
Population: 3,274,000
Area: 4,845 sq mi
    (12,549 sq km)
"Constitution State"

Delaware
Admitted: 1787
Capital: Dover
Population: 718,000
Area: 1,955 sq mi
    (5,063 sq km)
"First State"

Florida
Admitted: 1845
Capital: Tallahassee
Population: 14,210,000
Area: 53,997 sq mi
    (139,852 sq km)
"Sunshine State"

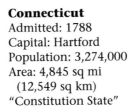

Georgia
Admitted: 1788
Capital: Atlanta
Population: 7,102,000
Area: 57,919 sq mi
    (150,010 sq km)
"Peach State"

Hawaii
Admitted: 1959
Capital: Honolulu
Population: 1,221,000
Area: 6,423 sq mi
  (16,636 sq km)
"Aloha State"

Kentucky
Admitted: 1792
Capital: Frankfort
Population: 3,851,000
Area: 39,732 sq mi
  (102,906 sq km)
"Bluegrass State"

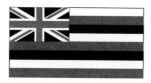

Idaho
Admitted: 1890
Capital: Boise
Population: 1,156,000
Area: 82,751 sq mi
  (214,325 sq km)
"Gem State"

Louisiana
Admitted: 1812
Capital: Baton Rouge
Population: 4,359,000
Area: 43,566 sq mi
  (112,836 sq km)
"Pelican State"

Illinois
Admitted: 1818
Capital: Springfield
Population: 11,853,000
Area: 55,593 sq mi
  (143,986 sq km)
"Prairie State"

Maine
Admitted: 1820
Capital: Augusta
Population: 1,236,000
Area: 30,865 sq mi
  (79,940 sq km)
"Pine Tree State"

Indiana
Admitted: 1816
Capital: Indianapolis
Population: 5,820,000
Area: 35,870 sq mi
  (92,903 sq km)
"Hoosier State"

Maryland
Admitted: 1788
Capital: Annapolis
Population: 5,078,000
Area: 9,775 sq mi
  (25,317 sq km)
"Old Line State"

Iowa
Admitted: 1846
Capital: Des Moines
Population: 2,861,000
Area: 55,875 sq mi
  (144,716 sq km)
"Hawkeye State"

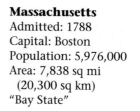

Massachusetts
Admitted: 1788
Capital: Boston
Population: 5,976,000
Area: 7,838 sq mi
  (20,300 sq km)
"Bay State"

Kansas
Admitted: 1861
Capital: Topeka
Population: 2,601,000
Area: 81,823 sq mi
  (211,922 sq km)
"Sunflower State"

Michigan
Admitted: 1837
Capital: Lansing
Population: 9,575,000
Area: 56,809 sq mi
  (147,135 sq km)
"Wolverine State"

Minnesota
Admitted: 1858
Capital: St. Paul
Population: 4,619,000
Area: 79,617 sq mi
  (206,208 sq km)
"North Star State"

New Hampshire
Admitted: 1788
Capital: Concord
Population: 1,132,000
Area: 8,969 sq mi
  (23,230 sq km)
"Granite State"

Mississippi
Admitted: 1817
Capital: Jackson
Population: 2,666,000
Area: 46,914 sq mi
  (121,507 sq km)
"Magnolia State"

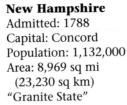

New Jersey
Admitted: 1787
Capital: Trenton
Population: 7,931,000
Area: 7,419 sq mi
  (19,215 sq km)
"Garden State"

Missouri
Admitted: 1821
Capital: Jefferson City
Population: 5,286,000
Area: 68,898 sq mi
  (178,446 sq km)
"Show Me State"

New Mexico
Admitted: 1912
Capital: Santa Fe
Population: 1,676,000
Area: 121,364 sq mi
  (314,333 sq km)
"Land of Enchantment"

Montana
Admitted: 1889
Capital: Helena
Population: 862,000
Area: 145,556 sq mi
  (376,990 sq km)
"Treasure State"

New York
Admitted: 1788
Capital: Albany
Population: 18,178,000
Area: 47,224 sq mi
  (122,310 sq km)
"Empire State"

Nebraska
Admitted: 1867
Capital: Lincoln
Population: 1,644,000
Area: 76,878 sq mi
  (199,114 sq km)
"Cornhusker State"

North Carolina
Admitted: 1789
Capital: Raleigh
Population: 7,150,000
Area: 48,718 sq mi
  (126,180 sq km)
"Tar Heel State"

Nevada
Admitted: 1864
Capital: Carson City
Population: 1,477,000
Area: 109,806 sq mi
  (284,398 sq km)
"Sagebrush State"

North Dakota
Admitted: 1889
Capital: Bismarck
Population: 637,000
Area: 68,994 sq mi
  (178,694 sq km)
"Flickertail State"

The States ● **R21**

Ohio
Admitted: 1803
Capital: Columbus
Population: 11,203,000
Area: 40,953 sq mi
(106,068 sq km)
"Buckeye State"

South Dakota
Admitted: 1889
Capital: Pierre
Population: 735,000
Area: 75,896 sq mi
(196,571 sq km)
"Coyote State"

Oklahoma
Admitted: 1907
Capital: Oklahoma City
Population: 3,271,000
Area: 68,679 sq mi
(177,879 sq km)
"Sooner State"

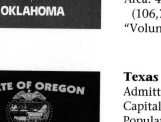

Tennessee
Admitted: 1796
Capital: Nashville
Population: 5,228,000
Area: 41,219 sq mi
(106,757 sq km)
"Volunteer State"

Oregon
Admitted: 1859
Capital: Salem
Population: 3,141,000
Area: 96,002 sq mi
(248,645 sq km)
"Beaver State"

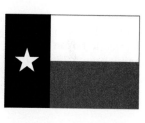

Texas
Admitted: 1845
Capital: Austin
Population: 18,592,000
Area: 261,914 sq mi
(678,357 sq km)
"Lone Star State"

Pennsylvania
Admitted: 1787
Capital: Harrisburg
Population: 12,134,000
Area: 44,820 sq mi
(116,084 sq km)
"Keystone State"

Utah
Admitted: 1896
Capital: Salt Lake City
Population: 1,944,000
Area: 82,168 sq mi
(212,815 sq km)
"Beehive State"

Rhode Island
Admitted: 1790
Capital: Providence
Population: 1,001,000
Area: 1,045 sq mi
(2,707 sq km)
"Ocean State"

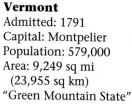

Vermont
Admitted: 1791
Capital: Montpelier
Population: 579,000
Area: 9,249 sq mi
(23,955 sq km)
"Green Mountain State"

South Carolina
Admitted: 1788
Capital: Columbia
Population: 3,732,000
Area: 30,111 sq mi
(77,987 sq km)
"Palmetto State"

Virginia
Admitted: 1788
Capital: Richmond
Population: 6,646,000
Area: 39,598 sq mi
(102,559 sq km)
"The Old Dominion"

Washington
Admitted: 1889
Capital: Olympia
Population: 5,497,000
Area: 66,581 sq mi
  (172,445 sq km)
"Evergreen State"

Wyoming
Admitted: 1890
Capital: Cheyenne
Population: 487,000
Area: 97,105 sq mi
  (251,502 sq km)
"Equality State"

West Virginia
Admitted: 1863
Capital: Charleston
Population: 1,824,000
Area: 24,087 sq mi
  (62,385 sq km)
"Mountain State"

District of Columbia
Population: 559,000
Area: 61 sq mi
  (158 sq km)

Wisconsin
Admitted: 1848
Capital: Madison
Population: 5,159,000
Area: 54,314 sq mi
  (140,673 sq km)
"Badger State"

The States ● **R23**

The Presidents

1. George Washington (1732–1799)
In office: 1789–1797
Federalist Party
Elected from: Virginia
Vice-President: John Adams

2. John Adams (1735–1826)
In office: 1797–1801
Federalist Party
Elected from: Massachusetts
Vice-President: Thomas Jefferson

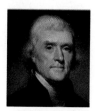

3. Thomas Jefferson (1743–1826)
In office: 1801–1809
Democratic-Republican Party
Elected from: Virginia
Vice-Presidents: Aaron Burr,
    George Clinton

4. James Madison (1751–1836)
In office: 1809–1817
Democratic-Republican Party
Elected from: Virginia
Vice-Presidents: George Clinton,
    Elbridge Gerry

5. James Monroe (1758–1831)
In office: 1817–1825
Democratic-Republican Party
Elected from: Virginia
Vice-President: Daniel D. Tompkins

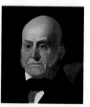

6. John Quincy Adams (1767–1848)
In office: 1825–1829
National-Republican Party
Elected from: Massachusetts
Vice-President: John C. Calhoun

7. Andrew Jackson (1767–1845)
In office: 1829–1837
Democratic Party
Elected from: Tennessee
Vice-Presidents: John C. Calhoun,
    Martin Van Buren

8. Martin Van Buren (1782–1862)
In office: 1837–1841
Democratic Party
Elected from: New York
Vice-President: Richard M. Johnson

9. William Henry Harrison* (1773–1841)
In office: 1841
Whig Party
Elected from: Ohio
Vice-President: John Tyler

10. John Tyler (1790–1862)
In office: 1841–1845
Whig Party
Elected from: Virginia
Vice-President: none

11. James K. Polk (1795–1849)
In office: 1845–1849
Democratic Party
Elected from: Tennessee
Vice-President: George M. Dallas

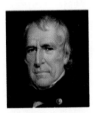

12. Zachary Taylor* (1784–1850)
In office: 1849–1850
Whig Party
Elected from: Louisiana
Vice-President: Millard Fillmore

13. Millard Fillmore (1800–1874)
In office: 1850–1853
Whig Party
Elected from: New York
Vice-President: none

14. Franklin Pierce (1804–1869)
In office: 1853–1857
Democratic Party
Elected from: New Hampshire
Vice-President: William Rufus de Vane King

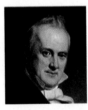

15. James Buchanan (1791–1868)
In office: 1857–1861
Democratic Party
Elected from: Pennsylvania
Vice-President: John C. Breckinridge

16. Abraham Lincoln† (1809–1865)
In office: 1861–1865
Republican Party
Elected from: Illinois
Vice-Presidents: Hannibal Hamlin,
        Andrew Johnson

*Died in office
†Assassinated

17. Andrew Johnson (1808–1875)
In office: 1865–1869
Democratic Party
Elected from: Tennessee
Vice-President: none

18. Ulysses S. Grant (1822–1885)
In office: 1869–1877
Republican Party
Elected from: Illinois
Vice-Presidents: Schuyler Colfax,
  Henry Wilson

19. Rutherford B. Hayes (1822–1893)
In office: 1877–1881
Republican Party
Elected from: Ohio
Vice-President: William A. Wheeler

20. James Garfield† (1831–1881)
In office: 1881
Republican Party
Elected from: Ohio
Vice-President: Chester A. Arthur

21. Chester A. Arthur (1830–1886)
In office: 1881–1885
Republican Party
Elected from: New York
Vice-President: none

22. Grover Cleveland (1837–1908)
In office: 1885–1889
Democratic Party
Elected from: New York
Vice-President: Thomas Hendricks

23. Benjamin Harrison (1833–1901)
In office: 1889–1893
Republican Party
Elected from: Indiana
Vice-President: Levi P. Morton

24. Grover Cleveland (1837–1908)
In office: 1893–1897
Democratic Party
Elected from: New York
Vice-President: Adlai E. Stevenson

† Assassinated

25. William McKinley† (1843–1901)
In office: 1897–1901
Republican Party
Elected from: Ohio
Vice-Presidents: Garret A. Hobart,
    Theodore Roosevelt

26. Theodore Roosevelt (1858–1919)
In office: 1901–1909
Republican Party
Elected from: New York
Vice-President: Charles Fairbanks

27. William H. Taft (1857–1930)
In office: 1909–1913
Republican Party
Elected from: Ohio
Vice-President: James S. Sherman

28. Woodrow Wilson (1856–1924)
In office: 1913–1921
Democratic Party
Elected from: New Jersey
Vice-President: Thomas R. Marshall

29. Warren G. Harding* (1865–1923)
In office: 1921–1923
Republican Party
Elected from: Ohio
Vice-President: Calvin Coolidge

30. Calvin Coolidge (1872–1933)
In office: 1923–1929
Republican Party
Elected from: Massachusetts
Vice-President: Charles G. Dawes

31. Herbert Hoover (1874–1964)
In office: 1929–1933
Republican Party
Elected from: California
Vice-President: Charles Curtis

32. Franklin D. Roosevelt* (1882–1945)
In office: 1933–1945
Democratic Party
Elected from: New York
Vice-Presidents: John Garner,
    Henry Wallace, Harry S Truman

* Died in office
† Assassinated

The Presidents ● **R27**

33. Harry S Truman (1884–1972)
In office: 1945–1953
Democratic Party
Elected from: Missouri
Vice-President: Alben Barkley

34. Dwight D. Eisenhower (1890–1969)
In office: 1953–1961
Republican Party
Elected from: New York
Vice-President: Richard M. Nixon

35. John F. Kennedy† (1917–1963)
In office: 1961–1963
Democratic Party
Elected from: Massachusetts
Vice-President: Lyndon B. Johnson

36. Lyndon B. Johnson (1908–1973)
In office: 1963–1969
Democratic Party
Elected from: Texas
Vice-President: Hubert Humphrey

37. Richard M. Nixon‡ (1913–1994)
In office: 1969–1974
Republican Party
Elected from: New York
Vice-Presidents: Spiro Agnew,
　　　　　　　　Gerald Ford

38. Gerald R. Ford (b. 1913)
In office: 1974–1977
Republican Party
Elected from: Michigan
Vice-President: Nelson Rockefeller

39. Jimmy Carter (b. 1924)
In office: 1977–1981
Democratic Party
Elected from: Georgia
Vice-President: Walter Mondale

40. Ronald Reagan (b. 1911)
In office: 1981–1989
Republican Party
Elected from: California
Vice-President: George Bush

† Assassinated
‡ Resigned

41. George Bush (b. 1924)
In office: 1989–1993
Republican Party
Elected from: Texas
Vice-President: J. Danforth Quayle

42. Bill Clinton (b. 1946)
In office: 1993–
Democratic Party
Elected from: Arkansas
Vice-President: Albert Gore, Jr.

The Presidents ● **R29**

Key Events in United States History

by 20,000 B.C. Earliest inhabitants spread across
   North America
7000 B.C. Agriculture begins in the Americas
600 Mound Builders establish the city of Cahokia
1000s Anasazis build cliff dwellings
1300s Aztecs establish their capital, Tenochtitlán
1419 Prince Henry's ships start to explore
   West African coast
1492 Christopher Columbus reaches the Americas
1497 Search for the Northwest Passage begins
1513 Ponce de León explores Florida
1519 Cortés begins the conquest of Mexico
1519–1522 Magellan's expedition circles the globe
1565 Spain founds St. Augustine in Florida
1570 League of the Iroquois formed
1607 Jamestown founded
1608 Champlain founds Quebec for France
1610 Spanish establish Santa Fe, New Mexico
1619 Virginia House of Burgesses first meets
   First Africans brought to Jamestown
1620 Mayflower Compact
   Pilgrims land at Plymouth
1630 Puritans found Massachusetts Bay Colony
1644 Roger Williams establishes religious freedom
   in colony of Rhode Island
1675–1676 King Philip's War
1676 Bacon's Rebellion
1681 Penn plans "holy experiment" in Pennsylvania
1682 La Salle explores the Mississippi for France
1730s The Great Awakening begins
1732 Georgia becomes the last English colony
1754 French and Indian War begins
1763 France gives up claims in North America
1765 Stamp Act
1769 Spanish build first mission in California
1770 Boston Massacre
1773 Boston Tea Party
1774 First Continental Congress
1775 Battles of Lexington and Concord
   Second Continental Congress
1776 Declaration of Independence
1781 Articles of Confederation ratified
   British surrender at Yorktown
1783 Britain recognizes American independence in
   Treaty of Paris
1787 Constitutional Convention
   Northwest Ordinance
1788 Constitution ratified
1789 **George Washington becomes first**
   U.S. President
1791 Bill of Rights ratified
1792 First political parties formed
1793 Eli Whitney invents the cotton gin
1797 **John Adams becomes President**
1798 Alien and Sedition Acts
Early 1800s Second Great Awakening sweeps the nation
1801 **Thomas Jefferson becomes President**
1803 *Marbury* v. *Madison*
   Louisiana Purchase
1804–1806 Lewis and Clark expedition
1809 **James Madison becomes President**

1812–1815 War of 1812
1817 **James Monroe becomes President**
1819 United States acquires Florida
1820 Missouri Compromise
1821 William Becknell blazes the Santa Fe Trail
1823 Monroe Doctrine
1825 **John Quincy Adams becomes President**
   Opening of the Erie Canal
1829 **Andrew Jackson becomes President**
1830 Indian Removal Act
1831 Nat Turner's Revolt
1832 Nullification Crisis
1833 American Anti-Slavery Society founded
1836 Texans declare independence from Mexico
   First families on the Oregon Trail
1837 **Martin Van Buren becomes President**
1838 The Trail of Tears
1841 **William Henry Harrison becomes President**
   John Tyler becomes President upon death
   of Harrison
1845 **James K. Polk becomes President**
   United States annexes Texas
1846 United States declares war on Mexico
1848 Treaty of Guadalupe Hidalgo
   Seneca Falls Convention on women's rights
1849 **Zachary Taylor becomes President**
   California gold rush begins
1850 The Compromise of 1850
   Millard Fillmore becomes President upon
   death of Taylor
1852 Harriet Beecher Stowe publishes *Uncle Tom's Cabin*
1853 **Franklin Pierce becomes President**
   Gadsden Purchase
1854 Kansas-Nebraska Act
1857 **James Buchanan becomes President**
   Dred Scott decision
1859 John Brown's raid on Harpers Ferry
1861 **Abraham Lincoln becomes President**
   Civil War begins
1862 Homestead Act
   Battle of Antietam
1863 Emancipation Proclamation
   Battles of Gettysburg and Vicksburg
1864 Sherman's forces seize Atlanta
1865 Lee surrenders at Appomattox
   Andrew Johnson becomes President upon
   assassination of Lincoln
   Thirteenth Amendment abolishes slavery
1866 National Labor Union organized
1867 Congress passes Reconstruction Act
   United States buys Alaska
1868 President Johnson's impeachment and trial
   Fourteenth Amendment defines U.S. citizenship
1869 **Ulysses S. Grant becomes President**
1870 Fifteenth Amendment defines rights of voters
1877 **Rutherford B. Hayes becomes President**
   Reconstruction ends
   Great Railroad strike
1881 **James Garfield becomes President**
   Chester A. Arthur becomes President upon
   assassination of Garfield

1882 Standard Oil trust formed
Chinese Exclusion Act
1885 Grover Cleveland becomes President
1886 Haymarket bombing
American Federation of Labor organized
1887 Dawes Act
1889 Benjamin Harrison becomes President
1890 Sherman Antitrust Act
1891 Populist party organized
1892 Homestead Strike
1893 Grover Cleveland becomes President
1894 Pullman Strike
1896 *Plessy* v. *Ferguson*
1897 William McKinley becomes President
1898 Spanish-American War
United States annexes Hawaii
United States acquires Philippines, Puerto Rico,
and Guam
1899 Open Door policy in China
**1901 Theodore Roosevelt becomes President upon
assassination of McKinley**
Progressive movement begins
1904 Construction of Panama Canal begins
Roosevelt Corollary to Monroe Doctrine
1909 William H. Taft becomes President
NAACP founded
1913 Woodrow Wilson becomes President
Federal Reserve Act
1914 World War I begins
1915 *Lusitania* sunk by German submarine
1916 U.S. troops sent to Mexico
1917 United States enters World War I
1919 United States rejects Treaty of Versailles
"Red Summer" and "Red Scare"
1920 Prohibition begins
Nineteenth Amendment gives women the vote
1921 Warren G. Harding becomes President
First immigration quota law passed
**1923 Calvin Coolidge becomes President upon
death of Harding**
1929 Herbert Hoover becomes President
Stock market crash
1933 Franklin D. Roosevelt becomes President
Good Neighbor policy proclaimed
New Deal begins
1934 Indian Reorganization Act
1935 Wagner Act and Social Security Act
1938 Congress of Industrial Organizations formed
1939 World War II begins
1941 Japan bombs Pearl Harbor
United States enters World War II
1942 Japanese-American internment
1944 Allies invade France
1945 Yalta Conference
**Harry S Truman becomes President upon
death of Roosevelt**
Germany surrenders
Atomic bombs dropped on Japan
Japan surrenders
UN charter goes into effect

1946 Philippines becomes independent
1948 Marshall Plan goes into effect
Berlin airlift begins
1949 NATO formed
1950 Korean War begins
1953 Dwight D. Eisenhower becomes President
Armistice in Korea signed
1954 *Brown* v. *Board of Education* decision
Army-McCarthy hearings
1955 Montgomery bus boycott
1956 Suez crisis
1961 John F. Kennedy becomes President
Peace Corps established
Berlin crisis
1962 Cuban missile crisis
1963 March on Washington for civil rights
Nuclear Test Ban Treaty
**Lyndon B. Johnson becomes President upon
assassination of Kennedy**
1964 Civil Rights Act of 1964
1965 U.S. troop buildup begins in Vietnam
Voting Rights Act of 1965
Immigration quotas based on national origins ended
1966 National Organization for Women founded
1968 Martin Luther King, Jr., and Robert Kennedy
assassinated
1969 Richard M. Nixon becomes President
American astronauts land on moon
1970 U.S. troops invade Cambodia
1971 Twenty-sixth Amendment lowers voting age
to eighteen
1972 President Nixon visits mainland China
Watergate break-in
1973 Cease-fire agreement with North Vietnam
**1974 Gerald R. Ford becomes President upon
resignation of Nixon**
1975 South Vietnam falls to North Vietnam
1977 Jimmy Carter becomes President
1978 Camp David Accords between Egypt and Israel
1979 Iranian hostage crisis begins
1981 Ronald Reagan becomes President
1983 U.S. troops invade Grenada
1986 Iran-contra scandal
1987 INF Treaty
1989 George Bush becomes President
U.S. troops invade Panama
Communist governments in Eastern Europe fall
1991 Persian Gulf War
Soviet Union collapses
1992 Los Angeles riots
Earth Summit
1993 Bill Clinton becomes President
1995 Republicans take over majority in Congress

Key Events in United States History ● **R31**

The Declaration of Independence

*W*hen, in the course of human events, it becomes necessary for one people to dissolve the political bands which have connected them with another, and to assume, among the powers of the earth, the separate and equal station to which the laws of nature and of nature's God entitle them, a decent respect to the opinions of mankind requires that they should declare the causes which impel them to the separation.

We hold these truths to be self-evident, that all men are created equal, that they are endowed by their Creator with certain unalienable rights, that among these are life, liberty, and the pursuit of happiness. That, to secure these rights, governments are instituted among men, deriving their just powers from the consent of the governed. That, whenever any form of government becomes destructive of these ends, it is the right of the people to alter or to abolish it, and to institute new government, laying its foundation on such principles, and organizing its powers in such form, as to them shall seem most likely to effect their safety and happiness.

Prudence, indeed, will dictate that governments long established should not be changed for light and transient causes; and, accordingly, all experience has shown that mankind are more disposed to suffer, while evils are sufferable, than to right themselves by abolishing the forms to which they are accustomed.

But when a long train of abuses and usurpations, pursuing invariably the same object, evinces a design to reduce them under absolute despotism, it is their right, it is their duty, to throw off such government, and to provide new guards for their future security. Such has been the patient sufferance of these colonies; and such is now the necessity which constrains them to alter their former systems of government. The history of the present King of Great Britain is a history of repeated injuries and usurpations, all having in direct object the establishment of an absolute tryanny over these states. To prove this, let facts be submitted to a candid world.

He has refused his assent to laws the most wholesome and necessary for the public good.

He has forbidden his governors to pass laws of immediate and pressing importance, unless suspended in their operation till his assent should be obtained; and when so suspended, he has utterly neglected to attend to them.

He has refused to pass other laws for the accommodation of large districts of people, unless those people would relinquish the right of representation in the legislature; a right inestimable to them and formidable to tyrants only.

He has called together legislative bodies at places unusual, uncomfortable, and distant from the depository of their public records, for the sole purpose of fatiguing them into compliance with his measures.

He has dissolved representative houses repeatedly, for opposing with manly firmness his invasions on the rights of the people.

He has refused for a long time, after such dissolutions, to cause others to be elected; whereby the legislative powers, incapable of annihilation, have returned to the people at large for their exercise; the state remaining in the meantime exposed to all the dangers of invasion from without, and convulsions within.

He has endeavored to prevent the population of these states; for that purpose obstructing the laws for naturalization of foreigners; refusing to pass others to encourage their migrations hither, and raising the conditions of new appropriations of lands.

He has obstructed the administration of justice, by refusing his assent to laws for establishing judiciary powers.

He has made judges dependent on his will alone, for the tenure of their offices, and the amount and payment of their salaries.

He has erected a multitude of new offices, and sent hither swarms of officers to harass our people, and eat out their substance.

He has kept among us, in times of peace, standing armies, without the consent of our legislatures.

He has affected to render the military independent of and superior to the civil power.

He has combined with others to subject us to a jurisdiction foreign to our constitution, and unacknowledged by our laws; giving his assent to their acts of pretended legislation:

For quartering large bodies of armed troops among us;

For protecting them, by a mock trial, from punishment for any murders which they should commit on the inhabitants of these states;

For cutting off our trade with all parts of the world;

For imposing taxes on us without our consent;

For depriving us, in many cases, of the benefits of trial by jury;

For transporting us beyond seas to be tried for pretended offenses;

For abolishing the free system of English laws in a neighboring province, establishing therein an arbitrary government, and enlarging its boundaries, so as to render it at once an example and fit instrument for introducing the same absolute rule into these colonies;

For taking away our charters, abolishing our most valuable laws, and altering fundamentally the forms of our governments;

For suspending our own legislatures, and declaring themselves invested with power to legislate for us in all cases whatsoever.

He has abdicated government here, by declaring us out of his protection, and waging war against us.

He has plundered our seas, ravaged our coasts, burnt our towns, and destroyed the lives of our people.

He is at this time transporting large armies of foreign mercenaries to complete the works of death, desolation, and tyranny already begun with circumstances of cruelty and perfidy scarcely paralleled in the most barbarous ages, and totally unworthy the head of a civilized nation.

He has constrained our fellow citizens, taken captive on the high seas, to bear arms against their country, to become the executioners of their friends and brethren, or to fall themselves by their hands.

He has excited domestic insurrections among us, and has endeavored to bring on the inhabitants of our frontiers, the merciless Indian savages, whose known rule of warfare is an undistinguished destruction of all ages, sexes, and conditions.

In every stage of these oppressions, we have petitioned for redress in the most humble terms. Our repeated petitions have been answered only by repeated injury. A prince, whose character is thus marked by every act which may define a tyrant, is unfit to be the ruler of a free people.

Nor have we been wanting in attentions to our British brethren. We have warned them from time to time of attempts by their legislature to extend an unwarrantable jurisdiction over us. We have reminded them of the circumstances of our emigration and settlement here. We have appealed to their native justice and magnanimity, and we have conjured them by the ties of our common kindred to disavow these usurpations, which would inevitably interrupt our connections and correspondence. They too have been deaf to the voice of justice and of consanguinity. We must, therefore, acquiesce in the necessity, which denounces our separation, and hold them, as we hold the rest of mankind, enemies in war, in peace, friends.

We, therefore, the representatives of the United States of America, in General Congress assembled, appealing to the Supreme Judge of the world for the rectitude of our intentions, do, in the name and by authority of the good people of these colonies, solemnly publish and declare, that these United Colonies are and of right ought to be free and independent states; that they are absolved from all allegiance to the British Crown, and that all political connection between them and the state of Great Britain is and ought to be totally dissolved; and that, as free and independent states, they have full power to levy war, conclude peace, contract alliances, establish commerce, and to do all other acts and things which independent states may of right do. And for the support of this declaration, with a firm reliance on the protection of Divine Providence, we mutually pledge to each other our lives, our fortunes, and our sacred honor.

Constitution Handbook

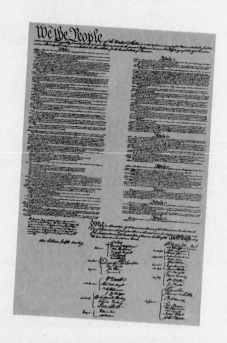

The Constitution, which was ratified in 1788, has seven articles, or parts. Since its ratification, 27 amendments have been added to the original document.

The Constitution is organized to serve as a user's manual for government. Long articles and amendments are broken into sections, each covering a single subtopic. Long sections are divided still further into clauses. This arrangement makes it easy to find your way around the Constitution.

Throughout this handbook, the original text of the Constitution appears in the right-hand column. Spelling and punctuation have been modernized where needed. The clauses have been numbered to help you identify them. You will see that some parts of the Constitution have lines drawn through them. These parts have been changed by amendments and are no longer in force.

The Constitution is written in a style of language that is more than 200 years old, making it difficult for people today to understand. To help you grasp its meaning, each section and clause has been rewritten in a simpler, more modern style. These translations appear in the left-hand column of each page, next to each section or clause.

On some pages, information appears below the Constitution text. There are explanations of what the Constitution means or how it works. Diagrams, tables, and photographs present interesting facts and help explain ideas.

Woven into the Constitution are three principles that shape how our government works:

- **Checks and Balances** Each branch of government can limit the powers of the other two.
- **Federalism** Power is divided between the federal government and the states.
- **Flexibility** General principles for running the government will survive the test of time better

than specific details. If necessary, the Constitution can be changed through amendments.

This handbook is organized to call your attention to these principles. You will see them, for example, in the titles of some explanations.

Guide to the Constitution

Preamble	R36
Article 1: The Legislative Branch	R37
Article 2: The Executive Branch	R48
Article 3: The Judicial Branch	R52
Article 4: States and Territories	R54
Article 5: The Amendment Process	R56
Article 6: National Supremacy	R57
Article 7: Ratification	R57
The Signers	R58
The Bill of Rights	R59
The Other Amendments	R62

Introducing the Constitution Handbook

Begin by reading the student page with the class. As they read, have them refer to pages in the handbook to make sure that they can identify the original text of the Constitution (in right-hand columns), the rewritten version (in left-hand columns), and the explanatory and enriching material (at the bottom of the pages).

Next, ask students to skim the handbook to get acquainted with its contents. Point out that skimming involves looking at titles, headings, illustrations, captions, and sometimes the first sentences of paragraphs. This process will help give students an overview of the handbook. Once they have the big picture of how the Constitution and this handbook are organized, they will be better able to delve into the details.

Ask students to use the table of contents on this page as a guide when skimming. Have them go to the page on which each article begins and read the title of the article. A glance at the boldfaced heads will give them important topics in the article.

Bonus Activity

Reciting the Preamble

Memorizing the Preamble will help students identify the purposes of the Constitution. One of the basic rites of passage in American education has been to memorize and recite the Preamble to the Constitution. Divide the class into small groups of three or four for the purpose of working together to memorize and prepare a group recitation of the Preamble. Remind students that the Preamble has six purposes, or goals. They can count off each goal in their minds as they memorize the Preamble. Provide time for each group to recite the Preamble.

✠ Constitutional Connections

Although the United States is a relatively new country, its Constitution is the oldest written national constitution in the world. It is very unlike the British constitution, which does not exist as a single written document. The British constitution consists of a variety of written documents and unwritten traditions establishing the powers of the monarchy, Parliament, and the courts. For example, the Magna Carta and the Declaration of Rights are two documents that are part of the British constitution. The form of constitution that Britain has is rare today. Most countries now have written constitutions that are single documents.

The Preamble to the Constitution

The Preamble

The Preamble is the introduction to the Constitution. It lists the six most important purposes of the new government. Those purposes are to:

- unify the states into a strong nation
- create a society based on law and justice
- keep peace among all Americans
- protect the nation from its enemies
- improve the lives of Americans
- ensure that all Americans, now and in the future, live in a free and democratic society

> We the people of the United States, in order to form a more perfect Union, establish justice, insure domestic tranquility, provide for the common defense, promote the general welfare, and secure the blessings of liberty to ourselves and our posterity, do ordain and establish this Constitution for the United States of America.

Why the Preamble is Still Important

If your parents or grandparents went to school in the United States, the chances are that by your age they had memorized the Preamble to the Constitution. For generations, American schoolchildren began their study of the Constitution by committing these words to memory. The reason is simple. This one sentence tells us where the power comes from under our Constitution and how it should be used.

Look at first words of the Preamble: "We the people." They tell us that in this country, the power to govern comes from the consent of the governed. The Constitution was "ordained and established" in 1788 only after that consent was given by the people of the United States. It remains in effect today because we still choose to live under this framework of government.

The Preamble also says what the power is to be used for. The first purpose, "to form a more perfect Union," was dear to the hearts of all who had struggled with the very imperfect union created by the Articles of Confederation.

The remaining five purposes are as important today as they were in 1787. We still want to live in a just and law-abiding society. We still want to feel safe in our homes and communities. We still want to be protected from foreign enemies. We still believe that government should help make our lives better. We still treasure the opportunities, rights, and freedoms that are the blessings of liberty. In the pages that follow, you will learn more about the government created by the Constitution and how it serves these purposes.

Article 1: The Legislative Branch

The Legislative Branch

Section 1. A Two-Part Congress

The legislative branch has the power to make laws. This power is given to both the Senate and the House of Representatives.

Section 2. The House of Representatives

Clause 1. Election of Members
Members of the House are elected every two years by the people of the states. Short terms allow the people to quickly get rid of a representative they don't like.

Clause 2. Qualifications of Representatives
A member of the House must be:
• at least 25 years old
• a U.S. citizen for at least seven years
• a resident of the state from which elected

Article 1.

Section 1.

All legislative powers herein granted shall be vested in a Congress of the United States, which shall consist of a Senate and House of Representatives.

Section 2.

Clause 1. The House of Representatives shall be composed of members chosen every second year by the people of the several states, and the electors in each state shall have the qualifications requisite for electors of the most numerous branch of the state legislature.

Clause 2. No person shall be a representative who shall not have attained to the age of twenty-five years, and been seven years a citizen of the United States, and who shall not, when elected, be an inhabitant of that state in which he shall be chosen.

Why Congress Comes First in the Constitution

The framers of the Constitution put the legislative branch at the center of the national government. Congress alone has the power to make laws. To indicate the importance of this branch, the framers put it first, in Article 1. Nearly half of the original Constitution deals with the organization and powers of Congress.

The structure of Congress is based on the Great Compromise of 1787. It is made up of two chambers: the House of Representatives, which represents the people, and the Senate, which represents the states.

The most important job of Congress is to make laws, the life blood of our political system. Laws do not just tell us what we can and cannot do. They also create government policies, programs, and agencies. Everything from the space agency to the school lunch program begins with a law passed by Congress.

Congress meets in the Capitol building in Washington, D.C.

Calculating House Representatives

To focus on how House representation can change over time, have students compare figures for their state after the 1980 and 1990 censuses. Provide national and state populations for each of those years, and then have students do the following steps for each year:
(1) Divide the national population by 435 to find the number of people represented by each House member. (2) Take that answer and divide it into the state's population to determine the number of House members for your state following that census. Conclude by having students compare the 1980 and 1990 figures. To expand the activity, have students also do calculations for earlier censuses and summarize trends.

⊕ Constitutional Connections

Since the first national census in 1790, the government has conducted a census every ten years, as directed in Article 1, Clause 3. Although the framers intended the census for purposes of determining representation in the House, today the Bureau of the Census collects many kinds of data, including information about housing, agriculture, government, and economic matters.

In the first census, enumerators traveled the country on horseback to count the fewer than four million Americans. In 1990 the Bureau of the Census used a process of "self-enumeration" in which people responded to census questions by mail. It also used enumerators to collect data from people who did not respond by mail or who made mistakes. Altogether the 1990 census employed 565,000 temporary workers.

Article 1: The Legislative Branch

Clause 3. The Number of Representatives
The number of representatives from each state is based on the state's population. Originally, slaves were counted as three-fifths of a person. When slavery was ended by the Thirteenth Amendment in 1865, the three-fifths rule became meaningless.

A census, or count of the people, must be taken every ten years. The results are used to apportion, or divide, House seats among the states. Each state must have at least one seat, no matter how small its population. Representatives within a state are elected from districts of roughly equal population. A typical House member now represents more than six hundred thousand persons.

Clause 4. Filling Vacancies
If a House seat becomes vacant between regular elections, the governor of that state can call a special election to fill the seat.

Clause 5. Impeachment Power
The Speaker of the House is the leading officer of the House. Only the House can impeach, or bring charges against, federal officials who have done wrong.

Clause 3. Representatives and direct taxes shall be apportioned among the several states which may be included within this Union, according to their respective numbers, ~~which shall be determined by adding to the whole number of free persons, including those bound to service for a term of years, and excluding Indians not taxed, three fifths of all other persons.~~

The actual enumeration shall be made within three years after the first meeting of the Congress of the United States, and within every subsequent term of ten years, in such manner as they shall by law direct. The number of representatives shall not exceed one for every thirty thousand, but each state shall have at least one representative; ~~and until such enumeration shall be made, the state of New Hampshire shall be entitled to choose three, Massachusetts eight, Rhode Island and Providence Plantations one, Connecticut five, New York six, New Jersey four, Pennsylvania eight, Delaware one, Maryland six, Virginia ten, North Carolina five, South Carolina five, and Georgia three.~~

Clause 4. When vacancies happen in the representation from any state, the executive authority thereof shall issue writs of election to fill such vacancies.

Clause 5. The House of Representatives shall choose their speaker and other officers, and shall have the sole power of impeachment.

Seats in the House of Representatives After the 1990 Census

The makeup of the House changed as a result of the census of 1990. Some states, mostly in the West and South, gained seats. The delegation from California, for example, swelled from 45 to 52 members. Other states, including New York, Ohio, Pennsylvania, and Massachusetts, lost seats.

✠ Constitutional Connections

When the first Congress convened, the Senate had 22 members. By the time it adjourned, the Senate had 26 members. North Carolina and Rhode Island senators had joined the Congress after those states ratified the Constitution in 1789 and 1790, respectively.

Checking Understanding

1. How many senators are there from each state? (Each state has two senators.)

2. Who has a longer term— a senator or a member of the House? (Senator, whose term is six years, as opposed to two years for a House term.)

Stimulating Critical Thinking

3. Why do you think the framers decided that the number of representatives "shall not exceed one for every thirty thousand"? (To make sure that the number was not too large and unwieldy. Point out, however, that the Constitution does not specify a maximum number. With the growth of the nation's population, there would be over 8,000 House members today if each member still represented 30,000 people. To avoid such a situation, Congress has set the number of House seats at 435.)

4. What do you think Washington meant by saying, "We pour legislation into the senatorial saucer to cool it"? (Senators, who represent whole states and have longer terms, are not as subject to the fluctuations of public opinion. With their longer terms, they may gain more experience and thus vote more cautiously. In Washington's day, senators were elected by state legislatures, and thus were further removed from the daily demands of voters than were representatives.)

Article 1: The Legislative Branch

Section 3. The Senate

Clause 1. Elections
The Senate is made up of two Senators from each state. Originally Senators were elected by their state legislatures. Amendment 17, ratified in 1913, calls for the direct election of Senators by the voters of each state.

Clause 2. Terms of Office
Senate terms overlap. Every two years, one-third of the Senators end their terms and must either leave or stand for re-election. As a result, there are always experienced lawmakers in the Senate.

Clause 3. Qualifications of Senators
A member of the Senate must be:
• at least 30 years old
• a U.S. citizen for at least 9 years
• a resident of the state from which elected

Clause 4. President of the Senate
The Vice-President serves as president of the Senate, but votes only in case of a tie.

Clause 5. Election of Officers
The Senate elects officers, including a temporary, or *pro tempore* president. The president pro tem leads the Senate when the Vice-President is absent.

Section 3.

Clause 1. The Senate of the United States shall be composed of two senators from each state, ~~chosen by the legislature thereof,~~ for six years; and each senator shall have one vote.

Clause 2. Immediately after they shall be assembled in consequence of the first election, they shall be divided as equally as may be into three classes. The seats of the senators of the first class shall be vacated at the expiration of the second year, of the second class at the expiration of the fourth year, and of the third class at the expiration of the sixth year, so that one third may be chosen every second year; ~~and if vacancies happen by resignation, or otherwise, during the recess of the legislature of any state, the executive thereof may make temporary appointments until the next meeting of the legislature, which shall then fill such vacancies.~~

Clause 3. No person shall be a senator who shall not have attained to the age of thirty years, and been nine years a citizen of the United States, and who shall not, when elected, be an inhabitant of that state for which he shall be chosen.

Clause 4. The Vice-President of the United States shall be president of the Senate, but shall have no vote, unless they be equally divided.

Clause 5. The Senate shall choose their other officers and also a president pro tempore, in the absence of the Vice-President, or when he shall exercise the office of President of the United States.

Giving States Equal Representation

The framers saw the Senate as a check on the House of Representatives. With longer terms in office and different interests in mind, Senators would see their role differently than Representatives. If the House passed a bill without fully considering its effects, the Senate might oppose it. When Thomas Jefferson asked George Washington why the delegates had established a Senate, Washington replied by asking, "Why do you pour your coffee into a saucer?" "To cool it," Jefferson answered. Washington replied, "Even so, we pour legislation into the senatorial saucer to cool it."

Article 1: The Legislative Branch

Clause 6. Impeachment Trials
The Senate serves as a jury in impeachment cases. A conviction requires a two-thirds vote of the members present.

Clause 6. The Senate shall have the sole power to try all impeachments. When sitting for that purpose, they shall be on oath or affirmation. When the President of the United States is tried, the Chief Justice shall preside. And no person shall be convicted without the concurrence of two thirds of the members present.

Clause 7. Penalty for Conviction
If an impeached official is convicted of wrongdoing by the Senate, that person is removed from office. The Senate cannot impose any other punishment. The convicted official can, however, be tried in a regular court.

Clause 7. Judgment in cases of impeachment shall not extend further than to removal from office, and disqualification to hold and enjoy any office of honor, trust, or profit under the United States; but the party convicted shall nevertheless be liable and subject to indictment, trial, judgment, and punishment, according to law.

Section 4. Elections and Meetings

Clause 1. Congressional Elections
Each state regulates its own congressional elections, but Congress can change the regulations. In 1872 Congress required that every state hold elections on the same day.

Section 4.

Clause 1. The times, places, and manner of holding elections for senators and representatives shall be prescribed in each state by the legislature thereof; but the Congress may at any time by law make or alter such regulations, ~~except as to the places of choosing senators~~.

Clause 2. Meetings
Congress must meet once a year. Amendment 20, ratified in 1933, changed the first day of Congress to January 3.

Clause 2. The Congress shall assemble at least once in every year, ~~and such meeting shall be on the first Monday in December,~~ unless they shall by law appoint a different day.

Checks and Balances: Impeachment

The framers worked hard to create a system of checks and balances that would keep any one branch of the government from misusing its power. One of the most important of those checks is the power of Congress to impeach and remove officials from office. To impeach means to accuse a government official of serious wrongdoing. Article 2, Section 4 defines such wrongdoings as "treason, bribery, or other high crimes and misdemeanors."

The first two offenses are clear. Treason is aiding the nation's enemies. Bribery involves giving gifts to a public official in exchange for special favors. Just what "high crimes and misdemeanors" means is less clear. The basic idea is that officials can be removed from office if they seriously abuse their power.

The House of Representatives has the power to impeach officials by charging them with such acts. Once impeached, an official is tried by the Senate. If found guilty by a two-thirds vote, the official is then removed from office.

Facing likely impeachment, Richard Nixon resigned from the presidency in 1974.

Constitutional Connections

In 1995, members of both houses of Congress earned an annual salary of $133,600. The president pro tempore of the Senate earned $148,400, as did the majority and minority leaders in the Senate. The Speaker of the House had an annual salary of $171,500, and the majority and minority leaders in the House of Representatives earned $148,400.

Discussion

Checking Understanding

1. **Which house of Congress conducts the trial of an impeached official?** (The Senate.)

2. **What publication contains the written records of the House and Senate?** *(The Congressional Record.)*

3. **Who determines the salaries to be paid to members of Congress?** (The members of Congress set their own salaries.)

Stimulating Critical Thinking

4. **What advantages might there be to having the power of impeachment divided between the House and the Senate?** (By reserving to the House the right to bring charges against a government official and to the Senate the right to try such an official, the framers of the Constitution probably increased the likelihood that the official charged would be granted a fair trial.)

5. **What might be a reason for the employment restrictions in Section 6, Clause 2?** (To avoid conflicts of interest for members of Congress and to ensure their objectivity about legislation before them.)

Article 1: The Legislative Branch

Section 5. Basics of Organization

Clause 1. Attendance
Each house can judge whether new members have been elected fairly and are qualified. A quorum is the minimum number of members who can act for all. While discussion can go on without a quorum, a quorum is required for voting.

Clause 2. Rules
Each house can:
• set up its own working rules
• punish members who misbehave
• expel a member with a two-thirds vote

Clause 3. Record-keeping
Each house must keep written records of what is done at meetings. Since 1873 the journals of the House and Senate have been published in the *Congressional Record.*

Clause 4. Ending Sessions
Both houses must agree to any adjournment, or ending of a session, for longer than three days.

Section 6. Privileges and Restrictions

Clause 1. Salaries and Privileges
The members of Congress can set their own salaries. When Congress is in session, members cannot be arrested except on certain criminal charges. While working on congressional business, members can write or say anything about anyone.

Clause 2. Employment Restrictions
Members of Congress cannot create new federal jobs or increase the pay for old ones and then leave Congress to take those jobs. Nor can a member of Congress hold a job in one of the other branches of the federal government while serving in Congress.

Section 5.

Clause 1. Each house shall be the judge of the elections, returns, and qualifications of its own members, and a majority of each shall constitute a quorum to do business; but a smaller number may adjourn from day to day, and may be authorized to compel the attendance of absent members, in such manner and under such penalties as each house may provide.

Clause 2. Each house may determine the rules of its proceedings, punish its members for disorderly behavior, and, with the concurrence of two thirds, expel a member.

Clause 3. Each house shall keep a journal of its proceedings and from time to time publish the same, excepting such parts as may in their judgment require secrecy; and the yeas and nays of the members of either house on any question, shall, at the desire of one fifth of those present, be entered on the journal.

Clause 4. Neither house, during the session of Congress, shall, without the consent of the other, adjourn for more than three days, nor to any other place than that in which the two houses shall be sitting.

Section 6.

Clause 1. The senators and representatives shall receive a compensation for their services, to be ascertained by law, and paid out of the Treasury of the United States. They shall in all cases, except treason, felony, and breach of the peace, be privileged from arrest during their attendance at the session of their respective houses, and in going to and returning from the same; and for any speech or debate in either house, they shall not be questioned in any other place.

Clause 2. No senator or representative shall, during the time for which he was elected, be appointed to any civil office under the authority of the United States which shall have been created, or the emoluments whereof shall have been increased, during such time; and no person holding any office under the United States shall be a member of either house during his continuance in office.

The veto gives the President the power to reject bills passed by Congress. At present, the President cannot veto a portion of a bill, nor can the President veto constitutional amendments. Six Presidents, among them Jefferson and John Adams, vetoed no bills. Washington vetoed two bills. The record holder for number of vetoed bills is Franklin D. Roosevelt. He vetoed 635 bills.

Article 1: The Legislative Branch

Section 7. How Bills Become Laws

Clause 1. Tax Bills

All tax bills must begin in the House. The Senate, however, can thoroughly revise such bills.

Clause 2. Submitting Bills to the President

After Congress passes a bill, it goes to the President. The President can do one of three things at that point:

- Sign the bill, which then becomes law.
- Veto the bill and then return it to Congress with objections. If Congress overrides the President's veto by a two-thirds vote of both houses, the bill becomes law.
- Do nothing. In that case the bill becomes law after 10 days (not counting Sundays), provided Congress is in session. If Congress adjourns within 10 days, the bill dies. This method of killing a bill is called a pocket veto. A President may use it to avoid an open veto of a controversial bill.

Section 7.

Clause 1. All bills for raising revenue shall originate in the House of Representatives; but the Senate may propose or concur with amendments as on other bills.

Clause 2. Every bill which shall have passed the House of Representatives and the Senate shall, before it becomes a law, be presented to the President of the United States. If he approve he shall sign it, but if not he shall return it, with his objections to that house in which it shall have originated, who shall enter the objections at large on their journal and proceed to reconsider it.

If, after such reconsideration, two thirds of that house shall agree to pass the bill, it shall be sent, together with the objections, to the other house, by which it shall likewise be reconsidered, and, if approved by two thirds of that house, it shall become a law. But in all such cases the votes of both houses shall be determined by yeas and nays, and the names of the persons voting for and against the bill shall be entered on the journal of each house respectively.

If any bill shall not be returned by the President within ten days (Sundays excepted) after it shall have been presented to him, the same shall be a law, in like manner as if he had signed it, unless the Congress by their adjournment prevent its return, in which case it shall not be a law.

**Checks and Balances:
How the Veto Works**

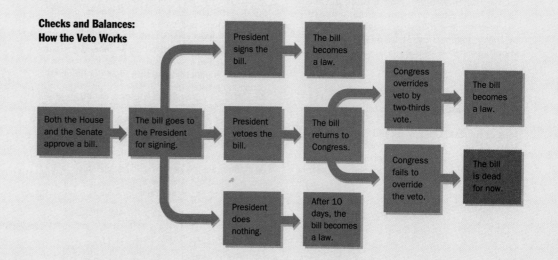

R42 ● *Constitution Handbook*

Article 1: The Legislative Branch

Clause 3. Submitting Other Measures
Any other measures that require agreement by both houses must go to the President for approval. Congress cannot avoid submitting bills to the President by calling them orders or resolutions. When such measures reach the President, they are treated as bills.

Clause 3. Every order, resolution, or vote to which the concurrence of the Senate and House of Representatives may be necessary (except on a question of adjournment) shall be presented to the President of the United States; and before the same shall take effect, shall be approved by him, or being disapproved by him, shall be repassed by two thirds of the Senate and House of Representatives, according to the rules and limitations prescribed in the case of a bill.

Section 8. Powers of Congress

Congress has the power to:

Clause 1. Taxation
- impose and collect taxes and excises (taxes on products, such as cigarettes)
- collect duties (taxes on imported goods)

Clause 2. Borrowing
- borrow money as needed

Clause 3. Regulating Trade
- control trade with foreign nations, with Indian tribes, and between states

Clause 4. Naturalization; Bankruptcy
- decide how foreigners can become citizens, a process called naturalization
- pass bankruptcy laws for the country (laws for those unable to pay their debts)

Clause 5. Coining Money
- coin and print money
- define weights and measures so that they are the same across the country

Clause 6. Punishing Counterfeiting
- punish people who make fake money or government bonds

Clause 7. Providing Postal Service
- set up a postal system

Section 8.

The Congress shall have power:

Clause 1. To lay and collect taxes, duties, imposts, and excises, to pay the debts and provide for the common defense and general welfare of the United States; but all duties, imposts, and excises shall be uniform throughout the United States;

Clause 2. To borrow money on the credit of the United States;

Clause 3. To regulate commerce with foreign nations, and among the several states, and with the Indian tribes;

Clause 4. To establish a uniform rule of naturalization and uniform laws on the subject of bankruptcies throughout the United States;

Clause 5. To coin money, regulate the value thereof, and of foreign coin, and fix the standard of weights and measures;

Clause 6. To provide for the punishment of counterfeiting the securities and current coin of the United States;

Clause 7. To establish post offices and post roads;

Discussion

Checking Understanding

1. **After Congress passes a bill, what three courses of action are open to the President?** (The President can sign the bill, veto the bill, or do nothing.)

2. **Who has the power to impose and collect taxes and duties?** (Congress.)

3. **What are the three ways in which a bill can become law?** (1. If the President signs a bill that has been passed by both the House and Senate, the bill becomes law. 2. If the House and Senate override a presidential veto by a two-thirds vote of both houses, the bill becomes law. 3. If after ten days the President has neither signed nor vetoed a bill sent by Congress, the bill becomes law, unless Congress adjourns within that ten-day period.)

Stimulating Critical Thinking

4. **Do you think the President should have the power to veto just a part of a bill (line item veto)? Explain.** (Yes: parts added for special interests or as pet projects of legislators could be deleted without vetoing the whole act; parts added often have little or nothing to do with the main issues of the bill. No: the act was approved as it is and should be passed or vetoed in its entirety.)

Congress in the News

To reinforce understanding of the roles of Congress, have students find stories about Congress in current newspapers and bring them to class. For each story that discusses congressional powers, have students identify the clause of Section 8 that authorizes Congress to exercise the specific powers mentioned.

✠ Constitutional Connections

In 1790, under powers granted in Section 8, Clause 8, Congress passed patent legislation to encourage inventors. As Secretary of State, Thomas Jefferson was the first patent officer. One of his last acts as patent officer was to write a letter to Eli Whitney, explaining that Whitney needed to submit a model as well as a sketch of his cotton gin before a patent could be granted.

Article 1: The Legislative Branch

Clause 8. Encouraging Invention
- grant copyrights to authors and patents to inventors as a way of encouraging progress in science and the arts

Clause 8. To promote the progress of science and useful arts, by securing for limited times to authors and inventors the exclusive right to their respective writings and discoveries;

Clause 9. Establishing Courts
- establish a federal court system

Clause 9. To constitute tribunals inferior to the Supreme Court;

Clause 10. Punishing Crimes at Sea
- punish piracy and other crimes committed on the seas

Clause 10. To define and punish piracies and felonies committed on the high seas and offenses against the law of nations;

Clause 11. Declaring War
- declare war
- authorize private ships to attack and seize enemy ships

Clause 11. To declare war, grant letters of marque and reprisal, and make rules concerning captures on land and water;

Clause 12. Raising an Army
- raise and support an army

Clause 12. To raise and support armies, but no appropriation of money to that use shall be for a longer term than two years;

Clause 13. Maintaining a Navy
- establish and maintain a navy

Clause 13. To provide and maintain a navy;

Clause 14. Regulating the Armed Forces
- make rules to govern the armed forces

Clause 14. To make rules for the government and regulation of the land and naval forces;

Clause 15. Calling Out the Militia
- call out state militia units, now known as the National Guard

Clause 15. To provide for calling forth the militia to execute the laws of the Union, suppress insurrections, and repel invasions;

Clause 16. Regulating the Militia
- organize, arm, and govern the National Guard. The states keep the power to appoint officers of state militias.

Clause 16. To provide for organizing, arming, and disciplining the militia, and for governing such part of them as may be employed in the service of the United States, reserving to the states respectively the appointment of the officers and the authority of training the militia according to the discipline prescribed by Congress;

Checks and Balances: Waging War

The Constitution gives Congress the sole power to declare war, to set up the armed forces, and to fund them. The framers gave these powers to Congress to make sure the nation would enter a war only if it was the will of the people. The President, however, was given the role of commander in chief of the armed forces. Under this authority, several Presidents have ordered American troops into battle without a declaration of war by Congress. In some of these cases, critics have charged that the President was going against the framers' intent.

Constitutional Connections
In 1790 George Washington selected a site on the Potomac River for a permanent national capital. Today Washington, D.C., has an area of approximately 70 square miles (180 sq km).

Article 1: The Legislative Branch

Clause 17. Controlling Federal Property
- make laws for the District of Columbia and for federal land used for forts, naval bases, national parks, and other purposes. In 1974, Congress gave citizens of Washington D.C. the right to elect their own mayor and city council and run their own affairs. Still, Congress can overrule the council's actions.

Clause 18. The "Elastic Clause"
- make all laws "necessary and proper" to carry out the powers listed above and any other powers of the federal government

Clause 17. To exercise exclusive legislation in all cases whatsoever over such district (not exceeding ten miles square) as may, by cession of particular states and the acceptance of Congress, become the seat of the government of the United States, and to exercise like authority over all places purchased by the consent of the legislature of the state in which the same shall be for the erection of forts, magazines, arsenals, dockyards, and other needful buildings; and

Clause 18. To make all laws which shall be necessary and proper for carrying into execution the foregoing powers and all other powers vested by this Constitution in the government of the United States, or in any department or officer thereof.

Flexibility: The Elastic Clause

The last law-making power given to Congress is known as the "elastic clause" because it gives Congress the flexibility needed to carry out its other powers. For example, Congress has the power to coin and print money. To do so, however, it must pass laws to build mints, buy supplies, and hire workers. None of these powers are listed in the Constitution. Instead, such laws are considered "necessary and proper" under the elastic clause. Over the years the elastic clause has been stretched to allow Congress to do everything from build dams to outlaw some kinds of guns.

Congress has the power to decide how foreigners can become citizens. Here two new citizens attend a naturalization ceremony.

Checking Understanding

1. What three reasons are given in Clause 15 for calling out the militia? (To execute the laws, suppress insurrections, and repel invaders.)

2. Why is Clause 18 called the "elastic clause"? (It provides flexibility by giving Congress the power to make all laws that are necessary to carry out the other powers given to Congress by the Constitution.)

Stimulating Critical Thinking

3. What might be the advantages of having the war-making power divided between Congress and the President? (It is more likely that war will be entered into cautiously and with time for reflection. The system of checks and balances makes it less likely that an impulsive act could launch the nation into a war that the people did not support.)

4. How might the President prevent Congress from abusing the "elastic clause"? (The President can veto bills, thus checking the power of Congress to stretch the elastic clause too far.)

A writ of habeas corpus is a court order commanding that a person held in custody be brought before a court to determine whether the detention is lawful. The purpose is to ensure that an accused person is granted due process under the law. Habeas corpus can be suspended only in time of rebellion or invasion. Early in the Civil War, President Lincoln used his constitutional power to suspend habeas corpus for pro-Confederate leaders in Maryland. As students will read in Chapter 18, this controversial action was part of Lincoln's strategy to prevent Maryland from seceding from the Union.

Article 1: The Legislative Branch

Section 9. Limits on Federal Power

Clause 1. Ending the Slave Trade
As part of a compromise between northern states and southern states, Congress was forbidden to end the importing of slaves before 1808.

Clause 2. Suspending Habeas Corpus
The government cannot take away a person's right to a writ of habeas corpus except in times of emergency. This right protects people from being held in jail without evidence.

Clause 3. Unfair Laws
Congress is forbidden from passing any:
• bill of attainder, or law calling for the punishment of a particular person
• ex post facto law, or law that makes an action done legally unlawful afterwards

Clause 4. Taxing Individuals
All taxes levied by Congress directly on land or people must be divided among the states according to their population. This was later changed by the Sixteenth Amendment.

Clause 5. Taxing Exports
Congress may not tax exports, or goods being sent to other countries.

Clause 6. Regulating Trade
Congress cannot favor one state over another in regulating trade and shipping.

Clause 7. Unlawful Spending
The federal government can spend money only when Congress authorizes the spending. This clause is meant to keep government officials or employees from misusing federal funds.

Clause 8. Creating Titles of Nobility
Congress cannot give anyone a title such as duchess or count. Federal officials cannot receive any gift of value from a foreign country. Such gifts are the property of the United States government.

Section 9.

Clause 1. ~~The migration or importation of such persons as any of the states now existing shall think proper to admit shall not be prohibited by Congress prior to the year 1808, but a tax or duty may be imposed on such importation, not exceeding ten dollars for each person.~~

Clause 2. The privilege of the writ of habeas corpus shall not be suspended, unless, when in cases of rebellion or invasion, the public safety may require it.

Clause 3. No bill of attainder or ex post facto law shall be passed.

Clause 4. No capitation or ~~other direct~~ tax shall be laid, unless in proportion to the census or enumeration herein before directed to be taken.

Clause 5. No tax or duty shall be laid on articles exported from any state.

Clause 6. No preference shall be given by any regulation of commerce or revenue to the ports of one state over those of another; nor shall vessels bound to or from one state be obliged to enter, clear, or pay duties in another.

Clause 7. No money shall be drawn from the Treasury but in consequence of appropriations made by law; and a regular statement and account of the receipts and expenditures of all public money shall be published from time to time.

Clause 8. No title of nobility shall be granted by the United States. And no person holding any office of profit or trust under them shall, without the consent of the Congress, accept of any present, emolument, office, or title of any kind whatever from any king, prince, or foreign state.

**Checking
Understanding**

1. Why did the Constitution's framers forbid Congress from ending the slave trade before 1808? (It was part of the compromise between the northern states and the southern states.)

**Stimulating
Critical Thinking**

2. Why do you think Congress is forbidden to pass ex post facto laws? (It would be unfair to be punished for an act that was not illegal when performed.)

Article 1: The Legislative Branch

Section 10. Limits on State Power

Clause 1. Forbidden Actions

The states are not allowed to:
- make treaties with other nations
- coin or print money
- pass bills of attainder, ex post facto laws, or laws excusing citizens from carrying out contracts
- grant titles of nobility

Clause 2. Taxing Trade

A state cannot tax any goods entering or leaving the state. A state can charge a small fee, however, to pay for inspection of the goods.

Clause 3. Foreign Dealings

Without the agreement of Congress, states cannot tax ships that use their ports. Nor can a state prepare for war or wage war unless there is a military emergency.

Section 10.

Clause 1. No state shall enter into any treaty, alliance, or confederation; grant letters of marque and reprisal; coin money; emit bills of credit; make anything but gold and silver coin a tender in payment of debts; pass any bill of attainder, ex post facto law, or law impairing the obligation of contracts, or grant any title of nobility.

Clause 2. No state shall, without the consent of the Congress, lay any imposts or duties on imports or exports, except what may be absolutely necessary for executing its inspection laws; and the net produce of all duties and imposts laid by any state on imports or exports shall be for the use of the Treasury of the United States; and all such laws shall be subject to the revision and control of the Congress.

Clause 3. No state shall, without the consent of Congress, lay any duty of tonnage; keep troops or ships of war in time of peace; enter into any agreement or compact with another state or with a foreign power, or engage in war, unless actually invaded, or in such imminent danger as will not admit of delay.

Limits on State and Federal Power

Concerned that the federal government might become too strong, the framers of the Constitution spelled out the limits on federal power shown on the left. They also made sure to deny to the states the powers shown on the right. Some of these powers were reserved for the federal government alone. Others were denied the federal government as well.

**What the Federal
Government Cannot Do**

- suspend the right to a writ of habeas corpus
- favor one state over another in trade
- spend money without approval by Congress

**What No
Government Can Do**

- pass bills of attainder
- pass ex post facto laws
- grant titles of nobility
- tax exports

**What State
Governments Cannot Do**

- make treaties with other nations
- coin or print money
- make war
- tax ships

Researching Vice-Presidents

To explore whether the vice-presidency is a stepping stone to the presidency, have students make a chart identifying all Vice-Presidents who later became Presidents. They may use information on Presidents and Vice-Presidents on pages R24–R29.

The chart should identify the Vice-Presidents who assumed the presidency upon the death or resignation of a President, those who became President by winning national elections, and those who did both (replaced a President and then ran successfully in the next election). Conclude the activity by having students speculate on why being Vice-President might or might not be an advantage to someone who wanted to become President.

Article 2: The Executive Branch

The Executive Branch

Section 1. The President and Vice-President

Clause 1. Term of Office
Executive power—power to carry out laws—is granted to the President, chief of the executive branch. The President serves a four-year term, as does the Vice-President.

Clause 2. The Electoral College
The people do not elect the President or Vice-President directly. Instead, both are chosen by a group of electors known as the electoral college. Each state legislature decides how electors are to be chosen in that state. Today electors are chosen by the voters. The number of electors from a state is equal to the number of senators and representatives from that state.

Clause 3. Electing a President
This clause describes the framers' original plan for electing a President and Vice-President. After the election of 1800 showed its weaknesses, the method was changed by the Twelfth Amendment. (See page R62 for more details.)

Vice-Presidents Who Have Taken Over for Presidents

Vice-President	President	Year
John Tyler	William Harrison	1841
Millard Fillmore	Zachary Taylor	1850
Andrew Johnson	Abraham Lincoln	1865
Chester Arthur	James Garfield	1881
Theodore Roosevelt	William McKinley	1901
Calvin Coolidge	Warren Harding	1923
Harry Truman	Franklin Roosevelt	1945
Lyndon Johnson	John Kennedy	1963
Gerald Ford	Richard Nixon	1974

Article 2.

Section 1.

Clause 1. The executive power shall be vested in a President of the United States of America. He shall hold his office during the term of four years, and, together with the Vice-President, chosen for the same term, be elected as follows:

Clause 2. Each state shall appoint, in such manner as the legislature thereof may direct, a number of electors, equal to the whole number of senators and representatives to which the state may be entitled in the Congress: but no senator or representative, or person holding an office of trust or profit under the United States, shall be appointed an elector.

~~Clause 3. The electors shall meet in their respective states and vote by ballot for two persons, of whom one at least shall not be an inhabitant of the same state with themselves. And they shall make a list of all the persons voted for and of the number of votes for each; which list they shall sign and certify, and transmit sealed to the seat of the government of the United States, directed to the president of the Senate. The president of the Senate shall, in the presence of the Senate and House of Representatives, open all the certificates, and the votes shall then be counted. The person having the greatest number of votes shall be the President, if such number be a majority of the whole number of electors appointed; and if there be more than one who have such majority, and have an equal number of votes, then the House of Representatives shall immediately choose by ballot one of them for President; and if no person have a majority, then from the five highest on the list the said house shall in like manner choose the President. But in choosing the President, the votes shall be taken by states, the representation from each state having one vote; a quorum for this purpose shall consist of a member or members from two thirds of the states, and a majority of all the states shall be necessary to a choice. In every case, after the choice of the President, the person having the greatest number of votes of the electors shall be the Vice-President. But if there should remain two or more who have equal votes, the Senate shall choose from them by ballot the Vice-President.~~

Every President, beginning with George Washington, has taken the same oath of office. Usually the Chief Justice of the Supreme Court administered the oath of office. Calvin Coolidge, however, was visiting his father in Vermont when he learned that President Harding had died. Coolidge's father, a local official, administered the oath of office. When the Attorney General pointed out that Coolidge's father had authority only in Vermont, Coolidge was sworn in a second time by a justice of the Supreme Court of the District of Columbia.

Article 2: The Executive Branch

Clause 4. Time of Elections
Congress sets the date for choosing electors, as well as the date for their voting. That date must be the same throughout the country.

Today Presidential elections take place every four years on the first Tuesday after the first Monday in November. Electoral votes are cast on the Monday after the second Wednesday in December.

Clause 4. The Congress may determine the time of choosing the electors and the day on which they shall give their votes, which day shall be the same throughout the United States.

Clause 5. Qualifications
Any American can be President who:
• is at least 35 years old
• is a natural born American citizen
• has lived in the U.S. for 14 years

Clause 5. No person except a natural-born citizen, or a citizen of the United States at the time of the adoption of this Constitution, shall be eligible to the office of President; neither shall any person be eligible to that office who shall not have attained to the age of thirty-five years and been fourteen years a resident within the United States.

Clause 6. Presidential Succession
This clause says that Congress can decide who should succeed, or replace, a President if the President dies, resigns, or is removed from office. In 1886 Congress said the line of succession would go from the Vice-President to members of the cabinet. In 1947 Congress changed it to go from the Vice-President to Speaker of the House, then to the president pro tempore of the Senate, and then to the cabinet. Amendment 25, ratified in 1967, prevents a long vacancy in the office of Vice-President. It also sets up procedures in case the President is disabled.

Clause 6. In case of the removal of the President from office, or of his death, resignation, or inability to discharge the powers and duties of the said office, the same shall devolve on the Vice-President, and the Congress may by law provide for the case of removal, death, resignation, or inability, both of the President and Vice-President, declaring what officer shall then act as President, and such officer shall act accordingly until the disability be removed or a President shall be elected.

Clause 7. Presidential Salary
The President gets paid like any other federal employee. That salary cannot be raised or lowered during a President's term in office. While in office, the President cannot receive any other salary from the U.S. government or a state government.

Clause 7. The President shall, at stated times, receive for his services a compensation, which shall neither be increased nor diminished during the period for which he shall have been elected, and he shall not receive within that period any other emolument from the United States or any of them.

Clause 8. The Oath of Office
Before taking office, the President must take an oath promising to carry out the duties of the Presidency and to preserve and protect the Constitution.

Clause 8. Before he enter on the execution of his office, he shall take the following oath or affirmation: "I do solemnly swear (or affirm) that I will faithfully execute the office of President of the United States, and will, to the best of my ability, preserve, protect, and defend the Constitution of the United States."

Checking Understanding

1. Who directly elects the President and Vice-President? (The members of the electoral college.)

2. What are the qualifications for a President? (A person must be a natural born citizen, at least 35 years old, who has lived in the U.S. for 14 years.)

3. What must the President-elect do before officially becoming President? (He or she must take an oath promising to carry out the duties of President and to uphold the Constitution.)

Stimulating Critical Thinking

4. Do you think the Constitution should be amended to drop the age requirements for members of Congress to 18, the same as the voting age? (Yes: a person old enough to vote for an office is old enough to hold that office. No: the age requirements ensure that someone with experience will hold these offices.)

Finding Examples of Presidential Roles

To focus on the importance of presidential roles, have students find current examples. Divide the class into groups and assign one presidential role to each group. Ask each group to bring in newspaper or magazine articles that show the President playing that role. The class might make a bulletin-board display titled "The President's Many Roles."

Article 2: The Executive Branch

Section 2. Presidential Powers

Clause 1. Military and Executive Powers
As head of the executive branch, the President has the power to:
- act as commander in chief of all the armed forces
- manage the federal bureaucracy
- grant a reprieve, or delay of punishment, to a person convicted of a federal crime
- grant a pardon, or excuse from punishment, to someone involved in a federal crime, except in impeachment cases

Clause 2. Treaties and Appointments
The President also has the power to:
- make treaties with foreign nations, with the approval of two-thirds of the Senate
- appoint Supreme Court justices, with the approval of a majority of the Senate
- appoint ambassadors and other important executive branch officials, with the approval of a majority of the Senate

Clause 3. Other Appointments
When the Senate is not in session, the President may make temporary appointments.

Section 2.

Clause 1. The President shall be commander in chief of the army and navy of the United States, and of the militia of the several states when called into actual service of the United States. He may require the opinion, in writing, of the principal officer in each of the executive departments upon any subject relating to the duties of their respective offices. And he shall have power to grant reprieves and pardons for offenses against the United States, except in cases of impeachment.

Clause 2. He shall have power, by and with the advice and consent of the Senate, to make treaties, provided two thirds of the senators present concur; and he shall nominate, and by and with the advice and consent of the Senate, shall appoint ambassadors, other public ministers and consuls, judges of the Supreme Court, and all other officers of the United States whose appointments were not herein otherwise provided for, and which shall be established by law; but the Congress may by law vest the appointment of such inferior officers as they think proper in the President alone, in the courts of law, or in the heads of departments.

Clause 3. The President shall have power to fill up all vacancies that may happen during the recess of the Senate, by granting commissions which shall expire at the end of their next session.

Checks and Balances: The Advice and Consent of the Senate

The framers hoped that the Senate would act as sort of an advisory board for the President on appointments and foreign policy. The Constitution requires that the President submit all treaties and appointments to the Senate for its "advice and consent." This is one of the checks on the President's power.

President George Washington took the idea of seeking advice from the Senate quite seriously. On August 12, 1789, he went to the Senate to discuss a proposed treaty with the Creek Indians. The Senators wasted so much time arguing over details that the President finally left in disgust. This was the last time a President went to the Senate in person for "advice."

Although the Constitution allows for a President or other officials to be removed from office for treason, there have been few prosecutions. One of the most famous trials involved Aaron Burr, the man who shot Alexander Hamilton and was a former Vice-President of the United States. Burr, accused of plotting to set up a separate country in the Southwest, was tried and acquitted.

Article 2: The Executive Branch

Section 3. The President's Duties

This section outlines the President's legislative duties. The President shall:

- Address Congress regularly on the nation's problems and recommend needed laws. This message is called the State of the Union Address.
- Call Congress into special session in times of national emergency.
- Adjourn Congress if needed.

The President shall also:

- Receive ambassadors from other countries. This duty puts the President in charge of the nation's foreign policy.
- Make sure the laws passed by Congress are "faithfully executed," or enforced.

Section 4. Impeachment

The President, Vice-President, and other federal officials including department heads and federal judges can be removed from office by the impeachment process.

Section 3.

He shall from time to time give to the Congress information of the state of the Union, and recommend to their consideration such measures as he shall judge necessary and expedient; he may, on extraordinary occasions, convene both houses, or either of them, and in case of disagreement between them with respect to the time of adjournment, he may adjourn them to such time as he shall think proper; he shall receive ambassadors and other public ministers; he shall take care that the laws be faithfully executed, and shall commission all the officers of the United States.

Section 4.

The President, Vice-President, and all civil officers of the United States shall be removed from office on impeachment for, and conviction of, treason, bribery, or other high crimes and misdemeanors.

The President's Many Roles

Chief of State
Acts as a symbol of the U.S. Performs ceremonial duties

Chief Executive
Appoints officials, runs federal bureaucracy

Chief Legislator
Proposes ideas for bills and urges Congress to support them

Chief Diplomat
Makes foreign policy

Chief of Law Enforcement
Enforces laws, appoints judges, grants pardons

Commander-in-Chief
Controls armed forces; determines military strategy

Chief Citizen
Stands up for the interests of all citizens

Chief of Party
Leads political party, supports party candidates

Checking Understanding

1. What is the State of the Union Address? (President's annual address to Congress on the nation's problems and goals.)

2. Who can be removed from office by the impeachment process? (President, Vice-President, and other federal officials, including department heads and federal judges.)

Stimulating Critical Thinking

3. Why does the President, rather than a military officer, serve as commander in chief? (In a democracy, decisions about war and peace should be made by someone answerable to voters. An officer in control of the armed forces might lead them in an attempt to overthrow the government.)

4. Why do you think Section 2, Clause 1, forbids the President from pardoning people who have been impeached? (Most officials subject to impeachment are presidential appointees; President might be likely to pardon his or her appointees.)

5. Why do you think the Constitution requires that the Senate approve appointments to the Supreme Court? (Maintains balance of power; if not, President could appoint supporters and the Court would not check presidential power.)

✠ **Constitutional Connections**

Perhaps the most important of the early Chief Justices was John Marshall, who presided over the Supreme Court from 1801–1835. Under his direction, the Court established many principles that continue to be observed today. For example, he established the principle of judicial review that enables the Supreme Court to review acts of Congress to determine their constitutionality.

Article 3: The Judicial Branch

The Judicial Branch

Section 1. Federal Courts

Judicial power is the power to decide legal cases in a court of law. This power is given to the Supreme Court and to lower federal courts established by Congress. A federal judge holds office for life unless impeached and found guilty of illegal acts. The salaries of judges cannot be lowered while they serve. This last protection prevents Congress from pressuring judges by threatening to cut their pay.

Section 2. Jurisdiction

Clause 1. Types of Cases
Jurisdiction is the power of a court to hear certain kinds of cases. The federal courts have jurisdiction over cases dealing with:
- the Constitution
- federal laws
- treaties with Indians or foreign powers
- ships and shipping on the seas
- disputes that involve the U.S. government
- disputes involving two or more states
- disputes between citizens of different states

Article 3.

Section 1.

The judicial power of the United States shall be vested in one Supreme Court, and in such inferior courts as the Congress may from time to time ordain and establish. The judges, both of the Supreme and inferior courts, shall hold their offices during good behavior, and shall, at stated times, receive for their services a compensation which shall not be diminished during their continuance in office.

Section 2.

Clause 1. The judicial power shall extend to all cases, in law and equity, arising under this Constitution, the laws of the United States, and treaties made, or which shall be made, under their authority; to all cases affecting ambassadors, other public ministers and consuls; to all cases of admiralty and maritime jurisdiction; to controversies to which the United States shall be a party; to controversies between two or more states; ~~between a state and citizens of another state;~~ between citizens of different states; between citizens of the same state claiming lands under grants of different states; and between a state, or the citizens thereof, and foreign states, ~~citizens, or subjects.~~

The Federal Courts and Judicial Power

The Constitution places judicial power in the hands of the Supreme Court and any "inferior courts" Congress decides to establish. Judicial power involves the authority to judge:
- **facts**—whether the accused violated the law
- **trials**—whether the case was tried properly
- **laws**—whether the law applied in the case is allowed by the Constitution

In the federal court system that has been set up since the ratification of the Constitution, there are two levels of "inferior" courts. The lowest level, made up of district and special courts, judges facts. The other level, made up of appeals courts, judges the fairness of trials. The Supreme Court is therefore left to judge matters of law, except in certain cases spelled out in the Constitution.

The photograph at the bottom of the page shows Ruth Bader Ginsburg at a Senate confirmation hearing. She was subsequently appointed to the Supreme Court. This hearing was part of the process by which the President must seek the advice and consent of the Senate to appoint justices to the Supreme Court. Students might refer back to Section 2, Clause 2, on page R50 to review the President's obligation. This process of advice and consent takes the form of public confirmation hearings held by the Senate. They are frequently televised.

Article 3: The Judicial Branch

Clause 2. Original and Appeals Cases

The Supreme Court has "original jurisdiction" in cases that involve the states or foreign countries. Such cases go directly to the Supreme Court. All other cases start first in the lower courts. The decisions of these courts may be appealed to the Supreme Court. Nearly all cases heard by the Supreme Court begin in the lower courts.

Clause 3. Trial by Jury

Anyone accused of a federal crime has a right to a jury trial. The trial is to be held in the state where the crime was committed. The only exception to these rules is impeachment trials.

Section 3. Treason

Clause 1. Defining the Crime

Treason is defined as making war against the United States or aiding its enemies. Convicting someone of treason is not easy. At least two witnesses must testify in court that they saw the accused commit an act of treason. Or the accused must confess to the crime in court. Talking or thinking about treason is not a crime.

Clause 2. Limits of the Punishment

Congress decides how to punish treason. It can only punish the convicted traitor, however. Punishments cannot extend to that person's family.

Clause 2. In all cases affecting ambassadors, other public ministers and consuls, and those in which a state shall be party, the Supreme Court shall have original jurisdiction. In all the other cases before-mentioned, the Supreme Court shall have appellate jurisdiction, both as to law and fact, with such exceptions and under such regulations as the Congress shall make.

Clause 3. The trial of all crimes, except in cases of impeachment, shall be by jury; and such trial shall be held in the state where the said crimes shall have been committed; but when not committed within any state, the trial shall be at such place or places as the Congress may by law have directed.

Section 3.

Clause 1. Treason against the United States shall consist only in levying war against them or in adhering to their enemies, giving them aid and comfort. No person shall be convicted of treason unless on the testimony of two witnesses to the same overt act, or on confession in open court.

Clause 2. The Congress shall have power to declare the punishment of treason, but no attainder of treason shall work corruption of blood or forfeiture except during the life of the person attainted.

Checks and Balances: Who Judges the Judges?

The power of the Supreme Court is checked in several ways. First, the other two branches of government decide who gets appointed to the Court. A candidate must first be nominated by the President and then approved by the Senate. Also, if Congress disagrees with the Court's interpretation of the Constitution, it can propose a constitutional amendment relating to the issue in question. If ratified, that amendment can overrule the Court's decision. Finally, Congress can remove a justice from office for wrongdoing.

Supreme Court nominee Ruth Bader Ginsburg answered questions at a Senate confirmation hearing in 1993.

Checking Understanding

1. Why is Congress not allowed to lower the salaries of federal judges while they are serving their terms? (To prevent members of Congress or other federal officers from pressuring judges by threatening pay cuts.)

2. How is the power of the Supreme Court checked? (The President appoints the justices, and the Senate approves or rejects the appointments; a constitutional amendment can override a Court decision; Congress can remove a Court justice for wrongdoing.)

Stimulating Critical Thinking

3. Why might trial by jury be seen as a basic democratic principle? (It ensures that the accused is tried, not by government officials, but by a group of fellow citizens. This protects the accused against persecution by government officials.)

Constitutional Connections

The nation's interstate highway system is a good example of federalism. The interstate highway system was built in the 1950s, during the Eisenhower administration. One of the largest public works programs in history, it would not have been possible without the cooperation of state and federal governments.

Article 4: States and Territories

States and Territories

Section 1. Relations Among States

This section outlines the responsibilities of the states to each other in a federal system. Each state must give "full faith and credit" to the laws, official records, and court decisions of another state. This means accepting them as legal. A marriage in one state, for example, is legal in all states.

Section 2. Treatment of Citizens

Clause 1. Equal Privileges
A state cannot discriminate unreasonably against citizens from other states except in special cases. Such cases include residency requirements for voting and higher fees for out-of-state students at state colleges.

Clause 2. Return of Fugitive Criminals
Criminals cannot escape justice by running across state lines. Anyone accused of a crime in one state, who flees to another state and is caught, is to be returned if the government of the state where the crime took place makes such a request.

Clause 3. Return of Runaway Slaves
Runaway slaves could not become free by escaping to another state. They were to be returned to their owners. The Thirteenth Amendment made this clause invalid.

Article 4.

Section 1.

Full faith and credit shall be given in each state to the public acts, records, and judicial proceedings of every other state. And the Congress may by general laws prescribe the manner in which such acts, records, and proceedings shall be proved, and the effect thereof.

Section 2.

Clause 1. The citizens of each state shall be entitled to all privileges and immunities of citizens in the several states.

Clause 2. A person charged in any state with treason, felony or other crime, who shall flee from justice and be found in another state, shall, on demand of the executive authority of the state from which he fled, be delivered up to be removed to the state having jurisdiction of the crime.

~~Clause 3. No person held to service or labor in one state under the laws thereof, escaping into another, shall, in consequence of any law or regulation therein, be discharged from such service or labor, but shall be delivered up on claim of the party to whom such service or labor may be due.~~

Federalism: Cooperation Among the States

Before the Constitution was adopted, the original 13 states behaved almost like independent countries. For the new nation to endure, the states had to give up some of their independence and agree to cooperate, not only with the new federal government, but with one another.

The Constitution spells out only a few ways in which the states must cooperate with one another. Under the principle of federalism, however, the states have worked together for their common good in many ways. Building the nation's railways and interstate highway system, for example, would not have been possible without state cooperation.

✠ Constitutional Connections

Puerto Rico is a Commonwealth of the United States, benefiting from the protection and assistance of the United States government. Its people are American citizens protected by the Constitution. In the 1960s, a commission studied whether to change Puerto Rico's status. Puerto Ricans have voted twice, in 1967 and 1993, to remain a Commonwealth rather than become a state.

Discussion

Checking Understanding

1. What happened to Section 2, Clause 3, of Article 4? (This clause was made invalid by the Thirteenth Amendment, which prohibits slavery.)

Stimulating Critical Thinking

2. What values or principles might the system of federalism encourage? (Cooperation would be vital to the success of a federal system, as would compromise, negotiation, and practicality.)

Article 4: States and Territories

Section 3. New States and Territories

Clause 1. Admitting New States
Congress has the power to add new states to the Union. No new states can be formed by dividing up existing states, however, unless both Congress and the states involved agree to the changes.

Clause 2. Governing Territories
Congress has the power to govern federal land and property. This includes federal territory not organized into states and also federal land within states.

Section 4. Protection of the States

The federal government promises that each state will have some form of representative government. It also promises to protect each state from invasion. The federal government also stands ready to send help, when requested, to stop rioting within a state.

Section 3.

Clause 1. New states may be admitted by the Congress into this Union; but no new state shall be formed or erected within the jurisdiction of any other state; nor any state be formed by the junction of two or more states, or parts of states, without the consent of the legislatures of the states concerned as well as of the Congress.

Clause 2. The Congress shall have power to dispose of and make all needful rules and regulations respecting the territory or other property belonging to the United States; and nothing in this Constitution shall be so construed as to prejudice any claims of the United States, or of any particular state.

Section 4.

The United States shall guarantee to every state in this Union a republican form of government, and shall protect each of them against invasion, and, on application of the legislature or of the executive (when the legislature cannot be convened), against domestic violence.

From Territory to State

The framers of the Constitution realized the new nation was likely to continue expanding as Americans settled new lands. They made it possible for territories to become new states and created some basic rules for this process.

Thirty-seven new states have been admitted to the union since the Constitution was ratified. Most gained statehood in the 1800s. The two newest states are Alaska and Hawaii, both admitted in 1959.

The two most recent states to be admitted to the union were Alaska and Hawaii, in 1959.

Article 5: The Amendment Process

Amending the Constitution

Article 5 outlines the process for amending the Constitution. As the diagram below shows, there are two ways to propose an amendment and two ways to ratify it. Congress decides which method of ratification to use.

Article 5.

The Congress, whenever two thirds of both houses shall deem it necessary, shall propose amendments to this Constitution or, on the application of the legislatures of two thirds of the several states, shall call a convention for proposing amendments, which, in either case, shall be valid, to all intents and purposes, as part of this Constitution when ratified by the legislatures of three fourths of the several states, or by conventions in three fourths thereof, as the one or the other mode of ratification may be proposed by the Congress; provided ~~that no amendment which may be made prior to the year 1808 shall in any manner affect the first and fourth clauses in the ninth section of the first article; and~~ that no state, without its consent, shall be deprived of its equal suffrage in the Senate.

Flexibility: The Amendment Process

The amendment process makes is possible to change the Constitution to meet changing needs and demands. Since 1787, the Constitution has been amended 27 times. Each of these amendments was proposed by a two-thirds vote of both houses of Congress. All but one of these amendments were ratified by three-fourths of the state legislatures.

The exception was the Twenty-first Amendment. For the first time, an amendment was being proposed that would repeal an earlier one—the Eighteenth Amendment. In this case, Congress required ratification by state conventions and set a deadline for ratification of seven years.

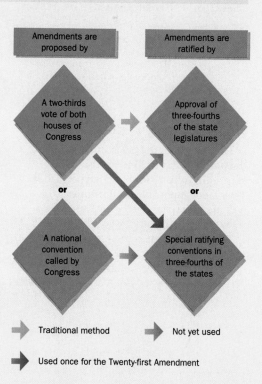

Amendments are proposed by

Amendments are ratified by

A two-thirds vote of both houses of Congress

or

A national convention called by Congress

Approval of three-fourths of the state legislatures

or

Special ratifying conventions in three-fourths of the states

Traditional method   Not yet used

Used once for the Twenty-first Amendment

✠ Constitutional Connections

The Articles of Confederation provided the structure of the government before the adoption of the Constitution. The central government under the Articles was ineffective in conducting foreign policy, quelling domestic disturbances, and maintaining economic stability. Demand for a stronger, more centralized government led to adoption of the Constitution.

Checking Understanding

1. **What does Article 5 of the Constitution cover?** (It outlines the process for amending the Constitution.)

2. **Which were the first nine states to ratify the Constitution?** (Delaware, Pennsylvania, New Jersey, Georgia, Connecticut, Massachusetts, Maryland, South Carolina, and New Hampshire.)

3. **What must state judges do when federal laws conflict with state laws?** (They must follow the federal laws.)

Stimulating Critical Thinking

4. **Why do you think the Constitution requires three-fourths of the state legislatures to ratify an amendment rather than a simple majority?** (The requirement ensures that the proposed amendment has widespread and general support of the people.)

Articles 6 & 7: National Supremacy, Ratification

National Supremacy

Clause 1. Federal Debts
This clause promised that all debts owed by Congress under the Articles of Confederation would be honored by the United States under the Constitution.

Clause 2. The Supreme Law of the Land
The Constitution and federal laws or treaties made under it are the highest laws of the nation. When federal laws conflict with state laws or constitutions, state judges must follow the federal laws.

Clause 3. Government Oaths of Office
All federal and all state officials must promise to support the Constitution. No federal official may be required to meet any religious standards in order to hold office.

Ratification

Nine states had to ratify the Constitution before it could go into effect. By June 21, 1788, the necessary nine states had approved the new framework. The Constitution went into effect on April 30, 1789.

Article 6.

Clause 1. All debts contracted and engagements entered into before the adoption of this Constitution shall be as valid against the United States under this Constitution as under the Confederation.

Clause 2. This Constitution and the laws of the United States which shall be made in pursuance thereof, and all treaties made, or which shall be made, under the authority of the United States, shall be the supreme law of the land; and the judges in every state shall be bound thereby, anything in the Constitution or laws of any state to the contrary notwithstanding.

Clause 3. The senators and representatives before-mentioned, and the members of the several state legislatures, and all executive and judicial officers, both of the United States and of the several states, shall be bound by oath or affirmation to support this Constitution; but no religious test shall ever be required as a qualification to any office or public trust under the United States.

Article 7.

The ratification of the conventions of nine states shall be sufficient for the establishment of this Constitution between the states so ratifying the same.

The Ninth PILLAR erected !
"The Ratification of the Conventions of nine States, shall be sufficient for the establishment of this Constitution, between the States so ratifying the same." *Art.* vii.
INCIPIENT MAGNI PROCEDERE MENSES.

This 1788 cartoon shows the first nine states that ratified the Constitution as upright pillars supporting a new national government.

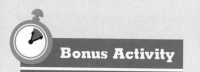
Sketches of Framers

To learn more about the framers of the Constitution, have each student prepare a biographical sketch of one of them. Each student should begin by creating an outline of the highlights of the person's life. The sketch should include basic information such as age when he signed the Constitution, his occupation, and the state he represented. Ask volunteers to present their findings to the class.

✠ **Constitutional Connections**

Although many people contributed to the ideas and language of the Constitution, James Madison of Virginia was its chief author. He was also a chief author of *The Federalist Papers,* which argued for the adoption of the Constitution. In light of his influence on the Constitutional Convention, Madison has been called "the architect of the Constitution."

The Signers

Done in convention by the unanimous consent of the states present the seventeenth day of September in the year of our Lord one thousand seven hundred and eighty-seven, and of the independence of the United States of America the twelfth. In witness whereof we have hereunto subscribed our names,

George Washington—
President and deputy from Virginia

New Hampshire
John Langdon, Nicholas Gilman

Massachusetts
Nathaniel Gorham, Rufus King

Connecticut
William Samuel Johnson, Roger Sherman

New York
Alexander Hamilton

New Jersey
William Livingston, David Brearley, William Paterson, Jonathan Dayton

Pennsylvania
Benjamin Franklin, Thomas Mifflin, Robert Morris, George Clymer, Thomas FitzSimons, Jared Ingersoll, James Wilson, Gouverneur Morris

Delaware
George Read, Gunning Bedford, Jr., John Dickinson, Richard Bassett, Jacob Broom

Maryland
James McHenry, Dan of St. Thomas Jenifer, Daniel Carroll

Virginia
John Blair, James Madison, Jr.

North Carolina
William Blount, Richard Dobbs Spaight, Hugh Williamson

South Carolina
John Rutledge, Charles Cotesworth Pinckney, Charles Pinckney, Pierce Butler

Georgia
William Few, Abraham Baldwin

Signing the Constitution

On September 17, 1787, the delegates to the constitutional convention met one last time to approve their work. Many were still not satisfied with parts of the document. Knowing this, Benjamin Franklin made this final plea for their support:

❝Mr. President

I confess that there are several parts of this Constitution which I do not at present approve, but I am not sure I shall never approve them. . . . I doubt, too, whether any other Convention we can obtain, may be able to make a better Constitution. . . . It therefore astonishes me, Sir, to find this system approaching so near to perfection as it does; and I think it will astonish our enemies.

Thus I consent, Sir, to this Constitution because I expect no better, and because I am not sure that it is not the best. The opinions I have had of its errors, I sacrifice to the public good. . . . I can not help expressing a wish that every member of the Convention who may still have objections to it would, with me . . . put his name to this instrument.❞

Of the 42 delegates present on that day, only 3 refused to sign the Constitution. Time has shown the wisdom of Franklin's words. The Constitution is not perfect. That it comes "so near to perfection as it does," however, continues to astonish those who study it today.

Constitutional Connections

The Second Amendment to the Constitution continues to be a source of controversy. Some argue that the amendment gives citizens the right to own guns for personal use. The Supreme Court and lower courts, however, have consistently ruled that the amendment only guarantees the right of states to keep militia, now known as National Guard units. In other words, the courts have declared that individual citizens do not have a constitutional right to possess guns. That is why gun control measures, such as the 1994 Brady Bill, have not been declared unconstitutional.

Amendments 1, 2, & 3

Amendments to the Constitution

The first ten amendments, called the Bill of Rights, were proposed as a group in 1789 and ratified in 1791. Other amendments were proposed and ratified one at a time. The dates in parentheses are the years of ratification.

Amendment 1 (1791)
Religious and Political Freedoms

Congress cannot establish an official religion or pass laws that limit freedom of worship. It cannot make laws that keep people from speaking or writing what they think. Nor can Congress stop people from holding peaceful meetings or from asking the government to correct a wrong.

Amendment 2 (1791)
The Right to Bear Arms

In order to maintain a state militia for their protection, citizens may own and use guns. Congress has outlawed the possession of certain firearms, however, such as sawed-off shotguns, machine guns, and assault rifles.

Amendment 3 (1791)
Quartering of Soldiers

In peacetime, citizens cannot be forced to provide a place in their homes for soldiers to stay. Even in wartime, this can only be done in a lawful manner.

Amendment 1

Congress shall make no law respecting an establishment of religion or prohibiting the free exercise thereof, or abridging the freedom of speech or of the press, or the right of the people peaceably to assemble and to petition the government for a redress of grievances.

Amendment 2

A well-regulated militia being necessary to the security of a free state, the right of the people to keep and bear arms shall not be infringed.

Amendment 3

No soldier shall, in time of peace, be quartered in any house without the consent of the owner, nor in time of war but in a manner to be prescribed by law.

The Bill of Rights

Amendments 1–10

1. Freedoms of religion, speech, press, assembly, and petition
2. Right to bear arms in a state militia
3. No quartering of soldiers without consent
4. Protection against unreasonable searches
5. Right to due process of law
6. Rights of the accused
7. Right to a jury trial in civil cases
8. Protection against unreasonable fines and cruel punishment
9. Other rights of the people and seizures
10. Powers reserved to the states and to the people

Checking Understanding

1. What are the first ten amendments called? (The Bill of Rights.)

2. What are the main freedoms identified in the First Amendment? (Freedom of religion, freedom of speech, freedom of the press, and freedom of assembly.)

Stimulating Critical Thinking

3. How do Benjamin Franklin's words on page R58 show his wisdom and common sense? (Franklin concedes that he does not approve of some parts of the Constitution, but he thinks it will be difficult to write a better Constitution. Further, he admits that he might be mistaken in his reservations about the document and thinks it sensible to sacrifice his minor objections to the public good.)

Bonus Activity

A Bill of Rights Skit

To underscore protections in the Bill of Rights, have students work in small groups to prepare short skits. Each skit should illustrate a situation in which a protection in the Bill of Rights is being violated. For example, a group might act out a scene in which officers enter a person's home without a search warrant. After each skit, the class should identify the right or rights being violated and discuss what actions should have been taken to avoid violating those rights.

✠ **Constitutional Connections**

One of the protections guaranteed by the Fifth Amendment is the right to refuse to incriminate oneself. This means that a person accused of a crime does not have to testify against him- or herself. Invoking the Fifth Amendment right implies neither guilt nor innocence.

Amendments 4 & 5

Amendment 4 (1791)
Search and Seizure

People are protected from arrests, searches of their homes, or seizures of their property without good reason. Authorities must get a warrant, or legal document signed by a judge, before making a search or an arrest. To obtain a warrant, they must explain to the judge why it is needed, where the search will take place, and who or what will be seized.

Amendment 5 (1791)
Due Process of Law

This amendment protects people from being abused by the legal system. It says:
- A person cannot be tried in a federal court for a serious crime without a formal indictment, or written accusation, by a grand jury. The grand jury decides whether there is enough evidence to make such an accusation.
- A person found not guilty of a federal crime cannot be tried again for the same offense in a federal court. This protection is known as the double jeopardy rule.
- Accused persons cannot be forced to say anything that might help convict them.
- The government cannot take away a person's life, liberty, or property without following correct legal procedures.
- The government cannot take away a person's property without paying a fair price for it. This power, called eminent domain, allows the government to acquire private property for public uses.

Amendment 4

The right of the people to be secure in their persons, houses, papers, and effects against unreasonable searches and seizures shall not be violated, and no warrants shall issue, but upon probable cause, supported by oath or affirmation, and particularly describing the place to be searched and the persons or things to be seized.

Amendment 5

No person shall be held to answer for a capital or otherwise infamous crime unless on a presentment or indictment of a grand jury, except in cases arising in the land or naval forces, or in the militia, when in actual service in time of war or public danger; nor shall any person be subject for the same offense to be twice put in jeopardy of life or limb; nor shall be compelled in any criminal case to be a witness against himself, nor be deprived of life, liberty, or property without due process of law; nor shall private property be taken for public use without just compensation.

Your Legal Rights and Protections

Before you are arrested, you are protected from:
- search without a warrant
- arrest without a warrant or sufficient cause (such as being caught in the act of committing a crime)

After your arrest, you have a right to:
- a writ of habeas corpus if held without charges
- remain silent
- consult a lawyer
- be indicted only by grand jury that weighs the evidence against you

(Continued on next page)

Amendment 6 (1791)
Rights of the Accused

Accused people have the right to:
- a prompt, public trial by a local jury
- know the charges against them
- face and question witnesses against them
- call witnesses to speak in their favor
- be represented by a lawyer

Amendment 7 (1791)
Right to a Jury Trial

When disputes involving more than $20 are tried in federal courts, either side can insist on a jury trial. If both sides agree, they can choose not to have a jury. Once a jury reaches a decision, it cannot be overturned simply because a judge disagrees with the jury's findings.

Amendment 8 (1791)
Bails, Fines, and Punishments

Bails, fines, and punishments must not be unreasonably high, cruel, or unusual. Bail is money or property given to the court by an accused person to guarantee that he or she will show up for trial. Usually, the more serious the crime, the higher the bail.

Amendment 6

In all criminal prosecutions, the accused shall enjoy the right to a speedy and public trial by an impartial jury of the state and district wherein the crime shall have been committed, which district shall have been previously ascertained by law, and to be informed of the nature and cause of the accusation; to be confronted with the witnesses against him; to have compulsory process for obtaining witnesses in his favor, and to have the assistance of counsel for his defense.

Amendment 7

In suits at common law, where the value in controversy shall exceed twenty dollars, the right of trial by jury shall be preserved, and no fact tried by a jury shall be otherwise reexamined in any court of the United States than according to the rules of the common law.

Amendment 8

Excessive bail shall not be required, nor excessive fines imposed, nor cruel and unusual punishments inflicted.

After you are indicted, you have a right to:
- know the charges against you
- reasonable bail
- a speedy trial by jury

At your trial, you have the right to:
- question witnesses against you
- call your own witnesses
- refuse to answer questions that might harm your case
- be represented by a lawyer

If you are found innocent, you are protected from:
- being tried again in federal court for the same crime

If you are found guilty, you are protected from:
- excessive fines
- cruel or unusual punishments

Checking Understanding

1. What is a warrant? (A legal document signed by a judge.)

2. What is double jeopardy? (Putting a person on trial again for an offense after he or she was found not guilty of that offense.)

3. What does the Seventh Amendment guarantee? (It guarantees the right to a jury trial in civil cases where $20 or more is disputed.)

Stimulating Critical Thinking

4. Do you think the framers of the Constitution were more concerned about protecting the innocent or convicting the guilty? (Students might suggest that the framers' care in protecting the rights of the accused suggests that they were aware that the innocent are sometimes falsely accused and that it was very important to protect the rights of someone wrongly accused of a crime.)

Amendments 9, 10, 11, & 12

Amendment 9 (1791)
Other Rights of the People

The listing of certain rights in the Constitution does not mean that these are the only rights the people have. Nor does it make those other rights less important.

Amendment 10 (1791)
Powers Reserved to the States or the People

The federal government is granted certain powers under the Constitution. All other powers, except those denied to the states, belong to the states or to the people.

Amendment 11 (1795)
Suits Against States

Citizens of other states or foreign countries cannot sue a state in federal court without its consent.

Amendment 12 (1804)
Election of the President

The Twelfth Amendment was passed after both candidates in the election of 1800 received an equal number of electoral votes. This occurred in part because electors voted only for President, leaving the second-place candidate to be Vice-President. (See page 283 for more details.) This amendment calls for electors to cast separate votes for President and Vice-President.

Amendment 9

The enumeration in the Constitution of certain rights shall not be construed to deny or disparage others retained by the people.

Amendment 10

The powers not delegated to the United States by the Constitution, nor prohibited by it to the states, are reserved to the states respectively, or to the people.

Amendment 11

The judicial power of the United States shall not be construed to extend to any suit in law or equity commenced or prosecuted against one of the United States by citizens of another state, or by citizens or subjects of any foreign state.

Amendment 12

The electors shall meet in their respective states and vote by ballot for President and Vice-President, one of whom at least shall not be an inhabitant of the same state with themselves; they shall name in their ballots the person voted for as President, and in distinct ballots the person voted for as Vice-President, and they shall make distinct lists of all persons voted for as President and of all persons voted for as Vice-President and of the number of votes for each, which lists they shall sign and certify and transmit sealed to the seat of government of the United States, directed to the president of the Senate.

The president of the Senate shall, in the presence of the Senate and House of Representatives, open all the certificates and the votes shall then be counted.

The Constitution does not specify the date of presidential elections. Article 2, Section 1, Clause 4 (page R49), says "Congress may determine the time of choosing the electors and the day on which they shall give their votes." Congress has set the election date as the first Tuesday after the first Monday in November. The electoral college votes on the Monday after the second Wednesday in December.

Checking Understanding

1. Which powers are reserved to the states or the people? (All powers not specifically given to the federal government by the Constitution are reserved to the states or the people.)

2. If no presidential candidate receives a majority of electoral votes, who decides the winner of the election? (The House of Representatives chooses a President from the top three candidates.)

Stimulating Critical Thinking

3. What do you think the "reserved powers" policy protects against? (It helps protect against the federal government taking too much power. It underscores that all power in the government flows from the people.)

Amendment 12

If no presidential candidate receives a majority of electoral votes, the House of Representatives chooses a President from the top three candidates. In the House, each state gets one vote.

If no candidate for Vice-President receives a majority of electoral votes, the election goes to the Senate. Two-thirds of either the House or Senate must be present when voting for President or Vice-President.

The person having the greatest number of votes for President shall be the President, if such number be a majority of the whole number of electors appointed; and if no person have such majority, then from the persons having the highest numbers not exceeding three on the list of those voted for as President, the House of Representatives shall choose immediately, by ballot, the President. But in choosing the President the votes shall be taken by states, the representation from each state having one vote; a quorum for this purpose shall consist of a member or members from two thirds of the states, and a majority of all the states shall be necessary to a choice. And if the House of Representatives shall not choose a President whenever the right of choice shall devolve upon them, ~~before the fourth day of March next following,~~ then the Vice-President shall act as President, as in the case of the death or other constitutional disability of the President.

The person having the greatest number of votes as Vice-President shall be the Vice-President, if such number be a majority of the whole number of electors appointed, and if no person have a majority, then from the two highest numbers on the list the Senate shall choose the Vice-President; a quorum for the purpose shall consist of two thirds of the whole number of senators, and a majority of the whole number shall be necessary to a choice. But no person constitutionally ineligible to the office of President shall be eligible to that of Vice-President of the United States.

Electing a President

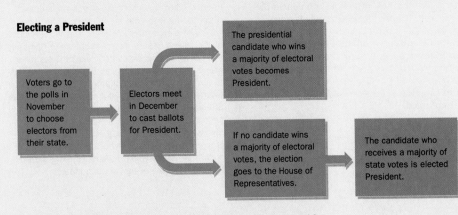

The process outlined in this chart was established by Amendment 12.

The "equal protection" clause of the Fourteenth Amendment continues to be important. It forbids states to discriminate against people on the basis of race, and also prohibits states from violating due process. The Supreme Court has interpreted the amendment to mean that states cannot make laws that prevent citizens from exercising rights under federal law.

Amendments 13 & 14

Amendment 13 (1865)
Abolition of Slavery

This amendment was the first of three passed shortly after the Civil War. It ended slavery forever in the United States and its territories. No one may be forced to work unless ordered to by a court as punishment for a crime.

Amendment 14 (1868)
Civil Rights in the States

The Fourteenth Amendment was designed to give full citizenship rights to former slaves.

Section 1. Citizenship

All people born or naturalized in this country are citizens of both the United States and the state in which they live. States cannot make laws that keep people from enjoying their rights as citizens. States may not deprive citizens of life, liberty, or property without due process of law. Nor may states deny citizens "equal protection of the laws" by discriminating against any one group.

Section 2. Representation and Voting

This section replaced the old rule, by which slaves were counted as three-fifths of a person in determining a state's representation in the Congress, with a new one. If a state denied the right to vote to some male citizens over age 21—except as punishment for crime or rebellion—those citizens would not be counted in determining representation. The purpose of this new rule was to force states to let former slaves vote. If a state did not, it would lose representation in Congress. This new rule, however, was never enforced.

Amendment 13

Section 1.

Neither slavery nor involuntary servitude, except as a punishment for crime whereof the party shall have been duly convicted, shall exist within the United States or any place subject to their jurisdiction.

Section 2.

Congress shall have power to enforce this article by appropriate legislation.

Amendment 14

Section 1.

All persons born or naturalized in the United States and subject to the jurisdiction thereof are citizens of the United States and of the state wherein they reside. No state shall make or enforce any law which shall abridge the privileges or immunities of citizens of the United States; nor shall any state deprive any person of life, liberty, or property without due process of law; nor deny to any person within its jurisdiction the equal protection of the laws.

Section 2.

Representatives shall be apportioned among the several states according to their respective numbers, counting the whole number of persons in each state, ~~excluding Indians not taxed.~~ But when the right to vote at any election for the choice of electors for President and Vice-President of the United States, representatives in Congress, the executive and judicial officers of a state, or the members of the legislature thereof is denied to any of the ~~male~~ inhabitants of such state, being ~~twenty-one years of age and~~ citizens of the United States, or in any way abridged, except for participation in rebellion or other crime, the basis of representation therein shall be reduced in the proportion which the number of such ~~male~~ citizens shall bear to the whole number of ~~male~~ citizens ~~twenty-one years of age~~ in such state.

Constitutional Connections

Although the Fifteenth Amendment was intended to protect the voting rights of African Americans, many states found ways to prevent them from voting. Two of the most commonly used means were the literacy test and the poll tax. A literacy test required voters to read and explain a difficult passage. If the readers failed to explain it to the satisfaction of the examiners, they could not vote. Some states also used a poll tax—a fee for voting. Since many African Americans were poor, this prevented them from voting. The Twenty-fourth Amendment abolished the poll tax in national elections. In 1966, the Supreme Court also outlawed the use of poll taxes in state and local elections. The Voting Rights Act, first passed in 1965 and later renewed, prohibited the use of literacy tests.

Amendments 14 & 15

Section 3. Punishing Rebel Leaders

Former state and federal officials who had supported the South in the Civil War were barred from voting or holding office again. In 1898, Congress removed this barrier.

Section 4. Legal and Illegal Debts

This section dealt with debts left over from the Civil War. The only legal debt was the federal government's war debt. No government, state or federal, was allowed to pay off rebel war debts. No payment was to be made to slaveholders for the loss of their slaves.

Amendment 15 (1870) Voting Rights

This amendment was intended to protect the voting rights of the freed slaves. It said that neither the United States nor any state can deny citizens the right to vote because of their race or color, or because they were once slaves. Despite this amendment, many states did find ways to keep African Americans from voting. You can read more about this in Chapter 19.

Section 3.

No person shall be a senator or representative in Congress, or elector of President and Vice-President, or hold any office, civil or military, under the United States, or under any state, who, having previously taken an oath as a member of Congress or as an officer of the United States or as a member of any state legislature or as an executive or judicial officer of any state to support the Constitution of the United States, shall have engaged in insurrection or rebellion against the same, or given aid or comfort to the enemies thereof. But Congress may by a vote of two thirds of each house remove such disability.

Section 4.

The validity of the public debt of the United States, authorized by law, including debts incurred for payment of pensions and bounties for services in suppressing insurrection or rebellion, shall not be questioned. But neither the United States nor any state shall assume or pay any debt or obligation incurred in aid of insurrection or rebellion against the United States or any claim for the loss or emancipation of any slave; but all such debts, obligations, and claims shall be held illegal and void.

Section 5.

The Congress shall have power to enforce, by appropriate legislation, the provisions of this article.

Amendment 15

Section 1.

The right of citizens of the United States to vote shall not be denied or abridged by the United States or by any state on account of race, color, or previous condition of servitude.

Section 2.

The Congress shall have power to enforce this article by appropriate legislation.

Tax Options

Have students work in groups to brainstorm methods for raising revenue for the government. Methods might include an income tax with different percentages for varying income levels, a flat income tax, a national sales tax, and other methods students think of. Have each group discuss the pros and cons of each method and then recommend which method, or combination of methods, they think is most reasonable, and why.

Amendments 16 & 17

Amendment 16 (1913)
Income Taxes

This amendment was passed to allow Congress to tax the incomes of individuals and businesses. The amendment was needed because Article 1, Section 9, Clause 4 says taxes levied on people must fall equally on the states based on their population. An income tax, however, taxes wealthy states more than poor states of equal population.

Amendment 17 (1913)
Direct Election Of Senators

Section 1. Regular Elections

The Constitution originally called for Senators to be elected by state legislatures. (See Article 1, Section 3, Clause 1.) This amendment gives the voters of each state the power to elect their Senators directly.

Section 2. Special Elections

If a senator dies or resigns before finishing his or her term, the governor must call a special election to fill that senate seat. The state legislature may let the governor appoint a temporary senator until such an election can be held.

Amendment 16

The Congress shall have power to lay and collect taxes on incomes, from whatever source derived, without apportionment among the several states, and without regard to any census or enumeration.

Amendment 17

Section 1.

The Senate of the United States shall be composed of two senators from each state, elected by the people thereof for six years; and each senator shall have one vote. The electors in each state shall have the qualifications requisite for electors of the most numerous branch of the state legislatures.

Section 2.

When vacancies happen in the representation of any state in the Senate, the executive authority of such state shall issue writs of election to fill such vacancies, provided that the legislature of any state may empower the executive thereof to make temporary appointments until the people fill the vacancies by election as the legislature may direct.

Section 3.

This amendment shall not be so construed as to affect the election or term of any senator chosen before it becomes valid as part of the Constitution.

The Federal Income Tax

The personal income tax is a progressive tax, which means that it taxes people with higher incomes at a higher rate than people with lower incomes. The theory is that the greater tax burden thus falls on the people who have the greatest ability to pay.

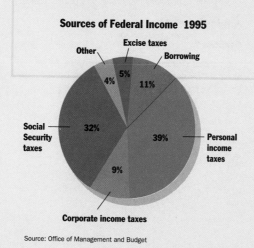

Sources of Federal Income 1995

- Other 4%
- Excise taxes 5%
- Borrowing 11%
- Personal income taxes 39%
- Corporate income taxes 9%
- Social Security taxes 32%

Source: Office of Management and Budget

Constitutional Connections

Prohibition resulted in massive lawbreaking during the 1920s. Gangsters and racketeers made millions of dollars selling illegal alcohol, and many citizens who were otherwise law-abiding broke the law to obtain alcohol. The Twenty-first Amendment made the sale and distribution of alcohol a local or state matter.

Amendment 18 (1919)
Prohibition of Alcohol

This amendment outlawed the making, selling, and transporting of alcoholic beverages in the United States and its territories. It was passed as part of a great reform effort to end the problems caused by the abuse of alcohol. The ban on alcohol, however, proved impossible to enforce. This amendment was repealed in 1933 by the Twenty-first Amendment.

Amendment 19 (1920)
Suffrage for Women

Until the passage of this amendment, most women in the United States were denied suffrage, or the right to vote. The Nineteenth Amendment says that women and men have an equal right to vote in both state and national elections.

~~Amendment 18~~

~~Section 1.~~

~~After one year from the ratification of this article the manufacture, sale, or transportation of intoxicating liquors within, the importation thereof into, or the exportation thereof from the United States and all territory subject to the jurisdiction thereof for beverage purposes is hereby prohibited.~~

~~Section 2.~~

~~The Congress and the several states shall have concurrent power to enforce this article by appropriate legislation.~~

~~Section 3.~~

~~This article shall be inoperative unless it shall have been ratified as an amendment to the Constitution by the legislatures of the several states, as provided in the Constitution, within seven years from the date of the submission hereof to the states by the Congress.~~

Amendment 19

Section 1.

The right of citizens of the United States to vote shall not be denied or abridged by the United States or by any state on account of sex.

Section 2.

Congress shall have power to enforce this article by appropriate legislation.

This 1919 cartoon, entitled "Almost Through the Dark Alley," criticizes senators who opposed woman suffrage. Many supporters believed that once the amendment was finally approved by Congress, ratification would follow quickly.

Discussion

Checking Understanding

1. **What is suffrage?** (The right to vote.)

2. **What did the Sixteenth Amendment authorize?** (An income tax on individuals and businesses.)

3. **What did the Eighteenth Amendment outlaw?** (The making, selling, and transporting of alcohol.)

Stimulating Critical Thinking

4. **Analyze the cartoon on page R67. What does it imply were the reasons for opposing suffrage for women? What do you think the senators feared?** (The cartoon identifies prejudice and tradition as two of the forces that led some senators to oppose suffrage for women. Fear of how woman suffrage might affect traditional roles of men and women may have caused many to oppose it. Students might suggest that the senators feared losing their jobs or having to address issues that were important to women.)

The term "lame duck" originally referred to a stockbroker or trader who could not pay his losses. William Makepeace Thackeray used the term in this sense in his novel *Vanity Fair:* "I don't like the looks of Mr. Sedley's affairs. . . . He's been dabbling on his own account I fear. . . . unless I see Amelia's ten thousand down you don't marry. I'll have no lame duck's daughter in my family."

Later the term came to mean anyone who defaulted on debts or who was disabled. Today, it is used almost exclusively in reference to a defeated elected official who continues to hold political office before the inauguration of a successor.

Amendment 20

Amendment 20 (1933)
The "Lame-Duck" Amendment

A "lame duck" is someone who remains in office for a time after his or her replacement has been chosen. The outgoing official is considered "lame," or without much power and influence. The main purpose of Amendment 20 was to reduce the amount of time "lame ducks" remained in office after national elections.

Section 1. New Term Dates

In the past, a new President and Vice-President elected in November waited until March 3 to take office. Now their terms begin on January 20. In the past, new members of Congress waited 13 months between election and taking office. Now they are sworn in on January 3, which is just a few weeks after their election.

Section 2. Meetings of Congress

Congress must meet at least once a year, beginning on January 3. Congress may, however, choose a different starting day.

Section 3. Death of a President-elect

If a newly elected President dies before taking office, the Vice-President-elect will become President.

Amendment 20

Section 1.

The terms of the President and Vice-President shall end at noon on the 20th day of January, and the terms of senators and representatives at noon on the 3rd day of January, of the years in which such terms would have ended if this article had not been ratified; and the terms of their successors shall then begin.

Section 2.

The Congress shall assemble at least once in every year, and such meeting shall begin at noon on the 3rd day of January, unless they shall by law appoint a different day.

Section 3.

If, at the time fixed for the beginning of the term of the President, the President-elect shall have died, the Vice-President-elect shall become President. If a President shall not have been chosen before the time fixed for the beginning of his term, or if the President-elect shall have failed to qualify, then the Vice-President-elect shall act as President until a President shall have qualified; and the Congress may by law provide for the case wherein neither a President-elect nor a Vice-President-elect shall have qualified, declaring who shall then act as President, or the manner in which one who is to act shall be selected, and such person shall act accordingly until a President or Vice-President shall have qualified.

Checking Understanding

1. When did a new President and Vice-President take office before and after the Twentieth Amendment? (In the past a new President and Vice-President elected in November took office in March; after the Twentieth Amendment passed, they began taking office in January.)

2. If a newly elected President dies before taking office, who becomes President-elect? (The Vice-President-elect.)

3. What did the Twenty-first Amendment do? (It repealed the Eighteenth Amendment.)

Stimulating Critical Thinking

4. Why do you think the Eighteenth Amendment was repealed? (It proved difficult to enforce. It resulted in massive lawbreaking and thereby led to disrespect for the law. Possibly most people came to feel that the use of alcohol in moderation should not be a crime.)

Section 4. Death of a Presidential Candidate in a House Election

Amendment 12 says that if no candidate for President wins a majority of votes in the electoral college, the House of Representatives must choose a President from the three leading candidates. If one of those candidate dies before the House votes, Congress can decide how to proceed.

Similarly, Congress can decide how to proceed in case a vice-presidential election goes to the Senate and one of the leading candidates dies before the Senate makes its choice.

Amendment 21 (1933) Repeal of Prohibition

Section 1. Repeal of Amendment 18

Amendment 18, which established a national prohibition of alcohol, is repealed.

Section 2. Protection for "Dry" States

Carrying alcohol into a "dry" state—a state that prohibits alcoholic beverages—is a federal crime.

Section 3. Ratification

Because this was such a controversial amendment, Congress insisted that it be ratified by state conventions elected by the people. This was the only time this system of ratification had been used since the Constitution itself was ratified.

Section 4.

The Congress may by law provide for the case of the death of any of the persons from whom the House of Representatives may choose a President whenever the right of choice shall have devolved upon them, and for the case of the death of any of the persons from whom the Senate may choose a Vice-President whenever the right of choice shall have devolved upon them.

Section 5.

Sections 1 and 2 shall take effect on the 15th day of October following the ratification of this article.

Section 6.

This article shall be inoperative unless it shall have been ratified as an amendment to the Constitution by the legislatures of three fourths of the several states within seven years from the date of its submission.

Amendment 21

Section 1.

The eighteenth article of amendment to the Constitution of the United States is hereby repealed.

Section 2.

The transportation or importation into any state, territory, or possession of the United States for delivery or use therein of intoxicating liquors, in violation of the laws thereof, is hereby prohibited.

Section 3.

This article shall be inoperative unless it shall have been ratified as an amendment to the Constitution by conventions in the several states, as provided in the Constitution, within seven years from the date of submission hereof to the states by the Congress.

Bonus Activity

Taking Sides on Term Limits

To review opinions about term limits, have student groups take positions for or against them. They should identify their positions and support them with reasons. A group may choose to take different stands on term limits for the President and term limits for members of Congress. Have each group summarize their position for the class.

✠ **Constitutional Connections**

Much of the original impetus for the Twenty-second Amendment came from Republicans who were unhappy with Franklin D. Roosevelt's long tenure. A proposal to limit the President to a single six-year term in office has also been made. Some proponents for a single-term presidency believe that the President could then make decisions without concerns about re-election.

Amendment 22

Amendment 22 (1951) Presidential Term Limits

This amendment made the long tradition that Presidents limit their stay in office to two terms part of the Constitution. It says that no person can be elected President more than twice. If a Vice-President or someone else succeeds to the presidency and serves for more than two years, that person is limited to one additional term.

Amendment 22

Section 1.

No person shall be elected to the office of the President more than twice, and no person who has held the office of President or acted as President for more than two years of a term to which some other person was elected President shall be elected to the office of the President more than once. But this article shall not apply to any person holding the office of President when this article was proposed by the Congress, and shall not prevent any person who may be holding the office of President or acting as President during the term within which this article becomes operative from holding the office of President or acting as President during the remainder of such term.

Section 2.

This article shall be inoperative unless it shall have been ratified as an amendment to the Constitution by the legislatures of three fourths of the several states within seven years from the day of its submission to the states by the Congress.

The Presidential Two-Term Tradition

1796
George Washington declines to run for a third term, beginning the two-term tradition.

1808
President Thomas Jefferson follows Washington's example by retiring after two terms.

1880
President Ulysses S. Grant runs for a third term but loses the Republican nomination on the thirty-sixth convention ballot.

1940
Democrat Franklin Roosevelt wins for a third and then a fourth term. Republicans begin pushing for a two-term amendment, which is ratified in 1951.

1985
After winning a second term, Ronald Reagan says: "I see no reason why the Twenty-second Amendment shouldn't be repealed."

Amendments 23 & 24

Amendment 23 (1961)
Voting in the District of Columbia

This amendment allowed residents of the District of Columbia to vote in Presidential elections. The District is given the same number of electors it would be entitled to if it were a state. But that number cannot be greater than the number of electors from the state with the smallest population.

At the time this amendment was ratified, more than 781,000 people lived in Washington, D.C. Capital residents paid taxes like all other citizens, but did not have the right to vote in national elections.

Amendment 24 (1964)
Abolition of Poll Taxes

A poll tax is a tax people have to pay in order to vote. For decades, poll taxes were used by some southern states to discourage poor people, especially poor black people, from voting. The Twenty-fourth Amendment says that neither the United States nor any state can require a citizen to pay a poll tax in order to vote in national elections.

Amendment 23

Section 1.

The district constituting the seat of government of the United States shall appoint in such manner as the Congress may direct: A number of electors of President and Vice-President equal to the whole number of senators and representatives in Congress to which the district would be entitled if it were a state, but in no event more than the least populous state; they shall be in addition to those appointed by the states, but they shall be considered, for the purposes of the election of President and Vice-President, to be electors appointed by a state; and they shall meet in the district and perform such duties as provided by the twelfth article of amendment.

Section 2.

The Congress shall have power to enforce this article by appropriate legislation.

Amendment 24

Section 1.

The right of citizens of the United States to vote in any primary or other election for President or Vice-President, for electors for President or Vice-President, or for senator or representative in Congress, shall not be denied or abridged by the United States or any state by reason of failure to pay any poll tax or other tax.

Section 2.

The Congress shall have power to enforce this article by appropriate legislation.

Why Did It Take an Amendment to Outlaw Poll Taxes?

Congress can outlaw many things by passing a bill into law. In the case of poll taxes, however, Congress faced a constitutional barrier. The Constitution gave the states authority over how to hold federal elections. So, if poll taxes were to be forbidden, an amendment specifically outlawing them had to be proposed and ratified.

Discussion

Checking Understanding

1. **Why did Republicans push for a two-term amendment for Presidents?** (Because Franklin Roosevelt had served for more than two terms, Republicans wished to prevent the possibility of a future Democratic President staying in office for so long.)

2. **What did the Twenty-third Amendment offer the residents of the District of Columbia?** (The right to vote in presidential elections.)

3. **What was the purpose of poll taxes?** (They were used to discourage poor African Americans from voting.)

Stimulating Critical Thinking

4. **Do you think the two-term restriction on Presidents is reasonable? Explain.** (Yes: helps guard against a President becoming overly confident in his or her use of power. No: voters should have the right to decide when a President has served long enough.)

Constitution Handbook • **R71**

R71

President Woodrow Wilson suffered a disabling stroke in September of 1919. He never fully recovered from the stroke, limiting his ability to serve as President. During the time he remained in office, a number of people made presidential decisions and exercised great influence over public affairs. Among them were unelected advisors such as Colonel E. M. House and Wilson's wife, Elizabeth Bolling Galt Wilson. Had the Twenty-fifth Amendment been in effect during his administration, the Vice-President could have acted as President.

Amendment 25

Amendment 25 (1967) Presidential Disability and Succession

Section 1. Replacing the President

If the President dies, resigns, or is removed from office, the Vice-President becomes President.

Section 2. Replacing the Vice-President

The President appoints a new Vice-President if that office becomes empty. That appointment must be approved by both houses of Congress.

Section 3. Temporary Replacement with the President's Consent

If the President notifies Congress in writing that he or she is unable to perform official duties, the Vice-President takes over as Acting President. The President may return to office after notifying Congress that he or she is again able to serve.

Section 4. Temporary Replacement Without the President's Consent

If a President is disabled and cannot or will not notify Congress, the Vice-President and a majority of the cabinet (or some other group named by Congress) can send such notice. The Vice-President will then become Acting President.

The Vice-President will step down when the President sends Congress written notice of renewed ability to serve. If the Vice-President and others disagree, they must notify Congress within four days.

Amendment 25

Section 1.

In case of the removal of the President from office or of his death or resignation, the Vice-President shall become President.

Section 2.

Whenever there is a vacancy in the office of the Vice-President, the President shall nominate a Vice-President who shall take office upon confirmation by a majority vote of both houses of Congress.

Section 3.

Whenever the President transmits to the president pro tempore of the Senate and the speaker of the House of Representatives his written declaration that he is unable to discharge the powers and duties of his office, and until he transmits to them a written declaration to the contrary, such powers and duties shall be discharged by the Vice-President as Acting President.

Section 4.

Whenever the Vice-President and a majority of either the principal officers of the executive departments or of such other body as Congress may by law provide, transmit to the president pro tempore of the Senate and the speaker of the House of Representatives their written declaration that the President is unable to discharge the powers and duties of his office, the Vice-President shall immediately assume the powers and duties of the office as Acting President.

Thereafter, when the President transmits to the president pro tempore of the Senate and the speaker of the House of Representatives his written declaration that no inability exists, he shall resume the powers and duties of his office unless the Vice-President and a majority of either the principal officers of the executive department or of such other body as Congress may by law provide, transmit within four days to the president pro tempore of the Senate and the speaker of the House of Representatives their written declaration that the President is unable to discharge the powers and duties of his office.

Congress must meet within 48 hours to discuss whether the President is still disabled. They have 21 days to decide the issue. If two thirds or more of both houses vote that the President is disabled, the Vice-President remains in office as Acting President. If they do not, the President resumes official duties.

Amendment 26 (1971)
Eighteen-Year-Old Vote

Neither the United States nor any state can deny the vote to citizens of age 18 or older because of their age. The effect of this amendment was to lower the voting age in most state elections from 21 to 18.

Amendment 27 (1992)
Congressional Salaries

If members of Congress vote to change their own salaries, that change cannot go into effect until after the next Congressional election. This change gives voters a chance to speak out on pay raises.

Thereupon Congress shall decide the issue, assembling within forty-eight hours for that purpose if not in session. If the Congress, within twenty-one days after receipt of the latter written declaration, or, if Congress is not in session, within twenty-one days after Congress is required to assemble, determines by two-thirds vote of both houses that the President is unable to discharge the powers and duties of his office, the Vice-President shall continue to discharge the same as Acting President; otherwise, the President shall resume the powers and duties of his office.

Amendment 26

Section 1.

The right of citizens of the United States, who are eighteen years of age or older, to vote shall not be denied or abridged by the United States or by any state on account of age.

Section 2.

The Congress shall have power to enforce this article by appropriate legislation.

Amendment 27

No law varying the compensation for the services of the senators and representatives shall take effect until an election of representatives shall have intervened.

The 26th Amendment passed mainly because many people believed that if 18-year-olds were old enough to fight for their country, they were old enough to vote.

Glossary

The Glossary defines terms that are important in the understanding of United States history. The page number at the end of the definition refers to the page in the text on which the term is first defined.

Pronunciation Key

In the text, words that are difficult to pronounce are followed by a respelling in parentheses. The respelling helps the reader pronounce the word. For example, Iroquoian (see page 28) has been respelled as IR-uh-KWOY-uhn. A hyphen separates the syllables. Syllables in large capital letters are stressed the most; syllables in small capital letters are stressed in a weaker tone.

The pronunciation key appears below. Letters used in the respelling of words are listed on the left side of each column. On the right side are commonly used words that show the pronunciation.

Pronounce			
a as in	hat	*j*	jet
ah	father	*ng*	ring
ar	tar	*o*	frog
ay	say	*ō*	no
ayr	air	*oo*	soon
e, eh	hen	*or*	for
ee	bee	*ow*	plow
eer	deer	*oy*	boy
er	her	*sh*	she
ew	new	*th*	think
g	go	*u, uh*	sun
i, ih	him	*z*	zebra
ī	kite	*zh*	measure

A

abolition putting an end to slavery (page 441)

aliens foreigners who are not yet citizens of the country in which they live (page 281)

allies helpers in times of trouble (page 182)

amendments changes, as in changes to the Constitution (page 248)

annex to take control of a territory and add it to a country (page 384)

anthropologists scientists who study human beings and how they live in groups (page 1)

archaeologists anthropologists who search for clues to how human beings lived in the past (page 1)

artifacts objects made by human work (page 1)

B

bias a one-sided or slanted view (page 309)

bicameral a legislature made up of two houses (page 129)

bill of rights a list of the rights and freedoms guaranteed to the people (page 234)

black codes laws passed by white southern politicians after the Civil War that limited the rights and opportunities of African Americans (page 529)

blockade blocking of a place by ships or troops to keep supplies from reaching it (page 185)

bond a piece of paper given in exchange for money with the promise to repay the loan plus interest by a certain date (page 269)

boycott to refuse to buy (page 189)

C

cabinet the department heads of the executive branch of government who advise the President and help carry out the nation's laws (page 267)

cape a piece of land sticking out into the sea (page 63)

carpetbaggers northerners, including teachers, ministers, businesspeople, and former Union soldiers, who moved to the South after the Civil War (page 532)

cash crops crops that are raised to be sold for a profit (page 150)

casualties soldiers killed, wounded, captured, or missing (page 500)

caucus a private meeting of political party leaders (page 350)

cede to give up terrritory (page 185)

checks and balances the system by which each branch of government can check, or limit, the power of the other two branches (page 252)

civilization a society in which a high level of art, technology, and government exists (page 14)

claim something that someone says is true (page 423)

colony settlement made by a group of people in a distant place that remains under the control of their home country (page 53)

confederation an alliance of independent states (page 234)

conquistadors conquerors (page 94)

constitution plan of government (page 234)

constitutional permitted by the Constitution (page 270)

corruption when public office is used for illegal purposes (page 535)

credibility believability (page 392)

culture the way of life of a group of people, including arts, beliefs, inventions, traditions, and language (page 13)

customs duties charges made on foreign imports (page 188)

D

depression a long, sharp decline in economic activity (page 238)

discrimination unfair treatment of a group of people compared with another group (page 417)

diversity variety (page 25)

draft system that requires people to serve in the military (page 508)

due process of law following the legal steps in a court of law (page 248)

E

emancipation freeing of slaves (page 440)

embargo to halt trade with one or more other nations (page 302)

evidence information given to support a claim (page 423)

excise tax a tax on the production or sale of a certain product (page 273)

executive branch the branch of government that carries out the laws (page 242)

expansionists people who believe that their country's prosperity depends on enlarging its territory (page 376)

expedition a journey organized for a definite purpose (page 63)

exports goods sent out of one country to sell in another (page 123)

F

Fall Line the eastern edge of the Piedmont, where the land drops sharply (page 127)

federalism the division of power between the states and national government (page 251)

feudalism a system of government in western Europe in which a vassal promised to serve a lord in exchange for a grant of land (page 50)

finance to supply the money for something, such as a project (page 63)

financial panic widespread fear caused by a sudden downturn in prices or change in property values (page 332)

freedmen former slaves, both women and men, who lived in the South during the Reconstruction period (page 526)

G

generalization a broad statement that is meant to sum up the specific characteristics of something (page 337)

glaciers vast slow-moving masses of ice (page 10)

grandfather clause provisions in southern voting laws stating that such laws did not apply to anyone whose father or grandfather could have voted before January 1, 1867 (page 540)

guerrillas soldiers who are not part of the regular army and who make hit-and-run attacks against their enemy (page 222)

H

habeas corpus right that protects people from being held in prison unlawfully (page 492)

historical interpretation a historian's opinion about an event or person (page 446)

hypothesis a theory that tries to explain an event (page 510)

I

immediate cause something that directly brings about an event (page 285)

immediate effect an effect that occurs right away (page 285)

immigration the movement of people from one country to make their home in another country (page 328)

impeach to accuse the President of wrongdoing and bring him to trial (page 531)

imports products brought in from another country to be sold (page 150)

impressed when someone is forced to serve in another nation's navy (page 276)

inauguration the ceremony that installs a new President (page 266)

income tax tax on money people earn from work or investments (page 509)

indentured servants people who signed a contract agreeing to work a certain number of years without pay for the person who paid their passage to England's American colonies (page 124)

Industrial Revolution the shift of production from hand tools to machines and from homes to factories (page 319)

infectious diseases illnesses that can be passed from one person to another (page 68)

invest to use your money to help a business get started or grow, with the hope that you will earn a profit (page 120)

irrigation supplying land with water by use of dams, ditches, and channels (page 19)

isolines lines on maps that mark off areas that are the same in some way (page 413)

J

Jim Crow laws laws that forcibly separated racial groups in public places in the South after Reconstruction (page 540)

joint-stock company a business that raised money by selling shares, also called stock, to investors (page 122)

judicial branch a system of courts to interpret the meaning of laws (page 242)

judicial review a court's power to decide whether or not an act passed by Congress is constitutional (page 293)

L

league a group of people with a common purpose (page 110)

legacy something handed down from past generations (page 71)

legislative branch the branch of government that makes the laws (page 242)

legislature a group of people chosen to make the laws (page 124)

libel printing statements that damage a person's good name (page 164)

literacy the ability to read and write (page 148)

long-range cause a cause that may take months or even years to bring about an effect (page 285)

long-range effect an effect that occurs months or even years after the cause (page 285)

loose construction the view that the government has broader powers than the ones specifically listed in the Constitution (page 270)

Loyalists colonists who did not want independence from Great Britain (page 213)

M

martial law rule by the army instead of by the usual government officials (page 492)

mass production using machines to make large quantities of goods faster and cheaper than they could be made by hand (page 320)

memoirs a person's written remembrances of the events of his or her life (page 460)

mercantilism the economic idea that a nation becomes strong by filling its treasury with gold and silver (page 102)

mercenaries soldiers who are hired to fight for a country other than their own (page 214)

migration movement of people from one region to another (page 10)

militia citizens trained to fight in an emergency (page 163)

minting the government process of printing bills or making coins to use as money (page 237)

minutemen militia volunteers in New England at the beginning of the War of Independence, so called because they were ready to fight on short notice (page 206)

monopoly complete control (page 194)

mudslinging making wild charges and lies about a candidate (page 352)

N

nationalism a strong feeling of pride in one's nation (page 308)

nativism the belief that immigrants threaten traditional American culture and institutions (page 421)

nativists people who believe in the ideas of nativism (page 421)

navigation the science of getting ships from place to place (page 46)

neutral when a nation does not take either side in a conflict (page 273)

nomads people with no permanent home who move in search of food (page 11)

nullify to declare that a certain law will not be enforced (page 282)

O

opinion an expression of a feeling or thought that cannot be proved or disproved (page 210)

oral history historical data in the form of personal recollections or stories passed on by word of mouth (page 341)

P

parallel time lines two or more time lines that cover the same time span but different sets of events (page 31)

Patriots strong supporters of American independence (page 213)

persecution a series of injurious actions—for example, attacking, imprisoning, torturing, or killing—carried out against members of a group for their beliefs (page 108)

plantation a large estate where a single crop that requires a large labor force is grown for profit (page 70)

plateau a large expanse of flat land at a higher elevation (page 24)

platform a statement of beliefs by a political party (page 476)

point of view the background or position from which a person observes something. Background includes such factors as age, culture, social position, and beliefs (page 249)

political parties organized groups of people who have similar ideas about government and society (page 279)

poll tax a fee enacted by state governments in the South that charged citizens for the right to vote and which successfully prevented black southerners from voting (page 540)

popular sovereignty when voters in a territory were given the right to decide whether to allow slavery or not (page 468)

population density the average number of people in a certain-sized area (page 271)

precipitation moisture from rain and snow (page 413)

prejudice a bad opinion of people based only on such factors as their religion, nationality, or appearance (page 154)

primary source an artifact or record from someone who has experienced the event described (page 193)

proclamation official announcement (page 187)

profiteers people who demand unfair profits for their goods (page 219)

proprietary colonies colonies in which the owners, known as proprietors, organized the colonies, controlled the land, and appointed governors (page 133)

protective tariff tax placed on imports aimed at discouraging the purchase of foreign goods (page 321)

R

racism the belief that one race of people is superior to another (page 156)

radiocarbon dating method of dating the remains of ancient plants, animals, and human beings by measuring the amount of radiocarbon remaining in them (page 2)

ratify to approve, as in to approve a plan of government or an amendment (page 245)

Reconstruction the task of bringing Confederate states back into the Union (page 529)

repeal to do away with a law (page 189)

representatives people who are chosen to speak and act in government for their fellow citizens (page 124)

republic a government run by elected representatives of the people (page 234)

revenue income (page 188)

revival a renewed interest in religion; a stirring up of religious faith (page 155)

royal colony a colony in which the monarch appointed both the governor and the council of advisors (page 125)

S

scalawags white southerners who joined the Republican Party during the Reconstruction period (page 532)

secede to break away from, as in a state breaking away from the United States (page 357)

sectionalism devotion to the interests of one's own section of the country over those of the nation as a whole (page 334)

secondary source an artifact or record made by someone who did not experience the event described (page 193)

sedition actions or speech that might be viewed as encouraging people to rebel against their government (page 281)

segregation the forced separation of races in public places and housing (page 540)

separation of powers the division of government power into legislative, executive, and judicial branches (page 252)

sharecropping a system where tenant farmers pay a part of their crop as rent, rather than using cash (page 539)

slave codes laws that tightened owners' control over slaves (page 417)

social reform the effort by individuals or organizations to make society better and more fair for everyone (page 433)

sovereignty the power of a government to control its affairs (page 357)

speculators people who buy something at a risk, hoping to make money if the price for it rises (page 269)

spoils system the practice of rewarding political supporters with government jobs (page 356)

statement of fact a word, phrase, or sentence that can be either proved or disproved (page 210)

states' rights the theory that states may nullify federal laws (page 282)

statistical table an orderly arrangement of facts in the form of numbers in rows and columns (page 139)

stereotype an oversimplified image of a person, group, or idea (page 369)

strait a narrow waterway connecting two larger bodies of water (page 74)

strict construction the view that government has the power to do only what is written in the Constitution (page 270)

strike employees refuse to work, the goal of which is to force their employer to meet their demands (page 419)

subsistence farming raising just enough food to survive on, with perhaps a little surplus to sell or trade (page 146)

suffrage the right to vote (page 351)

T

tariffs taxes on imports (pages 267)

temperance moderation in or abstinence from the drinking of alcohol (page 437)

tenant farmers people who pay rent for the use of land on which they grow crops (page 539)

terrain all the physical features of an area of land (page 100)

Tidewater waterways in the Atlantic Coastal Plain affected by the tide (page 150)

time line a chart that shows when, and in what order, events occurred in the past (page 31)

total war war conducted not only against armies but also against a people's resources and their will to fight (page 514)

trade union group of people who try to improve wages and working conditions in their trade, or craft (page 419)

transcontinental railroad a rail line extending across a continent (page 473)

tribute payment of money or goods made by one people or nation to another for peace or protection or some other agreement (page 16)

tyranny the harsh use of power (page 162)

U

utopias perfect societies (page 437)

W

writs of assistance general search warrants (page 188)

Index

The purpose of the Index is to help you quickly locate information on any topic in this book. The Index includes references not only to the text but also to special features, illustrations, and maps. *Italicized* page numbers preceded by an *f, i,* or *m* indicate a feature, an illustration, or a map. **Boldface** page numbers indicate pages on which glossary terms first appear.

A

abolition, 441. *See also* antislavery movement

Adams, Abigail, *i264;* advising the President, 280, *i281;* and election of 1796, 279; and election of 1800, *f284;* on Jay's Treaty uproar, 276; marriage partnership of, *f264–265,* 272, 280; on unity of states, 268, 282

Adams, John, *i192;* Boston Massacre and, 192; conflicts with Jefferson, 279–280; at Continental Congress, 197, 208; and election of 1796, 279–280; and election of 1800, 283, *f284;* as Federalist, 279–280, *f280;* judgeships, appointing, 292–293; marriage partnership of, *f264–265,* 272, 280; Olive Branch Petition and, 211; presidency of, 279–281, *f282,* 283, R24; and protests against British, 191, 192, 195; as Vice-President, 248, 266, 276; and War of Independence, 213

Adams, John Quincy, *i351;* and birth of National Republicans, 352; and election of 1824, *i346,* 350, *m353;* and election of 1828, 352, *m353;* and Panama Congress, *f351;* presidency of, 350–351, R24; as Secretary of State, 328–329, 331, *f331;* and slavery, *f335–336,* 445; and Treaty of Ghent, 307, 328

Adams, Samuel, 191, 192, *i192,* 194, 197

Adams-Onís Treaty, 329, *m330*

Adenas, 22

adobe, 20

Africa: cultures, 41–42, *f42, f43;* Europeans dividing up, *f542;* farming developed in, *f13;* piracy and, 300, *i301, m301;* slavery and, *see* slavery; trade, *f37,* 38–41, *m39, i40. See also specific countries and cultures;* West Africa

African Americans: in American Revolution, 192, 213, *i213,* 214, *f225;* in antislavery movement, 414, 418, *f422,* 440, 442–443; artists, *f454, f481;* black codes, 529–530; before Civil War, 417–418, *f417;* after Civil War, 526–529, *i528,* 532, 538; in Civil War, *f497,* 504, 505, *i505,* 507, 508, 514, *f516, f524–525;* in colonial America, *i142,* 157, 159–160; in Congress, 534, *i535, m540;* culture, development of, 41–42, 159–160, *f160, f415,* 441; education and, 448, 528, *i528,* 539, 543, *i543;* and Fifteenth Amendment, 533–534, 540; and Fourteenth Amendment, 530, 542; and gold rush, 398; immigration of, 328; as indentured servants, 157; Juneteenth, *f529;* and land ownership, 528–529, 531, 539; literature/narrative of, 452; migration of, 543, 553; racism and, 157, 160, *f166,* 417–418, *f497,* 505–506, 535, 536, *f544,* 552; religion of, 418, 433; and Republicans, 532, 533; resistance to segregation, 542–543; return to Africa of, 440, 543, *i554;* segregation and, 540–543, *f541, i542;* in Seminole War, 363; and social class, 102; tenant farming and, 538–539, *i539;* and Thirteenth Amendment, 527; voting rights of, 351, *f418,* 529, 530, 531, 532, 533–534, 534, 539–540; in War of 1812, 307; and white terrorism, 535, 536, *i536, f541;* in World War II, *i556. See also* Reconstruction; slavery

Africanus, Leo, 41

agriculture. *See* farming

AIDS, 560

airplane, 552

Alabama, 333, 482, *f534,* R19

Alabama (ship), 499

Alamo, *i373,* 382–383, *i382*

Alaska, 550, *i560,* R19, *iR55*

Albany Plan, 182–183

Alcott, Bronson, 454

Aleuts, 26

Alexander II (czar of Russia), *f483*

Algonkins, 28

Algonquians, 28

Alien Acts (1798), *i263,* 281, 282, 292

Allard, Andrew, *f173–175*

Allen, Ethan, 209

Allen, John, *f282*

Allen, Richard, 433

allies, 182

Allston, Washington, *f298*

amendments, constitutional, 248, *f248,* 251, *f251,* 284. *See also specific amendments*

America, naming of, 67

American Anti-Slavery Society, *i429,* 442, 450

American Colonization Society, 440

American Federation of Labor, 550

American Red Cross, *f490, f506*

American Revolution. *See* War of Independence

American System, 321

Amherst, Lord Jeffrey, 186

Amnesty Act (1872), 535

Anasazis, *i7,* 19, 20–21, *i20*

Anderson, Joe, 410

Anderson, Robert, 484

animals, 10, 71, *f87, f153,* 389, 515. *See also* horses; hunting and gathering

annex, 384

Anthony, Susan B., 450, *f450–f451*

anthropologists, *f1*

anthropology, *f1*

Antietam, Battle of, *i488, f490,* 497, 503, *i503*

Anti-Federalists, 246–247, *f247*

antislavery movement, 440–445, *i443, f446;* African Americans in, 414, 418, *f422,* 440, 442–443; colonization and, 440; and emancipation, 504; force used in, 443, 475, 480; Free Soil Party, 469, *i469;* opposition to, 445, *i445;* statehood debates and, 333–335, *f335–336,* 381, 384, 393–394, 468–469, 469–470; women in, 440, *i441,* 442, 447, 450

Apaches, 21, 30

Appalachian Highlands, *mP4–P7. See also* Appalachian Mountains

Appalachian Mountains, 149, 322, 326, *f485, i485,* 492

Appomattox Court House, *m501,* 516

apprentices, *f144–145,* 148

April Morning (Fast), *f228–229*

Arabs. *See* Middle East

Arawaks, *f82–83*

archaeologists, *f1*

archaeology: and African trade, 38; and ancient India, 45; and early Virginia, *f124;* and Indian cultures, *f1–3, i1–2, i8, f11–12, i12, m12,* 19, 21, 22, 23; and slavery, *f342–343;* and Viking settlement, 62, *i62*

architecture, 18, *f268*

Arctic and Subarctic culture area, 26–27, *m29*

Argentina, *m330,* 331

Arizona, 19, 20, 21, 99, 104–105, *m105,* R19

Arkansas, 492, *f534, i557,* R19

army, U.S.: in Civil War, 495–497, *i495–496, f497,* 504, 505–506, *i505;* Force Bill and, 358; and Reconstruction, 532–533, 534, 535, 536; in War of 1812, 305; in War of Independence, *f205, i205,* 208, 213, 215, 219

Arnold, Benedict, 209

art: African American, 42, 159; analyzing, *f107;* architecture, 18, *f268;* dance, 41, 159; early Indian, 14–15, *i14–16,* 19, *i19,* 20, 23, *i94,* 96; explorers and, *f75;* illustrated newspapers and, *f496, i521;* Indian, *i21,* 26, 27, 28, *i67,* 96; jewelry, *i67;* murals, *f329, f541;* music, 26, 42, *i143,* 159; painting, *f107, f217, f257–259, f298, f360, f378, f454;* poetry and spoken word, 41, 42, 452–453; quilting, *f149, f415;* sculpture, *f21, f42;* story-telling, 4, 26, 41; theater, 113; West African, 41, 42, *f42. See also* literature; *specific artworks*

Arthur, Chester A., R26

Articles of Confederation, *i230,* 234, 239, 242, *f245*

artifacts, *f1*

Ashley, Delos, *f399*

Asia: and farming, *f13;* piracy and, *f300;* roots in America, 48; route to, search for, 73–78, *m74, f75, m77,* 376–377; and trade, 44–48, *i44–47, m45, f48,* 406

Aspects of Negro Life: From Slavery Through Reconstruction (Douglas), *f541*

assassinations: of John Kennedy, 558; of Lincoln, 526; of McKinley, 552; of Martin Luther King, Jr., 558; of Robert Kennedy, 558

assemblies, colonial, 163

assembly, freedom of, 417, 433, R59

astrolabe, 53

astronomy, 15, 16

Atahualpa, 96

Atlanta, Battle of, *i489,* 515

Atlantic Ocean, fear of, *f37,* 53

atomic bomb, 556

Attorney General, 266

Attucks, Crispus, 192

Austin, Moses, 380

Austin, Stephen, 380, 381–382

Aztecs, *i7,* 16–17, *i16, f17,* 18, *i69, i100;* Cortés and, *i91,* 94–96, *i94, m98, m100*

B

baby boomers, 557, 560

backcountry, 152–153, 182

Bacon's Rebellion, 153

Bahamas, 65

al-Bakri, 39

balance of power, 334, 468–469

Balboa, Vasco Núñez de, 73

Baltimore, Maryland, 307

banks and banking: Federal Reserve Act, 553; national bank, 270, 292, 321; Panic of 1819 and, 332–333; Panic of 1837 and, 366; reserves of, 364; state, 364, 365. *See also* Bank of the United States

Bank of the United States, 321, 332, 333, 351, 364–365, *i365. See also* national bank

Banneker, Benjamin, 160, *i160, f269*

Baptist Church, 432

Barbary pirates, 300, *i301, m301*

Barbary States, 300, *m301*

Barré, Colonel Isaac, *f188*

Barton, Clara, *f490–491, i490,* 492, 497, 500, *f506,* 507, 516, *f516*

Basins and Ranges, *mP4–P7, f399, i399*

basket weaving, *i24,* 28, *f31*

Battle of Shiloh—April 6th, 1862, 462–463

Becknell, William, 379

Beckwourth, Jim, *i377,* 378

Belgium, 108

Bell, Alexander Graham, 550

Bell, John, 482, *m482*

Benin, *f42, f43*

Bennett, Robert, 125

Benton, Thomas Hart, *f374,* 376–377

Beringia, 10, 11

Berkeley, Lord John, 135

Berlin Wall, 558, *i560*

bias, *f309*

Bibb, Henry, 416

Bible and literacy, 148, 150, *f404*

bicameral, 129

Biddle, Nicholas, 364

bill of rights, 234; in state constitutions, 236; in U.S. Constitution, 246, 247, 248, R59–R62

Bingham, George Caleb, *i352*

birchbark canoe, *f26–27*

Birmingham, Alabama, 538

black codes, 529–530

Black Hawk War, 361, *m362*

Blackwell, Antoinette Brown, 448

Blackwell, Elizabeth, 448, 507

Blaine, James G., 534

Bleeding Kansas, 474–475, *f475*

blind, schools for the, 435

blockade, 185, 498, 499, 509

Bloody Massacre, The (Revere), *f191*

Bloomer, Amelia, *f448*

bloomers, *f448*

Blue Jacket, 274

Bolívar, Simón, *i330,* 331, *f351*

Bonaparte, Napoleon, 281, 294, *f296,* 301

bond, 269

Bonneville, Benjamin, 386

Boone, Daniel, 234–235

Booth, John Wilkes, 526

borderlands (Spanish), 97–99, *m98,* 104–106, *m105*

Border States of Civil War, 492–493, *m493, f497*

Boston, 128, *f191,* 192, *f193,* 195–196, 207, 209, *f210*

Boston Associates, *f316,* 320

Boston Massacre, *i179, f191,* 192, *f193*

Boston Tea Party, *i179,* 195–196, *i195*

Bowie, Jim, 382

boycotts, 189, 190, *f190,* 191, 195, *f196,* 198, *f198,* 208, 418

Braddock, General Edward, 183–184

Bradford, William, 121

Brady, Mathew, *f502*

Brazil, *f12, f65,* 73

Breckinridge, John C., 481, *m482*

Breed's Hill, 208, 213

Brendan, 62

Britain. *See* Great Britain

British East India Company, 194–195

"Broken Spears" (Aztec poem), 96

Brook Farm, 438, 454

Brooks, Preston, 475, *i476*

Brown, John, *i465,* 475, 480, *i481*

Brown, Moses, 319

Brown v. Board of Education, 542, 557

Bruce, Blanche K., 534

Buchanan, James, 476, 478, 483, R25

Buckner, Alice, *i507*

buffalo, 28, *f312,* 550

Bull Dance, Mandan O-Kee-Pa Ceremony (Catlin), *i360*

Bull Run, Battles of: First, 498–499, *f520–521, i521;* Second, 500, *m501*

Bull Run (Fleishman), *f520–521*

Bunker Hill, Battle of, 208–209, *i208,* 211, 213

Burgoyne, General John, 217–218

Burnside, Ambrose E., 511

Burr, Aaron, 283–284

Bush, George, *i479, i560,* R29

Buxton reunions, *f417*

C

Cabeza de Vaca, Álvar Núñez, 97–98, *m98, f113*

cabinet, 267

Cabot, John, 75

Cabral, Pedro Alvares, 73

Cabrillo, Juan Rodríguez, 99

Cahokia, 23

Calhoun, John C., 353, 357, *i358,* 470–471, *i471*

California, 398, 469, R19; Indian cultures of, 28, *m29;* Manifest Destiny and, 385, 391; Mexican,

i385, 386, 391; Mexican-American War and, 394–396, *m395;* and slavery debate, 469, 470; Spanish settlement in, *m105,* 106

California Trail, 386, *m387*

Californios, 386, 391

Calvert, Cecilius, 133

Calvert, George (Lord Baltimore), 133

Calvin, John, 108

camera, *f502*

camp meetings, 432, *i433*

Canada: British possession of, 185; free African Americans in, *f417;* French settlement in, 108–109, *m109;* and immigration, 328; Northwest Passage and, 76, 77–78, *m77;* and War of 1812, 304, 305, 306, *m306;* and War of Independence, 209, 223, 225. *See also* New France

Canadian Shield, *mP4–P7*

canals, *m323,* 324–325, *f324–325*

Canary Islands, 65, 70

Cane Ridge Revival, 432

canoes, *f26–27,* 27

Canyon de Chelly, *i4–5*

cape, 63

Cape of Good Hope, 63, 64

caravel, *i35,* 53

carbon dating. *See* radiocarbon dating

Carib, *f383*

Caribbean Islands, *i83,* 406

Carnegie Steel Company, 551

Carney, William, 506

Carolinas, 133–134

carpenters, 419

carpetbaggers, 532–533

Carson, Kit, *f374,* 378, *f392*

Carter, Jimmy, R28

Carteret, Sir George, 135

Cartier, Jacques, 77–78, *m77*

cash crops, 150

Cass, Lewis, 469

casualties, 500

Catholic Church. *See* Roman Catholic Church

Catlin, George, *f360, i363*

caucus, 350
Cayugas, 110
Cayuses, 386, 391
cede, 185
census, *f271*, R38
Central America, 25, *m330*. *See also* Mesoamerican civilizations
Central Lowlands, *mP4–P7*, *f240*
Central Park, *f439, i439*
Ceuta, *f36–37*
Champlain, Samuel de, 108, 109, *f113*
Chancellorsville, Battle of, 511, *i511, m513*
Charbonneau, Toussaint, 296
Charles I (king of England), 128, 133
Charles II (king of England), 133, 134, 135, 136
Charles I (king of Spain), 73, 101, 102, 103, 104
Charleston, 134, *i165*
Chase, Benjamin F., 495, 503, 511, 516
Chavez, Cesar, *f190, i190*
checks and balances, 246, 252–253, *f252, f253*, 294, R42, R44, R53
Cherokees, 23, 306, 359–361, 362–363, *i362, m362, f363*; and Civil War, 493, 516. *See also* Trail of Tears
***Chesapeake–Leopard* affair**, 301
Chesnut, Mary Boykin, 506
Cheyennes, 28, *f375*
Chicago, 110, 411, *i411*
Chickasaws, 23, 359–360, 493
children: in Civil War, *i495*, 496; in colonial America, 148, 150, 152, 153; and hunting, 28; as viewed by adults, 434–435; as workers, *i552*, 553
Chile, 96, *m330*, 331
China: emigration from, *f397, i397*; technologies, 46–47; trade and culture, *i35*, 46, *i46*, 47–48, *f48*, 407; as U.S. trade partner, *f238*; withdraws from the seas, 48, *f48*

Chinese Americans, *f397, i397*, 559
Chinese Exclusion Act (1882), 550
Chinooks, 27
Chipewyans, 26
Chisholm Trail, 550
Choctaws, 23, 359–360, 493
cholera, 68
Christianity, 50; African American churches of, 418, 433; antislavery movement and, 441; Bible and literacy, 148, 150, *f404*; explorers claiming land for, 65; Great Awakening, *i143*, 155–156; missionaries and Oregon, 386; New Testament, *f160*; Second Great Awakening, *i428*, 432–433, *i433*; slaves adopting, 160; and social reform, 433, 434, 441, 448, *f455*; traveling ministers, *i431*, 432; women ordained by, 448. *See also* Protestants; Roman Catholic Church; *specific churches or people*
Christy, Howard Chandler, *f243*
Chumashes, 28
Church of England, 121, 125, 128
Church of Jesus Christ of Latter-day Saints. *See* Mormon Church
Cimarrons, *f111*
Cincinnati, Ohio, 411
circuit riders, 432
cities and towns: early development, 13, 14; industry and, 409; Land Ordinance of 1785, 234–236, *f235*; New England and, 146, 148, 149; parks in, *f439*; planning and organization, 15, 23, 29–30, 45, 46, 102, *f439*. *See also specific cities or towns*
citizens, new, *iR45*
civilizations, 14; African, 38–41, *m39, i40*; Asian, 44–48, *m45*; early Indian, 14–18, *i14–16, m16, f17, i18, f113*; European, 49
Civil Rights Act (1866), 530
Civil Rights Act (1964), 558

civil rights movement, 557, *i557*, 558, *i558*
Civil War: advantages of North and South, 494–495, *i494*; African Americans in, *f497*, 504, 505, *i505*, 507, 508, 514, *f516*, *f524–525*; battles of, 498–503, *i499, m501, i503*, 511–515, *i511–512, m513, f520–521, i521*; blockade by Union, 498, 499, 509; costs of, 516; draft in, 508; economics of, 494, *i494*, 509; Emancipation Proclamation, *i489*, 504–505, *f510*; and farming, 494, *i494, f508*, 509, *f545*; Indians in, 493, 516; memoirs of, *f459–461*; opposition at home during, 507–508; photography of, *f502, i502, i503*; raising armies for, 495–497, *i495, f497*, 499, 508, 514; short war expected, 494, 495, 498; sides, choosing, 492–493, *m493*, 494–495; start of, *i465*, 483–484; strategies of North and South, 498; surrender at Appomattox, 516, *i516*; women in, *f490–491*, 496–497, 506–507, *i507*; wounded, treatment of, *f490–491*, 500, 506–507, *i507*
claim, *f423*
Clark, George Rogers, 222–223
Clark, William, *m295*, 296–297, *f297, f299, f313, i313*
class. *See* social class
Clay, Henry: American System and, 321; and bank bill, 364–365; and election of 1824, 350, *m353*; and election of 1832, 365; and election of 1844, 394; as Great Compromiser, 334, *f335, i335*, 470, *i470, i471*
Clem, Johnny, *i495*
Clermont, *i315*, 322–323
Cleveland, Grover, R26
Clinton, Bill, *f297, i479*, R29
Clinton, DeWitt, 324
Clinton, Henry, 209, 221
Clinton, Hillary, *i281*
clipper ships, *i403*, 407, *f409*
Clovis site, 11, *f11–12*

Coastal Lowlands, *mP4–P7, f127*

Coercive Acts, 195–196, *f197,* 198, 206

coins, minting, *f237*

Cold Harbor, Battle of, *m513,* 514

Cold War, 556, *f557,* 560, *i560*

Colombia, 96, *m330,* 331

colonies, the thirteen, *m135;* assisted by Indians, *f118–119,* 126, 130; and conflicts with Indians, 124–125, 131, 131–132, 134, 153, 156–157, *f156;* education in, *i142,* 148, *i148,* 150, 152, 153; freedom of religion and, 121, 126, 129–131, 133, 135, 136; government of, 124, 125, 126, 128, 129–130, 131, 133, 134, 135, 136, 138, 162–166; life in, 146–153, *i153, f166;* obedience to Britain, *f188,* 190; population of, 125, 128, *f139,* 149, *m155,* 162; postal service of, *f199;* products of, 146, *m147,*149, 150; reasons for starting, 120–121; roads of, *m199;* taxation by Britain, 187–192; trade, control of by Britain, 164–166, *f167;* unification, attempts at, 182–183, 189, 196–198, 207–208. *See also specific colonies*

colonization: Dutch, *m109,* 110–111; English, 111, 112–113, 118–138, 328; of freed slaves, 440; French, 78, 104; of India, *f185;* Portuguese, 53–54; Spanish, 66–67, 99, 101–106, *f107,* 108

colony, 53

Colorado, R19

Colorado Plateau, 20, *f24*

Colorado River, 99

Columbian Exchange, *i58,* 68–71, *f69, i70*

Columbus, Christopher, *i58,* 60–61, *i60–61,* 62, 63–67, *m66, f78;* legacy of, 68–71, *f69, i70;* and Manifest Destiny, 376–377

Comanches, 28

Command of the Army Act (1867), 531

Committees of Correspondence, 194, 195

Common Sense (Paine), *i202,* 211

communication, *f199, f207*

compass, 47, 53

Compromise of 1850, *i464,* 470–471, *i470, f471, m474*

Compromise of 1877, 536

computers, *i560–561,* 561, 563

Concord, Battle of, *i202,* 206, *i206,* 207, *f210,* 213. *See also* Lexington, Battle of

Confederate States of America, 482. *See also* Civil War

confederation, 234

Congress, *i333,* R37; African Americans in, 534, *i535, m540,* 561; under Articles of Confederation, 234–239; gag rule and abolition, 445; overriding vetoes, 530; representation in, 242–244; Republicans vs. Federalists in, 266; tax, power to, 214, 236, 238, *f250;* war declarations and, R44; women in, 561. *See also* Continental Congress; legislative branch of government

Connecticut, *i129,* 131, R19

conquistadors, 94–99, *i94, f97, m98,* 101, *f113*

constitution, 234; state, *i230,* 234, 534

Constitution, U.S., *i244;* amendments to, 248, 251, *f251,* R56, R59–R73; Articles of Confederation, compared, *i245;* branches of government in, 242; checks and balances in, 246, 252–253, *f253,* 294, R42, R44, R53; elastic clause, 251, 270, R41; federalism and, 246, *i250,* 251–252, R47, R54; flexibility of, 251, R35, R45; ratification of, *i231,* 246–248, *iR57;* separation of powers, 252; signing of, *i243,* 245, R58; slavery and, 244, *f446;* strict vs. loose construction of, 270, 295; text of, R34–R73. *See also* government; *specific amendments*

constitutional, 270

Constitutional Convention, *i231,* 238–239, 241–245, *f253*

Constitutional Union Party, 482

Continental Congress: First, 196–198; Second, 207–208, 209, 211, 212, 214

Continental Navy, 215

Convention of 1818, 328

Coolidge, Calvin, R27

Cooper, James Fenimore, 452

Cooper, Peter, 326

Coos, 27, *m29*

Copperheads, 508

corn, 13, 70

Cornish, Samuel, 441

Cornwallis, Charles, 221, 222, 224

corruption, 535

Cortés, Hernán, *i90,* 94–96, *i94, m98, m100, f113*

Costa Rica, 67

cotton, *i413;* Civil War and, *f508,* 509; and climate, *f413;* land settlement and, 381–382, 411; mills, *f316–317,* 318–320, *i318;* prices falling, 332; slavery and, 319, 412; South as region of, 411

cotton gin, *i314,* 319, *i319*

coureurs de bois, 108

courts, federal, 267, R52

Covey, Edward, *f404–405*

Crawford, William, 250, *m353*

credibility, *f392*

Creeks, 23, 138, 306, 359–360, 493

Crees, 26

creoles, 102

Crisis, The (Paine), 216

Crockett, Davy, 383

Crosby, Alfred, 68

Crows, 378, *f378*

Crusades, *i34,* 50, 52

Cuba, *f93,* 94, 551, 558

Cuffe, Paul, 440

culture, 13, 19–23, *i19–22,* 101

culture areas, 26–30, *m29*

Cunas, *i67*

Custer, George Armstrong, *f550*
customs duties, 188
Cuzco, 17

D

da Gama, Vasco. *See* Gama, Vasco da
Daugherty, Richard D., *f2, i2*
Davis, Jefferson, 206, 482, 484, 498, 507, *i509,* 516
Dawes, William, 206
deaf, schools for the, 435
debates, 479–480, *i479, f480*
debts and debtors: federal, 268–269; and Georgia colony, 137–138; Panic of 1819, 332–333; Panic of 1837, 366; prison and, 436; sharecroppers', 539, *f539;* states', 269; of War of Independence, 225, 236, 268–269
Decatur, Stephen, *i301*
Declaration of Independence, 4 July 1776, The (Trumbull), *f176–177*
declaration of independence, Texas, 383
Declaration of Independence, U.S., 212–213, *f212, f483;* text of, R32–R33
Declaration of Rights, 162
Declaration of Rights and Grievances, 198
Declaration of Sentiments, 449–450
Declaratory Act, 190, *f197*
Deerslayer, The (Cooper), 452
Deganawida, 110
de Las Casas, Bartolomé. *See* Las Casas, Bartolomé de
Delaware, 136, 149, 492, *m493,* R19
Delawares, 28, 136
Dellehay, Tom, *i12*
democracy: European alarm at spread of, 331; and French Revolution, 272; Gettysburg Address and, 512; Jacksonian, 351, 353, 356, 434; and Northwest Ordinance, 236; presi-

dential electors and, 351; and public education, 434; and religious revivals, 433; suffrage and, 351, *i352*
Democratic Party: beginning of, 351, *f368;* and election of Buchanan, 476; and election of Harrison, 366, 367; and election of Jackson, 352–353, *f369;* and election of Polk, 393–394; and Free Soil Party, 469; power regained in South, 535, 536; power shift to South, 476; split of, 481, 482
Department of War, 266–267
depression, 238
Description of the World (Polo), 44, *i44, f61*
desert farmer cultures, 19–20, *i19, i20*
de Soto, Hernando. *See* Soto, Hernando de
Detroit, 110, 186, 411
Dias, Bartolomeu, 63, *m64*
Díaz del Castillo, Bernal, 96
Dickerson, Susannah, 383
Dickinson, Emily, 453, *i453*
disabled persons, opportunities for, 435–436
discrimination, 417
disease, 68–69, *f69,* 132, 157, 158, *f420;* bubonic plague, 68; cholera, 388–389; measles, 68, 391; smallpox, 68, 69, *f69,* 96, 124, *f348, f360*
diversity, 25, 154–155, *m155, f161*
Dix, Dorothea Lynde, 435–436, *i436,* 507
Doña Marina. *See* Malinche
Doña Ysabel, 99
Donelson, Fort, 500
Donner party, 388
Dorris, Michael, *f82–83*
Douglas, Aaron, *f541*
Douglas, Stephen A., 470, 473–474, 476, 478, 479–480, 481, *m482*
Douglass, Frederick, *f404–405, i404, i443;* on African American soldiers, *f497;* antislavery move-

ment and, 414, 442, *f443;* escape from slavery of, *f405,* 406, 416, *f443;* on freedmen, 527, 538; *My Bondage and My Freedom, f422;* and northern racism, 418; observations of the North, 406, 408; as public speaker, 414; as wage earner, 419
draft, 508
Drake, Sir Francis, 104, 111–112, *f111, f113*
Dred Scott v. Sandford, 478
Du Bois, W. E. B., *i523,* 543–544
due process of law, 248
Duncanson, Robert S., *f454*
Duquesne, Fort, *f181,* 183, *m183,* 184, 185
Dutch West India Company, 110
dwellings: African, 38; early Indian cultures, 20–21, *i20;* Indian cultures, 25, 27, 28, 29, *i29;* Viking, 62, *i63*

E

Earth Summit, 561
East African trade, 38, *m39, i47*
Eastern Woodlands culture area, 28, *m29*
Eckford, Elizabeth, *i557*
economics and economy: of Civil War, 494, *i494,* 508; colonies and, 120–121, 146, *m147,* 149–152; depression, 238; differences between the North and the South, 406–412, *m407, f422,* 509; Great Depression, 555; mercantilism, 102, 121; of "New South," 538; Panic of 1819, 332–333; Panic of 1837, 366; and trade unions, 419; of War of Independence, 214–215, 218, 219
Ecuador, 96, *m330,* 331
Edelman, Marian Wright, 42
education: of African Americans after Civil War, 528–529, *i528,* 530, 539, 543, *i543;* colonial, 148, *i148,* 150, 152, 153, *f156;* Indian, *f156;* predictions about,

563; public schools, 235, *i428*, 434–435, *f434*, 539; of slaves, *f404*, 417, *f426–427*; women's right to, 447–448, *f447*

effect, 285

Egypt, 38

Eighteenth Amendment, R67

Eighth Amendment, R61

Eisenhower, Dwight D., R28

elastic clause, 251, 270, R45

election campaigns: "log cabin campaign" (1840), *i347*, 366–367, *i367*,; modern, *f480*

elections, presidential: of 1792, 270; of 1796, 279–280; of 1800, 283–284; of 1804, 300; of 1808, 302; of 1812, 305; of 1816, 328; of 1820, 332; of 1824, 350, *m353*; of 1828, 351, 352–353, *m353*; of 1832, 365; of 1836, 366; of 1840, *i347*, 366–367, *i367*; of 1844, 393–394; of 1848, 469, *i469*; of 1852, 473; of 1856, 476, 478; of 1860, 481–482, *m482*; of 1864, 515; of 1868, 533; of 1872, R26; of 1876, 536

Electoral College, 244, 351, 536, R62–R63

Eleventh Amendment, R62

Elizabeth I (queen of England), 111, 112, *i112*

emancipation, 440. *See also* antislavery movement

Emancipation Proclamation, *i489*, 504–505, *f510*

embargo, 301–**302**

Emergence of the Clowns (Swentzell), *f21*

Emerson, Ralph Waldo, 438, 454, 455

encomienda system, 103, *f103–104*

Enforcement Acts (1870, 1871), 535

England: Asia route, search for, 74–76, *f75*, *m77*; and colonization, 111, 112–113, 118–136; Declaration of Rights, 162; economic changes in, 120–121; in 1400s, 52; France, war with, *f164*; Magna Carta, 162; and the Netherlands, 134–135; and

Protestant Reformation, 108; religious conflict in, 121, *i121*; and Spain, 97, 104, 111–112, *i112*, 113, 133. *See also* Great Britain

English Americans, prejudice of, 154, 421, *f421–422*

entradas, 97–99, *f97*, *i97*

environmental movement, *f436*, 559

Equal Rights Amendment, *f251*

Equiano, Olaudah, 158, *i158*

Era of Good Feelings, 332, *f337*

Erie Canal, 324–325

Eries, 28

Estevan, 98, *m98*, 99

Ethiopia, *f542*

Europe: Africa divided up by, *f542*; beginnings of, 49–50, *i49*; Christianity, claiming land for, 65; emancipation and, 504, 505; farming developed in, *f13*; feudalism, 50–52; nations, development of, 52; Protestant Reformation, 108; Renaissance, 52, *f52*; trade, *f36–37*, 50–54, *m51*, *m53*, *f54*. *See also individual countries*

European Americans. *See individual heritages*

evidence, *f423*

exchange. *See* Columbian Exchange

excise tax, **273**

executive branch of government, **242**, 252–253, *f252*, 266–267, R48–R51. *See also* governors; President

Exodusters, 543

expansionists, **376**

expedition, **63**

exports, **123**

F

factories: child labor in, *i552*; distribution of, in Civil War, 494, *i494*; and immigrant labor, 420–421; mass production in, 320; and Northeast cities, 409; and trade unions, 420

Fall Line, *f127*

Fallen Timbers, Battle of, 275, *f290*

family: colonial, 148, 150, 153; of slaves, *i405*, 414–415; and the West, 386

farming: in Africa, 41; changes brought by, 13, 25, *f355*; in Civil War, 494, *i494*, *f508*, 509, *f545*; in colonial America, *i88*, 123, 124, 133, 134, 146, 149, 150, 152, 153, *f153*; early Indian, 14, 16, 18, *i18*, 19–20, 23; growing seasons/precipitation of U.S., *m413*; in Indian cultures, 26, 27, 28; Industrial Revolution and, *f316–317*; invention of, *i6*, 12–13, *f13*, *f31*; irrigation, 17, 19–20, 390; laborers in, *f190*, 559, *i559*; mechanization of, 319, *i319*, 410–411; Midwest and, 410–411; New France and, 109, *i110*; in Northwest Territory, *i240*; Panic of 1819, 332–333; potato famine, *f421*; Shays' Rebellion, 238, *i239*, 246–247; subsistence, 146; tenant farmers and sharecropping, 538–539, *i539*; Whiskey Rebellion, 273–274, *i274*; wool trade and, 120. *See also* plantations

Farragut, David G., *i499*, 500

Far West. *See* western settlement

Far West culture area, 28, *m29*

Fast, Howard, *f228–229*

federal government. *See* government

federalism, *i250*, **251**–252

Federalist, The (Madison, Hamilton, Jay), 246, 253

Federalists: beginnings of, 246, *i247*; differences between Republicans and, 266, 272, 274, 278, *i278*, 279, 279–280, *f280*; and election of 1796, 279; and election of 1800, 283–284; Hartford Convention, 307; and *Marbury* v. *Madison*, 293, *f294*

Federal Reserve Act (1913), 553

Federal style (architecture), *f268*

Ferdinand (king of Spain), 64–66, *f65*

feudalism, 50–52

Fifteenth Amendment,
533–534, *534,* 540, R65

Fifth Amendment, R60

Fillmore, Millard, 471, R25

finance, 63

financial panic, 332

Finley, James, 432

First Amendment, *f249,* R59

First Ladies: role of, *i281. See
also names of specific First Ladies*

fishing, 27, 108, 146

Fleishman, Paul, *f520–521*

Florida, R19; acquisition by U.S.,
328–329; early Indian trade and,
23; Indian removal from, *m362,*
363; and Reconstruction, 535,
f535; and secession of South,
482; Spanish settlement in, 97,
99, 104

Florida (ship), 499

Folsom site, 11

Force Bill (1833), 358

Ford, Gerald R., R28

foreign policy: alliances, avoiding, 278; of John Quincy Adams,
328–329, 331; neutrality,
272–273, 300. *See also* Monroe
Doctrine

forests, *f355*

Forten, Charlotte, *i441*

Forten, James, 440, *i441,* 442

forts. *See names of specific forts;*
presidios

Fourteenth Amendment, 530,
531, 534, 542, R64–R65

Fourth Amendment, R60

Fox (Indians), 361

France: American colonies of, 78,
104, 108–110, *m109, i110, m187,
m224,* 294, *f296;* Asia route,
search for, 74, 76–78, *m77;*
attacking U.S. ships, 276, 301,
302; in 1400s, 52; Great Britain,
war with, *f164, f180–181,*
182–185, *m183, i184,* 272–273,
276, 280, 300–301; "half war"
with U.S., 280–281; and
Louisiana Purchase, 294, *f296;*
Protestants (Huguenots) and,
108, 109, *f132;* revolution of,
272, *i273;* and Spain, 97, 104,
105–106, 294; and U.S. Civil
War, 503, 504, 505; after War of
Independence, 276, 280–281; in
War of Independence, 218,
m223, 224

Francis I (king of France), 76–77

Franklin, Benjamin: on canals,
324; at Constitutional
Convention, 243, 245, 250; on
signing the Constitution, R58;
before War of Independence,
i143, f144–145, 148, 154, 155,
162, 163, 165–166, 182; and War
of Independence, 213

Fredericksburg, Battle of,
i491, 511, *m513*

freedmen, 526–529, *i528,* 532,
538

Freedmen's Bureau, 528–529,
530

Freedmen's Bureau Act (1866),
530

freedoms. *See* Bill of Rights;
specific freedoms

Freeport Doctrine, 480

Free Soil Party, 469, *i469*

Frémont, Jessie, *f374–375, i374,*
376, 388, 398, *f398*

Frémont, John C., *f374–375,
i374,* 376, 398, *f398;* Bear Flag
Republic and, 394–396, *m395;*
and election of 1856, 476; expeditions of, *f374–375, i375,* 386,
388, 391, *f392*

French and Indian War, *i178,*
182–185, *m183, i184*

French Revolution, 272, *i273*

Frobisher, Martin, *f75,* 76

Fugitive Slave Law (1850), 472,
473, 476

Fuller, Margaret, 454

Fulton, Robert, 322–323

fur trade, 377–378, *i377;* mountain men and Indians, 378, *f378;*
New France and Indians,
108–109, *i110,* 182; rendezvous
and, 378; Russia and Indians,
f331; Vikings and Indians, 62

futurists, 562–564

G

Gadsden, Christopher, 189

Gadsden Purchase, 397, *m397,*
473

Gage, Thomas, 206, 208

Gallatin, Albert, 308

Gallaudet, Thomas Hopkins,
435

Galloway, Mary, 497

Galloway, Rebecca, *f291*

Gálvez, Bernardo de, 223

Gama, Vasco da, 64, *i64, m64*

Garfield, James, R26

Garnet, Henry Highland, 443

Garrison, William Lloyd, *i429,*
441–442, 442, *f442, f446,* 449

Genêt, Edmond, 273

generalization, *f337*

geography: Appalachian
Mountains, *f485;* Atlantic slave
trade, *f161;* basins and ranges,
f399; Central Lowlands, *f240;*
Civil War and southern agriculture, *f545;* Coastal Lowlands,
f127; colonial communication,
f199; of colonies, 146, 149, 150,
152–153; Colorado Plateau, *f24;*
first big city park, *f439;* from forest to farm, *f355;* horse, spread
of, *f72;* regions of United States,
P5; Rocky Mountains, *f299;* of
United States, P1–P7, *m224,
m235, m277, m396;* westward
expansion, *f327*

geology, 10, 146

George II (king of England), 137

George III (king of England),
192, 195, 211, 212

Georgia, R19; and Civil War,
482, 507, 514, 515; as colony,
i117, 137–138, 150, 197; and
Indian removal, 360–361, 362,
m362; and Reconstruction, *f534;*
and slavery, 244

German Americans, 154, *m155,*
421

Gettysburg, Battle of,
f459–461, i489, 511–512, *i512,
m513, m517*

Gettysburg Address, 512

Gettysburg National Military Park, *f517*
Ghana, 39
Ghent, Treaty of, 307, 328
Gilbert, Sir Humphrey, 112
Ginsburg, Ruth Bader, *iR53*
glaciers, 10, 11
Glass, Hugh, 378
Glorieta Pass, Battle of, 493
gold: conquistadors and, 94, 95, 96, *f96*, 97, 98, 99; fantasies of finding, 76, 94, 97, 98, 99, 113, 122; mercantilism and, 102; money and, 236, 364, 366; in trade, *f37*, 38, 39, 40, 53
gold rush, California, 397–398, *f397, i397*
Gooding, James Henry, 506
Goodyear, Charles, 408
government: Arctic peoples, 26; Articles of Confederation, *i230*, 234, 239, 242, *f245*; colonial, 124, 125, 126, 128, 129–130, 131, 134, 135, 136, 138, 153, 162–166; early Indian, 14, 15, 16–17, 23; endurance of, 250; feudalism, 50–52; funding of, 267–268; Jacksonian Democracy and, 353, 356; power, peaceful transfer of, 284, *f284*; self-government, 163, 186, 191, 196, *f253*; in Spanish colonies, 102–103, *f103–104*; of states, 234, 252, 529–530, 534–535, 539–543; of territories, 236. *See also* Constitution, U.S.; democracy
governors, 163, 186, 191, 194
Grady, Henry, 538
Grand Canyon, *f24*, 99
grandfather clause, 540
Grand Tetons, *i299*
Grandy, Charles, *f342–343*
Grant, Ulysses S., 493, 500, 512, 514, 515–516, *i515*; presidency of, 533, R26
Great American Desert, 385
Great Awakening, *i143*, 155–156; Second, *i428*, 432–433, *i433*
Great Britain: and American colonization, 137–138, 185, *f185*, 186, *m187, m224*; and Canadian colonization, 328; colonial resentment of, 187–192; France, war with, *f164*, *f180–181*, 182–185, *m183, i184*, 272–273, 276, 300–301; Indians, arming, 275–276, 304; and Oregon Country claim, 394; seizing U.S. ships, 276, 301, 302, 304–305, 307; slavery abolished by, *f442*; and Spain, 138; trade, banning, *f238*; trade, control of the colonies', 164–166, *f167*; treaties with U.S., 224–225, 236, 276, 307, 328; and U.S. Civil War, 498, 503, 504, 505, *f508*, 509, *f510*; War of 1812, 304–307, *m306, f309*; in War of Independence, 206–207, *i206*, *f207*, 208–209, *i208, f210*, 211, 213, 214, *i214*, 216, 217–218, 221, 223, *m223*, 224, *f348*. *See also* England
Great Compromise (1787), 243
Great Depression, 555, *i555*
Great Lakes, 305–306, *i305*, 324–325
Great Plains, *mP4–P7*, 298, 385
Great Serpent Mound, *i7*, 22
Greenville, Treaty of, 275, *i275*
Grenville, George, 188, 190
Grimké, Sarah and Angelina, 442, 447
Griswold, Roger, *i278*
Guadalupe Hidalgo, Treaty of, 396–397, *m396*
guerrillas, 222
Guidon, Niéde, *f12*
Gulf of St. Lawrence, 77
Gullah, *f160*
gunpowder, 46, 186
Gutenberg, Johannes, *f52*

H

habeas corpus, 492
Haiti, 294, *f296*
Hakluyt, Richard, 113
Hamilton, Alexander: debt plan of, 269; disagreements with Jefferson, 270; and election of 1800, 283–284; federal government, need for, 236, 246, *i247*; Federalists and, 246, 266, 272, 279, *f280*; and national bank, 270; as Secretary of Treasury, 267, *f267*, 269–270, 276; and Whiskey Rebellion, 274
Hamilton, Andrew, 164
Hammond, James, *f508*
Hancock, John, 212, 247
Hangzhou, 46
Hanson, Harriet, 420
Harding, Warren, R27
Harlan, John Marshall, 542
Harpers Ferry, 480
Harrison, Benjamin, R26
Harrison, William Henry, 303–304, 306, 366–367, R25
Hartford Convention, 307
Harvard College, *i142*, 148
Hawaii, *f275*, 406, 551, R20, *iR55*
Hawthorne, Nathaniel, 438, 452, *i453*
Hayes, Rutherford B., 536, R26
Hayne, Robert, *f357*
Hays, Mary Ludwig, 215
Heaten, John, *f88–89*
Helper, Hinton, 412
Henry, Fort, 500
Henry, Patrick, 191, 197
Henry (prince of Portugal), *i35*, *f36–37*, 38, 44, 52–54, *m53*
Hessian troops, 214, 216–217
Hiawatha, 110
Hicks, Edward, *f137*
Hidalgo, Miguel, 329, *i329*
Hidatsas, 28
Hispanic Americans. *See* Latinos
Hispaniola, 67, 70, *f92*, *f93*, 94
historical interpretation, *f446*
Hite, Daniel and Rebecca, 516
Hitler, Adolf, 555
hog killing, *i153*
Hohokams, 19–20
Holloway, Houston, 527
Homer, Winslow, *f496*
Homestead Strike, *i551*
Honolulu, 406

Hooker, Joseph, 511
Hooker, Reverend Thomas, 131
Hoover, Herbert, R27
Hopewells, 22, 23
Hopis, 28–29, 105
horses: and Civil War peace terms, 516; and Columbian Exchange, 28, 71, *f72;* Indians and, 28, 71, *f72, m72,* 96; spread of, *m72;* and trade, 38, *f43*
hospitals, Civil War, 506–507
House of Burgesses, *i116,* 124, 125
House of Representatives, U.S., 243, 244, *m540,* R37–R38
House of the Seven Gables, The (Hawthorne), 452
Houston, Sam, 382, 383–384, *m384*
Howe, Elias, 408
Howe, General William, 208, 209, 217, 218, 221
Howe, Samuel Gridley, 435
Hudson, Henry, *i59,* 76, *m77, f79*
Hudson River, 76, 324
Hudson River School, *f454*
Huguenots, 109, *f134*
human sacrifice, 17, 104
humor, *f467*
hunting and gathering, 10–11, 12–13, 22, 23, 26–27, 28
Hupas, 28
Hurons, 28, 109, 110
Hutchinson, Anne, *i116,* 130–131
Hutchinson, Governor Thomas, 194, 195
hydrogen bomb, 557
hypothesis, *f510*

I

ice age, 10–11, *f11–12*
ice trade, 406–407
Idaho, R20
Illinois, 333, R20
immediate cause, *f285*
immediate effect, *f285*
immigration, 328, 420–421, *f421,* 552; Asian, 48; and Canada, 328; Chinese, *f397, i397;* Irish, 152, 420, *i420,* 421, *f421;* Jewish, *f65;* low-cost labor and, 409, 420–421; mid-1800s, *i420,* 421–421, *f421;* nativism and, 421, *f421–422;* quotas for, 554. *See also* migration
Immigration Act (1924), 554
impeachment, 531, R40
imports, 150
impressed, 276
inauguration, 266, 292, 332, 354, *f354*
Incas, *i7,* 17–18, *i18,* 96
Incidents in the Life of a Slave Girl (Jacobs), 452
income tax, 509, 553, R66
indentured servants, 123–**124**
Independence, Missouri, 379, *m387,* 388
India, *f13,* 45–46, *m45, f185,* 194–195
Indiana, 22, 333, R20
Indiana Territory, 303–304, *i304*
Indian Removal Act (1830), 361
Indians: archeological sites, 1–3, *i1–2, i4, f11–12, m11, i12;* assisting settlers, *f118–119,* 126, 130, 138, 296–297; and Civil War, 493, 516; in conflict with Britain, 186–187; in conflict with colonists, 124–125, 131, 131–132, 134, 153, 156–157, *f156;* conflicts between tribes, 15, 16, 20–21, 23, 26, 28, 29, 110, 134; in conflict with U.S., 274–275, *i275, f290–291,* 303–304, *i304,* 306, *f308,* 361–363, *m362,* 391; conquistadors and, 94–99, *i94, f97, m98,* 101, *f113;* conversion to Christianity, 66, *i93,* 94, 95, 101–102, 105, *f119;* culture areas, 26–28, *m29;* disease and, 68–69, 70, 96, 124, 132, 157; diversity of, 25–26, *m29, f30;* early, 14–23, *i14–16, m16, f17, i18–22;* education and, *f156;* equal rights movement, 559, *i559;* and Far West expansion, *f375,* 390–391, *f391;* French and Indian War, 182–183, 184, 185, 186–187; fur trade of, *see* fur trade; and horses, 28, 71, *f72, m72,* 96; Iroquois League, 110; land as occupied by, 131–132, 377; land ownership and, 136, 156–157, *i157;* languages of, 25, 95, *i312;* life, traditional way of, *f82–83,* 156–157, *i157, f290,* 303, *f303, f360,* 550; Manhattan Island and, 111; paintings of, *f257–259;* Paleo-Indians, *f8–9, i8,* 10–13, *m11, i12, f30;* population, 25, 69, *f93,* 104; racism and, 156–157, *f156;* rebuilding nations of, *f363;* removal of, 359–363, *i362, m362;* resistance to removal, 361–363, *m362;* resistance to Spain, 95–96, 97, 98, 99, 105, 106, *f111;* slavery of, 70, *f92–93,* 94, 103, *f103–104,* 105, *i106, f107, f111,* 132, 134; social class and, 102; taken to Europe, 65, *f75, f92;* as term, *f10,* 65; territories, laws of regarding, 236; trade agreements of, 108–109, 111; treaties with U.S., 361; tribes, *m29;* unification of, *f291,* 303, 306, *f308;* voting rights of, 351; in War of 1812, 306, 307; in War of Independence, 213–214, *i214, f225. See also individual tribes, nations, or people*
Indian Territory, 362, *m362*
indigo, 150, 159, 319
Indonesia, 73
industrialization, 406–409, *m407,* 551, *i551,* 552; the South's lack of, 412, 494, 538
Industrial Revolution, 319–320; living conditions and, *f316–317,* 406
infectious disease, 68. *See* disease
Inman, Henry, *f258*
installment plan, 410
Interior Highlands, *mP4–P7*
Intermediate-Range Nuclear Forces Treaty, 560

Intolerable Acts. *See* Coercive Acts

Inuits, 26, *f75*

inventions and inventors, 46–47, *f258–259*, 318–319, *i319*, 322–323, 326, *i326*, 408–409, *f408–409*, *f502*, 550, 552. *See also individual inventions and inventors*

Iowa, R20

Iran-Contra scandal, 560

Iran hostage crisis, 559

Irish Americans, 152, 420–421, *f421*, 506, 508

iron-making, 538

Iroquoians, 28, 110, 182

Iroquois, 28, 109, *f156*, 182

irrigation, 17, **19**–20

Irving, Washington, 452

Isabela, 67

Isabella (queen of Spain), 64–66, *f65*

Islam, 39–40, 41, 64

isolines, *f413*

J

Jackson, Andrew, *i348;* background of, *f348;* and Bank of the United States, 364–365, *i365;* and birth of Democratic Party, 351; death of, 368, *i368;* and election of 1824, 350, *m353;* and election of 1828, *i346*, 352–353, *m353;* and election of 1836, 366; in Florida, 329; inauguration of, 354, *f354;* and Indians, 306, 329, 359, 361, 493; and nullification crisis, 357–358; presidency of, 356, 357–358, 364, 366, R24; Specie Circular order, 366; in War of 1812, 306, 307

Jackson, Jesse, 42

Jackson, Stonewall (Thomas J.), 498, 511, *i511*

Jacksonian Democracy, 351, 353, 356, 434

Jacobs, Harriet, 415, 452

Jamaica, *f442*

James I (king of England), 125

James II (king of England), 162. *See also* James, Duke of York

James, Duke of York, 135, 136

Jamestown, *f118–119*, 122, *m122*, *i123*, 125, 153

Jansson, Jan, *f85–87*

Japan, 406, 556

Japanese Americans, *i556*

Jay, John, 246, 276, *i276*

Jay's Treaty, 276, *i276*, 277, 280

Jefferson, Thomas: Alien and Sedition Acts, 282, 292; author of Declaration of Independence, 212; Constitutional Convention and, 239, 241; and democracy, 236; disagreements with Hamilton, 270; and election of 1800, 283–284; and Genêt affair, 273; home of, *f268;* inauguration of, 292; and Indians, *f297*, 304, *f308;* as inventor, *i293;* on Missouri Compromise, 335; and national bank, 270; peace medals of, *f297;* presidency of, 292–296, 300–302, 308, R24; Republicans and, 266, 272, 274, 279, *f280;* as Secretary of State, 267, *i267*, 269; as Vice-President, 279–280

Jeffersonian Republicans: differences between Federalists and, 266, 272, 274, 278, *i278*, 279, *f280;* and election of 1796, 279–280; and election of 1800, 283–284; and French Revolution, 272; and Jay's Treaty, 276; and *Marbury* v. *Madison*, *f294;* presidency of Jefferson, 292, 295

Jennison, Edwin, *i495*

Jesus, 50

Jews: in the colonies, 155; expulsion of, Spanish, 64, *f65*

Jim Crow laws, *i523*, **540**–542, *f541*

John I (king of Portugal), *f36*

John II (king of Portugal), 62–64, 73

John III (king of Portugal), *f71*

John Brown Going to His Hanging (Pippin), *f481*

Johnny Rebs, 495

Johnson, Andrew: impeachment of, *i522*, 531; presidency of, 526, 529, 530, R26

Johnson, Lyndon B., R28

Johnston, Joseph E., 500

Johnston, Samuel, 415

joint-stock company, 122

Joliet, Louis, *m109*, 110

Jones, Absalom, 433

Jones, John Paul, 215

judicial branch of government, 242, 252–253, *f252*, 293–294, *f294*, R52–R53. *See also* Supreme Court, U.S.; Supreme Court cases

judicial review, 293–294, *f294*

Judiciary Act (1789), 267, 293–294, *f294*

Judiciary Act (1801), 293

Juneteenth, *f529*

Jungle, The (Sinclair), 552

K

Kamehameha (king of Hawaii), *f275*

Kansas, 22, 99, 474–475, *f475*, 543, R20

Kansas (Indians), *f257*, 391

Kansas-Nebraska Act (1854), 474, *m474*, 476

Karlsefni, Thorfinn, 62

Kaskas, 27

Kearny, Stephen Watts, 394, 395–396, *m395*

Kennedy, John F., 558, R28

Kennedy, Paul, *f48*

Kennedy, Robert F., 558

Kentucky, 22, 278, 282, *f290*, 333, 492, 500, R20

Keres, 105

Key, Francis Scott, *i289*, 307

King, Charles Bird, *f257–259*

King, Edward, *f525*, 529, 538

King, Martin Luther, Jr., 42, *i435*, 558

King, Rufus, 334

King, William, *f417*

King Philip's War, *i117*, 132, *i132*

Kino, Eusebio, 105, *m105*

Kiowas, 28

Kitchen Cabinet, 356

kivas, 20–21, *i20*, 30

Know-Nothing Party, *i403,* 421, *f421–422*
Knox, Henry, 267, *f267*
Korean War, 557
Kosciusko, Thaddeus, 218
Ku Klux Klan, 535, *i536, f541*
Kush, 38
Kwakiutls, 27

L

labor. *See* indentured servants; slavery; trade unions; workers
Lafayette, Marquis de, 224
Lake Erie, 324–325
land: availability to freedmen, 528–529, 531, 539; booms, 332; ownership of, 136, 156–157, 234–236, *f235;* of United States, P1–P7
land bridge. *See* Beringia
land grants, 111, *m122*
Land Ordinance of 1785, 234–236, *f235*
Landscape with a Lake (Allston), *f298*
Landscape with Rainbow (Duncason), *f454*
language: Gullah, *f160;* used to describe United States, *f516*
L'Anse aux Meadows, 62
La Salle, Robert Cavelier de, *i91, m109,* 110
Las Casas, Bartolomé de, *f92–93, i92, f103–104, f113*
Last of the Mohicans, The (Cooper), 452
Latin America, 329, *m330,* 331, *f351*
Latinos, 102, *i102,* 559
Lawrence, Kansas, 475
Laws of the Indies, 102, 104
league, 110
League of the Five Nations, 110
Leaves of Grass (Whitman), 453
Le Boeuf, Fort, *f181*
Lee, General Charles, 221
Lee, Mother Ann, 437
Lee, Robert E.: background of, 494–495; Civil War battles of,

500, 503, 511–512, 514–515, 515–516, *i515;* and Harpers Ferry, 480; surrenders at Appomattox, 516
legacy, 71
"Legend of Sleepy Hollow, The" (Irving), 452
legislative branch of government, 242, 252–253, *f252,* R37–R47
legislature, 124
L'Enfant, Pierre, *f269*
León, Alonso de, 106
Leonard, Zenas, 386
Leutze, Emanuel, *f217, f344–345*
Levathes, Louise, *f48*
Lewis, Meriwether, *m295,* 296–297, *f297, f299, f312–313, i313*
Lewis and Clark expedition, *i288, m295,* 296–297, *f297, f299, f312–313,* 377
Lexington, Battle of, *i202,* 206, *f207,* 213, *i229. See also* Concord, Battle of
libel, 164
Liberator, The, 441, *i441,* 442
Liberia, 440, *f542,* 543
life expectancy, 150
Lincoln, Abraham, *i466–467, i508,* R25; on African American soldiers, *f497;* assassination of, *i522,* 526; background of, *f466–467;* and Border States, 492–493, *f497;* and Civil War strategy, 498, 499, 511, 514; and election of 1856, 476, *m482;* and election of 1860, 482; and election of 1864, 515; and Emancipation Proclamation, 504–505, *f510;* on end of Civil War, 516; Fort Sumter and, 483; Gettysburg Address, 512; inaugural addresses of, 483, 526; and Indians, *f422;* on Know-Nothings, *f421–422;* and Lincoln-Douglas campaign, 478–480, *i479;* on Mexican-American War, 394; opposition within Union, 507, 508; on secession, *f482;* on slavery, 482, *f484,* 504

Lincoln-Douglas debates, 479–480, *i479, f480*
Lindbergh, Charles, 554
Lisa, Manuel, 377, *i377*
literacy, 148
literature, *f82–83, f170–171, f228–229, f312–313, f426–427,* 452, 472–473, *f520–521*
lithography, *f258–259*
Little Elk, *f258*
Little Turtle, 274, *i275, f290*
Lone Star Republic, 384
Long, Stephen, 385
Longfellow, Henry Wadsworth, 452–453
long-range cause, *f285*
long-range effect, *f285*
loose construction, 270
Louis XIV (king of France), 110
Louisiana, 110, 333, 482, 504, *f534,* 535, R20. *See also* New Orleans
Louisiana Purchase, 294–296, *m295, f296*
L'Ouverture, Toussaint, *f296*
Love, Nat, *i550*
Lovejoy, Elijah, 445, *i445*
Lowell, Francis Cabot, 320, 408
Lowell, James Russell, 526
Lowell, Massachusetts, 320, *i321,* 409, 420
Loyalists, 213
Lucas, Eliza, 150
Lundy, Benjamin, 441
Luther, Martin, 108
lynchings, 508, 542, *f544*
Lyon, Mary, 447, 448
Lyon, Matthew, *i278, f285*

M

McClellan, George B., 500, 503, 511
McCormick, Cyrus, *i402,* 410–411
McDowell, Irvin, 498
McJunkin, George, 11
McKenney, Thomas, *f257–259*
McKinley, William, 552, R27
Madeira, 53, 70

Madison, James, *i232;* background of, *f232;* and Bill of Rights, 248; and creating the Constitution, 238–239, 241, 242, 243, 244, 245, *f253;* in Continental Congress, *f233;* and election of 1808, 302; and election of 1812, 305; and federal government, 238–239, 269; presidency of, 303, 305, R24; as Republican, *f280; The Federalist,* 246, 253

Magellan, Ferdinand, *i59,* 73–74, *i74, m74, f85–87*

Magna Carta, 162

Magoffin, Susan, *f399*

Maine, 131, R20

Makahs, *f1–3, i1–2*

Mali, 39, 40, *i40*

Malinche, *i94*

Manassas, Battle of. *See* Bull Run, Battles of

Mandans, 28, *f360*

Manhattans, 111

Manifest Destiny, 376–377, 393–394, *i393,* 396

Mankiller, Wilma, *f363*

Mann, Horace, 434–435, 471

Mansa Musa, *i35,* 40

manufacturing, 320, 356, *i357,* 406

maps: chart makers, 61; climate maps, *f413;* comparing historical and modern, *f55;* grid maps, *f517;* naming geographical features, *f85–87;* Oregon Trail, government issue, 386–388; population density maps, *f271;* terrain maps, *f100;* war maps, *f220*

Marbury, William, 293

Marbury **v.** *Madison, i288,* 293–294, *f294*

Marion, Francis, 222, *i222*

Marquette, Jacques, *m109,* 110

marriage, 124, 148, 390, 415, 437–438, 447, 450

Marshall, John, *i288,* 292, 293–294, *f294,* 361

Marshall Plan, 556

martial law, 492

Martin, Joseph, *f204–205,* 215, 216, 219, 221, 224, *f225*

Martin's Hundred, *f124*

Maryland, *i127,* 133, 150, 154, 159, 492, 503, R20

Massachusetts, R20; as colony, 126, 128–130, 195–196; Constitution of U.S., ratifying, 246–247, *f247;* Shays' Rebellion, 238; in War of Independence, 206–209, *i206, i208*

Massachusetts Antislavery Society, 414

Massachusetts Bay Company, 128

mass production, 320

Mayas, *i6,*15–16, *i15, m16,* 69

Mayflower, 126

Mayflower Compact, 126

Meade, George C., 511

meatpacking industry, 552

Mecca, 40

medicine, 18, *f50*

Meeker, Ezra, 388–389

Meltzer, David, *f12*

Melville, Herman, *f327, i453*

memoirs, *f460–461*

Menéndez de Avilés, Don Pedro, 104

mentally ill, reforms and the, 435–436

mercantilism, 102, 121, 165

mercenaries, 214

Merrimac, i488, 499, *m501*

Mesa Verde National Park, *i20*

Mesoamerican civilizations, 14–17, *i14–16, m16, f17,* 20, 23

mestizos, 102, *i102*

Metacomet (King Philip), 132, *i132*

Methodist Church, 432–433

Mexican Americans, 396–397

Mexican-American War, *i373,* 394–397, *m395*

Mexican Cession, 396–397, *m396*

Mexico: Spanish conquest of, 94–96; early agriculture, 13, *f13;* early civilizations of, 14–17, *i14–16, m16, f17;* independence of, 329, *f329, m330,* 379; population, 25; and Texas, 380–384, *i382, m384,* 394; war with U.S., *i373,* 394–397, *m395*

Miamis, 274, *f290*

Miantonomo, 156–157

Michigan, 22, R20

Middle Colonies, *m147,* 149–150. *See also specific colonies*

Middle East, *f13, f36–37,* 49, 51

Middle Passage, 158

midnight judges, 293

migration, 10–11, *f11–12, m11,* 71

militia, 163

mill girls, *f316–317, f320,* 322, 336, 420

Miller, Alfred Jacob, *f378*

mills, *f151, f316,* 318–320, *i318, i321,* 408, 420, *i551*

Minnesota, 468–469, R21

minting, *f237*

Minuit, Peter, 111

minutemen, 206

Mission San Diego, *f218*

Mission San Francisco, *f218*

Mississippi, 333, 482, 534, *f534,* R21

Mississippians, 22, *i22,* 23

Mississippi River and basin: and shipping, 236, 277, 294; in Civil War, 498, 500, *m501,* 512, 514; early Indians of, 23; Louisiana Purchase, 294–296, *m295, f296;* New France and, 110

Missouri, 474, 475, 478, 492, R21

Missouri Compromise (1820), *i315,* 334–335, *m334, f335–336,* 474, 478

Missouri River, 28, 296, 377

Missouris, *f257*

Missouri Territory, 334

Mobile Bay, Alabama, *i499*

Moby-Dick (Melville), 452

Moctezuma, 95

Mogollons, 19, *i19*

Mohawks, 28, 110

money: and Civil War, 509, 526; dependability of, 364, 366; minting coins, *f237, i450;* power to coin, 236–238, 252

Monitor, i488, 499, *m501*

Monmouth, Battle of, *m220*, 221

monopoly, 194

Monroe, James, 294–295, 328, 331, 332, *f337,* R24

Monroe Doctrine, *i315,* 331, *f331*

Montana, R21

Montcalm, General Louis Joseph de, 185

Montesinos, Antonio de, *f92–93, f103*

Montesquieu, Baron de, 252

Montgomery, Richard, 209

Monticello, *f268*

Montreal, 109, 110, 185, 209

moon landing, *i558*

Mormon Church, 389–390, *i390*

Morning Girl (Dorris), *f82–83*

Morse, Samuel F. B., 409

Mother Bethel African Methodist Episcopal (AME) Church, 433

Mott, Lucretia, 449, *i449,* 450

Mound Builder cultures, *i7,* 21–23, *i22*

mountain men, *i372,* 377–378, *i377*

Mount Holyoke Female Seminary, 448

mudslinging, 352

Muhammad (Prophet), 39

Muir, John, *i552*

Musgrove, Mary, 138

Muslims. *See* Islam

My Bondage and My Freedom (Douglass), *f422*

N

NAACP. *See* National Association for the Advancement of Colored People

Narragansetts, 28, 130, 156–157

Narrative of the Life of Frederick Douglass, 442, 452

Narrative of Sojourner Truth, 443, 452

Narváez, Pánfilo de, 97, *m98*

NASA. *See* National Aeronautics and Space Administration

National Aeronautics and Space Administration (NASA), *f76*

National Archives, *f173–175*

National Association for the Advancement of Colored People (NAACP), 543, 552

national bank, 270, 292, 321

nationalism, 308

National Organization for Women, 559

National Republicans, 352–353

National Road, 322

nativism, 421, *f421–422*

nativists, 421

NATO. *See* North Atlantic Treaty Organization

Navajos, *i4,* 21, 30

navigation, *f37,* **46**–47, *f47,* 53

navy, U.S.: in Civil War, 494, 498, 499, *i499, m501,* 505; Force Bill and, 358; and pirates, 300; in War of 1812, 305; during War of Independence, 215

Nebraska, R21

Necessity, Fort, *f181*

Netherlands: Asia route, search for, 76, *m77;* colonies of, *m109,* 110–111, 134–135; Jewish settlement and, *f65;* map making of, *f85–86;* and religion, 108, 111

neutral, 273

neutrality, 272–273, 278, 300

Nevada, R21

New Amsterdam, 111

New Bedford, Massachusetts, 406, 418

New Deal, 555

New England, *m131;* colonial, 146–148, *m147,* 163; education in, 148, *i148;* Hartford Convention, 307; Indians, conflicts with, 131–132; and Jefferson's embargo, 302, 304; Republican support in, 332; witch hunts in, *f170–171,* 452. *See also individual states*

Newfoundland, 62, *i63,* 75, 77, 108, 112

New France, 108–110, *m109, i110;* British and French war in,

m183, i184, 185; British governance of, 185, 186–187

New Hampshire, 131, R20

New Harmony, 438

New Jersey, 135, 149, 216–217, *i217, i220,* R21

New Jersey Plan, 242

New Mexico, R21; and Civil War, 493; early Indians of, 19, 20, 21; Mexican-American War in, 394; and slavery debate, 469; Spanish settlement in, 99, 104–105, *m105,* 297, 298

New Netherland, *m109,* 110–111, 134–135

New Orleans, 110, *i260–261,* 277, *m277,* 294

New Orleans, Battle of (1815), *m306,* 307; Battle of (1862), 500, *m501*

New Orleans (steamboat), *f327*

New Spain, 101, *m101,* 106

newspapers: antislavery, 441, *i441,* 442; freedom of the press, 163–164, *i163, f249,* 281, *f282, f285;* illustrated, *f496, i521*

New Sweden, 111

New York, *i88,* R21; British capture of, 216; as colony, 135, 149; founding of, 110–111; Jewish settlement in, *f65;* in War of Independence, 216, 217–218

New York City, 110–111, 135, 150, *i247,* 508

New York Times, f516

Nez Percés, *f378*

Niagara, Fort, 186

Niagara Movement, *i523,* 543

Nightjohn (Paulsen), *f426–427*

Niña, 65

Nineteenth Amendment, *f451,* 554, R67

Ninth Amendment, R62

Nixon, Richard M., 559, *i559,* R28, R40

Niza, Marco de, *m98,* 99

nomads, 11

Non-Intercourse Act (1809), 302

Norfolk Harbor blockade, 498, 499, *m501*

North: abolition, opposition to, 445; free African Americans in, 417, 418, *i418;* Fugitive Slave Law and, 472; industrialization and, 406–409, *m407;* moderate and radical views on slavery, 468; secession, response to, 483. *See also* Civil War

North American Free Trade Agreement (NAFTA), 561

North Atlantic Treaty Organization (NATO), 556

North Carolina, 77, 112, 133–134, 150, R21; in Civil War, 492, 515; and Reconstruction, *f534;* and slavery, 159, 244

North Dakota, R21

North Star, 442

Northwest Coast culture area, 27, *m29*

Northwest Ordinance of 1787, 236, 333

Northwest Passage, *i59,* 74–78, *m77,* 104

Northwest Territory, 236, *f240*

Noyes, John, 437–438

nullification, 282, 357–358, *f357, i358*

nullify, 282

Nzinga Mbemba (king of the Kongo), *f71*

O

Oberlin College, 441, 448

Oglethorpe, James, *i117,* 137–138

O'Gorman, Juan, *f329*

Ohio, 333, R22

Ohio River and Valley: Indians and, 22, 23, 274–276, *f290–291;* struggle for control of, *f180–181,* 182–183, 222; transportation to, 322, *m323,* 326; in War of Independence, 222–223, *m223;* Whiskey Rebellion, 273–274

oil spills, *i560*

Oklahoma, 362, 551, R22

Olive Branch Petition, 211

Oliver, Andrew, 189

Olmecs, 14–15, *i14, m16*

Olmsted, Frederick Law, *f439*

Omahas, *f257*

Oñate, Juan de, 104, *m105*

Oneida, 437–438

Oneidas, 110, 493

Onondagas, 110

opinion, *f210*

oral history, *f341–343*

Oregon, R22

Oregon Country, *m387;* annexation of, 394, *m396;* and Manifest Destiny, 377, 385; and slavery debate, 469; Spain gives up claims to, 329; U.S. and Britain share, 328, *m330*

Oregon Trail, *i373,* 386–388, *m387,* 389

Osceola, 363, *i363*

O'Sullivan, John, 376

Otos, *f257*

Ottawas, 275

overseers, *f159,* 414

Owen, Robert, 438

Ozette site, *f1–3, i1–2*

P

Pacific Mountains and Valleys, *mP4–P7*

Pacific Ocean, 73, 74, *f85–86*

Paine, Thomas, 211, 216

Paiutes, 28, 391, *i391*

Paleo-Indians, *f8–9, i8,* 10–13, *m11, i12*

Panama, 73, *m330,* 331

Panama Canal, 552

Panama Congress, *f351*

Panic of 1819, 332–333, 419

Panic of 1837, 366

Papagos, 20

Paraguay, *m330,* 331

parallel time lines, *f31*

Paris, Treaty of, 224–225, 236

Parker, Captain John, 206

Parliament, founding of, 162

Patagonia, *f87*

Patriots, **213**

patroons, 111

"Paul Revere's Ride" (Longfellow), 453

Paulsen, Gary, *f426–427*

Pawnees, *f257, i333*

Peaceable Kingdom, The (Hicks), *f137*

peace medals, *f297*

peninsulares, 102

Penn, William, 136, 149

Pennsylvania, R22; as colony, *i117,* 136, 149; early Indians of, 22; Panic of 1819 and, 333; prejudice in, 154; in War of Independence, 216, 218–219, 221

Pequots, 132

Peralta, Pedro de, 104–105, *m105*

Perot, Ross, *i479*

Perry, Matthew, 406

Perry, Oliver, 305–306, *i305*

persecution, 64, *f65,* **108,** 121, 125, 389–390

Persian Gulf War, 561

Peru, 14, 96, 101, *m330,* 331. *See also* Incas

Petalesharro, *i333*

Petersburg, Battle of, *m513,* 515

petition, right to, 162, R59

Philadelphia, *i242,* 419, 433; founding of, 136, 150

Philip II (king of Spain), 111

Philippines, 74, *f86,* 551

Pickett, George E., 512

Pierce, Franklin, 473, 474, R25

Pigafetta, Antonio, *f86–87*

Pike, Zebulon, *m295,* 297–298

Pikes Peak, 297

Pilgrims, and Plymouth, *i117,* 125–126

Pimas, 20

Pinckney, Thomas, 277, 300

Pinckney's Treaty, 277

Pinta, 65

Pippin, Horace, *f481*

pirates, 97, 104, 111, *i111,* 300, *f300, i301, m301,* 307

Pitt, Fort, 185, 186

Pitt, William, 184–185, 190

Pizarro, Francisco, 96, 99, *f113*

Plains culture area, 28, *m29*

plantations, **70,** 150, 151, *i412;* after Civil War, 528–529,

538–539; Indians owning, 359; living conditions of slaves on, *f404–405, i405,* 414, *f416,* 417, *f426–427;* use of slave labor, 70–71, 134, 157, 412

planters: after Civil War, 526, 528, 531; and Indian removal, 360–361; and tariffs, 356, *i357*

plateau, *f24*

platform, 476

Plessy v. Ferguson, 542

Plymouth Colony, *m122,* 125–126, *i125*

Pocahontas, *f118–119, i118,* 123, 124, *f138*

Poe, Edgar Allan, 453

Poems on Slavery (Longfellow), 453

point of view, *f249*

Polish Americans, 218

political parties: development of, *i262,* **279,** *f284. See also specific parties*

Polk, James K., 393–394, 394–396, R25

poll tax, 540, R71

Polo, Marco, *i35,* 44, *i44, f61*

Polynesians, *f47,* 62

Pomos, 28

Ponce de León, Juan, *i90,* 97, *m98*

Pontiac's Rebellion, 186–187

Poor Richard's Almanac (Franklin), *i143, f145*

Popé, 105

popular sovereignty, 468

population: agriculture and, 13, 14; Austin's colony, 380; and Civil War, 494, 514; of colonies, 125, 128, *f139,* 149, *m155,* 162; crop improvement and, 69; density, *m271;* and gold rush, 398; Indian, 25, 69, *f93,* 104, 359; of Louisiana Purchase, 296; predictions, 563; slaves, *m161,* 244, 412, 417; Spanish settlements in U.S., 106; of United States, 359; and westward expansion, *f327,* 386, 389, 390, 391, 411

population density, *f271*

Port Hudson, Battle of, *m513,* 514

Portolá, Gaspar de, 106

Portugal: Jews expelled from, *f65;* and slavery, 53–54; trade and exploration, *f36–37,* 53–54, *m53, f54,* 60–61, 62–64, 73

postal service, *f199*

Postmaster General, 266

potatoes, 70, *f421*

potlatch, 27

Potomac River, 236

pottery, 15, 19, *i19, i21, f31*

Powell, John Wesley, *f24*

Powers, Harriet, *f415*

Powhatan, *f118–119*

prairie schooners. *See* wagon trains

prayer, 243

Preamble to Constitution, R36

precipitation, *f413*

prejudice: among European Americans, **154–**155. *See also* racism

Prentiss, Clifton and William, 492–493

Presbyterian Church, 432

President: cabinet of, 266–268; checks and balances and, 252–253, R44, R50; election method of, 244; form of address for, 266; Jackson's influence on role of, *f368;* separation of powers and, 252; two-term tradition of, *iR70. See also* elections, presidential; *specific Presidents*

President's House: Abigail Adams on, 282–283; British burning, 307, *f309*

presidios, 102, *i106*

press, freedom of the, 163–164, *i163, f249,* 281, *f282, f285,* R59

Preuss, Charles, *f374, f392*

primary source, *f193*

Princeton College, *f232, i233*

printers, *f144–145,* 419

printing, invention of, 46

prison reform, 435–436

proclamation, 187

Proclamation of Neutrality, 273

Proclamation of 1763, 187, *f197*

profiteers, 219

Prohibition, 554.

Prophet, 303–304, *i303, f308*

Prophetstown, 303–304

proprietary colonies, 133

protective tariff, 321

protest, types of, *f196,* 559

Protestant Reformation, 108

Protestants: beginning of movement, 108; English, 111; fleeing persecution, 111, 121, 125–126, 128, *f134,* 136; French, 104, 109; Great Awakening, 155–156; hostility to Roman Catholics, 154, 421. *See also specific churches or people*

Ptolemy, Claudius, *f55*

public speaking, *f431, f435*

Pueblos, 21, *i21,* 28–29, 99, 104–105

Puerto Rico, 97, 551

Pulaski, Fort, *f524*

Pure Food and Drug Act (1906), 552

Puritans, 121, 125, 128, 135, 146, 147, 148; witch hunts by, *f170–171,* 452

Q

Quakers, 136, 150, 154, 160, 442

Quartering Act, 191

Quebec, 108, 109, *i184,* 185, 196, 209

Quebec Act (1774), 196

Quetzalcoatl, 95

quilting, *f149, f415*

R

racism, 156, *f166;* and African Americans, 157, 160, *f166,* 417–418, *f497,* 505–506, 535, 536, *f544,* 552; and Indians, 156–157

radiocarbon dating, *f2–3, f12*

railroad, 326, *i326,* 397, *m410,* 411, *i411;* and Civil War, 494, *i494;* transcontinental, 473–474, *i550*

Raleigh, Sir Walter, 112

ratify, 245

Reagan, Nancy, *i281*
Reagan, Ronald, 560, *i560,* R28
reaper, 410–411, 509
Reconstruction, 529, *f537;* end of, *i523,* 536; Johnson's plan, 529–530; legacy of, 538–544, *i540, f541, i542, f544;* under Reconstruction Act, 531, 532–536, *f534*
regions, geographic, P4–P5
religion: Buddhism, 45; Christianity, *see* Christianity; and colonization, 108, 121; early Indian, 14–15, *i14,* 17, *f17,* 20–21, 22, 23; freedom of, 121, 126, 129–131, 133, 135, 136, R59; Hinduism, 45; Islam, 39–40, 41, 64; prejudice and, 154–155, 156, 389–390, 418, 421; Pueblo cultures, 30; of slaves, 160; and social reform, 433, 434, 441, 448, *f455;* utopias based on, 437–438; West African, 41, 42, *f43. See also specific groups, churches, or people*
Religious Society of Friends. *See* Quakers
repeal, 189
representatives, 124
republic, 234, 250
Republican Party: establishment of, 476; Radicals, 530, 531, 532, 533–534; voting rights and, 532–533
Republicans. *See* Jeffersonian Republicans; National Republicans; Republican Party
research methods, *f79, f107, f173–175*
Revels, Hiram R., 534
revenue, 188
Revere, Paul, *f191,* 192, 206
revival, 155
Revolutionary War. *See* War of Independence
Reynolds, John Fulton, *f459–461*
Rhode Island, 130–131, 248, R22
rice, 134, 150, 159, 319
Richmond, Virginia, in Civil War, 492, 498, 500, 514,

515–516, *i527*
Rio Grande, 21, 99, 394, *m395*
"Rip Van Winkle" (Irving), 452
rivers: transportation and, 322–323. *See also specific rivers*
roads, 17–18, *m199,* 322, *m323,* 557
Roanoke Island, 112
Roaring Twenties, 554, *i554*
Rocky Mountains, *mP4–P7,* 297, *f299, i299*
Rolfe, John, *f119,* 123, 124
Roman Catholic Church: the Crusades, 50; explorers and, 52, 64, *f65,* 66, 94, 95; and freedom of religion, 121, 133, 154, 421; missionaries, 101–102, 105, 106, 110, *f218,* 386; Protestant Reformation and, 108; Texas settlers converting to, 380, 381. *See also specific people*
Roman Empire, *i34,* 49
Romantic period, *f298*
Roosevelt, Eleanor, *i555*
Roosevelt, Franklin Delano, 278, 555, *i555,* R27
Roosevelt, Theodore, 552, *i552,* R27
royal colony, 125
rubber, 408
Ruffin, Edmund, *f483*
Russia: land claims of, *f331;* serfs freed in, *f483;* settlements by, 106, *m187, m224, f331;* and Spain, 106
Russwurm, John, 441

S

Sacagawea, 295–297
Sagres, 53
St. Augustine, *i91,* 104, *m105, i106*
Saint Domingue. *See* Haiti
St. Leger, Barry, 217, 218
St. Louis, Missouri, 411
Salem, Massachusetts, 452
Salomon, Haym, 215
Sampson, Deborah, 215, *i215*
San Antonio, *i381*
San Martín, José de, *i330,* 331

San Salvador, 65, *i67*
Santa Anna, Antonio López de, 381–384, *m384,* 394
Santa Fe, New Mexico, *f379,* 394
Santa Fe Trail, *i372,* 379, 394
Santa María, i58, i61, 65
Santo Domingo, 67
Saratoga, Battle of, 218
Sauks, 361
Savannah, Georgia, 515, *f524–525*
sawmill, *f151*
scalawags, 532
Scandinavia, 50, 62, 108, 421
Scarlet Letter, The (Hawthorne), 452
scenario, 562
science and technology: birchbark canoe, *f26–27;* camera, *f502;* canal lock, *f324–325;* of China, 46–47; communication, *f207;* early Indian, 15, 16, 18; industrialization and, 408–409; moon landing, *i558;* predictions about, 562, 563; sawmill, *f151;* telegraph, *f408–409. See also* inventions and inventors
Scopes trial, 554
Scottish Americans, 152, 421
Scott, Dred, 478, *i478*
Scott, Winfield, *m395,* 396, 473
Sea Dogs, 111
Sea Islands, *f524–525*
search warrants, 188, R60
Sea Witch, 407
secede, 357
secession, 357–358, 482, *f482–483*
Second Amendment, R59
secondary source, *f193*
sectionalism, 334
sedition, 281
Sedition Act (1798), *i263,* 281, 282, *f282, f285, f292*
segregation, 540–543, *f541, i542,* 557, *i557*
Seguín, Juan, 382
self-government, 163, 186, 191, 196, *f253*

Seminoles, 23, 328–329, 359–360, 363, *i363,* 493

Seminole War, 363

Senate, U.S., 243, 468, 470, 475, *i476,* R39–R40

Seneca Falls Convention, *i429,* 449–450, *f450–451*

Senecas, 110, 493

"separate but equal" doctrine, 542–543

separation of powers, 252

Sepúlveda, Juan Ginés de, *f104*

Sequoyah, 359

serfs, 49–50, *i49, f483*

Serra, Father Junípero, 106, *f218*

Seven Cities of Gold, 98–99

Seven Pines, Battle of, 500, *m501*

Seventeenth Amendment, R66

Seventh Amendment, R61

Seward, William H., *i471,* 474

sewing machine, 408

Seymour, Horatio, 533

Shakers, 437, *i438*

sharecropping, 539, *i539*

Shawnees, 274, *f290–291,* 303–304, *i304*

Shays' Rebellion, *i231,* 238, *i239,* 246–247

sheep raising, *i24,* 120

shelter. *See* dwellings

Sherman, Roger, 243

Sherman, William Tecumseh, 514, 515

Sherman Antitrust Act (1890), 551

Shiloh, Battle of, *i462–463,* 500, *m500*

ships, 35, 47, 53, 146

shoemakers, 419, *f451*

Shoshones, 28, 296–297, *i312–313, f378*

Signing the Constitution (Christy), *f243*

silk trade, 46, *i46*

silver, 77, 95, 96, 97, 236, 364, 366

Singleton, Benjamin "Pap," 543

Singleton, Theresa, *f341–343, i341*

Singletry, Amos, *f247*

Sioux, 28, *f375, i550,* 551

Sitting Bull, *i550*

Sixteenth Amendment, 553, R66

Sixth Amendment, R61

Slater, Samuel, *i314,* 318–319

slave breakers, *f404–405*

slave catchers, 416, 443, 472

slave codes, 417

slave revolts, 294, *f296,* 417

slavery: in Africa, 40–41, *f43;* African American culture and, 41–42, 159–160, *f160;* in colonial America, *i142,* 157, 159, *i159;* Compromise of 1850, 470–471, *i470, f471, m474;* cotton gin and, 319; and Declaration of Independence, 212; education of slaves, *f404,* 417, *f426–427;* effect on Africa, *f71;* effect on Indian tribes, 134; Emancipation Proclamation, 504–505, *f510;* escape from, *f111,* 159, 363, *f405,* 415, 416, 418, *i426,* 443–444, *m444,* 472; in Europe, 53–54, 102; expansion of, 319, 333–335, *f335–336,* 412, *m474;* freed slaves before Civil War, 160, 415, 417, 440; of Indians, 70, *f92–93,* 94, 103, *f103–104,* 105, *i106, f107, f111,* 132, 134; Juneteenth, *f529;* Kansas-Nebraska Act, 474–475, *m474,* 476; language of slaves, *f160;* living conditions of slaves, 159, *f341–343, i343, f404–405, i405,* 414–415, *f415, f416,* 417, *f426–427, i427, f477;* Missouri Compromise, 334–335, *m334, f335–336,* 474, 476; origins of, 40–41; plantations' use of, 70–71, 134, 157, 412; resistance to, *i402,* 415–417, 443, 455; serfdom compared to, *f483;* in territories, 236, 468–469, 470, 474, 478, 480; in Texas, 381, 384, 393–394; Thirteenth Amendment, 527; Three-Fifths Compromise, 244; Vikings and, 50; and War of Independence, 212, 213, 214, *f225;* West Africa and, 41–42, *f43,* 53–54, 158, 440. *See also* African Americans; antislavery movement

slave trade, 40–41, 53–54, 71, *f71,* 134; Atlantic, 158, *i158, m161,* 412; Congress bans, 412; Constitutional Convention and, 244

Sloan, John Mather, 496

Smet, Pierre de, 389

Smith, Captain John, *f118–119,* 122, *f127*

Smith, Gerrit, 418

Smith, James, *f240*

Smith, Jonathan, *f247*

Smith, Joseph, 389–390

Smith, Margaret Bayard, 354

smuggling, 165, 186, 188

social class, 102

social reform, 433, *f455*

Social Security Act (1935), 555

Somalia, 561, *i561*

Songhai, 39, 40

Song of Hiawatha (Longfellow), 453

Sons and Daughters of Liberty, 189, 192, 195, *i195*

Soto, Hernando de, *m98,* 99

Sounding Reveille (Homer), *f496*

South: as cotton-growing region, 411; destruction of, 526, *i527,* 538; free African Americans in, 417–418; freedmen, 526–529, *i528,* 532, 538; moderate and radical views on slavery, 468; money of, 509, 526; after Reconstruction, 538–544, *i539, m540, f541, i542, f544;* secession of, 482, *f482–483;* slavery, spread of in, 412, 445; tenant farming, rise of, 538–539, *i539. See also* Civil War; Reconstruction; Southern Colonies

South America, 25, 69, *m330,* 331

South Carolina, R22; and Civil War, 482, 483, 504, 507, 515; as colony, 133–134, 150; and nullification crisis, 357–358, *f357;*

and Reconstruction, 534, *f534*, 535; and slavery, 159, 244, 417

South Dakota, R22

Southern Colonies, 150, 152, *f152*, 159. *See also specific colonies*

Southwest culture area, 28–29, *m29*

sovereignty, 357

Soviet Union, 556, 557, *i557*, 560

Space Camp/Academy, *f76*

Spain: Armada defeat, 111–112, *i112*; Asia route, search for, 73–74, *m74*; challenges to empire, 108; colonization of the Americas, 101–106, *m101*, *m105*, *m187*, *f218*, *m224*, 329, *m330*, 331, 379; and Columbus, 64–67; conquests of, *f92–93*, 94–99, *i94*, *m98*; and England, 104, 111–112, *i112*, 113, 133, 138; enslavement of Indians, 70, *f92–93*, 103, *f103–104*, 105, *i106*, *f107*, *f111*; Florida, cedes to U.S., 328–329; and France, 104, 105–106; Jews expelled from, 64, *f65*; Latin American revolutions and, 329, *m330*, 331; missionaries, 66, *i93*, 94, 95, 101–102, 105, 386; and Protestant Reformation, 108; treaties with U.S., 277, 329; and United States, 297, 551, *i551*; after War of Independence, 236; in War of Independence, 218, 223, *m223*

Spanish-American War, 551, *f551*

Spanish Armada, *i91*, 111–112, *i112*

Speare, Elizabeth George, *f170–171*

special artists, *f496*, *i521*

Specie Circular, 366

speculators, 269

speech, freedom of, *f249*, 281, *f282*

Spice Islands, 73, 74

spices, *f50*

spinning jenny, 318–319

spoils system, 356

Spotsylvania Court House, Battle of, 514

Springfield, Illinois, 479

Sputnik, 557

Squanto, 126

Stamp Act, *i178*, 188–190, *i189*, *f197*

Stamp Act Congress, 189

Standard Oil Trust, 550

Stanford, Dennis, *i8*, *f12*

Stanton, Edwin, 531

Stanton, Elizabeth Cady, *f448*, 449–450, *i449*, *f451*

"Star-Spangled Banner, The" (Key), 307

State Department, 266–267

statement of fact, *f210*

states: cooperation among, R54; government of, 234, 252, 529–530, 534, 534–535, 539–543; and nullification crisis, 357–358; powers of, *f250*, 251–252, R47; quarrels among, 236

states' rights, 282, 357–358, 367, 507

statistical table, *f139*

steamboats, 322–323, *f327*

steel mills, *i551*

stereotype, *f369*

Steuben, Baron Friedrich von, 219, 224

Stevens, Thaddeus, 528–529, 530, *i530*

Stewart, William, *f378*

stock market crash, 554, *i554*

Stockton, Robert, 395

Stone, Lucy, 450

stone points, *f8–9*, *i8*, 11

Stono Uprising, 417

Stowe, Harriet Beecher, 472–473, *i473*

strait, 74

Strait of Magellan, 74, *f87*

strict construction, 270

strikes, 419–420

Stuyvesant, Peter, 111, 134–135

subsistence farming, 146

suburbs, 557, *i557*

Sudan, 39

suffrage, 351

Sugar Act, 188, 192, *f197*

sugar cane, and slavery, 53–54, 70–71

Sumner, Charles, 475, *i476*, 530, *i530*

Sumter, Fort, 483–484

Supreme Court, U.S.: checks and balances and, R53; and Fifteenth Amendment, 540; and Indian removal, 361; under Marshall, 292, 293–294, *f294*, 361; and Missouri Compromise, 478; and states' rights, *f357*; women justices on, 560, *iR53*

Supreme Court cases: *Brown* v. *Board of Education,* 542, 557; *Dred Scott* v. *Sandford,* 478; *Marbury* v. *Madison,* 293–294, *f294*; *Plessy* v. *Ferguson,* 542

Sutherland, William, 207

Sutter, John, 397–398

Swamp Fox (Francis Marion), 222, *i222*

Sweden, 111

Swentzell, Roxanne, *f21*

Switzerland, 108, *f506*

T

Taft, William H., R27

Tainos, 65, 68, 70

Tallmadge, James, 334

Tallmadge Amendment (1819), 334

Tappan, Arthur and Lewis, 442

Tariff of Abominations (1828), 356–358, *i357*

tariffs, 267–268, 321, 356–358, *i357*

taxes and taxation: in Civil War, 509; on colonial trade, 165, 186–192, *i189*, *f191*; Congress's power of, 214, 236, 238, *f250*; federal, 267–268, 273–274, 292, 509, 553, R66; state, 535; and War of Independence, 188–189. *See also* tariffs

Taylor, Susie King, *f524–525*, *i524*, 527, 528, 529, 538, 543, *f544*

Taylor, Zachary, 394, *m395,* 469–470, 471, R25

Tea Act, 194–195, *f197*

technology. *See* science and technology

Tecumseh, *i289, f290–291, i290,* 303–304, 305, 306, *f308*

Tejas, 106

telegraph, *i403, f408–409,* 409

telephone, 550

television, 557, *i557*

temperance, 437, *i437*

Templo Mayor, *f17,* 95, *i95*

tenant farmers, 538–539

Tenkamenin (king of Ghana), 39

Tennessee, 278, 333, 492, 500, *f534,* R22

Tenochtitlán, 16, 95–96, *i96*

Tenskwatawa. *See* Prophet

Tenth Amendment, R62

Tenure of Office Act (1867), 531

Teotihuacán, 15

terrain, *f100*

territories: government of, 236; land division in, 234–236, *f235;* statehood of, R55

Tewas, *i21,* 105

Texas, R22; annexation of, 394, *m396;* and Civil War, 493; and Reconstruction, *f534;* as republic, 384; and secession of South, 482; Spanish settlement in, 105–106, *m105;* statehood debate, 384, 393–394; U.S. settlement in, 380–381, *i381;* war for independence, 381–384, *i382, m384*

Thames, Battle of the, 306, *m306*

Third Amendment, R59

Thirteenth Amendment, 527, 529, R64

Thoreau, Henry David, 454, 455

Three-Fifths Compromise, 244

Ticonderoga, Fort, 209, 218, *m220*

Tidewater, 150

Tierra del Fuego, *f85, f87*

Tilden, Samuel J., 536

Tillman, Ben, 536

Timbuktu, 40

time lines, *f31*

Tippecanoe, Battle of, 304, *f308,* 366

Tlaxcalans, 95–96

Tlingits, 27

tobacco, 123, 124, 150, 159, 319, 538

Todd, David, *f497*

Toleration Act of 1649, 133

Tolstoy, Leo, *f466*

Tompkins, Sally L., 507, *i507*

Tom Thumb, 326, *i326*

Tordesillas, Treaty of, 73

total war, 514–515

totems, 27

town meetings, 163

towns. *See* cities and towns

Townshend, Charles, 188, 190

Townshend Acts, 190–191, 192, *f197*

trade: African, 38–41, *m39, i40;* Asian, 44–48, *i44–47, f45,* 406; Britain banning, *f238;* British control of colonial, 164–166, *f167;* Constitutional Convention and, 244; early Indian, 13, 15, 17, 20, 22, 23; embargo, 301–302; European, *f36–37,* 50–54, *m51, m53, f54;* fur *see* fur trade; Indian, 27, 108–109, 111; of industrial Northeast, 406–407, *m407;* infectious disease and, 68; partners of U.S., *f238;* in slaves *see* slave trade; wool, 120

trade unions, 419–420, 550, 559

trading posts, 54, 108, 275–276

Trail of Tears, *i347,* 362–363, *i362, m362, f363*

transcendentalism, 453–455

transcontinental railroad, 473–474, *i550*

transportation: canals, *m323,* 324–325, *f324–325;* federal funding for, 321, 322; railroad *see* railroad; roads, 17–18, *m199,* 322, *m323,* 557; ships, 35, 47, 53, 146, 407; wagon trains, 388–389, *f388, i389;* and west-

ward expansion, 376, 411, *i411*

Trapper's Bride, The (Miller), *f378*

trappers. *See* fur trade

Travis, William, 382, *f383*

treasure ships, Spanish, *f96,* 97, 99, 104, 111

Treasury Department, 266–267

trends, 563

Trenton, Battle of, 216–217, *m220*

trial by jury, 162, 188, 194

tribute, 16

Trowbridge, C. T., *f525*

Troy Female Seminary, 448

Truman, Harry S, 557, R28

Trumbull, John, *f176–177*

Truth, Sojourner, *f430–431, i430,* 432, *f455;* "Ain't I a Woman" speech, *f430,* 450; in antislavery movement, 440, 442–443; in Civil War, 507; in women's movement, *f430,* 450

Tubman, Harriet, *i429,* 443, 507

Turks, 50

Turner, Nat, *i402,* 417

Tuskegee Institute, 543, *i543*

Twelfth Amendment, 284, R62–R63

Twentieth Amendment, R68–R69

Twenty-first Amendment, R69

Twenty-second Amendment, R70, *iR70*

Twenty-third Amendment, R71

Twenty-fourth Amendment, R71

Twenty-fifth Amendment, R72–R73

Twenty-sixth Amendment, R73

Twenty-seventh Amendment, *f248,* R73

Tyler, John, 366, 367–368, 393–394, R25

tyranny, 162

U

Uncle Tom's Cabin (Stowe), *i464*, 472–473, *i473*, *f477*

Underground Railroad, *i429*, 443–444, *m444*, 455

Union, 483. *See also* Civil War

unions. *See* trade unions

United Farm Workers union, *f190*, 559

United Nations, 556

United States: land use in, *mR9*; natural vegetation of, *mR8*; physical map of, *mR4*; political map of, *mR6*; population density in, *mR11*; recognition of, 224–225; territorial growth of, *mR10*

Upson, Ted, 495

Urban II (Pope), 50

Uruguay, *m330*, 331

Utah, 389, 390, *i390*, 469, R22

Utes, 28

utopias, **437**–438, 454

V

Valley Forge, *i203*, 218–219, *i219*

Van Bergen Overmantel (Heaten), *f88–89*

Van Buren, Martin, 351, 364, 365, 366, 366–367, 469, R24

vaqueros, *i385*

Vásquez de Coronado, Francisco, *m98*, 99

vassals, 50

Veil, Charles Henry, *f459–461*

Venezuela, *m330*, 331

Vermont, R22

Verrazano, Giovanni, 77, *m77*, *f127*

Very Brief Report of the Destruction of the Indies, A (Las Casas), *f113*

Vespucci, Amerigo, *i59*, 67

veto power, 252–253, *f252*, 530

Vice-Presidents who have taken over for Presidents, *iR48*

Vicksburg, Mississippi, 500, 511, 512, *m513*, 514

Vietnamese Americans, *i561*

Vietnam War, 558, *i558*, 559

View of New Orleans Taken from the Plantation of Marigny, A (de Woieseri), 260–261

Vikings, 50, 62, *i63*

Vinland, 62

Virginia, R22; Alien and Sedition Acts and, 282; and Civil War, 492, 498, 500, *m501*, 511, 514–515; as colony, 112, 122–125, 150, 196; first Africans brought to, *i142*, 157; prejudice in, 154; and Reconstruction, *f534*; and slavery, 159, 415, 417; in War of Independence, 224

Virginia Company of London, 122–125

Virginia Plan, 242

Virginia (ship, formerly *Merrimac*), 500

voting rights: of African Americans, 351, *f418*, 529, 530, 531, 532, 533–534, 539–540; of 18-year-olds, R73; Fifteenth Amendment, 533–534; under Reconstruction Act, 532–534, 535; using, *f533*; of women, 351, 447, 450, *f450–451*, 533, 553, *i553*, *iR67*

voyageurs, 108

W

wage earners. *See* workers

wages, 419–420, *f423*, 450

Wagner, Fort, 506

wagon trains, 388–389, *f388*, *i389*

Wakeman, Rosetta (Lyons), 496

Walden (Thoreau), 455

Waldseemüller, Martin, 67

Walker, David, 443

Walker, Joseph Reddeford, 386, 388

Wampanoags, 126

War of 1812, *i289*, 304–308, *i305*, *m306*, *f309*; events preceding, 300–302, 303–304

war bonds, 269, 509

War Hawks, 304–305

War of Independence: African Americans and, 213; beginning of, 206–209, *i208*, *f210*; end of, 221–225; events leading to, *i179*, 186–192, *i189*, *f191*, 194–198, *i195*, *f197*; foreign help, 218, 223; historical documents of, *f173–175*, *f204–205*; Indians and, 213; issues of independence, 211–215; in literature, *f228–229*; prisoners of war in, *f348*; progress of, 216–219, *m220*, 221–223, *i222*, *m223*; recruiting for, *f205*, *i205*; slave resistance compared to, 443; strengths and weaknesses of each side in, 214–215; surrender at Yorktown, *i203*, 224; Treaty of Paris, *i203*, 224–225, 236

Warner, Sarah Furman, *f149*

Washington, R23

Washington, Booker T., 528, 543

Washington, D.C., R23; burned by British, 306–307, *f309*; establishment of, *i263*, 269, *f269*, 282–283; and statehood, *f282*

Washington, George: in colonial militia, *f180–181*, 183–184; at Constitutional Convention, 241, 244; at Continental Congress, 197; in events leading to War of Independence, 191, 197, *f198*; Farewell Address of, 278; presidency of, 248, *i262*, 266, 267, *i267*, 270, 273, 275, 278, R24; views on the Senate, R39; in War of Independence, 208, 209, 211, 213, 215, 216–217, *i217*, 219, 221, 224, 225

Washington Crossing the Delaware (Leutze), 217

water power, 150, *f151*

Watie, Stand, 516

Wayne, General "Mad Anthony," 275

weapons: bow and arrow, *f31*; of Civil War, *f490*, 494, 500, 506, *i507*; mass production of, 320; Spanish vs. Aztecs, 96; of War of Independence, *f228–229*; women and, *i215*, 506, *i507*

Webster, Daniel, 354, *f357,*
i358, 470, 471, *i471*
Webster-Hayne debates, *i347,*
f357, i358
Weld, Theodore Dwight, 441
West. *See* western settlement
West Africa: colonization of
freed slaves, 440; culture, 41–42,
f42, f415; slavery and, 41–42,
f43, 53–54, 134, 158, 440; trade
and, *f37,* 39–41, *m39, i40*
western hemisphere, *m330*
Western Plateaus, *mP4–P7,* 20,
f24
western settlement, *m277,*
i344–345, i550; after Civil War,
550; and Civil War, 493; definitions of boundary of, 376;
expanded worldview following,
f398; farming and, *f240,*
273–274; government of, 236,
274, *i274;* Indians and, 274–276,
303–304, *i304,* 306, *f375,*
390–391, *f391,* 550; under
Jefferson, 294–297, *m295;* land
division in, 234–236, *f235;*
Manifest Destiny, 376–377,
393–394, *i393,* 396; Mexican-
American War, 394–397, *m395;*
mountain men and, 377–378,
i377, f378; revivals and, 432;
slavery and, 236, 381, 384,
393–394, 468–469, 470, 474,
478; steamboats and, *f326,* 376;
wagon train life, 388–389, *f388,*
i389
West Indies, 134
West Virginia, 492, R23; early
Indians of, 22
***Westward the Course of
Empire Takes Its Way***
(Leutze), *f344–345*
whaling, 406, *m407*
Whig Party, 365–366, 366–367,
i367, 393–394, 469, 476
Whiskey Rebellion, *i263,*
273–274, *i274*
White, John, *f75,* 112
Whitefield, George, *i143,* 155

White House. *See* President's
House
White League, 535
white terrorism, 535, 536, *i536,*
f541
**Whitman, Marcus and
Narcissa,** 386, 391
Whitman, Walt, 453, *i453*
Whitney, Eli, 319, 320, 408
Whittier, John Greenleaf, 438
Wilkins, James, 389
Willard, Emma Hart, 447–448
Williams, Roger, 130
Wilmot, David, 468
Wilson, Woodrow, R27
Winnebagos, 258
Winnemucca, Sarah, 391, *i391*
Winthrop, John, 128, 129, 130,
131, 156
Wisconsin, R23
Wisconsin Territory, Indian
removal from, 361, *m362*
Witch of Blackbird Pond
(Speare), *f170–171*
witch hunts, *f170–171,* 452
Wolfe, General James, 185
women: in antislavery movement, 440, *i441,* 442, 447, 450;
at the Alamo, 383; in Civil War,
f490–491, 496–497, 506–507,
i507; clothing of, *f448;* as
colonists, 124, 130–131; and
education, *f434,* 447–448; Equal
Rights Amendment, *f251;* fighting in wars, *i215,* 496–497; as
millworkers, *i316–317,* 320; pay
gap of, *f316, f320, f451;* in professions, 448; role of, as President's wife, *i281;* status of, in
early 1800s, 447; voting rights
of, 351, 447, 450, *f450–451,* 533,
553, *i553;* in War of Independence, 207, 215, *i215;* and the
West, *f375,* 391, *i391;* westward
journeys of, 386, 388–389, *f399;*
in workforce, *f316–317,* 320,
f320, 420, *f423, i556*
women's movement: African
American women in, *f430, f431,*

450; campaigning for rights, 450,
559, *i559;* education reform,
447–448, *i447;* hostile crowds
and, *i449,* 450; need for, 447,
449; professions and, 448;
Seneca Falls Convention,
449–450, *f450–451;* voting rights
and, 450, *f450–451*
Woolman, John, 160
wool trade, 120
workers: and boycotts, *f190;*
children as, *i552,* 553; in colonial America, 146, *m147,* 148,
150; farm, *i559;* predictions
about, 563; skilled vs. unskilled,
419; trade unions and, 419–420;
women, *i316–317,* 320, *f320;*
working conditions of, 320, 551.
See also indentured servants;
slavery
**World Anti-Slavery
Convention,** 449
World War I, 553, *i553*
World War II, 556, *i556*
Wounded Knee, 551
Wright, Jonathan J., 534
Wright brothers, 552
writs of assistance, 188
Wyoming, R23

X

XYZ affair, 280–281

Y

Yankees, 495
Yorktown, Battle of, *i203,* 224
Young, Brigham, 390
yucca, *i24*

Z

Zenger, Peter, *i143,* 163–164,
i163
zero symbol, 16
Zheng He, 47–48
Zimbabwe, 38, *m39*
Zunis, 28–29, 99, 105

Photo Acknowledgments

Front Matter: ii Terry Ashe*; **vT** Jerry Jacka Photography, 1996; **vC** *Van Bergen Overmantel* (detail), 1732–33 attr. to John Heaten. © New York State Historical Association, Cooperstown; **vB** *The Declaration of Independence, 4 July 1776* (detail) by John Trumbull. Yale University Art Gallery, Trumbull Collection; **viT** *A View of New Orleans Taken from the Plantation of Marignel, November 1803* (detail) by Boqueto de Woieser. Chicago Historical Society, **viB** *Westward the Course of Empire Takes its Way* (detail) 1861 by Emanuel Gottlieb Leutz. Bequest of Sarah Carr Upton, National Museum of American Art, Smithsonian Institution, Washington, D.C./Art Resource, NY; **vii** *Battle of Shiloh— April 6th 1862.* Chicago Historical Society; **xxiv** J. L. Atlan/Sygma

P1 David Muench/Tony Stone Images; **P4L** David Muench; **P4R** James Randklev/Tony Stone Images; **P5TL** Larry Lefever/Grant Heilman Photography; **P5TR** Robert Llewellyn; **P5B** Bob Burch/Bruce Coleman Inc.; **P6R** *On the Trail* by Theodore Gentilz. The Witte Museum, San Antonio, Texas; **P6L** California Section, California State Library, Photograph Collection; **P7TL** *Commanche Village, Women Dressing Robes and Drying Meat* by George Catlin 1834–35. National Museum of American Art, Smithsonian Institution. Gift of Mrs. Joseph Harrison, Jr. Photo: Art Resource, NY; **P7C** *Preparation for WAR to Defend Commerce* by William and Thomas Birch. Prints Division, The New York Public Library. Astor, Lenox and Tilden Foundations; **P7B** *A Cotton Plantation on the Mississippi* (detail) by Nathaniel Currier & James Merritt Ives. Library of Congress; **P7TR** *Man Looking at Steel Mills, Homestead, PA.* California Museum of Photography, University of California, Riverside; **P8** Terry Ashe* **1B** Makah Cultural and Research Center, Neah Bay, WA. Photo by Ruth & Louis Kirk; **1T** Cheryl Fenton*; **2T** Makah Cultural and Research Center, Neah Bay, WA. Photo by Ruth & Louis Kirk; **2B** Makah Cultural and Research Center, Neah Bay, WA. Photo by Ruth & Louis Kirk; **3** Cheryl Fenton*

Unit 1: 4–5 Jerry Jacka Photography, 1996

Chapter 1: 6L The Bettmann Archive; **6R** *A Ballgame Player.* Erich Lessing/Art Resource, NY; **7BCL** Peter French/Bruce Coleman Inc.; **7BCR** *God King Quetzalcoatl.* Boltin Picture Library; **7BR** Boltin Picture Library; **7BL** *Nursing Mother Effigy Bottle,* AD 1200–1400. St. Louis Museum of Science and Natural History, Missouri. Photo by Dirk Bakker; **7T** George Gerster/Comstock; **8L** Victor Krantz; **8R** Victor Krantz/ National Museum of American History; **12** Tom D. Dillehay; **14** Malcolm S. Kirk/Peter Arnold, Inc.; **15** *Mayan Seacoast Village,* a watercolor copy by Ann Axtell Morris of Mural in Temple of the Warriors, Chichén Itzá, Mexico. 800–1000 A.D. Peabody Museum—Harvard University. Photo by Hillel Burger; **16** *Codice Magliabechiano: Aztec game of "Patolli."* Scala/Art Resource, NY; **17** Kenneth Garett/Woodfin Camp, Inc.; **18** Janis E. Burger/Bruce Coleman Inc.; **19** Mimbres black-on-white bowls. Courtesy of Dennis & Janis Lyon. Jerry Jacka Photography, 1996;

20 Dave Wilhelm/The Stock Market; **21** *Emergence of the Clowns* by Roxanne Swentzell, 1988. The Heard Museum, Phoenix; **22** *Panorama of the Monumental Grandeur of the Mississippi Valley,* 1850. Detail: *Dr. Dickeson Excavating a Mound,* by John J. Egan. The Saint Louis Art Museum. Purchase: Eliza McMillan Fund.; **24T** Jack Couffer/Bruce Coleman Inc.; **24C** Rod Planck/Tom Stack & Associates; **24B** Woven Bag. White Dog Cave, Arizona, Basket Maker III, 450–700/750 A.D. Peabody Museum—Harvard University. Photo by Hillel Burger; **31** Cheryl Fenton*

Chapter 2: 34L Michael Holford; **34R** The Bettmann Archive; **35T** Photo from Louise Levathes' *When China Ruled the Seas* (1994); **35BL** The Bettmann Archive; **35BC** *Catalan Atlas* (detail) 1375 by Abraham Cresques. Robert Harding Picture Library; **35BR** *Arte de Navegae* (detail) by Pedro de Medinco, 1545. Rare Book Room & Manuscript Division, New York Public Library; **36** *Henry the Navigator* from 16th c. Portuguese manuscript. Michael Holford; **37** "Cantino" map of the world (detail). Scala/Art Resource, NY; **40** Wolfgang Kaehler; **42L** Werner Forman/Art Resource, NY; **42C** Michael Holford; **42R** Werner Forman/Art Resource, NY; **43** Cheryl Fenton*; **44** B.N. Ms. 2810 (detail). Photo by Bibliothèque Nationale de France, Paris; **46** Ming Dynasty vase (detail). Giraudon/Art Resource, NY; **47** *Tribute Giraffe with Attendant,* 1403–1424 by Shentu (1357–1434). Philadelphia Museum of Art. Given by John Dorrance; **49** Michael Holford; **52** The Bettmann Archive; **53** Werner Forman/Art Resource, NY; **55** Giraudon/Art Resource, NY

Chapter 3: 58R *Capsicum pepper* (detail) by William Blake, 1796. The John Carter Brown Library at Brown University; **58L** *Santa María in Palos de la Frontera.* Robert Frerck/Odyssey/Chicago; **59T** *Mapa Universal de 1507* (detail). Library of Congress, Geography & Maps Division; **59BC** Globe by Martin Behaim. Germanisches National Museum, Nürnberg; **59BR** *The Last Voyage of Henry Hudson* (detail) by John Collier. The Tate Gallery, London/Art Resource, NY; **59BL** Francisco Erize/Bruce Coleman Inc.; **60** *Portrait of Christopher Columbus.* Scala/Art Resource, NY; **61** Jon Levy/Gamma-Liaison; **63TL** Ed Degginger/Bruce Coleman Inc.; **63BL** André Cornellier/Canadian Parks Service; **63R** Canadian Parks Service; **64** *Vasco da Gama* from a Portuguese manuscript, c. 1558. The Pierpont Morgan Library/Art Resource, NY; **67** Adam Woolfitt/Woodfin Camp & Associates; **69** #4051 *Codex Florentino.* Department of Library Services, American Museum of Natural History; **70** Cheryl Fenton*; **72T** *Buffalo Chase with Bows and Lances,* 1832–33 by George Catlin. National Museum of American Art, Washington, D.C./Art Resource, NY; **72B** Coffrin's Old

West Gallery; **74** *Portrait of Magellan.* Museo Maritimo, Sevilla. Photo "ARXIU MAS"; **76L** *Eskimo man* by John White, © British Museum; **76R** *Eskimo Woman & Child* by John White, © British Museum; **79** Cheryl Fenton*; **82** © British Museum; **83** Adam Woolfitt/Woodfin Camp & Associates; **85L** Cheryl Fenton*; **85R** Library of Congress; **86L** Cheryl Fenton*; **86–87** Library of Congress

Unit 2: 88–89 © New York State Historical Association, Cooperstown

Chapter 4: 90R The Oakland Museum History Department; **90L** *Map of Florida from "Cosmographic Universelle,"* 1555, by Guillaume Le Testu. Giraudon/Art Resource, NY; **91T** Laurie Platt Winfrey, Inc.; **91BL** Jim Schwabel/Southern Stock; **91BR** Detail from George Catlin's: *La Salle Erecting a Cross and Taking Possession of the Land, March 25, 1682.* Paul Mellon Collection, © Board of Trustees, National Gallery of Art; **91BC** The Bettmann Archive; **92** Ampliaciones y Reproducciones Mas (Arxiu Mas); **93** Ampliaciones y Reproducciones Mas (Arxiu Mas); **94** Laurie Platt Winfrey, Inc.; **95** The Newberry Library; **97** Laurie Platt Winfrey, Inc.; **100** Bibliothèque Nationale de France, Paris; **102** Miguel Cabrera: *Depiction of Racial Mixtures: "1 De español y d India, Mestisa."* Copyright © by The Metropolitan Museum of Art; **103** Carved, painted & gilded ceiling of Santa Clara, Tunja, Columbia. Photo © Wim Swaan; **106** Wendell Metzen/ Southern Stock ; **107T** Cheryl Fenton*; **107B** Department of Library Services, American Museum of Natural History. Neg. #329340; **110** The New York Public Library; Astor, Lenox and Tilden Foundations; **112** Laurie Platt Winfrey, Inc., by kind permission of the Marquess of Tavistock, Woburn Abbey

Chapter 5: 116R Culver Pictures; **116L** Colonial Williamsburg Foundation; **117BC** Pie Plate, 1786. Attributed to Johannes Neis, American, Pennsylvania German. Philadelphia Museum of Art. Given by John T. Morris; **117T** The Bettmann Archive; **117BR** The Bettmann Archive; **117BL** American Antiquarian Society, Worcester, MA; **118** *Pocahontas.* Anonymous. English school, after 1616 engraving by Simon van de Passe. National Portrait Gallery, Smithsonian Institution/Art Resource, NY; **119** The Bettmann Archive; **121** *The English Conspirators, including Guy Hawkes.* Anonymous, 17th century. Art Resource, NY; **123** National Park Service, Colonial National Historical Park; **125** Cary Wolinsky/Stock, Boston; **127T** Bob Burch/Bruce Coleman Inc.; **127B** *Baltimore in 1752* by John Moale. Maryland Historical Society, Baltimore; **129** *Hooker and Company Journeying Through the Wilderness from Plymouth to Hartford in 1636* by Frederic Edwin Church. © Wadsworth Atheneum, Hartford; **132** Shelburne Museum, Shelburne, Vermont. Photograph by Ken Burris; **136** Rare Books and Manuscripts Division/The New York Public Library, Astor, Lenox and Tilden Foundations; **137** *The Peaceable Kingdom* by Edward Hicks. Abby Aldrich Rockefeller Folk Art Center, Williamsburg, VA; **139** Cheryl Fenton*

Chapter 6: 142R Embroidery of Harvard Hall. Attributed to Mary Leverett Denison Rogers. The Massachusetts Historical Society; **142L** American Antiquarian Society, Worcester, MA; **143T** Late 19th century handmade 5-string banjo, North Carolina. Aldo Tutino/Art Resource, NY; **143BL** *George Whitefield* by John Wollaston. The National Portrait Gallery, London; **143BR** Rare Books and Manuscripts Division/The New York Public Library, Astor, Lenox and Tilden Foundations; **143BC** Oliver Pelton engraving illustrating *Poor Richard's Almanack.* Franklin Collection, Yale University Library; **144** *Portrait of Benjamin Franklin* by Robert Feke. Harvard University Portrait Collection. Bequest of Dr. John Collins Warren, 1856; **145** Ed Bohon/The Stock Market; **147BL** The Newberry Library; **147BR** Library of Congress; **147T** Library of Congress; **148** *The School Room* by Jonathan Jennings, 1850s. Private collection; **149** Applique quilt (detail) by Sarah Furman Warner. From the collections of Henry Ford Museum & Greenfield Village. Accession #6341.1; **152** *The Rapalje Children* by John Durand. Collection of The New-York Historical Society, New York City; **153** *Mrs. Hausman killing a hog* (detail) by Lewis Miller. The Historical Society of York County, PA; **157L** From the collection of Gilcrease Museum, Tulsa, Oklahoma; **157R** *Indian Sugar Camp,* drawing by Captain S. Eastman. Collection of The New-York Historical Society, New York City; **158BL** National Maritime Museum, London; **158TL** The British Library; **158R** Collection of The New-York Historical Society, New York City; **159** *Overseer Doing His Duty* by Benjamin Henry Latrobe. Maryland Historical Society, Baltimore; **160** The Research Libraries/The New York Public Library; **163** The Bettmann Archive; **165** *Charleston Harbor* by Bishop Roberts. Colonial Williamsburg Foundation; **167** Cheryl Fenton*; **170** Free Library of Philadelphia; **171** The Bettmann Archive; **173** National Archives; **174** Victor Krantz/National Archives; **175** Cheryl Fenton*

Unit 3: 176–177 Yale University Art Gallery, Trumball Collection

Chapter 7: 178R Colonial Williamsburg Foundation; **178L** Library of Congress, Geography & Map Division. Photo by Breton Littlehales, National Geographic Society; **179BL** *Samuel Adams* (detail), ca. 1772 by John Singleton Copley. Deposited by the City of Boston, Museum of Fine Arts, Boston; **179BC** American Antiquarian Society; **179TL** Culver Pictures; **179TR** The Massachusetts Historical Society; **179BR** Library of Congress; **180** *George Washington in the Uniform of a Colonel in The Virginia Militia* by Charles Willson Peale. Washington/Curtis/Lee Collection, Washington and Lee University, Lexington, VA; **181** Culver Pictures; **184** *A View of the Taking of Quebec,* 1759. Royal Ontario Museum,

Toronto; **189R** Massachusetts Historical Society; **189L** Culver Pictures; **190T** Nina Berman/SIPA Press; **190L** Massachusetts Historical Society; **191** Massachusetts Historical Society; **192TL** *Paul Revere* (detail) by John Singleton Copley. Gift of Joseph W., William B., and Edward H. R. Revere. The Museum of Fine Arts, Boston; **192B** *John Adams* by Charles Willson Peale. Independence National Historical Park Collection; **192TR** *Samuel Adams* (detail) by John Singleton Copley. Deposited by the City of Boston/ Museum of Fine Arts, Boston ; **193** Cheryl Fenton*; **195** Library of Congress; **196** *The Bostonians Paying the Excise Man.* John Carter Brown Library at Brown University

Chapter 8: 202L Robert Weinreb/Bruce Coleman Inc.; **202R** The Bettmann Archive; **203T** Anne S. K. Brown Military Collection/Brown University Library; **203BR** The National Archives; **203BL** The Bettmann Archive; **203BC** The Bettmann Archive; **204B** *Pulling Down the Statue of George III at Bowling Green* (detail) by William Walcutt. Lafayette College Art Collection, Easton, Pennsylvania; **204T** The Bettmann Archive; **205** The Bettmann Archive; **206** *The Retreat from Concord.* John Carter Brown Library at Brown University; **208** *The Battle of Bunker Hill* by Howard Pyle. Delaware Art Museum, Howard Pyle Collection; **210** Cheryl Fenton*; **212** Michael Anderson/Folio Inc.; **213** Virginia Historical Society; **214** *Johnson Hall* by E. L. Henry. Collection of the Albany Institute of History and Art; **215** The Bettmann Archive; **217** *Washington Crossing the Delaware* by Emanuel Gottlieb Leutze, 1851. Oil on canvas, 149 x 225 in. (378.5 x 647.7 cm.) The Metropolitan Museum of Art, Gift of John S. Kennedy, 1897; **219** Robert Llewellyn; **220** *The Retreat through the Jerseys* by Howard Pyle. Delaware Art Museum, Howard Pyle Collection; **222** *Marion Crossing the Pedee* (detail) by William T. Ranney, oil on canvas, 1850, Amon Carter Museum, Fort Worth, Texas, #1983.126; **228** West Point Museum; **229** *The Battle of Lexington April 19, 1775.* Plate I by Amos Doolittle. The Connecticut Historical Society, Hartford, Connecticut

Chapter 9: 230R National Archives; **231BC** Independence National Historical Park Collection; **231BR** *Banner of the Society of Pewterers,* 1787. Collection of The New-York Historical Society, New York City; **231T** Independence National Historical Park Collection; **231BL** *Daniel Shays* (detail). National Portrait Gallery/Smithsonian Institution; **232** *James Madison* by Charles Willson Peale. Library of Congress; **233** Reverend Jonathan Fisher, American, 1768–1847, *A North-West Prospect of Nassau Hall with a Front View of the President's House in New Jersey* (detail), 1807. Oil on canvas, 66.6 x 150.8 cm., Princeton University. Presented by alumni headed by A.E. Vondermuhll; **237T** The American Numismatic Society; **237B** Cheryl Fenton*; **238** *Canton Factories,* ca. 1780/Peabody Essex Museum, Salem, Mass.; **239R** The Granger Collection, New York; **239L** Sam

Abell, © National Geographic Society; **240** Larry Lefever/ Grant Heilman Photography; **242** *2nd Street North of Market* by William Birch. Historical Society of Pennsylvania; **243** The Granger Collection, New York; **244** The Huntington Library, San Marino, California; **247** The Granger Collection, New York; **249** Cheryl Fenton*; **251** Jean Louis Atlan/Sygma; **257B** Cheryl Fenton*; **257T** *Young Omahaw, War Eagle, Little Missouri, and Pawnees* by Charles Bird King. National Museum of American Art/Art Resource, NY; **258B** Cheryl Fenton*; **258L** Lithograph, *Hoowaunneka [Little Elk], Winnebago,* by Charles Bird King, 1841. Peabody Museum, Harvard University. © President and Fellows of Harvard College. Photograph by Hillel Burger; **258R** Painting, *Hoowaunneka [Little Elk], Winnebago,* by Charles Bird King, 1824. Peabody Museum, Harvard University. © President and Fellows of Harvard College. Photograph by Hillel Burger; **259** Cheryl Fenton*

Unit 4: 260–261 Chicago Historical Society

Chapter 10: 262R Collection of The New-York Historical Society, New York City; **262L** *Portrait of George Washington (1732–1799), 1st President of the United States,* by Rembrandt Peale. National Portrait Gallery, Smithsonian Institution/Art Resource, NY; **263BL** The Bettmann Archive; **263BC** Collection of The New-York Historical Society, New York City; **263BR** Library of Congress; **263T** Cheryl Fenton*; **264** *Abigail Adams* by Benjamin Blyth. Massachusetts Historical Society; **265** Bruce M. Wellman/Stock, Boston; **267** The Bettmann Archive; **268** Photri Inc.; **269R** Alex S. MacLean/Landslides, Boston, MA.; **269L** Library of Congress; **271** The Bettmann Archive; **273** Bibliothèque Nationale de France, Paris; **274** *Washington reviewing the Western Army at Fort Cumberland, Maryland* by Kemmelmeyer. The Metropolitan Museum of Art, Gift of Edgar William and Bernice Chrysler Garbisch, 1963. (63.201.2); **275(B inset)** *Little Turtle (Michikinikwa), Chief of Miami tribe,* by Ralph Dille after a painting by Stuart in 1797. Chicago Historical Society; **275T** *King Kamehameha I (?1758–1819),* unknown artist. Bishop Museum, Hawaii; **275(B background)** *Treaty of Fort Greenville* (detail). National Archives; **276** New York State Historical Association, Cooperstown, N.Y. ; **278** Collection of The New-York Historical Society, New York City; **280L** *Portrait of Alexander Hamilton,* by John Trumbull, 1806. National Portrait Gallery, Smithsonian Institution/Art Resource, NY; **280R** *Thomas Jefferson* by Rembrandt Peale. Copyrighted by the White House Historical Association; photograph by National Geographic Society; **281R** Larry Downing/ Sygma; **281C** J. L. Atlan/Sygma; **281L** *Portrait traditionally said to be that of Abigail Adams,* artist unidentified. New York State Historical Association, Cooperstown, N.Y.; **283** Cheryl Fenton*; **285** Cheryl Fenton*

Chapter 11: 288R Smithsonian Institution, photo #83.3049; **288L** *Portrait of John Marshall* by John B. Martin. Collection of the Supreme Court of the United States; **289BR** Smithsonian Institution, photo #83.7221; **289T** *Battle of New Orleans* (detail). The Hermitage: The Home of Andrew Jackson, Nashville, Tennessee; **289BL** Culver Pictures; **289BC** Collection of The New-York Historical Society, New York City; **290** Field Museum of Natural History (Neg#A93851c), Chicago; **291** *An encampment of Potawatomis at Crooked Creek* by George Winter. Tippecanoe County Historical Association, Lafayette, Indiana. Gift of Mrs. Cable G. Bell; **293TL** *Thomas Jefferson* by Rembrandt Peale. Collection of The New-York Historical Society, New York City; **293TR** Obelisk clock designed by Thomas Jefferson and executed by Louis Chartrot. Private Collection; photo courtesy of Monticello/Thomas Jefferson Memorial Foundation, Inc.; **293B** Monticello/Thomas Jefferson Memorial Foundation, Inc.; **293TC** Sketch of obelisk clock designed by Thomas Jefferson. College of William and Mary, Earl Gregg Swem Library; **296** The Bettmann Archive; **297L** Oregon Historical Society. Negative number OrHi 38090; **297R** Oregon Historical Society. Negative number OrHi 38091; **298** *Landscape with a Lake* by Washington Allston. Gift of Mrs. Maxim Karolik for the M. and M. Karolik Collection of American Paintings, 1815–1865. Courtesy, Museum of Fine Arts, Boston; **299C** Chase Swift/Westlight; 299B James Randklev/Tony Stone Images; **299T** Larry Lee/Westlight; **301** The Naval Historical Foundation; **302** Prints Division/The New York Public Library. Astor, Lenox and Tilden Foundations; **303** *The Open Door, known as The Prophet, brother of Tecumseh,* by George Catlin. National Museum of American Art, Washington, D.C./Art Resource, NY; **304** The Bettmann Archive; **305** Beverley R. Robinson Collection, United States Naval Academy Museum; **309** Cheryl Fenton*; **312** Independence National Historical Park Collection; **313B** Independence National Historical Park Collection; **313T** Leaf of an evergreen shrub, from William Clark's journal. Missouri Historical Society, St. Louis

Chapter 12: 314L Slater Mill Historic Site, Pawtucket, Rhode Island; **314R** National Museum of American History/Smithsonian Institution, photo #73-11287; **315BL** *The Clermont on the Hudson.* I. N. Phelps Stokes Collection, Miriam and Ira D. Wallach Division of Arts, Prints and Photographs/The New York Public Library, Astor, Lenox and Tilden Foundations; **315BR** *Portrait of James Monroe* after an oil painting by John Vanderlyn, by James Herring. National Portrait Gallery, Smithsonian Institution/Art Resource, NY; **315T** Library of Congress; **315BC** Library of Congress; **316** Print Collection, Miriam and Ira D. Wallach Division of Art, Prints and Photographs/The New York Public Library, Astor, Lenox and Tilden Foundations; **317** Barfoot/Darton: *Progress of Cotton, No. 5* (detail). Yale University Art Gallery. The

Mabel Brady Garvan Collection; **318** The Bettmann Archive; **319** The New York Public Library, Astor, Lenox and Tilden Foundations; **321** *View of Lowell, Massachusetts.* I. N. Phelps Stokes Collection, Miriam and Ira D. Wallach Division of Art, Prints and Photographs/The New York Public Library, Astor, Lenox and Tilden Foundations; **326** Library of Congress; **329** *Panel of the Independence,* detail of center with Father Hidalgo. Mural by Juan O'Gorman. Schalkwijk/Art Resource, NY; **330L** *Portrait of Simon Bolívar,* 1859, by Arturo Michelena. Giraudon/Art Resource, NY; **330R** Culver Pictures; **333** Samuel Finley T. Morse, *The Old House of Representatives,* 1822, oil on canvas, 86 1/2 x 130 3/4 in (219.71 x 332.11 cm). In the Collection of the Corcoran Gallery of Art. Museum Purchase, Gallery Fund; **335** Joel T. Hart, *Portrait Bust of Henry Clay,* n.d., marble. In the Collection of the Corcoran Gallery of Art. Museum Purchase; **337** Cheryl Fenton*; **341B** Cheryl Fenton*; **341T** Terry Ashe*; **342** Cheryl Fenton*; **343** *Group at Drayton's Plantation (Hilton Head, South Carolina)* by Henry P. Moore. Moore Collection, New Hampshire Historical Society, Concord

Unit 5: 344–345 Bequest of Sarah Carr Upton, National Museum of American Art, Smithsonian Institution, Washington, D.C./Art Resource, NY

Chapter 13: 346L The Smithsonian Institution, National Numismatic Collection, Washington, D.C.; **346R** *Figurehead of Andrew Jackson,* carved for the frigate "Constitution." Museum of the City of New York, 52.11. Gift of the Seawanhaka Corinthian Yacht Club; **347BL** *Daniel Webster.* Hood Museum of Art, Dartmouth College, Hanover, New Hampshire; Gift of the artists; **347BCL** Stock Montage, Inc.; **347BC** *Endless Trail* by Jerome Tiger. The Philbrook Museum of Art, Tulsa, OK; **347BR** Political History Dept./Smithsonian Institution; **347T** *Chief Vann House.* Courtesy, the Georgia Department of Natural Resources; **348** *Andrew Jackson* (detail), ca. 1812, by Charles Willson Peale. Collections of The Grand Lodge of Pennsylvania on deposit with The Masonic Library and Museum of Pennsylvania; **349** The Bettmann Archive; **351** *Portrait of John Quincy Adams* (detail) by Pieter van Huffel. National Portrait Gallery, Smithsonian Institution, Washington, D.C./Art Resource, NY; **352** *Stump Speaking* (detail) by George Caleb Bingham, 1854. From the Art Collection of The Boatmen's National Bank of St. Louis; **354** The Granger Collection, New York; **355** Illustrations from O. Turner, Pioneer History of the Holland Land Purchase of Western New York (1850); **357** Library of Congress; **358** *Webster's Reply to Hayne* by G. P. A. Healy. Courtesy Cultural Affairs, Boston City Hall; **360** *Bull Dance, Mandan O-Kee-Pa Ceremony,* 1832, by George Catlin. National Museum of American Art, gift of Mrs. Joseph Harrison, Jr., Smithsonian Institution, Washington, D.C./Art Resource, NY; **362** *The Trail of Tears* by Robert Lindneux. Woolaroc Museum, Bartlesville, Oklahoma.; **363** *Osceola, the Black Drink, a warrior of great*

Acknowledgments • **R105**

distinction (detail), 1838, by George Catlin. National Museum of American Art, Smithsonian Institution, Washington, D.C./Art Resource, NY; **365** Collection of The New-York Historical Society, New York City; **367L** The Granger Collection, New York; **367R** Stanley King Collection; **369T** Cheryl Fenton*; **369B** The Granger Collection, New York

Chapter 14: 372L The New York Public Library, Rare Book Division, Astor, Lenox & Tilden Foundations; **372R** Louis— Rocky Mountain Trapper by Alfred Jacob Miller. Buffalo Bill Historical Center, Cody, WY. Gift of the Coe Foundation; **373T** Bulls. Feb. 1820 (detail) by Titian Ramsay Peale, American Philosophical Society, Philadelphia; **373C** Pioneer Women, 1927 by Bryant Baker. Gift of Bryant Baker, National Museum of American Art, Smithsonian Institution, Washington, D.C./Art Resource, NY; **373R** National Archives; **373L** US Postal Service; **374R** Jessie Benton Fremont by T. Buchanan Read. The Southwest Museum, Los Angeles. Photo #CT 18; **374L** Portrait of John Charles Fremont, 1856 by Bass Otis. On loan at the National Portrait Gallery, Smithsonian Institution, Washington, D.C./Art Resource, NY; **375** Library of Congress; **377BR** Colorado Historical Society; **377L** Trapping Beaver by Alfred Jacob Miller. The Walters Art Gallery, Baltimore; **377TL** Portrait of Manuel Lisa, 1818. Missouri Historical Society, St. Louis; **378** The Trapper's Bride by Alfred Jacob Miller. Joslyn Art Museum, Omaha, Nebraska (JAM. 1963.612); **381** East Side Main Plaza, San Antonio, Texas by William G. M. Samuel. Courtesy of Bexar County and The Witte Museum, San Antonio, Texas; **382L** David Muench; **382R** Collection of the Star of the Republic Museum, Washington, Texas; **385** Horse Race (detail), n.d. by Ernest Narjot. Collection of The Oakland Museum of California, gift of Mrs. Leon Bocqueraz, photo by M. Lee Fatherree; **389** Advice on the Prairie, 1853 by William Tyler Ranney. Buffalo Bill Historical Center, Cody, WY. Gift of Mrs J. Maxwell Moran; **390** Handcart Pioneers, 1900 by C. C. A. Christensen. Museum of Church History and Art, Salt Lake City, Utah; **391** Nevada Historical Society; **392** Cheryl Fenton*; **393** American Progress (lithograph) by John Gast. Library of Congress; **396** Rancho San Miguelito, California, 1852 by José Rafael. RG 49, Records of the Bureau of Land Management, California Private Land Claims, vol. 1, National Archives; **397** California Section, California State Library, Photograph Collection; **399** David Muench

Chapter 15: 402L Nat Turner by William H. Johnson. National Museum of American Art, Washington, D.C. Gift of the Harmon Foundation/Art Resource, NY; **402R** Culver Pictures; **403T** Paul Rezendes/New England Stock Photo; **403BL** National Maritime Museum, London; **403BC** Smithsonian Institution, negative #27979; **403BR** The Bettmann Archive; **404** J.R. Eyerman/Life Magazine, © TIME Inc.; **405** Culver Pictures; **407T** Culver Pictures; **407C** Culver Pictures; **407B** New York Public Library, Astor, Lenox and Tilden Foundations; **411** The Bettmann Archive; **412** Oakland House and Race Course, Louisville by Robert Brammer and Augustus A. Von Smith. J. B. Speed Art Museum, Louisville, Kentucky; **413** Rob Crandall/The Image Works; **415** National Museum of American History/Smithsonian Institution, photo #75-2984; **416** Library of Congress; **418L** Mrs. John Jones (Mary Richardson) by Aaron E. Darling. Chicago Historical Society (ICHI–18097); **418R** Mr. John Jones by Aaron E. Darling. Chicago Historical Society (ICHi–10896); **420** Library of Congress; **423** Cheryl Fenton*; **426** Culver Pictures; **427** Belair plantation quarter, Plaquemines Parish, Louisiana. Georges Francois Mugnier (ca. 1857–1938). Gold-chloride print, ca. 1884–1888. Louisiana State Museum, New Orleans

Chapter 16: 428L Henry Ward Beecher, attributed to Corbin. Abby Aldrich Rockefeller Folk Art Center, Williamsburg, VA; **428R** The New York Public Library, Astor, Lenox and Tilden Foundations; **429T** The Bettmann Archive; **429BL** The Bettmann Archive; **429BC** Culver Pictures; **429BR** Culver Pictures; **430** Sophia Smith Collection, Smith College; **431** Library of Congress; **434** The Country School by Winslow Homer. The Saint Louis Art Museum, purchase; **435** Flip Schulke/Black Star; **436** Dorothea Lynde Dix, 1802–1887. Daguerreotype. National Portrait Gallery, Smithsonian Institution/Art Resource, NY; **437** Library of Congress; **438L** Jim Schwabel/New England Stock Photo; **438R** Shakers near Lebanon. Color lithograph by Currier and Ives. Scala/Art Resource, NY; **439** Central Park Summer—Looking South, lithograph by John Bachmann. Museum of the City of New York. The J. Clarence Davies Collection (29.100.1944); **441TL** Moorland-Spingarn Collection, Founder's Library, Howard University, Neg. #146; **441TR** The Historical Society of Pennsylvania; **441B** The Bettmann Archive; **443** From the collection of Madison County Historical Society, Oneida, New York; **445** The Bettmann Archive; **446** Cheryl Fenton*; **447** Daguerreotype of the Emerson School by Southwath and Hawes. The Metropolitan Museum of Art, Gift of I. N. Phelps Stokes, Edward S. Hawes, Alice Mary Hawes, Marion Augusta Hawes, 1937. (37.14.22); **448R** The Bloomer Costume. Publisher: Currier and Ives. Museum of the City of New York. The Harry T. Peters Collection; **448L** Culver Pictures; **449L** Library of Congress; **449R** The Bettmann Archive; **450** Cheryl Fenton*; **451B** Hazel Hankin/Stock, Boston; **451T** Library of Congress; **453L** Library of Congress; **453C** By permission of the Trustees of Amherst College; **453BR** Culver Pictures; **453TR** Herman Melville, by Eaton. By permission of the Houghton Library, Harvard University; **454** Landscape with Rainbow by Robert Duncanson. National Museum of American Art, Washington, D.C./Art Resource, NY; **459** Courtesy Fred Veil; **460** Library of Congress; **461** Cheryl Fenton*

Key Events in United States History

by 20,000 B.C. Earliest inhabitants spread across
North America

7000 B.C. Agriculture begins in the Americas

600 Mound Builders establish the city of Cahokia

1000s Anasazis build cliff dwellings

1300s Aztecs establish their capital, Tenochtitlán

1419 Prince Henry's ships start to explore
West African coast

1492 Christopher Columbus reaches the Americas

1497 Search for the Northwest Passage begins

1513 Ponce de León explores Florida

1519 Cortés begins the conquest of Mexico

1519–1522 Magellan's expedition circles the globe

1565 Spain founds St. Augustine in Florida

1570 League of the Iroquois formed

1607 Jamestown founded

1608 Champlain founds Quebec for France

1610 Spanish establish Santa Fe, New Mexico

1619 Virginia House of Burgesses first meets
First Africans brought to Jamestown

1620 Mayflower Compact
Pilgrims land at Plymouth

1630 Puritans found Massachusetts Bay Colony

1644 Roger Williams establishes religious freedom
in colony of Rhode Island

1675–1676 King Philip's War

1676 Bacon's Rebellion

1681 Penn plans "holy experiment" in Pennsylvania

1682 La Salle explores the Mississippi for France

1730s The Great Awakening begins

1732 Georgia becomes the last English colony

1754 French and Indian War begins

1763 France gives up claims in North America

1765 Stamp Act

1769 Spanish build first mission in California

1770 Boston Massacre

1773 Boston Tea Party

1774 First Continental Congress

1775 Battles of Lexington and Concord
Second Continental Congress

1776 Declaration of Independence

1781 Articles of Confederation ratified
British surrender at Yorktown

1783 Britain recognizes American independence in
Treaty of Paris

1787 Constitutional Convention
Northwest Ordinance

1788 Constitution ratified

1789 **George Washington becomes first
U.S. President**

1791 Bill of Rights ratified

1792 First political parties formed

1793 Eli Whitney invents the cotton gin

1797 **John Adams becomes President**

1798 Alien and Sedition Acts

Early 1800s Second Great Awakening sweeps the nation

1801 **Thomas Jefferson becomes President**

1803 *Marbury* v. *Madison*
Louisiana Purchase

1804–1806 Lewis and Clark expedition

1809 **James Madison becomes President**

1812–1815 War of 1812

1817 **James Monroe becomes President**

1819 United States acquires Florida

1820 Missouri Compromise

1821 William Becknell blazes the Santa Fe Trail

1823 Monroe Doctrine

1825 **John Quincy Adams becomes President**
Opening of the Erie Canal

1829 **Andrew Jackson becomes President**

1830 Indian Removal Act

1831 Nat Turner's Revolt

1832 Nullification Crisis

1833 American Anti-Slavery Society founded

1836 Texans declare independence from Mexico
First families on the Oregon Trail

1837 **Martin Van Buren becomes President**

1838 The Trail of Tears

1841 **William Henry Harrison becomes President
John Tyler becomes President upon death
of Harrison**

1845 **James K. Polk becomes President**
United States annexes Texas

1846 United States declares war on Mexico

1848 Treaty of Guadalupe Hidalgo
Seneca Falls Convention on women's rights

1849 **Zachary Taylor becomes President**
California gold rush begins

1850 The Compromise of 1850
**Millard Fillmore becomes President upon
death of Taylor**

1852 Harriet Beecher Stowe publishes *Uncle Tom's Cabin*

1853 **Franklin Pierce becomes President**
Gadsden Purchase

1854 Kansas-Nebraska Act

1857 **James Buchanan becomes President**
Dred Scott decision

1859 John Brown's raid on Harpers Ferry

1861 **Abraham Lincoln becomes President**
Civil War begins

1862 Homestead Act
Battle of Antietam

1863 Emancipation Proclamation
Battles of Gettysburg and Vicksburg

1864 Sherman's forces seize Atlanta

1865 Lee surrenders at Appomattox
**Andrew Johnson becomes President upon
assassination of Lincoln**
Thirteenth Amendment abolishes slavery

1866 National Labor Union organized

1867 Congress passes Reconstruction Act
United States buys Alaska

1868 President Johnson's impeachment and trial
Fourteenth Amendment defines U.S. citizenship

1869 **Ulysses S. Grant becomes President**

1870 Fifteenth Amendment defines rights of voters

1877 **Rutherford B. Hayes becomes President**
Reconstruction ends
Great Railroad strike

1881 **James Garfield becomes President
Chester A. Arthur becomes President upon
assassination of Garfield**

Museum of American Art, Washington, D.C./Art Resource, NY; **555T** FPG International; **555BL** *White Angel Breadline* by Dorothea Lange, The Oakland Museum, The City of Oakland; **555BR** UPI/Bettmann; **556BC** Library of Congress; **556T** The Burns Archive; **556BL** UPI/Bettmann; **556BR** AP/Wide World Photos; **557BR** Los Alamos National Laboratory; **557T** Archive Photos/Lambert; **557BL** UPI/Bettmann; **557BC** The Bettmann Archive; **558BC** Dick Swanson/Black Star; **558BR** NASA; **558T** Lisa Law/The Image Works; **558BL** Matt Herron/Black Star; **559T** Bob Fitch/Black Star; **559BL** Peter Mitchel/© Sven Simon; **559BC** Diana Mara Henry; **559BR** Frank Johnston/Black Star; **560T** Paul Barton/The Stock Market; **560BC** J. L. Atlan/Sygma; **560BR** Eddie Adams/ The Stock Market; **560BL** AP/Wide World Photos; **561T** Bob Daemmrich/The Image Works; **561BL** Klaus Reisinger/ Black Star; **561BR** Jeffrey Markowitz/Sygma; **561BC** Liza A. Loeffler*; **562** Masahiro Sano/The Stock Market; **564** Anne Dowie*.

Rear Matter: R11 United States Department of Commerce, Bureau of the Census; **R24BL** *Portrait of James Madison* by Gilbert Stuart, oil on canvas, ca. 1820. Accession #1945.82. Mead Art Museum/Amherst College. Bequest of Herbert L. Pratt, Class of 1895; **R24TCR** *John Quincy Adams* by George Caleb Bingham. National Portrait Gallery/Smithsonian Institution/Art Resource, NY; **R24BCR** *Andrew Jackson* by James Tooley, Jr. National Portrait Gallery/Smithsonian Institution/Art Resource, NY; **R24BR** *Martin Van Buren* by George P. A. Healy. Copyrighted by the White House Historical Association; **R24TL** *Portrait of George Washington (1732–1799), 1st President of the United States,* by Rembrandt Peale. National Portrait Gallery, Smithsonian Institution/Art Resource, NY; **R24TCL** Independence National Historical Park Collection; **R24BCL** *Thomas Jefferson* by Rembrandt Peale. Copyrighted by the White House Historical Association; photograph by National Geographic Society; **R24TR** *Portrait of James Monroe after an oil painting by John Vanderlyn,* by James Herring. National Portrait Gallery, Smithsonian Institution/Art Resource, NY; **R25TR** *Millard Fillmore* by George Peter Alexander Healy. Copyrighted by the White House Historical Association; **R25TCR** *Franklin Pierce* by George Peter Alexander Healy. Copyrighted by the White House Historical Association; **R25BCR** *James Buchanan* by George Peter Alexander Healy. National Portrait Gallery/Smithsonian Institution/Art Resource, NY; **R25TL** *William Henry Harrison* by Albert Gallatin Hoit. National Portrait Gallery/Smithsonian Institution/Art Resource, NY; **R25TCL** *John Tyler* by George Peter Alexander Healy. National Portrait Gallery/Smithsonian Institution/Art Resource, NY; **R25BCL** *James Knox Polk* by Max Westfield after painting by George Peter Alexander Healy. National Portrait Gallery/ Smithsonian Institution/Art Resource, NY; **R25BR** Library of Congress; **R25BL** *Zachary Taylor* by James Reid Lambdin.

National Portrait Gallery/Smithsonian Institution/Art Resource, NY; **R26TL** Library of Congress; **R26TCL** Library of Congress; **R26BCL** Library of Congress; **R26BL** National Archives; **R26TR** Library of Congress; **R26TCR** National Archives; **R26BCR** Library of Congress; **R26BR** National Archives; **R27TL** Library of Congress; **R27TCL** Library of Congress; **R27BCL** Library of Congress; **R27BL** Library of Congress; **R27TR** Library of Congress; **R27TCR** Library of Congress; **R27BCR** Library of Congress; **R27BR** Reuters/ Bettmann; **R28TL** The Bettmann Archive; **R28TCL** UPI/Bettmann Newsphotos; **R28BCL** Bachrach Studios; **R28BL** Arnold Newman/L. B. Johnson Library Collection; **R28TR** Nixon Presidential Materials/National Archives; **R28TCR** Gerald R. Ford Library; **R28BCR** Jimmy Carter Library; **R28BR** Ronald Reagan Library; **R28C** The White House; **R28B** The White House; **R29T** National Archives; **R34** J. L. Atlan/Sygma; **R37** Andre Jenny/International Stock; **R40** Fred J. Maroon/Folio, Inc.; **R45** Elliott Smith; **R53** Dennis Brack/Black Star; **R55** Cheryl Fenton*; **R57** The Bettmann Archive; **R67** *Almost through the Dark Alley,* 1919 by Kenneth Chamberlain. Black crayon, pen and ink on paper. Grunwald Center for the Graphic Arts, University of California, Los Angeles. Gift of Mr. & Mrs. Kenneth Chamberlain; **R70TL** *Portrait of George Washington (1732–1799), 1st President of the United States,* by Rembrandt Peale. National Portrait Gallery, Smithsonian Institution/Art Resource, NY; **R70TR** *Thomas Jefferson* by Rembrandt Peale. Copyrighted by the White House Historical Association; photograph by National Geographic Society; **R70C** Library of Congress; **R70BL** Reuters/Bettmann; **R70BR** Ronald Reagan Library; **R73** Bob Daemmrich/The Image Works

Front cover and back cover inset: National Archives (Declaration of Independence); Wes Thompson/The Stock Market (flag); Randy Taylor/Liaison International (people)

Back cover: Dr. Viola photographed by Terry Ashe for Addison-Wesley Publishing Company, Inc.

*Photographed expressly for Addison-Wesley Publishing Company, Inc.

Art Acknowledgments

David Buisseret, ed., *From Sea Charts to Satellite Images,* The University of Chicago Press, 1990, plate 1.2a. Copyright © 1990 by The University of Chicago **55**
Kirk Caldwell **105, 109**
Nea Hanscomb Timelines, stars, and banners
Chet Jezierski **387, 388, 408–409, 444**
Peg Magovern **26–29, 29, 151, 324–325**
Sarah Woodward **P2–P3**

Maps: Maryland CartoGraphics

Unit 6: 462–463 Chicago Historical Society

Chapter 17: 464R Department of Special Collections and University Archives, Stanford University Library; **464L** The Bettmann Archive; **465BR** The Museum of the Confederacy, Richmond, Virginia, photo by Katherine Wetzel; **465T** Library of Congress; **465BL** The Bettmann Archive; **465BC** Boston Athenaeum; **466** Meserve-Kunhardt Collection; **467** *The Railsplitter,* 1860. Chicago Historical Society. Gift of Maibelle Heikes Justice; **469** Collection of The New-York Historical Society, New York City; **470** The Granger Collection, New York; **471TL** Collection of The New-York Historical Society, New York City; **471TR** The Bettmann Archive; **471BL** Meserve-Kunhardt Collection; **471BR** Chicago Historical Society; **473R** Schlesinger Library, Radcliffe College; **473** Smithsonian Institution; **475** Kansas State Historical Society, Topeka, Kansas; **476** The Granger Collection, New York; **476T** Cheryl Fenton*; **477B** Cheryl Fenton*; **478** *Dred Scott,* 1881, by Louis Schultze. Missouri Historical Society; **479R** Ira Wyman/Sygma; **479L** *Lincoln-Douglas Debate at Charleston, Illinois* (detail) by Robert Marshall Root. Henry Horner Lincoln Collection, Illinois State Historical Library; **481** *John Brown Going to His Hanging,* 1942 by Horace Pippin. The Pennsylvania Academy of the Fine Arts, Philadelphia. John Lambert Fund; **485** Robert Llewellyn

Chapter 18: 488L The Bettmann Archive; **488R** Library of Congress; **489T** Private Collection; **489BL** *Forever Free,* 1933 by Sargent Claude Johnson. Wood with lacquer on cloth, 36 x 11 1/2 x 9 1/2 in. San Francisco Museum of Modern Art. Gift of Mrs. E. D. Lederman; **489BC** *First Day of Gettysburg* (detail) by James Walker. The West Point Museum, United States Military Academy, West Point, New York. Photo by Karen Willis; **489BR** Library of Congress; **490** National Archives; **491** The Bettmann Archive; **494T** From *Echoes of Glory: Arms & Equipment of the Union.* Collection of Chris Nelson, photo by Larry Scherer. © 1991 Time-Life Books Inc.; **494BL** From *Echoes of Glory: Arms & Equipment of the Union.* Collection of Chris Nelson, photo by Larry Scherer. © 1991 Time-Life Books Inc.; **494BR** From *Echoes of Glory: Arms & Equipment of the Union.* Collection of Chris Nelson, photo by Larry Scherer, © 1991 Time-Life Books Inc.; **494BC** From *Echoes of Glory: Arms & Equipment of the Union.* Courtesy of The Museum of the Confederacy, Richmond, Virginia, photo by Larry Scherer. © 1991 Time-Life Books Inc.; **494C** The Museum of the Confederacy, Richmond, Virginia. Photo by Katherine Wetzel; **495** Library of Congress; **496** *Sounding Reveille,* 1865 by Winslow Homer. Oil on canvas, 13 1/4 x 19 1/2 in. Private Collection, photo courtesy of Gerald Peters Gallery; **499** *An August Morning with Farragut: The Battle of Mobile Bay, August 5, 1864,* 1883 by William Heysham Overend. Wadsworth Atheneum, Hartford. Gift of the citizens of Hartford by Subscription, May 24, 1886; **502L** Meserve-Kunhardt Collection; **502T** National Archives; **502CR** The Bettmann Archive; **503** Library of Congress; **505** Library of Congress; **507TL** The Granger Collection, New York; **507B** Culver Pictures; **507TR** Eleanor S. Brockenbrough Library/The Museum of the Confederacy, Richmond, Virginia; **508** Library of Congress; **509** National Archives; **510** Cheryl Fenton*; **511** *Stonewall Jackson at the Battle of Winchester, VA.* by L. M. D. Guillaume. R. W. Norton Art Gallery, Shreveport, Louisiana; **512** *First Day of Gettysburg* by James Walker. The West Point Museum, United States Military Academy, West Point, New York. Photo by Karen Willis; **514** Sam Abell, © National Geographic Society; **515** *Surrender at Appomattox* by Tom Lovell. © National Geographic Society; **517** David Muench; **520** Stephen Frisch*; **521** Culver Pictures

Chapter 19: 522L The Bettmann Archive; **522R** Library of Congress; **523BR** *William Edward B. DuBois* by W. Reiss. The Bettmann Archive; **523T** The Newberry Library ; **523BC** Library of Congress; **524** Photographs and Prints Division, Schomburg Center for Research in Black Culture/The New York Public Library, Astor, Lenox and Tilden Foundations; **525** Cook Collection/Valentine Museum, Richmond, Virginia; **527** Culver Pictures; **527** Cook Collection/Valentine Museum, Richmond, Virginia; **530** Culver Pictures; **531** Culver Pictures; **533** David Butow/Black Star; **535** Library of Congress; **536** Rutherford B. Hayes Presidential Center; **537** Cheryl Fenton*; **539** Brown Brothers; **541** *Aspects of Negro Life: From Slavery through Reconstruction* by Aaron Douglas. Photo by Manu Sassoonian. Arts and Artifacts Division. Schomburg Center for Research in Black Culture. The New York Public Library; Astor, Lenox and Tilden Foundations; **542** Elliott Erwitt/Magnum Photos, Inc.; **543** Library of Congress; **545** Old Court House Museum, Vicksburg, MS

Epilogue: 549R Ken Karp*; **549L** Culver Pictures; **550T** Nebraska State Historical Society, Solomon D. Butcher Collection; **550BL** Culver Pictures; **550BC** Denver Public Library Western History Department. Photo by David F. Barry; **550BR** Library of Congress; **551BR** *Destruction of the battleship maine in Havana harbor, Spanish-American War, 1898 Feb. 15.* Chromolithograph by Kurz & Allison, Chicago. Chicago Historical Society (ICHi–08428); **551T** University of Texas; **551BL** Brown Brothers; **551BC** Photoworld/FPG International; **552BR** National Air & Space Museum/Smithsonian Institution. Photo by Charles H. Phillips; **552T** Italian family supper, 1915. Photo by Lewis Hine. Culver Pictures; **552BL** Photo by Lewis Hine. The Bettmann Archive; **552BC** Culver Pictures; **553BC** Library of Congress; **553T** The Bettmann Archive; **553BL** The Bettmann Archive; **553BR** The Bettmann Archive; **554BC** Culver Pictures; **554BL** William Ransom Hogan Jazz Archive, Howard-Tilton Memorial Library, Tulane University; **554BR** FPG International; **554T** James Van Der Zee, courtesy Donna Van Der Zee; **555BC** *Construction of the Dam* by William Gropper. National

Project Team Acknowledgments

Editorial

Susan Hartzell
Jan Alderson
John Burner
Jeannie Cole
Bobbi Watkinson
Mark Landerghini

Design

Debbie Costello
Barbara Robinson
Pat Gavett

Product Management

Sharryl H. Davis

Market Research

Shirley Black

Photo Edit

Inge Kjemtrup
Lindsay Kefauver

Production Editorial

Ellen Williams
Elizabeth Halperin
Pam Suwinsky
Michael Walker

Production

Jenny Blackburn
Peter Boerboom
Lisa Chang
David Forrest
Bill Hollowell
Eric Houts
Laurel Patton
Laura Rosendahl
Don Shelonko
Cathleen Veraldi
Qin-Zhong Yu

Manufacturing

Lisa Bandini
Lynne Steele
Shelley Thesing

Marketing Services

Carol Wolf

Permissions

Marty Granahan

Electronic Media

Jack Hankin
Rob Cooper

Teacher's Edition Photo Acknowledgments

Terri Ashe: page T5
Jon Feingersh: page T4
Cheryl Fenton: page T3, T6–T7, T12, T14–T15, T17, T19, T21, T23, T24 (bottom), T25 (bottom), T26
Ken Karp: page T16, T18, T20, T22, T24–T25 (top)

Jeopardy!® is a registered trademark of Jeopardy Productions.

Printed in the United States of America.

ISBN 0-201-86938-1

2 3 4 5 6 7 8 9 10—VH—00 99 98 97 96

Addison-Wesley

Why We Remember

United States History
Through Reconstruction

Teacher's Edition

Herman J. Viola

Contributing Author
Diane Hart

Addison-Wesley Publishing Company

Menlo Park, California • Reading, Massachusetts • New York • Don Mills, Ontario
Wokingham, England • Amsterdam • Bonn • Paris • Milan • Madrid • Sydney
Singapore • Tokyo • Seoul • Taipei • Mexico City • San Juan